GCMM 2004

GCMM 2004

1ST INTERNATIONAL CONFERENCE ON MANUFACTURING AND MANAGEMENT

8TH TO 10TH DECEMBER 2004

EDITORS

PRASAD K D V YARLAGADDA
S NARAYANAN

VIT
VELLORE INSTITUTE OF TECHNOLGOGY
DEEMED UNIVERSITY
VELLORE – 632 014

Queensland University
of Technology
BRISBANE, AUSTRALIA

Narosa Publishing House
New Delhi   Chennai   Kolkata   Mumbai

Editors

Prasad K D V Yarlagadda
School of Mech., Mfg. & Medical Engg.
Queensland University of Technology
Brisbane, Australia

S Narayanan
Dept. of Mechanical Engineering
Vellore Institute of Technology
Vellore, India

N A R O S A P U B L I S H I N G H O U S E P V T. L T D.

22 Daryaganj, Delhi Medical Association Road, New Delhi 110 002
35-36 Greams Road, Thousand Lights, Chennai 600 006
306 Shiv Centre, D.B.C. Sector 17, K.U. Bazar P.O., Navi Mumbai 400 705
2F-2G Shivam Chambers, 53 Syed Amir Ali Avenue, Kolkata 700 019

www.narosa.com

Printed from the camera-ready copy provided by the Editors

ISBN 81-7319-677-X

Published by N. K. Mehra for Narosa Publishing House, 22 Daryaganj, Delhi Medical Association Road, New Delhi 110 002 and printed at Rajkamal Electric Press, New Delhi 110 033, India.

उप-राष्ट्रपति, भारत
VICE-PRESIDENT OF INDIA

MESSAGE

I am glad to know that International Conference on Manufacturing and Management – 2004 (GCMM – 2004) is being jointly organised by Vellore Institute of Technology, Vellore and Queensland University of Technology, Australia during December 8-10, 2004.

The industrial growth and all round development depends on the progress of the manufacturing sector. I am confident that the Conference will provide exposure and opportunity to different stakeholders to keep abreast with latest concepts and trends in the field of manufacturing and management to harness its vast potential.

My best wishes for the success of the Conference.

(BHAIRON SINGH SHEKHAWAT)

New Delhi
22nd September 2004

G. VISWANATHAN
CHANCELLOR,
VELLORE INSTITUTE OF TECHNOLOGY,
VELLORE 632 014.

FOREWORD

First Global Congress jointly organised by Queensland University of Technology, Australia & Vellore Institute of Technology, Vellore during 8th to 10th December 2004 is another great event in the history of VIT. This conference is desired to be a forum to discuss new ideas and technologies which will help the manufacturing professionals to attain global excellence.

I am pleased to note that around 200 manufacturing experts from all over the world are participating in this event. I hope this International Conference will motivate the academia and industry to go in the right direction to meet the global standards in quality and reliability.

I take this opportunity to thank GCMM Board members for permitting us to host this Global Congress at VIT, Vellore.

I congratulate the Staff members of VIT especially of Mechanical Engineering Department for their keen interest and commitment towards the success of this conference.

I wish the deliberations of this Global event a grand success.

G. VISWANATHAN

Preface

Manufacturing professionals across the globe are facing new challenges day-in and day-out and they are expected to make tough decisions using their expertise, knowledge and new ideas. Manufacturing firms are battling with their competitors for the ultimate prize and for survival in the global market. For this they must be able to adopt world class manufacturing technologies which will help them to improve productivity and profitability.

First Global Congress jointly organised by **Queensland University of Technology, Australia & Vellore Institute of Technology,** Vellore is a venture in the right direction to address the above issues faced by manufacturing community and will immensely benefit them to promote several frontier technologies towards manufacturing systems and their management.

This conference covers areas like **Manufacturing Process, Materials, Metrology, Finite Element Methods, Industrial Engineering, Optimization, Quality and Supply Chain Management** which will help the manufacturing enterprises to enrich their capability for effectively dealing with the new inter-disciplinary challenges.

In these three days we have Key Note addresses of 8 Eminent Manufacturing Professionals from countries like **U.S.A, Germany, Australia, U.K, Singapore and India.** Around 150 leading personalities from Academic and Research Institutes and Industry all over the world are going to present their valuable contributions in the above areas.

We take this opportunity to thank **GCMM** Board Members especially its **President Dr.Gim, Balzers Korea Coating Company,** Prof. **K.S. Taraman, Lawrence Technological University, U.S.A** and **Mr.G.Viswanathan, Chancellor, VIT** for their excellent guidance. We also deeply acknowledge the support provided by **Mr.Sankar Viswanathan and Mr.G.V.Sampath, Pro-Chancellors, VIT** and **Prof. P.Radhakrishnan, Vice-Chancellor VIT.** We are extremely thankful to **Prof. Peter Coaldrake, Vice-Chancellor, QUT** and **Prof. Martin Betts, Dean of Built Environment and Engineering Faculty, QUT** for their support and encouragement. Thanks are also due to sponsoring agencies such as **AICTE, DST** and **DRDO** and many other Industries. The efforts put in by the Staff members of VIT especially Mechanical Engineering Department are deeply appreciated and acknowledged. Lastly thanks are due to all organisations for their delegates.

Vellore
08.12.2004

Dr. Prasad KDV Yarlagadda
Dr.S.Narayanan

Contents

GCMM 2004
Editors: Prasad K D V Yarlagadda and S Narayanan
Copyright © 2005, Vellore Institute of Technology, Vellore, India
Publisher: Narosa Publishing House Pvt. Ltd., New Delhi, India

Global Manufacturing: Focus on New Product Development

Dr. Chanan S Syan

Warwick Manufacturing Group, International Manufacturing Centre
University of Warwick, Coventry, CV7 4AL, UK

Email: c.syan@warwick.ac.uk

Abstract

This paper presents a brief evolution and status today's manufacturing industry and the key role of product development / new product introduction. The product development and integration of downstream activities including manufacturing including associated processes and their management collectively known as integrated product development (IPD). Sometimes this is also known as integrated product and process development (IPPD). As numerous authors have used wide ranging terms for various aspects of these activities, an attempt will be made to rationalize these terms.

This paper plots the historical perspective of these developments and presents a current status of IPD presents major constituents of the domain both in industry (practice) and academia (research). Practice of Integrated Product development (IPD) will be discussed in automotive (high volume) and aerospace (low volume and high value) industries. A brief case study is reported showing benefits of effective NPI approaches. Finally areas of investigations and direction of advances in IPD will be outlined for automotive and advanced engineering products industry such as aerospace.

Keywords
Manufacturing, Integrated Product Development, Integrated Product and Process Development, Phase Review Process, Automotive, Aerospace, Lean, Value Stream Mapping, Value Stream Analysis.

1. INTRODUCTION

Innovation has driven the evolution of 'civilised society' by creating the means and environment for human existence. Technological innovation and their related socio-economic and political implications have totally dominated and shaped the world since industrial revolution. The pace of scientific and technological innovation has been accelerating and transfer of the knowledge and know-how to all parts of the world has also been gathering pace. All this has been fuelled by advances in materials, processes, transportation and communications leading to ever increasing global competition both in quality and magnitude.

The vehicle for innovation in today's industrial society is product design and development which will be included in the definition of IPD. Increased competition has put design and development of new products that satisfy the customers at the heart of the battle for survival of companies.

2. DRIVING FORCES FOR GLOBAL MANUFACTURING AND IPD

The increasing global competition, advances in technology and communications as well as expectations and needs of customers has resulted in compresses product lifecycles leading to higher levels of new product introduction (NPI, also considered to be part of IPD) activity in order to ensure survival and growth in the marketplace [1]. The key drivers for IPD and NPI today based on [2], [3] are:

1. Much more aware, demanding and sophisticated customers
2. Global competition
3. Fragmentation of markets
4. National and International legislation including safety, health and environmental
5. Technological, communications, materials and increase in knowledge of practitioners

Historically after World War II (1939-1945) the competitive advantage was innovation and marketing. In the seventies and eighties the focus of competition changed shifted to mass production in drive to reduce unit costs. With the rise of eastern economies with their lower base for labor and other manufacturing costs, the continuous drive to reduce unit costs, adoption of manufacturing control techniques such as MRP, JIT and OPT came to the fore in increasing the throughput and efficiency [4].

With the continuous progress of eastern economies (especially Japanese) quality, reliability and serviceability of products at competitive prices became the challenge. In 1970s, the Japanese had concentrated on these competitive attributes for engineered goods and secured large portions of worldwide markets in these products. The customers of engineered products such as cars were also becoming very discerning and demanded ever reducing prices and increasing features, safer and greener products. Driven by this "demand side" shift, "supply side" has followed by reducing development times whilst keeping the quality, reliability and other key aspects of products competitive edge in the markets.

These trends and their maturity are shown in figure 1, which is extended from the work of Macintyre, [5].

Traditional project management approaches tend to use three parameters of time, cost and quality for increasing performance A generally accepted views being that these three variables would be adjusted to bias selected parameter performance enhancement whilst reducing other(s), i.e. reaching a compromise. More recently time to market focus has shown that all the above mentioned parameters can be improved especially when improvements in product design and development are made [6].

3. KEY ELEMENTS OF AND TRENDS IN IPD

Effective operation and management of IPD in an organization needs a number of key elements to ensure that benefits are maximized by the oraganisation, these include:

- ➤ Multifunctional team approach
- ➤ Organisationally appropriate management and operational structures which can be tailored and reconfigured to suite changing requirements
- ➤ Emphasis on key competitive parameter in most industries of faster time to market (compared with other players)
- ➤ Tight coupling with key suppliers and partners to ensure the product quality and craftsmanship aspects are built into the operational structures and processes
- ➤ Innovative products produced to target identified markets and customising to take advantage of niche sectors (this in turn leads to effective management of product lifecycles and portfolios)
- ➤ Effective technology planning and product type (and differentiation) portfolios for ensuring long term survival
- ➤ Process models for product development and its management

A definition of IPD is that "it is a systematic, defined and continuously improving approach to integrated, design, development, manufacture and supply of products including all related processes and their effective management. This includes suppliers and support services and is intended to cause developers, from the outset to consider the through life implications of products and services". This is done to facilitate organizations to move a long way towards meeting all customer's needs and its own targets and goals. This Definition is consistent with the Concurrent Engineering (CE) definition accepted by many researchers and workers over the last decade [7], [8].

So what is new about IPD? In order to answer this question, you have to view the extent of influence and institutionalisation of concurrent Engineering practices in industry. It is common for practice for organizations based on integrated product teams to be leading product development projects in a wide range of industry nowadays. A lot of tools and techniques are also being used on regular basis. One could take the cynical view that the IPD and other terms for product design and development are merely to try and differentiate IPD practice to claim superior operations. However, I believe that this is a simplistic view.

The reality is that the IPD extends CE beyond the boundaries of the last decade and half and brings the more recent findings about what works and where in product development. It also allows more systematic and process based approach to its management as well as allowing integration of virtual product development and design automation aspects such as web assisted/based IPD (eIPD) and eSupplier /Partner integration support.

4. CONTINUOUES PROCESS IMPROVEMENT IN IPD

Process improvement activities in manufacturing have been long established. The lean manufacturing, JIT and use of a wide variety of Japanese approaches have been well documented. With the advent of model based IPD process management there has been a gradual and recently more rapid development in the models of product development.

4.1 PRODUCT DDEVELOPMENT MODELS

Many models and variations have been implemented in industry over time. Theses can be broadly categorized into three generations of product development models to date. These are introduced and explained in the following section.

4.2 GENERATION 0 MODELS – SEQUENTIAL ENGINEERING

Majority of the western world manufacturing companies until Second World War time had design, development and manufacturing process models which are known as sequential engineering. Typically, in a manufacturing organisation, marketing identifies the need for new products, the price ranges and their expected performance from the customers or potential consumers. Design and engineering receive the loose specification and commonly work alone and develop the technical requirements (e.g. materials, size, etc.) and final detail design as well as the associated documentation such as drawings and bills of materials etc.

As the design is done in relative isolation, manufacturing, test, quality and service functions only see the design in an almost complete state. As the process is sequential in progression, where each stage of product development follows completion of the previous stage, it is commonly known as sequential engineering. Since the design for any new product arrives in the manufacturing department with about as much warning and involvement as if it had been thrown over the factory wall it is also commonly known as "Over-The-Wall engineering". Figure 2 illustrates the sequential process of new product development, each design stage starts only when the previous one is completed. This type of approach is also known by many other names including Serial Engineering, Time-Phased Engineering, and Chimney Method.

In this sequential method of operation, a change required in a later stage will cause delay and additional costs in the upstream stages. Additionally, the subsequent stages are delayed until the current stage has been completed. This approach encourages a large number of modifications and alterations in the later stages of the product development phase when it is more expensive and difficult, as shown in figure 3. In many cases investment in tooling and equipment is usually committed and the product launch date may already be fixed.

There are many weaknesses of the over the wall engineering approach. In summary they include:

- Insufficient product specification, leading to excessive amount of modifications.
- Little attention to manufacturability issues of the product at the design stage.
- Due mainly to the uncontrolled late design change costs, the estimated costings are usually degrees of magnitude in error. This leads to a lack of confidence in the estimated costs of projects.
- The likelihood of late changes usually leads to expensive changes to tooling and other equipment.

Major advances took place from 1960s onwards as better understanding of project management and its relevance to IPD became clearer, especially in defense and high value product industries where the huge benefits of more efficient processes were potentially realisable. The following section describes the main models for product development as they evolved over the last four decades.

4.3 FIRST GENERATION PRODUCT DEVELOPMENT PROCESS MODEL - PHASE REVIEW

These are either broadly based on or are similar to the Phased Project Planning scheme (PPP) developed by NASA in early 1960s. First Phased Project Planning based model and often known as the Phase Review Process. This was a detailed scheme for working with suppliers and contractors on space projects. The US military adopted the approach and a number of organizations ended up using the PPP process.

The PPP broke development into discrete phases with review points at end of each phase. Payment to suppliers and funding for internal work was liked to completion of these phases and reviews. This system brought discipline to the previously under managed approaches to product development. It also reduced technical risk and for example Hewlett Packard still use modified version of this process [9].

This approach had a narrow focus on development and did not address the wider business and people issues. The process was still based on the departmental silo structures and was in essence better project managed and modified serial engineering process. There were further developments of PPP process which speeded the process and promoted integration between departments [10].

4.4 SECOND GENERATION IPD PROCESS MODELS- STAGE GATE / PHASE GATE

This, what I have called second generation IPD process models, were more that just process models. They included the underlying organization structure, people (team) and wider business issues. These included approaches such as:

I. **Concurrent Engineering based models**:
This approach is also known as Simultaneous Engineering as the phases of IPD are allowed to overlap in order to compress overall cycle time for product development. This approach involves all departments and suppliers in the project team.
Numerous publications have reported this approach in wide ranging industries who all achieved significantly reduced time to market at lower costs and with higher quality products [7].

4

II. **Innovation Units models**:

These have also been known as Skunk Works [11]. These approaches in essence take the innovative developments out of the organization to set up new venture companies with key skills and autonomy, technical and financial control. An example of this category approach is the Motorola's "Project Bandit" which produced the first ever pager in eighteen months [2].

III. **Stage Gate / Phase Gate models**:

This category is further development of the First Generation phase review process (PPP) which is widened to include all the IPD elements with review gates between each stage. Figure 3 shows this as described by Cooper [12].

This is the current practice for most automotive companies and variations of this are used widely throughout the world.

The process starts with the product/business idea. This is reviewed and refined at gate 1 and then stage 2 of preliminary assessment is undertaken. Each gate is characterized by a set of inputs, a set of exit criteria and output(s). This exit criteria is used for decision making typically go ahead with next phase or kill project or hold until matured or recycle back to refine. Senior managers (or sponsors) carry out these gate processes and multi-disciplinary teams are charged with carrying out the process with authority to approve resources and make decisions.

4.5 THIRD GENERATION IPD PROCESS MODELS- ADAPTABLE STAGE GATE

The first and second generation IPD process models, with the exception of the concurrent engineering framework, all have inherent deficiencies. These include:

➢ Overlapping of phases or stages is not possible
➢ Projects go through all stages and must pas through the gates/reviews, without flexibility this can lead to extended timescales
➢ Operational detail can be defined too precisely and too much detail which can lead to either blindly following procedures or non-compliance with the process as procedures may not be universally accepted
➢ Bureaucracy and increased unnecessary administration overheads

These and other deficiencies with the IPD process models lead Cooper to propose what he called the third generation process [9]. This process has four fundamental Fs as follows:

1) Fluidity – It is adaptable with overlapping fluid stages
2) Fuzzy Gates – The stage gates feature conditional GO decision rather than absolute ones to allow flexibility in the process
3) Focused – It builds in priority for techniques that consider all the portfolio of projects rather than just the task in hand
4) Flexible – Stage gates are tailorable and each project can have different routes through the gates

6. APPLICATION OF WORLD CLASS NPI PROCESS - A CASE STUDY

This work investigating NPI process and continuous learning to improve product and organizational performance is focusing on automotive and materials handling industries [17]. This innovative research has already developed a new NPI process at Cosworth Technology to design and develop the cylinder block, head, and bed-plate for a brand new incremental JCB diesel engine production facility at Wellingborough in the UK. The first three models of this engine will be in-line, four cylinder, direct injection diesels. The project contract was signed in July 2003 with the start of production date agreed to be October 2004 and end of production on December 2012. Production will be ramped up from 725 in year one to 34,000 in year three and is expected to peak at around 43,000 units in years 2010-12. It was acknowledged that the traditional NPI process for such projects at Cosworth Technology was based on the Advanced Product Quality Procedure (APQP) compliant approach (as typified by quality management system standards such as QS9000 and ISO/TS 16949) with limited capability for effective project monitoring, control and management. Therefore, it was agreed to re-engineer the process to enable better planning, monitoring and control to build-in the required quality whilst achieving timescale pressures to meet the customer launch plans.

The WMG project team worked closely with the Cosworth Technology Project Director to analyse the project requirements and existing NPI process. This enabled expertise and experience from international best practice approaches to be leveraged to develop an efficient and effective new NPI process for Cosworth, see Figure 4. The adapted NPI process was implemented and ensured effective monitoring and control of the JCB project in a multi-disciplinary team environment. Furthermore, supporting process documentation was developed by the team to ensure more effective communications with the customer and supply chain to deliver their expectations and objectives for the new product to agreed milestones with outputs agreed of which extended team had a shared understanding. The improved process has ensured visibility of activities for all involved and early identification and cost effective rectification of problems. The new Cosworth factory at Wellingborough has now been commissioned and is currently expected to meet the quality, production rate and cost targets demanded by JCB.

The achievements of this project to date are:
- Customer satisfaction and confidence in the organisation;
- Reduced cost of bringing production facility to completion on time. This is not the norm for such project, especially a novel work to the company such as the JCB project;
- Aggressive cost reduction targets for the project delivery and product cost

5. DISCUSSION AND CONCLUSIONS

This paper only looks at the process models for IPD. The concurrent engineering approach has been included in the second generation processes because this is how majority of the organizations have implemented it. The skunk works approach is also somewhat different from the very rigid process model approaches of second generation.

Key developments have taken place in methodologies, practice and efficiency of IPD I automotive (high volume) and aerospace (high value) industries. Lean product development has had significant impact on the aerospace industries both in USA [15] and UK [13]. This work has combined the lean approach [14], tools and techniques to project based, low volume, high value sector with increased business benefits. Other aspects of organisational structures, supplier involvement and integration as well as virtual IPD are not addressed. Also important is the close coupling of suppliers within the NPI process ([16]. These are all important aspects of managing and practicing effective IPD but are outside the scope of this paper.

Another key area of interest in IPD is the appropriate use of and integration of advanced quality tools in the IPD (or new product introduction – NPI) processes. An early case study work is presented to give an example of the benefits that industry can reap from focus on NPI and best practice. This paper is partly based on a keynote address by the author in July this year [18]. Further work on the aspects of process modeling and value stream mapping and analysis; this investigation is working closely with the automotive and material handling industries and the program is well into its first year.

6. ACKNOWLEDGEMENTS

The support for this work by Warwick Manufacturing Group is gratefully acknowledged. The Innovative Manufacturing Research Centre (funded by EPSRC, UK) is supporting the work on integration of advanced quality tools in NPI. Their support, as well as the support from all the industrial partners is also acknowledged.

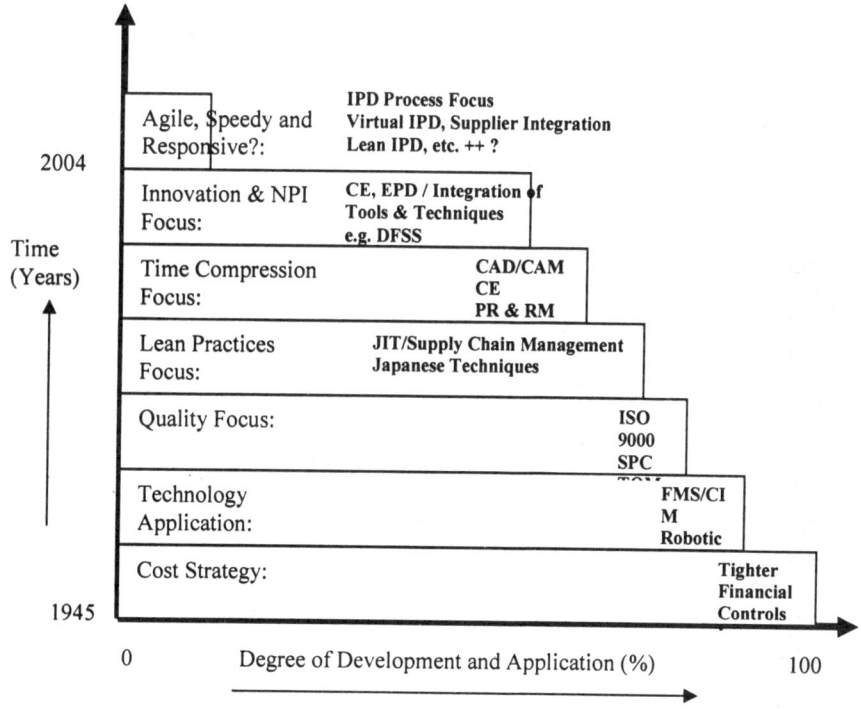

Fig. 1: IPD Maturity and Trends [18].

INFORMATION FLOW

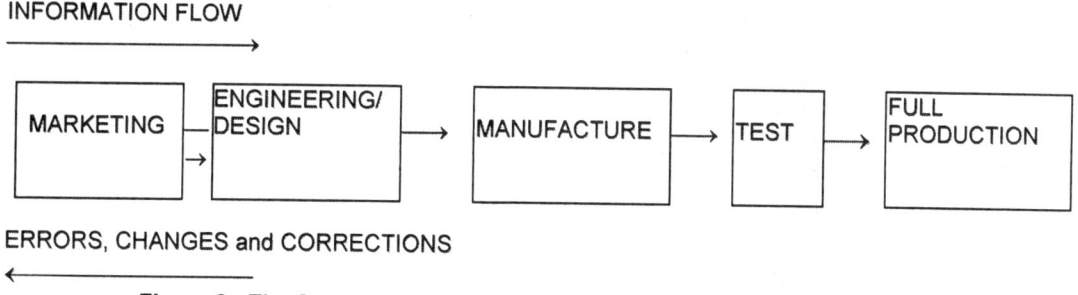

ERRORS, CHANGES and CORRECTIONS

Figure 2 - The Sequential Engineering Process (Syan et al, 1994)

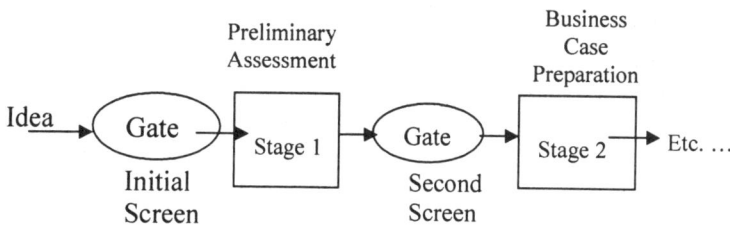

Fig. 3: - Stage Gate System

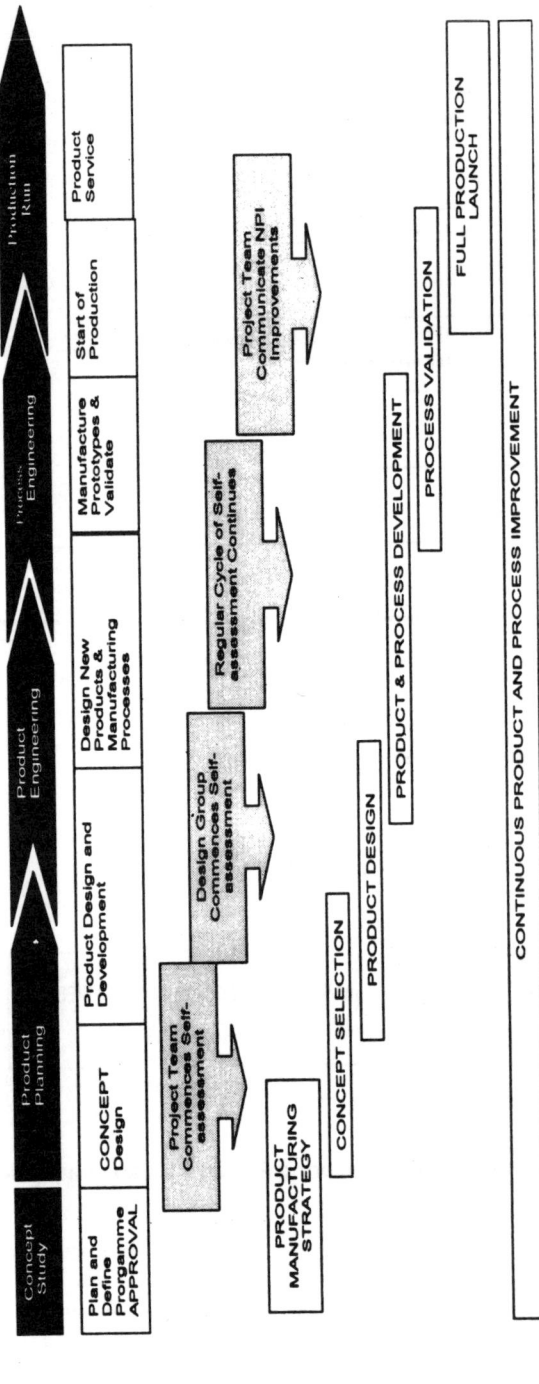

Fig. 4: Cosworth (JCB Engine Project) New NPI Process

7. REFERENCES

1. **Cardwell D,** "The Fontana History of Technology", *Fontana Press*, 1994.
2. **Wheelwright SC, Clark KB,** "Revolutionising Product Development, Quantum Leaps in Speed, Efficiency and Quality", *The Free Press*, 1992.
3. **Yazdani B,** "Design of Business Strategy", *Business Week Conference*, The Design Council, Warwick, UK, October 1997.
4. **Syan C,** "Concurrent Engineering: State of the Art", Invited keynote address at the *CARS & FOF Conference, Proceedings of the 11th Conference on CAD CAM,* Robotics and factories of the future, Ed. Hrishi Bera, Columbia, pp 37-42, ISBN 95782-1-7, 1995.
5. **Macintyre M,** "Introduction to Product Design and Development Management", MSc notes, Warwick Manufacturing Group, University of Warwick, Coventry, UK, 2004.
6. **Holmes C, Yazdani B,** "Models of Design Definition", Procs. of CE98: Advances in Concurrent Engineering, pp 525-535, July 1998
7. **Syan CS, Menon U,** "Concurrent Engineering: Concepts, Implementation and Practice", Chapman & Hall, London, 1994, ISBN 0412581302.

8. **Smith PG, Reinertsen DG,** "Developing Products in Half the Time", *Van Nostrand Publishing*, New York, 1991.

9. **Cooper RG,** "Third Generation New Product Processes", *The Journal of Product Innovation management*, Vol. 11 issue 1, pp 1-14, 1994.

10. **Coredo R,** "Managing for Speed to Avoid Product Obsolescence: A study of Techniques", *The Journal of Product Innovation Management,* Vol 8, pp 283-294, 1991.

11. **Bart CK,** "New Venture Units: Use Them Wisely to Manage Innovation", Sloan Management Review, pp 35-43, summer 1988.

12. **Cooper RG,** "Stage Gate Systems: A New Tool for Managing New Products", Business Horizons, pp 44-55, May-June 1990.

13. **Turner CE, Parry GC,** "Lean New Product Introduction", UK Lean Aerospace Initiative, University of Warwick, Spring 2003.

14. **Womack J, Jones D,** "The Machine That Changed the World: The Story of Lean Production", Harper Business Press, ISBN: 0060974176, 1991.

15. **Murman et al,** "Lean Enterprise Value: Insights from MIT's Lean Aerospace Initiative", Palgrave, ISBN: 0333976975, 2002.

16. **Petersen, KJ, Robert B, Ragatz H, Ragatz GL,** "A model of Supplier Integration into New Product Development", *The Journal of Product Innovation management*, Vol 20 pp 284-299, 2003.

17. **Bhattacharyya, S. K.,** World Cass New Product introduction: The Competitive Edge in the Manufacturing Supply Chain, To be published in the CBI Magazine and Professional Engineer, 2004.

18. **Syan, C. S.,** "Integrated Product Development: Practice and Advances", *Proceedings of the 20th International Conference* on CAD/CAM Robotics and Factories of the Future, Invited Keynote address, ISBN 980 12 0787 6, pp XII-XIX, Published by Nadie Nos Edita Editore, San Cristobal, Venezuela. 21-23 July 2004.

GCMM 2004
Editors: Prasad K D V Yarlagadda and S Narayanan
Copyright © 2005, Vellore Institute of Technology, Vellore, India
Publisher: Narosa Publishing House Pvt. Ltd., New Delhi, India

Micro supply chain management in manufacturing

John Paul

Bordeaux Business School, France

Abstract

Supply chain management (SCM) is the key to productivity and competitiveness of manufacturing and service enterprises. SCM links suppliers, manufacturers, retailers to the ultimate customers as a single "virtual" organization. SCM is a system approach to map the entire flow of information, materials, and services from raw materials suppliers through factories and warehouses to the end customer.

This session will present the Supply Chain Operations Reference-model (SCOR), a leading framework, that enables organisations to describe their simply or complex supply chain network easily using a common set of definitions and processes, which allows effective communication among supply chain partners. Business process reengineering, benchmarking, and best practices are integrated into the cross-functional framework. The model consists of 3 levels, and the scope and interdependency will be explained.

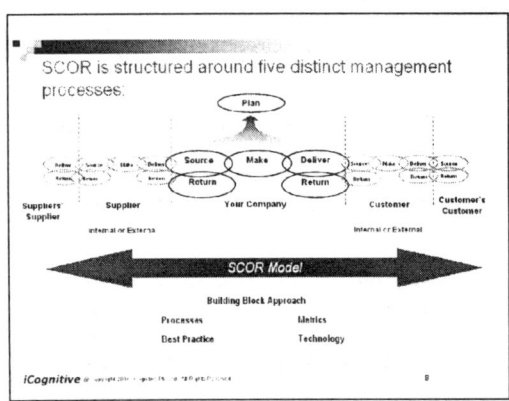
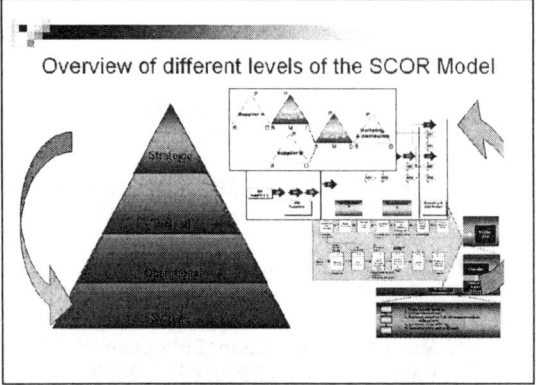

SCOR is structured around 5 distinct management processes: Plan, Source, Make Deliver and Return. At level 2 in the model, these processes are categorized according to different SCM strategies, and coded accordingly. For example: S1 means Source from Stock, M2 means Make to Order, etc. Using these different codes, a Supply Chain configuration can be mapped easily. This session shows how to decompose this configuration in a horizontal as well as in vertical way.

The SCOR model contains a set of metrics in 3 hierarchical levels. At level 1 there are thirteen metrics that are grouped in the SCORcard. These level 1 metrics measure performance in Delivery reliability, Supply Chain flexibility, Supply Chain responsiveness, Supply Chain Cost and Assets. A sample of these metrics will be explained, decomposed and analyzed using SCOR tools.

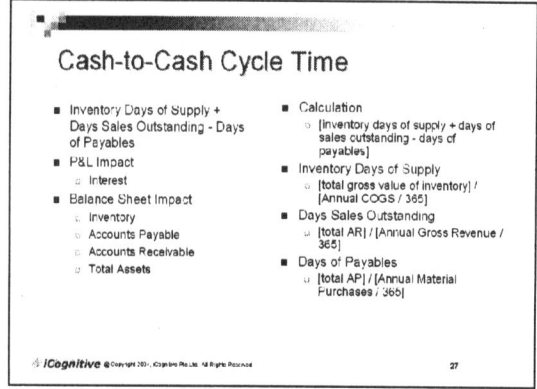

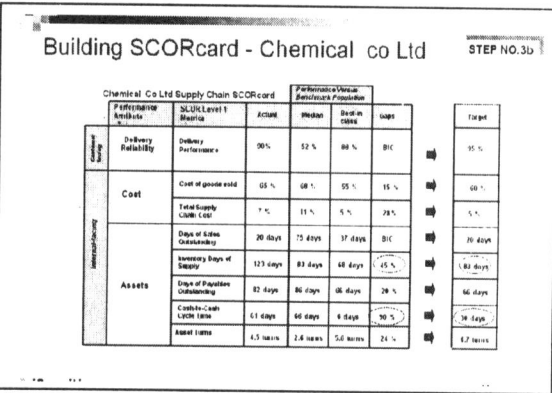

The SCORcard provides a process mea surement toolkit to set targets and track operational performance. Lower level objectives can be derived from the targets at level 1 in the SCORcard. This way, SCOR allows an organization to analyze its Supply Chain performance and link the results to its financial performance and vice versa.

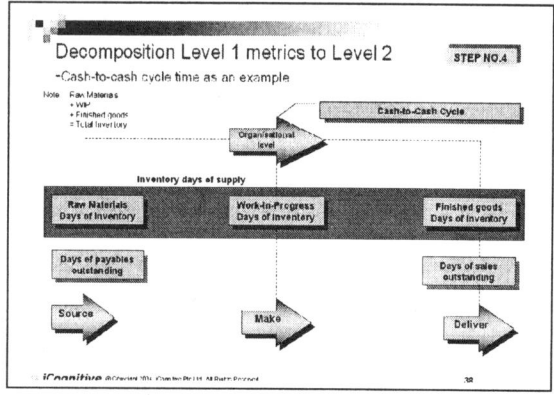

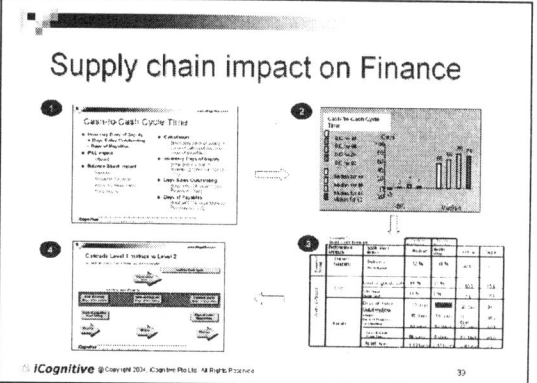

The model is flexible enough to be applied in different areas of SCM. For each particular process covered in the model it provides a series of best practices currently in use in the market, as well as suggestive technology in terms of both hardware and software.

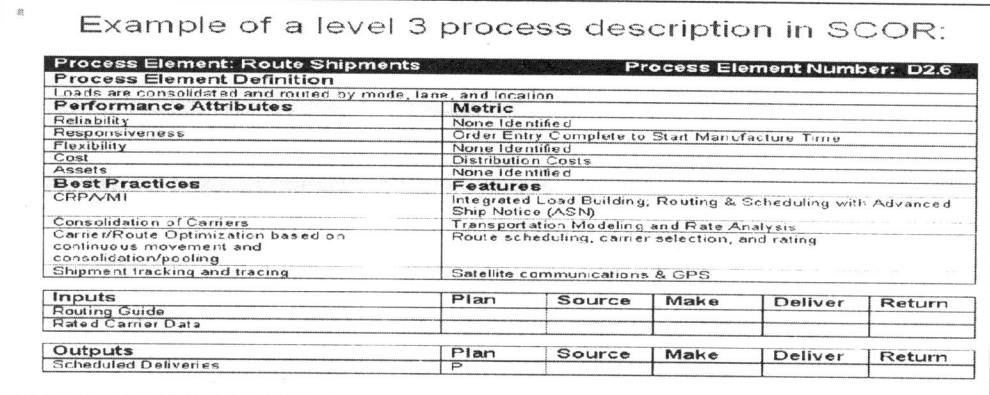

Since the launch of the SCOR-model in '96, it has been adopted as the cross-industry standard in Supply Chain Management by many well-known companies world-wide, which have achieved substantial improvements in delivery performance, forecast accuracy, and reduction in supply chain cost.

Information Technology

GCMM 2004
Editors: Prasad K D V Yarlagadda and S Narayanan
Copyright © 2005, Vellore Institute of Technology, Vellore, India
Publisher: Narosa Publishing House Pvt. Ltd., New Delhi, India

Customization the new mantra of e-manufacturing

Murali Manohar B

Debub University, Awassa, Ethiopia

Email: muralimb@hotmail.com

Abstract

Customization is the new mantra of the e-manufacturing i.e., the concept of conventional manufacturing has changed in the recent past. Many large manufacturing organizations adopt conventional manufacturing, in which the key word used is the "standardization" to reap the benefits of mass manufacturing i.e., the low costs of production. There is a see change in the business models adopted the companies like Dell Computers, General Motors of USA by moving towards customization where by enabling the customer to feed the design of the product and then develop it in to a full fledged product to suit the exact needs of him/her. The author is examining the changes to be adopted by the companies to move from standardization to customization. It is evident from the literature that the organizations need to re-engineer the manufacturing cycles to meet the expectations of the customer i.e., instead of maintaining the inventory, working with standard or dedicated production lines it needs to move totally in a different direction. In e-manufacturing environments the companies start their work when they receive the orders from the customers. Hence, the paper looks in to the issues of concern to the e-manufacturing firms.

Keywords

Customization, Agile manufacturing, Computer/automobile industry, SILS, E-Manufacturing

1. INTRODUCTION

Mass customization otherwise known as *agile manufacturing* has appears to have been used by the Iacocca Institute at Lehigh University which has been seeking ways in which US manufacturing can best respond to the Japanese. The emerging thinking appears be to combine lean and mass customization philosophy with high technology and also integrate manufacturing across the enterprise so as to create the manufacturing equivalent to TQM. Suppliers and distributors become part of the package (1).

2. E-MANUFACTURING

The rapid growth of internet-based and related systems is a dominant factor in business today and this work examines its impact on manufacturing.

The application of open, flexible, reconfigurable communications and computing for the enhancement of existing manufacturing practices and the creation of new business models and processes." (2)

Let us understand how, the manufacturing scenarios in the world's leading organizations are at this movement of time. The author is interested in presenting two manufacturing sectors viz., computers and automobile industry. Hence, the author is presenting the case studies of Dell Computers to represent the changes in computer industry and GM and BMW for Automobile sectors.

2. 1. Dell Computers

The company was founded in 1984 by Michael Dell on a simple concept: that by selling personal computer systems directly to customers, Dell could best understands their needs, and provides the most effective computing solutions to meet those needs. Today, Dell is enhancing and broadening the fundamental competitive advantages of the direct model by increasingly applying the efficiencies of the Internet to its entire business. Through the direct business model, Dell offers in-person relationships with corporate and institutional customers; telephone and Internet purchasing (the latter now exceeding $18 million per day); customized computer systems; phone and online technical support; and next-day, on-site product service.

Dell arranges for system installation and management, guides customers through technology transitions, and provides an extensive range of other services. The company designs and customizes products and services to the requirements of the organizations and individuals purchasing them, and sells an extensive selection of peripheral hardware and computing software. Nearly two-thirds of Dell's sales are to large corporations, government agencies and educational institutions. Dell also serves medium and small businesses and home-PC users. Dell's Unique Direct Model: Dell's award-winning customer service, industry-leading growth and consistently strong financial performance differentiate the

company from competitors for the following reasons:

2.2 Price for Performance

With the industry's most efficient procurement, manufacturing and distribution process, Dell offers its customers powerful, richly configured systems at competitive prices.

Customization

Every Dell system is built to order. Customers get exactly what they want.

Reliability, Service and Support

Dell uses knowledge gained from direct customer contact before and after the sale to provide award-winning reliability and tailored customer service.

Latest Technology

Dell introduces the latest relevant technology much more quickly than companies with slow-moving indirect distribution channels. Dell turns over inventory every six days on average, keeping related costs low.

The company's application of the Internet to other parts of the business including procurement, customer support and relationship management is approaching the same 30-percent rate. The company's Web received 25 million visits at more than 50 country-specific sites last quarter.

The company is committed to extending the advantages inherent in what is already the industry's most efficient business model. Current Dell initiatives include moving even greater volumes of product sales, service and support to the Internet; using the Internet to improve the efficiency of Dell's procurement, manufacturing and distribution process; and further expanding an already broad range of value-added services. By taking its direct business model and its associated customer experience to even higher levels, through the Internet and value-added services, Dell intends to continue to grow its business at a multiple of the high-growth rate anticipated for the computer-systems industry as a whole. Dell still has significant opportunity for expansion in all parts of the world, especially in markets outside of the U.S.; in all customer segments; and in all product categories, ranging from home PCs to enterprise products, such as network servers and workstations.

2. 2. Automobile Industry

For the automakers of Detroit, the first few years of the 21st century have been spent trying to avoid the competition from automakers from across the world. In the early 1990s, US automakers were plagued by stale product offerings and relentless competition from their Japanese counterparts.

In 1991 General Motors, Ford Motor, and DaimlerChrysler (then Chrysler Corporation) racked up a combined loss of $7.5 billion. The US automotive industry responded by cutting costs, improving quality, and introducing new products -- namely SUVs, minivans, and pickups.

2. 2. 1. General Motors

To bolster sales the US automotive industry (with GM leading the charge) began a campaign of heavy discounting in the form of 0% financing and huge cash-back incentive programs. At the same time they began cutting capacity to bring supply in line with decreased demand. But the combination of price war incentives and production cuts can be a dangerous duo. Incentives cease to be effective if the loss in revenue per vehicle is not made up for in volume. That volume can be difficult to attain if production is significantly reduced.

2. 2. 2. BMW

The South Carolina factory was created to be flexible and agile. Gathering the manufacturing technologies under one roof creates a flow of information, parts and knowledge throughout Body, Paint, Assembly, Logistics and Quality areas. It not only facilitates the production of multiple models and more complex vehicles, but supports BMW's goal to reduce the time between order and delivery.

BMWs are built in a specific manufacturing sequence, and suppliers deliver the parts to the plant to match the order in which the vehicles are manufactured. This practice saves actual production time and ensures accuracy, but also requires warehousing space and an excellent network of suppliers plus top-notch coordination of every detail from production schedules to placement of parts on the production line.

An Analysis Center allows BMW manufacturing to integrate its engineering and manufacturing functions by providing the tools to evaluate product issues on site. The Analysis Center covers three stages of vehicle development: pre-series, series and field. It contains testing labs for electrical analysis, endurance and reliability as well as noise reduction and road simulation, and enables engineers to check the dimensional accuracy of any part of any vehicle in order to make decisions "on the line" that helps ensure total quality.

State-of-the-art equipment provides in-depth analyses that help ensure excellence for vehicle interiors and exteriors, electrical systems, chassis and power trains, structure, dynamics and acoustics. On-site engineering supports problem solving and continuous improvements on the line.

The automotive industry's migration to a build to order paradigm is full of challenges, not the least of which is aligning the hundreds of component suppliers to an automotive OEM. The new manufacturing paradigm, Sequence In-Line Supply (SILS), is now being implemented at many OEM plants and their Tier 1 suppliers. But SILS is a new manufacturing model that can benefit other industry sectors including electronics, medical devices and aerospace & defense. At this time, best of breed Collaborative Production Management (CPM) suppliers provide the best functionality to enable SILS. (3)

The move to mass customization combined with the desire to take inventory out of the supply chain is having an enormous impact on the automotive industry.

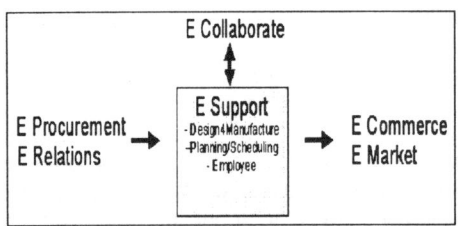

Automotive OEMs and their Tier 1 suppliers are moving from manufacturing large batches of identical components to having components delivered in sequence to manufacturing. That is, to deliver differently specified components in the order the OEM requires, to the point of fit on the final assembly line.

For OEM's, SILS solves three interrelated problems. First, how to provide a customized product for the customer without incurring excessive manufacturing expense. Second, rapidly identify and correct upstream errors particularly in the paint shop. Finally, compensate for inaccurate forecasts and schedules.

OEM's have reduced their Tier 1 supplier base, but outsourced a greater proportion of the vehicle's value. An OEM's long-term forecast and weekly schedules are notoriously inaccurate. OEM's generally regard long-term forecasts as a sales and profitability target, unfettered by realistic market assessments.

3. CONCLUSIONS

The improvements to existing manufacturing business processes are currently being achieved through the application of Internet technologies, the business processes and models and the systems that support them stem largely from manufacturing supply chain models developed in the early 20th century.

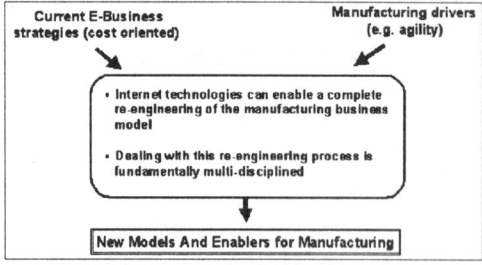

Classification of E Business Approaches Used in the Manufacturing Domain

There is some question about the extent to which these models and the supporting e-Business processes will apply manufacturing in the 21st century, where competition is entirely global, mass customization of products is commonplace and services are more critical than products. The research underway is examining a more integrated view of e-Manufacturing in which current e-Business strategies are examined in conjunction with emerging manufacturing drivers and new models and enablers for manufacturing are being developed.

4. REFERENCES

1. **John Bicheno, Brian B. R. Elliott** (2002), *"Operations Management: An active learning approach"*, Blackwell Publishers Inc., Massachusetts.
2. **Derek L. Waller** (2003), *"Operations Management: A supply chain approach"*, Thomson, London
3. **Davenport. T. H** (1990), "The new industrial Engineering: Information Technology and business process re-design", *Sloan Management Review, Summer,* 11-27
4. http://www.dell.com
5. http:// www.gm.org
6. http://www.altavista.org

GCMM 2004
Editors: Prasad K D V Yarlagadda and S Narayanan
Publisher: Narosa Publishing House Pvt. Ltd., New Delhi, India

IT Applications in Automotive Industry

Sivalingam T & Bhaskaran E

Presidency College, Chennai-600 005

Email: e_baskaran@vsnl.com

Abstract

IT penetration in most Indian manufacturing companies is considerably below global levels. For example, the annual IT spends of an average Indian auto-player is around 0.5 per cent of revenues against the comparable global figure of over 3-4 %. As a result, many Indian auto-companies continue to operate with little transaction support and little critical data that can form the basis for optimization of operations and decision-making.

The objective of the study is through UNIDO's Industrial Cluster Development Approach can automotive industry at Chennai will meet the global challenges in manufacturing by adopting latest IT applications like ERP on SCM, CRM etc. The methodology adopted is collection of primary data by well-structured questionnaire with three Major Car Manufacturers, one heavy / medium transport vehicle manufacturer, one tractor manufacturer and 30 Auto components manufacturers at Chennai and secondary data with Associations and Government Departments.

To conclude, by SCOT analysis (Strength, Challenges, Opportunities and Treats) some of the key processes that need to be optimized to meet the global challenges through IT applications include new Product Data Management Solutions (PDM), Supply Chain Management Process (SCM), Customer Relationship Management Process (CRM), Vendor Management process and E-procurement (COVISINT). In order to develop an effective IT capabilities, the company needs to develop its IT strategy inline with the company's vision, and then translate this into an information systems plan like ERP. This requires a comprehensive assessment of current and future information needs across divisions, functions and processes while considering in-house IT capability and commercially available solutions.

Keywords
Cluster Approach, CAD, E-marketing, E-commerce, E-tailing.

1. INTRODUCTION

IT penetration in most Indian manufacturing companies is considerably below global levels. For example, the annual IT spends of an average Indian auto-player is around 0.5 per cent of revenues against the comparable global figure of over 3-4 %. As a result, many Indian auto-companies continue to operate with little transaction support and little critical data that can form the basis for optimization of operations and decision-making.

It is important for organization to develop optimized processes that cut across multiple functions. Some of the key process that needs to be optimized includes customer management process, supply chain management process, new product development process and vendor management process.

2. NEED FOR NEW APPROACH

In Globalization the world economic environment and the industrial sector world over is undergoing rapid changes and in the process creating concern for the developing economies. Globalization is integration of economies and societies through flee flow of information, ideas, technologies, goods and services, finance and people. The challenge of globalization is formidable. For some, it holds a great potential and opportunity to grow, of course with no barriers. For others it represents a threat to their economy. Whatever it may be, for reasons for financial logic and economic compulsions, India may not opt out of globalization. However, the Government may be able to protect the manufacturing industries from global competitors. Automobile related industries have to compete with other global players to market their products locally as well as globally. In the global village quality and price will be the key factors for gaining market supremacy. Indian industry have to cope with the rapid transformation that is taking place in the areas of product quality and cost, technological leadership, capability to cater to the international market, product innovation and competition. India has to effect massive transformations of existing manufacturing system, put in place the necessary infrastructure and build up competitiveness.

3. CURRENT STATUS

With a total population of 42,00,000 Chennai city has approximately 7,50,000 workers employed in various industries. Chennai is a potential Industrial Metropolis in the Industrial map of India abounding with a variety of large, medium and small industries numbering well over 75,000 in the fields of Automobiles, General Engineering, Machine Tools, Metallurgy, Home Appliances, Farm Equipment etc., This city is renowned for Technical and Innovative Entrepreneurship.

Chennai has 3 major Car manufacturers, 1 Heavy/ Medium Transport Vehicle Manufacturer and 1 Tractor Manufacturer and 15 Large Scale and 340 SME Auto Component Manufacturers. Chennai is a major hub for the auto industry and its market share in India is around 30%. Total turnover of Automobile Industry of Chennai region exceeds 10,000 crores. This leads to growth of Auto Components Industry in Domestic and International market, which is positive and progressive. Auto components industry in Chennai region is becoming a major destination for component outsourcing of leading automobile manufacturers in USA and Japan.

Chennai Auto Cluster has 340 Small, Medium (SMEs) and 15 large Industries in Auto Component and Ancillary Category. The Turnover is 1350 crores for SMEs and Rs.550 crores for Large Enterprises totaling 1900 crores per annum. The direct and indirect employment from the industries is 48,000(approximately).

The various types of Auto components manufactured by the Auto Ancillary units are Piston rings, Engine Values and guides, Cylinder liners, Tappets and Push Rods, Rocker arm, Radiator, Water Pump, Oil Pump, Fuel Injection Parts, Starter Motors and Parts, Alternator and Parts, Wiring Harness, Transmission Parts, Clutch Assembly and Pars, Steering Parts, Brake Assembly and Parts thereof, Shock Absorber, Heat Exchanger, Rubber Mounts, King Pin and Shackle Pins, Ball Joints and Parts, Axels and Parts, Wheel Rims, Forged Parts, Cast parts, Aluminum Die Cast Parts, Plastic Molded Parts, Sheet Metal Pressed Parts, CNC Machined parts, Springs, Rubber parts, Oil Seals, Cable Parts, Friction Linings etc.

4. NEED FOR EXTERNAL INTERVENTION

Resolution of the problems of the small-scale sector, whose significant contribution to the national economy cannot be ignored, is of paramount importance to the national interest. This has promoted the international agencies and the Government concerned to

20

intervene with programmes to help the Small Scale Industries upgrade their technology and achieve competitiveness. The concentration of largely homogenous enterprises within a relatively limited geographical area facilitates the intervention because of the similarity of needs and support requirements, speeds up the dissemination of best practices because of the pervasiveness of demonstration effect, and allows for a distribution of the fixed costs of interventions among a large number of beneficiaries (UNIDO, Working Paper No.6). There is need of State-of-Art Infrastructure facilities for the common benefit and enlistment of the Industries in particular and the region in general.

5.ADVANTAGE OF CLUSTER APPROACH

An Industrial Cluster is basically a local agglomeration of small, medium and large enterprises, which are producing and selling a range of related and complimentary products and services. The enterprises in a cluster have similar needs and support requirements; they are faced with common opportunities and threats. The importance of efficient local business systems that is clusters, in determining competitiveness of a nation is now well recognized. Enduring competitive advantage in global economy lies increasingly in local factors- knowledge, relationships and motivation. By being near to the source of raw material, labour-force and availability of customized business development services from institutions like NSIC, clusters derive a clear competitive advantage.

A Cluster approach has an obvious advantage over the other forms of intervention.

- Clusters favour the emergence of specialized technical, administrative and financial services. Clusters create inter-firm and intra-firm cooperation to promote local production, innovation and collective learning. It builds up a successful enterprise and as such has a better chance to succeed.
- It facilitates process specialization among industrial units and improved quality. The internal rate of return (IRR)

is higher compared with any other investment in the virgin area for infrastructure.

- It develops strong roots in terms of improved local organization and Government structure (Public Private Partnership (PPP) Concept).
- It develops up strong wings in terms of necessary linkages with the external world (markets, competitors, regulatory frame work etc).
- It facilitates the Government and Non-Government Organizations to implement their Intervention/ promotional programmes more effectively and efficiently.

6. OBJECTIVES OF THE STUDY

The objective of the study is through UNIDO's Industrial Cluster Development Approach can automotive industry at Chennai will meet the global challenges in manufacturing by adopting latest IT applications like ERP on SCM, CRM etc.
1. To study the management perspectives on I.T. Applications on Automotive Industries.
2. To find out how far the Automotive Industries realize the importance of IT Applications.
3. To assess how far IT impact on Automotive Industries.
4. To suggest the Automotive Industries, the importance of IT applications through Cluster Approach.

7. DATA COLLECTION

The primary data have been collected through the interview conducted among Automotive Industries over the Phone, and Secondary data collected from reports, books and journals etc. The methodology adopted is collection of primary data by well-structured questionnaire with three Major Car Manufacturers, one heavy / medium transport vehicle manufacturer, one tractor manufacturer and 30 Auto components manufacturers at Chennai and secondary data with Associations and Government Departments.

8. SAMPLING DESIGN

Random sampling technique was adopted to select sample organizations. 23 Auto Component Manufacturing Industries of Small and Medium Scale from 355 Auto Component Manufacturing Industries located in Chennai city were selected for the purpose of the study.

The Personnel Manger or Production Manger of each of the selected industries was interviewed over the phone to collect the information regarding IT applications on manufacturing enterprises and its benefits. For the purpose of study, actually 30 Auto Components Manufacturing Industries were approached, but only 23 industries (77%) responded and cooperated with the study.

9. INTERPRETATION OF THE DATA

The industries participated in the study belonged to the product of water pumps, automotive oil pumps, air brake components, clutch assemblies, slip rings, brush holders, solenoids, rubber and plastic moulded parts, position rings for I.C.Engines, high tensile fasteners, wheels, starter motors, alternators, generators, wiper motor, axle shafts, manual and automatic slack adjuster, fan assemblies engine cooling, chilled grey iron castings of camshafts, tappets, rocker arms, machined aluminum components, bicycles, chains, roll form sections, tubes, rubber moulded components and value guide cam shafts etc.

Table 1: Number of Automotive Industries aware and apply IT

No. of Industries	Aware and apply IT	Aware and not apply IT	Total
Small Size	0	15	15
Medium Size	8	0	8
Total	8	15	23

The table 1 shows, the details of Industries awareness, applying and not applying IT applications in Automotive Sector. 8 Medium and 0 Small Scale Industries applies IT. All of these industries realized the benefits or importance of IT. Hence, they have much awareness of IT. All 15 Small Scale Industries still not take action

for implementing IT. The reasons for non-application of IT of Small Scale Industries are:

IT is costly as far as SSI is considered. The Small Scale Industry is not able to purchase CAD / CAM/ CAE, SCM, CRM / ERP Packages etc. Due to this there is no research and development facility in Small Scale Industries. They don't have own designs of goods for manufacturing. They have the right to manufacture goods from large-scale industries, like Lucas with out R & D improvement.

Table-2 Types of IT Applications in Automotive Industries

No. of Industries	e- M, e-Com, e-tailing user.	e- M, e-Com, e-tailing non-user.	Total
Small Scale	0	15	15
Medium Scale	8	0	8
Total	8	15	23

The table 02 express that 8 Medium Auto Components Manufacturing Industries have latest IT applications likes e-marketing, e-commerce, and e-tailing, while 15 Small Scale Industries is non-user of the above facilities. From the information indicated in table 01 and 02, all Small and Medium Scale Industries have awareness about IT applications and only Medium Scale Industries applies IT in their industries. The Small Scale Industries, which have awareness, don't go for implementation due to high cost of packages. These industries suggested to form Automotive Cluster at Chennai with Association as Special Purpose Vehicle so that they will get benefited by creating Common Facilities Centre, which involves CAD / CAM /CAE Centre, International Business Information Centre with facilities like e-marketing, e-commerce, e-tailing.

10. SCOT ANALYSIS

The SCOT analysis of the Auto components Cluster based upon the interactions during the interviews, and the insight developed thereon is highlighted below.

10.1. Strengths

- Presence of car and truck assembling plants that have been sourcing parts to "International standards" from local industries.
- Large number of Auto Ancillary Industries with background of more than 25 years of manufacture of Auto Parts.
- Good subcontracting "Net work" for various processes.
- Abundant availability of qualified engineers as well as skilled workmen with good work culture.
- Natural "Sea Port" with good "Container-ship" connectivity to all parts of the world.
- International airport with "Cargo-Flights" everyday to reach destinations world over

10.2. Challenges

1. Poor infrastructure in terms of Roads, Drainage, Water, Lighting communication facilities etc.
2. Only a few Test Laboratories with capability to test to International standards.
3. There is no Technical Library to refer to various International Standards.
4. There is no facility that offers at affordable rate "CAD / CAM" or "Rapid Prototyping" services.
5. There is good center to impart training to thousands of new recruit, particularly with reference to Quality and system needs.

10.3. Opportunities

1). U.S and European Car makers are not able to manage the onslaught of Japanese and Korean carmakers. They are desperately looking for sources that can deliver good quality parts at cheaper prices.

2). The "IT" revolution of nineties has created a good image of Indian Companies to be "Intelligent" and "Capable of working on cutting edge technologies". The US and European Car makers now look at India even for their "Design" needs.

3). The capability of all Indian Entrepreneurs and firms to transact in "English" language is a great advantage to them.

4). We have large source of qualified and skilled workers, who can easily adapt to needs

10.4. Threats

1. Stiff competition from China, East European Nations, Turkey, Brazil and Thailand.
2. Most of these countries have good infrastructure and ambience.
3. Geographically China and Brazil are closer to USA and East European Countries and Turkey are part of the European Zone itself.
4. Most of these countries enjoy a substantially lower "Energy" cost, which has an impact on all other inputs.

11. SUMMARY AND CONCLUSIONS

To conclude, by SCOT analysis (Strength, Challenges, Opportunities and Treats) some of the key processes that need to be optimized to meet the global challenges through IT applications include new Product Data Management Solutions (PDM), Supply Chain Management Process (SCM), Customer Relationship Management Process (CRM), Vendor Management process and E-procurement (COVISINT). In order to develop an effective IT capabilities, the company needs to develop its IT strategy inline with the company's vision, and then translate this into an information systems plan like ERP. This requires a comprehensive assessment of current and future information needs across divisions, functions and processes while considering in-house IT capability and commercially available solutions through Cluster Approach and Business Development Service Provider.

With the entire process of Industrial operations being computerized, it has become essential to adopt advanced techniques in production process. The study has found need of CAD / CAM Design Centre for design, development, simulation, Fabrication and testing of new products and modifications in existing products. CAD / CAM Designing is revolutionizing the industries to a large extent.

Every entrepreneur wants to develop an export market for his products at some point of his business career. With the changing world market, it becomes even more attractive to do business internationally. To equip the Auto Components units in the SSI sector, it was found necessary to establish an International Business Information Centre with facilities like e- Marketing, e-Commerce, and e-tailing. These facilities are intended to disseminate information on clients, trends, technology and assist the aspiring exporters of this region to develop suitable product to global market. It was also found to promote a common brand for Auto Components from Chennai region. This step helps in promoting the products jointly by the industry in National and International Markets.

Out of 23 Industries 8 Medium Auto Components Industries implemented IT successfully and 15 Small Scale Industries even though aware of IT applications were unable to implement due to heavy cost of IT packages, services (ITES) etc. Small Scale Industries suggested to form Automotive Cluster at Chennai with all SMEs as Stake Holders and Association as Special Purpose Vehicle so that they will get benefited by creating Common IT Facilities Centre, with CAD / CAM/ CAE / SCM/ CRM / ERP packages and International Business Information Centre with facilities like e-marketing, e-commerce, e-tailing to tap Global Market.

12. REFERENCES

1. **Sanjay Upendram** (2003), "Imperatives and Insights for Indian Automotive Industry-Towards Global Competitiveness" *Proc. of the Conference on Emerging Trends in Indian Auto Sector" organised by CII (Southern Region)*
2. **TUV Rheinland Group, Germany,** (2004) "*project report on Automotive Cluster at Chennai*"
3. **The Hindu,** dated 3-7-2004 "*Auto Cluster at Chennai.*"
4. **The Hindu,** "*Survey of Indian Industry 2003*".
5. **Tamil Nadu**- "*An Economic Appraisal-2001-2002*".

GCMM 2004
Editors: Prasad K D V Yarlagadda and S Narayanan
Copyright © 2005, Vellore Institute of Technology, Vellore, India
Publisher: Narosa Publishing House Pvt. Ltd., New Delhi, India

Managing Uncertainties using a Knowledge Management Approach

*Koh S C L, Saad S M, ***Arunachalam S

*Sheffield University Management School, UK

E-mail: S.C.L.Koh@sheffield.ac.uk

**School of Engineering, Sheffield Hallam University, UK

E-mail: S.Saad@shu.ac.uk

***School of Computing & Technology, University of East London, Dagenham, UK

E-mail: s.arunachalam@uel.ac.uk

Abstract

This paper discusses the use of a knowledge management approach in managing uncertainties. Results from a simulation study of a case company show significant reduction in tardy delivery as a result of deploying this approach. Some uncertainties are found to be more likely to result in tardy delivery than the others, and some are found to be more receptive to the effects of the knowledge management approach, but it is shown that interactions between uncertainties are generally difficult to manage due to their compounded effects. It can be concluded that a knowledge management approach enables uncertainties to be managed and the experiences learnt can be replicated in other similar situations.

Keywords
Knowledge management, Uncertainties, Simulation

1. BACKGROUND

Uncertainty can be defined as an unpredictable event in manufacturing environments that disturbs operations and performance of an enterprise [1]. Today's manufacturing enterprises must be responsive and be able to tackle uncertainty quickly and robustly in order to sustain and enhance business competitiveness. There are two main drivers for these needs: (1) the rapidly increasing power of mass customization market, which increases the bargaining and purchasing power of customers; and (2) the requirement for competing in a dynamic supply chain to ensure reliable supplies.

Following with the advent of IS and IT development, these systems are now envisaged to be more agile and responsive. Despite extensive research to find ways to tackle uncertainty and the emergence of web-enabled Material Requirements Planning (MRP), Manufacturing Resource Planning (MRPII) and Enterprise Resource

25

Planning (ERP) systems that were claimed to be responsive to change, yet many enterprises' underperformance are still reported [2, 3, 4]. MRP, MRPII and ERP have been widely implemented for controlling production-planning activities in modern manufacturing enterprises [5, 6, 7]. They become the central systems in manufacturing environments within which production data such as demand, supply, product, inventory, accounting, costing, lead-time and routing are kept in an integrated manner. The same MRP logic is used in MRPII and ERP in their production planning modules, thus their inability to cope and respond to uncertainty is still overruling given that the Planned Order Release (POR) schedules are indifferent to those that are generated from an MRP system [1, 8]. In this paper, we refer to those enterprises, which use these systems for production planning, as ERP-controlled manufacturing environment by following with the latest development of these systems.

Extensive research has been carried out in examining the effects of various types of uncertainty on the performance of ERP-controlled manufacturing environments, and also finding ways to tackle the effects of uncertainty. Comprehensive literature review in this area can be found in [4, 16]. The next generation of enterprises should be in a position to make use of information and extract knowledge from information system and the business environment to maximize their return [9]. This has resulted in the development and application of a knowledge management approach to improve enterprise's performance. This approach converts data to information and transforms information to knowledge so that business intelligence can be devised and used in the decision-making process. Knowledge management has been applied in new product development [10]; engineering design [11]; production management [12]; quality management [13]; supply chain management [14]; and maintenance management [15]. However, little research can be found in relation to the application of knowledge management approach in managing uncertainty. To this end, this research aims to examine how a knowledge-enriched ERP-controlled manufacturing environment could enable responses to and learning from uncertainty.

2. KNOWLEDGE MANAGEMENT APPROACH AND THE REFERENCE ARCHITECTURE

Since previous research [17] found that enterprises with similar characteristics tend to experience similar types of uncertainty, so learning from uncertainty could be feasible at both intra-enterprise and inter-enterprises levels. However, it has been found that enterprises do not measure uncertainty (no explicit knowledge), and uncertainty is usually tackled using ad-hoc manner and being treated as a one-off scenario [1]. The experiences of uncertainty and the methods used to tackle them can be referred as a type of tacit knowledge. No systems are available to protect and store this knowledge in tackling uncertainty at any one time. This puts the enterprise into a vulnerable position particularly when the same uncertainty happens again and the relevant experts are not available.

The types of uncertainty that are significant to delivery performance in ERP-controlled manufacturing environments are identified through the use of an uncertainty-diagnostic model [1]. In MM environments, changes in customer order batch size, changes in customer order due date, set-up time variations, operations time variations, purchase/external supply time variations, machine failure repair time variations, and changes in working shifts were found to be the main uncertainties affecting on-time delivery performance [18]. These uncertainties are defined as the problem factors investigated in this study and are stored in a reference architecture as the basic tacit knowledge. Lead-time allowance, capacity allowance and flexible routing are tested for their suitability to tackle each uncertainty considered in this study. These solutions (basic tacit knowledge) are also stored in the reference architecture.

The concept of a knowledge management approach is deployed as the basis to construct a knowledge-enriched ERP-controlled manufacturing environment in order to enable responses to uncertainty, to learn from uncertainty, and to adapt the knowledge for future use. To test the usefulness of a knowledge-enriched environment for uncertainty learning, a knowledge-based ERP planning module and a manufacturing simulation model are developed in order to construct a knowledge-enriched modeling environment. They are designed to be receptive to change and update of parameters, so that these reconfiguration of data and information provide a knowledge base for learning. To model availability of knowledge before the underlying causes of uncertainty to take effects for the second time, the following steps are executed:

- Record the event of uncertainty and measure against the affected parts or products in terms of lead-time variations.
- Compute the averages of the above performance records and feedback to the ERP-controlled manufacturing simulation model and ERP planning module to create explicit knowledge for future references.
- Update the planned lead-time, the original capacity of the affected resources, and planned routing to match with the explicit knowledge learnt from steps 1 and 2.
- Re-run the simulation experiments and compare the results with one that did not use the knowledge management approach.

Development details of the knowledge management approach can be found in [19]. The knowledge management approach is programmed within SIMAN simulation language in ARENA and using Visual Basic Applications (VBA). The decisions for updating the resources, quantities and lead-times to a correct level are made based on the explicit knowledge learnt and acquired from the tacit knowledge. The explicit knowledge in this approach is referred to the results of steps 1 and 2. For example, if we learnt that a broken down machine delays many parts, it will be more effective to re-route the affected parts to an alternative machine (if available) than reducing the repair time, which may or may not clear all affected parts at the queue of the broken down machine. Moreover, if a part is delayed and queued at the front of a broken down machine, it does not imply that its delay is merely due to machine failure repair time variations, because the part may have been delayed before it arrives at the broken down machine due to other uncertainty. This would mean that reducing machine failure repair time variations will not be suffice because the part will be released late. Therefore, tackling the first cause will prevent the part to arrive late and hence will less likely be affected by the machine failure.

After correcting the deviations resulted from uncertainties that are learnt from the explicit knowledge, the simulation experiments are run again. The knowledge management approach that is implemented onto the ERP-controlled manufacturing simulation model and the ERP planning module has created the knowledge-based characteristics within which knowledge of tackling significant uncertainties are stored for future reference in the reference architecture.

4. EXPERIMENTAL DESIGN

A real case company data is collected and used to model an ERP-controlled manufacturing environment. The case company is a medium-sized transformer manufacturer, based in London, UK, which use a commercial ERP system for production planning. The ten most popular products range, with two years Master Production Schedule (MPS), is modeled, which has resulted in some 50000 orders in the POR schedule. The company has a mixed demand pattern and hence the chosen products range reflects order from a combination of stranger, repeater and runner [20]. Since the initial simulation experiments aim to exclude the effects of buffering or dampening techniques on delivery performance, it is important to ensure that any slack, e.g. safety lead-time, safety capacity, etc are removed. Therefore, the resources modeled were attempted to match with the capacities required to produce the orders in the POR schedule. Ten types of machine-operated workstations and six types of labor-operated workstations were modeled. It was assumed that the case company is operated on a 24/7 three shifts system. A novel approach, called Part Tagging Method, is implemented to control the flow logic in the ERP-controlled manufacturing simulation model, but the discussions of the simulation model logic are beyond the scope of this paper [see 21, 22 for further details]. Simulation experiments are designed for the seven uncertainty factors that were found to be very likely to result in tardy delivery from the problems-driven approach as well as in the case company. Some details of the data and parameters can be found in [21]. This is different to the previous research from the perspective of the use of the knowledge management approach in the ERP-controlled manufacturing simulation model.

A half factorial design of experiments is made, which has resulted in 64 experiments for 7 factors each at 2 levels. Each experiment is replicated 5 times (pilot run) and it is found that for some experiments, the number of replications has to be increased to reduce the variance according to the set 5% error of the mean. The additional replications required is calculated using the formulae given in [23]. The total number of replications required for these experiments is found to be 445.

5. RESULTS, ANALYSIS AND DISCUSSIONS

To examine the effects of the uncertainty factors on product tardy delivery and the usefulness of such a knowledge-enriched ERP-controlled manufacturing environment, the simulation results before and after applying the knowledge management approach are analyzed using Analysis of Variance (ANOVA) and compared. A 95% confidence level is used in the ANOVA to determine the significant effects. Tables 1 and 2 show the ANOVA results.

The ANOVA results clearly indicate that changes in customer order batch size, changes in customer order due date, set-up time variations, and changes in working shifts are the uncertainties that significantly result in tardy delivery and hence significant reductions in tardy delivery can be obtained when explicit knowledge on the effects of these uncertainties is1. available to the ERP planning module and the ERP-controlled manufacturing simulation model. Operation time variations and purchase/external supply time variations are found not significantly affecting tardy delivery before the use of any explicit knowledge learnt. However, after adjustment has been made on the variations caused by these uncertainties, operation time variations are found to have significant effect on reducing the tardy delivery. This can be explained by the effective use of the explicit knowledge and the tacit knowledge in implementing the correct buffering or dampening techniques or solutions.

Table 1. ANOVA results before the application of the knowledge management approach

Source	Type III Sum of Squares	df	Mean Square	F	Sig. (p)
Corrected Model	312646.742	51	6130.328	149.748	.000**
Intercept	1562341.279	1	1562341.279	38163.952	.000**
Changes in customer order batch size	31565.436	1	31565.436	771.062	.000**
Changes in customer order due date	10742.557	1	10742.557	262.413	.000**
Set-up time variations	1355.148	1	1355.148	33.103	.000**
Operation time variations	82.004	1	82.004	2.003	.158
Purchase/external supply time variations	145.140	1	145.140	3.545	.060
Machine failure repair time variations	272.346	1	272.346	6.653	.010**
Changes in working shifts	1880.129	1	1880.129	45.927	.000**
Changes in customer order due date * Set-up time variations	5.321	1	5.321	.130	.719
Changes in customer order due date * Operation time variations	47.976	1	47.976	1.172	.280
Set-up time variations * Operation time variations	16.598	1	16.598	.405	.525
Operation time variations * Changes in working shifts	278.398	1	278.398	6.801	.009**
Machine failure repair time variations * Changes in working shifts	3062.530	1	3062.530	74.810	.000**
Error	16088.484	393	40.938		
Total	2933335.327	445			
Corrected Total	328735.226	444			
Corrected Model	312646.742	51	6130.328	149.748	.000**

Keys: ** p < 0.01 * p < 0.05

Machine failure repair time variations are found to have an insignificant effect on tardy delivery after using the knowledge management approach. Although there is an apparent reduction in tardy delivery, the variations in the experimental results do not justify the use of an appropriate buffering or dampening technique on tackling this uncertainty. More work has to be done in this area, but it has already been found from this study that using the knowledge management approach to update the status in ERP-controlled manufacturing environment appeared to be useful in tackling the uncertainty and reducing tardy delivery. Despite the reduction of the effect on tardy delivery from purchase/external supply time variations after using the knowledge management approach, yet its significance could not be identified. This may be due to some safety purchase lead-time that has not been entirely removed.

Some significant two-way interactions are identified from both experiments. Nevertheless, some differences between these interactions are found. Operation time variations and changes in working shifts are found to result in an additional level of tardy delivery when both of these uncertainties simultaneously affect the production process,

before the application of the knowledge management approach. A part that has an extended lead-time, if needs to be handled and processed using an extra shift, will result in an additional level of tardy delivery in the subsequent production process, as a result of knock-on and compound effects [21]. The use of the explicit knowledge and the tacit knowledge in updating the variations show some reductions in tardy delivery for tackling this interaction, but the variations in the experimental results do not justify the use of the buffering or dampening techniques or solutions on tackling this interaction. The additional level of tardy delivery due to the interaction between machine failure repair time variations and changes in working shifts is significantly reduced after the use of the knowledge management approach.

It is interesting to find that the interaction between changes in customer order due date and operation time variations to be significant even after the reduction of the level of these uncertainties. The additional level of tardy delivery is further increased after the use of the knowledge management approach. This is found to be an example of an out-of-control scenario where interactions between uncertainties are difficult to manage.

Table 2. ANOVA results after the application of the knowledge management approach

Source	Type III Sum of Squares	Df	Mean Square	F	Sig. (p)
Corrected Model	58201.744	51	1141.211	107.554	.000**
Intercept	254303.371	1	254303.371	23966.925	.000**
Changes in customer order batch size	3371.421	1	3371.421	317.741	.000**
Changes in customer order due date	1313.416	1	1313.416	123.783	.000**
Set-up time variations	683.125	1	683.125	64.381	.000**
Operation time variations	61.014	1	61.014	5.750	.017*
Purchase/external supply time variations	10.429	1	10.429	.983	.322
Machine failure repair time variations	24.573	1	24.573	2.316	.129
Changes in working shifts	161.993	1	161.993	15.267	.000**
Changes in customer order due date * Set-up time variations	31.958	1	31.958	3.012	.083
Changes in customer order due date * Operation time variations	190.236	1	190.236	17.929	.000**
Set-up time variations * Operation time variations	22.024	1	22.024	2.076	.150
Operation time variations * Changes in working shifts	.485	1	.485	.046	.831
Machine failure repair time variations * Changes in working shifts	226.665	1	226.665	21.362	.000**
Error	4169.964	393	10.611		
Total	473885.607	445			
Corrected Total	62371.709	444			

Keys: ** $p < 0.01$ * $p < 0.05$

6. CONCLUSIONS

A knowledge-enriched ERP-controlled manufacturing environment was created and a knowledge management approach was applied and tested to examine the viability of such an approach in learning from uncertainty and managing uncertainty. The tacit knowledge of the uncertainty factors (problems examined) and the buffering and dampening techniques (solutions evaluated) were presented in a reference architecture. This reference architecture is integrated with an ERP planning module and an ERP-controlled manufacturing simulation model, in order to create explicit knowledge from the acquisition of the tacit knowledge for updating any variations caused by uncertainty through the use of appropriate solutions and feedback to the models for subsequent learning. Explicit knowledge in the forms of differences between planned and actual release and due dates, planned vs. actual capacity requirements, and planned vs. actual routings, were used to update the planned parameters.

The results from the simulation experiments suggested that the proposed knowledge management approach was viable in tackling uncertainty in ERP-controlled manufacturing environment. ANOVA results showed significant reduction in product tardy delivery after the use of the knowledge management approach. Some uncertainties were found to be more likely to result in tardy delivery than the others, and some were found to be more receptive to the effects of the knowledge management approach. Some significant two-way interactions between the uncertainties were identified, but it was shown that interactions were generally difficult to manage due to their unstable effects.

The main conclusions from this study were that a knowledge-enriched ERP-controlled manufacturing environment that is supported by a reference architecture will be useful in providing tacit and explicit knowledge from the learning from uncertainty, to enable their management more effectively and efficiently. The knowledge management approach enables uncertainty to be tackled, not just on a one-off basis, but it is a sustainable approach, which allows the knowledge and experience

to be reused in the future when the same kind of uncertainty happens again in ERP-controlled manufacturing environments. Since both the problems-driven and the solutions-driven approach were used sequentially in a logical manner, the proposed approach and solution of managing and learning from uncertainty are envisaged to be fit-for-purpose.

7. REFERENCES

1. **Koh S.C.L.** and **Saad S.M.:** "Development of a business model for diagnosing uncertainty in ERP environments", *International Journal of Production Research*, Vol. 40, No.13, pp. 3015-3039, 2002

2. **Tinham B.:** "The MRP/ERP user satisfaction survey 1999", Manufacturing Computer Solutions, Vol. 5, No. 7, pp. 25-29, 1999.

3. **Koh S.C.L., Jones M.H.,** and **Saad S.M., Arunachalam A.** and **Gunasekaran A.:** "Measuring uncertainties in MRP environments", *Logistics Information Management: An International Journal*, Vol. 13, No. 3, pp.177-183, 2000.

4. **Koh S.C.L., Saad S.M.** and **Jones M.H.**: "Uncertainty under MRP-planned manufacture: review and categorisation", *International Journal of Production Research*, Vol. 40, No. 10, pp. 2399-2421, 2002

5. **Yusuf Y.Y.,** and **Little D.**: "An empirical investigation of enterprise-wide integration of MRPII", *International Journal of Operations and Production Management*, Vol. 18, No. 1, pp. 66-86,

6. **Davenport T.H.,** Mission Critical: Realising the Promise of Enterprise Systems, Harvard Business School Press, 2000.

7. **Hitt L.M., Wu D.J.,** and **Zhou X.:** "Investment in Enterprise Resource Planning: Business impact and productivity measures", *Journal of Management Information Systems*, Vol. 19, No. 1, pp. 71-98, 2002.

8. **Enns S.T.:** "MRP performance effects due to lot size and planned lead time settings", *International Journal of Production Research*, Vol. 39, No. 3, pp. 461-480, 2001.

9. **Davenport T.H.** and **Prusak L.,** Working Knowledge: How Organisations Manage What They Know, Harvard Business School Press, 1998.

10. **H.B. Ding** and **L.S. Peters**: "Inter-firm knowledge management practices for technology and new product development in discontinuous innovation", *International Journal of Technology Management*, Vol. 20, No. 5, pp. 588-600, 2000.

11. **Hicks B.J., Culley S.J., Allen R.D. and Mullineux G.**: "A framework for the requirements of capturing, storing and reusing information and knowledge in engineering design", *International Journal of Information Management*, Vol. 22, No. 4, pp. 263-280, 2002.

12. **Wagner W.P., Najdawi M.K. and Chung Q.B.:** "Selection of knowledge acquisition techniques based upon the problem domain characteristics of production and operations management", Expert Systems, Vol. 18, No. 2, pp. 76-87, 2000.

13. **Clarke A.J.**: "Knowledge management: implementation can benefit from quality experience", Quality Progress, Vol. 33, No. 11, pp. 67-74, 2000.

14. **Fan I.S., Russell S.** and **Lunn R..**: "Supplier knowledge exchange in aerospace product engineering", Aircraft Engineering and Aerospace Technology, Vol. 72, No. 1, pp. 14-17, 2000.

15. **Batanov D., Nagarur N.** and **Nitikhunkasem P.**: "EXPERT-MM: a knowledge-based system for maintenance management", Artificial Intelligence in Engineering, Vol. 8, No. 4, pp. 283-291, 1993.

16. **Guide V.D.R.** and **Srivastava R.**: "A review of techniques for buffering against uncertainty with MRP systems", *International Journal of Production Planning and Control*, Vol. 11, pp. 223-233, 2000.

17. **Koh S.C.L.** and **Saad S.M.:** "A holistic approach to diagnose uncertainty in ERP-controlled manufacturing shop floor", *International Journal of Production Planning and Control*, Vol. 14, No. 3, pp. 273-289, 2003.

18. **Koh S.C.L.** and **Saad S.M.**, Work order release under uncertainty in a manufacturing system with intelligent feedback, 13th International Conference on Flexible Automation and Intelligent Manufacturing, Tampa, Florida, USA, 9-11 June, pp. 165-176, 2003.

19. **Koh S.C.L.** and **Saad S.M.**, Learning from uncertainty in a knowledge-enriched ERP-controlled manufacturing environment, 14th International Conference on Flexible Automation and Intelligent Manufacturing, Toronto, Canada, USA, 12-14 July, 2004.

20. **Parnaby J.**: "A systems approach to the implementation of JIT methodologies in Lucas Industries", *International Journal of Production Research*, Vol. 26, 1988.

21. **Koh S.C.L.** and **Saad S.M.:** "MRP-controlled manufacturing environment disturbed by uncertainty", *International Journal of Robotics and Computer Integrated Manufacturing*, Vol. 19, No. 1-2, pp. 157-171, 2003.

22. **Koh S.C.L.** and **Saad S.M.:** "Design and implementation of ERP-controlled manufacturing in simulation", *International Journal of Advanced Manufacturing Systems*, Vol.6, No. 1, pp. 47-58, 2003.

23. **Pegden D., Shannon R.E.** and **Sadowski R.P.**, Introduction to simulation using SIMAN/C 2nd edition, Mc Graw-Hill,1995

GCMM 2004
Editors: Prasad K D V Yarlagadda and S Narayanan
Publisher: Narosa Publishing House Pvt. Ltd., New Delhi, India

Web Based Vibration Monitoring

Nesrin Akman, Prasad Yarlagadda, Vladis Kosse

Queensland University of Technology
QLD 4001 Australia.

Email: n.akman@qut.edu.au

Abstract

Advancing technology, easy access to the Internet, and the varying cost of global salaries and wages gives today's businesses the opportunity to minimise their cost without sacrificing quality. Outsourcing with minimal detrimental effect on local jobs is a priority because the local economy is becoming one of the most important areas of managerial responsibility. While keeping the company's and its stakeholders' interests foremost in their minds, managers must also consider the company's responsibilities in making decisions to outsource for expert services. One area of expertise outsourcing can easily be achieved is the web based condition monitoring.

Key Words:
Vibration Analysis, Coulomb Damping, Hysteretic Damping, Viscous Damping, Harmonic Frequencies

1. INTRODUCTION

The low cost of computers and the wide use of the Internet allow today's businesses to access service providers outside their countries. They can monitor machines and analyse component static and dynamic behaviour more efficiently and economically. These businesses do not need to have highly specialised staff to be able access the latest industry developments. A technician trained in the use of integrated portable data collectors is in most cases what the business needs. The raw data obtained from the system is transmitted through the internet to the service provider to be analysed.

One of the most common data analysed is the vibration data. All vibration is a combination of both forced and resonant vibration. Forced vibration is usually due to:

- Unbalances
- External loads
- Internally generated forces
- Ambient excitation.

Resonant vibration is caused by an interaction between the inertial and elastic properties of the materials within a structure. In other words, resonant vibration occurs when one or more of the resonances or natural modes of vibration of a machine or structure is excited. Resonant vibration is often the cause of, or at least a contributing factor to many of the vibration related problems that occur in structures and operating machinery, because it typically amplifies the vibration response far beyond the deflection, stress, and strain caused by static loading.

Modes (or resonances) are inherent properties of a structure and depend on the mass, stiffness, damping properties and the boundary conditions [1, 2]. The change in any of these properties will alter the modes of the system. Each mode is defined by its frequency, modal damping, and a mode shape. In very simple systems with linear approximation of the damping properties, the modal frequencies can be determined by solving a linear equation which contains the mass, stiffness and the damping properties of the system. In these properties the most challenging one is the formulation of the damping model.

2. DAMPING MODELS

2.1. Coulomb or Dry Friction Damping

In Coulomb damping, the damping force is constant in magnitude but opposite in direction to that of the motion of the vibrating body. It is caused by friction between rubbing surfaces that are either dry or insufficient lubrication. In vibrating structures when the components slide along each other in the absence of adequate lubrication, dry friction damping occurs internally and contributes to the overall damping of the system. The equation of motion for a lumped mass system can be written as:

$$[m]\vec{\ddot{x}} + [\mu N]sgn(\vec{\dot{x}}) + [k]\vec{x} = F(t) \underline{\quad\quad} (1)$$

Where,

$[m] =$ mass matrix

$\mu =$ coefficient of friction

$N =$ normal force on the sliding surfaces

$sign(\vec{\dot{x}}) =$ the signum function whose value

is 1 when $\vec{\dot{x}} > 0$, -1 when $\vec{\dot{x}} < 0$

and 0 when $\vec{\dot{x}} = 0$.

$[k] =$ stiffness matrix

$F(t) =$ forcing force

$\vec{x}$, $\vec{\dot{x}}$ and $\vec{\ddot{x}}$ are the displacement, velocity and acceleration vectors.

The equation 1 is a nonlinear differential equation for which a simple analytical solution does not exist. Numerical methods can be used to solve this equation. However, during the half cycle when $\vec{\dot{x}} > 0$, the equation of motion for a single degree of freedom in the absence of a forcing force can be written as:

$$m\vec{\ddot{x}} + \mu N + k\vec{x} = 0 \underline{\quad\quad} (2)$$

$$m\vec{\ddot{x}} + k\vec{x} = -\mu N \underline{\quad\quad} (2')$$

The equation $2'$ is a second order nonhomogeneous differential equation and the solution gives the displacement as:

$$x = X\cos(\omega t - \varphi) - \frac{\mu N}{k} \underline{\quad\quad} (3)$$

The energy loss per half cycle due to damping is

$$\nabla E_{loss} = \left| \int_0^{\lambda/2} F_{damping} .dx \right|$$

$$\nabla E_{loss} = \left| \int_0^{\pi/\omega} \mu N X \omega \sin(\varpi t - \varphi)dt \right| = \frac{A}{2}\mu NX$$

Where, $A = 4\cos\varphi$ and determined from the initial conditions. Hence the energy lost per cycle is

$$\nabla E_{loss} = A\mu NX \underline{\quad\quad} (4)$$

The energy dissipated in a Coulomb damping varies linearly with the amplitude and is independent of the frequency.

2.2. Viscous Damping

When a system vibrate in a fluid such as air, gas, water and oil (as is the case in most mechanical systems), the energy dissipated due to damping depends on the viscosity of the fluid, the size and the shape of the body, the frequency of the vibration. This type of vibration is termed the viscous damping and it is proportional to the velocity of the vibrating body. Viscous damping is the most commonly used damping mechanism in vibration analysis due to the linear nature of the equation of motion.

$$[m]\vec{\ddot{x}} + [c]\vec{\dot{x}} + [k]\vec{x} = F(t) \underline{\quad\quad} (5)$$

Where, $[c] =$ viscous damping matrix

In the case of a free harmonic motion with one degree of freedom, the solution is

$$x = Xe^{-\frac{c}{2m}t}\cos(\omega t - \varphi) \underline{\quad\quad} (6)$$

Where, $\omega = \sqrt{\frac{k}{m} - \left(\frac{c}{2m}\right)^2}$

In the first period, the displacement can be written as

$$x = X\cos(\omega t - \varphi)$$

The viscous damping force,

$$F_{damping} = -cX\omega\sin(\omega t - \varphi)$$

And the energy loss due to viscous damping force per cycle,

$$\nabla E_{loss} = \int_0^\lambda F_{damping}.dx = \int_0^{2\pi/\omega} cX^2\omega^2 \sin^2(\omega t - \varphi)dt$$

$$= B\pi c\omega X^2 \underline{\hspace{3cm}} (7)$$

Where, $\quad B = 1 + \dfrac{1}{2\pi}\sin(2\varphi)$

As seen from the above equation, the energy dissipated in a viscous damper varies linearly with the frequency and proportional to the square of the amplitude. According to the experimental evidence, the energy loss due to damping in most materials and structures does not follow the above linear dependence on frequency of the viscous model; rather it is almost independent of the frequency and approximately proportional to the square of the amplitude [3]. Hence using viscous damping to model energy dissipation in such materials leads the damping to be underestimated at low frequencies and overestimated at high frequencies.

2.3. Hysteretic or Material Damping

When components in a machine or a structure move relative to each other, elastic deformation takes place, which absorbs energy from the system. Using the energy lost with a viscous damper and the frequency independency of the energy as found in experiments, we can define the hysteretic damping coefficient as:

$$c_h = \dfrac{h}{\omega} \underline{\hspace{3cm}} (8)$$

The equation of motion for a single degree of freedom system is

$$m\ddot{\vec{x}} + \dfrac{h}{\omega}\dot{\vec{x}} + kx = F(t) \underline{\hspace{2cm}} (9)$$

The equation of motion for the hysteretic damping model is not linear as is the case in the Coulomb damping model. Obtaining experimental raw vibration data allows the damping of systems to be modelled in the

absence of analytical solutions. An understanding of the damping mechanism of structures allows the better management of the conditions that cause resonant vibration. At or near the natural frequency of a mode, the overall vibration shape (operating deflection shape) of a machine or structure will tend to be dominated by the mode shape of the resonance. The experimental modal parameters are obtained by artificially exciting a machine or structure, measuring its operating deflection shapes (motion at two or more DOFs), and post-processing the vibration data.

3. DATA ANALYSIS

The time based vibration data from a system of multiple degrees of freedom obtained using a filter to pass frequencies between 0 and 30 Hz is given in figure 1.

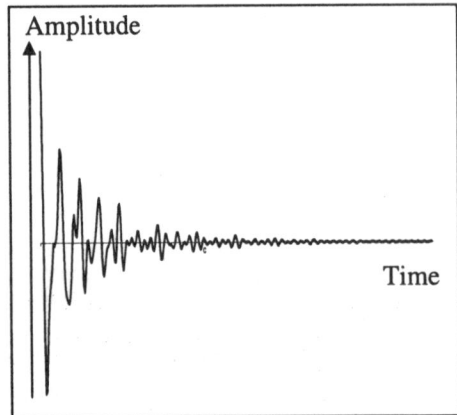

Figure 1: Time based vibration data of a system.

The fast Fourier transformation of the above data gives the system response in the frequency domain as shown in figure 2. It is important to note that when using FFT (Fast Fourier Transform) analysis to study the frequency spectrum of signals, there are limits on resolution between different frequencies, and on the ability to detect a small signal in the presence of a large one. In addition, the noise in the selected range of frequencies can not be eliminated. However, these signals are cleaned as much as possible after careful analysis of the data, use of various mathematical and numerical techniques and repeated experiments performed on the system to confirm the validity of these procedures.

In figure 2, it is seen that the fundamental frequency of the system is f_o and in the frequency range of measurement there are three harmonics. The frequencies f_1, f_2 and f_3 are not integer multiple of multiple each other and likely to result from the support mechanisms of the system and the external sources. Using a frequency-selective filter to eliminate the frequencies other than the fundamental harmonic frequency gives the time based data in the figure 3 below.

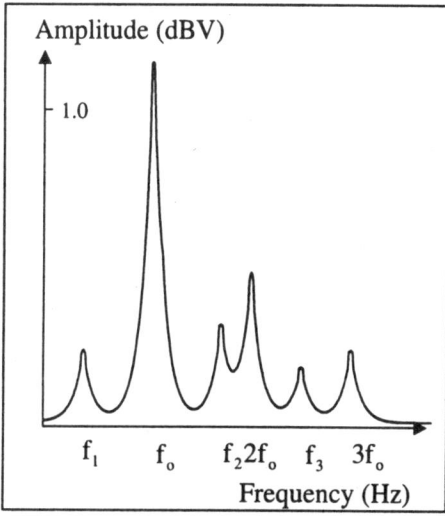

Figure 2: Frequency based vibration data.

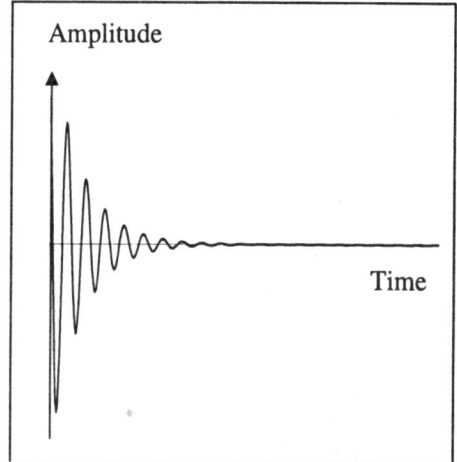

Figure 3: Vibration signal at the fundamental harmonic frequency of the system.

The equation 6 gives the coefficient of the viscous damping as:

$$c = -\frac{2m}{(t2-t1)}\ln\left(\frac{X_2}{X_1}\right) \qquad (10)$$

Where X_1 and X_2 are the amplitudes of two successive peaks. When the equation 10 is applied to the data at the fundamental harmonic frequency the damping coefficient, is found to be $0.71 \le c_1 \le 1.24$ with the average value being $c_1 = 0.99$. The large variations in the damping coefficient values indicate the presence of another signal/s with non-negligible amplitude/s in the vicinity of the fundamental harmonic frequency. The lack of these frequencies, in the figure 2 highlights the limits of using FFT analysis to study the frequency spectrum of signals.

Repeating the process of using the frequency-selective filter to eliminate the frequencies other than the second harmonic frequency give the time based data shown in figures 4. The damping ratio, c_2, obtained from the successive peaks of the vibration data shown in figure 4 as $0.49 \le c_2 \le 0.50$ with the average value being $c_2 = 0.50$. The smallness in the variation of the viscous damping coefficient indicates the lack of noise signals with non-negligible amplitude in the vicinity of the second harmonic frequency.

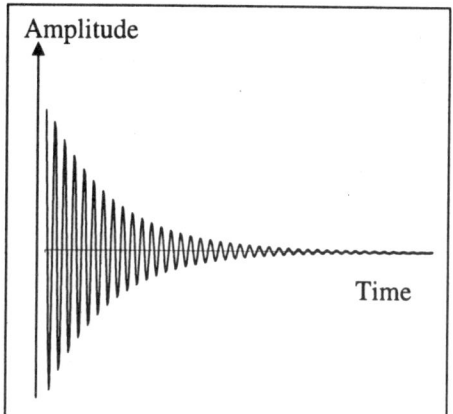

Figure 4: Filtered vibration signal at the second harmonic frequency.

Finally the filtered vibration at the third harmonic frequency using the same process is given in figure 5. The spikes on the amplitudes show that there are noise signals with comparable magnitude of vibration to that of the vibration at this frequency as well as possibly indicating the need of a smaller sampling interval.

The viscous damping coefficient once more is calculated by using successive peaks and the viscous damping model and is found to be $0.03 \leq c_3 \leq 0.51$ with the average value of $c_3 = 0.34$. Once more there is a large variation in the values of the damping coefficient. The large variation in the calculated damping coefficient using

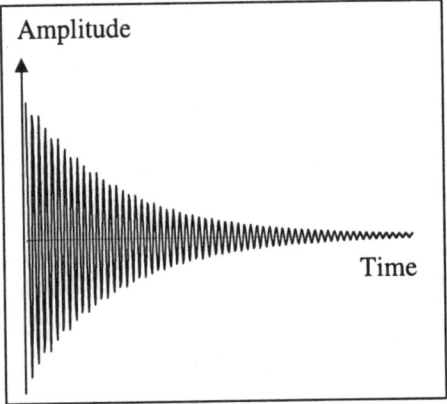

Figure 5: Filtered vibration signal at the third harmonic frequency.

successive two peaks in the time domain clearly shows the limitations of the FFT transformation in detecting closely spaced frequencies and to a lesser degree to detect a small signal in the presence of a large one. However, constructive and destructive superimpositions of these signals will cause a large variation in the calculated value of the damping coefficient. Numerical techniques are applied to smooth the data and eliminate the spikes. However, this process requires great care and specialised knowledge to maintain the integrity of the original data.

The vibration data obtained by numerically adding the vibration data for the three harmonic frequencies is shown in figure 6 above. The viscous damping coefficient of the system at the combined harmonic

frequencies is found as $0.16 \leq c \leq 0.76$ with the average value of $c = 0.47$. This average is very close to the average value obtained considering data at the second harmonic frequency which is found to be relatively free of noise signals. Using this comparison, one may argue that the viscous damping model is sufficiently accurate for describing the system

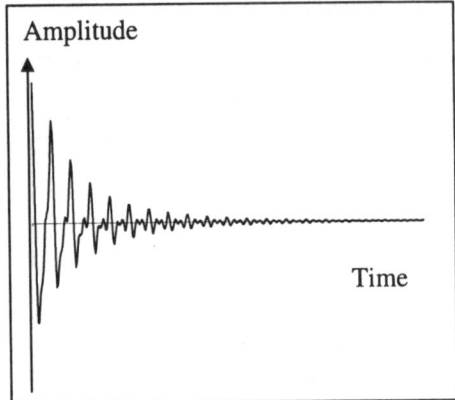

Figure 6: The sum of the vibrations of the first three harmonics.

response. However, the large variation in the calculated damping coefficient clearly indicates the noise signals with non-negligible amplitudes at closely spaced frequencies to those harmonic frequencies and to detect a small signal in the presence of a large one. In reality, the constructive and destructive superimpositions of these signals will cause a large variation in the calculated value of the damping coefficient using different pairs of consecutive peaks.

However, a closer inspection of the values obtained for the damping coefficient shows that the hysteretic damping model is equally likely for the system. Using $c_h = \dfrac{h}{\omega}$ (equation 8) gives:

$$h \approx 0.99 \times 2\pi f_0 \approx 0.50 \times 2\pi \times 2f_0$$
$$\approx 0.34 \times 2\pi \times 3f_0 \approx 2(2\pi f_0)$$

There is no clear evidence to conclude the existence of Coulomb damping. This conclusion is reasonable since Coulomb (Dry) damping does not occur in well lubricated systems. However, the data should be carefully analysed to eliminate the evidence of lubrication loss by detecting the possible presence of Coulomb friction in the system.

4. CONCLUSION

Resonant vibration is often the cause of or at least a contributing factor to many of the vibration related problems that occur in structures and operating machinery. It typically amplifies the vibration response far beyond the deflection, stress, and strain caused by static loading and might result in catastrophic failure. It is therefore important to know the dynamic behaviour of the system in order to manage adverse operating conditions. Analysing the vibration data, formulating a mathematical model to describe the dynamic behaviour of the system, validating and verifying the model by theoretical, numerical and experimental methods require considerable expertise at an equably considerable cost. This difficulty, to a small degree, .is demonstrated in the analysis given above.

However, the advancing technology, the easy access to Internet and the economical rates of professional services in non-western countries give unprecedented opportunities to today's businesses to have access to the latest know how at a minimal cost. The challenge now is for businesses requiring such services to show the initiative and outsource these services to the countries where the cost of providing these services is not outside the reach of ordinary businesses. Part of the economic benefit to the company can be used to train and skill the local work force.

5. REFERENCES

1.   **Schwarz B.J.** (1999), "Experimental Modal Analysis", *CSI Reliability Week*, Richardson M.H., Orlando, FL.

2.   **Potter R., Richardson M.H.** (1974), "Identification of the Modal Properties of an Elastic Structure from Measured Transfer Function Data", *20th International Instrumentation Symposium*, Albuquerque, New Mexico.

3.   **Rao S.S.** (2004) *Mechanical Vibrations*, (Fourth Edition), Pearson Prentice Hall, New Jersey.

4.   **Oppenheim. A.V.** (1996), *Signals and Systems*, Willsky A.S., (Second Edition), Prentice Hall, New Jersey.

Manufacturing Process

GCMM 2004
Editors: Prasad K D V Yarlagadda and S Narayanan
Publisher: Narosa Publishing House Pvt. Ltd., New Delhi, India

A Virtual Sheet Metal Bending Setup Planner

Kannan T R & Shunmugam M S

Manufacturing Engineering Section, Mechanical Engineering Department,
IIT Madras, Chennai - 600 036.

Email: shun@iitm.ac.in

Abstract

Sheet metal components vary to a vast extent in terms of planning and processing methods when compared with prismatic or rotational components. Sheet metal bending is one of the widely used methods in sheet metal processing. During progressive bending to form a 3D component from the flat pattern, any arbitrary bending sequence cannot be adopted as there is a possibility of tool-part collision. Normally, physical try-outs are done to arrive at a feasible bending sequence. Apart from a feasible bending sequence, part positioning, part reorientation and tool stacking details for each bend are also required for developing sheet metal bending setup plan. If the bending operations are tried out in a virtual environment, it will render setup planning easier and will save a great deal of time and money. Such a virtual sheet metal bending setup planner that determines all possible feasible sequences and chooses the optimal sequence requiring minimal number of tool changes is proposed in this paper.

Keywords
Sheet metal, Bending, Setup, DXF File

1. INTRODUCTION

Sheet metal components find their use in a variety of products. Sheet metal bending is a common process that is being widely used for manufacturing sheet metal components. Flat sheet metal blanks are progressively bent to form 3D components using press brakes. During progressive bending, there is a possibility of tool-part collision i.e. the previously bent faces or a portion of the component might collide with the tool hindering effective bending or forming of the component. For example, the component shown in Fig. 1(a) has two bends. If the bending sequence $b1,b2$ is adopted, then there will be tool-part collision while performing the bend $b2$ as shown in Fig. 1(b). Instead, if the bend sequence $b2,b1$ is adopted then there will not be any tool-part collision as shown in Fig. 1(c). Hence, it is not always possible to adopt any arbitrary bending sequence for a given component.

In order to arrive at a feasible bending sequence, physical try-out is adopted to check for any possible tool-part collision.

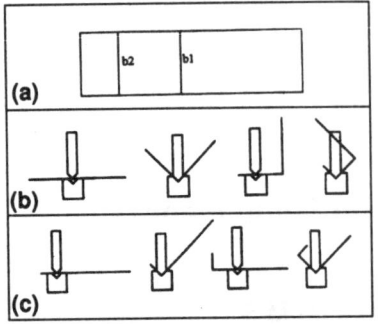

**(a) Flat Pattern, (b) Sequence b1, b2,
(c) Sequence b2, b1**
**Fig. 1. Typical Component with
Alternate Bending Sequences**

The number of tryouts grows exponentially with the number of bends. If there are n bends in a given component, then the number of alternate sequences will be $n!$.

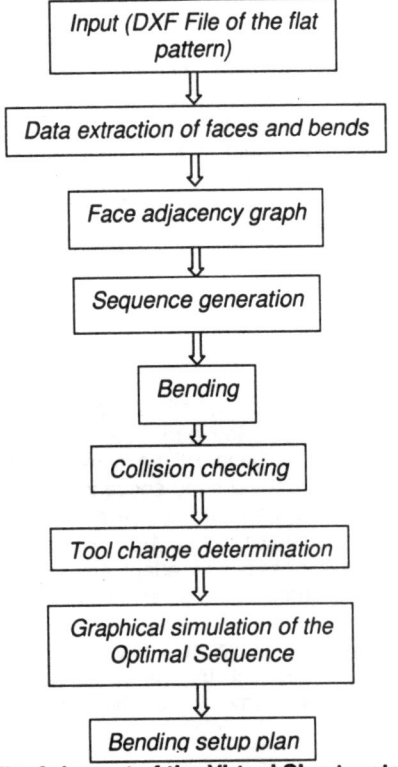

**Fig. 2. Layout of the Virtual Sheet metal
Bending Setup Planner**

Performing such a large number of physical try-outs is tedious. Moreover, physical try-outs are time consuming and in batch manufacturing units, it will have an adverse impact on the productivity as the effective utilization of the machine is reduced. In industries, feasible sequences are crudely determined using certain heuristics [1] and physical try-outs. Such feasible sequences may not be optimal in terms of the number of tool changes. If the bending operations are tried out in a virtual environment, it will save a great deal of time and money. All the possible sequences can be tried out and all possible feasible sequences can be determined. Among these feasible sequences, the solution with minimal number of tool changes can be determined as an optimal sequence. Such a virtual sheet metal bending setup planner is proposed in this paper.

2. BENDING SETUP PLANNER

Various modules of the virtual sheet metal bending setup planner are shown in Fig. 2. The flat pattern of the sheet metal component along with the bend lines and corresponding bend angles are drawn in Autocad and stored in DXF format. A typical input drawing for a component is shown in Fig. 3(a) and the corresponding final 3D component is shown in Fig. 3(c). The filename of the flat pattern is given as the input to the system. The face and bend details as shown in Fig. 3(b) are extracted from the DXF file and the component is represented as face-adjacency graph [2,3] as shown in Fig. 3(d) and the corresponding face-adjacency matrix is shown in Fig. 3(e). Detailed text about the DXF format is available in Autocad help. All possible bending sequences are generated and each bending sequence is virtually simulated on the sheet metal and checked for any tool-part interference till all feasible bending sequences are obtained. The number of tool changes required for all the feasible sequences are determined and the sequence which requires minimum number of tool changes is determined as the optimal sequence. Finally the bending setup plan with the optimal bending sequence, part positioning, part reorientation and tool stacking details is automatically generated.

2.1. Sequence Generation

Given a sheet metal component with n bends, all possible sequences have to be generated first in order to select the feasible bending sequences from among the generated $n!$ sequences. Consider S_{ij} is the bend number of the jth bend in the ith sequence, where j varies from 1 to n and i varies from 1 to $n!$. The algorithm for generating $n!$ sequences is as follows:

(a) Flat Pattern , (b) Face and bend details, (c) Final Component, (d) Face Adjacency Graph, (e) The Face Adjacency Matrix.
Fig. 3. Example Component

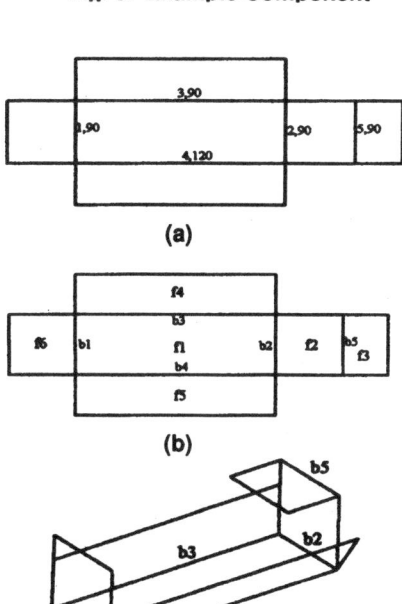

(a)

(b)

(c)

(d)

	f1	f2	f3	f4	f5	f6
f1	0	1	0	1	1	1
f2	1	0	1	0	0	0
f3	0	1	0	0	0	0
f4	1	0	0	0	0	0
f5	1	0	0	0	0	0
f6	1	0	0	0	0	0

(e)

Step 1: Initialize the first sequence $(i = 1)$ as

$S_{1j} = \{1,2,3, \ldots ,n\}$;

Step 2: Set $i = i + 1$;

Step 3: Set $j = 1$;

Step 4: IF $i = (n-j)!$ THEN set $S_{ij} = S_{(i-1)j} + 1$;

ELSE $S_{ij} = S_{(i-1)j}$;

Step 5: IF $S_{ij} \neq S_{ik}$; where $k = 1$ to $(j-1)$

THEN set $S_{ij} = S_{ij}$;

ELSE set $S_{ij} = S_{ij} + 1$;

Step 6: IF $S_{ij} = n + 1$ THEN $S_{ij} = 1$;

ELSE $S_{ij} = S_{ij}$;

Step 7: Set $j = j + 1$; and perform the steps 4,

5 and 6 till $j = n$;

Step 8: Repeat steps 2 to 7 till $i = n!$;

A partial list of the sequences generated for $n = 5$ is shown in Table 1.

Table 1. Few bend sequences out of 120 sequences for n = 5

Seq. No.	Bend Sequence	Seq. No.	Bend Sequence
1	1 2 3 4 5	111	5 3 1 4 2
2	1 2 3 5 4	112	5 3 1 2 4
3	1 2 4 3 5	113	5 3 2 4 1
4	1 2 4 5 3	114	5 3 2 1 4
5	1 2 5 3 4	115	5 4 3 2 1
26	2 1 3 4 5	116	5 4 3 1 2
27	2 1 4 5 3	117	5 4 1 2 3
28	2 1 4 3 5	118	5 4 1 3 2
29	2 1 5 3 4	119	5 4 2 1 3
30	2 1 5 4 3	120	5 4 2 3 1

2.2. Bending

After generating $n!$ sequences, the first bending sequence is chosen and the bends are made one by one as follows:

Step 1: Translate the component such that the start point of the bend line of Sij lies at the origin.

Step 2: Rotate the component about Z axis such that the bend line lies in the XZ plane.

Step 3: Rotate the component about Y axis such that the bend line lies in the X axis.

43

Step 4: Rotate the component about X axis such that both the immediate faces connected to the bend line lies in the XY plane.

Step 5: Determine both the face chains connected to the bend line.

Step 6: Determine the face chain lying in the negative Y direction and rotate that face chain by θr in the clockwise direction about the X axis, where $\theta r = (180 - \theta) / 2$; and θ – the bend angle as given in the input drawing.

Step 7: Rotate the other face chain by θr in the counter-clockwise direction about the X axis.

Step 8: Check for any tool-part collision with the intermediate component geometry. If any collision occurs then go to step 10.

Step 9: Repeat the steps 1 to 8 for all j values.

Step 10: Set $i = i + 1$; and repeat the steps 1 to 9.

Step 11: Repeat steps 1 to 10 till all sequences (i.e. $i = n!$) are analysed.

The above mentioned steps 1 to 10 are explained with the example component shown in Fig. 3. The first bending sequence for the component is $b1,b2,b3,b4,b5$. For performing the first bending operation ($b1$), the component is translated such that the start point of bend line $b1$ lies at the origin as shown in Fig. 4(a). Translation is done as follows:

$$[P'] = [P][T];$$

where $[P]$ is the point matrix of all vertices that form the component; $[T]$ is the translation matrix and $[P']$ is the translated point matrix.

In the next step, the component is rotated about the Z axis (using rotation matrices) by $90°$ to make the bend line lie in the XZ plane as shown in Fig. 4(b). The third step is not needed as the bend line is already lying in the X axis. Similarly the faces $f1$ and $f6$ that are connected to the bend line lies in the XY plane and hence step 4 is not needed. In step 5, the face chains connected to the bend line are determined from the face-adjacency graph as $f1,f2,f3,f4,f5$ and $f6$. In this case, the second face chain consists only of one face ($f6$). The first face chain i.e. $f1,f2,f3,f4,f5$ lies in the negative Y direction and hence these faces are rotated by θ_r in the clockwise direction about the X axis. In this case,

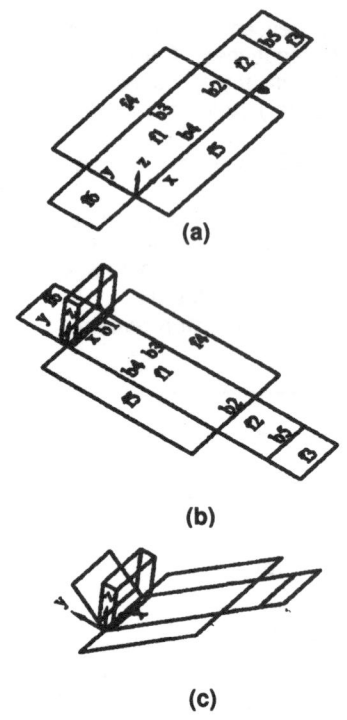

(a)

(b)

(c)

(a) **Translation to origin for the first bend,** (b) **Rotation to make the bend line parallel to XZ plane,** (c) **Rotation of the Face Chains.**
Fig. 4. Transformations done on example component

$\theta_r = 45°$. Similarly the face $f6$ is rotated by θ_r in the counter clockwise direction about the X axis as shown in Fig. 4(c). Then it is checked for any tool-part interference which is explained in the next section. In this case, there is no collision and hence the next bend $b2$ is performed. Instead if there is any collision, then all other bends in the particular sequence are discarded and the next sequence is chosen to perform the bends one by one. If there is no tool-part collision for any sequence even after completing all the bends, then that particular sequence is a feasible bending sequence for the given component. For the component shown in Fig. 3, the first eight sequences are not feasible sequences (Table 1) whereas the ninth sequence is a feasible sequence. Among 120 possible sequences, thirty sequences turned out to be feasible sequences, which are shown in Table 2.

44

Table 2. All Feasible Bending Sequences for the Component shown in Fig. 3.

Seq. No.	Bend Sequence	No. of tool changes	Seq. No.	Bend Sequence	No. of tool changes
9	1 3 4 5 2	3	78	4 1 5 3 2	4
10	2 3 4 5 2	4	86	4 3 1 5 2	2
16	1 4 3 5 2	3	89	4 3 5 1 2	2
18	1 4 5 3 2	5	90	4 3 5 2 1	2
21	1 5 3 4 2	3	91	4 5 1 3 2	4
23	1 5 4 3 2	3	95	4 5 3 2 1	4
49	3 1 4 5 2	4	96	4 5 3 1 2	4
51	3 1 5 4 2	4	98	5 1 4 3 2	3
63	3 4 5 2 1	2	101	5 1 3 4 2	3
64	3 4 5 1 2	2	109	5 3 4 1 2	3
66	3 4 1 5 2	2	110	5 3 4 2 1	3
69	3 5 4 1 2	4	111	5 3 1 4 2	5
70	3 5 4 2 1	4	115	5 4 3 2 1	3
71	3 5 1 4 2	4	116	5 4 3 1 2	3
76	4 1 3 5 2	4	118	5 4 1 3 2	5

2.3. Collision Checking

While bending, after rotating one face chain by θ_r in the clockwise direction and the other face chain by θ_r in the counter-clockwise direction, it should be checked for any tool-part collision. Collision check to be done between the tool and the sheet metal component is as follows.

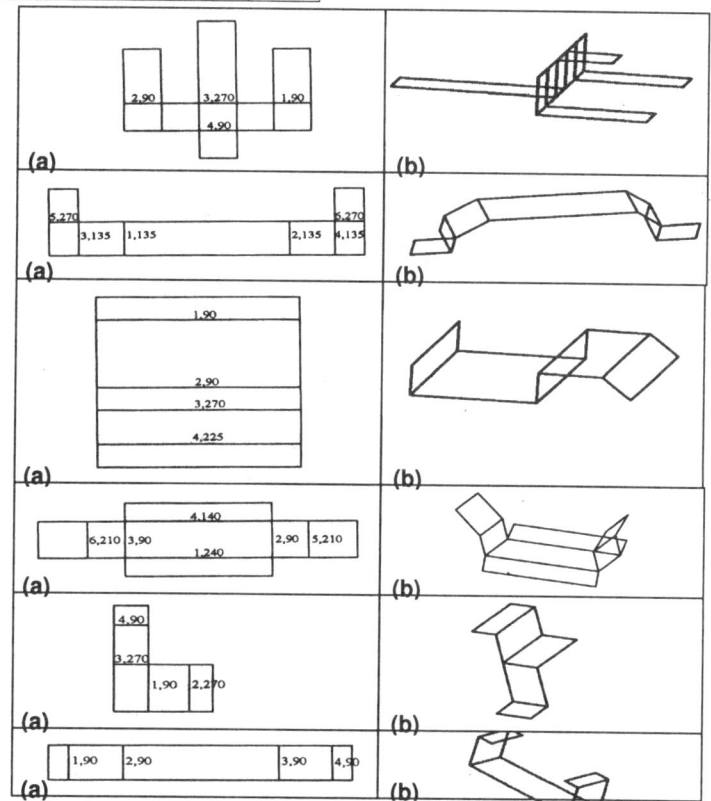

(a) Flat Pattern, (b) Final Shape after Bending.
Fig. 5. Six test components

Since the bend line is aligned with the X axis by the transformations performed before rotating the face chains, the punch and die cross-section profiles lie parallel to the YZ plane as shown in Fig. 4(c). The die profile is not shown in the figure for clarity. The component edges and the punch and die profiles are projected on to the YZ plane.

Then, it is checked whether there is any intersection between these projected component edges (other than the edges belonging to the immediate faces that are connected to the particular bend line) and the projected punch and die profile edges. If any component edge intersects with the punch and die profile edges then it is checked whether the X values of both the end points of the component edge is lesser than the lowest X value of the tool geometry or greater than the highest X value of the tool geometry. If this condition is not satisfied then it is concluded that there is tool-part collision. The tool length (along the X axis) is taken as the length of the bend line minus 2 mm [4].

2.4. Tool Change

The number of tool changes required for all feasible sequences are determined in order to find out the optimal sequence. Tool change can be found out by the fact that for a given sequence, if there is any change in bend length between consecutive bends, then it needs a tool change. The steps to be followed for finding out the number of tool changes required for a given sequence is as follows:

Step 1: Set *tool_change* = 1 and *j* = 2;

Step 2: IF *bend_length(j-1)* ≠ *bend_length(j)*

THEN set

tool_change = *tool_change* + 1;

Step 3: Set *j* = *j* + 1; and repeat step 2

till *j* = *n*;

The number of tool changes required for all feasible sequences for the part shown in Fig. 3 is shown in Table 2. After finding out the number of tool changes for all feasible sequences, the sequence with minimal number of tool changes is determined as the optimal sequence. In this case, six sequences have minimal number of tool changes (*3 4 5 2 1, 3 4 5 1 2, 3 4 1 5 2, 4 3 1 5 2, 4 3 5 1 2, 4 3 5 2 1*). Among these sequences, the first sequence (*3 4 5 2 1*) is taken as the optimal sequence.

2.5. Graphical Simulation and Bending Setup Plan

The system automatically generates an Autocad script file that can be executed in Autocad. On executing the Autocad script file, the graphical bending simulation of the optimal sequence can be viewed. Initially the flat pattern will be displayed in the Autocad screen followed by the display of repositioning of the component after completing step 4 of section 2.2. Then the component geometry after bending (rotating both the face chains) along with the tool is displayed. Similarly for all other bends, component repositioning, tool and bending

are displayed. For components having bend angles (θ) greater than *180˚*, the component has to be reoriented upside down. For example, if the bend angle between any two adjacent faces is *270˚*, then the component has to be reoriented upside down and the component is bent by only *90˚*.

The bending setup plan is generated for the optimal bending sequence. The part positioning, part reorientation and tool stacking details for each bend are derived from the bending simulation and a detailed drawing is generated. Six components taken for testing are shown in Fig. 5.

3. CONCLUSION

The developed system is tested with various sheet metal components and the system effectively generates the bending setup plan for all the components. The system reduces the setup planning time and the cost involved in setup planning. It renders a thorough analysis of all possible bending sequences for a given component to obtain an optimal sequence. As a bending sequence with minimal number of tool changes is obtained, the time for manufacturing a component is reduced, which in turn reduces the cost of manufacturing.

4. REFERENCES

1. **Ong, S.K., De Vin, L.J., Nee, A.Y.C.** and **Kals, H.J.J.** (1997), "Fuzzy set theory applied to bend sequencing for sheet metal bending", *Journal of Materials Processing Technology*, 69, 29-36.
2. **Shunmugam, M.S.** and **Kannan, T.R.** (2002), "Automatic flat pattern generation of sheet metal components from orthographic projections", *International Journal of Machine Tools and Manufacture*, 42, 1415-1425.
3. **Joshi, S.** and **Chang, T.C.** (1988), "Graph based heuristics for recognition of machined features from a 3D solid model", *Computer Aided Design*, 20(2), 58-66.
4. **Gupta, S.K., Bourne, D.A., Kim, K.H.** and **Krishnan, S.S.** (1998), "Automated process planning for sheet metal bending operations", *Journal of Manufacturing systems"*, 17(5), 338-360.

GCMM 2004
Editors: Prasad K D V Yarlagadda and S Narayanan
Copyright © 2005, Vellore Institute of Technology, Vellore, India
Publisher: Narosa Publishing House Pvt. Ltd., New Delhi, India

Capability of High Speed Milling (HSM) in CNC Machine & CAM Software

Madhusudhanan S*, Raja K** & Radhakrishnan P**

*PG Student, ** Senior Lecturer,
** Vice Chancellor, Vellore Institute of Technology, Vellore – 632 014

Email: madhu80shan@rediffmail.com

Abstract

Industries are moving towards emerging HSM technology for higher profit through higher productivity. There are many components to the successful implementation of high speed milling. High speed spindles, powerful CNC's, specifically designed cutting tools as well as finely tuned process knowledge are all important to master this specialised milling technique. Less recognised is the creation of tool path for high speed machining as it plays a major role. Nowadays many CAM software have recognised the need of this technology and incorporated HSM option. CAD/CAM software's such as CATIA and UNIGRAPHICS are considered for evaluating the HSM option in tool path creation.

The whence of chatter starts during machining a corner. The major issues such as design of the machine tool, tool path generation and process optimisation plays a major role in conjunction with chatter detection to optimise the cutting process. The engagement region of the tool is drastically increasing during machining of corners and this causes tool damage or tool wear and changes the dynamic characteristics of the total system. Novel approach has to be followed for acquiring tool paths for HSM rather than conventionally developed tool paths. This paper explains an algorithm for material removal during pocketing of four sided polygon shaped geometries by continuously monitoring the cutter engagement is developed.

CNC system should have the capability of reading the part program ahead, avoiding the error in tool motion and processing speed. The data transfer from CAM software to CNC machine is also an important consideration. These requirements are discussed in this paper.

Key Words
HSM, tool paths, tool engagement, look ahead and data transfer

1. INTRODUCTION

There are many opinions, many myths and many different ways to define high speed machining. Carl Salomon proposed the first definition of high speed machining in 1931. He

47

has assumed that at a certain cutting speed, which is 5 to 10 times higher than conventional machining, the chip tool interface temperature will start to decrease [3]. Later, McGee has disapproved the assumptions by showing that the cutting temperature of aluminium increases monotonically with an increase in the cutting speed [1]. Based on John Fish and Jay Foster [5], *High Speed Machining can be any CNC milling machine process that utilizes faster spindle rates, feed rates and better tooling technology for higher production rates than a conventional or previously developed machining process.* The ultimate aim of high speed and feed is to produce a workpiece that is accurate and precise.

HSM is relatively an emerging technology to industries. As a result of advances in machine tools and cutting tool technology, HSM became a cost-effective manufacturing process to produce parts with high precision and surface quality [6]. HSM has been widely applied to machining of aluminium alloys for manufacturing complicated parts used in the aircraft industry. Because of significant improvements, HSM has been extended for machining of various metallic workpiece materials such as cast iron, steels, titanium, bronze and brass, nickel alloys etc.,[5, 7].

Tool path planning has been traditionally approached from a geometric perspective. The majority of bulk material occurs in 2.5D operations. In this operation, tool path trajectories are generated through conventional strategies of using linear movement (G01) with non-continuous transition. Fig. 1 shows tool engagement conditions in spiral cutting from outside to inside. The tool engages for an angle of 180° in A during tool moves from one pass to the next pass, 0° in B at corner and 90° in C.

Fig. 1.1 shows tool engagement conditions in spiral cutting from inside to outside. The tool engages for an angle of 180° in D during tool moves from one pass to the next pass, 180° in E at corner and 90° in F. In both cutting the engagement of the tool is not maintained constant and it varies from 0° to 90° and 90° to 180°. Hence the machining of parts involves deceleration and acceleration of tool to stop at corners. When the dynamics and mechanics of the process and machine tool systems are considered, conventional tool path generation techniques are observed to be not ideally suitable for high speed milling which inturn causes chatter during machining.

When hard metals are cut during high speed machining the change in engagement angle causes the tool to hit at corners, which results in gouge and more importantly wear on the tool. Nowadays several softwares were giving HSM in manufacturing module. CAM softwares such as CATIA and UNIGRAPHICS are reviewed to evaluate the high speed milling capabilities. Tool path creation is considered to be important in High Speed Machining, which impacts the machining centre.

Fig. 1: Tool engagement in spiral cutting from outside to inside

2. STUDY OF HSM IN SOFTWARES

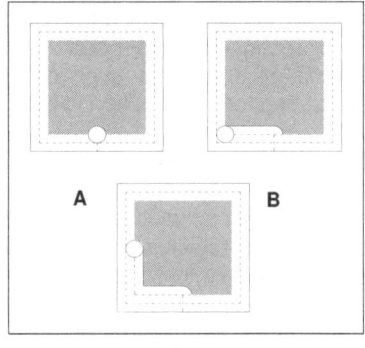

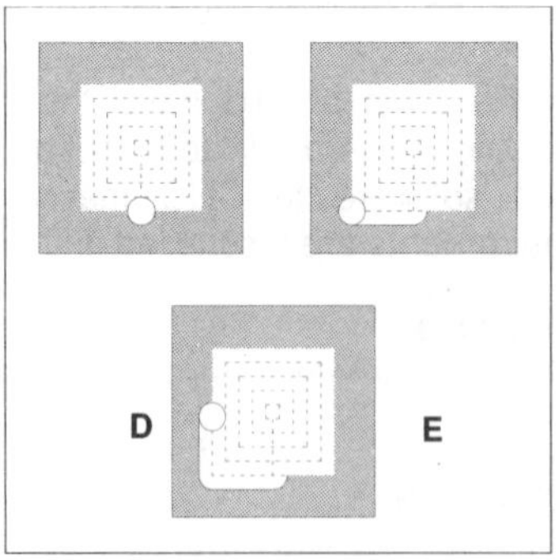

Fig. 1.1: Tool engagement in spiral cutting from outside to inside
F

CAM softwares have realised the importance of incorporating High Speed Milling (HSM) techniques inorder to meet the needs of industries for producing the parts precisely and quickly.

2.1. CASE AND ANALYSIS

A simple case with four pockets is modeled in SOLIDWORKS as in Fig. 2, and transferred to CATIA and UNIGRAPHICS and high speed milling is carried out. The cutter location paths obtained in these two softwares are shown in Fig. 2.1 and Fig. 2.2.

In case of traditional tool path, the transition between the two cutter pass in the CLPATH's are linear, where the cutter faces short stop. This is avoided by means of transition radius or fillet and angle in case of CATIA and UNIGRAPHICS. It also avoids sharp tool motions by providing radius and angle along the corner as in Fig. 2.1 & Fig.2.2. The tool is moved to next layer using helical ramping in UNIGRAPHICS as in Fig. 2.2 respectively. While in CATIA, the tool is directly plunged to the next layer for machining which results in recutting of chips as in Fig. 2.1.

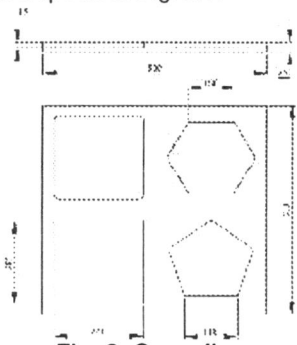

Fig. 2: Case diagram

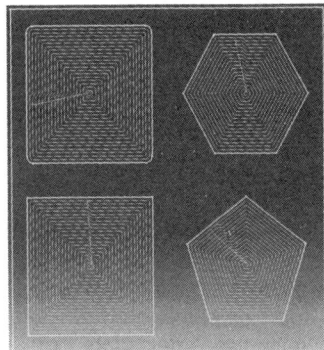

Fig. 2.1: CLPATH from CATIA

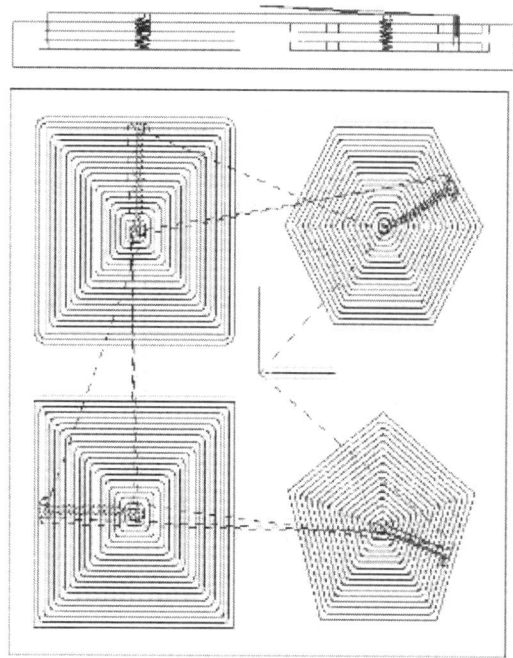

Fig. 2.2: CLPATH from UNIGRAPHICS

Apart from the CLDATA or part program developed from the two CAM software's, the CNC machines should process the tool to move fast and interpolate the intermediate points. The cutter paths are fed to CNC and load it into buffer for execution. Each block is interpolated, broken into pieces for different axis of the machine. These programmed motions are broken into smaller segments for interpolation. There are three crucial issues used in the CNC. They are block transfer time, interpolation time and servo cycle time.

2.2. Data flow to CNC

Block transfer time is the time that CNC is capable of absorbing block of program information. The ability to absorb program information quickly is very important for making the HSM to run smoothly. DNC stands for Direct Numerical Control (DNC), which distributes the cutter path data to CNC machine. It is the most common communications in use for CNC's today. It feed and transfers the block at 960 characters per second into CNC.

Considering a block from the part program obtained from CIMATRON as in Fig. 2.3 which has 20 characters or more including line numbers, feed rates, spaces, decimals, end of block etc. Hence the DNC can transfer about 48 program blocks per second only. CNC machine incorporating HSM option requires much faster input inorder to move the tool fast.

```
N216 G1 Z40.1
N217 X125. Y282. Z40.059
```

Fig. 2.3: Sample part program from CIMATRON

Direct CNC networking or DCN offers a much better solution to the data flow problems in high speed milling. Ethernet is the most common network architecture in use today. Ethernet has transferring capability of 1 million characters per second (10 megabits per second) can be the best throughput option for CNC. Hence the Direct CNC Networking eliminates data bottlenecks using DNC and space occupation using DNC.

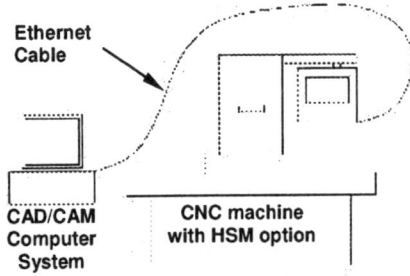

Fig. 2.4 Direct CNC Network (DNC)

2.3. Inference

Part program or cutter location data obtained from CAM software alone is not sufficient for incorporating HSM. The efficient HSM should eliminate the abrupt change of direction in tool path and increase the number of blocks throughput to CNC per time.

Considering tool path developed by CIMATRON and UNIGRAPHICS uses loops at corners and trochoidal loops along the paths.

CNC machine should have the capability to change the motor direction continuously. Ultimately, the tool path developed from the softwares suffers to gouging and overshoots on the tool path. The issue of engagement angle of the tool and its importance are not taken into consideration in these softwares.

3. METHODOLOGY ADOPTED

The strategies needed for successful incorporation of HSM tool paths are
a. Tool paths should be free from gouge
b. Smooth creation of tool path
c. Climb milling is favourable than conventional milling because of better quality, less noise, less vibration and higher tool life [4, 2].
d. When entering the material, feeding in at full depth and full feed rate can strain the tool and shorten the tool life. Ramping is the best way to approach the workpiece or part.

3.1. Role of engagement angle

The engagement angle is one of the important strategies, which represents the region contact between the tool and workpiece material. The source of chatter starts during machining a corner [8]. As in Fig. 3.1 engagement region of the tool is drastically increasing between B and C, which causes tool damage or tool, wear. Hence there are changes in dynamic characteristics of the total system.

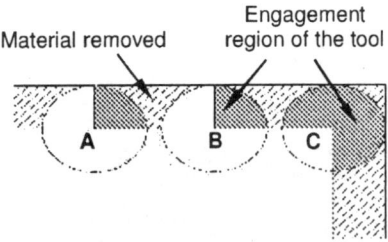

Fig. 3.1: Engagement of the tool

3.2. Spline based approach

The author adopted the approach of spiral cutting tool path as a starting point for developing the algorithm. The intent is to optimise the trajectory tool path segments so as to minimise deviation of the tool engagement angle along the path. The methodology adopted for generating the tool path is outlined below.

a. Continuous B- Spline curve is used to represent the tool path
b. Set of control points, which is obtained from the polygon vertices will uniquely determine the tool trajectory.
c. Engagement angle (θ) of the tool along the tool path is determined and variation along the tool path results from the effect of moving the control points accordingly and maintaining the consistent tool engagement angle.

3.2.1. Constant tool engagement

The tool paths required for HSM, should have constant engagement angle during machining by spiral cutting from outside to inside and inside to outside. In this approach, angle θ is kept constant. Fig. 3.2 shows a constant engagement angle during machining a corner with O as the centre point of the cutter. P and Q represent the intersection of the tool circumference with the previous and newly generated tool path respectively and OQ as the radius of the tool.

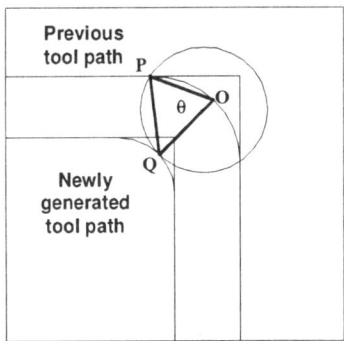

Fig. 3.2: Constant engagement angle during the corners

From the triangle OPQ,

$$ = [\quad [- \quad]] \quad --1.0 $$

4. SIMULATION MODULE

Simulation module for pocketing in High Speed Milling is developed by incorporating cutting tool database for the selection of cutting tools and machinability data and tool path generation for the pocket maintaining tool engagement angle constant throughout the path.

4.1. Cutting tool database

There are various methods for selection of cutting tool and machinability data. Sample rule adopted for selection criteria of cutting tool, speed and feed are shown in Table 4. The workpiece materials such as Low-C & free machining steels, alloy steels, cast iron, stainless steel, high temperature alloys, titanium alloys, aluminium alloys and copper alloys, appropriate cutting tool materials, feed and cutting speed are included in the database and is developed using "Turbo C".

Table 4: Sample rule for selection of cutting tool and machinability data

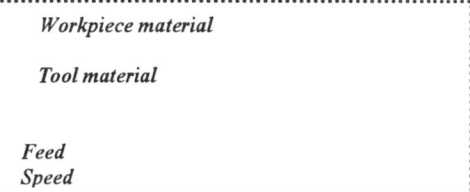

Workpiece material

Tool material

Feed
Speed

4.2. Pocketing module

Pocketing module is developed for a four sided polygon, which is constructed, by combination of horizontal and vertical lines (e.g. square & rectangle). This is further extended for 'n' sided polygon. The tool path is generated using offsetting method of
the part that maintains an ideally steady state-process by explicitly controlling the engagement angle of the cutting tool.

The procedures involved in the simulation of pocketing are
a. User inputs size of stock & part & the machining parameters such as step over distance & tool diameter.
b. User selects the cutting type (spiral outside to in or spiral inside to out).
c. The position vector along the tool path is calculated with polygon vertices as input for the B-Spline tool path creation & engagement angle is maintained constant throughout the tool path

d. The tool moves to the next layer by helical ramping and steps 4 & 5 are repeated until the required depth is reached.

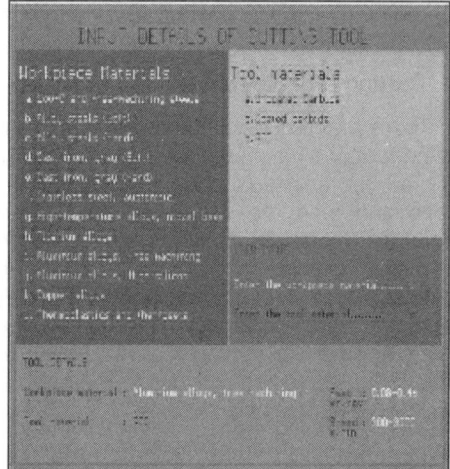

Fig. 4.1: Input screen of cutting tool database

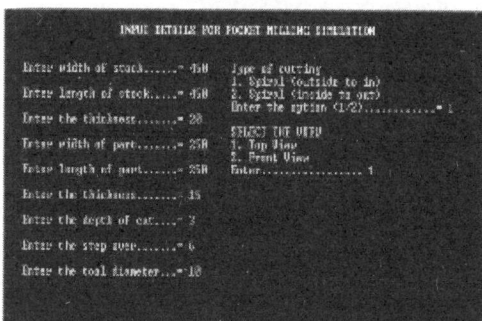

Fig. 4.2: Input Details for pocket milling

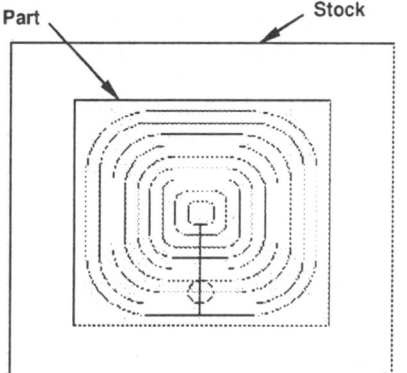

Fig. 4.3: HSM tool paths for spiral cutting (inside to outside) in front view

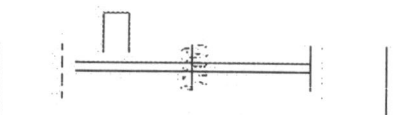

Fig. 4.4: HSM tool paths for spiral cutting (inside to outside) in front view

5. RESULTS & CONCLUSION

Fig. 4.3 reveals that the tool path generated for spiral cutting from inside to outside is smoother than conventionally developed tool path. The engagement angle obtained is maintained constant throughout the tool path by using the spline based approach as in Fig. 4.3. Fig. 5. reveals that there is a sudden rise in engagement angle from 90° to 180° along the transition between two tool paths. Hence it causes the tool to decelerate and accelerate between the transition path, which ultimately affects the tool leading to damage and wear. This sudden deviation of angle can be totally avoided by altering the tool path.

The tool path is modified by altering the polygon vertices in spline based approach as in Fig. 5.1. In spiralling from inside to outside the tool starts milling from periphery of the pocket and reaches the centre of the pocket thus avoiding unnecessary stepping between two cutter paths. The engagement angle along the tool path in spiralling from inside to outside is shown in Fig. 5.2 and varies between 1% and 2% from the required engagement angle. Hence the dwelling of the tool along the transition path is totally neglected using this novel approach. There are some unmachined portions along the corners, which are machined using smaller end mill tool further.

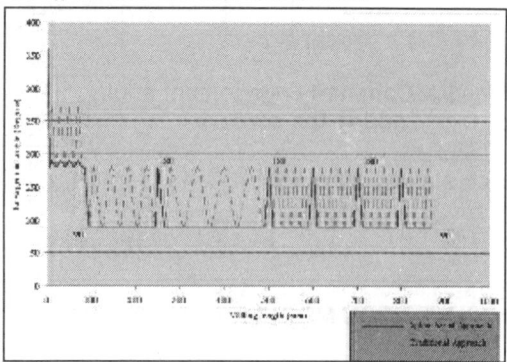

Fig. 5: Engagement angle in spiral cutting from inside to outside using spline based approach

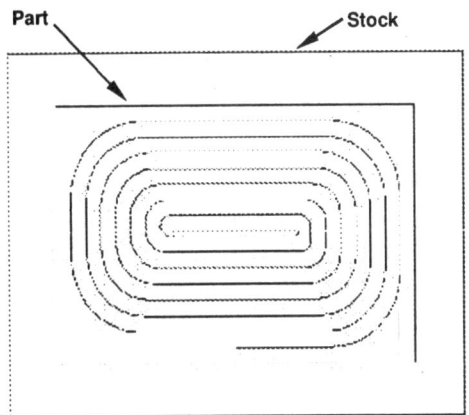

Fig. 5.1: Modified spline based approach for tool path generation using spiral cutting (inside to outside)

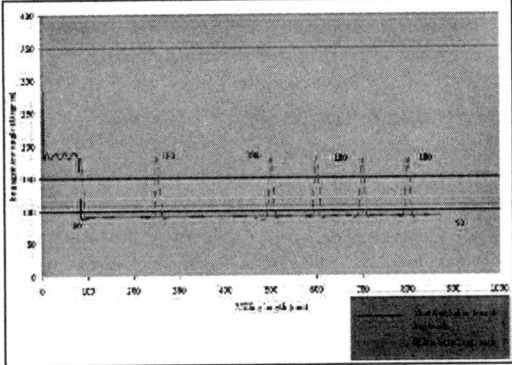

Fig. 5.2: Engagement angle in spiral cutting from inside to outside using modified spline based approach

6. REFERENCES

1. **Herbert Schulz, Toshimichi Moriwaki**. (1992). "High-speed machining", *CIRP Annals*, 41,2, pp 637-644.
2. **Manuel Monreal and Ciro A. Rodriguez.** (2003), "Influence of tool path strategy on the cycle time on high-speed milling", Computer-Aided Design, 35, pp 395-401.
3. **Przybylski Pasko, R. and Slodki, B.,** "High speed machining (HSM) – The effective way of modern cutting", *International Workshop on CA systems and Technologies*, pp 72-79.
4. **Dan Marinacm,** "Tool path strategies for high speed machining", http://www.mmsonline.com/articles/020004.html
5. **John Fish, Jay Foster, Duane Hilmar, Zachariah Horan and John Wabrek,** "High speed machining", http://aml2.eng.rpi.edu/GMPWeb/Sprojects Pwrpt/Fall2002/HighSpeedMachiningPrese ntation-Final2.ppt
6. **Sandvik tools** (Company article), "High Speed Machining and conventional die and mould machining". http://www.coromant.sandvik.com/Coroma nt/products/die&mould/new-pdf/HSM.pdf
7. **Taylon Altan, Peter Fallbohmer, Ciro A. Rodriguez and Tugrul Ozel,** "High-speed cutting of cast iron and alloy steels – state of research", http://www.rei.rutgers.edu/~ozel/pdf/cirp-vdi-98.pdf
8. **Urmaze Naterwalla,** *"Chatter-free milling and optimized material removal rates"*, http://www.mmsonline.com/articles.html

GCMM 2004
Editors: Prasad K D V Yarlagadda and S Narayanan
Copyright © 2005, Vellore Institute of Technology, Vellore, India
Publisher: Narosa Publishing House Pvt. Ltd., New Delhi, India

Comparison of Machining Characteristics of Titanium Alloys:

Effect of Slurry in Ultrasonic Machining Process

Rupinder Singh[*], Jaimal Singh Khamba[**]

*Mechanical and Production Engineering Dept. G.N.D.E.C, Ludhiana ,
**Mechanical Engineering Dept. T.I.E.T, Patiala

Email: rupindersingh78@yahoo.com

Abstract

In manufacturing process, finish machining of precision components constitutes one of the challenging tasks. Ultrasonic Machining Process (USM) is a non conventional machining process, which is capable of providing excellent surface finish and material removal rate on hard and brittle material. For tough materials like Titanium not much work hitherto been reported. This paper reports the results of an experimental study conducted on two Titanium alloys of different composition (i.e. with different toughness), when machined on USM with an objective to understand their machining characteristics with special reference to the effect of slurry. Machining properties of Titanium (TITAN15, TITAN31) ASTM Gr2 and ASTM Gr5 have been studied using 500W Sonic Mill Ultrasonic Drilling Machine with Boron Carbide, Silicon Carbide and Alumina Slurry at different power ratings, with fixed slurry concentrations.

Keywords
USM, Titanium, Slurry

1. INTRODUCTION

Titanium alloys are generally regarded as been amongst the most difficult of work piece materials to machine in-spite of their relatively low hardness (e.g. Ti 6/4 annealed ~350HV). Titanium and its alloys are very popular and are very widely used in aerospace, marine gas turbine engines and surgical applications. These alloys are branded as difficult to machine materials but have high utility in manufacturing sector [1]. Poor thermal conductivity of Titanium alloys retard the dissipation of heat generated, creating, instead a very high temperature at the tool work-piece interface and adversely affecting the tool life [2]. Titanium is chemically reactive at elevated temperature and therefore the tool material either rapidly dissolves or chemically reacts during the machining process resulting in chipping and pre mature tool failure [1]. Compounding of these characteristics is the low elastic modulus of Titanium, which permits greater deflection of the work piece and once again adds to the complexity of machining these alloys [3]. The conventional machining processes are unable to provide good machining characteristics on Titanium alloys. Commercially these alloys are machined by non-conventional Electric Discharge Machining, which is giving good material removal rate however accuracy and surface finish are some problematic area. Another non conventional machining process i.e. Ultrasonic Machining (USM) is widely used now a days for both conductive and non metallic materials; preferably those with low ductility [4-6] and

54

hardness above 40 HRC [1, 2, 7-9], e.g. Inorganic glasses, silicon nitride etc. [4-6, 10-13]. In this process tool is made of tough material, oscillated at frequencies of the order of 20-30 Kc/s with amplitude of about 0.02mm. An abrasive filled fluid flushed through the gap between master and work piece. The material removal mechanism involves both erosion and grinding [5]. The principle of stationary USM is clear from fig. 1.1.

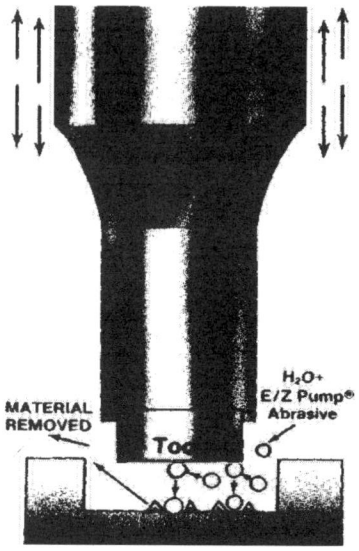

Fig. 1.1

The tiny abrasive chip off microscopic flakes and grinds a counter part of face. The work material is not stressed, distorted or heated because the grinding force is seldom over 2-lbs [11]. There is never any tool to work contact, and presence of cool slurry makes this a cold cutting process. The tool used for machining is prepared by Silver brazing process [14]. The amplitude of vibrations given to the tool also influences the cutting rate [12]. It has been found that the material removal rate is affected by amplitude of oscillations, size of abrasive [15]. There are number of applications of USM, ranging from the fabrication of small holes in alumina substrates, to engraving glass ware, to drilling large holes through laser blocks [11]. The fig. 1.2 shows the basic elements of USM set up using either a magnetostrictive or piezoelectric transducer with brazed and screwed tooling. It has been reported that ultrasonic assisted cutting can increase tool life by reducing both crater and flank wear [1,2,7,8,16]. In Ultrasonic assisted cutting the chip, and work face are periodically separated leading to lower

temperature/ forces there by increasing tool life. It has been observed in experimentation using Alumina as slurry and TITAN 15 as work material; material removal rate decreases from 150-300 Watt and increases further at 450 Watt of USM [6]. This experimentation set up can be used for commercial use of conventional tool material for machining titanium on USM. The profiles of tool used for machining with their preparation process are shown in fig 1.3.

From this discussion we came to conclusion that some practical work has been evidenced for machining brittle material using USM; for tough materials, very little effort has been put in to explore the USM capacity [17]. In the present experimental set up the typical value of amplitude and frequency of vibration used are 0.0254-0.0508 mm and 20Khz+/-200 Hz.

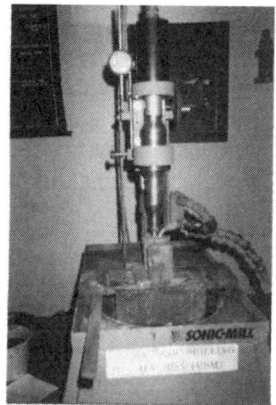

Fig. 1.2

The results of this experimental study conducted with the objective to understand material removal rate and tool wear comparison of TITAN 15 and TITAN31 of different composition, different toughness are reported; when processed by USM.

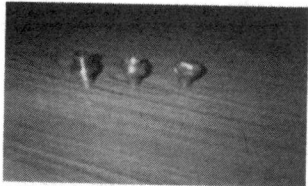

Fig. 1.3

The typical composition of titanium alloys (TITAN 15, TITAN3 I) to be used is listed in table 2.a and 2.b.

TITAN 15 {UTS 491 MPa} ASTM Gr 2
Chemical Analysis (%)
Table-2a

C	H	N	O	Fe	Ti
0.006	0.0007	0.014	0.140	0.05	Bal

TITAN 31 {UTS 994 MPa} ASTM Gr 5
Chemical Analysis (%)
Table-2b

C	H	N	O	Al	V	Fe	Ti
0.019	0.0011	0.007	0.138	6.27	4.04	0.05	Bal

-2b

From composition it is clear that TITAN31 is soft because of Al presence. The machining was performed on 500 Watt Sonic-Mill Ultrasonic Drilling Machine at three different power rating value [i.e. at 150W, 300Wand 450W]. High Speed Steel (H.S.S.) a conventional tool material has been used in combinations with three slurries of 320 Grit size namely silicon carbide, boron carbide and alumina at fix slurry concentration and temperature. The slurry concentration was fixed at 15% by volume and slurry temperature at 25.7 °C.

2.0 EXPERIMENTATION

The experiments were conducted in three setups. In the first setup, experiment was undertaken to determine the effect on TITAN 15 of H.S.S tool using silicon carbide slurry of 320 grit size with 15% concentration in distilled water as suspension media. The experiment started by setting power rating of the machine at 30% i.e. 150 Watt of ultrasonic drilling machine. The initial weight of Titanium work piece that is of TITAN 15 and tool that is of H.S.S was measured. Then machine was allowed to drill for fixed depth of one (1) mm with constant slurry flow rate and slurry temperature. The depth was closely watched using dial gauge. Correspondingly, time taken by USM for drilling was measured using stopwatch. The tool used was solid cylindrical cross section. After machining is complete again job (work piece) and tool weight is measured for finding difference in weight loss. Corresponding material removal rate (MRR) and tool wear rate are (TWR) calculated at 300 W, and 450 W, (i.e. at 60% and 90% of 500W). After this TITAN31 work piece was observed with H.S.S. tool using

same silicon carbide slurry of 320 grit size with 15% concentration in distilled water as suspension media. The experiment was performed on 500 W USM at 30%, 60%, and 90% rating. Corresponding MRR and TWR are calculated and tabulated. The same process is repeated in second and third set up with boron carbide and alumina slurry respectively. Corresponding MRR and TWR are calculated and tabulated.

3.0 RESULTS AND DISCUSSION

From repetitive number of experiments conducted under three different setups, the comparative results are plotted. From fig. 3.1 we can see that MRR of TITAN31 is higher than TITAN15 at 150 W, whereas TITAN15 has higher MRR at 300 W, then again at 450 W, TITAN31 MRR is higher. The increase of MRR with increase in power rating of machine is quite obvious because of higher value of power rating abrasive particles strikes with more momentum and kinetic energy with work piece. Hence more erosion of work piece but in certain cases, with increase in power rating, MRR decreases which may be because of strain hardening of work piece.

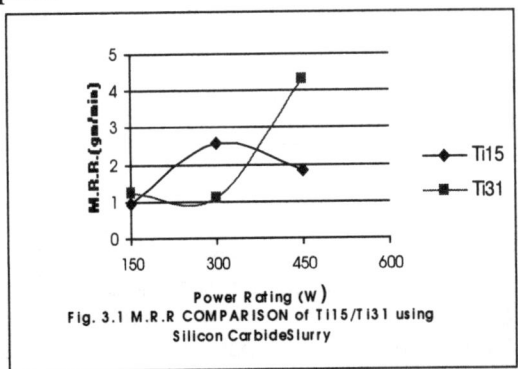

Fig. 3.1 M.R.R COMPARISON of Ti15/Ti31 using Silicon CarbideSlurry

From fig. 3.2 we can see TITAN31 has higher TWR at 150 W and 300 W but TITAN 15 has higher TWR at 450 W. But overall surface roughness of TITAN31 is more (refer fig. 2.7). From the outcome of this setup, TITAN 15 comes out to be better material than TITAN31 when processed by H.S.S tool up to 300W of Ultrasonic Power used; but there are certain power rating values in this combination itself where TITAN31 is proving better MRR and less TWR (like at 450 W better MRR and less TWR). The increase of tool wear rate with increase in MRR and power rating is quite obvious but sometimes TWR decreases with power rating increase/increase in MRR; the reason for this is again strain hardening of tool surface.

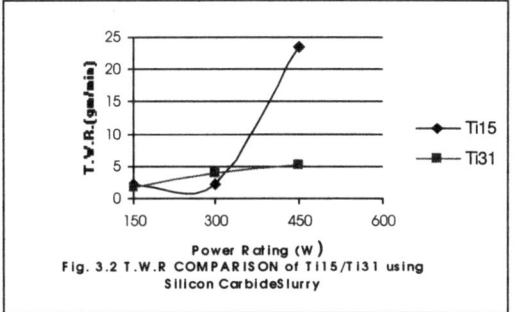

Fig. 3.2 T.W.R COMPARISON of Ti15/Ti31 using Silicon CarbideSlurry

From fig. 3.3 we can see that while using Boron Carbide MRR of TITAN31 is over all less than TITAN15 at 150,300 and 450W of Ultrasonic Power. The trend for variation is similar in both material cases. After 300W of Ultrasonic Power, MRR decreases which may be because of strain hardening of work piece.

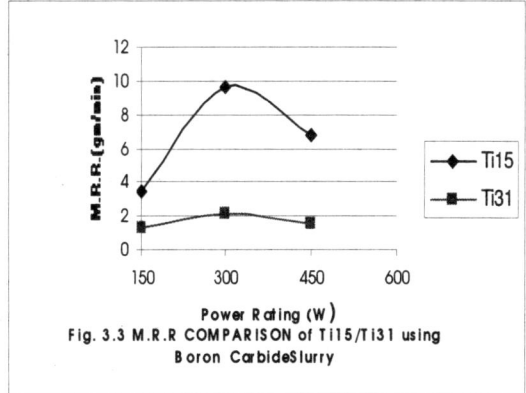

Fig. 3.3 M.R.R COMPARISON of Ti15/Ti31 using Boron CarbideSlurry

From fig. 3.4 we can see TITAN31 has higher TWR 450W and other segments of observation are similar. From the outcome of this setup, TITAN 15 comes out to be better material than TITAN31 when processed by H.S.S tool up to 300W of Ultrasonic Power used; but at 450 W less TWR makes a point for use of high Ultrasonic Power for machining Ti31. The variation in the results of observation points out that there is a strong need to use specific Ultrasonic Power rating value for specific material for specific slurry type choosen.

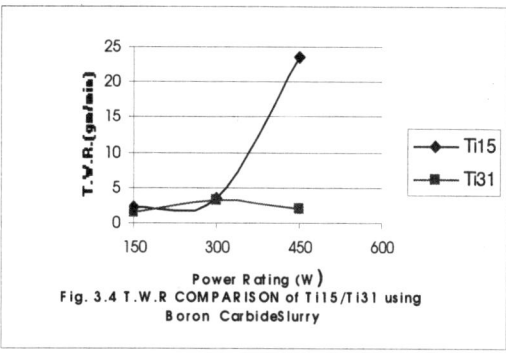

Fig. 3.4 T.W.R COMPARISON of Ti15/Ti31 using Boron CarbideSlurry

From fig. 3.5 we can see that while using Alumina MRR of TITAN31 is over all less than TITAN15 at 150,300 and 450W of Ultrasonic Power. The trend for variation is similar in both material cases and also like obtained while using Boron Carbide slurry .

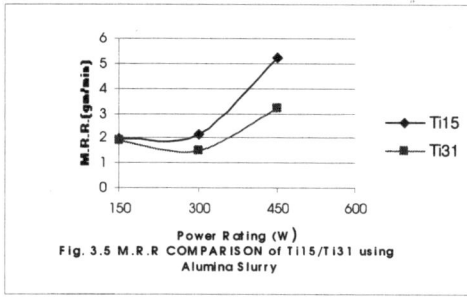

Fig. 3.5 M.R.R COMPARISON of Ti15/Ti31 using Alumina Slurry

From fig. 3.6 we can see that while using Alumina Slurry T.W.R of TITAN31 is over all more than TITAN15 at 150,300 and 450W of Ultrasonic Power. The trend for variation is similar in both material cases. Here we can say Titan15 should be machined by using alumina slurry only as it has not shown any significant nodel point for good M.R.R and T.W.R results for Ti31.

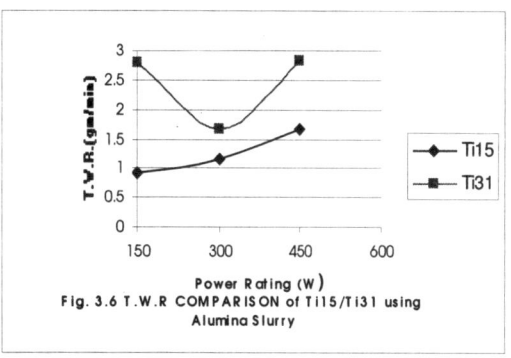

Fig. 3.6 T.W.R COMPARISON of Ti15/Ti31 using Alumina Slurry

4. CONCLUSIONS

1. From the experiment following conclusions were drawn:
2. It is possible to ultrasonically drill holes in TITAN15 and TITAN31 [ASTM Grade 2 and ASTM Grade.5] without causing excessive surface integrity damage, specifically cracking using ultrasonic assisted drilling .Higher surface finish is attained when machining on titanium alloy is undertaken by USM.
3. It is not always necessary that if work piece with higher toughness value is machined, it will have less MRR rather it is combination effect of material composition (hardness of work piece) relative of tool and work piece in other words selection of operating parameter levels is critical in order to achieve acceptable productivity.
4. No major fatigue problems were encountered with the carbide, titanium and high speed steel tools, any chipping/ fracture generally being due to tool/ hole misalignment during packing.
5. Ultrasonic drilling caused little or no deformation of the work piece microstructure.

5. REFERENCES

1. **Verma S V, NandaGopal, Srinivasulu K and Sudhakar Reddy S** (2003), " Effect of Pre- Drilled holes on Tool life in Turning of Aerospace Titanium Alloys", *Proceedings of National Conference on Advances in Manufacturing System. AMS-03*. Prod. Engg. Dept. Jadavpur University. Kolkata (INDIA), pp 42-47.
2. **Dornfeld D A, Kim, Dechow H, Hewsow J and Chen L J** (1999)," Drilling burr formation in Titanium alloy Ti-6Al-4V", *Annals of CIRP*. Vol. 48/1, pp 73-76.
3. Tool and Manufacturing Engineers hand- book Materials (1985), SME Vol.3.
4. **Koval Chenko, M.S., Paustovskii, A.V. and Perevyazko, V. A.** (1986), "Influence of properties of abrasive materials on the effectiveness of Ultrasonic Machining of Ceramics", *Sov. Powder Metallurgy and Metal Cer.* 25(7), pp. 560-562.
5. **Kremer D. and Mackie J.** (1988), "Ultrasonic Machining applied to ceramic materials", *Industrie Ceramique,* No. 830, pp.632-637.
6. **Moreland, M.A.** (1988), "Versatile performance of Ultrasonic Machining", *Cer. Bull.* 67(6), pp 1045- 1047.
7. **Drozda T.J and Wick C.**(1983)," Non traditional machining- Book Chapter 29",Tool and Manufacturing engineers hand book (Desk Ed.) Soc. Manuf. Engrs. Dearborn. MI, pp 1-23.
8. **Ezugwa E O and Wang Z M** (1997), "Titanium alloys and their machinability - A review", *Journal of Material processing technology*. Vol. 68, pp. 262-274.
9. **Gilmore R.** (1990), "Ultrasonic Machining of Ceramics", SME Paper MS 90-346. 12pp.
10. **Gilmore R.** (1991), "Ultrasonic machining: A Case Study", Proc. *of 7th Int Conf. on Computer Aided Prod. Engg.* pp. 139-148.
11. Instruction manual for stationary SONIC- MILL 500 W Model 2002 (U.S.A).
12. **Khamba J.S and Singh Rupinder** (2003), "Effect of Alumina (White fused) Slurry in Ultrasonic Assisted Drilling of Titanium Alloys (TITAN 15)", *Proceedings off National Conference on Materials and Related Technologies* (NCMRT-2003) at TIET Patiala (Pb.) INDIA. pp 75-79.
13. **Pentland, E.W. and Ektermanis, J.A.** (1965), "Improving Ultrasonic machining rates- some feasibility studies", *J. Engg. for Ind. Trans. of the ASME, 87 {Series B),* pp. 39-46.
14. **Singh Rupinder and Khamba J.S**. (2003), "Silver brazing for tool preparation in USM process", *Proc. of National Workshop of Welding Technology in India- Present status and future trends*, SLIET Longowal (Pb.) INDIA. pp.61-63.
15. **Singh Rupinder** (2002), "Ultrasonic machining for tough materials and its application in mechanical industry", *Proc. of fourth national symposium of research scholars on metal and materials* at IIT Madras. Chennai (INDIA), pp.31.
16 **Mantle A L and Aspinwall D K** (1995),Single point turning of titanium aluminide intermetallic", *Titanium 95- Proceedings of the eight world conference on Titanium*. Vol.1, pp 248-255.
17 . **Singh Rupinder and Khamba J.S.** (2003), "A Frame work for modeling the machining characteristics of titanium alloys using USM", *Proc. of Int. Conf. Digital aided modeling and simulation at CIT,* Coimbatore (INDIA), pp.31.

GCMM 2004
Editors: Prasad K D V Yarlagadda and S Narayanan
Copyright © 2005, Vellore Institute of Technology, Vellore, India
Publisher: Narosa Publishing House Pvt. Ltd., New Delhi, India

Cutting of 1.2 mm Mild Steel Using Nd:YAG Laser and 6 Axes Robot

K. Abdel Ghany, A. El-Batahgy and M. Newishy

Central Metallurgical Research and Development Institute (CMRDI), Egypt

Email: kghany@cmrdi.sci.eg

Abstract
In the recent years, laser cutting of metals has become a widely spread technology. Because the targeted optimum cutting quality is governed by different process parameters such as laser power, cutting speed, focus position, assistant gas pressure etc., research works tried to state correlations between process parameters and the resulted quality. This work discusses using Nd:YAG laser system connected via optical fiber to a cutting head mounted on a 6 axes robot to cut 1.2 mild steel sheets. The effect of different process parameters were investigated in addition to the effect of using robot. Results showed that optimum cutting quality of 1.2 mild steel was achieved at speed between 4 - 6 m/min, power between 440 – 1320 watt and oxygen pressure of 3 bars. High cutting speed provided low surface roughness, small kerf width, and small HAZ. Using robot showed noticeable instability especially at speed more than 3 m/min and prevents achieving good cutting of curved shapes under high speed conditions.

Key Words
Laser, Cutting Parameters, Quality, Mild_steel, Nd:YAG, Robot,

1. INTRODUCTION
1.1 General Information

Laser cutting of metals has become a commonly reliable technology and has gained increasing influence on the industrial production. Now, it is being considered as a feasible alternative to mechanical blanking due to its flexibility and ability to process variable quantities of sheet metal parts in very short time with no special die or fixture requirements, no tool wear because of the non-contact operation, high programmability, and total absence of mechanical force that can damage the work piece. Laser cutting is classified as a typical thermal process that has special advantages over other known thermal processes due to the high quality and very smooth cut surface, narrow kerf width, small heat affected zone (HAZ), small metal deformation, perpendicular and sharp cut sides, square corners of cut edges, little or no oxide layer.

Almost all materials can be cut by laser.

However, material properties such as absorption to electromagnetic wave length, thermal and electrical conductivity, melting temperature and surface condition govern the selection of laser and optics system [1]. Very thin Sheet metals and other non metals such as wood and polymers can be cut only by laser energy, where the focused laser beam elevates the material temperature up to the melting and evaporation temperature then the vapor is removed by the assistant gas. This is called "sublimation laser cutting". For thicker sheet metals, "laser fusion cutting" is dominating where metals are only melted and the molten materials are removed by the assistant gas jet. If the applied laser energy, cutting speed, focus position and assistant gas pressure are not controlled properly, incomplete melting occurs or traces of molten metal re-solidify over the cut sides forming undesired dross. For thick metal plates – specially mild steel – or high speed laser cutting the phenomena of "exothermic laser cutting" acts where the assistant oxygen gas

(i) adds additional exothermal energy to the cutting laser energy by its reaction with the material when heated by laser to the ignition temperature and (ii) generates a low viscosity, low surface tension molten metal particles which does not adhere to the parent metal and can be removed easily from the cut zone [1,2].

Oxidation of iron releases a certain degree of heat (100~150 J/molecular weight x degree) that is added to the focused energy of laser beam. As an average, the amount of energy supplied by the burning reaction is about 60% for mild and stainless steels and up to 90% for reactive metals such as titanium. The ignition temperature of pure iron is 1200°C and under exothermic cutting the oxygen forms iron oxide particles that have low melting point of about 1380°C comparing with that of 1530°C for pure iron. Also, iron oxide has high absorption coefficient up to 90% compared to only 8% of the pure iron. Both data makes the exothermic cutting of mild steel is easier and more efficient [3]. Powell et al. [4] examined the particles ejected during laser cutting and showed that the particles have size range from 50 ?m to 500?m and they are mainly spheres of iron surrounded by a shell of iron oxide or sphere of iron and iron oxide containing a suspension of iron and iron oxide and surrounded by a shell of iron oxide.

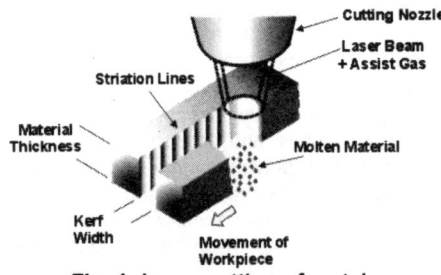

Fig. 1: Laser cutting of metals

Laser - Oxygen cutting of mild steel is accompanied by the formation of striation lines on the cut surface (Fig. 1). Miyamoto and Maruo [5] had firstly explained these striation lines by the model of ignition – extinction cycle. Later, Ivarson et al. [6] explained that the formation mechanism of striations is not due to one of the following: (i) re-solidification process; (ii) gas dynamics; (iii) melt boiling; (iv) optical effects; (v) time based fluctuations of power input, etc. They explained that the most likely sources of

formation mechanism are: (i) a cyclic variation in the driving force of the oxidation reaction, the variation being brought about by changes in the oxygen partial pressure in the cut zone melt; and (ii) viscosity and surface tension effects associated with melt removal [6]. The curvatures of the striation lines match the curvature of the laser beam cut front and so the inclination occurs when the energy flux velocity equal to the cutting rate. A surface roughness in the range of 10-20?m is usually obtained for thin sheets which increase dramatically in thick plates [7].

An optimized laser beam should have a parallel isotherm with deepest penetration and smallest cutting kerf. As shown in Fig. 1, the laser beam and the supplied gas melt and eject a cylindrical portion of the material through the cutting path. The highest melt surface temperature occurs in the bottom and the center of the kerf. The cutting speed plays the essential rule for determining the cutting quality. At low speed, more energy density is supplied to each $1mm^2$ of the material and more oxygen is supplied for reaction which leads to excessive melting and wide kerf width and much attached dross, also striation lines with large curvature appear at the cutting sides. Oppositely, laser cutting at high speed shortens the time for melting and reaction and heat diffusion to side ways. This reduces the HAZ and kerf width. However, very high speed leads to insufficient energy and incomplete melting and gouge cutting. There is an optimum range of cutting speeds for every material, thickness and laser configuration, below this range, the reaction front proceeds faster than the laser beam front leading to an oscillation in the cutting process and very rough surface because of the domination of self burning. In the optimum speed range, a thermal power balance is maintained between the exothermic burning and laser resulting in a parallel sided kerf and relatively. smooth surface. Behind this range, the thermal balance is not maintained and the cutting process becomes unstable [8].

Solid state lasers, specially Nd:YAG lasers, in comparison to the CO_2 lasers, have the advantages of less floor space, simple maintenance requirements, easy beam alignment, sharing, and delivery via optical fibers and smaller wave length (1.06 μm) that can cut materials having greater reflectivity to

CO_2 lasers. Moreover, using optical fibers to deliver Nd:YAG laser beam allows the using of robotic arms that can deliver laser beam through complicated and curved 3D paths, for example automobile and aircrafts bodies. Even so, using CNC movable heads and tables provides more cutting stability and accuracy comparing to robotic arms because of the effect of robot dynamic accuracy and the vibration induced during motion especially when high gas pressure is supplied [2].

Cutting quality is governed by many parameters; some of them are related to the laser system such as (1) maximum laser power and (2) wave length and (3) emerging beam waist diameter. Others are related to the transmitting optics such as (4) focused beam diameter (5) fiber diameter, (6) focal length of the focusing lens and the (7) amount of power loss in the delivery optics. The remaining are related to the operation such as the (8) cutting speed (m/min), (9) focus position related to the upper material surface, (10) nozzle tip diameter, (11) distance between the tip and the material (stand-off distance), (12) assistant gas type and (13) assistant gas pressure. (1) to (7) are system specifications that determine the type and thickness of material to be cut by that system and are not considered as operation parameters. (8) to (13) are the variable operation parameters that should be optimized in order to get the desired laser quality.

Hamoudi [7] showed a linear relationship between striation frequency and cutting speed and Kaebernick et al. [8] showed a linear correlation between striation frequency and increasing surface roughness of the cut surface. Increasing the assist gas pressure was shown to increase the cutting speed but to impair the surface roughness. HAZ and kerf width were found to decrease with increasing cutting speed and decreasing gas pressure. Rajaram et al. [9] showed that power had a major effect on the kerf width and HAZ while cutting speed played a minor role. Also, they showed that the cutting speed has a major effect on surface roughness and striation frequency and that power has a small effect on surface roughness and no effect on striation frequency.

As the technology of Nd:YAG laser beam deliverable via optical fiber and robot has been implemented since only few years, not many published works have discussed the optimization of the cutting quality of metals using this technology. This work presents experimental results for the effect of different operation parameters on the cutting quality of 1.2 mm mild steel and discusses the effect of cutting using 6 axes robot. 1.2 mm mild steel was selected as it is much applicable to the automobile industries and house appliances, where this laser technology is mostly used.

The objective of this work is to study the effect of the (1) Focus position relative to the material surface, (2) laser power and energy density, (3) cutting speed and (4) pressure and flow rate of the oxygen gas used as an assistant gas, on the quality of cutting by Nd:YAG laser.

2. EXPERIMENTAL WORK
2.1 Apparatus

For this experiments, the laser beam was generated by solid state diode pumped Nd:YAG laser (DY022 by Rofin) with maximum power up to 2200 watt, and transferred via 300?m diameter optical fiber to the cutting head that is mounted over a six axes robot (Motoman UP20) and equipped with automatic stand-off adjusting servo motor and electrostatic sensor. Roughness values, R_y (maximum height method) and R_a (arithmetical mean method) were measured using roughness meter (Mitutoyo) and kerf width was measured using profile projector equipped with edge detector (Nikon.) Roughness and kerf width data were averaged over three positions on every cut line. The laser's beam quality factor = 12 and M^2 = 36 that the beam cross section is near to multimode profile (Fig. 2-a). The theoretical minimum beam diameter at the focus spot = 0.18 mm.

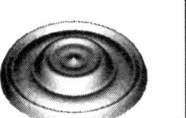

Fig. 2: (a) Multimode beam profile, (b) Experimental cutting path

2.2 Materials

1.2 mm thick cold rolled mild steel, specified as SPCC by JIS, made by NKK

Co., Japan. The chemical composition of the mild steel is given in Table 1. Specimens were cut using shear machine to rectangular shapes with dimension 100 mm x 100 mm and kept in dry box to avoid the formation of rust and swept by clean cloth to remove dust before start cutting process.

2.3 Procedure

Through the experimental work, the following parameters were constant: (1) laser mode = CW, (2) assistant gas is oxygen, (3) focal length of the final focusing lens = 120 mm, (4) nozzle tip diameter = 1.2 mm and (5) nozzle stand-off distance = 1 mm. The varied parameters were: (1) applied cutting speeds = 1, 3, 6 and 9 m/min, (2) applied laser powers = 220, 440, 660, 880, 1100, 1320, 1540, 1760, 1980, 2200 watt, (3) gas pressures = 3 and 6 bars, (4) focus positions relative to the upper material surface = 0, -0.5, +0.5, -1 respectively. Every specimen was cut by using only one combination of the above parameters. Total of 320 specimens were cut. Some tests were repeated for achieving consistent results. Specimen was mounted on specially designed jig to prevent vibration during cutting and the robot was programmed to move the cutting head as shown in Fig. 2-b. Line AB (incomplete specimen separation) was used to measure the kerf width and line CD (Complete separation) is to study the roughness and striation frequency. Preliminary tests were made to determine the location of minimum spot diameter where it defines the focus position = 0.

3. RESULTS AND DISCUSSION
3.1 Effect of mounting the cutting head on 6 axes robot

Mounting the cutting head over 6 axis robot that controls the cutting motion resulted with instable cutting especially when the cutting speed exceeds 3 m/min. Fig. 3 shows corrugated cutting lines and instable cutting section quality (areas of no dross and good cutting and others of dross and bad cutting). Comparing to the 2 or 3 axes CNC moving heads or tables, results proved that robots are not recommended to mount laser cutting heads especially when high speed is required to get optimum cutting quality.

3.2 Effect of changing laser parameters

Generally, the dross free surface was achieved at focus position between 0 and +0.5, oxygen pressure = 3 bars, power range between 660 watt and 1320 watt, cutting speed between 3 and 6 m/min. Testing at 9 m/min resulted with mirror like surface (small roughness) and small kerf width but cutting was instable due to the instability of the robot. Due to the high vibration of robot and the laser cutting head, the stand-off distance could not be kept = 1mm, thus the focus position and assistant gas pressure could not be trusted to be at the desired programmed location. It was shown that the dross formation is more sensitive to the focus position that other factors.

Fig. 4 shows the effect of changing the focus position on the roughness value, where the smallest roughness values were measured at focus position = 0 and 0.5. Over these focus positions the roughness value drastically increased. Roughness values (R_y and R_a) were averaged over 6 locations along the two sides of the cutting line. The measured roughness values agree with the acceptable range of R_y= 0.8 to 6 μm [1]. This curve shows that the roughness values are not much sensitive to the laser power, which agree with Refs. [9,10], but roughness values are a little higher because of the larger beam diameter of the Nd:YAG laser. Relation to the focus, can be explained by the increase of the diameter of the beam spot hit the upper surface, when out of focus, thus the wider area subjected to ignition temperature, oxidation and melting. If the lower laser power of 660 watt could ignite the material, then the effect of higher laser power slightly contributes to increase the reaction and this explains the slight effect of power on roughness. Fig. 5 also clarifies that laser power has no distinct effect of the measured roughness values.

Fig. 6 shows the effect of the focus position on the kerf width at two power and oxygen pressure levels. Because the material thickness 1.2 mm was relatively small, there is no large difference between the measurements of upper and lower kerfs, so only the upper kerf was considered. However, the top kerf is wider by few microns and this is due to the taper nature of the laser beam and also for the dynamics of the supplied gas [1]. Kerf increased a little with increasing of the cutting distance and this is due to heat accumulation from

Table 1 : Chemical composition of SPCC mild steel

C	Mn	P	S	Cr	Al	Cu	W	Ni
0.03	0.19	0.014	0.014	0.05	0.03	0.016	0.014	0.023

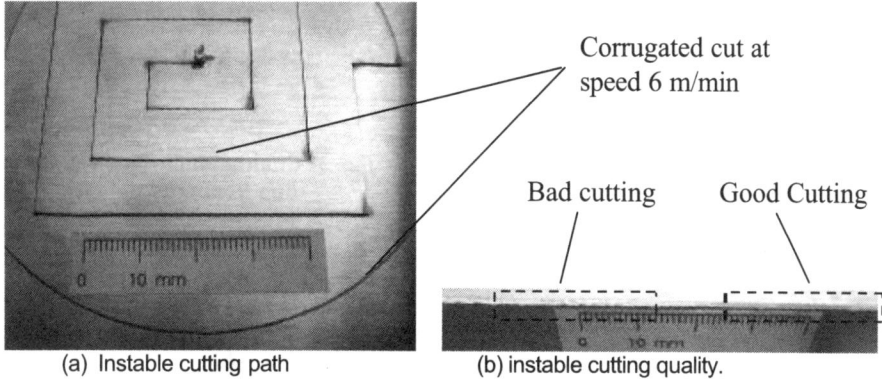

Corrugated cut at speed 6 m/min

Bad cutting   Good Cutting

(a) Instable cutting path   (b) instable cutting quality.

Fig. 3: Cutting instability due to using 6 axes robot at speed higher than 3 m/min.

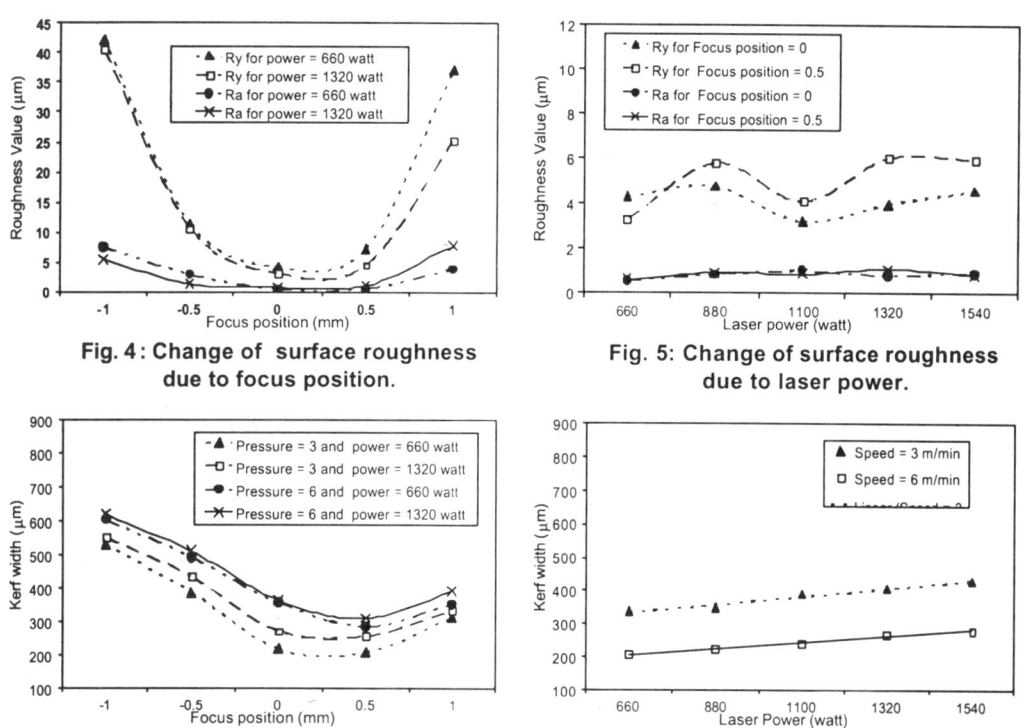

Fig. 4 : Change of surface roughness due to focus position.

Fig. 5: Change of surface roughness due to laser power.

Fig. 6: Change of upper kerf width due to focus position.

Fig. 7: Change of upper kerf width due to laser power.

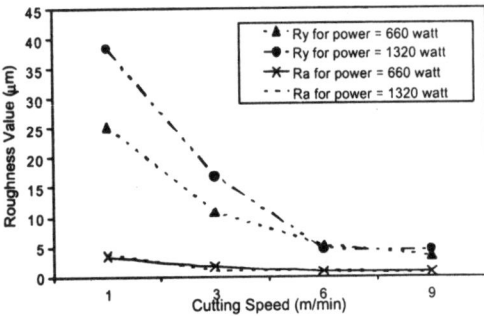

Fig. 8 : Change of surface roughness due to cutting speed.

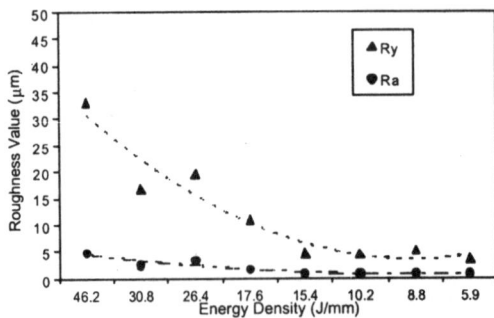

Fig. 9 : Change of surface roughness due to energy density.

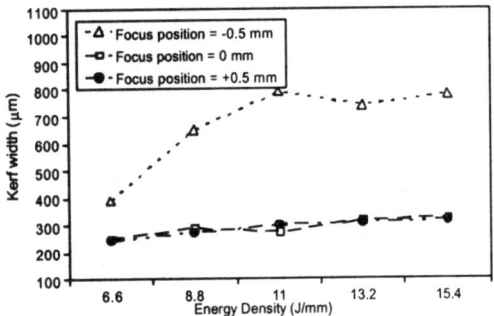

Fig. 10 : Change of kerf width due to energy density.

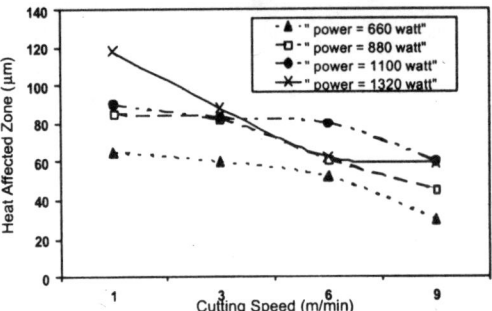

Fig. 11: Change of HAZ due to cutting speed.

previous cut which increased the total supplied energy. The minimum values of kerf width = 208? m was measured at focus position = +0.5, oxygen pressure = 3 bar and power = 660 watt. The increase in kerf width can be explained by the excessive melting due to high applied energy and oxygen However, increasing the power has a little effect comparing to increasing oxygen reaction and changing the focus position.

Fig. 7 shows the increase in kerf width with increasing the power at speed = 3 and 6 m/min and pressure = 3 bar. Kerf width is smaller at high speed. This result is also similar to that shown by Rajaram [9] and Dilthey [10]. Fig. 8 shows the increase of kerf width with the increase of power and reducing the speed. This is also explained by the increase of applied energy density and thus the volume of melted metals. Minimum kerf width of 207 mm was measured at speed 6 ? /min and power = 660 watt. Dilthey [9] proposed that in the case of lower cutting speeds, the materials is heated up to the ignition temperature within a relatively wide zone around the focus laser spot and results in the formation of a relatively wide cutting gap at the top surface. Due to the finite

thermal conductivity, the width of ignition zone, thus the top kerf width, decreases with an increase in cutting speed until the top kerf reach to the diameter of the focused beam.

Fig. 8 shows the drastic decrease of roughness with increasing the cutting speed. However, the best roughness should be achieved at speed more that 9 m/min – this is also confined with the reviewed literatures and manufacturer data – but due to the instability of robot at this speed, the practical cutting speed should be reduced to less than 3 m/min, as mentioned above. Fig. 9 and 10 show the effect of the calculated "Energy density" that is defined as the laser energy per unit length applied to the material (= Power / (thickness x speed x cut length)) on both the roughness and kerf width. Minimum roughness values are obtained at low energy density (5 to 15 J/mm), while increasing the energy showed increasing in the roughness values. Also, minimum kerf width was recorded within the above energy range. Fig 11 shows the decrease of the HAZ with increasing speed. HAZ was defined by microstructure examination. This result can be also explained by the effect of heat conductivity of the mild steel and the less time given to heat diffusion at high speed.

4. CONCLUSION

This work discusses cutting of 1.2 mild steel using Nd:YAG diode pumped laser and cutting head mounted on a 6 axes robot. High speed cutting could not be done using robot because it showed instability at speed more than 3 m/min. To cut complex curved geometries using robot, speed should be less than 3 m/min. The investigation of the effect of the different laser parameters on the cutting quality of 1.2 mm mild steel sheets showed that increasing the speed produced narrow kerf width, better surface roughness and narrow HAZ. Wide kerf is an indicator to high roughness and wide HAZ. High oxygen pressure up to 3 bars is needed to cut thin sheets of mild steel, but increasing the pressure of oxygen gas more than 3 bars leads to wide kerf and bad roughness.

5. REFERENCES

1. **Bass, M.** (1983), "Laser materials processing", *Materials processing theory and practices*, Vol. 3, North-Holland publishing company.

2. **Havrilla, D. and Anthony P.** (2000), *Laser cutting process fundamentals and troubleshooting guidelines*, Rofin Sinar Laser publications.

3. **Steen W. M.** (1991), *Laser materials processing*, Springer-Verlag, London.

4. **Powel J., Ivarson A. and Magnusson C.** (1993), "Laser cutting or steels: A physical and chemical analysis of the particles ejected during cutting", *Journal of laser applications*, Vol. 5, No. 1.

5. **Miyamoto I. and Maruo H.** (1991), "The mechanism of laser cutting", *welding world*, 29(9/10), 283-294.

6. **Ivarson A., Powell J., Kamalu J., and Magnusson C.** (1994), "The oxidation dynamics of laser cutting of mild steel and the generation of striations on the cut edge", *Journal of materials Processing Technology*, 40 359-374.

7. **Hamoudi W. K.** (1997), "The effect of speed and processing gas on laser cutting of steel using a 2kW Co_2 laser", *International journal of Materials*, 9 (1).

8. **Kaebernick H., Jeromin A., Mathew P.,** (1998) "Adaptive control for laser cutting using striation frequency analysis", *Annals of CIRP manufacturing technology*, 47 (1) pp. 137-140.

9. **Rajaram N., Sheikh-Ahmad J. and Cheraghi S. H.** (2003), "CO_2 laser cut quality of 4130 steel", *International Journal of Machine Tools and Manufacturing*, 43 - 351-358.

10. **Dilthey, M. and Weick, J.** (1992), "Laser cutting of steel – cut quality depending on cutting parameters", Welding in the world, UK, vol. 30, No. 9/10, pp. 275-278.

GCMM 2004
Editors: Prasad K D V Yarlagadda and S Narayanan
Copyright © 2005, Vellore Institute of Technology, Vellore, India
Publisher: Narosa Publishing House Pvt. Ltd., New Delhi, India

Design Assessment System for Sheet Metal Component Manufacturability

Ramana K V , Rao P V M

Mechanical Engineering Department, Indian Institute of Technology
New Delhi, INDIA

E-mail: kvramana@mech.iitd.ernet.in

Abstract

Design assessment for manufacturability is a key requirement in realizing complete integration of design and process planning. The purpose of such an assessment is to assist designers in their efforts to come up with manufacturable parts economizing in terms of cost and time, without compromising on quality and functional requirements. The present work deals with one such system developed for design assessment of sheet metal components for manufacturability. Unlike most of the work done in the past, which concentrates on specific domain manufacturability assessment, the present work is more comprehensive combining characteristics of all the existing methods manufacturability assessment. The prime modules of the present system are feature reasoning, design assessment and process planning, and data and knowledge modeling. Design evaluator and process planner use different types of data and knowledge to identify design violations and to generate process plan. Results of design assessment are presented for a typical sheet metal part to be produced by bending and shearing processes.

Key Words
Design assessment, Manufacturability, Feature reasoning, Process planning, Data and knowledge modeling

1. INTRODUCTION

Decisions made during design phase account for a significant portion of the total product cost. Requesting for design changes when manufacturing problems are encountered is extremely time and cost intensive. The later in the product design and development cycle the changes occur, the more expensive they become. Therefore, not only it is important to take manufacturing considerations into account during product design but also, these considerations must occur as early as possible in the design cycle [1].

When CAD/CAM tools are used to reduce the design lead times, accounting for manufacturability related considerations implicitly, is often difficult and the use of an explicit design assessment tool is always helpful. A good example for an explicit design assessment tool is one of the existing commercial DFMA (Design For Manufacture and Assembly) software [2] in the market. Assessing the manufacturability of a design with such a tool is always easier to modeling with implicit designer knowledge of manufacturing. Design assessment for manufacturability allows the designers to analyze the manufacturability during the design stage using computational tools.

Existing methods of manufacturability assessment can be classified as *rule-based* and *plan-based* [3]. In a rule-based assessment, rules are used to check the manufacturability of design from direct inspection of design description. An effort is made to generate a process plan in a plan-based manufacturability assessment. This paper presents a design assessment system for sheet metal component manufacturability. The proposed system uniting the features of both methods of manufacturability assessment is more comprehensive and holistic than the earlier proposed ones which deal with specific domain of manufacturability assessment.

The remaining part of the paper is organized as follows. Section 2 gives an overview of the existing design assessment systems in sheet metal for manufacturability. Section 3 describes the overall structure of the proposed design assessment system. Section 4 gives details of modules of the design assessment system. Integrated modules of the proposed system are feature reasoning, design assessment and process planning, and data and knowledge modeling. Section 5 presents the results of design assessment for a simple, yet typical sheet metal part demonstrating the effectiveness of the developed system. Section 6 concludes the paper.

2. RELATED WORK

Number of papers including reviews [3, 4, 5] has been published on the subject of design assessment for manufacturability. Relevant works are done by different groups which deal with design assessment of sheet metal components for manufacturability. Lin and Peing [6] studied a rule-based system to aid in the design of sheet metal bending and to alter the design whenever the design result is not satisfactory. Mantripragada et al. [7] developed a system for sheet metal forming that enables to perform formability analysis and output required design changes. Yeh et al. [8] developed a rule-based design advisor for sheet metal components that identifies design violations, suggests solution alternatives and estimates cost.

Tilley [9] dealt with manufacturing and production of sheet metal components for selection of machines, tools and methods, minimization of set-up, production time and cost. Cuesta et al. [10] developed a detailed time and cost analysis module for process-planning of sheet metal operations. Shpitalni and Saddan [11] formulated automatic tool selection and bending sequence determination to find an optimum path in terms of time and cost. De Vin et al. [12] discussed about tolerances, bending sequence determination and tool selection in sheet metal process planning. Ong et al. [13] described a methodology to determine the optimal set-up and bending sequences for the brake forming of sheet metal components. Gupta et al. [14] described a process planning system for sheet metal parts for generation of possible bending sequences and manufacturing costs, selection of punches and dies, interference checking, gripper selection and robot motion plan, near optimal plan development and feedback to improve the plan on operation by operation basis. Schmitz and Desa [15] established and implemented a methodology for manufacturing of stamped products for process plan generation, deriving punches and dies and manufacturing cost estimation. Tisza [16] developed a system for sheet and bulk metal forming for feature recognition, material selection, blank determination, optimum sequencing of operations, tool and machine selection.

De Vries et al. [17] focused on the integration of design and process planning using the functionalities of FROOM (Feature and Relation based Object Oriented Modeling), a design support system and PART-S (Planning of Activities, Resources and Technology-Sheet metal), a CAPP system as the basis for sheet metal components. Ramana and Rao [18] presented a system level architecture for automated manufacturability evaluation of sheet metal components.

67

Most of these works are dedicated to one of the rule-based or plan-based methods of manufacturability assessment and a very few have looked at both methods of assessment. It is felt that a hybrid system that combines the characteristics of both methods of manufacturability assessment is the need of hour. In the present work a more comprehensive and holistic design assessment system developed for sheet metal component manufacturability is presented. The proposed

be manufactured by shearing and bending processes.

3. DESIGN ASSESSMENT SYSTEM

This section gives salient features and overall architecture of design assessment system developed. The purpose of the proposed system is to check a given design of sheet metal component for manufacturability.

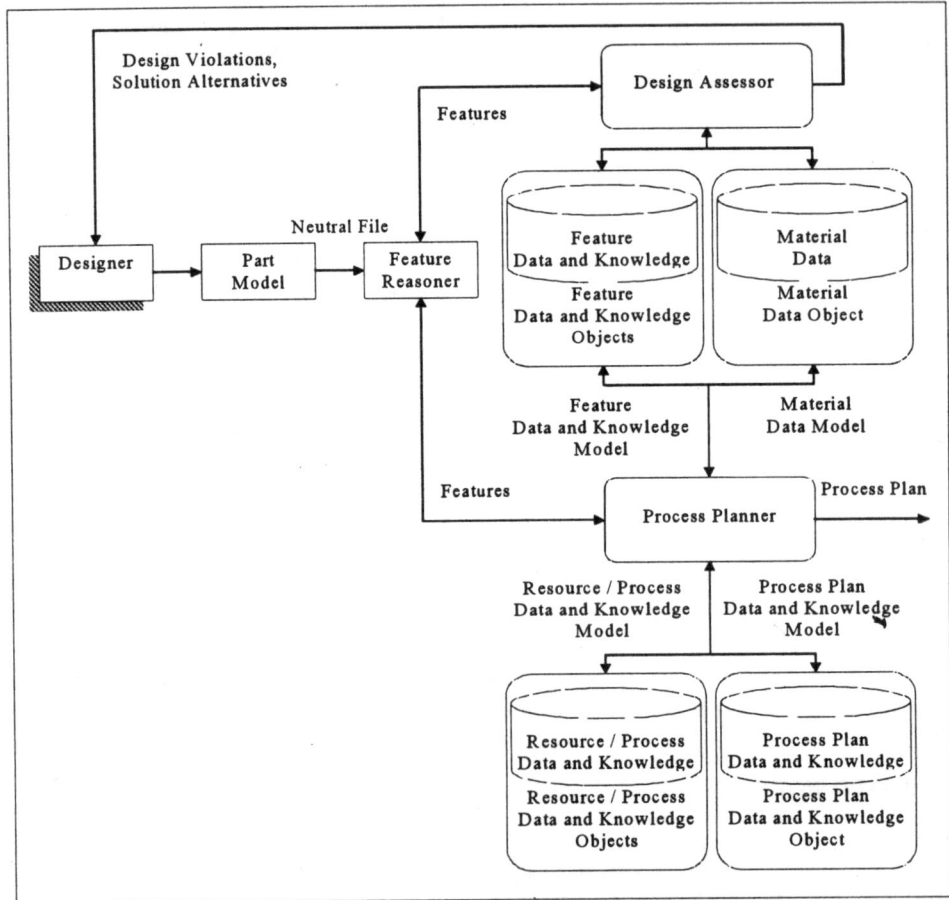

Fig.1: Design Assessment System Architecture

system differs from previous ones in the sense that it is a more complete system combining the characteristics of both rule-based and plan-based methods of manufacturability assessment. The scope of present system is restricted to those sheet metal parts which can

The system when used will advise in terms of possible design changes in order to overcome design violations and generates process plan. The architecture of proposed design assessment system is shown in figure 1.

Integrated elements of the proposed system are *part model, feature reasoner, design assessor, process planner, feature data & knowledge model, material data model, resource/process data & knowledge model* and *process plan data & knowledge model.*

The present system assumes that component design to be assessed is available as a CAD model which not only stores geometric information of the part, but also other design and manufacturing information such as material information, tolerances etc. Design assessment for manufacturability requires features to be recognized from CAD model by reasoning. Feature reasoner recognizes sheet metal features and extracts feature and part related information and makes it available to design assessor and process planner simultaneously for further use. Apart from feature data, design assessment requires material data, manufacturing resource/process data and process plan data.

Design assessor in relation with various data and knowledge models checks for design feature violations if any and corrects them by proposing design changes. During this process, according to the demands of feature knowledge, design assessor uses feature data and material data. The design violations along with solution alternatives are passed to the designer through the results display. Any design modification is followed by re-evaluation of the modified design for new violations if any that have been introduced. Process planner in relation with various data and knowledge models generates the process plan. Process planner along with feature data & knowledge and material data, also uses resource/process data & knowledge and process plan data & knowledge.

Design assessment system uses different types of data and knowledge to identify design violations and to generate process plan. Data and knowledge modeling methodology in this work is based on the Object-Oriented (O-O) approach, as this is more compatible with the intended implementation environment [19]. In this approach, the fundamental construct is the object or class that incorporates both data and functions. O-O modeling contains identification of objects, identification of relationships between objects and identifying data and functions in the objects. Data and knowledge models in this work consist of data and knowledge objects with relations via design assessor and process planner. A data and knowledge object incorporates both data and knowledge in the form of data and functions. Knowledge in the form of rules and expressions forms a part of the functions of a data and knowledge object. These knowledge rules and expressions form the basis for identifying data and functions of data and knowledge objects.

4. MODULES OF DESIGN ASSESSMENT SYSTEM

This section discusses major modules of the proposed design assessment system. These are feature reasoning, design assessment and process planning, and data and knowledge modeling.

4.1. Feature Reasoning

The process of design assessment for manufacturability starts with designer requesting for such an evaluation at some stage of the design process. This leads to reasoning about features taking part model as input. Part model in the form of a neutral file is passed to feature reasoner for feature recognition and extraction. Feature reasoner recognizes sheet metal features and extracts feature and part related information and stores it as feature data. This information is made available to design assessor and process planner simultaneously, in response to their demands for further use.

As the present work is concerned with sheet metal parts, representation of geometry does not pose any problem. It is enough to represent component geometry as a 3D model with uniform thickness. STEP (ISO10303) neutral files are used here to store sheet metal design information. The selection of STEP format has an advantage that the design assessment system developed here can be integrated with any commercial CAD system having STEP translator.

69

4.2. Design Assessment and Process Planning

The design assessor in relation with various data and knowledge models identifies design feature violations and finds solution alternatives in the form of design changes. The design violations along with solution alternatives are passed to the designer through the results display. Design assessor accesses feature knowledge to find violations caused by features. According to the demands of feature knowledge, design assessor uses feature data that is made available by feature reasoner after recognition and extraction. Material data is got by design assessor from available material information according to the requirements of feature knowledge.

The process planner in relation with various data and knowledge models generates the process plan. Process planner accesses feature knowledge, resource/process knowledge and process plan knowledge to generate the process plan. According to the demands of feature knowledge, process planner uses feature data that is made available by feature reasoner. Material data is got by process planner from available material information according to the requirements of various knowledge. Similarly resource/process data is got by process planner from available resource/process information according to the demands of resource/process knowledge. Process planner also gets process plan data according to the requirements of process plan knowledge.

4.3. Data and Knowledge Modeling

Data and knowledge models consist of data and knowledge objects with intra-object and inter-object relations via design assessor and process planner. A data and knowledge object incorporates both data and knowledge in the form of data and functions. Knowledge in the form of rules and expressions forms a part of the functions of a data and knowledge object. These knowledge rules and expressions form the basis for identifying data and functions of data and knowledge objects. Knowledge rules are of IF-THEN in nature. An actual rule checks one or more "Conditions" combined with Boolean operators "AND" or "OR" or both for correctness. If these conditions are true, the rule executes one or

more "Actions" again combined with Boolean operators. Knowledge expressions are simple mathematical expressions.

Design assessment system depicted in figure 1 shows various data and knowledge models and relationships among them. Data and knowledge models required are *feature data & knowledge model, material data model, resource/process data & knowledge model* and *process plan data & knowledge model*. Data and knowledge objects of different data and knowledge models are inter-related via design assessor and process planner components of the design assessment system. Also, data and knowledge objects of individual data and knowledge models are intra-related.

5. RESULTS

The design assessment system developed here uses STEP (ISO 10303) neutral file format as input to reason about the component features. Design assessment and process planning modules are written in C++. Data and knowledge required to execute the design assessment and process planning functions is modeled based on Object-Oriented methodology. Knowledge is represented in the form of IF-THEN rules and simple mathematical expressions.

The design assessment system developed here has been tested on many sheet metal parts which include typical industrial parts. To test the effectiveness of the system, design assessment was first carried out manually using part designs. Subsequently, the automated assessment results were obtained from part models and compared for correctness and completeness. Results of design assessment for the typical sheet metal part chosen (figure 2) for study are given below.

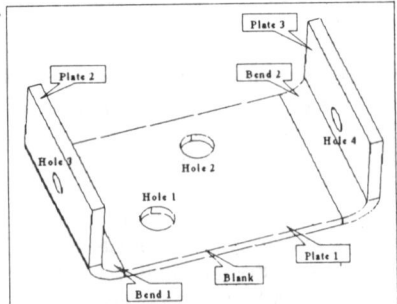

Fig.2: Typical Sheet Metal Part

5.1. Design Assessment Results for Typical Sheet Metal Part

- Hole 3 and Hole 4 should be avoided, otherwise they require expensive cams or additional dies or die stations
- Minimum diameter of Hole 3 should be 3.2 mm, otherwise it requires fragile punch which is susceptible to breakage
- Minimum distance (horizontal) between the edges of Hole 1 and Hole 2 should be 4.8 mm, otherwise die's resistance to the pressure of piercing is impaired
- Minimum distance between the edge of Hole 1 and Bend 1 should be 7.8 mm, otherwise die features will be weakened and so high die maintenance is required to avoid component distortion
- Minimum distance between the lowest edge of Hole 4 and the other surface should be 6.2 mm, otherwise hole distorts
- Minimum distance between the edge of Hole 2 and adjacent blank edge should be 3.2 mm, otherwise narrow section of the work piece distorts during piercing
- Two separate dies or die stations are required for Hole 1 and Hole 2
- Hole 1 must be created in a separate die or die station after Bend 1
- Hole 4 must be created after Bend 2 by using cam actuated tools and requires additional die or die station, otherwise it may not be held to true position
- Number of bend stages and the number of dies or die stations required to perform all the bends are 1
- Sequence of processes to be performed on separate dies is Shearing-Blanking (one die) - blank profile, Shearing-Piercing (one die, two punches) - Hole 2 and Hole 3, Bending (one die) - Bend 1 and Bend 2, and Shearing-Piercing (one die, two punches) - Hole 1 and Hole 4
- Sequence of processes to be performed on progressive die is Shearing-Piercing (one die station, two punches) - Hole 2 and Hole 3, Shearing-Blanking (one die station) - blank profile, Bending (one die station) - Bend 1 and Bend 2, and Shearing-Piercing (one die station, two punches) - Hole 1 and Hole 4
- Space allowed around the part on any die for securing of the die 5 cm, usable area

between the guideposts on any individual die 200.5961 cm^2, die set purchase cost for any individual die 192.2146 $
- Production volume 500 000, Shearing-Blanking die block thickness 28.4671 mm, Shearing-Blanking die making time 37.7569 h, Shearing-Blanking die making cost 1510.276 $
- Shearing-Piercing punch 1 and punch 2 making time 4.4 h, Shearing-Piercing die 1 making time 27.4789 h, Shearing-Piercing die 1 making cost 1099.156 $
- Bending die making time 32.9179 h, bending die making cost 1316.716 $
- Shearing-Piercing punch 3 and punch 4 making time 4.4 h, Shearing-Piercing die 2 making time 27.4917 h, Shearing-Piercing die 2 making cost 1099.668 $
- Part shearing time 6.3342 s, part bending time 4.7507 s, part processing time on individual dies 11.0849 s, shearing press force 85.8699 kN, part shearing cost 0.0968 $, bending press force 19.4109 kN, part bending cost 0.0726 $, part processing cost on individual dies 0.1694 $
- Usable area between the guideposts on progressive die 58.8042 cm^2, die set purchase cost for the progressive die 141.1695 $, progressive die making cost 10192.8015 $, progressive die making time 251.2908 h
- Press force 105.2808 kN, strokes per minute 100, part processing time on progressive die 0.6 s, part processing cost on progressive die 0.0092 $

6. CONCLUSIONS

A design assessment system for sheet metal component manufacturability is presented in this work. Existing methods of manufacturability assessment are discussed in detail along with a critical review on relevant works done in the area of design assessment system for sheet metal component manufacturability. Overall architecture of developed design assessment system is given. The prime modules of the system namely feature reasoning, design assessment and process planning, and data and knowledge modeling are described in detail. Towards the end, the effectiveness of the developed system is demonstrated by presenting the results of design assessment for a typical sheet metal part.

The proposed system is more comprehensive and holistic than the earlier proposed ones in the sense that it unites the features of both rule-based and plan-based methods of manufacturability assessment. It is expected that such a system will be extremely useful for designer to get quick feed back about improving manufacturing productivity without any detailed knowledge about the process. The method can be used to evaluate manufacturability at the completion of part design or incrementally during design process.

7. REFERENCES

1. **Boothroyd, Dewhurst** and Knight, (1994), *Product Design for Manufacture and Assembly*, Marcel Dekker, Inc., New York.
2. http://dfma.com/
3. **Gupta, S. K., Das, D., Regli, W. C.** and Nau D. S. (1997), "Automated manufacturability analysis: A survey", *Research in Engineering Design*, 9, 168-190.
4. **Van Vliet, J. W., Van Luttervelt, C. A.** and Kals, H. J. J. (1999), "State-of-the-Art Report on Design For Manufacturing", *Proceedings of the Design Engineering Technical Conferences*, ASME
5. **Ramana, K. V. and Rao, P. V. M.** (2002), "Automated Manufacturability Evaluation of Sheet Metal Components: A Review", *Proceedings of the Design Engineering Technical Conferences*, Montreal, Canada, ASME.
6. **Lin, Z. C. and Peing, G. -J.** (1994), "An investigation of an expert system for sheet-metal bending design", *Journal of Materials Processing Technology*, 43, 165-176.
7. **Mantripragada, R., Kinzel, G. and Altan, T.** (1996), "A computer-aided engineering system for feature-based design of box-type sheet metal parts", *Journal of Materials Processing Technology*, 57, 241-248.
8. **Yeh, S., Kamran, M., Terry, J. M. E.** and **Nnaji, B. O.** (1996), "A design advisor for sheet metal fabrication", *IIE Transactions*, 28, 1-10.
9. **Tilley, S.** (1992), "Integration of CAD/CAM and production control for sheet metal components manufacturing", *Annals of the CIRP*, 41, 177-180.
10. **Cuesta, E., Rico, J. C., Mateos, S.** and Suarez, C. M. (1998), "Times and cost analysis for sheet-metal cutting processes in an integrated CAD/CAM system", *International Journal of Production Research*, 36, 1733-1747.
11. **Shpitalni, M. and Saddan, D.** (1994), "Automatic determination of bending sequence in sheet metal products", *Annals of the CIRP*, 43, 23-26.
12. **De Vin, L. J., De Vries, J., Streppel, A. H., Klaassen, E. J. W. and Kals, H. J. J.** (1994), "The generation of bending sequences in a CAPP system for sheet-metal components", *Journal of Materials Processing Technology*, 41, 331-339.
13. **Ong, S. K., De Vin, L. J., Nee, A. Y. C. and Kals, H. J. J.** (1997), "Fuzzy set theory applied to bend sequencing for sheet metal bending", *Journal of Materials Processing Technology*, 69, 29-36.
14. **Gupta, S. K., Bourne, D. A., Kim, K. H. and Krishnan, S. S.** (1998), "Automated process planning for sheet metal bending operations", *Journal of Manufacturing Systems*, 17, 338-360.
15. **Schmitz, J. M. and Desa, S.** (1994), "Development and implementation of a design for producibility method for precision planar stamped parts", *Journal of Mechanical Design*, 116, 349-356.
16. **Tisza, M.** (1995), "Expert systems for metal forming", *Journal of Materials Processing Technology*, 53, 423-432.
17. **De Vries, J., Salomons, O. W., Streppel, A. H., De Vin, L. J. and Kals, H. J. J.** (1994), "CAD-CAPP Integration for Sheet Metal Products", *Proceedings of the 2nd International Conference on Sheet Metal*.
18. **Ramana, K. V. and Rao, P. V. M.** (2003), "An Automated Manufacturability Evaluation System Architecture for Sheet Metal Components", *Proceedings of International Symposium on Product Lifecycle Management*, Bangalore, India.
19. **Lee**, (1999), *An Overview of Information Modeling for Manufacturing Systems Integration*, NISTIR 6382, Gaithersburg, MD

GCMM 2004
Editors: Prasad K D V Yarlagadda and S Narayanan
Copyright © 2005, Vellore Institute of Technology, Vellore, India
Publisher: Narosa Publishing House Pvt. Ltd., New Delhi, India

Determination of Temperature Distribution in Metallic Layer during Selective Laser Sintering using FEM

Patil R B*, Patil M R* & Vinod Yadava**

*PG Student, Dept. of Mech. Engg.,MNNIT, Allahabad – 211004, India
**Asst. Professor Mechanical Engineering Department, Motilal Nehru National Institute of Technology, Allahabad (INDIA) – 211 004

Email: drvinody@indiatimes.com

Abstract

The selective laser sintering is used to make strong or hard metallic models for tools and dies directly from metallic powders. Thermal distortion is the serious problem after cooling of the solidified part rapidly. Uncontrolled temperature distribution in the metallic powder leads to undesirable properties in the solidified part. The study of temperature distribution within the metallic rapid prototyping model is important from the quality of the model point of view. Keeping this in view, a transient FEM based thermal model has been developed to calculate the temperature distribution within a single metallic layer formed on the powder bed during Rapid Prototyping using Selective Laser Sintering. This paper predominantly deals with the effects of laser power and time of scanning on temperature distribution within a model made of Ni based alloy during selective laser sintering.

Keywords

Rapid Prototyping, Selective laser sintering, Temperature distribution, FEM

1 INTRODUCTION

Rapid Prototype manufacturing is an emerging technology that provides an integrated way of manufacturing 3-D components from Computer Aided Design (CAD) files to finished parts [1], using only "additive processing". Additive processing implies that the structures are made by cumulative deposition of material, without using any hard tooling, dies, moulds, or machining operations. In SLS process parts are built by sintering a thin layer of powdered material using a CO_2 laser beam. The interaction of the laser beam with the powder raises the temperature to the point of melting, resulting in particle bonding fusing the particles to themselves and the previous layer to form the solid. The next layer is then built directly on top of the sintered layer after an additional layer of powder is deposited via a roller mechanism on top of the previously formed layer. The bulk powder material preheated to a temperature slightly below its melting point. Selective solidification happens by further heating, up to the "sintering temperature", by means of XY controlled pulsed laser beam [2].

Selective Laser Sintering is now in developing stage its exact nature of the behaviour is difficult to understand. This process is in its early stage of development and very few publications are available. Agarwala and Beaman. [3] have carried out experiments to find out the effects of process parameters on the density and strength of the part build. Materials affecting the process and resultant properties and microstructures of the parts are discussed.

Gibson and Shi [4] have given experimental details to study the effect of parameters on the density and the strength of the part build by SLS. In this paper it has been shown that the mechanical properties of SLS parts are influenced by powder properties and fabrication parameters.

Tontowi and Childs [5] have developed a FDM based numerical model to calculate density of sintered parts. Their experimental and predicted results for density shows that higher the powder bed temperature higher is the sintered part density.

Shiomi and Osakada. [6] have developed a FEM based heat conduction model to find temperature as well as weight of the solified part made of metallic powder. Their experimental and FEM based results show that weight of solidified part is effected by peak power rather than duration of laser irradiation. Further, Shiomi and Osakada. [7] have developed a thermal model to calculate temperature distribution and stress for various track lengths. They have shown that the cracking of layer can be avoided by using smaller track length.

In this paper a thermal model is developed to determine the non-uniform temperature distribution in the single layer of the part made of Ni based alloy due to laser irradiation for different laser power and pulse duration.

2 MATEMATICAL MODELING

In SLS, localized heating of a small volume of powder is shown schematically in Fig.1. The duration of laser beam at any powder particle is short, typically between 0.5 and 25 ms. Therefore, the thermally induced binding reactions must be kinetically rapid [8].

In principle, both single and two-component powders can be subjected to SLS processing [9]. However, two-component powders are more widely used for SLS. Usually two types of

two-component powders are used in SLS: powder mixtures and coated powders. In case of single-component powders the liquid phase arises due to the surface melting of particles and the powder is sintered by joining the solid non-melted cores of particles. Fig.2. shows the possible ways of contact formation during SLS of both single- and two-component powders (including powder mixtures and coated powders).

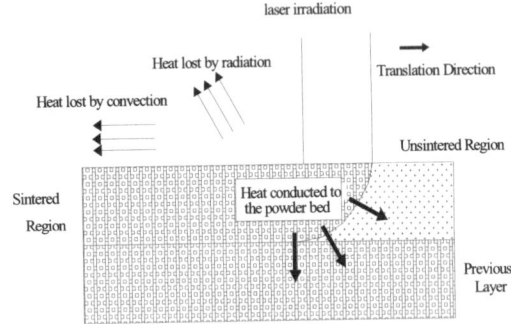

Fig.1: Interaction of the laser irradiation and powder bed

A. Single component metal powder

B. Two component metal/metal powder mixture

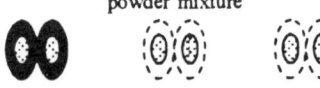

C. Two component metal/metal coated powder

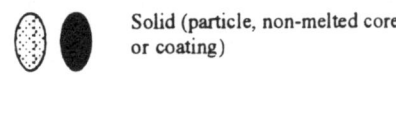

Solid (particle, non-melted core or coating)

Liquid (melt)

Fig.2 Schemes of inter-particle contacts formation during SLS of single- and two-component powders

Due to random and complex nature of SLS process, following assumptions are made to make the problem mathematically tractable.

1. The heat generation due to laser irradiation is treated as an internal heat generation in the modelling.
2. Laser beam spot is assumed to be circular in shape.
3. The heat caused by laser irradiation is given to the fully covered element under the laser beam. Here the laser beam is irradiated on one element at a time, but the laser beam is circular in shape and element is square in shape, so partial part of heat is also given to the elements neighbouring to the irradiated element.
4. To simplify the calculation the whole area is considered to be continuous neglecting the gap in the powder layer.
5. Only the part of powder material, which is coming in contact with laser beam spot, is melted.
6. Shrinkage due to solidification is assumed to result in only the change of the layer thickness.

The governing equation of heat conduction with heat convection from the powder material to the atmosphere in a cartesian domain is given by

$$\rho C \frac{\partial T}{\partial t} = k \left(\frac{\partial^2 T}{\partial x^2} + \frac{\partial^2 T}{\partial y^2} \right) + q_g - q_c \qquad (1)$$

in domain

Energy transferred to the work piece as heat input is considered as internal heat generation within the domain (Fig.3). Boundary condition on the surfaces AB, BC, CD, and DA assumed to be at such distance that there is no heat transfer across these boundaries.

$$K \frac{\partial T}{\partial n} = 0 \qquad (2)$$

on surface AB, BC, CD and DA.

The initial temperature is taken as the bed temperature, $T_i = T_0$ at t= 0.

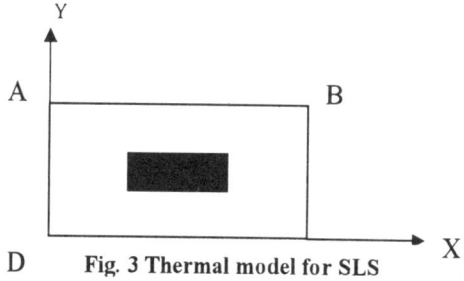

Fig. 3 Thermal model for SLS

Internal Heat Due to Laser Irradiation (q_g):

The heat generation due to laser irradiation is treated as an internal heat generation in the modelling. Because the heat supplied by laser beam is neither from X direction nor from Y direction, it supplied from Z direction which we are not considering in our modelling. So based on M.Shiomi and K.Osakada, in the present work, it is treated as internal heat generation because it is directly given to the middle elements.

The internal heat generation is given by [6],

$$q_g = \frac{2P\alpha}{\pi r^2} \qquad (3)$$

Where P= Laser power, = Absorptivity of the material, r= Radius of the laser beam

3 FINITE ELEMENT FORMULATION

The following expressions are obtained for elemental capacitance matrix [C]^e, conductivity matrix [K]^e and boundary flux vector {f}^{e} when Galerkin's method is applied to Eq. () ()

$$\left\{ \begin{aligned} \{K\}^e &= \int_D \{B\}^{eT}\{B\}^e kdxdy + h\int_D \{N\}^e \{N\}^{eT}dxdy \\ [C]^e &= \int_D \rho c\{N\}^e \{N\}^{eT}dxdy \\ \{f\}^e &= \int_D \{N\}^e q_g dxdy + \int_D \{N\}^e hT_0 dxdy \end{aligned} \right\} \quad (4)$$

Here, the matrix {B}^{e} relates the temperature derivatives with its nodal values. Above Eq. (4) when expressed in terms of global quantities takes the form as:

$$[C]\{\dot{T}\} + [K]\{T\} = \{F\} \qquad (5)$$

where [C] is global capacitance matrix, [K] is global conductivity matrix, [F] is global force vector, {T} is global temperature vector and $\left\{\dot{T}\right\}$ is time derivative of {T}.

Eq. (5) are solved after application of implicit Finite Difference Method (FDM). The solution marches in time, in steps of t until the desired final solidification time is reached.

4 RESULTS AND DISCUSSION

4.1 Validation of The Model

Fig.4 (a) shows the temperature contour plot within the powder, molten, and solidified parts in the beginning of third track scanning, for the laser power of 1kW using present model. Other data used are given in table 1. This figure shows similar pattern of temperature contour in comparison to the temperature contour given in ref [11] [Fig.4 (b)] at the beginning of the third track scanning. Both the results are matching with minor deviations.

4.2 Temperature Distribution

Effects of laser power and time of scanning on temperature distribution are discussed below.

Fig. 5 shows the effect of laser power on temperature distribution along x-axis at different y distance in the powder layer due to irradiation of laser beam in SLS process. The material properties and other data are given in table 1.The nature of temperature distribution graph shows that there is increase in temperature with increase in laser power and decrease in temperature due to decrease in laser power, along the length of the scanning track. This is because of fact that heat supplied to the powder layer is more with larger laser power and less with lower laser power. The solidus temperature of nickel base alloy is 1253 K and liquidus temperature is 1443 K.

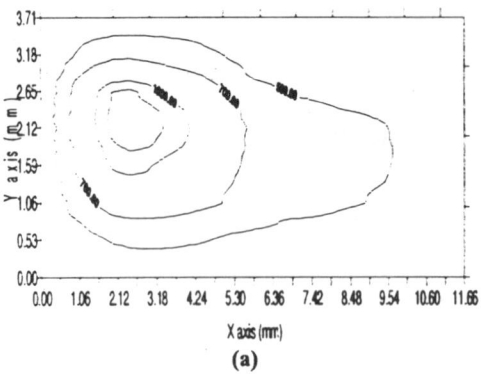

(a)

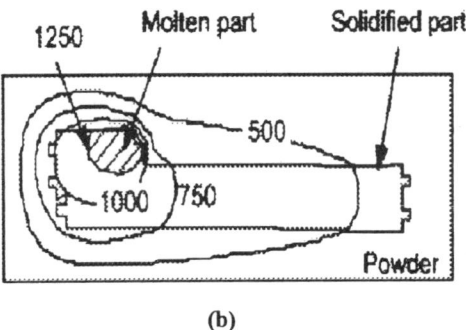

(b)

Fig. 4: Temperature contour plot (a) by using present model (b) Shiomi and Osakada [7] within powder, molten and solidified part in the beginning of the third track scanning for P=1kW. Other data are given in table 1

Table 1

Powder Material: Ni base alloy	
Laser power (kW)	1
Pulse Duration (ms)	1
Track Length (mm)	10
Laser Beam Diameter (mm)	0.75
Thickness of Powder Bed (mm)	1.5
Thermal Conductivity (W/m/K)	11.9
Heat Transfer Coefficient (W/m^2/K)	8.5
Specific Heat (J/kg/K)	444
Density (kg/m^3)	8200
Initial Temperature of Powder (K)	293
Thermal Expansion Ratio (1/K)	13.5x10^{-6}
Young's Modulus of Solid (GPa)	230 - 0.07 T
Poison's Ratio	0.32

76

In Fig.5 (a) the maximum temperature for the laser power of 1.5 kW is 1785 K high than the solidus temperature which is just below the laser beam. Fig. 5(a) shows the maximum temperature is 1298 K for laser power of 1 kW and 934 K for 0.7 kW. This shows the 0.7 kW power raises the temperature, which is insufficient for melting the powder material.

irradiation of laser beam in SLS process. The material properties and other data are given in table 1.The temperature plots are taken at the beginning of the third track, at the middle of the third track and at the end of the third track.

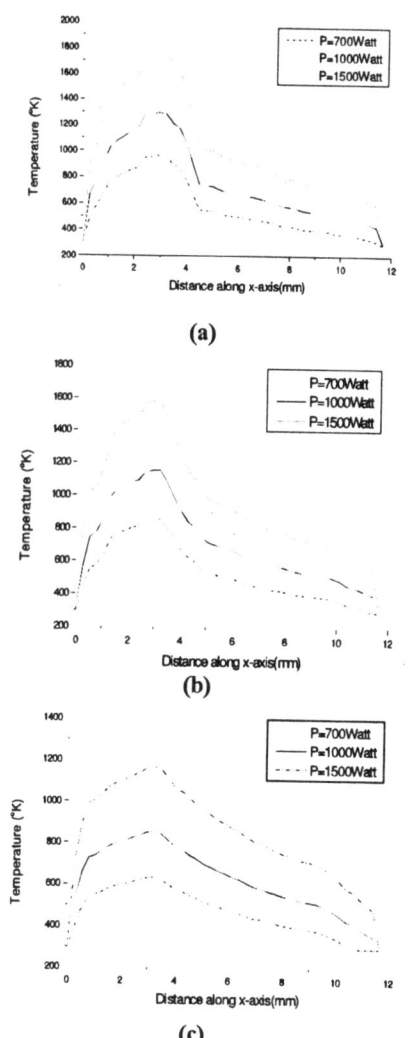

Fig. 5 Variation of temperature with laser power along x-axis in the powder of Ni base alloy at the beginning of the third track scanning during SLS at (a) y=2.12 mm, (b) y=1.59 mm, (c) y=1.06 mm.

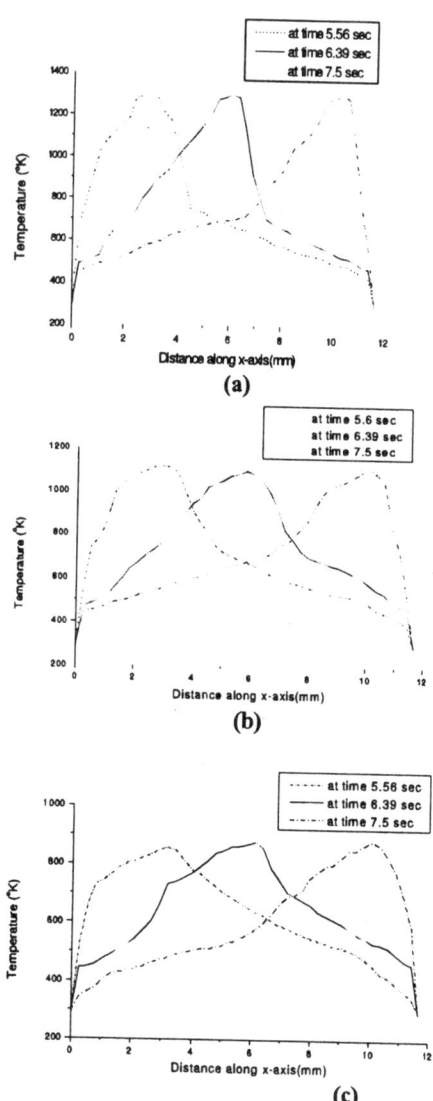

Fig. 6 Effects of scanning time on temperature distribution along x-axis in Ni base alloy powder during SLS with laser power of 1 kW at (a) y=2.12 mm, (b) y=1.59 mm, (c) y=1.06 mm.

Fig. 6 shows the effect of time of scanning on temperature distribution along x-axis at different y distance in the powder layer due to

Fig.6 (a) shows temperature distribution at different time position for the same laser power of 1 kW. The nature of temperature distribution graph shows that there is increase in temperature below the position of laser beam. This is because of fact that heat supplied to the powder layer is more at this position.

5. CONCLUSIONS

The finite element methods for heat conduction and for elastic deformation were employed in the simulation. A method for calculating the distribution of temperature and stress within the solidified layer on the powder bed in SLS process is proposed and the following conclusions were obtained.

1. The stress distribution in the solidified part caused by the temperature change during forming showed a stripe pattern of compressive and tensile stresses. The solid layer on the powder bed warped due to heating and cooling while the laser beam travelled on the track.

2. When the neighbouring track began to solidify, a large tensile stress between the solidified tracks appeared at the side end of solid part, which may cause the cracking of the layer.

3. The amount of the maximum temperature and stresses is affected by laser power. The temperature and stresses are increased as the laser power is increased. By decreasing the laser power, the temperature rise is insufficient to melt the powder material.

4. A suggested laser power should have the value to rise the temperature in between the solidus and liquidus temperature of the powder material. There should be appropriate peak power of the laser in rapid prototyping of metallic powders, to get best quality of the part without cracking.

7. REFERENCES

1. **Safari, A. and Danforth, S.**, Solid freeform fabrication of novel piezoelectric ceramics and composites for transducer applications Ferroelectrics, 2nd Ed. (1999).

2. **Kochan, D.**, Solid freeform Manufacturing, Elsevier Science Publicaters, 1st Ed. (1993).

3. **Agarwala, M., Beaman, J., Bourell, D. and Marcus, H.**, Direct Selective Laser Sintering of Metals, Rapid Prototyping Journal, 1, 1, (1995), 26-36.

4. **Gibson, I. and Shi, D.**, Material Properties and Fabrication Parameters in Selective Laser Sintering Process, Rapid Prototyping Journal, 1, 4, (1997), 129-136.

5. **Tontowi, A. and Childs, T.**, Density Prediction of Crystalline Polymer Sintered Parts at Various Powder Bed Temperatures, Rapid Prototyping Journal, 7, 3, (2001), 180-184.

6. **Shiomi, M., Abe, F. and Osakada, K.**, Finite Element Analysis of Solidifying Processes in Laser Rapid Prototyping of Metallic Powders, International Journal of Machine Tools and Manufacture, 39, (1999), 237-252.

7. **Matsumoto, M., Shiomi, M., Abe, F. And Osakada, K.**, Finite Element Analysis of Single Layer Forming on Metallic Powder Bed in Rapid Prototyping by Selective Laser Processing, International Journal of Machine Tools and Manufacture, 42, (2002), 61-67.

8. **Kai, C. and Fai, K.**, Rapid Prototyping Principles and Applications, John Wily & sons, New York, 3rd Ed. (1997).

9. **Tolochko, N., Mozzharov, S., Laoui, T. and Froyen, L.**, Selective Laser Sintering of single and two component metal powders, Rapid Prototyping Journal, (2003), 9, 2, 68-78.

GCMM 2004
Editors: Prasad K D V Yarlagadda and S Narayanan
Publisher: Narosa Publishing House Pvt. Ltd., New Delhi, India

Developing a Software to Optimise the Assembly Lines and increase their Flexibility

Manivannan K, & Narayanan S

Department of Mechanical Engineering,Vellore Institute of Technology,
Vellore-14, Tamil Nadu, India.

E-mail : manivannan_k@hotmail.com

Abstract

In the modern world optimisation is the key to success in product development in manufacturing arena. The way a manufacturer manages his resources can make or break the industry. The criterion today is not the technical superioritry but the production superiority. How a product is manufactured directly influences its costs and availability which, as is well known, is what the consumption of the product depends on. Hence, it stands to the reason that optimization is the need of the hour. This paper presents a software using set of heuristics to optimize the assembly line balancing problem. This is a user friendly software designed to aid the production engineer in making decisions regarding the management of production in accordance with the market demands.

Keywords

Assembly line balancing (ALB), Heuristics, Cycle time

1. INTRODUCTION

Assembly line balancing is all about balacing the assembly line in a way so as to maximise the production and minimize the idle time or the non productive period of the assembling process.Many companies, today want to set up assembly lines which give maximum efficiency within minimum time period without affecting the quality of the finished product.This paper provides an algorithm to develop a software which a company could use to optimize its assembly line either existing or new (to be setup). Here the optimization technique has been proposed using heuristic approach.

2. LITERATURE REVIEW

The balancing line problem has been extensively treated by the literature. Ghosh and Gagnon found more than 150 papers published on this subject in their comprehensive survey of the problem. Salveson was the first to present a mathematical formulation for the balancing line problem. Early work focused on the development of good heuristics for industrial problems. After Salveson followed by Jackson(1960),Bowman(1960),Spunik and Solinger(1960),white(1961)and Hu(1961) published papers ,since then the topic of assembly line balancing is of great interest for academicians. Although extensive research has been done in this area, the problem has consistently defined the development of efficient algorithms for obtaining optimal solutions Gutjahr and

Nemhauser(1964) with the growth on subject review articles are necessary to organise an summarise the findings for the research users and practitioners. The most of the review articles have been written by Baybars(1968) who reviewed the exact algorithms for the single model and deterministic problems and by Ghosh and Gagnon(1989) who represented comprehensive literature review of the subject.

The first computerised technique developed for sequecing operations of assembly lines called COMSOAL (Arcus 1966). Later another program CALB (Computerised Assembly Line Balancing) was deviced in 1969 (Magad, 1970, 1972). Then Ma (1997) devised a computerised technique for assembly line balancing which analyses the lines in their simplest form.Paneerselvam Oudayasankar(1993), Narayanan and Paneerselvam(2000) have developed heuristics for assembly line balancing problem in deterministic durations. In none of these researches can the assembly system be quantitatively linked with other types of mass production and jobshop production systems. Even the design of assembly lines deals with only a very limited number of issues at one time (Daganzo & Blumnfeld 1994, Shtub & dar-El 1989). Various assembly line issues such as economical cycle time, operating shift parameters, parallel line implementation and parallel workstation requirements, are directly regarded as pre-design requirements. It has been observed that various assembly line research activities appear to have very little inter-communication with each other, and because of this there is a shortage of general knowledge in manufacturing assembly line design (Bhattacharjee & Sahu 1987). It has even been suggested that the majority of manufacturing companies do not follow optimal design techniques for their production lines (Ma and Liu 1993). In addition, recent advances in product design such as Design For Manufacture and Assembly and the necessary flexibility in the market requirements has made the design of assembly systems even more complex and challenging. Thus, in order to maintain a competitive edge in today's World market, it is necessary to have a systematic software tool for generic design to achieve the required levels of production and the high standards of production quality.

3.BASIC TERMINOLOGY
3.1 Assembly Line

It can be defined as a moving platform on which the job is placed and all the machines are placed along the line which perform their tasks in a sequential order.

3.2 Assembly line balancing

It is defined as assigning number of tasks to various workstations so as to maximize balancing efficiency (BE) or to minimize number of workstations or to accomplish any other given objective function for a given volume of output without violating the precedence relationships.

3.3 Workstation

It is a location where a set of work elements is performed. Normally one operator manages one workstation. However under specific circumstances an operator may manage more than one station, sometimes workstations are frequently manned by several operators.

3.4 Cycle Time

It is defined as an effective time availible per period and production volume per period.

CT = produtive time / demand per period

3.5 Total Idle Time

Is the difference between time required by any assembly line to comlete the operation and the cycle time.

3.6 Balancing Efficiency

It shows the efficiency of all stations togather. This shows how much the stations are utilized.

BE(%) = {SACT/N*CT} *100

Where

CT   = Cycle time
SACT = sum of assigned cycle time
N   = Number of stations

3.7 Balance Delay

This is the calculation of idle time of all the statios put togather. The mathematical for balancing delay is given as below

BD (%) = {SUACT / N * CT} * 100

Where SUACT = sum of unassigned cycle time of the stations

4.CLASSIFICATION OF ASSEMBLY LINES

1. Single Model Deterministic (SMD)

2. Single Model Stochastic (SMS)

3. Multi/Mixed Model Deterministic (MMD)

4. Multi/Mixed Model Stochastic (MMS)

5. THE SOFTWARE

Designing a balancing line software to be used in industrial setting is not an easy task. The first challenge was to adapt the generic priority-based heuristic to the particularities of our assembly line. We will show that the key for the capability of the heuristic to generate good solutions is in making good use of logic and randomness in the algorithm. The second challenge was to provide an easy-to-understand code which could offer at the same time a good performance in terms of quality of solutions and execution speed. We first present an efficient algorithm for the programme and then describe the adaption of the heuristics and its implementation in the MATLAB

6. HEURISTICS

Many operations problems can be described verbally or formulated mathematically as optimization problems, yet there is no practical way to obtain the optimal solution in a reasonable amount of time, either because the problem is too large or the relationships are too complex. In these cases, solution methods called heuristics are ofter used. A **heuristic** is a rule of thumb or set of steps that produces a solution to a problem. The solution is not guaranteed to be optimal, but if the heuristic is well designed and tested over the long term the solutions produced should be better than those that would be obtained without the heuristic.

The heuristics commonly used in operations management have the following characteristics:

1. The are iterative : they repeat the same steps over and over.
2. They are usually "greedy" or "myopic". This means that at each step the heuristic makes a decision or selects an action based on the decision's immediate or "local" effect rather than its overall effect on the solution.

Heuristics have several desirable features:

1. They are simple and easy to understand because they are usually based on some intuitive ideas concerning the problem.
2. They solve problems quickly. Because they are based on simple rules and use a myopic evaluationat each step, little computaion is needed.
3. They can be combined with optimization techniques. It is common to break a large problem into pieces, solve the smaller subproblems with an optimization algorithm, and then use a heuristic to combine the subproblem solutions.

In devloping this software we used the following efficient heuristics to get the best line efficiency. They are

1. RPW (Ranked Positional Weight)
2. TF (Total number of work elements Following)
3. LC (Largest Candidate rule)
4. IF (Immediate Followers)
5. TL (Total number of Level)
6. NF (Number of unassigned jobs not Following)

Number of levels for number of tasks 55 is 12 and Cycle time is160Seconds

LEVEL	TASK	TASK TIMING	CONNECTORS	SUCCESSORS		
1	1	19	3	2	3	4
2	2	24	1	5		
2	3	21	1	6		
2	4	17	2	7	8	
3	5	10	2	9	10	
3	6	20	1	10		
3	7	22	2	11	12	
3	8	14	1	13		
4	9	21	1	14		
4	10	11	2	15	16	
4	11	12	2	16	17	
4	12	21	1	18		
4	13	20.	1	19		
5	14	16	1	20		
5	15	22	2	21	22	
5	16	23	1	23		
5	17	24	1	24		
5	18	16	1	26		
5	19	25	1	25		
6	20	18	2	27	29	
6	21	14	1	28		
6	22	23	1	31		
6	23	13	2	30	32	
6	24	10	1	31		
6	25	19	1	33		
6	26	9	1	34		
7	27	16	2	35	36	
7	28	12	2	36	37	
7	29	23	2	37	38	
7	30	25	2	38	39	
7	31	8	1	40		
7	32	18	1	40		
7	33	17	1	41		
7	34	21	1	41		
8	35	18	1	42		
8	36	20	1	43		
8	37	14	1	45		
8	38	24	1	44		
8	39	15	1	46		
8	40	9	1	47		
8	41	12	1	47		
9	42	22	1	48		
9	43	19	1	50		
9	44	15	1	51		
9	45	25	1	50		
9	46	17	1	49		
9	47	15	1	51		
10	48	11	1	52		
10	49	15	1	53		
10	50	22	1	54		
10	51	13	1	52		
11	52	11	1	55		
11	53	13	1	55		
11	54	17	1	55		
12	55	15	0			

OUTPUT OF THE PROGRAM

TASKS	DURATION	TL	IF	TF	RPW	NF
1	19	11	3	54	946	0
2	24	10	1	36	627	18
3	21	10	1	28	489	26
4	17	10	2	30	508	24
5	10	9	2	35	603	19
6	20	9	1	27	468	27
7	22	9	2	24	396	30
8	14	9	1	9	161	45
9	21	8	1	18	340	36
10	11	8	2	26	448	28
11	12	8	2	18	295	36
12	21	8	1	8	133	46
13	20	8	1	8	147	46
14	16	7	1	17	319	37
15	22	7	2	15	259	39
16	23	7	1	14	241	40
17	24	7	1	7	105	47
18	16	7	1	7	112	47
19	25	7	1	7	127	47
20	18	6	2	16	303	38
21	14	6	1	8	158	46
22	23	6	1	6	94	48
23	13	6	2	13	218	41
24	10	6	1	6	81	48
25	19	6	1	6	102	48
26	9	6	1	6	96	48
27	16	5	2	9	171	45
28	12	5	2	7	144	47
29	23	5	2	9	179	45
30	25	5	2	9	163	45
31	8	5	1	5	71	49
32	18	5	1	5	81	49
33	17	5	1	5	83	49
34	21	5	1	5	87	49
35	18	4	1	4	77	50
36	20	4	1	4	93	50
37	14	4	1	4	93	50
38	24	4	1	4	78	50
39	15	4	1	4	75	50
40	9	4	1	4	63	50
41	12	4	1	4	66	50
42	22	3	1	3	59	51
43	19	3	1	3	73	51
44	15	3	1	3	54	51
45	25	3	1	3	79	51
46	17	3	1	3	60	51
47	15	3	1	3	54	51
48	11	2	1	2	37	52
49	15	2	1	2	43	52
50	22	2	1	2	54	51
51	13	2	1	2	39	52
52	11	1	1	1	26	53
53	13	1	1	1	28	53
54	17	1	1	1	32	53
55	15	0	0	0	15	54

PROCEDURE

Step 1: Draw the precedence diagram

Step 2 : Clearly notedown the individual task time, cycle time, correct predecessors and successors

Step 3: Open the MATLAB FILE

Step 4 : Enter the number of levels, cycle time, individual task time and its connectors and successors correctly

Step 5: Run the MATLAB

Step 6: It gives the values of RPW,TF,LC,IF,TL,and NF individualy. Also it gives the efficiency of these heuristics separately.

Task allocation according to RPW

Workstation 1: 1 2 5 4 3 6 10
7 9 14 20 11 15
Workstation 2: 16 23 29 27 30 8 21
13 28 12 19 18 26
Workstation 3: 17 25 22 36 37 34 33
24 32 45 38 35
Workstation 4: 39 43 31 41 40 46 42 44

47 50 49 51 48 54 53 52
Workstation 5 : 55
Balancing efficiency using RPW is 79.4958%

Task allocation according to TF

Workstation 1: 1 2 5 4 3 6 10 7 9 11
14 20 15

Workstation 2: 16 23 8 27 29 30 12
13 21 17 18 19

Workstation 3: 28 22 24 25 26 31 32 33
34 35 36 37 38 39 40

Workstation4: 41 42 43 44 45 46 47 48 49
50 51 52 53 54

Workstation 5 : 55

Total efficiency using TF is 79.4958%
Task allocation according to IMF

Workstation 1: - 1 4 7 11 2 3 6 8 12
13 17 18
Workstation 2:- 5 10 15 9 14 16 19 21
22 25 26 31 33
workstation 3:- 20 23 27 28 29 30 32
34 35 37 38 39
Workstation 4:-   40 41 42 43 44 45 46
47 48 50 51 52 53 54
Workstation 5:-   55

Balancing efficiency using IMF is 79.498%

Task allocation according to NF

Workstation 1:- 1 2 5 4 3 6 10 7 9
11 14 20 15
Workstation 2:- 16 23 8 27 29 30 12 13
21 18 19
Workstation 3:- 28 22 24 25 26 31 32
33 34 35 36 37 38 39 40
Workstation 4:-   41 42 43 44 45 46 47
48 49 50 51 52 53 54
Balancing efficiency using NF is 79.4958%

Task allocation according to TL

Workstation 1:- 1 2 3 4 5 6 7 8 9
10 11 12 13
Workstation 2:- 14 15 16 17 18 19 20
21 22 23 24 25 26
Workstation 3:- 27 28 29 30 31 32 33
34 35 36 37 38 39 40
Workstation 4:- 41 42 43 44 45 46 47 48
49 50 51 52 53 54
Workstation 5:- 55

Balancing efficiency using TL is 79.4958%

PRECEDENCE DIAGRAM

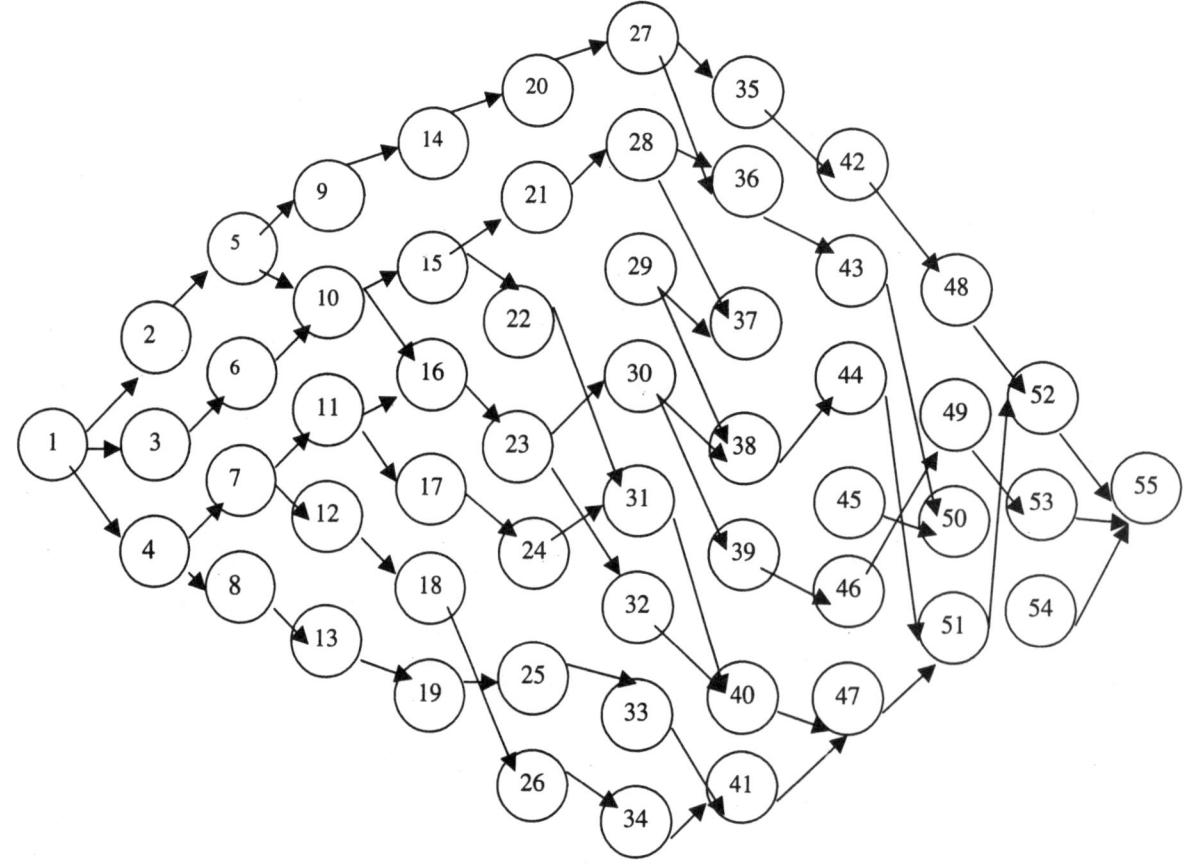

84

7. ALGORITHM TO SOLVE THE ASSEMBLY LINE PROBLEM

Step 1: Input the number of tasks(N), task timings (NT), Number of levels (L),precedence relationship and cycletime (CT)

Step 2 : Various heuristics such as RPW, TF, NF, TL and IF are calculated for each task.

Step 3: set RPW as heuristic 1, TF is heuristic 2 , NF as heuristic 3, TL as heuristic 4, IF as heuristic 5.

Step 4: set I=1

Step 5: solution due to heuristic 1

Step 6 : repeat steps 7 to 14 until if I<=5

Step 7: Assign new ranks to tasks for a given heuristic based on the values of the heuritic . Let the new rank be denoted by J and set cout = N

Step 8: Repeat steps 9 to 13 if count >=0

Step 9: Set workstation number W=1, time left = CT

Step 10: Repeat steps 11 abd 12 if time left >=0 and NT of task j<=ct and all predecessors of task J are assigned.

Step 11: Assign task J to W

Step 12: Set J = J+1 and time left = time left – NT of task J

Step 13: Set W = W+1

Step 14: Set Count = Count-1

Step 15: I = I+1

End of algorithm

8.CONCLUSION

We have developed a customized software package. We have taken a sample assembly line data and tested it with MATLAB. The efficiency of the assembly line based on the heuristics is printed here separately. To know the consistency of the result we can compare the output to the past resarch data. We hope that this will be useful to the researchers particularly those who are involved in this area. The computing time is less compared to other software and if any changes in the cycle time and precedence relations we can simply compute it and we can get the result which is not possible with other softwares.In future those who want to work in the area of ANN connected with ALB they can try this algorithm and source codes.

9.REFERENCES

1. **Ghosh S** and **Gagnon RJ** (1989) A comprehensive literature review and analysis of the design, balancing and scheduling of assembly line, *Internatioal Journal of Production research 27: 637-670*

2. **Arcus AL** (1966) COMSOL a computer method of sequencing operations for assembly lines, *International Journal of Production research 4:259-277.*

3. **Fleszar K** and **Hindi KS** (2003) An enumerative heuristic and reduction methods for the assembly line balancing problem, *European Journal of operational research 145: 606-620.*

4. **Lapierre S D** and **Ruiz AB** (2004) Balancing assembly lines, an industrial case study, *Journal of the operational research society 55: 589-597.*

5. MATLAB Version 6.1

6. **Asar Khan** and **Andrew J** (2002) A knowledge based design methodology for manufacturing assembly lines, Computers and Industrial engineering 41: 441-467

7. **Narayanan S** and **Pannerselvam R** (2000) New golbal search heuristic for assembly line balancing, *Industrial Engineering Journal 16-25*

8. **Pannerselvam R** and **Oudayasankar C** (1993) New heuristics for asembly line balancing problems, *International Journal of Management and Systems,9: 25-36.*

9. **Manivannan K** and **Narayanan** (2003) Assembly line balancing problem-A knowledge based gemba approach, *Proceedings on National Aerospace Manufacturing Seminar, 406-414.*

GCMM 2004
Editors: Prasad K D V Yarlagadda and S Narayanan
Copyright © 2005, Vellore Institute of Technology, Vellore, India
Publisher: Narosa Publishing House Pvt. Ltd., New Delhi, India

Effect of Ball Burnishing Parameters on Surface Finish and Surface Hardness using Factorial Design

Shirsat U M[*] , Ahuja[**]

*Rajarshi Shahu College of Engineering
Tathawade, Pune - 411033, Maharashtra, India
**Govt. College of Engineering   Pune- 411005.Maharashtra, India

e-mail : shirsatum@yahoo.com

Abstract

In present - day advanced technology, whole world is attracted towards the world-class manufacturing and surface finishing processes are becoming increasingly important. Considerable attention is being paid to the quality of the surface obtained, as surface finish is important not only on the cosmetic base but also because its affects the functional performance of the component and is important for process control. Burnishing is a cold working process, which is becoming popular as a finishing process. Special prototype combined turning and two ball burnishing tool is designed and fabricated to use on a Kirloskar Turn Master-40 lathe to turn and burnish the specimens simultaneously. Experimental work is based on 2^3 factorial design (Box method) to establish the effects of burnishing parameters on surface finish and on surface hardness of brass specimens. The results are analysed by analysis of variance technique and F-test and shows that force, speed, the feed and the lubricants have significant effects on surface finish and on surface hardness. A pre-machined surface roughness of 0.60 μm - 0.90 μm can be finished to about 0.10μm and improved surface hardness obtained.

Keywords
Burnishing, Kerosene, SAE-30 oil, Graphite, ANOVA, Statistical design.

1. INTRODUCTION

Burnishing is a cold working finishing process, where a highly polished and hard ball is pressed against a metallic surface of cylindrical component. The ball is feed in appropriate direction depending on the component surface. The finish machining processes like turning, grinding, milling, honing etc. will induce residual tensile stressing surface layer, which reduces the fatigue strength of the components. This can be prevented by inducing residual compressive stresses in the surface. This implies finishing of the components by press working or other chip less processes. In burnishing, initial asperities are compressed and modified. The deformation caused is a function of load applied. If the load is small, insufficient burnishing will take place. However, as load increases a stage will be reached when the burnishing loss may be

86

considered excessive, bulk deformation and metal displacement is likely to arise.

Wu [1] studied the tool life testing by statistical approach using response surface methodology on lathe by turning and for this surface roughness model equations are obtained. He considered three independent parameters namely; speed, feed and depth of cut and remaining parameters are considered constant. He found that the response surface model makes it possible to visualize overall metal cutting economy and to study optimum conditions. Loh, et al [2] ^{have} performed the experimental study by using 3^4 factorial design on vertical milling machine to find the effect of ball burnishing parameters on the surface roughness of AISI 1045 specimen. By using the analysis of variance technique and F-test, it is seen that the ball material, lubricant, feed and the depth of penetration have significant effect on the surface roughness. A pre-machined surface roughness could be finished up to 0.77μm. Baradie [3] has developed a surface roughness model for gray cast iron (154BHN) using carbide tool (turning) under dry condition and for constant depth of cut. The surface roughness models are developed in terms of speed, feed, and the nose radius of the cutting tool. These variables are investigated using design of experiment and response surface methodology (RMS). Ingole, et el [4] studied the effect of lubricants on surface finish of En8 specimens. Using 2^3 factorial design, the surface roughness models are obtained. The burnishing parameters considered are speed, feed and the force. The result obtained show improved surface finish. The contributing factors are force and lubricant.

Above information pertains to the separate turning and single ball burnishing. In this paper, parametric analysis of combined turning and two ball burnishing process (lubrication study) on surface roughness and surface hardness of brass specimens of cylindrical surfaces is presented. In this experimentation three independent parameters are considered namely force, speed, feed while the other burnishing parameters are kept constant. A combined turning and two ball-burnishing tool is specifically designed for Kirloskar Turn Master –40 lathe which is used for burnishing

of brass test specimen. Pre- machined surface hardness of brass is 130 BHN. Time required for this operation is less, due to combined operation. It gives more accuracy and out put owing to forces being balanced. With the help of this tool, cylindricity and circularity of the cylindrical component are maintained. Combined turning and two ball burnishing tool is shown in fig 1. Brass specimens are used for this experimentation mainly due to the following reasons:

- Brass cannot be heat treated properly for improvement of the material properties.

- For improving the properties of non-ferrous material, combined turning and two ball burnishing process is more suitable.

2. COMBINED TURNING AND TWO BALL BURNISHING TOOL

The combined turning and two ball burnishing tool is shown in fig.1. The balls are located inside an interchangeable adopter. Diameter of both the balls is 12.5mm and made from steel material. The balls are free to rotate with the movement of the work piece due to frictional engagement between their surfaces. When balls are pressed against the surface of metallic specimen, the adaptor compresses pre –calibrated springs. The springs are used to reduce the possible sticking effect of the balls and also to measure the applied vertical burnishing force with help of the depth nut. Rotating the depth nut in clockwise direction, the load is applied on spring through steel body. This tool includes two ball bearings (Bearing no 628X) and two flat-ended springs having stiffness 75 N/mm. The combined turning and two ball-burnishing tool is designed in a simple manner so that it can be mounted easily on lathe machine.

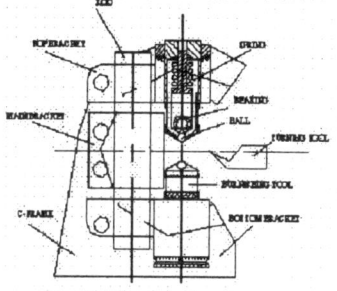

Fig. 1- Combined Turning and
Two Ball Burnishing Tool

3. DESIGN OF EXPERIMENT

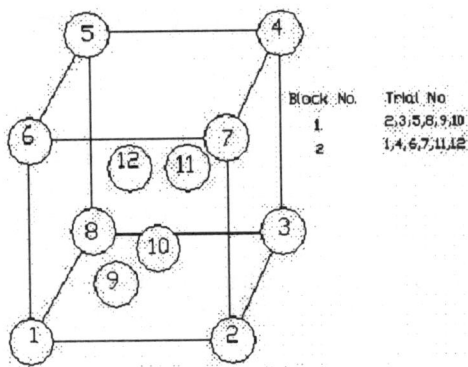

Fig. 1 Composite Design

Factorial design used in this work is a composite design, which has been initially proposed by Box [1,4,6]. There are numerous advantages associated with the use of factorial design in conducting of experiments. It is more efficient than the conventional one-factor-at-a-time experiments commonly employed by researchers, also, it ables to study both main and interaction effects among the different factors. Further, should a parameter (e.g. surface roughness) need to minimized with respect to the combination factors, factorial design will give a combination near to the minimum (or maximum), where as the one-factor-at-a-time procedure will not. A design consist of 12 experiments, are used to develop the surface roughness model equations. Eight experiments represent a 2^3 factorial design, where the eight experimental points are located at the vertices of a cube as shown in fig.2. Four experiments represent an added centre-point to the cube, repeated four times to estimate the pure error. This method classifies and identifies the parameters to three different levels (viz. low, center and high). In this experimentation twelve tests are carried out at these levels. These test values are divided in two group of six reading of each and one combined group (trial no. 1 to 12), for each group surface roughness model equations are obtained. (1) First block of six test (trial no. 2, 3, 5, 8, 9 and 10). (2) Second block of six tests (trial no. 1, 4, 6,7,11 and 12). (3) Combined blocks of twelve tests (trail no. 1 to 12).

The analysis of above blocks is carried out by using analysis of variance (ANOVA) technique and F-test. The trial nos.1 to 8 are at corner points and obtained by varying high and low values of the parameters. Center points (trial no 9 to 12) are obtained by keeping parameters at center values to minimize the error shown in fig. 2.

4. EXPERIMENTATION

Kirloskar Turn Master-40 lathe is used for machining that has wide range of parameter settings. Three level values for burnishing parameters are chosen (low, centre, high) [3,4] Table 1 gives the experimental values for burnishing. The lubricants used are (1) Kerosene (K) (2) SAE-30 oil (S) (3) 5 % graphite by weight in SAE-30 oil (G1). (4) Mixed lubricant (water + 20% coolant oil CUT 60EP, IOPL make (G2).
Ra – Surface Roughness in µm, F – Force (N), V – Speed (m/min), S – Feed (mm/rev)

In this experimental work, three burnishing parameters are considered i. e. speed, feed, force and the other burnishing parameters are considered as constant (i. e. ball diameter, nose radius, work piece material, number of passes etc.). The surface roughness is measured on SURFTEST 221 series 178, Mitutoya (Japan made). The surface roughness is taken perpendicular to the burnishing direction. In this work, the mean average surface roughness (Ra) values are measured by taking the average of three readings

Table 1: Three levels of variables and coding identification

Level	Force (F) N	Speed (V) m/min	Feed (S) mm/rev	Coding		
				X_1	X_2	X_3
Low	100	25	0.01	-1	-1	-1
Centre	200	35	0.04	0	0	0
High	300	45	0.1	+1	+1	+1

Table 2: Input parameters and out put response

Trial No	Force (X1)	Speed (X2)	Feed (X3)	Surface Roughness Ra in μm				Surface hardness Hv (BHN) SAE-30 oil
				SAE-30 oil	Kerosene	5% Graphite by weight in SAE-30	Mixed lubricant	
1	-1	-1	-1	0.1201	0.2563	0.486	0.3652	130
2	+1	-1	-1	0.1026	0.2353	0.6287	0.2435	133
3	-1	+1	-1	0.1346	0.2014	0.3122	0.2152	135
4	+1	+1	-1	0.1453	0.2320	0.4320	0.1526	136
5	-1	-1	+1	0.2025	0.1892	0.2131	0.1232	134
6	+1	-1	+1	0.1114	0.7837	0.6524	0.3251	133
7	-1	+1	+1	0.2582	0.1425	0.4016	0.1425	138
8	+1	+1	+1	0.1345	0.2562	0.3426	0.2132	134
9	0	0	0	0.1563	0.1893	0.6782	0.2311	132
10	0	0	0	0.1185	0.1752	0.4533	0.3452	139
11	0	0	0	0.1153	0.3253	0.7633	0.4356	134
12	0	0	0	0.1234	0.2151	0.3261	0.13240	136

Cylindrical brass specimen are turned up to 25mm diameter obtained is surface roughness in the range 0.60 μm to 0.90μm and after burnishing obtained is the surface roughness in the range 0.1004μm to 0.2012μm. For each reading surface hardness is measured in BHN.

From fig.3, when the force is increased up to 200N, the surface roughness is found to be decreased for SAE-30 base oil. Again when the force is increased above 200N, the surface roughness increased i.e. material get deteriorated. For 5% by weight in SAE-30 oil, the surface roughness is found to be increases. But the surface roughness is decreased rapidly for SAE-30 oil, as the force is increased. As compared to the kerosene, mixed lubricant and 5% graphite by weight in SAE-30 oil, the SAE-30 oil has greater effect on the surface roughness. From figs. 3,4,5, it is observed that the force has significant effect on the surface roughness as compare with speed and the feed. From fig. 6, as the force is increased up to 200N, surface hardness is increased. When the force is increased further, the surface-hardness started decreasing. The surface hardness varies from outer surface to the core of the element. Before burnishing hardness of brass component was 128 BHN.

5. RESULTS

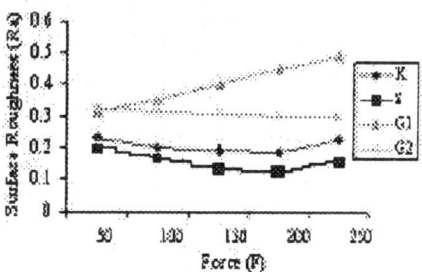

Fig. 3 - Effect of the Force(F) on Surface Roughness(Ra)

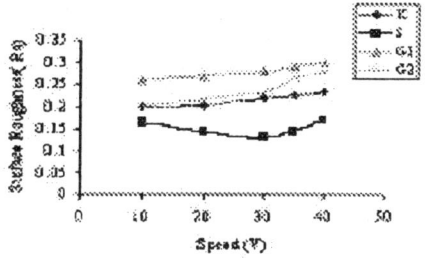

Fig. 4 - Effect of the Speed(V) on Surface Roughness(Ra)

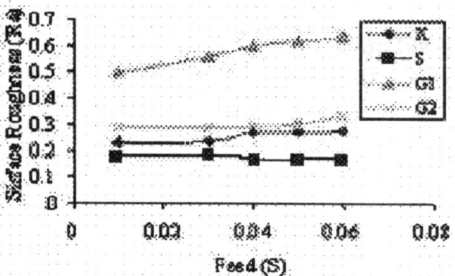

Fig. 5 - Effect of the Feed(S) on Surface Roughness(Ra)

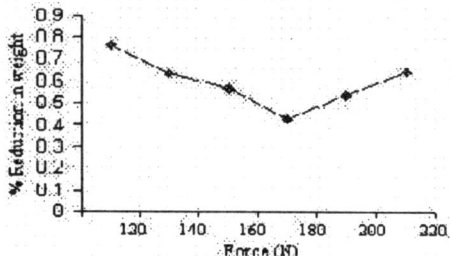

Fig. 6 - Effect burnishing Force on the Wear resistance

With the help of factorial design, total 12 experiments are conducted for each lubricant by considering all possible treatment combinations as stated in table 2. The mathematical surface roughness models are obtained for each lubricant. The models are

$Ra = 1.543\ F^{0.1199}\ V^{-0.4231}\ S^{0.231}$ ----- SAE-30

$Ra = 2.435\ F^{0.653}\ V^{0.4532}\ S^{-0.3422}$ ----- Kero

$Ra = 2.453\ F^{0.412}\ V^{-0.1422}\ S^{-0.3421}$ ----- 5% graphite in SAE-30 oil

$Ra = 4.342\ F^{-0.2634}\ V^{0.7642}\ S^{-0.4536}$ ---- Mixed lubricant

$Hv = 115.3\ F^{0.7863}\ V^{-0.2132}\ S^{0.6764}$ ----- Micro - hardness for SAE-30

The relationships amongst the burnishing parameters, model equations are developed and results are shown in fig. 3,4,5,6. The best surface finish is obtained by SAE-30 oil as a lubricant. Only for this lubricant surface hardness is measured, because surface finish obtained by SAE-30 oil is better than kerosene and mixed lubricant. For the rough surface finish, the surface hardness varies unevenly.

6. CONCLUSION

From fig. 3, 4, 5, 6, it is observed that (at 5% significance level)

1 Surface roughness is improved by 550% to 650% by using SAE-30 as a lubricant. At different values of force, speed, feed, the SAE-30 oil gives best surface finish than kerosene and mixed lubricants.

2 The force has a significant effect on surface roughness and surface hardness as compared to speed and feed.

3 With the help of this process, it is possible to turn the shafts of low rigidity by balancing the cutting forces.

4 This process gives more production due to combined operation.

7. REFERENCES

1 **Wu S. M.** (1964), " Tool- Life Testing by Response Surface Methodology- Part-I", *Trans. of ASME', J. Engg. for Indus.*, 116, 105 -110.

2 **Loh N. H., Tam S. C., Miyazawa S.** (1989)," A Study of the Effect of Ball Burnishing parameters on Surface Roughness using Factorial Design", *J. Mech. Working Tech.*, 18, 215-220.

3 **Baradie M. A.** (1993),"Surface Roughness for Turning Gray Cast Iron (154BHN)", *Proc. Instns. Mech. Egrs (India)*, 207, 43-54.

4 **Ingole M. W.** and **Bahedwar A. S.** (2002)," Parametric Analysis of Ball Burnishing – a potential metal cutting process", *J. Instns. Egrs. (India)*, 83, 69-71.

5 **Belov V. A.** (1987),"Technical and Economical Aspect of Ball Burnishing", *Russian Engg. J.,* IX, 79-85.

6 **Box G P E, K P Wilson** (1945),"On the Experimental Attainment of Optimum Condition, Some General Consideration and Examples", *Biometrics*, 10, 16-22

GCMM 2004
Editors: Prasad K D V Yarlagadda and S Narayanan
Copyright © 2005, Vellore Institute of Technology, Vellore, India
Publisher: Narosa Publishing House Pvt. Ltd., New Delhi, India

Experimental Investigations on Force Generation during Milling Operation using Staggered Teeth Cutter

Anthony Xavior M & Adithan M

Mechanical Engineering Dept., Vellore Institute of Technology
Deemed University, Vellore – 14

E-mail: Xavior_anto@hotmail.com

Abstract

In any machining operation, the cutting force generated is influenced by many factors such as cutting conditions, tool material & geometry, work-piece material, cutting fluid etc. The objective of this study is to determine the influence of cutting parameters on the force generation during machining. This article focuses on milling operation of non-ferrous alloy material namely brass using a staggered teeth cutter. A novel approach is the application of Taguchi technique for the design of experiments (DOE) and the experiments are conducted under different machining conditions. In the experiments certain important parameters such as spindle speed, feed, depth of cut, type of cutting fluid are considered as known parameters. The unknown parameter that is to be measured is the force generated during the cutting process. Analysis of variance (ANOVA) is carried out to establish the relative influence of various operating parameters on the force generation.

Keywords
Design of Experiments, Force Measurement, Signal to Noise Ratio, ANOVA

1. INTRODUCTION

Cutting parameters have marked influence on the force generated in all the three axis during the machining process. Cutting parameters includes feed rate, spindle speed, depth of cut, tool geometry and effect of cutting fluid. The factors that commonly contribute to force in practice include irregularities in the feed mechanism, defects in the structure of work material etc. In this article an attempt is made to identify mathematically, the influence of cutting parameters on force generated. In the proposed experiments, tool and work-piece material combination of staggered teeth cutter (HSS) and work- material (Brass) is considered. The tool geometry is kept constant for all the trails of experiment. The robust design method introduced by Taguchi provides a systematic and efficient approach for finding the near-optimum combination of operating parameters. This paper aims at predicting the influence of various operating parameters on force generation through experiments based on Taguchi's orthogonal array. Experiments were conducted on "Batliboi" universal milling machine under various conditions of spindle speed, feed, depth of cut and the type of cutting fluid as specified in the L9 array. Milling tool dynamometer will be used for measuring the force generated during the machining process for every experiment. Analysis of variance (ANOVA) is carried out to find out the factors that affect the force generated under various operating conditions. ANOVA is a tool for the quantitative evaluation of the influence of the known input variables on the unknown output variables. As a result of this investigation we can find the relative influence of various operating parameters on the force generated. The paper is organized into five parts namely, the methodology adopted, design of experiments using Taguchi's method, data collection, evaluating Signal to noise ratio, Analysis of variance and the conclusion.

2. METHODOLOGY ADOPTED

The actual machining process performed in this investigation is cutting of slot with a width of 18 mm and depth of 6 mm in a brass work piece of 25mm thick. The four parameters namely, spindle speed, feed, depth of cut, type of cutting fluid were identified as the influencing factor on force generation. There is a possibility of varying the above-mentioned parameters for experimentation. Levels are assigned to the parameters selected and an orthogonal array of experiments is designed using Taguchi technique. This experimentation focuses on selection of optimum levels of the controllable operating parameters such that the force generated is minimum. Experiments will be conducted with the combination of parameters as specified in the orthogonal array and data collected. Signal to noise ratio analysis is performed to determine the optimum level of the selected parameters. Analysis of variance is carried out to find out the degree of influence of the parameters on force generation

3. DESIGN OF EXPERIMENTS USING TAGUCHI'S METHOD

The technique of defining and investigating all possible conditions in an experiment involving multiple factors is known as the design of experiments (DOE). Taguchi developed methods to optimize the process of engineering experimentation. Parameter design is essential to produce the

best results of processes under study. The optimum condition is selected so that the influence of the uncontrolled factor causes minimum variation of overall performance. Taguchi constructed a special set of general designs for factorial experiment that consists of orthogonal arrays. The use of these arrays helps to determine the least number of experiments needed for a given set of factors. The orthogonal arrays provide a satisfactory solution for a number of experimental situations. An experimental design has the elements of number of trials and condition for each trial. In this work surface roughness value is the parameter to be studied and the objective is to minimize the force generated by choosing the optimum value of controllable parameters. Four parameters are identified and selected for experimentation. Each of these parameters form a factor and each factor is assigned three levels.

Table 1: Factors and Levels

S.No	Factor	Factor levels		
		Level – 1	Level – 2	Level – 3
1	Spindle speed (rpm)	125	180	250
2	Feed rate (mm/min.)	40	56	80
3	Depth of cut (mm)	0.5	0.75	1.00
4	Cutting fluid	No cutting fluid	Direct cutting oil	Coconut oil

The factors considered and their levels are listed in **Table–1**. The standard orthogonal array for the present configuration is L9 array shown in Table–2.

Table 2: L9 Array

Trail No.	Spindle speed	Feed rate	Depth of cut	Cutting fluid
1	1	1	1	1
2	1	2	2	2
3	1	3	3	3
4	2	1	2	3
5	2	2	3	1
6	2	3	1	2
7	3	1	3	2
8	3	2	1	3
9	3	3	2	1

4. DATA COLLECTION

The details of 9 experiments conducted as per L9 orthogonal array are listed in Table – 3 along with the force generated in the X-axis alone during the machining process. Online data of force generated is monitored from the dynamometer and recorded.

5. SIGNAL TO NOISE RATIO

The change in the quality of the outcome of the process under investigation, in response to a factor introduced in the experimental design is the signal of the desired effect. However, when an experiment is conducted, there are numerous external factors not designed into the experiment that can influence the outcome. These external factors are called as noise factors and their effect on the outcome of the quality characteristic under test is termed "the noise". The signal to noise ratio (S/N) measures the sensitivity of the quality characteristic, which is being investigated in a controlled manner to those external – influencing factors not under control. From the force generated value recorded in the experiments, the signal to noise ratio is found out and is presented in the last column of Table – 3. The effect of a factor level is defined as the deviation of the individual S/N ratio from the overall mean. The average S/N ratio for the experiments which are conducted for the spindle speed of 125 rpm (factor A, Level – 1) is defined as A1 = 1/3 (η1 + η2 + η3). In a similar manner the effect of each factor at each of its level namely A2, A3, B1, B2, B3, C1, C2, C3, D1, D2 and D3 are found out.

These averages are shown graphically in **Figure – 1 to Figure – 4**. The optimum level for a factor is the level that gives the highest value of the experimental region. The figures indicate that the S/N ratio plot of depth of cut on force generation has the maximum slope. This implies that the depth of cut has the largest effect on force generation. From the plots it is evident that the best combination of factor levels for getting minimum force in X-axis is as follows.

Table 3: Experimental data & dB value

Ex No	(A)	(B)	(C)	(D)	Max. cutting force	η(dB)
1	125	40	0.5	No Cutting oil	24	- 27.60
2	125	56	0.75	Direct cutting oil	28	- 28.94
3	125	80	1.00	Coconut oil	36	-31.13
4	180	40	0.75	Coconut oil	28	- 28.94
5	180	56	1.00	No cutting oil	34	- 30.63
6	180	80	0.5	Direct cutting oil	20	-26.02
7	250	40	1.00	Direct cutting oil	21	- 26.44
8	250	56	0.5	Coconut oil	18	- 25.11
9	250	80	0.75	No cutting oil	27	- 28.63

Spindle speed : 250 rpm
Feed rate : 40 mm/min.
Depth of cut : 0.5 mm
Cutting Fluid : Direct Cutting oil

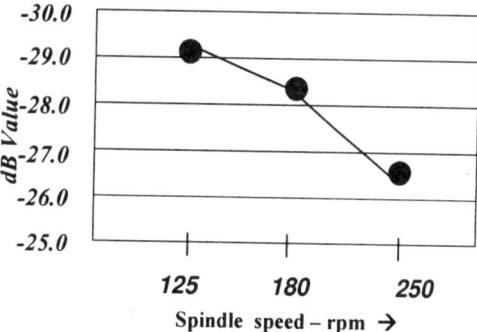

Fig. 1: Relation between dB value & Cutting speed

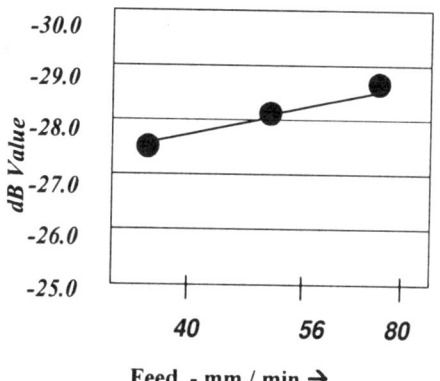

Fig. 2: Relation between dB value & Feed

93

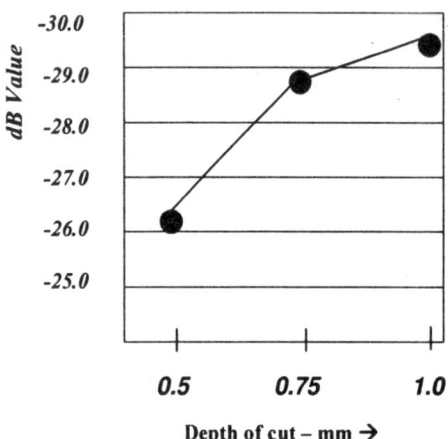

Depth of cut – mm →

**Fig. 3: Relation between dB value
& Depth of cut**

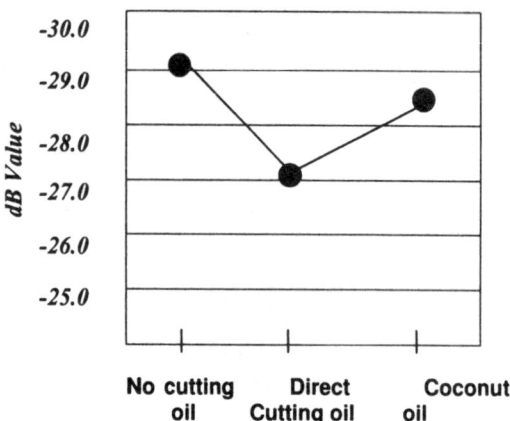

No cutting   Direct   Coconut
oil   Cutting oil   oil

**Fig. 4: Relation between dB value
& Type of Cutting oil**

6. ANALYSIS OF VARIANCE

The analysis of variance is a tool for the quantitative evaluation of the influence of the independent variables on the dependent variable. In a machining operation various factors effect the force generated. The relative magnitude of the different factors can be obtained by the decomposition of variables, which is commonly called as analysis of variance (ANOVA). ANOVA is also needed for estimating the error variance, factor effect variance of the prediction error and percentage contribution.

The steps involved in estimating the effects of the four factors from the calculated values of η for the nine experiments are as follows.

$$\text{Overall mean (m)} = 1/9 \left(\sum_{i=1}^{9} \eta_i \right)$$

$$=1/9 \, (-253.44) = -28.16$$

$$\text{Grand total sum of squares} = \sum_{i=1}^{9} \eta_i^2$$

$$= 7170.72$$

Sum of squares due to mean = (Number of Experiments) X m^2 = 7136.87

Total sum of squares = (Grand total sum of squares) – (Sum of squares due to mean)= 33.85

Sum of squares due to factor – A = 3[$(A1 – m)^2 + (A2 – m)^2 + (A3 – m)^2$] = 9.916
The sum of squares due to each of the remaining three factors are calculated using similar relationships and are found to be 1.319, 17.059 and 5.152 for the factors B, C & D respectively.

Degree of freedom for the error = (Degrees of freedom for the total sum of squares) – (Sum of the degrees of freedom for the various factors) = 8 – 8 = 0

Mean squares = (Sum of squares due to each factor)/(Degrees of freedom for each factor)

Variance ratio = (Mean squares due to the factor) / (Mean squares error)

Percentage of contribution = (Sum of squares for each factor X 100) / (Total sum of squares) = (9.916 X 100) / (33.85) = 29.65 for factor – A. Similarly the percentage contribution can be calculated for other factors also. The results of the ANOVA are summarized in **Table – 4**. It shows the relative influence of various operating parameters on surface roughness value.

Table 4: ANOVA Table for Factor effects

S.No	F	DoF	SoS	MS	% C
1	Spindle speed (A)	2	9.916	4.958	29.65
2	Feed (B)	2	1.319	0.659	3.94
3	Depth of cut (C)	2	17.059	8.526	51.00
4	Cutting fluid (D)	2	5.152	2.576	15.4
5	Error	0	0.404	-	-
6	Total	8	33.85	-	99.99

7. CONCLUSION

From the calculations it is observed that the Factor – C (Depth of Cut) has more influence on force generated during machining. The results obtained from ANOVA are in agreement with those obtained from the signal to noise ratio analysis. Factor – B (Feed) has a relatively small effect on the force generated. Speed and cutting fluid has some influence on force generation. When the cutting fluids used for the experiments were compared, direct cutting oil has significant influence on force generation. The results of this work can be used to establish a relationship between force generation and the operating variables.

8. REFERENCES

1. **Varadarajan A.S., Philip P.K. and Ramamoorthy B.**, "Comparison of Hard Turning with Minimal fluid application with dry turning and conventional wet turning" Manufacturing technology, *Proc. of 19 th AIMTDR Conf.2000*.
2. **King J.A., Michalek D.J., Sutherland J.W., Zuidema K. and Eppert J.,** " Development of a database of cutting fluid properties and establishment of a classification system for cutting fluids. Machine tool agile manufacturing research institute; National science foundation.
3. **Loan I. Steranescu, Camelia Calomir, George Chirita**, "On the future of biodegradable vegetable lubricants used for industrial tribosystems". The annals of university " Dunarea De Jos" of Galati Fascicle VIII, 2002.
4. **Suthetland J.W., Gandhi A., Zheng Y. and Li H.,** "Characterizing the role of cutting fluids in machining processes". Machine tool agile manufacturing research institute; National science foundation.
5. **Nicolo Belavendran** "Quality by design – Taguchi techniques for industrial experimentation, prentice Hall International (U.K.) Ltd.

GCMM 2004
Editors: Prasad K D V Yarlagadda and S Narayanan
Copyright © 2005, Vellore Institute of Technology, Vellore, India
Publisher: Narosa Publishing House Pvt. Ltd., New Delhi, India

Fabrication and Characterisation of Welding Parameters of Aluminium Hybrid Composites – An Overview

Venugopal* P & Murugan** N

*Asst. Professor, **Professor, Department of Mechanical Engineering,
TamilNadu College of Engineering, Coimbatore – 641 659, TamilNadu, India.

E-mail: venu_gp@yahoo.com

Abstract

Metal matrix composites are a class of materials with a wide variety of structural and thermal management applications. Metal matrix composites are capable of providing higher temperature operating limits than their base metal counterparts, and they can be tailored to give improved strength, stiffness, thermal conductivity, abrasion resistance, creep resistance or dimensional stability. Unlike resin matrix composites, they are nonflammable, do not outgas in a vacuum, and suffer minimal attack by organic fluids such as fuels and solvents. This paper presents an overview of (1) the various methods available to fabricate hybrid composites (2) Stir casting method of manufacturing hybrid composites with a special focus to the factors to be considered during fabrication (3) friction stir welding of composites, the experimental set up, operating process parameters (4) developing mathematical models for predicting the welding parameters such as penetration and weld bead by varying the process parameters such as speed, feed and Volume % of dispersoid using Design of Experiments (5) optimizing the mathematical model and (6) micro structural examination of the friction weld zone.

Keywords
Metal Matrix Composites, Friction Stir Welding, Welding Parameters, Design of Experiments

1. INTRODUCTION

The continuous evaluation of emerging trends and stimuli to introduce novel materials and to meet the requirements of various strategic applications leads to development of functionally gradient materials and composites. Composite materials have proved their worth as engineering materials for a variety of structural and non-structural applications due to their mechanical and thermo-physical properties [1,2]. The performance of the composites basically depends [3] on the microstructures. Higher stiffness, toughness and yield strength is obtained as a result of equiaxed [4] grain structure. Metal matrix composites are steadily gaining importance because of their potential for the production of components with high specific strength, stiffness [5], good wear resistance and improved elevated temperature properties. With continuing improvements in process technology, MMC have become quite cost-competitive with conventional materials and they have been recognized as potent advanced engineering materials for their commercial exploitation in aerospace, automotive [6], general engineering and recreational industries.

The processing methods [7] for discontinuous MMCs include stir casting, squeeze casting, rheocasting (compocasting), liquid metal infiltration, spray deposition, powder metallurgy (P/M) and extrusion. Discontinuous Al-SiC-MMCs are being developed by the aerospace industry for use as airplane skins, intercostals ribs and electrical equipment racks. This paper deals with various methods for manufacturing metal matrix composites, welding of the composite, creating a mathematical model for machining parameters using design of experiments and microsructural examination of friction weld zone.

2. METHODS OF MANUFACTURING COMPOSITES

There are several methods for manufacturing metal matrix composites, out of which major methods are discussed below

2.1. Stir casting

Stir casting technique includes melting of aluminium alloy in a crucible with an induction furnace. Melting under an inert cover gas is at the discretion of the caster. Degassifying tablets are plunged for nucleation of gas bubbles on the SiC particles and subsequent dewetting of the ceramic. Close control of melt temperature is needed to avoid overheating and subsequent formation of aluminium carbide. The melt is gently stirred using a stirrer-motor arrangement to maintain a uniform dispersion of SiC particles. The ceramic particles do not melt and dissolve in the matrix alloy, and because they are denser than the host alloy, they want to sink to the bottom of the furnace or crucible. The molten metal is tapped to the die using a bottom outlet attached to the crucible and argon gas is passed over the pouring area to avoid oxidation.

2.2. Squeeze casting

Squeeze casting, also known as liquid metal forging, is a process by which molten metal solidifies under pressure within closed dies positioned between the plates of a hydraulic press. The applied pressure and the instant contact of the molten metal with the die surface produce a rapid heat transfer condition that yields a pore-free, fine grain casting with mechanical properties approaching those of the wrought product.

Squeeze casting of Al-MMCs involve placing a porous ceramic preform in the preheated die, which is later filled with the liquid metal; pressure is then applied. The pressure in this case, helps the liquid metal infiltrate the porous ceramic perform, giving a sound metal ceramic composite. The squeeze casting process minimizes material and energy use and can produce net shape components, and offers a selective reinforcement capability. With proper casting conditions, high moduli and strengths (both room temperature and high temperature) of SiC fiber reinforced MMCs can be obtained.

2.3. Rheocasting

Rheocasting, also referred to as compocasting, is similar to the melt stirring route, but instead of particulates being stirred into a fully liquid melt, it is stirred in a semi-solid state. Particles and discontinuous fibers of SiC, Al_2O_3, TiC, silicon nitride, graphite, mica, glass, slag, MgO and boron carbide have been incorporated into vigorously agitated, partially solidified aluminium alloy slurries by this technique. The discontinuous ceramic phase is mechanically entrapped between the proeutectic phase present in the alloy slurry, which is held between its liquidus and solidus temperatures.

2.4. Liquid Metal Infiltration

The pressureless metal infiltration process is based on material and process controls that allow a metal to infiltrate substantially non-reactive reinforcements without the application of pressure or vacuum. Reinforcement level can be controlled by the starting density of the material being infiltrated. As long as interconnected porosity and appropriate infiltration conditions exist, the liquid metal will spontaneously infiltrate into the preform.

Key process ingradients for the manufacture of reinforced aluminium alloy, a nitrogen atmosphere, and magnesium present in the system. During heating to infiltration temperature (-750ºC or 1380ºF), the magnesium reacts with the nitrogen atmosphere to form magnesium nitride (Mg_3N_2). The Mg_3N_2 is the infiltration enhancer that allows the aluminium alloy to infiltrate the reinforcing phase without the necessity of applied pressure or vacuum. During infiltration, the Mg_3N_2 is reduced by the aluminium to form a small amount of aluminium nitride (AlN). The AlN is found as small precipitates and as a thin film on the surface of reinforcing phase. Magnesium is released into the alloy by this reaction. The pressureless metal infiltration process can produce a wide array of engineered composites by tailoring of alloy chemistry, particle type, shape, size and loading. Particulate loading in cast composites can be as high as 75 vol% given the right combination of particle shape and size.

2.5. Spray Deposition

Spray deposition involves atomizing a melt and rather than allowing the droplets to solidify totally as for metal powder manufacture, collecting the semi-solid droplets on a substrate. The process is a hybrid rapid solidification process, because the metal experiences a rapid transition through the liquidus to the solidus, followed by slow cooling from the solidus to room temperature. This results in a refined grain and precipitation structure with no significant increase in solute solubility. The process has been developed mainly for difficult-to-cast steels, nickel super alloys, and copper, with aluminium developments now showing considerable promise.

The alloy to be sprayed is melted by induction heating in a crucible which is pressurized and the metal is ejected through a nozzle into an atomizer. The atomized stream of metal is then collected on a substrate placed in the line of flight. A solid deposit is built up on the collector. Atomized powder that is not deposited is separated from the exhaust gas by a cyclone and collected. Typical recovery efficiency is in the range of 60 to 90%, depending on the product form. The shape of the final product depends on the atomizing conditions and the shape and motion of the collector

A number of aluminium alloys containing SiC particulate have been produced by spray deposition. These include aluminium-silicon castings alloys and the 2xxx, 6xxx, 7xxx and 8xxx series wrought alloys. Products that have been produced by spray deposition include solid and hollow extrusions, forgings, sheet and remelted pressure die castings

2.6. Powder Metallurgy

Powder metallurgy is especially suited for the production of discontinuous fibre, whisker or particulate reinforced metals. Powder metallurgy processing of Al-MMCs involves both SiC particulates and whiskers. With particulate reinforcement, processing involves: (1) blending of the gas-atomized matrix alloy and reinforcement in powder form (2) compacting (cold pressing) the homogenous blend to roughly 80% density and (3) hot pressing, forging or extruding the cold-pressed billet to full density.

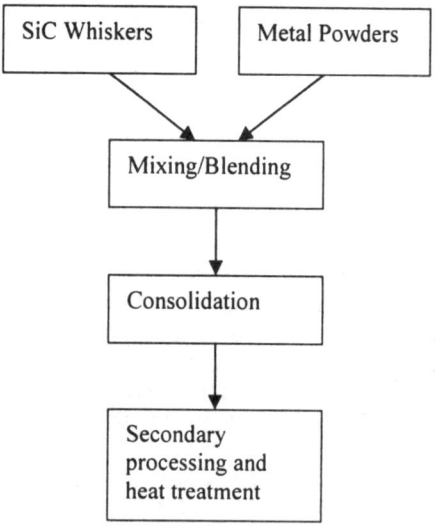

Fig.1: Powder metallurgy process flow to produce SiC whisker reinforced MMCs

The powder metallurgy process begins with mixing and blending prealloyed metallic powder and SiC whiskers, followed by heating and degassing, and consolidation in to intermediate or final product forms.

The Fig. 1 illustrates the manufacture of SiC whisker-reinforced MMCs in a dense, gas-free condition using powder metallurgy technique.

Composites with up to 50% reinforcement can be produced by powder metallurgy, but most manufacturers limit the reinforcement to a maximum of about 25% because of damage to fibers during processing and loss of toughness at high volume fractions. In the case of discontinuous fibers and whiskers, some alignment of their axes perpendicular to the applied load takes place during pressing. This leads to anisotropic behavior with improved longitudinal properties.

3. STIR CASTING METHOD

In the stir casting method, the matrix alloy is stirred in a furnace above liquidus temperature using a mechanical impellar and the dispersoids added while stirring the molten metal. The experimental setup is shown in the Fig. 2. The experimental setup consists of an electrical resistance holding furnace and a stirrer assembly. The stirrer consists of a three bladed impeller attached to a variable speed D.C motor, where the speed can be varied between 0-1500 rpm. The stirrer and the motor assembly are of adjustable type and it could be set at any height and at any angle from the vertical. A bimetallic thermometer composed of Invar and Tin is used to measure the temperature and constant temperature is maintained by a temperature controller device. Aluminium alloy is first melted in a graphite crucible, which has a provision of bottom pouring. During the process, the molten metal is well agitated by a mechanical impeller to create vortex motion. The depth of the immersed impeller is approximately one third of the height of the molten metal from the bottom of the crucible and the speed of the impeller is maintained at 760 rpm. Preheated reinforcement is added into the vortex created by the impeller. Vortex produces uniform suspension of solid particles in the melt due to centrifugal acceleration. The dispersoid being added ranges from 4-15% by weight and the size of the particles dispersed are from 25 m to 100 m. A holding time of 15 minutes at a maximum temperature of 750°C is given to get maximum dissolution of reinforcement in the alloy. After completion of quartz addition, the mixture is degassed with nitrogen. The crucible containing the melt and dispersoids is taken out and placed in a hot refractory brick. The melt is hand stirred with a graphite rod and then tapped into permanent steel moulds through bottom pouring.

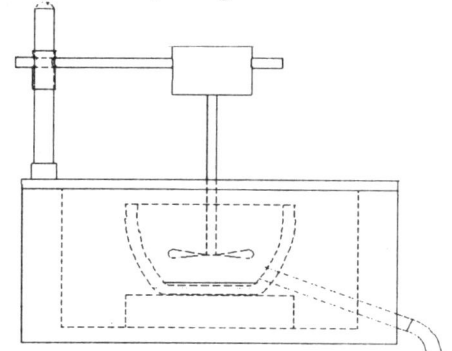

Fig. 2: Experimental set up for manufacturing metal matrix composite

4. FRICTION STIR WELDING

Friction stir welding has offered a great welding quantity to the joining of mainly Al, Mg, Ti and Fe alloys, since it was invented in 1991 [8]. FSW enables long Al alloy butt joints, which are often difficult to join by fusion welding without producing porosity (voids), cracking or distortion. Although it was one of the welding techniques, it was also used for such methods that can acquire ultra fine grain size of Al alloys. Basically FSW process uses a non-consumable tool with a specially designed rotating pin inserted into the abutting edges of the sheet or plate to be welded. Once entered, the rotating tool produces frictional heat and plastic deformation in the weld zone. The tool is then translated along the joint to complete the joining process.

Microstructural changes in the friction stir weld zone have been described in recently published papers. With regard to age hardenable Al alloys, there have been some microstructural studies of welds in alloys 7075-T651 [9,10], 6061-T6 [11,12], and 6063-T5.[13,14] These have demonstrated that the weld zone consists of fine, equiaxed grains and elongated, recovered grains. A heat affected zone thus formed decides the weld zone. These reports also explained the behaviour of precipitates and dislocations associated with the temperature profile caused by frictional heat. The precipitates originally present in the base metal disappeared in the stir zone and coarsened in the heat affected zone. This precipitate and dislocation is considered to be the reason why a softened region is observed near the weld zone.

However, the effects of FSW parameters, especially welding speed, on the microstructural changes and mechanical properties of FSW Al alloy have not been rigorously studied. The objective of the present study is to evaluate the microstructure in the near weld zone and the distribution of strengthening precipitates and dislocations linked to the hardness profile, and the effects of FSW parameters like tool tilt angle, tool rotation speed and welding speed on microstructural changes and mechanical properties.

5. DEVELOPING MATHEMATICAL MODEL FOR MACHINING AND WELDING PARAMETERS USING DESIGN OF EXPERIMENTS

Mathematical model is developed to obtain equations for machining and welding parameters. There are mainly three methods for increasing the accuracy of experiments [15]. The first is to increase the size of the experiment, either through the provision of more replicates or by the inclusion of additional treatments. The second is to refine the experimental technique. Third is to handle the experimental material so that the effects of variability are reduced. This may be done by careful selection of the material, by taking additional measurements that provide information about the material, or finally by skillful grouping of the experimental units in such a way that the units to which one treatment is applied are closely comparable with those to which another treatment is applied. Other methods for increasing the accuracy of the experiments are measurement of relative efficiency, selection of treatments, refinements of technique, selection of experimental material, additional measurements, planned grouping.

In a formal analysis of the results, the first step is to set up an equation for every observation. This equation expresses the observation as the sum of four components. (i) a general average about which the observations are presumed to be fluctuating: (ii) a component representing the effect of the treatment applied: (iii) a component representing certain environmental effects which the design of experiments enables us to isolate: and (iv) a residual component, representing all other sources that influence the observation, and generally referred to as the experimental error.

6. OPTIMISING THE MATHEMATICAL MODEL

The mathematical model created for machining and welding parameters is optimized using robust design of experiments. A response y is thought to be affected by a number of quantitative factors $x_1, x_2 \ldots x_k$. An experimental program is undertaken so as to discover the level at which each of these factors must be set in order to maximize the response. The investigator seeks various ways in industries to manufacture a new product with certain desired characteristics, or to obtain an old product more economically. The response may be the actual amount of product or a measure of the quality of the product. Sometimes the object is to minimize y, as when y represents the amount of an undesirable by-product or the cost of manufacture per unit of output.

7. MICRO STRUCTURAL EXAMINATION OF FRICTION WELD ZONE

Friction stir welding of composites produces microstructural characteristics that are typical of friction stir welds in general: namely a fine grain recrystallized zone (the nugget), a thermo-mechanically affected zone (TMZ) and a heat affected zone (HAZ).Microstructural changes from the weld zone to the unaffected zone are examined with OM (optical microscopy)and SEM (scanning electron microscopy). An etching reagent may be used to observe the microstructure.

8. CONCLUSIONS

In recent years critical consolidation has occurred in the understanding of basic mechanical behaviour in Dis-continuous metal matrix composites (DMMC) particularly with respect to bulk strength, for which an improved understanding of many key physical processes would now appear to be established. The availability of increasingly powerful numerical modeling methods would appear to be particularly valuable in optimizing the machining and welding parameters. Major methods for manufacturing the metal matrix composites have been discussed within the literature. Although various key issues as Friction stir welding, mathematical modeling for machining and welding parameters are identified, but not systematically quantified.

In terms of general utilization of DMMC materials, a broader appreciation of novel combinations of physical properties has proved to be important. Continued experimental and theoretical investigation of the physical properties of DMMC in homogeneous and heterogeneous forms is a prerequisite for their further effective exploitation.

9. REFERENCES

1. **Taya M. and Arsenault R.J.**, *Metal Matrix Composites, Thermomechanical behaviour* (Pergamon Press, Elmsford, Newyork), 1989.
2. **Rohatgi P.K. and Surapa M.K.**, *Mater. Sci, Engg.*, 62, 154, 1984.
3. **Gupta M., Lai M.O., and Soo C.Y.**, *Mater. Sci, Engg.*,A210, 114-122, 1996
4. **Asthana R. and Rohatgi P.**, *Z Metal*, 1Kd.84, 1, 1993.
5. **Ohri K., Watanabe H. and Takeuchi Y.**, *Mater. Sci. Technology*, 4, 41-51, 1988.
6. **Surapa M.K.**, *J. Mater. Process Technol.*, 63, 325-333, 1997.
7. ALUMINIUM ALLOY ASM HAND BOOK, 160-178.
8. **Dawes C.J.**, *Weld.Met.Fabr.*, 1995, 63, 13-16.
9. **Rhodes C.G., Mahoney M.W., Bingel W.H., Spurling R.A. and Bampton C.C.:** *Scr. Mater.*, 1997, 36, 69-75.
10. **Mahoney M.W., Rhodes C.G., Flintoff J.G., Spurling R.A. and Bingel W.H.:** *Metall. Mater. Trans.* A. 1998, 29A, 1955-1964.
11. **Liu G., Murr L.E., Niou C.S., Mcclure J.C. and Vega F.R.:** *Scr. Mater.* 1997, 37, 355-361.
12. **Murr L.E., Liu G. and Mcclure J.C.:** *J. Mater. Sci.*, 1998, 33, 1243-1251
13. **Sato Y.S., Kokawa H., Enomoto M. and Jorgan S.**, *Metall. Mater. Trans.A*, 1999, 30A, 2429-2437.
14. **Sato Y.S., Kokawa H., Enomoto M. and Jorgan S.:** *Metall. Mater. Trans.A*, 1999, 30A, 3125 – 3130
15. **Cochran W.G. and Cox G.M.**, *Design of Experiments*, 15-43, 1950

GCMM 2004
Editors: Prasad K D V Yarlagadda and S Narayanan
Copyright © 2005, Vellore Institute of Technology, Vellore, India
Publisher: Narosa Publishing House Pvt. Ltd., New Delhi, India

Fiber Orientation with Flow Condition during Injection Molding of Reinforced Thermoplastics – A Review

Parvin Shokri[*] & Naresh Bhatnagar

Mechanical Engineering Department
Indian Institute of Technology- Delhi 110016, India

E-mail: nareshb@mech.iitd.ernet.in , narbhat@hotmail.com

Abstract

Injection molding process is one of the most versatile production methods in plastic manufacturing industry. It is capable of producing molded parts of relatively intricate configuration at a high production rate with good dimensional accuracy. Following this development of technology the industry is now looking for high specific strength, high specific stiffness and low cost materials to meet the demands of structural design and economic benefit. Amongst them the reinforced plastic material is one that cannot be ignored. Fibers of glass or carbon are often used as reinforcing agents in polymers with the weight fraction of the dispersed phase depending on the desirable mechanical, thermal and sometimes electrical properties of composites. In this process the molded product can be orthotropic or anisotropic due to the fiber orientation by the governing flow state. The mechanical properties of the final part are affected by fiber orientations. Thus there is a considerable interest in predicting the fiber orientation in order to control tailor made properties. In this paper a review of all the experimental studies investigating the influence of different parameters on fiber orientation in injection molding of fiber reinforced thermoplastic has been covered. The effects of different parameter such as melt and mold temperature, matrix and fiber properties, volume fraction of fibers, part geometry, flow rate, gate type, and gate location on the detailed distribution of fibers in final product are presented. In spite of all of these investigations still this process offer challenges on a fundamental level to the understanding of the relations between material parameters, processing, structure development, and final properties. This review paper reveals the areas of problem related to the sources of fiber orientation, which is still not in common agreement between various scientists and introduces this field for further investigations.

Keywords:
FRP composites, Injection molding, Fiber orientation

1. INTRODUCTION

Injection molding is capable of producing intricate net shapes without requiring finishing treatment and thus is being used widely in the electronic, automotive, aerospace and various other industries.

Recently, with increasing demands for geometrically complex and precision products, possessing superior mechanical and chemical properties, processes such as powder injection molding, which is a mixture of metal or ceramic powders and an organic binder is rapidly growing. Conductive-filler filled plastic composites fabricated by injection molding are now a topic of growing research interest and fibrous conductors are found to improve conductivity much more than spheres, flakes, or irregular particulates. When coupled to the resin matrix, fibers offer a number of advantages in terms of end-use performance, however their use can also create several processing-related problems.

The differential shrinkage between the in-flow and cross-flow directions of fiber-reinforced polymers can be significantly different. This anisotropic behavior can make it more difficult to determine the appropriate cavity dimensions unless it is properly understood and taken into account in tool design. Anisotropic behavior of fiber-reinforced polymers can be attributed to the fact that the fibers become oriented during injection molding process. However, with the proper prediction of flow fields and states of fiber orientation, it should be possible to control the fiber orientation and the anisotropy, resulting in lightweight short fiber reinforced polymeric products with improved mechanical properties and reliability. Many experiments have been conducted to investigate the relation between mold design, molding geometry, process conditions and fiber orientation during injection molding. Different compound of materials were taken under different process conditions. Although there are some agreements between scientists in describing the sources of fiber orientation, it could be found that still there. are some ambiguities in solving the problem properly. In this review paper, by describing briefly the process of different experiments, the gained results are compared and the field of disagreements is clarified.

2. MATERIALS

Major constituents in a fiber-reinforced composite material are the reinforcing fibers and a matrix, which acts as a binder for the fibers. Other constituents that may also be found are coupling agents, coatings, and fillers. Coupling agents and coatings are applied on the fibers to improve their wetting with the matrix as well as to promote bonding across the fiber/matrix interface. Both in turn promote a better load transfer between the fibers and the matrix. Fillers are used with some polymeric matrices primarily to reduce cost and improve their dimensional stability [1].

Ogadhoh & Papathanasiou [2] used polystyrene filled with glass particles of various sizes. This material was chosen, as polystyrene is transparent and thus allows easy visual observation of the particle arrangement within and glass remains solid at the melting temperature of polystyrene. The beads also remain unaffected at the temperature of 550°C, which was used to completely degrade polystyrene during burning. Since the polymer powder has a density significantly lower than that of the glass beads (1.05 versus ~2.5 g/cm^3), it was not possible to produce a uniform mixture by dry mixing routes as such a solution of propanol in distilled water was used to wet the polymer powder prior to mixing. This composite was used by the same authors [3] to study the microstructure at the weld-line in injection molded particulate composites.

Natural fibers are renewable resources, which are both biodegradable and CO_2-neutral. But there are lots of differences between the conventional and natural fibers. For example the shape and the dimensions of natural fibers vary. Sometimes the bundles of natural fibers are not completely separated or unwanted ingredients are not removed from the fiber surface. Owing to the limited thermal stability of natural fibers, thermoplastics with low melting temperatures are preferred matrix materials. A compound of flax fibers with polypropylene was prepared by Aurich & Menning [4] and 2-wt% maleic anhydride grafted polypropylene was added to the polypropylene matrix. The advantage of this composite was the low hardness and brittleness of flax fibers, which made it possible to prepare thin-cut sections parallel to the surface for analyzing fiber orientation angle.

Transparent polymers for easy visual observation were chosen in many investigations. Hine et al. [5] used long glass fiber-reinforced Nylon 6/6 from the VERTON family of materials manufactured by ICI Ltd. Chang et al. [6] used polycarbonate reinforced with 30-wt% short glass fibers and polystyrene was used by Lee et al. [7]. Pontes et al. [8] and Neves et al. [9] used 10% by weight glass fiber reinforced grade of polycarbonate fitting into the range $(d / L)^2 < V_f < (d / L)$ which is a semi-concentrated regime.

Bijsterbosch & Gaymans [10] used an injection moldable grade polyamide (PA-6) with a glass fiber roving. The glass fibers had a diameter of 20 m and were treated with a proprietary sizing (0.2 wt%). Pellets of PA-6 with long glass fiber (9 mm) were produced by a continuous melt impregnation process. They produced pellets with different fiber concentration and degree of impregnation to analyze the effect of these parameters on structure and properties of the injection molded samples.

Yang et al. [11] used an injection grade ABS 900 (Toray, Japan) and two types of conductive fibers (stainless steel fibers and nickel-coated graphite fibers) to analyze the effects of conductive fibers and processing conditions on the electromagnetic shielding effectiveness of injection molded composites.

3. MOLD & MOLDING GEOMETRY

Common molding geometry used for fiber orientation analysis is a simple plate in the form of rectangle or circle.

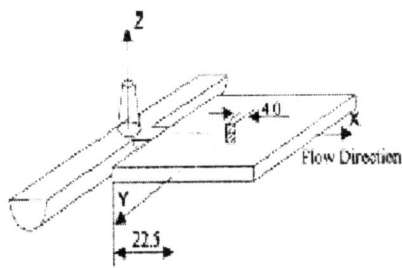

Fig.1: Configuration of the cavity and the runner [6]

This is produced under different conditions of injection molding, where different samples are cut out of these plates in desired directions and locations. One of these molding geometries is shown in Fig. 1.

A four-cavity mold with different filling times was designed by Lee et al. [7] for studying the effects of compressibility of the polymer melt. In this mold, relative location of

the gate for its two identical cavities was also designed differently. Sometimes moldings have the exact geometry of standard tensile specimens [10,12].

Different types of gates were used for analyzing their effects on fiber orientation. Both, top-gated and edge-gated rectangular cavities were used by Ogadhoh & Papathanasiou [2] and a film-gated rectangular strip was designed by Bay & Tucker [13]. Circular center-gated plates imply a radial divergent flow and were used for analyzing the effects of different parameters such as interaction coefficient [8] and circumferential stretching [13] on fiber orientation. A ring-gated circular plate was used by Yang et al. [11]. This ring gate, which was adjustable from 120° to 240° at 60° intervals, was set to facilitate observation of the relation between melt entrance and the fiber dispersion and its orientation.

4. PROCESSING CONDITIONS

Different sets of processing conditions were chosen for analyzing the effects of each parameter on fiber orientation. For example different melt temperatures and flow rate were used by pontes et al. [8] and Neves et al. [9] while other parameters such as mold temperature, holding pressure, holding time and cooling time were kept constant. Fast and slow constant speed injection speed were used by Folkes & Russell [14] as the process variables while barrel temperature on all zones, screw speed, backpressure and mold temperature were kept constant. Different filling time were also used by Larsen [15], Lee et al. [7] and Yang et al. [11] while the other parameters were kept constant.

Three different combinations of cavity thickness and filling time were examined by Gupta & Wang [16] while melt and mold temperatures were kept constant.

To minimize fiber degradation, the lowest possible back-pressure (~ 0 bar) and screw speed (50 rpm) were used by Bijsterbosch and Gaymans [10] and Barrel temperatures were set to 290 °C. A low injection speed was used to obtain the highest possible orientation in the direction of flow.

5. RESULTS

Fig. 2, which is reprinted in Handbook of Molded Part Shrinkage and Warpage [17] by permission of Oxford Science Publication [18], shows micrographs of sections taken through a glass-fiber-filled polypropylene molding.

The upper view shows the section parallel to the flow direction. Near the part surface (at the top and bottom of the micrograph) a skin layer is found where the fibers are frozen into a random pattern. Just inside the skin layer is a region, a shell layer, of highly oriented fibers. This oriented layer is seen to extend toward the center of the part, with more random orientation resulting at further distance from the wall and forms transition layer. Finally, core layer in the center of the part is a randomized area of fiber orientation.

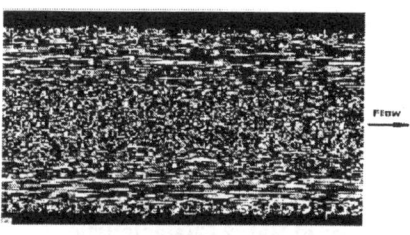

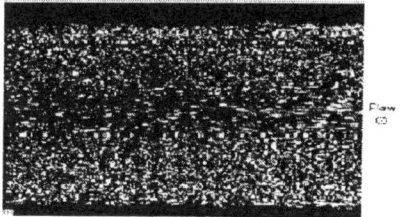

Fig. 2: Glass- filled polypropylene sections parallel and perpendicular to the flow [17]

Planar orientation state of fibers in injection-molded parts is also observed in conclusion of other studies [4,16,19,20,21]. Alignment of fibers with the flow due to shear-dominated flow near the surface was also in the conclusion of Gupta & Wang [16], which is in agreement with fluid mechanical modeling of the mold-filling process [22,23]. Nearly a random orientation in the skin layer directly under the surface of the part and a high alignment in main flow direction below skin

layer was also observed by Aurich & Menning [4] and Bay & Tucker [13].

As can be seen there are common conclusions between scientists about the condition of fiber orientation in the skin and shell layers.

Although frequently it is reported that the fibers in the core of injection-molded parts lie predominantly in the plane of the plate and perpendicular to the mold-fill direction [4,9,19,20], There are a few observation in contrast with cross-flow alignment of fibers at core. For example Zhang et al. [24] proposed an open-ended injection molding method so that the majority of fibers align parallel to the flow direction throughout the section and Folkes & Russell [14] in the case of slow injection, observed that the fibers are aligned parallel to the axis of the strip in the core. The important problem is the completely different explanations, which were presented for describing the state of fiber orientation at core region. For example Gupta & Wang [16] concluded that the in-plane stretching flow causes the fiber at the mid-plane to align transverse to the flow. Folkes & Russell [14] concluded that the major contribution to the condition of the core comes not from flow induced molecular alignment but from columnar spherulitic growth that is known to occur around fibers in the absence of an externally applied flow field. Different crystallization characteristic of matrix due to the presence of fibers was also mentioned by Larsen [15]. The author believes that fibers have an effect on nucleation and resulting fiber orientation. In [17], the author explained that in the core of the part, the melt being pushed forward develops a flattened profile and fibers within this region do not orient without a well-developed shear flow. Malzhan & Schultz [25] concluded that the complete transverse alignment at the core region develops only after the instant of fill, while Gupta & Wang [16] believe that the fiber orientation should be only weakly dependent upon the post-filling stage of injection molding because of a decreased flow field. Effects of each parameter on the state of fiber orientation are summarized as follows:

5.1. Effect of Filling Time

A tendency for a more random in-plane orientation is observed by Neves et al. [9] in the inner layers if a slower injection speed is used and by increasing the injection speed, transverse alignment would result. Folkes & Russell [14] observed that for fast injection in the core of the molding, fibers were aligned at 90° to the overall flow direction whereas in the case of slow injection, the fibers were aligned parallel to the axis of the specimen in the core. Larsen [15] concluded that decreasing of core thickness downstream at slow filling rates depends on increased crystallization during filling.

5.2. Effect of Mold Design

Ogadhoh & Papathanasiou [2] found that there is an increase in the concentration of glass beads as the distance from the injection gate increases. This was observed in both edge-gated and top-gated cavities and was more pronounced for the larger particle size as shown in Fig. 3. Regarded to the gate design Bay & Tucker [13] concluded that if the mold geometry causes strong in plane stretching motions just inside the gate (e.g., a center-gated disk or a point gate in a large cavity) then the three-dimensional details of the flow near the gate could probably be neglected. The gate flow is more important for parts like the straight specimen strip, where there is no in-plane stretching and the gate effects are carried throughout the cavity.

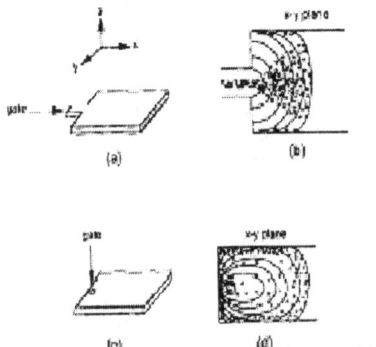

Fig. 3: Schematic of the edge-gated and top-gated cavities and the mechanisms

5.3. Effect of Mold Temperature

Gupta & Wang [26] believe that under isothermal condition, which means replacing the cold-wall temperature with the injection temperature, a change in injection speed has no effect on fiber orientation and this means that the mold temperature is a parameter which should be considered in studying the fiber orientation; While Bay & Tucker [13] found that the mold temperature T_{wall} has little effect on the fiber orientation. Although the authors believe that the mold temperature could have a large effect on molecular orientation or crystallinity in some polymers.

5.4. Effect of Melt Temperature

It was observed [8,9] that the skin is more oriented in the flow direction for lower melt temperatures, whereas the core shows a higher fiber orientation transverse to the flow direction. Raising the melt temperature [8,9] seems to favor a nearly random state of fiber orientation in the core and throughout the thickness. Bay & Tucker [13] through simulating concluded that despite the importance of heat transfer; injection temperature does not have a large effect on the final orientation pattern.

5.5. Effect of Matrix Characteristic:

In studying the effect of thermal conductivity of the polymer upon predicted fiber orientation Gupta & Wang [16] concluded that as the thermal conductivity of the polymer is increased, thereby increasing the thickness of the cold boundary layer, fibers at the mid-plane become more flow-aligned and the thickness of the core region decreases. Considering compressibility of polymers Lee et al. [7] concluded that changes in fiber orientation occur after complete filling of the cavity and prominently in the transition region when the fiber flow rate is low. Bay & Tucker [13] used three materials (PP, PC, and PA 6,6) in their predictions and explained that because the polypropylene has a flatter velocity profile, so the shearing occurs mainly close to the wall and causes the formation of thicker core layer. Also the large heat of fusion of the polypropylene delays the formation of the frozen layer, allowing the shear flow behind the flow front to erase the effect of the fountain flow. This is why there is no skin layer predicted for polypropylene. The polycarbonate, with its more pointed velocity profile, has a smaller core than even the nylon moldings.

5.6. Effect of Fiber Characteristic

Measurements in the study of Folkes & Russell [14] indicated that close to the fibers, molecular reorganization during flow is inhibited leading to excessively long relaxation times for the molecular network and as the concentration of fibers increases; the molecular orientation in the matrix becomes dominated by the orientation of the fibers. Larsen [15] believes that fiber length, as the length both relative to the gradients of the flow field and to the distance from the surface of the mold can play a role. Bijsterbosch & Gaymans [10] observed that with increasing fiber concentration, the fiber orientation remains constant but the fiber length decreases considerably. Voids are also common imperfections in composites [27,28,29] especially at high fiber concentrations. The a_{11} values which are the degree of alignment in the direction of flow, measured in the core of the moldings [9] are lower than those reported by Bay & Tucker [13] and to other authors [30,31]. The authors concluded that this might result from a less intense fiber interaction in the much less reinforced material used in their work (10 wt% vs. 40 wt%).

5.7. Effect of Mold Geometry

In analyzing the effect of cavity thickness as a parameter of mold geometry it was concluded that [16] the relative extend of solid layer is larger for thinner cavities and increases as the injection speed is reduced.

7. REFERENCES

This affects the thickness of different layers and the state of fiber orientation. No large fiber concentration difference could be observed by Bijsterbosch & Gaymans [10] due to the convergence in the tensile bar. By ignoring fiber fragments in analyzing fiber lengths [10], in a typical manner has been done by Doshi & Charrier [32], it was observed that the fiber length is fairly constant over the samples and the convergence in the dumbbell does not degrade the fibers. It was further concluded that [10] a fiber orientation perpendicular to the main flow direction develops at the gate due to compressional flow. Near the convergence in the tensile bar, fibers align parallel to the flow lines, resulting in a higher orientation. The observed orientation can be understood from general flow models [33,34].

6. CONCLUSION

• The primary factors controlling fiber orientation are the process condition, the shape of the cavity and the location of the gate. Among them different shapes of cavities strongly influences the predictive simulation for use in mold design.

• Despite many restrictions that exist for predicting accurately the flow behavior it is possible to introduce guidelines in designing molds and resulting products provided the understanding on the fundamentals of fiber orientation in injection molding of reinforced thermoplastics becomes clear.

1. **Mallick, P.K.**, Fiber Reinforced Composites – Materials Manufacturing and Design, 2nd Ed. Marcel Dekker Inc, NY, 1993.
2. **Ogadhoh, S.O. & Papathanasiou, T.D.**: Particle rearrangement during processing of glass-reinforced polystyrene by injection molding, *J. Composites*, 1996, 27A, 57-63.
3. **Ogadhoh, S.O. & Papathanasiou, T.D.**: On microstructure at the welding in injection moulded particulate composites, *J. Scripta Materialia*, 1997,37,1143-1149.
4. **Aurich, T. & Menning, G.**: Flow-induced fiber orientation in injection molded flax fiber reinforced polypropylene, *J. Polymer Composites*, 2001, 22, 680-689.
5. **Hine, P.J., Davidson, N., Duckett, R.A. & Ward, I.M.**: Measuring the fiber orientation and modeling the elastic properties of injection-moulded long-glass-fiber-reinforced nylon, *J. Composites Science and Technology*, 1995, 53, 125-131.
6. **Chang, S.H., Hwang, J.R., & Doong, J.L.**: Optimization of the injection composites, *J. Polymer Composites*, 2002,23, 1003-1013.

7. **Lee, S.C., Yang, D.Y., Ko, J., & Youn, J.R.:** Effect of compressibility on flow field and fiber orientation during the filling stage of injection molding, *J. Materials Processing Technology*, 1997, 70, 83-92.

8. **Pontes, A.J., Neves, N.M., & Pouzada, A.S.:** The role of the interaction coefficient in the prediction of the fiber orientation in plannar injection moldings, *J. Polymer Composites*, 2003, 24, 358-366.

9. **Neves, N.M., Isdell, G., Pouzada, A.S. & Powell,** P.C.: On the effect of fiber orientation on the flexural stiffness of injection molded short fiber reinforced polycarbonate plates, *J. Polymer Composites*, 1998, 19, 640-651.

10. **Bijsterbosch, H., & Gaymans, R.J.:** Polyamide 6-Long glass fiber injection moldings, *J. Polymer Composites*, 1995, 16, 363-369.

11. **Yang, S.Y., Chen, C.Y., & Parng, S.H.:** Effects of conductive fibers and processing conditions on the electromagnetic shielding effectiveness of injection molded composites, *J. polymer Composites*, 2002,23,1003-1013.

12. **Tsui, C.P., Tang, C.Y., & Lee, T.C.:** Tensile properties and damage behaviors of glass-bead-filled modified polyphenylene oxide under large strain, *J. Polymer Composites*, 2001,22, 742-751.

13. **Bay, R.S., & Tucker III, C.L.:** Fiber orientation in simple injection moldings. Part II: Experimental results, *J. Polymer Composites*, 1992, 13, 332-341.

14. **Folkes, M.J. & Russell, D.A.M.:** Orientation effects during the flow of short-fiber reinforced thermoplastics J. *Polymer,* 1980, 21, 1252-1258.

15. **Larsen, A.,** Injection molding of short fiber reinforced thermoplastics in a center-gated mold, *J. polymer Composites*, 2000, 21, 51-64.

16. **Gupta, M. & Wang, K.K.:** Fiber orientation and mechanical properties of short-fiber-reinforced injection-molded composites: simulated and experimental results, *J. Polymer Composites*, 1993,14, 367-382.

17. **Fischer, J. M.,** Handbook of Molded Part Shrinkage and Warpage, Plastic Design Library / William Andrew / Inc., USA, 2002.

18. **McCrum, N., Buckley, C., & Bucknall, C.,** Principles of Polymer Engineering, Oxford Science Publ., 1988.

19. **Friedrich, K.:** Fracture mechanics characterization of glass fiber reinforced thermoplastic polyesters, Kunststoffe, 1982, 72, 290-296.

20. **Lhymn, C. & Schultz, J.M.:** Fracture behavior of collimated thermoplastic poly (ethylene terephthalate) reinforced with short E-glass fiber, J. *Material Science*, 1983, 18, 2029-2046.

21. **Bay, R.S., & TuckerIII, C.L.:** Fiber orientation in simple injection moldings. Part I: Theory and numerical methods *J. Polymer Composites,* 1992, 13, 317-331.

22. **Ballman, R.L. & Toor, H.L.:** Orientation in injection molding, Modern Plastics, 1960, 38, 113-207.

23. **Tadmor, Z.:** Molecular orientation in injection molding, *J. Applied Polymer Science*, 1974, 18, 1753-1772.

24. **Zhang, T., Evans, J.R.G. & and Bevis, M.J.:** J. Composites Science and Technology, 1996, 56, 921.

25. **Malzahn, J.C. & Schultz, J.M.:** Transverse core fiber alignment in short-fiber injection molding, *J. Composites Science and Technology*, 1986, 25, 187-192.

26. **Gupta, M. & Wang, K.K.:** SPE ANTEC Tech. Papers, 1993, 39, 2290.

27. **Denault, J., Vu-Khanh, T. & Foster, B.:** *J. Polymer Composites*, 1989, 10, 313.

28. **Darlington, M.W. & Smith, G.R.:** J. Polymer, 1975, 16, 459.

29. **Vaxman, A., Narkis, M., Siegmann, A. & Kenig, S.:** *J. Polymer Composites*, 1989, 10, 449.

30. **Lian, B., Nothe, A., Ladewig, J. & McGrath,J.**J. SPE ANTEC Tech. Papers, 1995,41,608.

31. **Jones, R. M.,** Mechanics of composite Materials, Taylor & Francis, PA,USA, 2nd Ed.,1999.

32. **Doshi, S.R. & Charrier, J.M.:** *J. Polymer Composites*, 1989, 10, 28.

GCMM 2004
Editors: Prasad K D V Yarlagadda and S Narayanan
Copyright © 2005, Vellore Institute of Technology, Vellore, India
Publisher: Narosa Publishing House Pvt. Ltd., New Delhi, India

Modeling and Prediction of Tool Life in Turning Operation

Noorul Haq A

Head, Department of Production Engineering,
National Institute of Technology, Tiruchirappalli – 620 015,
Tamilnadu, India

E.mail - anhaq@nitt.edu

Tamizharasan T

Senior Lecturer, Department of Mechanical Engineering,
A A M Engineering College, Kovilvenni – 614 403, Tiruvarur district,
Tamilnadu, India

Abstract

The life of cutting tool in metal cutting plays an important role in the quality and cost of product. In this present study, an empirical model for the prediction of cutting tool life in turning operation is developed. The performance of the system has been studied under varying operating conditions such as speed of cutting, feed rate and depth of cut. This study describes the operation of the experimental system and presents the measured data. The required turning operation is performed on a Kirloskar lathe machine with hardened material used as engine crank pin for workpiece and Polycrystalline Cubic Boron Nitride(PCBN) for cutting tool. For developing the required empirical model, log transformed linear regression analysis, Linear cross product regression analysis and Linear regression analysis are employed. The values predicted from empirical model are compared and verified with the experimental values. Metal turning experiments and statistical tests demonstrate that "the empirical model developed in this work is best fit with acceptable range of deviation".

Keywords

Tool life, Linear regression, Log transformed linear regression, Linear cross product regression, prediction, Design of experiments

1. INTRODUCTION

The primary goal of this work is to establish the process relationships for the cutting process and to build an empirical model. This analysis focuses on the effects of various parameters on the cutting tool life in turning operation. The empirical model is developed to locally approximate the relationship between outputs and inputs based on collected data. The Taylor's tool life equation[1] shows that the tool life 'T' and cutting speed 'V' are related to each other as,

$$VT^n = C \text{ ------------------(1)}$$

where,

n – tool life exponent
C – Taylor's constant

The above Taylor's equation(1) is linearised to convert the nonlinear form of equation into linear form and rewritten on a log-log scale as,

$$\log V + n \log T = \log C \text{ --------(2)}$$

Therefore the Taylor's equation represents a straight line. In order to include the effects of feed rate 'f' and depth of cut 'd' in the above equation, it is generalized and the relationship[1] is of the form,

$$VT^n f^{n_1} d^{n_2} = C_1 \text{ --------------(3)}$$

where n, n_1, n_2 and C_1 are the constants which depend on tool and work materials, tool geometry, types of coolant used, etc.,.

Since the Taylor's equation does not fit the actual tool life data for many materials, with the experimental data, it is analyzed to estimate these various parameters for the first-order model and since the first-order model determines some statistical evidence of lack of fit, a general second-order linear equation in the form of logarithmic terms has also been proposed with additional data collected. i.e. the parameters in the first-order model are estimated using multiple regression analysis and the analysis of variance performed for this model reveals some lack of fit, so that the second-order model is developed on log-log scale[2]. It is expressed as,

$$\log T = n_0 + n_1 \log V + n_2 \log f + n_3 \log d$$
$$+ n_{12} \log V \log f + n_{13} \log V \log d$$
$$+ n_{23} \log f \log d \text{ ------------------(4)}$$

where n_0, n_1, n_2, n_3, n_{12}, n_{13} and n_{23} are the constants determined from the experimental data by curve fitting.

For simplicity, the second-order empirical model is postulated from equation (4) as,

$$T_p = n_0 + n_1 x_1 + n_2 x_2 + n_3 x_3 + n_{12} x_1 x_2$$
$$+ n_{13} x_1 x_3 + n_{23} x_2 x_3 \text{ ------------------(5)}$$

where
T_p - Predicted value of tool life

x_1, x_2, x_3 - Cutting parameters

The experimental deviation or residual is the difference between the predicted and observed values of the tool life.

2. LITERATURE REVIEW

A considerable number of studies had been investigated on the general effects of speed of cutting, feed rate and depth of cut on the tool wear and the surface finish. The basic numerical prediction methods were described by Chapra et al.[1]. Chang-Xue (Jack) et al.[2] presented the various methods of developing mathematical models. Kevin Chou et al.[3] explained the modeling methods of hard turning. Feng [4]., Feng and Kusiak[5] and Feng and Kusiak[6] developed empirical models with some data mining techniques such as regression analysis. A surface roughness model was developed for a turning operation by Groover[7]. A mathematical model was developed and the nose radius and feed rate were related by Boothroyd and Knight[8]. The effects of built-up-edge on surface roughness and tool wear was presented by Shaw[9]. Karmakar[10] considered the effects of speed in the performance of empirical model. Petro poulos[11] developed the relationship between surface roughness and tool wear. Montgomery[12] presented various design and analysis of experiments. Geometric modeling and regression analysis were compared by Sata[13]. The simple linear regression analysis was discussed by Smith and Mason[14]. The method of fitting the equations to data with statistical modeling methods is presented by Sundaram et al.[15]. The various effects of cutting conditions on bearing area parameters were well defined by Grieve et al.[16]. The effect of cutting speed was clearly explained by Chandramani et al.[17]. Different types of mathematical models were studied by Box and Draper[18].

So many surface roughness empirical models were developed by the past researchers with the machining parameters such as speed, feed rate, depth of cut etc.,. Few of the authors developed models for tool wear but no author had been considered the most practically used machine component material as specimen. So, in this study, the commercially available engine crank pin material is selected for workpiece.

3. EXPERIMENTAL DETAILS

The PCBN cutting tool inserts of same CBN content [3] are selected and the required hard turning operations are performed on eighteen engine crankpins, having same hardness values. The different test conditions are shown in Table1.

Table 1. Experimental Test Conditions

Test Condition Number	Speed in m/min.	Feed in mm/rev.	Depth of Cut in mm	Flank Wear in mm	Tool Life in min.	S/N Ratio for Tool Life
1	100	0.06	0.3	0.2	43	32.67
2	100	0.10	0.3	0.2	40	32.04
3	100	0.06	0.4	0.2	39.5	31.93
4	100	0.10	0.2	0.2	38.5	31.71
5	150	0.06	0.2	0.2	37	31.36
6	100	0.14	0.4	0.2	35	30.88
7	100	0.14	0.3	0.2	35	30.88
8	150	0.06	0.3	0.2	34.5	30.76
9	150	0.10	0.4	0.2	34	30.63
10	150	0.14	0.4	0.2	33	30.37
11	150	0.10	0.3	0.2	32.5	30.24
12	200	0.06	0.3	0.2	31	29.83
13	150	0.14	0.2	0.2	31	29.83
14	200	0.06	0.4	0.2	28	28.94
15	200	0.10	0.4	0.2	27.5	28.79
16	200	0.10	0.2	0.2	26.5	28.46
17	200	0.14	0.3	0.2	25.5	28.13
18	200	0.14	0.2	0.2	25	27.96

The required hard turning operations are performed on a PSG141 lathe of 177.5 mm centre height, 520mm swing gap, 1600 rpm speed, 0.05-3.5 mm/rev of feed range and main motor power of 3.7 kW. The geometry of the selected cutting inserts is 80° diamond shape, with a 20° edge chamfer and 0.102 mm wide[3]. The outermost layer of the workpiece is turned off first by using mixed alumina cutting insert in order to avoid the hard turning of oxidized layer. For the test cut, suitable length is selected and the number of cuts vary depending upon the depth of cut. At regular intervals of time, the tool wear and surface roughness are measured and when the flank wear of the cutting tool comes to 200 microns, the turning operation is stopped because, most of the tools fracture with a flank land measurement between 180 and 200 microns(0.18mm and 0.20mm)[3]. Similarly, the other turning operations with different cutting conditions are also performed with different cutting inserts[3]. The flank wear and surface roughness values are measured at regular intervals of time until the flank wear reaches 0.2mm.The measured tool life and flank wear values are tabulated in Table1, for all the eighteen test conditions. The values of speed, feed rate and depth of cut are properly utilized for developing the empirical tool life model. The Microsoft Excel and Origin software are used in this work.

4. REGRESSION MODELING

The model development is that of the dependence of the model on the data collected to construct the model, termed as "construction sample"[4]. The assumption for the linear regression models is the estimated linear functional form, while dependence is the determination of the slope and intercept parameters using the construction data set. The empirical models are more specific than analytical models. These models are approximate only under certain conditions or for certain products. These empirical modes depend on data-its abundance, integrity, completeness and timeliness[5].

Three levels of interest for the factors are selected and this paper concentrates on modeling methodology[6] and the related model validation procedures. For constructing the model by regression analysis, the factorial experimentation approach to design of experiments(DOE)[2] is followed. The study of empirical modeling is sometimes restricted because of more number of parameters. The number of experiments to be conducted is calculated as,

$$(L-1)p+1 = (3-1)3+1 = 7 \quad \text{------(6)}$$

where, L – Number of levels

p – Number of parameters

The nearest available array is L_9, but for cross checking the trend, 18 experiments (2x 9) are conducted.

The order of the 18 experiments is randomized and the experiments are conducted on the specified lathe. The arithmetic average value of surface roughness in all the experimental conditions does not exceed 5 microns. Both the high adjusted R^2 value and the close to zero P value in the analysis of variance(ANOVA) are presented by the regression analysis.

5. RESULTS AND DISCUSSIONS

The effect of each individual factor and factor interactions on tool life[9] are examined with a reasonably small amount of time and cost. This research is able to include all parameters simultaneously with more accurate experimental data. The positive signs of the regression analysis mean that the tool life value goes in the same direction and the negative signs mean the opposite. The magnitude of impact of each term on the tool life is studied based on the values of their coefficients. The model suggests with 't' and 'p' values that the effect of cutting speed[10] on tool life is more and the effects of other parameters are comparatively lower.

Table2. (a,b,c and d) Prediction of RMS differential percentage for Tool Life with log transformed linear regression analysis.

(a) SUMMARY OUTPUT

Regression Statistics	
Multiple R	0.955005423
R Square	0.912035358
Adjusted R Square	0.893185791
Standard Error	0.022960319
Observations	18

(b) ANOVA

	df	SS	MS	F	Significance F
Regression	3	0.076522192	0.025507397	48.3849 5199	1.23021E-07
Residual	14	0.007380467	0.000527176		
Total	17	0.08390266			

$$\log T_p = 2.39 - 0.49 \log V - 0.17 \log f - 0.01 \log d \quad \_\_(7)$$

(c) t AND p TESTS

	Coefficients	Standard Error	t Stat	P-value	Lower 95%
Intercept	2.39030	0.104343	22.9081	1.69E-12	2.1665084
V	-0.48718	0.043826	-11.1164	2.48E-08	-0.5811781
f	-0.16589	0.035773	-4.63743	0.000384	-0.242619
d	-0.01202	0.043826	-0.27437	0.787808	-0.106021

Upper 95%	Lower 95.0%	Upper 95.0%
2.614096273	2.166508405	2.614096273
-0.393184966	-0.581178102	-0.393184966
-0.089168681	-0.242619018	-0.089168681
0.081972183	-0.106020952	0.081972183

Observation	Predicted(T_p)	Residuals	Observed(T_o)	Residuals.sq
1	1.62704	0.00643	1.62061	4.131E-05
2	1.58812	0.01394	1.57418	1.943E-04
3	1.56238	-0.01831	1.58068	3.352E-04
4	1.54125	0.02695	1.51430	7.262E-04
5	1.50233	0.00955	1.49278	9.123E-05
6	1.47659	0.04193	1.43466	1.758E-03
7	1.47827	0.01309	1.46517	1.715E-04

Observation	Predicted(T_p)	Residuals	Observed(T_o)	Residuals.sq	RMS Diff%
8	1.43996	-0.00063	1.44059	3.958E-07	
9	1.41934	-0.02139	1.44074	0.0004579	
10	1.62342	-0.02682	1.65025	0.0007195	
11	1.59024	-0.00478	1.59501	2.28205E-05	
12	1.56388	-0.01981	1.58369	3.92461E-04	
13	1.53914	-0.00132	1.54045	1.73253E-06	
14	1.50083	0.03065	1.47018	9.39375E-04	
15	1.48021	0.01115	1.46905	1.24413E-04	
16	1.47677	-0.02961	1.50637	8.76584E-04	
17	1.44358	-0.02034	1.46392	4.13540E-04	
18	1.41722	-0.01068	1.42790	1.14110E-04	
			1.51503	0.02025	1.33655

Since the depth of cut is not having a significant individual effect on tool life[11], it is increased to some extent in order to improve the material removal rate. All the values in connection with the empirical model are presented in Table2 and Table3.

Table3. (a,b,c and d) Prediction of RMS differential percentage for Tool Life with Linear Cross Product regression analysis.

(a) SUMMARY OUTPUT

Regression Statistics	
Multiple R	0.985348941
R Square	0.970912535
Adjusted R Square	0.955046645
Standard Error	1.120031419
Observations	18

(b) ANOVA

	df	SS	MS	F	Significance F
Regression	6	460.6036036	76.76726727	61.194962 1	8.23546E-08
Residual	11	13.79917417	1.254470379		
Total	17	474.4027778			

$$T_p = 72.39 - 0.17V - 183.92f - 42.78d$$
$$+ 0.31Vf + 268.24fd + 0.09Vd \quad \text{-------(8)}$$

(C) t AND p TESTS

	Coefficients	Standard Error	t Stat	P-value
Intercept	72.38753754	5.78370665	12.5157692	7.53916E-08
V	-0.16686486	0.035646237	-4.68113555	0.000670322
F	-183.918919	48.27397339	-3.80989809	0.002893274
D	-42.7792793	15.68620473	-2.72719119	0.019676893
V x f	0.313513514	0.211551597	1.481971856	0.166418274
f x d	268.2432432	105.7757987	2.53596046	0.027678261
V x d	0.094594595	0.084620639	1.117866701	0.287443661

Lower 95%	Upper 95%	Lower 95.0%	Upper 95.0%
59.65767859	85.11739648	59.65767859	85.11739648
-0.24532174	-0.08840799	-0.24532174	-0.08840799
-290.169272	-77.6685661	-290.169272	-77.6685661
-77.3044006	-8.25415798	-77.3044006	-8.25415798
-0.15210865	0.779135676	-0.15210865	0.779135676
35.43216216	501.0543243	35.43216216	501.0543243
-0.09165427	0.280843459	-0.09165427	0.280843459

(d) RESIDUAL OUTPUT

Observation	Predicted(Tp)	Residuals	Observed (T_o)	Residuals. sq	RMS Diff%
1	43.10195	-0.10195	43.2039	0.010394	
2	38.49565	1.504354	36.99129	2.263082	
3	36.03529	-1.03529	37.07057	1.071816	
4	36.6452	0.354805	36.29039	0.125886	
5	33.13889	-0.63889	33.77778	0.408179	
6	31.77853	1.221471	30.55706	1.491993	
7	29.41186	1.588138	27.82372	2.522183	
8	28.07853	-0.57853	28.65706	0.334695	
9	24.78303	0.216967	24.56607	0.047075	
10	39.65691	-0.15691	39.81381	0.02462	
11	39.1452	-0.6452	39.79039	0.416277	
12	35.61186	-0.61186	36.22372	0.374375	
13	35.39565	-0.89565	36.29129	0.802181	
14	32.96231	1.037688	31.92462	1.076796	
15	29.98574	1.014264	28.97147	1.028732	
16	28.63529	-0.63529	29.27057	0.403587	
17	27.48574	-0.98574	28.47147	0.971675	
18	26.1524	-0.6524	26.8048	0.425629	
	33.13889		0.875569		2.64212

Similarly the tool life is predicted by using Linear regression analysis and the model is given as, $T_p = 77.35 - 0.17V - 122.82f - 39.81d$ ------(9)

This analysis shows some higher values of percent relative deviation and RMS differential percentage when comparing with other models. The output tables are not shown due to page limit.

Figure1.represents the tool life calculated with various models such as experimental, log transformed linear regression, linear cross product regression and Linear regression for all the eighteen test conditions. This figure shows that the deviation in tool life calculated with various models is within the acceptable range.

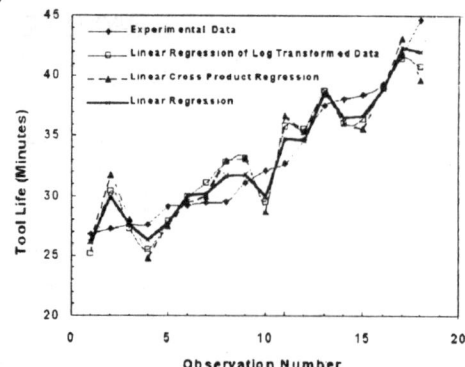

Fig 1: Tool Life with various models Vs. observation numbers.

114

The percent relative deviations[2] between the values of tool life with various models in all the test conditions are calculated as,

$$\frac{\text{Predicted value - Observed value}}{\text{Observed value}} \times 100$$

----------(10)

The calculated values of absolute percent deviation are plotted in Figure2 which shows the relative deviation in tool life of various models in different test conditions. From the study of various models, it is known that all the models have a statistically satisfactory goodness of fit from the modeling point of view.

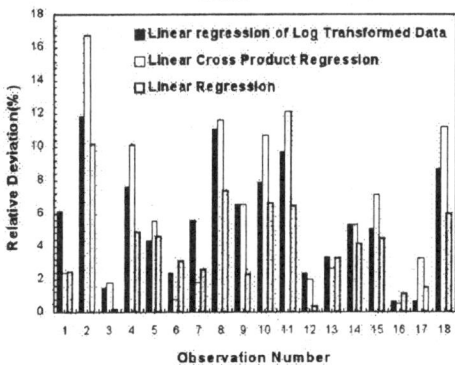

Fig 2: Relative deviation in Tool Life Vs. Observation numbers.

By using one of the optimization techniques, Taguchi's design of experiments[12], the best values of speed as 100ml/min, feed rate as 0.06 mm/rev and depth of cut as 0.2 mm are identified but not included in this paper due to page limit. With these best values of parameters, an experiment is conducted as validation and the tool life is getting improved from 43 min to 43.25 min which is also not shown in this paper. Then an empirical model and another analytical model are developed and compared[13]. The models developed are validated with experimental data and the results are shown in Table4.

Table 4. Validated Results

SI.No	Method	Experimental Tool Life	Predicted Tool Life	Residual	Percent Relative Deviation
1	Log Transformed Linear Regression Analysis	43.25	41.9704	-1.2796	2.95862
2	Linear Cross Product Regression Analysis	43.25	42.67768	-0.5723	1.32328
3	Linear Regression	43.25	45.0188	1.7688	4.08971

This analysis shows that the model is well suited not only to the parameter range of experimental conditions in model construction, but also to the range of experimental conditions in model validation.

6. CONCLUSION

This paper presents the various multiple linear regression analysis methods used to develop empirical models for estimating cutting tool life. The results obtained from various models are compared with each other. The values of percent relative deviation predicted by these models are then verified and it is concluded that the developed models provide a statistically satisfactory prediction. These developed models aid to improve the tool life and for the selection of various cutting parameters. It is once again concluded that these empirical models developed are well suited for all the experimental conditions.

7. REFERENCES

1. **Chapra** and **Canale,** "Numerical Methods for Engineers", *Tata McGraw-Hill*, Third edition, 2002.

2. **Chang-Xue(Jack)** and **Xianfeng Wang**, "Development of empirical models for surface roughness prediction in finish turning", *International journal of advanced manufacturing technology*, 20(5), pp. 1-24, 2002.

3. **Kevin Chou Y, Chris.J.Evans** and **Moshe.M.Barash,** "Experimental investigation on CBN turning of Hardened AISI-52100 steel", *Journal of material processing technology*, 124, pp. 274-283, 2002.

4. **Feng**, "An experimental study of the effect of turning parameters on surface roughness in finish turning", Proceedings of the 2001 industrial engineering research conference, paper 2036, Noreross, 2001.

5. **Feng C X** and **Kusiak K**, "Robust tolerance design with the design of experiments approach", Transactions of ASME journal of manufacturing science and engineering, 122(3), pp. 520-528, 2000.

6. **Feng C X** and **Kusiak K**, "Robust tolerance design with the integer programming approach", Transactions of ASME *journal of manufacturing science and engineering*, 119(4A), pp. 602-610, 1997.

7. **Groover M P**, "Fundamentals of modern manufacturing", *Prentice Hall*, John Wiley, NewYork, 1996.

8. **Boothroyd G** and **Knight W A**, "Fundamentals of machining and machine tools", Marcel dekker, NewYork, 1970.

9. **Shaw M C**, "Metal cutting principles", Oxford university press, NewYork, 1984.

10. **Karmakar A**, "Factors influencing surface finish during fine turning", Proceedings of fourth all India machine tool design and research conference", India, pp. 123-128, 1970.

11. **Petropoulos P G**, "Statistical basis for surface finish assessment in oblique finish turning of steel components", International journal of production research, 12, pp.345-360, 1974.

12. **Montgomery D C,** "Design and analysis of experiments", John Wiley, NewYork, Fifth edition, 2001.

13. **Sata T,** "Surface finish in metal cutting", Annals of CIRP, 12(4), pp. 190-197, 1964.

14. **Smith A E** and **Mason A K**, "Cost estimation predictive modeling:regression Vs neural network", *The engineering economist*, 42(2), pp. 137-161, 1997.

15. **Sundaram R M** and **Lambert B K**, "Mathematical models to predict surface finish in fine turning of steel: Part I and II", International journal of production research, 19, pp. 547-564, 1981.

16. **Grieve D J, Kaliszer H** and **Rowe G W**, "The effects of cutting conditions on bearing area parameters", Proceedings of ninth international machine tool design and research conference, UK, 2, pp. 989-1004, 1968.

17. **Chandramani K L** and **Cook N H**, "Investigation on the nature of surface finish and its variation with cutting speed", Journal of engineering for industries, Series B, pp. 134-140, 1964.

18. **Box G E P** and **Draper N R**, "Empirical model building and response surfaces", John Wiley, NewYork, 1987.

GCMM 2004
Editors: Prasad K D V Yarlagadda and S Narayanan
Copyright © 2005, Vellore Institute of Technology, Vellore, India
Publisher: Narosa Publishing House Pvt. Ltd., New Delhi, India

Operations Sequencing for Machining Prismatic Components using Ant Colony Optimization

Muthukumar T*, Kumarasamy G S** & Rajmohan B***

*PG Student, **Senior Lecturer, ***Professor
Dept. of Production Technology, Madras Institute of Technology Campus,
Anna University, Chennai, India – 600044

Email: kumarasamy@mitindia.edu

Abstract

Computer aided process planning (CAPP) is considered as the key technology in computer aided design and manufacturing (CAD/CAM) and is crucial for implementation of Computer Integrated Manufacturing (CIM) systems. In developing such systems, Operation Sequencing is regarded as one of the critical activities in CAPP. It is a combinatorial optimization problem with specified precedence constraints. A methodology for Sequencing of Machining Operations using Ant Colony Optimization (ACO) Algorithm is proposed. The objective function considered is minimization of total machining cost. ACO is applied to construct a near optimal sequence and local search to improve the solution further. The various instances of Travelling Salesman Problem (TSP) problems are tested and the results are promising. The proposed algorithm is applied for a typical prismatic component and proved to give better results.

Keywords
CAPP, ACO, CAD/CAM, Optimization.

1. INTRODUCTION

Mechanical design means the design of components and assemblies that involve creative thinking, experience, intuition and quantitative analysis. Computer Aided Design (CAD), Computer Aided Process Planning (CAPP) and Computer Aided Manufacturing (CAM) are now commonly used.

Process Planning has been defined by the Society of Manufacturing Engineers as 'the systematic determination of the methods by which a designed product is to be manufactured economically and competitively'. It is a mixture of complex tasks which are accomplished by using suitable forms of process technology and geometric reasoning. (Markopoulos, 1995) A number of process planning problems can be defined and solved analytically, and in those cases a solution or number of optimal solutions are obtained by applying algorithms and technological constraints.

One of the important bottleneck problems in Computer Aided Process Planning (CAPP) is to sequence the selected machining operations to manufacture the part. The nature of the operation sequence generation is to develop a feasible and optimal sequence of operations for a part based upon the technical requirements, the given manufacturing resources and certain goals such as cost or time targets.

2. LITERATURE REVIEW

There are a number of research papers on various operation sequencing problems, viz Graphic constraint representation techniques such as Hamiltonian path analogy, the Latin multiplication method (Irani et al, 1995). Bhaskara Reddy et al (1999) introduced the use of genetic algorithm to obtain the best machining sequence for rotational components. Dong-Ho lee et al (2001) suggested Branch and Fathoming algorithm to solve the operation sequence problem.

3. METHODOLOGY

The following are the various steps involved in obtaining the optimal operation sequence for the given component.

1. Recognizing the various manufacturing features from the CAD model of the part.
2. Determining the overall dimensions of the feature and its tolerance requirements.
3. Determining the various constraints existing between the features, setup details regarding the number of setups required and in each setup, the number of features that can be machined.
4. Selection of machining operations corresponding to each feature.
5. Generation of Feature Precedence Graph based on the constraints and setup details.
6. Generation of Precedence Cost Matrix.
7. Applying ACO algorithm for operations sequencing.

4. OPERATIONS SEQUENCING

The main task in operations sequencing is to identify the various machining operations that are required to manufacture the various features of the part. The selection is done by matching the type of feature and its specifications such as geometry, surface finish and tolerance requirements to the appropriate operation or a set of operations for machining each feature.

4.1 Manufacturing Constraints

The operation sequencing is a complex task, which is influenced by two major factors: the constraints imposed by the part on the use of each operation and their possible interaction. The various precedence constraints are Locating constraint, Accessibility constraint, Non-destruction constraint and Geometric tolerance constraint.

4.2 Feature Precedence Analysis

Once the various machining operations required to machine the component is selected, a Feature Precedence Graph (FPG) is generated by incorporating the various constraints in it. In a FPG, a node represents an operation and each path, a constraint among operations. The construction of a FPG constitutes the following stages:

1. For each constraint, parent child relationships are generated for the relevant features.
2. From the above parent-child relationship, the final FPG is generated by refining the relationship using the following rule: If feature A and Feature B have precedence relationship with feature C and feature B has precedence relationship with feature A, they can be represented in a form C→B→A.

In the final process plan, each feature can precede or succeed the other depending upon the cost of each pair, since cost tend to rule all decisions in all sequence optimization problems. The relative costs are approximated as the number of tasks that need to be performed in each category of physical effort such as machine parameter change, tool change, setup change and machine change.

Intuitively, it is desirable to try to design a process plan that minimizes the changes in the higher cost categories between operations. The Precedence cost matrix (PCM) is a square matrix with equal number of rows and columns equal to the number of machining operations to be performed on the part and the cost values of each operational change are represented in the corresponding cells.

5. ANT COLONY OPTIMIZATION

Evolutionary algorithms which are inspired by biological systems are gaining more importance for solving combinatorial optimization problems. Ant Colony Optimization (ACO) Algorithms proposed by Dorigo et al., (1992) belong to this class of evolutionary algorithms which are based on the natural behaviour of ants.

Ants are capable of selecting the shortest pathway amongst a set of alternatives, from their nest to food source. They deploy a chemical trail (Pheromone) as they walk; this trail attracts other ants to take the path that has the most pheromone.. This provides positive feed back and results in the selection of the shortest path. The basic idea is to imitate the cooperative behaviour of ant colonies in order to solve combinatorial optimization problems.

6. PSEUDO CODE

1. Initialization phase ACO
For each edge (r, s), t(r, s) = t0
2. Find operations without precedence constraints
For operation = 1 to n, do
    Let start[i] be operations without precedence constraints where ants start their tour
3. Ants build feasible operation sequence in this step. Sequence for each ant is stored in seq[j][k], where 'j' represents starting operation of kth ant
For K = 1 to m, do
For op = 1 to n, do
    Find possible operations that can be selected (Which doesn't violates precedence constraints and also not yet visited)
    Choose the next operation according to Ant Transition Rule (exploration or Exploitation)
    Do local pheromone updating Update seq[j] [k]
End For
End For
4. Global Pheromone Updating
For k = 1 to m, do

Compute the cost for each ant's sequence and find the minimum cost.

Update those edges belonging to global best sequence.
5. Stopping Criterion
If (stopping Criteria is met)
Print Best Sequence and its associated cost.
Else
Goto Step 2
End if.

7. COMPUTATIONAL RESULTS

The algorithm is applied to a typical industrial prismatic component. (Fig. 1)

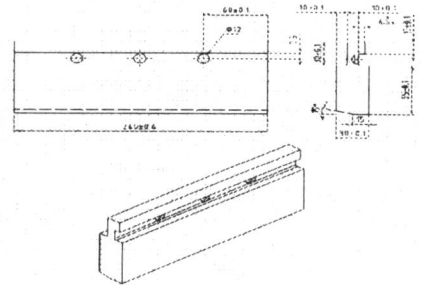

Fig.1 Prismatic Component

7. 1 Selected Operations

Operation No	Operation
1	End Milling I
2	End Milling II
3	End Milling – Finish
4	End Milling I
5	End Milling II
6	End Milling – Finish
7	Drilling
8	End Milling of Slot
9	Plain Milling - Flat Surface
10	Plain Milling Finish – Flat Surface
11	Plain Milling I – Tapered Surface
12	Plain Milling II – Tapered Surface
13	Plain Milling – Finish – Tapered Surface
14	Radius Forming

7.2 Precedence Constraints Details

The various features associated with the component have the following precedence relationship among them.

Table.2. Precedence Constraint Details

Sl.No	Constraint	Details
1	Accessibility	$2\rightarrow1, 3\rightarrow2,$ $5\rightarrow4,6\rightarrow5$ $10\rightarrow9,12\rightarrow11,$ $13\rightarrow12,$ $14\rightarrow10,13$
2	Geometric	$7\leftrightarrow8,8\rightarrow3,$ $10\rightarrow3,13\rightarrow10$
3	Non-Destructive	$8\rightarrow6,7$
4	Location	NIL

7.3 Optimal Machining Sequence

The optimal machining operation sequence of the component generated by Ant colony optimization algorithm is 1,2,4,5,6,3,7,8,11,12,9,10,13,14 and the corresponding cost value is 229 units.

8. CONCLUSION

In a CAPP system, an efficient search is required to explore the large solution space of feasible operation sequences under various operation constraints. The present work describes a heuristic procedure based on ACO. This heuristic procedure is best suitable for solving Sequential ordering problems with multiple starting points (which does not have any precedent constraints).

And also it is capable of finding the optimal operations sequence in less number of iterations quickly as compared to existing heuristic procedures. This procedure helps the process planner to obtain the optimal operation sequence in a dynamic industrial production environment.

9. REFERENCES

1 **BhaskaraReddy, S.V., Shanmugam, M.S.,** and **Narendiran, T.T.** (1999), "Operation Sequencing in CAPP using Genetic Algorithms", *International Journal of Production Research*, Vol.31, No.5, 1063-1074.

2 **Dong-Ho Lee, Kiritsis, D.,** and **Xirouchakis, P.** (2001),"Branch and Fathoming algorithm for Operation Sequencing in Process Planning", *International Journal of Production Research*, Vol.39, No.8, 1649-1669.

3 **Gambardella, L.M,** and **Dorigo, M.** (2000)," An Ant Colony System Hybridized with a New Local Search for the Sequential Ordering Problem", *INFORMS Journal on Computing*, Vol.12 (3), 237-255.

4 **Irani, S.A., Koo, H.Y.,** and **Raman, S.** (1995),"Feature-based operation generation in CAPP", *International Journal of Production Research*, Vol.33 No.1, 17-39.

5 **Marco Dorigo, Vuttirio Maniezzo,** and **Alberto Colorni**(1996),"The Ant System: Optimization by a colony of cooperating agents", *IEEE Transactions on Systems, Man and Cybernetics*-Part B, Vol.26, No.1, 1-13.

6 http://softlib.rice.edu/softlib/tsplib/.

GCMM 2004
Editors: Prasad K D V Yarlagadda and S Narayanan
Copyright © 2005, Vellore Institute of Technology, Vellore, India
Publisher: Narosa Publishing House Pvt. Ltd., New Delhi, India

PRODUCT AND PROCESS OPTIMIZATION FOR METAL FORMING AND MODAL ANALYSIS OFA RECTANGULAR PAN

Raghu Echempati

Mechanical Engineering Department
Kettering University
1700 West Third Avenue
Flint, MI-48504 (U.S.A.)
rechempa@kettering.edu

Abstract

Product and process optimization involves the integration of all the activities from product concept through production/field support to simultaneously optimize the product and its manufacturing processes to meet cost and performance objectives. This paper describes the use of a numerical computational method for the design and manufacture of an example sheet metal component. The goal is to optimize the product parameters (e.g., die and punch geometry, blank material and thickness), and process parameters (e.g., punch velocity, binder pressure, friction) in order to improve the chances of success for a stamping operation. With the increasing power and availability of computational tools, simulation of stamping operations may be the best way to optimize these parameters rather than the trial and error method of real forming often used in industry. Some sample results of this study are presented.

Keywords:

Metal forming simulations, FEA, Vibration Analysis

1. INTRODUCTION

Design is the process of converting information about the application into technical specifications for the product and its implied processes. It is an iterative activity. The way in which products are produced has evolved during the last decade. Terms like Concurrent Engineering, DFX, Life-cycle Engineering, and Lean Manufacturing have been used to indicate that an improved method was being implemented to design and manufacture products. Optimum Product and Process Development involves the overlapping, interacting, and iterative nature of all the aspects that impact the product realization process. It is a continuous process that leads to a company's increased profitability and market share based on a product's cost, performance and features, value, and time-to-market [1].

As is well known, optimizing the process parameters in the early stages of design helps avoid costly changes due to manufacturability problems. However, when Computer Aided Engineering (CAE) is used the efficiency of the approach depends on the accuracy of simulation, which is complicated by the large number and interdependency of product and process parameters.

Once the product concept (e.g., a rectangular pan in this paper) has been determined with an initial geometry and material for the final product, the tool geometry and the process models can be parameterized with an appropriate CAE tool. Selection of the material model for the part is critical for an accurate simulation of the entire process. The model must describe the mechanical response of the material, in terms of mechanical properties like elongation, anisotropy, and elastic recovery (springback).

Both real and virtual forming experiments were performed for the work presented in this

121

paper. Appropriate CAE tools (DYNAFORM© and LS-DYNA©) were used for the virtual forming experiments. The process parameters like the friction between the tools, binder pressure, and punch velocity were virtually optimized using the Design of Experiments (DOE) method. Simulations were run until the process parameters were optimized, thus integrating product and process development.

1.1. Importance of Optimum Design Engineering

Evolution toward the Optimum Engineering in part are brought about by the realization that within the first 10% of the total time it will take to design, manufacture, and deliver a product, numerous decisions will have been made that effectively commit 85% of the funds to be expended for the project. Thus, the cost of a change in the product at the final production run stage can be many times the cost of making the change at the design stage. In summary, the overall goal of optimum design engineering is to convert a product concept into a manufacturable, salable, and profitable product in such a way that the design of the product and the corresponding processes result in high customer satisfaction, short lead-times, high quality and reliability [2]. This is accomplished by optimizing the product parameters and process parameters using CAE tools that are available today. In fact, many OEMs now require that their suppliers perform virtual simulations of the stamping process in order to reduce the more costly try-outs.

1.2. Current Industry Status

In a manufacturing environment like metal forming industry, the scope and implications of optimum engineering are far-reaching. The metal forming industry is a several hundred billion dollar industry in the United States, with a large portion being accounted for by the automotive industry. New dies for stamped parts for a car model typically cost several hundred million dollars, with costs for an entire car line approaching in excess of $2B/year, and the typical time to production for a new car model is around 36-40 weeks. The time for producing and try-out dies can be on the order of 25-28 weeks.

The current die fabrication costs are quite high because design processes are typically sequential operations involving little concurrent communication among the various technical functions involved in the process.

The product/production development cycle used by many metal-stamping operations is described below.

- *Styling* defines what the car should look like using a computer or clay model.
- *Product Engineering* designs and creates computer models or drawings for the parts.
- *Manufacturing Engineering* performs the metal performing analysis and creates computer models or drawings for tooling.
- *Tool & Die-makers* fabricate the tooling.
- *Tool-setters* setup the tooling for "try-out" operations.
- *Product Engineering and the Customer* inspects the try-out panels and eventually give their "buy-off."
- *Production* performs Production Process and Planning (PPAP) runs. If PPAP runs are successful, the tooling is released for production.
- *Quality Engineering* sets up a Customer feedback loop system used for all internal and external Production facilities.
- *The Customer feedback* loop system might be a web-based (e-Product) system, which can be used to resolve Customer concerns as well as monitor the performance of Production facilities.

As can be seen from the above product/production development cycle, the preliminary design stage usually dictates the cost to manufacture the product. Dixon and Poli [3] outlined the relative cost estimates for redesign of stamped parts, which shows that the entire process can be very expensive.

Figure 1 shows the sectional outline view and basic definitions and parameters involved in a typical stamping operation for an example rectangular pan. The typical product and process design parameters in a sheet metal stamping process are outlined below.

Product design parameters

- Blank material

122

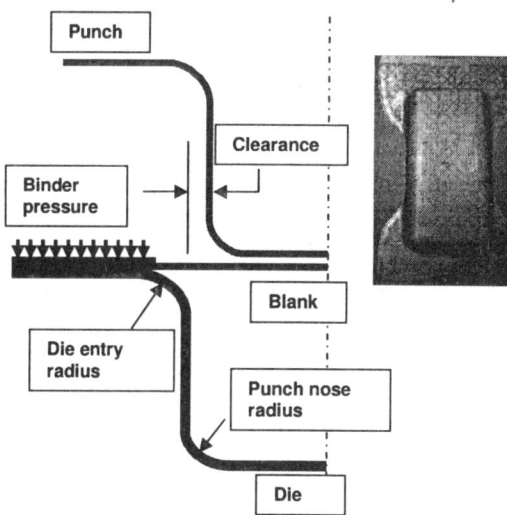

Fig. 1: Basic Forming Tool Set Up

- Blank thickness
- Blank geometry
- Die geometry
- Punch geometry

Process design parameters

- Stages of forming
- Pre/post heat treatment requirement for the blank
- Punch velocity
- Binder pressure
- Selection of lubricant

Simulation of the sheet metal forming process can be done with a wide variety of CAE tools. Choosing the best computational tool depends on the type of the simulation. There are Finite Element Analysis (FEA) packages that include solid modeling and linear solvers and nonlinear, large deformation FEA programs such as incremental solvers and one-step solvers with limited solid modeling capabilities. A typical sheet metal forming analysis might include solid modeling using I-DEAS©, transfer of the geometry to DYNAFORM© for preprocessing, LS-DYNA© for solution, and back to DYNAFORM© for postprocessing.

As pointed out by Magrab [4], it is always better to structure the concept generation process by first organizing the general search space with the aim of finding all conceivable solutions that satisfy each functional requirement. As explained in their book, one method of doing this is the morphological method, where the goal is to find as many solutions as possible that theoretically satisfy each functional requirement. In the context of metal stamping, this means that once the product concept has been defined, multiple combinations of part geometries and materials are considered. Optimum Engineering implies that multiple punch and die geometries are also considered for the various part geometry and material combinations.

The best part design will include the part geometry/material combination that meets the functional requirements of the product and can also be manufactured efficiently at an acceptable cost. Material selection cannot be made independently of the manufacturing process parameters, and the optimal process parameters depend on the part's size and shape. Once a material has been chosen, an appropriate material model is chosen or developed, which describes the material behavior in terms of mechanical properties like elongation, anisotropy, elastic recovery, etc. Choosing the material model is a major consideration for metal forming analysis.

1.3. Integrating Process Parameters

The selected material model and part geometry serve as the basis for the product development process. An initial set of process parameters is considered, operating bands are mapped for each parameter, and a detailed DOE study can be carried out. Experimental designs are used to identify or screen important factors affecting the process, and to develop empirical models of those processes [5]. Following a designed experiment, a computer model can be made to visualize and predict a response as a function of the factors varied. The important outcome of this procedure is that the number of influencing factors can be significantly reduced from the "trivial many" to the "vital few," which are critical to efficient processes and product quality.

For the metal forming industry, forming defects and springback or elastic recovery, are perennial problems. Issues like these can efficiently be handled using a numerical tool-based optimization procedure. Reasonably accurate predictions for the magnitude of wrinkling or thinning or springback can be made after carrying out optimization trials using DOE. In this paper a trial and error optimization of the various parameters has been carried out to obtain many potential solutions. A more sophisticated method might be to use Response Surface Methodology (RSM), in which a response of interest is influenced by more than one variable and the objective is to optimize the response [6].

In the present study, a successful draw is the response of interest. This is influenced by three factors, viz., binder pressure, punch velocity, and the coefficient of friction, which is controlled by the choice of lubricant used in between the blank and the die.

2. ILLUSTRATIVE EXAMPLE

In order to illustrate the use of numerical optimization process described in this paper, the example of a rectangular pan is considered. Both experimental and computer simulations were undertaken for validation purposes. The effects on the drawing operation were studied numerically for several combinations of geometric and process parameters. The *geometric parameters* are explained earlier in the paper and are given in Table 1. The material parameters used in the program were determined from experimental tests conducted at *Kettering University*. In addition to these parameters, there are FEA modeling parameters (such as the mesh size, type of element, and yield criterion) that affect the computer simulation of the stamping process. Due to their large size, detailed results will only be presented in the conference.

2.1. Criterion for a Successful Draw

A few optimum combinations of the process parameters result in a successful "full-draw" depth of the part. Other combinations result in excessive thinning, wrinkling, or rupture. In this example, a full-draw depth of around

24.00 *mm* was considered a successful draw if the thickness strain was less than 20%.

2.2. Real experiments

Experiments were performed by changing only the friction coefficient on a 60-tonne hydraulic press to stamp the pan and noting whether or not each draw was successful. The punch speed and the binder force can not be altered on this machine. Many part samples were stamped to check the consistency of the results. Thinning was measured at critical locations using an ultrasonic gage. The first set of forming results are all for the same tool geometry and lubricant (Polythene paper) with a coefficient of friction of approximately 0.08. Other lubricants such as tissue paper were also used in the experimental study.

Table 1: Geometric parameters used to draw the rectangular pan

Blank (mm)	Length	177.8
	Width	101.6
Binder (mm)	Outer Length	177.8
	Outer Width	127.01
	Inner Length	114.6
	Inner Width	63.8
Punch (mm)	Outer Length	107.081
	Outer Width	56.281
	Nose Radius	6.5
	Height	25.4
Die (mm)	Outer Length	177.8
	Outer Width	127
	Entry Radius	6.5
	Height	25.4

Echempati and Sathya Dev obtained similar results for a cylindrical cup draw as presented in reference [7]. MATLAB© software was used in the development of a fitted surface from a set of 9 experimental data points.

Figure 2 shows the actually drawn rectangular part (steel pan) in the laboratory. As can be noticed, this pan is instrumented for conducting modal analysis, which is briefly

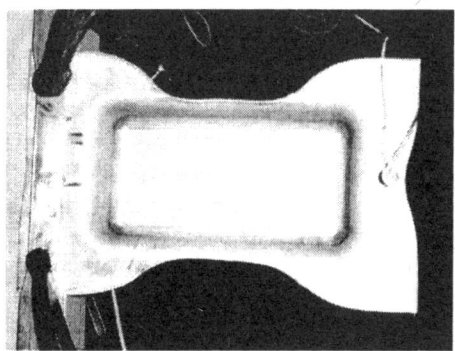

Fig. 2: Instrumented Rectangular Pan Drawn In the Laboratory

explained later in this paper. Modal analysis of real automotive parts is needed some times to study crash behavior of formed parts.

2.3. Virtual Experiments

If the degree of confidence in the simulations is high enough, then DOE can be done using simulation results instead of real experiments to determine the optimum process parameters. In this way, the number of real experiments and the cost of die revisions can be minimized.

A simulation was done to see if the strains could be accurately predicted for a set values binder pressure, punch velocity, and coefficient of friction. Figure 3 shows the tool set up for virtual forming using the DYNAFORM©. Figure 4 shows the results of fully drawn pan using LS-DYNA©.

Output from the simulations includes predictions for the major strains, minor strains, thinning, Forming Limit Diagrams (FLDs), and springback that may be compared with measurements from the real stamping. This information can be used to predict whether or not a successful draw would be achieved for a specific combination of binder pressure, punch velocity, and

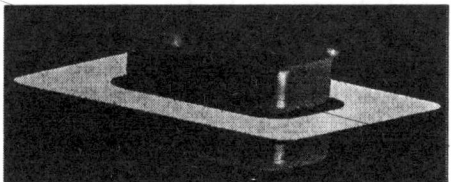

Fig. 3: Tool Set Up In DYNAFORM©

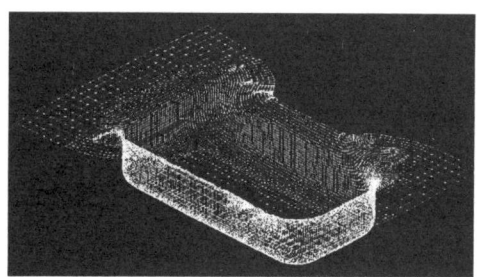

Fig. 4: View of the Fully-drawn Pan

coefficient of friction. The predicted values are checked for consistency with the measures

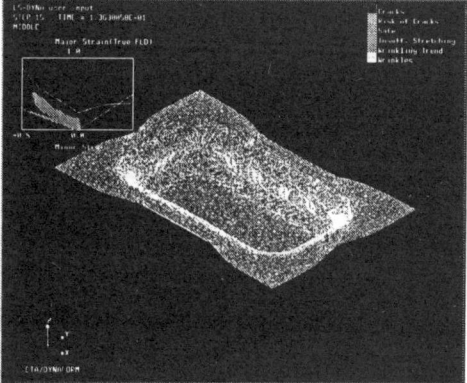

Fig. 5: Thinning Contours and FLD Plot

strains at critical points. Figure 5 shows the thinning plots of the optimized rectangular pan.

3. MODAL ANALYSIS OF THE PAN

3.1. Simulation Results

The final solution step of the formed pan in LS-DYNA© was exported as a NASTRAN© (.nas) meshed file which is then imported into I-DEAS© to perform the modal analysis with the appropriate boundary conditions. The exported file, however, does not include all the stresses and strains locked in the pan when it was imported into I-DEAS©. Figure 6 shows the meshed file after applying the necessary clamped boundary conditions on one edge. The model is then solved in I-DEAS© to obtain the modal frequencies of vibration of the formed rectangular pan. The picture in Figure 2 shows the instrumented pan for carrying the modal analysis using the OROS24© software.

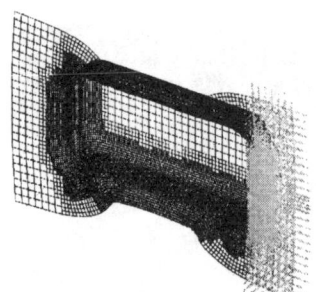

Fig. 6: Meshed Pan using the I-DEAS© software'

Figure 7 shows the fundamental bending mode of the pan with a frequency of 45.3 Hz compared to an experimental value of around 44 Hz. Several other frequencies have been computed numerically and verified experimentally for this pan.

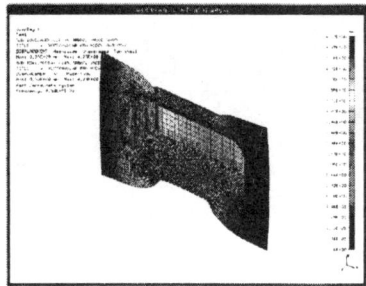

Fig.7: The First Bending Mode

4. CONCLUSION

Due to growing pressure to decrease product development time and the increased awareness that decisions made early in the product design phase have a huge impact on the total cost of the product, industries are integrating the design of the processes with the design of their products. A numerical optimization methodology was described in this paper, where CAE, FEA, and DOE can be integrated to predict the manufacturability of stamped metal parts. Changes might be made to the product design if it would be difficult to manufacture. An example of a rectangular pan was presented, where optimum sets of process parameters were determined for its successful full-depth draw using virtual and real experiments.

Computer simulations are becoming a necessary part of the stamping design process, particularly in the early stages of the product design. With a proper understanding of the forming process and material modeling, the number of costly and time-consuming try-outs (prototypes) can be reduced using high-speed computers and sophisticated computational software. For this purpose, DOE plays an important role in minimizing the number of experiments – real and virtual – needed to identify optimum combinations of "vital" process parameters.

5. ACKNOWLEDGMENTS

The author acknowledges the help extended by William J. Riffe, Professor of Manufacturing Engineering, Kettering University

6. REFERENCES

1. **Thangaraj, A.R.**, et al., editors, (1995), "Concurrent Product and Process Engineering", *ASME International Mechanical Engineering Congress and Exposition.*

2. **Nevins and Whitney,** (1989), "Concurrent Design of Products and Processes", *McGraw-Hill.*

3. **Dixon and Poli,** (1995), "Engineering Design and Design for Manufacture", *Field Stone Publishers.*

4. **Magrab, E.B.** (1997), "Integrated Product and Process Design and Development: The Product Realization Process", *CRC Press.*

5. **Hundal, M.S.** (1997), "Systematic Mechanical Designing: A cost and management perspective", *ASME Press.*

6. **Montgomery. D. C.** (2000), "Design and analysis of experiments", *John Wiley and Sons.*

7. **Echempati and Sathya Dev,** (2002), "Statistical Design Study of Aluminum Forming", *Proceedings of NUMISHEET2002 Conference, Vol. 1.*

GCMM 2004
Editors: Prasad K D V Yarlagadda and S Narayanan
Copyright © 2005, Vellore Institute of Technology, Vellore, India
Publisher: Narosa Publishing House Pvt. Ltd., New Delhi, India

Punch Load of Non-Axisymmetric Deep Drawing Product According to Blank Shape

Dong Hwan Park, Prasad K D V Yarlagadda

Queensland University of Technology, 2, George Street,
GPO Box 2434, QLD 4001

Email: dh.park@qut.edu.au

Abstract

Deep drawing process, because of its efficiency is very much sought in sheet metal forming industries. The production of optimal products using this process is dependent on the process variables such as blank shapes, profile radii of punch and die and formability of the material. Out of these variables, blank shape is very important since it controls the formability factor. This paper reports the investigations on three kinds of blank shapes and the friction test on these three conditions. The punch load distributions for non-axisymmetric forming processes were measured under different conditions of profile radii of punch and die and discussed here.

Keywords
Deep drawing, Blank shapes, Friction test, Punch load

1. INTRODUCTION

The sheet metal forming processes have an important role in industries such as automobile, aeronautical and electric appliance due to their reduced development time and low cost. This process involves either one or a combination of stretching, drawing and repetition of bending and unbending. Many studies have been carried out on the process variables of deep drawing for producing cylindrical, rectangular, elliptical and non-axisymmetrical shapes. Most of the research work in deep drawing is directed towards the formability of axisymmetrical shapes. There have been very few reports on the formability of non-axisymmetric shapes.

For determining the drawabilty of a non-axisymmetrical product, various process variables such as material property, profile radii of punch and die, lubrication condition, ram speed, blank holding force, clearance etc must be considered. The profile radii of the punch and die and blank shape are the important variables since these can influence the formability of the process [1-4]. If appropriate profile radii of the punch and die and blank shape can be selected, then the lead time and cost of the product can be reduced [5, 6].

2. DEEP DRAWING EXPERIMENT
2.1. Materials

The material used in this study was SECD (Korean Standards) with high quality formability and a thickness of 1.6□. Specimens were galvanized with Zinc of 20□. Tensile tests were carried out in the directions of 0°, 45°, and 90°to the rolling direction. The gauge length and width of the tensile specimens were 25 and 50□ respectively. The mechanical properties of the material in the tensile direction are indicated in Table 1. The specimens for the tensile tests were cut by a wire-electric spark machine. The tensile strength of the specimens was measured by the tensile test using UTM with setting load speed as 10□/min.

2.2. Equipment and Conditions

Fig. 1 shows the equipment used hydraulic press (100 Ton) with a die-cushion to control blank holding force and limit switch to determine a stroke of upper ram according to the processes. A computer with a linear variable differential transformer (LVDT) was used to measure the punch load with respect to the punch stroke when the steel sheet was formed.

Table 2 shows the experimental conditions for profile radii of the punch and die. The punch profile radius (R_p) was fixed on 6.4□, the die profile radius (R_d) was selected based on two different conditions. The punch stroke for the experiment consists of three strokes which are (a) 46□ in the first process; (b) 62□ in the second process; and (c) 74□ in the third process. The blank holding pressure was fixed at 2N/□. Soluble oil was used as lubricant for plastic working.

Table 1: Mechanical properties in the tensile direction

Direction	Yield strength [MPa]	Tensile strength [MPa]	Elongation [%]
0°	182	426	48.4
45°	200	433	41.4
90°	205	412	48.2
Average	195.7	423.7	46

Fig. 1: Experimental equipment for deep drawing

2.3. Friction Test

The friction test was divided conditions into three types, non lubrication, full lubrication, and film lubrication. This was to obtain mean the friction coefficient according to the pin load [7]. Table 3 shows the mean friction coefficient of each condition. This consists of a load cell that could measure the friction coefficient, personal computer that calculates and saves the measured signal, and a pneumatic cylinder that transforms the energy of compressed air into a mechanically reciprocating straight line motion.

Table 2: The experimental conditions for punch and die Profile radii

	First Process R_{d1} [□]	Second Process R_{d2} [□]	Third Process R_{d3} [□]
Blank type (A, B, C)	11.2	11.2	11.2
			16
		16	11.2
			16
	16	11.2	11.2
			16
		16	11.2
			16

Table 3: Mean friction coefficient of each test

Type	150N	200N	250N	Mean value
Non lubrication	0.24	0.26	-	0.25
Full lubrication	0.08	0.15	-	0.12
Film lubrication	0.09	0.07	0.08	0.08

3. BLANK SHAPE DESIGN

Generally, the trial-and-error method based on previous experience is used for developing the blank shape. This will increase the production time and cost. Hence, to design the blank shape (which is equivalent to the surface area of the final product) the surface area of the final product was determined by means of 3D modelling [8-12]. Three kinds of blanks, which have an equivalent surface area to the final product, were used. Fig. 3 shows the geometrical shapes of the blanks used. The outline of the type A blank is larger than the type B and C blanks. The short side length of the type B blank is smaller than the type C blank. On the contrary, the long side length of the type B blank is a little larger than the type C blank. The process of the applied product in the experiment consists of 7 stages of the deep drawing process and 3 stages of trimming and restriking.. Hence, the total number of multi-deep drawing stages is 10. In this study, the experiment to measure punch load was performed from the first process to the third process. Fig. 4 shows the product shape of each type blank according to process.

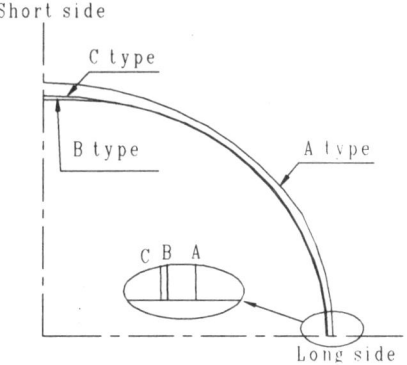

Fig. 3: Geometry of blank shapes

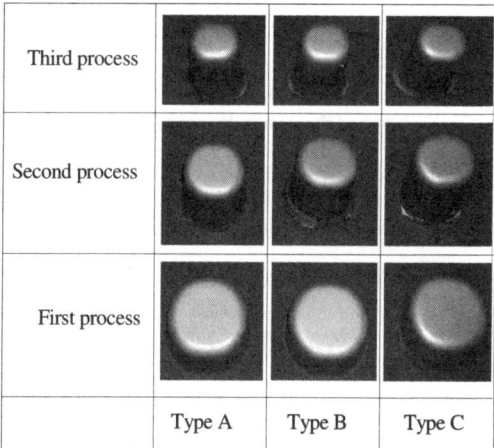

Fig. 4: Product shapes of each type blank

4. RESULT AND DISCUSSIONS

Fig. 5 and Fig. 6 show the comparison of the punch load along the blank types in the first process. R_p was fixed at 6.4□, R_{d1} of the first process was selected under two conditions, such as 11.2□ and 16□. The punch load of the type A blank measured relatively large in comparison with the type B and C blanks, and the punch loads of the type B and C blanks were similar. The area of the type A blank is on the whole large in

comparison with the type B and C blanks. In other words, the contact surface area of blank holder of the type A blank is larger than that of the type B and C blanks. Therefore, it is considered that the largest value of the punch load is measured at the type A blank where the high blank holding force is needed due to the large contact surface area of the blank holder. Table 4 shows the maximum punch load of the blank shapes along the die profile radii in the first process. The maximum punch load when $R_{d1}=16$□ is smaller than when it is $R_{d1}=11.2$□.

Table 4: The Max. punch load of blank shapes in the first process (R_p=6.4)

	Type A	Type B	Type C
Max. Punch load (ton)	R_{d1}=11.2 : 13.1	R_{d1}=11.2 : 10.9	R_{d1}=11.2 : 11.4
	R_{d1}=16 : 11.2	R_{d1}=16 : 9.8	R_{d1}=16 : 9.9

Fig. 7 and Fig. 8 show the comparison of the punch load along the blank types in the second process. R_p was fixed at 6.4□, the die profile radius of the first process (R_{d1}) was fixed at 16□ and the die profile radius of the second process (R_{d2}) was selected under two conditions, such as 11.2□ and 16□. The maximum punch load was measured at 80 percent of punch stroke when the type A, B blanks were used, and was measured at 60 percent of punch stroke when the type C blank was used. The punch load in each process was compared and it is seen that the punch load of the second process was smaller than the first process and the results of experiments showed that the punch load of the three types of blanks was similar. The punch load is small while the blank draws from the first to the second process due to the reduced drawing length.

R_p was fixed at 6.4□, compared the two conditions, the one, R_d of the first, second and third process was fixed at 16 , the other die profile radii (R_{d1}) of the first, second and third process was fixed at 11.2□.

The punch load of the type A blank was relatively large in comparison with the type B and C blanks while the punch stroke made progress. We attributed some difference of the punch load to friction between the punch and the steel sheet. If the maximum punch load is larger than the fracture force (P_F) to shear the steel sheet when forming a non-axisymmetric product, then the fracture will occur at that time. Theoretically P_F is calculated as follows.

$$P_F = Lt\sigma_b = 210 \times 1.6 \times 43.29$$

The fracture force (P_F) was calculated using the drawing length (L) of the blanks. It is 14.5ton. Therefore, the maximum punch load measured in the experiments, 13.1ton, was performed without the fracture of the non-axisymmetric product.

C blanks is smaller than that of the type A blank, the blank holding force was found to be decreased. Therefore, the punch load of the type B and C blanks shows a small value for every process due to the reduced blank holding force. Although the punch load is similar to that in the type B blank, a good product that has no discontinuous section could make from the type C blank. Hence it is advantageous to use type C blank in the industrial field.

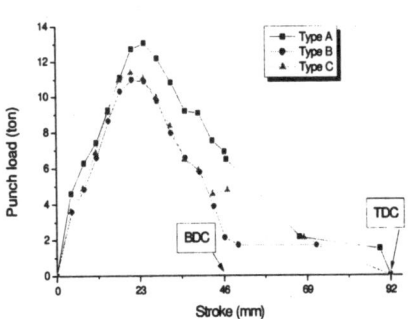

Fig. 5: Punch load-stroke curve of each blank type (R_{d1}=11.2□)

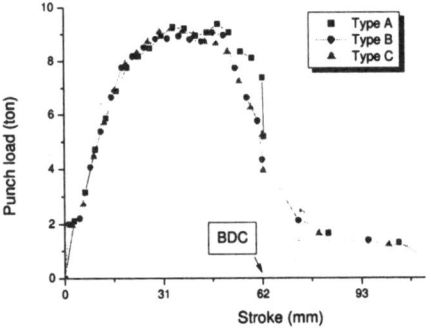

Fig. 7: Punch load-stroke curve of each blank type (R_{d1}=16□, R_{d2}=11.2□)

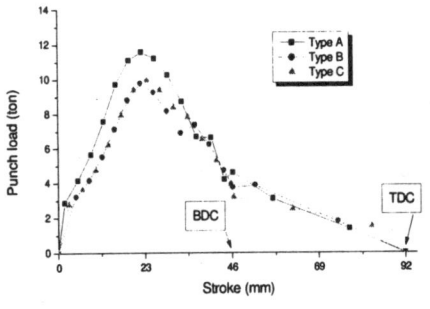

Fig. 6: Punch load-stroke curve of each blank type (R_{d1}=16□)

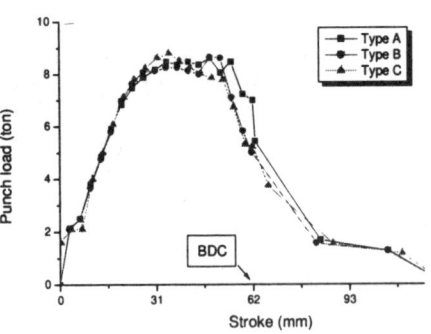

Fig. 8: Punch load-stroke curve of each blank type (R_{d1}=16□, R_{d2}=16□)

Because the type A blank is larger than the type B and C blanks, the blank holding force has increased. Therefore, the punch load of the type A blank shows a large value in every process due to an increase in the blank holding force. In contrast to the type A blank, since the punch load of the type B and

130

5. CONCLUSIONS

In this study, experiments were carried out for tensile and friction with steel sheets for drawability for a non-axisymmetric product. The experiments clarified the influence of the profile radii of the punch and die and the blank shape on the punch load distribution for non-axisymmetric deep drawing products. From the results the followings conclusions are drawn.

(1) Under the friction test conditions of three types, non lubrication, full lubrication, and film lubrication, the results of friction test showed that the mean friction coefficient measured the smallest value, 0.08, when film lubrication was used. Better results were obtained with the applied film lubrication to the non-axisymmetric product as compared to full lubrication.

(2) The maximum punch load was reduced gradually as the process progressed.

(3) The maximum punch load of the type A blank had the largest value among the three kinds of blanks during the process and although the type C blank's punch load is similar than that of the type B blank, good products without discontinuous section could be obtained from the type C blank.

6. REFERENCES

1. **Kim D H**, (1998), "Experimental study on minimizing wall thickness thinning for deep drawing of circular shells", *Korean Society for Technology of Plasticity*, 7(4), 393-399.

2. **Majlessi S A** and **Lee D**, (1993), "Deep drawing square-shape sheet metal parts, Part 1: Finite element analysis", *ASME J. of Eng. for Industry*, 115, 102-109.

3. **Majlessi S A** and **Lee D**, (1993), "Deep drawing square-shape sheet metal parts, Part 2 : Experimental study", *ASME J. of Eng. for Industry*, 115, 110-117.

4. **Kim D H**, (1999), "Influence of die shoulder radius and punch to die clearance for multistage deep drawing of complex cylindrical shell", *Korean Society for Technology of Plasticity*, 8(3), 262-268.

5. **Park D H, Bae W R, Park S B** and **Kang S S**, (1999), "An experimental Study on optimization of blank shape in elliptical deep drawing process", *Korean Society of Precision Engineering*, 16(10), 101-108.

6. **Eary D F** and **Reed E A**, (1974), Techniques of pressworking sheet metal, Prentice-Hall.

7. **Ernest Rabinowicz**, (1995), Friction and wear of materials, 2nd ed., John Wiley & Sons.

8. **Park D H,.Bae W R, Park S B** and **Kang S S**, (2000), "Application surface area calculating system for design of blank shape of deep drawing product", *Korean Society of Precision Engineering*, 17(4), 97-105.

9. **Park D H, Park S B** and **Kang S S**, (2000), "An Experimental Study on Improvement of Formability for Elliptical Deep Drawing Process", *Transaction of Materials Processing*, 9(2), 120-127.

10. **Marumo Y** and **Saiki H**, (1998), "Estimation of the deep drawability of aluminum square cups by fracture forces", *Metals and Materials International*, 4(3), 372-375.

11. **Zhou S, Chin K S, Xie Y** and **Prasad KDV Yarlagadda**, (2003), "Internet based distributive knowledge integrated system for product design", *Inernational. Journal of Computers in Industry*, 50, 195-205.

12. **Chin K S, Zhou S, Krishnamurthy R, P. KDV Yarlagadda**, (2003), "An intelligent approach of knowledge searching within Internet-based distributive knowledge integrated environment", *J. Eng. Appl. of AI*, 1~12.

GCMM 2004
Editors: Prasad K D V Yarlagadda and S Narayanan
Copyright © 2005, Vellore Institute of Technology, Vellore, India
Publisher: Narosa Publishing House Pvt. Ltd., New Delhi, India

Some Studies on Tool Wear and Tool Life of PVD Coated Tools while Machining (Turning) of Inconel 718

Shingan[*] V T, Madhekar[*] Y S, Purva[*] D S, Thakur[**] D G & Sadaiah[***] M

[**] Senior Lecturer, [*] B. Tech. Student, [***] Asst. Professor
Department of Mechanical Engineering
Dr.Babasaheb Ambedkar Technological University
Lonere, Raigad-401203. (Maharashtra)

E-mail – msadaiah@yahoo.com
dinnu74@yahoo.com

Abstract

Nickel based alloys are high temperature super alloys and these are hard to machine materials. It has wide range of applications in high temperature and high stressed regions. In the present study an attempt has been made to study the tool wear while machining Inconel 718 with PVD coated carbide tool for turning operation. Experiments are performed on heavy duty Precision lathe HMT NH22. The cutting tool used in the experiments is a multilayer PVD (TiN/TiAlN) coated carbide tool. The insert is designated as SNMM 120408 GC1025 manufactured by Sandvik Coromant. The chip reduction coefficient and power consumption are also measured and which are used as the machinabilty criteria for the Inconel 718. Speed, feed and depth of cut were varied and its effect on the tool wear is studied. The optimum machining parameters for semi finish turning of Inconel 718 are found as speed (Vc) is 38.70 m/min, feed (s) is 0.12 mm/rev and depth of cut (t) is 0.4 mm. Tool life for PVD coated tools is also investigated for the above optimum parameters. The tool life obtained is 6 minutes for the flank wear of 0.3 mm.

Keywords
Tool wear, Tool life, Turning, Inconel 718

1. INTRODUCTION

Nickel based alloys are high temperature super alloys and these are hard to machine materials. It has wide range of applications in high temperature and high stressed regions like aerospace industries steam turbine power plants etc. Heat resistance super alloys possess some characteristics that are detrimental to their machinability. The metallurgical characteristics responsible for the good strength and creep resistance of Nickel based super alloys at high temperatures are responsible for their being difficult to machine. The aspects of these alloys are: i) Elevated temperature strength ii) High hardness iii) High work hardening rates at machining strain rates leading to high machining force iv) Low temperature diffusivity leading to high temperature v) Presence of highly abrasive carbide particles and vi) Strong tendency to weld to the tool and to form build-up edge [7]. From the various variables affecting in any machining operation the cutting tool is one of the most critical, although it is small and relatively inexpensive. The requirements for any cutting tool materials used for machining Nickel-based alloys should include i) Good wear resistance ii) High strength and toughness iii) High hot hardness iv) Good thermal shock properties and iv) Adequate chemical stability at elevated temperatures.

2. LITERATURE REVIEW

Choudhury I.A., et al [7] has conducted studies on machining of Inconel 718. At the cutting speeds of 36 and 48 m/min, wear progression is almost linear and very rapid and the tool life is very short which less than five minutes is observed. When the cutting speed has been changed to 20m/min, initial wear is rapid. Uncoated carbide cutting tools give a better performance with respect to different cutting speeds and feed rates. The use of coated tools is justified only when the depths of cut exceed 1.0 mm. The effect of cutting speed on tool life is more pronounced than the effect of feed rate and depth of cut for coated tools.

H G. Prengel, et al [8] has conducted study on new class of high performance PVD coated carbide cutting tools and investigated the cutting characterization and metal cutting performance of various monolayer and multilayer PVD inserts. Inconel 718 turning tests were performed with a coolant. The TiAlN-multilayer coating shows some performance advantage over the TiAlN-monolayer and the TiN/TiCN/TiAlN-multilayer coating particularly at higher speed.

P.C. Jindal, et al [9] did some study on the performance of PVD TiN, TiCN, and TiAlN coated cemented carbide tools in turning by taking in account coating microstructures and adhesion evaluation, coating composition, residual stresses in coatings, hot hardness and metal cutting performance of coated tools.

Y.S.Liao et al [10] have investigated about carbide tool wear mechanism in turning of Inconel 718 superalloy under high speed machining condition. In most cases, the tool wears uniformly and the flanks wear progresses uniformly as cutting time increases up to the point where the tool fails.

L. Li, et al [11] in their study on high speed cutting of Inconel 718 with coated carbide and ceramic tools has shown that cutting speed is an important factor influences the tool wear and the tool life when cutting Nickel-based alloys with carbides.

A. A. Minevich, et al [12] in their case studies on tribological behavior of coated cutting tools have tried to focus on various points such as the application of tribological coating to the extend the life of cutting tools has proved to be successful.

E. O. Ezugwu, et al [13] did some investigation on wear of coated tools when machining Nickel (Inconel 718) and Titanium based alloys, and they have found that flank wear is the dominant failure mode at slow cutting speed (42 m/min) for the Inconel 718.

M. Rahman, et al [14] has discussed about the problems encounter during machining of Inconel 718 in their study.

3. EXPERIMENTATION

In the present study an attempt has been made to study the effect of the various machining parameters such as cutting speed (V_c), feed (s), and depth of cut (t) on tool wear of Inconel 718. The experiments were conducted using a precision lathe (NH22, HMT) 7.5 HP motor, maximum spindle speed 1020 rpm, and feed range- 0.02-1.12 mm/rev. In the present study three experiments were performed, and in every experiment two parameters are kept constant and one parameter is varied. In the first experiment, feed (s) (from 0.02-1.12 mm/rev) is varied, while cutting speed (Vc) and depth of cut (t) is kept constant at 37.78 mm/min and 0.5 mm respectively. Similarly, in the second and third experiments cutting speed and depth of cut are varied from 3.46-176.5 m/min and 0.1-1.6 mm respectively. In second experiment feed and depth of cut are kept constant at 0.12 mm/rev and 0.5 mm respectively. In third experiment cutting speed and feed is kept constant at 46.65 mm/rev and 0.12 mm/rev respectively.

The cutting tool used during the experiments is a multilayer PVD (TiN/TiAlN) coated tool. The insert is designated as SNMM 120408 GC1025 manufactured by Sandvik Coromant. This tool is used for semifinish turning operations. The nose radius of the insert is 0.8 mm, and which can be used for good surface finish. Power consumption is also measured during experiments with the help of a digital wattmeter. The range of wattmeter is 0-16 kW and accuracy is 0.1%. The chip reduction coefficient (ζ) and power consumption (P) are kept as parameters to decide the machinability of the Inconel 718. The chip reduction coefficient is determined by calculating cut and uncut chip thickness. Further, the types of chips and nature of them also extensively studied in order to ascertain the machinability of Inconel 718. Optimum machining parameters are found out from the each experiment on the basis of the chip reduction coefficient and power consumption and those are as follows: cutting speed (Vc) is 38.70 m/min, feed (s) is 0.12 mm/rev and depth of cut (t) is 0.4 mm. The surface finish obtained for these machining parameters is, Ra = 1.41 µm.

Tool flank wear is measured during the experiments. Maximum flank wear that is allowed during the experiments is 0.3 mm. The flank wear is measured with the help of Toolmaker's microscope. Least count of the instrument is 0.02 mm.

Tool life is investigated for the optimum parameter for that two experiments are carried out for two different cutting speeds. The maximum tool life achieved is 6 minutes.

4. RESULTS AND DISCUSSION

4.1 Effect of various machining parameters on chip reduction coefficient:

In the variable feed the rate of increase in cut chip thickness is greater than the rate of increase of uncut chip thickness, hence the chip reduction coefficient decreases as the feed increases which is shown in Fig.1.

Fig.2 shows the cutting speed Vs chip reduction coefficient. It is observed that as speed increases, there is decrease in chip reduction coefficient. This is because of

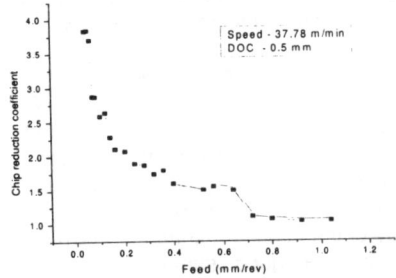

Fig.1: Feed Vs Chip Reduction Coefficient

decrease in chip thickness with increase in speed at constant uncut chip thickness. It is

also observed that chip reduction coefficient increases with increase in depth of cut.

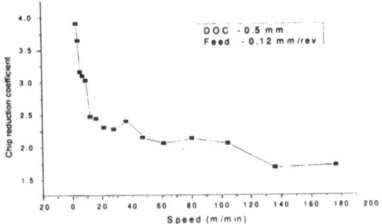

Fig.2: Speed Vs Chip Reduction Coefficient

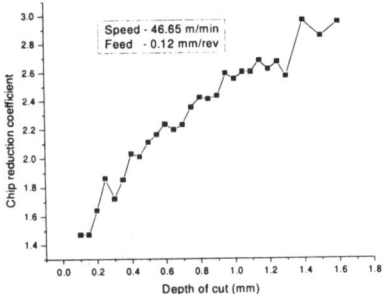

Fig.3: Depth of Cut Vs Chip Reduction Coefficient

This is because of constant uncut chip thickness there is increase in chip thickness as shown in Fig.3. There is good surface finish when the chip reduction coefficient is in the range of 2.0 to 2.3.

4.2 Effect of Various Machining Parameters on Power Consumption

As the feed increases the power consumption increases. This is because of increase in cutting forces, which leads to increase in the power consumption as shown in Fig. 4. Here, theoretical cutting forces are calculated using the empirical relations available in the literature [2]. Further, these forces are compared with experimental cutting forces.

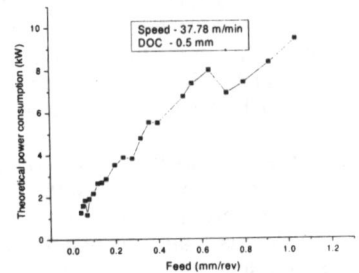

Fig. 4: Feed Vs Theoretical Power Consumption

The Fig. 5 shows the variation of theoretical and experimental power consumption with variation in cutting speed respectively.

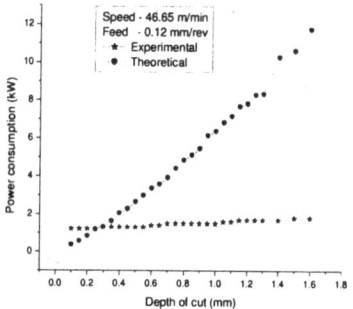

Fig. 6: Depth of Cut Vs Power Consumption

It has been observed from the Fig.10 that as has the cutting speed increases, both the theoretical and experimental power consumption increases, as the power consumption is directly proportional to the cutting speed.

The Fig.6 shows the difference between experimental and theoretical power consumption.

It is observed that both experimental and theoretical power consumption increases as depth of cut increases. The increase in power consumption is due to corresponding increase in cutting forces.

4.3 Tool Wear

During the experimentation the flank wear is measured after every feed variation. Fig. 7 shows the graph of cutting length Vs flank wear for the variable feed. It is observed that as the feed increases the rate of flank wear increases, hence the tool life decreases. The larger the feed, the greater is the cutting force per unit area of chip tool contact, on the rake face and the flank face and also the increase in cutting temperature, increases the wear of the tool. Increase in cutting force because of large feed increases the chipping of the cutting edge, which is observed while machining.

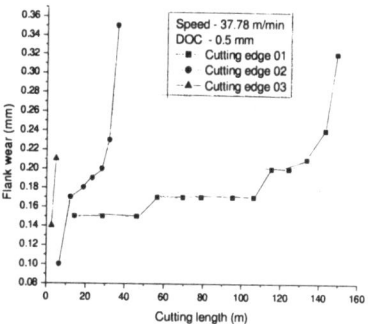

Fig. 7: Cutting length Vs Flank wear

Fig. 8 shows the graph of cutting length Vs flank wear for variable speed. It is observed that with increase in cutting speed there is increase in flank wear. This is because of that, as speed increases, tool temperature increases, which soften the tool material. It thereby aids abrasive, adhesive and diffusion wear. The combine effect of these causes an increase in flank wear. Fig. 9 shows the graph of cutting length Vs flank wear for variable depth of cut. It is observed that there is increase in flank wear as depth of cut increases.

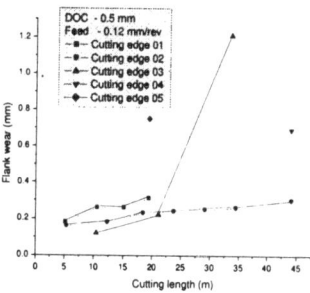

Fig. 8: Cutting length Vs Flank wear

An increase in depth of cut causes an increase in chip-tool contact area thus increases the friction between the work piece and tool, thereby accelerates the abrasive, adhesive and diffusion wear and thus increases the flank wear rate.

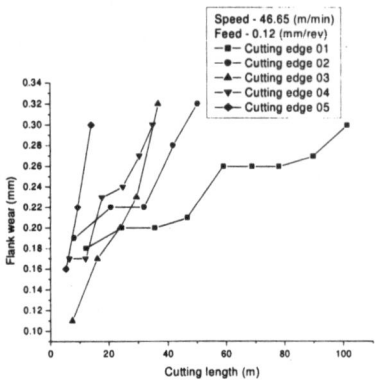

Fig. 9: Cutting length Vs Flank wear

4.4 Tool Life

For tool life investigation of PVD (TiAlN/TiN) coated tool two experiments were carried out for two cutting speeds while keeping depth of cut and feed constant. Fig. 10 shows the graph of time Vs flank wear for two experiments conducted for determination of tool life and the details are given below:

Experiment no. 1

Cutting speed, V_c = 33.79 m/min
Diameter, D = 51.2 mm
Feed, S = 0.12 mm/rev
Depth of cut, t = 0.4 mm

Tool life for the above parameters (T_1) = 360 sec .
Corresponding flank wear = 0.30 mm

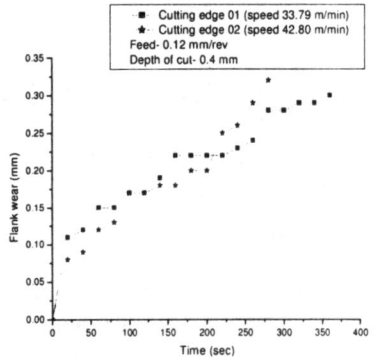

Fig. 10: Time Vs flank wear

Experiment no. 2
Cutting speed, V_c = 42.8 m/min
Diameter, D = 49.6 mm
Feed, S = 0.12 mm/rev
Depth of cut, t = 0.4 mm

Tool life for The above parameters (T_2) = 280 sec.
Corresponding flank wear = 0.30 mm
Tool life equation for PVD coated carbide tool during machining of Inconel 718:

$$V T^n = C$$
$$\therefore V_1 T_1^n = V_2 T_2^n = C$$
$$\therefore \log V_1 + n \log T_1 = \log V_2 + n \log T_2 = \log C$$
$$\therefore \log V_1 - \log V_2 = n (\log T_2 - \log T_1)$$
$$\therefore \log 33.79 \log 42.80 = n (\log 280 - \log 360)$$
$$\therefore n = 0.94$$

Therefore, the tool life equation for Inconel 718 with PVD coated carbide tool is,

$$V T^{0.94} = 8550$$

5. CONCLUSION

The following conclusions are drawn from the present study.
1. The recommended machining parameters for doing semi finishing turning operation on Inconel 718 with PVD coated tool are:
   Cutting speed (V_c) = 38.70 m/min.
   Feed (s) = 0.12 mm/rev.
   Depth of cut (t) = 0.4 mm
2. It has been found that for the above machining conditions the maximum tool life found is 6 minutes. In the present study the maximum flank wear allowed is 0.3mm.

Nomenclature

o	=	Orthogonal rake angle (degree)
ζ	=	Chip reduction coefficient
t	=	Depth of cut (DOC) (mm)
V_B	=	Flank wear (mm)
s	=	Feed (mm/rev)
V_c	=	Cutting speed (m/min)
L	=	Cutting length (m)

6. REFERENCES

1. **Brietzig R. W.**, INCO AlloysInternational, "Machining of Nickel and Nickel alloys", *ASM Handbook*, 16, 835-843.
2. **Bhattacharya A**. (2000), *Metal Cutting Theory and Practice*, New Central book agency Pvt. Ltd. Calcutta.
3. **Edward M. Trent and Paul K. Wright** (2000), *Metal Cutting*, Butterworth Heinemann Publications.

4. **Shaw M. C.** (2002), *Metal Cutting principles*, CBS Publishers and Distributors, New Delhi.

5. **Geoffrey Boothroyd, Winston A. Knight** (1989), *"Fundamentals of Machining and Machine Tools"*, 2nd Ed., Marcel Dekker, USA.

6. **Basu S. K., Pal D. K.** (1995), *Design of Machine Tools,* Oxford and IBH Publishing Co. Pvt. Ltd., New Delhi.

7. **Choudhary A., El-Baradie M.A.** (1998), "Machinability of Nickel base super alloys: A general review", *Journal of Material Processing Technology*, 77, 278- 284.

8. **H .G. Prengel, P.C. Jindal, K. H. Wendt, T. Santhanam, P. L. Hegde, R.M. Peinich** (2001), "A new class of high performance PVD coating tools in turning", *Surface and Coating Technology,* 139, 25-34.

9. **Jindal P.C., Santhanam A.T., Schleinkofer U., Shuster A. F.** (1999), "Performance of PVD TiN, TiCN and TiAlN coated cemented carbide tools in turning", *International Journal of Refractory Metal and Materials*, 17, 163-170.

10. **Lion Y. S., Shine R. H.** (1996), "Carbide tool wear mechanism in turning of Inconel 718 superalloys", Wear, 193,16-24.

11. **Li I., Wang N. He., Wang Z. G.** (2002), "High speed cutting of Inconel 718 with coated carbide and ceramic inserts", *Journal of Material Processing Technology*, 129, 127-130.

12. **Minevich A. A., Eizner B. A., Gick L. A., Popok N. N.** (2000), " Case studies on Tribological behavior of coated cutting tools", *Tribological Transactions*, 43, 740-748.

13. **Ezugwu E. O., Wang Z. M., Machado A. R.** (2000)," Wear of coated carbide tools when machining Nickel (Inconel 718) and titanium base alloys", *Tribological Transactions*, 43, 912-918.

14. **Rahman M., Seah W. K. H., Teo T. T.** (1997), "The machinability of Inconel 718", *Journal of Material Processing Technology*, 63, 199-204.

GCMM 2004
Editors: Prasad K D V Yarlagadda and S Narayanan
Copyright © 2005, Vellore Institute of Technology, Vellore, India
Publisher: Narosa Publishing House Pvt. Ltd., New Delhi, India

The State of the Art Research of Burr Minimization in Drilling

Gaitonde[*] V N, Achyutha[**] B T & Siddeswarappa[**] B

*B. V. B College of Engineering & Technology, Hubli – 580 031, India
**U.B.D.T. College of Engineering, Davangere – 577 004, India

Email: vngaitonde@rediffmail.com, gaitondevn@yahoo.co.in, vngaitonde@bvb.edu

Abstract

The state of the art of burr minimization in drilling is reviewed. Burr formation in drilling is one of the serious problems in precision engineering and mass production. The exit burr, which results from drilling of holes, degrades the precision of products and causes additional cost of deburring. Since deburring processes are not yet well automated, the productivity of advanced manufacturing systems is often reduced. Burr formation in drilling is a complex process to analyze because it is fundamentally a three-dimensional process in which many parameters are involved. Understanding the drilling burr formation and its dominant parameters is essential for predicting and reducing burr. A lot of research on the burr formation mechanism and burr minimization has been done experimentally and several attempts have been made analytically. The present paper aims at bringing out the state of art of burr minimizing techniques in drilling including some recent works of authors.

Keywords

Drilling Process, Burr, Burr Formation, Burr Minimization

1. INTRODUCTION

As one of the size error during drilling, projection of material, defined as "Burr" is formed. Burr is plastically deformed material, generated on the part edge during cutting or shearing [1]. These burrs cause several problems for product quality and functionality as they can interfere with assembly of parts and can cause jamming and misalignment. Burrs produced on components lead to many undesirable features in practice, such as improper contact between current carrying members and improper seating of mating surfaces. Burrs are injurious even during machining because they hit the cutting edge and cause the groove wear [2]. Exit burr strongly affects product quality and assembly

process. Due to this reason, additional deburring process is required. Usually, this deburring process is done manually because of difficulties in automation, requires additional time and may damage the edges resulting in workpiece rejection. It also may cause high cost in edge finishing of precision parts [3,4]. Since deburring processes are not yet well automated, the productivity of advanced manufacturing systems is often reduced. Understanding the drilling burr formation and its dominant parameters is essential for predicting and reducing burr. Deburring of small holes is especially difficult due to bad accessibility and tight tolerances. When the exit burr is formed inside a cavity, there are no tools available for deburring. In this case, very special tools must be used, thus increasing the deburring cost.

An attempt has been made to avoid the formation of a drilling burr or at least to minimize it, or sometimes, to control the type of the burr. It is very difficult to develop reliable analytical models for prediction and control of drilling burr formation. Drilling burr formation is a very complicated phenomenon affected by many parameters such as drill geometry, material property and process conditions.

Edge finishing and deburring operations are often neglected in the design and process planning of precision parts. These finishing operations are often the source of many dimensional discrepancies and they usually occur in the final stages of manufacturing, after the completion of a series of processes, which add value to a precision part. When the deburring of a precision part is not considered until the final stages of manufacturing, the potential loss due to any failure in the selection, planning or execution of the edge-finishing process is great. The cost of deburring these components may contribute as much as 30% to the cost of finished parts [3]. The selection of capable deburring and finishing processes for precision components is highly dependent upon knowledge of burr properties. Burr size, shape, location and the allowable surface finish, are the primary determinants in the selection of a deburring process.

This paper is an attempt to summarize the state of the art of burr formation and its minimization in drilling, as well as that of some of the authors work in this area.

2. LITERATURE REVIEW

Gillespie L.K. [5,6] was one of first researchers to study burr formation at an academic level in drilling. He studied the effects of process conditions, tool geometry and material properties on burr formation over a wide range of test conditions and proposed a basic model of burr formation in drilling. No influence was found in that study. Importantly most of Gillespie's tests were done with hand fed drills (un known and un controlled feed rates). So, the influence of feed rate is

confounded with other parameters studied. Gillespie L.K. and Blotter P.T. [7,8] identified four different types of burrs, namely, poisson burr, roll over burr, tear burr and cut off burr. Poisson mode is predominant for the entry burr while the roll over and tear mode are predominant for the exit burr produced in drilling. They reported that the basic factors like thrust, uncut chip thickness, relative energies for bending and shearing the chip etc., govern the mechanism of burr formation.

Pande S.S. and Relekar H.P. [9] observed burr formation tendency especially to burr height and thickness at entry and exit of holes during drilling by changing the drill diameter, feed rate, length of hole to drill diameter ratio and BHN of the work material. They found that the effect of length of hole to drill diameter ratio has the least effect. In addition, an attachment has been designed to provide continuous modification of feed during drilling and cause significant reductions in the sizes of burrs at the entry and exit of holes. Sofronas A. and Taraman K. [10,11] carried out theoretical and experimental investigations to study the exit burr thickness as a function of drill geometry. It was reported that, increasing helix angle and lip clearance angle and decreasing feed and point angle on drills could reduce the exit burr thickness. Similar trend of results have also been reported under different experimental conditions in carbon steel sheet drilling by Shikata H. et al., [12].

Sugawara A. and Ingaki K. [13] found that the quantity of the burr increases with a decrease in drill diameter in the case of diameters ranging from 0.2 mm to 2.5 mm, where as the quantity of the burr decreases with a decrease in diameter in the case of Drills having a diameter of less than 0.2 mm. The behaviour in the former case can be well explained by the drill edge becoming effectively duller with a decrease in drill diameter. They reported that dullness of shapes causes the larger burr formation so that cutting ability becomes worse. The cause was not clear for the latter case. Again, the burr formation process was investigated, through model experiment, using model tool by Sugawara A. and Ingaki K. [14]. Workpieces of different structures were drilled with several size drills and the difference in workpiece structure on the burrs produced was examined by Sugawara A. and Ingaki K. [15]. The characteristics results are that, burr formation is reduced when the grain size of the workpiece increases, and this effect of grain size becomes especially important when the drill diameter is very small and its tool edge is dull or worn.

Sofronas A. [16] experimentally investigated the influence of work material properties like shear strength and hardness on the size of exit burrs while drilling steels. Results of the experimental investigations show that exit burr size increases with increase in hardness of the workpiece. Takazawa K. [17] has studied several elements of burr formation during drilling. Stein J. M. [18] observed the effect of the feed rate, cutting speed, pecking and tool material on burr height, thickness and shape using micro drill in stainless steel and the influence of workpiece exit angle on burr formation in drilling intersecting holes. Sung-Lim Ko and Jing-Koo Lee [19] investigated the effects of elements of drill shape, point angle, helix angle, length of chisel edge etc. on cutting force, hole accuracy and burr formation as well. Sung-Lim Ko and Jae-Eun Chang [20] also performed several experiments to observe burr formation in each material with modified drill with chamfer, round and step at the corner of the drill edge. Another approach given by Adachi K. [21] and Takeyama H. [22,23], involves a modification of the drilling process, which makes use of ultrasonic, or low frequency vibratory techniques to reduce burr formation. Lee G. B. [24] has also used method of controlling thrust force by changing cutting conditions during drilling.

Kim J. S. [25] has carried out preliminary experiment to investigate drilling burr formation on Ti-6Al-4V, which is most widely used titanium alloy in aircraft industry because of its high specific strength. This experiment was a preliminary study to investigate the drilling burr formation of the material. Two different types of carbide drills were used to observe the effects of variation of feed rate and cutting speed on drilling burr formation. No coolant was used for the above experiments. Quantitative measurement of height and thickness of burrs

did not yield much useful information because relatively uniform and small burrs were formed under all conditions.

Kim J. S. [26] has developed a control chart for prediction of burr type and size in drilling of stainless steel by split point twist drills. One of the two parameters used for the chart was found by the concept of similarity. The other one was the indicator of the cutting speed of the process. It was shown that the chart could predict burr type [27] and size with feed rate and spindle speed even if the drill diameter changes. Water-based coolant was used. Stein J. M. and Dornfeld D.A. [28] studied the burr formation of miniature holes drilling in stainless steel. Increase in feed, cutting speed and drill wear were found to increase the burr height and thickness.

However, the burrs are categorized as several groups based on their shape [29], such as, uniform, uniform learned-back, rolled-back and rolled-back widened exit small height, which is more important in studying the burr formation mechanism and deburring issue. Heat generation due to friction between the drill and workpiece during drilling was believed to be the main influence that decides the final burr shapes. A ring type burr was observed when drilling titanium alloy with coolant [29]. They found that cutting conditions had little effect on the burr sizes formed. The drill geometry (helix angle, split point vs. helical point, lip relief angle and point angle) affected burr thickness and height.

An experimental study was carried out by Stein J. M. and Dornfeld D.A. [30] to investigate the mechanism of the burr formation in drilling of intersecting holes with a gun drill and twist drills. It was found that geometric parameters played the most dominant role in determining burr size. The geometric characteristics [31] are the variation of the exit angle, which is defined as the angle between the drill axis and the exit surface. It was found that burr sizes decreased almost linearly with increasing exit angle regardless of drill type. The cutting conditions did influence the burr size as much as exit angle. However an increase in feed rate tended to increase the burr size for twist drills. The analytical expressions for the exit angle and the gradient of the exit angle in intersecting hole of drilling were developed by Kim J. S. [32]. The analytical expressions will provide the information on the geometry in intersecting hole drilling and its effect on the drilling formation.

Hewson J. [33] has carried out analysis in drilling operations on titanium alloy, Ti-6Al-4V, to identify the relationship between exit burrs, cutting fluid, supporting backplate material and tool geometry allowing a further understanding of the formation modes of burrs between layered materials. Uniform burr shapes would not have been formed at these cutting conditions without the backplate and fluid. Burrless regions were the direct result of the support provided to the workpiece by the backplate. Exit burr sizes were found to be significantly lower than those found in Kim's experiment, which was done without cutting fluid or a backplate.

A simplified analytical model was proposed by Sofronas A. [34], employed various feed control schemes to minimize burr size using the thrust force. This model cannot predict the burr geometry because a closed form analytical solution for drilling burr formation is extremely difficult to derive. Guo Y. B. [35] developed a finite element model of drilling burr formation process. The nonlinear thermo elastic- plastic model accounts for dynamic effects, strain hardening, strain rate, automatic mesh contact with friction and material ductile failure. Guo's finite element simulation gave an insightful description of drilling burr formation. He divided drilling formation mechanism into four stages: initiation, development, pivoting point and formation stages. Cap formation and removal greatly affected burr size and shape. The burr height was determined by the positions of the pivoting point and the cap formation.

Park I. W. [36] conducted preliminary FEM simulation on the effect of backup material and concluded that the burr can be effectively minimized by backup material in 2-D orthogonal cutting. However, Park used a backup material whose material properties are twice as stiff (Young's modulus) and twice as strong (yielding and ultimate strength) as those of the workpiece material in his simulation. This

is not done in practice because it produces a shock at the tool tip and reduces tool life. Guo Y. B. and Dornfeld D. A. [37] developed 3-D FEM drilling models with two sets of backup materials to investigate the influence of backup material on drilling burr formation and showed that burr size is best minimized by use of a bushing having a hole with the same diameter as that of the drill.

Guo Y.B. and Dornfeld D.A. [38] proposed an integrated CAD/FEA system for drill design and drilling burr formation process. Various drills from the industrial collaborators can be modeled parametrically with a commercial CAD program and be incorporated into a finite element input file automatically with workpiece geometry and, material, cutting conditions and process data.

3. CONCLUDING REMARKS

Based on the analysis of the various literatures, certain areas have been identified for further investigations, it is very much indicative from the literature that many investigations have been done in past to identify the process parameters which influence burr formation, but still some improvements are expected to minimize it. All the investigations have centered on the size of the exit burr while drilling a hole of constant diameter. No information is available regarding the influence of cutting speed, drill diameter, work material properties while drilling non-ferrous metals. The investigations which have been performed under a large variety of experimental conditions dealt with the effect of each of the independent variables on burr size, changing one independent variable while fixing the other independent variables at constant levels. None of these studies has considered the interaction effects of these variables on burr size. So far many experiments have been carried out in minimizing the burr formation in drilling, but no work has been done on the mathematical modeling, analysis and optimization of various parameters considering cutting conditions, drill geometry, different work materials and tool materials responsible for burr formation. It is quite difficult to establish a general relation for predicting burr geometry under any known set of conditions (process parameters). In order to understand the effect of different process parameters and the interactions on the burr geometry, Response Surface Methodology can be proposed. Response Surface Methodology is combination of mathematical and statistical techniques used in the empirical study of relationships, where several independent variables or factors influence a dependent variable or response. Response Surface Methodology makes use of Statistical Design of Experiments to conduct minimum number of experiments, which is a time saving means of establishing relationships between drilling process parameters and geometry. For obtaining better parametric combination of process parameters to minimize burr size in drilling Taguchi approach can be suggested which could optimize one parameter at a time. Considering the complexities involved in setting the process parameters so as to satisfy the multi objective optimization for minimization of burr formation, several other methods such as Artificial Neural Network, Genetic Algorithm and Memetic Algorithm can be designed to optimize process parameters.

4. REFERENCES

1. **Gillespie, L.K.** (1975), "The $2 Billion Deburring Bill", *Manufacturing Engineering and Management*, Vol.74, No.2, 20-21.
2. **Arai, M. and Nakayama, K.** (1986), "Boundary Notch on Cutting Tool Caused by Burr and its Suppression", *J. Bull Japan Society of Precision Engineering*, Vol.52, 864-866.
3. **Gillespie, L.K.** (1979), "Deburring Precision Miniature Parts", *Precision Engineering*, Vol.1, No.4, 189-198.
4. **Gillespie, L.K.** (1981), "Deburring Technology for Improved Manufacturing", *SME*, Dearborn, MI.
5. **Gillespie, L.K.** (1975), "Burr Produced by Drilling", *Bendix Corporation*, Unclassified Topical Report, BDX-613-1248.
6. **Gillespie, L.K.** (1976), "Effects of Drilling Variables on Burr Properties", *Bendix Corporation*, Unclassified Topical Report, BDX-613-1502.
7. **Gillespie, L.K. and Blotter, P.T.** (1976), "The Formation and Properties of Machining Burrs", *Trans. ASME, J.*

8. **Sung-Lim, Ko and Dornfield, D. A.** (1991), " A Study on Burr Formation Mechanism", *Trans. ASME, J. Engineering for Materials and Technology*, Vol. 113, 75-87.
9. **Pande, S. S. and Relekar, H. P.** (1986), "Investigations on Reducing Burr Formation in Drilling", *Int. J. Machine Tool Design Research*, Vol.26, No.3, 339-348.
10. **Sofrnas, A., Spurgeon, M.M. and Taraman, K.** (1975), "Reduction of Burr Formation in Drilling", *SME Technical Paper*, MR 75-376, 1-14.
11. **Sofrnas, A. and Taraman, K.** (1976), " Model Development for Exit Burr Thickness as a Function of Drill Geometry and Feed", *SME Technical Paper*, MR 76-253, 1-12.
12. **Shikata, H., DeVries, M.F. and Wu, S. M.** (1980), "An Experimental Investigation on Sheet Metal Drilling", *Annals of CIRP*, Vol.29/1, 85-88.
13. **Sungawara, A. and Ingaki, K.** (1978), " The Effect of Shape of Tool Point with Dwindling of Drill Diameter on Drilling in the Case of 0.02% of C Steel", *J. Bull Japan Society of Precision Engineering*, Vol.44, No. 2, 179-184.
14. **Sungawara, A. and Ingaki, K.** (1981), " Burr in Micro Diameter Drill Working", *J Bull Japan Society of Precision Engineering*, Vol.15, No. 1, 21-26.
15. **Sungawara, A. and Ingaki, K.** (1982), " Effect of Workpiece Structure on Burr Formation in Micro drilling", *Precision Engineering*, Vol.4, No. 1, 9-12.
16. **Sofrnas, A.** (1976), " The Effect of System Stiffness, Workpiece Hardness and Spindle Speed on Drilling Burr Thickness", *SME Technical Paper*, MR 76-132, 1-14.
17. **Takazawa, K.** (1988), "The Challenge of Burr Technology and Its Worldwide Trends", *J. Bull. Japan Society of Precision Engineering*, Vol.22/3, 165-170.
18. **Stein, J. M.** (1995), "*Burr Formation in Precision Drilling of Stainless Steel*", Ph.D. Dissertation, University of California, Berkeley.
19. **Sung-Lim, Ko and Jing-Koo, Lee** (2001), "Analysis on Burr Formation in Drilling with New Concept Drill", *J. Materials Processing Technology*, Vol.113, 392-398.

20. **Sung-Lim, Ko and Jae-Eun, Chang** (2001), "Development of Drill Geometry for Burr Minimization in Drilling ", *LMA Annual Reports*.

21. **Adachi, K.** (1987), "A Study on Burr in Low Frequency Vibratory Drilling", *J. Bull. Japan Society of Precision Engineering*, Vol.21, No.4, 258-264.

22. **Takeyama, H. and Kato, S.** (1991), "Burrless Drilling by Means of Ultrasonic Vibration", *Annals of CIRP*, 83-86.

23. **Takeyama, H.** (1993), "Study on Oscillatory Drilling Aiming at Prevention of Burr", *J. Bull Japan Society of Precision Engineering*, Vol.59, No.10, 1719-1724.

24. **Lee, G.B.** (1989), "*Digital Control for Burr Minimization in Drilling*", Ph.D. Dissertation, University of California, Berkeley.

25. **Kim, J. S.** (1998), "Preliminary Experiment of Drilling Burr Formation in Titanium Alloy", *LMA Annual Reports*.

26. **Kim, J. S.** (1998), "Control Chart of Drilling Exit Burr in Stainless Steel", *LMA Annual Reports*.

27. **Stein, J. M. and Dornfield, D. A.** (1995), "An Analysis of Burrs in Drilling Precision Miniature Holes using Fractional Factorial Designs", *ASME Symposium on Production Engineering*, Winter Annual Meeting.

28. **Stein, J. M. and Dornfield, D. A.** (1997), "Burr Formation in Drilling Miniature `Holes", *Annals of CIRP,* Vol. 46, 63-66.

29. **Dornfield, D.A., Kim, J. S., Dechow, H., Hewson, J. and Chen, L.J.** (1999), "Drilling Burr formation in Titanium", *Annals of CIRP*, Vol. 48/1.

30. **Stein, J. M. and Dornfield, D.A.** (1999), " Influence of Workpiece Exit Angle on Burr formation in Drilling Intersecting Holes", *Trans. North American Manufacturing Research Institute, SME*.

31. **Kim, J. S., Furness, R. and Dornfield, D.A.** (1999), "Experimental Study of Burr formation in Drilling of Intersecting Holes with Gun and Twist Drills", *Trans. North American Manufacturing Research Institute, SME*.

32. **Kim, J. S.** (1998), "Geometric Characteristics of Drilling of Intersecting Holes", *LMA Annual Reports*.

33. **Hewson, J.** (1998), "Exit Burr Size and Shape in Backplate Assisted Drilling of Ti-6Al-4V ", *LMA Annual Reports*.

34. **Sofronas, A.** (1975),"*The Formation and Control of Drilling Burrs*", Ph.D. Dissertation, University of Detroit.

35. **Guo, Y. B.** (1997), "*Finite Element Modeling of Drilling Burr Formation Process*", M.E. Dissertation, University of California, Berkeley.

36. **Park, I.W.** (1996), "*Modeling of Burr Formation Processes in Metal Cutting*", Ph.D. Dissertation, University of California, Berkeley.

37. **Guo, Y. B. and Dornfield, D.A.** (1998), "Finite Element Analysis of Drilling Burr Minimization with a Backup Material", *Trans. North American Manufacturing Research Institute, SME*, Vol. 26, 207-212.

38. **Guo, Y. B. and Dornfield, D.A.** (1998), "Integration of CAD of Drill with FEA of Drilling Burr Formation", *Trans. North American Manufacturing Research Institute, SME*, Vol. 26, 201-206.

GCMM 2004
Editors: Prasad K D V Yarlagadda and S Narayanan
Publisher: Narosa Publishing House Pvt. Ltd., New Delhi, India

Time Standards for Garment Manufacturing

Prasad P S S[*] & Thanenthran M[**]

[*] Assistant Professor, Department of Mechanical Engineering,
P.S.G College of Technology.

Email: pssai@yahoo.com

[**] M.E (Industrial Engineering) student, P.S.G College of Technology.

Email: thanen_thran@yahoo.com

Abstract

Factories using scientific methods for setting production standards and adapting suitable production strategies were more productive. Time study method is one of the tools in industrial engineering mostly used for finding the time required for various operations and subsequently developing the time standards. The present work attempts to carry out time study on various operations involved in manufacturing a garment named "Polo-shirt". Dividing the total work content of product into elements, the time required to complete each element of the total work was recorded using a stopwatch through continuous observation. Then using various allowances suitable for garment industry, standard times were estimated. The standard time was estimated for two different production systems and compared for the best one. The full paper presents detailed time study process carried out and results.

Keywords
Productivity, Time Study, Garment Industry, Standard Times

1. INTRODUCTION

The productivity performance of an average Indian Apparel Industry is one of the lowest in Asia [1]. The present day Indian and other Asian garment manufacturers are facing the increasing competition, raising costs and falling sales prices. To retain its competitiveness, Indian apparel industry will have to pay increased attention to productivity improvement. Factories using scientific methods for setting production standards and adapting suitable production strategies were more productive [2]. Time-based performance measures are essential for the competitive apparel and sewn-products industry. The production cycles have become shorter and shorter while the number of styles has increased. To make matters even better (or worse), the increased competition has ensured that for every garment manufacturer there are ten who will be willing to adopt the rigorous standards demanded by the buyers while delivering consistent quality [2]. There is no doubt that technology has a major role to play in optimizing the entire production process. It is important that productivity should be maximized at the highest degree of economic efficiency. As a result more and more garment manufactures have to concentrate in technologies to optimize their production standards to enable them to come at par with the accepted standards of production while delivering a high quality.

Setting of realistic time standards for the operations in assembly line will help the supervisor to balance the line effectively and increase the productivity. Basic Polo-Shirt, which is widely manufactured in Tirupur, South India was considered for the studying the suitability of different production systems and to set the time standard for productivity enhancement.

The different types of production systems implemented in garment industries are Synchro System, Progressive Bundle System (PBS), Unit Synchro System and Hanger System or Unit Production System (UPS). In synchro system workers were divided according to the process and piece by piece transfer by hand occurs between operators. In PBS, again the workers were divided according to the process and but the lots were transferred by hand rather than pieces. These two systems will have the layout according to the process. In Unit synchro system workers were divided according to the group and lots were transferred by hand and they have the layout according to the unit. In UPS, workers were divided according to the process and pieces were transferred by the conveyor. UPS was very much suitable for assembly operations to decrease the lead time and increase the productivity. Productivity of the systems will be influenced by the bottleneck operations that take highest processing time among all operations in the assembly line and the line balancing. As the size of line increases, the balancing become very difficult and may be difficult manage and maintain the productivity.

2. METHODLOGY

Production systems namely Progressive Bundling System (PBS) and Unit Production System (UPS) were considered to identify the best one for Polo-Shirt production [3]. Time study was carried out to find the basic time of the operations. The time measured in accordance with the "continuous time observation method" using stop-watch. Each observation was recorded as lap time and recording was stopped at the end of the observation cycle. Upon completion of all the work components (the operation under study), subtract the value recorded at the

start of each work component from the value observed at the end of each work component so as to obtain the time required for each work component [4]. Table 1 shows the time study form for recording basic times. The sample sizes of observations were chosen from International Labor Office, Geneva standards [5] and are reproduced in the Table 2.

The allowance rate was determined by operation rate research method as shown in Table 3. Worker was observed for every five seconds and his action at that particular time was recorded. This was carried out for 100 times. The frequencies of main operations (MF) and additional operations (AF) were considered to be basic time frequency. Other frequencies (OF) are considered as the allowance frequency and allowance is calculated as shown in the equation 1.

Allowance rate = $OF/(MF+AF)$ -------- 1

The allowance was added with basic time to arrive at standard processing time.

Standard Processing Time = Basic time + Allowance rate

3. CASE STUDY

As it was already mentioned above, the present work considers the manufacture of polo-shirt for study to find suitable production system and compare the current performance with standards. The following sections detail the various steps involved in the study.

3.1 Analysis of the Systems

In the process of garment manufacturing a sequence of operations involved are partly dependent. In the progressive bundling system (PBS) of manufacturing the independent operations are carried out simultaneously and then they were brought into the assembly process.
The precedence diagram was drawn to represent various operations, listed in Table 4 on a Polo-shirt of basic style and is shown Figure 1.

3.2 Time Study on PBS System

The time study was conducted as per the standard procedure and the time taken for the operations of Polo-shirt manufacturing

Table 1: Time study form [4]

		Product No	Product name		workshop	Study date	researcher

Operator's name; Skill & effort	Process name	Observation Number									total	max	mini	average	remark
		1	2	3	4	5	6	7	8						

Table 2: Sample sizes

Time per cycle in Minutes	0.50	0.75	1.0	2.0
No of cycles	60	40	30	20

Table 3: operation rate research form

operations	Operation allowance								Office allowance				Fatigue and physiological needs		Miscella neous
Main work	Additional work	Establishing the condition	Arranging the	Thread replacements	Recording	Trouble	judgment	correction	Preliminary work arrangements	transport	moving	Waiting for work	fatigue	Physiological needs	Neglect of duty

Table 4: Operations on Polo-shirt

Sub assemblies

1.	Pocket – P	4.	Back - B
	Hem pocket mouth - P1		Attach half moon patch to back – B1
2.	Front – F		Cover stitch on the moon patch – B2
	Attach pocket to front – F1		Attach label on the moon patch - B3
3.	Moon patch – M	5.	Sleeve - S
	Serge moon patch – M1		Attach ribs – S1
			cover stitch on rib – S2

Assembly process	
Join shoulder – A1	set button – A9
set left and right placket – A2	set sleeve – A10
topstitch shoulders – A3	topstitch sleeves – A11
set collar at ends – A4	close side seams – A12
Tape collar at ends – A5	tacking sleeves – A13
Topstitch collar + add label – A6	hem bottom – A14
topstitch placket double top row A7	topstitch vent - A15
button hole –A8	thread trimming and inspection – A16

Finishing – FS

Table 5: Basic Times of Polo-shirt manufacturing operations in PBS

Operation No	Description	No of operators	Basic time in min	Time allocated in sec
1	Join shoulder	1	0.60	36
2	Set left and right placket	3	2.50	50
3	Top stitch shoulder	1	0.60	36
4	Set color at ends	1	0.50	30
5	Tap color at ends	1	0.60	36
6	Top stitch color + add label	1	0.70	42
7	Top stitch placket + V box	4	3.20	48
8	Button hole	1	0.55	33
9	Set button	1	0.45	27
10	Set sleeve	2	1.20	40
11	Top stitch sleeves	1	0.70	42
12	Close side seam	2	1.15	35
13	Tacking sleeve	1	0.60	36
14	Hem bottom	1	0.60	36
15	Top stitch vent	3	2.20	44
16	Thread trimming and inspection	1	0.70	42
	Total	25	16.05	

Table 6: Basic Times of Polo-shirt manufacturing operations in UPS

Operation No	Description	No of operators	Basic time in min	Time allocated in sec
1	Loading	1	0.30	18
2	Join shoulder	1	0.50	30
3	Set left and right placket	3	2.00	40
4	Top stitch shoulder	1	0.50	30
5	Set color at ends	1	0.40	24
6	Tap color at ends	1	0.50	30
7	Top stitch color + add label	1	0.60	36
8	Top stitch placket + V box	4	2.50	37
9	Button hole	1	0.50	30
10	Set button	1	0.35	21
11	Set sleeve	2	1.00	30
12	Top stitch sleeves	1	0.60	36
13	Close side seam	2	1.05	31
14	Tacking sleeve	1	0.50	30
15	Hem bottom	1	0.50	36
16	Top stitch vent	3	2.00	44
17	Thread trimming and inspection	1	0.55	42
	Total	26	14.35	

147

Table 7: Comparison of UPS and PBS System for Polo-shirt manufacturing

S no	Condition of sewing line	PBS	UPS	Remarks
1	Daily working hours(D) (sec)	28,800	28,800	Overtime not included
2	Basic total processing time (sec)	963	861	Only assembly operations
3	No of Operators(N)	25	26	Included trimming
4	Basic pitch time	38	33	
5	Bottleneck processing time(B) in(sec)	50	40	Set left and right placket
6	Allowance rate %	25	17	UPS is motivating tool
7	Standard total processing time(S) = Basic total time X (1+Allowance rate)	1204	1007	
8	Possible daily output in pcs = (D x N) / S	598	744	
9	Actual organization efficiency = Bpt / bottle neck processing time	76%	82.5%	
10	Bottle neck daily output(BP) in pcs = (D x N) / (B x allowance)	455	614	
11	Bottleneck productivity (pcs/operator) = BP / N	18.2 pcs per operator	23.6 pcs per operator	

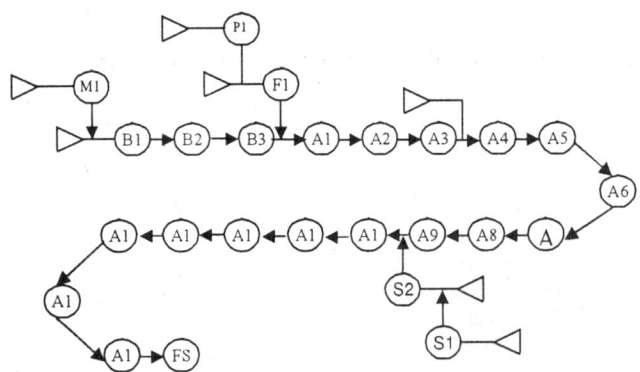

Fig 1: Precedence diagram for a basic Polo-shirt

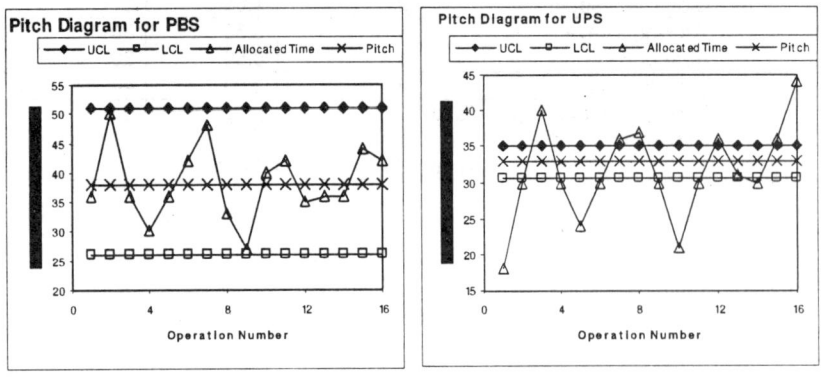

Fig. 2: Pitch diagram for PBS   Fig. 3: Pitch diagram for UPS

were tabulated in Table 5. Since the preparatory work on subassemblies will be carried out separately, there is no influence of these operations on productivity of the system. Hence time study was limited to assembly operations only.

Total basic time (Bt) = 16.05 minutes
No of operators (N) = 25
Basic pitch time(Bpt) = Bt/N = 0.64 min

On an average, one Polo-shirt will be produced within 0.64 min or 38 sec in Progressive Bundling System.

Target organization efficiency = 75%
Upper control limit (UCL)
= Bpt / target organization efficiency
= 0.85 minutes or 51 sec
Lower control limit (LCL) = 2 X Bpt – UCL
= 0.43 min or 26 sec
Main frequencies (MF) = 20
Additional frequencies (AF) = 60
Other frequencies (OF) = 20

Allowance rate for PBS as per factory efficiency = OF/ (MF+AF) = 20/80= 25% Bottleneck operation was identified as "set right and left placket" which determines the production output.

3.3 Time Study On UPS System

The time study was conducted as per the above methods and the operations time for manufacturing polo-shirt were tabulated along number of operator. Time study was limited to assembly operations only.

Total basic time(Bt) = 14.35 minutes
No of operators (N) = 26
Basic pitch time(Bpt) = Bt/N = 14.35/26
= 0.55 minutes

On an average each machine should have 0.55 min or 33 sec in Unit Production System

Target organization efficiency = 94%
Upper control limit(UCL)
= Bpt / target organization efficiency
= 0.59 minutes or 35 sec
lower control limit(LCL) = 2 X Bpt – UCL
= 0.51 minutes or 30.5 sec
Allowance rate for UPS as per factory efficiency = 15 / 85 = 18 %

Bottleneck operation was identified as 'set right and left placket' which determines the production rate.

4. RESULTS

It can be observed from the Table 7 that UPS was better production system than PBS. The efficiency of the UPS was 82.5% where as in PBS it is 76%. The increase in the efficiency was 15%. Allowance rate also reduced form 25% to 17%. This reduction was due to better control in UPS. Polo –shirt SAM value in the assembly line reduced form 963 to 861seconds. This savings in the SAM value can be effectively utilized for more production.

Time study results show that the productivity per operator in PBS at 75% efficiency was 18 pieces in one shift where as in UPS; the same was 24 pieces at 82.5% efficiency. This difference may be due to elimination of bundling and unbundling of batches in UPS.

5. CONCLUSION

Current competitive market environment thrust upon garment industry to improve productivity. Higher productivity can be achieved in the garment industry by choosing suitable production systems for given product and establishing time standards. The present work considers Polo-shirt as product and studies are conducted to identify the appropriate production system and establish time standards. Time study was conducted on two different production systems for chosen product type of garment and it reveals that performance of UPS was about 15% better than PBS. Even though the parallel processing of some of the elements have to be sacrificed by implementing UPS, SAM value reduction due to the better material handling compensates the drawback.

6. REFERENCES

1. **Rajesh Bheda.(2002)**, "*Productivity in Indian Apparel Industry: Paradigms and Paragons*", *Journal of Textile and Apparel Technology and Management*, Vol. 2,Issue 3.

2. "*Time standards in Production: A Synopsis*", Apparel views, Vol. II, Issue 10, 2003.
3. **Thiyagarajan.N.(2003)**, "Effect of UPS Implementation on Throughput Time"-, Presented on "Innovation for Garment Productivity", NIFT Delhi.

4. JUKI Corporation, *"seminar on sewing production control Textbook on the Management Development Course"*, Apparel Manufacturing Research Laboratory, chofu-city, Japan, 1992.

5. *"Introduction to Time Study"*, International Labor Office, Geneva, 1996.

6. **Zvonko Drageeive, Dubravoko Rogale, Daniela Zavee and Jelka Gersak,(2002.)** *"Workloads and Standard Time Norms in Garment Engineering"*, *Journal of Textile and Apparel Technology and Management"*, Vol. 2, Issue II.

GCMM 2004
Editors: Prasad K D V Yarlagadda and S Narayanan
Publisher: Narosa Publishing House Pvt. Ltd., New Delhi, India

Use of Concurrent Engineering Tools for Product and Process Improvement in Manufacturing

Radharamanan R* & Ansuj A P**

*Mercer University, Macon, GA 31207 USA
**Federal University of Santa Maria, Santa Maria, Brazil

Email: radharaman_r@mercer.edu

Abstract

At present, every manufacturing industry that is involved in making complex products must work towards constantly reducing product costs, shorten time to place the product in the market and continuously improve product quality. Today, the first acceptable design must be close to optimum and rapidly made with little or no need for quality induced modifications. The concurrent engineering design process provides a stable, repeatable process by which increased accuracy is achieved in a shorter time with less variation. In this paper, the concurrent engineering design concepts, the tools that are used to achieve the concept of design for manufacturability, quality standards (ISO-9000), and quality function deployment (QFD) are applied for product and process improvement in an electronic manufacturing industry. The results are presented and discussed.

Keywords

Concurrent engineering, Electronic manufacturing, Product and Process improvement, Quality function deployment, Design for manufacturability, and Quality standards.

1. INTRODUCTION

Concurrent Engineering (CE) is defined as the earliest possible integration of overall company's knowledge, resources, and experience in design, development, marketing, manufacturing, and sales into creating successful new products, with high quality and low cost, while meeting customer expectations (Figure 1). The most important result of applying CE is the shortening of the product concept, design, and development process from a serial to a parallel one. The general concepts when applied in an integrated manner are very powerful and can be applied in any type of organization [2]. The basic purpose of CE is to be more effective by means of cooperation among all departments involved in the creation of a product [3]. The CE design process [17, 19] in its simplest form is the integrated execution of basic principles, such as process management, design, manufacturability and automated infrastructure support. Process management is probably the most important of the four principles, since it coordinates and facilitates the CE design process [10, 14]. The design phase is the execution of the design process for developing a product and its manufacture, and many different people that are involved in the project execute this phase. Manufacturability involves

151

the interaction of the people involved in the actual production of the product with its designers, so that different parameters of the product can be reviewed and discussed and any problems quickly identified and solved. Finally, automated infrastructure support provides all the processes that facilitate all the other processes, such as computers, data transfer and retrieval systems, and the like. A very basic and important ingredient of CE is Design for Manufacture (DFM). DFM is the practice of designing products with manufacturing in mind so that they can be designed in the least time with the least cost. Also, DFM allows a smoother transition from the design of a product into its production as well as minimizing the cost of assembling and testing the product. Quality and reliability are also affected by DFM in a positive way, and therefore the needs and satisfaction of the customers are met and the product automatically becomes more competitive in the market [6, 7, 18].

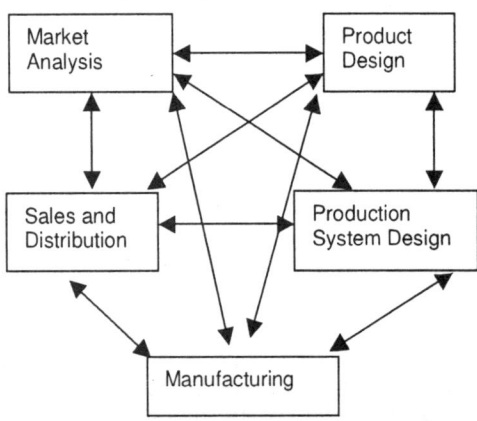

Fig 1: Concurrent Engineering Model.

This paper provides an overview of concurrent engineering design concepts and quality tools. These tools are applied for product and process improvement in a small electronic manufacturing company located in the State of Rio Grande do Sul, Brazil to reduce the rate at which defective parts are produced, increase the quality of manufactured products, increase productivity, minimize product cost, supply products on time to customers, provide customer satisfaction, and keep the company competitive in the market place.

2. CE/DFM TOOLS

A simple definition of DFM is the comprehension and optimization of interactions between different facets of the complex manufacturing systems for effective quality, cost and delivery, with the ultimate aims of producing products with better quality, lower cost, and a reduced time-to market [3, 16]. The design process is the heart and foundation of DFM. It is an iterative, decision-making activity involving the use of scientific and technological information to produce a system, device, or process intended to meet specific needs [3, 6].

The DFM design process should immediately and accurately identify the problem at hand, namely, the production of a product within certain specifications, usually design constraints and criteria set by the engineering teams, marketing, and consumer surveys, for example. Once the problem has been identified, iteration takes place where different ideas are exchanged and methods tried in order to completely define and design the product. This part of the DFM design process is very important since at this stage the major decisions will be made regarding the production and marketing of the product. This iteration period can vary in length, and the length is usually subjected to a deadline in order to meet an optimal time-to-market for the product. In addition to that, the iteration period allows the design to be continuously improved and optimized over time as better and more complete design information becomes available and all the teams involved in the design process communicate their discoveries and ideas.

A comprehensive planning, research and development reduces the amount of iteration and makes any engineering change possible at a reduced cost
in the event that a product is being revised and redesigned. As a result the quality, cost and delivery of the product are greatly improved thanks to early design decisions and increased communication among all members involved in the design, production, and marketing of the product [5, 12]. A typical product design cycle for manufacture is shown in Figure 2.

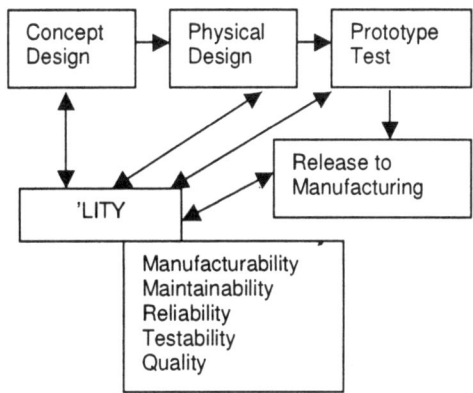

Fig. 2: Product Design Cycle.

2.1. DFM Tools

There are two axioms that can be applied when using DFM tools to improve a product or process. This approach operates under the belief that fundamental principles (axioms) exist for any product to have a good design and that the use of those principles will guide and evaluate design decisions that will ultimately lead to a good design. The axioms must be applicable to the full range of design decisions and to all stages, phases and levels of the design process. Axiom 1: in good design, the independence of functional requirements is maintained. Axiom 2: among the designs that satisfy axiom 1, the best design is one that has the minimum information content. In order to apply both axioms first the team must identify the functional requirements and constraints to be used when designing the product. Once those requirements and constraints have been found, the axioms should be applied to each individual design decision to ensure the success of the project under the DFM guidelines [7, 15]. The condensed listing of the DFM guidelines includes [11, 15]: 1. Design for a minimum number of parts; 2. Develop a modular design; 3. Minimize part variations; 4. Design parts to be multifunctional; 5. Design parts of multiuse; 6. Design parts for ease of fabrication; 7. Avoid separate fasteners; 8. Minimize assembly directions (design for top-down assembly); 9. Maximize compliance (design for ease of assembly); 10. Minimize handling (design for handling and presentation); 11. Evaluate assembly methods; 12. Eliminate or simplify adjustments; and 13. Avoid flexible components.

2.2. Quality Tools and ISO-9000 Standards

Quality is a competitive advantage in the marketplace. This means that a company must have the same or better quality than its competitors. The quality of competitors, however, is improving continuously. This situation keeps a company improving quality continuously to remain a viable force in the market place. Companies can no longer tolerate adverse gaps in product quality between their products and those of their competitors. To prevent this, a viable program of continuous improvement must be developed and put into practice [20].

ISO-9000 standards exist principally to facilitate international trade. The driving forces that have resulted in widespread implementation of ISO-9000 standards can be summed up in one phrase: "the globalization of business". Expressions such as "post-industrial economy" and "the global village" reflect profound changes during recent decades. These changes include: new technology in virtually all industry/economic sectors; widespread worldwide travel; dramatic increase in world population; worldwide electronic communication network; depletion of natural resource reserves; more intensive use of land, water, energy, and air (widespread environmental problems/concerns); downsizing of large companies and other organizations; number and complexity of language, culture, legal, and social frameworks encountered in the global economy with diversity being a permanent key factor; and developing countries becoming a larger proportion of the total global economy with new kinds of competitors and new markets. These changes have led to increased economic competition, increased customer expectations for quality, and increased demands upon organizations to meet more stringent requirements for quality of their products [13].

Vision 2000 report proposed four goals that relate to maintaining the ISO-9000 standards so that they continually meet the needs of the market place. These goals are *universal acceptance,* being adopted and used worldwide; *current compatibility,* combined use without conflicting requirements; *forward compatibility,* with successive revisions being accepted by users; and *forward flexibility,* using architecture that allows new features to be incorporated readily [8, 13].

ISO-9000 certification occurs when a neutral and independent "registrar" uses one of the ISO-9000 standards to certify a supplier. This results in an official designation of the supplier as an "ISO-9001 or ISO-9002 or ISO-9003" certified supplier. A supplier registered in this manner is in the enviable position of being seen as a reliable worldwide supplier of quality products and services; its customers can reduce or eliminate inspection of purchased parts thereby resulting in an efficient system of global trade [9].

The ISO quality standards do not refer directly to the products or services delivered, but rather to the production and administrative processes that produce them. It is generic enough to be applicable to any industry type. Specifically, the standards focus on the need for organizational structure, well-documented procedures, and management's commitment of resources to implement quality management [20]. The 20 clauses of ISO-9001 standard, the most comprehensive of the three standards are found in [9, 13].

2.3. Quality Function Deployment

Measurement and evaluation of product quality is not difficult, since one can establish conformance standards, inspect and test products, identify defect rates, correct errors, and impose performance level. The quality function deployment (QFD) permits to assemble a considerable amount of information in a concise form, in a small number of documents - QFD diagrams. The graphical format is more effective in simplifying complex information [1, 4].

The QFD aims at the customer. It is necessary to hear the "voice of the customer" during the development of the products and processes, identify and focus on the details and decide what is important. This tool simplifies a set of information through the use of graphs based on matrices. The QFD is a system that translates the requirements of the customer, identifies necessary modifications before major expenses take place, reduces risks during the development phase, creates basic knowledge of the product, and introduce the "voice of the customer" in the development process [4, 14]. This method permits to collect a large quantity of information in the form of graphs. Each customer differs in his/her expectations and necessities, consequently, in the requirements. QFD identifies customers in the various stages of development life cycle, and employs techniques to compile their requirements. The QFD demands a list of "WHATS" AND "HOWS", where the items "WHATS" are the necessities of the customers and the "HOWS" are the measurable requisites that can affect the understanding of the requisites of the customers [1, 4].

Quality function deployment – specifically, the house of quality – is an effective management tool in which customer expectations are used to drive the process under consideration. Some of the advantages and benefits of implementing QFD are: an orderly way of obtaining information and presenting it; shorter development cycle; considerable reduction in costs; fewer process changes; reduced chance of oversights during process execution; an environment of team work; consensus decisions; and preserving everything in writing. QFD implementation results in a satisfied customer [1, 15].

3. ELECTRONIC MANUFACTURING

A study has been conducted for implementing some of the CE/DFM tools in a small size electronic manufacturing industry located in the southern part of Brazil. The main products of this industry are: sirens and alarms for the cars. These products are distributed to the car manufacturers and retail auto shops located in several states. The initial study with the management, design and manufacturing teams indicated the following:
1. Types of problems with respect to the product: defective plastic parts from supplier, visual external finish, defective raw material,

defective circuit board, and improper use of the product. 2. Factors affecting the product cost: raw material, employees training, transportation, quality program, rework, idle time in the assembly line, marketing, taxes, and product warranty. 3. Problems related to the production process: burnt resistance and motors, obsolete machines and equipment, lack of preventive maintenance, and insufficient tools. 4. Types of complaints from the consumer: delay in product delivery, high cost of the product, better product from the competitors, and defective products.

4. RESULTS AND DISCUSSIONS

Over a period of three months, 625 units installed and sold through two car manufacturers have been monitored. Out of these 625 units installed, 248 units (39.7% of total units sold) were returned from the customers to the manufacturer for repair and rework. The units were inspected before they were sent for repair and/or rework. Table 1 shows the inspection results on the 248 returned units.

Table 1: Inspection Results

Reason for Repair/ Rework	No.of Units	Percentage
1. Burnt resistance/motor	112	45.16
2. Defective plastic part	67	27.02
3. Defective raw material	42	16.93
4. Improper use	21	8.46
5. Visual external finish	16	6.45
Total	248	100.00

Table 2: Results of Customer Complaints

Customer Complaints	No. of complaints	Percentage
1. Defective units	154	44.77
2. Low Quality	82	23.84
3. High cost	67	19.47
4. Delay in delivery	41	11.92
Total	344	100.00

It is observed from Table 1 that burnt resistance/motor is responsible for 45% of repair and rework. About 44% of repair/rework are due to defective plastic parts and raw materials. The customer complaints received along with the returned 248 units were analyzed and 344 responses were registered as shown in Table 2. It is clear from Table 2 that defective units and low quality (68%) are major causes for return of the products from the customers for repair and rework.

Based on the preliminary study results, the following actions were taken to minimize the number of defective units reaching the customers, increase product quality, minimize unit cost of the product, and deliver the products on time to the customers. *Defective Units:* Some of the concurrent engineering tools have been adapted and applied to this industry. First the DFM guidelines were used for redesigning the existing products. The assembly line has been redesigned incorporating new tools and equipment. An intensive training program has been arranged for everyone in the shop floor on the new tools and equipment. The existing raw materials and plastic parts suppliers have been changed to ISO-9000 certified suppliers. The above changes significantly reduced repair and rework and increased productivity. *Product Quality:* Final product testing procedures have been modified. Everyone in the enterprise starting from the shop floor employees to top management personnel has been trained in total quality management concepts. Product quality is improved through ISO-9002 certification. *Product Cost:* The selling price/unit is reduced to that of the competitors in the market. This was made possible due to reduced repair and rework, and increased productivity. *Delivery Time:* Product delivery time is significantly reduced due to the incorporation of DFM guidelines and increase in productivity. *Customer Satisfaction:* Quality function deployment (QFD) concepts have been incorporated to meet the customer needs and requirements. This also provided continuous feedback from the customers.

Before the incorporation of the concurrent engineering concepts almost 40% of the items manufactured and sold were sent back by the customers for repair and rework within three months time of purchase. This has been significantly reduced after the incorporation of quality standards, design of assembly, and QFD concepts. The customer complaints have been significantly reduced, and the repair and rework dropped to 5-10%. At present, the company is selling their products in several states of Brazil and also exporting them to neighboring Latin American Countries.

5. CONCLUSIONS

In this paper, many concepts have been listed that when properly applied will lead a design team to an optimal design of any product or service. The guidelines and methods explained here have been proved to be highly effective when applied in a small electronic manufacturing industry. Any industry that is not currently applying CE/DFM in its design and production phases is urged to do so. The benefits that can be obtained by correctly applying and implementing CE/DFM, QFD, and ISO-9000 are great when compared to other methods of design and production. From this study, it is very clear that only by the skillful integration of design, manufacturing, and marketing an industry today can survive in this highly competitive world where cost, time-to-market, and good quality are imperative for survival.

6. REFERENCES

1. **Akao Y.** (1990), *Quality Function Deployment – Integrating Customer Requirements into Product Design,* Productivity Press, Cambridge, MA.
2. **Allen W. C.** (1990), *Simultaneous Engineering: Manufacturing and Design,* SME, Dearborn, MI.
3. **Anderson D. M.** (1990), *Design for Manufacturability: Optimizing Cost, Quality, and Time-to-Market,* CIM Press, Lafayette, CA.
4. **Besterfield D. H. et. al.** (1999), *Total Quality Management,* Second Edition, Prentice Hall, Englewood Cliffs, NJ.
5. **Boothroyd G.** (1994), *Product Design for Manufacture and Assembly,* Marcel Dekker, New York, NY.
6. **Corbett J. et. al.** (1991), *Design for Manufacture: Strategies, Principles and Techniques,* New York, NY: Addison-Wesley Publishing Company.
7. **Helander and Nagamachi,** (1992), *Design for Manufacturability: A Systems Approach to Concurrent Engineering and Ergonomics,* Taylor & Francis, Washington D. C.
8. **Juran J. M. and Godfrey A. B.** (1999), *Juran's Quality Handbook,* Fifth Edition, McGraw-Hill, New York, NY.
9. **Lamprecht J. L.** (1992), *ISO 9000: Preparing for Registration,* ASQC Quality Press, Milwaukee, WI.
10. **Miller, L. C. G.** (1993), *Concurrent Engineering Design: Integrating the Best Practices for Process Improvement,* SME, Dearborn, MI.
11. **Nevins J. L. and Daniel E. W.** (1989), *Concurrent Design of Products and Processes: A Strategy for the Next Generation in Manufacturing,* McGraw-Hill, New York, NY.
12. **Norman R.** (1990), *Concurrent Product and Process Development (CP/PD) - A Current Design Methodology: Making it Happen,* Revised Ed., Int. TechneGroup Incorporated.
13. **Peach R. W.** (1997), *The ISO 9000 Handbook,* Richard D. Irwin, Chicago, IL.
14. **Radharamanan R.** (1993), "Concurrent Engineering and Design for Manufacture", Keynote Speech, *XIII Encontro Nacional de Engenharia de Produção,* Florianópolis, Brazil.
15. **Shina S. G.** (1991), *Concurrent Engineering and Design for Manufacture of Electronics Products,* Van Nostrand Reinhold, New York.
16. 16, **Stoll H. W.** (1998), "Design for Manufacture", *Journal of Manufacturing Engineering,* January.
17. **Susman G. I.** (1992), *Integrating Design and Manufacturing for Competitive Advantage,* Oxford University Press, New York.
18. **Tanner J. P.** (1989), "Product Manufacturability", *Journal of Automation,* May.
19. **Turtle Q. C.** (1994), *Implementing Concurrent Project Management,* Prentice Hall, Englewood Cliffs, NJ.
20. **Winchell W.** (1991), Continuous Quality Improvement: A Manufacturing Professional's Guide, SME, Dearborn, MI.

GCMM 2004
Editors: Prasad K D V Yarlagadda and S Narayanan
Copyright © 2005, Vellore Institute of Technology, Vellore, India
Publisher: Narosa Publishing House Pvt. Ltd., New Delhi, India

Virtual Manufacturing: A New Paradigm in Manufacturing

Radharamanan R

Mercer University
Macon, GA 31207 USA

Email: radharaman_r@mercer.edu

Abstract

In this paper, Virtual Manufacturing (VM), an emerging technology, that provides the capability to "Manufacture in the Computer", and the modeling approaches necessary to realize VM are presented and discussed. VM has the ability to interchange models between their use in simulation and control environments. The use of VM concepts improves decision-making and quickly achieves products with high performance and quality at a low cost. VM can provide accurate and realistic means to predict schedule, cost, and quality; address affordability as an iterative solution; and bridge the gap between engineering (design) and manufacturing in an interactive fashion. The benefits, costs, limitations, and risks associated with adopting VM are highlighted and discussed.

Keywords
Virtual manufacturing, Virtual organization, Agile manufacturing, Virtual reality, and Web-based learning in engineering education.

1. INTRODUCTION

It is known that acquisition strategies require the capability to prove the manufacturability and affordability of new products/systems prior to the commitment of large production resources and/or to shelving the system for restart in the future. Loosing the manufacturing capability and experience in production is a major risk in the current manufacturing environment [6, 8]. Maintaining the state-of-the art manufacturing proficiency without actually building/manufacturing the products is a major challenge. Virtual Manufacturing meets the above challenges by providing the capability, in essence, to continue manufacturing in the virtual world of the computer. Through the use of distributed manufacturing modeling and simulation, VM enables the enterprises to evaluate the producibility and affordability of new product and/or process concepts with respect to risks, their impacts on manufacturing capabilities, production capacity, and cost.

Virtual Manufacturing is one of the key technologies that allow going beyond the assumptions driving the old acquisition strategies. It provides the following fundamental changes: VM can be used to *"prove out"* the production processes, resulting in *"pre-production hardened systems"* - i.e., the systems which are developed and verified but never actually undergo actual production

157

runs; VM can significantly improve production flexibility, and hence, reduce the fixed costs; and VM can substantially improve the decision making process of acquisition managers by reliably predicting schedule, risks, and costs.

2. BACKGROUND

According to the Air Force Man Tech *"Virtual Manufacturing is an integrated, synthetic manufacturing environment exercised to enhance all levels of decision and control"* in a manufacturing enterprise [6, 10].

It is clear from the results of the Virtual Manufacturing Workshops organized by Air Force Man Tech [11, 12] that a single definition of VM is inappropriate. A definition of VM is proposed to capture design, production, and control aspects of manufacturing: The Design-Centered VM adds manufacturing information to the Integrated Product and Process Design (IPPD) process with the intent of allowing simulation of many manufacturing alternatives and the creation of many *"soft"* prototypes by *"Manufacturing in the Computer"*. The Production-Centered VM adds simulation capability to manufacturing process models with the purpose of allowing inexpensive, fast evaluation of many processing alternatives. The Control-Centered VM uses machine control models in simulations, the goal of which is process optimization during actual production.

Vision of VM: The vision of Virtual Manufacturing is to provide a capability to *Manufacture in the Computer*. VM will ultimately provide a modeling and simulation environment so powerful that the design, fabrication/assembly of any product including the associated manufacturing processes, can be simulated in the computer. A comparison between the physical and virtual manufacturing is shown in Figure 1.

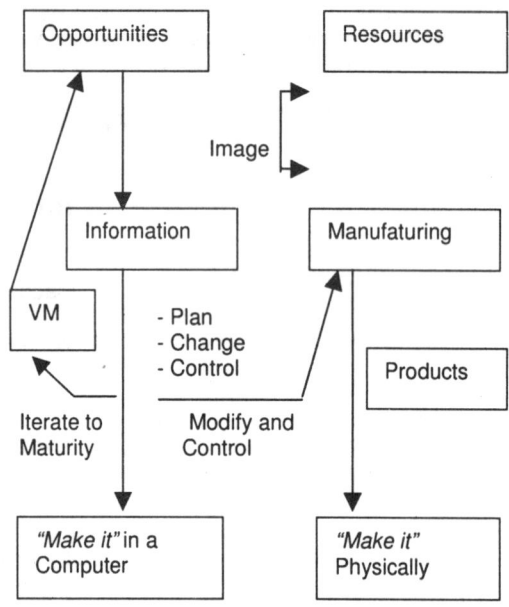

Fig. 1: Comparison between Physical and Virtual Manufacturing

VM Concepts: VM supports implementation of lean/agile manufacturing to achieve improvements in enterprise flexibility and economy. The use of simulation results in manufacturing systems those are less risky to change. Computer assisted model-based planning and control systems require less coordinating communications. The models provide a basis for sharing knowledge between organizations. VM based systems are expected to enhance operations by providing timely answers to the questions: Can we make the product? What are the alternatives? What is the best way to produce the product? When can we deliver the product? How much will it cost?

The relation between the existing enterprise and the market force in creating a new product, the needed changes, the bottlenecks, and the requirements for the new product development are highlighted in Figure 2.

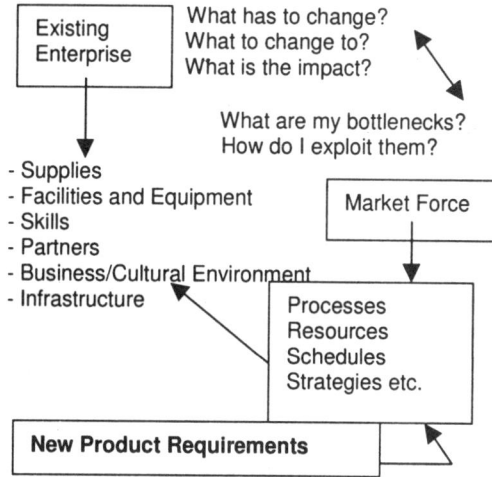

```
Existing
Enterprise

What has to change?
What to change to?
What is the impact?

What are my bottlenecks?
How do I exploit them?

- Supplies
- Facilities and Equipment        Market Force
- Skills
- Partners
- Business/Cultural Environment
- Infrastructure              Processes
                              Resources
                              Schedules
                              Strategies etc.

New Product Requirements
```

Fig. 2: Requirements for New Product Development

VM relies on modeling and simulation technology to simulate the production process and to enable us *"make it virtually."* It is an application of modeling and simulation, but extends that discipline beyond the conventional use. VM supplements the IPPD process since it provides a pathway for the manufacturing knowledge to be migrated to the early phases in the life cycle. VM also adds simulation to the Virtual Enterprise (VE) concept and Virtual Prototyping. VM must be integrated with all the relevant enterprise functional areas via a trade-off mechanism (IPPD process) as shown in Figure 3.

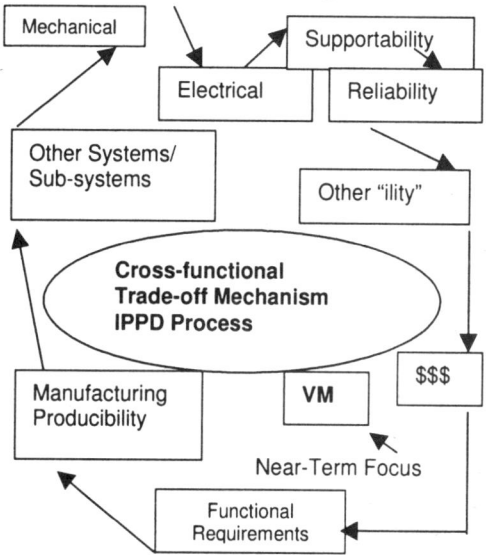

The expected benefits of VM are summarized below: preparedness for market trend, affordability, shorter cycle times, producible prototypes, flexibility, quality, responsiveness, and customer. Virtual Manufacturing as an emerging technology looks for the development of appropriate new tools and techniques for its successful implementation and realization.

Some of the existing tools that can be effectively incorporated for realizing VM include [9]: Design tools, production tools, quality tools, artificial intelligence (AI) tools, computer science tools, management tools and mathematical tools.

The Technical Workshop results indicated that the technologies critical to VM could be organized into the following major categories [12]: Visualization; Environment construction technologies; Modeling technologies; Representation; Meta-modeling; Integrating infrastructure and architecture; Simulation; Methodology; Integration of legacy data; Manufacturing characterization; Verification, validation, and measurement; Workflow; and Cross-functional trades.

VM environment enables a shortening and simplification of the life cycle, by improving the reliability of analyses and accelerating decisions through the use of modeling and simulation. VM helps to evaluate product making using simulation and supports operations to provide timely response to the Integrated Product and Process Design (IPPD) functions in the development of new products and/or processes. Collections of objects in a VM environment may also simulate the entire manufacturing enterprise to provide rapid response to customer requirements. Customers with multiple VM-based supplier organizations can use models of their suppliers' enterprises to provide knowledge to an Enterprise Capabilities Expert. Vertical partners can contribute to capabilities models for use in the knowledge-based computer programs that will evaluate customer requirements and supplier capabilities to establish the organizations desirous of responding to specific customer needs. VM also will support rapid technology

159

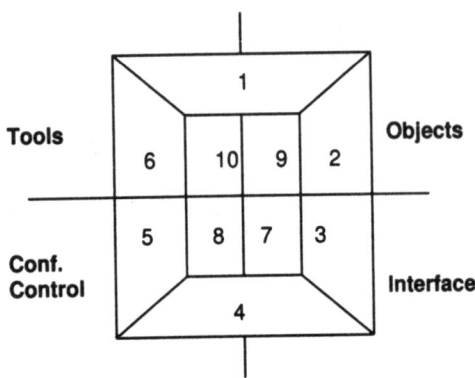

1. Product performance; 2. Process simulation;
3. Producibility simulation; 4. Production control;
5. Supportability, Maintainability, Disposability;
6. Assembly Visualization; 7. Unit & Component
Models; 8. Assembly Models; 9. Factory Models;
and 10. Enterprise Models.

Fig. 4: Architecture of VM Technology

transfer by enabling the sharing of the advanced manufacturing capabilities between cooperating organizations. VM applications and VM tools of one organization may be shared by means of the National Information Highway to the operations of manufacturing partners. Some of the specific areas of applications are: corporate memory, capital investment, supplier management, product design, cost estimation, risk management, customer interface, functional interface, and shop floor. The components of VM architecture are shown in Figure 4.

3. RESULTS AND DISCUSSIONS

Based on the literature search to identify the key issues for realizing VM, it can be summarized that new integration technologies and philosophies are emerging. Visualization hardware and software is becoming more affordable and widespread. New modeling and model abstraction techniques are appearing. The most important set of technologies centers on modeling and simulation. Some of the key areas that require attention in modeling and simulation are: model object selection (what to model); degree of abstraction; level of depth; flexibility and maintenance of models; integration of different

models; and model validation. The results are discussed under the following headings:

Flexible Manufacturing: The discussion with a National Research Group from Oak Ridge National Laboratory, Sandia National Laboratories, and Los Alamos National Laboratories indicated that the research in telerobotics and flexible manufacturing systems though showed progress, it would be practically impossible to totally replace human with robots. Maturity in existing and emerging technologies (both hardware and software) is needed to see potential success in this area.

Lean Manufacturing: Womack et al. [13] in their book on *"The Machine that Changed the World"* addressed the future of the automobile and extensively discussed the importance of lean production. A team spent five years exploring the differences between mass production and lean production in one enormous industry. They have been both insiders with access to vast amounts of proprietary information and daily contact with industry leaders, and outsiders with a broad perspective, often very critical, on existing practices. In this process they have become convinced that the principles of lean production can be applied equally in every industry across the globe and that the conversion to lean production will have profound effect on human society - it will truly change the world.

Virtual Prototyping: The discussion with a rapid prototyping user group revealed that the customers have difficulty is accepting *"Virtual Prototyping"* as one of the means of acquisition for the following reasons: There exists a significant difference in the prototype they see *"virtually in the computer"* and the real product they receive; One can show a colorful, attractive, and high quality products *"virtually in the computer"*; however, the real product may differ in various aspects - including functional and aesthetic aspects - of what was seen in the computer. Virtual Prototyping is still in the experimental stage and it will take a few more years to mature in terms of technology (visualization, representation, abstraction, and appropriate hardware and software) and be used by vendors and consumers.

Virtual Quality: The discussion with the users of TQM, and ISO/QS 9000 showed that virtual manufacturing concepts will aid significantly the way business will be done in the future for the following reasons: Once the VM technologies mature, the concept of building quality in the product is much easier even before the product is made and hence the concept of *"Right First Time"* will have much more meaning in term of Quality Standards. Quality is defined as *"Fitness for Purpose"*, and the VM technologies will make it happen since the customers can make *"changes virtually"* in the product and make it fit for the intended purpose even before the product is made. In terms of quality, VM can go beyond the customer satisfaction and help in achieving Quality Function Deployment (QFD).

Virtual Reality: Despite the enthusiasm surrounding virtual reality (VR), there is a substantial gap between current technology and that needed to bring virtual environments closer to reality. That is the conclusion of a National Research Council committee report on 3D computer-generated worlds with which people can interact. According to the committee, certain areas hold the most promise for practical uses of VR: training, hazardous operations, medicine and health care, design, manufacturing, and marketing. Using VR and telerobotics, one can or will be able to explore the ocean floor and outer space, dig up a 10-ton container of hazardous waste, take a submarine trip through the human circulatory system, and try out products not yet manufactured, for example.

Virtual Organization and Agile Manufacturing: In the search for agility, companies will rely increasingly on virtual enterprises, virtual manufacturing, and virtual reality. Goals of virtual manufacturing include analyzing design, product, and process alternatives for viability, cost and risk; integrating product and process development; improving customer response time and cost estimates; and retaining corporate knowledge. The Society of Manufacturing Engineering

developed a videotape on *"Agile Manufacturing: Moving to the Next Level"* [1]. The video addressed *"agility"* as the new survival concept for global manufacturing competitiveness and indicated that the emerging concept of agility is based on the factors: markets of all nations are combining into a single global economy; rapid change in the global market place is inevitable; the explosion of technology makes every country a potential competitor; customers are demanding customized products with short lead times. Goldman et al., [3] in their book on *"Agile Competitors and Virtual Organization: Strategies for Enriching the Customer"* addressed how to confront and thrive on change and uncertainty.

VM Concepts in Engineering Education: The increasing access to Internet and the World Wide Web has expanded the variety of media by which universities are able to offer distance learning opportunities. Most recently courses and whole degree programs are being developed for delivery via the Internet. At present, VM concepts and web-based tools are effectively being used in engineering education for training, distance learning, laboratory education, and testing of students. Some of the other VM concepts/tools such as virtual reality [7], virtual prototyping, virtual quality, virtual laboratory, virtual factory system [2], and modeling and simulation technology are being tested for effective use in engineering education.

Realization of VM: The STEP standard [5] is intended for long-term development and uses a widely available language called Express to describe the complexities of solid geometry. STEP, also referred to as ISO-10303, is an international standard for the exchange of product model data. Designers and engineers should be aware of its capabilities, how it might be used, and what developers have planned for it. The super-model database, in progress, will be Web compatible and it can be accessed by the entire supply chain. The Web based languages such as SGML (Standard Generalized Markup Language), HTML (Hyper Text Markup Language), and XML (eXtensible Markup Language) are helpful in implementing

VM. SMMS software [4] developed by RTSe (USA), Inc., is an ideal product for creating, managing, and publishing metadata to improve overall management of large data archives. SMMS can also be used in the realization of VM.

Research Relevant to VM: The Virtual Manufacturing Technical Workshop [12] identified technologies that are critical to virtual manufacturing. The technologies were classified under Core Technology, Enabling Technology, Show Stopper Technology, and Common Technology. The Core Technologies identified and reported are: VM methodology for process characterization; technologies to simulate assembly operations; declarative representation of product and processes; natural language for VM meta-model; cost database and integration; VM user interface (communication between VM knowledge base and user); VM verification & validation methods, algorithms & tools; process model and simulation validation; methodology for using a VM system; VM framework (guidelines, integration standards, etc.); methodology for design abstraction; tools to relate conceptual design with possible manufacturing methods and processes and cost estimates based on manufacturing features; manufacturing engineering automation (knowledge-based computer applications to perform manufacturing engineering decision making); and simulation architecture.

It is seen that some of the technologies listed above and other related technologies are being studied by government agencies, academia, and industry in the U.S. and other nations. It is necessary to coordinate and bridge the gaps in randomly emerging technologies related to VM and mature them. Some of the technologies that need immediate attention are: selective addition to animation, shop floor based generic models, metrics, representation, and integration.

4. CONCLUSIONS

The potential scope of VM is very large. What is important is that a time phased, realizable scope for VM be defined. VM should be implemented incrementally starting at unit product/process level, then at subsystem level and finally at system level. The manufacturing process and the scope of VM products should be improved in the *"big M"* manufacturing domain: concept through production including marketing, sales, and service. Disagreement remains on what VM is and the key issues for realizing VM - there is a need to define VM more precisely.

5. REFERENCES

1. **Agility** (1994), "*Agile Manufacturing: Moving to the Next Level*", A Manufacturing Insight Video by SME, VT516-2393.
2. **Dessouky M. M. et al.** (1998), "Virtual Factory Teaching System in Support of Manufacturing Education", *Journal of Engineering Education,* Vol. 87, No. 4, pp. 459-467.
3. **Goldman S. L., Nagel, R. N. and Preiss, K.** (1995), *Agile Competitors and Virtual Organizations: Strategies for Enriching the Customer*, Von Nostrand Reinhold, New York.
4. **Goodchild M. F.** (2000), "Manage Your Metadata", *Geo Info Systems,* Vol. 10, No. 5, pp.43-45.
5. **Hardwick M.** (2000), "What You Should Know About STEP", *Machine Design,* Vol. 72, No. 13, pp. 98-102.
6. **Hitchcock, Baker and Brink,** (1994), "The Role of Hybrid Systems Theory in Virtual Manufacturing", *Proc. IEEE Symposium on Computer-Aided Control Systems Design (CACSD),* IEEE, New York, pp. 345-50.
7. **Impelluso T. and Metoyer-Guidry T.** (2001), "Virtual Reality and Learning by Design: Tools for Integrating Mechanical Engineering Concepts", *Journal of Engineering Education,* Vol. 90, No. 4, pp. 527-534.
8. **Kessler W. C., Shumaker G. C. and Hitchcock M. F.** (1993), "*Early Manufacturing Consideration in Design*", In AGARD, Integrated Airframe Technology, Dec., 7p.
9. **Radharamanan R.** (1994), "*A Study on Virtual Manufacturing*", Report, AFOSR Summer Faculty Research Program at Wright Laboratory, Aug., 19p.
10. **VM** (1993), "*Virtual Manufacturing; A Methodology for Manufacturing in a Computer*", Report: An Air Force Man Tech Perspective, CNCPTFRN.DOC, October, 15p
11. **VM** (1994), "*Virtual Manufacturing User Workshop*", Report, Lawrence Associate Inc., Dayton, Ohio, August 1994.
12. **VM** (1995), "*Virtual Manufacturing Technical Workshop*", Report, Lawrence Associate Inc., Dayton, Ohio, January 26, 1995.

Management

GCMM 2004
Editors: Prasad K D V Yarlagadda and S Narayanan
Publisher: Narosa Publishing House Pvt. Ltd., New Delhi, India

Challenging Issues in Managing New Product Development

Shajahan C A & Kumanan S

Department of Production Engineering
National Institute of Technology, Tiruchirappalli, India

Email: cashaji@yahoo.com

Abstract

Product development (PD) is a complex business process of transforming new ideas into marketable new products, processes or services. It gets more importance in business due to stiff competition and fast changing business environment. It is a complex activity that requires better management. This paper focuses on the challenging issues in managing new product development and the means to address them.

Keywords
Product development (PD), New Product Development (NPD), Product Life Cycle (PLC), Quality function deployment (QFD), Design Structure Matrix (DSM).

1. INTRODUCTION

A PD process is the entire set of activities required to bring a new concept to a state of market readiness. It is a complex business process of transforming new ideas into marketable new products, processes or services. Its activities involve more than engineering. It is fraught with risks and opportunities, and it requires effective judgment over technology, the market, and time [1]. Successful PD requires the collaboration of many constituencies. The contending activities and the resources needed are to be represented and to be timed for better estimation and control.

Speed in developing products or services allow companies to obtain a differential advantage over their competitors with the result of increased profit margins. Therefore to maximize a company's profitability, it is necessary to get quality product to market in as little time as possible.

The steps involved in PD process are intellectual and organizational rather than physical. Some organizations define and follow a precise and detailed development process, while others may not even be able to describe their processes. Furthermore every organization employs a process at least slightly different from that of every other organization. In fact the same enterprise may follow different processes for each of several different types of development projects. PD involves many people performing many different tasks. Successful PD projects result in high quality, low cost products while making efficient use of time, money and other resources. Development of products that meet the customer or human needs is a priority area in the PD process.

It is an interdisciplinary and complex activity involving different set of tasks that require the participation of hundreds or even thousands of engineers, managers and technicians over a period of several years. This paper addresses the various challenging issues and the means to meet the challenges.

2. PHASES OF PRODUCT DEVELOPMENT PROCESS AND ISSUES

There are six phases of generic product development process as shown in Figure 1.

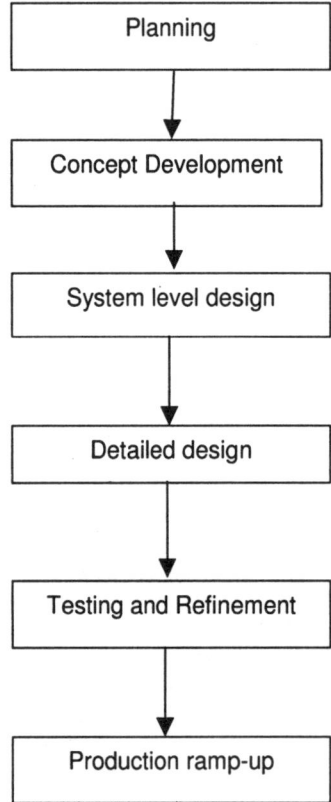

Fig. 1: Phases of PD

2.1 Planning

The planning activity is often referred to as "phase Zero" since it precedes the project approval and launch of the actual product development process. This phase begins with corporate strategy and includes assessment of technology developments and market objectives. The output of the planning phase is the project mission statement, which specifies the target market for the product, business goals, key assumptions and constraints. Determining the user needs is probably the most important step in the planning phase [2]. Information about the customer needs and their priorities can be gained through various marketing methods like questionnaires, interviews, brainstorming techniques etc.

The first step in planning a PD project is to list the tasks, which make up the project. In most of the PD projects the team will not be able to list every task in great detail, too much uncertainty remain in the subsequent development activities. To be most useful in project planning the task list should contain from 50-200 items.

The different traditional tools used in planning and scheduling are PERT, CPM etc. The limitations of such models are
1.   The traditional tools are inadequate for regenerating and rescheduling activities automatically.
2.   Existing tools are not capable of representing inter dependencies.

2.2 Concept development

In this phase the needs of the target market are identified, alternative product concepts are generated and evaluated, and one or more concepts are selected for further development and testing. A concept is a description of the form, function, and features of a product and is usually accompanied by a set of specifications, and analysis of competitive products and an economic justification of the project.

2.3 System level design

This phase includes the definition of the product architecture and the decomposition of the product into subsystems and components. The final assembly scheme for the production system is usually defined during this phase as well. The output of this phase usually includes a geometric layout of the product, a functional specification of each of the product's subsystems and a preliminary process flow diagram for the final assembly process.

2.4 Detailed design

This phase includes the complete specification of the geometry, materials and tolerances of all of the unique parts in the suppliers. A process plan is established and tooling is designed for each part to be fabricated within the production system. The output of this phase is the Control Documentation for the product- the drawings or computer files describing the geometry of each part and its production tooling, the specifications of the purchased parts and the process plans for the fabrication and assembly of the product.

2.5. Testing and refinement

This involves the construction and evaluation of multiple production versions of the product. Early (Alpha) Prototypes are usually built. Parts with the same geometry and material properties as intended for the production version of the product, but not necessarily fabricated with the actual processes to be used in production. Alpha prototypes are tested to determine whether or not the product will work as designed and whether or not the product satisfies the key customer needs. Later (Beta) prototypes are usually built with parts supplied by the intended production process but may not be assembled using the intended final assembly process. Beta prototypes are extensively evaluated internally and are also typically tested by customers in their own environment. The goal for the beta prototype is usually to answer questions about performance and reliability in order to identify necessary engineering changes for the final product.

2.6. Production ramp-up

In the production ramp–up phase, the product is made using the intended production system. The purpose of the ramp-up is to train the work force and to work out any remaining problems in the production processes. Products produced during production ramp–up are sometimes supplied to preferred customers and are carefully

evaluated to identify any remaining flaws. The transition from production ramp-up to ongoing production is usually gradual. At some point in this transition, the product is launched becomes available for widespread distributions

3. THE CHALLENGING ISSUES

The various challenging issues in PD process are discussed below and is summarized in Table 1.

3.1 The tasks are parallel, sequential or coupled

A product development effort is the process of transforming input information about customer needs into output information corresponding to manufacturable design and tooling for production. Each individual development activities is an information processing unit that receives information from previous activities and transform it into information suitable to be used by subsequent tasks. Information needs create dependencies between tasks that determine the product development structure and the most appropriate task sequencing. According to the information dependencies between them task can be classified (Fig 2) as parallel if there is no information exchange and can thus be performed simultaneously, serial if there is unidirectional information flow and coupled tasks if they are mutually dependent and information flows both ways.

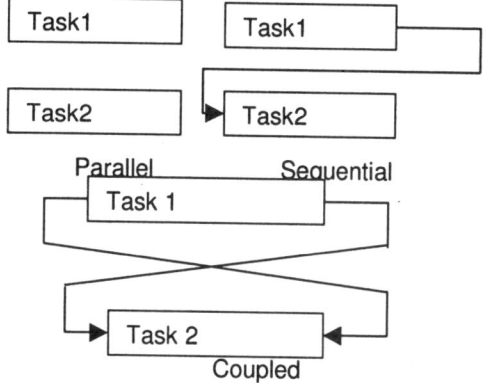

Fig. 2: Parallel, sequential & Coupled tasks

Scheduling, monitoring and controlling the tasks are essential in managing PD projects because of the uncertainty and diversified nature inherent in PD. The PD projects are often delayed either due to delay in task or due to iteration of a group of tasks. Task delay may occur in a PD project either due to non-availability of resources or due to breakdown of a machine or due to uncertainties.

Iteration occurs in PD ' for several reasons. An upstream task may need to be repeated when the downstream task discovers some sort of error or incompatibility. Similarly, downstream tasks may need to be repeated when modified information is passed along from upstream, perhaps as a result of correcting an earlier error or reflecting a change in the project duration.

Design Structure Matrix (DSM) is a useful tool for representing and analyzing task dependencies. This representation was originally developed by Steward in 1981 [3] for the analysis of design descriptions and has more recently been used to analyze development projects modeled at task level [4]. It is a useful tool for analyzing highly complicated dependencies, inclusive of feedback and coupled tasks. This is extremely important, since most PD process exhibits such as cyclic property.

3.2 Product Life Cycle

Product life cycles are shrinking day by day. If a product becomes obsolete sooner, it must be developed faster or it will become stale by the time it reaches the market. By exploiting management techniques that allow activities to start sooner and run concurrently with formerly sequential activities, a company can build a strategic advantage based on speed. This advantage pays off in product development because early product introduction can dramatically enhance market share and product margins while building the company's image as an innovation leader.

Techniques like cross-functional development team and concurrent engineering can be used for shortening PD cycle time [5].

3.3 Technically Complex Products.

The market place has necessitated development of products that are technically more complex, and in several instances this development is required to be completed in a period of time shorter than traditionally usual. Strong market pressure and increased technical sophistication of products necessitate experimental technologies be incorporated at earlier stages of the product cycle. Consequently projects will have technological uncertainty of the technology employed. Therefore it is extremely difficult to precisely define the tasks and estimated completion time of the projects. Project planning and control techniques available today are useful with projects with well-defined tasks and reasonably easy to predict start and completion times time of the tasks. This situation creates a significant challenge for NPD activities where very large numbers of tasks are involved [6].

3.4 Cost-Time trade off.

Today new products do not remain new for long. The technologies going into our products change more quickly than they have in the past. If a product becomes obsolete sooner, it must be developed faster or it will become stale by the time it reaches the market. By exploiting management techniques that allow activities to start sooner and run concurrently with formerly sequential activities, a company can build a strategic advantage based on speed. This advantage pays off in product development because early product introduction can dramatically enhance market share and product margins while building the company's image as an innovation leader.

The pressure is on to accelerate product development partly because product life cycles are shrinking.

Speedy development of the product can increase R&D expense and inflate product cost. It can also degrade product performance or quality. Managers must take trade-off decisions among these variables daily, but often their decisions are made without good rules of thumb or true appreciation of what is being given up in the trade [7]. The value of development time is to be taken into account in managing a NPD. This can be calculated by building a financial model for a specific product. Using a cash flow approach, we can model the revenue generated by the product each year of its life by projecting selling price and unit sales. The cash out flow can be calculated by projecting product's cost each year. These costs include relatively heavy development expense over the development period and smaller maintenance engineering expenses later. They also include manufacturing costs and sales and marketing expenses annually. The output of the model is cumulative before tax profit over the life of the product.

3.5 Effective Risk Management

As product development cycles shrink, and the products themselves grow more complex, managing risk in a product development project becomes increasingly critical. The risk can be either technical risk or market risk. If the developers are unable to develop a product that satisfies the specifications, we have a technical risk issue. On the other hand if the specification is satisfied but we are still unable to achieve commercial success, then we have a market risk issue. The risk management starts at the same time the project schedule, budgets and specifications are created and these items are managed throughout the project by a customized risk management plan. Managing these plans include addressing the toughest issues first and providing a productive role for failure.

3.6 Ergonomics and Safety aspects

Ergonomics has a wide application to every day situations, but there are even more significant implications for efficiency, productivity, safety and health. Even a simple product can be a nightmare to use if poorly designed. These days the designers of products are often far removed from the end users, which make it vital to adopt ergonomic user- centered approach to design, including studying people using equipment, talking to them and asking to them to test objects. Quality as well as ergonomics aims at meeting the demands of the customers. A high quality product therefore may be regarded as an ergonomic product–a product adapted to human abilities and limitations. In the area of quality technology, a number of methods have been developed, among other things, aimed at simplifying and making the PD more efficient. Quality Function Deployment (QFD) is a well-known tool, which is based on the idea of adapting technology to people. This method can also be used for developing ergonomic or usable products [8].

3.7 Customer involvement

The economic success of firms depends on their ability to identify customer needs and to profitably develop and market products that meet these needs. While NPD has always been challenging, a number of trends have emerged in recent years, which have increased the stakes for firms and their NPD efforts.

Customer involvement in NPD may provide access to innovative product ideas, new technologies, market information, and development capabilities that the manufacturer lacks in house. Customer orientation has proven to be a crucial success factor for organizations both in routine operations as well as in innovation projects [9]. Customer orientation can be viewed, as a bridging strategy to gain access to critical information about customer needs, acquiring information about customer needs and user experience is particularly important in the context of new product development. Customer orientation in NPD activities addresses the likely severe information asymmetry between potential customers and innovating company and thus reduces market related risk.

Developing the right product requires an accurate understanding of customer needs. The economic success of manufacturing companies depends on their ability to identify the needs of the customers and quickly create products that meet their needs and that can be produced at a low cost. All available customer need information should be carefully assessed in the early phase of PD and utilized effectively in the NPD [10].In a customer driven market customers will buy what will satisfy their needs and wants. Only those companies that sell what the customer wants and needs will survive and prosper [11].

4. CONCLUSION

Literature review reveals that project management approach is preferred in managing new product development. The limitations of the traditional tools necessitate new tools in product development process. This paper has focused on the limitations of traditional tools, challenges in PD, and the means to address the various challenging issues in managing NPD.

Table1: Issues, existing methods and scope of work

Issue	Existing method	Scope of work
Planning and scheduling of tasks	Gantt chart, PERT,CPM etc.	DSM, Decision support systems, simulation, Petri nets etc.
Shortened PD cycle	Concurrent Engineering, Rapid prototyping etc.	Adopt Japanese manufacturing philosophy into the PD setting.
Cost-Time trade off	CPM, Cash flow approach etc.	Development of appropriate financial accounting system.
Risk management	Identifying and resolving risk proactively	Customized risk management plan
Ergonomics and customer involvement	QFD, Customer analysis, Interview method etc.	Total quality Function Deployment, Decision support systems for QFD systems.

5. REFERENCES

1. **Chun-Hsien Chun, ShihFu Ling, Wei Chen** (2003), "Project Scheduling for Collaborative Product Development Using DSM", *International Journal of Project Management*.

2. **Plmmer TU, Eppinger SD**(2000). Product Design and development, *Boston Irwin McGraw- Hill;*

3. **Steward D.V** (1981), "Systems Analysis and Management, Structure, strategy and design". *Princeton: Petrocelli Books.*

4. **Preston Smith G and Donald Reinertsen G.** (1992), "Shortening the Product development cycle", *Research Technology management.,*

5. **CeciliaTemponi** and **Rajiv Malhotra** (2002) "Project Management challenges of *High technology product development,IEEE Transactions".*

6. **Preston G Smith**(1990)," Fast Cycle product Development", *Engineering Management Journal, .*

7. **Thomas Ritter and Achim Walter**(2003). "Relationship-specific antecedents of Customer involvement in new product Development", *Int. Journal of Technology management.*

8. **Kahn,K.B** (2001), "Market orientation, Interdepartmental integration and product Development performance"', *The Journal Of product innovation Management, Vol.18.*

9. **Karin Bergquist** and **John Abeysekera** (1996),"Quality Function deployment (QFD)- a Means for developing usable products", *International Journal of Industrial ergonomics*

10. **Kalle Elfvegren, Hannu Karkkainen, Marko Torkkeli and Markku Tuominen** (2002)," A GDSS based Approach for the assessment of customer Needs in industrial markets", *International Journal of Production Economics.*

11. **Kevin Otto** and **Kristin Wood** (2003), *Product Design, Techniques in Reverse Engineering and New Product Development*, Pearson Education.

GCMM 2004
Editors: Prasad K D V Yarlagadda and S Narayanan
Copyright © 2005, Vellore Institute of Technology, Vellore, India
Publisher: Narosa Publishing House Pvt. Ltd., New Delhi, India

Evaluating E-business Readiness for United Kingdom Companies

Kay Hooi Keoy* Khalid Hafeez** and Robert Hanneman**

*PhD Researcher, School of Computing and Management Sciences,
Sheffield Hallam University, UK

E-mail : kay.h.keoy@student.shu.ac.uk

**Principal Lecturer and Research Leader in Information Systems Computing and Management
Sciences, Sheffield Hallam University, UK

E-mail : K.Hafeez@shu.ac.uk

*** Professor of Sociology, Department of Sociology in the College of Humanities, Arts, and
Social Sciences at the University of California, Riverside, USA

E-mail : robert.hanneman@ucr.edu

Abstract

This paper analyzes the e-business readiness of 177 United Kingdom companies from 6 key industrial sectors. Success of E--Business adoption is linked with 4 dependent elements namely Supply Chain Strategies, Business Strategies, E--Business Ripeness and E--Business Readiness via a theoretical model. Each of these were further decomposed and related to People, Technological and Organizational factors. Structural equation modelling (SEM) was used to test the hypothesis using AMOS 4.0 software. Results show that the proposed 6 tested hypotheses were positively significant which validate our hypothesis that efficient supply chain management is crucial for successful E-commerce adoption. The analysis also reveals the strategic and investment gaps with regards to People, Technological and Organizational factors. Overall results also suggest that there is a high degree of readiness among United Kingdom companies for e-business development.

Keywords
Business Strategy, Supply Chain Strategy, Business Excellence, E-Business Readiness, Structural Equation Modelling

1. INTRODUCTION

Electronic Commerce (E--Commerce) represents a new way of conducting business transactions, including buying, selling, or exchanging products, services, and information, usually through communication networks such as the Internet, intranet, and extranet (Chou 2001). The competitive landscape in the E-business arena consists primarily of three types of players: clicks (Internet pure plays), click and mortar (brick and mortar companies with online operations), and service providers. Organizations that preferred a "wait and see" approach will be cast away because they could not compete in this fast and dynamic market will led to an environment where investors are caught up in this irrational exuberance and have been willing to go without the basics in search for the promised land (Ravindra 2001). Recent E-business failures have changed dramatically the evaluation the Internet opportunities and how will companies exploit them. They must respond in unique ways by leveraging both online and offline parts of their business to effectively build tight linkages between the technological, organizational, and people factor across the companies and their supply chain network as it does for new economy start--ups (Ravindra 2001). To avoid any E--business failures, an important question is: How can organizations survive in the post dot.com meltdown era? It is important, however, to not get caught up in the hype, but instead to understand the reasons why some succeed while others fail. Further, for those companies that are still competing in an already crowded space, there is a need to understand the factors that will determine their survival in the immediate future. Supply chain and business strategies have been shown to interact in the development of e--business readiness in UK companies, which will directly affect the performance of doing business online. It is our view that in order for companies to build a successful e--business environment, they need to combine and align Supply chain and business strategies to develop value-added processes that deliver innovative, high-quality, low-cost products on time with greater responsiveness.

2. RESEARCH METHODOLOGY

Stevens (1989)'s model outlines a sequence for moving from poor supply chain performance toward the seamless supply chain.(Table 1). As such, the Stevens Reference Framework can be used to assess a supply chain's evolution and maturity level. The model takes consideration of three main elements namely Organizational, People and Technological that are inter-dependent. Without the right people in place, creating a sustainability position within the industry would be impossible. But without the right enabling tools and the right organisational processes, the best people in the world will still come up short (Quinn,2004). Companies that consider implementing e-business in Asia need to look carefully at the market potential for each country by having the suitable business strategies and supply chain strategies to access e-businesses readiness and ripeness of the company. They need to assess how the organisation reacts to the implementation of e-business (Organisational), the support or reaction of their customers and business partners (People), and necessary infrastructure to serve each market (Technological). Hence, there is a need to perform a balancing act among these three elements. We have proposed to correlate supply chain strategy, business strategies and e-business readiness and evaluate the direct link to business excellence. The goal of this research was to prove/disprove our proposed hypotheses (Fig 1)

An integration model was developed which consists of first order factors (Organization, People and Technology). Supply Chain Strategies, Business Strategies, E-Business Readiness and Business Excellence constructs are then operationalized as second order factors, which were related to each other in a structural model (Fig 1). E-Business Readiness define as the readiness of a company (i.e. brick and mortar, click and mortar, pure dot com) in assessing their current business operation and assist in defining at a basic level how easy and how applicable e-business initiatives may be for them. How 'ready' a company is for e-business i.e. how easy it will to be introduced Internet technology to the existing infrastructure?

Table 1: A Modified Steven's Framework (Steven, 1989)

	Stage of Supply Chain Integration	Supply Chain Characteristics
Technological	Baseline	Reactive short-term planning. Fire fight. Large pools of inventory. vulnerability to market changes
Organizational	Functional Integration	Emphasis still on cost, not performance. Focus inward and on goods. Reactive towards customer. Some internal trade-offs
Organizational	Internal integration	All work processes integrated. Planning reaches from customers back to supplier. EDI wide used. Still reacting to customer
People	External Integration	Integration of all suppliers. Focus on customer. Synchronized material flow. SC covers extended enterprise

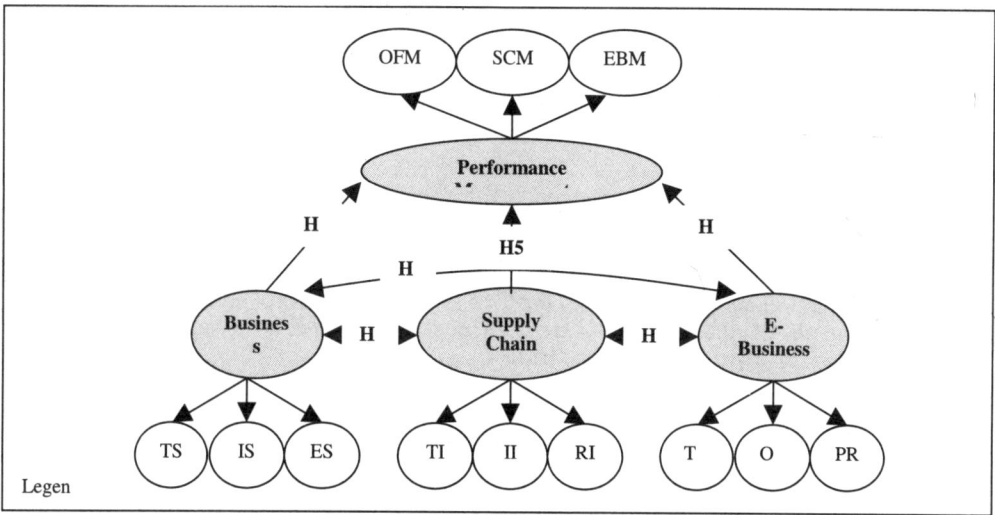

Legen

TS	Technological Strategy	TI	Technological Integration	TR	Technological Readiness	OFM	Operational Measures
IS	Internal Strategy	II	Internal Integration	OR	Organizational Readiness	SCM	Supply Chain Measures
ES	External Strategy	RI	Relationship Integration	PR	People Readiness	EBM	E-Business Measures

Fig. 1 Structural Equation Model of the Hypothesized Relationship

3. DATA COLLECTION AND ANALYSIS

Structural Equation Modelling (SEM) is a multivariate statistical process that allows testing of theoretical models using latent variables and multiple indicators. Structural Equation Modelling is a confirmatory data analysis approach requiring a priori assignment of inter-variable relationships (Winser, 2003). Structural equation modelling was used to assess the propositions of the research model using Arbuckle (1997) approach implemented in the SPSS AMOS 4.0 computer program This model simultaneously analyzed the first-order and second-order measurement model as well as the structural model. Methodological emphasis was placed on developing expanded conceps of these strategy constructs by modelling them as second order factor and express their defining

173

constituent domains of content as first order factor (Gerbing and Hamilton, 1994).

The study design was cross sectional because this research method allows researchers to capture "snapshots of practices at a particular point in time" (Galliers, 1985). Data were collected by the was of a questionnaire was posted and e-mailed either to CEO or the supply chain manager of the firm. 390 organizations were randomly selected from the sample of large-sized firms. A total of 177 questionnaires were completed and usable for analysis giving a response rate of 45.4 %. The sample includes various industries sectors including manufacturing and Information Technology (IT) industries (Table 2)

Table 2: Respondents by Sectors

Sectors	No of Respondents
Information Technology	29
Travel and Services	30
Retail, Distribution & Trading	33
Construction	30
Retailing, wholesaling and warehousing	25
Computer and Accessories	30
Questionnaire mail send	65 Questionnaire (send to each sector) *6 = 390
Responded	177
% Responded	45.4 %

4. RELIABILITY AND VALIDITY OF MEASURES

The values of Cronbach's alpha range from 0.749 to 0.954 suggesting an adequate measurement of reliability (Table 3). As for convergent validity, standardized factor loadings for all items were above the suggested cut-off of 0.60, and all were significant, most of them being above 0.80 with a minimum of 0.701. This shows strong evidence of convergent validity. Lastly discriminant validity shows that correlation matrix of first-order and second order constructs were significant at 99 % confidence interval ranging from 0.271 to 0.970. Discriminant validity is therefore considered to be at an acceptable level.

Table 3: Chronbach Alpha Reliability

Constructs of 1st order	No of questions	Chronbach Alpha Reliability Coefficient	Standardized item alpha
		UK Cases	
EBR			
1. TR	3	.906	.906
2. OR	3	.762	.760
3. PR	3	.804	.806
BE			
4. OF	4	.894	.897
5. SC	3	.746	.749
6 EB	3	.777	.784
BS			
7. TS	4	.895	.899
8. ES	4	.822	.825
9. IS	4	.848	.850
SCS			
10. II	4	.953	.954
11. TI	4	.871	.875
12. RI	3	.850	.850

Whereas all the measurement errors are assumed to be independent of one another, a multivariate Lagrange multiplier test indicated that allowing the measure errors in certain of the variable to correlate would provide a significant improvement in the model fit (Bentler, 1995). However, it was not decided not to re-specify the model in such a manner because this would conceal the meaning of the variables (Anderson and Gerbing, 1988).

As summary, the earlier evaluation of the measurement model thus provides the necessary foundation for testing the hypothesis of the theoretical model.

4.1 Overall Model Fit

In structural equation modelling, there is no single test of significance test that can absolutely identify a correct model given the sample data (Byrne 1998; Shumacker, Randall and Lomax 1996). Many goodness-of-fit criteria have been established to assess an acceptable model fit. Consequently, several authors recommend present a number of indices to support a model fit (Bentler 1992; Garver and Mentzer 1999) An analysis of the direct effects business strategy, supply chain strategy and e-business readiness: (higher order factors) (including path coefficients) on business excellence (N = 177), revealed a χ^2 of 904.808, df = 761with 100 parameters and fit

indices of TLI = 0.973, CFI = 0.975, RMSEA = 0.033. The model fit indices are in an acceptable range (> 0.900) and the Root Mean Square Error of Approximation is less than .05. This model is nested within the first order model, in that it has been generated by imposing restrictions on the parameters of the first order model. However, the remaining indices goodness of fit (GFI), adjusted goodness of fit (AGFI), Normed Fit Index (NFI) and did not meet the minimum requirements for a good fit suggested by Chin and Todd (1995) and Hair et al.(1998). However, according to Hair et al. (1998) the GFI obtained was considered to be marginally acceptable. Moreover, the model had a high degree of freedom (761) relative to a sample size of 177 and with the relatively small number of parameters (100); there was a tendency for GFI to be downward bias Gadson (1997). Hence, the model justified a good overall fit (Table 4)

Table 4. The primary goodness of fit statistics

GOODNESSOF-FIT MEASURES	Default Model (χ^2 = 904.808, df = 761)
Absolute Fit Measures	
GFI	0.816
RMSEA	0.033
Incremental Fit Measures	
AGFI	0.791
NFI	0.862
TLI	0.973
Parsimonious Measures	
χ^2/df	1.19

The parameters of the estimated model, along with their significance are shown in Figure 2 below.

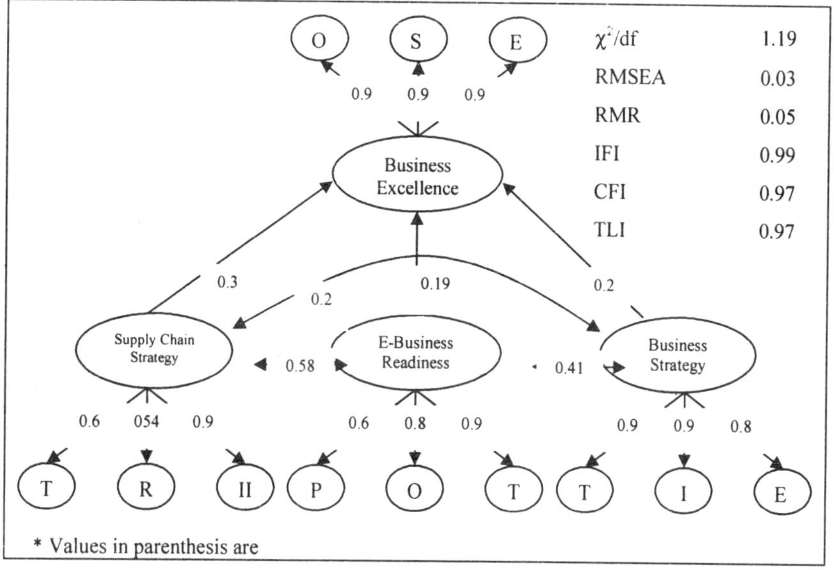

Fig. 2: Testing for country effect - UK sample (n = 177)

175

5. DISCUSSIONS

The paper makes several theoretical contributions. First, it proposes a model identifying the correlation among supply chain strategy, business strategy and e-business readiness influencing the success of company. It also validates our claim that in order adopt a successful e-business, it is vital to consider these three factors. Previous studies have focused on what dimensions are important in supply chain strategies and business strategies. By contrast, our model measures the influence of e-business readiness in order to become a successful e-business company. Our analysis suggest that most of the companies in our sample are very much in the first wave of development, seeking operational excellence through improvement in individual elements of the supply chain (Gattorna, 2000). The challenge for the companies is to move up to a whole new level of performance - the second wave - on the back of e-business - e-procurement, e-fulfilment, and shared services that will lead to Internet-enabled supply chain

Table 5: Hypothesis Testing Results

	Hypothesis	Standardized estimate	Is Hypothesis Supported?
H1	Business Strategy is positively correlated with Supply Chain Strategy	0.26	Hypothesis Supported because Critical Ratio (CR) is > 1.96 for a standardized regression weight and path is significant at the 0.05 level
H2	Supply Chain Strategy is positively correlated with E-Business Readiness	0.58	
H3	Business Strategy is positively correlated with E-Business Readiness	0.41	
H4	Business Strategy has direct positive effect on the Success of the company	0.20	
H5	Supply Chain Strategy has direct positive effect on the Success of the company	0.32	
H6	E-Business Readiness has direct positive effect on the Success of the company	0.19	

Significant value results supporting our hypotheses suggests that UK companies enjoy favourable conditions for e-commerce development, including a highly open, competitive economy with a good mix of advanced manufacturing activities, sophisticated financial, telecommunications infrastructure, a compact, mixed and wealthy population with multicultural regional, a relatively large pool of specialized IT talents and high penetration of IT literacy among the general population. Companies that had not adopted e-business preferred to "wait and see." because they are still not convinced there is a compelling need to adopt e-commerce, due at least in part to the lack of proven models. The lack of readiness of their business partners as well as lack of readiness by the firm itself also appears to be important impediments to the adoption of e-commerce.

All of the key factor weightings contributed to the second-order factors of in this model. In-depth analysis reveal overall that the standardized regression weights for People factor in supply chain strategy (Relationship Integration, 0.54) and e-business readiness (People Readiness, 0.64) is substantially weaker in terms of contributing the prediction of business excellence at the structural higher-order level especially in e-business measure (0.97).(Table 5) Results reveal overall UK still lack of consideration in People factor. They lack to acknowledge that collaboration among supply chain partners represents another good opportunity are In order to facilitate collaboration, companies must re-engineer and integrate their internal supply chain planning processes and technology to develop unified solutions. Organizational factor can be viewed to UK companies as the choice pertaining to the particular configurations and internal arrangements intended to support the organization's chosen position in the market (Marton, 1991). Kaplan and Norton (2004) described organization capital as the company's culture, its leadership, how aligned its people are with its strategy goals and employees ability to share knowledge. Technology factor imposes genuine interests in IT both inside and outside the organization (Croteau, 2001). The success of any E-business depends on whether it has an E-strategy acquiring the right technology at the right time (Broad, 1999). Therefore, UK companies need to keep up—to—date on the latest technology and have sufficient organizational knowledge and technology skills to make the best possible technological investments for their firm (Croteau and Bergeron, 1999). In our view supply chain strategy must align business overall strategy. A company must develop objectives for the management for their supply chain strategy based upon corporate objectives (Keoy, Hafeez and Drake 2002).

6. CONCLUSIONS

This study employs a structural equation modelling to link the theory construction and testing in the e-commerce domain. Methodologically, this paper established the feasibility of constructing a large scale model constructs as second-order factors which are then amenable to a structural analysis of their casual relationships. This contributes to the construction of supply chain strategy, business strategy and e-business readiness. Furthermore, an array of three first order constructs (factors) to determine e-commerce success is posited, namely, organisational, people and technological elements. Indeed, the sequence of causality depicted suggests that supply chain strategy ,business model and e-business readiness are positively influencing each other at the same time contributing to the attainment business excellence. Results show that the six tested hypotheses (H1 - H6) were positively significant which validate our hypotheses that efficient and careful planning of supply chain strategy, business strategy and e-business readiness are crucial for successful E-business adoption. Overall results also suggest that there is a high degree of readiness among UK companies for e-business development. Further research will be performed for a comparative study by industry to find out which will perform and relate better to three factors and is more successful e-business adoption.

7. REFERENCES

1. **Arbuckle, James AMOS** Users' Guide Version 3.6. Smallwaters Corporation. (1997) (ISBN: 1-56827-125-5).
2. **Anderson, J. C., & Gerbing, D. W.** "Structural equation modelling in practice: A review and recommended two-step approach", Psychological Bulletin, (1988), 103 (3), 411-423
3. **Byrne, B. M.** Structural Equation Modeling with AMOS: Basic Concepts, Applications, and Programming, Mahwah, NJ: Lawrence Erlbaum(1998)
4. **Bentler, P. M.,** EQS Structural Equations Program Manual. Encino. CA: Multivariate Software, Inc. (1995)
5. **Broad Vision** , Business-to-Business E-Commerce: Finding the 80-20 Solution, White Paper, August (1999)
6. **Chin, W.W., Todd, P.A.** (1995) On the use, usefulness, and ease of use of structural equation modelling in MIS research: A note of caution. *MIS Quarterly* 19, 2 (1995), 237-246.
7. **Croteau A.M., Bergeron F,** "La trilogie de l'harmonisation technologique: Stratégie d'entreprise, déploiement des technologies de l'information et performance organisationnelle", *Proceedings of thé Administrative Sciences Association of Canada Conférence*, St John, New Brunswick, , pp. 57-67, (1999)
8. **Chou, David,** "Integrating TQM into E-Commerce", *Information Systems Management*, Fall, C (2001), Vol. 18 Issue 4, p31, 9p, 1 diagram; (AN 5472699)
9. **Gerbing, David W, Hamilton, Janet G.** "A large-scale second-order structural equation model of the influence of management participation". *Journal of Management*, Winter, (1994)Vol. 20 Issue 4, p859, 27p, 7 charts, 2 diagrams; (AN 9503274399).
10. **Graham, C. Stevens,** "Integrating the Supply Chain. International", *Journal of Physical Distribution*, (1989) Vol 19, Issue 8.
11. **Galliers R.D.** "In Search of a Paradigm for Information Systems Research.", Research Methods in Information Systems, E. Munford et al. Eds., (1985), pp. 281-297.
12. **Gattorna John L ,** "The E-Supply Chain Reaches Asian Shores", (2002), Ascet, Volume 2, Accenture.

13. **Garver, M. S. and Mentzer, J. T.** "Logistics research methods: Employing structural equation modelling to test for construct validity", *Journal of Business Logistics*, (1999). 20(1), 33-57

14. **Hair, J., Anderson, R., Tatham, R., Black, W,** Multivariate data analysis. Englewood Cliffs: NJ: Prentice Hall. (1998)

15. **Keoy Kay Hooi, Hafeez Khalid and Drake Robert** "Supply Chain Management Strategies for E-Commerce Companies", ICT Research & Application Innovation at Work, *Conference on IT Research and Applications*, (2002), Malaysia.

16. **Quinn, Francis J**. "People, Process, Technology". *Supply Chain Management Review*, (2004) Vol. 8 Issue 1, p3, 3/4p; (AN 11997449).

17. **Ravindra Krovi,** "Surveying the E-Landscape : New Rules for Survival ", *Information Systems Management*, Fall, (2001)Vol. 18 Issue 4, p22, 9p, 3 diagrams; (AN 5472642)

18. **Schumacker, Randall E.** and **R.G. Lomax.,** A Beginner's Guide to Structural Equation Modelling, Hillsdale, N.J.: Lawrence Erlbaum Associates.(1996) ISBN: 0-8058-1766-2; 0-8058-1767-0

GCMM 2004
Editors: Prasad K D V Yarlagadda and S Narayanan
Copyright © 2005, Vellore Institute of Technology, Vellore, India
Publisher: Narosa Publishing House Pvt. Ltd., New Delhi, India

Management of Machine Tool Accessories

Prasad P S S[*]

Neelakandan M[**], Mike Agustus Richards R X[**], & Vasanth.G[**]

* Assistant Professor, ** BE Students
Department of Mechanical Engineering,
PSG College of Technology,
Coimbatore – 641004, India.

E-mail: pssai@yahoo.com

Abstract

Inventories are materials and supplies that a business or institution carries either for sale or to provide inputs to the production process. Mismanagement of inventories can result in a huge loss for the concerned company. There are various types of inventory that may exist in an industry and spares inventory is important among them. Insurance spares are those which have high reliability i.e. spares with long life namely lathe centers, collets etc. Since, these items are not maintained in the inventory; failure of these parts may lead to downtime of the machine, hence affecting the production rates. This work is an attempt to identify the insurance spares that are present in M/s. Rane TRW steering systems and suggest suitable inventory plans. The insurance spares were identified with the help of the spares/tool purchase indent and classified according to their cost value as A, B and C type. The optimum lot size was calculated for A and B type spares by economic order quantity rule. Since the number of spares found to be very high (about 300), maintaining records and monitoring the stock levels that too over a longer periods will be difficult and error prone. Hence simple user-friendly software has been recommended to overcome this problem. The expected benefits from implementation are highlighted.

Keywords
Inventory, Spares, Economic Order Quantity, ABC analysis

1.0 INTRODUCTION

Inventories are materials and supplies that a business or institution carries either for sale or to provide inputs to the production process. There is a cost for carrying inventories, which increases operating costs and decreases profit. Hence there should be continuous efforts to either eliminate the inventory or optimize the costs associated with it. Due to several real world factors, it will be highly difficult to work with zero inventories. So the minimization of inventory costs is under prime focus in the industry as well as in academia. The main objective of this focus is to minimize total (actual or expected) cost [3]. There are several parameters which influence the total cost of inventory. Among them, the variables that can be controlled, separately or in combination, are;

- The quantity acquired (by purchase, production, or some other means); i.e. How much to order? This may be set for each type of resources separately or for all tools collectively.
- The frequency or timing of acquisition; i.e. how often? Or when?

Any organization, in general, may maintain different types of inventory namely;

raw materials, spares, bulk inventory, consumables, parts.

The spares control is an important activity in manufacturing organizations to reduce equipment (namely machine tools) downtimes. Spare part is defined as a part, identical to the part of the machinery, which needs replacement due to wear and tear as the life of the part is less than the Operating life of the equipment. The spares can be classified under various categories as given below [1].

The various types of spares are;
- Commissioning Spares
- Overhauling Spares
- Rotable Spares
- Insurance Spares.

1.1 Insurance Spares

Expensive and renewable spares are known as insurance type spares. These are those components which have a small probability that any will be needed at all. If these components are not available when needed then the company will suffer a major loss [4]. Even though the reliability of these components is very high, the non-availability of insurance spare units may prove catastrophic; resulting in downtime of the machine until those parts are replaced. [3].

Managers are often required to estimate the spare parts requirements for a system, (a fleet of aircraft, for example) or a set of equipment for a particular function (moving oil, producing electricity, etc.). A typical operating system has various components (motors, valves, pumps, etc.). When those components fail, they must be replaced with spare parts (spares) before operations can continue.

The Logistics Management Institute's [5] has developed the system based approach for spares requirements explicitly on each item's effect on overall system performance as well as the item's unit cost. The overall system performance is measured in terms of availability, which can be quantified as below.

- The probability that the system will be operating within normal parameters,
- The probability the system does not become inoperative over a period for lack of a spare.

The following questions needed to be answered in any spares management programme [5]. How many spares should be maintained? How are they tracked and managed? Can they be used as "common spares" for more than one facility? What alternatives exist today? How large is the investment in capital spares? How is it managed? How are critical spares identified? What is the process to stock and maintain these items? What alternatives exist? Are they repairable? Are they used on multiple pieces of equipment? What is the mean/average time between failures?

The aim of the spares management is to acquire and allocate the correct mix and amount of spares to fulfill the availability requirements of the system [4]. The present work study the current practices of insurance spares control in a batch manufacturing type industry namely M/s RANE TRW Valve Plant, Trichy, and propose suitable spares-management procedures.

1.2 About the Organization

M/s. RANE TRW is a major manufacturer of power steering components for Indian cars like Hyundai Santro, Tata Indica, Tata Indigo, Opel Corsa, Honda City and Ford Ikon. This particular plant produces Valve assemblies for the Power Steering mechanism. Currently the production rate is 48000 valve assemblies per month. The company has a Standard Operating Procedure (SOP) for each machine. They contain information like the spares item code, name, life, and the operating procedure for that machine. (Collet, Hob, Cam, Collet housing, Base plate, Arbor were some of the insurance components that were present in the industry).

Table 1: Identification of spare parts and related data

SI. No	Item Code	Description	Transaction (2001-2004)	Total Production (2001-2004)	Life In Terms Of Number Of Components Produced	PRICE
VALVE SLEEVE						
COMPONENT - Valve sleeve; OPERATION -Pin hole Drilling MACHINE - KMB Pinhole SPM;						
1	T010200112	Adjustable adaptor with collet holder	2	365232	260880	1050.28
2	710436004	Fixture	2	365232	260880	5721.00
3	710436014	Special bush	4	365232	107422	345.00
4	T010100043	Collet	5	365232	83008	473.00

Currently, the industry has not adopted any particular system for spares control. Due to this policy, the industry experiences frequent breakdown of machines. This directly affects the production rate and thereby affecting the company's goodwill.

The following section detail the methodology followed to identify the insurance spares and recommend suitable spares control mechanism for the above organization.

2. METHODOLOGY

The following plan was adopted to systematically identify and propose a suitable approach to maintain the insurance spares in the above stated organization.

➤ *Identification of the insurance spares* (non-stock items), in the industry, with the help of Standard Operating Procedure.

➤ Collection of data for insurance spares. The data collected are the annual demand, price, inventory carrying cost, production rate (month-wise), purchase indent and ordering cost for the past three years. Also calculation of life for the insurance spares with the help of the data on the production rate for the past three years.

➤ *Determining the priority of the insurance spares*, according to their money value, with the help of ABC Analysis.

➤ *Calculation of Economic Order Quantity (EOQ) for insurance spares* for the A & B types system of the ABC analysis.

➤ *Recommendations for suitable computer based monitoring systems* to help users to maintain and track the status of insurance spares in the organization.

3. CASE STUDY

The following paragraphs discuss, in detail, each step applied to M/s. RANE TRW.

3.1 Identification:

The insurance spares of each machine are identified with the help of the Standard Operating Procedure chart of machine and the purchase indent for the past three years. The components that come under the inventory are given in the chart and the components that do not included in the SOP are considered as the insurance spares (Non-Stock items).

By comparing the SOP chart with the purchase indents of the past three years, it can be segregated the insurance spares from other inventory items. Likewise, the insurance spares are identified for all the machines present in the Valve plant.

3.2 Data Collection

The organization industry is maintaining organized data about all major manufacturing activities with the help of Enterprise Resource Planning (ERP) package. With the help of a step , 303 components were identified as insurance spares in the above mentioned plant. The annual demand for these components was obtained with the help of the ERP package. The inventory carrying cost for each component was obtained by the rent for the storage space, tax on the items, and price of each component. The life of each component was found out with the help of purchase indent and the ERP package. Table 1 indicates the sample information available for each spare part.

Production rate, for every month, varies according to the challenges faced by the industry. Production rate depends on the following;

❖ Number of workers present
❖ Skill of the worker
❖ Number of machines, in working condition
❖ Condition of the machine
❖ Companies shift in policies
❖ Type of component manufactured.

Ordering cost can be calculated from the data on salary for the clerical staff, cost incurred to place the order through post or e-mail.

Among the identified insurance spares, some may be more valuable than the others, in terms of monetary value. The spares of higher value must be separated from the lower value spares in order to design optimal inventory policies for higher valued items. In this context, the role of ABC analysis will be highly appreciable as its working on simple principles. The following section highlights the important findings applied of ABC analysis in the current application.

3.3 ABC Classification

Every organization consumes several items from store. Since, all the items are not of equal value/importance, a higher level of control on each items inventory is neither useful/needed nor applicable. So, it becomes necessary to classify items into groups depending upon their utility value/importance. Such type of classification is named as the *Principle of selective control* [7].

Type A components are those which account for the highest rupee inventory investment. Such items have large investments but are few in number. So more careful and closer control is needed for such items [6].

Type B components are those which account for a moderate share of investment. These items cannot be overlooked and require lesser degree of control than *Type A* [6].

Type C components are those large remaining group of stock-keeping items, which account for a small fraction of the total investment [6].

The objective of this classification is to separate out the third group which is large in number and also may potentially require a large amount of record keeping and attention but which is relatively unimportant from the point of view of keeping the inventory at reasonable levels [5].

The graph given in Figure 1, is indicated the ABC analysis for the given set of tools. Table 2 shows various parameters considered in ABC analysis with a sample data.

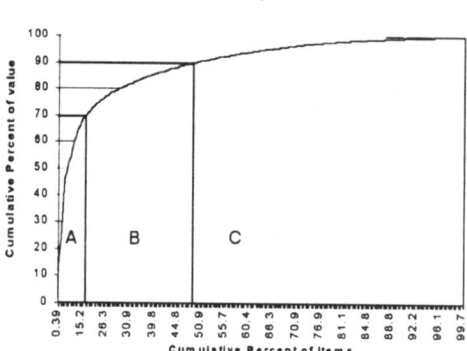

Figure.1 ABC Analysis

☞ *Type A* Components are those which constitute *70 % of the total cost* but only *18.46%* of the total Quantity of consumption of all spares.

☞ *Type B* components are those which constitute *20 % of the total cost* and *30.56 %* of the total Quantity of consumption of all spares.

☞ The remaining *55.981% of the components* which contribute only *10% of the total cost* are classified as *Type C*
☞ Components.

3.4 Economic Order Quantity

It is the amount of a product which should be purchased or manufactured at one time in order to minimize the total cost involved, including the ordering cost (setup of machines, writing orders, checking receipts, etc.) and carrying cost (cost of capital invested, insurance, taxes, space, invested, insurance, taxes, space, obsolescence, and spoilage). Also called "optimum lot size" [3]. The traditional Wilson formula for calculating the Economic Order Quantity is given as

182

Table 2: ABC Analysis

Name Of The Component	Price/unit Rs.	Expected Consumption in the current Year	Annual Usage value in Rs.	Cumulative annual usage value in Rs.	% Cumulative Annual Usage	% of item	Cumulative % of Items	Type
Tool Body	66583.24	2	133166.5	133166.5	9.447	0.385	0.385	A
Helical Guide (RH)	104800	1	104800	237966.5	16.882	0.192	0.577	A
Helical Guide (LH)	102939.2	1	102939.2	340905.7	24.184	0.192	0.769	A
Helical Guide	102939.2	1	102939.2	443844.9	31.487	0.192	0.961	A
Helical Guide For RH Pinion	101939.2	1	101939.2	545784.1	38.718	0.192	1.153	A
Helical Guide For LH Pinion	101939.2	1	101939.2	647723.3	45.95	0.192	1.345	A

$$Q = \sqrt{\frac{2 \times A \times S}{R}}$$

Where

Q= quantity to be ordered
A= annual demand
S= ordering cost
R= carrying cost/unit/unit time
V= unit cost.

For example, an 'A' type component has been chosen and the corresponding data given in the Table 3.

Tool Code	- 810331114
Name of the tool	- Input shaft collet
Unit Cost, **V**	- Rs. 4590/-
Annual demand, **A**	- 7
Obsolescence cost,**O**	- Rs. 0.10*V
Rent, Tax, Insurance, **T**	– Rs. 0.0*V
Interest on capital, **C**	- Rs. 0.06*V
Ordering Cost, **S**	- Rs. 987 /-

Carrying Cost, R
= Obsolescence Cost +Rent, Tax, Insurance + Interest on capital
= (0.10 + 0.01 + 0.06) * 4590
= 0.17 * 4590 = Rs. 780.3

Economic Order Quantity,

$Q = \sqrt{(2 * 7 * 987) / (4590 * 0.17)}$
$Q = 4.20809$ units
$Q \approx 5$ units.

So, the EOQ for Input Shaft Collet has been found as 5 units. Similarly economic order quantity for all A and B type

components can be calculated. This step helps the users in optimizing the inventory costs. But at the same time there should be proper monitoring system to keep track of the status of the inventory levels of various spares. Since insurance spares are having long life, regular checking of stock may not be needed and can lead to total ignorance if manual stock maintenance is adopted. Hence simple user friendly software can be recommended for this problem. Or if the organization already runs with standard ERP packages, the spares control module can be planned to introduce into the main system.

3.5 Computer Based Monitoring System

The following are the objectives, in general, of any inventory program.

¬ To maintain a proper inventory
¬ Assist the user in calculating the economic order quantity for each item
¬ To maintain a record of all the items in the stock
¬ To indicate the items whose stock level is less than the critical limit?

Hence the software must be provided with the features to achieve above objectives. The following features can be incorporated into computer based monitoring of spares inventory.

☞ User must be able to search the spares by name, code number etc.

☞ User must be able to enter the data related to spares without much computer knowledge.

☞ User must be provided with automatic alerts on out of stock details, stock

183

addition and deletion at regular intervals or whenever appropriate.

☞ Software must be capable of generating lists/tables highlighting the spares which needs placing of an orders or which falls below safety stock etc.

4.0 CONCLUSION

Spares control, in particular insurance spares, is an important issue in any manufacturing organization to reduce machine downtimes and achieve higher productivity. But unlike raw material or part inventory, the consumption of insurance spares is very negligible and tends get ignored till the need occurs. Also very limited focus and minimal or no records will be maintained of these items.

Hence the present work focuses on identifying the insurance spares in an automotive spares producing organization and proposes a suitable inventory control methodology. The insurance spares are identified from the purchase orders of the organization by comparing with standard operating procedure charts of each machine. The data related to life and costs are derived from the above procedure. ABC analysis was carried out to classify the components according to their money value and classified into three groups as A, B and C. The economic order quantity was calculated for A and B type components using Wilson formula. The need for computer based monitoring of these items was discussed and the important features those must be provided with software are recommended.

5.0 REFERENCES

1. **Gopalakrishnan.P,** 1999, "*Handbook of Materials Management*", Prentice Hall, New Delhi, pp 225-230.
2. **Joseph Buchan**, 1963, "Scientific Inventory Management", Prentice Hall, New Jersey, pp 284-285.
3. **Datta.A.K.,** 1998, "*Material Management*", *Prentice Hall, New Delhi, pp 199-210.*
4. **Gopalakrishnan.P and Sunderesan.M,** 2002, "Materials Management-an integrated approach", *Prentice Hall, New Delhi, pp 32-36.*
5. http://citrix1.lmi.org/asm/IntroSys.pdf.
6. www. houndware.com
7. www. sentai.com
8. www. pinnacle-online.com
9. www. distinction-systems.com

GCMM 2004
Editors: Prasad K D V Yarlagadda and S Narayanan
Copyright © 2005, Vellore Institute of Technology, Vellore, India
Publisher: Narosa Publishing House Pvt. Ltd., New Delhi, India

Total Quality Management System for Greek Public Sectors

Arunachalam S, * Bofakou M,** Thoburn J G***

*Senior Lecturer in Manufacturing Systems Engineering;
School of Computing & Technology, University of East London
Longbridge Road, Dagenham, Essex, RM8 2AS, UK

E-mail: s.arunachalam@uel.ac.uk

*General Secretariat of Research and Technology
Ministry of Development
Athens, Greece

***Director, Seven Sigma Training (UK), Coventry CV3 4BA, UK

Email: jg.thoburn@ntlworld.com;
URL: http://www.seven-sigma.co.uk

Abstract

Like most of the public sectors around the world, Greek public sectors too are faced with change, challenge, and uncertainty. The factors driving change are include: an increasingly global economy; significantly expanded use of technology; organisational pressures to do more with less as senior government economic transfers are reduced; and, an increased awareness of the concept of customer in service delivery. In response to these factors of change, the public sector, including local government, has moved towards a more output oriented, customer-focused approach to service delivery. In many respects, this movement has followed the principles of total quality management. TQM is now becoming recognized as a generic management tool, just as applicable in service and public sector organizations. This paper attempts to analyse the need for public sectors in Greece to implement TQM systems to provide highly successful quality services to its citizens and to maintain its status quo among the European nations.

Keywords

TQM, Public sector, Greek, Quality, Management, Government

1. INTRODUCTION

Total Quality Management, TQM, is a method by which management and employees can become involved in the continuous improvement of the production of goods and services. It is a combination of quality and management tools aimed at increasing business and reducing losses due to wasteful practices. Although originally applied to manufacturing operations, and for a number of years only used in that area. Total Quality Management has become more popular since the early 1980's. Total Quality is a description of the culture, attitude and organization of a company that strives to provide customers with products and services that satisfy their needs. The culture requires quality in all aspects of the company's operations, with processes being done right the first time and defects and waste eradicated from operations or activities. Total Quality Management, TQM, is a method by which management and employees can become involved in the continuous improvement of the production of goods and services [1]. It is a combination of quality and management tools aimed at increasing business and reducing losses due to wasteful practices. TQM is a management philosophy that seeks to integrate all organizational functions (marketing, finance, design, engineering, and production, customer service, etc.) to focus on meeting customer needs and organizational objectives [2]

2. PRINCIPLES OF TQM

TQM introduces systematic and continuous improvements to an organisation's process, products and services. It seeks to involve all stakeholders and ensure that their experience and ideas contribute to on-going improvement in quality. Underlying such an approach are some fundamental principles such as promoting a quality-focussed environment where there is open communication and employee ownership; rewards and recognition systems; ongoing training and education; and employee empowerment [4,5]. The key principles of TQM are listed below in table 1:

• *Management Commitment*
    o Plan (drive, direct)
    o Do (deploy, support, participate)
    o Check (review)
    o Act (recognize, communicate, revise)
 	
 • *Fact Based Decision Making*
    o SPC (statistical process control)
    o DOE, FMEA
    o The 7 statistical tools
    o Team Oriented Problem Solving)
 	
 • *Customer Focus*
    o Supplier partnership
    o Service relationship with internal customers
    o Never compromise quality
    o Customer driven standards
	• *Employee Empowerment*
	    o Training
	    o Suggestion scheme
	    o Measurement and recognition
	    o Excellence teams
	
	 • *Continuous Improvement*
	    o Systematic measurement and focus on CONQ
	    o Excellence teams
	    o Cross-functional process management
	    o Attain, maintain, improve standards

Table 1:Key principles of TQM

TQM is a client-oriented approach that introduces systematic management changes and continuous improvements to an organisation's processes, products and services. As the diagram below indicates, the TQM process begins with the customer and ends with the customer [7]. The TQM process takes specific inputs (the customer's wants, needs and expectations), transforms (processes) these inputs within the organisation to produce goods or services that, in turn, satisfy the customer (output).

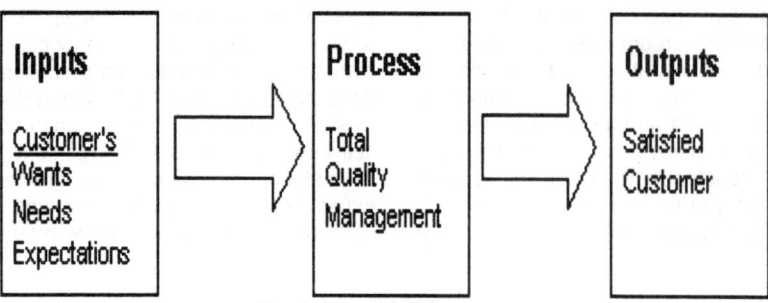

Fig. 1: The TQM Process

TQM views an organization as a collection of processes and maintains that organizations must strive to continuously improve these processes by incorporating the knowledge and experiences of workers. Although originally applied to manufacturing operations, TQM is now becoming recognized as a generic management tool, just as applicable in service and public sector organizations [8]. While TQM has its roots in industrial and corporate models, its usage is now influencing the management structures of both government departments and non-profit organisations [9,10]. It is not only the private sector, that is responding to a rapidly changing economic environment but governments are also under increasing pressure to improve services in response to budgetary restrictions and growing public dissatisfaction with the quality of service provision. Many of the ideas, programmes and approaches for improving services such as promoting competition between suppliers, customer satisfaction and to achieve competitive advantage that were pioneered in the private sector are now having an impact on how public sector services are being provided. Osborne D. and T. Gaebler [15] identified that the following features that are increasingly characteristic of public sector organisations:

- Promoting competition between providers;
- Empowering citizens by pushing control out into the community;
- Measuring performance;
- Focusing not on inputs but on processes for their outcomes;
- Driven by their goals (vision)-not by their rules and regulations;
- Redefining clients as customers;
- Offering citizens/customers real choices;
- Preventing problems before they occur rather than rectifying them afterwards;
- Decentralising authority and embracing participatory management;
- Putting energy into earning money, not simply spending it.

Organisational cultures are very hard to change whether in the private sector or in the public sector. Factors that shape organisational culture include positional hierarchy structures, administrative systems, work processes, leadership, employees' pre-dispositions and management practices [16]. Greek government organisations are slowly transforming to a decentralised bottom up system. This change in future will enable TQM to address many of the constraints to more client-oriented and participatory service provision. The primary, long-term benefits of TQM in the public sector include better services, reduced costs and satisfied customers. Progressive improvement in the management systems and the quality of services offered result in increasingly satisfied customers. In addition a number of other benefits are observable including improved skills, morale and confidence among public service staff, enhanced relationships between governments and its constituents, increased government accountability and transparency and improved productivity and efficiency of public services [17].

3. PROBLEMS DUE TO UNSATISFIED CUSTOMERS IN PUBLIC SECTORS

The difference between private and public sector is that public sector has responsibilities and constraints that do not seem to be part of private sector organizations. So, the translation of TQM concepts to government is more complicated Ron Hikei [19], partner in the KPMG Centre of Government suggests that citizens may not be well served by considering the users of government service as customers for the following reasons:

- o Since users of government services don't usually have the choice of going elsewhere, treating them as customers may not convince them that we value them as customers.
- o Private sector companies often gather information from customers to improve service as private sector agencies. operational problems occurs because resolving the complaints of customers is often not in the power of civil servants, but can only be undertaken by senior officials or politicians.
- o Equating the concepts of citizen and customer does not take into account the responsibilities of citizenship, nor the role of government. Customers have very few obligations, citizens do.
- o The author also suggests that simply referring to citizens as

customers,without undertaking more encompassing structural changes to government, will be ineffective.

According to Hikel [20], members of the public should be treated as valued customers, even in situations where they are subject to regulatory or law enforcement control. The notion of "customers" suggests that they are important enough to not be considered as nuisances, but are the focus of our organizational existence. In addition, government organizations, focusing on customer satisfaction, can reduce the cost of poor customer service, in terms of redoing work, and handling complaints. Even where a government employee can't change the laws or policies, there is considerable benefit to treating the "customer" in a polite, helpful and respectful way. Hikel also suggests that if we want to treat government users as true customers, we must restructure our organizations to operate in this new way. On this point, there is considerable evidence to suggest that TQM and customer service improvements succeed when there is a willingness to address the larger organizational issues, rather than simply telling staff to treat people like customers. To address these types of concerns it is important to adapt quality principles to fit the unique context of public sector organisations [21,22].

Quality movement started from a private sector, primarily manufacturing orientation. As a result, some fundamental concerns about the adaptation of TQM to the public sector are frequently raised and these concerns must be addressed based on the following issues: The nature of TQM itself inhibits public sector applications:

o The nature of the public sector is inimical to the reception of TQM applications;
o The work cultures of professional groups that characterise the public sector are inimical to the public sector;
o In the public sector, the "customer" is a more problematic concern; and,
o Public sector provisions (decision-making) are much more complicated than manufacturing.

4. OBSTACLES AND DISCOURAGEMENT FACTORS TO ADOPTING TQM PUBLIC SECTORS

Many government organisations often have multiple and even conflicting missions; few are accountable to their clients; there are rarely sanctions for poor performance and there is little direct competition. This is in direct contrast to organisations in the private sector that exist in more "functional" systems, such as the market economy, have clearer missions, and are accountable to their customers. In many public sectors senior managers have considerable authority. The adoption of TQM will calls for a change for this structure. It is also identified that many of senior managers in the public sector are very reluctant in considering TQM for fear of losing the positional power [23].

5. CHARACTERISTICS TO FOLLOW FOR SUCCESSFUL IMPLEMENTATION OF TQM IN PUBLIC SECTORS.

TQM connects organizations with their customers, service receivers, employees, and suppliers in times of difficulties. This can be summarised as five characteristics that government institutions must adopt if they are to have successful total quality management today:

o *Leadership with a clear improvement vision.*
This vision must recognize the fact that an organization's culture is the collective result of the organization's actions and can be affected only by hands-on changes in these actions and a deep confidence in the capabilities of men and women throughout the organization to bring about these changes.

o A unrelenting focus on identifying the goals required for full achievement of the necessary improvement for the organization.

What sets the successful organizations apart is that their goals and the supporting steps are based on analysis and planning by people from the bottom to the top of the organization who really understand the details of what has to be accomplished

○ Effective use of human resources through the kind of empowerment.

○ This should not be just an emphasis on increasing employee responsibility in the workplace. It is building among all employees the openness, trust, and multi-channel communication that create the environment for individual job entrepreneurship-encouraging people to develop their own forms of teamwork and their own personal ownership of competitive improvement. Development and setting up teamwork management processes that drive improvement and that everyone in the organization understands, believes in, and comes to be part of.

○ Insistence that what is measured correctly will be managed correctly for improvement, particularly in terms of the three fundamental metrics of user service quality satisfaction, cost effectiveness, and human resource utilization [24,25].

6. A STUDY INTO THE PUBLIC SECTOR IN GREECE

The Greek government has recognised the deficiencies afflicting the operations of the public sector and the need to take appropriate measures to make it more responsive to the nation's development needs. The strategies taken aim to eliminate the identified deficiencies in the system and instituting measures that will raise the sector's productivity, efficiency, and effectiveness. The strategic activities can be grouped into two categories: those already adopted and implemented or in the course of implementation, and those that are being proposed. It is abundantly clear that in Greece, there is a huge need in the public and the private sectors for well-trained managers. Much of the organisational dysfunction encountered. In public organisations in Greece is rightly attributed to a lack of skilled professional managers. As a consequence, vast amounts of time and money have been invested by governments and donor agencies in management training and development with relatively little tangible return on this investment [26].

Greek public sectors are centr5alised and need s decentralisation to allow employees to influence their own destiny.

Increasing local participation in decision making can make government more immediately transparent and accountable. Decentralisation can result in more efficient use of resources because projects that are locally conceived and implemented are more likely to meet local needs and are subject to local control. Importantly, decentralisation will provide a conducive setting for the emergence of NGOs and voluntary activities. It can improve economic participation by encouraging local entrepreneurship and can reduce disparities in development between regions as long as central governments are prepared to devise formulae for the redistribution of tax revenues. But effective decentralisation is dependent mostly on the reform of existing power structures. Considering the above facts, the authors suggest sectors it is important for the Greek public sectors to adapt quality principles to fit the unique context of public sector organisations which are summarised as follows [27]:

○ Customer Satisfaction should be the primary goal and ultimate measure of service quality.

○ Ensure the definition of "customer" includes both internal (employees in other departments); and, external dimensions (vendors, taxpayers, suppliers, service users etc.).

○ Develop and communicate a common vision of the organisation based on an extended view of the customer.

○ Reward teamwork, encourage innovation, and work process improvement at all levels.

○ Provide expanded training and self-improvement opportunities.

○ Employee involvement at all levels is very important.

○ Acknowledge and reward success at both individual and team levels.

○ Eliminate fear in the work place and remove barriers to developing pride in service (empowerment).

○ Make the necessary changes to successfully implement the preceding goals [28].

7. APPLICATION OF TQM IN PUBLIC SECTORS CASE STUDIES

Recently it is quite clear that there are significant public sector quality initiatives and total quality management programs that have been introduced in a variety of authorities. A survey on quality systems US public sector has identified a series of lessons of "best practices" for consideration by other jurisdictions interested in pursuing quality initiatives or TQM. First, it is important to start with a customer orientated service area that is prepared to adapt new methods to improve service. The most important strategies to adopt was found to be obtaining and maintaining managerial support, identifying customer needs, and involving employees with implementation" [29].

In the United Kingdom, local authorities have had "...an increasing interest in quality and quality management" [30]. To some extent, the expanded interest in and use of quality techniques in the UK may be attributed to the work of the Audit Commission. This Commission produced a paper entitled Putting Quality on the Map: Measuring and Appraising Quality in the Public Service (1993), which has served as an important document for local authorities

In the United Kingdom, public sectors have an increasing interest in quality and quality management [30]. To some extent, the expanded interest in and use of TQM quality techniques in the UK may be attributed to the work of the Audit Commission. This Commission produced a paper entitled Putting Quality on the Map: Measuring and Appraising Quality in the Public Service (1993), which has served as an important document for public sectors. The commission identified that there are four key areas that together will contribute to a quality service: Quality of Communication –

Does the public sector communicate with, listen to, and understand its users?

  o Quality of Specification – Is this understanding converted into clear standards for service delivery?

  o Quality of Delivery – Are the standards actually delivered, and is remedial action taken when failure occurs?

  o Quality of People and Systems – Are staff motivated, trained, well-managed, and supported by good management systems and processes?

The relationship of these components is illustrated in Figure 2.

8. CONCLUSION

Like most of the public sectors around the world, Greek public sectors too are faced with change, challenge, and uncertainty due to changes in global economy, technological advances and organisational pressures to do more with less as senior government economic transfers. In response to these factors of change, the public sector, including local government, has moved towards a more output oriented, customer-focused approach to service delivery. In many respects, this movement has followed the implantations of QM principles in public sectors. This paper has highlighted the need for Greek public sectors to consider improving the quality management systems and analysed the obstacles in the Greek public sectors to provide the customer-orientated quality service.

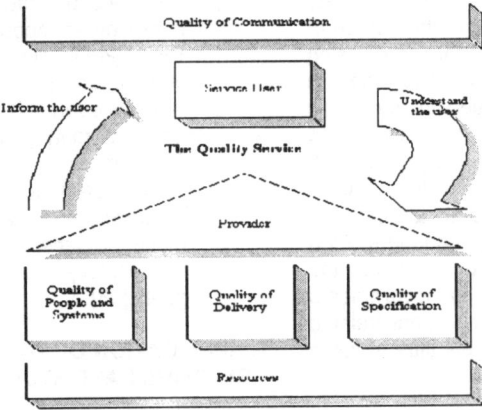

Fig. 2:The Quality Map
[Source: Audit Commission, Putting Quality on the Map: Measuring and Appraising Quality in the Public Service, Audit Commission, London, UK No. 18 March 1993 p. 3]

9. REFERENCES

1. **Gilbert, G.** (1992). Quality Improvement in a Defence Organization. Public Productivity and Management Review, 16(1), 65-75.
2. **Hyde, A.** (1992). The Proverbs of Total Quality Management: Recharting the Path to Quality Improvement in the Public Sector. Public Productivity and Management Review, 16(1), 25-37.
3. **Martin, L.** (1993). "Total Quality Management in the Public Sector," National Productivity Review, 10, 195-213.
4. **Swiss, J.** (1992). Adapting TQM to Government. Public Administration Review, 52, 356-362.
5. **Tichey, N.** (1983). Managing Strategic Change. New York: John Wiley & Sons.
6. **Hill Stephen, 1991.** "Why Quality Circles failed but Total Quality management might succeed." *British journal of industrial relations*, 29(4), 541-568.
7. **Ishikawa, K**, 1985.What is Total Quality Control? The Japanese way. Englewood Cliffs, New Jersey, Prentice- Hall.
8. Smith, AK, 1993. Total Quality Management in the Public sector. Quality Progress, June
9. **Barkley, Bruce T. & Saylor, James H.** , Customer Driven Project Management - A New Paradigm in T Q Implementation. USA : McGraw-Hill Inc., 1994
10. **Caroselli, Marlene**, Quality Games for Trainers - 101 Playful Lessons in Quality and Continuous Improvement. USA : McGraw-Hill Inc., 1996
11. **Delp, Peter ; Thesen, Arne ; Motiwalla, Juzar & Seshadri, Neelakantan**, Systems Tools for Project Planning. Program of Advanced Studies in Institution Building and Technical Assistance Methodology, 1997
12. **Morgan, Colin & Murgatroyd, Stephen,** Total Quality Management in the Public Sector. USA : Open Univ. Press, 1994
13. **Stamatis, DH.,** Total Quality Service - Principles, Pratices and Implementation. USA : St. Lucie Press, 1996
14. **West, J., E. Berman,** and **M. Milakovich** 1994. Total Quality Management in Local Government. The Municipal Yearbook, Washington, DC: ICMA, 10-30.
15. **West, J., E. Berman,** and **M. Milakovich** 1995. Implementing TQM in Local Government: The Leadership Challenge. Quality Management Today: What Local Governments Need to Know, Washington, DC: ICMA.
16. **David Osborne** and **Ted Gaebler**, Reinventing Government - How the entrepreneurial spirit is transforming the public sector, Penguin Books 1992.
17. **David Osborne** and **Peter Plastrik,** Banishing Bureaucracy - The five strategies for reinventing government, 1997, Penguin Books
18. The Partnership for Governance Reform in Indonesia - The Partnership Secretariat, UNDP, Jl MH Thamrin 14, Jakarta 10240. Tel: 021 314 1308 Fax: 021 31903160.
19. **Gore, A**. 1993. Creating a Government that Works Better and Costs Less: Report of the National Performance Review, Washington, DC: U.S. Government Print Office.
20. The Support for Decentralisation project (GTZ) - Department Dalam Negeri Republic Indonesia, Ministry of Home Affairs, 2nd floor, West Wing, Jalan Veteran No. 7, Jakarta. Mail: P.O. Box 4813 Jakarta 10110, email: gtzsfdm@server.indo.net.id
21. Ref: http://www.work911.com/articles/tqm4.htm
22. **M.E. Milakovich,** Improving Service Quality: Achieving High Performance in the Public and Private Sectors, St. Lucie Press, Delray Beach, FL 1995 p. 162.
23. The Capacity Building to Support Decentralised Government Project (ADB)
24. **Audit Commission,** 1993. Putting Quality on the Map: Measuring and Appraising Quality in Public Services. 18 (March): 2.
25. **Ball, R.** 1998. Performance Review in Local Government, Aldershot, UK: Ashgate Publishing.
26. **Bensley, F.** and **B. Wortman** 1994. ISO Primer, Terre Haute, IN: Quality Council of Indiana.
27. **Brown, S., E. Gummesson, B. Edvardsson, B. Gustavsson** 1991. Service Quality: Multidisciplinary and Multinational Perspectives, Lexington, MA: Lexington Books.
28. **City of Vancouver** 1995. Better City Government: The Next Steps. City of Vancouver Staff Report (April): 2.

Composites

GCMM 2004
Editors: Prasad K D V Yarlagadda and S Narayanan
Publisher: Narosa Publishing House Pvt. Ltd., New Delhi, India

Design of Composite Sandwich Panels for Crack Growth Path Control

Paiboon Limpitipanich[1] and Pichai Rusmee[2]

Sirindhorn International Institute of Technology, Thammasat University, Thailand
[1] Mechanical Engineering Department, Burapha University, Thailand
[2] Fabrinet Company Limited, Thailand

Email: paiboonl@buu.ac.th

Abstract

Composite sandwich panels have been used in many applications because of high strength-to-weight ratio comparing to other composite configurations. The panels are usually made by sandwiching a layer of foam or any lightweight materials between two faceplates. Usually the core layer is much lighter and weaker than the face layers thus more susceptible to damages. One of the more serious types of damages is fracture or crack since this will dramatically decrease strength of the panels. In addition, a crack located in the middle of the core layer is more difficult to detect via non-destructive means such as acoustic emission. It would be ideal to be able to direct the crack toward the faceplates where detection can be made more easily.

A design method for composite sandwich panels is introduced so that the crack path can be directed. The method is demonstrated in foam-core, double cantilever beam specimens. The specimens were manufacturing from 16 kg/m^3 density EPS foam and aluminum plates of varying thickness. Under the normal crack-opening-type condition, the crack path would normally grow in the direction perpendicular to the applied load. However, on a local scale, the direction of the crack path was not predictable as the crack may propagate either through or around the bead structure of the EPS foam.

Key Words:
Composite Sandwich Panels, Crack Path Control

1. INTRODUCTION

The use of sandwich structures can be found in many applications, e.g., aircrafts, automobiles, and other lightweight structural elements. The uses of sandwich panels are very attractive because they generally have high strength-to-weight ratios compared to other composite configurations. They also possess good thermal insulation sound absorption characteristic. A basic sandwich panel can be made by sandwiching any lightweight material between two faceplates. The function of the material is to keep the faceplates separate and reduce the total weight of the panel. Materials having cellular structure, i.e., honeycomb, reticulated foam, and non-reticulated foam, can be used for this purpose. The face materials can be single-component solid such as aluminum plate or laminates such as fiberglass. A physically assembled sandwich panel will require a use of compatible adhesive to hold the faceplates and the core together.

Damage of composite sandwich panels can be in any of the three components: faceplate, core, or adhesive. For the panel that has a polymeric foam core, one of the most serious types is fracture or crack in the core since this will dramatically decrease strength of the panels.

Foam usually has better sound absorption characteristics than other engineering solids. A panel with foam core that has a crack in the core layer is more difficult to detect via non-destructive means such as acoustic emission. It would be ideal to be able to direct the crack towards the faceplates where detection can be made more easily.

The purpose of this study, as a part of a bigger study, is to design and manufacture double cantilever beam specimen that can be used in fracture study of the core of composites. The resulting specimen is a double cantilever beam specimen modified from that used in the study of laminate strength or adhesive fracture strength. The modified specimen has an added foam core as shown in Fig. 1. The same specimen configuration can be used in the next phase of the study where the stress field is manipulated so that the crack will propagate in a desired direction.

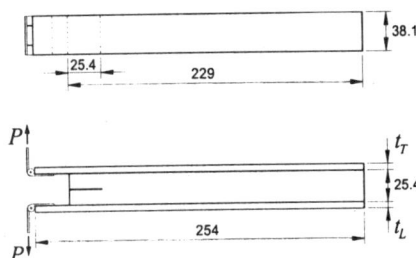

Fig. 1: Foam-core, double cantilever beam specimen geometry (Dimensions are in millimeter.)

2. MATERIAL SELECTION

In the current study, foam core, double cantilever beam specimens were tested under the normal crack-opening-type loading. This specimen is widely used for the study of interfacial fracture toughness of composite sandwich panels.[1, 2, 3] Adaptation of such specimen for a sandwich beam by adding foam core introduces additional level of complication in specimen fabrication and testing. The current discussion is restricted to one particular paring of specimen materials but should be applicable to other composites system as well.

2.1 Core Selection

Expanded polystyrene (EPS) foam of 16 kg/m^3 density was used as the core material. EPS foam is two component composites consisting of polystyrene matrix and gas filler.

The matrix and the filler are encased into beads that are later processed into a piece of foam. Unlike engineering solids or other homogeneous foams, crack in EPS foam do not have a clear path through the material. Instead, the crack may propagate either around the bead or through the foamed beads.[4, 5] However, the overall tendency of the crack path is to propagate in the direction normal to the maximum resultant tensile loads.

2.2 Faceplate Selection

Faceplates of the foam-core, double cantilever beam specimen can be either laminated plates or solids. The purpose of the faceplate in this study is to control the crack path in the foam core propagating toward the desired location. Aluminum, which is more rigid than foam, was used for this purpose. Any laminated plates can also be used as faceplate of the specimen. However, they do not offer any advantage since the faceplates are not the focus of the current study. In actual application, the importance of the system is reversed where faceplates are more important and the foam core is there to lighten the weight and keep the faceplates apart.

2.3 Adhesive Selection

The purpose of the adhesive layer is to adhere faceplates and the core. Failure in a composite sandwich panel can occur at the interface layer. However, the strength of the adhesive glue is usually higher than that of the foam core. Cracks in the core will propagate before any damage at the adhesive occurs. Then, any adhesive that does not affect the material being testing can be used. High peel strength epoxy adhesive (3M DP-460 Off-White) was used for this purpose. The epoxy can bond the polymeric foam and aluminum without excessive curing temperature and without affecting the material being test.

3. SPECIMEN PREPARATION

In order to obtain the foam core, double cantilever beam specimen in a size as shown in Fig. 1, the following procedure are used.

3.1 Foam and Faceplate Preparations

The specimen had EPS foam core and aluminum faceplates. The sandwich beam specimens are machined from a composite sandwich plate. The specimen preparation in the current study could not follow the same procedure since the foam core is too soft and has much lower melting point comparing with the aluminum faceplates. Traditional machining process such as grinding, cutting, and milling can generate enough heat to damage the foam core. Liquid-cooled tile saw with a diamond blade can be used for this purpose. It can solve the heating and tearing problems.[3] However, softness of the foam core remains an issue because the force from the cutting operation may still be large enough to damage the foam core. For this reason, it may not be desirable to manufacture the sandwich panel first then cut the beam specimens from the panel. An alternative is to machine the components of the beam specimen separately then assemble them afterward.

Faceplates of 38.1 mm wide and 254 mm long were cut from an aluminum sheet. The core material was cut from a 25.4 mm thick foam stock using a band saw. The core was cut to the desired length but nominally wider than the desired width of 38.1 mm. This excess width will be cut after the specimens are assembled.

3.2 Assembly Process and Surface Finish

The function of the adhesive layer is to hold the core and the faceplates together. It is desirable to minimize the effect of introducing this extra element since the primary factor being study is the foam core and its interaction with the faceplates. A high strength epoxy such as the 3M DP-460 was selected for this reason. This epoxy, with the modulus of 1760 MPa, can be assumed to be infinitely rigid comparing to the rigidity of the foam core.

The effect of the epoxy layer will have to be minimized as much as possible. This is accomplished by applying the adhesive layer as thinly as possible. To maintain a thin, constant thickness of the adhesive layer, a plastic scraper is used to evenly spread the epoxy on the foam surface. Then the aluminum plates are affixed to the foam. It is imperative that the adhesive is applied to the foam surface to fill in the surface unevenness. Had the epoxy been applied to the plate instead, the foam surface will not get adequate epoxy coverage resulting in poor adhesion.

After the epoxy cured, the foam core was cut flush with the faceplates using a band saw. It is not recommended that additional sanding or surfacing be done to the foam core. Doing so may damage the core or otherwise impart foreign matters on the surface thus changing the core properties.

3.3 Loading Points

Testing of the specimen is to be done by pulling in direction perpendicular to the longitudinal direction of the specimen. Pull-tabs must be affixed to the specimen. Sometimes in composites or adhesive testing where the total fracture load is low, reinforced cellulose tape can be used successfully. To use tape for the pull-tabs, adequate length of the tape is affixed to the underside (foam core side) of the faceplate. Extra length of the tape is folded over itself to cover the adhesive side and serve as reinforcement for the tab.

A simple pull-tab made form tape may not be suitable for foam core specimens depending on the pull strength required. If this is the case, small hinges can be used as pull-tabs. Hinges can be affixed to the specimens in two possible locations, outside or inside face of the faceplates. Affixing the hinges to the outside has an advantage in that there is slightly .larger surface area on the hinge leaf to affix to the specimen. In addition, location of the loading point can be adjusted by placing the hinges at different locations along the length of the specimen. The disadvantage of the hinge on the outside is that the peel strength of the epoxy used to affix the hinges becomes the controlling factor since the hinges can peel off the faceplates. From preliminary tests, specimens made with the hinge pull-tabs on the outside all fail at this adhesive joint making such hinge placement not usable for the purpose.

Affixing the hinge to the inside of the faceplates was the only solution that works for this particular beam specimen. Instead of peeling, failure mode is now a combination of peeling and shearing. Peeling will occur near the edge of the hinge where there was a strain mismatch between free surface and the glued surface of the hinge. The part of the glue joint closest to the applied load will experience a shear and compressive load instead of peeling load. There is no pull force

197

directly peeling the hinge off the specimen as in the other configuration.

3.4 Precracking

Precracking of metal fracture specimens is normally done via a laborious fatigue loading steps. Fortunately, soft material such as acrylics or foam does not require this same operation. Precrack can be satisfactorily simulated by a sharp notch generated be a razor blade. In polymeric material, the length of the precrack is not that critical. A hard tap on the razor blade is usually sufficient to generate an acceptable precrack. This is not the case for foam core. The length of the precrack must be sufficiently long to avoid any end effect from such a soft material. In order to introduce a precrack of sufficient length in the mid-plane of the foam core specimen, a band saw was used to cut into the EPS foam core to make a deep but blunt notch. Then, a razor blade was used to introduce a simulated crack tip at the end of the notch.

Keeping track of the crack front by visual means requires painting and marking of the surface since the foam surface and the crack have a very low contrast ratio. Selection of the paint or dye used on the foam surface is also a critical factor. Foam is very sensitive to many solvents, so solvent-based markers will not be usable. If they were used, the surface of the foam core could be partially dissolved thus ruining it in the process. Certain water-based ink is also not usable. Water does not wet plastic sufficiently. Any water-based dye used must contain wetting agent that will wet the surface the foam. Watercolor paint turns out to possess adequate wetibility to be used successfully on the foam surface. Finally, endorsing ink can be used to mark the specimen at regular interval to assist in visual observation of the crack.

The finished specimen made for this study consisted of the EPS core layer made of foam glued to the aluminum faceplate material with a thin layer of 3M DP-460 epoxy. Pull-tabs made of hinges affixed to the inside of the faceplates using the same high strength epoxy. A profile view of a completed specimen is shown in Fig. 2.

Variation in the test specimen can possibly be made to obtain similar effect to its counterparts in composite or adhesive test specimens. For example, the width or thickness of the faceplates can be varied to obtain a beam of constant strength making extraction of fracture data easier, but at a cost of making manufacturing step being more difficult. It was deemed that the effort in designing and manufacturing such a specimen did not justify it.

Fig. 2: Foam-core, double cantilever beam specimen

4. TESTING

The finished specimen can be tested in any tensile testing machine with adequate capacity. The specimens made for this study required machine capacity of ±1 kN.

There are two similar, important quantities in fracture mechanics: Stress Intensity Factor, K, and Strain Energy Release Rate, G. The cantilever beam specimen discussed here is suitable for determining G. Testing for this quantity using this particular specimen requires a rate control feature of the testing machine. The machine must apply the load at a constant displacement rate. Other types of specimen or quantities desired may require a constant loading rate.

One additional part of the fixture not used in other tensile type testing is a supplementary pulley. Because of the weight of the ungripped end of the specimen and the free pivot of the hinges, the end of the specimen will not stay horizontal. A simple string cannot be used to hold the specimen horizontal since that end must move at half the speed of the crosshead to stay centered to the two "free" ends being pulled. A system of pulleys was device to support the free end so that the specimen stayed level during the test. The system is shown schematically in Fig. 3. Fig. 4 shows a picture of testing of this beam specimen in progress.

Fracture surfaces of a foam-core, double cantilever beam specimen are shown in Fig. 5. This specimen was pulled crack opening mode as discussed. It is expected that the crack should grow perpendicular to the direction of the applied load.

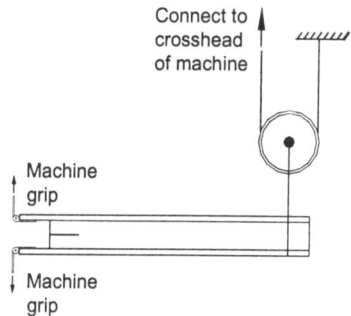

Connect to crosshead of machine

Machine grip

Machine grip

Fig. 3: Test configuration holding the specimen to be in the horizontal level

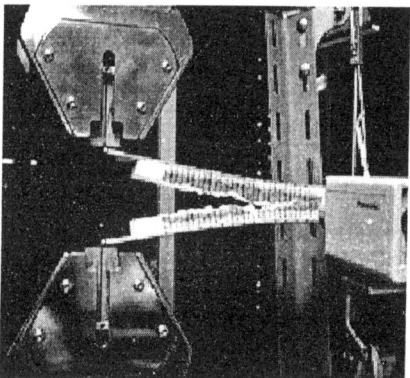

Fig. 4: Foam-core, double cantilever beam test setup

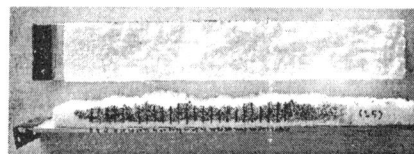

Fig. 5: Fracture surface of the foam-core specimen.

From the figure, it can be seen that the crack did not quite propagate in a straight line perpendicular to the applied load. Instead, the crack profile is jagged and uneven. This is because EPS foam is not a homogeneous material. It consists of plastic matrix and gas encased in beads that are thermally bonded together. A propagating crack has two possible crack paths: through or around the beads. Good quality foam would produce a crack surface going through both as the crack front weaves around finding the weakest point in the foam. However, the overall path of the crack remains perpendicular to the pull direction.

The results from these specimens showed that the EPS foam does not behave in the exact same manner as other solid material in which the fracture properties are studied. Locally, the crack front may or may not propagate in the direction as predicted by elementary fracture mechanics. However, the overall crack path being horizontal illustrates that fracture mechanics theories predicting the crack path on a non-localize scale will be applicable. This will be an important factor to consider in the next phase of the study where the overall crack path will be manipulated.

5. CONCLUSION

The method to manufacturing the foam-core, double cantilever beam specimen of the composite sandwich panel to be used in fracture study was presented. The specimen was produced from 16 kg/m^3 density EPS foam, aluminum plates, and high modulus epoxy. The precrack in soft material such as foam can be successfully simulated using a razor blade instead of long and laborious fatigue pre-crack technique.

Testing technique of the fracture beam specimen was discussed. Excessive weight of the hanging end of the specimen required the use of a supplementary pulley system to ensure that the specimen remains horizontal during the entire duration of the test.

The resulting crack path and crack surfaces were jagged and uneven. This was due to the special nature of the EPS foam that was not truly homogeneous. However, the overall path of crack was as expected in a normal crack-opening-type test.

6. REFERENCES

1   **Ural, A., Zehnder, A. T., Ingraffea, A. R.** (2003), "Fracture Mechanics Approach of Facesheet Delamination in Honeycomb: Measurement of Energy Release Rate of the Adhesive Bond", *Engineering fracture Mechanics*, 70, 93-103.

2   **Prasad, S., and Carlsson, L. A.** (1994), "Debonding and Crack Kinking in Foam Core Sandwich Beams-I. Analysis of Fracture Specimens", *Engineering Fracture Mechanics*, 47(6), 813-824.

3   **Smith, S. A.** (2001), "Vacuum Assisted Resin Transfer Molding of Sandwich Structures: Material Processing, Evaluation, Fracture Testing and Analysis", *Doctoral Dissertation, North Carolina A&T State University*.

4   **Stupak, P.R., Frye, W. O., and Donovan, J. A.** (1991), "The Effect of Bead Fusion on the Energy Absorption of Polystyrene Foam", *Journal of Cellular Solids*, 27, 484.

5   **Ramsteiner, F., Fell, N., Forster, S.** (2001), "Testing the Deformation Behavior of Polymer Foams", *Polymer Testing*, 20, 661-670.

GCMM 2004
Editors: Prasad K D V Yarlagadda and S Narayanan
Copyright © 2005, Vellore Institute of Technology, Vellore, India
Publisher: Narosa Publishing House Pvt. Ltd., New Delhi, India

Experimental Studies on the Curing of Alternate Un-reinforced Mould Materials using Microwave Heating

Prasad K D V Yarlagadda

School of Mechanical, Manufacturing and Medical Engineering,
Queensland University of Technology, Brisbane, Qld. 4001, Australia

Abstract

There is an increasing interest of using microwave technology for curing resins. The heating of the epoxy resins greatly relies on various factors which includes the dielectric properties, kind of waveguide used and the frequency and power used. The majority of curing via microwaves were normally performed on epoxy resins like diglycidyl ether of bisphenol-A (DGEBA) with hardeners like 4,4' diaminodiphenylmethane (DDM). This paper investigates the experimental use of materials such as Casting Resin ADR 2512, High Temperature Resin ADR 2515 and Laminating Resin GPR 2516. Two high temperature hardeners were used together with the resins, mainly ADH 2403 and ADH 2409. Microwave curing resulted in a shorter curing time to reach the maximum percentage cure. Two moulding techniques were studied, mainly curing by placing the mould in the cavity or by preheating the resins prior to pouring the resin into the mould. By preheating the resin, it decreases gel time and improves production rates.

Keywords
Microwave Heating, Mould Materials, Curing, Epoxy Resins

1. INTRODUCTION

Microwave technology has been adopted in the industry working on the principle of releasing heat to cure a wide range of materials. Advantages of using microwave curing over thermal curing are that the process speeds are increased, uniform heating may occur throughout the material, efficiency of energy conversion, better and more rapid process control, precise and controlled heating [1]. Currently moulding processes make use of conventional heating devices like the convection oven or eating coils. Numerous researches have been carried out in the harnessing of microwave power in the curing or joining of various materials.

2. THEORY

Microwaves are electromagnetic waves with wavelengths ranging from 1 mm to 1 m and frequency that ranges from 300 MHz to 30 GHz. According to international agreement, industrial microwaves operate at a frequency of 2.54 GHz, which is powered by a variable power generator up to 1.26kW. The microwave oven uses a magnetron to create intense microwaves that are channeled to the microwave cavity using electromagnetic waves with a frequency of 2.45 GHz. However, if greater power penetration is required, a system with a frequency of 915 MHz can be used.

Important properties that are involved in the theory of microwave curing of materials include the wave propagation, microwave instrumentation (which includes the magnetron, impedance matching and tuning, waveguides used and the microwave cavity) and the dielectric properties of the material. The heating pattern of a sample that is heated by microwaves will depend on the dissipation factor which can be expressed by Eq (1) and the dielectric may be assumed to have a complex dielectric constant as shown in Eq. (2)

$$\tan \delta = \frac{\epsilon''}{\epsilon'} \text{----------} \quad (1)$$

$$\epsilon = \epsilon' + j\epsilon'' \text{------} \quad (2)$$

The energy that is absorbed by the sample as the microwave energy penetrates it, is dependent on the sample's dissipation factor. Materials that are transparent to microwave energy, penetration is considered to be infinite. As in the case of reflective materials such as metals, penetration is considered to be zero. However, the dissipation factors for absorptive materials are finite.

3. EQUIPMENT USED

Two sets of equipment were used in this study. The first set of equipment used was for the curing and post-curing of the materials and the second set used was for the testing of material properties like tensile strength, flexural strength and hardness tests were conducted. In addition, tests to find the glass transition temperature of the materials were also conducted and the morphology of the fracture surface were studied.

4. MICROWAVE INSTRUMENTATION

A magnetron as shown in Fig. 1a is used to generate intense electromagnetic waves with a frequency of 2.45 GHz. This 2.45 GHz magnetron tube is one of the most commonly used tubes in the industry. The microwave generator that is used has digital displays, which outputs the forwarded, and reflected wave power that could be adjusted by a dial on the microwave generator.

The stub tuners Fig. 1c are used for the impedance matching for the unnecessary loss of power or the tuning of the microwave

system. Impedance matching is required to minimise the reflectance of the travelling waves travelling from one medium to another. Ideally, the system would be perfectly matched if the microwaves that travel from the magnetron to the sample in the microwave cavity are not reflected back. However in many cases, mismatching occurs. Tuners are used for impedance matching to provide the maximum absorption and minimise the reflected power back to the magnetron. This is important as the reflected microwaves could cause the magnetron to overheat excessively and change the output of the magnetron. The absence of an absorber in the cavity will also increase any minor leakage of microwaves from the system because the microwave intensity inside the cavity will be much higher than normal.

The waveguide Fig. 1 is a device that channels the microwaves generated by the magnetron to the cavity with little loss and virtually no leakage hazard. There are many cross sectional shapes of waveguides available. Cross sections of almost any shape can be used. However, the analysis of odd shaped cross sections would prove to be difficult. Round cross sectional waveguides are rather common.

4.1. Tensile

The Hounsfield tensile machine was used and it consists of the following apparatus: a fixed member, a moveable member and grips on both sides. The material to be tested are held together by the grips on both the fixed and moveable member. With reference to the ASTM D638-00 standards, for test specimens of moulded plastics that are rigid or semi-rigid, the test specimen shall conform to certain dimensions as directed. The specimen thickness used in this study has a thickness of 6mm. The recommended number of specimens to be tested is at least five per sample. The speed of testing is the relative rate of motion of the grips during the test. In this case, the speed of testing for rigid or semi-rigid specimens of Type 1 is at 5 ± 25% mm/min. The controls were done by using a Windows based software that was connected to the Hounsfield machine. A graph of Force vs Extension was plotted on the screen and the force would be taken at the point where the sample fails. The Hounsfield Flexural three point tester utilises the same Hounsfield machine as the Hounsfield Tensile test. This test determines

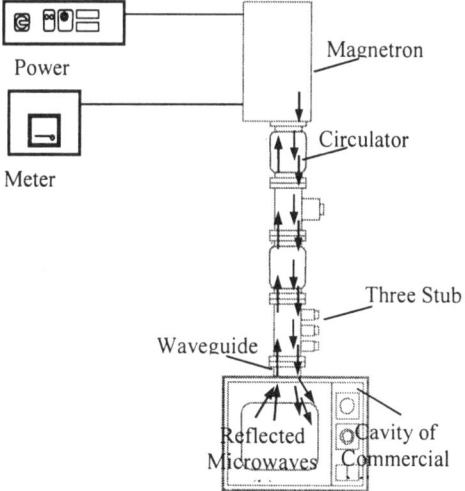

Fig. 1: Setup of Microwave Curing Apparatus

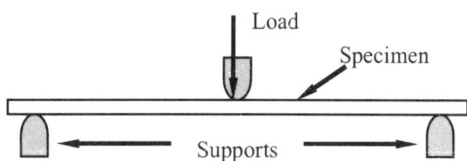

Fig. 2: Three-point loading system on a simply supported beam

4.2. Flexural Strength

The test method uses the theory of a three point load acting on a simply support beam as shown in Fig. 1. There are mainly two procedures of testing the flexural properties as stated in the ASTM D 790-00 Standards. At least five specimens for mould materials have to be done with a recommended specimen size of 127 mm x 12.7 mm x 3.2 mm. They are then placed on a three point support jig that utilises the Hounsfield machine. As recommended, a support span-to-depth ratio of 16:1 has to be used unless specified.

4.3. Rockwell Hardness

The Rockwell Hardness tester is used to test the indention hardness of plastics. With accordance to various Rockwell Hardness (HR) Scales available, conversions to different Rockwell Hardness Scales or hardness standards like the Brinell hardness numbers (BHN) can be done. This test

the flexural properties of the unreinforced rigid or semi-rigid plastics that were moulded. method consists of indenting the test material with a diamond cone or hardened steel ball indenter and corresponds to ASTM D 785-98 Standards.

The results gathered from this test is not a measure of the abrasion or wear resistance of the material but mainly as an indication of cure of the samples at room temperature.

4.4. Glass Transition Temperature

The tests to find the various glass transition temperatures for the samples were conducted by using the Differential Scanning Calorimeter (DSC). The Differential Scanning Calorimeter measures the amount of energy (heat) absorbed or released by a sample as it is heated, cooled or held at constant temperature.

4.5. Fracture Surface

The viewing of non-conducting specimens like epoxy resins usually causes problems when analysing it in the SEM. It is virtually impossible to record photography detail due to the specimen's charging effect.

A common technique used to overcome this problem to coat the specimen with a thin film of conductive material such as gold which should follow the irregularities that appear on the fracture surface of the specimen.

5. EXPERIMENTAL PROCEDURES
5.1. Resin Composition

The resins used are R2512, which consists of Bisphenol-A, Bisphenol-F and Aliphatic Glycidylether. Resin R 2515 is a reaction product of Bisphenol-A based epoxy resin and epichlorohydrin. The final resin used was R2516 with ingredients that include Bisphenol-A, Bisphenol-F and Hexandiol Digcidyl Ether. The hardeners used fall into the chemical category of Cycloaliphatic Amine. The hardeners used are H2403 which has Isophoronediamine ingredients. Another hardener used is the H2409 with ingredients that includes Dimethyl Methylene Di (Cyclohexylamine). Mixture of mould materials of resin and hardener were mixed using parts by weight as shown on Table 1.

Table 1: Mix Ratio of resin and hardener

Material	Parts by Weight					
R2512	100	100				
R2515			100	100		
R2516					100	100
H2403	25		25		25	
H2409		33		33		33

5.2. Tensile

The material's tensile properties were determined by using procedures based on ASTM D638-00. The tests were conducted on a testing machine with both fixed and movable member with specimen Type I as referenced from ASTM. The tests were carried out with the aid of a Hounsfield Mechanical testing machine with a speed of testing to be 5 ± 25% mm/min. The specimens of Type I were of thickness 6 mm and other dimensions are given in the standards. In the tensile test, the specimen was subjected to a continually increasing uniaxial tensile force while simultaneous observations were made on the elongation of the specimen. The tensile strength is the maximum tensile stress of the material and can be found by applying Eq. (3).

$$Tensile\ Strength\ (MPa) = \frac{Force\ (N)}{Cross\ Sectional\ Area\ (m^2)} \quad -- (3)$$

It is also necessary to note the percentage elongation of the specimen. This shows the relative ductility of the material. The percentage elongation, %EL is the percentage of plastic strain at fracture point. The percentage elongation can be found by applying the formula as shown in Eq. (4). Where l_f and l_o are the final and original length respectively.

$$\%EL = \left(\frac{l_f - l_o}{l_o}\right) \times 100 \quad ----- (4)$$

5.3. Flexural Strength

The specimen is then deflected at a strain rate of 0.01 mm/mm/min with a load applied at the center until it breaks or until a maximum strain of 5.0% is reached. The load at yield is the sample material's flexural strength. The thickness of the material used is 3.2 mm and the support span, 100 mm.

Obtaining the material's flexural strength, $\sqcup_M$ is the maximum flexural stress sustained by the test specimen. The maximum flexural stress can be found by applying the formula:

$$\sigma_f = \frac{3PL}{2bd^2} \quad -------- (5)$$

Whereby the flexural stress at midpoint, σ_f is three times the load at yield, P times the support span L divided by two times the width and the square of the depth.

The Bio-Rad SC500 sputter coater was used in the coating process. The specimen were affixed onto a stand and placed into the sputter coater. The chamber of the sputter coater is then void of all air and an inert gas is then allowed to enter the chamber. This whole process takes an approximate time of 40 minutes. The surfaces of the samples were coated with a thin ion deposited layer of gold to improve its reflectivity. This technique gives a uniform coating and covers the surface of the specimen fully. The coated specimens are then carefully placed in the Quanta 200 SEM for analysis

6. RESULTS AND DISCUSSIONS
6.1. Tensile Strength

Tensile tests were done and the final mean results for each specimen at typical room temperatures were tabulated in Table 4. From the results shown, the three different materials exhibit tensile strengths of different values. In general, out of the three epoxy resins tested, results on the tensile strength properties of the microwave cured unreinforced epoxy resins shows rather encouraging results. However for the case of Resin R2515, results proved to be unsatisfactory and were found to be rather brittle.

Table 4: Results for Tensile Strength

Specimen	Tensile Strength (MPa)
R 2512 / H 2403	46
R 2512 / H 2409	28
R 2515 / H 2403	15
R 2515 / H 2409	12
R 2516 / H 2403	45
R 2516 / H 2409	50

Another important factor in the tensile properties of the material is it's percentage elongation. The values tabulated in Table 5 shows in general that resin R 2515 experiences very little elongation before it fails as compared to resins R 2512 and R 2516. In general, resin R 2515 is considered to be a brittle resin as is exhibits very little plastic deformation upon fracture. As compared to certain materials like metals, epoxies are not as ductile.

Table 5: Results for % Elongation

Specimen	Percentage Elongation (%)
R 2512 / H 2403	3.21
R 2512 / H 2409	2.54
R 2515 / H 2403	1.04
R 2515 / H 2409	1.14
R 2516 / H 2403	3.25
R 2516 / H 2409	3.32

6.2. Flexural Strength

Flexural strength tests are carried out on the proposed sample to find out the ability of the specimens to resist deformation under a load. Results of the flexural strength tests are shown in Table 6. For specimens that do not break, the load at yield, typically measured at 5% deformation/strain of the outer surface, is reported as the flexural strength.

Table 6: Results for Flexural Strength

Specimen	Flexural Strength (MPa)
R 2512 / H 2403	167
R 2512 / H 2409	135
R 2515 / H 2403	70
R 2515 / H 2409	17
R 2516 / H 2403	177
R 2516 / H 2409	145

As the results show, resin R 2515 is a rather brittle resin which exhibits low flexural strength. Resin R 2516 gives an overall tougher flexural strength and has a greater ability to resist deformation.

6.3 Rockwell Hardness

The higher the Rockwell hardness number, the harder the material is. From the results shown in Table 7, it can be seen that resin R 2515 is of a harder material as compared to the other two. R 2516 is also harder than resin R 2512. The results obtained from this test are a useful measure of relative resistance to indentation of various grades of plastics. However, the Rockwell hardness test does not serve well as a predictor of other properties such as strength or resistance to scratches, abrasion, or wear,

and should not be used alone for product design specifications.

Table 7: Hardness Properties

Specimen	Rockwell Hardness Number (HRE)
R 2512 / H 2403	57
R 2512 / H 2409	58
R 2515 / H 2403	60
R 2515 / H 2409	63
R 2516 / H 2403	58
R 2516 / H 2409	60

6.4. Glass Transition Temperature

The Glass Transition Temperature test was done to compare if samples cured by microwave improves the material's Glass Transition Temperature. The results show improvement in the Glass Transition temperature as compared to the epoxy resins cured using the conventional oven.

Table 8: Glass Transition Temperatures

Specimen	Conventional Oven	Microwave Oven
R 2512 / H 2409	71.74	80.22
R 2515 / H 2409	54.04	86.06
R 2516 / H 2409	78.30	85.92

In general, the T_g for resin R 2512 has increased an average of 11.82%, resin R 2515 experiences and increase of 59.25% and T_g for resin R 2516 has improved by 9.73%. It is therefore important to increase the material's Glass Transition temperature, so as to have a general increase in the temperature where the material starts to degrade. This is important as the material would then perform and would not fail in higher temperatures as compared to the same material with a low T_g.

6.5 FRACTURE SURFACES
6.5.1 R2512 H2403

The fracture surface of Resin and Hardener Mix R 2512 / H 2403 were observed under a magnification of 76 times. The overall surface exhibits a rather smooth texture. In Fig. 3, bowed-out crack fronts and trailing river lines can be seen. The river lines are on cleavage cracks of the fracture surface. Splinters or filaments in Fig. 3 of material that have separated at the steps and lie at random angles on the surface are also observed. Dust specks can bee seen on the fracture surface which could be due to dust particles in the air or filaments of material that have landed on the fracture surface.

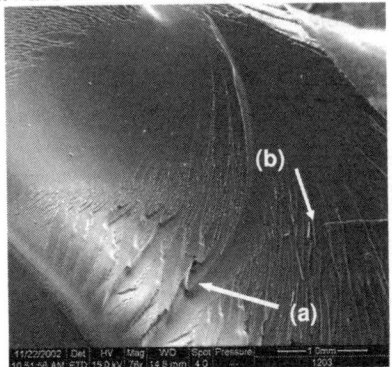

Fig. 3: SEM Image of R 2512 / H 2403

6.5.2   R2512 / H 2409

The fracture surface of R 2512 / H 2409 in Fig. 4 shows a progressive increase in

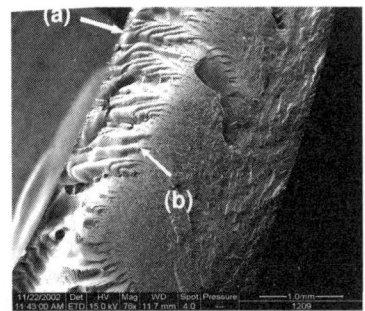

Fig. 4: SEM Image of R 2512 / H 2409

roughness. The crack propagated from the edge and the difference on the fracture surface could be due to compression on one end and tension on the other. Closer examination of the surface shows that river lines and terraces cover particular section of the fracture surface.

7.   CONCLUSION

The ability of using microwave energy to cure alternate un-reinforced mould materials were investigated. Satisfactory results were obtained and only three alternate mould materials were researched on. However, the process of moulding and it's materials go far beyond than just casting. The effects on using microwave heating to develop and cure the mould materials clearly shows a great improvement in the time taken to cure. Material properties were not greatly affected with the exception of Resin R 2515 which turned out to be very brittle even after

reaching it's "C state". In general, comparing both the results of the time taken to cure mould materials with the use of microwave heating has improved tremendously and could increase the overall productivity of productions. However, further research need to be done on the feasibility of implementing microwave heating to be used in the industry.

8.   REFERENCES

1. **Clark, D. E.,** and **Lewis, D.A.,** "Microwaves: Theory and Application in Materials Processing IV", 80.
2. **Yarlagadda, P K.D.V.** and **Chong, T. S.** (1998), *Journal of Materials Processing Technology* 84 162 – 174.
3. **Olofinjana, A., Yarlagadda, P K.D.V.** and **Oloyede, A.** (2001), *Int. J. of Machine Tools &Mfg.*41(2001)209– 225.
4. **Jacob, J., Chin, L. H. L.** and **Boey, F. Y. C.** (1995), *J. Mtrl. Science* 30 5321-5327.
5. **C. Nightingale** and **Day R.J.** (2002), Composites : Part A 00, *Manchester Materials Science Centre, University of Manchester & UMIST*, 000 – 000.
6. **DuBois, J. H.** and **Pribble, W. I.** (1966), *Plastics Mold Engineering,* Revised Edition, Reinhold Publishing Corporation, Chapman & Hall, Ltd., London.

GCMM 2004
Editors: Prasad K D V Yarlagadda and S Narayanan
Copyright © 2005, Vellore Institute of Technology, Vellore, India
Publisher: Narosa Publishing House Pvt. Ltd., New Delhi, India

Flow Behavior of Fiber Reinforced Thermoplastic Composites During Injection Molding

Parvin Shokri * & Naresh Bhatnagar

Mechanical Engineering Department
Indian Institute of Technology- Delhi 110016, India

E-mail: nareshb@mech.iitd.ernet.in , narbhat@hotmail.com

Abstract

The successful development of injection molded plastic parts is one of the greatest challenges faced by engineers today. This may seem like an extraordinary statement, however, by considering the number and variety of unique injection molded parts developed every day, and the complexity and the risk associated with their development, the statement becomes more understandable. Once the mold is built, a processing condition must be found that satisfactorily produces the product to specification using the mold and material. There are several programs available for simulating the melt flow during mold filling. Details of injection mold design can also be simulated before manufacturing of any part. Designing a mold with computer-aided procedures may lead to produce a part with acceptable residual stress levels. Parameters such as required pressure, mold temperature, melt temperature, rate of injection filling, and cooling time are a few among so many which can be setup before any metal is cut for making the mold, the level of research in this area is rather limited. During the injection molding of short fiber composites, not only the processing parameters and part geometry affect the mechanical properties of the molded parts but also the mold design as these mechanical properties depend on the fiber orientation, which is primarily produced by the flow state. The flow of polymer melts into the mold cavity therefore depends on the mold design, molding conditions and part design. One of the most important features of mold design is the selection of gate type and its geometry. In this work a design and fabrication of a modular spiral mold and MOLDFLOW simulation are proposed for investigating the effect of gate type and gate size on mechanical properties of molded part.

Keywords
Injection molding, Mold flow, gate type, shear stress, reinforced thermoplastics

1. INTRODUCTION

Injection molded parts are best designed through use of injection molding simulation. These programs provide a unique opportunity to evaluate mold filling, packing, cooling, product shrinkage, warpage, and structural characteristics before a mold is ever built. Although it may not be able to predict changes in the mold, process, and material that will occur with time, it can help identify designs and processes that are robust and are more tolerant of these changes.

207

Simulating programs are tools that only provide information. Success comes from using them proficiently, combined with the cooperative efforts of a skilled team. Evaluation of the advancing flow-front shows the filling pattern and makes it possible to predict weld-line location, the last point to fill, and other locations of potential air entrapment where vents are needed. Moreover it is possible to predict mechanical properties such as tensile modulus, shear stress, shear rate, Poisson's ratio, and volumetric shrinkage in different locations of the molded part. Enhancement of mechanical strength usually is the object of structural part production and it could be provided through proper design of the part and the mold. Considering mechanical properties such as shear rate and shear stress can provide sufficient information to produce products with higher quality. For example forcing a shear-rate insensitive polymer through an opening of incorrect size will cause degradation of polymer.

Gates are one of the most important elements in designing injection moulds and their type, location and size have significant effects on flow pattern. By simulating with Moldflow it was found [1] that the properly determined gate location for an automobile junction box cover leads to a better resin flow and shorter hesitation time at hinges, where the cross sectional area of the part reduces significantly. Due to increased fluidity resistance at hinges during molding several defects such as short shot or premature failure can occur with the improper selection of gate locations. In another study [2] it was seen that the type of the gate affects the arrangement of particles near the gate and particles tend to accumulate towards the free surface which results in a marked increase in part density as the distance from the gate increases so gate type and its arrangement strongly affects the microstructure of the molding. It can also be seen that [3] in injection molding of composite thermoplastics, near the midplane, fibers are aligned in the principal stretching direction provided there is significant in-plane stretching as happens in a center-gated disk while fibers are more likely to have random in-plane orientation in a film-gated strip in which there is no in-plane stretching. According to another study [4] fiber orientation

distribution across the thickness of the injection-molded parts affects tensile modulus in the flow and across flow direction. The tensile modulus for parts with thicker shell region, in which the fibers are aligned in the flow direction, is larger in the axial direction compared to the transverse direction.

In this study Moldflow software (Flow and Fiber module) is used for simulating flow pattern in injection molding of reinforced Nylon66 into a modular spiral through different types and sizes of gate design.

2. SHEAR STRESS

When a viscous material flows through a tube, the layer adjacent to the wall sticks to it and does not move. The next layer moves and slides over the wall-adhering layer. The remaining layers move with respect to each other at an increasing rate as the distance from wall to center increases. This type of shearing takes place in the injection or extrusion cylinder, and in the nozzle, sprue, runners, gates, and cavities. The unit pressure on the fluid that is subjected to the action of shearing is the shear stress. The speed of the movement of layers with respect to each other is the shear rate.

While shear stress results presented in Moldflow are not the actual residual stress in a part, it is indeed indirectly related to it. It is a measure of the factors affecting the degree of orientation of the frozen layer. Oriented materials tend to shrink more than unoriented materials, so a large amount of orientation near the edge of the melt compared to near the center will lead to higher residual stress. Higher residual stresses can result in parts stress cracking during ejection or in service. Wall-shear stress is the shear force at the solid-liquid interface, per unit area, and is proportional to the pressure gradient at each location. The polymer melt is a liquid and the first solid-liquid interface is at the mold wall. Under the current viscous flow formulation, shear stress is zero at the center of a runner or near the mid-plane of a part, and linearly increases to the solid-liquid interface at the mold wall. Thus, the wall-shear stress is the maximum value at any cross section. The shear stress should be less than the maximum recommended for the material in the material database. Considering the upper recommended limit prevents polymers from degradation. The shear-rate sensitive materials respond to the pressure by having their molecules readily shifted and aligned with the direction of flow. Their viscosity decreases and as a result flow becomes easier. They are normally of lower molecular weight and usually possess lower properties. On the other hand, the shear-rate insensitive materials consist of long chain molecules, which are so intertwined that the application of shear stress only causes greater entanglement. The net result is that the viscosity does not change with increased application of force. In addition, a danger of affecting properties may exist due to the perturbation of entanglements formed in the polymerization [5]. For reducing the shear stresses, following suggestions are presented in Moldflow manual [6].

- Local thickening at the end of flow or in thin sections
- Increasing injection speed which can result in increasing temperature, with decreasing viscosity subsequently decreasing the shear stress
- Increasing melt temperature or changing the material to a less viscous material

Since, according to the end use of product in some cases changing the material is not possible, and for each material a maximum melt temperature is defined such that increasing the melt temperature and injection speed cannot be used over a specific limit and also local thickening which affects the geometry of molding is not usually possible, additional choice for reducing shear stress could be altering the gate design. Maximum shear stress and shear rate usually occur at gate locations and different gates offer different conditions.

3. GATE DESIGN

The gate is the link between the part and the runner system. It is normally a restricted area that facilitates separation of the runner from the part. The size, shape, and placement of the gate can significantly affect the ability to successfully mold a product. The key feature of the gate is to allow for easy, or automatic, separation of the part from the runner system, while allowing for filling and packing of the part. For designing gates the following factors should be taken into consideration [6]:

- Quality of the appearance of the molded parts
- Removal of the gate
- Complexity of the cavity
- Material used
- The volume of the material injected

For parts where appearance is important, the gates should be narrow to prevent large blemishes on the surface of the part. A smaller opening will also make degating simpler. Short gate lands prevent large pressure drops and sharp angles between gates and runners should be avoided in order to prevent further pressure drop in the system. By making corners round easy flow of melt results.

3.1. Gate Size:

Gates should be large enough for suitable fill rate and small enough to seal off and prevent backflow as in packing [7]. Too small a gate may freeze off too early and can restrict the packing of the part, causing overshearing of the material, jetting and other gate related defects [8]. Larger cross-section gates are used for plastics, which are shear-sensitive, and for semi crystalline plastics in order to minimize shrinkage. The minimum gate dimension must be at least one-half of the part thickness. In Ref. [7] the gate thickness is suggested to be around 40 to 60% of the part thickness and in Ref. [8] it is recommended that the thickness of a gate, or the diameter of a gate, should be 30% to 70% of the wall thickness of the part to which it is attached. Thin parts may require gates that are thicker in proportional to the wall thickness. An inadequate gate size can cause higher mold shrinkage. A good practice suggested is to start with a gate approximately 0.625 mm, in depth and then gradually open the gate by removing metal from the mold until a good part is obtained. This should be done while varying the pressure and temperature on the molten plastic material in the injection machine. This process demands frequent loading and unloading of the mold from the machine leading to

209

expensive unproductive time of the injection-molding machine. The same process can be done easily during simulation with Moldflow in order to optimize the gate size. If proper gate size and land length are incorporated some of the molding defects such as short shots, sinks, air traps, cloudy appearance, weak parts, jetting, and shrinkage could be minimized.

3.2. Gate Types:

Gate types that are usually employed are shown in Fig.1. Each of them has its own advantage and application. Some of the commonly employed gates in unreinforced thermoplastics are described as under.

3.2.2. Fan Gate:

They are similar to a basic edge gate in that they are attached to the product at the parting line and require manual degating. The difference is that the fan gate expands out from the runner in the shape of a fan with its widest end opening to the cavity. This design spreads and slows the melt as it enters the cavity and reduces the chances of jetting. The major disadvantage is that its width causes a problem with degating.

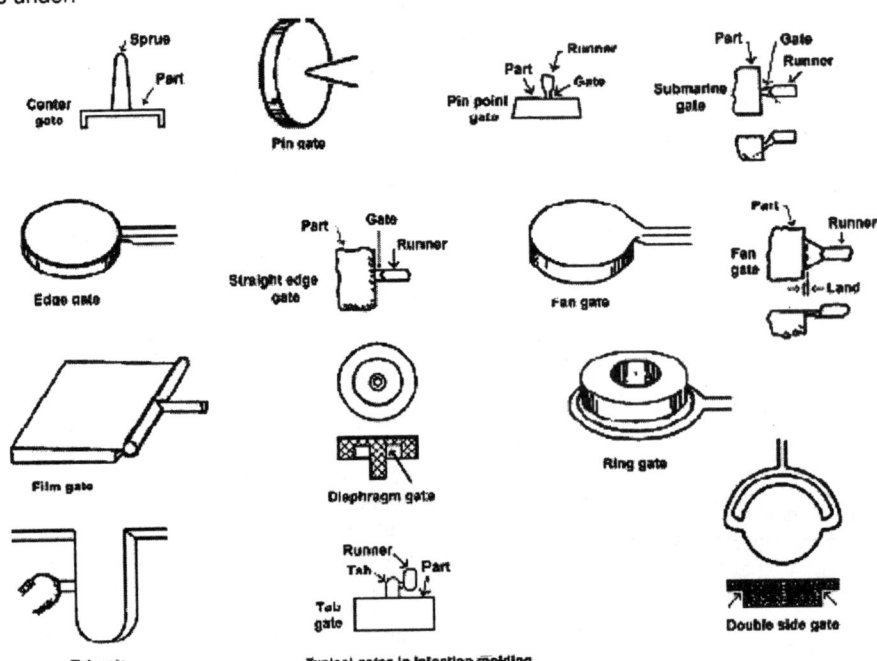

Fig. 1: Typical gates used in injection molding [9]

3.2.1. Edge Gate:

These are normally rectangular in cross section and attach to the part, along its perimeter, at the parting line of the mold. An edge gate is desirable in a multi cavity mold where parts are to be positioned for automated post-molding assembly. The primary disadvantage of the edge gate is the need for manual degating. One of the

variations of edge gate is lapped gate, which reduces the possibility of jetting.

3.2.3. Film Gate:

The film gate attempts to capture the advantages of the fan gate but utilizes less space and material. Here, the runner is attached to a gate manifold that distributes the melt along a broad thin gate and that is attached directly to the part. The disadvantage compared to the fan gate is that the flow of melt through it is less predictable. The melt entering the manifold from the runner can hesitate at the gate land in that immediate location. It then can proceed down the manifold and enter the part at the ends of the manifold where there will be no hesitation. Increasing injection rate can potentially reverse this situation. The result is that filling from this gate can be somewhat sensitive to process variations. Film gates normally work best at fast fill rates where hesitation is minimized. Fig.2 shows a few types of film gates [9].

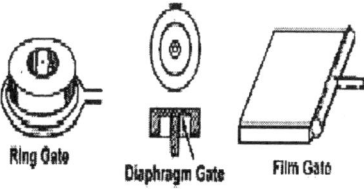

Fig. 2. Film gate designs [9]

4. MATERIAL

The material used in this work is PA66 (Polyamide 66, or Nylon 66, or poly (hexamethylene adipamide)) homopolymer that is produced by the polymerization of hexametylene diamine and adipic acid (a dibasic acid). Among commercially available polyamides, PA66 has one of the highest melting points. It is a semi crystalline-crystalline material. The grades have strength and stiffness, which is retained at elevated temperature. It does absorb moisture after molding, but the retention is not as much as in the case of PA6. Moisture absorption depends on the composition of the material, wall thickness, and environmental conditions. Dimensional stability and properties are all affected by the amount of moisture absorption, which must be taken into account for product design. Various modifiers are added to improve mechanical properties; glass is one of the most commonly used filler. The viscosity is low and therefore, it flows easily (but not as easily as PA6). This allows molding of thin components. The viscosity is very sensitive to temperature. Shrinkage is of the order of 0.01 - 0.02 mm/mm (1 - 2%). Addition of reinforcing glass fibers reduces the shrinkage to 0.2 - 1%.

Differential shrinkage in the flow and cross-flow directions is quite high. Mineral fillers yield more isotropic moldings. PA66 is resistant to most solvents but not to the strong acids or oxidizing agents. PA66 is heavily used in the automotive industry, appliance housings, and generally where impact resistance and strength are required [6].

TUFNYL S13 33% Glass fiber filled (SRF made) is a reinforced PA66, which is selected for simulations in this work. Recommended process conditions for this material by Moldflow are as follows:
Mold surface temperature = 90 °C
Melt temperature = 265 °C
Maximum shear stress = 0.5 MPa

5. SIMULATION

For analyzing the effects of gate types on mechanical properties of molded part, all the parameters except injection pressure in process setting are kept constant. In addition to recommended process conditions for TUFNYL S13 the other parameters selected are as follows:
- Injection time = 2 sec
- Velocity / pressure switch-over at 50, 75, and 100 MPa
- Cooling time = 20 sec
Fiber parameters:
- Fiber orientation boundary condition: Aligned at skin / transverse at core
- Closure approximation model: Orthotropic 3
- Micro-mechanics model: Tandon-Weng
- Thermal expansion coefficient model: Chamberlain

Injection pressures were selected in the range, which cover the recommended range for PA66 by Moldflow.
Different gate types including trapezoidal, circular, rectangular, and fan gates with equal cross sectional areas are designed for the spiral model. In addition the area of rectangular gate was increased by 50% in two different cases. In all cases land length is considered 1 mm. In Fig. 3 the FE based simulation model created in Moldflow can be seen.

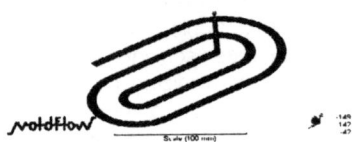

Fig.3: Moldflow simulated model

6. RESULTS & DISCUSSION

The results of simulations for analyzing the effects of gate type and size on flow length, tensile modulus, shear modulus, Poisson's ratio and volumetric shrinkage were obtained. The study indicates that the shear stress at wall for which the results are summarized in Table 1, is the only parameter that varies significantly with designed gates. All the other mechanical properties do not vary considerably with change of gate design. In Fig. 4 one of the sample result of simulation with Moldflow is shown. The fan gate gives the lowest shear stress at wall as compared to other gate types. The benefit of the slower flow with uniform melt flow front improves the melt orientation along with fibres thereby reducing stresses in the gate region of the part.

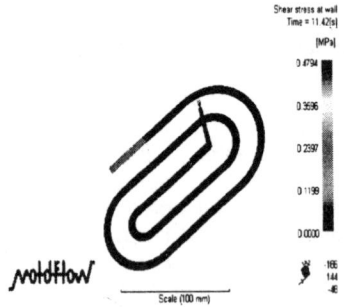

Fig. 4: Moldflow result for shear stress at wall (circular Gate 50 MPa V/P)

Reducing the residual stresses due to orientation, which is much more critical for fiber reinforced thermoplastics, and preventing materials from degradation are the two important factors for maintaining high quality production. Upper limit of shear stress at gate location, which may usually be ignored comparing to other mechanical properties of molded part or process conditions for the injection molding of unreinforced thermoplastics, has to be considered for fiber-reinforced plastics in order to reduce residual stresses and subsequent warpage.

7. CONCLUSIONS

- Gate types have significant effect on shear stress only.
- Fan gates could be a best solution in the case where changing other process parameters are not easily possible for fiber reinforced thermoplastics.

8. REFERENCES

1. **Kim, H.S, Son, J.S, Im, Y.T,** Gate location design in injection molding of an automobile junction box with integral hinges, J. *Material Processing Technology*, 2003, 140, 110-115.
2. **Ogadhoh S.O. & Papathanasiou T.D.,** Particle rearrangement during processing of glass-reinforced polystyrene by injection molding, J. *Composites - Part A*, 1996, 27A, 57-63.
3. **Bay R.S. & Tucker C.L. III,** J. *Polymer Composites*, 1992, 13, 317-331.
4. **Gupta M. & Wang K.K.,** Fiber orientation and mechanical properties of short-fiber-

GATE TYPE	AREA mm²	INJECTION PRESSURE			
		50 MPa	75 MPa	100 MPa	
(r.5 / 2.545)	4.909	0.2400	0.3771	0.5258	SHEAR STRESS AT WALL AT GATE LOCATION (MPa)
(R.25)	4.909	0.2159	0.3465	0.4838	
(4.909 / 1.0)	4.909	0.2543	0.4064	0.5606	
(8-1.0 / 4.909)	4.909	0.06-0.16	0.12-0.255	0.15-0.35	
(4.909 / 1.5)	2x4.909	0.1373	0.3063	0.4307	
(7.364 / 1.0)	2x4.909	0.2125	0.3381	0.4751	

Table1. Shear stress at gate location for different types and sizes of gates

reinforced injection molded composites: Simulated and experimental results, *J. Polymer Composites*, 1993, 14, 367-382.

5. **Dym J.B.**, Injection molds and molding (a practical manual), *Van Nostrand Reinhold Co.*, New York, 1987. MoldFlow Software Manual, V4.1, Moldflow Inc, USA

6. **MoldFlow Software Manual, V4.1**, Mold flow Inc, USA

7. **Ronald D. Beck**, Plastic Production Design, *Van Nostrand Reinhold Co.*, New York, 1980.

8. **Beaumont J.P., Nagel R., Sherman R.**, *Successful Injection Molding*, Hanser Publishers, Munich, 2002.

9. **Fisher J.M.**, Handbook of Molded Part Shrinkage and Warpage, *Plastics Design Library/ William Andrew*, Inc USA, 2003.

GCMM 2004
Editors: Prasad K D V Yarlagadda and S Narayanan
Publisher: Narosa Publishing House Pvt. Ltd., New Delhi, India

High Speed Orthogonal Machining of FRP Composites

Bhatnagar N, Kokane N G & Nayak D

Mechanical Engineering Department,
Indian Institute of Technology, Delhi 110016

E-mail: narbhat@hotmail.com, nareshb@mech.iitd.ernet.in

Abstract

The present study is conducted to understand the mechanism of chip tool interaction during machining of FRP composites. Usually laminated composite plates are used for orthogonal machining studies; however, they have a limitation of slow cutting speeds. In order to cut FRP laminates at high speed, little work has been done and as such a novel technique of fabricating filament wound tubes with different fiber orientations was developed for the purpose of work specimen. Orthogonal cutting was performed with HSS tools of two different rake angles at 3 cutting speeds and 3 feeds with constant depth of cut. Cutting forces were measured at all various combination of statistically designed full factorial experiment (2x3x3) for obtaining governing equation of thrust and cutting forces. Suitable force models based on ANOVA were developed and validated.

Keywords
FRP Composite, Machining, Filament Winding, ANOVA, Cutting Forces

1. INTRODUCTION

The genesis of composite materials lies in using the best properties of the respective constituents to the best of advantage to make a customized product. FRP composites are one of them, which use polymers, either thermoplastics or thermosets, as matrix and fibers of various types as reinforcement. The fibers of FRP composites give them their unique mechanical characteristics. The purpose of the matrix material is to bind the fibers together. By virtue of their adhesive characteristic the resins (matrix) give FRP composites the ability to transfer load to and between fibers and to protect them from environmental conditions and handling. The most common thermoset matrix materials are epoxy & polyester.

The fiber orientation has a significant influence on the cutting forces, tool wear and possible friction behavior of FRP composites. Today, fiber-reinforced plastics (FRP) occupy an important place as high performance engineering materials. Although in most of the fabrication processes FRP machining is avoided, but sometimes it is unavoidable in order to achieve the required shape and dimensional tolerances. Machining of FRP parts includes turning, drilling, milling, grinding etc.

Machining may also be desirable for making high precision components from standard shapes, prototype development and when the production volume is not large enough to justify the investment for molds and molding equipment. The FRP machining methods now in use utilize the existing machines and tools developed for machining conventional metals. Owing to the vast possible variability of material properties such as types of fibers, their orientation and also the type of the matrix material, the basic understanding of the machining characteristics of FRP is rather limited and also data on the machinabity of FRP composites is scarce.

FRP composites usually contain fibers of glass, carbon or aramid. Of these, glass and carbon fibers are brittle whereas aramid is ductile. These qualities of fibers influence the machining characteristics of composites, making dimensional and surface quality control difficult. This study presents an experimental analysis of cutting forces during orthogonal machining operation of filament wound laminated FRP composites tubes using HSS tools.

2. LITERATURE REVIEW

Though polymeric composites are being used for a long time, study of their machining characteristics started only in 1980s. Koplev et al [1] was among the first to report the orthogonal machining study on CFRP laminated composites. Most of the later researchers [2-9] also presented machining studies during the orthogonal cutting of UD-FRP composites. Some of commonality is a reduced cutting force with tool rake and lower thrust force for higher relief angle. The cutting force decreased from 0° fiber orientation to around 30° and then increased to 90° [2-5, 9]. However, the thrust force increased from 0° fiber orientation to 45° and then decreased to 90° [3-5, 9]. Some form of analytical and empirical formulations were presented to compute the cutting forces from process variables in orthogonal machining [2-4, 6-8]. The chip geometry was found to be highly fiber orientation dependent [3-5]. However, all of these publications were about the orthogonal machining operation, which is seldom found in a real life situation. Most of

these cutting were performed at a very slow cutting speed [3-9], which was well below the industrially acceptable cutting speed limits and was aimed at gaining fundamental knowledge.

Some researchers have also reported results of turning operations performed on the FRP composites [10-14]. The cutting force was found to increase with increased feed rate and depth of cut and reduced marginally with cutting speed [10, 13]. Feed force was noticed to be higher as compared to cutting force [11, 13]. Lower surface roughness was seen at low feed rate [10-11] and cutting speed. However, cutting speed and depth of cut didn't affect the roughness [10]. Higher tool wear was observed at higher cutting speed [12]. Tool geometry was reported to have more influence than tool material [10].

However, most of the turning operation was carried out for 0° fiber orientation only [11-13]. GFRP cylinder of 45° fiber orientation was used by Sang-Ook et al [10] as a unique study. On the other hand Ramulu et al [14] used a multi-directional CFRP disc for such experiments. There seems to be a dearth of a complete study taking process parameters, tool and work material geometries into consideration.

In this paper, a comprehensive study of orthogonal cutting of GFRP tube is conducted. The GFRP specimen is manufactured for different fiber orientations by changing the wind angle in the filament winding process. Tool rake, cutting speed, and feed rate are varied for the cutting experiment for a constant depth of cut equivalent to the tube thickness.

3. MANUFACTURING FILAMENT WOUND GFRP TUBES

The material for this study is glass fiber roving with epoxy as filament wound tubes. The tubes were made using the conventional filament winding process. Passing the fiber strand through an epoxy resin bath system wet the glass fiber roving. Before winding, the mandrel is properly covered with release agent so that cured tube does not get stuck to the mandrel. The mandrel speed was kept constant at 38 rpm. Three tube specimens were manufactured with different fiber angles of ±50º, 60º & 70º.

4. MEASUREMENT OF FORCES

Various researchers concluded that the machining forces while machining FRP composites vary according to the fiber orientation. The process parameters like feed, speed and rake angle of tool may also affect the machining forces. Therefore, the orthogonal machining tests were conducted on a lathe machine at high speeds to cut glass fiber filament wound tubes of various fiber orientations. The HSS cutting tool of Zero deg inclination angle was mounted on the dynamometer, the tools were ground to two different rake angles for orthogonal cutting of GFRP specimen. The work pieces prepared in the tubular shape with a wall thickness of 3mm were machined from one end. The cutting and thrust force components were measured using a Kistler type 9257A three-component piezoelectric dynamometer. The induced charge signals of cutting and thrust forces were amplified by two Kistler type 5001-charge amplifiers and send to the digital storage oscilloscope for display, storage and further analysis.

5. TREATMENT DESIGN

A full factorial design was used with different ranges of feed, rake angle, cutting speed and fiber orientation as the four factors. Specifically, three levels of feed (0.04, 0.07 and 0.1mm /rev) were tested at three levels of cutting speed (11, 19 and 32 m/min) and two levels of tool rake angle (10° and 20°). Three levels of fiber orientation (50°, 60 ° &70°) were also taken to see the effect of fiber orientation on the forces. Each of the 54 treatment combinations of feed, speed, and fiber orientation and rake angle was assigned to two replicates. Feed is in mm/rev, fiber orientation is in degree, cutting speed is in m/min and rake angle is in degree.

6. RESULTS & DISCUSSIONS

Fig.1 to 6 shows in general the individual trends of one parameter variation while all other parameters were maintained constant. Fig 1 shows the effect of fiber orientation on thrust force, which continuously increases with increase of fiber orientation. Fig.2 and Fig.3 shows the effect of cutting speed and feed on thrust force, both the figures show an increasing trend with increase of either speed or feed. Similar type of plots for cutting forces is shown in Fig 4, 5 and 6.

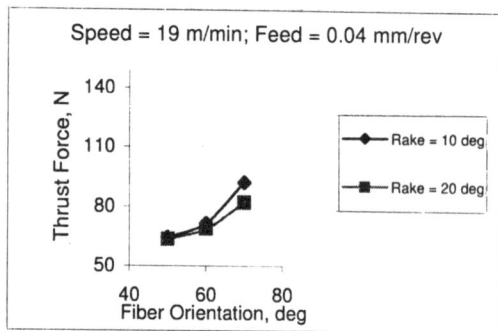

Fig .1: Effect of fiber orientation on thrust force

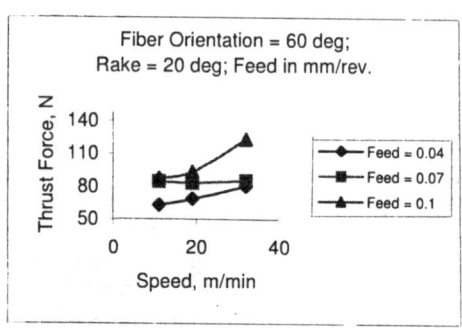

Fig .2: Effect of cutting speed on thrust force

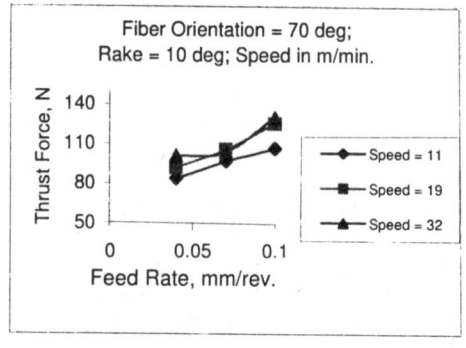

Fig .3: Effect of feed on thrust

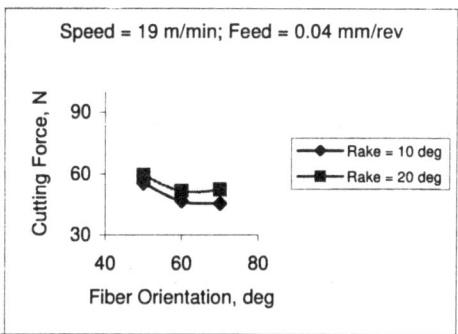

Fig. 4: Effect of fiber orientation on cutting force

Fig 4. Shows the variation of cutting force w.r.t fiber orientation, which decreases with the increase of fiber orientation, this behaviour is just opposite to the thrust force variation and is found typical for filament wound tubes as the cutting force usually increases with the increase of fiber orientation in a laminated plate specimen.

In Fig 5 and 6 the variation of cutting forces with the cutting speed and feed increases continuously similar to the thrust force variation.

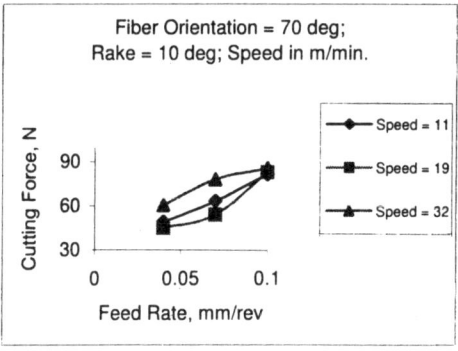

Fig .5: Effect of cutting speed on Cutting force

From the statistical results it is shown that the effect of feed on both the forces is highly significant. Forces increase with the increase in feed and cutting speed from 11m/min to 32m/min. One way and two way ANOVA was conducted and results tabulated. In order to give a brief understanding, the expanded analysis of variance is summarized as sample in Table 1

after completing one way and two-way ANOVA for thrust force that is found to be higher than the cutting forces with all process parameter variation. ANOVA has shown that the effect of rake angle is not much significant in case of both the forces. But the interaction effects of rake angle along with the other factors do exists. Similar table of cutting force parameter was also developed and analyzed based on which the cutting force and thrust force prediction models are evolved and the following conclusions are derived.

7. CONCLUSIONS

1. In orthogonal machining of glass fiber filament tubes the chip formation is in the form of powder and no continuous chip is obtained at any speed, feed combination.

2. The thrust force while machining composite tube with $\pm 70^\circ$ fiber orientation is maximum and it is minimum with $\pm 50^\circ$ whereas cutting force is less while machining fibers at $\pm 70^0$ fiber orientation but is higher for $\pm 50^\circ$ fiber orientation.

3. ANOVA shows a marked effect of three factors viz. feed, cutting speed, and fiber orientation with maximum effect of feed, next fiber orientation and then cutting speed respectively on **Thrust Force**. The effect of rake angle is very less compared to other factors at high cutting speeds. But the interaction effect of rake angle along with other factors is found significant.

4. From the expanded analysis of variance it is seen that both linear and quadratic effects of cutting speed are also significant whereas for remaining three factors viz. feed, fiber orientation and rake angle, linear effect itself is significant.

5. From a similar table it was seen that the effect of feed, fiber orientation and cutting speed is significant whereas the effect of rake angle is negligible in case of **Cutting Force**.

6. From the expanded analysis of variance it is seen that both linear and quadratic effects of fiber orientation are significant whereas the remaining three factors viz. feed, cutting speed and rake angle linear

Table 1. A sample two-way ANOVA showing linear and quadratic effects for *Thrust Force*

Source of variation	SOS	DOF	MS	Fo	F0.01
Feed (mm/rev) f	17088.21	2	8544.105	249.3448	5.02
f_L	17017.51	1	17017.51	496.6263	7.13
f_Q	70.69806	1	70.69806	2.063199	7.13
Fiber orientation (degree)	5942.533	2	2971.266	86.71122	5.02
L	5779.738	1	5779.738	168.6715	7.13
Q	162.7951	1	162.7951	4.750892	4.02[a]
Cutting speed (m/min) s	7264.926	2	3632.463	106.0071	5.02
S_L	6946.668	1	6946.668	202.7264	7.13
S_Q	318.2574	1	318.2574	9.287786	7.13
Rake angle (degree) r	850.392	1	850.392	24.8172	7.13
F interaction	274.2578	4	68.56445	2.000934	4.11
f $_{L \cdot L}$	135.5088	1	135.5088	3.954588	2.8[b]
f $_{L \cdot Q}$	63.97334	1	63.97334	1.86695	7.13
f $_{Q \cdot L}$	8.865506	1	8.865506	0.258724	7.13
f $_{Q \cdot Q}$	65.91016	1	65.91016	1.923473	7.13
Fs interaction	1590.57	4	397.6424	11.6045	4.11
$fs_{L \cdot L}$	606.6252	1	606.6252	17.7033	7.13
$fs_{L \cdot Q}$	206.7604	1	206.7604	6.033942	4.02[a]
$fs_{Q \cdot L}$	518.4729	1	518.4729	15.13073	7.68
$fs_{Q \cdot Q}$	258.7111	1	258.7111	7.55003	4.02[a]
Fr interaction	66.33146	2	33.16573	0.967884	5.49
S interaction	175.6498	4	43.91246	1.281508	4.11
S $_{L \cdot L}$	160.4545	1	160.4545	4.682585	4.02[a]
S $_{L \cdot Q}$	0.3969	1	0.3969	0.011583	7.13
S $_{Q \cdot L}$	1.428025	1	1.428025	0.041674	7.13
S $_{Q \cdot Q}$	13.37037	1	13.37037	0.390191	7.13
r interaction	295.1606	2	147.5803	4.306873	3.17[a]
Fs interaction	579.9777	8	72.49722	2.115705	2.12[a]
f $^2 s^2$	113.3623	2	56.68114	1.65414	5.02
f $^2 s$	356.9199	2	178.4599	5.208042	5.02
f s^2	109.6811	2	54.84056	1.600426	5.49
F s	0.014453	2	0.007227	0.000211	5.49
Sr interaction	215.1389	2	107.5694	3.139226	3.17[a]
F r interaction	102.5521	4	25.63803	0.748201	3.68
Fsr interaction	393.1953	4	98.29883	2.868679	3.68
sr interaction	211.9444	4	52.98609	1.546307	3.68
f sr interaction	347.4297	8	43.42872	1.267391	2.86
Error	1850.376	54	34.26623		
Total	37248.64				

[a] and [b] are significant at 5 and 10 percent

To find the above coefficients general regression method was used. In this study MATLAB 6.1 is used to find these coefficients.

After finding the coefficients the final **Thrust force model** is given as under;

$$F_T = 1.3825 + 855.68f - 0.94279\theta + 0.022986\theta^2 + 0.042503s + 0.06772s^2 + 2.1663r$$
$$- 0.70176f\theta + 55.681fs - 2.9872fs^2 - 580.84f^2s + 28.264f^2s^2 - 7.4194fr - 0.037215\theta r - 0.0017409f t^2 s$$

And the **Cutting force model** is given as;

$$F_C = 6.17 + 1283.32f - 2090.58f^2 + 0.78s - 0.27\theta + 0.8r - 0.21f^2\theta^2 - 6.99fs$$
$$- 15.69fr + 0.0000382s\theta^2$$

effect for feed and cutting speed are significant, but effect of rake angle is not significant.

7. Based on design of experiments new force models for thrust force and cutting forces for GFRP filament wound tubes are proposed.

8. REFERENCES

1. **Koplev A., Lystrup Aa. & Vorm T.**: The cutting process, chips, and cutting forces in machining *CFRP, Composites Part A*, 1983, 14, 4, 371-376.
2. **Takeyama H. & Iijima N.**: Machinability of glass fiber reinforced plastics and application of ultrasonic machining, *Annals of CIRP*, 37, 1, 93-96.
3. **Bhatnagar N., Ramakrishnan N., Naik N. K. & Komanduri R.**: On the machining of fiber reinforced plastic (FRP) composite laminates, *International Journal of Machine Tool manufacture*, 35, 5, 701-716.
4. **Wang D. H., Ramulu M. & Arola D.**: Orthogonal cutting mechanisms of Graphite/Epoxy composite. Part I. Uni-directional Laminate, *International Journal of Machine Tool manufacture*, 35, 12, 1623-1638.
5. **Arola D., Ramulu M. & Wang D. H.**: Chip formation in orthogonal trimming of graphite/epoxy composite, Composites Part A, 27A, 121-133.
6. **Caprino G. & Nele L.**: Cutting forces in orthogonal cutting of uni-directional GFRP composites, *Journal of Engineering Materials Technology*, 118, 3, 419-425.
7. **Caprino G., Santo L. & Nele L.**: On the origin of cutting forces in machining unidirectional composite materials, 3rd Biennial Engineering Systems Design and Analysis Conference (ESDA'96), Montpellier, 1-4 July, 83-89.
8. **Caprino G., Santo L. & Nele L.**: Interpretation of size effect in orthogonal machining of composite materials. Part I: Unidirectional glass fiber reinforced plastics, Composites Part A, 29A, 887-892.
9. **Zhang L. C., Zhang H. J. & Wang X. M.**: A force prediction model for cutting unidirectional fiber reinforced plastics, Machining Science and Technology, 5, 3, 293-305.
10. **Sang-Ook An., Lee E. S. & Noh S. L.**: A study on the cutting characteristics of glass fiber reinforced plastics with respect to tool materials and geometries, *Journal of Materials Processing Technology*, 68, 60-67.
11. **Rahman M., Ramakrishna S., Prakash J. R. S. & Tan D. C. G.**: Machinability study of carbon fiber reinforced composite, *Journal of Materials Processing Technology*, 89-90, 292-297.
12. **Ferreira J. R., Coppini N. L. & Miranda G. W. A.**: Machining optimization in carbon fiber reinforced composite materials, *Journal of Materials Processing Technology*, 92-93, 135-140.
13. **Satheesha, M., Jain V. K. & Kumar P.**: Investigation into machining of GFRP composites, *Processing of Advanced Materials*, 1, 1-10.
14. **Ramulu M., Faridnia M., Garbini J. L. & Jorgensen J. E.**: Machining of graphite/epoxy composite materials with polycrystalline diamond (PCD) tools, *Transaction of ASME Journal of Engineering materials and Technology*, 113, 430-436.
15. **Montgomery D.C**, "Design And Analysis of Experiments", 1976, 2nd Ed. *John Willy and Sons, NY.*

219

GCMM 2004
-Editors: Prasad K D V Yarlagadda and S Narayanan
Copyright © 2005, Vellore Institute of Technology, Vellore, India
Publisher: Narosa Publishing House Pvt. Ltd., New Delhi, India

Statistical Modelling of Thin Epoxy Resin Layers curing using Microwave Energy

Klaus Berg & Prasad K D V Yarlagadda

School of Mechanical, Manufacturing and Medical Engineering
Queensland University of Technology, Brisbane, Q 4001, Australia

E-mail: y.prasad@qut.edu.au

Abstract

In this research microwave curing is used to support fast curing in order to prevent changes to the form and shape of a selective applied layer. In this investigation the layer consists of a liquid mixture of epoxy resin with aluminium particles is cured using microwave heating and is further used in rapid product development. The issue of statistical modelling of the fast curing process of thin epoxy resin layers using microwave heating is addressed in this paper. The modelling by a linear regression method is based on information available from the curing process as well as from data collected performing the Dynamic Scanning Calorimetry analysis. To reach the state of dimensional stability, the curing temperature of the layer material was controlled using two options. First, through the reduction of the microwave power and second, through altering the turntable speed so that the microwave exposure time of the layer was monitored. This operation was controlled using appropriate computer software.

Keywords

Epoxy, Resin Layers, Microwave Energy

1. INTRODUCTION AND BACKGROUND

The main objective of this study is to determine whether microwave heating could facilitate rate of curing of epoxy resins, thus achieving rapid solidification. Experiments were carried out to determine how quickly a thin layer of resin could be cured to the point that it is not flowing any more, which is important in the building a new product by using one of the rapid product development techniques. Curing is a result of exothermic reaction that increases the material's temperature, which in turn accelerates the curing. Therefore temperature change of a thin layer of resin exposed to a microwave field was measured. The temperature change

was due to exothermic curing reaction and absorption of energy through interactions with microwave field.

Statistical models of the processes studied have been developed based on number of experiments designed by using statistical composite design of the experiments. Regression analysis has been used to determine relationships between the variables and the experimental outcome. In this case the variables were mixture composition of the resin, power of the microwave field applied and exposure time of the specimens to the microwave field. In all cases linear regression models using stepwise approach have been developed using SPlus software. The quality of all models was assessed using graphical diagnostic tools and descriptive estimates of the coefficients. The graphical diagnostic tool is a set of plots that summarises the basic statistical properties of the model derived from the data.

2. EXPERIMENTAL DETAILS

Specimens in the form of a thin layer of epoxy resin were exposed to a microwave field. The time of exposure and the mixture composition of the specimens are shown in

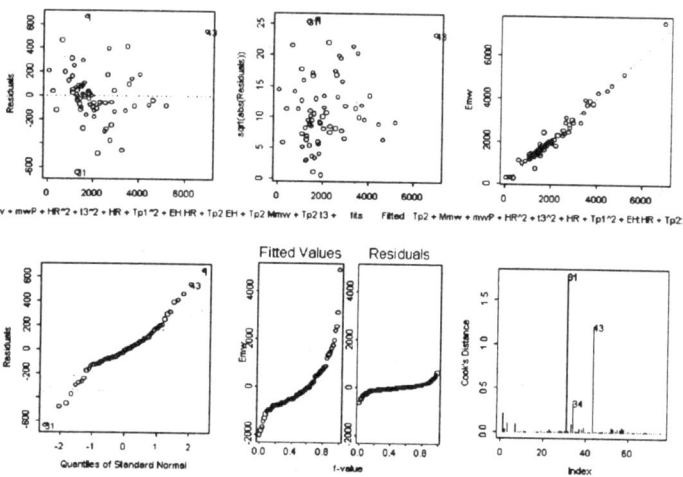

Fig. 1: Example of diagnostic plots

Table 1. The microwave heating system used in these experiments is shown in Figure 2. Each sample was manually applied to a thin laboratory glass slide forming 0.4 to 0.55mm thick layer of epoxy resin. The specimen was placed 3mm below the tapered waveguide inside the microwave cavity, layed horizontally across a glass tube that was used as support structure. The surface temperature of each sample was measured using an IR thermopile that was positioned alongside the tapered waveguide. Figure 3 shows diagrammatically the temperature change of the specimen during the experiments.

The temperature was measured at the surface of the specimen. There are three distinctive stages. The first one reflects the rise of the specimen's temperature due to the heat transfer from the environment after the sample was placed in the microwave cavity. At this stage the sample's temperature increased during the time t_x. The area "E_{heat}" is proportional to the amount of heat absorbed. The value of E_{heat} varied with each experiment as the starting temperature varied. The manual tuning of the microwave system made it difficult to

maintain, over time, the appropriate impedance resulting in loss of significant portion of the microwave energy, which affectively diverted to heat the microwave system's hardware rather than the sample.

By continuously using the cavity for heating one specimen after the other, the temperature inside the cavity was gradually rising so the next sample placed in the cavity quickly absorbed heat to equilibrate the temperature. The time elapsed from placing the sample inside the cavity until starting the experiment was not recorded. However, it was estimated that it took on average approximately 10sec to the moment of commencing microwave heating. Thus the temperature T_{p1} was variable and the heat energy absorbed by the specimen prior to microwave exposure (E_{heat}) is proportional to:

$$E_{heat} \sim 1/2 \cdot t_x \cdot T_{pl} \text{ ------ (1)}$$

Where t_x is time of heating the specimen prior the microwave heating (sec) and T_{p1} is temperature at the beginning of the microwave exposure (°C).

The equation 1 describes the heat transfer to the specimen by conduction and radiation. Maintaining fixed temperature T_{p1} would require controlled cooling of the microwave cavity after each experiment.

The second stage starts at the temperature (T_{p1}) when the specimen is heated by microwave radiation until it reaches the predetermined maximum temperature (T_{p2}) of 240°C. The heat energy absorbed by the specimen is proportional to the area "E_{mw}":

$$E_{mw} \sim 1/2 \cdot (t_2 - t_1)(T_{p2} - T_{p1}) \cdots (2)$$

Table 1: Summary of test-table includes mw-power, exposure time and mixture ratios

Test	MW-power	Exp-time	Hardener	Aluminum	Resin	Hardener	Aluminum
No	(W)	(sec)	(ml)	(grams)	(wt%)	(wt%)	(wt%)
1	325	37.5	0.475	0.475	51.2	24.4	24.4
2	775	37.5	0.475	0.475	51.2	24.4	24.4
3	325	92.5	0.475	0.475	51.2	24.4	24.4
4	775	92.5	0.475	0.475	51.2	24.4	24.4
5	325	37.5	0.825	0.475	20.6	35.9	43.5
6	775	37.5	0.825	0.475	20.6	35.9	43.5
7	325	92.5	0.825	0.475	20.6	35.9	43.5
8	775	92.5	0.825	0.475	20.6	35.9	43.5
9	325	37.5	0.475	0.825	43.4	20.7	35.9
10	775	37.5	0.475	0.825	43.4	20.7	35.9
11	325	92.5	0.475	0.825	43.4	20.7	35.9
12	775	92.5	0.475	0.825	43.4	20.7	35.9
13	325	37.5	0.825	0.825	37.8	31.1	31.1
14	775	37.5	0.825	0.825	37.8	31.1	31.1
15	325	92.5	0.825	0.825	37.8	31.1	31.1
16	775	92.5	0.825	0.825	37.8	31.1	31.1
17	1000	65.0	0.650	0.650	43.4	28.3	28.3
18	550	120.0	0.650	0.650	43.4	28.3	28.3
19	550	65.0	1.000	0.650	37.7	37.7	24.6
20	550	65.0	0.650	1.000	37.7	24.6	37.7
21	100	65.0	0.650	0.650	43.4	28.3	28.3
22	550	10.0	0.650	0.650	43.4	28.3	28.3
23	550	65.0	0.300	0.650	51.3	15.4	33.3
24	550	65.0	0.650	0.300	51.3	33.3	15.4
25	550	65.0	0.650	0.650	43.4	28.3	28.3

Where t_2, t_1 are finishing and starting time of microwave exposure (sec) and T_{p2}, T_{p1} are maximum and starting temperature of microwave exposure (°C). Rise of the temperature from T_{p1} to T_{p2} over time t_e represents the heating rate (HR) of the specimen. This heating rate is determined by the interaction of the specimen with the microwave field, which in turn depends on mixture composition of the specimen. Thus HR should uniquely describe the reaction of specimens with the microwave field. Therefore E_{mw} that is proportional to microwave energy absorbed by the specimen can be described as follows:

$$E_{mw} \cong 1/2 \cdot HR \cdot t_e^2 \; \text{------ (3)}$$

Where HR is heat rate coefficient (°C/sec) and t_e is time of exposure (sec). The heat rate coefficient (HR) can be calculated using the data from the experiments.

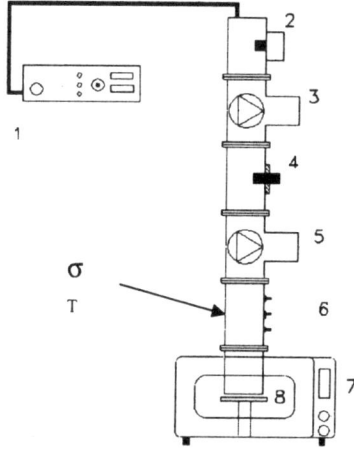

(1) Microwave power control unit,
(2) Magnetron,
(3) First circulator,
(4) Attenuator,
(5) Second circulator,
(6) Three stub tuner,
(7) Modified commercial microwave oven,
(8) Sample holder or modeling table

Fig. 2: Schematic diagram of microwave system for curing epoxy resin

The third stage relates to holding the temperature (T_{p2}) at a predetermined value of 240 °C. The experiments were designed based on mixture composition, exposure time and microwave power. It was found that in some cases specimens would be heated to high temperatures and burnt. To avoid this, at a predetermined temperature the microwave power was switched on and off to maintain constant temperature. The maximum temperature of 240°C was chosen after it was found that exposing the specimen up to 240°C for a limited period of time would not damage the material. The

temperature was controlled by the IR-thermopile through switching the microwave power on and off. The microwave heat energy balanced the energy lost through radiation to the environment until the experiment was completed. After completing the experiment, the specimen was cooled rapidly and stored at -10°C in order to prevent further curing reactions.

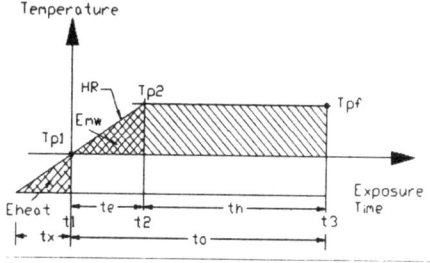

Fig. 3: Temperature profile of microwave cured sample

3. MODELLING OF HEATING RATE COEFFICIENT

The following linear relationship has been determined.

$$HR = 59.7 - 0.541 \cdot T_{p1} - 2.77 \cdot H +$$
$$0.02694 \cdot M_{mw} + 0.01359 \cdot H^2 +$$
$$0.01785 \cdot (T_{p1} \cdot H) + 8.3 \cdot 10^{-4} \cdot (mwP \cdot H)$$
$$- 7.9 \cdot 10^{-4} \cdot (H \cdot M_{mw}) - 8.74 \cdot 10^{-6} \cdot$$
$$(mwP \cdot M_{mw}) - 4.1 \cdot 10^{-4} \cdot (mwP \cdot Al)$$
$$+ 0.01205 \cdot (H \cdot Al) \qquad \text{------------ (4)}$$

Where HR is heating rate coefficient (°C/sec), T_{p1} is temperature of the specimen at the commencement of the microwave heating (°C), H is weight percent of hardener in the epoxy mixture (wt%), M_{mw} is mass of the specimen in grams, mwP is nominal microwave power applied in the experiment (W) and Al is weight percent of the aluminium powder in the mixture (wt%).

The diagnostic plot of the "Partial residual plot (top left) indicates a normal, independent distribution. The "Square root of absolute residuals against fitted values", (top centre) does not indicate a specific structure. There are some outliers but not of major influence to the regression model. The "Response versa the Fit" plot (top right) indicates the usefulness of the fit as a model. Most of the values are superimposed on the dotted line, indicating a normal distribution. The "Normal quantile plot of residuals" (bottom left) shows that the residuals are superimposed the zero mark (dotted line), indicating that the errors distribution is normal. The "Residual–Fit Spread or r-f plot" (bottom centre) shows the proportion of the variability between the fitted values and the residuals. In our case, the spread of the fitted values is larger than the residuals confirming that our model is valid. The "Cook's Distance" plot is useful for observation of individual regression coefficients. In this model there is no large value that would affect the model negatively and require isolation.

4. MODELING OF ABSORPTION OF MICROWAVE HEAT ENERGY

Following relationship for E_{mw} has been determined.

$$E_{mw} = 50.1278 \cdot T_{p2} - 9.005 \cdot M_{mw}$$
$$+ 55.9499 \cdot HR^2 + 0.2425 \cdot t_h^2$$
$$- 1506.9196 \cdot HR + 0.1727 \cdot T_{p1}^2$$
$$+ 1.311 \cdot (EH \cdot HR) - 0.0822 \cdot (T_{p2} \cdot EH)$$
$$+ 0.0365 (T_{p2} \cdot M_{mw}) + 0.0014 \cdot (mwP \cdot t_h)$$
$$- 0.0015 \cdot (T_{p2} \cdot t_h) \text{-------------} \quad (5)$$

Where E_{mw} is proportional to microwave heat energy absorbed by the specimen, HR is heating rate coefficient (deg/sec), EH is proportional to energy absorbed by the specimen due to microwave exposure, t_h is time during which the temperature was held constant (sec), T_{p1} is temperature of the specimen at the commencement of the microwave heating (°C), T_{p2} is temperature of the specimen at the end of the microwave heating (°C), M_{mw} is mass of the specimen in grams, mwP is nominal microwave power applied in the experiment.

Analysing the diagnostic plots at the "absolute residuals against fitted values" (top left) identifies values that do not fit inside the visualised structure of the residuals. The plot "Square root of absolute residual against fitted values" (top centre) compares the spread of the fitted values with the spread of the residuals. The distribution of values identifies some

concentration that could have an affect on our result. The plot of "quantities of standard normal-residuals" (left bottom) superimposes the zero or normal distribution line of model errors. The plot of "partial residual" (top right) confirms the linearity and has indicated some incompatible residuals. The "Cook's distance plot" (right bottom) reflects that most of the values have been useful for the regression model, and also reflects the standard deviation. In both regression models the heat rate HR-model is based on variables, however, the absorption of microwave produced heat energy E_{mw} includes in the structure the heat rate function (HR) and therefore makes the E_{mw} function more complex. The absorption of microwave energy progresses exponentially with the square of the exposure time. Analysing the model of the heat rate coefficient (HR), it was noticed that five variables are important. These five variables were used as single values and in combination to develop the model shown for the heat rate (HR). The important variable, absolute value, is the hardener (H) with 82%, followed by the starting temperature (T_{p1}) with 16%. The variables such as mass of specimen, aluminum content and microwave power share the remaining 2% of the HR-model. The absorbed microwave heat energy (E_{mw}) is a combination of the heat rate (HR) and additional variables as shown in the model. Most of the model parameters are not material related, where the main contribution comes from the heat rate (HR) followed by the final temperature (T_{p2}) and the mass of the specimen (M_{mw}) with 7.7%, together they share 98.3% of the model. The starting temperature (T_{p1}) which was still an important variable for modeling (HR) slipped to 0.15% and hardly contributes to the E_{mw}-model. The rest of variables participate in combination at the absorbed microwave heat energy (E_{mw}) and achieved about 1.7% of the model.

5. MICROWAVE EXPOSURE ESTIMATE

The mathematical analysis of microwave heating involves equations that are coupled to Maxwell's equations of electromagnetic radiation. The closest conventional heating method equivalent to microwave heating is the method of 'transient heat flow in systems with negligible internal resistance', under the assumption that the internal thermal resistance of the system is low and that the temperature at any point of the system is uniform through thermal diffusion. Based on the analytical modelling performed in this chapter, we know that the heat rate (HR) multiplied with the exposure time (t_e) will cure a layer of epoxy resin. The heat energy absorbed by the sample that is proportional to the microwave energy, was calculated in the following paragraph under the assumption of no heat loss to the environment. The heating process of any material is represented in equation 6.

$$-c_p \cdot \rho \cdot VdT = \overline{h} \cdot A_s \cdot (T - T_o) \cdot d\theta$$
---- (6)

Where c_p is specific heat of dielectric(J/kg °K), V is volume of the dielectric(m^3), h is average heat transfer coefficient (J/m^2 sec °K), A_s is surface area of dielectric(m^2), T, T_0 are temperature change (°C) and $d\theta$ is time factor at temperature change(sec).

We consider that the temperature within a material is substantially constant at any instant and the energy balance over a small time period is zero. Microwave energy is converted into heat by the dielectric material property at a temperature rate following distinct parameters. The relationship between the microwave power (P) and the amount of heat (Q_h) produced over time (t) is presented in the equation 7

$$P = \frac{Q_h}{t} = M_a c_p (T - T_o)/t \ (W) ---- (7)$$

Where P is power(W), Q_h is amount of heat(kJ) and t is time(sec)

The temperature rate is calculated using the following equation [7]:

$$(T - T_o)/t = \frac{0.556 \cdot 10^{-10} \varepsilon_{eff}^{''} f E_{rms}^2}{\rho c_p} \ (°C/sec)$$
-- (8)

Where M_a is mass of dielectric(kg), c_p is specific heat(kJ/kg °C), T is final temperature (°C), T_o is starting temperature (°C), and ε_{eff} is affective loss factor (farad/m). The power consumed by the dielectric material can be calculated using the temperature difference versa the time factor, as indicated in eqn.8. This calculation, however, presents an average value of the power consumption consumed by the dielectric material. For a more

accurate calculation we should consider the electric field strength before calculation of the average power consumption.

6. CONCLUSIONS

The outcome of the models confirms a close relationship between thermodynamic equations of transient heat flow in systems with negligible internal resistance (see Eqn.6) and analytical modelling presented in two regression models such as the heating rate (HR) and the microwave energy absorbed (Emw). It can be observed that over the exposure time the heat of the sample increases, based on the heat rate over exposure time. Finally, the epoxy resin mixture is cured at the glass transition temperature. The intention was to design and develop a new technique of fast curing the material mixtures using microwave heating. A major part of this research is focused on determining the optimal material combination to enable fast curing. To this end it was important to generate an extensive experimental data set in order to understand the relationship between microwave power, exposure time and the material for fast curing. Therefore, a special waveguide was designed to cure samples of epoxy resin amine mixtures. In order to understand and to specify the curing state of microwave exposed samples, samples were analysed using Dynamic Scanning Calorimetry. In line with the curability of epoxy resin amine layers.

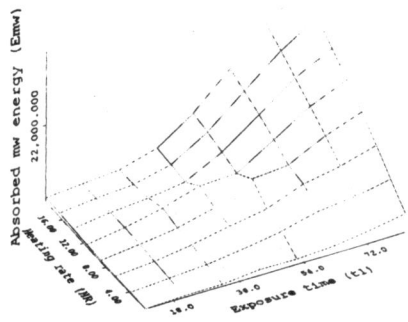

7. REFERENCES

1. **Chan L. and Gourdenne A.** (1992), *Polymeric Materials: Science and Engineering, Proceedings.*
2. **Ciriscioli P.R. and Springer G.S.** (1989), Proc. of *34th Int. SAMPE Symposium.*
3. **Demeuse M.T.** (1992), *Polymeric Materials: Science and Engg., Proc.,* 66, pp. 428 - 429.
4. **George G.A., Cole-Clarke P., and F. G. John N. St.** (1991), *Journal of Applied Polymer Science,* vol. 42, pp. 643 - 657.
5. **Iskander M.F., Lauf R. J., and Sutton W.** (1994), *Materials Research Society Symposium Proceedings,* Sab, California.
6. **Lam L.** (1999), "S-PLUS," S-PLus for Windows ed. Amsterdam: CSIRO, Sydney.
7. **Metaxas R. and Meredith R.J.** (1983), *Industrial Microwave Heating.* London: Peter Peregrinus Ltd.
8. **Yarlagadda P. and Loon N.H.** (1999), *AFDM'99, Korea,*Sept 99, pp. 609-616.
9. **Zhao H., Turner I., Yarlagadda P., and Berg K.** (2001), *Int. J. of Advanced Manufacturing Tech.,* vol. 17, pp. 916-927.

GCMM 2004
Editors: Prasad K D V Yarlagadda and S Narayanan
Copyright © 2005, Vellore Institute of Technology, Vellore, India
Publisher: Narosa Publishing House Pvt. Ltd., New Delhi, India

Strain Toughening of Composites for Thrust Minimization during Drilling

Arul S, Vijayaraghavan L, & Malhotra, S K*

Department of Mechanical Engineering
* Composites Technology Centre
Indian Institute of Technology Madras
Chennai – 600 036, India.

Email: sa_arul@yahoo.com

Abstract
Drilling of polymeric composites calls for online monitoring of process indicators, least the drilling of composite parts should experience delamination / debonding. The main contributing factor for such defects is drill thrust. Hence for thrust constrained drilling techniques such as modifying drill point, including web-thinning, Zherov point, tripod drill and vibration assisted drilling have been implemented. The present study illustrates a new method for defect constrained drilling. By inducing strain toughening in polymeric composite, it was possible to bring down the drill thrust and consequently the defects.

Keywords
Delamination, thrust, delamination factor, strain toughening

1. INTRODUCTION

Composite materials consist of two or more microconstituents that differ in form and chemical composition and which are insoluble in each other. However, many composite materials are composed of only two phases: one termed the matrix, which is continuous and surrounds the other phase, often termed the dispersed phase. The objective of having two or more constituents is to take advantage of the superior properties of both materials without compromising on the weakness of either.

Fiber reinforced composites are well recognized for their superior properties and are widely used in various field of science and technology. Composite materials possess problems such as, delamination, debonding, fiber pull-out, matrix crazing and thermal alterations during machining due to their anisotropic, inhomogeneous and abrasive nature. The quality of the machined parts is strongly dependent on drilling parameters. Many researchers have examined the delamination in drilling has been recognized as one major problem [1-2]. It is generally regarded as a resin or matrix dominated failure behavior, which usually occurs in the interply region. It appears as peeling away of the bottom ply or plies and is attributed to the thrust of the drill which pushes the layers apart rather than cutting through them.

227

The presence of delamination reduces the stiffness and strength of a laminate and hence its load carrying capacity. Delamination can often be the limiting factor in the use of composite materials for structural applications, particularly when subjected to compressive, shear and fatigue type of loads and when exposed to moisture and other aggressive environments over a long period of time. Thrust generated during the drilling operation is identified as responsible for delamination [3]. And it is believed that there is a 'critical thrust force' below which the damage can be constrained / eliminated. Thus, searching for new drilling methods to control the delamination is imperative. Hence for thrust constrained drilling techniques such as modifying drill point, including web-thinning, Zherov point, tripod drill and vibration assisted drilling have been implemented.

The present study illustrates a new method for defects constrained drilling. Polymeric composites subjected to low frequency fatigue loading, exhibited a marginal rise in the stiffness, depending upon the loading [4]. By inducing strain toughening in polymeric composite, it was possible to bring down the drill thrust and consequently the associated defects.

2. EXPERIMENTAL WORK

The experimental set up is shown in Fig.1, in which the workpiece had been mounted on the dynamometer of the Deckel milling machine, and the spindle was fed to the workpiece. The thrust force and toque during drilling were monitored by Kistler two-component dynamometer (model 9271A). The resulting charge signals were converted into output voltages proportional to the forces sustained and then these voltage signals were amplified by two charge amplifiers (model 5015) and managed via a data acquisition system.

The low frequency high amplitude fatigue test rig is shown in Fig.2. In that the work piece was subjected to low frequency high amplitude fatigue loads as per Table 1. The main concept of induced vibration to the work piece before drilling was to develop strain in the material before drilling. The Experimental details are shown in Table 1.

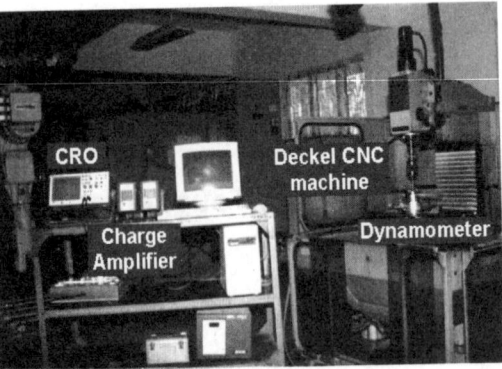

Fig.1: Experimental set-up

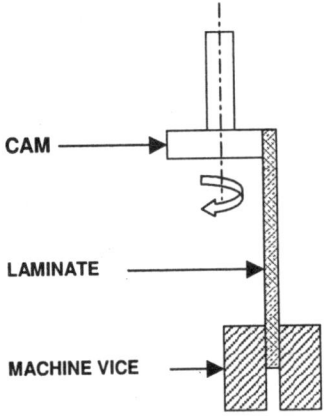

Fig.2: Schematic representation of low frequency high amplitude fatigue test rig

Table 1. Experimental details

Workpiece and	Woven glass fabric/Epoxy
Fiber volume fraction	0.40
Cutting speed	9.43 - 30.16 m/min insteps
Feed rate	0.02 - 0.06 in steps
Drill material	HSS
Drill diameter	6 mm

3. RESULTS AND DISCUSSION
3.1 Load deflection curve

An important physical parameter for indicating the flexural response of any beam specimen is deflection. The specimens exposed to different duration of low frequency fatigue loading were subjected to post impact flexural bending by static loading.

The glass epoxy polymeric composite is a heterogeneous material and hence the

228

response of the material to any flexural test can be non-linear. In order to evaluate this, data on load deflection characteristics during flexural bending of glass/epoxy composites subjected to low frequency, high amplitude fatigue loading was acquired. Typical load-deflection characteristics of the epoxy composite coupons are exposed to fatigue loading is illustrated in Fig.3.

The observations on load-deflection characteristics of glass epoxy composite, indicates that exposure to low frequency high amplitude fatigue loading has resulted in marginal rise in the stiffness (fig.4).

3.2 Strain Toughening on Drilling Performance

Fig.5 shows the relationship between the thrust force and cutting parameters for drilling normal workpiece. For a given cutting speed, the thrust is seen to increase with feed rate and it is ascertained that for the drilling of woven fabric GFRP, the optimum cutting parameters are 18.85 m/min cutting speed and 0.02 mm/rev feed rate for minimum thrust force.

From Fig.6, the optimum cutting condition for toughened workpiece are 23.56 m/min cutting speed and 0.02 mm/rev feed rate for minimum thrust force.

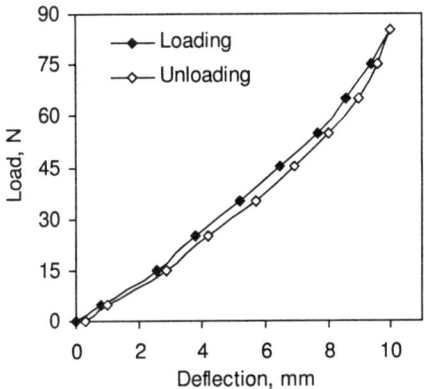

Fig.3: Load deflection characteristics

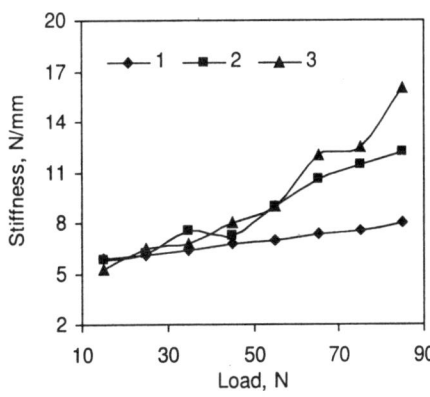

Fig.4: Influence of flexural bending loads on stiffness
1. Stiffness Average $= y_a / x_a$
2. Stiffness Loading $= y_1 / x_1$
3. Stiffness Unloading $= y_2 / x_2$

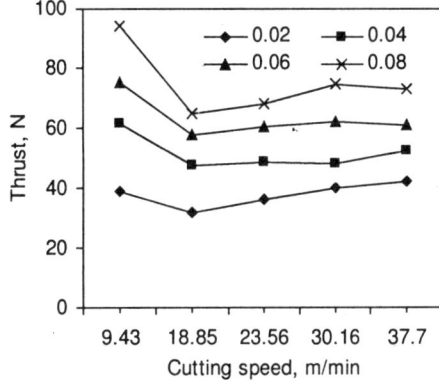

Fig.5: Parametric influence of cutting parameters on thrust in normal workpiece

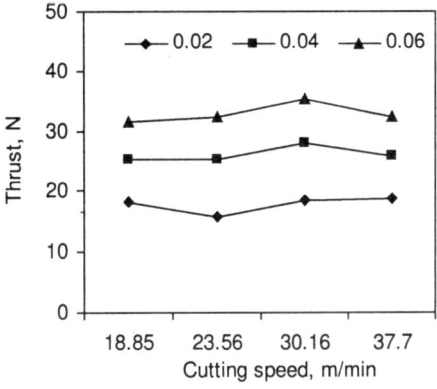

Fig.6: Arametric influence of cutting parameters on thrust in toughened workpiece

3.3 Observation on thrust

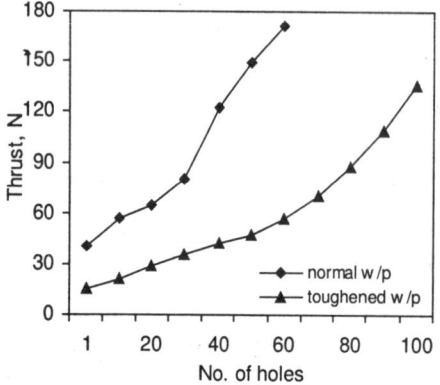

Fig.7: Typical variation of thrust with number of holes drilled

Fig.7 shows that thrust force with toughened workpiece is smaller than for normal workpiece for the same drilling conditions. It can be explained by the features of strain toughening. Polymeric composites subjected to low frequency fatigue loading, exhibited a marginal rise in the stiffness, depending upon the loading. By inducing strain in polymeric composite, it was possible to bring down the drill thrust.

3.3 Observation on delamination factor

To determine the differing extent of intrinsic hole machining defects caused by drilling, specimens were examined using optical microscope coupled with image analyser (Fig.8). Ultrasonic 'C' scan imaging method was adopted to characterize the defects at exit side of the holes and the results were analysed through image analyser.

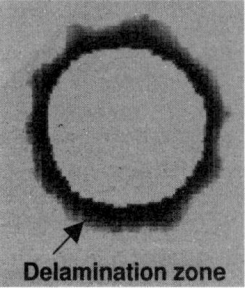

Fig.8: Delamination zone at exit of hole through C-scan

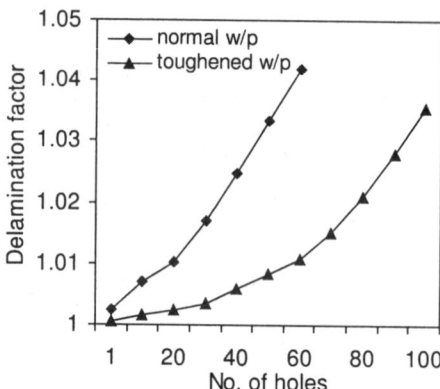

Fig.9: Typical variation of delamination factor with number of holes drilled

The value of delamination factor (F_d) can be obtained by the following equation:

$$F_d = \frac{D_{max}}{D} \qquad (1)$$

where, D_{max} is maximum diameter of the damage around the hole and D is the diameter of the hole.

In drilling normal workpiece, the maximum tolerance is attained up to 30 holes, while for drilling of strain toughened workpiece the same tolerance is reached around 70 holes. The trend is almost similar to that of thrust with feed rate.

4. CONCLUSIONS

Some of the important observations are:

- The thrust in toughened workpiece is smaller than that in the normal workpiece, which indicates that inducing strain before drilling is suitable for defect constrained drilling polymeric composites.

- The trend of variation of thrust and delamination factor with number of holes for both work pieces is similar.

- In normal workpiece, increase of thrust and delamination factor around 30 holes, indicated that 30 is the limiting number of holes to be drilled and in strained toughened work piece 70 is the limiting number of holes to be drilled for defect tolerancing.

5. REFERENCES

1. **Dharan,C.K.H. and Won M.S.** (2000), "Machining Parameters for an Intelligent Machining System for Composite Laminates", *Int. J. Mach. Tools Manuf.,* 40, 415-426.

2. **Konig,W. and Graβ.P.** (1989), "Quality Definition and Assessment in Drilling of Fiber Reinforced Thermosets", *Annals of the CIRP,* 38, 119-124.

3. **Jain and Yang.** (1984), "Delamination-Free drilling of composite laminates", *Transactions of the ASME, J. Engg. Ind,* 116, 475–481.

4. **Rema Abraham Thomas.** (1999) *Ph.D. Thesis,* IIT Madras.

Industrial Engineering

GCMM 2004
Editors: Prasad K D V Yarlagadda and S Narayanan
Copyright © 2005, Vellore Institute of Technology, Vellore, India
Publisher: Narosa Publishing House Pvt. Ltd., New Delhi, India

An Evaluation of Production Performance Benefits of Selected Indian Industries from JIT Implementation

Dhanraj B. Waghmare[*]

[1]M.E. (Production Engg.)(Student), Department of Mechanical Engineering,

Government College of Engg,, Karad (M.S.) – 415 124 India.

E-mail: dhanraj_wb@yahoo.co.in

Prof. Telsang M T [**]

[2]Professor and Head, Mechanical Engineering Department, Rajarambapu Institute of

Technology, Rajaramnagar, Sakhrale (M.S.) – 415 414 India.

E-mail: telsang1@rediffmail.com

Abstract

The basic idea of JUST-IN-TIME Manufacturing was originally developed and brought to a high level of sophistication by the Toyota Motor Company in Japan. JIT is by now a very widely discussed, researched and applied manufacturing philosophy, in a variety of industries across the globe. This study evaluates the production performance benefits of the performance parameters related to selected JIT implemented Indian industries. The production performance parameters are selected from the literature of JIT manufacturing. A JIT survey instrument is designed to collect the data related to, selected JIT implemented Indian industries. This survey instrument was sent to various Indian industries. Depending on the responses an evaluation is carried out to comment on the benefits from JIT implementation. It is found that JIT manufacturing can be beneficially implemented in India. JIT can reduce raw material, WIP as well as finished goods inventory, control defects efficiently, stabilize production; and crate a flexible, multi-skilled work force.

Keywords
JIT, JIT Survey Instrument, WIP.

1. INTRODUCTION

The basic idea of JUST-IN-TIME Manufacturing was originally developed and brought to a high level of sophistication by the Toyota Motor Company in Japan. JIT is by now a very widely discussed, researched and applied manufacturing philosophy, in a variety of industries across the globe. Its ultimate aim is to achieve 'perfection' in manufacturing through continuous improvement and elimination of all waste. JIT can be defined as, " JIT is a system of production control that seeks to minimize raw material and WIP inventories: control (eliminate) defects; stabilize production; simplify production process; and create a flexible, multi-skilled work force." By making

235

itself eminently suitable for adoption in any type of manufacture, that is, mass production, batch production, continuous process production or custom oriented job order production, JIT holds a true potential to become, what can be termed as a "Universal Manufacturing Philosophy" of the future. By eliminating all wastes and seeking continuous improvements, it aims at creating a manufacturing system that is responsive to the market needs. JIT enables organizations to achieve simultaneously the goals of high quality, quick delivery, low cost and a high degree of flexibility for quick response.

2. LITERATURE SURVEY

Rosemary R. Fullerton et al. [1] carried out literature search to identify all of the US manufacturing firms known to be formally practicing JIT. A sample study was carried to better understand the benefits through JIT adoption, and whether a more comprehensive implementation is worthwhile. Nazim U. Ahmed et al. [2] carried a comparative study of US manufacturing firms at various stages of JIT implementation. The findings of this study suggest that some of the issues such as supplier proximity and the lead-time of the supplier, which have been traditionally considered important, are not major impediments to JIT implementation. James P. Gilbert [3] carried out an empirical study to discover the organizational design configuration of a broad base of US firms that are currently implementing and developing the JIT philosophy. It shows that, smaller and mid-size manufacturers have started to enjoy the benefits of JIT implementation.

Sadao Sakakibara et al. [4] carried out survey of JIT-implemented industries, in order to study the impact of JIT manufacturing and its infrastructure on manufacturing performance. The results of this study show that, there is not a significant relationship between the use of JIT practices, alone, and manufacturing performance. There is a very strong relationship between JIT practices and infrastructure practices. Richard E. White et al. [5] carried out research about JIT implementation in U.S. manufacturers. In this study, it was investigated that JIT implementation differences between small and large U.S. manufacturers, and the changes in performance attributed to JIT

implementation in two groups of manufacturer size. D Chang et al. [6] carried out an empirical study, The results of the study show that JIT firms have not achieved better organizational performance in terms of sales in dollar/employee, operating profit margin, and return on investment than non JIT firms, but achieved better performance in terms of finished goods inventory turnover, raw materials inventory turnover, and WIP inventory turnover.

M. S. Spencer, et al. [7] surveyed manufacturers and logistics executives to determine their attitudes and understanding about JIT. In this study, the manufacturer respondents indicated a much broader view of JIT as a management philosophy whose general goal is to eliminate waste throughout an organization. In contrast, the logistics respondents were more likely to view JIT as largely an inventory reduction policy. The literature survey shows that, there is a need to carry out survey of some Indian industries, which have implemented JIT manufacturing. Considering this need, comparative study of some Indian industries has been done.

3. JIT SURVEY INSTRUMENT

Initially, the performance parameters have been selected from the literature of JIT manufacturing. And the survey instrument is designed. This survey instrument is used to collect data for the evaluation of production performance benefits. It is divided into, two measure sections (i) general information, and (ii) questions related to JIT practices. The section of general information is used to collect information like, name of the company, status of the company, status of JIT manufacturing etc. While the other section was divided into five categories like product, equipment and processes, work force, suppliers and miscellaneous.

3.1 Product

Within each section the questions are primarily close ended. Many of the questions are single-response items except for questions such as "Have you arranged your equipments in U cells for JIT implementation?" Other questions are on a five-point scale such as "Benefits from the flexible workforce", with 1 being very low to 5 being very high. The performance parameters considered under this section are accuracy of short-term forecasting, reduction of, raw material inventory, WIP (work in progress), finished goods inventory, set up times.

3.2 Equipment and Processes

Within this section the questions related to arrangement of the equipments into U cells, use of group technology to improve scheduling efficiencies, lead time, level of automation, percentage of equipments on which preventive maintenance is done, ease of adjustment to design changes due to JIT implementation.

3.3 Work Force

The multi-skilled work force is beneficial for JIT manufacturing. This program would attempt to formally cross train employees on several different machines and in several different functions. Within this section questions related to number of multi-skilled workers; before and after JIT implementation, benefits from flexible work force, cost of cross training for flexible work force. Other questions are related to group decision-making, problem solving network, employee suggestions, and life-long employment.

3.4 Suppliers

Traditionally, JIT implies that the suppliers are to be located within close proximity, which helps reduce lead-time for delivery. Companies also generally have a small number of suppliers for their major parts. They are also involved in relationships with suppliers for improving quality. The questions under this section are related to these assumptions. In addition, questions are related to evaluation of suppliers based on reliability, product flexibility and product quality.

3.5 Miscellaneous

This section is related with the JIT practices like Kanban system, quality circles, JIT purchasing. The program of Kanban system would attempt to eliminate the "push" system of material flow and develop a "pull" system which is dependant upon the operators at downstream workstations to initiate material movement and control material flow for upstream work stations versus the traditional management control of the initiation of material movement. Quality circles, is an employee participation program. JIT purchasing is a supplier participation program

4. METHODOLOGY
4.1 Sample Selection

From the population of Indian industries, a sample is selected randomly. This sample contains the Indian industries located in a typical geographical area. The Indian industries located in the western industrial zone of India particularly in Maharashtra have been selected. This geographic industrial area covers Mumbai, Pune, Satara, Kolhapur, and Belgaum-industrial area. Initially the survey instrument was send to 96 industries. Most of these industries have been selected from the Internet. The survey instrument was send personally or either by post or by e-mail. Among the responding managers, some are operations managers, some are production managers, and some are vice presidents or the owners of the manufacturing firms. Out of these firms only 25 manufacturing firms responded. So the response rate is 26.04%. These responding firms are grouped under three major groups, depending upon the status of JIT implementation,

(i) Full/partial implementation, 52% of respondents are coming under this category,
(ii) Pilot program/learning process, 8% firms are reported under this, and,
(iii) JIT considered but not feasible/JIT not considered, remaining 40% are grouped under this category.

4.2 Validation of the Survey Instrument

The survey instrument was designed and validated in several steps. A preliminary survey instrument was developed consisting of questions concerning the above performance parameters. Various business managers and the academic professionals validated the preliminary survey instrument, in a limited pretest. Depending upon the suggestions from these people, it is modified and a final survey instrument is designed.

4.3 Data Collection

A packet containing a cover letter of the college, a copy of the JIT survey instrument and a letter describing the objective of the study, need of the study and other details was mailed to these thirteen industries, selected as the sample. To encourage the managers were also asked if they were interested in receiving the survey results. The selected industries are, KCL, SIL, MSL, PAL, PES, DIL, PPL, CIL, SIP. SML, RIL, BIL and IE (The names of these industries are abbreviated for the purpose of confidentiality). Out of these, IE and PES are small-scale units while others are medium to large-scale industries. KCL, PPL, IE are manufacturers of engineering equipments and CIL is a food industry. The remaining nine industries are automobile industries.

5 RESULTS AND DISCUSSION
5.1 Product

After JIT implementation industries like PPL and KCL have achieved about 61-80% increase in accuracy of short term forecasting. JIT is mainly related with reduction of waste in the form of inventory, which does not add any value. The percentage decrease in raw materials inventory (RMI) ranges from 0-20% to 81-100% as shown in fig.1 Industries like PAL has achieved reduction in RMI up to 41 to 60%. Initially PAL, which is producing castings, used to keep raw materials in huge quantities to meet the market demands. Hence it was possible for PAL to reduce their RMI up to 50%.

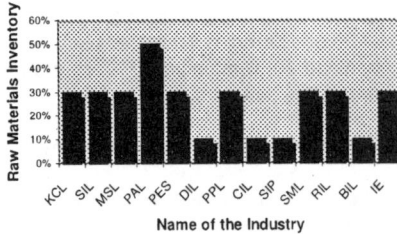

Fig. 1: Percentage Reduction in RMI

The industries like CIL, a milk processing industry, used to keep raw materials inventory as low as possible, hence the fig.1 shows only 10% decrease. The industries like DIL, SIP, and BIL have already implemented JIT from their start and they are keeping inventory as low as possible, hence the graph of these industries shows only 10% decrease. The remaining industries showing 30% decrease in raw materials inventory still have a large scope to

reduce their raw materials inventory. There is 30% average decrease in raw materials inventory due to JIT implementation.

WIP (Work In Progress Inventory) resembles to the buffer stock kept in between the workstations to ensure continuous flow of products. JIT manufacturing attempts to reduce WIP, as it is considered as non-value adding activity. Fig. 2 shows percentage decrease in WIP of selected Indian industries.

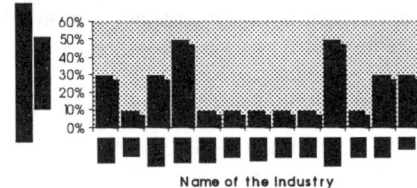

Fig. 2: Percentage Decrease in WIP

The graph of decrease in WIP shows variation from industry to industry depending upon certain parameters like buffer stock, bottleneck etc. In certain cases, the industries like PAL and SML have achieved 41 to 60% reduction in WIP. Initially PAL and SML used to keep large stock in between processes, but JIT implementation made it possible to reduce WIP up to 50%. As it is very critical to reduce WIP, the remaining industries are able to reduce WIP up to 10% only. The graph shows average decrease in WIP is about 22.31%. Hence JIT reduces WIP depending upon various forms of industries like food, automobile, engineering industries etc. The fig. 3 shows the percent decrease in finished goods inventories (FGI).

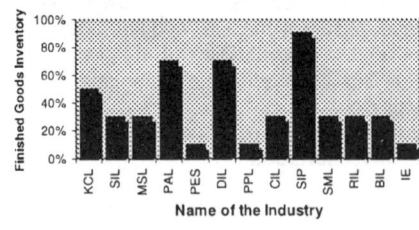

Fig. 3: Percentage Decrease in FGI

The industries like SIP have achieved the decrease of FGI up to 81 to 100%, PAL and DIL up to 70%. This is because previously their customers (other cooperate industries) have not implemented JIT or supply chain management, and due to the increased awareness of lean manufacturing in their customers. KCL has reduced FGI up to 50%, the reason behind this is, they are keeping large stock of FGI to meet seasonal demands. Industries like PES, PPL and IE shows decrease in FGI as 10% only, because previously they were having very less stock of FGI. Thus, on an average JIT decreases FGI up to 37.7%.

Reduction in set up time attempt to reduce the time and costs involved in changing from the tooling, layout, etc., required to produce one product to that required producing other products. Reducing the setup times will allow for reduced economic lot sizes produced and reduced need for buffer inventories. Thus various industries shows percentage reduction in set up times depending up on the product, equipment and processes and the multi skilled work force. The table 1 shows percent reduction in set up times after JIT implementation.

Table 1: Industry Wise Percent Reduction in Set-up Time

Industry	KCL	SIL	MSL	PAL	PES	PPL	CIL	SML	RIL	BIL	IE
Set-up time	15 to 20 %	0 to 15 %	10 %	60 %	0 to 20 %	10 to 20 %	0 to 10 %	10 to 20 %	30 %	0 to 10 %	5 to 10 %

As the industries like PAL and RIL are using SMED (Single Minute Exchange of Dies), they have reduced their set up times up to 30% to 60%. The remaining industries are still struggling to reduce their set up times and able to reduce set up times up to 10 to 15%. There is on an average 19% reduction in set up times after JIT implementation. Thus, it is a very challenging job for JIT implemented industries to reduce their set up times.

5.2 Equipment and Processes

The literature on JIT manufacturing shows that, JIT implementation, affects the various parameters related to equipments and processes of the particular industry. Certain case studies related to JIT show that arranging the equipments in U cells leads increase in productivity. As 61.54% of respondents have not arranged their equipments in U cells, and only 38.46% respondents have arranged their equipments partially in U cells. Hence this study does not provide any validation for the said assumption.

The average percent reduction in lead-time after JIT implementation of these industries is 30.73%. KCL uses ERP software for JIT purchasing and other shop floor activities; hence they have reduced lead-time up to 57%. Though automation helps to increase productivity 85% of respondents have partial automation only, and remaining 15% are implementing JIT without automation. It was asked, if the respondents were using group technology to improve scheduling efficiencies, 53.85% of the respondents said that, they had implemented it. This was because of the different types of the products, impossible to be grouped under certain features. Majority of the respondents (46% industries) have done preventive maintenance on 81 to 100% equipments. These industries are KCL, SIL, MSL, PAL, CIL and SIP. Due to preventive maintenance these industries have achieved continuous flow of production. About 31% respondents (industries like, PES, SML, RIL, BIL) have done preventive maintenance on 61 to 80% equipments and remaining 23% respondents have done preventive maintenance on about 40% equipments. These industries are attempting to increase the percentage of equipments on which preventive maintenance is to be done.

5.3 Work Force

The questions involving work force centered around: number of multi-skilled workers, benefits from flexible work force, cost of cross training for flexible work force, etc. All the respondents have indicated that flexible work force is beneficial in JIT environment. When the respondents were asked about the benefits from multi-skilled workers, by mentioning the options as none, very little, not sure, some, a lot on a five point Likert scale. From the responses available 77% are getting a lot of benefits and remaining 23% are up to the mark of some benefits. The industries, getting some benefits, can increase their benefits by increasing flexibility of the workers. The respondents, getting lot of benefits from flexibility of the workers, are investing very low to moderate cost for cross training the workers to achieve flexibility.

When asked about the benefits from implementation of performance parameters like group decision-making, problem-solving network, employee suggestion scheme and life long employment of employees the results shows, 93% respondents have implemented group decision making and employee suggestion scheme beneficially. Problem solving network program involves the employees at lower levels as well as managers of higher levels and this is implemented up to 62%. The industries are not interested in employing the workers for life long period because only 38% industries have implemented life long employment programs. Remaining 62% industries are going for employment of workers on contract basis only as they do not find it beneficial to use life long employment.

5.4 Suppliers

The concept of JIT manufacturing believes in single sourcing, hence the industries are making attempts to reduce the number of suppliers. The industries, which are able to reduce number of suppliers, are nine in number. The industries like PAL are purchasing raw material in the form of sand, scrap, etc. hence these have to rely upon more number of suppliers. The industries like KCL, SIL, MSL etc. are purchasing sub assemblies and due to standardization of products, they have reduced their suppliers up to 50%. Thus the average percent reduction in number of suppliers is 26.63%.

Hundred percent respondents agree that JIT implementation leads to small lot sizes. When the respondents were asked to rate their suppliers based upon the performance parameters like, maintaining delivery schedule, maintaining product quality, and flexibility to schedule and production changes, 68% of the respondents responded that their suppliers are excellent in maintaining delivery schedules, 62% respondents responded that their suppliers are excellent at maintaining product quality, Many times due to the bad quality of the products, product lots get rejected. After implementation of JIT, the respondents find their suppliers maintaining excellent product quality. About 77% of respondents find their

suppliers can cope up with schedule and design changes flexibly

The percentage of respondents saying proximity to customer is beneficial is 76.92%. There is less number of respondents saying single sourcing is beneficial and these are 46.15%. This shows still Indian companies are not able to change their attitude to their suppliers. Still 53.85% industries find long-term contract with suppliers is beneficial, which is a first step towards single sourcing. Apart from this, 85.62% respondents insist on suppliers training to implement JIT beneficially. Thus the part of suppliers in JIT implementation plays a very important role.

5.5 Miscellaneous

The percentage of respondents, which have implemented Kanban system beneficially, is 61.54%. These industries have implemented Kanban system in some of its sections only. For example PAL has implemented Kanban system in its stores department only. As these industries are implementing Kanban systems initially in some of its departments and then depending upon its results, they are going for over all implementation.

A quality circle is an employee participation program, which attempts to involve employees in decision making and problem solving activities. About 76.92% respondents have implemented programs like quality circles to improve product quality. Implementation of quality circles helps to achieve flexibility of the work force. Remaining 23.08% industries are taking steps towards implementation of quality circles. There is not much awareness of the programs like JIT purchasing. This is a supplier participation and partnership program. This program involves suppliers in long range mutually rewarding cost reduction efforts such as value analysis, and the implementation of JIT management practices. About 39% respondents are using JIT purchasing, while others are not able to distinguish this program as JIT purchasing as it involves suppliers training programs.

6 CONCLUSIONS AND DIRECTIONS FOR FUTURE RESEARCH

Manufacturing managers are confronted daily with the tasks of reducing costs and improving productivity. JIT as a manufacturing strategy can be implemented to do both, through its various practices. Now JIT is not monopoly of Japanese and US manufactures. The study shows that Indian manufacturers can also avail all the benefits of JIT manufacturing. JIT can reduce raw material, WIP as well as finished goods inventory, control defects efficiently, stabilize production; and crate a flexible, multi-skilled work force. In future, the scope of this research can be widened to increase the sample of the respondents, and more accurate results can be achieved. There is a strong need to design a generalized measurement system to measure the performance of JIT There is a need to carry out the same study, by adding certain other performance parameters, throughout all the Indian manufacturers.

7. ACKNOWLEDGEMENTS

The valuable inputs, from Prof. Dr. P. M. Khodke, Principal GCOE, Amravati (M. S.) and Mr. S. D. Nigade, Astt. Manager (PPC), Universal Luggage Mfg. Co. Ltd. Satara (M.S.) are gratefully acknowledged.

8. REFERENCES

1. **Rosemary R. Fullerton, Cheryl S. McWatters**, "The production performance benefits from JIT implementation", *Journal of Operations Management,* 2001, Vol. 19, pp. 81-96

2. **Nazim U. Ahmed, E. A. Tunch, R. V. Montagno**, "A comparative study of US manufacturing firms at various stages of just-in-time implementation", *International Journal of Production Research*, 1991, Vol. 29, no. 4, pp. 787-802.

3. **James P. Gilbert**, "JIT implementation and development in USA", *International Journal of Production Research,* 1990, Vol. 28, no. 6, pp. 1099-1109.

4. **Sadao Sakakibara, B. B. Flynn, R. G. Schroeder, and W. T. Morris,** "The impact of just-in-time manufacturing and its infrastructure on manufacturing performance", *Management Science,* September 1997, Vol. 43, no. 9, pp. 1246-1257.

5. **Richard E. White, John N. Pearson, Jeffery R. Wilson**, "JIT manufacturing: A survey of implementation in small and large U.S. manufacturers", *Management Science,* 1999, Vol.45, no.1, pp. 1-15.

6. **Chang. D, Lee S.M,** "Impact of JIT on organizational performance of US firms", *International Journal of Production Research*, 1995, Vol. 33, no. 11, pp. 3053-3068.

7. **Spencer M.S, Daugherty P.J** and **Rogers D.S**, "Logistics support for JIT implementation", *International Journal of Production Research,* 1996, Vol. 34, no. 3, pp. 701-714.

GCMM 2004
Editors: Prasad K D V Yarlagadda and S Narayanan
Copyright © 2005, Vellore Institute of Technology, Vellore, India
Publisher: Narosa Publishing House Pvt. Ltd., New Delhi, India

An Intelligent Mobile Agent Frame work for

Distributed Manufacturing Network Management

Rao B.V.A* , Iyengar N.Ch.S.N** & Kannammal A***

*Director, **Faculty, ***Research Student
Vellore Institute of Technology, Deemed University
Vellore – 632 014, India

Email: nchsniyr@vit.ac.in

Abstract

The goal of this paper is to show how we will apply mobile agent technology to an integrated network management framework in the field of distributed manufacturing. A virtual clustering application framework is proposed, which is intended to show the integration of the manufacturing enterprise information and production system. In addition, a mobile agent framework will be required to provide a discussion regarding the ideas of mobile agent application in terms of the distributed network management.

Key Words
Manufacturing ,Network Management, Intelligent mobile agent,

1 INTRODUCTION

Manufacturing industries are facing increasingly competitive challenges in maintaining their existing markets and improving their capability to respond efficiently to rapidly changing customer needs. As a result, it is inevitable that modern manufacturing will move towards integrating their activities with their customers, suppliers and competitors into a supply chain through a computer network. This, thus, reflects the increasing complexity of computer network which supports the overall organisational and manufacturing environment(Wu et al., 2000).

Existing centralised client-server based network management frameworks have suffered from numerous problems such as insufficient scalability, interoperability, reliability, and flexibility. Hence, Network Management (NM) becomes a critical issue in today's rapidly changing distributed network environment. (Feridun et al., 1999; Gavalas et al., 1999; Puliafito et al., 2000; Rubinstein et al., 1999).

Intelligent Mobile Agent (IMA) is an emerging paradigm that is gaining momentum in several applications. (Sliva et al, 1999; Shen et al., 1999). From the viewpoint of network management, the idea of IMA reduces the complexity of the managing entity by delegating part of the management responsibility to the managed network entities. It represents a challenging approach to provide advanced network management functionalities, due to the ability to easily implement decentralised and active monitoring of the system (Puliafito et al., 2000).

In recent· years, a number of distributed agent approaches to concurrent design and manufacturing have been proposed (Maturana et al., 1997; Papaioannou et al., 1999). However, most of them focus their attention on the alignment between IT systems and the real manufacturing processes they support. Several commercial implementations of mobile agents exist in the industry such as Aglet from IBM, Condoria from Mitsubishi etc.[1] . We believe that they are much too general-purpose for most network management applications.

In this project, therefore, our purpose is to present a framework using the concepts of mobile agents for achieving efficiency in the acquisition of network management data and enhancing network performance, particularly in the distributed manufacturing network system. In order to demonstrate the real applicability of the introduced concepts, we have introduced the concepts of **function management domains** by using a **virtual clustering** mechanism. The function management domains are virtual domains built from resources and relationships between organisational and manufacturing activities. The designed model will be tested with a state-of-the-art simulator - OPNET.

The structure of this paper is organised as follows: ·

Section 2 - Provides a background analysis of the integration of distributed manufacturing system.

Section 3. Provides an overview of the network management and the importance of Intelligent Mobile Agent (IMA) in terms of distributed network management.

A mobile agent framework based on integrated distributed manufacturing architecture will be demonstrated in Section

4. This will be followed by a brief overview of further implementation and evaluation. ·
Section 5 – A closing discussion and conclusion.

2. FEASIBLY ANALYSIS OF THE DISTRIBUTED MANUFACTURING SYSTEM
2.1 Background

Manufacturing enterprises in the 21 st century will be in a competitive environment where markets are shifting frequently, new technologies are continuously emerging, and competitors are increasing dramatically and globally. It appears that new architectures for next-generation manufacturing need to be distributed, intelligent and incorporate concurrent design and manufacturing principles. Hence, moves towards the convergence of Engineering, Business, Manufacturing and Office Systems etc., which are, typically, in the heterogeneous software and hardware environments. (Umar,1993).

An integrated manufacturing system includes the management of all activities and processes from the customers' order to product delivery

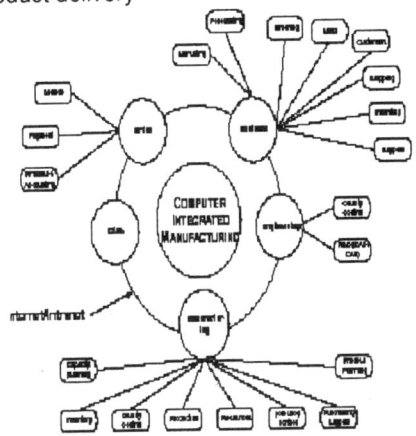

Fig. 1: Integrated Manufacturing management Architectural Framework

Figure 1 shows an integrated framework of distributed manufacturing management system. In order to accomplish the manufacturing mission successfully and efficiently, the relevant functions could be clustered into specified domains and be done collaboratively.

2.2 Virtual Clustering Mechanism

This method of clustering is among the oldest techniques used in data mining (Berson. 1997,Berson et al., 1997; Jain et al., 1999; Talluri, 2000). It is a method in which like records are grouped together and put into the same category. In this framework, the clustering approach is employed to cluster the manufacturing processes and subtasks into various domains, in which the correlated functions will most likely .be clustered together. Hence, it could be used to identify different domains for an abstract high level overview of the whole manufacturing or business. Figure 2 shows a virtual clustering framework in an integrated manufacturing management system, which is modified from Wu et al., (2000).

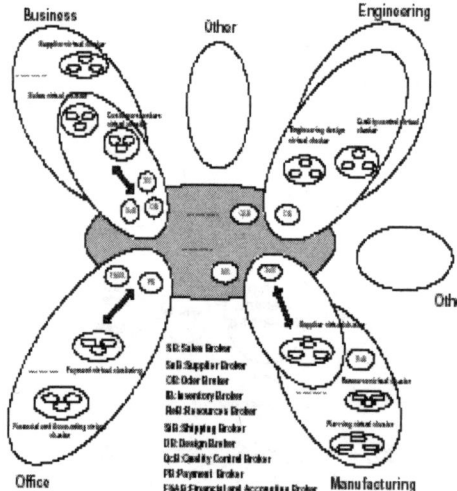

Fig. 2: A virtual clustering framework in integrated manufacturing management system

In this paradigm, one or several manufacturing activities could be virtually clustered into several virtual function management domains. For each cluster, there is a process broker (e.g., Production Broker, Sales Broker, Resource Broker etc...). Brokers may co-operate with similar or dissimilar brokers into harmonious decision groups. Suitable communication and co-ordination protocols could be used to efficiently maintain the stability of these clusters.

Virtual clustering is a dynamic, emergent function-driven group behaviour of the multi-broker system. To accomplish a certain activity, relevant brokers will be grouped together. For example, the OB (Order Broker) and SB (Sales Broker) can be dispatched to the customer and sales cluster with their expected actions to perform the manufacturing plan. Through the virtual clustering mechanism, brokers can dynamically participate in a problem-solving group (cluster). This clustering process provides scalability and aggregation functionality to the system.

2.3 Analysis of Functional Dependence

The organisational structure of a manufacturing we described above is function-driven, which implies that the relationships between functions are significant. In this section, we will discuss the importance of functional dependence within the manufacturing environment.

For a certain function or manufacturing (business) plan, several designed processes are required. The definition of dependencies is used to identify the relations between processes as well as those related work units which are used to implement the processes. The work units can be regarded as the tasks or resources for implementing one or more specified activities. Relevant research can be found in Jin et al., (1999). With this generic definition, "manager" or "engineer" can characterise certain relations within activities and work units.

Moving the above scenario to network management, we can regard these work units or resources as network elements. It is essential for a network manager to achieve effective and efficient coordination with network monitoring if the dependencies between work units have been well understood. This information may come from the best knowledge of the process designers and engineers.

Researches showing the significance for analysing dependencies from processes or resources are suggested in (Jin et al., 1999; Kim, 2000). Jin et al. (1999) proposed a method to capture emergent dependencies dynamically between activities and work units. Similarly, Kar et al., (2000) proposed a model for analysing the dependency relationships pertaining to physically monitored domains in the network management layer. In this model, there are two distinct classes of dependencies,

i.   Intra-System Dependencies: These dependencies normally occur within a single domain. A specific service (or activity) requires another service that is installed on the same system.
ii.   Inter-System Dependencies: These are dependencies between services (or activities) across different domains.

3. DISTRIBUTED NETWORK MANAGEMENT
3.1 The Current System

It is now widely recognised that the use of decentralisation potentially solves most of the problems that exist in centralised client/server solutions (Gavalas et al., 1999). A form of decentralised network management (provided in the first version of SNMP) is the mechanism of notification of asynchronous events (Puliafito et al., 1999). However, in SNMPV1, no management action can be performed locally, because any decision is made centrally by the Network Management System (NMS) (Stallings, 1999). In addition,

SNMPv2 introduces another decentralization feature: the concept of proxy agent, which leads to a structure of hierarchical management. However, SNMPv2 has not been used widely as SNMPv1, due to the few implementations available. Another approach to decentralisation is Remote MONitoring (RMON), which has been proposed by the IETF (Waldbusser, 1995). RMON assumes the existence of appropriate devices called probes, whose task is to provide indications concerning the network traffic in a specific sub network.

3.2 The Emergence of Intelligent Mobile Agent (IMA)

The use of approaches based on mobile code for network management allows us to overcome some limitations of current centralised management system.

The ideas of Intelligent Mobile Agent (IMA) started with early work on Management by Delegation (MbD) based on static agents (Yemini et al., 1991) and has been recommended as a promising solution to distributed network management in several papers (Simoes et al., 1999; Zapf et al., 1999).

When applied in the area of network management, the IMA provides an efficient way to delegate part of the responsibility from a managing entity to managed entities. Rather than sending the same agent code in parallel to a set of managed entities, a single mobile agent can be launched from the managing entity with pre-assigned itinerary plan and required actions.

4.IMPLEMENTATION OF DISTRIBUTED MANUFACTURING NETWORK MANAGEMENT SYSTEM (DMNMS)
4.1 Framework of DMNMS

In our implementation, we employ the hierarchical model to present a framework of our distributed manufacturing network management system. Figure 3 shows the framework of our implementation. Prior to the design of the mobile agent platform, the functional management domains are divided into multiple clusters in terms of their functional missions. This is, for example, customers' order virtual cluster, sales virtual cluster and production virtual cluster.

We designed an application –agent manager to launch mobile agents (MAs), which can define the itinerary of MAs, monitor and control the network situation, and display their results. For each virtual cluster group, we assign a Virtual Mobile Agent Platform (VMAP) and one sub-master agent can be launched. VMAP is a platform for developing and managing mobile agents and give all the primitives needed for their creation, execution, communication, migration and even security concerns. Once a sub-master agent arrives at each virtual cluster platform in the first layer, the processes will be expanded into the second layer. At this stage, one or several slave agents will be created to execute the local management tasks.

A slave agent will travel around several managed network elements. The list of nodes that are visited by the mobile agent are specified by a pre-defined itinerary object. In each managed object, the agent can choose different migration strategies depending on its task and the current network conditions, and then change its strategies as network conditions change. Hence, a set of planning algorithms that allow an agent or a small group of cooperating agents to identify the best migration path through a network is required. It will permit a mobile agent to navigate among a series of remote managed objects in specific sequence to solve network problems by processing information or by supplying information to the remote management agents. Thus, without transferring large amounts of unnecessary data from remote nodes to the central station, only high-level information will be transferred to the central station.

4.2 Agent Itinerary

In our implementation described above, we launch several sub-master agents to each pre-defined manufacturing function clustering and then these agents could send out a wave of slave agents to visit destination machines in parallel. However, in reality, we may want to use fewer network resources by sending fewer agents than the number of possible destination machines. Hence, there is a need for planning that decides the best sequence (itinerary) of machines to be visited by each agent so that the desired

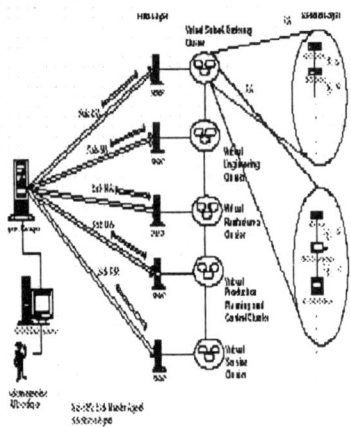

Fig 3: Framework of DMNMS

information can be found in minimum time. Hence, we initially define our agent itinerating problem as follows:

Definition

There are $(n+1)$ sites of data servers, S_i with $0 \leq i \leq n$. There are k function management domains, which are pre-clustered depending upon their functional dependence with a certain function (or activity). We then assign a Virtual Mobile

Agent Platform (VMAP) to each functional cluster, A_j with $0 \leq j \leq k$. Each VMAP takes charge of the number of data servers which will need to be accessed to implement a certain activity. Each data server has a known probability of dependence, P_d with $0 \leq P_d \leq 1$ showing the frequency of being accessed by its functional domain manager. In addition, a known probability PE_i, with $0 \leq PE_j \leq 1$ of being able to complete the management task successfully. These data servers might locate at a single physical domain or across multiple domains in different physical sites. We cluster these data servers depending on their functional correlation as well as location separations. In addition, a time t_i is required for the agent to execute the task at S_i regardless of whether it is successful. Travel time or latencies for the agent to move between sites are also known and given by $l_{ij} \geq 0$ for moving between site i and site j. When the agent completes its itinerary, it must return to the site from which it started (i.e., A_0). The Agent Itinerating Problem is to minimise the expected time to travel and successfully complete the task.

The formal definition of the Agent Itinerating Problem has been described above. A solution consists of pre-defined ordering of sites, $<i_1, i_2, \ldots i_n>$ called a **tour T** which is permutation of 1 through n. In this scenario, an agent with a specified itinerating plan will be run under different criteria. The directory service identifies relevant information, for example, locations of the tour, the probability of functional dependence P_d, and the probability of complete task successfully, PE_i, for finding the required data at the corresponding data servers. If there is only an agent and all sites must be visited, then the problem will become

the classical travelling salesman problem (TSP) which is known to be NP-Complete. (Jin et al., 1999)

Basic Assumptions:

i. We assume that there is a greater need to access a certain data server if there is a high probability of dependence within a pre-defined function cluster for a certain activity.

ii. Due to the limited time of our system implementation, the current management system is unable to deal with capturing functional dependencies between processes. Hence, we set up the static dependencies data. This data is kept in a database maintained by the application dependency analysis stage.

iii. Computer times t_i and latencies l_{ij} are obtained from network status monitors. They could be assumed as constants or average time with a given distribution.

4.3 Evaluation

The performance of an agent itinerary is determined by the number of agents employed; the size of a mobile agent; and the time spent on locating the managed agent. These evaluation criteria are also affected by the number of times that the managed nodes are accessed. Therefore, the well-planned travel plan using the probability of functional dependencies for those data servers would probably consume less search time and network overhead than blind search strategies.

SCENARIO 1: SINGLE DOMAIN
1-1: SINGLE AGENT

The expected time to visit the required nodes (tour T) within the same domain and complete the tasks by using a single agent is:

$$C_r = 2l_{R_0 A_i} + l_{A_i i_1} + t_{i_1} + \sum_{k=2}^{n} \left\{ \left(\prod_{j=1}^{j=k-1} PE_{i_j} \right) \right\} (i_{k-1} i_k) + l_{i_n A_i}$$

There is one or more tasks to be executed in each node within the **tour.** The required travel time for dispatch a sub-master agent to VMAP, and return to Root Agent after it completes its tasks is $l_{R_0 A_i}$ and $l_{A_i R_0}$.

The first site, S_{i_1} is the node with the highest functional dependence for this particular function and requires $l_{A_i i_1}$ time to reach. Upon arrival, time t_{i_1} must be spent here regardless of success or failure. For each site, here is a probability of success PE_{i_n}. As there is only one agent travelling within a cluster, the agent might need to complete each task successfully before it travels o the next destination. Hence, an optimal travel agent algorithm and well-defined travel policy will be needed.

The use of this model brings the advantages of simplicity in planning the agent itinerary and monitoring dispatched mobile agents. However, there is a considerable increase in the size of mobile agents once the number of visited nodes grows, which would cause slow migration among nodes. In addition, if the agent is failed, the travel plan might not be completed. The VMAP would need to assign another agent or restart the travel plan.

THEOREM 2-1: MULTIPLE AGENTS

To solve the above problems, more agents could be employed to decentralise processing and control and improve management efficiency.

i.   The advantages of using multiple agents are:
ii. It allows some concurrent execution for parallelism.
iii. If one agent is found to be faulty, then the VMAP only has to re-assign the task, so the others may reliably continue.

However, the complexity of managing mobile agents will be increased and the consumption of network bandwidth might be high. Hence, a careful consideration regarding the tradeoffs of the number selection of mobile agents will be evaluated.

Scenario 2: Multiple Domains

In this scenario, the effect of the latencies across sub- networks should also be considered. Hence, it can be defined as follows:

The relevant sites belong to two physical subnetworks or more, S_1 and S_2, Sites in S_i are S_{ij} where $1 \leq j \leq n_i$. There are three latencies $L_1, L_2, L_{12} \geq 0$, which are latencies in S_1, S_2 and between them. In theory, latencies within a single sub-network are smaller than latencies across sub networks and to the home sites.

To optimise the outcomes of the project, we will evaluate the prototype model by conducting a series of experiments using alternative test situations. All experiments will be based on the same conditions and under the same environment. In order to increase the accuracy of our test, the machine would need to be rebooted for operating system rejuvenation. The agents will also be restarted before each experiment.

5. CONCLUSION

We firstly employed a mechanism of virtual clustering to analyse the manufacturing and organisational environment collaboratively. We then described a mobile agent framework on network performance management issues, particular, in distributed manufacturing network systems. Mobile agents are becoming an increasingly attractive alternative to traditional centralised architectures. They offer better support for robustness, scalability, re- configurability, and reusability, especially in network systems where problem solving and decision making must be distributed.

6.REFERENCES

1. **Berson A. and Smith J.**, (1997), Data Warehousing Data Mining and OLAP, McGraw-Hill, USA.
2. **Feridun M., Kasteleijn W., and Krause J.,** (1999),Distributed Management with Mobile Components, in he Integrated Network Management VI-Distributed Management for the Networked Millennium, Boston, A, U.S.A., pp.857-870
3. **Gavalas D, & Greenwood D, & Ghanbari M and 'Mahony M.**, (1999), "An Infrastructure for distributed and Dynamic Network Management based on Mobile Agent Technology", in the IEEE International Conference on Communications, p.1362- p.1366.
4. Jain K.A., Murty M.N., and Flynn P.J., (1999), Data Clustering A Review, in the ACM Computing Surveys, VOL 31, Issue 3, pp.264-323.
5. **Jin Y., Zhao L., and Raghunath A.,** (1999), Activeprocess: A Process-Driven and Agent-Based Approach to Supporting Collaborative Engineering, in the Proceedings of DETC'99-ASME Design Engineering Technical Conferences.
6. **Kar G., Keller A., and Calo S., (2000),** Managing Application Services over Service Provider Networks: Architecture and Dependency Analysis, in the 2000 IEEE/IFIP Network Operations and Management Symposium "The Networked Planet: Management Beyond 2000" NSOM 2000, pp.61-74.
7. **Kim Hee-Woong,** (2000), Business Process Versus Coordination Process in Organizational Change, in the International Journal of Flexible Manufacturing Systems, Vol.12, No.4, pp.275-290.
8. **Maturana, F., Balasubramanian, S. Norrie, D.H., (1997),** "Learning Coordination Patterns from Emergent Behavior in a Multi-Agent Based Manufacturing System", in the ISAS 97, Intelligent Systems and Semiotics '97: A Learning Perspective, Gaithersburg, Maryland, September 23-25, 1997, pp. 225-232.
9. **Papaioannou T. and Edwards J.,** (1999),"Using Mobile agents to Improve the Alignment Between Manufacturing and its IT Support Systems", in the Journal of Robotics and Autonomous Systems, Vol 27, pp.45-57.
10. **Puliafito A. and Tomarchio O., (1999),** "Advanced Network Management Functionalities through the use of Mobile Software Agents", in the Proceedings of the 3rd International Workshop on Intelligent Agents for Telecommunication Applications-IATA'99, LNCS vol. 1699, pp. 33-45, August 1999.
11. **Puliafito A. and Tomarchio O., (2000),** "Using Mobile Agents to Implement Flexible Network Management Strategies" in the Computer Communications, Vol. 23, p.708-719.
12. **Rubinstein, M. G. and Duarte, O. C. M. B., (1999),** "Analyzing Mobile Agent Scalability in Network Management", in the IEEE Latin American Network Operations and Management Symposium - LANOMS'99, pp. 64-74, Rio de Janeiro, RJ, Brazil, December 1999.
13. **Shen W. and Norrie D.H,** (1999), "Agent-Based Systems for Intelligent Manufacturing: A State-of –the-Art Survey", in the Knowledge and

Information Systems, and International Journal, p.129-156.

14. **Silva L.M., Batista V., Martins P., and Soares G.,** (1999), "Using Mobile Agents for Parallel Processing", in the DOA' 99 International Symposium on Distributed Objects and Applications, 5-7 September, UK: Edinburgh.

15. **Simoes P., & Silva L.M., and Fernandes F.B.,** (1999), "Integrating SNMP into a Mobile Agent Infrastructure", in the Active Technologies for Network and Service Management 10 th IFIP/IEEE International Workshop on Distributed Systems: Opertions and Management, DSOM'99, pp.148-163.

16. *Stallings, W.,* (1999), SNMP, SNMPv2, SNMPv3, and RMON 1 and 2 Third Edition, *Addison Wesley Longman Inc., Massachusetts, USA.*

17. **Talluri S.,** (2000), A benchmarking Method for Business-Process Reengineering and Improvement, in the International Journal of Flexible Manufacturing Systems, Vol.12, No.4, pp.291-304.

18. **Umar A.,**(1993), Distributed Computing and Client-Server Systems, New Jersey, PTR Prentice Hall.

19. **Waldbusser S., (1995),** Network Monitoring Management Information Base, RFC 1757, in the Puliafito A. and Tomarchio O., (2000), "Using Mobile Agents to Implement Flexible Network Management Strategies" in the Computer Communications, Vol. 23, p.708-719.

20. **Wu J., Cobzaru M., Ulieru M., and Norrie D.,** (2000), "SC-web-CS: Supply Chain Web-Centric Systems", in Proceedings of the IASTED International Conference on Artificial Intelligence and Soft Computing (ASC2000), Banff, July 24-26, 2000, pp. 501-507.

21. **Yemini Y., Goldszmidt G. and Yemini S.,** (1991), "Network Management by Delegation", in Proceedings of the 2 nd International Symposium on Integrated Network Management, April.

22. **Zapf M., Herrmann K., and Geihs K.,** (1999), "Decentralized SNMP Management with Mobile Agents", in the Proceedings of the Sixth IFIP/IEEE International Symposium on Integrated Network Management, Boston, MA, U.S.A., p.623-635.

23. http://www.trl.ibm.co.jp/aglets

24. http://www.meitca.com/HSL/Projects/Concordia

GCMM 2004
Editors: Prasad K D V Yarlagadda and S Narayanan
Copyright © 2005, Vellore Institute of Technology, Vellore, India
Publisher: Narosa Publishing House Pvt. Ltd., New Delhi, India

CIP-Application to Automobile Industries

Jayant K Singh

Professor, Mechanical Engineering Dept.,College of Technology
Pantnagar- 263 145 (Uttaranchal), India

E-mail: jayantksingh@rediffmail.com

Abstract

Quality systems based on ISO – 9000 series of standards have become a coveted status in all sectors of economy. With the rapid industrialization and economic liberalization, the world is undergoing a phase of transition from fragmented market to a global one. To survive in a highly competitive world, it is imperative for these to be identified with and integrated in to the business environment. A standard implies a qualified goal and when it is reached to employees and managers, a like will become satisfied and complacent. A business enterprise must earn profit in order to realise satisfactory growth and to stablize its existence. This could only be possible provided a company tries to make continuous improvement of its system and structure. A quality system is crucial for its survival as a supplier and is a signal for export.

A Japanese concept 'Kaizen' has proved to be the key of success for automotive industries. The main objective of 'Kaizen' is not on a qualified goal expressed as a standard but rather on a 'Continuous Improvement in Performance'. This paper will elaborate this concept for easy understanding with case studies related to shop floor common problems of an automobile industry. The paper will also discuss the implementation and possible developments of CIP concept.

Keywords
Quality Improvement, CIP, Automobile,

1. INTRODUCTION

Continuous Improvement Performance (CIP) has proved to be the key to Japanese success. A wide array of tools and techniques is at the disposal of Kaizen Practitioners like Total Quality Control, Quality Circle, Just-in-time[1], Quality Improvement, Manufacturing Automation, Productive Maintenance and New Product Development etc. For these tools to unleash the power of 'CIP', they must be used with an understanding of how the combination of human needs and engineering provide the essential connection between people and their aspiration.

The International business environment can be characterized by:

1. Sharp increase in cost of material, energy and labour.
2. Changing customer values and more emphasis on quality requirements.
3. Increased competition among companies in saturated market.
4. Over capacity of production facilities.
5. A need to lower the break even point.
6. A need to introduce new product more frequently.

Any business house can earn profit in order to realize satisfactory growth and to stabilize its existence. This could only be possible provided the house tries to make continuous improvement of its system and structure to improvement in both product quality and workers motivation.

2. CIP – THE CONCEPT

Continuous Improvement in Performance concept covering most of the Japanese practices[2]. The implication of Kaizen is to generate a process oriented way of thinking and to develop strategies that assures continuous improvement of involving people at all levels of organizational structure. The 'CIP' message is that "not any day should go waste without some kind of improvement being made in the organization". In CIP, we assume that all concern developments should lead to increase the customer's satisfaction.

3. TECHNIQUE FOR PROBLEM SOLVING

The avenues through which CIP may be applied are endless. Kaoru Ishikwa[3] and Roger slater[4] emphasis on customer where as Deming[5] stresses on the importance of constant interaction among research, design, production and sales in conducting the company business. The problem solving phases for such concept as realized by Deming[4] is presented in fig (2), recast from the PDCA cycle shown in fig (1).

4. CASE STUDIES

Rejection due to production of defective products were considered as the subject for this investigation.

4.1 Case – 1

Consider the problem associated with the assembly of rear axle drive shaft for Maruti 800 CC vehicle. This assembly consists of bearing, retainer and a spacer onto the shaft. The existing workstation is designed to assemble and press fit the bearing, retainer and the spacer. It appears that akle of the vehicle after the complete final assembly gives some abnormal sound. This lead to rejection of the shaft. After the problem was examined and studied, it was detected that

the worker often skipped the assembling of the spacer to the axle shaft fig (3).

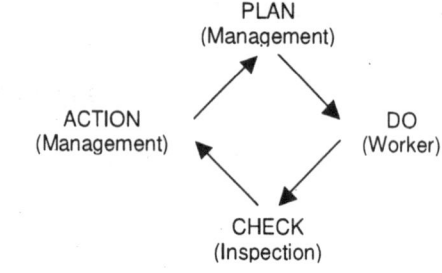

Fig. 1   PDCA   CYCLE

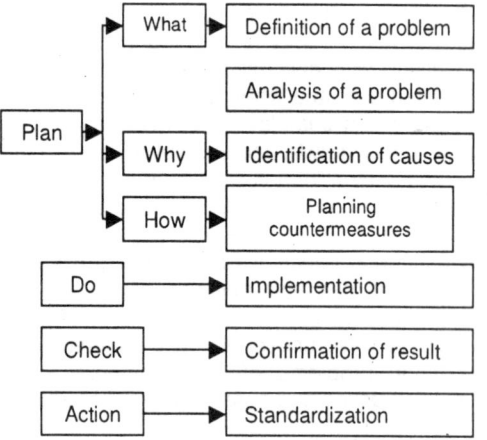

Fig. 2   PROBLEM SOLVING CYCLE

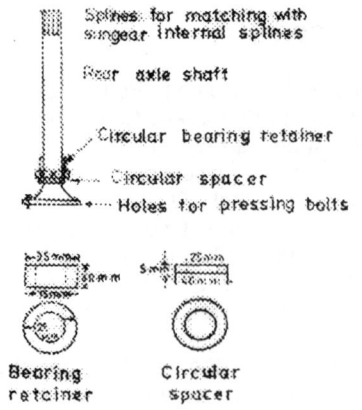

FIG.3 VARIOUS COMPONENTS OF REAR AXLE

252

Solution

Once spacer was mounted integral with the ram such that when it presses the OK condition shaft, it will move to the position as shown in Fig (4).

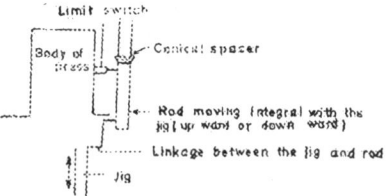

Fig:4 Setting of Spacer relative to Limit switch

In the absence of spacer of 3mm, the ram has also to travel a distance of 3mm to fix at the proper position. Consequently the bush provided in the rod strikes the limit switch which in turn will complete the electrical circuit and give a signal to the operator to make him alert that the spacer is missing.

Result:

Proposed solution after implementation not only increases the quality leading to customer satisfaction but also eliminates completely the occurrence of the problem.

4.2 Case – 2

Consider the two separate assembly lines for production of two different models of vehicle. The problem encountered by one of the assembly lines is the shortage of items to discontinue the operation in the assembly line. Due to this total man hour loss may occur for the assembly line.

Solution

After discussing with the people responsible, it was found that since the size of the hangers were same for both the models. In the shortage line over head area other models can be stored, say 15 Nos so that these stored models can be processed during the shortage period say 12 Nos.

Result

Total saving by keeping the line on for the shortage period is quite significant.

5. CONCLUSION

If implemented properly the benefits of CIP are more Productivity of any organization will increase by 20% without any further capital investment. It will also help to lower the break even point and help management to become more attentive towards customer needs and built a system that takes customers requirements. Thus Continuous Improvement in Performance, if applied to shop floor, will definitely make business more profitable and competitive.

6. REFERENCES

1. **E-milo Bartezzaghi, Turco Francesco** "The Impact of Just in-time in Production System performance – An Analytical Framework", *International Journal of Operations and Production Management*, Vol. 9(8), 1990.
2. **Kaizen Ramond Cheser**, " Kaizen is more than Contineous Improvement", *Journal of Quality Progress*, April 1998, pp 23-25.
3. **Kaoru Ishikawa**, " What is TQC?", The Japanese Way", *Eagel Wood Cliffs*, N.J., 1992.
4. **Roger H. Slater**, " The Pursuit of Quality through Personal Charge", Part- II, *Journal of Quality Progress*, May 1994, pp 76-80.
5. **Deming W.E**, "Kaizen – The Key to Japanese Competitive Success", New York Random House, 1986

GCMM 2004
Editors: Prasad K D V Yarlagadda and S Narayanan
Copyright © 2005, Vellore Institute of Technology, Vellore, India
Publisher: Narosa Publishing House Pvt. Ltd., New Delhi, India

Design and Optimisation of Collapsible PET Water Fountain Bottles

KeshavaMurthy V, Masood S H and Kosior E

Industrial Research Institute Swinburne,Swinburne University of Technology,
Hawthorn, Melbourne, Australia 3122

Email: smasood@swin.edu.au

Abstract

15-litre water fountain bottles, made of polycarbonate, providing clean drinking water in many offices and homes, have become a common sight in many developed and developing countries. This paper presents the development of a collapsible 15-litre water bottle made of an alternative material, PET, which offers several advantages including lightweight, use-and-throw concept and recyclability. The paper details the process and results of design, analysis and optimisation of the bottle shape using Pro/Engineer parametric modelling software and Pro/Mechanica Finite Element Modelling software. Some of the main criteria used in the design and development of this collapsible bottle include: light weight, collapsibility, identical neck dimensions to fit standard size water coolers and manufacturing by one step injection stretch blow moulding process. Results are supported by graphs and pictures of the final designed bottle.

Keywords

PET, Design, Optimisation, Collapsible bottle, FEA

1. INTRODUCTION
1.1 General Information

Refillable, 15-litre water fountain bottles, mounted downwards on water coolers, have become a common but pleasing sight in most commercial places and also households over the past decade or so. The main reason for the successful introduction of these bottles was largely due to contaminated, impure drinking water in many parts of the world. It has been quite a number of years since the introduction of these bottles, which are placed downward on water coolers with hot and cold-water faucets in them, making it really convenient and safe for people to drink. These bottles are made from Polycarbonate (PC) material and have been a very popular choice for manufacturers because it offers a flexible production alternative even though it is more expensive than other plastics. PC bottles are designed to normally withstand an average 25 trips to the refilling plant. While about 700,000 of these bottles were sold in Western Europe in 1999, industry experts expected the consumption to triple by the year 2004 to about 2.3 million bottles [1].

Extensive research and development is in full swing to penetrate the market and gradually replace the 15-litre PC water bottles with the use of a cost effective plastic material, Poly Ethylene Terephthalate (PET). This is because PET offers excellent mechanical and barrier characteristics along with superior recyclability. Also, the process of cleaning and refilling of PC bottles, which involves bleaching and caustic treatment, poses extreme health hazards, which is of prime concern.

1.2. Nature of Problem

PC water bottles are taken in contract collection trucks by refilling companies for cleaning and refilling. However more recent news from various parts of the world report about residual chemicals in the bottle after the process of refilling which involves cleaning the bottle with caustic and chemicals and bleaching. This has raised serious hygiene and health safety issues. It is also a known fact that plastics are made from fossil fuels, thereby having a serious effect on global warming.

There are however, other problems to be taken into account. PC bottles, after the final use, most often find their way into the trashcans. It can be readily pictured that two or three of these 15-litre jumbos can fill up any bin. This gives rise to problems in collection, transportation and storage before progressing on to recycling. Apart from these issues, a bottle made of PC weighs approximately 750 grams and the cost of recycling is considerably high and varies from country to country. In Australia, the cost of recycling is around A$750/tonne. All these may well add up to the final cost of the bottle.

2. RESEARCH
2.1. Introduction

One effective solution to the afore-mentioned problem would be a bottle, which can be used only once and can be collapsed and crushed after its first and final use. This would mean that the so designed bottle should be of optimum wall thickness so as to provide enough strength to store 15 litres of water and still collapse under normal load by a human being. Cost effectiveness of the material, design and processing also plays a quintessential role in such a venture. Investigation into material characteristics reveal that Poly Ethylene Terephthalate or PET offers excellent mechanical and barrier characteristics, ease of processing, superior clarity, great impact resistance,

leak resistance and is nearly 1/4th of the cost of PC.

2.2. Global Practices

Extensive research is presently being carried out in many countries around the globe to effectively introduce 15-litre PET containers into the market and gradually replace PC bottles. In 1999, Sterling Containers, a company in the USA has produced the largest stretch-blow moulded 5-gallon (18 litres) PET bottle for home delivery [2]. PET is a felt to be a better choice by designers when there are complex shapes to be considered. It was observed that a company in the UK was distributing PET bottles in an unusual triangular shape [3]. Due to low cost, better aesthetic appearance and savings in transport and handling, PET is being preferred over PC. Also, areas where the collection and recycling system is not so well organised, the latter too do not live out the number of cycles. It has been estimated that the market for 5-gallon water containers is increasing at an annual rate of 20% to 25% and research has showed that Europe alone will need 5 to 7 million units by the year 2007 [4].

2.3. Technological Advancements

Stretch blow moulding technique has been employed to produce PET bottles. This is conventionally a two-step process wherein the preform is injection moulded in the first step, reheated, blown and stretched simultaneously in the second step [5]. To achieve this, two machines are used leading to double the cost and wastage of energy because of the need to reheat the preforms. There is also an observed risk of surface damage resulting from knocking of preforms during storage and transportation.

There are many stretch blow-moulding machines currently available in the market, that are able to roll out 30 to 40 bottles an hour. AOKI, a Japanese company, manufacturer of ASB (Aoki Stretch Blow-Moulding) machines, developed an innovative one-step process, which eliminates the need for two machines and the whole process of blowing of the bottle takes place in one single step. Hot preforms are moved between open blow moulds. After the mould closure, the stretch rods stretch the preform to the required length and simultaneously high-pressure air inflates the preform similar to the inflation of a balloon. This results in a high precision injection moulded neck finish [6].

Even though technological innovations in terms of manufacturing process and the material research has made consistent and considerable progress over the years to address the issues of contamination, residual chemicals and health concerns, the call for a one way fully collapsible 15-litre PET bottle is loud and clear. This paper presents the design and development of a collapsible 15-litre water bottle made of PET.

3. COLLAPSIBLE 15-LITRE PET BOTTLE
3.1. Design preview

The design and development of a bottle is a very long but interesting process, with great attention paid to minute details such as neck dimensions, radii of curvature along the bottle etc. This process has become far easier since the introduction of CAD and parametric modelling techniques. There are several parametric modelling software available today, which not only provide design flexibility but also the facility by which design parameters like thickness volume, density, mass etc can also be calculated and altered to suit our needs. This paper illustrates the use of Pro/Engineer parametric modelling software, which has been chosen in this case to design the 15-litre collapsible PET bottle.

3.2. Objectives of Research

The primary aims here were to design a bottle which is preferably half the weight of the existing PC bottle, which weighs around 750 grams, have identical neck dimensions to the conventional 15-litre PC bottles so as to fit the water coolers readily available, should be of optimum wall thickness so as to facilitate easy collapsing and light-weight and finally, be able to be made from one step injection stretch blow moulding production process.

3.3. Design Methodology

The design process started with measuring the critical dimensions of the existing bottle, that are the neck and shoulder portions, so as to incorporate it in the new design to make it suitable for existing coolers. The normal collapsing technique of a bottle is longitudinal collapsion but here a lateral collapsion was attempted. This gave a certain degree of flexibility in design and a template for consideration of various shapes for the bottle.

A body diameter of 250 mm was maintained and a square body of side 250 mm was constructed. The length of the body 350 mm, the distance between the start of the shoulder to the start of the neck 70 mm and neck dimension of 45 mm were all maintained as per the existing bottle. The collapsibility of the bottle heavily depended on the wall thickness, as did the stability of the bottle. Initially a thickness of 0.5 mm for the entire bottle was assigned and the bottle was modelled in Pro/Engineer CAD software.

3.4. CAD model of collapsible PET bottle

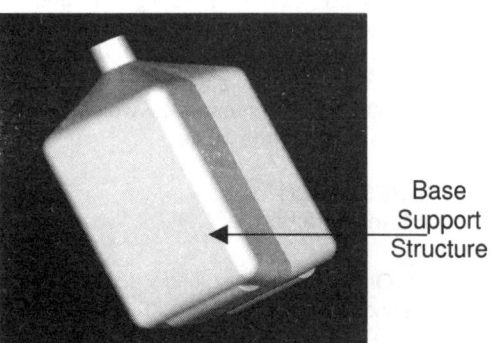

Base Support Structure

Fig. 1: CAD Model of the bottle

Figure 1 shows a CAD model of the collapsible PET bottle. The details of the model is summarised as follows. Feature based modelling technique was used to model the bottle. Physical properties like mass, volume, etc. were computed from the program. First the volume of the 'solid' bottle was determined. The bottle was then 'shelled' (removal of material to the desired wall thickness) and the volume of the 'shell' bottle was determined. The difference between the two values gave the volume occupied by the water, which is 15 litres.

The base support structure prevents the bottle from rocking while standing upright, during transportation and handling.

This model was then exported in IGES format to Pro/Mechanica software to perform the FEM structural analysis.

4. FINITE ELEMENT ANALYSIS OF THE BOTTLE

4.1. Finite element modelling (FEM)

The exported CAD model consisted of lines, curves and innumerous nodes. This model was converted to a finite element model using the tools available in the software. Surfaces and Shells were generated to prepare the model for analysis.

Figure 2 shows a Finite Element Model generated in the Pro/Mechanica software. After the shell model was generated, material and mechanical properties of PET such as density, Poisson's ratio, Young's modulus, co-efficient of thermal expansion values etc., were input into the Pro/Mechanica system. Appropriate shell thickness was assigned for different sections of the bottle to carry out structural analysis.

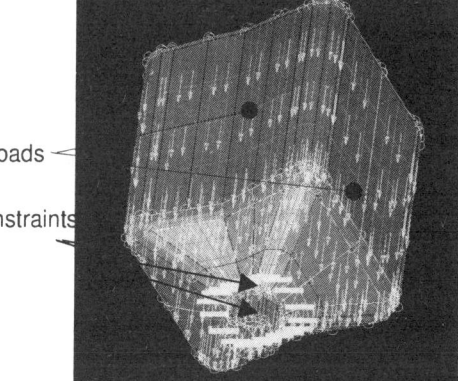

Loads

Constraints

Fig. 2: FE Model under 15-litre water load

4.3. Structural Analysis for stability of the PET bottle

Boundary conditions such as constraints and loads were applied to the model reflecting the real time situation the bottle operates under. It can be seen from Figure 2 that the model is constrained halfway up the shoulder and then remaining portion is left free. This is because, in reality the bottle, when placed on the cooler with full water in it, the neck being completely concealed rests on half the shoulder and then other half is not constrained. So the constraints as shown in the figure above resembled the real condition. Figure 2 also shows the model is subjected to load as indicated by the arrows pointing downwards which represents the load acting on the bottle applied by 15 litres of water, which amounts to 157.2 N. Using single pass convergence method the analysis was run and results were observed.

4.2. Results for 15 litre water load

Figure 3 shows the structural analysis results generated by the Pro/Mechanica system under a load of 15 litres water. The result shows a maximum displacement of 6.63 mm for an optimum shoulder thickness of 0.35 mm and body thickness of 0.2 mm.

The results are shown as a fringe of colours with the intended result value ranging from the lowest to the highest in a colour range of blue to red in that order, as shown in Figure 3.

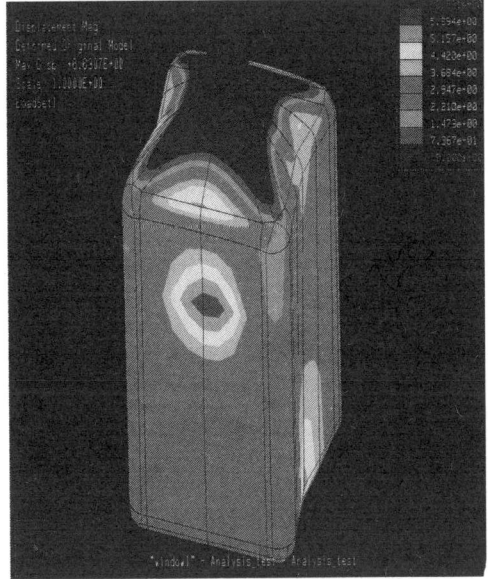

Fig. 3: Result window 15 litre water load

4.4. Structural Analysis of Collapsion of the PET bottle

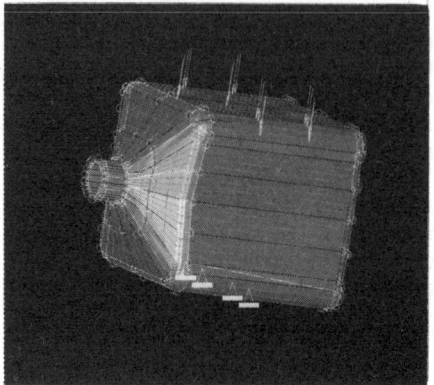

Fig. 4: F.E. Model under crushing load

Figure 4 shows the finite element model of the collapsible bottle under the application of a normal load by human foot on one surface with the other constrained as fixed on all the three axes. A minimum static load of 300 N was applied on the top surface and the analysis was run to check for the collapsion.

Figure 5 shows the structural analysis results generated by the Pro/Mechanica system under the load of 300 N for a shoulder thickness of 0.35 mm and body thickness of 0.2 mm.

The simulated results showed a maximum displacement of 8.77 e+01 mm or 87.7cm. It was also observed that the crushing pattern was uniform about the model and followed a particular sequence from the neck to the base of the bottle as can be observed from result window in Figure 5. The weight of the PET bottle was calculated to be 311 grams, which is less than half the weight of the existing PC bottle that is around 750 grams.

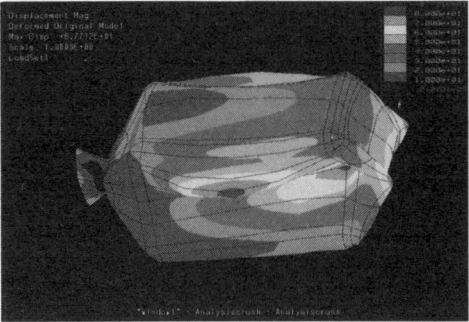

Fig. 5: Result window 300N crushing load

5. OPTIMISATION OF PET BOTTLE

One of the main areas of concern in this attempt was the effect of the load on the shoulder and neck portions because these two portions bear the maximum weight of the bottle under load. Several runs of the analysis carried out with different values of varying wall thickness provided clearer understanding of the behaviour of PET material under different conditions. Comparative test results and testing for average values of shoulder and body thickness optimised the design and satisfied the criterion of stability and collapsibility of the bottle.

With the results obtained from the analysis of the bottle and with the awareness of the many ill-effects the existing PC bottle poses, it was proven that a collapsible one-way 15-litre PET water fountain bottle would be practicable in terms of manufacturing and marketing in a global scenario.

A summary of comparisons between the existing 15-litre PC bottle and the newly designed 15-litre PET collapsible bottle is shown in Table 1.

6. CONCLUSIONS

The proposed design of collapsible PET bottle offers an effective alternative to existing PC bottles meeting all the intended design objectives and advantages. It is expected that such a design will overcome the problems associated with the existing PC water fountain bottles and the inherent hazards that come along with its usage.

There are however, many other issues that have to be taken into account such as incorporating a handle to the PET bottle, which is a difficult feat to achieve because of process incompatibility, future research into material properties, investigation of other manufacturing techniques and machinery.

Table 1: Comparison of New PET bottle and the existing PC bottle

Features	PET bottle	PC Bottle
Material Cost	Low	High
Production Process	Injection stretch blow moulding	Extrusion moulding
Type of process	Single step	Multiple steps
Collapsible	Yes	No
Weight	311 grams	750 grams
Recycling cost	Low	High
Market	Rising	Stagnant
Drop testing performance	High	Lesser than PET
Refilling	Unnecessary	Necessary
Washing and cleaning	Unnecessary	Necessary

The use of 15-litre PET water bottle for one-way application is becoming a crucial reality in today's competitive market. Clear, lightweight and cost effective 15-litre collapsible PET water bottles may ultimately replace PC bottle once and for all in the immediate future.

7. REFERENCES

1. **Arnaldo Siniga** and **Michael Thielen**, (2001), "Polycarbonate Water Bottles On The Advance", http://www.petnology.com
2. "PET makes debut in 5-gallon water bottles", *Plastics Technology*, New York: May 1999, Vol. 45 (5); pp. 59.
3. "Filling the big ones", www.petpla.net
4. **Matthew T. Defosse**, (2000), "PET is low-cost alternative to PC in 5-gal water containers", *Chemical Week Publishing, L.L.C, Modern Plastics.*
5. **Martin L. et.al.** (1999), "Modelling And Experimental Validation of the Stretch Blow Molding of PET", *ANTEC Proceedings*, 982-987.
6. "Direct Heat Conditioning Stretch-Blow Moulding Machines", *AOKI Product Catalogue,* 2003.

GCMM 2004
Editors: Prasad K D V Yarlagadda and S Narayanan
Copyright © 2005, Vellore Institute of Technology, Vellore, India
Publisher: Narosa Publishing House Pvt. Ltd., New Delhi, India

Effective JIT Implementation using 5's Philosophy

Rane S B*, Bhonsale A V**, Mantha S S***, Aravandekar S G****

Lecturer*, Professor**, Dept. of Mech. Engg., Sardar Patel C .O.E.,
Mumbai – 400 058, India

Email- ranesantoshb@yahoo.co.in, ourpapers2003@yahoo.co.in

Professor & Head***, Dept of Mech . Engg.,V.J.T.I., Mumbai, India

Email- vjtirobotics@vsnl.com

Dy. Manager****, Field Quality,
Mahindra & Mahindra Ltd. Tractor Division, Mumbai, India.

Email- aravandekar.sadashiv@mahindra.co

Abstract
Global business market has become more sophisticated and challenging due to Liberalized economy, Privatization and Globalization. The products and / or services therefore must be provided with World-class level. It is therefore necessary to emphasis on waste elimination, waste reduction by implementing Just-In-Time (JIT) technique. Using 5S philosophy can further enhance the effectiveness of JIT.

The effective JIT implementation focuses on systematically managed supply chain of products and / or services. It is necessary to manage all work centers efficiently in synchronization to give the requisite output. This is possible when 5'S philosophy is adopted and inculcated in the organization.

Paper describes the concept of Effective JIT Implementation Using 5'S Philosophy to enhance the effectiveness of supply chain. It also presents the case study in support of the concept.

Key Words
Just-In-Time (JIT), 5S - SEIRI, SEITON, SEISO, SEIKETSU, SHITSUKE

1.SEIRI

Sorting, keep the necessary items in work area, dispose off less frequently used items or keep them at a distance storage area, unneeded items are discarded.

Parts are kept as per their frequency of usage. Following criteria can be used to decide on requirements of the parts: -
1. Item is not needed.
2. Item is needed however quantity in stock is more than what is needed for consumption in near future.
3. Critically decide the quantity of contingency parts to be retained and criteria for such parts.

Seiri helps to keep work area tidy, improves searching and fetching efficiency, and generally clears much space. Seiri is also excellent way to gain valuable floor space and eliminate old broken tools, obsolete jigs and fixtures, scrap and excess raw material. Proper Arrangement means sorting what you have, identifying the needs and throwing out those unnecessary. One example is using red-tags. This is a little red-bordered paper saying what the production is, how many are accumulated and then stick these red tags on every box of inventory. It enhances the easiness to know the inventory status and can reduce cost.

Success Indicators can be taken as Area saved or percentage of space available , Reduction in inventory

2. SEITON

Systematic arrangement for the most efficient and effective retrieval. A good example of Seiton is the tool panel. Effective Seiton can be achieved by painting floors to visualize the dirt, outlining work areas and locations, shadow tool boards. To reduce machine downtime through Total Productive Maintenance (TPM) it is necessary to have tools at hand. So a specific mobile tool cart was designed. Orderliness means keeping things in order. Examples include keeping shelves in order, keeping storage areas in order, keeping workplace in order, keeping worktables in order and keeping the office in order.

Seiton saying would be: "A place for everything and everything on its place."

Success Indicators can be taken as Time saved in searching ,Time saved in material handling.

In short these means : Arrange correctly in accordance with the correct method of doing activities.

3. SEISO

Cleaning. After the first thorough cleaning when implementing 5'S, daily follow-up of Cleaning is necessary in order to sustain this improvement. Cleanliness is also helpful to notice damages on equipment such as leaks, breakages and misalignments. These minor damages, if left unattended, could lead to equipment failure and loss of production. Regular cleaning is one type of inspection. Seiso is an important part of basic TPM; Total Productive Maintenance (TPM) and Safety matter through cleanliness is obvious.

Success Indicators can be taken as Reduction in machine down time, Reduction in no. of accidents

4. SEIKETSU

Standardizing. Once the first three 'S' have been implemented, it should be set as a standard so to keep these good practices at work area. Without it, the situation will deteriorate right back to old habits. Have easy-to-follow standards and develop a structure to support it. Allow employees to join the development of such standards. The first 3 'S' are often executed by order. Seiketsu helps to turn it into natural, standard behavior. Here the Visual Management is used as indicators. Success Indicators can be taken as Less inventory, Less documentation

5. SHITSUKE

Finally, to keep first 4 S alive, it is necessary to keep people educating, maintaining standards. Set up a formal system, with display of results, follow-up. Keep '5S' alive in an ongoing improvement way; the Kaizen way. The effect of continuous improvement leads to less waste, better quality and faster lead times.

Success Indicators can be taken as High employee morale, Involvement of all people.

EFFECTIVE 'JIT' IMPLEMENTATION USING '5S' PHILOSOPHY

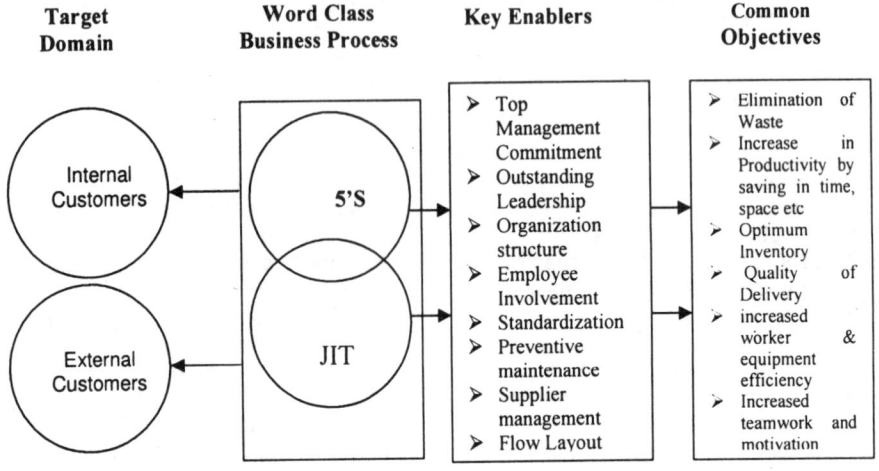

VARIOUS FUNCTIONAL AREAS OF JIT INFLUENCED BY '5S' PHILOSOPHY

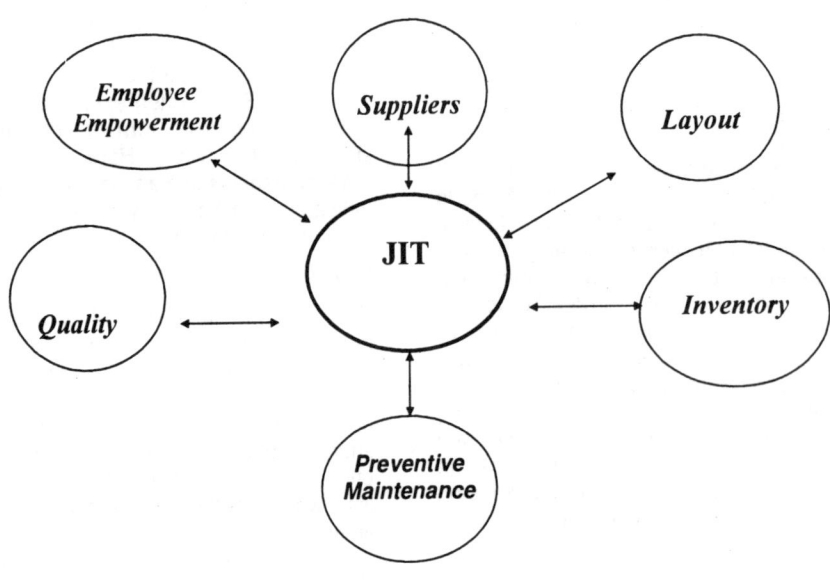

262

Taking the complete advantage of JIT the organization intending to implement JIT needs to integrate '5S' in all the levels of JIT.

An integrated Model is as shown in figure. On one side it shows the outcome needed to be achieved by integrating JIT and 5S.

On the other side it shows the key enablers & objectives to be achieved. In order that this model be effective & efficient following key enablers are of importance.

6.TARGET DOMAIN

➢ JIT focuses on internal as well as external customers. JIT concentrates on smooth flow of the material from one person to another, from one department to another and takes care of internal customer's satisfaction. JIT also deliver the quality products to cater the changing needs of the external customer and increase the satisfaction level. It increases the responsiveness of the organization to the dynamic market.

➢ 5S philosophy focuses on internal customer. It also increases the external customer satisfaction level by systematically functioning the entire organization.

7.KEY ENABLERS

Top Management commitment:

Management of the organization should be committed to effective JIT implementation using 5'S philosophy. It should create a base for the same. Top Management should create conducive environment in the organization for it. It should eliminate all obstacles in the execution of the theme. Management should take lead & take the employees in confidence, provide essential training to them, increase awareness among them. The management must make it as an integral part of the system. Thus top management commitment is one of the most important key enablers for concept.

Outstanding leadership: Outstanding leadership is must for effective implementation of Jit with 5S. Leadership is very important driving force on which all the activities of the organization depends. Leadership of exceptionally high caliber is essential to bring into sharp focus all those desirable forces that can transform an organization into a competitive responsive organization offering services that can consistently delight its customers. The success or failure of any programme depends to a great extent on its Leadership. It is the leader of the Organization who can decide on the implementation of the above process model. Leaders should demonstrate their capabilities to motivate people to achieve the organizational goals in an enthusiastic manner. Thus outstanding leadership is must for effective implementation of JIT And 5S.

Organization structure: Organization structure is one of the most important key enablers for the JIT implementation. Appropriate, structured organization not only smoothens the flow of the information and material but also enhances the effectiveness. Goals and objectives of organization are achieved by appropriate organization structure like flat organization.

Employee Involvement : JIT and 5 S insists on involvement of all employees to their best possible extent. It focuses on training of the people to fulfill their individual roles in the movement of change, then empowering them to act accordingly & finally recognizing, rewarding the best performance to encourage increased involvement.

Standardization and simplification: JIT emphasizes on small-standardized containers. This simplifies movement of material and use of material handling equipments. JIT and 5S concentrate on standardization of the parts, simplification of manufacturing processes.

JIT also concentrates on rationalization of product range. This finally reduces the set up time .

Preventive maintenance: JIT and 5S focus on the routine inspection and service operations designed to detect potential failure conditions and make major adjustments or repair s that will avoid break down of the machine or accidents.

Supplier management: JIT suggests single but highly reliable vendor. Suppliers are considered and are treated as partners. They are expected and trained to achieve quality, production by suitable methodology including 5S so that there is no error in the delivery commitment. Extreme care is taken in selection and development of the vendor.

Flow Layout: The physical layout of manufacturing facilities must be arranged in order to keep th4e process flow streamlined. i.e. For each part the proportion of value added time should be more, there should be minimum queuing and non-value added times. Preference must be given to the use of dedicated lines, U-shaped or Parallel lines, use of small machines. Flexibility of the system is the key requirement for responding to the changing demand in the market. The 5 S philosophy increases the smoothness of the flow pattern.

As a sample, various elements of JIT and effects of implementation of some of the 'S' in respective domain and benefits out of implementation are discussed as follows.

a) **Inventory: -**
   - Seiri (sorting): It classifies the material as per their usage, quantity & location from workplace.
   - Seiton (Systematic arrangement): It helps to maintain the optimum inventory by defining the proper location.
   - Siketsu (Standardization): It helps to get visual control over inventory.

b) **Layout :-**
   - Seiri (sorting): It removes unwanted items, machinery from the workplace. Thus it helps to layout the plant effectively.

   - Seiton (Systematic arrangement): It ensures the availability of all equipments whenever required which reduces the set-up time, waiting time, rework time & total lead time. Thus increases productivity.

c) **Scheduling: -**
   - Seiton (Systematic arrangement): It provides the space for material storage as per its re-order quantity . It helps to schedule effectively.
   - Siketsu (Standardization): It helps to have visual control over inventory as per signals received from the visual control Mechanism.

d) **Preventive Maintenance: -**
   - Seiso (Cleaning): As Seiso calls for inspection, many probable defects can get detected, identified during cleaning of machinery. This is the basic principle of Total productive maintenance. 'My machine' concepts get realized by workman, which helps in better maintenance of machinery & reduction in down time.

e) **Quality: -**
   - Seiso (Cleaning): As Seiso calls for inspection. Many probable defects, which may lead to the variation in performance of the machine, can get detected during cleaning of machinery. Thus the reduction in process variation will be helpful in achieving the consistency in operation & in turn improvement in quality.

f) **Employee Empowerment: -**
   - As all '5S' calls for total employee involvement, the belongingness in people increases which results into highly motivated & committed workforce.

g) **Suppliers: -**
   - If the '5S' is implemented at supplier end then, parent organization will be benefited in many ways. e.g. lower inventory level, timely delivery of right quantity with right quality.

Thus 5'S plays a vital role in incasing JIT effectiveness.

Table-1.

Sr. No	Area	Parameter	Without '5S'	With '5S'	Average % Improvement
1	Inventory Level	1. Control on re-ordering	50 %	95 %	200 %
		2. Visual control	25 %	85 %	
		3. Control over non-moving, slow moving	25 %	95 %	
2	Layout	1. Storage	75 %	95 %	40 %
		2. Material handling	More	50 % less	
		3. Space utilization	Low	25 % Max	
3	Scheduling	1. Control on re-ordering	50 %	95 %	200 %
		2. Visual control	25 %	85 %	
		3. Control over non-moving, slow moving	25 %	95 %	
4	Down time	1. Response time	High	85 % Less	140 %
		2. Visual control.	25 %	85 %	
		3. Reactive approach	Yes	No	
5	Quality	1. Visual control	25 %	85 %	135 %
		2. Reactive Approach	Yes	No	
		3. Rework	High	75 % less	

8.CASE STUDY

The concept was implemented in a Public Ltd. Automotive company. Prior to implementation, sufficient inputs were given at various levels by conducting training sessions. The progress was periodically tracked and after a period of two years of implementation, the comparison was done to evaluate success and benefits obtained in various functional areas of the organization. The evaluation done in March 2004 is as given in Table-1.

9.CONCLUSIONS

The **5S** are prerequisites for any improvement activity. Avoiding waste is a potential gain. **5S** Philosophy focuses on effective workstation organization, simplifies work environment, reduces waste while improving quality and safety. There is no hope for improvements in efficiency or quality with disorderly dirty work place, waste of time and scrap. They are the features, which are common to all locations and are the meters of how well an organization is functioning.

Case study conveys the Potential benefits obtained in a short span of two years. This clearly indicates that successful implementation of JIT by inculcating '5S' philosophy can give an edge over others in competitive environment and therefore necessary for competitive growth.

10.REFERENCES

1. **Alonso, R.L**. and **Frasier, C.W.**, " JIT hits home : a case study in reducing management delays ", *Sloan Management Review*, 59 –67
2. **Chu C** and **Shin W**,/ 1992, "Simulation studies in JIT production", *Int. J. of Production Research,* Vol. 30(11), pp.2573-2586.
3. **Funk, J.L.**, " A Comparison of Inventory Cost Reduction strategies in a J I T Manufacturing System," *International Journal of Production Research*, Vol.27,No. 7,pp.1065-1080,1989.
4. **Hayes, R.H.**, 1981, "Why Japanese Factories Work", *Harvard Business Review,* Vol. 59 No. July-August pp. 56-66
5. **Lu. D.J.(translator)**, 1986, Kanban Just In Time at Toyota, Edited by Japan Management Association (Productivity Press).
6. **Levitt. T** ., " Production line approach to service.,"***Harward Business review.***,pp.42 -52, Sep-Oct 1972.
7. **Less., J.** and **Date,B**.," Quality Circles in Service Industries: A study of their use," The *Service Industry Journal*, Vol. ,no.2 ,1988.
8. **Mejabi, O,** and **Wasserman G.S.**, 1992, "Basic concepts in JIT modeling". **Int. J.of production Research**, Vol.30(i) pp 141-149
9. **Mejabi, O**, and **Wasserman G.S.**, 1990, *"Simulation Contructs for JIT Modelling"*, Technical Report, Department of Manufacturing And Industrial Engineering, Wayne State University, Detroit U.S.A.
10. **Monden, Y**, 1983, Toyota Production System: Practical Approach to Production *Management Industrial Engineering And Management Press,* Atlanta, Georgia.
11. **Ohno, T.**, 1982, How the Toyota Production System was Created, *Japanese Economic Studies*, Vol. 10 No. 4, Summer 1982, pp.83-101
12. **Schonberger, R.J.** , Japanese Manufacturing Techniques Nine Hidden Lessons in Simplicity. The Press, New York.
13. **Schonerberger, R J** .," Some Observations on the Advantages and Implementation Issues of Just –in-Time production Systems." Journal of Operations Management, Nov 1994.
14. **Shinohara, I.**, " New production systems: J I T crossing industry boundaries." Productivity Press, Cambridge , May 1988.
15. **Shankar, R.** (2000), *Industrial Engineering and Management,* Galotia Publishers, New Delhi.

GCMM 2004
Editors: Prasad K D V Yarlagadda and S Narayanan
Copyright © 2005, Vellore Institute of Technology, Vellore, India
Publisher: Narosa Publishing House Pvt. Ltd., New Delhi, India

M.O.S.T.- Productivity Improvement through New Technique

Siddharth K Tated* & Chopde I K**

***Student, M.Tech (I.E.), **Professor, Dept. of Mech. Engg.
VNIT, Nagpur**

Email: siddharthtated@rediffmail.com

Abstract

The paper is concerned with the introduction of work Measurement technique called "Maynard's Operation sequence technique" essential for planning & controlling operations. Every work measurement technique aims at improving the productivity by reducing work content. With MOST training, Engineers & analysts will become more productive. They will spend less time on data collection and will be able to transform the work processes for improvement in much shorter time. MOST is breakthrough work measurement technique that allows greater variety of work for Manufacturing, Engineering to Administrative service activities to be measured quickly with accuracy and ease.

Keywords

MOST, Sequence Models, TMU

1. INTRODUCTION

H B Maynard and Company had introduced MOST system after they found the application of PMTS, MTM, detailed in data collection. This new system brought into practice in USA in 1975.

2. CONCEPT OF MOST WORK MEASUREMENT TECHNIQUE

A MOST analysis is a complete study of every activity. MOST is a system to measure work, therefore it concentrates on movement of objects1. It was noticed that the movements of the object follow certain consistent repetitive patterns such as reach, grasp, move & position the object. To move an object, its movement is described by a universal sequence model.

Objects can be moved in only one of two ways, either they are picked up and moved freely through space or they are moved and maintain contact with another surface. For example, a box can be picked up and carried from one end of a workbench to other or it can be pushed across the top of workbench. For each type of a move, a different sequence of event occurs, therefore a separate MOST activity sequence model applies.

The use of tools is analyzed through a separate activity sequence model that allows the analyze the opportunity to follow the movement of a hand tool through a standard sequence of events, which in fact is combination of the two basic sequence models.

Consequently, only three basic MOST activity sequence are needed for describing the manual work plus a fourth for measuring the movements of objects with manual cranes l

1) The general move sequence (for spatial movement of an object freely through air)-

The activity sequence is made up of four sub activities -

A - Action distance (Mainly horizontal)
B- Body Motion (Mainly Vertical)
G- Gain control
P - Placement

2) The controlled move sequence (for the movements of an object when it remains in contact with a surface or is attached to another object during the movement)

In addition to A, B & C parameters from General move sequence; the sequence model for controlled move contains the following sub activities.

M - Move controlled
X - Process time
I - Align

3) The Tool use sequence (for the use of common hand tools).

This sequence model covers the use of hand tools for activities such as fastening or loosening, cutting, cleaning, gauging and recording. Also certain activities requiring the use of the Brain for mental processes as reading & thinking. The tool use sequence model is combination of general move & controlled move. It consists of following additional sub activities -

F - Fasten
L- Loosen
C - cut
S - surface treat
M- Measure
R - record
T - think

All the sub activities mentioned above are assigned a time related index numbers as per the motion content of sub activity.

3. MOST SYSTEM FAMILY

MOST is divided into various systems as follows:

3.1 Mini MOST

At the lowest level, Mini MOST provides the most detailed and precise method analysis. In general, this level of detail & precision is required to analyze any operation likely to be repeated more than 1500 times per week. An operation in this category may range from 2 to 10 seconds. The index value total for a sequence model is multiplied by 1 and converted to minutes or seconds

Area of Application: Light press shop operation, Manufacturing of PCB etc.

3.2 Basic MOST

At the intermediate level, operation that is likely to be performed more than 150 but fewer than 1500 times per week should be analyzed with Basic MOST. An operation in this category may range from few seconds to 10 min. in length. The index value total for a sequence model is multiplied by 10 and converted to minutes or seconds

A fully indexed general move sequence for example may appear as follows -
A6 B6 G1 A3 B3 P3 A3.

Where -
A6 - walk three four steps to object location.
B6 - Bend and arise
G1- Gain the control of one light objects
B3- partial bending
P3- Place & adjust the objects
A3- return back

This example could for instance represents the following activity,
Walk 3 steps to pick up a box from floor level, walk 2 steps & place the box on rack.

Areas of Application: General Manual work

3.3 Maxi MOST

At the highest level, Maxi MOST is used to analyze operations that are likely to be performed fewer than 150 times per week. An operation in this category may be just less than 2 minutes to more than several hours in length. The index value total for a sequence model is multiplied by 100 & then converted as required.

Area of Application: Maintenance Work, Ship Building, Rail Car Fabrication etc.

4. TIME UNITS

The Time units used in MOST are identical to those used in basic MTM system & are based on hours & parts of hours called Time Measurement units (TMU) 2 thus,

1 TMU = 1/28 of seconds = 0.036 second
$$= 0.0006 \text{ minute}$$
$$= 0.00001 \text{ hour}$$

Adding the index numbers & multiplying the sum by 1 for Mini MOST, 10 for Basic MOST & 100 for Max MOST, calculate the time value in TMU for each sequence model. (2) In our example of Basic MOST general move sequence, the time would be (6+6+1+3+3+3+3) * 10 = 250 TMU approx. = 0.15 minutes.

All the time values established by MOST reflect the activity of an average skilled operator working at an average performance level or normal pace. This time represents pure work content at 100 % performance level.

5. METHODOLOGY

The following methodology is used for carrying our MOST study -

1) The operation or assembly line on which the study is to be carried out is notified.
2) Rapid information is collected of the operation under sight.
3) The observer notes down the major stages of Operation.
4) On his desk he redefines the operation in detail by means of MOST data card / sheet
5) Any operator's motions are checked according to the principles of motion economy and Industrial Engineer makes corrections.
6) If required, Layout changes are carried out.
7) The recent MOST sheet is recorded for future references.

6. ADVANTAGES OF MOST OVER OTHER WORK MEASUREMENT TECHNIQUES

1) It is faster than other work measurement technique and easy to learn & understand easily.
2) It is compact in nature and reduces the paper work.
3) Rating factor is not required[2].
4) The time can be calculated in advance.
5) It is method sensitive so non-value added activities could be easily detected.
6) The staff required is less than other methods and hence economical.
7) It is universal in application.

7. CONCLUSION

It is possible to achieve the dramatic improvement by Productivity by imopementing MOST in less time with less paper work & by giving proper training to associates without disturbing the production system.

8. REFERENCES

1) **Kjell B Zandin** ," MOST - Work measurement systems", Second edition., McGraw Hill Publications.
2) **Venketesh Subramanian, Narkhede B.E.,** June 2003, " Productivity Improvement", *Industrial Engineering Journal* volume XXXII , P.14-17.

GCMM 2004
Editors: Prasad K D V Yarlagadda and S Narayanan
Copyright © 2005, Vellore Institute of Technology, Vellore, India
Publisher: Narosa Publishing House Pvt. Ltd., New Delhi, India

Reverse Engineering of Ka-Band Antenna- A Case Study

Bhardwaj R K, Atul Dev & Dutta V P

DEAL, Def. R&D Organisation
Min. of Defence, Govt. Of India, DEHRADUN – 248001

E- Mail: dealdrdo@del2.vsnl.net.in

Abstract

The development process of product has been influenced by the present technologies like CAD/ CAM/CAE. Time to market is another factor, which governs the reduction in development time to achieve the profitability of the company. The new and revised goals in the competitive environment such as drastic reduction of product development time and increase of customized features of product require innovative strategies & support tools. To cope up with these challenges Reverse Engineering (RE) techniques are effective which helps in the implementation of concepts such as Concurrent Engineering (CE). RE is basically the process by which a physical object is converted into a virtual CAD model. Traditionally it has been carried out by taking the measurements from product itself with certain probes and then transfering it into mathematical surfaces by means of some CAD softwares. RE also uses non-contact digitizers and other modern accessories to digitize the object. This paper describes the emerging methodologies devoted to the applications of RE considering their Impact on mechanical design process. A brief description of the method is outlined with a case study in which a Ka-Band antenna was reverse engineered. The hardware and software's used for RE are also described. It has been concluded that RE is a very effective technique for R&D Organizations and small-scale industries because of reduction in time to market and labour among many other advantages.

Keywords

Reverse Engineering, Concurrent Engineering

1. INTRODUCTION

It is very necessary and important to reduce the product development time in order to survive in the competitive world because of product diversity, time to market, manufacturing process diversity, economy of machining, complexity of product and quality of product etc. CAD/CAM/CAE has improved a lot by which the changes in product can be brought to market fast. The stringent requirements of the customers necessitate the industries to adopt the best techniques and machines available and feasible for the development of their products. Product development using CAD/CAM/CAE [1] starts with geometric modeling of the part using standard CAD software's like Unigraphics, Inventor, Pro-E, I-DEAS, and Auto CAD etc. The model is analyzed and optimized using CAE tools [2] and finally it is produced using CAM softwares and CNC machines [3]. This is an iterative process for the final optimized product. During the iterative process there are many changes and CAD/ CAM/ CAE tools help a lot for the faster development. There are many cases where the geometrical modeling is not feasible because of non-availability of dimensions or when the physical part is required to be reproduced as in our case study. RE is the appropriate solution for such problems in which the function of design, manufacturing and measurements are integrated to reduce the total elapsed time & to bring the product to market faster. Surface models are generated from point clouds captured by 3-D scanning digitizers or 3-D Co-ordinate Measuring Machines (CMM)[4]. When CAD geometrical models are not available or they are not usable for parts, which are required to be modified or reproduced, RE is used for reproduction of such parts. There are many reasons for non-availability of the CAD models such, as CAD was not used in the original design, inadequate documentations of original design, no record of the in process changes, existing CAD model is insufficient. In such cases RE techniques are helpful for product development in short time compared to the traditional methods.

2. CASE STUDY

Electromechanical components are used in wide range of communication equipments, computer peripherals and various space applications. These components are very precise, small in size and complex in geometry [5]. It is therefore important that product development must be of highest quality and RE can play a major role in ensuring high accuracy. An antenna of Ka-Band was required to be re-engineered. The design documentation of the antenna was not available and the profile was to be made as per the given part. RE was effectively used to reproduce the antenna using the hardware and softwares as described in the subsequent sections.

3. PRODUCT DEVELOPMENT TECHNIQUE:

The techniques used for development can be traditional or non-traditional as described below [6][7].

4. TRADITIONAL TECHNIQUES

Traditional techniques start with geometrical 2D/3D modeling using CAD softwares and then transferring the data among different application softwares, which involves data loss. The process in outlined in Fig. 1 shown below.

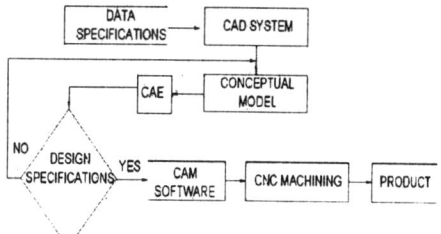

Fig. 1: Traditional techniques for product development

5. NON-TRADITIONAL TECHNIQUES

When a part is to be reverse engineered from an exiting physical part, the conventional techniques cannot be applied because of non-availability of dimensional values. Hence it is essential to apply techniques, which allows capturing the geometrical information of the product to generate a conceptual numerical model from the physical part, which could be used further for CAM/CAE applications. This is where RE is an appropriate technology for reproduction. The technique is shown as flow diagram in Fig.2.

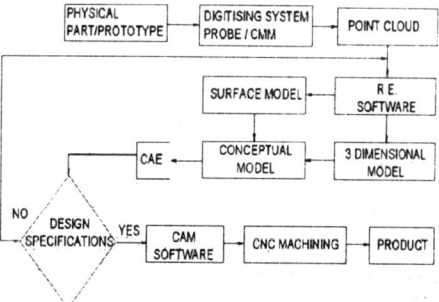

Fig. 2: Non-Traditional technique of product development

6. REVERSE ENGINEERING

The basic of reverse engineering is to develop a conceptual model from a given physical part or its prototype. The methodology is described in the flow diagram shown in Fig. 3 and the various steps involved are described thereafter.

271

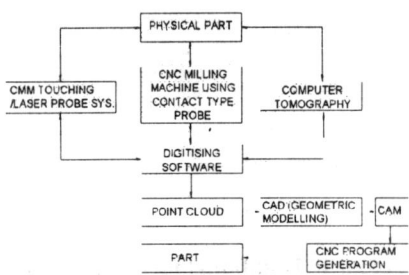

Fig.3: Flow diagram of Reverse Engineering

6.1 Digitization of the Physical Part

It involves the digitization/measurement of the physical part using the digitizers. The profile Co-ordinates of the antenna were measured using optical probe along with image processing software to provide high accuracy. The point cloud was directly transferred to CAD Software thus completely removing the human transcription errors form the measurement process. Measurements can also be taken directly on CNC Machine using touch probes. The measurement station used for digitization of antenna is shown in Fig.4. The RE software should have large data handling capability, hole filling and merging, primitive detection, plane and cylinder detection, polygon creation and editing etc. The softwares can be proprietary items of the scanner manufacturers or standard softwares like Geomagic.

Fig. 4: Multisensor 3-D Measurement station with Optical probe

6.2 Geometrical Modeling (CAD)

Three-dimensional model was created from the digital point cloud data generated by the digitizer using AutoDesk Inventor software. The various entities of the software were used so as to create the model having least data size to define features of the model as shown in Fig 5.

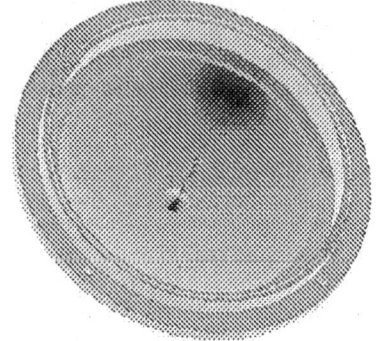

Fig. 5: 3-D model

6. 6.3 CNC Programming and data transfer (CAM & DNC)

CNC program is a set of instructions in terms of G and M codes sent to the machine for executing the cutting process under control of the operator [8][9]. The cutting parameters are defined based on the capability of machine tool, available tooling and work material. The CNC program thus created was transferred to Schaublin 125CCN, CNC lathe machine having Fanuc 18i controller using Remote access DNC software through RS 232 cable. The machining is shown in Fig.6.

Fig. 6: Schaublin 125 CCN, CNC Lathe Machine with Fanuc 18i Controller

6.4 Measurements

The component reproduced using RE was inspected to verify the dimensional accuracy. All the linear dimensions were found within the desired tolerances of ± 10 μm. The surface finish of the order of 0.08 μm Ra value was measured on the profile. The profile accuracy was measured within 0.012 mm.

6.5 Applications of RE

- Tool and die making.
- Plastic industries.
- Complex Casting.
- Automotive and Aerospace industry.
- Consumer products like Toys, Foot- wear & Jewelry.
- Medical instruments.
- Preservation of Cultural heritages by Archeological departments.

7.0 DISCUSSIONS

Reengineering of the product from the physical part has become the only solution in case the design parameters or the dimensions of the part are not available. The product development with RE in research and development can be very helpful to deliver the products in short time. If this methodology is integrated with new rapid manufacturing technologies, it has the capability to reduce the product development time. In addition to this the transcription errors can also be minimized and in process product changes can be incorporated into the final product.

8.0 ACKNOWLEDGEMENT

We are thankful to Director DEAL for providing us the required resources to carryout the work. We would also like to thank Mr. RP Dobhal, VVS Panwar, SR Singh & Mahipal of QC&M [DEAL] for the digitization of the antenna, Mr.Yogesh Kumar & Anup Dutt of NC CENTRE [DEAL] for CNC Programming using CAM machining.

9.0 REFERENCES

1. **John Stark**, What every engineer should know about Practical CAD /CAM Applications, *MARCEL DEKKER.INC, NEW YORK* and BASCEL. 1986.
2. **Rembold U, Nnaji B O** and **Storr A**, *Computer Integrated Manufacturing*, Addison-Wesley Publishing Company England-1993.
3. **Constantine Spyrakos**, *Finite Element Modeling in Engineering Practice*, Algor Publishing Division Pittsburgh. 2001.
4. **Worth**, Users manual for Winworth Measuring Programme Version 6.21.002, April 2002, Germany
5. **Marwah PP**, *"Manufacturing Technology in Millimeter Wave and Microwave Components"*, IETE-26th Mid-Term Microwave and millimeter wave –Recent trends, DEAL Dehradun, April 1995.
6. **Sunil K Semani, Vijay K Karma, Samita Manipatil** and **Al Khandwawala**,*"Reverse Engineering: The design with CAD/CAM/CAE tools"*, 13th National Conference OF ISME Dec.2003.
7. **Dr. Sinha A N, Ojha R P** and **Choudhary B S**", Desk *Top digitization of Human Body parts and its CAD Modeling*", Advances in metrology for manufacturing technology, IEI and CMERI Durgapur Jan. 2004.
8. **Pathtrace**, Edge CAM Basic Training Guide, Pathtrace Engineering Systems, 2001.
9. **Bhardwaj R K, Dutta V P** and **Marwah P P**,*"Machining of MMW Components using CAM Software –A Case Study*", 18th National Convocation of Production Engineers, IEI Jabalpur, Dec.20

GCMM 2004
Editors: Prasad K D V Yarlagadda and S Narayanan
Copyright © 2005, Vellore Institute of Technology, Vellore, India
Publisher: Narosa Publishing House Pvt. Ltd., New Delhi, India

Web Based Prediction of Optimal Tool Parameters using Immune Genetic Algorithm

Alwarsamy T[*], Dr. Balasubramaniam R[**], Deepak Ramakrishnan[**'], Karthik S[***]

Assistant Professor, ** Professor, *** Students

Government College of Technology (Anna University), Coimbatore, 641013, India

E-Mail: alwar_samy@yahoo.co.in

Abstract

This study aims to investigate the dynamic stability of manufacturing systems by the use of Immune Genetic Algorithm. A computational procedure is developed to predict the stability margin using Routh-Hurwitz criteria. The present investigation also involves the implementation of advanced operators like dominance, inversion in Genetic Algorithm and development of source code for Immune Genetic Algorithm to predict the best stability margin at global optima. The paper presents the design and development of a software for web based stability analysis. Software is developed to facilitate the industrial users worldwide to determine the stability boundary of the components of the system. The software is developed to be highly interactive and user friendly so that any user with little or no knowledge of chatter can perform a stability analysis.

1. INTRODUCTION

Developments in manufacturing systems during the past few decades have raised a growing number of vibration problems. Although the importance of the question of vibration as it affects manufacturing systems is widely recognized, few practicing engineers have kept up to date with the results obtained in machine tool chatter research.

The purpose of this study is to use computer intelligence to investigate and improve the stability of manufacturing systems. In the present investigation, an **Immune Genetic Algorithm** is developed to determine the optimal system parameters of tool and workpiece in turning.

2. IMMUNE SYSTEM

Immune system is a learning mechanism that rivals the complexity and computational power of the nervous system. It is responsible for recognizing & defending against pathogens, toxins and other foreign molecules, collectively called **Antigens**. The immune system produces special molecules, called **Antibodies**, which bind to antigen and lead to their elimination.

2.1 Baldwin Effect

Individuals that learn or acquire useful characteristics during their lifetime tend to survive and Baldwin claimed this would cause succeeding generations to have a higher probability of acquiring the same characteristics, even though the characteristics themselves were not genetically propagated. Baldwin called this **"a new factor in evolution"**, and it has come to be known as the **Baldwin effect**.

In this work, a binary model of the immune system is formulated to include **"Clonal Selection"**, which is the learning process used by the immune system. Once this learning mechanism is incorporated into the model it becomes possible to observe the Baldwin effect in the evolution of our binary immune system.

In typical applications, Genetic Algorithms (GA) process populations of potential problem solutions to evolve a single population member that specifies an **"optimized"** solution. The majority of GA analysis has focused on these optimization applications. To eliminate this problem, the analysis is done considering a simplified genetics based machine-learning model of an immune system. In this model, the GA must discover a set of pattern matching antibodies that effectively match a set of antigen patterns. The Analysis shows how the GA can automatically evolve and sustain a diverse, cooperative population. The cooperation emerges as a natural part of the antigen antibody matching procedure. This emergent effect is shown to be similar to fitness sharing, an explicit technique for multimodal GA optimization.

3.0 WORKING OF AN IMMUNE GENETIC ALGORITHM

➤ Antigen recognition is a form of template matching – when the shape and charge of the antibody and antigen molecules match in a complementary fashion, the molecules can bind and the antigen is recognized.

➤ The closer the match is between the antibody and antigen, the stronger is the molecular binding and the better is the recognition.

3.1 Clonal Selection

➤ B cells produce a specific type of antibody, which can recognize only specific types of antigen.

➤ When the antibody receptors of a B cell recognize an antigen, that B cell is stimulated to reproduce.

➤ In the presence of antigen, the daughter cells of a stimulated B cell will also become stimulated and reproduce.

➤ Thus, the presence of antigen will cause the proliferation of those B cells best suited to recognizing that antigen.

➤ Fittest clones recognize the antigen; these survive and grow, whereas clones that do not recognize the antigen die and are replaced by others.

➤ A bit string of length L represents an antigen. A bit string of length L also represents an antibody.

3.2 Antigen Universe

The antigens are contained in the antigen universe. The antigen universe is taken to be 4. One antigen is chosen at random and this antigen is then matched for all the antibodies (which is 30 in this case). The length of the antigen and the antibody are to be equal so that they can be matched. After the size of the antigen universe is fixed and the number of antibodies is determined, then antigens and antibodies are generated at random.

3.3 Antigen – Antibody Matching

In this binary immune system model, antibodies and antigen are simply bit strings: the match between them is defined as the number of bits that complement each other in the two strings. The match score is then compared and this is the basis for the selection of strings. The matching process is described below:

➤ Antibody   :1100100100010010

- Antigen   :01111100111001011
- Complement   :101101011111011111
- Length of contiguous substrings: 1, 2, 1, 5, 5
- A family of matching functions is defined over the lengths of contiguous substrings.

4. TYPES OF FUNCTIONS

- Linear or Nonlinear,
- Exponential, and
- Threshold functions (sum of lengths of substrings)

We have taken a linear function, which can be defined as

$F(x)$ = length of the maximum contiguous substring

Each string (antibody) has a particular value for its function and such value is evaluated.

- The top 20(population size) is chosen from the given antibodies (which is taken at 30) and the fitness function is evaluated for this selected 20 strings.
- These strings are evolved using the genetic algorithm with the reproduction, mutation and crossover operators.
- The best solution in each generation is chosen and iterated for convergence.

5. STRUCTURE OF IMMUNE GENETIC ALGORITHM

{

Generate Antigen universe

Generate Antibodies

While matching is not done for all the antibodies

{

Match the Antibody with the randomly selected antigen from the Antigen universe

Compute the match score

Substitute the match score in the function

}

Select antibodies required (corresponding to the population size) from the antibodies

Initialize population as selected antibodies

{

Evaluate population;

While termination criteria not reached

{

Select solutions for next iterations;

Perform crossover;

Perform mutation;

Evaluate population;

}

}

}

6. WEB BASED IGA

The aim is to develop a web based software to cater the needs of the industrial users. The software gives the results directly in graphical form from which the optimal parameters of the cutting tool system can be obtained. The software facilitates the industrial users to determine the stability boundary of effective cutting damping. From the computed graphs the optimal tuned tool stiffness can be obtained and it is possible for users to work on approaches to design a damped tool holder for the existing machine tools at their facility.

6.1. Design Of Software

A software is designed and developed in Microsoft Visual Basic. Designing consists of creating a form to give the user an option to vary one of the system parameters and view its effect on the stability margin. When a particular parameter is selected for study, a form is setup to get data such as lower and upper limits of the parameter, increment, and other system parameters. An example of the values to be input illustrating the units is also included in the form. An "Analyze" button is included to start the dynamic analysis. After the analysis is performed the next screen is coded with a chart to display the results graphically. An option is given in the output screen to switch between two-dimensional and three-dimensional graphs.

6.2. Development Of Software

The software uses the well-known Routh's criteria to find the stability boundary of the given cutting tool. It takes input values according to the user's choice. The software uses an ActiveX control MSChart20.ocx, a plug-in control provided by Microsoft Corporation to plot the graphs. The graphs can be viewed in two formats either two or three dimensions. The software is developed with an aim to enable users from all over the world to access it through the Internet. dimensional graphs.

6.3. System Requirements

The following configuration lists the minimum requirements of the software.

1. Processor with 300MHz clock speed.

2. 32MB RAM.

3. 1MB of unused disk space.

4. Operating system – Windows 95 and above.

5. An Internet connection (optional) to download the software.

6.4. Graphical Representation Of Results

The chart control receives all the output values of the analysis, i.e., the stability boundary values and plots them. The software plots 2D or 3D graphs (as required) between the stiffness of the tool and the stability boundary values by changing the damping ratio of the tool in the range of interest of the user. The results in graphical form can be used to tune the stiffness of the tool to an optimal value.

The graph is plotted taking the stiffness of the tool in the X-axis and the stability boundary in the Y-axis, for various values of the damping factor of the tool. Depending on the testing range and the increment step the user selects, graphs are drawn. From the curves obtained, the user can choose the value of the damping factor of the tool, for which his system is to be optimized for improved working conditions

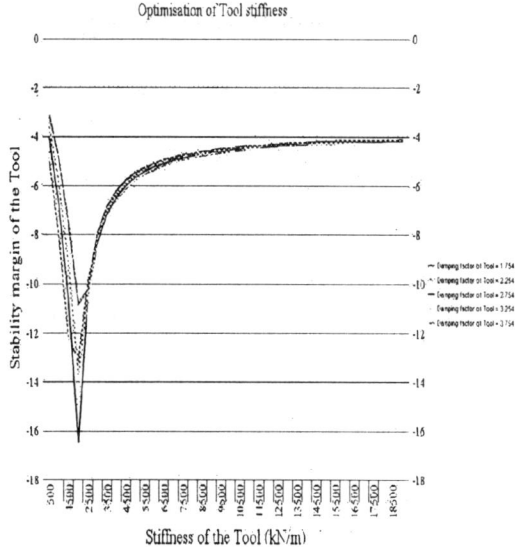

Optimisation of Tool stiffness

Stiffness of the Tool (kN/m)

Fig.1: Effect of damping factor of the tool on stiffness of the tool

7. IGA INPUT PARAMETERS

In this study, two-degree freedom mathematical model connecting workpiece and cutting tool is used.

The equations of motion of the two DOF system are :

$$M_w \ddot{X}_w = -C_w \dot{X}_w - K_w X_w - C_c (\dot{X}_w - \dot{X}_t) - K_c (X_w - X_t)$$

$$M_t \ddot{X}_t = -C_t \dot{X}_t - K_t X_t - C_c (\dot{X}_t - \dot{X}_w) - K_c (X_t - X_w)$$

$$M_w \ddot{X}_w + C_w \dot{X}_w + K_w X_w + C_c (\dot{X}_w - \dot{X}_t) + K_c (X_w - X_t) = 0$$

$$M_t \ddot{X}_t + C_t \dot{X}_t + K_t X_t + C_t (\dot{X}_t - \dot{X}_w) + K_c (X_t - X_w) = 0$$

The system parameters K_t, M_t, K_w, M_w and also effective stiffness K_c are given as input values The main objective is to predict optimal values of these parameters for the best stability margin. The input values for IGA Test are given as shown in Table 1.

Table 1 – IGA Test Input Values

Input Parameters	Test1	Test2	Test3	Test4
Number of Parameters	7	7	7	7
Population Size (Pop)	20	20	20	20
Number of Antigens	4	4	4	6
Number of Antibodies	20	25	30	20
Chromosome Length	14	14	14	14
Crossover Probability (P_c)	0.8	0.8	0.8	0.8
Mutation Probability (P_m)	.001	.001	.001	.001

8. IMMUNE GENETIC ALGORITHM TEST

The IGA test is performed by keeping the chromosome length, crossover probability (P_c), Mutation Probability (P_m) and population size (POP) constants and varying the number of antigens and number of antibodies

8.1. IGA – Test

The IGA Test is performed with the values corresponding to Test 1 of the genetic parameters and the test results are shown in the fig.2. Similar graphs are obtained for the other three tests.

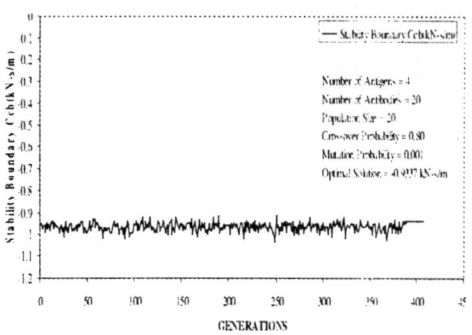

Fig.2: Generation Vs Average Stability Boundary

8.2. Discussion of Results

1. The Test indicates the stability boundary reaching a value nearly Ccb=-0.9337 kN-s/m for an antigen = 4 and anti-bodies = 20

2. The antigen value is kept constant and by increasing the anti-bodies to 25 the stability boundary Ccb=-0.9665 kN-s/m has been improved further which indicates the antibodies play an important role in the convergence of Ccb.

3. The solution is further improved when the anti-bodies are increased to 30 but there is a constraint for the computational considerations. The combination of Antigen = 4 and Anti-bodies = 30 gives a better stable margin Ccb=-0.9790 kN-s/m. When the antibodies are further increased the convergence solution remains the same whereas the computational time increases.

4. The computation of the immune Genetic algorithm is investigated when the antigen value is increased to 6 and by keeping the antibodies as 20. The results indicates that the stability margin is reduced to Ccb=-0.9160 kN-s/m

9. REFERENCES

1. **S.S Rao**, Mechanical Vibrations, Addison Wesley Limited (1985)

2. **Kalyanmoy Deb**, Optimization for Engineering design Algorithms and examples, *Prentice Hall India Limited* (2000)

3. **David E. Goldberg**, Genetic Algorithms, Addison- Wesley Longman Inc(1999)

4. **Vijayarangan et-al** , Design Optimization of Leaf Springs, **Institution of Engineers (India) Journal**.(1999)

5. **Chiou, R.Y** and **Liang, S.Y.**, 1998, "Chatter stability of slender cutting tool in turning with tool wear effect" *Int.J.Mach.Tools Manufact.* Vol38, No.4 pp.315-327

6. **Rao, J.S.**, and **Gupta.K**, 1984, "Ind. Course on theory and practice of Mechanical vibration", *New age international (P) Ltd.*

7. **Rivin, E.I** and **Kang, H.L.**, 1989, "Improvement of Machining conditions by tuned dynamic stiffness of tool", Int. J. Mach. Tools Manufact, Vol 29, No.3, pp 361-376

Manufacturing Systems

GCMM 2004
Editors: Prasad K D V Yarlagadda and S Narayanan
Copyright © 2005, Vellore Institute of Technology, Vellore, India
Publisher: Narosa Publishing House Pvt. Ltd., New Delhi, India

Joint Operation and Tool Schedule in an Automated Manufacturing System / FMC using GA

Prabaharan T

Department of Mechanical Engineering, Mepco Schlenk Engineering College,
Mepco Engineering College, Tamilnadu, India.

E-mail: prabaharan_369@yahoo.co.in

Nakkeeran P R

Department of Mechanical Engineering, College of Engineering, Guindy,
Anna University, Chennai, Tamilnadu, India.

Jawahar N

Department of Mechanical Engineering, Thiagarajar College of Engineering,
Madurai, TamilNadu, India.

E-mail:jawahartce@yahoo.co.uk

Udhayakumar K

Lecturer, Department of Mechanical Engineering,
K.L.N. College of Engineering & Technology, Madurai, India.

Abstract

The concern of this paper is to generate joint operation – tool schedule in a Flexible manufacturing cell (FMC) consisting of several identical machines and a common tool magazine (CTM). To this aim, the jobs and tools must be sequenced and scheduled in a tool constrained environment. Since these problems are NP-hard even without additional resources, their solution calls for suitable heuristic approach. Genetic Algorithm (GA) is proposed to derive optimal or near optimal solutions and they adopt the new procedure (PNJ_SCH) for active feasible schedule generation. As investment cost in FMC is high it is proposed to schedule each single operation to maximize hardware utilization which is measured by a performance measure such as makespan. The performance of the proposed algorithm is compared with makespan and computational time. The GA based heuristic provides an optimal solution.

Keywords
Sequencing, Scheduling, GA, Heuristics, Flexible Manufacturing

1. INTRODUCTION

Flexible manufacturing system (FMS/FMC) is an integrated manufacturing system that consists of multi-functional numerically controlled machine tools connected with an automated material handling system, all controlled by a computer system. The aim of an FMC is to achieve the efficiency of high-volume mass production while retaining the flexibility of low-volume production. To achieve this efficiency, various decisions must be made. One of these decision problems is to allocate parts (or operations) and required tools to machines with exact time spans, which is often called the loading and scheduling problem [1]. Scheduling literature addresses wide range of problems described with machine environment, job description, and objective function [2, 3]. Determining an efficient schedule for the general job shop problem has been the subject of research for more than 50 years. Although, the evolution of FMS/CIM has complicated the issue, because of its complex nature of working; it will be best suited to produce variety of parts with flexibility of even small lots [4]. Part and tool flows, two major dynamic entities, are the key factors and their management play important roles in the operation of a FMS. Most of the researches done in this field consider part and tool flow as separate issues and often, the effects of one of the pair on the other is neglected.

There are basically two approaches of machine loading and scheduling problem in FMS: (a) part movement approach and (b) tool movement approach. In part movement approach, the parts move and the objective of tool allocation is to find the suitable combination of tool sets on machines which will require least processing times [5, 6]. The majority of research conducted on the scheduling problem of FMS generally assumes a part movement policy. [5] Researchers using this part movement approach have focused on a number of issues that are specifically related to the flow of work pieces [7]. Part movement approach can be justified in many cases, where the cost of parts is very high in comparison with the cost of cutting tools required. However in many batch machining applications, the cost of cutting tools is a significant proportion of the total production cost, sometimes as much as 25%-30% [8]. Therefore, by adopting appropriate tooling strategies and economizing on the tooling cost, large reductions in the total cost are feasible [9]. In the tool movement approach, the parts are assigned to machining centres using some priority rule and tools required for processing the parts move to the required machining centre from either the central tool magazine or other machining centres. Each part is fixed to one machining centre throughout its total processing time and only the tools are transported to perform different operations [5,6]

In this context, the concern of this paper is to generate joint operation-tool schedule for an FMC consisting of two number of identical work centres (WC) and a common tool magazine (CTM). Conflicts may arise whenever same tool is required by two or more jobs/WC at the same time. In those circumstances, one of the jobs will be served first and others have to wait for the release of tool. Further, the loss of productivity due to some WC being idle (waiting for tool availability) may be reduced by means of proper scheduling under shared tool magazine and may well traded-off by the cost saving we obtain by sharing tools on different WC. This type of manufacturing system is necessary for manufacturing environment in which tools are particularly expensive. Scheduling in such environment requires taking three types of decisions:

1. The jobs waiting for the operation must be sequenced
2. Each job must be assigned to any of the available WC.
3. Each operation of a job must be scheduled, taking tool availability into account.

Since the operations of a job are executed during a single machine visit, the problem is essentially an identical parallel machine problem with additional resources; since these problems are NP-hard even without additional resources, their solution calls for suitable heuristic approaches [10]. Genetic algorithm which belongs to a class of heuristics and stochastic search techniques based on the mechanism of natural selection and natural genetics. A large number of applications of GA for Sequencing and Scheduling of FMS/Job Shop problems have been published over the last decade [4, 11, 12]. A new algorithm PNJ_SCH which uses similar procedure of Giffler and Thompson algorithm [13] for job shop problem is proposed to generate active feasible joint operation-tool schedule. In order to find optimal schedule, alternate to resolve all the conflicts one by one and enumerating all possible feasible schedules, GA is proposed for the above problem to find optimal schedule and adopts the procedure of PNJ_SCH for active feasible schedules. The rest of the paper addresses the followings in detail: Problem description, Proposed Heuristics, Performance comparison and conclusion.

2. PROBLEM DESCRIPTION

The usage of common tool storage is traditionally followed in many manufacturing systems with one tool grip serving many manufacturing facilities in order to reduce tool inventory. This paper considers a FMC that has a CTM which serves all the WC in the cell by means of tool handling system. This section presents the description of the joint operation-tool schedule problem of FMC. The description includes the operation environment, assumptions, objectives and definition of the problem under consideration.

2.1. Operation Environment

The WC of the cell are capable of doing many operations and identical in nature. They can process a group of parts or part variety. The CTM has necessary tool varieties for all WC and one tool in each variety (that is required for all the WC). These tools are shared among all the WC. The operating environment of FMC is shown in Figure 1. The processing requirements of the jobs are:
- Any job can be processed in any WC.
- Each job involves a set of operations and each operation requires a specific tool.
- Sequence of operations and respective tools vary from job to job.

2.2. Assumptions

- The sequence of operations and its corresponding processing time and tools of the job are pre-specified.
- The operations of a job are executed during a single WC visit.

- Each WC/tool can process only one job at a time.
- Each job once started, must be completed (Interruption is not allowed).
- The operation time "t_{ik}" of a job includes the loading, unloading, tool changeover and setup times (both tool and job) along with processing time.
- WC failure is not considered
- All the jobs that require processing are available at time zero.
- Once an operation is over, the tool returns to the tool magazine with negligible transfer time immediately and is available for the next operation.

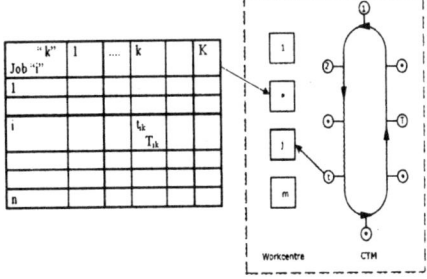

Fig. 1: Operation environment of FMC

2.3. Objective

Manufacturing systems are designed to meet the demands efficiently. The efficiency / performance of the system can be measured by any one or more of the following scheduling objectives such as machine utilization, due date, lead time, setup time or cost, work-in-process inventory (WIP), etc. The selection of performance measure purely depends on the type of manufacturing system, business environment and competition. As FMS requires very high investment cost, maximum hardware utilisation is highly essential to have a competitive manufacturing cost. Considering this aspect, minimum makespan that increases the utilisation of hardware is considered as the appropriate measure of system performance.

2.4. Problem Definition

"Determination of optimal or near optimal joint operation – tool schedule of 'n' jobs, available at time zero in an FMC, which has

283

two identical workcenters and a common tool magazine, for minimum makespan criterion."

3. PROPOSED HEURISTICS

Two heuristics that use PDRA and GA are proposed for the problem under consideration to find optimal or near optimal solution. Both the methods employ new algorithm (PNJ_SCH) which is based on the logic of GT algorithm, for the generation of active feasible schedules.

3.1. Active Feasible Joint Operation-Tool Schedule Generation Algorithm (PNJ_SCH)

The GT algorithm, which was originally designed to generate all active feasible schedules for the traditional job shop model, can still provide good results for an FMS model [14]. This algorithm is a numerical version of the procedure described for drawing a Gantt chart to arrive at an active feasible schedule. Using similar procedure a new algorithm (PNJ_SCH) is proposed for the generation of active feasible schedules for joint operation and tool schedule. This requires to resolve tool conflicts that arises whenever two or more workcentres/jobs require the same tool at one instant (*datum time*). When the choice is made arbitrarily an active féasible schedule is obtained. By enumerating all possible choices, which occur at different stages one by one, the entire set of active feasible schedules can be obtained, including the optimal one. The optimal solution is obtained by evaluating the feasible schedules with the desired objective criterion.

3.2. Priority Despatching Rules Algorithm (PDRA) based Heuristic

Priority dispatching rules (pdrs) are probably the most popular method in the scheduling of complex real job shops, and are very often embedded in schedule generation algorithms and in commercial scheduling packages. A priority rule is one which assigns a value to each waiting job, the maximum/minimum of which, among the job waiting at a machine, determines the job to be selected over all other jobs for scheduling. In case of a tie, the job with a secondary parameter may be used. Many scholars have come up with several scheduling rules [15]. Two priority rules

Shortest Processing Time (SPT) and Longest Processing Time (LPT) which are very popular in heuristics and found applications in many scheduling problems are proposed.

3.3. Genetic Algorithm

Genetic algorithms are stochastic search techniques based on the mechanism of natural selection and natural genetics. A large number of applications of GA for Sequencing and Scheduling of FMS/Job Shop problems have been published over the last decade.[4, 11, 12] The proposed GA evaluates the active feasible schedules of each population that are generated by resolving the conflicts accordingly to the priority sequences represented as chromosomes and evolves the best priority sequence. The coding adopted in this GA is as follows: a gene denotes the job number; position of the gene represents the priority rank of the job; one chromosome describes a priority sequence; number of chromosomes forms a population. The optimal or near optimal solution is obtained through number of generations with the genetic procedure of random generation of members for initial population and generation of members for new population based on selection of fittest members of previous population, crossover and mutation [16]. The fitness parameter 'makespan time' is found out by generating an active feasible schedule using the concept and adaptation of New Algorithm (PNJ_SCH) and resolving the conflicts with priority sequence as argued in the chromosome. The values of the various parameters and operators used in this GA process are: population size = twice the number of jobs; probability of cross over = 0.40; probability of mutation = 0.05; fitness parameter = $e^{-0.05 \cdot f(c)}$ where $f(c)$ is the makespan time; cross over operator = PMX operator with cyclic exchange; mutation operator = exchange mutation. The structure of the proposed GA is shown in figure 2.

4. PERFORMANCE COMPARISON

Ten data sets have been randomly generated for the performance analysis of the proposed methodologies. The problems considered address a typical range of problems of smaller to medium size. The makespan time of the schedules of the ten problems obtained with both methodologies is given in Table I and their computation experience is shown in Figure 3. The direct application of pdrs for resolving conflict does not guarantee optimal or near optimal solutions and no generalisation is possible. There is no specific priority despatching rule to provide best solution. It varies from problem to problem and is data dependent. The application of a GA to this problem is useful as the values of the objective function are optimal or very close to the optimal and it can be obtained with reasonable computational time. However, the computational time increases exponentially with the problem size. Hence the proposed GA can be used to find better schedule in manufacturing environment considered under CTM.

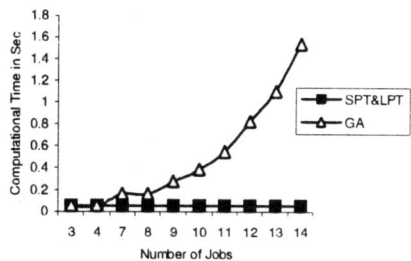

Indicates best solution   # Indicates next best solution
P.NO- Problem Number

Fig. 3: Computational Time Chart

5. CONCLUSION

A joint operation-tool scheduling problem of FMC that operates with limited number of tools in a CTM, which serves two WC in the cell by means of tool handling system, with minimum makespan criterion has been addressed in this paper. Two different classes of heuristics, GA and PDRA are proposed for the above problem which uses a PNJ_SCH procedure for active feasible schedule generation. The performance of these two algorithms is compared in terms of makespan performance measure and computational time. The comparison reveals that GA is capable of providing optimal or near optimal solutions compared to PDRA. Also the computational time is reasonable for the problems concerned and very well can be applied to the FMS/FMC environment considered in this paper. However, further research is needed for larger size problems and to other hardware configuration consisting of more workcentres.

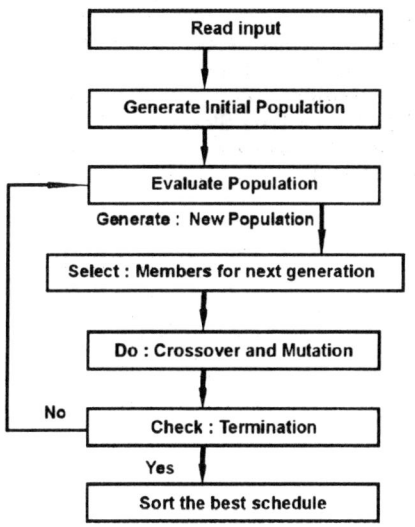

Fig. 2: Structure of GA

Table 1: Makespan Time Comparisons of Proposed Heuristics

P.No	Job Size	Tool Size	SPT MT(in sec)	LPT MT(in sec)	GA MT(in sec)	Best Solution GA/PDRA Rule
1	3	3	39 #	38 *	38 *	GA
2	4	3	113	103 #	100 *	GA
3	7	5	248	238 #	215 *	GA
4	8	7	385	349 #	329 *	GA
5	9	5	283 #	301	251 *	GA
6	10	6	407 *	448	412 #	SPT,GA
7	11	5	332 #	324 #	302 *	GA
8	12	4	309 #	347	281 *	GA
9	13	5	820 #	892	717 *	GA
10	14	6	658	602 #	545 *	GA

6. ACKNOWLEDGEMENT

The authors thank the Management, Principal and Head of Mechanical Engineering Department of Mepco Schlenk Engg. College, Sivakasi; Anna University, Chennai; Thiagarajar college of Engineering, Madurai; and K.L.N.College of Engg&Tech., for the cooperation and encouragement given to the authors, providing all the facilities needed to carry out this work.

7. REFERENCES

1. **Roh HK, Kim YD** (1997) Due-date based loading and scheduling methods for a flexible manufacturing system with an automatic tool transporter. *International Journal of Production Research* 35(11): 2989-3003.
2. **French S,** (1982) Sequencing and Scheduling, 5th edition. Ellis Hardwood, London.
3. **Brucker P,** (1995) Scheduling Algorithm, 1st edition. Springer Verlag-Heidelherg, Berlin, USA.
4. **Jawahar N, Aravindan P,** Ponnambalam SG (1998) A Genetic Algorithm for scheduling flexible manufacturing systems. *International Journal of Advanced Manufacturing Technology* 14: 588 – 607.
5. **Mukhopadhyay SK, Nandi PK** (1999) Solving tool allocation problem in Flexible Manufacturing System. *Industrial Engineering (India) Journal* 80: 16-20.
6. **Hong-Bae Jun, Yeong-Dae Kim, Hyo-won suh** (1999) Heuristics for a tool provisioning problem in a flexible manufacturing system with an Automatic Tool Transporter. *IEEE Transactions on Robotics and Automation* 15(3) June: 488 – 496.
7. **Rahimifard S, Newman ST** (1997) Simultaneous scheduling of work pieces, fixtures and cutting tools with in FMCs. International *Journal of Production Research,* 35(9): 2379-2396.
8. **Selim Akturk M, Siraceddin Oxen** (1999) Joint lot sizing and tool management in a CNC environment. *Computers in Industry* 40: 61 – 74.
9. **Gray AE, Seidmann A, Stecke KE** (1990) A synthesis of decision models for tool management in automated manufacturing. *Management Science* 39: 249-567.
10. **Alessandro Agnetis, Arianna Alfieri, Paolo Brandimarte, Paolo Prinsecchi** (1997) Joint job/tool scheduling in a FMC with no on-board tool magazine. *Computer Integrated Manufacturing Systems* 10(1): 61 – 68.
11. **Tiwari M. K., Vidyarthi N. K.** (2000) Solving machine loading problems in a flexible manufacturing system using a genetic algorithm based heuristic approach. *International Journal of Production Research* 38(14): 3357 – 3384.
12. **Sridhar J., Rajendran C.** (1996) Scheduling in Flowshop and Cellular manufacturing with multiple objectives a genetic algorithmic approach. *International Journal of Production Planning and Control* 7(4): 374 – 382.
13. **Giffler B, Thompson GL** (1960) Algorithms for solving production scheduling problems. *International Journal of Operations Research* 8: 487-503.
14. **Nascimento MA** (1993) Giffler and Thompson algorithm for job shop scheduling is still good for flexible manufacturing systems. *Journal of the Operational Research Society* 44(5): 521-524.
15. **Waikar AM, Sarkar BR, Lal AM** (1995) A Comparative study of some priority dispatching rules under different shop loads. *International Journal of Production Planning Control* 6(4): 301-310.
16. **Michalewicz Z.** (1992) Genetic Algorithms + Data Structures = Evolution Programs, Springer – Verlag, Berlin-Heidelherg, USA.

GCMM 2004
Editors: Prasad K D V Yarlagadda and S Narayanan
Copyright © 2005, Vellore Institute of Technology, Vellore, India
Publisher: Narosa Publishing House Pvt. Ltd., New Delhi, India

Machining Feature Recognition based on ISO10303

Kumar Amaresh

Lecturer, Production, National Institute of Technology, Jamshedpur-14

Saha J

Professor, Production Engg., Jadavpur University, Kolkata – 32,

E-mail: amaresh_nitjsr@yahoo.co.in

Abstract

IGES considered as a widely used neutral file for reading solid models generated in CAD Data base and has been used for machining feature recognition for integrating CAD and CAM. Over the years, IGES has got diluted as different countries started using IGES like product data exchange and they deviated from IGES standard some way or other. IGES is also considered as a neutral file initially designed for 2D objects and then modified to Incorporate 3D objects .To over come these problems and to have a single International Standard format for product data exchange a new standard called STEP (Standard for Exchange of products) is developed which is ISO 10303 Within these standards there are Several Industry specific standards called Application Protocol (AP), which are also International standards. Some of them used for Mechanical and Industrial Engineering Applications are STEP AP203, which defines the geometry, topology and configuration management data for solid models of mechanical parts. STEP AP 214 goes beyond STEP AP203 and is for automotive application. STEP AP 224 is Mechanical part definition for process planning using machining features. The paper here is to see the application of these STEP AP standards for feature recognition from 3D solid model.

Keywords

STEP, Feature Recognition.

1.INTRODUCTION

ISO 10303, informally known as the Standard for the Exchange of Product Model Data (STEP), was developed upon the lessons learnt from the previous standards for product data exchange and was published in 1994. STEP is the third-generation methods of data exchange. STEP is a formal standard being developed by the International Standards Organization (ISO) and is the effort to overcome the many de-facto standards that currently exist. The primary goal of the standard is to provide a neutral format for product data exchange over the entire life cycle of a product, from realizing the need for a product, through product design, process design, manufacturing, and maintenance. STEP is different from the other standards in several aspects. First, it is not restricted to a particular industrial sector or discipline, such as automotive design, electrical industry, or aerospace. It describes data at all stages of a product and provides a standardized framework for product data, regardless of the kind of product. Besides the geometry information, it also has specifications for the communication of information concerning the material, tolerances, and the relation to other parts. Second, STEP has benefited from the development of its prior standards by using a number of formal methods in its development. It has used activity and information modeling to capture the requirements. The EXPRESS language, which is a part of the standard, reduces the ambiguity of natural language definitions. STEP consists of an infrastructure and method for conformance testing, and has defined standard application protocols. STEP uses application protocols (AP's) to specify the representation of product information for one or more applications. AP 203 defines the geometry, topology, and configuration management data of solid models for mechanical parts and assemblies. AP 214, designed for the automotive industry, defines the core data for the automotive mechanical design process. AP 214 goes well beyond AP 203, providing a far more comprehensive model for automotive applications and covering the lifecycle of a design from engineering through manufacturing. It also covers such design issues such as colors and layers, geometric dimensioning and tolerancing, and design intent. AP 214 is considered an extension of AP203. AP-203, along with AP-224, (Mechanical Parts Definition for Process Planning Using Machining Features) has a significant cost savings impact on mechanical parts manufacturing. The paper here explains the STEP format, extraction of data from the STEP file and recognizing manufacturing features like form features based totally on the data available in STEP.

2 LITERATURE REVIEW

STEP uses Boundary representation as a basis for defining solid model, hence review here is based on the methods that take B-Rep data as input and use geometric and topological relations between the boundary entities. The B-Rep tree is scanned and comparing the tree structure with the structure required for a feature identifies the features. This approach can be broadly classified as graph based method, cell based decomposition method, convex hull based decomposition method and hint-based methods. Feature extraction and recognition has been a widely researched field with a lot of work done in this area. "Joshi and Chang "[1] have done pioneering work in this field.

They used the concept of attributed adjacency graph (AAG) to recognize machining features from a boundary representation (B-Rep) of the solid but in this work they limited themselves to polyhedral features." Gavankar and Henderson" [2] have developed a graph-based feature extraction technique to identify protrusions and blind holes from boundary models. It uses the Edge-Face relation of the solid to represent a graph and then recognize features but limits itself to pocket and blind holes opening in one face. "Ferreira and Hinduja "[3] have used the method of convex hull to recognize features. "Qamhiyah"[4] presented a boundary-based procedure for the sequential extraction of form features of objects with planar surfaces from CAD model. All the above mentioned research have developed feature extraction schemes using various techniques input, however the extracted features do not render themselves easily to data exchange as warranted by the needs of Agile Manufacturing. The features are also not stored in a standard format. Then feature like form features were recognized using neutral format of the model generated in CAD like IGES as input, which also use B-Rep as one of the basis of solid representation. "Liu"[5] had designed form-feature extraction method taking the IGES format as input to the feature extractor, and classifying all the features present on the work piece based on information in the IGES file. The extracted form-features are stored in an object-oriented format. As the IGES format could not be recognized as international standard, the new area is meant to use STEP file as input (based on B-Rep) for feature recognition."An and Leep "[6] used STEP as product data exchange structure for manufacturing application At this time STEP was at developing stage, hence not much use of this was done. "Liang and Ahamed"[7] used STEP file for feature data extraction and then using this data for CL file and NC code generation. Here the features are not recognized. "Lau and Jiang" [8] used STEP data for generating GT codes to be used for Process Planning. "Bhandarkar"[9]," Dereli" [10], "Fu and Ong"[11] have also used STEP file for feature recognition and process planning.

3 REPRESENTATION OF SOLID

The most common way to create a geometric representation is through the use of neutral file format standards such as IGES and STEP Among the various methods of geometric representation provided by STEP AP 203, the most interoperability is achieved through the transfer of a geometric representation of a part or assembly, commonly referred to as a boundary representation, or B-rep. STEP data transfer today uses Boundary Representation (B-rep) of the part geometry. B-rep is a necessity for high-precision manufacturing operations requiring exact boundary locations needed to drive NC cutting and quality checking processes. Using neutral file format standards, the advantage of B-rep translations is that they are fairly simple to use. In a B-rep format, an object is represented in terms of its shells, Surfaces, loops, edges and vertices. The boundary of a surface is defined by a cyclic set of edges referred to as the outer loop. An inner loop on the other hand consists of a cyclic set of edges contained within the boundaries of a surface. An edge is shared between two loops on the object. The loop is selected herein as the descriptive wilt for object representation, since a form feature exists as a geometric formation (i.e. a set of vertices. edges, loops and surfaces) on the object, the utilization of loops as a descriptive unit would automatically lead to the representation of form features in terms of their loops. In this work a loop is defined as a cyclic set of edges that is essentially restricted to be convex or concave depending on the types of edges that form the loops.

3.1 Classification of Edges

Edges are being classified in different ways to be used for feature recognition but the most common classification is based on the angle between the faces sharing the edges as convex and concave edges. In B-Rep form of representation the outer loops bounding the faces are in counter clockwise direction and the inner loops in clockwise direction. In fig.1 if es be the edge shared by two faces F1 and F2, then to decide the convexity and concavity based on the STEP data is, I) the direction vectors f1 and f2 normal to the two faces F1 and F2 respectively is considered and its cross (vector) product (c)=f1 x f2 is calculated, where order is from right to left of the edge view perspective. By the right hand rule and face vector geometry the direction of edge c will be parallel to the direction of edge es .If

the direction (c) and edge es is same, the edge is concave otherwise it is convex. II) The direction of (c)

Will be the dot product (d) of the resulting cross product (c) with the directional vector of the common edge es as in equation d=c.es=||c|| ||es|| cos where ||c|| is the magnitude of (c), ||es|| is the magnitude of es and is the angle between (C) and es. The feature considered here can have as 0 or 180, if is 0 then the value of d is positive indicating concave edge es otherwise it is convex.

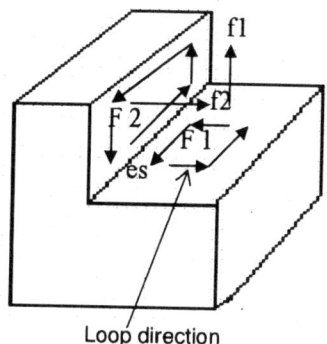

Loop direction

Fig.1: showing direction vector

3.2 Classification of Loops

The presence and type of loop indicates the feature. Loops in a target surface can be identified and classified as inner or outer from the data available in STEP file. Then edges of this loop are identified and can be categories broadly as convex or concave and based on the classification of edges loop can be identified as convex loop (where all the edges are convex) and can be both internal and external. Similarly concave loops (where all edges are concave) can also be internal or external.

3.3 Classification of Form Features

Form features are features, which are identified by the combination of geometric and topological entities. The classification of form features can be done in many ways. Here it is based on the effect of the features in changing the basic shape of the solid. The form features can be classified into four basic types:

1. Void features,
2. Inner form features
3. Outer form features, and
4. Connectivity modifying forms features.

Form features belonging to the type void features form voids within the solid. Voids are areas, which are totally enclosed within the outer shell of the solid. Voids are represented as solid shells within the solid and the solid is represented as b-rep- with- voids in the STEP format. The form-features of the type inner are the ones, which modify the internal shape of one or more surfaces and can be detected by having more than one loop i.e. external loop and internal loop in the target surface. Each Internal loop represent a feature. These features are classified as through features which go right through the solid and create a path from one outer face of the solid to another outer face, e.g., through holes and through-pockets, and blind features which alter the internal shape of a surface but do not penetrate through the solid; these types of features begin at one of the outer surfaces of the solid and end inside the solid, e.g., blind-holes and blind pockets. Inner form features can also be grouped on the basis of internal loop in the surface i.e. concave or convex loop. These types of features are represented in STEP as MANIFOLD_SOLID_BREP. Form features belonging to the type outer modify the external shape of the solid, e.g., steps, slots, external pockets, etc. Outer form features are further classified in the three sub-types Edge modifying: these features modify an edge of a face or between a pair of faces to create a feature. Face modifying: these features split up a single face to create a feature on that face. However, these features may not be restricted to a single surface only. Vertex modifying: these types of feature modify the vertex between adjacent faces, Connectivity modifying form features are those, which alter the "joint" between the various faces of the part, e.g., chamfers and rounded edges.

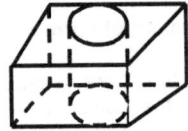

Fig.2: Example of feature type inner(through)

4 STEP DATA STRUCTURE

Every STEP data has at least one schema and three types of data: descriptive, geometrical and topological. STEP data is hierarchal in the form of closed-shell, face-surface, face-bound, Cartesian point and is exchanged as ASCII text. The STEP format of a rectangular block with a through hole is used here for explaining STEP data structure.

```
ISO-10303-21;
HEADER;
FILE_DESCRIPTION((''),'1');
FILE_NAME('PRT0001','2004-06-
29T',('p4ht1'),(''),
'PRO/ENGINEER    BY    PARAMETRIC
TECHNOLOGY CORPORATION, 1999140',
'PRO/ENGINEER    BY    PARAMETRIC
TECHNOLOGY            CORPORATION,
1999140','');
FILE_SCHEMA(('CONFIG_CONTROL_DESI
GN'));
ENDSEC;
DATA;
#1=DIRECTION ('',(0.E0,-1.E0,0.E0));
#2=VECTOR ('',#1,6.583262350937E0);
#3=CARTESIAN_POINT ('',(0.E0,0.E0,0.E0))
.............................................
#27=DIRECTION ('',(-1.E0,0.E0,0.E0));
#28=DIRECTION ('',(0.E0,1.E0,0.E0));
#29=AXIS2_PLACEMENT_3D('',#26,#27,#28
);.............................................
#84=VERTEX_ POINT ('',#83);
#85=CARTESIAN_POINT('',(0.E0,0.E0,2.82E
0));.............................................
#105=PLANE ('',#104);
.............................................
#114=EDGE_LOOP('',(#107,#109,#111,#113
));.............................................
#115=FACE_OUTER_BOUND ('',#114,.F.);
#116=ADVANCED_FACE ('',(#115),#105,.F.)
.............................................
#128=ORIENTED_ EDGE ('', *, *, #127,.F.);
#129=EDGE_LOOP('',(#122,#124,#126,#128
));.............................................
#136=FACE BOUND ('',#135,.F.);
.............................................
#201=CYLINDRICAL_SURFACE
('',#200,7.090150743384E-1);............
#223=CLOSED_SHELL
('',(#116,#137,#151,#171,#184,#196,#210,#2
22)); ..........
#224=MANIFOLD_SOLID_BREP ('',#223);
);.............................................
#25=CIRCLE ('',#24,7.090150743384E-1);
.............................................
#125=EDGE_ CURVE ('',#87,#88,#56,.T.);
```

290

ENDSEC;
END-ISO-10303-21;
#N is an entity identifier can be used as pointer. HEADER; information of STEP translator. CARTESIAN_ POINT: address of point in Cartesian space (x, y, z). VERTEX POINT: a point defining the geometry of a vertex. CLOSED_ SHELL: a collection of one or more faces, which bounds a region. MANIFOLD_SOLID_BREP: solid object representation and has a closed shell. EDGE_ CURVE: a type of edge, which has its geometry, defined. EDGE_ LOOP: a path in which start and end vertices are same. and bounds the faces by collection of edges. ORIENTED_ EDGE: an edge constructed from another edge and containing the orientation information. ADVANCED_FACE: a type of face in which geometry is defined by associated surfaces and it shares an edge with one other face to form a closed set of faces. FACE_BOUND: bounded by a loop with orientation for representing each face. FACE_OUTER_BOUND: a sub type of face-bound and defines the outer loop of the face. AXIS2_PLACEMENT_3D: location of Cartesian point. PLANE: it defines the surface and has its position in AXIS2_PLACEMENT_3D. CYLINDRICAL SURFACE: it is sub type of plane with radius.

5. DATA EXTRACTION

The data extraction method proposed here uses the geometric and topological sections of the STEP file. As the first step, the number of pointers used to construct the CLOSED-SHELL is the number of pointers used to form a EDGE-LOOP determines the number of ORIENTED-EDGES that have to be traced. The number of associated pointers also indicates the shape of the surface (e.g., a four- pointer EDGE-LOOP indicates a four-sided polygon and a five-pointer EDGE-LOOP indicates a five- sided polygon, etc.:).
An example taken in section 3 is used to illustrate the data extraction process of internal feature. The functional elements of the block such as CLOSED-SHELL etc. are explained in section 3. The block is represented as a CLOSED-SHELL. It is shown in the STEP file as "#223 = CLOSED_SHELL
(",(#116,#137,#151,#171,#184,#196,#210,#222));. Here, #223 is the address of the block. The pointers nested in the statement: #116, #137, etc. leads ADVANCED_FACE, which has the address of the surfaces representing

the solid. In the example taken it leads to PLANE and FACE_OUTER_BOUND. FACE_OUTER_BOUND pointer leads to EDGE LOOP, here the pointers lead to ORIENTED_ EDGE, again the pointer here lead to EDGE_ LOOP where it is lead to EDGE_CURVE of these surfaces then it is lead to the coordinates of the vertices of the block.. For example, a pointer #116 of closed shell leads to Cartesian pointer #85. In address #85, the coordinate values of a vertex can be located. The output of this extraction can have Coordinate of vertices, number of vertices in each face, number of edges in each face, number of faces in each feature, internal and external loops, type of edges and loops.

6. FEATURE RECOGNITION

After obtaining geometric data and its relationship from the STEP file as explained in above section, feature recognition of form features can be dome. We like to concentrate here on inner form features like type of hole, pockets, grooves etc. representing convex type internal loop in the target surface and boss representing concave type internal loop. It can be seen that inner features having convex internal loop in the target surface can pass through the entire solid or can penetrate to some distance in the solid. Looking at the data can recognize the presence of these features.

I). A face of the solid is represented FACE_OUTER_BOUND representing the outer loop of edges and FACE_BOUND representing the inner loop of edges. The ADVANCED_FACE entity showing these two entities together indicates of a face having another internal face indicating presence of an internal feature.

II). If the internal faces present in the outer faces are more than one it indicates the presence of" through" feature i.e. STEP file will have more than one ADVANCED_ FACE entity showing FACE_OUTER_BOUND and FACE_BOUND this indicate two inner loops in different surfaces.

III). If there is only one ADVANCED_ FACE entity showing FACE_OUTER_BOUND and FACE_BOUND, and the internal loop is of convex loop type it indicates "blind "feature.

IV). If the conditions (i) is satisfied and the STEP has the inner edges of the internal loop bounded by four straight edges, the feature that is formed is an internal-pocket. The existence of an inner loop with two edge elements bounding the loop with cylindrical surfaces or NURBS surfaces of cylindrical nature indicates that the internal feature is a hole. The presence of curved edges would indicate that the feature being formed is a rounded or circular pocket with the conditions (ii) or (iii) deciding the "through" or "blind" nature.

V). If there is only one ADVANCED_ FACE entity showing FACE_OUTER_BOUND and FACE_BOUND, and the internal loop is of concave loop type it indicates Boss feature.

7. CONCLUSIONS

The paper here explains the STEP format and extraction of data. Here the feature recognition of inner form features is based totally on the available data in STEP file, which is generated using PRO/E solid modeler and the format of STEP used is based on AP 214. The feature recognition can be similarly expanded to other type of form features and the feature recognized can be used for process planning.

8. REFERENCES

1. **Joshi and Chang**, (1988) "Graph-based heuristics for recognition of machined features from a 3D solid model", *Computer Aided Design* v 20(2) 81–86.
2. **Gavankar and Henderson**, (1989),"Graph based extraction of protrusions and depressions from Boundary Representation", *Computer Aided Design* v 22, 81–86.
3. **Ferreira and Hinduja,** (1990),"Convex hull based feature recognition methods for 2.5 D components", *Computer Aided Design* v 22(2) 81–86.
4. **Qamhiyah and Venter,** (1996) "Geometric reasoning for the extraction of form features", *Computer Aided Design* v 28(11) 857–903.
5. **Liu and Gonzalez**, (1996) , " Development of an automatic part feature extraction and classification system taking CAD data as input", *Computers in industry* v 29,137-150.
6. **An and Leep**, (1995), "A product data Exchange Integration structure using PDES/STEP for automated

manufacturing application", *Computers industrial Engineering* v 29(1-4), 711-715.
7. **Liang and Ahamed,** (1996) " A STEP based tool path generation for rough machining of planar surfaces", *Computers in industry* v 32, 219-231.
8. **Lau and jiang,** (1998)," A generic integrated system from CAD to CAPP: a neutral file –cum-GT approach", *Computer integrated manufacturing,* v11 (1-2), 67-75.
9. **Bhandarkar and Nagi,** (2000), " STEP based feature extraction from STEP geometry for Agile manufacturing" *Computers in industry* V 41 ,3-24.
10. **Dereli and Filz**, (2002), " A note on the use of step for interfacing design to process planning", *Computer aided Design* V 34, 1075-1085.
11. **FU and Ong**, (2003), " An approach to identify design and manufacturing features from a data exchanged part model". *Computer Aided Design* V 35, 979-993.

GCMM 2004
Editors: Prasad K D V Yarlagadda and S Narayanan
Copyright © 2005, Vellore Institute of Technology, Vellore, India
Publisher: Narosa Publishing House Pvt. Ltd., New Delhi, India

Modeling of Flexibility and Rapid Response in a Production System: A Conceptual Frame Works, Approaches and Technology

Lokesh Kumar

Lecturer, Department of Mechanical Engineering & Technology ,
J.M.I , New Delhi – 110025.

E-mail : lokeshkrsax@yahoo.com

Amrik Singh

Asst. Professor , Department of Mechanical Engineering , SLIET Sangrur.

Prof. Khan R A

Department of Mechanical Engineering , Faculty of Engg. & Tech.,
J.M.I , New Delhi – 110025.

Abstract

This paper deals with development of a model of a production system to improve flexibility and rapid response of system to highly turbulent environment. This requires strategy formulation, structuring and integration of all functions of a production system right from the moment customer expresses a need for a product and the Production system have undergone revolutionary changes. With WTO agreement and consequents opening up of world market, there is ever-growing competition in the market. The costumers are the king of the market. They are very demanding in nature today. They seek high quality, large variety, low cost products responsive to their specific and rapidly changing needs Also, they are seeking speedy deliveries, reliability, supportability, innovativeness and customized products concept to market time has become critical factor in market competition. It forced the companies to launch new products , updates their design , make design changes more frequently , manufacturing products quickly and produce at lower volume than ever before, moment that product goes into use, This involves integration and flexibility creations in organizational process , business functions , product development and design, manufacturing planning , execution and control in order to improve dynamism of system. This paper also explores tools and technology available.

To meet these challenges, companies should be flexible and fast responding to highly uncertain market conditions. The companies needs to understand their, objectives , develop corporate and manufacturing strategies with operations , develop core competency and capabilities and plan to change .They need quick management of information and knowledge , integration of all functions and flexibility creations in all functions to have fast responses. Flexibility can be achieved both internally and externally. Important flexibility factors are modular product design manufacturing technology flexibility, employee flexibility and flexibility in organization structure.[4]

1. FLEXIBILTY IN ORGANIZATIONAL PROCESS

In the changing global scenario, the organization must be able to adapt to change and respond quickly to meet threat and opportunities, Core competence of an organization is an vital factor. It is a collective learning process that imparts information, synthesized technology that involves people from all functions that enables a company to provide particular benefits to customers. Therefore, it is hard to script, imitates or even document.

There is need for flexibility creation in management which implies openers in thinking, adeptness to environment, responsiveness to change, freedom, informal attitudes, broading of mind etc. The greater attention and more flexibility to people is keys to successful management.

In the past management was inward looking operation were function driven. Flexibility was low structured was hierarchal, and decision making was centralized , now management , operations has to be people orientated flexibility has to be high structure has to be flat and decision making decentralized high commitment and encouragement of risk taking also supportive reward system.[9]

There is need of communication, involvement, deep commitment to working across organization. The goal is to build a strong feeling of community among the competency carrier so that precious idea across the corporation are traced frequently.

Flexibility in terms of individuals as well as team improvement is reported to be a dominant factor for success in promoting collaboration problem solving culture among team members.

Performance appraised cells for adequate flexibility in human resources practices , particularly in rewards and reorganization in order to promote creativity , innovation and risk taking.

Technology is an important parameter for corporate growth and performance. An organization that can discover a better technology for performing an activity than its competitor gain competitive advantage.

Timely and accurate information flow within system is a critical aspect for success of firms. Flexible system requires real time control with help of high level computer based status monitoring and decision automation Information flow and flexibility can be improved by investing type of computer – aided technology to gather , process and present the information to choose appropriate course of action.

2. FLEXIBILTY IN PRODUCT DEVELOPMENT

Flexibility in context of product development refers to ability of firm to change or react with little penalty in time , effort , cost or performance w r t change in business environment , during the period of product development and introduction to market.

Firms should use structured , flexible , integrated , product development process so that appropriate corrections deviations may be made depending on market environment .

Key factor of I.P.D are multifunctional development teams, overlapping development phases and collective consideration of product design and process through which it will be manufactured, tested, marketed and supported at later stages.

2.1 Use of Cross Functional Products Development Teams

Products development teams should includes people from marketing, costumer care, purchase production quality, finance, H.R,M , etc .besides design people . Team based consideration of down stream issues from area like production, quality, test, marketing at upstream stages like design facilities better trade off decision higher customer focus, enhanced product quality and reduced cycle time and costs.

Team should import elements of strength such as functional integration, quick and open information sharing, collaboration problems solving. Individuals should be committed to team task and team goal and shared vision. Qualities of mutual trust, good team spirit, cooperation, high goal-commitment, quick / free communication and encouragement of risk – taking result in high level of team performance with positive effect on project success.

Managerial flexibility in terms of decentralization, financial delegation and non rigid H R practices facilitates smooth and quick flow of product and project formation among the team members therefore, improving development process.

2.2 Conceptulisation & Dev. Phase

In this phase, aim is to understand ways and means for delivering maximum valve to customer by generating most appropriate definition of product.

It involves analysis of internal and external factors , the customers requirements / preferences , Market competition, available resources similar product form competitors , competitors strength / weakness , existing core competencies of company , new technology required , vendors identifications and selections.[1]

While design phase account for only16% of total development cost , decision making during conceptual design stage have direct impact on over 70% of production cost.

Firms should have flexible product development process and technology to enables the firms to take corrective actions to keep pace with fast changing market environment including technology , competition and customers preference.

Flexibility in technology reduces incremental costs and time required to include design modification in the product. Firms also adopt flexible approaches in selection of suppliers and employ several criteria for supplier – selection, namely technical compatibility, matching aims and

objectives, development speed, strategies positioning, management ability, cost of development, security of business information and cultural compatibility. [2]

Modular product architecture is used as flexible platforms for leveraging a large product variety [3, 9] in minimum time frame. In order to get low cost product variety advantages one should work towards maximizing the product modularity right form concept development phase. [3]

In Modular product design group components into modules by localizing maximization of interaction within each module and minimization of interaction between modules. Other characteristics are potential to become standardized and stand alone sub system , commonality , functional interaction design for manufacturing and assembly.

3. FLEXIBILITY IN MANUFACTURING

System flexibility is a function both of technology and how effectively the system is managed .Modular design and flexible manufacturing allowed SONY to producing a high variety of modulus with high quality and how costing and hence to capture nearly 50% of world market for walkman.

3.1 RMS / FMS

A Flexible manufacturing system (FMS) is a highly automated system consisting of a group of automated work centers, inter connected by an automated and integrated material handling and storage system and controlled by distributed (supervisory) computer system. This system is flexible enough to suit changing market conditions and product type without buying other equipment. FMS is useful to low verity and high volume production.[5]

Currently attempts are made to improve flexibility by developing new types of manufacturing system known as Reconfigurable Machining System (RMS).

Reconfigurability can be defined as ability to adjust the production capacity and operation to new circumstances through the rearrangement or change of systematic components. Components could be machines and conveyors in the whole system, mechanism controller in individual's machines, new sensors or new controller Reconfigurable manufacturing system will be open – ended, so that they can be improved and upgraded rather than replaced.

RMS Technology requires a system approaches to creating new design knowledge and manufacturing system. The system must contain the following elements:- Some of which have already developed.

- A system - level process planner , that one gives a part family , Volume and Mix chooses the best system. ·
- A life – cycle economic modeling methodology that can blend dynamic programming to recommend the most profitable system.
- A reconfigurable machining tool , consist of numerous module that can be replaced on basic machine to allow it to be modified quickly to suit the job.
- A control system for sequencing and coordinating large manufacturing system.
- A measurement scheme solution that ensures highest quality production.

3.2 Quality Information System

After making a parts , parts should be inspected for conformity towards quality. An inspection should also be flexible as well as integrated with manufacturing system fully. A Flexible Inspection system is defined as a highly automated inspection work cell consisting of one or more Coordinating Measuring Machines (CMM) and other types of inspection equipments plus parts handling system needed to move into , within , and out of cell [6] .

4. INTREGRATED SUPPLY CHAIN MANAGEMENT

Manufacturing paradigms are changing with time. Traditional concepts and methods for business management were focused or

optimization of internal activities (such as FMS , MRP – I , MRP – II , ERP and so on) in a company. Companies must drive an integrated approach to mange their entire business including procurements , inventory , manufacturing , logistics , distribution and sales known as Supply Chain Management. It implies optimization of whole process from suppliers to end users.

A Supply chain may be defined as an integrated manufacturing process where in a member of various business entities i.e. suppliers , manufacturers , distributors , and retailers work together in an effort to :-
1. Acquire raw materials.
2. Convert these raw materials into specific products.
3. Deliver these final products to retailers.

A supply is comprised of two basic:-The Production and Inventory Control Process and The Distribution and Logistic process.

5. PROPOSED MODEL

The process to develop an upgraded or a new product is shown in fig.1.

Top Management formulates vision and goal for enterprises. It formulates corporate and manufacturing strategies. HRM take responsibilities of development of competency by recruiting & training and rewards system. With inputs from customers , customer support service and other seller (Competitors) and market researches, marketing department prepare voice of customer and competitors strength and weakness. This information is given to product development team. Purchase department provides information regarding vendor's identification and selection to I.P.D. FINANCE representative provides inputs to decides financial availability to products of the company. Design Engineers or R & D an engineer creates new designs or modifies their design. Manufacturing department conducts manufacturability assessment, provides inputs regarding quality aspects for product , also conduct rapid prototyping of products. Thus with combined efforts of all , most appropriate products definition is created by I.P.D. team.

After the product is designed , prototype is made to test the performance. After successfully completion of all stages , Commercial production of product is formally launched. Parts are manufactured by flexible manufacturing system. Then parts are inspected by FIS. If parts found non – conforming, it is sent to either rework facility (if Possible) or to dispose off. If parts is conforming to standards it is shipped to the customer by distribution network.

6. APPROACHES AND TECHNOLOGY

Tools and techniques for I.P.D. are QFD , DFA , DFM , FMEA ,Value engg. , axiomatic Design . There are numbers of tools available for designers as rapid prototyping and tooling technology besides CAD.

To help in manufacturing there are many CAM technology available such as CAPP , CAS , Group Technology , FMS , FIS , etc.

7. CONCLUSION

This paper an integrated discussed various issues to improve dynamisms of a production system. An integrated conceptual framework of the production system is also proposed. Lastly , available tools and techniques is also briefly presented. The proposed conceptual framework has potential to enables an organization to improve its dynamism by devising means to implement it.

In next step in this direction is to conceive the step by step ways to implement it. Also , One should explore appropriate technology available , improvement in available technology and development of new unavailable technology for rapid response production system and hopes future researches will extend this attempt to realize proposed model.

8. REFERENCES

1. **Bailetti A J, Callahan J.R , Mcclusley S** (1988) coordination t different stages of product design , R&D management , 28(4) , 237-243.
2. **Bailey W J , Masson R** and **Raesid R** (1998) choosing successful technology Development Partners : A Best Practice Model , *Int J. of Tech. Management.*
3. **Baldwin C.Y.** and **Dark K.B** (1997) , Managing in Age of Modularity HBR , (Sept , Oct) 84-93.
4. **Das T.K** and **Elango B** (1995) , Managing strategies Flexibility: Key to Effective Performance , *J. Gen. Management* , 20(3) , 60-75
5. **Groover M.P** (2002) Automation Production System and Computer integrated Manufacturing, *Second Edition , Printice Hall of India Pvt. Ltd.* , New Delhi.
6. **Hamel G.** and **Prahalad CK** (1991) The Core competence of corporation HBR , May- June , 79-91.
7. Development : A Canadian Survey , Res Management , 27 (1) , 5 – 15.
8. **Robertson** and **Ulrich K** (1998) Planning For Product Plateform , Sloan Management Review Summer, 19-31.
9. **Saleti S D** and **Wrang C K** (1993) The Management of Innovation Strategies , Structure and Organization Climates, *IEEE Transaction on Engineering Management* , 40 ,(1) , 14-20.
10. **Schilling M A** and **Hill CWL** (1998) Amnaging the new Product Development Process: Strategies Imperative , Academy of Management Review , June.
11. **Stalk G , Evans P** and **Shulman L E** (1992) Computing on Capabilities , SLOAN Management Review , fall
12. **Takenchi T H** and **Nonaku J** (1986) The New Product Development Game, HBR, Jan-Feb , 130-137.

GCMM 2004
Editors: Prasad K D V Yarlagadda and S Narayanan
Copyright © 2005, Vellore Institute of Technology, Vellore, India
Publisher: Narosa Publishing House Pvt. Ltd., New Delhi, India

Need for an Improved Worker Training System to offer Production Flexibility in Manufacturing Companies

Maki Ichimura, Arunachalam S, & Jalahankhani H,

School of Computing & Technology, University of East London,
Longbridge Road, Dagenham, Essex RM8 2AS, UK

Abstract

In order to be competitive in the global, rapidly changing market, worker flexibility has become a central issue in the organisation of manufacturing enterprises. Researchers have concluded that worker training affects shopfloor productivity directly. However, there is only a little research on training in the manufacturing environment and no systematic training method proposed [1]. This paper proposes an intelligent systems approach for the selection of the most suitable training of shopfloor workforce for given tasks. The proposed intelligent system uses a Holonic approach, which allows both cooperation and autonomous control.

Keywords

Worker flexibility, Productivity, Holonic Manufacturing System, Cross-training

1. INTRODUCTION

As a consequence of the structural transformation of the market, traditional organizational structures and systems have become rigid and hierarchical in terms of flexibility and responsiveness. Therefore, it is crucial to adapt "old-fashioned" high volume, low variety manufacturing systems to the new market demands – competitiveness in the global, rapidly changing market depends upon adaptability. Adaptability is defined as the ability to change or be changed to fit changed circumstances. An important viable integral to the organization of manufacturing systems is worker flexibility. The employees are required to be capable to adapt to the complexity of changes in work environment, orders, and rapid technological development. Shopfloor labour skills thus need to be updated regularly [2]. Training is generally recognized as a vehicle to develop labour skills such as flexibility and quality of work.

Indeed, there seems to be empirical evidence that the quality of training provided to the employees within a given manufacturing system significantly affects the efficiency and productivity of the enterprise [1] [3] [4]. Despite this link between training and productivity, there is no consensus of what training methods are most productive. Most research models of efficient/productive training propose is either oversimplified or require improvement within a scope of intelligence system.

It is the thesis of this paper that the development of an intelligent training system entails an increase in shopfloor productivity as a logical consequence of improved worker flexibility. Worker flexibility is a skill integral to the intelligent training system that allocates the most suitable worker for each task based on one's individual profile and preference. However, the success criteria of such intelligent training system depend on the realization of positive learning transfer [5]. Training activities would become mere waste of money, time and resource if the knowledge obtained from the training was not applicable to the real working situation [6]. The extent to which the criteria of a successful intelligent training system are fulfilled defines the development of performance in a wide range of changing situations concerning future production planning and unexpected disturbances. The proposed intelligent system introduced in this paper draws upon Holonic Manufacturing concept. Holonic Manufacturing System has emerged to develop an architecture which is highly flexible and decentralized in order to overcome the difficulties with frequent changes and disturbances facing traditional manufacturing systems.

2. TRAINING REVIEW
2.1 Training needs

Many companies are recognizing that one of the most difficult things to maintain their competitiveness is well-trained labours [7]. In recent years, some researches conclude that the labour training is essential [1] [2] [7]. Moreover, it has been shown that quality of training provided to the employees will significantly affect an organization's efficiency and productivity [1] [3] [4] [5]. It is also crucial to upgrade labour skills as they become outdates due to development of new technology and adapting of new technology to manufacturing environment [2] [8].

As technology has improved, the manufacturing environment has changed. Today's Manufacturing systems operate within a short-term production cycle, a small lot size and a changing environment. In uncertain situations, however, organizations strive to improve the productivity in order to strengthen the compatibility with other organizations. Within the scope of intelligent training systems, shopfloor workers are expected to adapt immediately to the difficulties that arise from both unexpected situations and changes without halting production or reducing productivity. Table 1 summarises a number of manufacturing situations where training is required:

Table 1: Manufacturing situations requiring training

Expected Changes	Unexpected Changes	Requirements
Add new machines Replace machines Introduce new products Future orders Skills become outdated [1]	Sudden absence Sudden retirement Breaking down Interruption by high priority jobs	Managers decision to improve productivity

In order to response to both expected changes and unexpected changes, shopfloor workers need to be trained according to the each change. A characteristic of expected changes is that the required skill is clear. Therefore, a labourer or a group of labourers attend a training session in order to gain new skills according to production planning, order schedule and/or machining schedule. However, on the other hand, as for unexpected changes, required skills are uncertain. In an unexpected situation, cross-trained workers are capable of covering other workers' tasks and handling more than their regular job. Workers can be cross-trained in all skills within a small group. Nowadays, many organizations' line workers in shopfloor are divided into a small number of labours. Team working and cross-training are known as the efficient way to improve the productivity [9]. Moreover, it has been shown that a small cross-training group can increase the productivity and motivation of labourers [10] [11].

2.2 Cross-training

It is simply believed that the more workers are trained more skills, the more shopfloor will have flexibility. In general, cross-training is aimed at increasing the flexibility of workforce and improving the shopfloor performance [11]. For example, it enables that the labours to help the other workers to finish the tasks on time where the queue is long and to minimize the idle time. Moreover, when the early due date job is assigned to the shopfloor, workforces are able to move to the high priority job. In other words, the more workers are cross-trained, the more shopfloor managers have opportunities for job rotation [12]. Molleman and Slomp (1999) discuss the importance of focusing on the distribution of skills within teams.

Some researchers mentioned that the advantages of implementing cross training are
1) The capacity of dealing with absenteeism, attrition, turnover, illness and day off will be increased as cross-trained worker can be assigned to the task rather than his/her work being held [12] [13] [14].
2) When the more labour can perform the task, the more possibilities that the deadline can be achieved with accuracy [13].

A research carried out at the Toyota Tsutsumi plant concludes that cross-training and job rotation within a small group increase productivity and quality of the plant [10]. In this research, the workers have been trained many different skills (maximum eight skills), while rotating from one job to the other. Hence, the workers did not loose their acquired knowledge even though a particular skill may not be required in the first job.

Even though cross-training seems to be great benefits for the company in improving its worker flexibility, there are some concerns. The major concern of cross-training is that it is costly. In addition, worker flexibility which is the result of cross-training might present a trade-off in both technical and behavioural [15]. Moreover, it is not practical to train all the tasks on the shop floor for all of the workforces [16]. Hottenstein [17] (1998) has mentioned that cross-training more than two or three skills per labour do not always promise to improve the shopfloor productivity. For the reason that a labour who is trained more than his/her first job might not be able to show same quality, efficiency or productivity among the jobs.

2.3 Chained cross-training

Only a little research has tried to identify the most effective way to organize cross-training and the necessary amount of cross-training [18]. As the answer to this question, chaining concept has been applied to cross-training [16] [18]. The concept of "Chained Cross-training" aims to organize cross-training simply. A labour will be trained skill of his/her first task and one more additional skill of downstream task. Therefore, it will promise that the entire task has at least one backup worker. Moreover, chained cross-training is very simple and easy to understand. However, this chained cross-training totally ignore if the task is fit to the worker and his/her job preferences.

3. HOLONIC MANUFACTURING SYSTEM (HMS)
3.1 Concepts of HMS

The HMS concept was proposed in 1994 by the HMS consortium as an experiment under the international Intelligent Manufacturing Systems Research Program. HMS is a new approach designed to develop an architecture for highly decentralized manufacturing system, which attempts to overcome the difficulties faced by traditional manufacturing systems. The word "Holon" was proposed by Arthur Koestler in order to describe a basic unit of organization in biological and social systems over three decades ago [19]. "Holon" is a combination of holos, which means whole in Greek and the suffix on meaning particle or part as in proton or neutron [20].

HMS is one of the burgeoning manufacturing systems, which every entity is the system such as machines, robots, persons, products, or any other element of a process (modelled as holon) have autonomous and cooperative properties. Hence each holon is enable to communicate and collaborate with each other. The word "holon" represents the methodology to harmonize individual parts as holon with the whole system [20]. This means that while systems are comprised of individual functions, these individual functions are related to, and are coordinated in the whole system. Moreover, HMS is able to switch between hierarchical control and heterarchical control in order to try and take the best features from those two approaches [20]. Hence, HMS combines the high and predictable performance accomplished by hierarchical systems with the strength of the agility of heterarchical systems against disturbances. This approach is known as "holarchy."

3.2 Basic structure of HMS

PROSA is a holonic reference architecture for manufacturing systems developed at PMA-KULeuven. In this architecture, there are three types of basic holons, which built up a holonic manufacturing system: product holon, resource holon and order holon [20]. Each of them has responsibility for one feature of manufacturing process. The basic building blocks of holonic manufacturing system and their relations are shown in Figure 1.

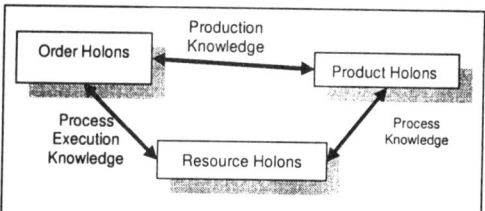

Fig. 1: Holonic Manufacturing System, Basic building blocks and their relations [20]

An *order holon* is created for each manufacturing orders. It is responsible for performing the work correctly, efficiently, and on time. It is inevitable to have clear responsibilities before things go wrong and/or tasks get delayed. It may contain customer orders, stock orders, maintenance and repairing tasks. It can deal with more than one order concurrently.

A *product holon* holds information about the process status of product components during manufacturing, time variables, quality status, and decision-making knowledge against the order request in order to ensure that the product is produced with sufficient quality. Furthermore, a product holon provides up-to-date engineering information relating to the product life cycle such as configuration, bill of material, process plans and design. A product holon perform as information server within holonic architecture.

A *resource holon* consists of a physical part (production resource) and of an information processing part that controls the resource. The physical part contains a production resource of the manufacturing system such as machine, conveyor, tool, raw material, and end product etc. together with controller components. The information processing part contains planning and scheduling components.

4. HOLONIC WORKFORCE TRAINING SYSTEM
4.1 Aims of Holonic workforce training system

Planning process is the vital phase in order to carry out a successful training. However, in the past, organizations did not have a strategy of choosing the right person, the right time, and the right planning for training [6]. In order to carry out the most effective training, these elements need to be systematically and deliberately encapsulated in strategies and/or policies adapted by companies. Moreover it is important that the labourers' job preference is carefully considered during the selection process as an incentive to increase motivation, particularly if the labourer is interested in gaining new skills and meeting new challenges.

The development of an intelligent training system aims to maximize the productivity of shop floor and to maximize the flexibility of the workforce through selecting the most suitable labour for each task based on job analysis, their profile and preference and the best training according to the production schedule, customer orders and/or machining schedule. Hence, *"Holonic Workforce Intelligent Training System"* is capable of selecting the best training method, task to be trained and the most suitable labour through Holonic concept in accordance to production schedule, labour information, task analysis and labour interests.

4.2 Components of Holonic workforce training system

In order to develop an effective training system, holonic architecture characterised as distributed, autonomous and cooperative is applied. Holonic Workforce Intelligent Training System comprises of six holons, Order Holon, Labour Holon, Shopfloor Holon, Product Holon, Training Holon, and Schedule Holon. Table 2 summarize the information that each holon is holding and is responsible. Fig. 2 shows the entire system as a whole.

Table 2: Information held in each holon

Holon	Information
Order Holon	Customer order plans
Labour Holon	Labour information (age, physical information, gender, education level, past experiences, skill level, training record, personnel interests, performance quality, and time availability)
Shopfloor Holon	Task information *Job classification* (e.g. material processing, assembly, inspection, maintenance and troubleshooting, material handling and transfer, storage, and quality control and inspection) *Skill requirements* (e.g. skill-based level, rule-based level, and knowledge-based level) *Physical requirements* (e.g. carry heavy stuff, lift up heavy stuff, and standing long hours)
Product Holon	Product information
Training Holon	Training delivery methods (cross-training or same training for all labours)
Schedule Holon	Production schedule

4.3 Decision-making search engines

Holonic workforce intelligent training system consists of two search engines, 1) labour search engine and 2) training search engine as shown in Figure 2. They will help to make the beat decisions according to the information received from the six holons. The labour search engine is responsible for selecting the most suitable workforce for a certain task based on criteria such as gender, age, job preference, time availability, educational level, past experiences, previous training level, and performance quality. It is also liable for the selection more than one labourer when the shopfloor management is going to carry out a cross-training. The training search engine is employed to select the best training from the options held in the Training Holon according to task analysis performed by Shopfloor Holon, production schedule, product information and customer order. The proposed six holons and two search engines interact among themselves by sending and receiving information in order to achieve the aims of the system.

5. CONCLUSION

In the past, the companies did not have knowledge and skills of worker training in organizing and upgrading their skills. As a consequent of this mismanagement of workforce, organizations failed to transform themselves to contemporary companies. This paper proposes a new training system based on holonic manufacturing architecture. Published research has invoked the importance of focusing on training as there is empirical evidence that training has a direct influence on shopfloor productivity. However, not much research has contributed to systematic training methods. The proposed intelligent training system provides an effective approach towards executing training for shopfloor workers. The proposed intelligent training system contains six different holons, which comprise two decision-making search engines. Furthermore, each holon will interact with one another in order to select the best training and the most suitable labour for the training. This systematic, decision-making approach proves to have the potential of meeting challenges in manufacturing environments affected by constant changes and disturbances.

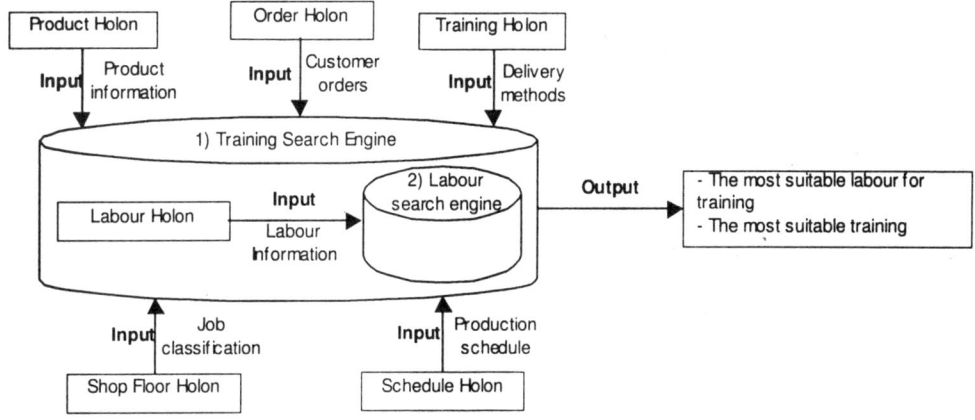

Fig 2: A conceptual model for holonic workforce intelligent training system

6. REFERENCES

1. **Pennathur, A. and Mital, A.** (2003) "Worker mobility and training in advanced manufacturing", *International Journal of Industrial Ergonomics*, Volume 32, Issue 6, Pages 363-388

2. **Ntuen, A.C. and Chestnut, A.J.** (1993) "An Expert System for Selecting Manufacturing Workers for Training", *Expert Systems with Applications*, Vol. 9, No. 3, 1995, pp309-332

3. **O'Connor, P.E.** (1993) "Getting Down to Basic" *Training & Development*, pp62-63

4. **Goldstein, L.I. and Buxton, M.V.** (1981) "Training and Human Performance," in *"Human performance and productivity, Vol.1: Human capability assessment"* Marvin D. Dunnette, Edwin A. (ed.), Hillsdale, L. Erlbaum Associates

5. **Salvendy, G. and Karwowski, W.** (1994) "Design of work and development of personnel in advanced manufacturing," New York, Chichester

6. **Reid, M. A. and Barrington, H.** (1999) "Training Interventions, Promoting learning opportunities", *Chartered Institute of Personnel and Development*, Sixth Edition

7. **Stewart, B. D., Webster, D. B., Ahmad, S., and Matson, J.O.** (1994) "Mathematical models for developing a flexible workforce", *International Journal Production Economics*, 36

8. **Molleman, E. and Slomp, J.** (1999) "Functional flexibility and team performance," *International Journal of Production Research*, Vol. 37, No. 8, pp1837-1858

9. **Takeyama, T., Kawata, S. and Ohta, H.,** (2003) "Self-organizing Map for Group Technology Oriented Plant layout Planning," *IEICE Trans. Fundamentals*, Vol. E86-A, No. 11, pp2747-2754

10. **Muramatsu, R., Miyazaki, H. and Ishii K.,** (1987) "A successful application of job enlargement/enrichment at Toyota", *IIE Transactions*, Vol. 19, No. 4, pp451-459

11. **Jensen, John B.** (2000) "The impact of resource flexibility and staffing decisions on cellular and departmental shop performance", *European Journal of Operational Research*, 127, pp279-296

12. **Slomp, J. and Molleman, E.** (2002) "Cross-training policies and team performance," *International Journal Production Research*, Vol. 40, No. 5, pp1193-1219

13. **Ebeling, A.C. and Lee, C.Y.** (1994) "Cross-training effectiveness and profitability," *International Journal of Production Research*, Vol. 32, No. 12, pp2843–2859

14. **Van Der Beukel, A. L. and Molleman, E.** (1998) "Multifunctionality: the driving and constraining forces," *Human factors and Ergonomics in Manufacturing*, Vol. 8, Issue 4, pp303-321

15. **Kenneth L. Schultz, John O. McClain and L. Joseph Thomas** (2003) "Overcoming the dark side of worker flexibility", *Journal of Operations Management*, Volume 21, Issue 1, Pages 81-92

16. **Inman, R. R., Jordan, W. C. and Blumenfeld, D. E.** (2004) "Chained cross-training of assembly line workers," *International Journal of Production Research*, Vol. 42, No. 10, pp1899-1910

17. **Hottenstein, M. P. and Bowman, S. A.** (1998) "Cross-training and worker flexibility: A review of DRC system research", *Journal of a High Technology management Research*, Volume 2, Number 2, pp157-174

18. **Hopp, W. J., Tekin, E. and Van Oyen, M. P.** (2004) "Benefits of skills chaining in serial production lines with cross-trained workers," *Management Science*, Vol. 50, No.1, pp83-98

19. **Arthur Koestler**, (1967) "The Ghost in the Machine", London, Hutchinson, pp45-58

20. **Brussel, V.H., Wyns, J., Bongaerts, L. and Peeters, P.** (1998) "Reference architecture for holonic manufacturing systems: PROSA," *Computers in Industry*, Vol. 37, Issue 3, pp. 255-274

21. **Simmonds, D.** (2003) "Designing and Delivering Training", *Chartered Institute of Personnel and Development*

GCMM 2004
Editors: Prasad K D V Yarlagadda and S Narayanan
Copyright © 2005, Vellore Institute of Technology, Vellore, India
Publisher: Narosa Publishing House Pvt. Ltd., New Delhi, India

Non-Contact Measurement of Spur Gear Parameters

by Image Processing Technique

Ramesh Kumar P

Senior Lecturer, Department Of Mechanical Engineering
Adhiparasakthi Engineering College, Melmaruvathur-603 319
E-Mail: pandianramesh1967@rediffmail.com

Jothilingam* A , Rajmohan** B

*Selection Grade Lecturer, **Professor & Head
Department of Production Technology, Madras Institute of Technology,
Anna University, Chrompet, Chennai-600044

E-Mail: ajothilingam@yahoo.co.in, rajmohan@mitindia.edu

Abstract

Since the advent of digital computer there has been a constant effort to expand the domain of computer applications. Some of the motivations for this effort come from important practical needs to find more efficient ways of doing things. Some of the motivation comes from sheer challenge of building or programming a machine to do things that machines have never done before. Both of these motives are found in that area of artificial intelligence and called as machine perception. In Manufacturing and Assembly Line Environments, where there is a need for Precise Measurement as a part of the Inspection Process, a Vision Measurement System can be used in a Real-Time Environment to achieve 100% Inspection. In the Manufacturing of Gears, where it is necessary to maintain strict tolerances of the Parameters, Machine Vision Technology, which is adopting image-processing technique, can be used as a Computer Enhanced Measurement Device that is fast and reliable. And, this measurement can be fed back to a Control Device to regulate the Production Process more efficiently.

In line with that thought, here gears are considered. Gears play vital role in this era of automation. Gears are used without any exception, in almost all applications such as automobile vehicles, clocks, wristwatches, and toys. Gears play important role in mechanisms used in different machines. So, the accuracy of the gear in its dimensions, determines the performance of one such a mechanism or a system, to a large extent. Hence, 100% inspection of gears is essential, to find different parameters of it. But, measuring different parameters of a gear is not an easy job. Different instruments are needed. Also, it is a time consuming process. To tackle all these troubles, a non-contact method of measurement, in the name of machine vision, is considered.

In this paper, a spur gear is selected and its axial image is acquired for further processing. The acquired image is first subject to image enhancement and processed further to extract the different parameters, including the number of teeth. This project work deals with these processes in a sequence, towards achieving the objective.

Keywords
Machine Vision, Image Processing Technique, and Image Enhancement

1. IMAGE PROCESSING METHODOLOGY

The standard methodology of image processing is shown in figure 1.1. In the process of image sampling, a scene of environment is projected onto a one-or-two-dimensional sensor, which digitizes and stores the image. Much attention has to be paid for lighting, in order to extract the maximum useful and the minimum useless information from the scene.

Image sampling followed by image conditioning, where frames averaging or low pass filtering can be employed to improve noisy images, and by feature enhancement, where edge and contour filters are applied in order to highlight the important features of the image. The next step is segmentation of the image and the extraction of information relating to the segments, such as dimensions, areas etc. The next step is the analysis of the features arising from this information. The last step is the action / actuation.

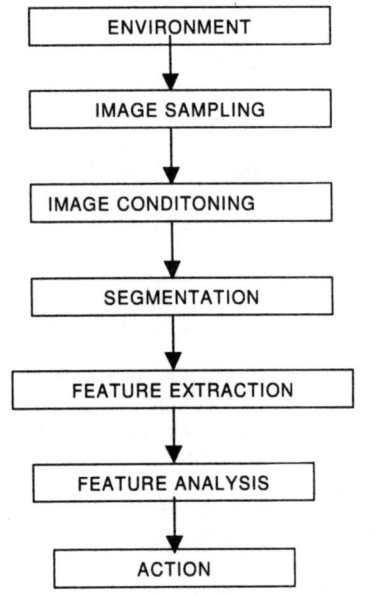

Figure 1.1
Image processing methodology

2. BASIC IMAGE PROCESSING SYSTEM

A basic image processing system consists of personal computer aided with a video graphic adapter card or a super video graphic adapter card. The images to be tested and the required algorithms are provided on a storage device. Then a display device that supports VGA or SVGA would be required. It may also consist of a pc equipped with an image grabber. Attached to the input port of the image grabber is a video camera and to output port a display device. Initially, most of the studies were carried out on gray level images, and a black and white monitor.

2.1. Image

Images can have either digital or analog representation. In the digital representation of gray level images, the images are represented as two-dimensional array of numbers. Each number represents the intensity or gray level of image at that relative position. If each gray level is represented by 8-bits, then gray levels allowed are 2^8 or 256 possible values. These levels are usually assigned integer values ranging from 0-255, with '0' representing the darkest intensity level and '255' the brightest intensity level. Each element in the matrix is called a picture element, which is usually referred as 'pixel'.

2.2. Camera

In general there are two types of cameras viz. vacuum tube devices and the solid-state devices. These solid-state cameras are also known as CCD cameras due to their usage of special analog shift register called charge-coupled device. These CCDs transfer electric charge from the light transducer, located in front of the camera, to the electronic circuit that encodes the resultant current into a TV video signal.

3. DIGITAL IMAGE PROCESSING SYSTEMS

The elements of the general-purpose system capable of performing the image processing operations are namely,
- Image acquisition
- Image storage
- Pre processing
- Communication
- Display

4. EXPERIMENTATL WORK
4.1. Image Acquisition

Image acquisition is an important and difficult task. Acquiring a right image will reduce the difficulties in processing the image further. An axial image of the gear is needed for analyzing and finding the parameters of the gear.

To get an image perpendicular to the axis of the gear, the camera viewing direction should be exactly perpendicular to the cross section of the spur gear specimen. Otherwise, it results in elliptical images from which parameters cannot be extracted.

4.1.1. Hardware / Software Used
Camera:

CASIO-QV – 5000 SX
Software used: QV – LINK
Lighting used : RING NEON LIGHT
Specimen : GEARS USED IN WATCHES

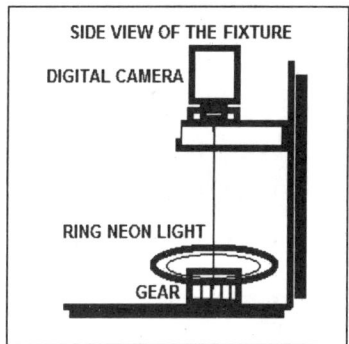

Fig 4.1: Fixture used in Image Capturing

In the arrangement shown above, the planer table and planer tool head are used as fixture elements. Placing the gear on the planer table and keeping the camera in the planer tool head, which is exactly perpendicular to the planer table, the axial image of the spur gear is captured.

4.2. Different Images Captured

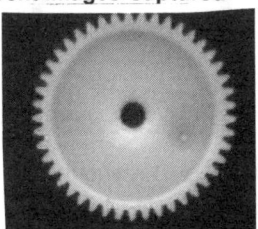

Fig 4.2.1: Gear3.Jpg

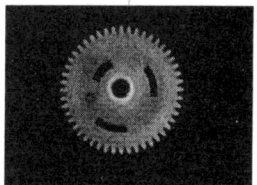

Fig. 4.2.2: gear7.jpg

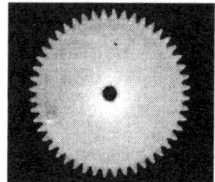

Fig 4.2.3: Gear2.bmp

Fig 4.2.4: Gear1.bmp

4.3. Difficulties In Image Capturing

- Obtaining a perfect circular cross section of the spur gear
- The shadows formed because of the fixture elements
- Improper lighting

4.4. Flow Chart

Showing the steps involved in processing the image and extracting the features from the image.

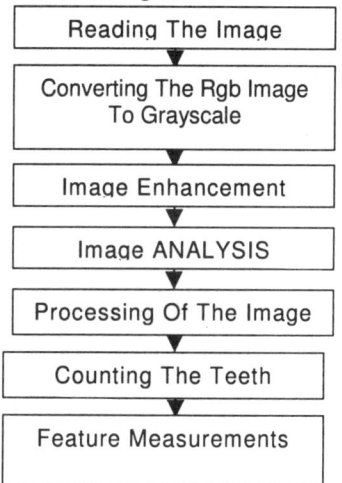

Reading The Image

Converting The Rgb Image To Grayscale

Image Enhancement

Image ANALYSIS

Processing Of The Image

Counting The Teeth

Feature Measurements

4.5. Processing the Image

For processing the image and counting the teeth of the gear from selected gear image gear3.jpg, different functions and subroutines available in MATLAB PROGRAMMING SOFTWARE are used. The following functions used.

Imread   imshow
imopen   imsubtract
bwlabel   bwperim
imresize

IMAGES OBTAINED AFTER PROCESSING

FIG.4.5.1: Selected Image Gear3.Jpg

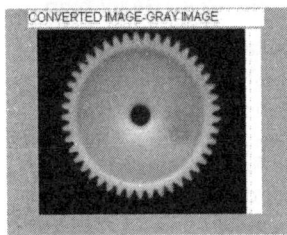

FIG.4.5.2: Converted Image

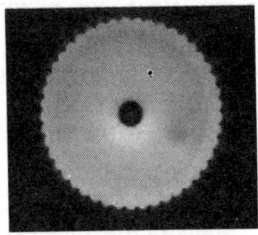

FIG.4.5.3: Background of the Gray Image

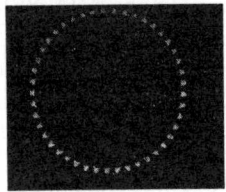

FIG.4.5.4: Image After Subtraction

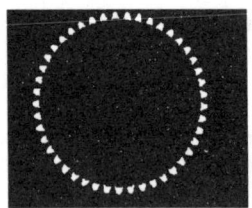

FIG.4.5.5: Thresholded Subtracted Image

By counting the number of Bounded Regions, MATLAB CODING is giving the count, that is, the number of teeth of the selected spur gear.

The Number Of Teeth Is   45.

4.6. Functions Used

Imread   imshow   Imopen
imsubtract   Imadjust   graythresh
im2bw   edge   imdilate
imfill   imclearborder imerode
bwperim   bwoutline   rgb2gray

4.7. Post Processing Images

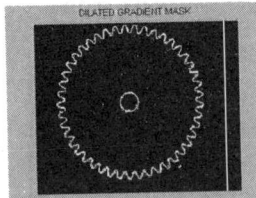

FIG .4.7.1: Dilated Gradient Mask

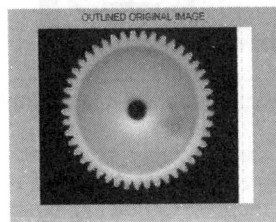

FIG4.7.2: Outlined Original Image

FIG.4.7.3: Thresholded Gear

FIG.4.7.4: Thresholded Hole-Filled Image

FIG.4.7.5: Final Boundary Image

After processing the image, the thresholded hole-filled image is used to extract the parameters of the gear.

Here, JAVA PROGRAMMING is used to extract the listed parameters of the spur gear from its image. JAVA coding is developed for radial scanning of the image. Using Radial Scanning Approach, three circles namely, teeth tip circle, teeth root circle and pitch circle, are obtained.

4.8. Parameters of The Gear

Outside Diameter
Root Diameter
Pitch Circle Diameter
Addendum
Dedendum
Module   M
Pitch
Teeth Thickness
Face Width
Number Of Teeth

The following images are obtained after executing the java coding.

FIG.4.8.1: Gear Image with Teeth Tip Circle

FIG.4.8.2: Gear Teeth Root Circle

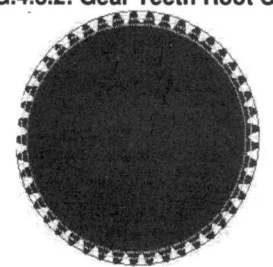

FIG.4.8.3: Tip Circle, Root Circle and Pitch Circle

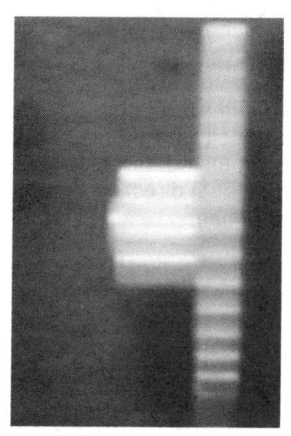

309

FIG.4.8.4:
Gearthick.Bmp

FIG.4.8.5:Gearthick After Thresholding

5. EXTRACTING THE PARAMETERS

First, the four extreme points are obtained.

Then, the center of the gear is obtained by drawing a square, which contains the gear.

Then, after obtaining the required circles, the pitch of the gear is obtained by counting the number of pixels along the teeth tip circle, between two successive teeth.

Then, the tooth thickness of the gear teeth is obtained by counting the number of pixels along the pitch circle, between two successive teeth.

In the same way, the diameters of the tip circle, pitch circle and root circle are found by counting the number of pixels along a diagonal direction, from the center of the gear image.

Finally, gear face width is obtained, using MATLAB programming.

6. RESULTS
6.1. Calibration

Tip Circle Diameter = 8.627 X 2 mm
                    (From The Profile Projector)
17.25mm = 213 Pixels
I Pixel = 0.081mm

6.2. Obtained Parameters

PARAMETERS	PIXELS	mm
Outside Diameter	252	20.412
Root Diameter	228	18.468
Pitch Circle Diameter	240	19.44
Addendum	6	0.486
Dedendum	6	0.486
Module M	5	
Pitch	17	0.112
Teeth Thickness	5	0.405
Face Width	23	1.863
Number of Teeth	45	

7. REFERENCES

1. **Janakiraman P. A.** (1995), Robotics And Image Processing, Tata McGraw-Hill Publishing Company.
2. **Mikell P. Groover, Mitchell Weiss, Rogel N. Nagel And Nicholas G**. Odrey (1986), Industrial Robotics Technology, Programming And Applications, McGraw-Hill International Edition.
3. **Rafel C. Gonzalez** And **Rafel E. Woods** (1993), Digital Image Processing, Addison – Wesley Publishing Company.
4. **Chanda B. and D. Dutta Majumder**, Digital Image Processing And Analysis
5. **Parker J. R.**, Algorithms For Image Processing And Computer Vision
6. **Anil K. Jain**, PHI Publishers, 2002, Fundamental Of Digital Image Processing
7. www.Mathworks.Com
8. www.zygo.com

GCMM 2004
Editors: Prasad K D V Yarlagadda and S Narayanan
Copyright © 2005, Vellore Institute of Technology, Vellore, India
Publisher: Narosa Publishing House Pvt. Ltd., New Delhi, India

Optimization of Manufacturing System – A Case Study

Anthony Xavior M & Narayanan S

Mechanical Engineering Department, Vellore Institute of Technology,
Deemed University, Vellore – 632 014, Tamil Nadu.

E - Mail: Xavior_anto@hotmail.com

Abstract

Increased competition in many industries has resulted in a greater emphasis on optimizing the manufacturing system A company, which is involved in design and manufacture of textile machinery parts want to add a new product in their product's list. In order to cater the machinery requirement an additional manufacturing facility is to be installed. The major problem associated with manufacturing system is to identify the optimum number of machines required at each workstation. Based on the number of major components, five workstations had been identified. Initially the number of machines required at each workstation is estimated using the fundamental formulae of queuing model. Next Taguchi technique is being adopted to find the optimum number of machines at each workstation, considering the average waiting time of jobs in the system as the major factor. The basic idea is to minimize the waiting time of jobs in the entire system, which can be done by optimizing the number of machines. Finally the workstation that is having more influence on the total waiting time has been identified.

Keywords
Manufacturing, Queuing analysis, Waiting time

1. INTRODUCTION

A company, which is involved in design and manufacture of textile machinery parts want to add a new product in their product's list. The product is a subassembly of a large textile-processing machine, which consists of five major components and some bought-out items. In order to cater the machinery requirement an additional manufacturing facility is to be installed. The sequence of processing each of these components and the machine tool required for processing had been identified. It is decided to keep identical machines in a particular workstation i.e. the machines in different stations are dissimilar. Reducing the waiting time of jobs in the system is one way of improving the throughput, which also reduces the in-process inventories. Here an attempt is made to optimize the number of machines required at each workstation in this manufacturing setup. Accordingly five workstations are to be installed with identical machines at each workstation. The task is to determine the number of machines needed in each workstation. Taguchi's orthogonal array is used to evaluate the optimum number of machines at each workstation, which will minimize the total waiting time in the system. Various combinations are formed by varying the number of machines at each workstation and the total waiting time for each combination were calculated. Further the workstation that has the largest effect on the waiting time of jobs in the system is also identified.

2. DESCRIPTION OF THE MANUFACTURING SYSTEM

Manufacturing system with an input / output (receiving / shipping) station and five workstations were considered. Assuming that jobs arrive at the input / output station with inter-arrival times that are independent exponential random variables with a mean of 12 jobs for 8 hrs (i.e.) 1.5 jobs arrive in typical hour. The five components are referred as job 1,...,5 and their respective probability are 0.14, 0.14, 0.14, 0.29 and 0.29. The job types 1,...,5 require 4,4,2,2,2 operations to be done respectively and each operation must be done at a specified workstation in a prescribed order.

If a job is brought to a particular workstation and all machines there are already busy or blocked, the job joins a single FIFO queue at that station. Each job begins at the input / output station on its routing and then leaves the system. The time to perform an operation at a particular machine depends on the job type, the nature of the machining process and the workstation to which the machine belongs. The routings for the different job types and the mean service time for each job type and each operations are given in table – 1.

Table – 1 Routing for the different job types and mean service time.

S.no	Job type	Workstation routing	Mean service time for successive operations (hrs.)
1	1	2, 4, 3, 5	4, 3, 8, 2
2	2	2, 4, 3, 5	4, 3, 5, 1
3	3	3 ,5	2, 3
4	4	6 ,5	1, 1
5	5	2 ,5	2, 2

3. QUEUING MODEL ANALYSIS

Optimization of the proposed manufacturing facility can be done to determine how may machines are needed at each work station to achieve an expected throughput of 12 jobs per day which is the minimum requirement. To determine a starting point for the optimization process, a simple queuing type analysis of the system is performed. In particular for workstation I(where I = 1....5) to be well defined in the long run, its utilization factor $\rho = \lambda / S W$ must be less than 1. The arrival rate to station 2 is 12 per day. Using conditional probability the mean service time at station 2 is 1.12 hrs which implies that the service rate at station 2 is 0.893 jobs / hr. Therefore, assuming the utilization factor as 1, it is found that the required number of machines at station 2 is 1.68 (i.e.) 2 machines. A summary of the calculations for all the workstations is given in the table – 2.

Table – 2 Summary of calculations for all workstations.

S.n	Work station	Arrival rate (Jobs / hr)	Service rate (Jobs / hr / machine)	Required no. of machines
1	2	1.5	0.893	1.68 ~ 2
2	3	1.5	0.476	3.15 ~ 4
3	4	1.5	1.19	1.26 ~ 2
4	5	3	0.585	5.12 ~ 6
5	6	3	3.45	0.87 ~ 1

The best system design can be chosen on the basis of measures of performance such as average time in system, Queue sizes, proportion of time each workstation is busy. The summary table depicts that 2, 4, 2, 6, 1 machines were required for stations 2, 3, 4, 5, & 6. For this situation the performance measures were evaluated and presented in the table – 3.

4. TAGUCHI'S TECHNIQUE

Taguchi developed methods to optimize the process of engineering experiments. This is a concept that has produced a unique and powerful quality improvement discipline that differs from traditional practices. The Taguchi's approach can also applied for manufacturing system optimization process. The focus of the system is to determine suitable number of machines at each workstation to minimize the total waiting time of the jobs in the system. Taguchi constructed a special set of general designs for factorial experiment that consists of orthogonal arrays.

The use of these arrays helps to determine the least number of combinations needed for a given set of values. The orthogonal arrays provide a satisfactory solution for a number of situations. Taguchi has established orthogonal arrays to a large number of experimental situations. An experimental design has the elements of number of trials and condition for each trial. In this work the total waiting time in the system is the parameter to be studied and the objective is to minimize the waiting time by choosing the optimum values of the number of machines in each workstation. Five workstations are identified and for each workstation two levels for the number of machines were assigned which is shown in **table – 4.**

The details of 8 combination of number of machines at each workstation as per L8 array are listed in **table – 5** along with the total waiting time evaluated for the combinations of machines.

Table – 4 Two levels for number of machines

S.No	Work station	No. of machines [level – 1]	No. of machines [level – 2]
1	2	2	3
2	3	4	5
3	4	2	3
4	5	6	1
5	6	1	2

A response table is constructed using the total waiting time obtained for various combination of number of machines. Difference between the waiting time for the levels were calculated and they were ranked to find the workstation effects due to the number of machines. The difference and the ranking is shown in the response table [Table – 6] of workstation effects.

Table – 5 Total Waiting time for various combination of machines in L8 Array

Trial No.	W.S. - 2	W.S. - 3	W.S. – 4	W.S. - 5	W.S. - 6	Total Waiting Time
1	1	1	1	1	1	13.85
2	1	1	1	2	2	11.31
3	1	2	2	1	1	12.25
4	1	2	2	2	2	9.71
5	2	1	2	1	2	9.14
6	2	1	2	2	1	8.23
7	2	2	1	1	2	8.45
8	2	2	1	2	1	9.72

Table – 6 Response table of workstation effects

From the response table the optimum set of waiting time for each workstation is identified by choosing all factor levels with the lowest time, since the waiting time is lesser – the – better parameter characteristic. The effects of level – 1 and level – 2 can be compared by taking the average of waiting time in those combinations at each level. The response table indicates that if the number of machines in workstation – 2 is increased from 2 to 3 the average waiting time falls from 11.78 hrs to 8.35 hrs. Similarly the reduction of average waiting time in the system due to the variation of number of machines at each workstation is calculated and presented in the response table. The difference between the highest and the lowest values for each workstation is also calculated. Since this difference represents the significance of a workstation a ranking is done comparing all the workstations. Workstations 2, 6 & 4 are more significant than 3 & 5. While ranking gives the order of significance / importance, it does not indicate the relative magnitude of importance. A response graph can also be drawn using the values obtained in table –6, which is shown in Figure – 1. Graph is drawn by taking the waiting time in vertical axis and the levels for each workstation in the

S.No	Performance Measure	Workstation				
		2	3	4	5	6
1	Proportion the machines are busy	0.839	0.79	0.63	0.86	0.87
2	Average number in the queue	3.997	2.13	0.824	3.68	5.82
3	Average number in the system	5.676	5.28	2.084	8.80	6.69
4	Average waiting time in the queue	2.665	1.42	0.549	1.22	1.94
5	Average waiting time in system	3.784	3.52	1.389	2.93	2.23

Average total time in the queue is 7.8 hrs & Average total time in the system is 13.85 hrs.

Table – 3 Performance measures.

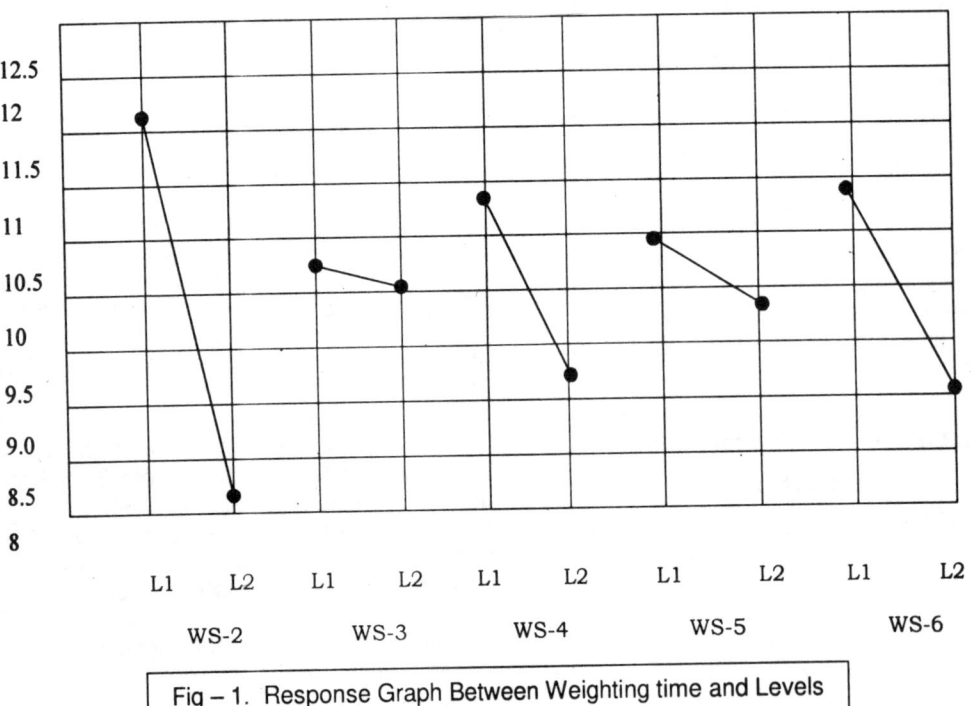

Fig – 1. Response Graph Between Weighting time and Levels

horizontal axis. The workstation, which has more slope is considered to be having more effect on the total waiting time of job in the system.

5. CONCLUSION

From the calculations it is observed that the workstation – 2 has more influence on the total waiting time of jobs in the system. The results obtained from the response graph is in agreement with those obtained from the response table of work station effects. Workstation –3 has a relatively small effect on overall waiting time of job in the system. So the company may choose either level –1 or level – 2 for workstation – 3 based on other criteria, such as cost of the machine, labor cost involved, etc. The response table of workstation effects has specified the optimum number of machines to be installed at each workstation. When level – 1 is considered the total waiting time of jobs in the system is found to be 13.85 hrs and if level – 2 is considered then the total waiting time of jobs in the system is found to be 7.36 hrs. This work helps in making a decision about the number of machines to be installed at each workstation based on one factor viz. the total waiting time of the jobs in the system.

6. REFERENCES

1. **Thyla P R, Kumaraswamidhas L A, Rudramoorthy R,** "Optimization of operating conditions in worm gearbox using Taguchi's orthogonal array", *Industrial Engineering journal,* Vol.XXXII, No.9.
2. **Joe D.Hoffman,** "Numerical Methods for Engineers and Scientists" *McGraw Hill,* 1993.
3. **Henry W. Stoll,** "Product Design Methods & Practices" Marcel Dekker Inc., Newyork.
4. **Nicolo Belavendram**, *"Quality by Design, Taguchi Techniques for Industrial Experimentation",* Prentice Hall International (U.K.) Ltd.
5. **Averill M. Law, W. David Kelton,** "Simulation modeling & Analysis", *McGraw Hill International Editions*, Industrial Engineering series.

GCMM 2004
Editors: Prasad K D V Yarlagadda and S Narayanan
Copyright © 2005, Vellore Institute of Technology, Vellore, India
Publisher: Narosa Publishing House Pvt. Ltd., New Delhi, India

Selective assembly for components with Multi characteristics

*Kannan S M., **Asha A & ***Gayathri, N

*Thiagarajar College of Engineering, Madurai - 625015.
²K.L.N.College of Engineering, Pottapalayam – 6306116.
³ Sudharsan Engineering College, Sathyamangalam- 622501

Email : soma_kannan@yahoo.co.in.

Abstract

Quality is an important aspect of any manufacturing process. Only high quality products can survive in the market. The consumer not only wants quality, precision and trouble-free products, but also he wants them at attractive prices. When a product consists of two or more components, the quality of that product depends upon the quality of the mating parts. The mating parts are manufactured in different machines, different processes and with different standard deviations. Variability is inevitable in any manufacturing process. Therefore, the dimensional distributions of the mating parts are not similar. This results in clearance or interference between the mating parts. In some high precision assemblies, it may not be possible to have closer assembly clearance variation with interchangeable system. Selective Assembly meets the above requisite and gives an enhanced solution. In this paper, a new selective assembly method is proposed for Piston &Cylinder assembly by considering Multi-characteristics of components. Non-dominated Sorting Genetic Algorithm (NSGA) is used to find out the best combination to obtain the minimum clearance variation and to minimize the surplus parts.

Keywords
Quality, Clearance Variation, Selective Assembly, Genetic Algorithm

1. INTRODUCTION
1.1.Selective Assembly

Quality is an important aspect of any manufacturing process and only high quality products can survive in the market. When a product consists of two or more mating components being assembled, the quality of the product may then depend on the clearance or, perhaps, interference between the mating parts. When the components are assembled radially[3], the resulting variation will be the sum of the component tolerances.

To achieve high precision assembly, the parts have to be manufactured with close tolerances, increasing the product cost. If the variation acceptable is less than the sum of the available component tolerances, it is not possible to assemble interchangeably. Selective assembly is the only solution. In selective assembly high precision assemblies are obtained from relatively low precision components. The mating parts populations are partitioned with respect to their dimensional distributions to form groups. The corresponding groups of mating parts are assembled interchangeably.

2. THE PROBLEM

A complex assembly –the case of the piston and cylinder as shown in Figure 2 is considered for analysis. The piston and cylinder consists of three components namely the piston, piston ring and cylinder. The dimensional distribution of the components is equivalent to the process capability (6) of the process as shown in Figure 1. The process capability '6 ' of the process is considered for analysis.

Component

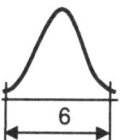

Fig: 1 Dimensional Distribution of Component

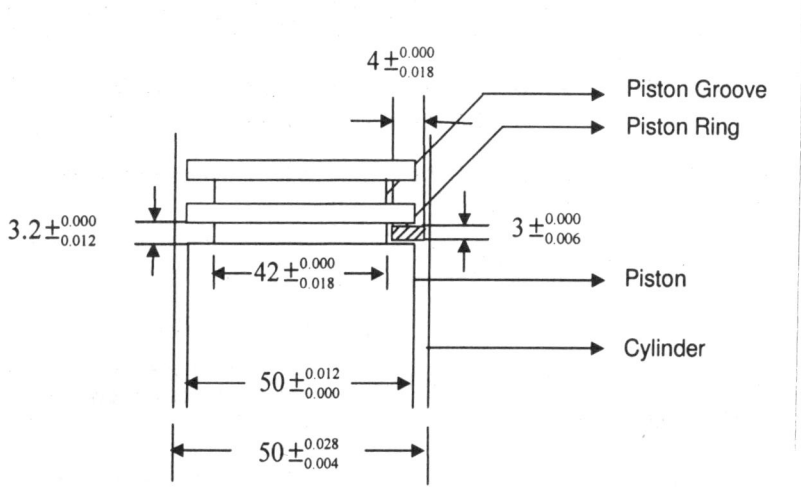

Fig: 2   Piston and Cylinder Assembly

These parts are manufactured in different machines and different processes resulting in different standard deviations. If the parts are assembled interchangeably, the clearance variation is high. In this paper the authors propose a method of grouping which satisfies the clearance variation.

3.0. Quality Characteristics For Analysis

The quality characteristics, which are contributing to the assembly clearance variation of piston and cylinder assembly, are

Quality Characteristic	Represe-ntation	Tolerance
i) Piston groove diameter	Char A	18
ii) Piston diameter	Char B	12
iii)Piston groove thickness	Char C	12
iv)Piston ring width	Char D	18
v) Piston ring thickness	Char E	6
vi)Piston ring diameter	Char F	24
vii)Cylinder inner diameter	Char G	24

By considering all the above quality characteristics of Piston and Cylinder assembly components four possible combinations contributing for the assembly clearance variation of the assembly product is obtained. The four possible combinations are

Piston groove diameter ⎤
Piston ring width } Combination 1
Cylinder inner diameter ⎦

Piston groove thickness ⎤ Combination 2
Piston ring thickness ⎦

Piston diameter ⎤ Combination 3
Cylinder inner diameter ⎦

Piston groove diameter ⎤
Piston ring diameter } Combination 4
Cylinder inner diameter ⎦

The four possible combinations are considered as the objective functions which are minimized using the proposed Non dominating sorting algorithm

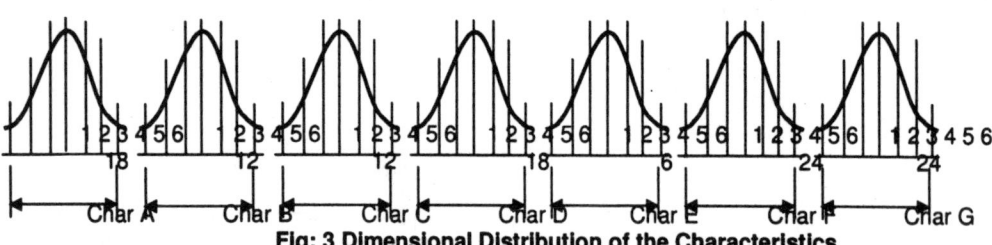

Fig: 3 Dimensional Distribution of the Characteristics

The dimensional distribution of the quality characteristics are shown in figure 3. Selective group tolerance value for characteristic A is 3 , B is 2 , C is 2 , D is 3 , E is 1 , F is 4 and G is 4 respectively. The clearance variation is calculated as follows

Clearance Variation =
Maximum clearance – Minimum clearance

4. PROPOSED METHOD

In this paper, a new method is proposed using *Non-Dominated Sorting Genetic Algorithm (NSGA)* [7] for finding out the best combination of the selective groups of components having multi-characteristics for minimizing the assembly clearance variation and the surplus parts to a great extent.

5. SELECTION OF BEST SELECTIVE GROUP USING NSGA

5.1 Input Module

The following data are given as input;

i) Number of quality characteristics[C] = 7
ii) Number of groups [Group_size]   = 6
iii) Number of initial population[pop_size] = 42

5.2. Initialization Module

All the possible combinations of the selective group numbers given in the input are taken as the chromosomes. Samples are shown in Table 1.

5.3. Evaluation Module

Four fitness values based on the multi-characteristics are evaluated and represented by *fit(c)*.
Clearance variation =
(Maximum clearance - Minimum clearance)
Where,
Max. Clearance = (Selective group number)
x Group tolerance value
Min. Clear. = (Selective group number – 1) x
Group tolerance value

For example the Clearance Variation calculation for the combination 1 for chromosome 1 (*fit1*) is shown in Table 2.
The maximum clearance for the assembly;
1 x 3 + 5 x 3 + 6 x 4 = 42μ
The minimum clearance for the assembly;
(1-1) x 3 + (5 -1) x 3 + (6-1) x 4 = 32 μ
The clearance variations for the initial population corresponding to all combinations are shown in Table 3.

318

Table 1: Initial Population

Chro No.	Char A	Char B	Char C	Char D	Char E	Char F	Char G
1	134652	654213	324516	524631	362154	634512	643521
2	513642	215436	213465	124635	326154	364512	123546

Table 2: Calculation of Fitness Value

Char			Clear μ		Range μm
A	D	G	Max	Min	
1	5	6	42	32	
3	2	4	31	21	
4	4	3	36	26	56-3= 53
6	6	5	56	46	
5	3	2	33	22	
2	1	1	13	3	

Table 3: Evaluation Module

Chro No.	Fitness Values			
	Fit 1	Fit 2	Fit 3	Fit 4
1	53	12	32	51
2	49	16	34	38

5.4. Non-Dominated Sorting Genetic Algorithm; (NSGA)

5.4.1. Sorting of Fronts:

By following the rule of dominance the initial population is divided into number of non-dominated fronts The rule of dominance produces a set of pareto optimal solutions.

Example:

The initial population set P = { 1,2,3.. 42 } is divided in to four fronts of non-dominated sets P₁, P₂, P₃ & P₄ as shown below.

Front 1 = { 3, 4, 10, 15, 19, 26, 33, 34, 38, 39, 40, 41, 42 }
Front 2 = { 7, 8, 9, 11, 14, 16, 20, 22, 23, 24, 27, 28, 29, 36, 37 }
Front 3 = { 2, 5, 6, 12, 13, 18, 21, 25, 30, 31, 32, 35 }
Front 4 = { 1, 17 }

5.4.2. Shared Fitness Calculation:

The shared fitness preserves the diversity among solutions of each non dominated front.
i) Assigned fitness for front 1 is assigned as 42,(equal to the population size).

ii) For each solution i in the front P_1, the *normalized Euclidean distance* d_{ij} from another solution j in the same front is calculated as below.

$$d_{ij} = \sqrt{\sum_{k=1}^{|P_1|} \left(\frac{x_k^i - x_k^j}{x_k^{max} - x_k^{min}} \right)^2} \quad .....(1)$$

where $|P_1|$ is the number of fronts.

iii) Based on d_{ij} & $_{share}$ values *sharing function* value $Sh(d_{ij})$ is calculated. Here n is the number of decision variables and q is the number of optimal solutions.

$$share = \frac{0.5}{\sqrt[n]{q}} \quad .....(2)$$

$$Sh(d_{ij}) = \begin{cases} 1 - \left(\frac{d_{ij}}{\sigma_{share}} \right)^\alpha, & .....(3) \\ 0, & \text{otherwise.} \end{cases}$$

iv) After all $|P_1|$ sharing function values are calculated, they are added together to calculate the *niche count* nc_i of the ith solution.

$$nc_1 = Sh(d_{34}) + Sh(d_{310}) + \cdots$$

v) From the assigned fitness of the i-th solution and its niche count, the shared fitness is obtained.

Sharedfitness= Assignedfitness/niche count
.....(4)

The above calculations are done for the population based on the front and are tabulated as shown in the Table 4.

Table 4: Shared Fitness Calculations

Chromo some	Front Id.	Assigned fitness	Niche count	Shared Fitness
1	4	1	1.8072	0.5533
2	3	1	7.1829	0.1392
3	1	42	8.0826	5.1963

5.5. Selection For New Population Generation

The selection of which individuals will be copied into the next generation is done probabilistically based upon relative fitness[4]. This new population generation module consists of selection module, crossover module and mutation module.

i) Calculation of New Fitness Values:

Fitness value for all chromosomes is calculated in the evaluation module. The fitness is calculated as shown below

$$New\ fit(c) = e^{(-k\,fit(c))} \qquad .....(5)$$

The value of the constant k, after many trials, is assumed as 0.05 to scale the fitness function reasonably so that at least half or more than half of the good chromosomes in the population find place in the new population. The probability of selection is calculated for all chromosomes as follows:

$$p(c) = newfit(c) / \sum_{c=1}^{c=pop\_size} newfit(c) \ .....(6)$$

ii) Random Selection:

The random number r between 0 and 1 is then used to match with cp(c) and the corresponding chromosome is selected, if r satisfies the following condition

$$C_{p(c-1)} < r \le C_{p(c)} \qquad .....(7)$$

This selection process is repetitive as many times equal to population size.

Newfit(c),p(c)& cp(c) of above population are calculated by using the equation 6& 7 and the values are given in Table 5.

Table 5: Parameters for the generation of new population

Chro No.	New fit(c)	p(c)	Cp(c)
1	0.972712	0.029194	0.029194
2	0.993063	0.029805	0.058998

New Population before Crossover and Mutation:

The random number r is compared with the cumulative probability of selection $C_{p(c)}$ and it selects a new population for the next generation. The random numbers generated and the chromosomes selected are shown in Table6.

Table 6: New populations before crossover and mutation

New.C.No. (c')	Random number (r)	Selected chro.(c)
1'	0.022000	1
2'	0.528000	20

5.6. Crossover Module:

The crossover module consists of 2 steps;

i) Selection of Chromosome for Crossover:

The value of probability of crossover [p_cross] is taken as 0.60 so that 60% of the chromosomes selected in the earlier module will undergo crossover operation and produce offspring.

ii) Crossover Operation:

Crossover operations are carried out by the operator called Partially Mapped Crossover (*PMX*). It's working with the cutting point crossover, which changes the feasibility of the sequence. The crossover operations are carried out between the substrings only. Selection of chromosome for crossover is shown in Table 7.

Table 7: Selection of chromosome for Crossover

Chro No.	Random No.(r)	Selected / Not selected
1'	0.022000	Selected
2'	0.528000	Selected

The selected chromosomes (parents) 1', 2', ... 41' and 42' are undergoing crossover operation and generate offspring. The cutting points (P1, P_2 and P_3) selected randomly along the chromosome length. Parent and children are given in the Table 8 & Table 9.

5.7. Mutation Module:

The value of probability covering the mutation operation [p_mut] is taken as 0.05. The mutation exchanges the gene with in the chromosome only. In this problem, it is assumed that the mutation is carried for all genes within the substring only.

The new population with the crossed chromosomes is given Table 10. The mutated reproduction population is shown in Table 11.

Table.8: Selected chromosomes before crossover (parent)

Cutting points P1   P2   P3   P4   P5   P6   P7   P8

Chro No.	Char A	Char B	Char C	Char D	Char E	Char F	Char G
1"	134652	654213	324516	524631	362154	634512	643521
2"	513462	564213	234516	562431	326154	364512	634152

Table 9: Chromosomes after crossover (child)

Chro No.	Char A	Char B	Char C	Char D	Char E	Char F	Char G
1'''	513462	654213	324516	524631	362154	634512	643521
2'''	134652	564213	234516	562431	326154	364512	634152

Table 10: Crossed chromosome before mutation

Chro No.	Char A	Char B	Char C	Char D	Char E	Char F	Char G
1'''	513462	654213	324516	524631	362154	634512	643521

Table 11: New population after Mutation

Chro No.	Char A	Char B	Char C	Char D	Char E	Char F	Char G
1	153462	652413	324516	524631	326154	643512	643521

5.8. Termination Module:

The whole process of evaluation, shared fitness calculation, selection, crossover and mutation are repeated until the objective criterion gets least value.

5.9. Output Module:

The objective criterion is determined for the new population after mutation. The best chromosome in each iteration is stored and the best among the best stored as the optimal one.

6. RESULTS AND CONCLUSION
6.1. Results:

The best chromosome having minimum clearance variation corresponding to four possible combinations is given below:

513642   654231   234516 562431
326154   364512   234156

The clearance variation obtained is reduced for all combinations taken for analysis. The results are given in Table 12.

Table 12: Results

Assembly	Clearance Variation (in m)			
	C_1	C_2	C_3	C_4
In Interchangeable Assembly	60	18	36	66
In Selective Assembly using NSGA	20	12	24	18

6.2. Conclusion:

Selective assembly is used for minimizing the assembly clearance variation. Non-dominated Sorting Genetic Algorithm (NSGA) is used for finding the best combination of the selective groups for minimizing the assembly clearance. The components are assembled as per the combination obtained using NSGA. The best possible selective group with the lowest possible clearance range is obtained and there will be no surplus parts. A computer program is written in 'C' language for Non-dominated Sorting Genetic Algorithm (NSGA) to calculate the optimum combination in the assemblies The paper can be further developed for optimization of the clearance variation using constraints.

7. REFERENCES

1. **Fang X.D. and Zhang Y,** (1995), "A new algorithm for minimizing the surplus parts in Selective Assembly", *Computers and Industrial Engineering,* 28, 341-350.

2. **Kannan SM and Jayabalan V,** (2001-02), "A new grouping method for minimizing the surplus parts in Selective Assembly", *Quality Engineering,* 14(1), 67-74.

3. **Kannan SM, Jayabalan V, Jeevanantham. K,** (2003), "Genetic algorithm for minimizing assembly variation in selective assembly", *International Journal for Production Research, Vol.41, No 14, 3301-3313*

4. **David E. Goldberg,** (1989), "Genetic Algorithms in Search Optimization and Machine Learning", *Addition Wesley publishing Co. Inc,* New York.

5. **Kalyonmoy Deb,** (1996), "Optimization for Engineering Design", *Prientice Hal, India private Ltd.*

6. **Lazzerini B and Marcelloni F,** (2000), "A Genetic Algorithm for Generating Optimal Assembly Plans", *Artificial Intelligence in Engg 14,* 319-329, 2000.

7. **KalyanmoyDeb,** (2003), "MultiObjective Optimization using Evolutionary Algorithms", *John Wiley & Sons, Ltd. England,* 1-216.

Scheduling

GCMM 2004
Editors: Prasad K D V Yarlagadda and S Narayanan
Copyright © 2005, Vellore Institute of Technology, Vellore, India
Publisher: Narosa Publishing House Pvt. Ltd., New Delhi, India

Heuristics Development for Hybrid Parallel Line Scheduling

Balasubramanian K

Research Scholar, Anna University, Chennai

E-mail: bala_manu2002@yahoo.co.in

Noorul Haq A

Head of the Department, Production Engineering, NIT, Trichy.

Amala Rajesh M

Student, Production Engineering Department, Sethu Institute of Tech., Madurai.

Abstract

This paper presents a scheduling problem for hybrid parallel line machines with sequence independent setup times where the objective is to minimizing the maximum makespan. Then the problem is formulated into a mathematical model, an integer-programming model. There have been many difficulties in course of solving large scale hybrid parallel line scheduling problem with too many jobs, machines and lines. Furthermore, the mathematical model is solved by the meta-heuristic in order to get the optimal solution. Performance of the suggested algorithm is tested through computational experiments on randomly generated test problems and the results demonstrate the genetic algorithm proposed is efficient and fit for larger scale hybrid parallel line scheduling problem for minimizing the maximum make span.

Keywords
Hybrid Parallel, Genetic Algorithm, Tabu Search, Optimization

1. INTRODUCTION

Identical parallel machine scheduling problem for minimizing the make span has been proved to be a NP problem. The objective is subjected to the machines with sequence dependent set up time. The individual job routings or the dependence of a job over the completion of another makes the hybrid parallel line scheduling as a remedy. There are various published papers in parallel machine scheduling problems, as mentioned in Cheng and Sin's review. The common objectives studied in this area include the minimization of completion time, tardiness, and make-span. Ho and Chang also showed that a similar parallel machine scheduling problem was NP-hard. Due to the difficulty, it is a general and acceptable practice to find an appropriate heuristic rather than an optimal solution in complex parallel scheduling problems. Recently, meta-heuristics, which were developed to solve complicated combinatorial problems, have been applied to scheduling problems. Tamimi and Rajan used a Genetic algorithm to find a scheduling policy for identical parallel machines with setup times. In general, there are two essential issues to be dealt with for the parallel line machine scheduling problems, minimizing the total lateness of individual jobs, utilization of the machines with respect to aggregate time spent by the jobs in the system. Genetic Algorithm (GA) has been applied in those fields such as combinatorial optimization successfully in view of its characteristic such as near optimization, high speed and easy realization. And it has also shown great advantages in industrial production scheduling.

2. PROBLEM DEFINITION AND ENVIRONMENT

In the hybrid parallel line scheduling process, number of flow lines each having similar set of machine but with different capabilities is considered. It is assumed in such a way that the job requires processing in all the machines of the flow line. And the processing time differs from line to line and the setup time. The reason for variation of processing time is due to the varying capability and functionality of machines of each flow line. The setup time of machines are varied for every sequence of the jobs. Also, each flow line is composed of identical machines having the same functional performance but different functional capabilities so the setup time are varied. Job has a deterministic processing time, if it is schedule on line with all machines. No preemption is considered in this case, since no interruption of jobs between the flow lines occurs. The jobs are processed any one of the line and each line can process at most one job at a time.

The following assumptions are made in solving the problem.
- All the jobs require same operation sequences as arranged in the flow line. i.e. first operation in machine

one, second operation in machine two, k_{th} operation in machine k and so on...
- Any job could be processed in any line.
- The individual job processing time is deterministic and included in transportation time between two workstations.
- Breakdown of machine is not allowed.
- The jobs once assigned to particular line should flow in the same line.
- All the jobs should follow the same sequence of operations.
- The sequence is independent and there is no any prescribed priority between individual jobs.
- Machines are identical and they are always available
- Setup times are sequence dependent

The following notations shall be used to define the problem.

i-job identifier {i= 1,2,3...n}
l-line identifier {l= 1,2,3...j}
k-machine identifier {k= 1,2,3...m}
t_{ilk}-process time for job i at line l in machine k
q-batch quantity of job i
T_{cil}-total processing times for job i in line l.
s_{ik} – set up time for job i in machine k

The objective function of our problem is to determine which job is to be allocated in which line and in what sequence so as to minimize makespan and hence to minimize the number of machines and lines.

$$\text{Min} \sum T_{cil} = \sum_{i=1}^{n} \sum_{l=1}^{j} \sum_{k=1}^{m} t_{cilk} + (q_i-l) \max (t_{ilk}) + s_{ik}$$

3. GENETIC ALGORITHM (GA)

In recent years GA is gaining popularity for its easy searching process. Global optimality independence of searching space and probabilistic nature, GA is a multiple point probabilistic search technique characterized by the mechanisms of natural selection and natural genetics. It is the general-purpose optimization algorithm that is distinguished from conventional algorithm by the use of concept of population genetics to guide the optimum research. GA searches from population to population. Each member of population is a randomly selected binary string of definite length called chromosome.

New population is evolved from older one through reproduction, crossover and mutation. Reproduction is the probabilistic selection of two parent strings. Crossover between two individual chromosomes is done by crossing over the bits around a randomly selected bits position to generate two child strings. Mutation is the process complementing 0's and 1's of the newly born child strings probabilistically in order to introduce variety in the child strings.

3.1. Representation and initialization

We form a list of *job symbol and partitioning symbol* as the coding scheme for multiple parallel machines scheduling problem, which can be essentially viewed as a kind of extended permutation representation. The job symbols, denoted with integer, represent all possible permutation of jobs (or sequence of jobs) and the partitioning symbols, denoted with slash, designate the partition of jobs to lines. With an example of 10 jobs and 3 lines, the chromosome can be represented as follows:

4 3 3 / 2 7 5 1 4 8 3 6 9 10
2 4 4 / 5 2 7 1 4 3 10 9 8 6

3.2. Crossover

We anticipate our genetic algorithm to use such crossover to maintain building blocks in the offspring in much the same manner as Holland described [11]. Some common crossover operations are one-point crossover, two-point crossover, cycle crossover and uniform crossover. The proposed crossover takes two parent and creates two offspring by propagating at single point from partition symbol " / ". Both the sides from "/ " and we got offspring as shown in below.

P1   4 3 3 / 2 7 5 1 4 8 3 6 9 10
P2   2 4 4 / 5 2 7 1 4 3 10 9 8 6

Off 1   4 3 3 / 5 2 7 1 4 3 10 9 8 6
Off2   2 4 4 / 2 7 5 1 4 8 3 6 9 10

3.3. Mutation

We use *random exchanging as* our mutation, *i.e., se*lect two random genes and then exchange their positions which only one side from slash. The randomly selected genes may be either job or line. The different combinations of job and line result in two basic types of mutation. One case is that two selected jobs are exchanged and to form offspring 1 another case is that two lines are exchanged and to form offspring 2 as shown in Figure.

P1   4 3 3 / 2 7 5 1 4 8 3 6 9 10
Off 1   4 3 3 / 2 7 5 6 4 8 3 1 9 10
Off 2   3 4 3 / 2 7 5 1 4 8 3 6 9 10

Now we summarize our implementation of genetic algorithms as follows:

Step 0 (parameters): Set evolution environment, such as *pop_size, pc, Pm and max_gen.*

Step 1 (initialization): Generate an initial population containing *pop_size* chromosomes using proposed procedure.

Step 2 (crossover): Make *pop_size* offspring using proposed procedure.

Step 3 (mutation): Make *pop_size, n* offspring using proposed procedure.

Step 4 (evaluation): Calculate fitness for expanded population (parents and offspring) and make s roulette wheel. Spin it *pop.size* times to get next generation.

Step 5 (stop test): If generation equals to *max_gen,* stop the evolutionary process; otherwise return back to step 2.

4. EXPERIMENTAL STUDIES

The computational experiments are conducted and tested with sample problem as shown below **Table – 1.**The setup time matrixes for each line are shown below **Table - 2**. We have to run our GA program in different parameters such as cross over probability and mutation probability with variation of iteration. The first tested problem is simple which consist of 3 jobs 3 lines. The basic parameters of GA is pop_ size = 10, and max_gen = 200. After running the program we got the results are shown in the following Table – 3.

Table 1: Processing Time

		M1	M2	M3
J1	L1	2	7	3
	L2	4	5	6
	L3	5	4	6
J2	L1	6	6	5
	L2	4	2	2
	L3	3	4	3
J3	L1	1	7	5
	L2	2	8	6
	L3	4	2	8

Table 2: Setup matrix

	Line 1			Line 2			Line 3		
j	1	2	3	1	2	3	1	2	3
1	--	5	6	--	6	5	--	4	5
2	4	--	7	5	--	4	5	--	6
3	2	5	--	3	4	--	7	4	--

Table 3: Result

Iteration	Minimum makespan
10	143
20	140
30	139
40	136
50	136
62	132

We found the best result from 62 iteration with the best sequence for the three lines with optimal makespan time. We have to try with increase the number of jobs and lines with machine, and also got the best results at minimum number of iteration.

5. CONCLUSION

This paper develops a genetic algorithm that optimally solves the problem of scheduling identical jobs with hybrid parallel uniform machines to minimize the maximum makespan of the jobs. The genetic algorithm is used for solving the scheduling problem because of its easy reliability, no demand for differentiability and convex of objective function. The performance of the proposed algorithm was not affected by an increase in the number of machines, increase in the number of lines, and by an increase in the number of jobs.

6. REFERENCES

1. **Sethi R**. (1977) On the complexity of mean flow time scheduling. *Mathematics of Operations Research*; 2(4): 320–30.
2. **C.Y.Lee,** (1991) Parallel m/c Scheduling with non-simultaneous m/c available time, *Discrete Applied Mathematics* 30, 53-61.
3. **Cheng, T.C.E.,** (1989), A Heuristic for common due date Assignment and Job Scheduling on Parallel machines. *Journal of Operational Research Society* 40(12); 1129-1135.
4. **Baker, Kenneth R. and Gary D.Scudder**, (1990) Sequencing with earliness & tardiness penalties: a review, *Operations research*, 3822-27.
5. **Cheng, T.C.E and C.C.S.Sin**, (1990) A state-of-the art review of parallel m/c scheduling research, *European Journal of Operational Research*, 47271-292.
6. **Michalewicz Z.** (1992). *Genetic Algorithms + data structure = evolution programs*, Berlin: Springer,
7. **Sannomiya N, Lima H.** (1996) Application of Genetic Algorithm to scheduling problems in manufacturing processes. *Proceedings of the IEEE conference on Evolutionary Computation*,.pp.523-8.
8. **Tamimi SA, Rajan VN.** (1997) Reduction of total weighted tardiness on uniform machines with sequence dependent setup. *Industrial Engineering Research Conference Proceedings.* Pg181–5.
9. **Ho JC, Chang YL.** (1995) Minimizing the number of tardy jobs for m-parallel machines. *Euro. Jour. Opera Res*; 84:343–55
10. **Holland, J.** (1975) *Adaptation in Natural and Artificial Systems,* University of Michigan Press, Ann Arbor.

GCMM 2004
Editors: Prasad K D V Yarlagadda and S Narayanan
Copyright © 2005, Vellore Institute of Technology, Vellore, India
Publisher: Narosa Publishing House Pvt. Ltd., New Delhi, India

Lot Streaming and Scheduling Multiple Jobs in Two-Machine Flow Shop

Marimuthu S

Department of Mechanical Engineering, K.L.N.College of Engineering, Madurai - 630 611, India.

E-mail: marimuthushree@yahoo.co.in

Ponnambalam S G

School of Engineering and Science, Monash University, 46150 Petaling Jaya, Selangor, Malaysia.

E-mail: sgponnambalam@engsci.monash.edu.my

Abstract

The objective of this paper is to propose and evaluate heuristic search algorithms for two machine flow shop problem with multiple jobs requiring lot streaming that minimizes makespan and total flow time of jobs. A job here implies many identical items. Lot streaming creates sub lots to move the completed portion of a production sub lots to down stream machine. The two heuristic search algorithms evaluated in this paper are Hybrid evolutionary algorithm (HYBRID) and Simulated annealing algorithm (SA). A wide variety of data sets are randomly generated for comparative evaluation. The Hybrid evolutionary algorithm found to perform well for lot streaming in the two machine flow shop scheduling.

Keywords
Flow Shop, Heuristic algorithms, Lot streaming, Scheduling

1. INTRODUCTION

This paper addresses the problem of making sequencing, lot sizing and scheduling decisions for two machines n jobs manufactured in a flow shop environment, so as to minimize the makespan and total flow time of jobs. This problem has attracted the attention of many researchers. A lot consists of many identical items. Lot streaming (Lot sizing) is the process of creating sub lots to move the completed portion of a production sub lots to down stream machines. However, the planning decisions become more complex when lot streaming is allowed. In this paper the performance of two heuristic algorithms viz. Hybrid evolutionary algorithm and Simulated annealing algorithm for lot streaming in the two machine flow shop scheduling problem are evaluated.

2. LITERATURE SURVEY

Baker [1] used scheduling models with time lags and setup times to analyze the lot streaming of multiple products in two machine flow shop with setup times. He also discussed the extensions to special cases with more than two machines. Sriskandarajah and Wagneur [2] studied two machine flow shops with both continuous and integer lot sizes in a no-wait environment. Subodha Kumar et al. [3] considered the problem of finding optimal integer sub lots for a single product. Marimuthu and Ponnambalam [4] studied two machine multi job flow shop. There is a scope for developing heuristic search algorithms for lot streaming problem in two machine flow shop.

3. NOTATIONS

The notations used in this paper are,

S_{1j} Setup time for machine 1
S_{2j} Setup time for machine 2
a_j Processing time for machine 1
b_j Processing time for machine 2
n_j number of identical items for job j
T1 Initial temperature
T2 Final temperature
r Reduction factor
n Number of iterations to be performed at a particular temp
SAP Simulated annealing algorithm with pair wise exchange
SAI Simulated annealing algorithm with insertion
SAR Simulated annealing algorithm with random insertion

4. ASSUMPTIONS FOLLOWED IN THE MODELS

1. All jobs are available at time zero.
2. Each job has a unit size sub lot.
3. Different jobs are having different setup times.

5. HYBRID EVOLUTIONARY ALGORITHM

In recent years, much attention has been devoted to heuristics that are applicable in particular for solving combinational optimization problems. In this paper, Hybrid evolutionary algorithm (Hybrid) heuristic to solve lot streaming in the two machine flow shop scheduling problems is tried.

5.1. The Hybrid algorithm

Hybrid evolutionary algorithm (Luciana Buriol [5]) also known as hybrid genetic algorithm are recognized as being meta heuristics that belong to the class of population based algorithms. A population based algorithm uses several individuals to search the solution space of a problem. Hybrid evolutionary algorithms (Hybrid) are similar to genetic algorithms (GA) in terms of operators commonly used (as crossover and mutation) to explore the solution space of a problem. However, differently from genetic algorithms, Hybrid uses a local search phase to improve genotypes. Like genes that goes through mutation, Hybrid also participates in the evolutionary process and therefore replicates itself in the population.

However where a genetic algorithm models biological evolution, the Hybrid algorithm models cultural evolution of biological ideas and a population of ideas can be maintained. Ideas can be combined to form new ideas, they can be mutated and good ideas are likely to be used then bad ideas. The main difference between this model and the biological model is that the owner can improve upon ideas. This improvement is obtained by incorporating local search into the genetic algorithm. In the Hybrid evolutionary algorithm mutation with local search is employed instead of mutation in GA.

5.2. Hybrid procedure
5.2.1. Population structure

The sequence of the jobs is represented as a chromosome which in turn is members of a population. The objective function used in the problem is to minimize the makespan and total flow time of jobs. Population size is equal to number of jobs.

5.2.2. Position based cross over

The crossover operators explore the search space a problem by combining features from different individuals. Crossover is an operation to generate a new string (i.e. child) from two parent strings. One-point crossover, Two-point crossover and Position based crossover operators turned out to be effective for the flow shop scheduling problem by computer simulation (Goldberg

[6], Murata and Ishibuchi [7]). In this paper, Position based crossover are employed. The crossover operators are explained in Figure.1.

In Position based crossover, the jobs at randomly selected (positions marked by *) are inherited from one parent to the child, and the other jobs are placed in the order of their appearance in the other parent. In this number of positions is selected as two and then positions are randomly selected.

5.2.3. Shift change mutation with local search method

Mutation is an operation to change the order of n jobs in each string generated by a crossover operator. Adjacent two-job change, Arbitrary two-job change, Arbitrary three-job change, Shift change mutations were found to be good for flow shop scheduling problem (Goldberg [6], Murata and Ishibuchi [7]). In this paper shift change mutation are employed. The mutation operators are explained in Figure.1.

In shift change mutation, a job at one position is removed and put at another position. The two positions are randomly selected.

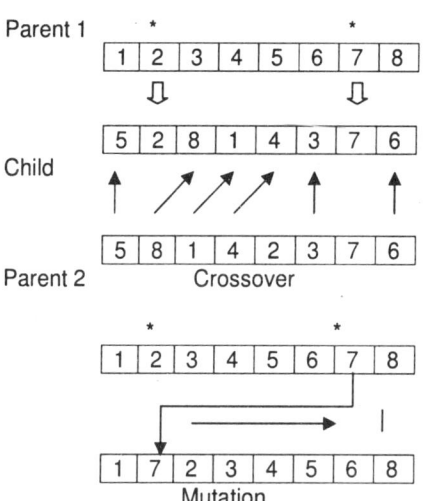

Fig. 1: Genetic operators

The local search technique is applied in this place. In this local search technique, Insertion perturbation scheme (refer 7.2.) is used after mutation. Then the improved sequence from the local search method is added to the population set.

5.2.4. Stopping criterion

The stopping criterion is based on the number of generation that the algorithm may run. Initial parents will be selected randomly and then the offspring will be obtained by crossover and mutation operations. Due to the selection of large number of parents (equal to the number of jobs), algorithm ending in local optima can be avoided.

6. SIMULATED ANNEALING ALGORITHM

In recent years, much attention has been devoted to heuristics that are applicable in particular for solving combinational optimization problems. In this paper, the SA heuristic to solve Lot streaming in the m-machine flow shop scheduling problems is tried. For more extensive bibliographies of application please refer to Van Laarhoven and Aarts [8].

6.1. The SA Algorithm

The SA approach is based on the ideas from statistical mechanics and motivated by an analogy to the behaviour of a heat bath. It can be viewed simply as an enhanced version of the familiar techniques of local optimization or iterative improvement, in which an initial solution is repeatedly improved by making small local perturbations until no further improvements.

The algorithm begins with an initial solution and at high temperature T. A second point is created by using a perturbation scheme. The difference in the function values (delta) at these two points is calculated. If the second one has a smaller function value, that is accepted, otherwise that is accepted with a probability exp (-delta /T). This completes one iteration of the SA procedure. The algorithm is terminated when a sufficiently small temperature is reached or a small enough change in function values is found.

6.2. General Schema of SA

The structure of the SA is as shown below.

Step 1. Get an initial solution S
Step 2. Set an initial temperature, T > 0
Step 3. While not frozen do the following:
Step 3.1. Do the following n times:
Step 3.1.1.Sample a neighbour S' from S
Step 3.1.2. Let delta = time (S') - time (S)
Step 3.1.3. If delta <= 0
then (i.e. downhill move) set S = S'
else (i.e. uphill move) set S = S' with
the probability of exp (-delta/T)
Step 3.2. Set T = r * T, where r is the
reduction factor
Step 4. Return S.

6.3. SA Operators

The best solution obtained in SA depends on the SA operators such as initial temperature, final temperature, reduction factor and number of iterations to be performed at particular temperature. The initial temperature and temperature reduction factor are fixed such that a reasonable number of iterations can be carried before the algorithm freezes. An initial temperature of 300 is chosen and temperature reduction factor is fixed as 0.75.

7. PERTURBATION SCHEMES

The three perturbation techniques used in this paper are,
(i) Pair wise exchange (Ogbu and Smith [9]);
(ii) Insertion (Ogbu and Smith [9]);
(iii)Random insertion perturbation scheme (RIPS), (Parthasarathy and Rajendran [10]).

7.1. Pair Wise Exchange

The proposed perturbation scheme pair wise exchange can be best explained with an example, consider the sequence 1,2,3,4,5 as a seed sequence and that the integers i,j (i,j <= 5) are randomly generated. Suppose in the first instance that i = 1 and j = 4 (i.e. i < j), the pair wise exchange technique will generate the new sequence 4,2,3,1,5 ; which is the result of exchanging the first and fourth integers in the starting sequence.

7.2. Insertion

Consider the sequence 1, 2,3,4,5 as a seed sequence and that the i,j (i,j < = 5) are randomly generated. Suppose in the first instance that i = 1 and j = 4 (i.e. i < j). The insertion technique will generate a new sequence 2, 3,4,1,5. i.e. the result of inserting the first integer in the sequence in the fourth position.

7.3. Random insertion perturbation scheme (RIPS)

To solve the conflicts between jobs on the same machine, we have to randomly select the priority dispatching rules (pdr). For example, the pdr rule is 2, 3, 1, 5, 4 with the five machines, call this sequence S. The pdr in the first (i.e. extreme position) can be inserted at any position to its right. Hence, the job in the first position is inserted in any position between 2 and n (here n = 5), and a random number generated between 2 and n is used to select the job position. Suppose the selected position is 3. Job (1) is inserted in position 3, yielding a new sequence, S1', as 3, 1, 2, 5, 4.

8. DATA GENERATION

Five test problems for 2 machine 50 job problems are generated randomly to evaluate the algorithms.

8.1. Test Problem Instances Generation

The test problem instances are generated by a proposed random generation method. In this method, for each job j, integer setup time for machine (s_j) is generated based on two parameters namely, lower bound of setup time (s_l) and upper bound of setup time (s_u) and an integer setup time is generated as a random number from the range (s_l, s_u). Similarly processing time for machine (a_j), number of identical items for each job (n_j) is generated based on two parameters lower bound and upper bound limit. It is given in the table.

Notation	Lower bound limit	Upper bound limit
S_{1j} & S_{2j}	1	6
A_j & b_j	1	8
N_j	2	10

The generated values of setup time for machine, processing time for machine and number of identical items for each job will form the problem instances of lot streaming in the two machine flow shop scheduling problem.

9. RESULTS AND DISCUSSION

The two algorithms are coded in C and executed on a Pentium III-750MHz - 192MB RAM system. The Results for Makespan are given in table 1 to 4 and Total Flow times are given in table 5 to 8. The average CPU times obtained are given in each table. The CPU times are for the following parameters.

HYBRID Parameters:
Population size = Number of jobs
Crossover operator = Position based crossover
Mutation operator = Shift change mutation
Number of generation = 350 for 50 job Problem
Number of Local search = No. of job
Probability of crossover = 1
Probability of Mutation = 1
SA Parameters:
Initial temperature = 300
Temperature reduction factor = 0.75
Freezing temperature = 30
Number of iterations to be performed at particular temperature = number of jobs

Table 1: Makespan value for two machines 15 jobs problems

Problem No.	Makespan			
	HYBRID	SAP	SAI	SAR
1.	429	429	429	429
2.	363	363	363	366
3.	249	249	249	250
4.	291	292	291	292
5.	305	307	305	307

Average CPU time for HYBRID = 0.88 sec. Average CPU time for TA = 0.06 sec.

Table 2: Makespan value for two machines 25 jobs problems

Problem No.	Makespan			
	HYBRID	SAP	SAI	SAR
1.	648	648	648	648
2.	581	581	581	582
3.	436	437	438	436
4.	489	489	489	490
5.	671	673	671	671

Average CPU time for HYBRID = 9.44 sec. Average CPU time for TA = 0.06 sec.

Table 3: Makespan value for two machines 35 jobs problems

Problem No.	Makespan			
	HYBRID	SAP	SAI	SAR
1.	914	915	914	934
2.	772	772	773	775
3.	709	709	709	710
4.	720	721	720	720
5.	892	894	892	892

Average CPU time for HYBRID = 15.15 sec. Average CPU time for TA = 0.06 sec.

Table 4: Makespan value for two machines 50 jobs problems

Problem No.	Makespan			
	HYBRID	SAP	SAI	SAR
1.	1258	1258	1262	1260
2.	1153	1156	1154	1153
3.	1013	1017	1013	1017
4.	1035	1035	1035	1035
5.	1250	1250	1251	1255

Average CPU time for HYBRID = 30.11 sec. Average CPU time for TA = 0.11 sec.

Table 5: Total flow time value for two machines 15 jobs problems

Problem No.	Total flow time			
	HYBRID	SAP	SAI	SAR
1.	637	652	683	714
2.	562	570	694	698
3.	368	392	387	393
4.	468	539	604	566
5.	507	541	501	543

Average CPU time for HYBRID = 1.35 sec. Average CPU time for TA = 0.05 sec.

Table 6: Total flow time value for two machines 25 jobs problems

Problem No.	Total flow time			
	HYBRID	SAP	SAI	SAR
1.	1032	1132	1274	1172
2.	957	1200	1475	1302
3.	653	667	643	729
4.	857	1153	1242	1081
5.	1046	1562	1392	1712

Average CPU time for HYBRID = 6.37 sec. Average CPU time for TA = 0.06 sec.

Table 7: Total flow time value for two machines 35 jobs problems

Problem No.	Total flow time			
	HYBRID	SAP	SAI	SAR
1.	1484	1789	1858	1800
2.	1290	1556	1899	1577
3.	1016	1103	1180	1095
4.	1357	2260	2226	2003
5.	1395	1760	2002	2204
Average CPU time for HYBRID = 11.38 sec. Average CPU time for TA = 0.06 sec.				

Table 8: Total flow time value for two machines 50 jobs problems

Problem No.	Total flow time			
	HYBRID	SAP	SAI	SAR
1.	1919	2386	2625	2486
2.	2016	2864	3092	2544
3.	1607	2315	2330	2469
4.	1694	2269	2112	2298
5.	1980	3005	2823	2962
Average CPU time for HYBRID = 27.8 sec. Average CPU time for TA = 0.06 sec.				

9.1. Discussion

The results presented in the tables 1 to 8 indicate that the HYBRID outperforms SA in almost all problems. We can conclude that HYBRID performs better over SA.

10. CONCLUSION

In this paper, two heuristic algorithms HYBRID and SA for minimizing makespan for two machine flow shop that uses lot streaming are presented. The performance of HYBRID is compared with SA. The results indicate that HYBRID performs better over others. The CPU time required for SA is less compared with the time of HYBRID. But with the availability of high speed systems, we conclude that Hybrid evolutionary algorithm is found to perform well for lot streaming and scheduling in flow shop.

11. REFERENCES

1. **Baker K.R.**, (1995), Lot streaming in the two –machine flow shop with setup times, *Annals of operations research*, 57, 1-11
2. **Sriskandarajah C. & Wagneur E.**, (1999), lot streaming and scheduling multiple products in two-machine no-wait flow shop, *IIE Transactions*, 31, 695-707
3. **Subodha Kumar, Tapan P.Bagchi, C.Sriskandarajah,** (2000), Lot streaming and scheduling heuristics for m-machine no-wait flow shop, *Computers & Industrial engineering*, 38, 149-172
4. **Marimuthu S. & Ponnambalam S.G.,** Heuristic search algorithms for lot streaming in two machine flow shop, *International journal on advanced manufacturing technology*, (To appear)
5. **Paulo M.Franca, Gilberto Tin Jr., Luciana Buriol**, Genetic algorithms for the No-wait flow shop sequencing problem with time restrictions.
6. **David E.Goldberg,** (2000), *Genetic algorithms in search, Optimization and Machine Leaning*, Addison Wesley Limited, U.S.A.
7. **Tadahiko Murata, Hisao Ishibuchi and Hideo Tanaka,** (1996), Genetic algorithms for flow shop scheduling problems, *Computers and Industrial Engineering*, 30, 4, 1061 - 1071.
8. **Van Laarhovan P.J.M. and Aarts E.H.L.,** (1987), *simulated annealing: Theory and applications,* Dordrecht, Kluwer academic.
9. **Ogbu F.A. and Smith D.K.,** (1990), The application of the simulated annealing algorithm to the solution of the n/ m/ Cmax flow shop problem, *Computers and Operation research*, 17, 243-253
10. **Parthasarathy S. and Rajendran C.,** (1997), An experimental evaluation of heuristics for scheduling in a real life flow shop with sequence -dependent setup time of jobs, *International journal of production economics*, 49, 255-263.

Computer
Numerical Control

GCMM 2004
Editors: Prasad K D V Yarlagadda and S Narayanan
Copyright © 2005, Vellore Institute of Technology, Vellore, India
Publisher: Narosa Publishing House Pvt. Ltd., New Delhi, India

Robust Design for Optimizing Case Depth on CNC Hardening Machine

Rane S. S. *

*Senior Lecturer, Mechanical Engineering Department, Padre Conceicao College of Engineering, Verna Goa, 403 722, India.
Email: rsurajs@yahoo.com

Mariappan V. *

*Lecturer, Mechanical Engineering Department, College of Engineering, Ponda Goa 403 401. India

Abstract

Sufficient hardening of automobile components determines its period of useful life and reduces its wear and tear when in use. Hence effective and optimum hardening is critical for its durability. Taguchi Methodology optimizes performance characteristics, which yields a set of process parameters, which makes product robust. This paper reports determination of robust condition using application of Taguchi Methodology, for maximizing Case Depth of Spring Pin used in automobiles. S/N ratio plots and raw data plots were used to select the levels of the parameters.

Keywords
Design of Experiments, Taguchi methods, Orthogonal Array, Control parameters, Noise parameters, S/N ratio.

1. INTRODUCTION

Surface hardening is an important operation used for imparting impact resistant properties in the component. Result of this operation is harder surface and tough interior, which will offer resistance to wear and impact forces when in use. Surface hardening is carried out on Induction Hardening Machine.

If the required Case depth is not attained while hardening, then problems like surface wear, surface crack occurs. Case Depth is a critical quality characteristic, which attained properly will ensure high quality product, through proper parameter settings.

If the operators were not getting the required case depth when passed through the machine, then they were adjusting the parameters till it falls within the specification limits. It was therefore decided to study the process for a 20mm diameter Spring Pin.

There are various approaches to investigate the effects of different testing parameters. The simplest one is single parameter approach i.e., only one parameter is changed for a given test run. But this is a time consuming and costly approach as number of parameters increase. The Taguchi methods [1], by developing a set of standard orthogonal arrays and a methodology for the analysis of results, can extract information from experiment more precisely and more efficiently than other approaches; also fewer tests are needed even when the number of parameters being investigated is quite large [2].

This paper presents use of Taguchi methods to investigate systematically the effect of hardening parameters and obtains optimum combination for maximum case depth.

2. PROBLEM FOR STUDY

The study was carried out on a Computer Numerically Controlled (CNC) Induction Hardening Machine shown in Fig. 1.The parameters are set on the machine through a interactive computer system and verified for mistakes. The component to be hardened was placed on the rollers, which takes it into the heater coil. As soon as the component enters the coil, induction heating starts and

Fig. 1: CNC Induction Hardening Machine

3. THE CASE STUDY

Case Depth of 20mm diameter Pin was found to be as low as 1.3 mm. Pin is expected

simultaneously coolant impinges on it through inner core of the coil. Once the component comes out of the coil another wave of coolant impingement starts, which is aimed at quenching.

The component, called Spring Pin selected for the study is used in automobiles to secure the Leaf Spring to the axle. Fig. 2 shows the Spring Pin. To prevent ill effects due to constant rubbing action at the axle, the Pin (referred henceforth) should have hard surface with wear resistant properties. As mentioned earlier to obtain case depth within specified limits the operators were adjusting the parameters with trial and error. Even then some of the readings obtained were below limits forcing them to pass the Pin again through the machine.

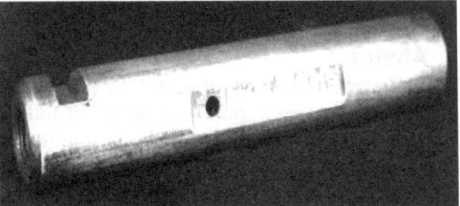

Fig. 2: Spring Pin

to have a case depth in the range of 2.4 – 3.4 mm. Also it was observed that there was variation in case depth from one end of Pin to other. These measurements were carried out after hardening operation. Low case depth resulted in faster wear out of Pin.

The objective of the study was to get settings of process parameters, which will give maximum case depth within specified limits and also reduce variation within the Pin.

The quality characteristic of interest is Case Depth of the Pin. The Pin was cut at both the ends and solvent was applied on its cut cross-section. Then the case depth was measured with a vernier caliper. The flow diagram for the Pin processing is shown in Fig.3.

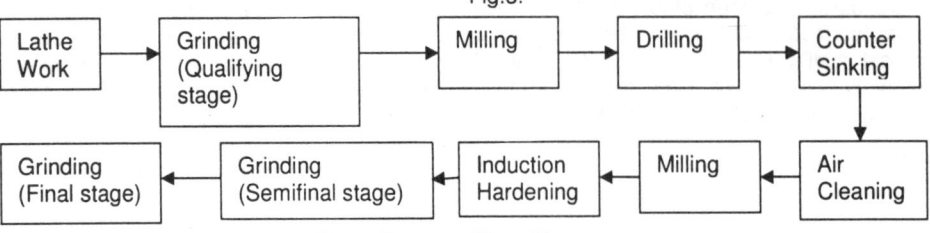

Fig.3: Process Flow Chart

4. PARAMETER SELECTION

A detailed brain storming session was carried with persons concerned with the problem of interest. The result of this session is the Cause Effect Diagram shown in Fig. 4. The following four parameters were considered to be most important to control:
(i)   Power level (A); the amount of heat required for heating the Pin,
(ii)   Feed/Scan Speed (B); the rate, at which the Pin is passed through the heater coil,

(iii) Quench Temperature (C); the temperature of cooling media and
(iv)   Quench Pressure (D); the pressure at which the coolant strikes the Pin.

Even though Pin material influences case depth, it was not considered here as Pins were procured from another unit, which was beyond the scope of this experiment.

Variation of case depth along the axial length was difficult to control and thus measuring position on the Pin was selected as Noise Parameter.

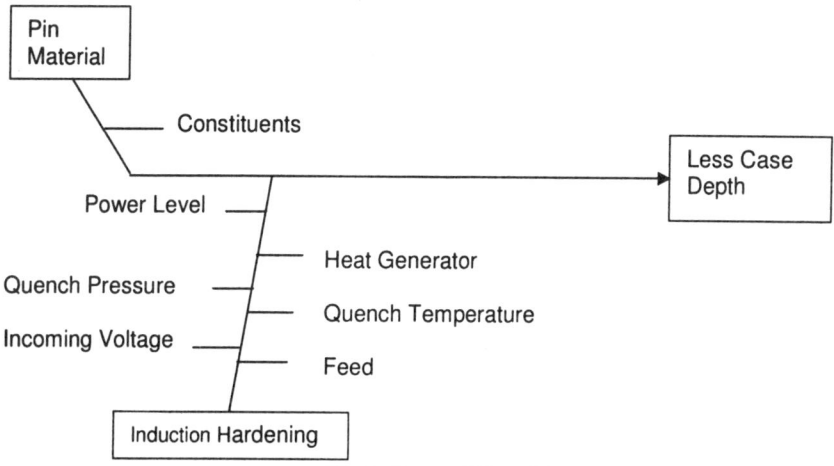

Fig.4: Cause Effect Diagram

5. EXPERIMENTAL DESIGN

Since this was an initial attempt to find the direction for optimization of this process, only two levels for each parameter was considered [2]. Previous experiments have shown that Power level is around 75% for hardness to be within limits; so for this study, range for Power level is taken as 70 – 95 %. Scan speed is selected in the range of 5 – 6 mm/min. Room temperature of 30°C is selected as one level of Quench

Temperature. To study the effect of lower temperature, lower level (25°C) is obtained by cooling the quench medium. Quench pressure was selected so as to prevent overheating of heater coil and at same time does enough quenching. Since we wanted to control variation within a pin, position on the pin is taken as noise parameter. Table 1 shows the four parameters and their two levels.

Table 1. Chosen parameter and their levels

Level	Parameters			
	A: Power level (%)	B: Feed (mm/min)	C: Quench Temp. (°C)	D: Quench Press.
1	70	5	30	Low
2	95	6	25	High
Position on the job: Level 1--- Front; Level 2 --- Rear				

Main effects A, B, C and D of the four parameters along with their different interactions were studied to find which of these treatment combinations exert significant influence on the hardness [3]. It was found that main parameters A, B, C, and D, two-parameter interaction AB, AC and BC need to studied here. Using linear graph these parameters can easily fit into standard Taguchi Orthogonal Array (L8 OA) shown in Table 2.

Table 2. Standard L8 OA used in Taguchi method

Run	A	B	AXB	C	CXA	CXB	D
1	1	1	1	1	1	1	1
2	1	1	1	2	2	2	2
3	1	2	2	1	1	2	2
4	1	2	2	2	2	1	1
5	2	1	2	1	2	1	2
6	2	1	2	2	1	2	1
7	2	2	1	1	2	2	1
8	2	2	1	2	1	1	2

6. PLANNING THE EXPERIMENT

The layout used for the experiment consists of the inner array for control parameters and outer array for noise parameter (only one parameter in this case).

7. CONDUCTING THE EXPERIMENT

Even though complete randomization is the best strategy, it was not possible in this case as it required temperature levels to be changed from one test run to other. So experiments were conducted with temperature setting at one level. Within this block, complete randomization was done [4]. Then experiments were conducted for second block of temperature. A sample size of 1 was selected which gives one standard deviation at 90% confidence level. Results of this experiment are shown in Table 3.

8. EXPERIMENTAL ANALYSIS
8.1. Signal to Noise (S/N) Ratio

S/N ratio is an important concept used by Taguchi to analyze the test run. It represents both mean and scatter of the experimental results [5]. Selecting the proper

S/N ratio depends on the physical properties of the problem, need of experimental results etc. Here, maximum case depth is the objective function, so higher the better S/N ratio is chosen, the relation of which is given by,

$$S/N_{HTB} = -10 \ log \ [(1/n)\Sigma \ (1/y_i^2)] \ \forall \ i = 1 \ to \ n \text{--(1)}$$

Where
n= Number of observations in the test run
y_i= i^{th} response value
Table 3. also shows the values of S/N ratios for different test runs.

8.2 Response Analysis

Averages of each parameter at a particular level were considered for analysis. Each level of each parameter is contained in four test runs. When we consider one level of a parameter, all the influences from different levels of other parameters will be counterbalanced because every other parameter will appear at each different level once. Thus the effect of one parameter at one level on the experimental results can be separated from other parameters. Result of the analysis on response data [6] is shown plotted in Fig.5. Similarly results of level average response analysis using S/N ratio is plotted in Fig.6.

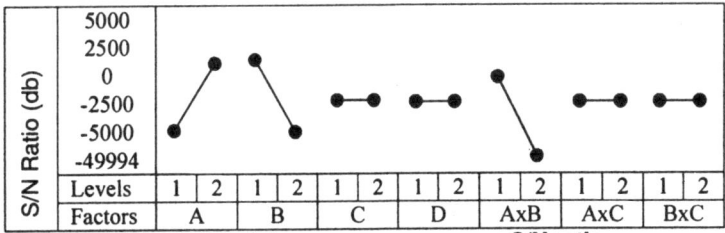

Fig. 5: Level Average responses on S/N ratio

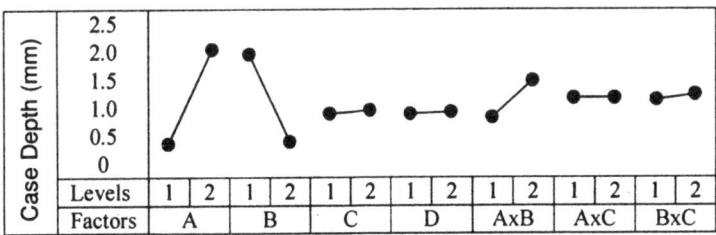

Fig. 6: Level Average responses on Data

9. ANALYSIS OF VARIANCE

ANOVA is a statistically based objective decision making tool for detecting any differences in average performance of groups of items tested. It estimates relative contribution of each control parameter towards overall measured response. The ANOVA was carried out on this work and presented in another paper by the authors. The results of this ANOVA on raw data and S/N ratio are shown in Fig.7.

Table 3. Response and S/N ratio table

	L8 Orthogonal Array						Noise		Avg.	S/N
Run	A	B	AxB	C	AxC	CxB	D	Front	Rear	mm	dB
1	1	1	1	1	1	1	1	0.6	0.8	0.7	-3.36
2	1	1	1	2	2	2	2	0.7	1.1	0.9	-1.56
3	1	2	2	1	1	2	2	0	0	0	-9999
4	1	2	2	2	2	1	1	0	0	0	-9999
5	2	1	2	1	2	1	2	3.0	3.4	3.2	10.05
6	2	1	2	2	1	2	1	3.1	3.5	3.3	10.32
7	2	2	1	1	2	2	1	0.8	1.2	1.0	-0.52
8	2	2	1	2	1	1	2	1.0	1.2	1.1	0.72

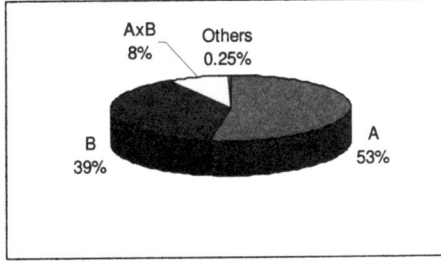

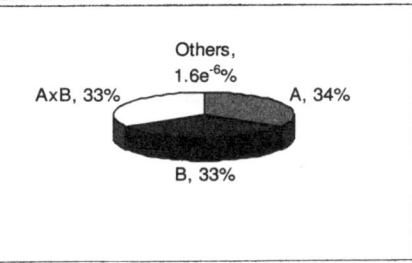

Others include contribution of C,D and AxC, BxC towards Sum of Squares

Raw Data   S/N Ratio

Fig.7: Percentage contribution of Parameters in ANOVA

10. INTERPRETATION OF RESULTS

ANOVA on raw data and S/N ratio show that parameters A, B and AxB are significant and need to be controlled carefully. From the response plot and S/N ratio plot, the levels for the four parameters can be selected [1]. Coincidently both the plots show same results for level selection except for AxB. For this interaction plots of S/N ratio are referred before response plots while settings the levels.

Parameter A (Power level) is the most significant parameter. It is responsible for affecting the mean case depth as well as variance. It should be set at a higher level, i.e. level 2 (95%). Higher power level always provides higher case depth.

Parameter B (Feed/Scan level) is also responsible for affecting the mean case depth as well as variance. The lower level i.e., 5 mm/min. is selected for parameter B.

Parameter interaction A × B also plays important role in change of mean. Appropriate levels combination for A × B is 2 x 1, i.e. higher Power Level combined with lower Feed.

Parameter C (Quench Temperature.) doesn't contribute much towards affecting variance but it definitely affects mean. Level 2, i.e. low quench temperature is selected as it gives more case depth.

Parameter D (Quench Pressure) affects only the mean and the level setting should be 2, i.e. higher quench pressure. This helps in quenching the pin and improves case depth.

11. CONFIRMATION EXPERIMENT

The confirmation experiment was carried out with parameter combination $A_2B_1C_2D_2$ i.e., Power level – 95%, Feed – 5mm/min, Quench Temp. – 25°C and Quench Pressure – High. The maximum case depth achieved was 3.3 mm. Almost all measurements were falling within specified limits of 2.4 - 3.4 mm.

With only eight runs we could establish the optimum combination for the Spring Pin. Taguchi methods helped in identifying the parameters affecting the response and setting them at appropriate levels. The trials conducted over a period of time always conformed to the results of this study. The result obtained didn't affect the Hardness of the Pin.

12. REFERENCES

1. **Bendell T.,** *(1989), Taguchi Methods: Proceedings of the 1988* European Conference; *Elsevier,* New York,.
2. **Taguchi G., Chowdhary S.and Taguchi S.,** (2000), *Robust Engineering,* McGraw-Hill, New York,.
3. **Montgomery D. C.** (1997), *Design and Analysis of Experiments,* John Wiley &Sons, New York.
4. **Box G. E. P., Hunter W. G. and Hunter J. S.,** (1996), *Statistics for Experimenters-An Introduction to Design, Data Analysis and Model Building,* John Wiley &Sons, New York.
5. **Kang J. and Hadfield M.** (2001),"Parameter optimization by Taguchi methods for finishing advanced ceramic balls using a novel eccentric lapping machine." *Proc. Instn. Mech. Engrs.,* Vol. 215, Part B, 69-78.
6. **Ross P. J.** (1996), *Taguchi Techniques for Quality Engineering,* McGraw hill, New York.

GCMM 2004
Editors: Prasad K D V Yarlagadda and S Narayanan
Copyright © 2005, Vellore Institute of Technology, Vellore, India
Publisher: Narosa Publishing House Pvt. Ltd., New Delhi, India

Use of CNC Equipment and the Operator's Skill: A Survey of Selected Queensland Industries

Mahalinga R, Iyer and McMillan R C

School of Mechanical Manufacturing & Medical Engineering
Queensland University of Technology
2 George Street, Brisbane, Australia

Email: m.iyer@qut.edu.au

Abstract

Australia has over 40% of the manufacturing industries in the small to medium enterprise category, employing less than 20 persons. This is much higher for Queensland. Small firms tend to undertake less formal training with flexible working arrangements. This leads to the use of outdated equipment and there is a reluctant to invest in computer numerically controlled equipment (CNC). A preliminary survey was undertaken in 2003 within selected Queensland manufacturing industries to determine the use of CNC equipment, operators' skill level and future investment intentions. Two hundred survey questionnaires were sent with a return of 34.5%. The main findings of the survey indicate that 57% of the companies do not own any kind of CNC equipment and that most of these companies are not intending buy one either. Companies that currently own CNC equipment are intending to buy additional CNC equipment and that the workers do not have formal CNC training and learnt it on the job. The survey indicates that there is a need for educating the organizations in the benefit in using CNC equipment. An expanded survey with interviews are planned to confirm the results of this preliminary survey.

Keywords
CAD/CAM, CNC, Survey, SME

1. INTRODUCTION

The world trend in manufacturing is moving rapidly towards automated systems (1). Current state of technology is capable of producing situations where human intervention is not necessary. However, not all companies are able to adopt this fast changing technology. In many parts of the world, the shift from conventional machines to basic numerically controlled machines (CNC) is not taking place. CNC machine was first introduced in metal working around fifty years ago (2). Since then CNC has advanced considerably from the machine tools, cuttings

tools and controllers points of view. Spindle speed of up to 30,000 rpm and cutting speeds exceeding 5000 mm/min are not uncommon.

Australia has over 40% of the manufacturing industries in the Small to Medium Enterprise (SME) category (3), employing less than 20 people. This figure is even higher in Queensland. Patterson and Henderson (4) reported that "it became evident that there was little information available as to what proportion of the industries own CNC machines". Australian Bureau of Statistics (ABS) identified (5) that

343

only 17% of all machine tools are CNC. This is a national average and would have been much lower in Queensland due to the nature of Queensland Industries which are predominantly primary production and mining. There is hardly any evidence available in literature on the training requirements or the skill level of the operators using the CNC machines. In order to gauge the training requirements and the skill level of the workers operating CNC machines, a preliminary survey was undertaken. The following sections describe the survey methodology, the results obtained and the conclusions from the survey.

2. SURVEY METHOD
2.1 Questionnaire Design

Proper design of questionnaire is essential for a successful survey and to obtain unbiased information. McLennon (6) detailed the following areas that must be considered when designing a questionnaire:
- Sequence of questions should be logical
- Simple and minimal instructions
- Provide for all possible variations.
- Avoid leading questions
- Make questions simple

In order to get a quick response and a good representative answer, it was decided to use the closed type questionnaire design with provision for open response at the end as an optional item. Another aspect of the survey design is the layout. A clear and logical presentation is essential for a good response. McLennon (6) points out that the sequence of the questions should be laid out such that the "sequence of material presented must match the sequence that the respondents are expected to follow". To facilitate the logical flow, the questions for this survey were grouped in three sections as follows:
- General information about the organization
- Specific CNC equipment and training related questions
- CAD/CAM specific questions

The reason for this grouping is that some companies may not be operating any CNC machines as such do not have to answer any questions from the other two sections. Similarly there may only be few companies

who use CNC equipment also use CAD/CAM software to assist in their NC programming. Those who do not use CAD/CAM software need not fill the last section of the questionnaire. The groupings will, therefore. cater for all possible variations.

The survey method adopted for this investigation is to conduct a pilot survey to determine the weakness in the questionnaire design and to conduct the survey proper with a modified questionnaire. McLennon (6) also reinforces the importance of conducting a pilot survey by saying "pilot testing is an invaluable tool for maximizing, within resource constraints, the quality of results obtained from the final survey". The next step is to select the sample size. Approximately 400 organisations were identified from yellow pages and other trade publications as possible candidates for the survey. Thus, for a 95% confidence level with a confidence interval of ±5% the sample size is about 200. Assuming a 30% return, it was decided to send the questionnaire to 200 randomly selected organizations from the list. Out of this ten organizations were selected for the pilot survey. This number was arbitrarily chosen.

2.2 Pilot Survey

Four of the ten organizations returned the completed questionnaire. It was found that there was some confusion in answering questions that require ranking. Youtie et.al. (7) based on their experience indicated that most ranked type questions are to be given extra clear but brief directions, detailing that the respondents are to rank the parameters in order and not give them a level of importance. They suggested to include "do not give the same rank to more than one parameter" in the instructions. One factor that was not considered in the pilot survey was the possibility of outsourcing CNC work. This was pointed out by one of the respondents. An additional question on outsourcing CNC work was included in the main survey questionnaire. Pilot survey also indicated that it is possible to have the number of dedicated CNC operators could be zero (One or two workers use the machine without dedicated operator). This option was also included in the final questionnaire. The question on company's intention to purchase CNC equipment in the near future was moved from the CNC specific questions to the general section because it is possible that a company who do not own CNC equipment now is intending to purchase in the near future. Pilot survey did not consider CAD/CAM usage in detail. Several questions were added to the final questionnaire to gather this information. The modified questionnaire was sent to 200 selected organizations. Sixty nine completed forms were returned within four weeks. This equates to a return rate of 34.5%. This return rate was considered more than adequate to make reasonable conclusions regarding the training requirements and CNC usage in Queensland.

3. RESULTS AND DISCUSSION

The response to selected questions from the general section is shown in Table 1. The number of respondents in this category is 69. It can be seen from Table 1, that 43% of the companies surveyed operate CNC equipment. This is to be expected. This is a rise from 17%, national average as reported by ABS Survey, 1999 (5) to 43%. This is expected and will higher in the other capital cities due to much wider industrial activity. It is interesting to note that 79% of the respondents are not inclined to buy CNC equipment in the near future.

Table 1: Response to general questions

Question	Category	%
1. No. of Employers	<25	84
	25	16
2. No. of Engineers	0	62
	>0	38
3. Do you operate CNC equipment?	Yes	43
	No	57
4. Do you outsource CNC work?	Yes	50
	No	50
5. Intention of purchasing new CNV equipment	< 5 yrs	18
	5-10 yrs	3
	No	79

This may be due to the fact that majority of the industry in Queensland is in primary production. The many small organizations that service these primary industries may not require CNC equipment. This needs further investigation. The survey also indicated that outsourcing of CNC work was predominantly from organizations that do not own CNC equipment.

The result from the main part of the survey on the use of CNC equipment and training requirement is shown in Table 2. The

number of respondents in this category is 29. It is evident from the survey that majority of the organizations use small number of CNC equipment and that most of the skills in using such equipment is learnt on the job. This suggests that there is a need to have formal training in the operation and programming of CNC machines. Increased profit is listed as the major impact of CNC equipment by all CNC users. The rating is an average of 3.46 on a four point scale. They also indicated (85%) that they have plans to buy more (or replace) CNC equipment in the next five years.

Table 2: Response to CNC related questions

Question	Category	%
1. No. of CNC equipment	< 5	83
	5 – 10	14
	>10	3
2. Main source of technical support for CNC	Manufacturer	34
	Distributor	41
	Other	25
3. No. of staff with prior experience in CNC	<25%	28
	25 – 50%	52
	>50%	20
4. Source of CNC skills (Staff may have prior training on different equipment)	On the job	96
	TAFE*/University	7
5. Intention of purchasing more CNC equipment	< 5 yrs	85
	Not in the near future	15
6. Programming CNC equipment is done	Manually	46
	CAD/CAM	19
	Combination	35

*TAFE – Technical and Further Education

The survey also rated the need for general machining skills along with blue print reading as far more important for the organization.

Out of the 29 organisations that use CNC equipment, only 15 use CAD/CAM software to assist in their programming. The results also indicates that only a small number of staff (<25%) are involved in the use of CAD/CAM software. This is to be expected in any SME with few workers. However, 87% of the CAD/CAM users reported that they learnt the skills on the job and only 27% has some formal training from TAFE or University. It must be noted that those who obtained the skills on the job may also have had some prior training on a different system.

CAD/CAM users reported that understanding coordinate systems and proficiency in the use of CAD/CAM software are the important skills required and not overly concerned about the theory of NC/CNC. In general, the survey indicated the need for some training in the areas of general machining, CNC operation and the use of CAD/CAM software as well as principles of programming.

In addition to qualitative analysis of the survey results some statistical analysis was done to find the correlation between some key questions. The following strong correlations were found:
1. CNC ownership influences strongly the intention to purchase CNC equipment. (Test statistic 29.08, ^{2}<0.1%)
2. Operation of CAD/CAM software influences the employment of engineers. (Test statistic 6.0, ^{2}<0.1%)
3. Outsourcing of CNC work is influenced by the ownership of CNC equipment. (Test statistic 17.78, ^{2}<0.1%)

There is also inconclusive evidence on whether a company operates CNC equipment or not influences the employment of engineers. Although the outsourcing of CNC work is predominantly by non-CNC users, It can be argued that outsourcing indirectly leading to increased utilization of CNC equipment. A major reason for the high proportion of CNC operators are trained in-house is that the company may feel that the training they receive is for the equipment the operators are going to work on. Whereas the TAFE University training programs would be more generic or on the CNC machines they have. Even though this will give the operators some skills, it may not be directly transferable in their organization. Thus, the TAFE and Universities must provide the training that is transferable immediately to their operation. The survey indicates strongly that the organizations are finding it difficult to find staff with right skills in the operation of CNC equipment using CAD/CAM software. It is also evident that the organizations want their CNC and CAD/CAM operators to be skilled machinist. This may be attributed to the size of the workforce in the organization where flexibility of staff is imperative.

4. CONCLUSIONS AND FUTURE WORK

A preliminary survey of the CNC usage and training skills requirements was conducted successfully. The 34.5% response rate was considered adequate to make reasonable conclusions. The survey also indicates that only 43% of SME's operate CNC machines. Just over 50% of these companies use CAD/CAM software for their NC programming. Observing from the trend, it is reasonable to expect that more companies will operate CNC equipment and use CAD/CAM software to assist in their programming. The companies that do not own CNC equipment are unlikely to purchase CNC equipment in the near future. The companies prefer skilled CNC, CAD/CAM operator who is a skilled machinist, but increasingly finding it difficult to find such person. Most of the skills in using CNC equipment as well as CAD/CAM software is learnt on the job. It is clear that TAFE and Universities must develop training courses that will enhance the skill level of the machine operators in general and some CNC, CAD/CAM skills.

Further investigation must be undertaken to find the exact nature of training required. This could be done by using a more detailed survey with face-face interviews. It may be worthwhile to find out if there is a need for the management of SME's to understand the benefits of providing a wider training in NC/CNC to their operators before they buy the equipment to better prepare for the operation of the CNC machines.

5. REFERENCES

1. **Williams B.** (1996), "Australia: Metal Working Machine Tool Market", *Industry Sector Analysis*, NY, Jan. 17.
2. **Groover M.P.** (1987), "Automation Production Systems and Computer Integrated Manufacturing", *Prentice Hall International*, USA, Part III, pp197 – 296.
3. **Pappas, Carter, Evans & Kopp** (1990), *The Global Challenge: Australian Manufacturing in the 1990's*, Australian Manufacturing Council, Melbourne, Australia.
4. **Anderson B. & Patterson D.** (1996), "Use of Statistical Process Control in Furniture and Cabinet Industries", *Forest Products Journal*, Vol. 46, January, pp36 – 39.
5. Australian Bureau of Statistics (1991), *Manufacturing Technology Statistics, Australia*", ABS Cat. No. 8123, Canberra, ABS

6. **McLennan W.** (1999), *"An Introduction to Sample Surveys: A Users Guide"*, ABS Cat. No. 1299, Canberra, ABS.

7. **Youtie,J. Shapira,P. Brice,K. Hedge,D. Changen,D. & Wang,J.** (2002), Manufacturing Needs, Practices and Performance in Georgia 1999 – 2002, Atlanta, Georgia Institute of Technology (accessed from the web site http://www.cherry.gatech.edu/survey/finrept02.pdf)

Supply Chain Management

GCMM 2004
Editors: Prasad K D V Yarlagadda and S Narayanan
Copyright © 2005, Vellore Institute of Technology, Vellore, India
Publisher: Narosa Publishing House Pvt. Ltd., New Delhi, India

A Simulated Annealing Methodology for Multi - Stage Logistics in Supply Chain Network

Manimaran P

Kamaraj College of Engineering & Technology
Virudhunagar – 626 001, Tamilnadu, India

E-mail: manimarantce@yahoo.com

Selladurai V

Coimbatore Institute of Technology
Coimbatore - 641 014, Tamilnadu, India

E-mail: profvsdcit@yahoo.com

Parthiban V

Seethai Ammal Polytechnic College
Sivaganga - 630 561, Tamilnadu,India

Abstract

Supply chain networks have gained prominence in the last decade. In multi stage logistics, supply chain network involves multiple suppliers, multiple plants, multiple distributors and multiple retailers with different capacities. The objective is to find out the set of plants, distribution centers and retailers to be opened and determine the quantities to be supplied so that the total supply chain cost of distribution network are minimized. The supply chain cost includes transportation cost for distributing the products from one stage to another stage and fixed overheads and variable overheads for maintaining the plants, distribution centers and retailers. This paper proposes a mathematical model and a solution procedure that incorporates a Simulated Annealing methodology that is proven to be effective in dealing with such NP hard problem designed to find near optimal distribution network for this problem

Keywords

Logistics, supply chain, simulated annealing

1. INTRODUCTION

A global economy and increase in customer expectations in terms of cost, quality, and services have put a premium on effective supply chain management. The customers in business sectors have come to expect faster reaction, high reliability, and greater flexibility to ever-changing requirements.[6] Supply chain is a network of facilities that performs the procurement of raw materials, the transformation of raw material to intermediate and end products and the distribution of finished products to retailers or directly to customers. It is also considered as

351

a network of autonomous business entities that are collectively responsible for procurement, manufacturing and transportation activities associated with one or more families of related product groups[4]. The chain links suppliers and customers beginning with the supply of raw material by a supplier and ending with the consumption of a product by the customer. Multi stage logistics supply chain network involving multiple suppliers, multiple plants, multiple distribution centers and multiple retailers with different capacities. These entities are highly interdependent when it comes to improve supply chain performance in terms of objectives such as cost minimization, quality assurance, and on-time delivery. The objective is to find out the set of plants, distribution centers and retailers to be opened and determine the quantities to be supplied so that the total supply chain cost is minimized. The supply chain cost includes transportation cost for distributing the products from one stage to another stage and fixed and variable overheads for maintaining the plants, distribution centers and retailers. Heuristics solution development has risen to new heights with the successful progression of decision support system technology. This paper proposes a mathematical model and a solution procedure and incorporates a Simulated Annealing methodology. The overall system generates globally feasible, near optimal distribution system design and utilization strategies utilizing the simulated annealing methodology.

2. LITERATURE REVIEW

Many problem variants and solution methods have been proposed for the single-echelon problem of designing a supply network. The location of facilities and the allocation of demand to the facilities have been an area of considerable research. The typical location-allocation problem involves choosing p facilities among n potential locations and allocating demand to the open facilities (Hakimi, 1965). Geoffrion and Graves (1974) was one of the first to solve the version of the multi-commodity location problem that is characterized by multiple products, capacitated plants and warehouses, product flow and customer assignment. Golden and Skiscim (1986) have reported an application of simulated annealing to a location-allocation problem (namely the p-median problem), but initial results of this application were unsuccessful and the process was deemed not worthy of further investigation. Eglese (1990) describes the general simulated annealing methodology. Kirkpatrick etal. were the first who applied SA to solve combinatorial optimization. Revelle and Laporte (1996) have suggested new problems and models in the field of plant location. They also have encountered researchers to consider and create new and more realistic decision tools for plant location.

Pirkul and Jayaraman (1998) studied two-echelon distribution problem with multiple plants and multiple capacitated distribution centers. The objective is to decide product flow quantity from plants to distribution centers and from distribution centers to customers in order to minimize system's overall cost. Jayaraman and Pirkul (2001) studied an integrated logistics model for locating production and distribution facilities in a multi-echelon environment. Jayaraman and Ross (2002) addresses distribution network design consists of multiple product families, central plant, distribution centre, cross-docking sites and retail outlets using a simulated annealing algorithm. Admi Syarif (2002) studied choice of the facilities to be opened and the distribution network design to satisfy the demand with minimum cost and proposes spanning tree based GA using prufer number representation.

Many models in the literature are concerned with material procurement, production or distribution activities. In this multi stage logistics supply chain network system, multiple suppliers supply the raw materials to multiple plants. The output of the products that can be transported to different distribution centers. These distribution centers supply the multiple products to the customers based on their demands to satisfy them through the retailers. The distribution network design system described is a part of the supply chain management structure.

3. MATHEMATICAL FORMULATION

The integrated model presented aims to minimize the total supply chain cost which includes the transportation cost for distributing the products from one stage to another stage and fixed and variable overheads for maintaining the plants, distribution centers and retailers.

We present a mathematical model

$$\text{Min } Z = \sum_i \sum_j t_{ij} . X_{ij} + \sum_j \sum_k t_{jk} . X_{jk} + \sum_k \sum_l t_{kl} . X_{kl} +$$
$$\sum_l \sum_m t_{lm} . X_{lm} + \sum_j U_j . f_j + \sum_k V_k . g_k +$$
$$\sum_l W_l . h_l + \sum_j F_j + \sum_k G_k + \sum_l H_l$$

Subject to constraints

$$\sum_j X_{ij} \leq a_i \qquad \text{for all i}$$

$$\sum_k X_{jk} \leq b_j . U_j \qquad \text{for all j}$$

$$\sum_j U_j \leq P$$

$$\sum_l X_{kl} \leq c_k . V_k \qquad \text{for all k}$$

$$\sum_k V_k \leq Q$$

$$\sum_m X_{lm} \leq d_l . W_l \qquad \text{for all l}$$

$$\sum_l W_l \leq R$$

$$\sum_l X_{lm} \geq e_m \qquad \text{for all m}$$

$$U_j, V_k, W_l = \{0,1\} \qquad \text{for all j,k,l}$$
$$X_{ij}, X_{jk}, X_{kl}, X_{lm} \geq 0 \qquad \text{for all i,j,k,l,m}$$

The objective function involves three types of costs

    1. Transportation costs
    2. Fixed overhead cost
    3. Variable overhead cost.

The model minimizes" the sum of the costs to send the raw materials from suppliers to plants, the costs to distribute the products from plants to distribution centers, the costs to transport the products to the retailers from distribution centers and the costs to distribute the products from retailers to customers and the fixed overhead cost and variable overhead cost associated with locating and operating plants, distribution centers and retailers".

4. PROPOSED METHODOLOGY- SIMULATED ANNEALING APPROACH

4.1. Introduction

Combinatorial optimization problems are encountered in many areas of science and engineering. Most of these problems are too difficult to be solved optimally, and hence heuristics are used to obtain good solutions in reasonable time. One heuristic that has been successfully applied to a variety of problems is simulated annealing. Simulated annealing has attracted significant attention as suitable approach form large optimization problems where a desired global extremum is concealed among inferior, local extreme.

While the results show promise, these studies used a single set of SA parameter settings to compare with other studies on the same or similar datasets. The SA search process changes potential networks by reassigning the facilities and customers. The attraction of the simulated annealing method is simple to apply. Solving a problem with it requires only that one provide an adequate way of generating neighbors of solution points.

The table relates standard simulated annealing terminology to the current problem environment being studied. SA provides near optimal solutions to combinatorial problems. During its search process, and this is a defining characteristic of SA, there are times when an incumbent solution found is replaced by an inferior solution.

Table 1: Terminology relationship

SA terminology	Problem equivalent	Purpose/definition
System	Cross-dock network	To be reconfigured through annealing
Energy state	Network	An arrangement of retailers, cross-docks, and customer zones
Energy	Network cost	The total cost of the system as configured
Atoms/particles	Cross-docks, retailers, and customers	Assignments are randomly changed during the search for their lowest-cost arrangement
Temperature	Temperature	Influences the acceptance probability for inferior solutions.
Cooling	Cooling	Decreases probability of accepting
Perturbation	Perturbation	A change in network

4.2. Input module

Input data for this distribution network is the number of suppliers, number of plants, number of distribution centers number of retailers and number of customers. Capacity, Demand, Fixed and Variable Overheads are given and unit transportation cost for each stage in Rupees are given as input for multi stage logistics supply chain network.

Step 1: Initialization

Initial control parameter T_i and final values of the control parameter temperature T_f are specified. The rate at which systematically lower it, called alpha. Both alpha and temperature determine the acceptance of inferior solutions. Alpha the cooling rate is specified along with the maximum number of iterations at each temperature value. An initial solution is randomly generated by assigning customer's demand between distribution centers through retailers, and finally from the manufacturing plants. Status indicators on the facilities and product family assignments are set. The objective function

value of the this solution becomes the objective value for both the best network, $C(\psi)$, and the newest network, $C(\psi')$. All counters are set to 1.

Step 2: Check feasibilities

The algorithm now evaluates product flow assignments for distribution centers and retailers to ensure no capacity violations exist. We also check that demand in the customer zones is satisfied. If the network is not feasible, then return to step 1.

Step 3: Generate a feasible neighboring solution

Once the problem has been initialized an objective function value is computed, and feasibility ensured, the current feasible distribution centers system network is then modified by selecting a customer zone and reassigning its demand between a distribution centers and retailers. This is accomplished by randomly selecting a customer zone to perturb. Its flow is

randomly assigned to another retailer/distribution centers combination. All feasibilities are checked once again. The objective function value of the neighboring solution, $C(\psi')$, is finally determined.

Step 4: Evaluate incumbent solution with neighboring solution

If the objective function value of the neighboring solution is greater than that of the incumbent ($C(\psi') < C(\psi)$), proceed to step 5. Otherwise, if the objective function value of the newest network improves over the incumbent ($C(\psi') < C(\psi)$), the neighboring solution becomes the incumbent. We then compare this solution to the best solution found thus far. If the objective function value of the newest network is less than that of the best one found so far, then replace the best solution with that of the neighboring solution. Proceed to step 6.

Step 5: Examine condition

Determine the difference, $\Delta COST$, between the neighboring solution and the incumbent solution

$$\Delta COST = C(\psi') < C(\psi)$$

The Metropolis criterion is then used to determine the probability at which the relatively inferior solution should be accepted, PROB (A). This probability is computed as

$$PROB(A) = \exp(\Delta COST/T_i)$$

where T_i is the current temperature. A random number is then generated from the interval (0, 1). If this random number is less than PROB (A), then the neighboring solution replaces the incumbent. Proceed to step 6.

Step 6: Increment counter

Update memory and status variables. Increase the counters by one. If the iteration counter value is less than or equal to the maximum iterations for the temperature level, then return to step 3. Otherwise go to step 7.

Step 7: Adjust temperature

Adjust temperature by the cooling rate. Mathematically this is $T_{i+1} = T_i * \alpha$, where T_i is temperature used to compute acceptance probability at iteration I and α is the cooling rate in (0, 1). The rate at which T_i is decreased. If the new value of T_i is greater than or equal to the stopping value, T_f, then reset iteration counters to one and return to step3. Otherwise stop.

5. CONCLUSION

The integrated model described in this paper has proven to be a cost minimization procedure for analyzing facility logistics strategies in the context of production and distribution system design. We have proposed a simulated annealing methodology for this integrated model. The structure of the proposed method is very simple, we believe this method will be an efficient method to solve multi-stage supply chain logistics network design problem.

6. REFERENCES

1. **Admi Syarif, YoungSu Yun, Mitsuo Gen** (2002), "Study on multi-stage logistic chain network: a spanning tree –based genetic algorithm approach", *Computers and Industrial Engineering,* 43, 299-314
2. **Andreas Bolte, Ulrich Wilhelm Thonemann** (1996), "Optimizing simulated annealing schedules with Genetic programming", *European Journal of Operational Research,* 92, 402-416
3. **Anthony D.Ross** (2000), "A two-phased approach to the supply network renetwork problem", *European Journal of Operational Research,* 122, 18-30
4. **Geoffrion, A.M., Graves, G.W** (1974), "Multi commodity distribution system design by benders composition", *Management science,* 20, 822-844.
5. **Vaidyanathan Jayaraman, Hasaan Pirkul** (2001), "Planning and coordination of Production and Distribution facilities for multiple commodities", *European Journal of Operational Research,* 133, 394-408
6. **Vaidyanathan Jayaraman, Anthony Ross** (2002), "A simulated annealing methodology to distribution network design and management", *European Journal of Operational Research ,* 144, 629-645

Nomenclature

I   – number of customers (i = 1,2...I)
J   – number of plants (j = 1,2...J)
K   – number of distribution centers (k =1,2...K)
L   – number of retailers (l = 1,2...L)
M   – number of suppliers (m = 1,2...M)
a_i – capacity of supplier i
b_j – capacity of plant j
c_k – capacity of distribution centre k
d_l – capacity of retailer l
e_m –demand of customer m
t_{ij} – unit transportation cost from supplier i to plant j
t_{jk} – unit transportation cost from plant j to distribution centre k
t_{kl} – unit transportation cost from distribution centre k to retailer l
t_{lm} – unit transportation cost from retailer l to customer m
F_j – fixed overhead for plant j
G_k – fixed overhead for distribution centre k
H_l – fixed overhead for retailer l
f_j – variable overhead for operating plant j
g_k – variable overhead for operating distribution centre k
h_l – variable overhead for operating retailer l
P – upper limit on total no. of plants that can be opened

Q – upper limit on total no. of distribution centers that can be opened
R – upper limit on total no. of retailers that can be opened
X_{ij} – amount of raw materials transported from supplier i to plant j
X_{jk} – amount of products transported from plant j to distribution centre k
X_{kl} – amount of products transported from distribution centre k to retailer l
X_{lm} – amount of products transported from retailer l to customer m
U_j = 1, if production takes place at plant j
    0, otherwise
V_k = 1, if distribution centre k is opened
    0, otherwise
W_l = 1, if retailer l is opened
    0, otherwise

GCMM 2004
Editors: Prasad K D V Yarlagadda and S Narayanan
Copyright © 2005, Vellore Institute of Technology, Vellore, India
Publisher: Narosa Publishing House Pvt. Ltd., New Delhi, India

Achieving World-Class Excellence in Contract Processing in a Manufacturing Firm: A Case Study

Manmohan Bhoomkar ,

PVS's COET, Pune.

Kallurkar S P,

AISSMS COE, Pune.

Abstract

Manufacturing sector in India has undergone a sea change since the commencement of economic reforms in 1991. Competition has increased and manufacturing competence is identified as an important ingredient in the strategy for enhancing Indian firms' competitiveness. In order to achieve business excellence, quality and process improvements are very important aspects in manufacturing firms today. Achieving Competitive Excellence (ACE) indicate a continuous improvement that is designed to utilize the resource of the firm to achieve a quality driven culture. Implementation of ACE process means achieving a level of quality and productivity improvement that will delight the customers and allow the firm to satisfy increased workloads more efficiently [1,2]. A case study was carried out on process improvement in 'Contact Processing' of a manufacturing firm in Bhosari Industrial area Pune.

1.0 INTRODUCTION

During the past few decades, there has be an exponential improvement in every field of business like never before, especially in the knowledge sector. Manufacturing sector is still a big brother and knowledge of the best practices in manufacturing has grown to become today's World Class Manufacturing. This knowledge will surely be an integral part of the tomorrow's World Class Management.

2.0 ABOUT THE INDUSTRY

NAND composites Pvt. Ltd. is in the business of Polyurethane since 1979, has attained expertise in handling and processing

polyurethane and engineering plastic materials. Company belongs to family of Leles' with professional support from Chartered Accountants and Management persons. NAND established engineering plastics processing unit by Injection Moulding in 1997. It has developed different products for Auto Industries.

Nand Composites Pvt. Ltd., an ancillary firm is associated with manufacturing of screwdriver grips, which is one of the components of toolkit of Bajaj Automobile vehicles.

3.0 ABOUT SCREWDRIVER GRIP

The initial stage of manufacturing the screwdriver grip is done by injection moulding process of Polypropylene

356

Copolymer material. It has a diameter of 18mm at the base (holding portion) and 19mm in the top portion. It is 84mm in height and it has got serrations throughout its circumference at the base of the grip. (See Fig. 1)

3.1 About the clips which are to be inserted in grip

The clips that are inserted in the slot provided at the top end of the grip are made of mild steel. The clips get inserted in the grip in such a way that they shear the walls of the grip so as to fit tightly inside the grip. The tool driver which fits in the grip as shown in Fig.2 forces the clips on the circumference, thus receiving a reaction from the clips to make the tool driver fit tightly inside the screwdriver grip. The clips dimensions are found to be varying to a large extent as they are manufactured from the scrap material.

3.2 Survey of Clips

Following is the survey of dimensions of 10 clips, which was taken with the help of Vernier Calipers Instrument.

Clip No.	A	B	C	D	E	F
1	12.9	0.8	3.42	6.22	3.26	13.54
2	12.02	1.2	3.35	5.27	3.4	13.52
3	12.8	0.82	3.32	6.2	3.28	13.56
4	12.98	1.21	3.54	5.98	3.46	13.5
5	12.84	1.02	3.7	5.64	3.5	13.52
6	12.99	0.7	3.28	6.47	3.3	13.55
7	13.2	-	-	-	-	-
8	12.88	0.84	3.38	6.3	3.2	13.58
9	12.7	0.91	3.32	5.87	3.51	13.72
10	13.1	0.89	3.4	6.32	3.38	13.59

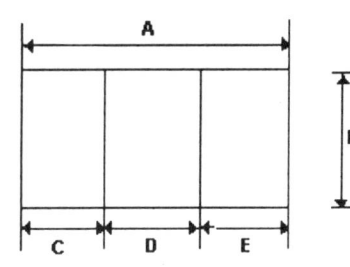

4.0 PROBLEMS ASSOCIATED

Problems associated are of two types:
- Customers' complaint about toolkit
- Contract Processing unit's problem of screwdriver grip

Conventionally the work of insertion of clips is carried manually and More man power is required since one person can insert clips in only one grip at a time.

- More time is required, as it requires two operations of insertion of a clip in a handle.
- Wastages are there since the accuracy cannot be maintained.

5.0 PROBLEM SOLVING

A special purpose machine is needed to be manufactured which eliminates the problems mentioned above but at the same time considers the following constraints:

1. Daily requirements of fulfillment of 4000 screwdrivers.
2. Minimum manpower needed to be used.
3. Clip dimensions need to be checked at the initial stage and should be removed if not matching the desired specifications.
4. Cost of the special purpose machine should be as minimum as possible.
5. Idle time of machine should be minimum.
   - More cost since maximum manpower is required.

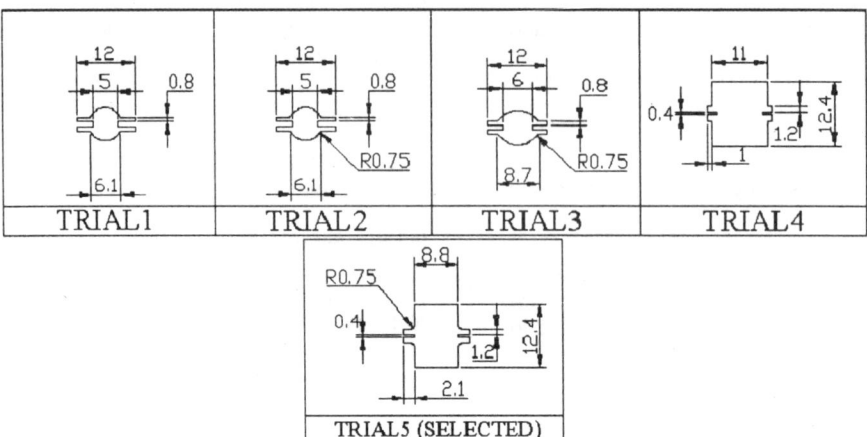

| TRIAL1 | TRIAL2 | TRIAL3 | TRIAL4 |

TRIAL5 (SELECTED)

5.1 Trials for Clip Slot

The trials for clip slots were done on the basis of statistical data that was collected for various clips.

The clip slot had to perform following functions in the machine:

- To hold the clip in order to make them available for punching.
- To locate the clips exactly above the clip slot in screwdriver grip.
- To keep a distance of 0.4mm between two clips.
- To accommodate clips of variable sizes.

The trials 1,2 and 3 were conducted for clips that were later changed due to more unevenness in the dimensions and trial 4 and 5 were conducted according to the new dimensions as shown in the statistical data. The analysis of the data is done by plotting the graphs of 'A' value vs. clip no. and 'B' value vs. clip no.

The 'A' values as well as the 'B' values are the critical values in terms of design of the clip slot and hence we collect data for 'A' and 'B' for 150 Clips.

The following table gives the values of the collected data and the corresponding graphs showing the range and distribution of these values:

Clip No.	A	B	Clip No.	A	B	Clip No.	A	B
1	12.84	0.89	51	12.17	0.98	101	12.62	1.03
2	12.12	1.1	52	12.8	1	102	12.44	1.08
3	12.8	0.9	53	12.9	1.2	103	12.84	1.09
4	12.21	1.1	54	12.95	0.85	104	12.99	1.19
5	12.8	1.08	55	12.54	0.75	105	12.94	0.84
6	12.98	1.15	56	12.86	0.98	106	12.84	0.95
7	12.88	1.07	57	12.98	0.96	107	13.1	1.1
8	12.7	1.3	58	13	0.84	108	13	1.2
9	12.83	0.88	59	12.94	0.84	109	12.38	0.98
10	12.8	0.84	60	12.92	1.15	110	12.56	0.99
11	12.7	1.06	61	12.96	1.1	111	13.05	0.81
12	12.8	0.99	62	12.84	1.08	112	12.84	0.84
13	12.5	1	63	12.76	1.2	113	12.15	0.75
14	12.52	0.98	64	12.45	1.19	114	12.34	0.99
15	12.85	1.2	65	12.54	1.2	115	12.68	1.2
16	12.17	1.1	66	12.59	1.3	116	12.73	1.3
17	12.3	0.86	67	12.9	1.15	117	12.8	1.2
18	12.8	1.11	68	12.84	0.84	118	12.91	1.23
19	12.85	1.16	69	12.81	1.79	119	12.75	1.15
20	12.82	0.8	70	12.95	0.84	120	12.78	0.93
21	12.8	1.02	71	12.68	0.79	121	12.91	1.16
22	12.9	0.83	72	12.53	0.9	122	12.84	0.96
23	12.98	0.94	73	12.9	0.8	123	12.62	0.94
24	12.35	0.88	74	12.99	1	124	12.74	1.1
25	12.83	1.1	75	12.38	1.2	125	12.71	0.95
26	12.9	0.96	76	12.64	1.22	126	12.786	0.97
27	12.4	1.2	77	12.46	1.14	127	12.98	1.23
28	13.02	0.85	78	12.37	1.13	128	12.5	0.98
29	13	0.94	79	12.44	1.12	129	12.65	1.2
30	12.74	0.8	80	12.4	1.15	130	12.85	0.92
31	12.28	0.76	81	12.86	1.16	131	12.84	0.91
32	12.39	1.1	82	12.84	0.98	132	12.94	1.19
33	12.39	1.23	83	12.99	0.84	133	12.5	0.98
34	12.5	1.21	84	13	0.81	134	12.3	0.96
35	12.8	0.85	85	12.54	1.2	135	12.62	0.8
36	12.9	1	86	12.68	1.25	136	12.83	0.95
37	12.3	1.3	87	12.88	1.01	137	12.53	1.11
38	12.9	1.19	88	12.94	1	138	12.79	0.94
39	13.08	0.8	89	12.92	1.2	139	12.98	1.18
40	12.86	1.1	90	12.62	0.94	140	12.99	0.99
41	13	0.98	91	12.97	0.98	141	13.1	0.99
42	12.84	0.99	92	12.93	0.8	142	13.12	1.15
43	12.5	0.97	93	12.3	1.14	143	13.19	0.84
44	12.68	0.9	94	12.41	0.86	144	13	0.99
45	12.7	0.86	95	12.58	0.81	145	12.56	0.91
46	12.8	0.92	96	12.94	0.94	146	12.68	1.11
47	13.02	1.05	97	12.96	0.96	147	12.54	1.15
48	13	1.08	98	12.88	1.2	148	12.89	0.94
49	12.8	1.09	99	12.44	1.26	149	12.4	1.2
50	12.82	1.2	100	12.31	0.95	150	12.38	0.91

'A' Values Vs Clip No.

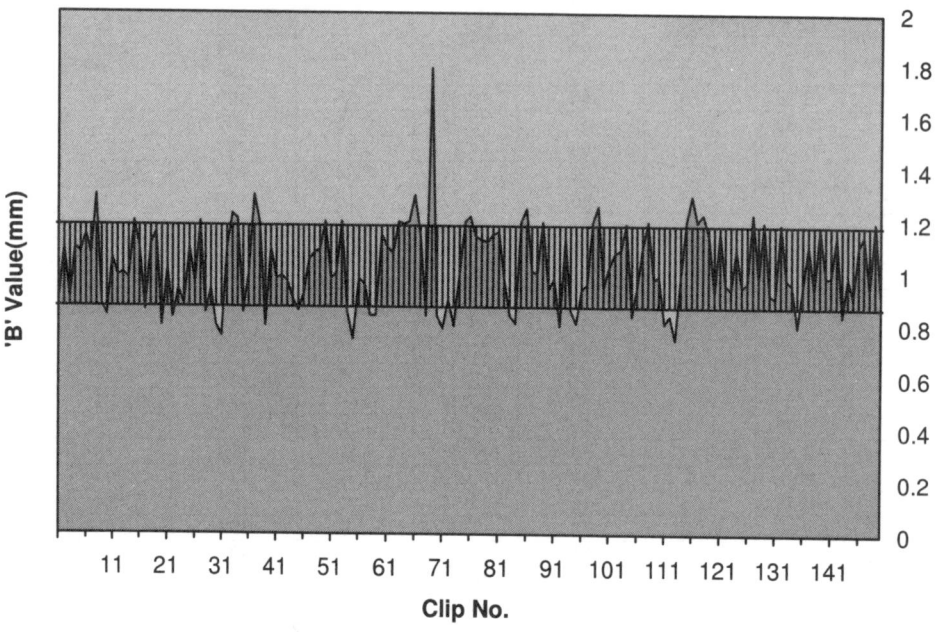

'B' Values Vs Clip No.

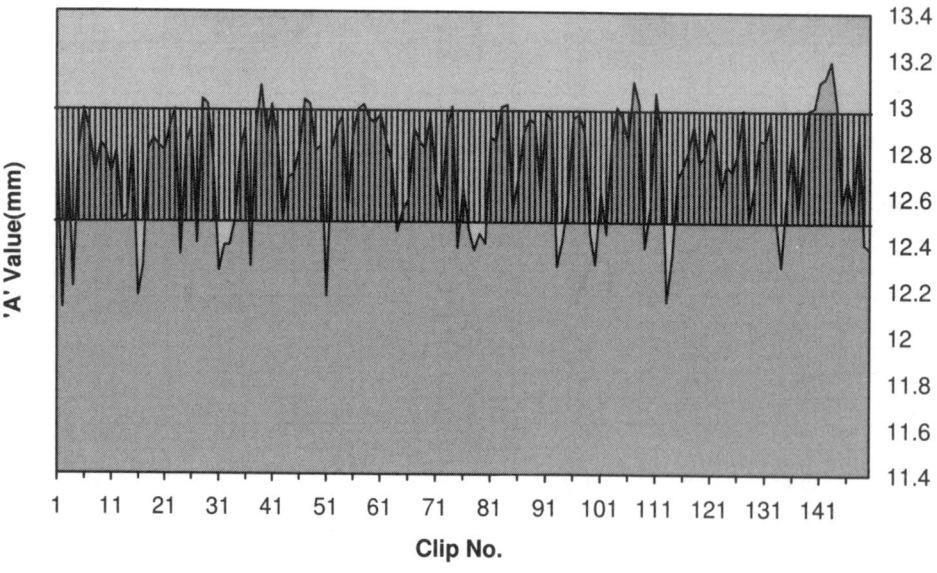

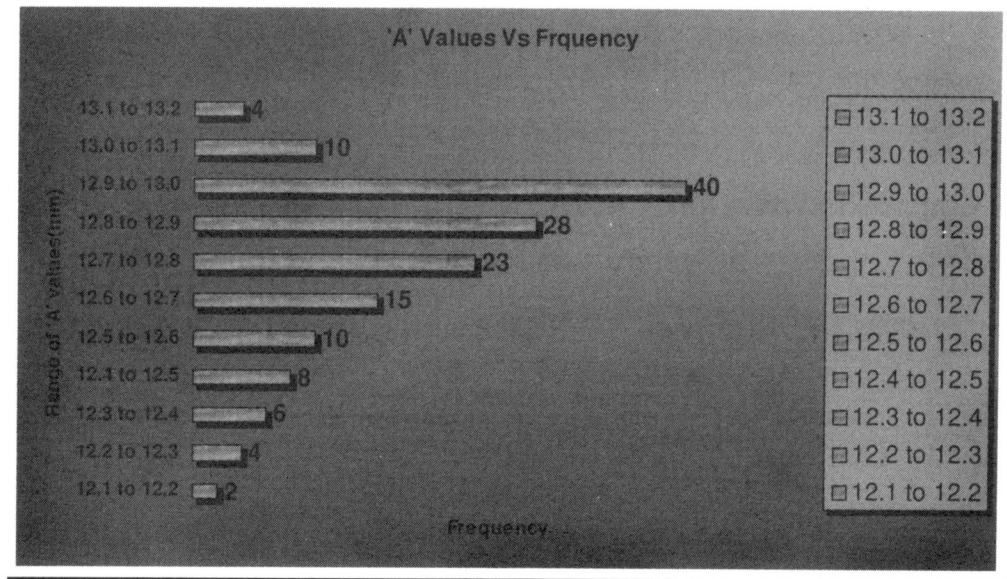

'A' Values Vs Frquency

Range of 'A' values (mm)	Frequency
13.1 to 13.2	4
13.0 to 13.1	10
12.9 to 13.0	40
12.8 to 12.9	28
12.7 to 12.8	23
12.6 to 12.7	15
12.5 to 12.6	10
12.4 to 12.5	8
12.3 to 12.4	6
12.2 to 12.3	4
12.1 to 12.2	2

6. CONCLUSION

An optimum alternative is selected which satisfy the requirements of the company as well as that of the manufacturing firm; as the product is of world class standard and achieves the competitive excellence in the international market.

6. REFERENCES

1. **Bhoomkar M. M.,** March 2004, World-class manufacturing, *A National conference on World-class manufacturing*, ABS 39, B.D. College of Engineering, Sevagram, Wardha
2. **Roland Toone,** 1999, World Class Manufacturing: Myth or Reality", *MIOM Journal*, pp 24-35
3. **Bhoomkar M. M and Dr. Kallurkar S.B.** ,"Manufacturing excellence through world-class manufacturing" , June 2004, *National conference on recent trends in CAD/CAM/CAE (NCRTC-2004)*, Rajarambapu Institute of Technology, Rajaramnagar, Sakharale, Sangli

GCMM 2004
Editors: Prasad K D V Yarlagadda and S Narayanan
Publisher: Narosa Publishing House Pvt. Ltd., New Delhi, India

Composite Value Index (CVI) for Performance Measurement of a System - An Intuitive Method

Parthiban P*, Narayanan S**, Rohit Ranjan*", Jaiguru N*" & Satya***

*Faculty, ***Student, **Prof. & Head,
Mechanical Engineering Department, Vellore Institute of Technology, Vellore-14.

Ganesh K

Research Scholar, Ph.D, Department of Management Studies, IIT Madras, Chennai.

Abstract

The basic purpose of any measurement system is to provide feedback, relative to your goals, that increases your chances of achieving these goals efficiently and effectively. Measurement gains true value when used as the basis for timely decisions. The ultimate aim of implementing a performance measurement system is to improve the performance of the organization. If you can get your performance measurement right, the data you generate will tell you where you are, how you are doing, and where you are going. Performance measurement involves, determining what to measure, identifying data collection methods, and collecting the data. Evaluation involves assessing progress toward achieving performance expectations, usually to explain the causal relationships that exist between program activities and outcomes. Performance measurement and evaluation are components of performance-based management, the systematic application of information generated by performance plans, measurement, and evaluation to strategic planning and budget formulation. The Composite Value Index (CVI), an intuitive method is a framework to evaluate the entities or products of the system according to the profitability rank order and then compare the weightage of the entities or products with the actual performance level and the result of their product (multiplication) suggest an overall index to the total performance of the system. So, CVI is a technique which is used to evaluate the performance of a system with its alternative / substitute / competitive system and indicate the performance in terms of an index. It is also termed as a scaffold for designing a set of measures for products / activities chosen by you as being the key drivers of your business and it involves four distinct perspectives (financial, customer, internal process and innovation and learning) to promote a more holistic view of the business. Successful organizations "manage by fact." They do not rely upon anecdotes, rumors, assumptions, or wild guesses to make their business decisions. But, CVI can be used to make fact-based decisions and resource allocations. A case study of Brakes Indian Limited validates the above statement. The performance of an automated system for their shop floor is evaluated by considering the measures such as profitability range and processing time of the products. The conventional manual system is compared with the automated system. The result index of instinctive method CVI will help the Brakes Indian Limited to improve their automated system.

Keywords
Composite Value Index, Performance Measurement, Intuitive Method.

1. INTRODUCTION

Customers have changed the landscape for suppliers when it comes to quick delivery response, quality and price. The customers-driven demand for quick response, no excuses on-time delivery performance and perfect quality has caused many managements to focus on order-to delivery lead time reduction by streamlining internal internal operations and quicker response expectations you lose! Many companies have trouble delivering products on time, never mind quickly, and are plugged with excessively long order to delivery lead times and cannot seem to find a solution. In addition, the desire to reduce inventories, lower over head costs and to stabilize erratic production schedule performance are profit improvements benefits that put further emphasis on the need and desirability for reducing the lead times. Often more than 50 of order-to-delivery time consist of waiting. Waiting of sales order to processed. Waiting in manufacturing bottleneck. Waiting for material. Waiting for production process to be corrected. All of this waiting just keeps the order-to-delivery time scretching, ballooning inventories, increasing cost and alienating expense in the mad scramble to correct the problem we never should have created in this first place. It's a vicious circle that feeds on it self. It's the lead that you should stop.

Prices and over head pressures have forced to many companies to focus soley on cost- cutting often at the expense of delivery and quality. Some companies are engrossed in cost-cutting that they have lost sight of value equation. The value equation consists of quick, on time delivery and competitive price. Even though customer ask for better pricing this is often the higher priority in what the customer needs.

Paramount to reducing lead times and increasing on-time predictability is to be keep material and information flowing at high velocity through value added processes. This means eliminating time wasting queues that constrain flow and prevent balance between various manufacturing operations. As the same time, get rid of (as much as possible) the non value added (NVA) tasks that are likely performed in all the function areas. Those NVA tasks not only slow work flow velocity, increases lead times desired predictability, but these operations has

ballooned operating expenses, once accepted as normal, to un predicted level. Often not recognized as critical to lead time reduction is the need top improve the quality and velocity of the information flow. Reducing lot size can also cut lead times must simultaneously and at least proportionately cut change over times to effectively cut lot sizes.

Balance and flow must be maintained in order to reduce the bottleneck in every area of the company. Production bottleneck generally occur due to poor scheduling routine created them, resulting in the need to expedite orders and disruption in the flow of production. Lead time reduction can mean lower cost, reduced inventories, improved production predictability, increased customer satisfaction and better quality. If a company had the pick up single operational issue to focus on time compression across the entire operation would be an excellent one to start with.

2. EFFECTS OF LONG LEAD TIME
2.1 Poor Quality

To much time is spent fixing flaws, recycling the wastes, handling complaints and trying to keep customers from going to your competitors. The practice improved quality must led to lower operating expenses. Perfect quality products and information to be very high quality to the manufacturers. Customers demand perfect products and not afraid to let u know in when think there something less often resulting in search of new suppliers. For the suppliers it actually takes less time and cost reduce high quality products.

2.2 Low Throughput

When the lead times are extended you can be assured that the causes are also depressing total production throughput which reduces profit and cash flow.

2.3 Falling Sales

Lead times that are too long will inevitably leed to a drop in sales revenue. Customers when became to seek other suppliers as delivery time grows and become erratic.

2.4 Too Much Inventory

Excessive amount in raw material or working process or finished inventories are prime indicators that the company is not adequately and effectively balancing production output with customer demands.

2.5 Too Much Non Value Activities

Moving inventory, storing waiting, rework, expediting orders, lots of paper works etc, balloons operating expenses when consumes lot of lead time to produce a product in many companies. The actual value added activity is much less than NVA.

2.6 Poor Delivery and Unhappy Customers

On time delivery and customer satisfaction go hand in hand. Lead time that are too long lead to delivery delays, which leads to dissatisfied customers and eventually loss of business and profits.

3. CAUSES OF LONG LEAD TIME

Most lead time problems can be traced back to root causes. Identify and collecting the root causes impediments must be done in order to achieve significant lead time improvements. Some are the common causes of the poor lead time.

3.1 Bottlenecks

Think of the order-to-delivery process as similar to the six lane highway. when you introduce any type of impediment on the highway, be it toll booth, construction , and accidents, a slow vehicle or poor weather. traffic begins to slow and queue up until it eventually stops completely. These bottlenecks can be fixed by taking action, like adjusting toll booth capacity or adjusting flow capacity. In manufacturing , too much queue form work-in-process inventory will clog work centers slowing velocity and creating bottlenecks.

3.2 Poor Supplier Relation

Close ties to suppliers are critical to lead time reduction. Suppliers must be your goals and needs and production and business process that can support nothing less than 100% of your needs. On-time-delivery of materials is essential to reduce lead times, decreasing inventories and lowering costs.

3.3 Improper Performance Metrics

Frequently, management rewards production practices that actually results in longer leads times. For instance , if the success of the shop floor is measured simply by efficiency, utilizations and/ or standard hours , you can be sure that parts be produced even when they are needed, resulting in too much inventory of unneeded material and possible of what is needed.

3.4 Overly Complicated Business Processes

Ineffective practices and slow , fragmented systems for handling sales orders, acquiring materials, scheduling production and other information are often big contributors overly long order-to-delivery lead times. Complication needs to be replaced with effectiveness to reduce lead times and costs whenever possible.

4. METHODOLOGY
4.1 Critical Value Index

In this paper we propose to two methods for the reduction of lead time.

1. Ordering the production process based upon profitably rank order.
2. Estimating the efficiency of automated production line so as to find out the potential for improvements in the production process.

These two methods are presented as the case study of a foundry unit.

Table: 1

Components	Number of components	Rate of products	Total sales	Profitably rank order
A	100	20	2000	2
B	20	3	60	4
C	30	4	120	3
D	40	60	2400	1

Critical value to customers

Table: 2

1-sales lost.   **2**-slight delay acceptable.   **3**-larger delay acceptable.

Components	Profitability rank order(X)	Critical value to customers(Y)	Product X*Y	Order of production
A	2	1	2	4
B	4	2	8	1
C	3	1	3	2
D	1	3	3	3

By proposed methodology the manufacturing industry can reduce the lead time by 23 hours in a month considering the lesser pattern change.

By monthly plan of may-2004.

No of types of components to be produced = 224, average pattern change time = 7 mins. Average no of pattern changes per month = 420 (15 per day).

Therefore reduction in lead time due to pattern change = (420-224)*7=23 hours.

1. Reduction of lead time by estimating the efficiency of the automated line.

Time study was conducted for seven components which are common to fully automated line and semi automated line.for example:

Table: 3

Part no: 5026.   **No of castings: 230.**

S.no	Process description	Date	Starting time	Finishing time
1	Loading on tractor	30/05/04	04:00am	06:00am
2	Transportation to yard	30/05/04	-	7.11mins
3	Down loading from tractor	30/05/04	-	3.00mins
4	Derisering	30/05/04	10:30am	03:30pm
5	Loading on tractor to weigh	31/05/04	11:25am	12:03pm
6	Transportation for weighing	31/05/04	12:03pm	12:18pm
7	Transportation to DA	31/05/04	12:18pm	12:24pm
8	Transportation to subcontractor	31/05/04	12:32pm	12:52pm
9	Downloading	31/05/04	12:52pm	01:00pm
10	Shot blasting	31/05/04	02:00pm	04:0pm

Total time taken for this series of processes mentioned above in a semi automated line :

(30/05/04)- 04:00am to (31/05/04)-04:00pm = 36 hours.

Similairly time study for seven components were carried out for the semi automated line and the timings were to found as follows:

Table: 4

Part no	Starting time	Finishing time	Total time	Ratio
5046	26/05/04 (05:00am)	27/05/04 (06:00pm)	37 hours	0.12
2288	27/05/04 (09:30am)	28/05/04 (11:30am)	14 hours	0.047
5078	26/05/04 (10:05am)	28/05/04 (06:30pm)	60 hours	0.203
6180	29/05/04 (07:05am)	02/06/04 (07:00am)	72 hours	0.244
5026	30/05/04 (04:00am)	31/05/04 (04:00pm)	36 hours	0.12
5045	31/05/04 (00:35am)	02/06/04 (08:00pm)	36 hours	0.122
1045	30/05/04 (01:30am)	01/06/04 (03:00pm)	40 hours	0.135

Starting time: this denotes the commencement of the process.

Initial time: this denotes the completion of the process.

Total time: this is the time taken for completion of all the processes studied.

Ratio: It is the normalization of the time for a particular component in the scale of 1.

For example : for part no 5046, ratio = 37/(37+14+16+72+36+36+40) = 0.12

Table: 5

Part no	Total time	Ratio	Efficiency Ratio	Performance level
1045	4.6 hours	0.149	1.08	108 %
2288	2.5 hours	0.08	1.702	170.2%
5026	4.2 hours	0136	0.788	78.8%
5045	4.4 hours	0.143	0.778	77.8%
5046	4 hours	0.13	1.13	113%
5078	5 hours	0.16	1.172	117.2%
6180	6 hours	0.19	1.103	110.3%

The above tabular column provides the time study of fully automated line for similar components as in semi automated line.

Ratio: It is the normalization of the time for a particular component in the scale of 1.

Efficiency ratio: It is the ratio of the normalization ratio of two lines namely semi automated and automated.

Therefore the performance index for the automated line = 0.108 + 0.1702 + 0.0788 +0.113 + 0.1172 + 0.1103 = 0.7753.

5. CONCLUSION

Many companies have trouble delivering products on time, never mind quickly, and are plugged with excessively long order to delivery lead times and cannot seem to find a solution. In addition, the desire to reduce inventories, lower over head costs and to stabilize erratic production schedule performance are profit improvements benefits that put further emphasis on the need and desirability for reducing the lead times. . Lead time reduction can mean lower cost, reduced inventories, improved production predictability, increased customer satisfaction and better quality.

Two methods proposed in the paper namely, estimation of efficiency of the automated line i.e, how much more can be extracted from an automated line and profitability rank order has been studied with respect to a manufacturing industry.

6. REFERENCES

1. **Cox, A.,** 1997. Business Success. *Earlsgate Press*, Midsomer Norton, Bath.
2. **Harland, C.M.**, 1996. Supply chain management: relationships, chains and networks. British Academy of Management 7 (Special Issue), S63-S80.
3. **Hines, P.**, 1995. Network sourcing: a hybrid approach. International *Journal of Purchasing and Materials Management 31* (2), 18-25.
4. **Houlihan, J.B.**, 1987. International supply chain management. *International Journal of Physical Distribution and Materials Management 17* (2), 51-66.
5. **Houlihan, J.B.**, 1988. International supply chains: a new approach. Management Decision: Quarterly Review of Management Technology 26 (3), 13-19.
6. **La Londe, B.J.,** Masters, J.M., 1994. Emerging logistics strategies: blur print for the next century. *International Journal of Physical Distribution and Logistics Management 24* (7), 35-47.
7. **Lamming, R.C.,** 1993. Beyond Partnership: strategies for innovation and lean supply. *Prentice-Hall,* Hemel Hempstead.
8. **Martin Christopher**, Logistics and Supply Chain Management, Financial Times, *Pitman Publishing,* 2000.
9. **New, S.J.**, 1997. The scope of supply chain management research. Supply Chain Management 2 (1), 15-22.
10. **New, S.J.**, Payne, P., 1995. Research frameworks in logistics: three models, seven dinners and a survey. *International Journal of Physical Distribution and Logistics Management 25* (10), 60-77.
11. **Sako, M.,** 1992. Prices, Quality and Trust: Interfirm Relations in Britain and Japan. Cambridge University Press, Cambridge.
12. **Tan, K.C., Handfield, R.B., Krause, D.R.,** 1998a. Enhancing firm's performance through quality and supply base management: an empirical study. *International Journal of Production Research 36* (10), 2813-2837.
13. **Thorelli, H.B.,** 1986. Networks: between markets and hierarchies. *Strategic Management Journal 7* (1), 37-51.
14. **Wind Y.** and **Saaty T.L.,** Marketing Applications of the Analytic Hierarchy Process, Management Science, 26(7), 641-658, (1980).

GCMM 2004
Editors: Prasad K D V Yarlagadda and S Narayanan
Copyright © 2005, Vellore Institute of Technology, Vellore, India
Publisher: Narosa Publishing House Pvt. Ltd., New Delhi, India

Evaluation of Health Care Quality based on Hospital Resource Performance and Customer Service Preferences Using Analytic Hierarchy Process

Parthiban P*, Ganesh K**, Narayanan S*, Udayakumar K*

* Faculty, Department of Mechanical Engineering,
Vellore Institute of Technology, Deemed University, Vellore-632014, TN, India

E-mail ID:parthee_p@yahoo.com

** Research Scholar, (Ph.D.), Industrial Engineering and Management Division,
Humanities and Social Sciences Department, Indian Institute of Technology, Chennai,

Email ID: koganesh@yahoo.com

Abstract

The future success of health care supply chain relies on the aspect of better service quality to the customers. The growing health care providers should take into account the customer service preferences for providing the services in a competitive business environment. The kaizen approach of health care is needed in customer service aspects to serve to the people by developing the infrastructure, clinical arrangements and by reducing the mortality rate through eminent doctor professionals. Smart shoppers look for low prices and top quality when buying cars, televisions, internet services, or any other product or service. In case of health care services, it can often be difficult to find the information which needs to choose on the aspect of quality, distance traveled, time taken to travel, as well as cost. In choosing an operation or other procedure in a particular hospital, depends upon the both qualitative and quantitative attributes. The quality of health care in America varies a lot. But, that quality can be measured, and it can be improved. Moreover many public and private groups are working on ways to measure and report on the quality of health care. In regard with the certain customer service based preferences information, hospitals can improve the quality of health care. With an effort to develop set of guidelines for competitive benchmarking and to measure the health care quality of medical hospitals, this paper proposes an analytic hierarchy process that can help the customers to choose the better hospitals in aspect of service preferences.

Keywords
Supply Chain, AHP, Health Care

1. LITERATURE REVIEW: HEALTH CARE INDUSTRY

During the last decade, the health care industry in the United States has seen the dramatic increases in competitive environment. The most critical factor for health care providers becomes the health care quality according customer service preferences. Health acre reform based on quality, reliability and affordability is of real world concern. The Quality Service Model, a 22-item survey tool called the ServQual is used to collect information from customers on five factors of quality service namely reliability-the ability to provide what was promised, dependably and accurately, assurance—the knowledge and courtesy of employees, and their ability to convey trust and confidence, tangibles—the physical facilities, equipment, and the appearance of personnel, empathy—the degree of caring and individual attention provided to customers, responsiveness—the willingness to help customers and provide prompt service. These five factors account for much of the variation of customer's perception of quality service across industries [3] But the technical aspect of service quality has been omitted. The main aim of this paper is to develop an analytical approach for evaluating the health care quality of hospitals in the aspect of qualitative and quantitative customer service preferences. The mortality rate versus operations is taken into consideration for the evaluation, so that the Health Maintenance Organization (HMO) can prescribe the concern hospitals as a quality one. The model called Analytic Hierarchy Process (AHP) has been presented for the evaluation. The process was carried over by identifying and prioritizing heath care service attributes affecting customer service preferences of health care quality, by measuring and comparing the distance, time taken to travel, cost level of the hospitals, by identifying the

2. DEFINING HOSPITAL PERFORMANCE

Hospital Performance (HP)
    = Hospital Resource Performance (HRP) + Customer Service Preferences (CSP)
Where
HRP = Hospital Management (HM) + Operations Vs Mortality Rate Performance (OMP)

CSP = Hospital Infrastructure Preferences (HIP) + Critical Decision Factors (CDF)

3. RESEARCH APPROACH FOR EVALUATING HEALTH CARE QUALITY

Quality health care is defined as doing the right thing, at the right time, in the right way, for the right person and having the best possible results. Every health plan, doctor, hospital, and other providers cannot provide the same customer preferred-quality care. Quality varies, for many reasons. Health professionals are mostly used these tools and they use measures to check on and improve the quality of health care. But there is some quality information that can used to compare the health care choices. Many public and private groups are working to improve and expand health care quality measures. The goal is to make these measures more reliable, uniform, and helpful to consumers making health care choices. There are two main types of quality measures that can help to choose quality health care. They are customer ratings and clinical performance measures. Customer ratings or "customer satisfaction" information look at health care form the customer's point of view. Clinical performance measures, are also called "technical quality" measures, look at how well a health care organization prevents and treat illness and reduces the mortality rate. In this paper the two aspects, tangible and intangible criteria is taken into account and the alternatives (hospitals) are evaluated according to customer service preferences using AHP by the Heath Maintenance Organization of United States Hospital [2]

4. COMPETITIVE ADVANTAGE OF HEALTH CARE IMPROVEMENT TOOL

Benchmarking is a continuous quality improvement process by which an organization (hospitals) can assess its internal strengths and weakness, evaluate comparative advantages of leading competitors, identify best practices of industry or functional leaders, and incorporate these findings into a strategic action plan geared to gain a position of superiority [1]

369

5. CUSTOMER SERVICE BASED HEALTH CARE QUALITY MEASURES (QMS) VERSUS QUALITY INDICATORS (QIS)

Quality indicators are not direct measures of quality; they are pointers that indicate potential problem areas that need further review and investigation. Quality indicators are the starting point for a process of evaluating the quality of care though careful investigation. A true measure of quality identifies an aspect of care where there definitely is a problem and describes the extent of the problem. Quality measures are their own end points; no further investigation is needed in order to make judgments about the quality of care. Customers, policy-makers and many others who are interested in the quality of care provided by a facility are not able to conduct clinical investigations. They need information that clearly relates to actual problems. They need true quality measures, which , unlike quality indicators, become the sole judge of quality [5]

6. ANALYTIC HIERARCHY PROCESS APPROACH FOR EVALUATION OF HOSPITALS

An extensive survey on multi criteria decision problem solution results as follows. The complication of a multi attribute decision problem, which demands each alternative must be judged on a multidimensional scale spanning risk, performance, time, and cost, can be resolved by the application of two approaches. The first is linear weighting scheme developed by Saaty known as the Analytic Hierarchy Process (AHP). It uses pair-wise comparisons and a ration scale to arrive at a cardinal ranking of the alternatives [4]

6.1 Algorithm of Solving Multi Criteria problems by AHP

1. Define the problem and determine the objectives.
2. Identify the factor, which influences the decision.
3. The factors are groups based on their interdependence as criteria sub-criteria, sub-criteria criteria etc.
4. Formulate the hierarchical structure i.e., the criteria on the top level and sub criteria

and sub-sub criteria are arranged in the intermediate and lower levels.
5. This can be done by, writing all factors in row wise and column wise. Compare the first factor in the first row with all the factors in the column. During comparing if factor 1 in the row dominate over the factor 2 in the column then the whole integer (ranging for 4 to 9 based on the preference of one over the other is assigned in the cell (1,2) and the reciprocal is entered in cell (2,1). If elements being compared are equal 1 is assigned to both the positions. Otherwise integer 2 or 3 is assigned in the cell 1,2 the reciprocal is assigned in cell 2,1. This pair wise comparison is based on the Thomas L.Saaty scale for AHP.
6. There are n (n-1) judgments are required to develop the set of matrices in step
7. Having made all the pair-wise comparisons of the data the consistency ratio (C.R) is determined. The consistency ratio (C.R) is an approximate mathematical indicator, or guide, of the consistency of pair-wise comparisons. It is a function of what is called "maximum eigen value" and size of the matrix, "n" (called a consistency index) which is then compared against similar values if the pair-wise comparisons had been merely random (called a "random Index" R.I, see the Random Index table) . If the ratio of the Consistency Index to the Random Index is no greater than 0.1 (with in 10%), saaty suggests the consistency is generally quite acceptable for pragmatic purposes. The Consistency index (C.I) can be calculated using the equation
8. $C.I. = (\lambda max-1) / n - 1$. Here "$\lambda max$" s the maximum eigen value of the pair-wise comparison matrix and "n" is the size of the pair-wise comparison matrix.
9. Steps 5 to 7 are performed for all levels and clusters in the hierarchy.
10. Hierarchical composition is now used to weight the eigen vectors by the weight the criteria and the sum is taken overall weighted eigen vectors entries corresponding to the next lower levels of hierarchy.

Hierarchy of Health Care Quality

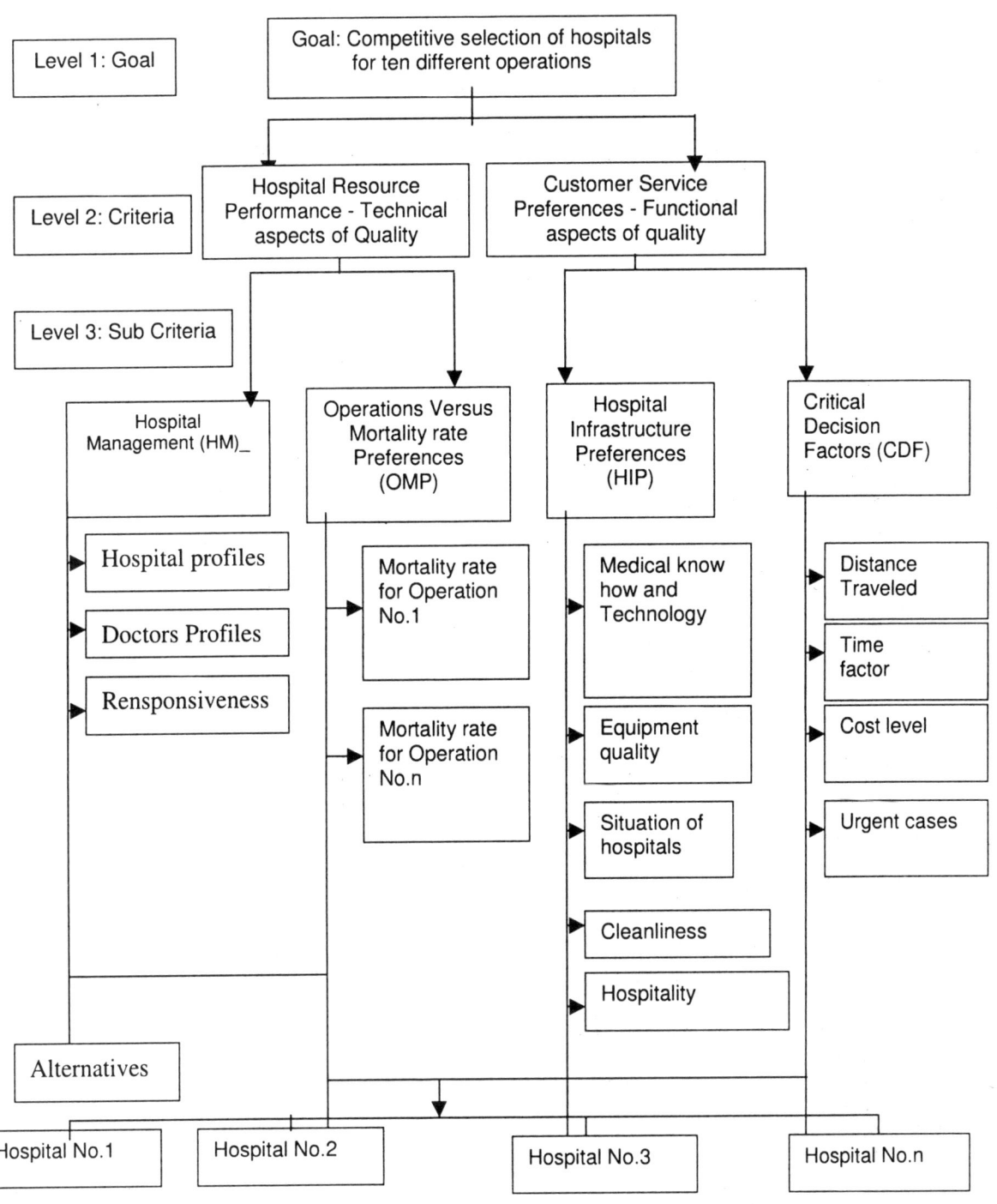

6.2 Findings the Priority of Hospitals using Pair-Wise Comparison Matrix:

The priority values of the pair-wise comparison matrix are found by multiplying the pair-wise comparison matrix with the unit column vector repeatedly until we get the maximum priority value same to the previous iteration. For example we have considered two alternative hospital 1 and hospital 2 with the consideration of all criteria.

Technical Aspects of quality	Hospital 1	Hospital 2
Hospital 1	1	5
Hospital 2	0.25	1

The priority values for the remaining criteria in the second level of the hierarchy are as shown in the table. From the results, the hospital.1 carries more priority than the hospital 2. Likewise it can be applicable to finite number of hospitals to evaluate the priority.

CRITERIA	Technical Aspects	Functional Aspects	TOTAL Priority
WEIGHTS	0.29	0.07	
Hospital 1	0.83	0.80	0.841
Hospital 2	0.17	0.20	0.159

7. CONCLUSION

In today's competitive arena, quality health care is a vital goal to be accomplished at an affordable price. This paper illustrates the use of competitive benchmarking for quality measurement. This approach is used for setting service standards for public and private sector hospitals We have developed the software using Turbo 'C' for AHP and it is useful for the Health Maintenance organizations to evaluate the hospitals according to both technical and functional aspects in accordance with customer service preferences.

8. REFERENCES

1. American Productivity and Quality Center, The Benchmarking Management Guide. *Productivity Press,* Portland, Oregan (1993).
2. **Y.Wind** and **T.L.Saaty,** Marketing Applications of the Analytic Hierarchy Process, Management Science, 26(7), 641-658, (1980).
3. **Woodside, L.Frey** and **R.Daly**, Linking Service Quality, Customer Satisfaction, and Behavioral Intention, *Journal of Health care Marketing*, 9(4), 5-17, (1989).
4. **F.Zahedi**, The Analytic Hierarchy Process-A survey of the Method and Its Applications, Interfaces, 16(4), 96-108, (1989).
5. **W.D.Cook** and **M.Kress**, A Multiple Criteria Decision Model with Ordinal reference Data, *European Journal of Operational Research*, 34, 191-198, (1991)

GCMM 2004
Editors: Prasad K D V Yarlagadda and S Narayanan
Copyright © 2005, Vellore Institute of Technology, Vellore, India
Publisher: Narosa Publishing House Pvt. Ltd., New Delhi, India

Supply Chain Management in India – A Perspective

Rupa S Bindu & Prashant M More

P.E.S College of Engineering,Nagsenvana
Aurangabad-431002

E-mail :rsbindu31@rediffmail.com, moreprashant_in@yahoo.com

Abstract

The paper discusses about the various factors that can result in effective management of SCM in Indian context and brings out the hurdles and suggests the remedies in the hardware and software aspects of SCM. Hardware aspects of SCM means the physical elements of logistics which include transportation, inventory,warehousing and packaging.The various problems related to hardware aspect Handling Damages & Losses,oil crisis and fuel bills,theft and pilferage,excessive lead time on certain vendors,uncertain vendors,poor packaging/excessive packaging costs.The various problems related with the software aspects are Communication and the philosophy to deal with its suppliers.The paper also discusses a Case Study related to the importance of communication.

Keywords

ITR,RFP,PLS,CFM,JIT,Win-Win.

1.INTRODUCTION

Global competitiveness is the measure of a country's advantage or disadvantage in selling its product in international markets. It is also the measure of overall economic performance of a nation, particularly its level of Productivity, its ability to export goods and services and its maintenance of high standards of living of its citizens.For India to withstand the Global competition and to improve its rank in World Economic Forum every effort needs to be directed towards "customer is supreme" approach,since in the coming years only those enterprises will be successful which will be able to provide goods and services to the customer in timely cost effective manner with quality which not only satisfies the customer but delights him.

Application of Supply Chain Management (SCM) in an effective way in Indian context will definitely upgrade India's present position. For India to achieve excellence in SCM the first step is to evaluate the present position and to identify the hurdles and improvement areas. The paper discusses about the various factors that can result in effective management of SCM in Indian context and brings out the hurdles and suggests the remedies in the hardware and software aspects of SCM.An effort is made to analyse some aspects of the present scenario which may provide useful feedback that will help us to survive the race of digital economy.

2.HARDWARE ASPECTS

Hardware aspects of SCM means the physical elements of logistics and purchase.

2.1 Transportation

The first and the foremost of the hardware aspects is the transportation. We are fortunate to have a vast network of :
Railways : Route km length: 62,915 km;7068 stations(terminals).
Roadways : National highway : 34,000 km.
Ports :Coastline of about 6,000 km ,11 major ports and 139 minor ports.
Air: 6 major International airports and 86 domestic airports.
Inspite of this infrastructure the Indian industries are facing the problems of :

2.1.1 Handling Damages & Losses:
2.1.2 Improvement Opportunities

Proper identification of material handling damages can determine appropriate corrective actions adding longevity to the damage problem. We have to train the material handling operators in the proper techniques for their products. We should help the operators to understand the total cost of damage including the hidden cost of poor material handling techniques.
Process re-engineering of material handling should start with :

1. Selection of proper material handling equipment.
2. Operator Training
3. Standardised procedure of training, testing and certification for material handling.
4. Optimising the method of loading different products and vehicles configuration and to optimise the vehicle loading patterns to use appropriate placement of all the blocking and bracing material.

2.2 Oil Crisis and Fuel Bills

As the oil prices are governed by the prices of crude oil in international markets, still we can exercise some control by reducing the cost of bills by duly considering the following factors:
• Delays at the Tollbooths.
• Fuel saving/energy conservation through better maintenance of vehicles.
• Use of non-conventional method of transportation Ex.pipeline transportation wherever applicable.

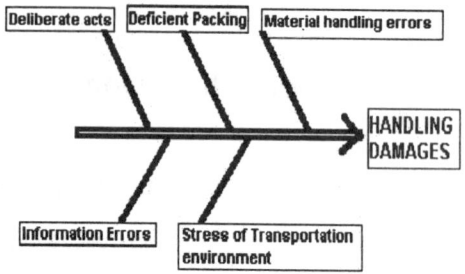

Fig 1 : CAUSE-EFFECT DIAGRAM

2.3 THEFT AND PILFERAGE
2.3.1 Use of Securement Devices

Cargo loading should focus on the products you ship with separate reviews for safety done for each mode of transportation used by company. The company should determine the most cost effective securement device applicable.The securement devices suppliers should provide a set of good options for the shipment.s. Once the final selection is made on the product/device to be used,the technical directions are needed to be given and documented to the concerned crew for proper application of securement devices.Proper training of the loading crews should be done to ensure that all blocking and bracing devices are properly installed to reduce theft and pilferage.

2.3.2 Use of Information Technology

1. 1.Now a days Geographical Information systems(GIS) are widely used for accurate map production and quick updation.
2. Proper planning for routing and scheduling can be done using real time interactive planner.
3. 3.Moblie communication – Fast transmission of voice/data via radio,cellular and satellite devices.
4. 4.Global positioning system(GPS) for accurate location,specification and references with effective tracing systems.

All the above technologies can be integrated effectively with internet,intranet option, so that communication among the supplier,customer and the carriers become easier and faster.

374

3. INVENTORY

Inventories may be taken as the barometer of effectiveness of materials management function.Inventory turn over ratio(ITR) tells how often a business inventory turns over during the course of the year.It is defined as cost of goods sold divided by average value of inventory.High inventory turn over ratio is generally preferable.Inventory turn over ratio in indian scenario is very low due to variety of reasons.In one of the comparisions of ITR in automobile companies of india is 16.0 and that of an auto company in USA is 19.0 (in the same sector).

ITR can be improved by implementing the following strategies.

3.1 Reduction in Lead Time

To conduct the business in timely cost effective manner "management of time" is the key,for withstanding the global competition.Among various activities of a business,procurement lead time consumes valuable transaction time.Lead time analysis must be done to find out exactly where the waste of time exists,so that we can go about eliminating or reducing it.

Some key points related to this activity are :
1. Pinpoint the activities where waste of time occurs.
2. Identification of value added and non-value added activities.
3. Recognise that time is money and a key to competitive advantage.
4. Ask question how much value addition is in process being studied, then look back when determined.(usually less than 5%to VA).
5. The value in this way being monitored by an organisation should be displayed in the work area.
6. Methods of lead time reduction :
   • Reduce
   • Combine
   • Eliminate
7. For flow visual impact on the employees display the processes which are re-engineered.

3.2 UNCERTAIN VENDORS
3.2.1.Strategic sourcing

The appropriate method to resolve the problem of uncertain vendors is strategic sourcing.Strategic sourcing group should identify the universe of potential vendors big or small.The vendor database should rapidly expand allowing sourcing team to get a clear picture of the marketplace and identify the most innovative and competitive suppliers. Steps to strategic sourcing:

1. Purchasing profiles and prioritising : Strategic sourcing team should gather as much information as possible about what, when and how the business buys. Priorities should be set in areas such as cost,service and quality.
2. Identifying strategic sourcing products : Develop specifications for the product to be purchased,identifying how a product is used and which features are most and least important.
3. Solicit bids and negotiate with suppliers: Once the sourcing team understands what the user need, a detailed RFP(Request for proposal) should be sent out based on vendor database.Each bid should be rated using weighted criteria agreed to by the sourcing team.The lowest price may be overshadowed by speedy delivery or quality depending upon specific product or service.
4. Applying sound business principles,the sourcing team should review payment terms,any value added programs and delivery issues. Strategic sourcing team then should meet with the successful bidder vendor and award him the purchase relationship. Everyone involved should be notified of the results with feedback.It should be made available to unsuccessful bidders so they can make improvements and bid again next time.

4. WAREHOUSING AND PACKING
4.1 Excessive material retrieval time

Packing, storage and retrieval methods employed in Indian situations are not the best and there is tremendous room for improvement in packing and warehousing function.Many times,poor storage of materials leads to damage,loss,pilferage and even hazards.There is a need to update the quality of storage methods with a high degree of mechanisation and automation. Unfortunately, most stores/warehouses in India are conventional with poor maintenance and little technological innovation.

Material handling equipments in the international arena has a wide range of products and equipments available such as electro-hydraulic cranes fitted to cargo trucks.Need for more robust ,versatile,secure and reusable systems is felt and are being improved upon.Palletised load system(PLS) is fast becoming accepted neccessity with use of computers.Industries in Sweden are leaders in the class of manual and electric warehouse trucks,having a very wide range such as hand trucks,powered pallet trucks,stackers,order selectors,reach trucks and very narrow aisle trucks.

4.2 Poor Packaging/Excessive Packaging Costs

Value Analysis

Either poor packaging or excessive packaging cost, both are the present day hurdles faced by packaging department of many industries. It is required to have optimality in design and development of packaging.

Value =(Performance +Capability)/Cost

Value Analysis defines a "basic function" as anything that makes the product work or sell. "Secondary functions" are also called supporting functions could be modified or eliminated to reduce packing cost, ultimately increasing the value.

A cost function matrix(CFM) or value Analysis matrix is prepared to identify the cost of providing each function by associating the function with a mechanism or component part of the packaging. Packaging function with high-cost function ratio are identified as opportunities for further investigation and improvements. Improvement opportunities are then brainstormed, analysed and selected.

A number of questions as framed by Miles[4] at G.E. The packaging is analysed in light of these questions (tests).
(1) Does packaging contribute value to end product ?
(2) Is its cost proportionate to its function ?

(3) Can some of its features be combined or elliminated ?
(4) Would there be a better packaging?
(5) Can a packaging be produced by less costly process ?
(6) Can one go for an available standard packaging?
(7) Taking into account the quantity required, Is the packaging being made with proper tools?
(8) Does the packaging has resonable resale price?
(9) Can the packaging be procured at less cost from elsewhere?
(10)Is anybody purchasing the packaging at lower rates ?

4.3 Procedure

(1) Blast → Identify the packaging
→ Collect relevant information
→ Define function
→ Create alternatives.
(2) Create ► Critically evaluate alternatives
► Develop the best alternative
(3) Refine ► Implement the alternative.

5. SOFWARE ASPECTS

Software aspect relates to the overall philosophy of business enterprises dealing with the suppliers.

5.1 Communication

Co-ordination and communication are very important software aspects of SCM.Unfortunately one of the weakest links in the developing countries is communication. Both in terms of software and hardware terms the current developments in IT(internet,e-mail,EDI) have made it possible for electronic connectivity, but in the nation like India because of high cost involved in this upgraded technology most of the business enterprise have financial constraints to afford it and therefore lack behind due to time factor.

5.1.1 Importance of Communication
5.1.1.1Case Study

In multi-plant locations of manufacturing and warehousing there is a need to increase information sharing for the latest developments in the transportation.

A company US filters had more than 200 shipping locations and 20 thousand employees an annual freight spent of more than 100 million dollars.

Day today transportation purchasing decisions were made at each of more than 200 sites. To reduce the freight charges of 200 locations, the logistics staff negotiated a corporate transport tariff at a significant discount to the tariffs in use by the local facilities. This tariff was projected to provide significant savings and was made available at all the locations. But despite of this the company's freight cost did not drop, and the amount of freight tendered to the corporate carrier did not increase why?

(1) There was no means to communicate constantly changing corporate rates to all the locations. The updated carrier service times data was not communicated constantly to all the locations.

(2) Lack of access to all the companies shipping data due to which under negotiations took place.

To resolve these challenges, a transportation management system was developed which included :

- Transportation service rating module
- Transaction management database
- Optimisation modules
- Order status module
- Data warehouse

The user can access the system using a web browser. There was no software to install or hardware to buy.

With the tariff loaded in the web-based TMS all the companies field managers could quickly and easily view the company best rate when ever they were ready to ship simply by logging in. As the shipment are entered in to the system tariff manager can request quotes, the quotes come back instantly from the rating module and show all the carriers and their rates who can meet the service requirement of the shipments.

6. PHILOSOPHY TO DEAL WITH IT'S SUPPLIERS
6.1 Enterprise Supplier Relationship

The enterprise supplier relationship must be based on the understanding that both the buyer and the seller actively participate in the transactions and business should be viewed as social co-operation rather than being equated to the game or war.(see Table no.1).

Table 1. Enterprise –Supplier Relationship

FACTORS AFFECTING RELATIONS	CONVENTIONAL RELATIONS	CO-OPERATIVE RELATIONSHIP
Competition	• Less competition • Friendly relationship • More business	• Collaborative but Dynamic
Basic of sourcing decisions	• Price based	• Performance history and price
Information sharing	• Minimium	• Maximum
Delivery of goods	• Large Quantities	• Small Quantities • JIT concept
Prices changes	• General negotiations annually • A game of Win / Lose	• Planned reduction and rise considering the inflation rate. • A game of Win/Win
Attitude toward Quality	• Inspection • Argument	• 100 % O.K • Quality checked at the suppliers end
Level of Pressure	• Low/Medium	• Very high but predictable.

Table 2 : Hardware and Software Aspects

377

Building up of innovative and creative culture within enterprise has become today's ultimate need for effective implementation of SCM in India.

7. REFERENCES

1. **Vittal N.** (1999), "Supply Chain Management for Global Competitiveness", *Proc. of the International Conference on Supply Chain Management for Global Competitiveness*, India.

2. **Vijayaraghavan T.A.S.** (1999), "Tranportation Logistics in India – Problems,Issues and Strategies for competitive advantage", *Proc. of the International Conference on Supply Chain Management for Global Competitiveness*, India.

3. **Rao A.K., and Chetty B.S.** (1999), "Customer-Supplier Relationship", *Proc. of the International Conference on Supply Chain Management for Global Competitiveness*, India.

4. **Khanna O.P.** (1992), *Industrial Engineering and Management*, Dhanpatrai and sons, Delhi.

Materials

GCMM 2004
Editors: Prasad K D V Yarlagadda and S Narayanan
Copyright © 2005, Vellore Institute of Technology, Vellore, India
Publisher: Narosa Publishing House Pvt. Ltd., New Delhi, India

Challenges and Goals in Scaffolds for Tissue Engineering

Sreejith P S & Yarlagadda P K D V

Queensland University of Technology
2, George Street, GPO Box 2434, QLD 4001

E-mail: p.sreejith@qut.edu.au

Abstract

Tissue engineering (TE) is a multi disciplinary subject, which includes the restoration of the biological functions, either through repair or regeneration. Many of the tissues and organs to be replaced serve important biomechanical functions, and despite early successes, tissue engineers have faced challenges in repairing/replacing tissues that serve predominantly biomechanical roles in the body. In fact, the properties of these tissues are critical to their proper functioning *in vivo*. In order for tissue engineers to effectively replace these load-bearing structures, they must address a number of significant questions on the interactions of engineered constructs with mechanical forces both *in vivo* and *in vitro*. This paper presents the state of arts in scaffold guided tissue engineering.

Keywords
Tissue Engineering, Scaffolds, Extra Cellular Matrix, Biomaterials

1. INTRODUCTION

A biomaterial can exhibit specific interactions with cells that will lead to stereotyped responses. This is partly because of the physical properties of the biomaterial, microshape, and ability to transmit stresses to cells and ability to adsorb proteins to its surface in complex arrays and super physiological concentrations. The biomaterials used to create scaffolds for tissues should be able to deliver fixed and soluble drugs to guide the regeneration process. At the same time the biomaterial should be degradable and should be stress responsive. The chemical, mechanical and architectural properties of the scaffold over time *in vivo* will affect the physiological response of the cells. As a result, the mechanical influence on the cells will be related to the mechanical properties of the scaffold, the mechanical boundary conditions acting on the construct, and the interaction between the cells and the scaffold. In addition, the shape and morphology of the cells will be related to the cell/scaffold interactions.

In the past decade, significant scientific advances have been made in establishing therapeutic methods for treatment of diseases that require reconstructive surgery or organ replacement. Soft and hard tissue engineering has emerged as one of the most exciting areas of research in healthcare product engineering [1-3]. These approaches have been effective in regenerating functional tissues or organs ranging from bioartificial skin to functional urinary bladder and blood vessels using cell-scaffold-based approaches.

Once implanted in the body, engineered constructs of cells and matrices will be subjected to a complex biomechanical environment, consisting of time-varying changes in stresses, strains, fluid pressure, fluid flow and cellular deformation behaviour

381

[4, 5]. It is now well accepted that these various physical factors have the capability to influence the biological activity of normal tissues and therefore may play an important role in the success or failure of engineered grafts [6, 7]. In this regard, it would be important to better characterize the diverse array of physical signals that engineered cells may experience *in vivo* as well as their biological response to such potential stimuli. This information may provide an insight into the long-term capabilities of engineered constructs to maintain the proper cellular phenotype [8].

Scaffold-guided TE has been developed to regenerate specific and functional human tissues or organs [1, 2]. As the scaffolds form the platform for cells to develop and to be organized into tissues and organs, TE scaffolds should facilitate the colonization of cells and possess properties and characteristics that enhance cell attachment, proliferation, migration and expression of native phenotypes. Scaffold characteristics and properties such as porosity, surface area to volume ratio, pore size, pore interconnectivity, structural strength, shape (or overall geometry) and biocompatibility [3, 4] are often considered to be critical factors in their design and fabrication.

2. REQUIREMENTS OF BIOMATERIALS

Biomaterials used in tissue engineering can be broadly divided into two categories; synthetic or naturally derived, with a third category of semi-synthetic materials is rapidly emerging. A particular challenge in addressing materials is that the processes are not yet completely understood well enough to allow a clear set of design parameters to be specified *in priori*. Adaptation of already used materials can have some advantages from the regulatory perspective, as the safety and toxicity profiles of the materials in humans are already defined, but other performance aspects such as cell material performance interactions and degradation properties however are not assured. This need for substantially higher performance characteristics is pushing research and development in the design of new materials that meet specific performance criteria in tissue engineering.

The field of biomaterials and scaffolds for tissue engineering is in an adolescent phase and maturing rapidly. One of the most important changes coming in the field is the strong need to integrate basic polymer science and engineering with molecular cell biology and stem cell biology in the design of new materials that carry out very sophisticated signaling needs.

3. TITANIUM BIOMATERIAL

The outstanding biocompatibility of titanium was already recognized by many researchers [9, 10, 11]. The mechanical properties of titanium compare favourably with those of other implantable metals and alloys. The yield strength is approximately the same as that of surgical quality 316L stainless steel and almost twice that of the familiar cast Co-Cr-Mo alloy used in orthopedic implants. The elastic modulus is approximately half that of the other common metal alloys used in surgery. This low modulus results in a material that is less rigid and deforms elastically under applied loads. This is important in the development of orthopedic products where a close match is desired between the elastic properties of long bone and the surgical implant. The fatigue strength is about twice that of stainless steel. Titanium has an extreme low toxicity and is well tolerated by both bone and soft tissue.

Animal experiments have revealed that the materials may be implanted for an extensive length of time; fibrous encapsulation of the implants is minimal to nonexistent. Porous titanium structures may be used as permanent implants with healthy bone growing around and into the pores and the implant remaining in place in the body as a framework for the bone. Titanium also offers great promise as a permanent scaffold as wire mesh [12, 13].

4. SCAFFOLDS IN TISSUE ENGINEERING

Today, tissue engineers are attempting to engineer virtually every human tissue. Potential tissue-engineered products include cartilage, bone, heart valves, nerves, muscle, bladder, liver, etc. Tissue engineering techniques generally require the use of a porous scaffold, which serves as three-dimensional template for initial cell attachment and subsequent tissue formation both *in vitro* and *in vivo*.

Scaffolds play an important role in manipulating cell functions. Isolated and expanded cells adhere to the temporary scaffold in all three dimensions, proliferate, and secrete their own extracellular matrices (ECM), replacing the biodegrading scaffold. Therefore, in addition to permitting cell adhesion, promoting cell growth, and allowing retention of differential cell functions, the scaffold should be biocompatible, biodegradable, highly porous with a large surface to volume ratio, mechanically strong, and capable of being formed into desired shapes. The scaffold structures can be classified as adapted or designed. The structure of a scaffold plays an important role in guiding tissue development. Three very general types of scaffold are structural. scaffolds with an imposed pore structure; gelatin type scaffolds formed *in situ* in the presence of cells or tissues, and natural tissue derived gels. For most tissues, the key requirement that can be defined at present is that interconnected porosity of larger dimensions than the cells is required or desired.

5. ISSUES IN TISSUE ENGINEERING

Tissue engineering is a multidisciplinary science to restore biological function, either through repair or regeneration and has led to a lot of potential products involving

1. Human tissues or organs
2. Animal tissues or organs
3. Human or mammalian cells
4. Totally synthetic biomaterials

The above-mentioned products are in different stages of development. In a little over a decade more than $3.5 billion are invested in worldwide research and development in tissue engineering [14].

Many of the tissues and organs to be replaced serve important biomechanical functions and despite early successes, tissue engineers have faced challenges in repairing or replacing tissues that serve predominantly biomechanical roles in the human body [15]. Due to their complex nature and composition, most biological tissues can be classified from a material standpoint as inhomogeneous, viscoelastic, nonlinear and anisotropic materials. The fundamental basis for these behaviors is not fully understood, and may differ among different tissues. Also it remains to be determined, which aspects of these

mechanical properties are essential for the normal, healthy functioning of different tissues and also for the replacements [14].

Assessment of the outcome of successful functional tissue engineering will require quantitative measures of graft properties, structure and composition. Given the biomechanical nature of many tissue-engineered products, there have been surprisingly few reports of the material or structural properties of engineered tissues. For example, several investigators have reported either mechanical properties of grafts prior to implantation [15] or at sacrifice [16, 17]. An important direction in this field will be the development of new methodologies that will allow assessment of the material or structural properties of engineered tissues in a non-invasive or minimally invasive manner.

It is anticipated that the control of cellular development *in vitro* will require the interaction of tens if not hundreds of molecular species varying in concentration and location in time. Biomimetics and tissue engineering depend then upon the capacity to expose cells to permutations of reactive molecule concentrations in high throughout models in real time. For this reason, *in vivo* models alone will be untenable. However, there are very good *in vitro* models that fully reflect events *in vivo*, partially because of the multiplicity of *in vivo* stimuli and the difficulty in reproducing them *in vitro*. A new approach to assay design consists of control elements in place to govern a sufficient number of potential species in their interaction with desired target cells. These assays should correlate in their responses with experiments performed *in vivo*. Potential enhancements of *in vivo* models that will also be valuable include the development of appropriate transgenic animal models for the study of matrix protein and growth factor deficiencies. Animal models of stem cell excess and depletion should also be considered. Also it will be important to develop methods to track signals and cells from their generation step to their end stage fate. The first step towards this is to develop methods digitally record and track events in tissue development in a non-destructive fashion as possible. The second is to use this information to build virtual models of cellular and tissue behavior to enable the testing of theories as a prelude to *in vitro* or *in vivo* assays using live cells and animals. Important elements to be explored include the mechanical forces acting upon the cells, the spatial location and frequency of stem cells and their daughters, the repeating structures of tissues and the role of apoptosis in the regulation of tissue structure. This information will lead to the development of accurate three-dimensional models of tissue that will enable the effects of perturbations to be understood quickly and virtually, thus setting the stage for appropriate correlative experiments using live tissue. The latter may include the development of novel bioreactors for three-dimensional tissue growth.

6. GOALS IN SCAFFOLDS

A number of fabrication technologies have been applied to process biodegradable and bioresorbable materials into 3D scaffoldsof high porosity and surface area. The conventional techniques for scaffold fabrication include textile technologies, solvent casting, particulate leaching, and membrane lamination and melt molding. Froma scaffold design point of view and function viewpoint each processing methodology has its own advantages and disadvantages.

The ultimate goal in tissue engineering is to develop effective substitute or replacements for bone, cartilage, enamel, dentin, cementum and the periodontal ligament. Approaches for achieving this goal will consist of three strategies.

1. Using stem cells and their lineage to regenerate missing or damaged tissue *in vitro* or *in vivo*.
2. Developing new classes of biomaterials that may be either biologically derived or wholly synthetic.
3. Developing innovative physical/chemical stimuli to induce existing adult tissues to regenerate missing or damaged body parts.

It is important for an improved understanding of interfaces between cells, between cells and matrix, between different kinds of matrix and between cells, matrix and minerals. Interfaces between organic-inorganic compounds need to be more thoroughly investigated to determine the environment needed for physiological calcification and to achieve new approaches to designing hard tissues. Improved understanding of factors that affect regeneration and repair of tissues and the effect of nutrients, hormones, age and gender on such factors is needed. This kind of understanding will allow polymeric delivery systems to be developed and will provide new ways of influencing bone cells and other cell types.

Many of the present generation biomaterials are still based upon the early concept that implantable materials should be bioinert and therefore designed to evoke minimal tissue response, if none [18, 19]. However, a growing body of clinical data demonstrates that the long survivability of these materials is hampered by high rates of failure, which is primarily attributed to interfacial instability. Biomaterials developed should actively interact with tissues and thereby induce their repair/regeneration [20]. It is a far gone conclusion that old cells must die and be replaced [21]. Biomaterials enable the repair and replacement of deteriorated bones and joints [22, 23]. The first generation of biomaterials selected was chemically inert in the body. These include special medical grades of stainless steel, cobalt-chrome alloys, titanium alloys and polymer materials such as polyethylene and poly-methyl-methacrylate and are still the dominant materials in orthopedic surgery. However such implants are reported to fail before the patient die [24]. The reason for failure is the progressive deterioration of the bone in contact with the biomaterial. Many factors contribute to the gradual breakdown of this interface; micromotion, wear debris, infection, stress-shielding etc. [25]. Creating new biomaterials is now the greatest challenges in material science.

7. CELL GROWTH ON MICROSTRUCTURED TITANIUM SURFACES

In recent years it has been understood that tissue reactions are determined mainly by surface parameters of the biomaterials used [26]. A detailed understanding of these reactions is the basis for targeted approaches towards implant improvement. Various studies have demonstrated that it may be possible to enhance the performance of an implant by designing the texture of the surface [27]. Beyond variation of irregular surface roughness parameters, surface designs with defined microstructures, especially groove ridge designs have been proposed for a number of applications. Investigations of cellular relations to microstructured surfaces have been greatly enhanced by the development of semiconductor technology. It is also evidenced that bone ingrowth into porous implant surface may result in improved soteointegration and mechanical stability by interlocking the surrounding bone tissue with the implant [28]. A study conducted by Gotz et al [29], showed that textured implants with pores resulted in a good profound improvement in osseointegration after 12 weeks of implantation.

Earlier in vitro were concerned with effect of diverse biomaterials on cell adhesion, proliferation and differentitation withoput much significance being given to surface characterization. But recently, much attention has been given to the surface topography of the implants. A large body of evidence indicates that surface roughness of titanium implants strongly affects the behaviour of cells. Clearly, more experimentation is required to demonstrate that both surface textured and porous implants are superior in terms of osseointegration and mechanical stability in different models.

8. FUTURE WORK

A surface engineering method has to be developed which will achieve surface modifications that promote biological interactions occurring at the scaffold surface tailored for tissue growth whilst still maintaining the bulk properties of the biomaterial. For achieving the above, the authors are investigating the possibility of ion implantation on titanium surface to create ridge patterns similar to the arc-like ridges which are aligned longitudinal like the human hair. Another investigation is based on using titanium wire mesh construct as scaffold for tissue growth that will remain permanently in the new bone.

9. CONCLUSIONS

Tissue engineering is set to revolutionize the treatment of patients and contribute significantly to life sciences in the coming years. Clearly, the field of TE needs to establish functional criteria that will help those who seek to design and manufacture these repairs and replacements. Scale-up, packaging, storage and handling properties are also critical. The implants must be capable of retaining their mechanical, structural, and biological integrity during surgical implantation. Understanding those conditions that preserve the character of the implants may be essential for the success of the tissue-engineered products. It is important to consider the principles of functional TE in the light of the role of novel growth factors and new biomaterials.

10. REFERENCES

1. **Long-Hao Li, Young-Min Kong, Hae-Won Kim, Young-Woon Kim, Hyoun-Ee Kim, Seong-Joo Heo, Jai-Young Koak**. (2004), "Improved biological performance of Ti due to surface modification by micro-arc oxidation", *Biomaterials*, 25, 2867-2875.

2. **Clark R.A.F**, (1996), The molecular and cellular biology of wound repair, 1-35, (2nd ed.) Plenum Press New York.

3. **Babensee J.E** and **Anderson J.M.**(1998), "Host response to tissue engineered devices", *Advanced Drug Delivery Review*, 33(1-2).

4. **Perka C** and **Sittinger M**, (2000) "Tissue engineered cartilage repair using cryopreserved and noncryopreserved chondrocytes", *Clinical Orthopedics*, 378: 245-254.

5. **Anseth K.R** and **Shastri V.R**, (1999), "Photopolymerizable degradable polyanhydrides with osteocompatability", *Nature Biotechnology*, 7(2), 156-159.

6. **Rachael H. Schmedlen, Kristyn S. Masters and Jennifer L. West**, (2002) "Photocrosslinkable polyvinyl alcohol hydrogels that can be modified with cell adhesion peptided for use in tissue engineering", *Biomaterials*, 23, 4325-4332.

7. **Lacouture M.E, Schaffer J.L, Klickstein L.B.** (2002), "A combination of type I collagen, fibronectin and vitronectin in supporting adhesion of mechanically strained osteoblasts", *J Bone Miner Res*, 17(3), 481-492.

8. **Cavallaro T.F**, and **Kemp P.D**, (1994), "Collagen fabrics as Biomaterials", *Biotechnology and Bioengineering*, 43, 781-791.

9. **Ramoshebi L.N, Matsaba T.N, et al**, (2002), "Tissue engineering: TGF-superfamily members and delivery systems in bone regeneration", *Exp. Rev. Mol. Med.*

10. **Lange R, Luthen F, Beck U, Rychly J, Baumann A, Nebe B.** (2002) "Cell-

extracellular matrix interaction and physico-chemical characteristics of titanium surfaces depend on the roughness of the material", *Biomolecular Engineering*, 19(2-6), 255-261.

11. **Ching-Hsin Ku, Dominique P. Pioletti, Martin Browne, Peter J. Gregson.** (2002), "Effect of different Ti-6Al-4V surface treatments on osteoblasts behaviour", *Biomaterials*, 23(6), 1447-1454.

12. **Johan W.M. Vehof, Paul HM. Spauwen, John A. Jansen.** (2000), "Bone formation calcium phosphate-coated titanium mesh", *Biomaterials*, 21, 2003-2009.

13. **Van den Dolder J, Farber E, Paul HM. Spauwen, Jansen J A.** (2003), "Bone tissue reconstruction using titanium fibre mesh combined with rat bone marrow stromal cells", *Biomaterials*, 24, 419-423.

14. *Proceedings of the WTEC Workshop on Tissue Engineering Research in the United States*, (2000), 175-178.

15. **Peter S. Donzelli, Robert L. Spilker, Gerard A. Ateshian and Van C. Mow,** (1999), "Contact analysis of biphasic transversely isotropic cartilage layers and correlations with tissue failure", *J. Biomech.*, 32(10), 1037-1047.

16. **Vunjak-Novakovixc G, Martin I** and **Obradovic B,** (1998), *J Orthop Res*, 17, 30-138.

17. **Hench L.L, Polak J.M, Xynos I.D** and **Buttery L.D.K,** (2000), "Bioactive materials to control cell cycle, *Mat. Res. Innovat*, 3, 313-323.

18. **Hench. L.L and Ethridge E.C** (1982), "Biomaterials: An interfacial Approach", *Academic Press*, New York.

19. **Kwan M.K, Coutts R.D, Woo S.L and Field FP,** (1989). *J Biomech*, 22: 921-930.

20. **Komi P.V,** (1990) J. Biomech. 23: 23-44, Simon S. R., (ed.) (1994) Orthopedic basic Science, *Am Acad Orthopedic Surgeons,* Rosemong, IL.

21. **Ham W,** (1969) *Histology*, J B Lippincot, Co., Philadelphia.

22. **Davies J.E,** (ed.) (1991) *The Bone-Biomaterial interface,* University of Toronto Press.

23. **Ratner B.D, Hoffman A.S, Schoen F.J** and **Lemons J.E,** (eds.) (2000), *Biomaterials Science* (2nd edition) Academic Press.

24. **Davies J.E,** (ed.) (1991) The Bone-Biomaterial interface, *University of Toronto Press.*

25. **Ratner B.D, Hoffman A.S, Schoen F.J, and Lemons J.E.** (eds.) (2000), Biomaterials Science (2nd edition) *Academic Press.*

26. **Scheideler L, Geis-Gerstorfer J, Kern B, Pfeiffer F, Rupp F, Weber H, Wolburg H.** (2003) "Investigation of cell reactions to microstructured implant surfaces", *Materials Science and Engineering*, C23, 455-459.

27. **Bigerelle M, Anselme K, Noel B, Ruderman I, Hardouin P, Iost A.** (2002), "Improvement in the morphology of Ti-based surfaces: a new process to increase in vitro human osteoblast response", *Biomaterials,* 23, 1563-1577.

28. **Stangl R, Pries A, Loos B, Muller M, Erben R.G.** (2004), "Influence of pores created by laser superfinishing on osteointegration of titanium alloy implants", *J Biomed Mater Res,* 69A, 444-453.

29. **Gotz H.E, Muller M, Emmel A, Holzwarth U, Erben R.G, Stangl R.** (2004), "Effect of surface finish on the osseointegration of laser treated titanium alloy implants", *Biomaterials,* 25, 4057-4064.

GCMM 2004
Editors: Prasad K D V Yarlagadda and S Narayanan
Copyright © 2005, Vellore Institute of Technology, Vellore, India
Publisher: Narosa Publishing House Pvt. Ltd., New Delhi, India

Challenges in Manufacturing Miniaturized Active Implants with Shape Memory Alloy Wires

Butsch M & Scafaru C

University of Applied Sciences Konstanz

E-mail: butsch@fh konstanz.de

Abstract

The purpose of this research is to manufacture and commercialize a miniaturized active implant by using shape memory alloy wires. These results are important for the extension of the bones when reconstructing the face and jaw (craniofacial skeleton) after e.g. an accident or resection of a tumour /1/. The previous work deals with devices that are activated by external hand tools. This sometimes causes infections because of the open wound. The manufacturing of such miniaturized active implants is a challenge owing to the special methods which are required for medical devices. The wires have to be connected to the housing. When heating the wires, the distinct shortening of the wires is used for the drive unit. On the other hand, the shortening of the wires is a problem for the connection to the housing. A solution to overcome this problem will be presented. The components of a ratchet mechanism that are driven by the shape memory alloy wires have to be machined in order to realize a smooth surface which is essential for the device to function. All metal parts are made of titanium. Finally, the assembly of the device and the testing have to be performed in a clean room according to the specifications which are established for medical devices. The sterilization has to be done with regard to the electronic components that are used for the device. Future work involves in producing a commercially viable implant.

Keywords

Active Implant, Shape Memory Alloy Wires, Machining of Titanium, Sterilisation of Active Implants

1. INTRODUCTION

The distraction of the craniofacial skeleton can be done by fully implantable, mechatronic distraction plates with wireless, percutaneous supply of energy. The drive unit of such a distraction plate can be miniaturized by using shape memory alloy wires which have a diameter of .2 mm (79 mil).

The innovation brought by this development is, among others, the drive by means of shape memory alloy wires, as well as the possibility to implant completely the device (**Fig.**). Shape memory alloys can be deformed in cold conditions with small energy consumption. If they are subsequently heated up, the alloys "remember" their original form and take back their initial non-deformed state. Therefore, very high tensions, close to the limit of elasticity of the memory alloy material, can be realized /2/.

387

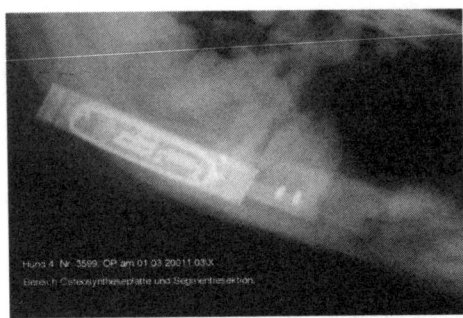

Fig. 1: Radiograph of a dog jaw implant /1/

Fig. 2: Distraction Plate (length 70 mm, width 10 mm, height 5 mm) /2/

The target of this new development is to minimize the infection hazard and the patient's risk, and to enhance the treatment comfort by the complete closure of the operated area. In addition, the cosmetic result is improved by minimizing the scar formation.

2. DESIGN OF THE MINIATURIZED ACTIVE IMPLANT /2/

The extension of the bone is performed by slowly separating the two neighbouring bones fragments. In this process, one of the bone fragments is connected to the tongue and the other one to the lower part of the housing. The separation is realized by means of a ratchet mechanism, consisting of several toothed parts, which engage alternatively, thus pushing the rack out of the housing. A lock blocks the mechanism, which prevents the tongue from slipping back into the housing. The teeth allow distraction steps of 0.45 mm. The maximal possible distraction displacement is about 15 mm.

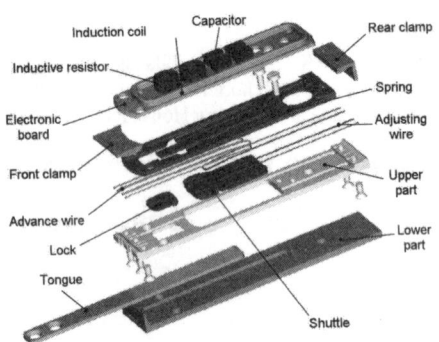

Fig. 3: Exploded view of the active implant /2/

A distraction speed of 1 mm per day enables the growth of the bone material and entrails.

The drive is generated by means of internally strained shape memory wires. These shape memory wires are heated by electrical current and are shortened by exceeding a certain temperature due to a phase transformation. During this wire shortening, forces are released, which can be mechanically used. In order to bring the wires to their initial length, external forces are necessary.

3. SHAPE MEMORY ALLOY WIRES
3.1 Characteristics of the Used Shape Memory Wires

The used shape memory wires were provided by the Company of Memory Metalle /3/, which at their turn procured the material from Dynalloy, Inc., the USA.

The wires are made of a nickel titanium alloy. The mass proportion of these elements determines considerably the transformation temperature A_f from martensite into austenite. At this temperature the wire is fully contracted. For the implant, an alloy with a transformation temperature of 95 °C was selected. This alloy is mainly used in actuator applications, where electrical current is used as actuation energy. The measured compositional average is around 49.6 to 49.4 at-% Ni. The Flexinol™ process can be applied to thin wires for use in straight wire actuators with maximum performance.

Further on, the most important mechanical characteristics are listed:

- Modulus of elasticity E: at body temperature 28,000 to 41,000 N/mm^2 above 95 °C 83,000 N/mm^2;
- Limit of elasticity: at body temperature 70 to 140 N/mm^2 above 95 °C 195 to 690 N/mm^2;
- Shortening of the wire above 95 °C approx. 3.5% of the length.

3.2 Electric Current Supply of the Shape Memory Wires

The advance wires and the adjusting wires are alternatively supplied with electrical current wirelessly by electronics. The advance wire is used for driving the tongue of the active implant, the adjusting wire assures the return movement of the ratchet mechanism into the starting state and stretches the advance wire (stretches it again as far as the original length). The adjusting wire is stretched by the advance wire. The strength developed during the functioning process amounts to 12 N per wire. To bring the wire to its initial form, a force of maximum 4 N is required.

The wireless control of the shape memory wires is achieved by means of integrated electronics, a sending coil and a transmitter. The integrated electronics is placed directly on the active implant and will be implanted along with it. It consists of two-coupled oscillating circuits with different resonant frequencies. Both oscillating circuits are electrically connected with advance wire and adjusting wire. The energy connection takes place by means of an induction coil, which serves as a receiver, and a sending coil. The sending coil is found in a hand piece that will be placed in the vicinity of the implanted device so as to initialize a distraction step from outside the body. The sending coil is connected to the sender with power electronics and control electronics. The control adjusts the sending frequency optimally, so that independently of the distance between sender and receiver, the oscillating circuits are each time in resonance. The switching between the two oscillating circuits, i.e. between the advance and adjusting wires, is realized by shifting a switch on the sender.

3.3. The Connection Method

A particular manufacturing challenge is the connection of the shape memory wires to the relating parts. There are the following requirements, considering the special characteristics of the wires, as described at 1.1:
- secure connection during the load cycles;
- stretching and shortening of up to 5% of the wire length;
- temperatures above 100 °C;
- loads close to the limit of elasticity of the material (up to 20 N per wire with 0.2 mm in diameter).

3.3.1. Crimping /3/

Using crimping techniques is a cost effective way, and special types of terminators are provided for example by Memory Metalle Company /3/.

The problems with crimping are the process security and the achievable strength. By using wires of 0.2 mm in diameter for active implants, it was not possible to obtain reliable results for the above mentioned stress.

3.3.2. Soldering

The soldering process is discarded due to the necessary biocompatibility of the assigned materials and the high loads.

3.3.3. Welding

Welding NiTi alloys is possible. For the connection of the small-diameter wires to the parts the laser welding is appropriate. As regards the laser welding, the energy is locally targeted, thus the different heat discharge in the wire and in the parts does not play any role. The disadvantage is represented by the complex technology at small diameters, which at the time of the prototype manufacturing was not available.

3.3.4. Clamping

The shape memory wire is led through a hole in the upper part which, after the detour in a groove of the upper part, is clamped by means of a clamping plate that will be fastened with M1 Bolts. In the upper part there are the pierced holes for the bolts, in the clamping plate is the M1 thread.

The wires must also be put into contact with the electronics. Since no great forces arise in this case, a crimping process was adopted.

389

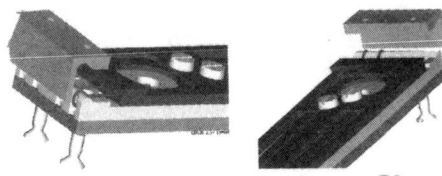

Fig. 4: Clamps of the shape memory wires /2/

4. PARTS MADE OF TITANIUM
4.1. Biocompatible Titanium Alloys /4,5/

For the parts of the active implant the medically certified TiAl4V alloy is used. The most important mechanical characteristics are specified, as follows:

- Modulus of elasticity E: 105.000 to 120.000 N/mm^2;
- Limit of elasticity $R_{p0.2}$: 885 N/mm^2;
- Tensile strength R_m: 985 N/mm^2.

An important factor for the biocompatibility of titanium and titanium alloys is the formation of a stable and pure titanium oxide layer. In many clinical investigations the biocompatibility of the TiAlV connections was confirmed.

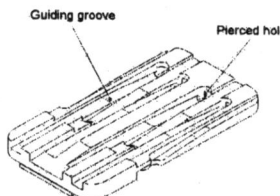

Fig. 5: Example of a construction part: the shuttle with the dimensions 10 mm x 7 mm; Thickness: 2.5 mm

4.2. Machining of the Titanium Parts /6/

The titanium and titanium alloys can be machined through procedures similar to those of the austenitic steel, however the following must be considered:

- The cutting tool is highly thermally stressed, because the titanium and its alloys possess considerably worse heat conductivity;
- Compared to steel, titanium has a much smaller elasticity module and, therefore, breaks due to strong shear forces;
- Titanium tends to weld with the tool.

Therefore, titanium must be machined with slower cutting speed, relatively ample and even advance motion and under plentiful supply of cooling fluid. The tool must be fastened as vibration-free as possible and possess a very sharp cutting edge. Hard surface layers lead to increased wearing of the tools, but owing to biocompatibility, they should not be removed by pickling.

For the drill heads are used high-speed steels and hard alloys. Amongst the hard alloys, the tungsten carbide with cobalt bond has proved to be the best.

Due to the tendency of the titanium to weld with the tool, the climb milling is preferred to the conventional milling. Thus, the comma-shaped splinter is detached in its thinnest spot, and damages to the drill head, due to the forming of the build-up edge and sticking of the splinters, are reduced to the minimum. The effective cutting angle of the drill head should be by tungsten carbides 0° and the draft angle of 12°. For the parts presented above, drill heads of 1mm diameter were also used.

5. ASSEMBLING IN THE CLEAN ROOM AND STERILIZATION /4/

The presented active implants are so-called long-term implants, which remain implanted in the body longer than 29 days. Having in view the USA regulations of the FDA, the assembly is necessary to be made in a clean room with high cleanness standard.

Considering the electronics and plastics used, the steam sterilization and the gamma radiation sterilization are less appropriate. A proper procedure is the gas sterilization with ethylene oxide, which, nevertheless, needs a long exhalation.

6. REFERENCES

1. **Kremer, M., Butsch, M., Schnell, M., Genecov, CD, Salyer, K.,** (2001), "Miniaturized Mechatronic Distraction Plate for University-Directional Internal Distraction - Technical Concept, Design feature and Preliminary Experimental Results", *3rd International Congress on Cranial and Facial Bone Distraction Process,* Paris.

2. **Butsch, M., Schnell, M.,** (2001) "Mechatronic Osteosynthesis Plate", *Final Report at the Federal Ministry for Education and Research,* Germany.

3. **Memory Metalle GmbH** www.memry.com (2004) *Info Sheets No.2* ("Shape Memory Alloys"), *No.8* ("The NiTiNOL Soldering Kit – Product Description"), *No. 10* ("Standard Crimping Techniques"), *No. 13* ("NiTinol Alloy Types, Conditions and Surfaces").

4. **Wintermantel, E., Suk-Woo, H.,** (1998) "Biocompatible Materials and Building Methods", *Springer Publishing House*, Berlin, Germany.

5. **Peter, M., Leyens, C, Kumpfert, J.** (1998) "Titanium and Titanium Alloys", *Material Information Society*, Frankfurt, Germany.

6. **ThyssenKrupp www.deutschetitan.de** (2004) References to the Machine Cutting Treatment of Titanium and Titanium Alloys.

GCMM 2004
Editors: Prasad K D V Yarlagadda and S Narayanan
Copyright © 2005, Vellore Institute of Technology, Vellore, India
Publisher: Narosa Publishing House Pvt. Ltd., New Delhi, India

Effect of Cryogenic Treatment on Corrosion Resistance of Ball Bearing Steel

Hariharan P & Sangeeth Kumar P

Department of Manufacturing Engineering, College of Engineering,
Anna University, Chennai-25, India

Rajadurai A

Department of production Technology, MIT Campus,
Anna University, Chennai-44, India

Mohanlal D & Renganarayanan S

Department of Mechanical Engineering, College of Engineering,
Anna University, Chennai-25, India

Email: hari@annauniv.edu, psangeeth@yahoo.com

Abstract

Rolling element bearings are of paramount importance to almost all forms of rotating machinery. Bearings that are exposed to corrosive fluids or a corrosive environment require corrosion resistance. Cryogenic Treatment after hardening is a one time permanent process that influences the entire section of the component and causes improvement in tribological properties and dimensional stability.

In this paper an attempt has been made to study the effect of cryogenic treatment on corrosion resistance of bearing steel. Two treatment procedures namely, conventionally Heat Treated (HT) and Cryogenically Treated (HCT) were considered. Electrochemical corrosion testing of HT and HCT samples was performed. It was found that the corrosion rate of the HT specimens is 10 to 15% lesser than that of HCT specimens. Salt Spray test was also conducted on HT and HCT samples as per ASTM B117 standard. Test duration was varied between 24 and 72 hours. The weight loss on corrosion was measured. The formation of very fine mixture of carbide and ferrite in HCT specimens in comparison with the presence of coarse mixture of carbide and ferrite in HT specimens could be the reason for the better corrosion resistance of HT specimens.

Keywords
Ball Bearing Steel, Cryogenic Treatment, Corrosion Resistance, Salt Spray Test, Potentiostat.

1. INTRODUCTION

Rolling element bearings are used in almost all forms of rotating machinery. Bearings are generally exposed to corrosive fluids or a corrosive environment hence they require corrosion resistance. Cryogenic Treatment of steels after hardening is a unique process that influences the entire section of the component and causes improvement in tribological properties and dimensional stability.

Cryogenic treatment involves cooling the hardened samples to 80 K (-193 °C) slowly from room temperature, held at that temperature for a long time and then brought back to room temperature and finally a low temperature tempering is done.

Recently, interest in cryogenic treatment of ferritic and non-ferritic alloys has increased due to the large potential for enhanced performance. Potential property enhancements include increased hardness, wear resistance, dimensional stability and intergranular corrosion resistance [1].

Corrosion is defined as the destruction or deterioration of a material because of reaction with its environment [2]. The wear resistance of bearing steel was improved after cryogenic treatment [3]. The fatigue properties of cryogenically treated AISI 304L cruciform welded joints have shown improvement. The strain induced martensites formed during the cryogenic treatment and the associated generation of compressive stresses in the weld metal are considered to be effective in fatigue life extension of welded joints in the high cycle regime [4].

The present study seeks to investigate the effect of cryogenic treatment on corrosion resistance of AISI 51100 bearing steel.

2. EXPERIMENTAL WORK

2.1. Material Selection

Many of the bearings produced today are made of AISI 51100 high – carbon, chromium bearing steel. The bearings made out of this steel is conventionally hardened and tempered prior to application. Due to the presence of carbon about 1%,there is a possibility of retention of austenite in considerable quantity after the heat treatment and this retained austenite may affect service behavior of the bearing. Cryogenic treatment after hardening could nullify the retained austenite and improve tribological behaviour. So AISI 51100 bearing steel was selected for the investigation. AISI 51100 bar stock of 17 mm diameter was purchased. Spectrometric analysis of the sample was carried out and

found to be as per the requirements of the standard. The test result is shown in Table 1.

Table 1: Spectrometric analysis of the bearing steel

Element	C	Cr	Mn	P	S
% Weight	0.977	1.15	0.499	0.024	0.035
Element	Mo	Ni	Cu	Si	Fe
% Weight	0.008	0.17	0.062	0.201	Balance

2.2. Sample Preparation

Specimens for corrosion test were prepared as per ASTM G3, G5 standards for electrochemical testing and ASTM B117 for salt spray test. For electrochemical testing the specimen was brazed with a current conducting copper rod on one of its face. Then the brazed side of the specimen was covered with epoxy resin (Araldite). The exposed face of the specimen was ground with abrasive paper up to 1200 grit. The polished specimens were cleaned with double distilled water, acetone and then dried.

2.3. Conventional Treatment

For the conventional heat treatment (HT) namely, hardening and tempering, specimens were placed in a pre heated electric resistance furnace to a temperature of 873K (600 °C). They were then heated to the austenitizing temperature of 1123K (850 °C) and kept at this temperature for one hour (soaking period). They were then quenched in an oil bath maintained at a temperature of 323K (50 °C). They were then tempered by heating them to 473K (200 °C) with one hour soaking period followed by air cooling to room temperature.

2.4. Cryogenic Treatment

Cryogenic treatment of the hardened specimens was done in the cryogenic chamber where the cooling medium used is liquid nitrogen. The samples were cryogenic treated at a temperature of 80K (-193 °C) for a period of 24 hours.

The basic steps involved are

a. Ramp Down: The ramp down in temperature is an important part of the process. When the ramp down is too quick there is a possibility of inducing residual stresses into the part. Ramp down is critical in that it is possible to induce cracks in the part by cooling it too quickly.

b. Hold: The micro structural changes are realized in this part of the treatment. Typical hold times are in the range of ten to 30 hours.

c. Ramp Up: Ramp up time is also important. A quick rise in temperature may result in fissure, therefore a gradual rise in temperature is to be followed. Typical ramp up times can be anywhere from ten to twenty hours. The Cryogenic Treatment cycle is shown in Figure 1.

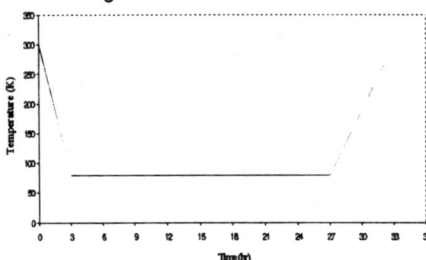

Fig.1: Cryogenic Treatment Cycle

2.5. Corrosion Testing

1) Hardened Tempered (HT) and 2) Hardened Cryogenic treated and Tempered (HCT) samples were tested for electrochemical corrosion and salt spray.

2.5.1. Electrochemical Corrosion Testing

Since most corrosion is electrochemical in nature, electrochemical techniques were used to monitor corrosion. The test was carried out using the equipment "Potentiostat Galvanostat 12", AUTOLAB. Seawater taken from Bay of Bengal was used as electrolyte. Test samples were made as anode in a special electrochemical cell, and corrosion "finger print " of the metal in the seawater environment was obtained by electronically monitoring corrosion current as the cell

potential was varied. These tests are called polarization studies.

In electrochemical studies, a metal sample with a surface area of a few square centimeters is used to model the metal in a corroding system. The metal sample is immersed in a solution typical of the metal's environment in the system being studied. Additional electrodes are immersed in the solution, and all the electrodes are connected to a Potentiostat. A Potentiostat allows us to change the potential of the metal sample in a controlled manner and measures the current that flows as a function of potential. In this study, the cell used was a conventional three-electrode Pyrex glass cell with a platinum counter electrode and a Saturated Calomel Electrode (SCE) as reference. The working steel rod electrode was embedded in araldite, so that its cross section area was in contact with the solution. The Current Vs Potential was recorded by changing the electrode potential automatically with the scan rate of $1mVs^{-1}$. Electrochemical Impedance Spectra (EIS) were carried out at E_{corr} with the electrochemical system Frequency Response Analyser (FRA) that included a Potentiostat model PGSTAT 12. AISI 51100 Bearing steel with the exposing surface was used as the working electrode.

2.5.2. Salt Spray Test

The purpose of an accelerated corrosion test, such as the salt spray test, is to duplicate, in the laboratory, the corrosion performance of a material in the field. Basically, the salt spray test procedure involves the spraying of a salt solution onto the samples being tested. This is done inside a temperature-controlled chamber. Typically, the solution is a 5% salt (sodium chloride) solution. The samples being tested are inserted into the chamber and then the salt-containing solution is sprayed as a very fine fog mist over the samples. The temperature within the chamber is maintained constant. Since the spray is continual, the samples are constantly wet, and thus, constantly subject to corrosion. Through the years, there have been some new twists added to better simulate special environmental conditions, but the most common procedure is as described in ASTM B 117 Standard Practice for Operating Salt Spray (Fog) Apparatus. Within the chamber, the samples are rotated frequently so that all samples are exposed as uniformly as possible to the salt spray mist.

Salt spray test was carried out on 1) Hardened and Tempered (HT), 2) Hardened, Cryogenic treated and Tempered specimens (HCT) to find out the weight loss due to corrosion. Specimens in each type were taken for test and the tests were carried out in three different time period i.e., 24 hrs, 48 hrs and 72 hrs.

The specimens were cleaned as specified in the ASTM B117 standard and then the weight of the specimens was taken, before test in a digital balance with an accuracy of 1mg. After weighing the specimens were given for salt spray test. The samples were withdrawn from the salt spray chamber after the prescribed period of testing and cleaned as specified in the ASTM B117 Standard. After cleaning, weights of samples were measured. The percentage weight loss was computed for both the treated samples (HT, HCT).

The details of the testing parameters are given below.

PH of salt solution : 6.5 – 7.2
Solution concentration : 5% NaCl
Test temperature : 35°C

The weights of the samples before and after salt spray test were measured in electronic weighing machine

3. RESULTS AND DISCUSSION

3.1. Electrochemical Testing

The results of electrochemical corrosion studies are shown in Figure 2 and 3.

The Open Circuit Potential (OCP)-time measurements curves for HT and HCT samples are shown Figure 2.

The Open Circuit Potential for Hardened Cryogenic Treated (HCT) sample is almost constant whereas for the Hardened and Tempered (HT) sample the Open Circuit Potential decreases with time till it attains the steady state potential. The HCT sample behaves like a noble potential than HT sample.

The result of polarization studies is shown in Figure 3. The I_{corr}, E_{corr} and Corrosion rates were calculated from the curves using GPES V 4.9 (General Purpose Electrochemical System) software. They are tabulated in Table 2.

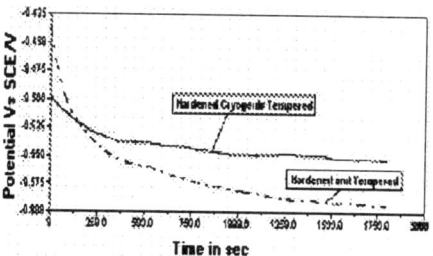

Fig. 2: OCP-time measurements of HT and HCT samples.

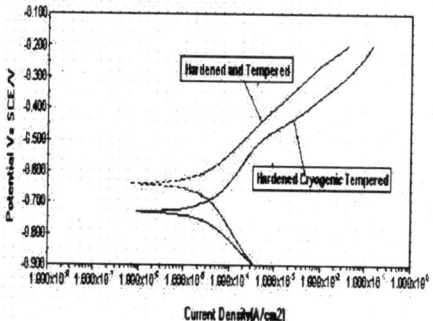

Fig.3: Cathodic and Anodic Polarization curve observed on the samples

Table 2: Results from Electrochemical

Treatment	I_{corr} A/Cm^2	E_{corr} V	Corrosion Rate mm/year
HT	3.791x 10^{-6}	-0.643	4.78E-2
HCT	4.187 x 10^{-6}	-0.732	5.279 E-2

Testing

It was found that the corrosion rate (Table 2) was slightly higher for Hardened Cryogenic and Tempered sample (HCT) than HT sample. It means that cryogenic treated samples offer less resistance to corrosion when compared to HT samples. But only marginal difference in corrosion rate between the two treated samples were observed.

Scanning Electron Micrographs of HT and HCT samples were taken at different positions of the samples and at different magnifications after electrochemical corrosion testing and are shown in Figure 4 and 5 respectively.

Figure 4 Scanning Electron Micrographs of AISI 51100 Ball Bearing Steel after Hardening and Tempering (a,b&c)

Figure 5 Scanning Electron Micrographs of AISI 51100 Ball Bearing Steel after Hardening Cryogenic treatment and Tempering (a,b&c)

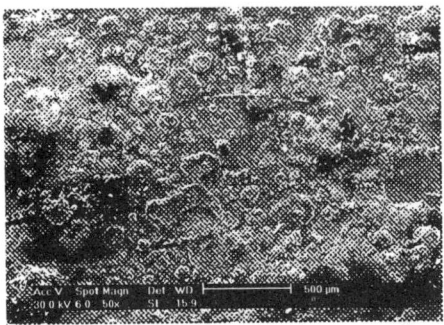

Fig.4 a): SEM Micrograph of HT sample shows distributed semi adherent cracked corroded particles coarser in size

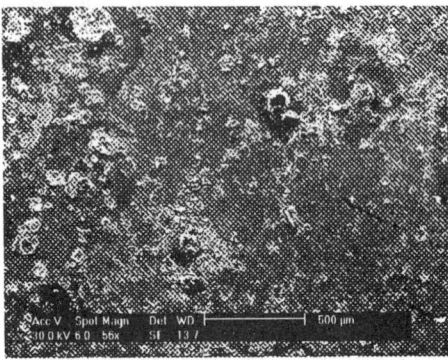

Fig.5 a): SEM Micrograph of HCT sample shows the presence of fine corroded particles widely spread and uniformly distributed

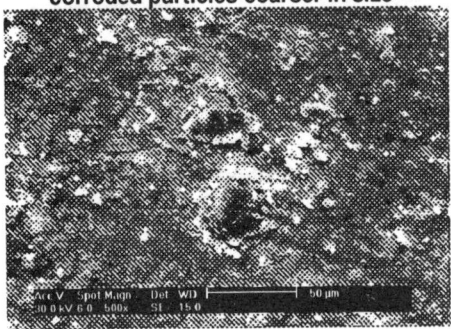

Fig.4 b): SEM Micrograph of HT sample shows corrosion is intensive at selected location but only at few parts, due to the presence of coarser carbides

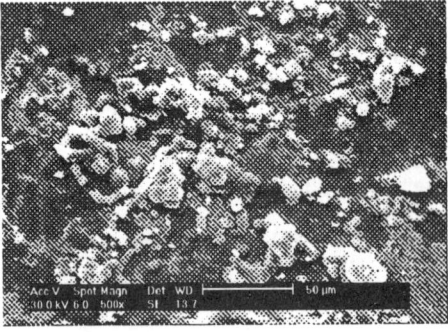

Fig.5 b): SEM Micrograph of HCT sample shows Distributed corrosion on a fine scale, due to the presence of fine carbides

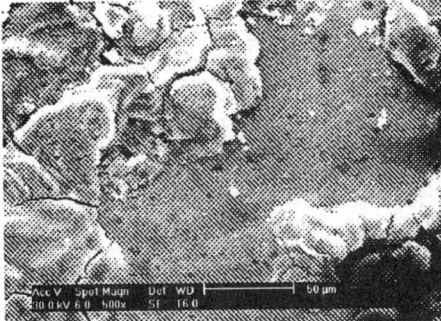

Fig.4 c): SEM Micrograph of HT Sample shows the presence of cracked corrosion product, which exposes the new parent material for further corrosion.

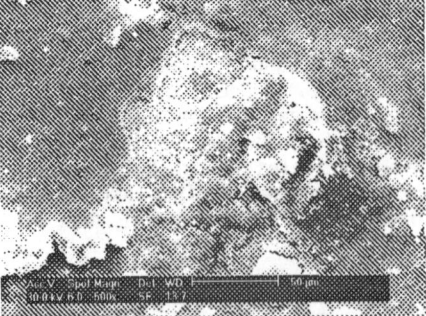

Fig. 5 c): SEM Micrograph of HCT sample shows the presence of lose deposits of corroded particles and spalling of corrosion products away.

From the micrographs it is inferred that corrosion is more widely spread in the HCT samples than HT samples. This may be due to the precipitation of fine eta carbide particles in HCT samples which leads to the distributed corrosion on a fine scale. Hence the micrographs results correlate with the one obtained by Electro chemical corrosion test. Moreover it is observed that there are loosely adhered corroded particles on the surface of both the treated samples.

3.2. Salt Spray Test

The percentage of weight loss of the HT samples and HCT samples are shown in the Figure 6.

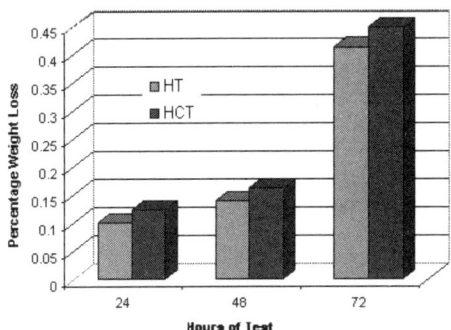

Fig.6: Percentage weight loss due to corrosion for HT and HCT samples.

Red rust was noticed after 72 hours on both HT and HCT samples. It can be inferred from the chart that the percentage weight loss for HCT samples are more when compared to HT samples. But the difference in percentage weight loss is only marginal. Hence it can be inferred from the salt spray test that cryogenic treated samples offer less resistance to corrosion when compared to HT samples.

4. CONCLUSION

The effect of cryogenic treatment on corrosion resistance of AISI 51100 bearing steel was studied and the following conclusions were made.

1) Electrochemical corrosion test reveals that Hardened, Cryogenic treated and Tempered (HCT) sample behaves like a noble potential than Hardened, Tempered (HT) sample but I_{corr} value of HT is lower than that of HCT sample.

2) Corrosion rate of HT sample is 4.78×10^{-2} mm/year whereas the corresponding value for HCT sample is 5.279×10^{-2} mm/year.

3) Micrographs from SEM reveal that corrosion is more widely spread in HCT samples than HT samples. This is due to the precipitation of fine η carbide particles in HCT samples. Hence the results correlate with the one obtained by Electro chemical corrosion test.

4) The salt spray test indicates that HT samples have comparatively better corrosion resistance than HCT sample. Red rust was noted on both the treated samples after 72 hours of salt spray test.

Thus the Cryogenic treatment of AISI 51100 bearing steel reduces corrosion resistance marginally.

5. REFERENCES

1. **Collins D.N.**, Deep Cryogenic Treatment of Tool Steels- a Review, Heat Treatment of Metals, 1996, pp 40-42.
2. **Mars G. Fontana**, Corrosion Engineering, McGraw-Hill International Book Company, Third Edition, 1987.
3. **Fanju Meng**, Kohsuke Tagashira and Hideaki Sohama, Wear Resistance and Microstructure of Cryogenic Treated Fe-1.4 Cr-1C Bearing Steel, Scripta Metallurgica et Materialia, Vol 31, No.7, 1994,pp 865-868.
4. **Johan Singh.P**, Fatigue life improvements of AISI 304L cruciform welded joints by cryogenic treatment, Engineerig Failure Analysis, 2003, pp 1-12.
5. **Sidney H. Avner**, Introduction to Physical Metallurgy, McGraw-Hill International Book Company, Second Edition, 1979.

GCMM 2004
Editors: Prasad K D V Yarlagadda and S Narayanan
Copyright © 2005, Vellore Institute of Technology, Vellore, India
Publisher: Narosa Publishing House Pvt. Ltd., New Delhi, India

New Multiphase Steels used for Car Body Applications

Gümpel, P. and Strittmatter, J.

Fachhochschule Konstanz, University of Applied Sciences, D-78464 Konstanz, Germany
Institut für Werkstoffsystemtechnik Thurgau an der Fachhochschule Konstanz, CH-8274
Tägerwilen, Switzerland

guempel@fh-konstanz.de and info@witg.ch

Abstract

In recent years a lot of new developments in lightweight construction for car bodies have been done. One development was the use of aluminium in designing the whole car body with this light material. Another development, which leads to an extremely good relationship between lightweight construction, safety, easy to repair and easy to recycle, was the development of new steels, the so called multiphase steels with new hardening mechanism. Tensile strengths reaching from 500MPa to more than 1400MPa can be achieved by a specific combination of the microstructure components in combination with individual process parameters. The differences in the properties of these materials like mild steel, dual phase steel, duplex steel and TRIP (transformation induced plasticity) steel are presented. Comparisons of the ductility-strength relation and also the specific energy absorption, between these different steel grades and aluminium and magnesium based materials, give the data basis for engineers for modern car body design.

Key Words:

Lightweight construction, aluminium, multiphase steels, mild steel, TRIP steel, dual phase steel

1. INTRODUCTION

The greater environmental awareness of the European population and an economic pressure gave considerable pressure on the automotive industry. The demand for lighter vehicles with reduced fuel consumption was the main incentive for the development of light automobiles through the combination of design, new materials and optimised joining technology. In order to fulfil the customers expectations and the legal requirements and standards, car manufacturers focus the main design criteria of a modern car on reduced weight and high safety. **Table 1** gives a comparison of an old fashioned and a most recent approach to a small sportive car, the 1959 Austin Mini with the 2001 BMW Mini. It demonstrates the trend of the automotive industry and the significant role of weight reduction in the development of current cars. The main design criteria for modern car bodies are safety and light weight, both targets can be supported by new steels [1].

Table 1: Comparison of 1959 and 2001 Mini car

	Austin Mini 1959	BMW Mini 2001	Change %
Length overall, m	3,05	3,62	19
Width overall, m	1,41	1,69	20
Kerb weight, kg	587	1050	79
Engine	4 cylinder, 8V, petrol	4 cylinder, 16V, petrol	-
Engine displacement, ml	848	1598	88
Max. power, bhp	37	90	143
Compression ratio	8,5:1	10,6:1	25
Max. torque, Nm	59,6	149	150
Gearbox (manual)	4 speed	5 speed	-
Power assisted steering	No	Yes	-
Seat belts	No	Yes	-
Max. speed. Km/h	115	185	60
Acceleration 0-100 Km/h, s	28,7	9,2	-68
Fuel consumption, mpg	45 (touring)	42,2 (EU cycle)	-6
CO2 emissions	Not required in 1959	163 g/km	-
Power/weight ratio, bhp/kg	0,063	0,086	37
Crash requirements	Not required in 1959	EuroNCAP	-

Automotive lightweight design can be achieved in several ways which could be associated with each other: materials lightweight selection and constructive lightweight design. With the material lightweight selection a material is selected on the basis of the occurring loads, the selected materials resist better these loads than the standard materials. In this way, material and therefore mass can be economised in some places, when e.g. the load bearing cross section area is reduced. In the case of the constructive lightweight design, the topology or the final shape of the component is adapted. By disappearing of unloaded material areas the mass of a component can be reduced without any loss or the function. In the recent years both ways for reducing weight have been used and especially the substitution of steel by lighter materials such as aluminium or magnesium could be observed. Depending on the lower Young's Module a lot of design works have to be done to give the necessary stiffness to these components. Another problem which was solved during the developments in the last years was the technique for joining parts of different light materials, but nevertheless this is still a problem especially in the case of repairing the vehicles.

Nowadays a multi-material design is used, this means complying the demands of every part by an optimised material selection. The result is a mixture of different materials as shown in **Figure 1**. The innovative competition between the materials as steel, aluminium and polymer materials has a big importance for automotive lightweight design. A full aluminium car body is an alternative development which will not be realised in a wide range. According to the average aluminium application in automobiles **Figure 2**) in Western Europe, the part of aluminium in the whole automobiles (car body, motor, chassis.....) will be rising from 100 kg in 2000 up to about 220 kg in 2015. In a full aluminium car body the weight rate of aluminium is even now in the range of 258 kg (AUDI A2).

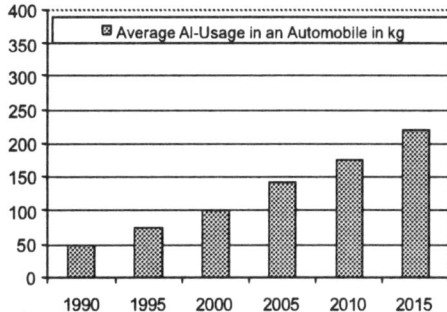

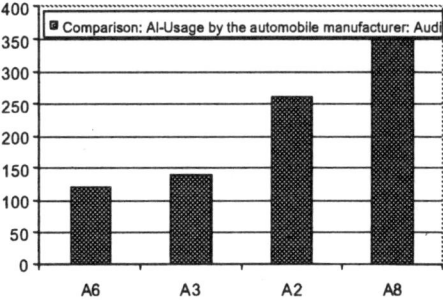

Figure 2: Average aluminium application (kg) in automobiles in Western Europe [3]

In this context, new materials should be developed not only for weight reduction but also to improve the crash safety of vehicles. These materials must combine an increased formability with a high strength level at a wide temperature and strain rate spectrum. Multiphase steels, among them especially dual phase and TRIP steels, feature promising results in this field, while their extraordinary mechanical properties can be tailored and adjusted by processing.

Parallel to the demand for stronger steels, the formability of the newly developed steel types acquired increasing importance, because the constructional requirements called for growing complexity of the geometries which had to be implemented with these materials. The more exacting demands for passive vehicle safety constituted a further driving force for material developments in recent years. A new family of steel grades, called the "multiphase steels", was devised in the course of time to meet these more exacting requirements. In the last years a lot of new developments in steel materials have been done and some of these new developments, especially in the field of high strength steels, are reported below.

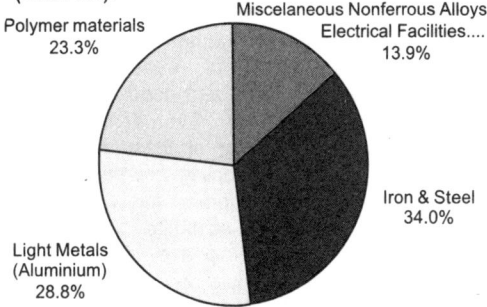

Figure 1: Shares of different materials at the total weight of AUDI A2 (895 kg) [2]

2. MODERN HIGH STRENGTH STEELS

Many steels have been developed in order to match the requirements of the automotive industry which can shortly be summarised as a sufficient combination of strength and formability. An example for the chemical composition of several cold-rolled steels for car bodies is given in **Table 2**. These steels have been thoroughly investigated with regard to formability and dynamic behaviour [4]. The family of multiphase steels include Dual-phase (DP), Residual-austenite (RA), Complex-phase (CP), Martensite-phase (MS) and Partly-martensite-phase (PM) steels. Amongst the well-known hardening mechanisms like precipitation hardening, solid-solution hardening and grain refinement this steel category make use of the particular characteristic of steel to transform into various microstructures in dependency on the composition and temperature. **Figure 3** schematically shows the micro structural components of multiphase steels.

Table 2: Examples for designation and chemical composition of cold-rolled steels for car bodies

Steel designation	Steel type	C	Si	Mn	P	Al	misc.
DC04	LC	0,025	0,01	0,19	0,008	0,054	-
DC06	IF	0,005	0,01	0,11	0,008	0,033	0,05 Ti
H260YD	IF-HS	0,003	0,01	0,35	0,050	0,030	0,04 Nb, 0,02 Ti
H180B	BH	0,006	0,01	0,02	0,018	0,054	-
H260B	BH	0,076	0,02	0,44	0,086	0,041	
H250G1	HSLA	0,035	0,01	0,02	0,008	0,036	0,03 Ti
H260P	Rephos	0,080	0,50	0,70	0,100	0,02	-
H320LA	HSLA	0,006	0,01	0,04	0,007	0,038	0,04 Nb
H300X	DP	0,082	0,07	1,48	0,017	0,059	
TRIP 700Z	TRIP	0,200	0,05	1,60	0,015	1.800	-
DOCOL 1400	Marten-sitic	0,170	0,50	1,59	0,010	0,046	

The different steel types can be characterised by their microstructure or their alloying concept:

LC: low carbon unalloyed Al-killed low carbon steel; extra deep-drawing grade.
IF: interstitial free steel; micro alloyed extra deep-drawing grade.
IF-HS: high-strength interstitial free steel, strengthened by P addition.
BH: bake hardening steel grades, which show additional strengthening during paint bake treatment by controlled C ageing.
HSLA: high strength low alloy steel, strengthened by micro alloying with Nb or Ti.
Rephos: P alloyed high strength steels.

DP: dual phase steels with a microstructure of ferrite and martensite islands, also called duplex steels.
TRIP: transformation induced plasticity steels with a microstructure of ferrite, bainite and retained austenite.
Martensitic: partly (PM) or fully martensitic steels (MS).

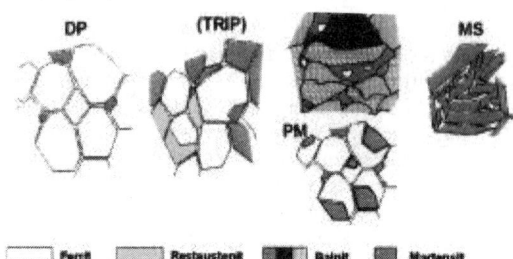

Figure 3: Microstructural hardening of multiphase steels [5]

The material properties are essentially defined by the combination of the microstructural components with different degrees of hardness. With these materials tensile strength values between 500MPa and 1400MPa can be realised. The tensile/ductility-ratio is much better compared to the conventional steels (**Figure 4**). While in Dual-phase steels the soft ferritic phase is prevailing, a Martensite-phase steel consists of very hard martensitic phase. A particular steel type are the Residual-austenite steels (TRIP-steels) where a small proportion of austenite remains in the ferritic-bainitic basic matrix. The austenite transforms into hard martensite during forming to a component which leads to a significant improvement of the formability and high component strengths. The Complex-phase steels consists of bainite with some traces of ferrite and martensite. Especially the combination of hard and soft components in the microstructure of these multiphase steels enables this extraordinary combination of tensile strength and ductility. The development of the desired microstructure is difficult and needs a special cooling path in the Time-Temperature-Transformation behaviour of these materials. **Figure 5** shows the cooling course through the respective TTT-diagram for hot rolled Dual-phase, Residual-austenite, Complex-phase and Martensitic-phase steels. The formation of pearlite would be detrimental and therefore must be avoided.

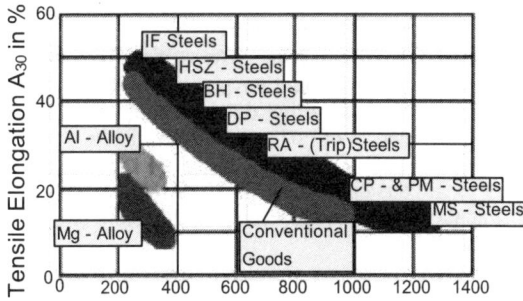

Figure 4: Increasing tensile/ductility-ratio by using multiphase steels [5]

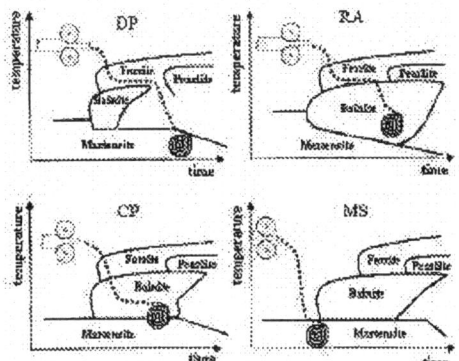

Figure 5: Temperature-time-schedule for producing different microstructures of hot rolled steels [6]

For dual phase steels, which consists of 70 to 90 vol.-% of ferrite and 5 to 20 vol.-% of martensite in the shape of fine islands (**Figure 3**), the cooling rate must be low enough to enable the transformation of this high rate of austenite to ferrite to take place. This transformation rate has to be associated with a carbon enrichment of the austenite, and at the same time has to be high enough to avoid the formation of pearlite and higher amounts of bainite and to ensure the formation of martensite at low coiling temperatures of about 200 °C. Hence, a holding step has to be inserted in the temperature range of the maximum ferrite formation kinetics or the alloying concept has to be adapted in order to accelerate the ferrite formation. In practice most Duplex steels contain small amounts of bainite and or retained austenite.

Numerous alloying concepts have been developed for Dual-phase steels in order to adjust the desired microstructure and properties [7]. The alloying elements change the thermodynamic stability of the phases and

the kinetics of the transformations whereby the transformation temperatures are shifted (**Figure 6**). The transformations are either promoted or hindered and the phase distribution is altered. Additionally, the elements might act as solid solution or precipitation hardeners and affect the grain size. In the modern CP-steels all kinds of hardening mechanism such as grain refining, precipitation hardening, solid solution hardening come into operation.

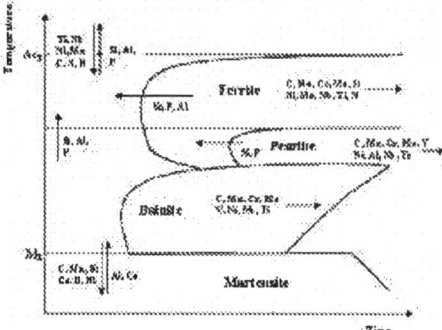

Figure 6: Influence of alloying elements on the transformation behaviour of steels [6]

Figure 6 shows the effect of various alloying elements on the transformation behaviour. The alloy design is of decisive importance for the transformation behaviour and for setting the desired microstructure. Different phase transformations during hot rolling, intercritical annealing, cooling, isothermal holding in the temperature range of bainite formation, and straining are modified thus resulting in superior mechanical behaviour.

The material properties of these steels can be optimised by using the micro-alloying elements niobium and titanium. They act in solid solution and in precipitated condition, in combination with the elements carbon or nitrogen. Niobium and titanium exert a remarkable influence on grain size development, transformation behaviour, carbon enrichment of the austenite, and martensite nucleation. This renders process control much easier and allows less demanding process routes. The benefit of using niobium in comparison with the traditional P-alloyed DP-steel is shown in **Table 3**. The Nb-alloyed variant showed considerably higher strength values with a acceptable reduction in the elongation values. Due to the finer grain size, the yield strength ratio is similar, even at this higher strength level. Furthermore , the fine grain size of the Nb-alloyed variant thereby has an extremely favourable effect on hole expansion value [6].

Table 3: Material properties of two different types of DP-steel [6]

			Nb	P
Microstructure	Ferrite	%	70	75
	Pearlite	%	-	10
	Bainite	%	10	-
	Martensite	%	20	15
	Mean Grain Size	µm	2,5	4,2

Mechanical Properties, transversal	Y.S	MPa	496	364
	T.S	MPa	618	487
	T.E	%	26,8	35

3. TRIP AIDED STEELS

The transformation induced plasticity means a phase transformation behaviour induced by mechanical stresses. Materials with a low strength and good plasticity for car body parts can be used and if there is a crash situation an excellent energy adsorption behaviour (**Figure 7**) is shown. Benefits of the TRIP-steels are the extraordinary strength-ductility relationship, the high strain hardening potential, the temperature sensitivity and the stress state dependency of the mechanical properties. The pre-requisite for the TRIP-effect is a high amount of transformable austenite in the microstructure.

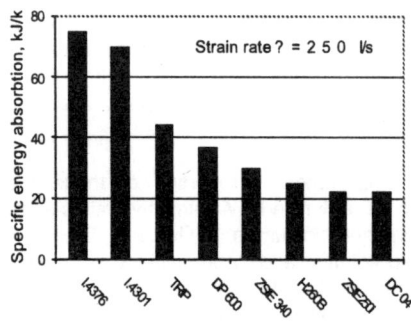

Figure 7: Specific energy absorption during tensile testing of different cold-rolled steels [8]

As it can be seen in **Figure 7** the high alloyed metastable austenitic stainless steels 1.4376 and 1.4301 offer a greater energy absorption than mild steels. The best values for ferritic steels are obtained with multiphase microstructures; especially TRIP steels seem to be very promising in this regard. The combination of the high elongation values and the high work-hardening rate of TRIP aided steels is expected to result in this good crash-

worthiness behaviour. As the crash-worthiness is important for pressformed parts, it will be necessary that during manufacturing of the part not all of the äustenite is transformed. By leaving a significant amount of rest austenite for transformation during impact, energy is absorbed in the event of a crash.

A comparison of the crash behaviour of different steel types is presented in **Figure 8**. The TRIP-steel offers a much better energy-absorption behaviour than the classical P-alloyed steel.

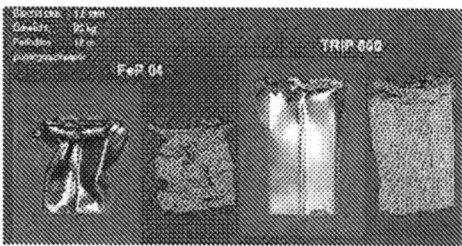

Figure 8: Simulation of crash behaviour and real results [9]

For producing cold rolled multiphase steels the materials have to undergo a heat treatment, which can be realised in continuous annealing lines and in hot dip galvanising lines. The result in phase composition, which means the volume fractions of the different phases of the final products are almost similar to those of hot rolled multiphase steels. Depending on the total different processes the details in microstructure, such as distributions of elements as well as precipitates in and between the phases, are most likely to differ from each other. Typical temperature-time-schedules for cold rolled multiphase steels are shown in **Figure 9** for TRIP and dual phase steels. TRIP aided steels offer an extremely attractive combination of higher strength together with high ductility (**Figure 4**) and remarkable high strain hardening (**Figure 10**) [10, 11, 12].

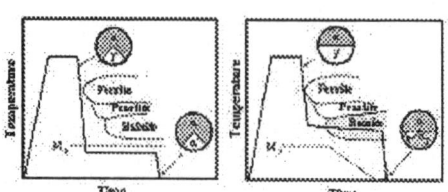

Figure 9: Temperature-time-schedule for cold rolled TRIP (right) and dual phase steel (left) [12]

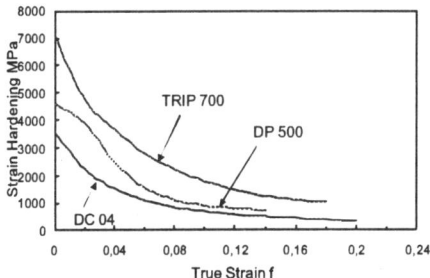

Figure 10: Strain hardening as determined in tensile tests for different cold rolled steels [12]

In the international Project **U**ltra **L**ight **S**teel **A**uto **B**ody (ULSAB) new concepts for the usage of steel in lightweight design for car bodies have been developed. The lightweight car body of the ULSAB advanced vehicle concept is designed completely with high-strength steels, dual phase steels are forecasted to become the dominant car body material. **Figure 11** gives an overview of steel grades used and developed within the ULSAB midsize passenger car.

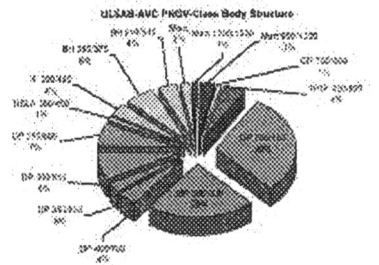

Figure 11: Steel usage in the international project ULSAB [2]

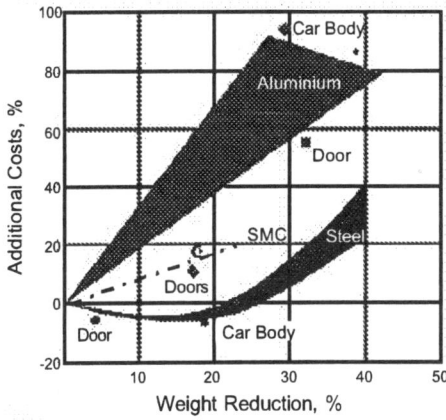

Figure 12: Relationship between weight reduction and costs [5]

In this project it could be shown, that a reduction of weight in the range of 25 % can be realised by the usage of high strength steels with getting the same or better mechanical and safety properties (**Figure 12**).

4. CONCLUSION

The application of modern multiphase steels in car bodies together with a multi material design offers extremely good possibilities for saving weight and obtaining better safety standards. Increased usage of high strength steels seems to be the best economic solution in reducing weight. Especially the usage of complex phase and TRIP-aided steels with their extraordinary formability combined with a good energy absorption behaviour offers a lot of new possibilities.

REFERENCES

1. **N N.** (2002), Conference report: "The automotive industry in the future: The role of UK steel, Iron and Steel making", Vol. 29, No 6, p.407
2. **N. N.** (2000), ATZ/MTZ Sonderausgabe, März 2000
3. **N. N.** AUDI AG
4. **Bleck W., Frehn F. and Ohlert, J.** "Influence of temperature and prestraining on the plastic material behaviour of modern sheet steels for autobody applications", to be published in Stahl & Eisen
5. **Schaumann T. W., Heller T. and Palkowski H.** (2001), "Anwendungs-potential warm- und kaltgewalzter Mehrphasenstähle", in Verlag Meisen-bach GmbH, Bamberg UTF science, Heft III. Quartal 2001, p. 17-22
6. **Engl B., Heller T. and Nuss A** "Improvement of Materials properties by Microalloying in the Case of Multiphase Steels", Thyssen Krupp Stahl AG, Germany
7. **Bleck W.** "Using TRIP effect – the dawn of a promising group of cold formable steels", Int. Conf. On TRIP-Aided High Strength Ferrous Alloys
8. **Bleck W. and Schael I.** (2000), steel res 71 (2000) No. 5, p. 173/78
9. **Engl B., Heller T. and Kawalla R.** (1999), "Stand und Potential der Werkstoffentwicklung am Beispiel der Stähle für die Automobilindustrie", Technische Mitteilungen ThyssenKrupp forum, April 1999, p. 20
10. **Engl B. and Drewes E. J.** (1997), "From 450 MPa dualphase to 1100 MPa complex phase steels: development of a new generation of automotive sheet steels", in Proc. IBEC'97 Congr., Automotive body materials, p. 127/32
11. **Heller T. and Engl B** (2000), "Thermomechanical rolling of hot-rolled multiphase steels", in Proc. Conf. on Thermomechanical Processing of Steels, London, 24.-26. May 2000, p. 438/45
12. **Bleck W.**, "Using the TRIP effect – the dawn of promising group of cold deformable steels", Paper at: Int. Conf. On TRIP-Aided High Strength Ferrous Alloys

Welding

GCMM 2004
Editors: Prasad K D V Yarlagadda and S Narayanan
Copyright © 2005, Vellore Institute of Technology, Vellore, India
Publisher: Narosa Publishing House Pvt. Ltd., New Delhi, India

Improving Performance of Shielding Gases through Helium

Praveen P & Yarlagadda P K D V

Queensland University of Technology
QLD 4001

Kang B Y*

Korea Institute of Industrial Technology
Chonan 330-820, South Korea

Email: p.posinaseeti@qut.edu.au

Abstract

The selection of the welding process variables directly affects the economics of welded structures and determines the performance of the welded joint. Often shielding gases importance is under estimated and solely the province of welder. The selection criteria used for the selection of shielding gases often is only cost which results in poor performance of welding joints in terms of economics as well as performance of welded joint. This paper explores how adding helium to shielding gases results in improving productivity and performance.

Keywords
Argon, Helium, Shielding Gases Blend, Alternate Supply of Shielding Gases

1. INTRODUCTION

A successful welding should result in a welded joint, which performs its function adequately, safely and economically. This goal can only be achieved with correct selection of welding parameters. Often shielding gases are selected to save pennies. However, this poor selection of shielding gas often results in more expenses as shielding gases can have a major effect on welding speed, penetration, mechanical properties, weld appearance and shape, fume generation, and arc stability. At present, almost exclusively mixtures of two or three different gases are used to protect the arc and the molten weld pool. The most frequently used gas is argon and carbon dioxide. A small portion of oxygen, in some cases also helium is often added to these two gases. The intention of this paper is to study the effects of adding helium to shielding gases.

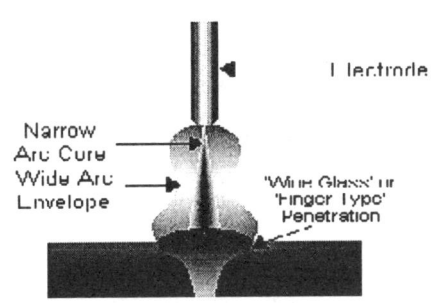

Fig. 1: Argon Arc [1]

* - Working as a research fellow in school of MMME, QUT, Australia at the time of submission of Paper

2. BASIC CHARACTERISITCS OF PURE ARGON AND HELIUM ARC

Argon is the most widely used shielding gas in the industry for welding a wide range of materials. Some relevant properties of argon are summarized in table 1.

Table1: Properties of Argon

Density	Heavy (1.784 kg/m^3)
Ionization Potential	Low (15.75 eV)
Thermal Conductivity	Low (0.02J/m-sec-deg)

Argon is non-toxic, chemically inert, monoatomic and readily available in high purity form. The main advantage of argon as shielding gas is that it produces low arc voltages and promotes good arc initiation characteristics and arc stability due to its low ionization potential. The other advantages are: High density results in efficient shielding around the arc as well as lower flow rate of gas required, produces fast freezing weld pool having finger type profile shown in figure 1 because of high energy inner core and an outer zone of less energy and concentrated inner arc, automatically cleans the surface by removing oxides. The disadvantage of an argon atmosphere is that the arc column is quite narrow which can lead to difficulties with arc stability.

Helium is the second lightest inert and monoatomic gas. Some relevant properties of helium are summarized in table 2. It has the highest ionization potential of all the shielding gases used in industry for welding. The main advantage of helium as shielding gas is high ionization potential and thermal conductivity, which results in hotter arc and more uniform arc energy distribution. As a result, the weld bead produced has following characteristics: Deep, broad and lenticular weld pool, improved wetting-in weld pool, low level of reinforcement and increased depth of sidewall fusion. Fig. 3 shows weld bead produced by helium arc.

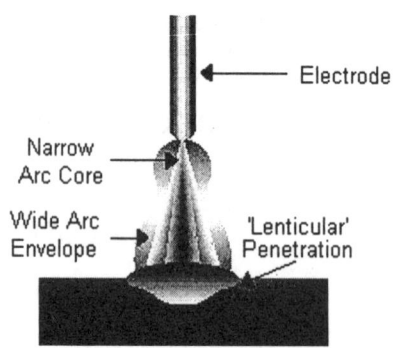

Fig. 2: Helium Arc [1]

Helium increases melting efficiency. Thus achieving higher welding speeds and reduced wire consumption without sacrificing weld metal integrity [2]. Helium arc being broader is less likely to wander around [3]. The stable helium arc is most conducive for conductive materials [4] and shielding welding operations in the overhead position.

Table1: Properties of Helium

Density	Light (0.166 kg/m^3)
Ionization Potential	High (24.58 eV)
Thermal Conductivity	High(0.15J/m-sec-deg)

3. ADDING HELIUM TO SHIELDING GASES

Pure helium as shielding gases suffer from following drawbacks: Commercial disadvantage due to higher cost of helium than argon, difficulty often experienced in initiating the arc [5], need for high flow rate and vulnerability to cross drafts due to lower density of helium, and sometimes produces more spatter and rougher bead surfaces than argon-shielded gases [6].

However, the weld profile character (Lenticular penetration), increased melting efficiency and welding speed, reduced wire consumption and improved weld mechanical properties are often desirable.

In order to overcome drawbacks of helium while achieving maximum benefits, helium is generally added to shielding gas in two ways as: constituent of shielding gas blend (Ar/He mixture) or alternate supply of shielding gases (Ar:He).

3.1 Constituents os Shielding Gas Blend or Argon-Helium Mixture (Ar/He)

Shielding gas blends generally used are of two types: two-part blends and three-part blends.

Two-part blend generally used is argon/helium mixture. Increased heat input into the weld pool can be achieved through the addition of helium. The helium content in this mixture ranges from 25% to 75% [2], which combines the advantages of the higher arc power with ease of arc initiation [5]. Preference of helium over carbon dioxide for some materials is due to the fact that it produces stable arc, reducing spatter and does not adversely affect the mechanical properties of the deposit. Figure 5 shows the effect of adding helium to pure argon. Helium addition improves penetration and width of weld, fluidity of weld pool and voltage tolerance [7].

| Pure Ar | 67%He – 33%Ar |

Fig. 5: Section of single pass deposits showing the effect on the weld profile of adding helium to argon

Small amount of oxygen added to argon improves arc stability[8], reduces arc wander, and broadens the deep penetration finger at the center of the weld. Oxygen lowers surface tension of the molten droplets and weld pool. As a result, improves metal transfer, bead counter, and degree of weld reinforcement and wetting angle. Excess oxygen addition leads to the formation of heavy oxides, with often porosity, lack of sidewall fusion and undercutting defects observed.

Carbon dioxide is chemically active gas and produces higher voltage than carbon. Carbon dioxide's higher thermal conductivity transfers heat to the base material and produces a deep, broad fusion area. Compared to Argon-Oxygen mixtures, the seam is wider. Use of carbon dioxide in the argon – carbon dioxide

mixture is restricted by chemical reactivity. Excess of carbon dioxide reduces the recovery of reactive metals due to oxidation produces more spatter and particulate fume and reduced arc stability.

Three-part blend of argon, helium and oxygen or carbon dioxide is useful for achieving high deposition rates. Small amounts of oxygen or carbon dioxide results in smoother metal transfer and increase in arc stability. Detrimental effect on wire melting can also be observed. However, presence of helium in the gas mixture improves the wetting characteristics and welding speed. Helium neither affects stability of the arc nor change the oxidation potential of the gas. As a result, this gas mixture is a versatile, low oxidizing, highly energy efficient gas suitable for wide variety of material. Figure 6 clearly shows improvement in welding profile as a result of presence of helium in this gas mixture.

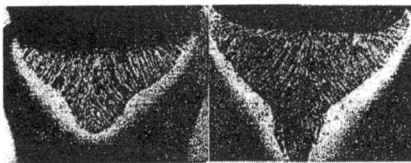

| Ar – 2%O_2 | 50%He: 50%Ar-2%O_2 |

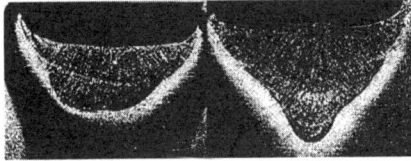

| Ar – 2%CO; | 25%He:75%Ar-2%CO_2 |

Fig. 6: Section of single pass deposits showing the effect on the weld profile of adding helium to argon-oxygen and argon-carbon dioxide mixture [8]

For the majority of mixtures of shielding gases, supply methods for mixture of shielding gases are of two forms:

- Compressed pure or pre-mixed gases in cylinders. Method of filling up of mixture of gases in shown in figure 7.

- Pure gases in cryogenic vessels fitted with vaporizing units and mixing panels for the additions of other component gases.

3.2 ALTERNATE SUPPLY OF SHIELDING GASES OR ARGON-HELIUM ALTERNATE SUPPLY (Ar:He)

Novikov et al. [9-11] suggested for the first time an advanced technology related to alternate supply of shielding gases. Several researchers continued his work and found several advantages: Reduction in defect incidence such as porosity, cracks, distortions etc., increased strength and improved ductility of welded joints.

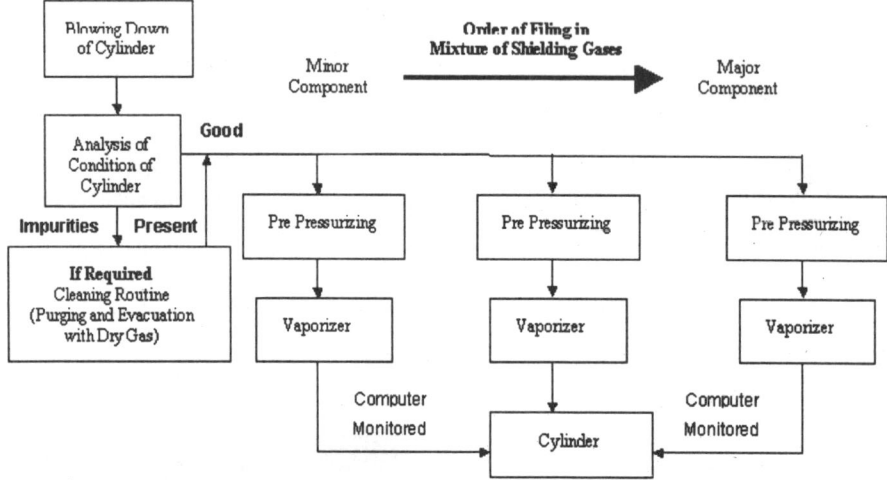

Fig. 7: Method of filling of mixture of shielding gases

Collins [12] and Hilton et al. [13] explained that reduced porosity levels with the argon and helium mixture are attributed to a more efficient oxide removal mechanism as well as providing a more stable spray transfer than argon alone. Improved protective gas atmosphere and increased fluidity of molten pool is observed in supply of shielding gases. Weld profile obtained is similar to as shown in Fig. 5 but deeper and broader penetration compared with argon is observed.

Alternate supply of shielding gases allows increased welding speed and improves weld penetration for welding of nonferrous materials. It overcomes some of the restrictions of the argon and helium mixture by reduction in helium consumption and lesser distortions because of reduced heat input.

Supply method for alternate supply of shielding gases employs KR301 (KR301 is a trademark of KR precision Co. Ltd. in South Korea) for alternately supplying pure argon and pure helium. The main control unit of alternate supply of shielding gas is an electromagnetic valve, which is shown in figure 8. The sequence of supply of shielding gases is depicted through figure 8 (a) to figure 8(c). When the electromagnetic valve is in the extreme left (Fig. 8(a)) or right (Fig. 8(c)) side, pure Ar or He is supplied from their respective cylinders. When the electromagnetic valve is in the centre, Ar and He is simultaneously supplied as shown in Fig. 8(b).

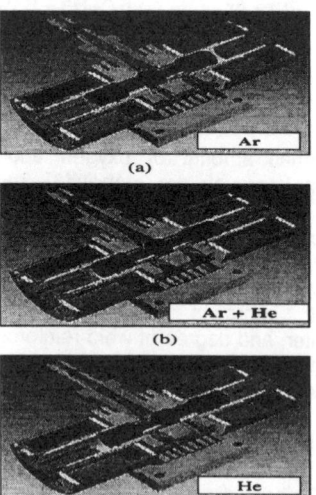

Fig. 8: Schematic diagram showing sequence alternate supply of shielding gases by electromagnetic valve [7]

4. CONCLUSION

Helium arc releases 50% more energy in the arc zone because of its electrical property. But helium use in the welding industry has been restricted because of cost and problems of pure helium arc. In order to overcome these difficulties helium needs to be added in form of constituent of mixture or supplied alternately with another shielding gas. Addition of helium to shielding gas for welding offers many advantages while overcoming the drawbacks of pure helium as shielding gas.

5. REFERENCES

1. **Praxair Technology Inc.** (1998), "Shielding Gas Selection Manual", Praxair, USA.
2. **Hilton, D. E, and Norrish, J** (1988), "Shielding gases for arc welding", *Welding and Metal Fabrication*, 5(6), 189-196.
3. **Hilton, D** (1990), "Shielding gases for gas metal arc welding", *Welding & Metal Fabrication*, June, 332-336.
4. **Norrish, J** (1992), *Advanced welding processes*, Institute of Physics Publishing, UK.
5. **Lucas, W** (1992), "Shielding gases for arc welding – part I", *Welding & Metal Fabrication*, June, 218-225.
6. **O'Brien, R. L** (1991), "Welding Handbook Vol. 2 – Welding processes" *American Welding Society*, USA.
7. **Kang, B. Y, Prasad, K. D. V. Y, Kang, M. J, Kim, H. J, Kim, J. H, and Kim, I** (2004), "The meaning of alternate supply of shielding gases in aluminium GMA welding", *Proc. of the Third International Conference on Advanced Manufacturing Technology*, Kuala Lumpur, Malaysia, International Islamic University Malaysia
8. **Lucas, W** (1992), "Shielding gases for arc welding – part II", *Welding & Metal Fabrication*, July, 269-276.
9. **Novikov O.M. et al.** (1989), Russian Patent No. 1808563.
10. **Novikov O.M.et al.** (1991), Russian Patent No. 1816596.
11. **Novikov O.M.et al.** (1992), Russian Patent No. 2008153.
12. **Collins, F.R** (1958), "Porosity in aluminum alloy welds", *Welding Journal*, 37(6), 589-593.
13. **Hilton, D. E, and McKeown D** (1986), "Improvement in Mild Steel Weld Properties by Changing the Shielding Gas – Theory or Practice?", *Metal Construction*, 18(10), 617-619.

GCMM 2004
Editors: Prasad K D V Yarlagadda and S Narayanan
Copyright © 2005, Vellore Institute of Technology, Vellore, India
Publisher: Narosa Publishing House Pvt. Ltd., New Delhi, India

Progress in Control of Pulsed Gas Metal Arc Welding

Praveen P & Yarlagadda P K D V

Queensland University of Technology
QLD 4001

Kang M J

Korea Institute of Industrial Technology
Chonan 330-820, South Korea

Email: p.posinaseeti@qut.edu.au

Abstract

In recent years there has been a spurred interest in development of synergic systems for Pulsed Gas Metal Arc Welding (GMAW-P). Achieving best quality in welding at faster rate and economically is the key need of today's industries. Modern welding has become complex due to need for setting up of combination of large number of welding parameters to achieve best quality of weld. Also there are many facets of disturbances and each has its own source and mitigation techniques. Hence this calls for an automatic GMAW-P machine with inbuilt automatic control of metal transfer. Such a system would provide wide range of operational and control features. This paper describes some of the improvements in control of GMAW-P technology.

Keywords
GMAW-P, Metal Transfer Mode, One Knob Control, Microcomputer Control

1. INTRODUCTION

Gas metal arc welding (GMAW) achieves coalescence of metals by melting continuously fed current-carrying wire. Its wide popularity is due to practical advantages offered like: continuously fed electrode, flux free operation, relatively low operator skills required, ease of automation, can weld wide range of metals and welding in any position possible.

The attractive looking GMAW suffers from need for continuous adjustment to achieve good quality. This need is due to a feature in GMAW, which is called mode of metal transfer.

Due to existence of number of metal transfer modes, good process stability and quality of weld fillet can only be obtained by controlling the mode of metal transfer [1]. This area has received a wide attention from researchers since late 1950s.

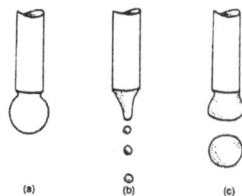

Fig. 1: Different modes of metal transfers in GMAW (a) Globular, (b) Spray, (c) Pulsed

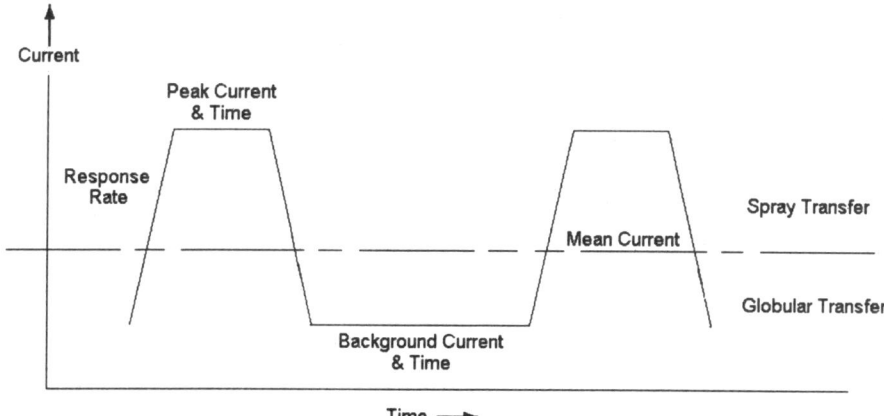

Fig. 2: Pulse waveform

With the advent of electronics, saw significant progress has been made in the development of high performance arc welding equipment. This paper describes some of the developments in control technology of GMAW-P.

2. MODE OF METAL TRANSFERS IN GMAW

At relatively low currents, GMAW operates in the globular metal transfer mode. It is characterized by periodic formation of big droplets at the end of electrodes, which detach due to gravitational force in to the weld pool. This metal transfer mode suffers from lack of control over molten droplets and arc instability due to formation of big droplets.

At higher currents, the process transits to spray mode. This mode offers high mode of deposition rate but due to tapering of electrode smaller diameter drops are formed. Continuous metal deposition in form of drops produces smooth bead and stiffer arc. Drawbacks of this metal transfer are: Minimum current for spray mode is too high for some materials, large heat input to workpiece, wide bead, and only downhand positional capability.

During the mid 1960's, an alternative transfer technique of GMAW-P was invented. This mode of metal transfer overcomes the drawbacks of globular mode while achieving the benefits of spray transfer. This mode is characterized by pulsing of current between

low-level background current and high-level peak current in such a way that mean current is always below the threshold level of spray transfer as shown in figure 2. The purpose of background current is to maintain arc where as peak currents are long enough to make sure detachment of the molten droplet.

3. CONTROL FEATURES

With increasing use of automated of welding systems, need for automatic control system for achieving better quality and improved control has grown. In a welding system, principal sources of disturbances are welding parameters, which need constant control and adjustments.

For achieving controlled transfer during pulse welding, it is essential that wire feed rate is balanced by burn rate [2]. This means achieving one drop per pulse condition all the time, which involves constant control of all the pulse parameters. Synergic control [3] is defined as – 'any system by which pulse parameters (or wire feed speed) can be manipulated to achieve equilibrium over a wide range of wire feed speeds (or mean current levels)'. Synergic has been practically implemented into modern welding machine in two forms: one knob control and microcomputer control.

3.1 One Knob Control

One knob control basically achieves manipulation of all pulse variables by using a single control or knob. This type of control

413

eases the job of welder allowing him to manipulate all welding parameters over wide range of wire feed rate and current. This system uses tachogenerator reading as input to hardwired electrical unit, which generates appropriate square waveform on the basis of the input. Logic of one knob control is implemented in two ways:

3.1.1 Synergic Control

This mode can also be regarded as wire feed speed control of mean current [4]. Power supply and wirefeeder are directly linked in such a way that means current is determined by wire feed rate to ensure stable arc. The circuit arrangement for this system is shown Fig. 3.

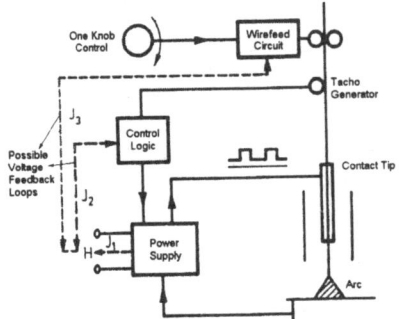

Fig. 3: Synergic control [4]

3.1.2 Self-Regulating Control

This mode can also be regarded as voltage control of mean current or error voltage system [4]. The welding voltage varies according to the arc length in GMAW. This system always tries to restore arc length to set reference voltage by automatically modifying the burn off rate. The circuit arrangement for this system is shown in Fig. 4.

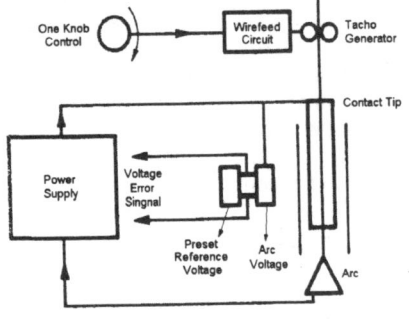

Fig.4: Self-regulating control [4]

One knob control suffers from need for calibration at the start that requires considerable operator skills [6], no means to store preset conditions or display parameters, cannot incorporate other system variables such as arc force control etc. [6], slower response time to changes in welding parameters, simpler design gives poor flexibility as it restricts implementation of complex control strategies [6] and difficult to integrate with other forms of automation like robots.

3.2 Microcomputer Control

Microcontroller or microprocessor controlled welding power sources brought a revolution in the control of welding. They have replaced traditional hard-wired systems for controlling, sequencing and timing of operations to achieve optimum output. The microprocessor increases efficiency, flexibility and consistency by quick retrieval of predetermined process parameters specific to different welding conditions. Algorithms, which can compute relationship between various pulsing parameters, can be stored in some form of memory system, e.g., EPROM, EEPROM (electrical erasable programmable read only memory) or FLASH ROM etc [5].

Fig. 5 shows microcomputer control for synergic systems. This system first takes wire material and diameter as input to compute molten metal droplet volume. Based on droplet volume, pulsing parameters, wire feed rate and arc length is automatically selected from memory. The possible disturbances in the system can be extinguishment of arc and change in wire feed rate or arc length. Former is overcome by initiating the arc again by supplying a high level of DC current. Latter is automatically corrected by resetting freshly calculated values of pulsing parameters from synergic relationships defined in the memory.

4. RECENT DEVELOPMENTS

It has been generally observed that disturbance in the welding system causes deviation to occur from pre-determined parameters settings. These deviations are due to non-linear relationship between average current and resistance melting of wire and generally results in poor quality of weld. Fig. 5. shows some of the non-linear relationships between average current and wire feed speed.

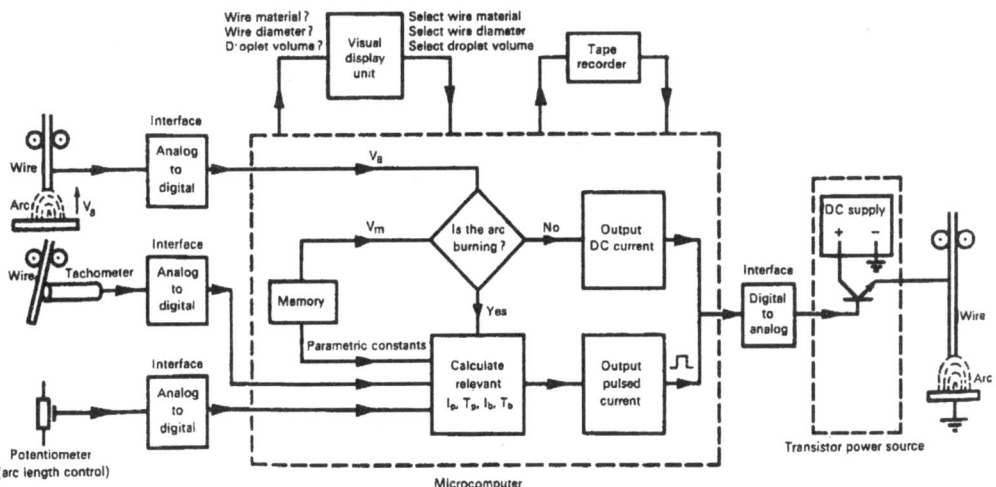

Fig. 5: Microcomputer Controlled Pulsed Synergic System [6]

During the last ten years, the use of intelligent microprocessors has grown. Features of this type of control use artificial intelligence to implement refined control strategies. It can self diagnose the system and can easily setup the downloaded system variables with ease. This feature also improves process consistency by elimination of need for trim control to counter deviations from pre-determined parameters.

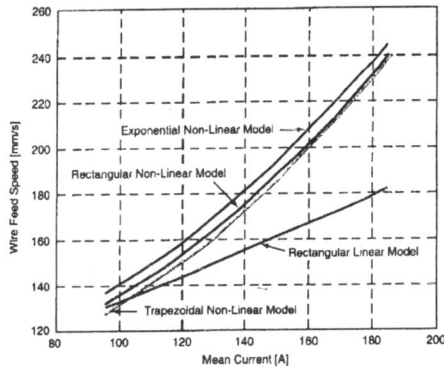

Fig.6: Non-Linear Models between Mean Current and Wire Feed Rate [7]

Improved external control is obtained by implementation of non-linear relationships (as shown below) between welding parameters taking into account power source dynamics.

Physical Equations for Controlled Transfer

Wire Melting Rate [8]:

$$W = \alpha I_m + \beta L I_m^2 + \frac{(I_p - I_b)^2 t_p t_b}{(t_p + t_b)^2} - \frac{(I_p - I_b)^3}{3(t_p + t_b)} \frac{dI}{dt}$$

where W is the wire feed rate

α and β are arc and resistance heating constant

I_m is the mean current

I_p and I_b are pulse peak and base current

t_p and t_b are pulse peak and base time

dI/dt is the response rate

Droplet detachment criterion [2]:

$$I_p^n T_p \geq c$$

In order further achieve control of metal transfer, waveforms can now be tailor made to suit different welding conditions as the power sources respond to changes demanded by the software instantaneously.

5. CONCLUSION

Significant progress has been made in the controlled transfer welding through GMAW-P. The use of intelligent microprocessor control in conjunction with automatic feedback control systems can provide the user various benefits like increased flexibility and improved productivity and quality. With advent of technology and increase in the knowledge base about the

415

welding processes, future trend of GMAW-P machines is likely to be improved performance at affordable price.

6. REFERENCES

1. **Norrish, J., and Richardson, I. F** (1988), "Back to Basics: Metal Transfer Mechanisms", *Welding and Metal Fabrication*, Jan-Feb, 17-22.
2. **Amin, M** (1983), "Pulse Current Parameters for Arc Stability and Controlled Metal Transfer in Arc Welding", *Metal Construction*, 15(5), 272-278.
3. **Needham, J.** (1985), "Synergic Power Supplies – Classification and Questionnaire", *International Institute of Welding, IIW Doc XII-905-85.*
4. **Elliott, S** (1985), "Using Synergic MIG Successfully", *Metal Construction*, 17(3), 148-151.
5. **Pixley, M** (1999), "The Microprocessor Revolution – Synergic Pulsed MIG/MAG Welding", *Welding & Metal Fabrication*, March, 17-18.
6. **Amin, M** (1986), "Microcomputer Control of Synergic Pulsed MIG Welding", *Metal Construction*, 18(4), 216-221.
7. **Vilarinho, L., O, and Scotti, A** (2000), "An Alternative Algorithm for Synergic Pulsed GMAW of Aluminium", *Australasian Welding Journal*, 45(2), 36-44.
8. **Richardson, I. M., and Bucknall, P. W., and Stares, I** (1994), "The Influence of Power Source Dynamics on Wire Melting Rate in Pulsed GMA Welding", *Welding Research Supplement*, February, 32s-37s.

GCMM 2004
Editors: Prasad K D V Yarlagadda and S Narayanan
Copyright © 2005, Vellore Institute of Technology, Vellore, India
Publisher: Narosa Publishing House Pvt. Ltd., New Delhi, India

Synergic Effects of Hybrid Welding

Praveen P & Yarlagadda P K D V

Queensland University of Technology, Queensland, Australia

Email: p.posinaseeti@qut.edu.au

Abstract

In modern world, industries are constantly under dual pressure from demands made by the customers for an ever-higher product quality and for achieving higher production efficiency. Continuous innovations are considered to be absolutely decisive for being successful. This especially applies to the welding technology, and therefore the goal is to develop newer welding processes offering better quality and more flexibility. The biggest problem faced by today's industries to achieve in case of welding are: increase depth of penetration, speed of welding and bridging ability while achieving better quality. Existing conventional welding processes provides solution to only some of the above problems individually. However combination of two welding processes can overcome the drawbacks of individual welding processes and provide advantages not found in either of them. New possibilities and synergic effects, however, are based on the combination of both processes. This paper shows how synergic benefits are achieved through hybrid welding processes.

Keywords
Hybrid Welding, Laser Welding, Arc Welding

1. INTRODUCTION

In recent years, two of the welding processes, namely Laser welding and arc welding, are being combined together to achieve benefits found in neither of them. The new welding process developed as a result of this combination is named as 'hybrid welding process'.

The hybrid welding process was first investigated way back in the 1970's. Hybrid welding processes are capable of achieving higher welding speed, good quality, increased depth and improved bridging ability. Hybrid welding was developed to solve the problem, where one of the welding processes is able to achieve greater depth while other process provides good bridging ability.

2. TRADITIONAL WELDING METHODS

Laser welding is a low heat input process capable of producing deep, narrow and less heat-affected zone (HAZ) welds at high rate. This feature makes it ideally the best available solution to the industry. The principal limitations to the wide application of laser welding in industry are restriction to small gap between workpieces, stringent joint preparation and high operating cost.

Arc welding is a higher heat input process having good bridging ability. The weld obtained is wider and shallow in penetration. Arc welding is widely used for all types of welding due to high flexibility and lower operating cost. The inability to produce deep penetration is a major drawback of this process.

417

3. SYNERIC EFFECTS OF HYBRID WELDING PROCESS

Hybrid welding can be achieved by coupling laser and arc in a single weld pool simultaneously. This combination produces synergic effects that overcome drawbacks of individual processes.

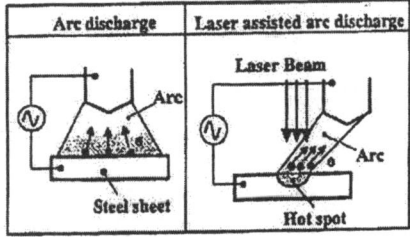

Fig. 1: Effect of the Laser on Arc Discharge [1]

An arc is an electric discharge between two electrodes that takes place through ionised gas known as 'plasma'. The space between the electrodes can be divided into three regions: arc column, cathode and anode. Arc column is the central region having uniform potential gradient. Two regions, namely cathode and anode, are classified based on the direction of current and are categorized by rapid drop in potential.

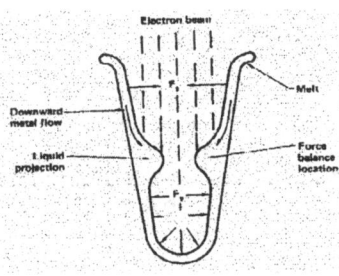

Fig. 2: Keyhole observation during laser welding [2]

From the practical point of view great importance is attached to the property of arc stability. Arc is greatly influenced by the forces and emissions taking place at the arc roots. Cathode of a welding arc play is a major influence in electric arc by influencing field emissions. Generally, in arc welding workpiece acts as cathode, which takes the form of a relatively large cathode area. This large area is categorized by many small cathode spots that are active and in a constant state of movement.

If large current is passed in arc welding to improve emissions and achieve greater depth, it results in disappearance of cathode spots and poor weld appearance due to loss of cathodic cleaning. One of the ways of achieving improved emissions without affecting weld quality is through use of external means like laser. In hybrid welding, the arc is constricted because of the effect of laser (as shown in Fig. 1) [1, 3]. As a result, increase in the current intensity is observed while resistance decreases. Temperature in the arc column also increases which results in improved metal transfer frequency.

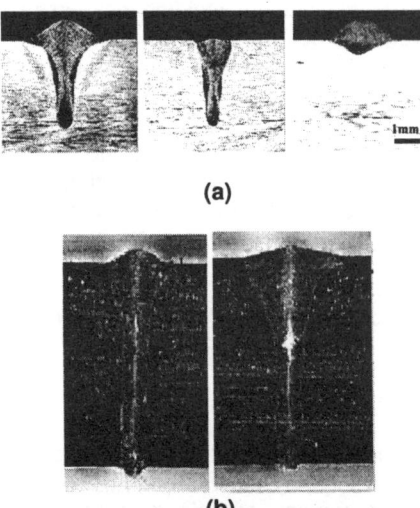

(a)

(b)

Fig. 3: Cross Section of Weld Beads for Different Welding Processes – (a) Laser MAG Hybrid Welding [4] (b) Laser Plasma Hybrid Welding [5]

Laser is able to achieve greater depths by producing keyhole during welding in the workpiece. At high speeds of welding, the keyhole collapses resulting in porosity. Major factor contributing to collapse of keyhole is large surface tension on the walls of keyhole that results in formation of small projections as shown in Fig. 2 [2]. Porosity is present at the bottom of the keyhole because molten metal is not able to fill the region completely due to collapse of keyhole.

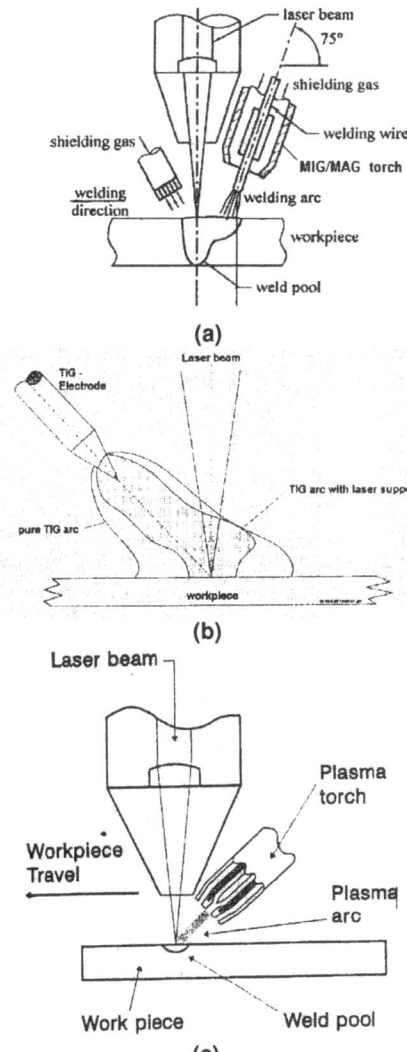

(a)

(b)

(c)

Fig. 4: Schematic Illustrations of Various Hybrid Welding Processes – (a) Laser MIG/MAG Hybrid [3], (b) Laser TIG Hybrid [6], and (c) Laser Plasma Hybrid [7]

In hybrid welding keyhole formed is relatively wider than in laser welding as seen in Fig. 3(b). Reduction of porosity in hybrid welding process is attributed to wider keyhole and suppression of gas bubbles, both of which are effect of arc acting on the surface of keyhole [8]. Hybrid welding also reduces reflections of laser light that results in cost savings by reducing consumption of laser power [9]. Improved beam absorption is because of the arc acting on the surface of keyhole.

4. CLASSIFICATION OF HYBRID WELDING PROCESSES ON THE BASIS OF ARC WELDING PROCESES EMPLOYED

In recent years, numbers of versions of hybrid welding processes are available in the market. While analysing the studies devoted to different hybrid welding systems, one can identify that researchers have focused on hybrid welding systems that differ in arc welding processes. Schematic illustration and classification of different hybrid welding processes is shown in Fig. 4 and 5.

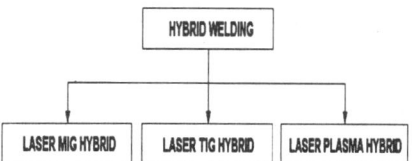

Fig. 5: Classification of Various Hybrid Welding Processes

Arc welding processes are of 3 types: Metal inert gas (MIG) or metal active gas (MAG) welding, tungsten inert gas (TIG) welding and plasma welding.

MIG/MAG welding is a process that employs welding wire to transfer the metal to the workpiece. An electric arc is struck between the welding wire and workpiece. Ohmic heating in the wire causes the wire to melt and create droplets that are transferred to the workpiece. This phenomenon is commonly referred to mode of metal transfer. Based upon the welding conditions different modes of metal transfer like short circuit, globular, pulse, spray and rotating modes can be observed. Hybrid MIG/MAG welding is also characterized by the appearance the appearance of different modes of metal transfer [10]. Spray transfer is preferred over the short circuit for hybrid welding to avoid unstable molten weld pool and achieve deeper penetration [10]. Microstructure variation that results in variation of properties of weld is also found in the Hybrid MIG/MAG welding due to use of external metal wire [11].

TIG and Plasma are similar in nature to eachother. TIG uses non-melting tungsten. Electric arc is struck between

419

the tungsten electrode and work piece, which is used to melt the workpiece and form molten weld pool. Hybrid Laser TIG loss of popularity is due to because its performance lies in between TIG and Laser [6] and due to inherited which are present in TIG like erratic arc starting, lack of directionality etc. [7]. Plasma welding artificially constricts the TIG arc to achieve higher velocities and stiff arc in high temperature ionized gas stream. Good directionality helps in achieving greater tolerance to mis-match. Plasma arc in keyhole mode can achieve good depths at reasonable speeds (less than laser welding speed) at much lower costs when compared to laser welding. When coupled with plasma, this hybrid system produces surpasses the productivity obtained by the laser. It is able to achieve large depths (as shown in Fig. 3(b)) as well high speeds. The graph (shown in in Fig. 6.) shows the interaction between the plasma arc and laser [7].

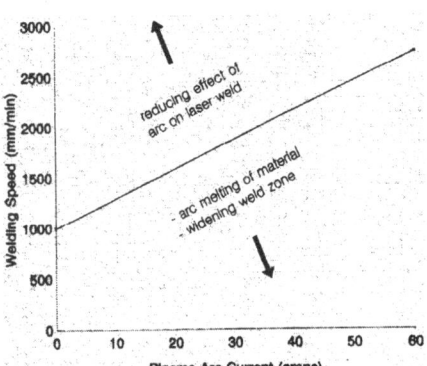

Fig. 6: Relationship between Plasma Arc Current and Welding Speed [7]

5. CONCLUSION

Hybrid welding process is a process with an exciting future. From the present research it can be concluded that coupling of laser and arc is ideal solution for joining thicker material at higher speed and better quality. Significant progress has been made in the area of hybrid welding processes. Hybrid welding with different configurations have been produced, researched and commercialised up to certain extent. Different configurations of hybrid welding vary depending upon the secondary heat source (or arc welding process) used and the properties of the

final weld are influenced by the secondary heat source. Table 1 compares different hybrid welding processes.

Table 1: Comparison Between Various Hybrid Welding Processes

	Laser Plasma Hybrid	Laser MIG Hyrbid	Laser TIG Hybrid
Purpose of Arc Welding Source	Heat	Heat	Heat & Fill Weld Pool
Microstructure Variations	Not Present	Present	Not Present
Cost	High	Low	Low
Depth of Penetration	High	Low	Low

Hybrid welding as a process that has received wide interest but much research is still needed to explore its true potential in advanced welding applications. The extent to which both laser and arc welding process is influenced by each other still need to be ascertained completely. From the previous research it can be clearly seen that properties and microstructure is influenced by the secondary heat source. Further research is needed to study how variation in individual parameters of welding processes affects the synergic benefits of hybrid welding process. Most of the developments in hybrid welding process are based on practical experimentation, which becomes very costly. Hence there is a need for development of mathematical models, which can simulate the interaction between two welding processes and predict the weld quality obtained. New developments in welding torch technology are also required which can fit two different welding processes together and meet the long-term durability, as heavier demands will be put on the performance of hybrid welding process.

6. REFERENCES

1. **Cho, K, Fukuyama, and Hiroshima** (2002), "Welding Properties of Thin Steel Sheets by Laser-Arc Hybrid Welding: Laser-Focused Arc Welding", *Proc. of First International Symposium*

on *High-Power Laser Macro processing*, I. Miyamoto et al. (Eds.), SPIE – The International Society for Optical Engineering.

2. **Ducharme, R, and Giedt, W. H** (1978), "Prediction of Electron Beam Welding Spiking Tendency", *Welding Journal (Miami)*, 57(7), 189-200.

3. **Tusek, J, and Suban, M** (1999), "Hybrid Welding with Arc and Laser Beam", *Science and Technology of Welding and Joining*, 4(5), 308-311.

4. **Moriaki Ono, M., Shinbo, Y., Yoshitake, A.m and Ohmura, M.** (2002), "Development of Laser-arc Hybrid Welding", *NKK Technical Review*, 86, 8-12.

5. **Briand, F, Chouf, K, and Lefebvre, P, and Matile, O**, "Hybrid Laser/Arc Welding", *Air Liquide Welding/CTAS*, France.

6. **Wendelstorf, J, Decker, I, and Wohlfahrt, H** (1994), "Laser-Enhanced Gas Tungsten Arc Welding (LASER-TIG)", *Welding in the World*, 34, 395-396.

7. **Walduck, R. P, and Biffin, J** (1994), "Plasma Arc Augmented Laser Welding", *Welding & Metal Fabrication*, April, 172-176.

8. **Naito, Y, Katayama, S, and Matsunawa, A** (2002), "Keyhole Behavior and Liquid Flow in Molten Pool during Laser-Arc Hybrid Welding" *Proc. of First International Symposium on High-Power Laser Macro processing*, I. Miyamoto et al. (Eds.), SPIE – The International Society for Optical Engineering.

9. **Graf, T and Staufer, H** (2002), "LaserHybrid Process at Volkswagen", *International Institute of Welding, IIW-Doc. XII-1730-02.*

10. **Kutsuna, M, and Chen, L** (2002), "Interaction of Both Plasmas in CO_2 Laser – MAG Hybrid Welding of Carbon Steel", *Proc. of First International Symposium on High-Power Laser Macro processing*, I. Miyamoto et al. (Eds.), SPIE – The International Society for Optical Engineering.

11. **Metzbower. E. A, Denney, P. A, Moon, D. W, Feng, C. R, and Lambrakos, S. G** (2003), "Thermal Analysis and Microhardness Mapping in Hybrid Laser Welds in a Structural Steel", Materials Science Forum, 426-432, 4147-4152.

Maintenance

GCMM 2004
Editors: Prasad K D V Yarlagadda and S Narayanan
Copyright © 2005, Vellore Institute of Technology, Vellore, India
Publisher: Narosa Publishing House Pvt. Ltd., New Delhi, India

Autonomous Maintenance for Vehicle Maintenance

Prasad P S S

Assistant Professor, Department of Mechanical Engineering,
PSG College of Technology, Coimbatore – 641 004. TN.

E-mail:pssai@yahoo.com

Eswaramoorthi M

Senior Assistant Engineer,
TN State Transport Corporation (Coimbatore) Ltd. (Erode Division)
Erode – 638301. TN.

E-mail:shanthimoorthi@yahoo.com

Abstract

Passenger transport in India is managed by public transport operated by state government and private transport. Since maintenance is an important activity in the transport sector, there is a huge scope for applying some of maintenance strategies like Total Productive Maintenance (TPM) to reduce costs and autonomous maintenance, the important element of TPM can be considered for implementing in transport maintenance. Even though many standard procedures are proposed by practitioners at industry, they can not be applied to transport maintenance as it falls under service sector. The equipments in the transport maintenance are buses, which will be on move most of the time in a day and away from the maintenance department. Hence it will be necessary to train the personnel attached to the vehicle namely; driver and conductor to carry out the minor maintenance activities to reduce the downtimes of the vehicle. In this context, the present work proposes four key steps of autonomous maintenance suitable for transport maintenance. They are Conduct initial checking, Standardize maintenance activities, Develop general inspection skill, and Strive for autonomous management. The various activities could be carried in each step are identified and recommended for implementation.

Key Words
Transport Maintenance, Autonomous Maintenance, Vehicle Operators

1. INTRODUCTION

Passenger transport in India is characterized by wide variety of vehicles and can be divided in to two categories namely; public transport operated by state government and private transport. Among these, state transport comprises 30% of buses. Safety will be the prime concern in public transport systems. The number of road accidents increased by more than 100% between 1975 and 1995. Vehicle condition is found to be one of the major causes in accidents (Maunder et. al., 1999). Vehicle condition will depend on the life and maintenance policies of the organization. Also there is a stiff competition between public and private sectors. Hence cost

425

savings at various levels is an important issue for the very survival of these transport organizations. Even though quite a large number of productivity enhancement concepts are evolved over the decades applied to manufacturing sectors; very few concepts are extended to service sectors like public transport. Since maintenance is an important activity in the transport sector, there is a huge scope for applying some of the developments in maintenance strategies. Total Productive Maintenance is one of the maintenance strategies, which is getting increased attention from the manufacturing sector since its promotion began two decades ago by the Japan Institute of Plant Maintenance (JIPM) (Suzuki, 1994). TPM is actively adopted in fabrication, production and process industries.

In the traditional preventive maintenance approaches which minimizes equipment deterioration with scheduled maintenance to minimize wear and breakdowns, only technicians carry out the maintenance activities. But the fast changing global marketing scenario demands the changes in the traditional maintenance approach. Even preventive maintenance does not guarantee complete elimination of machine downtimes. At the same time it is also not economical to use large number of maintenance personnel for simple maintenance activities. Hence to overcome these limitations of traditional; approach, it will be a good idea to train the operators to do some possible minor maintenance works to eliminate the losses, failures and maximize the effectiveness of the existing equipment. So the need for new approaches in maintenance like TPM is increasing. One of the important steps in successful TPM is the establishment of autonomous maintenance. Autonomous maintenance is an operator equipment management fosters ownership of equipment through participation and technical knowledge (www.diecasting.asn.au/nissan/tpm.html). It increases the operator's knowledge, participation and responsibility for their equipment. The purpose of autonomous maintenance (Shirose,1992) is to teach operators how to maintain their equipment by performing daily checks, lubrication, replacement of parts, repairs, precision checks and other maintenance tasks including the early detection of abnormalities. It is about raising awareness of the operators on the knowledge and understanding the operation principles of their machines. The same is true for service sectors also. But the maintenance activities in industry and transportation differ considerably. Some of the major differences are as below.

1. The equipment means the vehicle in transport which is very complex and consists of number of sub assemblies: engine, suspension, transmission systems, tyres, bus body etc. In case of industry, the equipment is a machine which is less complex.
2. The vehicles are in moving on various road and load conditions. But machinery is static.
3. In transport, the equipment (vehicle) will be away from the maintenance team most of the time, whereas the equipment is readily accessible to the maintenance department in industry.
4. The equipment efficiency not only depends on the operator's skill and vehicle condition, but also on the road and other traffic conditions. In case of machines the equipment efficiency depends on operators and machine condition only.
5. The vehicle operator (driver) has to take care of passengers' safety, road and traffic conditions and equipment behavior whereas machine operators can focus solely on operations.

The above discussion clearly shows that the autonomous maintenance steps that were practiced in production industries cannot be fully implemented in transport sector. The drivers (operators) have to concentrate on multiple activities. So the conductor who is always accompanying with the driver also has to be trained to help drivers in the autonomous maintenance.

2. DEVELOPING AUTONOMOUS MAINTENANCE STEPS

The autonomous maintenance activities were broken down into number of steps. Various books and implementations recommend 7 or 8 steps depend up on the nature of equipment. The 8 step procedure for implementing the autonomous maintenance described in the "Training for TPM" by Nachi-Fujikoshi Corporation and Japan Institute of plant maintenance are as follows.

1. Conduct initial cleaning
2. Address causes of dirty equipment
3. Improve areas that are hard to clean
4. Standardize maintenance activities
5. Develop general inspection skill
6. Conduct autonomous inspection
7. Organize and manage the workplace
8. Strive for Autonomous Management

Considering the various maintenance activities and breakdowns in the vehicle the following four steps from above the list are found to be suitable for autonomous maintenance in the present application. The proposed four steps in the development of autonomous maintenance are described in the following paragraphs.

Step1: Initial checking

In this step the emphasis is on putting motto "checking is inspection" into practice. The physical act of touching the equipment and shifting it around helps in the discovery of abnormalities. Checking discovers the passenger seat looseness, body sheet looseness, front, rear, side glass loose mountings and poor painting areas. The passenger seat, body sheet looseness can be corrected by tightening the screws. Checking glasses reveals the loose mountings and avoids future damages. The results of this step are the improved vehicle appearance, which is one of the important strategies to attract the passengers. Driver and conductors have to be involved in this, since these two only attached to the vehicle during operation.

Step 2: Standardize maintenance activities

In this step the past experiences of failures are used to standardize the maintenance activities. The main purpose of this step will be to impart knowledge about basic function and structure of equipment. Some of the maintenance activities that can be standardized are:
- Checking diesel oil, engine oil level in engine, power steering system and arresting minor leakages
- Checking water level in radiator and arresting leakages
- Checking tyre inflation and changing tyres
- Checking the clutch pedal play
- Checking the alternator function and fan belt tension
- Changing electrical bulbs

The important failure areas are listed in the Table 1. These failures may recur due to poor and/or neglected maintenance. Engine failure and excess oil consumption leads to changing the piston, rings, liners and bearings. It will cost around Rs.15, 000/- per engine. The leakage occurring in the enroute will damage the engine. The operator has to be trained to attend minor leakages of oil and water. So the operator has to check the oil, water levels in the engine before starting the engine. He has to monitor the temperature gauge and oil pressure gauge which are fixed in the panel board frequently while the vehicle is running. Possible areas of water leakage and oil leakage in a vehicle are as shown in Fig. 1, 2 and 3. The engine life and re-ringing details of two vehicles are compared and listed in Table 2.

Ring service work in the engine of N1334 is attended only after 5.4 lakhs Kms. But in N1450 engine it was attended at an engine life of 4.5 lakhs Kms. It clearly shows that N1450 engine life is poor. Due to insufficient coolant the wear and tear of piston rings were more in N1450. Any leakage in the engine should be attended as quickly as possible so as to improve the engine life and to reduce the maintenance cost. So the operators may be trained to concentrate on important oil, water leakage areas as shown in Figures 1, 2 and 3.

Tyre failures occur due to the following reasons.
1. Failures after covering the life (Normal)
2. Failures due to damage of tyre walls (Stone/metal hit)
3. Failure due to improper air pressure (leakage of air)

This work mainly focuses attention on failures due to variation in the air pressure. By properly doing the tyre maintenance we can avoid such type of failures. Maintenance staffs doing air pressure checkup in all vehicles once in two days. When the vehicle is running there may be possibilities for reduction in air pressure due to leakage in the tube mouth, weak tube and nail hit punctures. In such a situation the vehicle driver is only able to find out the under inflated tyres. He has to inflate the tyre or change the punctured tyres. Every vehicle is provided with stepney tyre and tools for changing the tyres. It is necessary to educate and train the drivers to identify the under inflation tyres. Inflation of tyres should be checked at the intermediate bus stands where ever time is available.

The physical act of touching the tyres leads to discovery of defects in the tyres like uneven wear, one side wear and wavy wear. Reporting and correcting the defects will give good results in terms of increased tyre life.

The data collected showing the tyre condemnation is listed in Table 3.

Clutch play: Inadequate clutch pedal pre play will leads to clutch slip. So the driver should ensure the proper clutch pre play of ½" to 3 ¾". Clutch play cannot be adjusted by the operator. So he has to report the problems to the technicians immediately.

Table 1: Types of failures

S.No.	Type of failures & reason	Corrective action to be taken	Standardized activity
1	Engine failure	Sufficient coolant oil should be maintained in the engine.	- Check water level and correct minor leakage in the coolant line. -Watch temperature gauge frequently. - Check oil level and correct minor leakages.
2	Excess oil Consumption		
3	Tyre failures due to over inflation, under inflation of tyre pressure	Tyre air pressure should be checked in the bus stands	Check air pressure
4	Loss of power due to clutch slip	Clutch pedal pre play should be ½" to 3¾"	Check clutch pedal pre play
5	Checking electrical parts	The alternator function, fan belt condition and bulb conditions should be checked.	Watch the ammeter function, check the fan belt tension and bulb condition.

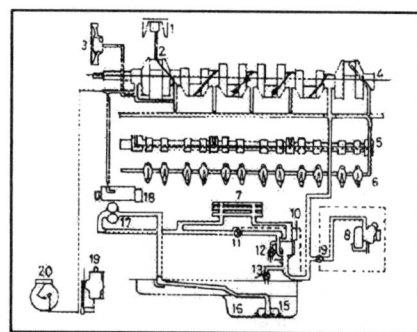

Fig 1: Lubrication system

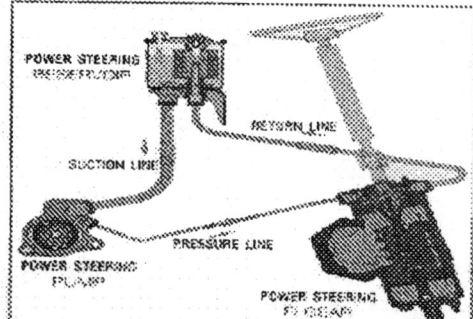

Fig 2: Power steering system

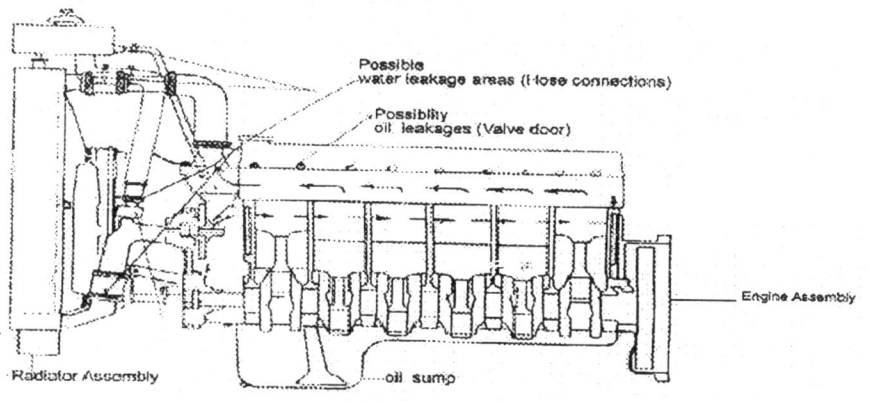

Fig 3: Cooling system

Table 2: Vehicle ring service details

	TN 33 N1334		TN 33 N1450
Engine No	CBH 149776	Engine No	ZLH 167950
Engine Type	HINO	Engine Type	HINO
Engine life	5.48 Lakhs	Engine life	4.50 Lakhs
Ring service		Ring service	
attended on	9.8.03	attended on	10.7.03
Reason	Below bye	Reason	Below bye
Findings	Normal wear	Findings	2,3 Piston siege
Branch	Nambiyur	Branch	Nambiyur
Route	Palani – Tirupur	Route	Coimbatore - Madurai

Table 3: Failure of tyres

Month	No. of tyres condemned	Average condemn life (Kms)	Tyre condemn due to air pressure difference		% of tyres condemn
			No's	Life(Kms)	
Jan 03	321	170922	59	150502	18%
Feb 03	275	174468	59	146495	21%
Mar 03	359	176477	74	170403	21%

Checking Alternator Functions and Fan Belt: While starting the vehicle the alternator function can be checked by ensuring the working of ammeter in the panel board. Any failure of alternator will lead to discharge of battery and light failure. Any looseness in the fan belt tension is also leads to the above problem and less coolant circulation in the engine block. This again damages the engine performance, since the water pump is driven by the fan belt. The alternator and fan belt location in an engine is shown in the Fig..4.

Fig 4: Engine fan belt arrangement

Changing Bulbs: Training should be given to change head light and other electrical bulbs. It will avoid the breakdown of vehicles at enroute. Standardizing maintenance activities helps operators to understand the need for improvements aimed at raising standards.

In this step the past experience of failures in engine and tyres are exposed to draft work standards for its maintenance. This will help the operators to decide which parts of equipment need regular observation, how to inspect the equipment, judge the abnormalities and so on. Educating these maintenance standards to the operators will help them to carry out their tasks with greater confidence and ability.

looseness in bolts and nuts. The general inspection can mostly focus on the following issues. They are

- Engine sound
- Gear box, crown sound
- Smoke emission
- Tyre wear pattern
- Steering hardness
- Spring leaves broken
- Loose bolt and nuts

Example: Broken spring leaves may damage the tyres if it came out from the spring assembly since they are located very close the tyres as shown in the Fig 5. Hence Training enables operators to perform

Table 4: Maintenance inspection chart

Date :	Signature :	PLACE : 1		PLACE : 2		PLACE : 3	
SL.NO	Description	Yes	No	Yes	No	Yes	No
1	Water level in radiator						
2	Water leakages						
3	Engine oil level						
4	Oil leakages						
5	Tyre air pressure						
6	Spring leaves broken details						
7	Fan belt condition						

Step 3: Develop general inspection skill

The procedures for carrying out general inspection are proposed as follows.

- Basic training in equipment function.
- Teaching equipment failures.
- Training operator in trouble shootings to find abnormalities.

Basic training in equipment function: Teach the structure of equipment, its function, proper adjustments and use, structural problem points and daily checks to the operator.

Teaching equipment failures: The details about the failed parts may be taught to the operators in consultation with technicians so as to improve the level of understanding. This will improve the knowledge and enhance the inspection skills.

Training operator in trouble shootings to find abnormalities: For operators to understand their equipment they must be educated and trained in the common trouble shootings of each of the important components. Viz engine, gear box, crown assembly, smoke emission levels, tyre wear, steering hardness, spring leaves broken,

inspections on components/elements of prime importance rather than casual checking of just tyres.

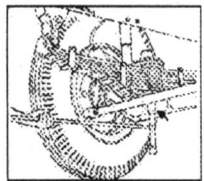

Fig 5: Spring assembly

Step 4: Autonomous maintenance

It encourages the equipment operators to discover what needs to be done to improve their equipment, make firm decisions on what to do and preserve their gains. In other words, it teaches them an approach and skills that will enable them to take maintain their equipment independently. To have autonomous management, standard format check list is proposed to equipment operators to check, ensure the important functions and to take decisions about the equipment. The check list is shown in the Table 4. Equipment operator (driver) has to check the above areas at the each destination and the findings should be recorded in the check list. Any abnormality

430

noticed in the equipment should be corrected then and there. This will definitely avoid the failures. Necessary tools should be given to promote the autonomous maintenance in transport maintenance. The partial list of tools to be provided to operators is as follows.

- ➢ Double end and ring spanners
  - o 10 – 11 mm   12 – 13 mm
  - o 14 – 15 mm   16 – 17 mm
  - o 18 – 19 mm   20 – 21 mm
- ➢ 8" screw driver, Wheel nut spanner
- ➢ Tyre lever, pipe, Hydraulic jack

3. CONCLUSIONS

Autonomous maintenance is presented as an important means to prevent the failures at the initial stage itself. The result expected will be improved equipment life. Implementing the proposed autonomous maintenance steps will definitely reduce the maintenance cost. There may be initial resistance from the operators(drivers).It is necessary to impart training to the operators so as to realize them as taking pride of our machine. Finally it is suggested that installing on board sensors in future will assist the operators to have a health monitoring. It is concluded that autonomous maintenance for transport vehicles offers the first defense against the failures and down time.

4. REFERENCES

1. **Shirose K. (1992),** "*TPM for Workshop Leaders*", Productivity press.
2. **Logothetis N. (2002),** "*Managing for Total Quality*" Prentice-Hall of India, New Delhi.
3. **Ansuini S. J. (1995),** "*The Improvement Engine*", Productivity Press.
4. **Suzuki, T. (1994),** "*TPM in Process Industries*", Productivity Press.
5. ***Roberts, J.* (1997),** "*Total Productive Maintenance (TPM)*"
6. http://www.blomconsultancy.nl/tpm-english.htm
7. http://www.main2k.com/what-is-tpm.html
8. www.tpmclubindia.org
9. http://et.nmsu.edu/~etti/fall97/manufacturing/tpm2.html

GCMM 2004
Editors: Prasad K D V Yarlagadda and S Narayanan
Copyright © 2005, Vellore Institute of Technology, Vellore, India
Publisher: Narosa Publishing House Pvt. Ltd., New Delhi, India

Evaluation of Total Productive Maintenance Implementation using O- MAX Tool

Rane S B* & Bhonsale A V**

*Lecturer, **Professor,Dept. of Mech. Engg., Sardar Patel C .O.E., Bhawan's Campus, Mumbai – 400 058, India.

Email: ranesantoshb@yahoo.co.in, ourpapers2003@yahoo.co.in

Mantha S S

Professor & Head Dept of Mech. Engg., V.J.T.I., Mumbai, India

Email: vjtirobotics@vsnl.com

Dalvi D S

Deputy Manager, Mahindra & Mahindra Ltd. Tractor Division, Mumbai, India.

Email: dalvi.deepak@mahindra.co

Abstract

Industries all over the world are facing fierce competition due to the Globalization, Privatization and Liberalization. To remain in market competition it is very essential for corporate bodies to implement strategies like TPM, SCM, BPR, RPD etc to keep the cost and quality optimum.

Total Productive Maintenance (TPM) is a maintenance program concept. Philosophically TPM resembles Total Quality Management (TQM) in several aspects, such as
(1) Total commitment to the program by top-level management is required,
(2) Employees must be empowered to initiate corrective action, and
(3) A long-range outlook must be accepted as TPM may take a year or more to implement and is an on-going process.

Changes in employee mind-set toward their job responsibilities must take place as well. TPM brings different departments into focus as a necessary and vitally important part of the business. Contrary to the old concepts, MAINTENANCE, QUALITY ASSUARANCE are no longer regarded as a non-profit activity. After institutionalizing phase of TPM it is necessary to evaluate the effectiveness of the TPM implementation. It is vital to study the depth of TPM culture and the ease with which it is being followed in industry. Unless the effectiveness of TPM is tracked, there is danger of deterioration of TPM culture. There could be different tools for evaluating the TPM. Here Objective Matrix (O-Max) is described.

O-Max is a tool, which focuses on all components of the object to be evaluated. O-Max gives the performance improvement index for current and previous period. The performance levels used in this technique are easily applicable to all parameters and are of World- class level. The method of rating for quantifying weights for parameters is realistic and focuses more on top priority parameters. Scores of these parameters reflect the true picture of present status of industry performance. Performance Improvement Index shows the actual improvement in percentage and helps us to set the target for next performing year.

The evaluation of TPM using O-Max tool could set the industry at World- class level and will act as a BENCHMARK for other aspiring industries. This paper describes the model of evaluating TPM performance parameters using O-Max tool.

Keywords
MTBF- Mean Time Between Failure, MTTR- Mean Time To Repair, SYS DT – System Down Time, OEE- Overall Equipment Effectiveness, LTB – Line Throw Back

1. INTRODUCTION

TPM activities in organizations throughout the world have brought numerous performance achievements, which have in turn increased the profit of an organization. The Return On Investment (ROI) on TPM project outplays the actual investment in project, be it man-power or any capital investment.

The TPM can give the dying organization a new life and can turn a sick unit into a profit-making establishment. Following points showing TPM outcomes explain the need of TPM to organizations.

❖ Better understanding of the performance of their equipment (what they are achieving in Overall Equipment Effectiveness (OEE) terms and what the reasons are for non-achievement,
❖ Better understanding of equipment criticality and where it is worth deploying improvement effort and potential benefits,
❖ Improved teamwork and a less adversarial approach between Production and Maintenance,
❖ Improved procedures for changeovers and set-ups, carrying out frequent maintenance tasks, better training of operators and maintainers, which all lead to reduced costs and better service,
❖ General increased enthusiasm from involvement of the workforce.

2. MEASURE OF PERFORMANCE

Performance indicators, or measures, for best practices are misunderstood and misused in most companies. Performance indicators should not be used for ego gratification; that is to be used for benchmarking against another company to show how much better one company is than another.

Properly used, performance indicators should highlight opportunities for improvement within companies and outside the companies as well. Performance measures should highlight "critical spots " in a company, then enable further analysis to find the problem that is causing the low indicator, and then ultimately point to a solution to the problem.

The ladder for performance indicators is as follows.

❖ The first layer of indicators might be at a corporate strategic level and is applicable to top management.
❖ A supporting level would be the financial performance indicator for a particular department or process.
❖ A third level would be an efficiency and effectiveness indicator that highlights what impacts the financial indicator.
❖ A fourth level would be a tactical level indicator that highlights the departmental functions that contribute to the efficiency and effectiveness of the department.

The fifth level of indicator is the measurement of the actual function itself.

The correct way to develop performance indicators is to work from the top, or corporate level, and develop indicators at each subsequent level to allow the indicators to be connected. This is in the same manner as the policy formulation and deployment that begins at the top of the organization and ends at the lower i.e. operational level. If the indicators are selected at the bottom and then built upward, they may be conflicting rather than supportive and it may not produce the desired effective results.

3. STRATEGIC FIT & PERFORMANCE

❖ The first step in achieving strategic fit between competitive and a TPM strategy is to understand how the TPM is helping to increase the organization's performance.

❖ The second step is to understand the each pillar of TPM and map it on the performance spectrum.

❖ The third and final step in achieving strategic fit is to ensure what the TPM does particularly well in consistent with the targeted organization goals and then perform the gap analysis if required.

4. PERFORMANCE MAP

➤ How much responsive is the company?

➤ Is there any improvement in performance because of any strategic change?

➤ If yes, then what is the level or percentage of improvement?

These are the important aspects in performance measurement of any management strategy. All the above questions are answered by O-Max technique, which is useful for measuring the performance of the company.

5. OBJECTIVE MATRIX (Omax)

A measurement method called the Objectives Matrix (O-Max) is particularly appropriate to basic work units such as crews, departments and staffs, although it can also represent a complete organization. It is conveniently applied to knowledge based activities that are considered difficult to measure, as well as skill based work that can be metered by more conventional measures. It has been positively received in manufacturing, services and government sectors by both large and small organizations.

4. PERFORMANCE SCORES

Performance scales in the body of the Objectives Matrix run 1 to 5. There are 5 levels of accomplishments for each criterion occupy a column that stretches from top to bottom. Levels of accomplishments extend across the body of the matrix as indicated by the rows marked from, 1 through 5. The assignment of the results expected at each level is the crucial part of scaling because the results set specific hurdles that reflect the accomplishment of a work unit of performance measurement objectives.

• **Level 1:** The lowest level recorded for the a recent period of time, say, the last year in which normal operating conditions existed is normally the worst performance reading and we never want that readings again.

• **Level 3:** These operating results indicative of performance proficiency are the time of rating scale establishment.

• **Level 5:** A realistic estimate of results that can be attained in the foreseeable future , with essentially the same resources that are now available.

Level 5 is the challenge, while level 1 or 3 is the present case.

An overly optimistic objective may later prove to be discouraging by its difficulty in achievement and a conservative goal may inhibit motivation if it is too easily achieved. Determining the appropriate entries for the cells between the benchmark levels completes the scoring columns for all the criteria. These are often equal –interval scaled. By using the above data we can get the score for the each criterion. The final phase lays together criteria scores and weight to determine performance index. Data for criteria are collected. Results are entered on the performance line of the matrix and translated into scores according to rating scale of each criterion.

5.1 Scores, Weight, Value and Indicators

All the criteria of performance do not have equal effect on overall performance of the work unit. Therefore assigned weights, generally 100 points are distributed among the criteria with consideration of performance objectives.

The final phase lays together criteria scores and weight to determine performance index.

Data for criteria's are collected. Results are entered on the performance line of the matrix and translated into scores according to rating scale of each criterion.

Scores are entered in the score line and are multiplied by the weight immediately below each score to complete the value row.

The sum of the numbers in the value row is entered in the first box below it. This is the current performance indicator.

An index of performance is calculated by designing the difference between the current and previous performance in by the previous performance indicator.

Scores are entered in the score line and are multiplied by the weight immediately below each score to complete the value row.

Now the **Performance Index** is calculated as below.
(Current Performance -- Previous Performance) / Previous Performance

6. DEFINIG THE PERFORMANCE CRITERIA

To achieve complete strategic fit, a firm must consider all functional strategies within the TPM; it must ensure that all functions in the TPM have consistent strategies that support the competitive strategy. All functional strategies must support the goals of the competitive strategy and all sub strategies of TPM such as Manufacturing, Maintenance, Purchase, and Quality Assurance etc.

Fair weightage should be given to each sub strategy, as their effect on performance is not same. Some points must be considered as critical, high value parameters and must be treated with top priority. Financial gains in terms of productivity, quality must be given high priority. Employee related strategies such as training is must but can be given a second row.

However a point is to be noted that these parameters are applicable to different departments. All parameters cannot be applicable to all departments.

7. QUANTIFYING THE SCORES, WEIGHT, VALUE AND INDICATORS OF PERFORMANCE

The eight pillars of TPM are considered as sub strategies of TPM. These pillars are treated as a base for performance criteria. Successful implementations of these pillars reflect the success of TPM and these all strategies together will bring the benefit to the organization. It is now required to distribute 100 points among these strategies depending upon their importance. In all Business management functions, finance is important parameter for performance evaluation of industry.

Effect of these parameters on industry performance are different, the weight given to these parameters are not same. The parameters, which can seriously affect the financial aspects, are treated with high priority.

These points are further distributed among separate sub points. Their individual weights, performance nature are summarized in following table-2 and table-3

435

Table-1

A Sample Objective Matrix

DEFINE STRATEGY						
						PERFORMANCE
QUANTIFY THE PERFORMANCE						
						SCORES
MONITOR THE PERFORMANCE						
						SCORES
						WEIGHT
						VALUE
	Performance Indicators			Present	Previous	INDEX

Table –2

S No	SUB STRATEGY	POINTS
1	5 S	10
2	ZISHU HOZEN	5
3	KOBETSU KAIZEN	15
4	PLANNED MAINTENANCE	25
5	QUALITY MAINTENANCE	25
6	TRAINING	5
7	OFFICE TPM	5
8	SAFETY	10
TOTAL		100

Table-3

AREA	PARAMETERS	REQUIRED PERFORMANCE NATURE	POINTS
1. 5 s			
Housekeeping score	Neatness and cleanliness	Increasing	5 %
Leakage proof machining cells	Zero leakage from machines	Increasing	3 %
Documentation	Easy availability	Increasing	2 %
2.ZISHU HOZEN (AUTONOMOUS MAINTENANCE)			
No of machines for AUTONOMOUS MAINTENANCE	All machines of manufacturing cells to be covered.	Increasing	5%
3.KOBETSU KAIZEN			
Improvement projects	No of projects / employee.	Increasing	15 %
4.PLANNED MAINTENANCE			
MTBF	Availability of machine	Increasing	10 %
MTTR	Break down Time	Decreasing	10 %
System Down Time	Work Stoppage	Decreasing	5%
5.QUALITY MAINTENANCE			
Rejection	Acceptable Quality Level	Decreasing	15 %
Rework	Defective components	Decreasing	5 %
Line Throw Back	Rejection from assembly	Decreasing	5 %
6. OFFICE TPM			
Customer Satisfaction	Customer Satisfaction Index	Increasing	5%
7. TRAINING			
Functional Training	Man days / Calendar Year	Increasing	2.5 %
Managerial Training	Man days / Calendar Year	Increasing	2.5
8. SAFETY			
ACCIDENTS/ HAZARD	Zero accidents / Zero Hazards	Decreasing	5 %

8. MONITORING THE RESULTS

After successful implementation of TPM and quantifying the values for performance criteria, it is now necessary to calculate the scores for these performance criteria.

TPM pillar	5 S	Zishu Hozen	Kobetsu kaizen	Planned Maintenance			Quality Maintenance		Train ing	Office TPM	Safety	SCORE
PER-FOR-MANCE PARA	House-keeping Score %	No. machines covered %	No. of improve-ment projects %	MTTR %	MTBF %	SYS DT %	Rejection/ Rework %	Line Throw Back %	Man Days/ Year %	Customer Satisfac tion Index %	Zero Acci-dents %	
	80.00	80.00	80.00	120.00	80.00	80.00	120.00	120.00	120.00	120.00	120.00	1
	90.00	90.00	90.00	110.00	90.00	90.00	110.00	110.00	110.00	110.00	110.00	2
	100.0	100.00	100.00	100.00	100.00	100.00	100.00	100.00	100.00	100.00	100.00	3
	110.0	110.00	110.00	90.00	110.00	110.00	85.00	90.00	90.00	90.00	90.00	4
	120.0	120.00	120.00	80.00	120.00	120.00	70.00	80.00	80.00	80.00	80.00	5
	10	5	15	10	10	5	20	5	5	5	10	weight

The table shows the score level of every TPM strategy. It shows the improvement required in parameters over the target value. 100 % performance is when the TARGET value meets ACTUAL value and it qualifies for score 3. Performance over this value is eligible for score 4 or 5 and performance below this is score 2 or 1.

For some parameters (MTTR, SYSTEM DOWN TIME,REJECTION,LTB) actual value is required to be less than target value for qualifying higher performance.

Let us consider the PLANNED MAINTENANCE STRATEGY.
For MTTR

> Actual = 80 minutes
> Target = 60 minutes.

Performance Improvement =
(60 / 80) X 100   = 75 %
As the improvement is 5 % less than 80 % , the score is 5.

For MTBF

> Actual = 240 Hrs
> Target = 192 Hrs
Performance Improvement =
(240 / 192) X 100   = 125 %
As the improvement is 25 % i.e. more than 20 % , the score is 5.

For SYSTEM DOWN TIME

> Actual = 4.2 minutes / day
> Target = 7 minutes / day
Performance Improvement =
(4.2 / 7) X 100   = 60 %
As the improvement is 20 % less than 80%, the score is 5.

Hence the score for PLANNED MAINTENANCE STRATEGY is 5.

By assuming the some score for remaining strategies as

STRATEGY	SCORE
5 s	4.2
ZISHU HOZEN	3.5
KOBETSU KAIZEN	4.5
PLANNED MAINTENANCE	5.0
QUALITY MAINTENANCE	4.2
TRAINING	5.0
OFFICE TPM	3.5
SAFETY	5.0

Now calculated performance index is =
4.2*10+3.5*5+4.5*15+5*25+4.2*25+5*5+5* 3.5+5*10 = 449.5

Considering initial performance index is = 300 (considering score 3)

Performance Improvement Index =
((449.5 – 300) / 300) X 100   = 49.84%

9. CONCLUSION

Omax is the tool for measuring the performance of any organization as well as it is useful for finding the best strategies to achieve the strategic fit. The theory behind the Omax tool is that effectiveness of TPM is a function of several performance factors, each with distinct dimensions such as quality , productivity, and cost. Strategic decisions made by companies include the implementation and continuation of TPM culture throughout the life cycle. Also the horizontal deployment of this strategy is possible across the sector if the group has diversified itself in different businesses.

TPM phases may be categorized as preparatory, introductory, initializing and institutionalizing stages and for each stage the time frame is required

The performance of larger organizational units can be represented by an appropriate collection of performance factors. A sophisticated weighting system would be required to measure the performance parameters of the departments. Therefore a more practical procedure is to measure directly the performance factors that collectively indicate the performance of each unit of interest in the organizational hierarchy, regardless of size.

10. REFERENCES

1. **Ahmed Khan:** T Q M in INDUSTRY
2. Arthur Andersen Best Practices Handbook.
3. Chrysler/Ford/General Motors Supplier Quality Requirements Task Force: Quality Systems Requirements Qs 9000.

4. **Kapgate Er.R.A., Deshpande Dr. N. V.** "Omax – The Responsiveness Measurement Tool For Supply Chain". *International Conference on Responsive Supply Chain and Organizational Competitiveness (RSC2004)* At Coimbtore Institute of Technology , Coimbtore.

5. **Hayes, Bob E.:** How to "Measure Empowerment", Quality Progress (Feb. 1994)

6. **James Riggs:** Productivity measurement; Page 647-659, Tata McGraw-Hill publications, 1998

7. **Ken Green, Jr.:** Supply chain management –Literature review, Page 51-57, *Supply Chain management review Journal*, April 8,1998.

8. **Michael S Malone,**"New Metrics for a New Age,"Fobes, April 7,1997

9. **Makajima, Seichi,** Total Productive Maintenance, Portland, Productivity Press Inc., 1988.

10. **Scholtes, Peter R.,** The Team Handbook. How to Use Teams to Improve Quality. Madison, WI: Joiner Associates,Inc.,1992.

11. **Takezawa ,Shin-ichi,:** "The Quality of Working Life", Trends in Japan, : Research Series, No 11 , International Institute of for labour Studies, Geneva , 1976.

12. **Zavala, A:** "Development of the Forced Choice Rating Scale Technique". Psychological Bulletin, 63,1965.

13. www.jipm.com : T P M Implementation.

14. www.ManagementSupport.com : 5'S for workers.

15. www.MaintenanceWorld.com: Best practices in Maintenance Management.

GCMM 2004
Editors: Prasad K D V Yarlagadda and S Narayanan

Fractal Dimension Approach in Wear Particle Analysis for Machine Condition Monitoring

* Kumar V, **Ghosh S, ***Sarkar B, ** Saha J

* M.E. student, ** Research Associate, *** Professor and Head, **** Senior Professor
Department of Production Engineering, Jadavpur University,
Kolkata – 700 032

Email: bijon_sarkar@email.com , surojit_ghosh@email.com

Abstract

Machine condition monitoring is a proven and cost effective maintenance management technique. Whenever moving surfaces interact, wear particles are produced. Microscopic examination of wear debris is an accepted method for machine condition monitoring and fault diagnosis. Nevertheless, used oil analysis has shown the extremely effective results in predicting the potential machine failures and accordingly fault diagnosis can be done properly. Applying wear particle analysis in industry, the expert interpretations of particle morphology and assessment criteria are very much essential. Consequently, the methods are quite time consuming and are not always consistent. In the present work CCD camera has been used to detect the wear particles present in an oil sample. Some techniques of fractal dimension have used to analyze the wear particles more efficiently present in lubricating oil and some numerical parameters have also been described briefly in the proposed method for machine condition monitoring.

Keywords
Condition monitoring, Fractal dimension, Image processing, Wear analysis.

1. INTRODUCTION
1.1 Condition Based Monitoring

Machine condition monitoring involves continuous analysis of operational equipment and identification of the problems before component breakage or machine failure. Generally vibration, lubrication, wear, degradation by–product, performance monitoring etc. are quite efficient and popular techniques for condition monitoring. Increasing the application of condition monitoring, the machinery and equipment characteristics can be well understood and the operation of machinery can be optimized to reduce the costs rather than improving product and service quality. The majority of monitoring system for machineries relies [5] on some periodic diagnostic test methods by means of electrical, physical and chemical phases. There are some common methods, which are generally used for machine condition monitoring such as, electrical test method includes insulation resistance, dielectric dissipation factor, polarization (dispersion), applied and induced high voltage, partial discharge etc., physical test methods included temperature, vibration, acoustic emission, proximity / displacement etc. and chemical test methods included chemical analysis of degradation by-products, wear particle analysis, high performance liquid chromatography, degree of polymerization, oil interfacial tension etc. As a hole to obtain the accurate measure of the condition of any machinery, a wide range of approaches can be employed to extract features indicative of condition. By comparing these features, the known normal and probable fault conditions and the machine's condition can be estimated. The approaches used vary from measuring vibrations to oil debris analysis where the metal worn off the machine can be analyzed [4]. Modern technology for condition monitoring technique based on integrated systems like, continuous monitor and estimation of condition with the help of some software application etc.

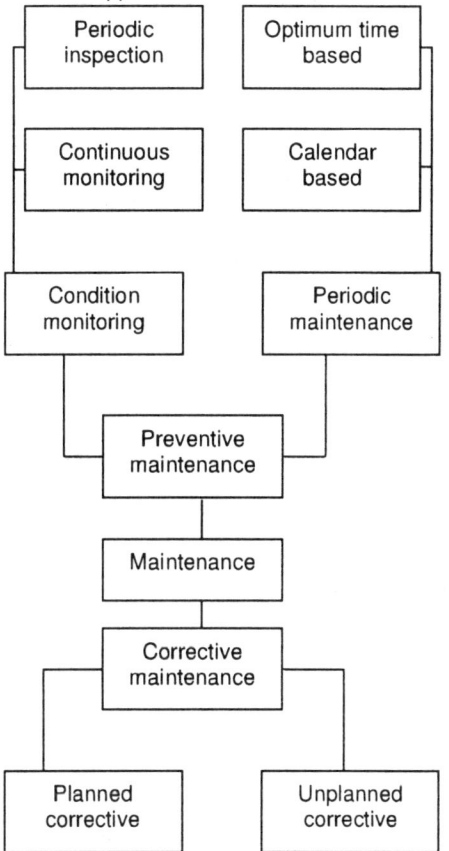

Fig. 1: Condition Monitoring with Different Strategies of Maintenance

Generally, pro-active maintenance strategy focused on identifying repetitive problems that shorten component life and eliminating them through design modifications, therefore, preventive maintenance can be the first step towards the pro-active maintenance strategy. Various maintenance strategies have been depicted in fig. 1 for condition monitoring purpose.

1.2 Wear Debris Analysis

Wear created when damage to a particular surface involves progressive loss of material and due to relative motion between that surface and a contacting substance or substances [1]. Plastic shear deformation of a surface is one sign of wear. Wear can also be accompanied by a number of other surface damages such as, extrusion, chip formation, tearing, brittle fracture, etc. There are certain wear for which the loss of material occurred due to contact mechanism, which can be understandable with the help of Table 1.

Table 1: Different types of wear

Wear	Material loss due to a force that act slides surfaces relative to one another
Abrasive wear	Presence of abrasive particles in the contact zone
Sliding and adhesive wear	Sliding of one surface over another with no abrasive
Polishing wear	Wear leading to polished surface
Fretting wear	Wear due to small amplitude oscillatory lateral movement between two surfaces
Rolling contact Wear	Wear due to rolling contact between two solids

Apart from wear generated under various conditions as shown in Table 1, there are some wear like corrosive wear, cutting wear etc. that also would be the critical factors for detecting the condition monitoring.

2. IMAGE PROCESSING TECHNIQUE

Wear debris analysis is quite well known phenomenon in condition monitoring of any tribosystem [2]. The conditions of machine operation generally related to the process of wear debris generation. Finally, considering different morphological classes can make classification of wear debris. Morphological analysis usually based on shape, texture and color of debris. Various colors or shape of the particles are allowed to decide the type of wear. The present work deals with color CCD camera embedded with the microscope and the images of different ferrograms acquired and finally those images have been analyzed with the help of certain mathematics.

Hi resolution PC

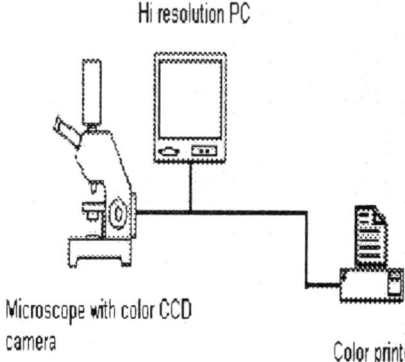

Microscope with color CCD
camera
Color printer

Fig. 2: Schematic Diagram of the Proposed System

Some of the effects of measurement for condition like, resolution, noise, defocusing, smoothing etc. on the image of any particle are being investigated in order to get the optimal conditions of wear, thus obtained reliable results. Images of the same surface can be acquired with different resolutions, i.e., with different numbers of pixels per measurement unit [6]. Fractal surface can be represented by different size images like, 256 X 256, 128 X 128, 64 X 64 pixels etc. Generally, the resulting images of 128 X 128 and 64 X 64 pixels have lower resolutions than their original image of 256 X 256 pixels. 1023 X 916 pixels have found in the proposed work from 1280 X 1024 pixels for chunk wear particle. At the same time noise present in a wear particle image can be considered as local variations in pixel brightness values, which do not represent real features in images of wear particles. Generally any image with 15% noise contains 85% of the noise-free image especially when fractal images are taken into consideration. Hence, all precautions must have to be made during the image acquisition to ensure that the highest possible signal-to- noise ratio is obtained. Defocusing factor sometime may arise during the image acquisition process as some parts

of the surface images could be out of focus, which may create difficulties in subsequent surface characterization. The effect of defocusing on fractal dimension can be analyzed the relationship between the percentage changes in fractal dimension against the level of image 'smoothness'. It has been seen that the fractal dimension decreases rapidly for smoothed images. Though in the present work both noise and defocusing factors have not taken into consideration as the main focus has been given mainly on the fractal dimension approach.

3. FRACTAL DIMENSION TECHNIQUE

Fractal is an irregular geometric object with an infinite nesting of structure at all scales. Fractal objects can be found everywhere in the nature such as trees, ferns, clouds, snowflakes, mountains, bacteria, coastlines etc. But it is very much useful for characterizing the roughness of wear particles for machine condition monitoring [8]. The term "fractal" (for fractional dimension) was first used by *Benoit Mandelbrot* who proposed the concept as an approach to problems of scale in the real world. Basically three most important properties of fractals are there, such as,

- Self-similarity
- Chaos
- Non-integer fractal dimension (FD)

If N = No. of self-similar pieces and

$1/r$ = Magnification factor, then

$$FD = \frac{\ln N}{\ln (1/r)} \qquad \text{------------------- (1)}$$

There are many concepts of fractal, which are used in practical application but among them *Koch Curve* and *Sierpinski Triangle* are most helpful to understand.

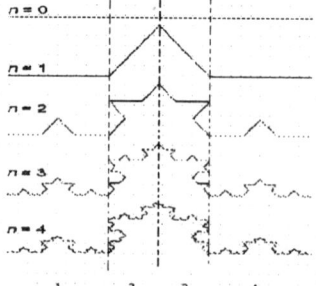

Fig. 3: Fractal Dimension using Koch Curve

In fig. 3, N = 4 and r = $^1/_3$ hence,

FD = $^{\ln 4}/_{\ln 3}$ = 1.261

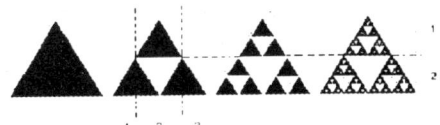

Fig. 4: Fractal Dimension using Sierpinski Triangle

In fig. 4, N = 3 and r = $^1/_2$, hence

FD = $^{\ln 3}/_{\ln 2}$ = 1.584

Both the cases in Koch curve and Sierpinski triangle the magnification factor [7] always been kept as $\dfrac{height}{width}$ ratio. The main objective of the present work is to detect the machine condition monitoring by wear analysis using fractal dimension technique and accordingly the proper maintenance planning can be carried out further. The proposed method tries to show the fractal dimension approach to wear analysis. The fractal analysis can be carried by different techniques such as vector-based method, matrix based etc. But EXACT method, FAST method, FAENA method etc. are quite useful in vector based fractal analysis.

3.1 EXACT Method

EXACT method is based on *Richardson's hand and dividers* technique, which is a computerized technique.

Fig. 5: Piece-wise linear assumption and the EXACT algorithm

In fig. 5 piece-wise linear assumption has been considered as the step length unable to match with the digitized coordinates. To overcome this situation P (X_P, Y_P) has considered and by taking the step length of 'ϵ'. Q (X_Q, Y_Q) and T (X_{Q+1}, Y_{Q+1}) have been detected so that every time ϵ falls in between Q and T i.e. on R.

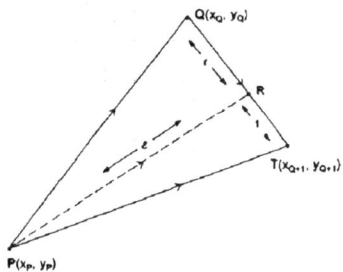

Fig. 6: Geometry of Vector Interpolation (P Is the Current Pivot Point; Q and T are the Consecutive Profile Co-Ordinates, R is the next Pivot Point, ϵ is the known Step Length)

Usually P, Q, T and ϵ are maintained their relationship as Euclidean distances,

$$\sqrt{(X_Q-X_P)^2+(Y_Q-Y_P)^2} < \epsilon < \sqrt{(X_{Q+1}-X_P)^2+(Y_{Q+1}-Y_P)^2}$$
$$\text{------------- (2)}$$

the step sizes kept as,

Step length = step length + trunc (10^{10} (number loops*0.015)) ------------- (3)

where, 'number loops' indicates the number of step size increments.

3.2 FAENA Method

FAENA method typically known as *fractal analysis by estimation – normalized approach*. Here the step length value has set up and the edge points are searched until this length is exceeded. The exact distance between these two points then recorded. This point then becomes the pivot point for the next step length. In this way, the step lengths are accumulated until the last full step has been determined and the average step length being calculated. Generally, step length of this method varies from ϵ to $[\epsilon + (\sqrt{2})$ x]. Fig. 7 shows how FAENA method can be carried out.

Fig. 7: FAENA Algorithm

3.3 FAST Method

The FAST algorithm, or the equipaced method avoids the problem of interpolation associated with the EXACT algorithm by choosing a fixed number of points as the step length. The distance from the starting point to the point destination point calculated and stored, which represents the first side of a polygon. The procedure repeated for the next set of points. Suppose the initial point be (X_O, Y_O) and the first destination point be (X_m, Y_m). Then the Euclidean distance between these two points being calculated and stored, which represents the first side of a polygon, then next point would be (X_{2m}, Y_{2m}) and again Euclidean distance between (X_m, Y_m) and (X_{2m}, Y_{2m}) to be calculated and stored, which represents second side of the polygon. The method continues until all the sides of the polygon have been defined properly. The sum of all sides of that polygon represents the perimeter, i.e., L ($\in$). This technique is substantially quicker than the EXACT method but can be considerably inaccurate, especially with regard to profiles with various degrees of ruggedness.

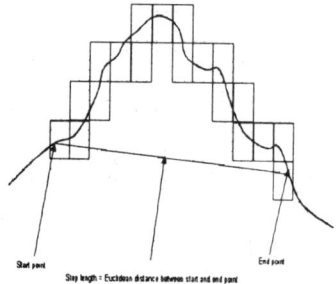

Fig. 8: Difference between Step Size and Step Length in FAST Method

4. FRACTAL DIMENSION APPROACH IN WEAR ANALYSIS: CASE STUDY

The present work deals with color wear particle analysis through fractal mathematics for condition monitoring purpose. Color CCD camera has used for this purpose which is embedded with the microscope and the ferrograms placed on it so that the image acquisition can be done. The proposed work tries to show the relationship between length of step and perimeter and finally by line of best-fit technique FD has been calculated.

Fig. 9: Image of Chunk Wear Particle

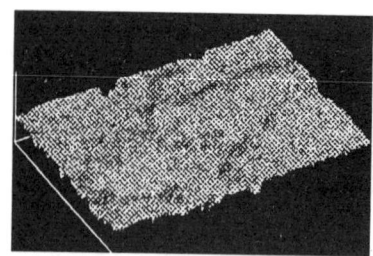

Fig. 10: Surface Texture of the Chunk Wear Particle

The boundary nature of the image in fig. 9 being highlighted and accordingly fractal dimension has calculated. Depending on the tabulated data, logarithmic relationship between length of step and their corresponding perimeter has plotted. The slope of the curve represented as fractal dimension. In this way by considering several fractal dimensions for different wear particle like, cutting wear, wear due to sliding contact etc. can be recognized. Apart from fractal parameters there are some more parameters such as, area, roundness, height aspect ratio etc. can be calculated. Finally, by considering those parameters, the type of wear can be easily recognized.

Table 2: Data observed for FD calculation

Length of step (LOS)	Perimeter (PER)	log (LOS)	log (PER)
2	1958.736	0.301	3.291
4	1858.604	0.602	3.269
6	1705.074	0.778	3.231
8	1649.333	0.903	3.217
10	1537.690	1.000	3.186
12	1509.333	1.079	3.178
14	1501.174	1.146	3.176
16	1479.392	1.204	3.170
18	1452.958	1.255	3.162
20	1444.756	1.301	3.159
22	1419.525	1.342	3.152
24	1394.135	1.380	3.144
26	1392.728	1.414	3.143
28	1351.808	1.447	3.130
30	1360.376	1.477	3.133
32	1273.002	1.505	3.104
34	1230.611	1.531	3.090
36	1210.312	1.556	3.082
38	1227.400	1.579	3.088
40	1233.429	1.602	3.091

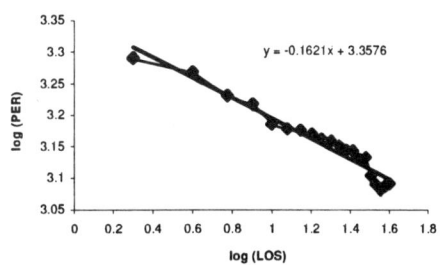

Fig. 11: Fractal Dimension using Length of Step and Perimeter

The slope of the of the curve as shown in the fig. 11 has calculated and by following the relationship,

$$D = 1 - m \qquad \text{.......................... (4)}$$

where, D = fractal dimension and m = slope of the curve, FD has found as,

$$D = 1 - (-0.162) = 1 + 0.162 = 1.162$$

In this way for different type of particles fractal dimension can be calculated.

5. DISCUSSION

The objectives of condition based monitoring through oil analysis is to identify the potential failures in their early stages when repairs can still be initiated and costly secondary damage is avoided. Another objective is to monitor the quality of the lubricants. The net benefits may be to reduce the maintenance costs, increase the equipment availability and life, reduce the lubricant usage and improve the safety. The proposed method tries to show an approach of condition monitoring through wear analysis. Wear particles have been characterized by fractal parameter though there are some other parameters like area, height aspect ratio, roundness etc. can also be considered. This would be used to reduce the expert interpretation of wear particles morphology and further the industry may be able to utilize it for their future development.

6. REFERENCES

1. **Kirk T.B., Pauzera D., Anamalay R.V., Xu Z.L.** (1995), "Computer image of wear debris for machine condition monitoring and fault diagnosis", *Wear*, 181-183, 717-722.

2. **Peng Z, Kirk T.B.** (1997), "Two-dimensional fast Fourier transform and power spectrum for wear particle analysis", *Tribology International*, 30 (8), 583-590.

3. **Podsiadlo P, Stachowiak G.W.** (1999), "3-D imaging of surface topography of wear particles found in synovial joints", *Wear*, 230, 184-193.

4. **Peng Z, Kessissoglou N** (2003), "An integrated approach to fault diagnosis of machinery using wear debris and vibration analysis", *Wear*, 255, 1221-1232.

5. **Yin Y, Wang W, Yan X, Xiao H, Wang C** (2003), "An integrated on-line oil analysis method for condition monitoring", *Measurement Science and Technology*, 14, 1973-1977.

6. **Russ J.C.**, (1995), *Image Processing Handbook*, CRC Press, Boca Raton, FL.

7. **Shirong G, Guoan C, Xiaoyun Z** (2001), "Fractal characterization of wear particle accumulation in the wear process", *Wear*, 251, 1227-1233.

8. **Podsiadlo P, Stachowiak G.W.** (2003), "Fractal-wavelet based classification of tribological surfaces", *Wear*, 254, 1189-1198.

9. **Ellinas J.N., Sangriotis M.S.** (2004), "Stereo image compression using wavelet coefficients morphology", *Image and Vision Computing*, 22, 281-290.

GCMM 2004
Editors: Prasad K D V Yarlagadda and S Narayanan
Copyright © 2005, Vellore Institute of Technology, Vellore, India
Publisher: Narosa Publishing House Pvt. Ltd., New Delhi, India

MQFD: A Model for Integrating Customer's Reaction in Maintenance Engineering

Pramod V R

Lecturer, Department of Mechanical Engineering, N.S.S.College of Engineering, Palakkad,Kerala State,Inidia.

Email: pramodvram@yahoo.com

Devadasan S R & Muthu S

Assistant Professor, Department of Production Engineering, P.S.G.College of Technology, Coimbatore, Tamil Nadu State, India,

Abstract

Total Productive Maintenance (TPM) is considered as a new strategy for enhancing quality in maintenance. But it is inefficient in taking care of customer views which is not worthy especially in the era of globalization where customer ("God of Business") has an important role in the success of a business. In Total Quality Management (TQM) projects, the technique Quality Function Deployment (QFD) facilitates the translation of customer views into technical language. Hence it would be a prudent proposition if QFD principles are integrated in TPM. For this purpose a model named as Maintenance Quality Function Deployment (MQFD) is introduced in this paper. MQFD has been developed by merging QFD principles in TPM. In a nutshell, this paper deals with the principles of TPM, QFD and MQFD and the feasibility of implementing MQFD in a hypothetical company.

Keywords
TPM, QFD, MQFD, House of Quality

1. INTRODUCTION

The modern concept of maintenance is to ensure that the equipments are capable of doing what users want them to do at required time Total Productive Maintenance (TPM) was one among the strategies for the organizations achieve it. TPM aims to increase the over all equipment efficiency. But as the new philosophy that "Customer is the god of business" is to be taken into consideration, It was found that there are some inadequacies of for TPM. In this world of competition it is absolute

necessary that this research gap has to be filled. Quality Function Deployment (QFD) aims to convert the voice of customers into technical requirements. Therefore it has become customary that QFD principles have to be implemented in TPM and also redirect the concept of maintenance in that direction.

2. TPM

TPM is a systematic approach to understand the equipments function, the equipments relationship to product quality and the likely cause and frequency of failure of the critical equipment components [1] TPM is aimed at maximizing equipment effectiveness through the optimization of equipment availability, performance, efficiency and product quality. It establishes a maintenance strategy for the life of the equipment. It involves all staff members from top management down to shop floor workers. It promotes improved maintenance through small group autonomous activities. It aims to improve over all equipment efficiency by eliminating major losses The success or failure of implementing TPM needs the whole hearted cooperation of every body in the organization.

3. EIGHT PILLARS OF TPM

Bundgaard, [2] made an Eight pillar modeled TPM. Eight pillars are

1. Jishu – Hozen (Autonomous Maintenance)
2. Kobetsu Kaizen (Individual Improvements)
3. Planned Maintenance
4. Quality Maintenance
5. Office TPM (TPM In Non- Shop Floor Areas)
6. Education & Training
7. Safety / Health & Environment
8. Initial Control (Development Management)

When these eight pillars are implemented We can say that TPM is in full swing. Fig. 1 shows the eightpillar modeled TPM.

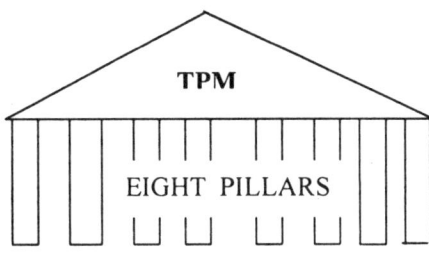

Fig.1: TPM

4. QFD

QFD is a technique which was born in Japan as a strategy for assuring that quality is built in to new products. Yoji Akao, "The Father of QFD" defined it as "A method for developing a design quality

aimed at satisfying consumer and then translating the consumers' demands into design targets and major quality assurance points to be used throughout the production phase"[3]. QFD generally considers customers as internal and external customers. Internal customers refer to the personnel who work inside the organization, who depend upon the outputs contributed by fellow personnel. The external customers refer to the buyers of the products and services offered by the organization. Both customers often use languages, which are not always understood without ambiguity and confusion by the practitioners.

5. HOUSE OF QUALITY

The House of Quality is the most commonly used matrix in QFD The House of Quality includes the following components: an Objective Statement, the Voice of the Customer, Importance Ratings, a Customer Competitive Assessment, and the Voice of the Supplier, Target Goals, a Correlation :Matrix, a Technical Assessment, Probability Factors, a Relationship Matrix, Absolute Score, and Relative Score. For convenience of interpretation it is divided in to six sections. Fig. 2 shows the six sections of the house of quality. They are as follows.

Section 1
This contains a list of input requirements. Generally that will be the voice of customers that drives for the current matrix of the QFD analysis. These input requirements have to be translated in to output technical requirements
Section 2
This section shows how input requirements are to be satisfied in new product or services. The method will be finding out the possible technical requirements which can fulfill the input requirements .
Section 3
This section shows the technical correlations among the output technical requirements. Here each of the output requirements are compared with others and some quantifiable measures will be given for each.
Section 4
This is called Relationship matrix. This shows the relationship between input and output in quantifiable measures.

Section 5

This section shows the Comparative evaluation of inputs in quantifiable measures.

Section 6

This section shows the Comparative evaluation of outputs in quantifiable measures

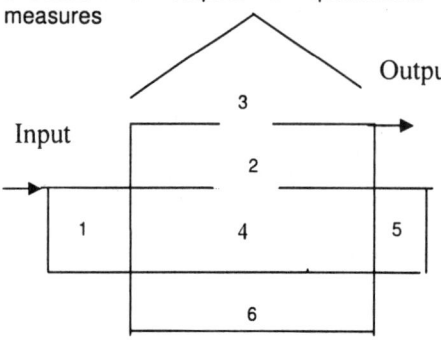

Fig. 2: QFD

6. MQFD MODEL

On realizing the deficiencies of TPM despite of its unique merits, we developed interest to assess the penetration of TPM in practical arena. The enormous volume of literature available on TPM leads to an impression that, TPM lacks to take care of the customer views properly[4,5,6]. Zero defect concept of TPM has to be upgraded in the view of product for customers. It essential that the views of the customer's especially potential customers should be taken care of. The pity thing is that QFD is still lying in the hands of theoretical researchers and very rarely it is brought into the real time application[7]. In this context, we developed a notion that if an improved model of TPM is developed to overcome the above deficiencies and also with an aim to make it viable for easy practical implementation, then such model would be a useful contribution to both theoreticians and practioners. The model is as shown in Fig. 3.

7. PLANNING AND IMPLENENTATION OF MQFD

MQFD being a new philosophy cannot be implemented at once to the entire plant. There for first We have to find a critical area where it can be implemented on a trial basis. Critical area is the place which influences the overall performances of the firm. Before the implementation a target, which can be achieved by some effort will be fixed. The porous of this target is to have a base for the work and to have easy comparison feasibility at ant stage.

Step 1

MQFD experts have to convince the top management benefits can be reaped by the implementation of MQFD. This has to be done as seminars and brain storming sections

Step 2

Top management has to announce the implementation of MQFD as a decision. They have to state the objectives either in company news letter or by some other media such that it will reach every body. Different sorts of educational campaigns are to be done for people at different levels in order to make the people fit to the policies.

Step 3

Form an MQFD team consisting of 7-8 members of different departments. They meet once in a week and plans for the implementation.

Step 4

Identify the customer language

Step 5

Rank customer language. This can be done either by Analytical Hierarchy Process (AHP) or by some other suitable means.

Step 6

Develop HOQ. For that find how customer languages can be converted to technical languages.

Step 7

Send the output of HOQ through eight pillars of TPM.

Step 8

Direct the results to the production system.

Step 9

Evaluate the results based on six parameters (OEE, MTBF, MTTR, Performance quality, MDT and Availability).

Step 10

Compare the results with the set targets.

Step 11
Check that by means of tactical suggestions. In this way matrix can be improved and targets can be achieved.

Step 12
After achieving the target, revise the target and revise the matrix. If there is change in customers languages, that also has to be considered while revising the matrix.

Step 13
Thus by means of continuous trial, full efficiencies can be achieved.

8. A HYPOTHETICAL CASE STUDY

In order to illustrate the implementation aspects of MQFD, a hypothetical case study is presented here. For this purpose a company manufacturing sanitary paper products has been considered. The products of this company are facial tissues, pocket tissues, lady napkins and diapers. The efforts that are carried out to apply MQFD model are presented below.

MQFD expert delivers seminar to the top management personnel who subsequently agree to implement MQFD in the company. Then MQFD experts and top management personnel undergo brainstorming sessions on MQFD implementation. At the end of the session, they decid to apply MQFD in the production process of diapers because its sales volume is the highest of all the other three products produced.Top management forms MQFD team consisting of 8 members. The structure is as follows.

I Works manager
II Engineer "A"
III Engineer "B"
IV. Foreman A
V. Foreman B
VI. Quality controller
VII. Factory Accountant
VIII. Marketing Manager

Top management permits the MQFD team to meet once in a week in the training hall. The top management instructs the concerned personnel to reserve the training hall for meeting of MQFD team members to be held once in a week.

The MQFD experts conduct a half a day seminar to both management and employees on MQFD.The MQFD team identifies the following four customer languages.

Customer language 1." Eva tape (used for tying diapers on babies) is getting peeled off." Customer language 2."Other companies are making T shape diapers .Diapers produced by our company are X shaped which are difficult to handle".

Customer language 3. "Packing of diapers produced by competitor companies tri fold which are attractive after packing whether as diapers produced by our company are bi fold. Customer language 4. The diapers produce by competitors last long.

The MQFD team ranks the customer languages according to their importance. and decides to choose the customer language 1 for subsequent consideration. MQFD team conducts brainstorming session and develops house of quality. The highest ranked for technical languages is brought out of house of quality is as follows. "It was found that oil used at the cutter knife flows the tape while cutting. It caused it to get peeled off. They replace the oil system by artificial chiller unit. The MQFD team submits the results to the top management personnel.

The top management personnel along with MQFD experts undergo a brain storming session. Concludes that the results reported by the MQFD team are to be fed in to appropriate TPM pillars. Once the construction of eight TPM pillars are completed, then the results must have to be directed towards the operation of the production system. In this regard. MQFD team computes the six parameters namely OEE, MTBF, MTTR, Performance quality, MDT and availability.

The overall results indicates 60%, increase in organizational performance. The MQFD members compare this result with the set target. They find that the target set is 70%. MQFD members conduct brainstorming sessions among themselves and conclude that the performance quality has to be improved. For this purpose they evolve tactical suggestions. Tactical suggestions of

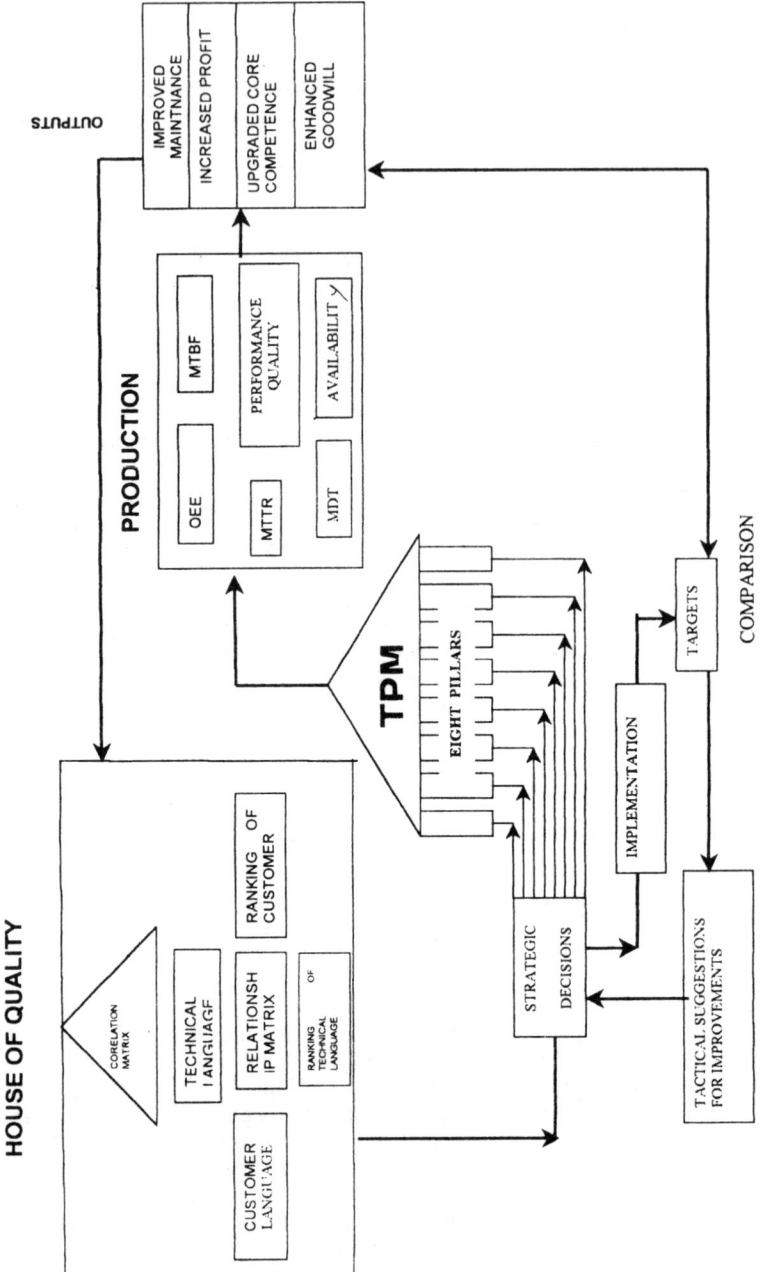

MQFD MODEL

Fig. 3: MQFD Model

MQFD team members are submitted to the top management for taking strategic decisions. The strategic decisions lead to the approval of implementing the tactical suggestions.

The tactical suggestions are implemented. The overall maintenance quality reaches the set target of 70%.On observing the powers of MQFD, management revises the target for attaining maintenance quality as 80%.In this background the MQFD members are preparing them selves to work along with Quality Engineers to proceed towards the next cycle of MQFD which begins by the construction of new house of quality. Thus MQFD leads to overall maintenance quality improvement with a particular reference to choice of customers.

9. CONCLUSION AND SCOPE FOR FUTURE RESEARCH

It has been found out that QFD has been implemented in companies only to a limited extent, whereas TPM implementation has just now been started. A strategy has to be adopted to get higher benefits by merging QFD in TPM journey. Till now, no research has been done in this direction. On recognizing this lacunae, in this paper we have brought out a model called MQFD. This model has been developed by linking QFD's HoQ with TPM principles. In order to configure this model so that it fits in practical situations we have integrated the business performance results namely profit, core competence and good will. Further with the MQFD model in order to direct the MQFD program along the streams of management's mission and policies, the provision for taking the strategic decision has been included. Though MQFD's practical validity is yet to be checked we have presented the hypothetical case study which illustrates it's implementation steps. We believe that this model will be an useful vehicle for today's organizations to achieve business results coupled with continuous maintenance quality improvement. As a next step, we wish to implement MQFD, at least on trial run basis in a company and study its practical validity. Right now one of the companies surveyed has agreed to data and opinion on the implementation feasibility of MQFD in its environment. We believe that enormous potential exists for future researchers to work on the implementation aspects of MQFD. Practical case studies on implementing MQFD in non manufacturing fields like hospitals, finance, agriculture and service sectors will also offer very valuable contribution to the society. This article is concluded by claiming that MQFD model could be a basis for future researchers seeking strategies for perfection in maintenance.

10. References

1. **Nakajima S.(1993)**, "Introduction to TPM", Productivity Press, Chennai.
2. **Blanchabrd, B.S.** (1997), "An enhanced approach for implementing Total Productive Maintenance"
3. http:// www.shef.ac.uk/ ~ibberson/ QFD-Introduction.html
4. **Cua, K.O., Mc Kone, K.E. and Schroeder, R.G.** (2001), "Relationship between TQM, JIT ,and TPM, and manufacturing performance", *Journal of operations management* 19, 675-694.
5. **Mc Kone, K.E., Schroeder, R.G. and Cua, K.O.** (1999), "Total productive maintenance: a contextual view", *Journal of operations management* Vol.19, 123-144.
6. **McKone,K.E., Schroeder, R.G. and Cua, K.O.** (2001), "The impact of total productive maintenance practices on manufacturing performance", *Journal of operations management* Vol.19,pp.39-58.
7. **Rho, B-H., Paark, K., and Yu, Y-N.** (2001), "An international comparison of the effect of manufacuring strategy – implementation gap on business performance", International Journal of production economics Vol. 70, pp 89-77.
8. **Terziovski, M. and Sohal, A.H.** (2000), "The adoption of continuous improvement and innovation strategies in Australian manufacturing firms", *Technovation* Vol.20,pp.539-550.

Artificial Neural Networks

GCMM 2004
Editors: Prasad K D V Yarlagadda and S Narayanan
Copyright © 2005, Vellore Institute of Technology, Vellore, India
Publisher: Narosa Publishing House Pvt. Ltd., New Delhi, India

A Neural Network based Prediction of Catastrophic Failure in an Inserted Tool Bits

Parivendhan Inbakumar J

M.S by Research, Department of Production Technology, Madras Institute of Technology, Chennai, Tamilnadu, India.

Email: inbakumar@yahoo.com

Rajmohan B

Professor and Head, Department of Production Technology, Madras Institute of Technology, Chennai, Tamilnadu, India.

Abstract

Catastrophic failure is being so predominant in the field of growing industries, detection of tool breakage during machining is important for automation. This approach to the tool breakage detection has focused on the development of signal processing techniques that has enhanced the effect of tool breakage on measurements of sound level. A neural network technique was used to predict the failure.

Keywords
Neural Network, Back Propagation, Sound Level.

1. INTRODUCTION

The realization of proper usage of the tool and failure of the tool shows a predominant effect in the growing industries. Thus spoiling the surface texture of the work piece and reducing the tool life. Thus this needs to be analyzed and the failure or the breakage of the tool should be reduced in order to minimize the tool cost as well as the work piece cost. Action is to be taken for process monitoring of the tool.

A neural network based system is used to predict the condition of the tool in the turning process. Specifically the relationship between the sensor's reading and the tool failure states are analyzed by neural network approach. In this approach the neural network serves as analyzing mechanism for the generated data that is consistent with the behavior of the process. And it logically provides a transparent view of the relationship between the measured variables and the tool states. The methodology used in this paper incorporates prediction driven scheme in conjunction with the neural network based model.

The prediction is associated with the tool condition monitoring; the analysis reflects the true experimental nature of the inter-relationship between the sound level sensor

455

readings and the tool conditions. Special emphasis is placed on the incorporation of varying cutting conditions, which is being seen on a sound level meter. A feed forward rule, training algorithm is used. Some attempts were made to predict the tool failures. The trained neural network is then taken to be sufficiently accurate model for tool failure based algorithm for estimating catastrophic failures in inserted tool bits. Performance strategies is developed and compared.

2. STATEMENT OF THE PROBLEM

A skilled operator can often predict the condition of the tool by observing the machining conditions and by utilizing his sensory perceptions. But an unskilled operator may not be able to predict the situation of the operation when there is a tool failure.

3. ARCHITECTURAL AND METHODOLOGICAL BASIS

The methodology used in this research paper basically uses a multilayered neural network to develop the model for prediction of the catastrophic failure of the tool bit. A supervised, feed forward, back propagation technique was used. A relatively sparse set of data was obtained during actual machining tests, performed on a heavy duty turning machine.

An accurate sound measuring instrument, a sound level meter was used to measure the sound level produced by the machine. Since the lathe machine produces noise more than the surrounding environment, the environment noise is neglected when the machine is on. The sensor was placed 10 centimeters to the tool shank because sound produced would be recorded easily while machining. In turn this sensor was connected to data acquisition chord and these data are brought to the computer system for neural network analysis.

The cutting parameters like speed, feed and depth of cut is also taken as the input for the network to learn. The experimental setup

is shown in the fig.1 and the architecture of the system is shown in fig.2.

Basically three steps are involved for the prediction.
- Determining the data
- Develop the software
- And at the last adapting the network to learn.

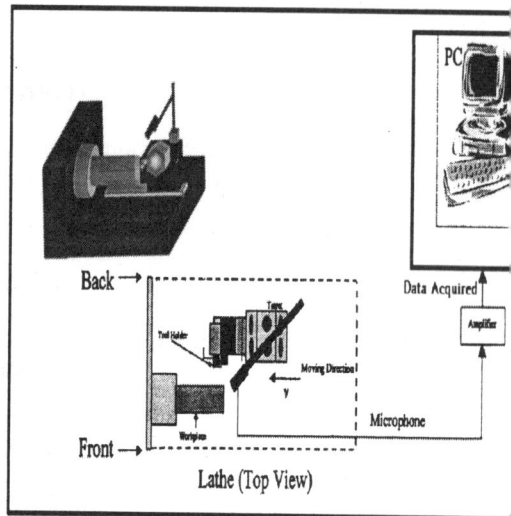

Fig. 1: Experimental Setup

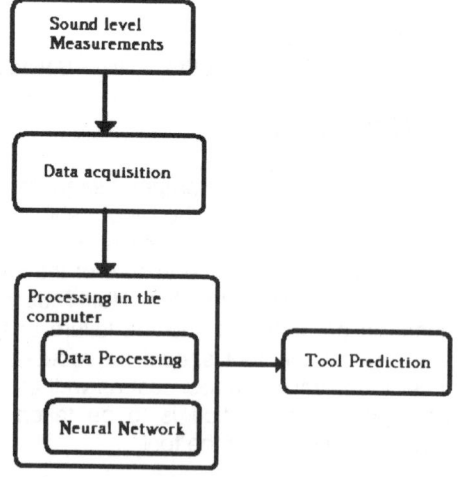

Fig. 2: Architecture of the system

456

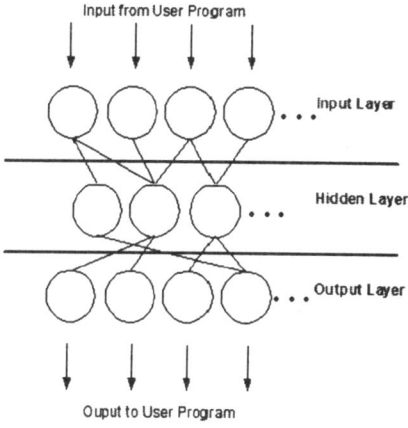

Fig. 3: Structure based model

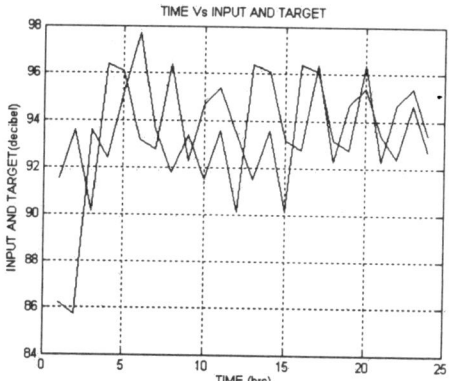

Fig. 4: Time vs Input and Target

4. STRUCTRE BASED MODEL ON NEURAL NETWORK

Neural networks are composed of computationally simple processing elements and their connections. Each of the processing elements receives input from the sensor and the cutting conditions. It operates on its input with a transfer function to produce the output [4]. The inputs are processed in the network; it forms the input to hidden layers in turn to the output layer.

This paper gives out the structural model based on neural network as shown in fig.3. The network structure composes of three individual layers, input layer, hidden layer and the output layer.

The inputs are fed forward in the network as described in the methodology.

Figure 4 & 5 gives the relationship between the input, output and the target.

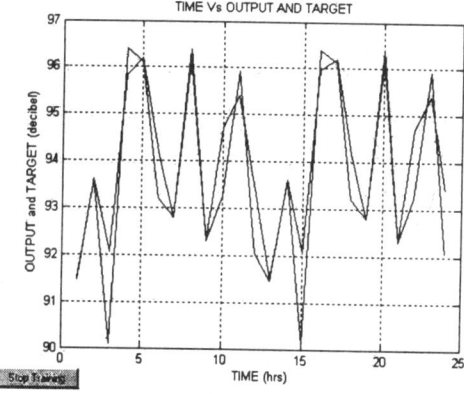

Fig. 5: Time vs Output and Target

The initializations are done to the network, layers, and to every neuron in the network. Each weights and biases are initialized for smooth performance. The layers are connected as required. These processing elements are processed in the hidden layer and the output layer. A correct transfer functions is selected for the network. The interconnected connections feed the information in a single direction towards the output end.

$$H_j = f\left(\sum_{i=1\ to\ n} W_{1j} * I_j + _j\right)$$

H_j = Hidden Layer output Signal
f = Activation Function Known as Sigmoid
W_{1j} = Weights of the input layer
$_j$ = Threshold of jth processing Element

$$O_k = f\left(\sum_{k=1\ to\ m} V_{jk} * H_j + _k\right)$$

O_k = Output Layer output Signal
H_j = Hidden Layer output Signal
f = Activation Function Known as Sigmoid
V_{jk} = Weights of the Output layer
$_k$ = Threshold of kth processing Element

By appropriately adjusting the weights and threshold of these above two equations, the network would be able to predict the failure of the tool bit. The training of the network is possible when this structure is processed.

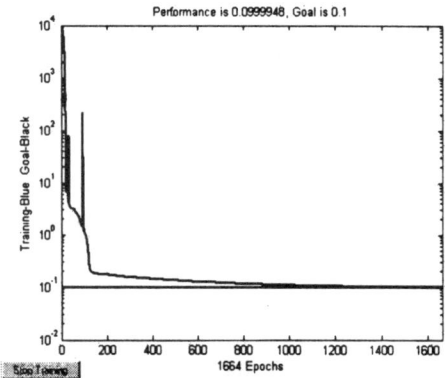

Fig. 6: Training Process

5. DEVELOPMENT OF TRAINING PATTERN

Training involves some form of teaching to force subsequent system behavior to meet specification. It involves the corrections or adjustment of the system parameters to make system response in the next iteration or experiment closer to the desired value. The training patterns have been developed by experimental work in which mild steel work piece and carbide tool are used. For the

example production cost and production time are calculated for various combinations of speeds and feeds amiable in the machine.

First data is presented, and output is computed. An error is obtained by comparing the output with the desired response, and it is used to modify the weights with the training algorithm. This procedure is repeated using all the data in the training set until a convergence criterion is met.

CONVERGENGE CRITERIA

Maximum number of layers produces slow convergence to the network, which may lead to over fitting when large neurons are used.

Some measures have been taken to accelerate the convergence of the gradient. The network training time can be improved by some tricks, such as joggling the weight or slightly noisy data. It has been found that if the activation level is restricted to the range from negative half to positive half, convergence time may be reduced by half compared ranges.

6. CONCLUSION

The prediction is associated with the tool condition monitoring; the analysis reflects the true experimental nature of the inter-relationship between the sound level sensor readings and the tool conditions. Range of sound produced during the catastrophic failure was predicted above 90 db. (reading taken on the sensor placed at 10 cm from the tool bit). Special emphasis is placed on the incorporation of varying cutting conditions, the neural network machining parameters. The program developed here is useful in predicting the catastrophic tool bit failure in turning process.

This is shown that tool failure can be predicted by monitoring the sound level.

7. REFERENCE

1. **Kare. M.K and Amit Agarwal**, 1997,"Development of neural

network software for the optimization of cutting speed and feeds in single pass turning", *17th AIMTDR*, REC.

2. **Myon-Woong Park, HYung_ Min Rho, Byoung Tae Park**, 1996, "Generation of modified cutting condition using neural network for an operation planning system, *Annals of CIRP*, Vol. 45, No. 1, pp. 475-478.

3. **Sakakura. M, Inasaki. I,** 1992, "A neural network approach to the decision-Making process for Grinding Operations", *Annals of CIRP*, Vol. 41, No. 1, pp. 353-356.

4. **Toshio Teshima, Toshiroh Shibasaka, Masannori Takuma, Akio Yamamoto,** 1993, Estimation of cutting tool life by processing tool image data with neural network", *Annals of CIRP*, Vol. 42, No.1, pp. 59–62.

GCMM 2004
Editors: Prasad K D V Yarlagadda and S Narayanan
Copyright © 2005, Vellore Institute of Technology, Vellore, India
Publisher: Narosa Publishing House Pvt. Ltd., New Delhi, India

Applications of Fractal Robots in Flexible Manufacturing System

Samleo L Joseph* & Chandrasekaran N**

*B.E.-Final year, **HOD
Department of Electronics & Instrumentation Engineering, Arunai Engineering College,
Thiruvannamalai-606603,

E-mail:lev_win@yahoo.co.uk

Abstract

The aim of this paper is to develop an autonomous fractal shape shifting robots in the application of manufacturing processes. Our proposal is to implement solar power panels for the electric drive mechanism (actuators) in these robots to make it autonomous for the possibility of telepresence in the Flexible Manufacturing System. Fractal robots are cubic bricks with inbuilt motors that can move under computer control by shuffling the cubes & hence change its shape to do unlimited tasks in accordance with its software. Motors are energized by electrical contact pads that also allow power & data signals to be routed from one robotic cube to another and thereby establish communication between robotic cubes by plate mechanism & 45 degree wedges provides their Sliding, Locking, Attaching and Detaching through screw mechanism. There are many amazing properties of a shape changing robot including a form of self-repair, fractal operation and possibly even self-manufacturing. One of the faces of the cube can be implemented by an end effector so that it can provide various kinds of machines which can be used in the application of the manufacturing process. If the operation is done once, then the project file will be merely downloaded into the manufacturing site and waited for the manufactured product to be delivered. Fractal robots implement the manufacturing processes to produce the goods placed on order with a turn around time of a few minutes to a few hours. So, a factory to produce factories can be made possible only with fractal robots. There are many proposed ways concepts through which manufacturings are processed but fractal robotics proves to be the best-chosen way to achieve every aspects of manufacturing.

Keywords
Solar Power Panels - Telepresence, Inbuilt Motors, Plate & Screw Mechanism, Self Repair,

1. INTRODUCTION

The rapidly changing demands and possibilities on the world market need high level flexibility and adaptability of production systems. For this reason all methods, technologies, tools that increase the modernity, quality, reliability of the products and satisfy the customers' individual needs and at the same time decrease the price, and delivery deadlines, have strategic importance. Highly automated production systems, such as computer controlled Systems can respond to this challenge. [5] Fractal robot is a new kind of robot made from motorized cubic bricks that move under computer control. These cubic motorized bricks can be programmed to move and shuffle themselves to change shape to make objects, potentially in few seconds, because of their motorized internal mechanisms. The shuffling movements of fractal robots are shown in figure-1. A minimal design requires 6 motors per cube. A maximal system requires 36 motors per cube if each mechanical function is implemented separately. One master cube has power and it routes the power from one cube to the next as and when needed. The voltage is about 10V. The cubes we implement at present are 400mm in size. The same design can be scaled from 100mm to 800mm. These robots are mainly used to carry tools on them and move to the workspace rather than take the work to the robot, so that they can be implemented for a wide range of applications. The advantage of using fractal robot is that they require far less energy to operate. Instead of moving a large robotic arm and its entire mass, only one robotic cube and the work piece attached to needs to be moved. If the work is more delicate, then even less power is required as smaller fractal robots having less mass and consuming even less power are used. So, solar power panels can be used to generate power for this fractal robots .The proposal of this paper is to implement solar power panels for the electric drive mechanism (actuators) in these robots to make it autonomous for the possibility of telepresence, so that it can be implemented in the Flexible Manufacturing Systems (FMS).

2. CONSTRUCTION OF FRACTAL ROBOTS

A shape-changing robot is built of a series of identical cubic bricks with electrical motors and computer chips. They have the ability to move under computer control by themselves such that their final structure is completely controlled by a computer program. Movement in fractal robots is by electrical motors that are present inside the cube. Motors are energized by electrical contact pads that also allow power and data signals to be routed from one robotic cube to another. This is referred to as active plate mechanism, shown in figure-2. The contact pads are placed in the outer surface of all the faces of these cubes. They also have 45-degree wedges, which are controlled by the electric motors that push in and out of the surfaces to engage the neighboring face that allows one robotic cube to lock to its neighbor through screw mechanism as shown in figure-3.

The locking mechanisms are classified into two types:
- o Face lock mechanism
- o Complementary lock mechanism

(When one robotic cube has locked all four of its locks into another cube it will be referred to as a face lock condition. Where one pair of lock engages from one face into another and vice versa, it will be referred to as a complementary lock.) These are the various sliding and locking mechanisms for these cubes to slide over one another and perform their right movement. [3]

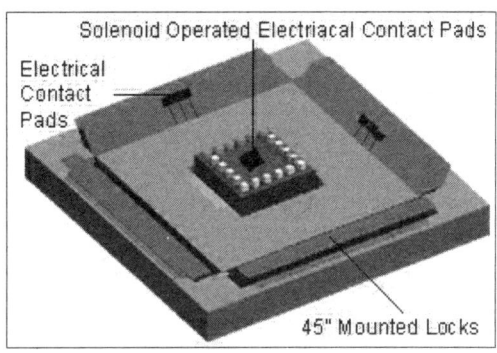

Figure .2:Plate Mechanism

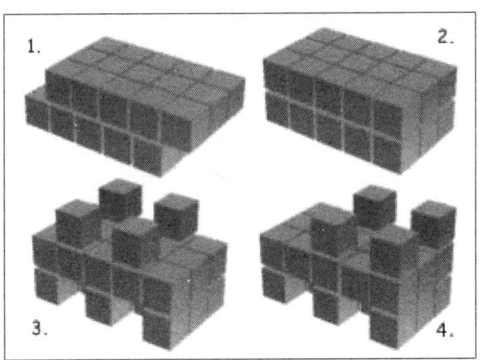

Figure. 1: Movements in Fractal Robots

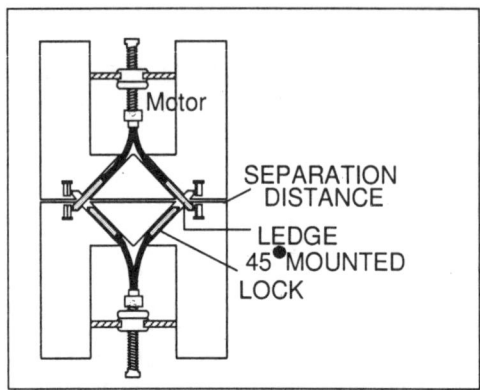

Figure. 3:Screw Mechanism

3.WORKING OF FRACTAL ROBOTS:

For proper operation of fractal robots power and data should be supplied and exchanged between robotic cubes properly. Power and data routing from face to face is implemented through the contact pads on the surface of the robotic cubes. Figure-4 illustrates how power and data is routed between two cubes. There are two layers of contact (copper strips) in this contact pad design. The two layers of contacts are kept apart by springs, which push the outer strips of contacts away from the inner strip. In this position, the outer contacts are effectively relayed out and isolated. When the contact pad is pushed out by the motor rotating screw against a nut, the spring is no longer able to keep the two sets of contact strips from touching and all the contacts from the lower strip make connections to the outer strip. When the motor in the bottom cube tends to push the contact pads still further, a situation arises when the contact pads of the bottom cube comes in contact with the top cube through all four levels of contact strips allowing power and data to be conveyed across the gap between the two faces. This is the working principle of fractal robots. [1]

4.SOLAR POWER PANELS

Photovoltaic (PV) materials convert sunlight into electricity & produces direct current (DC) electricity like a battery ranging from a few mill watts (mW) to several megawatts (MW). PV cells made of

semi-conductor silicon produce electrons when photons from sunlight strike them. This flow of electrons creates an electric current in the wire, which may be used directly or "stored" for later use. Electricity storage is important for PV cells because they obviously

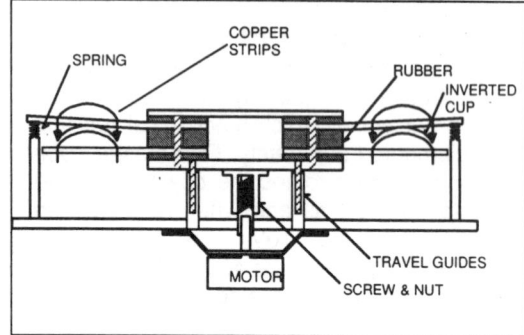

Figure. 4:Power Transmission

only generate electricity when the sun is shining. In remote locations, not served by electric transmission grids, PV cells coupled to batteries in Fractal Robots are often the least expensive method of providing electricity, as it requires only 10V per cell. So, Fractal Robots implemented with solar power panels for its electric drive mechanism (actuators) makes it autonomous for the possibility of telepresence.

4.1 Solar Photovoltaic Module

Solar cells generate an output of approximately 1 Watt per cell. This output is quit small for most of the applications. For our convenience in the system, solar modules in convenient packs of 10 Watt peak is manufactured, using its own manufactured high efficiency Mono-Crystalline solar Cells. The cells used in a given Module are carefully matched for maximizing the Module output. The aluminium frame construction is corrosion resistant and allows for lightweight module that is easy to transport across rugged terrains. The state-of-Art encapsulation ensures high insulation resistance and maximum moisture resistance. These Modules can be stacked in series and parallel to obtain desired power output in accordance with the tools implemented on the Fractal Robots. [4]

4.2 Technical Specifications:

Sl No.	Module Type	BE 100R61
1.	Peak Power (W)	10.0
2.	Peak Current (A)	0.61
3.	Peak Voltage (V)	16.5
4.	Normal Voltage (V)	12.0
5.	Open CKT VOL (V)	21.0
6.	Short CKT CT (A)	0.71
7.	DIM. L×B×W (mm)	365×365×40

5.TELEPRESENCE & SELF-REPAIR:

When damaged, the fractal robots move the faulty parts to elsewhere in the machine. Ideally there is a telemetry link that sends one picture every hour to a central point where operators are kept aware of the progress of the machines. (They also control the machines). There are many amazing properties to a Shape-changing robot that does not immediately spring to mind including a form of self-repair, fractal operation and possibly, which is really a wonder because it eliminates human intervention for repairing the cubes damaged and thereby they could be called immortal structures. There are three kinds of self-repair mechanisms. The easiest to implement in all the three is cube replacement. In large and complex structures, it's not always possible to ensure that all cubes are functioning. However, unlike those positional devices, shape-changing robots can repair themselves from almost any kind of isolated fault. Any cube that becomes faulty is simply picked up by a functioning cube and deposited else where in the structure. It can alternatively be ejected altogether. A second level of repair involves the partial dismantling of cubes and re-use of the plate mechanisms used to construct the cubes. In this case the entire structure involves a robot assembly station. If any robotic cubes get damaged, they can be brought back to the assembly station by other robotic cubes, dismantled into component plates, tested and then reassembled with plates that are fully operational to restore the cubes normal function. The third scheme for self-repair involves smaller robots servicing larger robots. Since the robot is fractal, it could send some of its fractally smaller machines to affect self-repair inside large cubes. With large collections of cubes, self-repair of this kind becomes extremely important. It increases reliability and reduce down time. Self-repairing capability of fractal robots can provide a better support of implementation in telepresence. [2]

6.APPLICATIONS

Fractal robots have application in every field of engineering activity and would possibly be the ultimate machine for improving safety in all aspects of manufacturing as well being the ultimate machine for dealing with all kinds of natural and human made disasters such as earthquakes, avalanches and nuclear accidents. One of the faces of the cube can be implemented by an end effector so that it can provide various kinds of machines which can be used in the application of the manufacturing process. Operations such as pressing, cutting, drawing, grinding and lapping can be implemented in machinery. The application include Mine clearance, Terra forming, Bridge building, Fractal road maintenance, Methyl hydrate extraction, Nuclear handling emergency, Neuron digitization and in Electronics. Everything from building space stations to managing nuclear accidents with 100% automation can be implemented with this technology. [3]

Manufacturing Through Fractal Robots:

If the operation is done once, then the project file will be merely downloaded into the manufacturing site and waited for the manufactured product to be delivered. They have many applications in the manufacturing sector from light assembly to complete productions lines that are automatically assembled and cabled ready to manufacture products on demand. The general direction this technology allows us to move is a new phenomenon called mass customisation. Mass customisation allows products to be tailored to individuals by making full use of the flexibility found in fractal robots to customise products in a most detailed way that requires a great deal of human intervention. Every manufactured product will go this way as computers take control of the order generating process through Internet, shopping terminals, voice recognition systems and tele-linked conventional retail outlets while fractal robots implement the manufacturing processes to produce the goods placed on order with a turn around time of a few minutes to a few hours. Of all these applications fractal robotics proves to be the best-chosen way to achieve every aspect of Flexible Manufacturing System.

6.1 Flexible Manufacturing System (FMS)

FMS have continuously increasing importance not only in big factories but in SMEs as well, and not only in the small and medium serial production, but in one-of-a-kind production, too. The reason is that in a well-organised FMS the production costs and delivery times are relatively low, keeping the appropriate quality at the same time. An FMS may consist of similar or different types of machine tools, robots or cells, such as manufacturing, warehouse, transportation, cleaning, measuring and assembly cells, etc. The cell elements have their own local controllers (RC, CNC, PLC, etc.) and each cell can be controlled separately [6].

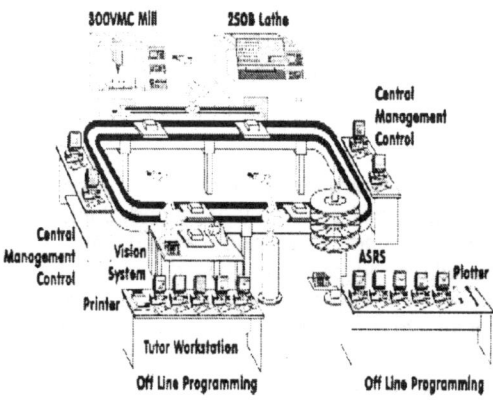

Figure. 6: Flexible Manufacturing System

6.2 FMS WITH FRACTAL ROBOTS

Here FMS with fractal robots replaces all the robots and cells such as warehouse, transportation, cleaning, measuring and assembly cells, etc. into a single cell with all these features revolving around the whole manufacturing system.

The Fractal Robotic technology involved in the FMS follows:

Minitek-1:
Definition of the production lots may be executed automatically. A pick and place robot arm on Fractal Robots is responsible for loading and unloading the parts on the lathe.

Minitek-2:
The integration of machines with the fractal robots allows a bigger flexibility in the type of the parts to be produced. The route of the parts to be produced can have operations in both machines and as many phases as desired.

Minitek-3:
The inclusion of a storage tray on this Fractal Robot allows the introduction of an additional concept of the CIM philosophy, which is the management of the parts storage. This revolving warehouse replaces the AS/RS (Automatic Software/ Retrieval system) cell.

Minitek-4:
With this fractal configuration, a new concept (Robot transport concept) is introduced with the Machine Vision System, and on the other hand the capacity of the warehouse is enlarged. Besides, this configuration provides a pallet or part fixturing system managed in automatic way with high speed by the software control of the cell.

Minitek-5:
This configuration introduces the assembly like one more operation to be made with a group of parts in order to build a mechanical assembly. This cell combines the possibilities of the Flexible Manufacturing Cells (FMS) with the Assembly ceils (FMA).

In future, if the precision and accuracy of the fractal robots are improved high in the machining operations, then even the CNC lathe machines can be replaced by fractal robots, along with the virtually real machining stimulation in Flexible Manufacturing System.

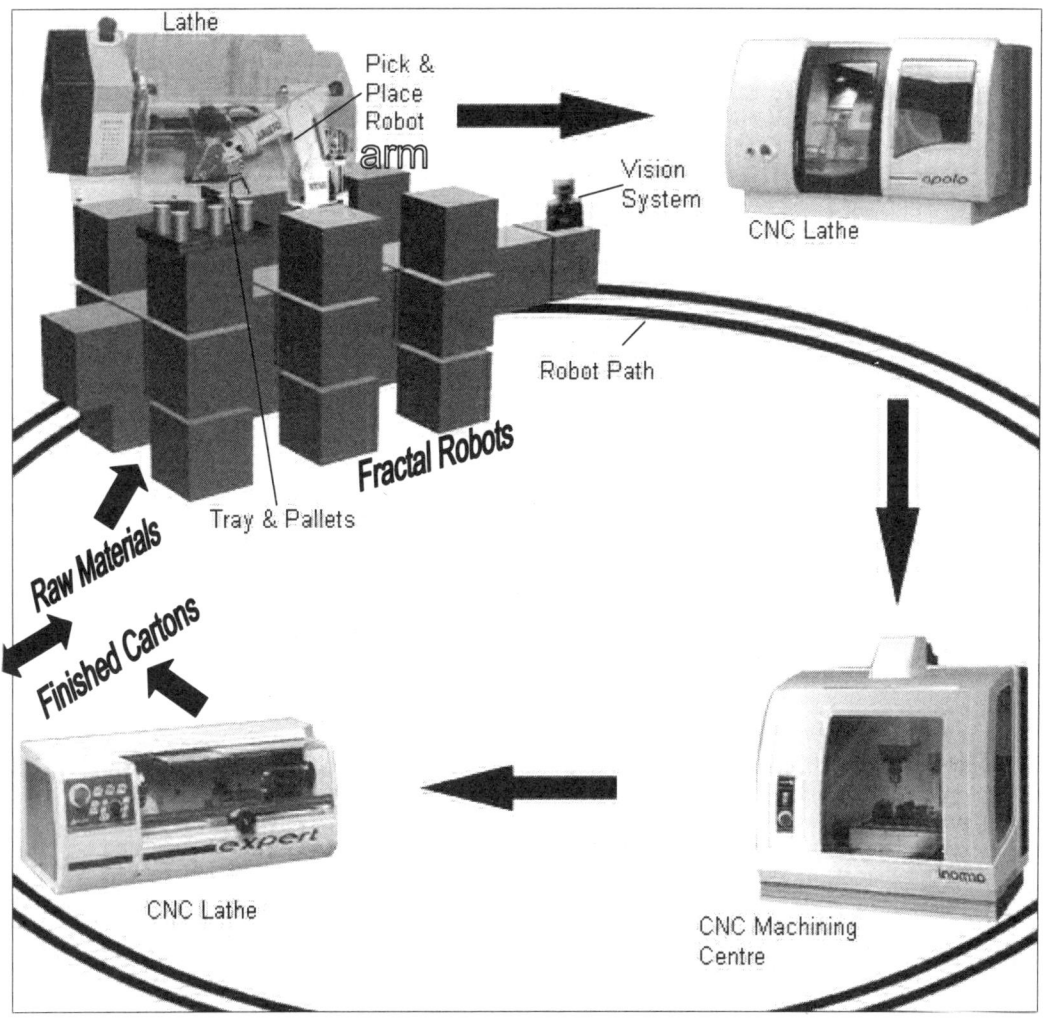

Figure. 6:Typical Flexible Manufacturing System with FRACTAL ROBOTS

7.CONCLUSION

From the above descriptions, it is very sounding that we are projected towards the manufacturing era. So, shape-changing robots can be implemented in every aspect of manufacturing, assembly, personal safety and environmentally friendly applications with telepresence. People will look back on today's technology with the same feelings we have towards medieval times when technology was primitive. All previously intractable mechanical problems in robotics have now been solved with this new branch of robotics. No doubt, fractal robotics is the newest weapons in engineering armory. [2]

8.REFERENCE

1. Digital matter control website www.fractal-robots.com
2. **J. Michael**, Advanced Manufacturing Temporary Bridges and Dams,Robodyne Cybernetics Ltd,1995. <http://www.ecu.pwp.blueyonder.co.uk/>
3. Solar Photovoltaic Modules, Bharat Electronics, Bangalore.
4. **Ránky P,** Components and Planning of Flexible Manufacturing Systems, Introduction to CIM Systems, Centre, Budapest, 1985
5. **A.S. Carrie**, Introducing a flexible manufacturing system. In: Int. J. of Prod. Research, Vol.22, No.6, 1984, pp.907-916.

GCMM 2004
Editors: Prasad K D V Yarlagadda and S Narayanan
Copyright © 2005, Vellore Institute of Technology, Vellore, India
Publisher: Narosa Publishing House Pvt. Ltd., New Delhi, India

Intelligent Control of the Motion and Path of a Robotic Arm

Srikant R R

Lecturer, Dept. of Mechanical Engg. RIT, Adavipolam, Yanam.

Email: srikant_revuru@yahoo.com

Srinivasa Rao Ch

Associate Professor, College of Engineering, GITAM,Visakhapatnam-530045

Email: csr_gitam@yahoo.co.in

Nageswara Rao D

Professor, Dept. of Mechanical Engg. A.U. College of Engineering,
Visakhapatnam-530003

Abstract
With the growth of computer-integrated manufacturing and the urge for automation, robotics are finding their application in almost all fields of engineering. Proper utilization and application of the robotics can be achieved by proper control of the motion characteristics and path of the robotic arm. Over many years, much work is dedicated in this direction. But the complexities in the modeling and solving of the related calculations limit the success of such work. The present paper is concerned with the application of Artificial Neural Networks to find the motion characters and the trajectory planning of the manipulator. The network is trained in two ways: to calculate the joint variables in inverse kinematics and to calculate the final position in direct kinematics. The trajectory of the manipulator is also calculated in the present work.

Keywords
Path, Robot, Manipulator, Neural Networks, Welding, Kinematics, Back Propagation Neural Networks, Inverse Kinematics

1. INTRODUCTION

The growth and urge for flexible manufacturing systems has led to the growth in the field of robotics. The successful utilization of robotic manipulator is determined by the successful understanding and proper control of the motion characteristics of the manipulator is inevitable. The control of the manipulator is studied in two ways: Inverse and direct kinematics. In direct kinematics, by using the joint angles and the link lengths and orientations, the final position of the end-effecter is calculated. Inverse kinematics deals with the calculation of the orientation and link characteristics based on the final position of the end-effecter. This is particularly useful in pick and place manipulators wherein the final position is known and the link characteristics are to be calculated for achieving the desired position [1]. The calculations involved are complex and their complexity increases with the number of degrees of freedom of the manipulator. Also, in applications like welding and painting, the speed of the manipulator plays a major role in the success of the process. The trajectory planning occupies a very prominent place in the calculations. Every care has to be taken to ensure that the robotic arm in no way causes any harm to the other equipment or men by following a collision free path [1]. The calculation of all the above mentioned quantities and related concepts demands highly complicated and strenuous calculations [2-4].

2. ARTIFICIAL NEURAL NETWORKS

In the present age of automation, where the human element is needed to be replaced, artificial intelligence has gained immense importance. Artificial Neural Networks is a very popular technique used to replace the intelligent human operator who takes decisions based on past experience and relevant data. Artificial neural networks are modelled closely following the brain. Some neural network structures are not closely associated with the brain and some does not have a biological counterpart. However, neural networks have a strong similarity to the biological brain and therefore a great deal of terminology is borrowed from neuroscience.

Back Propagation Neural Networks (BPNNs) are one of the most common neural network structures, as they are simple and effective, and have found home in a wide assortment of machine learning applications, such as character recognition. . The network is a multi layer network (multi layer perceptron) that contains at least one hidden layer in addition to input and output layers. Number of hidden layers and number of neurons in each hidden layer is to be fixed based on application, the complexity of the problem and the number of inputs and outputs. Use of non-linear log- sigmoid transfer function enables the network to simulate non-linearity in practical systems. Due to its numerous advantages, back propagation network is chosen for present work.

BPNNs start as a network of nodes arranged in three layers--the input, hidden, and output layers (fig 1). The input and output layers serve as nodes to buffer input and output for the model, respectively, and

the hidden layer serves to provide a means for input relations to be represented in the output. Before any data has been run through the network, the weights for the nodes are random, which has the effect of making the network much like a newborn's brain-developed but without knowledge.

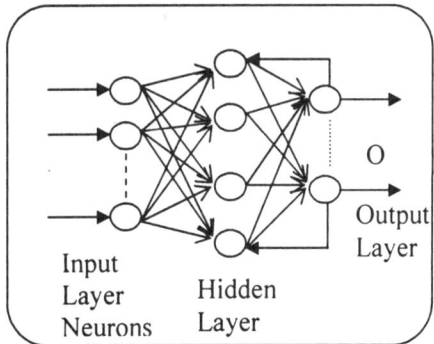

Fig.1: Back Propagation Neural Network

When training the network, once a classification has been given, it is compared to the actual target value. The error in the result is then ``back propagated'' through the network, which causes the hidden and output layer nodes to adjust their weights in response to any error in classification, if it occurs. The modification of the weights is done according to the gradient of the error curve, which points in the direction to the local minimum near the instance. Unfortunately, the local minimum is not always the global minimum, which causes the network to settle in an non-optimal configuration. The network can sometimes be deterred from settling in local minima by increasing or decreasing the number of hidden layer nodes or even by rerunning the algorithm (this is because the weights will be reinitialized to a different set of random numbers, which may keep them from falling into a local minimum that is not the global minimum [3-6].

The present work uses heuristic methods of optimization to obtain the global minimum. The process necessitates the use of 'momentum' to facilitate prevention of getting trapped in local minimum. For inverse kinematics the inputs are taken as the final position and orientation of the end-effecter. Thus in total the network has six inputs. The

467

outputs being the orientations of the links. The number of the outputs depends on the number of the joints. In direct kinematics, the inputs are taken as the orientations and link lengths while the outputs are the position and orientation of the end-effecter. Besides the above-mentioned outputs, the speed required based on the application is also presented as output in either of the cases.

3. RESULTS AND DISCUSSIONS

To study the validity of the proposed model, a simple two-degree of freedom serial manipulator is taken up for study. The various characteristics of the manipulator are calculated for various positions and orientations and positions of end-effecter. This data is normalized and is used for training the network. For direct kinematics, the inputs are the lengths and orientations of the links, thus the inputs are four. The outputs are the orientation and the position of the end effecter in all three directions. The network is trained for various number of hidden layer neurons and is optimized to have 4 hidden layer neurons. Based on the base position and the position of the end-effecter, the trajectory can be planned keeping in view the man and machine locations in the industry. The type of the application, the speed of the manipulator is determined. The obtained results are compared with the calculated ones and an error of less than 10% is found. Similar strategy is adopted in case of inverse kinematics, wherein the final position of the arm is known; the link orientations are calculated.

It may be observed that to implement the system proposed, it is necessary to provide some data like that pertaining to the type of application, positions and orientations of links or end effecter as the case may be. To facilitate the easy and fast understanding and implementation of the system, a user-friendly interface is developed using Microsoft Visual Basic 6.0. the required data may be entered through the screens and the C++ programs are implanted in the back end. Sample Screens are shown in fig2 and fig 3.

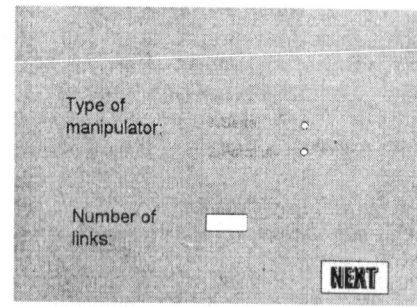

Fig. 2: A Sample screen from the developed package

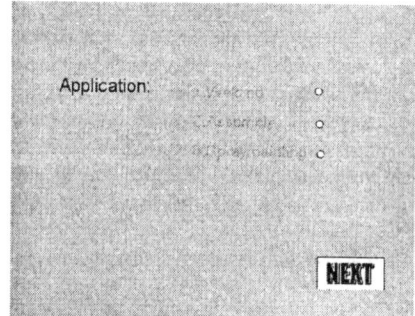

Fig. 3: A Sample screen from the developed package

4. CONCLUSIONS

❖ The applications of robotics in present day world are manifold.

❖ Artificial neural networks can be successfully implemented to overcome the difficulties in calculations of kinematics of robotics.

❖ Use of a properly optimized and well-trained network produces results with very reasonable error.

5. SCOPE FOR EXPANSION OF WORK

➢ The possibility of using various other networks may be explored.

➢ More complex manipulators may be studied and the results may be further generalized for an 'n' DOF manipulator. This would require extensive calculations to be performed.

➢ The package developed may be further improved by incorporating other suggestions and features related to each and every application.

6. REFERENCES

1. **Shuli Sun and Pingyuan Cui**," Path tracking and a practical point stabilization of mobile robot.", *Robotics and Computer-Integrated Manufacturing* 20 (2004) 29-34.

2. **Ill- Soo Kim, Joon-Sik Son, Sang-Heon Lee, Prasad K.D.V.Yarlagadda,** "Optimal design of neural networks for control in robotic arc welding", *Robotics and Computer-Integrated Manufacturing* 20 (2004) 57-63.

3. **Martin T. Hagan, Howard B. Demuth, Mark Beale,** "Neural Network Design." Thomson Learning, Vikas Publishing House, (1996)

4. **James A.Freeman, David .M.Skapura,** "Neural Networks Algorithms, and Programming Techniques." Addison-Wesley (1999).

5. **Bose N.K. and Liang P.,** "Neural Networks Fundamentals with Graphs, Algorithms and Applications." Tata Mc. Grawhill Publishing Co. Ltd. (1998)

6. **Junhong and Dereklinkens**, "Fuzzy Neural Control: Principles, Algorithms and Applications." Prentice hall of India Pvt. Ltd. (1998).

GCMM 2004
Editors: Prasad K D V Yarlagadda and S Narayanan
Copyright © 2005, Vellore Institute of Technology, Vellore, India
Publisher: Narosa Publishing House Pvt. Ltd., New Delhi, India`

Logical Reasoning with Neural Network in Decision Making Analysis

Ghosh S*, Sarkar B** & Sanyal S***

* Research Associate, ** Professor and Head, *** Professor
Department of Production Engineering, Jadavpur University
Kolkata – 700 032, India

Email: bijon_sarkar@email.com
surojit_ghosh@email.com

Abstract

The recent developments that offer promises for enhancing the ability to solve any logic-based decision making problems. Some of the promising directions for elaborating the innovative works may be viewed from artificial intelligence and operation research point of view. Propositional logic techniques have been considered effectively, so that the controlled randomization, learning strategies, induced decompositions etc. can be understood properly. As a matter of fact, the complementary strength, optimization as well as constraint programming can be profitably merged since their integrations have been subject of increasing commercial and research activity. The proposed approach tries to enlighten on the use of logical inference in different ways and their connectivities to neural network technique. Among various logical operators, the most useful logical operator has been trained by neural network in the present work. Depending on the results obtained by applying learning rule, the decision has been made properly.

Keywords
Propositional Logic, Normal Form, Neural Network.

1. INTRODUCTION

Modern technology has been given several efforts for incorporating the logic concept in decision-making analysis especially in optimization methods. Logical deduction is one of the better alternatives in solution techniques of optimization problems. Integer programming can be another option for logical inference. Various logical statements can be established in optimization problems and with the help of integer programming solution can be made. For problem representation usually Boolean logic i.e. 0-1 variables are considered as a discrete choice. Accordingly various logical propositions can be formed. The propositions involved some logical operators like, AND, OR, NOT, IMPLICATION etc. But when these operators are used in Propositional calculus, these are treated as "disjunctive" or "conjunctive" operators. Recent advancement of logical reasoning showed a lot of effort on incorporating this with neural network (NN). Artificial neural network presents a new integrative approach in decision-making analysis. Though they have been highly inspired by biological neuron systems. But NN method has been widely used in prediction and classification problems. For decision makers it will be easier if they are able to use some logical reasoning techniques embedded with neural network. To overcome some of the critical situation, logic can be established by some atomic sentences so that the predictions can be made with the help of NN method. The purpose of the present work is to show the alternative approach of optimization techniques using logical reasoning methods and its integrated view with neural network for decision makers.

2. LOGICAL REASONING
2.1 Forms of Logical Inference

A proposition is a declarative sentence that is either true or false, but it cannot be both. Propositional logic is a mathematical model for reasoning about the truth of the logical expressions. Logical expressions can be determined by some deductive concepts, resolution techniques etc. Propositional variables depend on mainly two constants such as *true* and *false* statement. The proposed method tries to show the logical approach toward the decision-making analysis and for this reason neural network can be used as a tool. Some of the logical operators have used in the present work such as, NOT, AND and OR. There are some symbols, which have been used for logical expression. Some of the expressions can be depicted with the help of fig. 1.

¬ : NOT
: OR
∧ : AND
: IF ... THEN (Conditional)
: IFF and only IFF (iff) (Biconditional)

Fig. 1: Logical Operators

2.2 Truth Table Concept

In a truth table, the column for each variable in the expression and each row in the table corresponds to an assignment of values to variables. The final column gives the value of the expression for the particular set of variable assignments given in the row. If A and B are two atomic propositions then truth table would be able to show their interrelationship which is shown is Table 1.

Table 1: Truth table for two propositions

A	B	¬ A	A ^ B	A B	A B	A B
1	1	0	1	1	1	1
1	0	0	0	1	0	0
0	1	1	0	1	1	0
0	0	1	0	0	1	1

In the Table 1 '0' stands for false and '1' stands for true values. Some equivalent forms of the relationship stated in Table 1 can be written as,

A   B: ¬ (A   B)
A   B: (A → B) ∧ (B → A)
¬ (A ∧ B): ¬ A ∨ ¬ B
¬ (A ∨ B): ¬ A ∧ ¬ B

2.2.1 Normal Form of Logical Expression

Normal forms generally are being used in logical modeling. Two types of normal form are quite useful such as conjunctive normal form (CNF) and disjunctive normal form (DNF). If A, B and C are three propositions, then their normal form can be considered as,

$$(A) \wedge (B \vee C'): CNF$$
$$(A \vee \neg B) \to C = \neg (A \vee \neg B) \vee C$$
$$= (\neg A \wedge \neg (\neg B)) \vee C \quad \} \quad DNF$$
$$= (\neg A \wedge B) \vee C$$

2.2.2 Tautologies

A 'tautology' would be the logical expression that is always TRUE, regardless of the assignment of truth-values to the variables in the expressions. If A and B are two propositions then they may be related so that their combination must be giving the outcome TRUE.

Table 2: Tautologies

a)

A	¬ A	A ¬ A
1	0	1

b)

A	¬ A	¬ (A ^ ¬ A)
1	0	1

c)

A	B	A (¬ (A ^ B))
1	1	1

3. NEURAL NETWORK

Neural network concept has been adapted from the structure of brain, which consists of a set of interconnected entities called nodes or units. Each unit has been designed by biological counterparts called neurons. This concept has been used in medical diagnosis, target recognition, character recognition, speech recognition, process modeling, data modeling, machine diagnosis, financial forecasting etc. where weighted set of input can be responded by outputs.

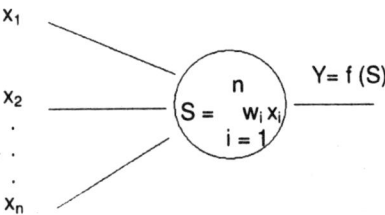

Fig. 2: Neural Network Structure

In the fig. 2, x_1, x_2, ..., x_i etc. have been considered as inputs and w_1, w_2, ..., w_i etc. associated as weight vectors corresponding the input vector X. Neural network can be composed of defined units and their corresponding weights through some connectivity, sometime it has a thousand of units. Neural net can have some layers may single, double or multilayers. Single layer network can have the structure as shown in fig. 3.

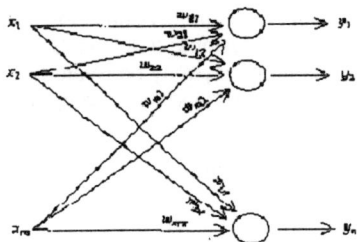

Fig. 3: Single Layer Network

If $X = (x_1, x_2, ..., x_m)$ are the input vector and the weight vector can be given as,

$$W = \begin{pmatrix} w_{11}\ w_{12}\ w_{13} \cdots w_{1n} \\ w_{21}\ w_{22}\ w_{23} \cdots w_{2n} \\ .... \\ .... \\ w_{m1}\ w_{m2}\ w_{m3} \cdots w_{mn} \end{pmatrix} \quad ... (1)$$

then, output y_k can be written as,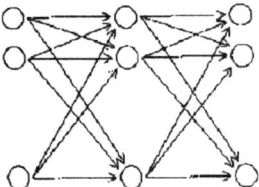

$$y_k = (w_{1k}, w_{2k}, w_{3k}, ..., w_{mk}) \qquad ... (2)$$

Finally, the output vector $\overline{Y} = (y_1, y_2, y_3,..., y_m)^T$ can be written as,

$$\overline{Y} = W^T * \overline{X} \qquad .... (3)$$

Whereas in multilayer net, two or more layers can be added to the input vector. This can be shown in fig. 4.

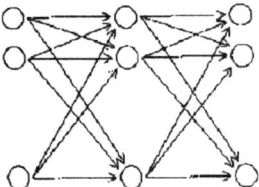

Fig. 4: Multilayer Neural Network

4. LOGICAL REASONING WITH NEURAL NETWORK

The proposed method tries to show the boolean-based exclusive OR (XOR) function with the help of neural network tool. Only two inputs have been selected for the problem. Let us consider x_1 and x_2 are two input variables in the present work and they are related by boolean logic.

Table 3: Two inputs XOR function

x_1	x_2	Y (output)
1	1	0
0	0	0
1	0	1
0	1	1

For building up the neural net one learning rate would be the most important component, which can be associated with certain weights for making relationship between input and output. During training period weights have adjusted so that the relationship, $Y = W^T * X$ can be built up. Generally weights are to be adjusted by following the relationship,

$$dw_{ij} = r * x_i * (t_j - y_j) \quad \ldots\ldots\ldots\ldots (4)$$

where, dw_{ij} = change in weights
  r = learning rate
  t_j = target output

This rule can be helpful for minimizing the error by making difference between target out and actual output. Neural net for Table 3 can be described by fig. 5.

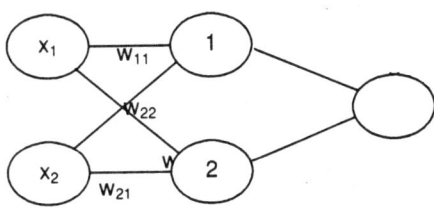

Fig. 5: Neural Net for XOR

Certain weights have been given in the proposed approach so that the network can be formed properly. The target error has fixed up till 5% and learning cycle has been terminated after 100 cycles. The relationship between learning cycle and normalized error has been plotted graphically.

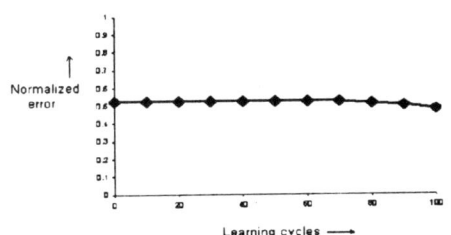

Fig. 6: Average Error after 100 Cycles

Table 4: Relative error after 100 cycles

Row	Output	Normalized error	Relative error
1	0	0.522	
4	1	0.520	
3	1	0.519	
2	0	0.478	

After learning after 200 cycles, the average error became 0.122, which can be shown in fig. 7 and the relative error shown in Table 5.

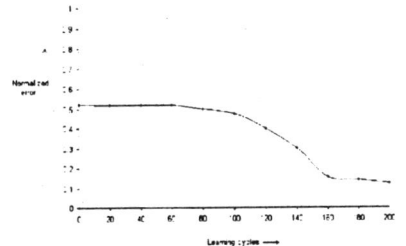

Fig. 7: Average Error after 200 Cycles

Table 5: Relative error after 200 cycles

Row	Output	Normalized error	Relative error
1	0	0.519	
4	1	0.475	
3	1	0.299	
2	0	0.122	

Learning after 250 cycles the curve can plotted as shown in fig. 8 and corresponding relative error shown in Table 6.

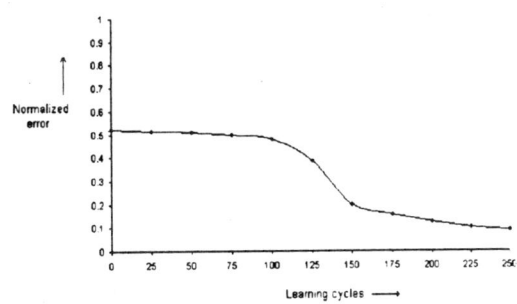

Fig. 8: Average Error after 250 Cycles

Table 6: Relative error after 250 cycles

Row	Output	Normalized error	Relative error
1	0	0.519	
4	1	0.275	
3	1	0.199	
2	0	0.098	

The average error has found 0.098 at the end of 250 cycles and finally, after 300 cycles target error of 5% have found.

473

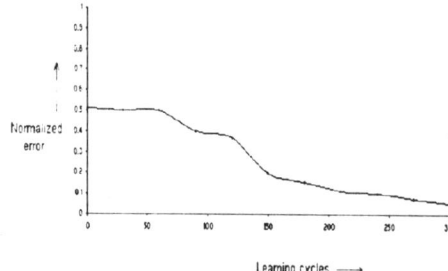

Learning cycles ⟶

Fig. 9: Average Error after 300 Cycles

Table 7: Relative error after 300 cycles

Row	Output	Normalized error	Relative error
1	0	0.419	
4	1	0.256	
3	1	0.099	
2	0	0.051	

4.1 Discussion

The result found in the training has reached 5% (approx.) of the targeted error. On the basis of this result decision makers would have choice to decide the most optimal result among all learning results. Accordingly the corresponding proposition has to be selected.

Let us consider, A be an atomic sentence, which has defined with help of some boundary conditions in an optimization problem. If those boundary conditions are not satisfied then that proposition cannot be defined properly. Error minimization by neural network can be able to give decision of choosing the optimal proposition. In the present work only XOR logical reasoning has been learned by neural network. But in case of conjunctive normal, disjunctive normal form etc. these can also to be performed by neural network.

5. CONCLUSION

Artificial neural networks present a new paradigm for decision support system that integrates knowledge and learning. They have been highly inspired by biological neural systems where the nodes of the network represent the neurons and the arcs, the axons and dendrites. The proposed work tries to show the application of neural network in logical reasoning method especially in propositional logic. Depending on the results of these method decision makers can also be able to decide the optimal solution any strategy.

6. REFERENCE

1. **Bjorkqvist J., Westerlund T.** (1999), "Automated reformulation of disjunctive constraints in MINLP optimization", *Journal of Computer and Chemical Engineers*, 23, 11 – 14.
2. **Turkay M., Grossmann I.E.** (1996), "Logic based algorithm for optimal synthesis of process networks", *Journal of Computer and Chemical Engineers*, 20 (8), 959 – 978.
3. **Vecchietti A., Grossmann I.E.** (1999), "A disjunctive 0 – 1 nonlinear optimizer for process system models", *Journal of Computer and Chemical Engineers*, 23, 555 – 565.
4. **Denton J.W., Hung M.S.** (1996), "A comparison of nonlinear method for supervised learning in multilayer feedforward neural network", *European Journal of Operation Research*, 93, 358 – 368.
5. **Liebowitz J.** (2001), "Knowledge management and its link to artificial intelligence", *Expert Systems with Applications*, 20 (1), 1 – 6.
6. **Freeman J., Skapura D.** (1991), *Neural Networks Reading* MA: Addison-Wesley.
7. **Shea P., Lin V.** (1989), "Detection of explosives in checked airline baggage using an artificial neural system", *International Journal of Neural Networks*, 1 (4), 249-253.
8. **Baumgartner J., Laver R.** (1979), "Iterated perfect set forcing", *Annals of Mathematical Logic*, 17, 271 – 288.
9. **Kurilic M.S.** (2002), "Unsupported boolean algebras and forcing", *Bulletin of Symbolic Logic*, 8 (1), 146.
10. **Emden V., Kowalski M.H.** (1976), "The semantics of predicate logic as a programming language", *Journal of ACM*, 23, 733 – 742.
11. **Robinson J.A.** (1965), "A machine oriented logic based on the resolution principle", *Journal of ACM*, 12, 23 – 41.
12. **Miller D.** (1986), "A theory of modules for logic programming", *IEEE Comp. Soc. Press*, 106 – 114.

GCMM 2004
Editors: Prasad K D V Yarlagadda and S Narayanan
Copyright © 2005, Vellore Institute of Technology, Vellore, India
Publisher: Narosa Publishing House Pvt. Ltd., New Delhi, India

Modeling the Process Parameters to Predict the Surface Qualities of RP / FDM using Artificial Neural Networks.

Devika D

Dr M G R Educational and Research Institute,
Chennai.

Email: ddevika39@yahoo.co.in

Abstract

Rapid prototyping (RP) has a profound impact on the way to produce models, prototype parts and tooling. Companies are now extending the application of the technology for producing the finished goods. Rapid manufacturing (RM) may rapidly grow and ultimately overshadow the rapid prototyping and rapid tooling markets, which will assist the companies to remain competitive. Fused Deposition Modeling (FDM) is a complex RP technology involving many different process parameters. This paper uses Artificial Neural Networks (ANN) approach to evolve an efficient model for estimation of output parameters such as porosity, surface roughness and dimensional accuracies, based on three levels of input parameters such as slice thickness, road width, model temperature and air gap. Multilayer feed forward network and supervised learning algorithm is used to predict the product quality by experimenting the models of ABS plastic on Stratasys FDM 2000 RP machine. The training and validation of the network is performed with experimentally measured data. The result obtained from the above proves that, this model can predict accurately the surface quality of the product.

Keywords
Rapid Prototyping, FDM, ANN, Modeling, Responses.

1. INTRODUCTION
1.1 General Information

In recent years, wind of change in opening up local markets for worldwide competition has led to a fundamental change in product development of manufacturers. Introducing new products at ever-increasing rate is crucial for remaining successful in a competitive global economy [1]. In order to stay competitive, manufactures should be capable in delivering products in fulfilling the total satisfaction of customers, or more specifically, products in higher quality, right time to market and at reasonable costs.

Decreasing product development cycle time and increasing product complexities require new way to realize innovation ideas [2]. Many technologies are being developed and one of the newest technologies is Rapid Prototyping and manufacturing system.

Nowadays RP technology has become an increasingly important part of the manufacturing industry. It provides almost direct translation of a design into a manufactured component and that; compared to most traditional manufacturing processes it has a low lead-time. The right product being developed in a prompt lead-time is the most important winning ingredient [3].

1.2 Rapid Prototyping (RP)

Current RP systems are based upon a layered manufacturing paradigm. In this method, a solid 3D CAD model of the object is first decomposed into cross-sectional layer representations in the process planner. The planner then generates trajectories for guiding material additive processes to physically build up these layers in an automated fabrication machine to form the object. Supporting layers are also simultaneously built up to fixture the object. Each physical layer, which consists of the cross section and a supporting layer, is then deposited and fused to the previous layer using one of several available deposition and fusion technologies. The initial concept of RP was, to use it as a prototype model. But advances in the technology have widened the scope of its application.

Practical implementation of layered manufacturing for modern manufacturing needs have been made possible by several enabling technologies, including CAD based solid modeling, lasers, ink-jet printing and high performance motion controllers integrated with more traditional manufacturing processes such as powdered metallurgy, extrusion, welding, CNC machining and lithography into novel arrangements.

1.3 Rapid Manufacturing (RM)

Economic and industrial communities worldwide will be subjected to the increasing impact of competitive pressures resulting from the globalization of markets and supply chains to satisfy the customers [4]. Now RP is a technology racing towards its finishing line with other emerging branches of Rapid Tooling and Rapid Manufacturing. Current RP processes are unable to (1) produce parts with the accuracy and surface finish required for many engineering models, (2) build with a wide variety of engineering materials, and (3) directly produce high quality product for functional and structural applications. Creation of parts with satisfactory key issues such as surface finish, strength and dimensional accuracies are the barrier for creating visually, functionally and structurally suitable product in direct RP Manufacturing. A good surface finish on the parts helps to eliminate dimensional inaccuracies, costs and lead-time to market, which is defeated by the time delays involved in post processing.

So process improvements are necessary before any of the techniques can be successfully commercialized for structural and functional applications [5].

1.4 Fused Deposition Modeling (FDM)

One of the most widely used RP process is the Fused Deposition Modeling. Extruding freeform shapes was first developed and commercialized by Stratasys, Inc. (U.S.). This system consists of the main 3D modeler unit, slicing software and a workstation. The process starts with the creation of a part with a CAD system as a solid or surface model. This approach called FDM, deposits a continuous filament of a thermoplastic polymer or wax through a resistively heated nozzle. The material is delivered as a wire in the extrusion head and heated slightly above its flow point so that it solidifies relatively quickly after it exists the nozzle.

2. PROCESS PARAMETERS

Process parameters are listed in four categories [6].

- Operation specific parameters such as slice thickness, road width, head speed, model extrusion temperature, envelope temperature and fill pattern.
- Machine specific parameters such as nozzle diameter, filament feed rate, roller speed, flow rate and filament diameter.
- Material specific parameters such as powder characteristics, binder characteristics, viscosity, stiffness, flexibility and thermal conductivity.
- Geometric specific parameters such as fill vector length and support structure.

Once material specific parameter has been developed, the other parameters are interdependent and optimized concurrently.

Otherwise, it will severely limit the structural properties of the parts thus produced. Hence the FDM is a layer addition process; the following are the main expected internal and external defects. Internal defects to be considered are porosity and voids and external defects are normally surface roughness and dimensional inaccuracies. These defects are caused by layer slice thickness, road width, model temperature, air gap and build orientation.

The accuracy is usually different in horizontal and vertical directions; hence part orientation may be an important factor. The tessellation or triangulation of the solid model itself introduces some inaccuracies, which is compounded by the step like surfaces produced during fabrication. So dimensional accuracy is also thus one of the main goals for improvement in RP technology. Due to layering process and non application of pressure to improve the fusing between adjacent particles, roads or layers which will cause porosity and voids in between them. These defects can be overcome by adjusting model temperature and air gap setting. This will result in part strength. It is confirmed that the surface quality problem cannot be completely eliminated but it can be reduced to certain percentages by carefully controlling the process parameters.

3. ARTIFICIAL NEURAL NETWORKS (ANN)

The current FDM system results in parts with several surface and internal defects that limit the structural properties of the parts produced. This aims modeling the process parameters of a part built by the Fused Deposition Modeling process in order to get good quality by predicting the output parameters after efficient training using ANN technique.

When certain crucial parameters like slice thickness, road width, model temperature, air gap etc. are varied or even modified slightly, it might lead to large variations in the output responses, which is of paramount importance in the fabrication of the product. This might may result in heavy loss and hence, in order to prevent such losses, ANN developed provides the more accurate results which are incorporated in the FDM machine.

ANN is a computational structure inspired by the study of biological neural processing and stemming from the basic mathematical principles. The basic attributes of neural networks may be divided into the architecture and the functional properties or neurodynamics. Architecture defines the network structure, that is, the number of artificial neurons in the network and their interconnectivity. Neural network consist of many interconnected neurons, or processing elements, with familiar characteristics, such as inputs, synaptic strengths, activation, outputs and bias. The neurodynamics of neural networks learns, recalls, associates, and continuously compares new information, and how it develops new classifications if necessary [7].

Learning in neural networks is highly important and is undergoing an intense research in both biological and artificial networks. It is the process by which the neural network adapts itself to a stimulus, and eventually it produces a desired response. During the process of learning, the network adjusts the synaptic weights, in response to an input stimulus so that its actual output response converges to the desired output response. Neural network paradigms observe learning rules desired by mathematical expressions called learning equations. Learning equations describe the learning process for the paradigm, which in equality is the process for self-adjusting its weights.

With the help of ANN as a prediction tool, it is possible to predict the output responses namely porosity, surface finish, thickness deviation and width deviation for any specific combination of input parameters.

The desired accurate models can be obtained by proper modeling, resulting in improved part characteristics with simultaneous minimization of time and cost on predicting before fabricating the model.

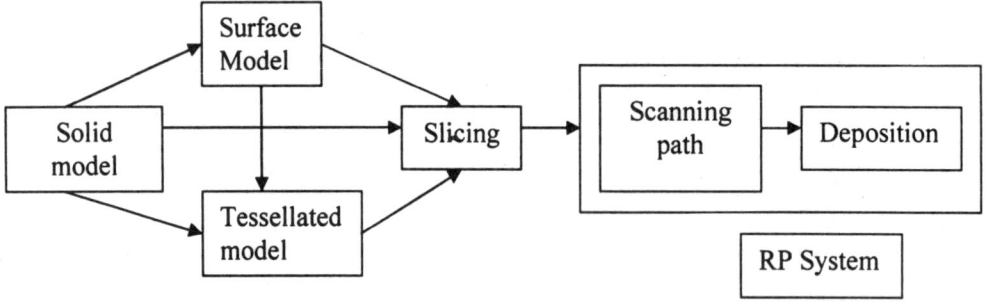

Fig. 1: Transfer of CAD model to RP machine

4.FABRICATION OF THE COMPONENTS USING FDM MACHINE

The important aspect of Artificial Neural network is training. For training the network, it needs lot of experimental data. Hence, experimental measures of various output responses were made from the component fabricated using FDM 2000 machine with three levels of different input parameters.

Table 1: 3 levels of input parameters

Parameters	Level 1	Level 2	Level3
Slice thickness (ST) mm	0.178	0.216	0.254
Road width (RW) mm	0.305	0.643	0.98
Model temperature (MT) ° C	250	270	290
Air gap (AG) mm	-0.01	-0.005	0.00

The table 1 shows the input parameters with three levels. A suitable model was chosen for fabrication.

After choosing the model, the CAD format of the model was converted to STL format using PRO-E 2000i software. STL format is the standard format, which many modeling software provide for exporting the CAD models to a neutral format, so that other software could use the models. Transfer of CAD model to RP machine is shown in the fig. 1.

The above procedure was repeated for various values of slice thickness, road width, model temperature and air gap. 81 components were produced using the RP

machine. The output responses such as surface roughness, porosity and dimensional accuracies such as % thickness deviation and % width deviation are measured using Surtronic-3+, Electronic-weighing machine and CMM respectively and the values are assigned [8].

5. TRAINING AND TESTING

Artificial neural networks consist of a large number of processing elements, called neurons that operate in parallel. For modeling the process parameters, three layer feed forward neural networks were used. They contained four neurons in the input layer, four neurons in the hidden layer and four neurons in the output layer. The number of neurons in the hidden layer was varied in different experiments. Network training involves the process of interactively adjusting the interconnection weights in such a way that the prediction errors on the training set are minimized.

The back propagation algorithm is applied to each pattern set, input and target for all pattern sets in the training set. Since the learning process is iterative, the entire training set will have to be presented to the network over and over again, until the global reaches the minimum acceptable values. The training was supervised. The desired output values of the network also being supplied during training. Training of the ANN was made with raw experimental data of 65 full training examples. Tan-h non-linearities were applied to the neurons.

After the neural network had been trained it was applied to 16 examples that did not take part in the training process. This time solutions of the examples were not supplied, so that the network had to estimate them. It appeared that the test set error for the 16 examples was slightly higher than the training error.

6. TOPOLOGY OF ANN AND ITS ADAPTATION TO MODELING

Varying the number of neurons in hidden layers varies the topologies. To evaluate the individual effects of training parameters on the performance of neural networks, different networks were trained, tested and analyzed. The network performances were evaluated by the number of training cycles. The number of neurons in the input and output layers are determined by the number of input and output parameters.

Learning rate that will give overall optimum performance (i.e.) to minimize the number of training cycles and obtain low prediction errors is 0.1.

To minimize the estimation errors, momentum rate selected is 0.7.

The number of hidden layer assumed is one with four nodes.

The number of neurons in the input layer is four (slice thickness, road width, model temperature and air gap).

The number of neurons in the output layers is four (porosity, surface roughness, Thickness-deviation and width-deviation).

1000 number of iterations was made to achieve the minimum error.

Networks trained with optimum training parameters give the best overall performance.

7. RESULTS AND DISCUSSION

An extensive number of tests were made on the FDM 2000 RP machine to confirm the neural model with different input process parameters. This presents, the results of experiments and the comparison between the experimental and ANN model. The effect of network parameter on validating values for output parameters prediction is shown in the table 2. The results are graphically represented as shown in figs. 2 to 9.

Table 2: The effect of network parameter on validating values for output parameters prediction

S. No	Responses	Average error / training pattern (%)	Average error / testing pattern (%)	Deviation
1	% Porosity	1.0584	1.9080	-0.8496
2	Surface roughness (Ra)	4.7566	8.0134	-3.2568
3	% Thickness deviation	0.6933	1.2720	-0.5787
4	% Width deviation	1.1061	0.5454	0.5607

From the table 2, the errors found on all output responses are within ± 10 %. The deviation for surface roughness is –3.2568, this large could occur due to the range of Ra value obtained from experiment lies in between 7.47μm and 34.73μm. Also, instead of training one output, all the four output parameters were trained and tested in the same network for the necessity of application areas where, all the four responses are considered while manufacturing.

From the graphs and tables, it is inferred that the error is the deviation of output parameter values predicted using ANN from those of Experimental values. Comparing the results of ANN with Experimental indicates that the developed ANN model can be used to predict

- % Porosity
- Surface roughness (Ra) μm
- % Thickness deviation
- % Width deviation

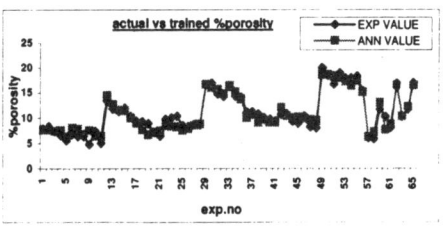

Fig. 2: Comparison of %porosity between Experimental and trained ANN

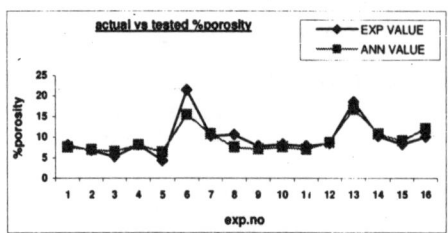

Fig. 3: Comparison of %porosity between Experimental and tested ANN

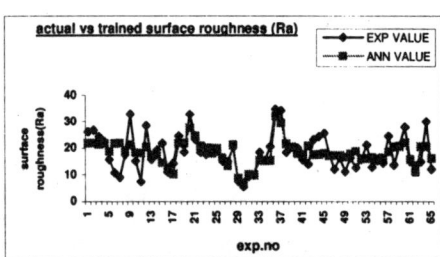

Fig. 4: Comparison of surface roughness between Experimental and trained ANN

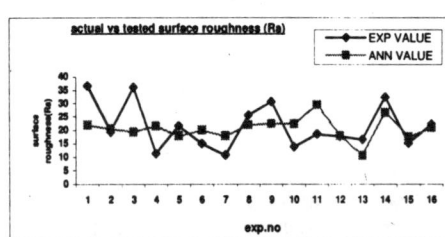

Fig. 5: Comparison of surface roughness between Experimental and tested ANN

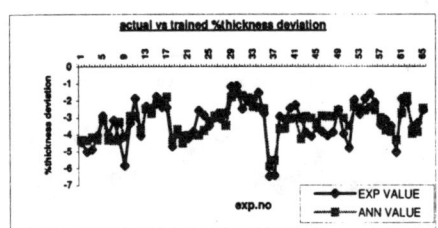

Fig. 6: Comparison of %thickness deviation between Experimental and trained ANN

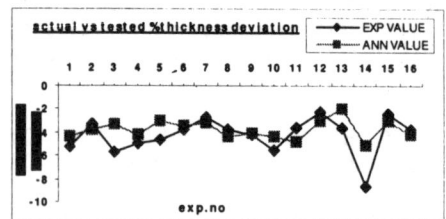

Fig. 7: Comparison of %thickness deviation between Experimental and tested ANN

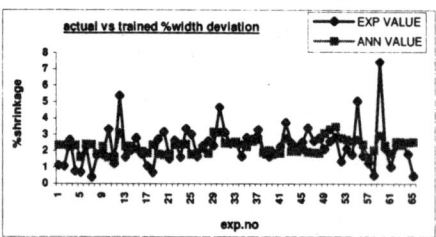

Fig. 8: Comparison of %width deviation between Experimental and trained ANN

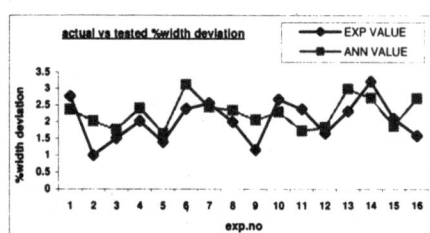

Fig. 9: Comparison of %width deviation between Experimental and tested ANN

with less error. Also, the values from prediction coincide well with values from Experiment.

8. CONCLUSION

FDM is one of the most widely used layer-by-layer additive RP processes of producing parts directly from a CAD model. In using this technology, the designer is often confronted with a host of conflicting options including achieving desired accuracy, surface finish and strength for fulfilling structural as well as functional requirements.

480

The network was trained using 80% of the experimental values. While training the network, weights are assigned to the input parameters to generate the output parameters. These stored weights are used to predict the output for a given set of input pattern in the test mode. The remaining 20% of the experimental values were used for testing the network. The output patterns predicted from the NN are accurate with the deviation of $\pm(10 - 15)\%$ from the experimental value.

Hence Artificial Neural Network can be used as a prediction tool to predict either the input or output parameter to improve the surface quality of the components.

9. REFERENCES

1. **Onuh S.O.,** Rapid prototyping integrated systems, *Rapid prototyping journal, volume 7. Number 4. 2001, pp220-223.*
2. **Bullinger H.J.,** Rapid product development an overview, *Computers in Industry 42 (2000)* pp 99- 108.
3. **Martin C M Wong,** Business driver behind Rapid Prototyping and Manufacturing thro' *Internet.*
4. *Bharat Vasudevarao,* (2000), Sensitivity of RP surface finish to process parameter variation, *SFF Symposium, Arizona state University.*
5. **Too M.H.,** Investigation of 3D non-random porous structures by FDM, *Int J Adv Manu Technol (2002)* 19:217-223, 2002.
6. **Mukesh K. Agarwala,** Structural quality of parts processed by fused deposition, *Rapid Prototyping Journal,* volume 2. Number 4. 1996. pp 4-19.
7. **Gautham Kattethota,** A design tool to control surface roughness in Rapid Prototyping. *SFF Symposium Arizona State University.*
8. **Arumaikannu G.,** Development of ANN for process optimization of RPT using FDM, II *National Symposium on RP&RT technologies,* Nov 9-10, 2001 pp 23-28.

Non-Traditional Manufacturing

GCMM 2004
Editors: Prasad K D V Yarlagadda and S Narayanan
Publisher: Narosa Publishing House Pvt. Ltd., New Delhi, India

Development of the Aspherical Lens using the Euler's Method

Lee J Y, Kim M J, Lee S S, Park J H, Jeon EC & Seo Y K

Dong-A University, Busan, Korea

Email : ppidae@donga.ac.kr

Abstract

This thesis is about designing, manufacturing, and measuring the aspherical lens. The aspherical lens are used in many optical devices today, and Euler's Method has been tested as a new approach to create such lens instead of the Taylor's theorem which has usually been used. The geometrical figure of the large-caliber aspherical lens was created using a high-speed prototyping machine. The precision of the lens was tested measuring straightness of the light and the aberration, and the method to create a new, non-conventional aspherical lens is presented.

Keywords

Aspherical lens, Euler's method, CAM(Computer Aided Manufacturing), Aberration

1. INTRODUCTION

The optics industry, together with the precision machinery industry and the digital-electronic industry, is a very valuable, high-tech industry.

Optical equipments such as digital cameras and camcoders are spreading rapidly to everyday life, and thus the need for high-precision, light-weight, and highly-functional optical devices rise.

The aspherical lens is the core technology in many optical equipments, and is used in everything from digital optical products, multi-purpose OA appliance, and medical devices to satellite cameras.

An aspherical lens can achieve high transmissivity without the complicated arrays of lenses, and to achieve the same distance-to-focus it may have smaller thickness, thus allowing an optical equipment the lens is used in may be lighter and smaller.

On the other hand, a spherical lens inevitably contains aberration, and this spherical aberration is the biggest factor which obstructs imaging when the focus gets larger. The methods to lessen the spherical aberration are; a) to lessen the aberration by applying a higher degree mathematical formula; b) to use a new material so that one lens can have many different refractive indices; and c) to use an aberration-correcting lens with an aberrant lens, thus compensating aberration of an optical device. These methods, however, do not completely eliminate aberration, and as the recent effort to eliminate aberration, the industry has continuously tried to improve focusing efficiency.

Therefore, to solve the fundamental problem that is the spherical aberration, development of the aspherical lens is much needed, but the domestic optics industry is

485

limited in technology to only cutting and manufacturing of such lens, and research needed for designing and creating such lens is slim to none. When designing an aspherical lens, one creates the curved surface with a formula, or eliminates the spherical aberration by using a ray back-tracer thus correcting the aberration. These methods, however, can have many variables and with the changes in the variables precision of the aspherical lens suffers. Furthermore, Many formulas are available for designing the aspherical lens, but these formulas are difficult to access for the licensing matters.

Therefore it is desperately needed to possess our own unique, original technology that will allow us to develop and precision-manufacture an aspherical lens. To satisfy this need, an original formula was used to design, to model, and to prototype an aspherical lens out of the acryl. The object of this study is to test and to verify the genuineness and precision of the so-created lens by testing its light straightness and aberration.

2. DESIGNING AN ASPHERICAL LENS
2.1. The Snell's Law

Fig. 1 shows the Snell's law. The Snell's law is also called the law of refraction, and it was discovered by W. Snell of the Netherlands in 1615, and this formula has been proven valid for not only the light wave, but also for other waves.

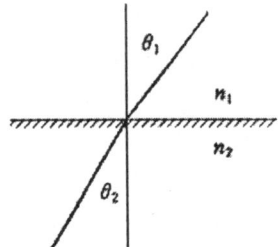

Fig.1: Principle of Snell's law

When the wave goes into an isotropic medium to another, the surface of entry (the surface which contains the direction of the entering wave and the surface which contains the boundary normal) and the refraction surface (the surface which contains the direction of the refraction wave and the boundary normal) are on the same surface;

and if the entry angle were θ_1 and the refraction angle θ_2, the following relationship is valid:

$$\frac{\sin\theta_1}{\sin\theta_2} = n$$

In this, n is called the index of refraction of the refraction medium to the entry surface medium, and can be defined with the formula:

$$n \equiv \frac{c \cdot}{v_{phase}}$$

where, c is the speed of light, and v_{phase} is the phase velocity

$$c \equiv 2.99792458 \times 10^8 \, m/\sec$$

☐ Therefore, the Snell's Law can be defined as:

$$n_1 \bullet \sin\theta_1 = n_2 \bullet \sin\theta_2$$

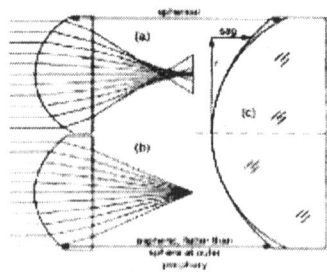

Fig. 2: Comparison between a Spherical and an Aspheric Lens

Fig. 2 shows the difference between a spherical and an aspherical lens when applied the Snell's Law. With the spherical lens the light rays that are parallel to the lens' axis do not focus on one point, whereas the aspherical lens does not show any aberration.

2.2. Mathematical Modeling of the Aspherical Lens

The Taylor's theorem is used in designing the conventional aspherical lens, but in this study the Euler's method was used to model the geometrical shape of the aspherical lens. Fig. 3 shows the schematic diagram for the aspherical lens.

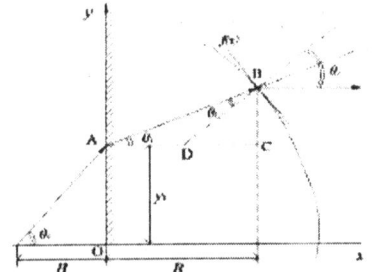

Fig. 3: Schematic Diagram of Modeling for the Aspherical Lens

The object here is to get the value. First, consider the y-axis as a surface of the lens, and as the maximum angle for the laser sheet generator. Finally, H is the distance between the lens and the point where the laser sheet generator is originated. The data for these values are gathered from experiments.

The laser ray generated from the laser sheet generator must project parallel to the x-axis through the lens, and the formulas (1) to (5) are hypothesized for calculation.

$$y_0 = H \tan\theta_0 \qquad \text{-------------------- (1)}$$

$$\sin\theta_1 = \frac{\sin\theta_0}{n} \qquad \text{-------------------- (2)}$$

$$\tan\theta_1 = \frac{(y - y_0)}{x} \qquad \text{-------------------- (3)}$$

$$\sin\theta_3 = n\sin\theta_2 \qquad \text{-------------------- (4)}$$

$$\frac{dx}{dy} = -\tan\theta_3 \qquad \text{-------------------- (5)}$$

The above are the fundamental formulas to get the value, and the *n* defined by the Snell's Law is the index of refraction where the laser or the light transmit an object; and as for the acryllic object used in this experiment, the value *n* can be calculated from measurement. The value is found to be around 1/0.65.

In this study the above formulas are developed using the Euler's method, and the aspherical coordinates were acquired with a Visual C++ program; and the result is displayed in a text window in Fig. 4.

2.3. The Geometrical Modeling for an Aspherical Lens

VisualLISP, the AutoCAD authoring tool, was used to develop the software which geographically models the aspherical point data in accordance of the Euler's Method; and with this software the geographical point data were plotted in a three-dimensional space.

The point data plotted were connected as a polyline and the final model product is shown in Fig. 4, and its detailed drawing is shown in Fig. 5.

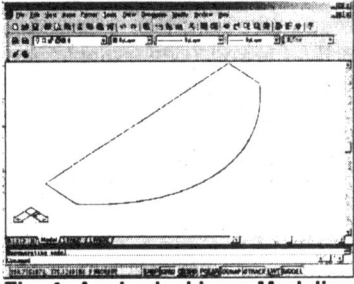

Fig. 4: Aspherical Lens Modeling

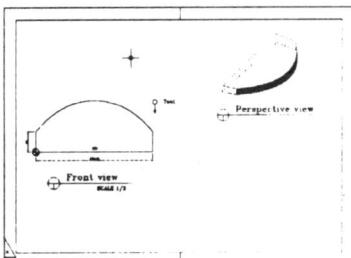

Fig. 5: Drawing of an Aspherical Lens

3. PROCESSING AND CUTTING OF THE ASPHERICAL LENS
3-1. CAM and the Process Simulation

To verify the validity for the aspherical lens modeling with the Euler's method point data, an actual aspherical lens was created using reinforced acryl, and Fig. 6 shows the process within a CAM software and the process simulation.

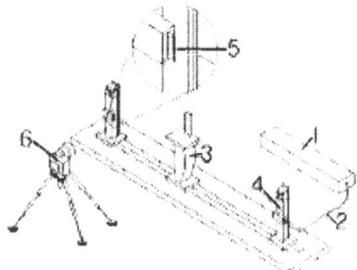

Fig. 11: Experiment Apparatus for Aberration Measurement

The test is performed after the optical axis, using the linear guide set up on the side, are lined up to the size of the aspherical lens; and then focusing the laser on the center of the micro-scale. The distance-to-focus for the aspherical lens in this experiment is 22.5cm, and the height of the laser was moved at a millimeter from the bottom. For accurate observation of the laser light the test was performed in a dark room.

4.2. EXPERIMENT RESULTS
4.2.1. Straightness of the Laser Light

The result for the experiment of the aspherical lens precision is shown in Fig. 12. The laser light is very visible in the middle of the artificial mist, and as shown in Fig. 12, when the light coming out of the laser generator hits the aspherical lens it projects itself straight and it also is well visible. The width of the ray is 23.5cm, both at 1m from the lens and at 5m.

Fig. 12: Result of the Experiment

4.2.2. Aberration in the Aspherical Lens

After measuring the aberration as in Fig. 11, the aberration in this aspherical lens was almost zero. The distance between the glass surface and the aspherical lens, or the distance-to-focus was 22.5cm, and the width of the laser light was 2mm. The height of the laser was moved at a millimeter using the linear guide, and since the total length of the aspherical lens is 300mm, the height of the lens itself was recorded as the values between -150 and 150mm. The measurement for the aberration of this experimental aspherical lens is displayed in Fig. 13.

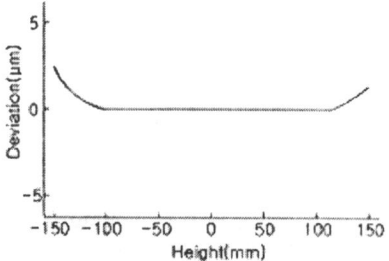

Fig. 13: The Experiment Result for the Aberration of the Aspherical Lens

It is concluded with this study that the aberration was almost non-existence, and observed that at each end of there was 2 to 2.5 μm of deviation. This can be regarded as astigmatism, and the error is thought to have occurred for the lens at the polishing process. Additionally, the deviation was little bigger at the bottom, and within the -100 to 100mm range there were no deviations.

5. CONCLUSIONS

The aspherical point data was gathered using the Euler's method, and the data was modeled using AutoCAD. The design became a prototype using a high-speed prototyping machine, and the experiment was performed, which gave us the following conclusion:

1. Designed and developed a large-caliber aspherical lens (300mm in diameter) using the Euler's method, instead of the more conventional Taylor's theorem.
2. Tested and validated the possibility of cutting and processing an aspherical lens with a high-speed prototyping machine.
3. Invented and developed an equipment which tests straightness of light, and with this equipment the light that passed through the lens was measured and verified that it had the constant width of 23.5cm.
4. Invented and developed an aberration-testing equipment, and with this equipment it is verified that, except for the 2 to 2.5 μm of deviation at the tip of the lens, the deviation did not exist in the range between -100 to 100mm.
5. By designing and creating an aspherical lens; the new formulas used to develop the lens were found to be valid.

6. ACKNOWLEDGEMENT

This paper was supported by grant No. R12-2002-004-01-004 from the Center for Advanced Net Shape Manufacturing and Clean Processes of the Korea Science & Engineering Foundation, and supported by Brain Korea 21 Team of Division of Mechanical Industrial & Systems Engineering, Dong-A University.

7. REFERENCE

1. **Beamonte J.I.**, "Stability of the spherical aberration up to the fifth order in cemented doublets", *J. Opt. A: Pure Appl. Opt. 2*, pp. 161-168, 2000.
2. **Roman Ilinsky**, "Gradient-index meniscus lens free of spherical aberration", *J. Opt. A: Pure Appl. Opt. 2*, pp. 449-451, 2000.
3. **Park K., Han C. Y.**, "Flow Simulation and Deformation Analysis for Injection Molded Plastic Lenses using Solid Elements", *Proceeding of KSPE*, pp. 784-787, 2003.
4. **Kim W. B., Lee S. J., Kim Y. J., Lee E. S.**,"Ultra-precision Polishing Technique for Micro 3 -Dimensional Structures using ER Fluids", *Journal of KSPE*, Vol. 19, No. 12, pp. 134-141, 2002.
5. **Jesus Atencia, Manuel Quintanilla**, "Ray tracing for holographic optical element recording with non-spherical waves", *J. Opt. A: Pure Appl. Opt. 2*, pp. 387-397, 2001.
6. **Kim H.S., Park K.Y., Lee W.K., Jeon J.U.**, "Design of Spherical Aberration Free Aspherical Lens by Use of Ray Reverse Tracing Method", *Journal of KSPE*, Vol. 20, No. 10, pp. 191-198, 2003.

GCMM 2004
Editors: Prasad K D V Yarlagadda and S Narayanan
Copyright © 2005, Vellore Institute of Technology, Vellore, India
Publisher: Narosa Publishing House Pvt. Ltd., New Delhi, India

Evaluation of Rapid Tooling for Electric Discharge Machining using Electroforming and Spray Metal Deposition Techniques

Ricky Blom, Prasad K D V Yarlagadda and Iyer R M

School of Mechanical, Manufacturing and Medical Engineering
Queensland University of Technology
Brisbane, Q 4001, Australia

Email: y.prasad@qut.edu.au

Abstract

Electroforming and spray-metal deposition offer an alternate option to traditional machining of electrodes. Electroforming is one method of producing electrodes for EDM. The fact that electroforming can be used to produce multiple electrodes simultaneously gives it the advantage of saving on costs when multiple electrodes are needed. Spray-metal deposition offers another alternative that is much cheaper and relatively faster to manufacture. In this paper the use of these non-traditional manufacturing methods are compared to the performance of traditional solid electrodes in terms of machining time, material removal rate, tool wear rates and surface roughness at several standard machining settings.

Keywords
Rapid Product Development

1. INTRODUCTION

To compete in today's industry environment, companies must keep up with the leading technologies and processes and also push the boundaries and develop new and improved products and processes. Electro-Discharge Machining (EDM) is a manufacturing process that has been affected by developments in Rapid Prototyping and Tooling. EDM is commonly used by toolmakers for complex injection moulds, punch dies and cavities made from hardened tool steels. EDM is ideal for materials and complex shapes that traditional machining processes are unable to perform. In die and mould production, the EDM cycle can account for 25 to 40% of the tool room lead-time [1, 2]. The electrode production represents over 50% of the cost and time of an EDM operation [2]. The goal is to reduce the time and cost of the EDM cycle and to do this, alternate methods of electrode production is a key area of research. Since conception EDM electrodes have been manufactured from solid conductive metals including copper and tungsten, and also from non-metals mainly graphite. Using traditional machining operations in producing complex electrodes from solid copper or graphite may require the production of several smaller electrodes and joining them together, or running several machining cycles to get the required cavity or shape. Therefore increasing the complexity of the electrode increases the electrode production time and also increases the machining time if several machining cycles are required. In this paper attempts made by the authors in investigating the alternate methods of electrode production in order to reduce cost and time are presented.

2. LITERATURE REVIEW AND BACKGROUND

Rapid Prototyping (RP) and tooling is a continuation from three-dimensional CAD modelling. RP uses the CAD data to produce layer information that is feed into RP machines to produce a three dimensional solid model from a chosen process and material. Common RP processes include Stereolithography (SL), Selective Laser Sintering (SLS), Laminated Object Manufacturing (LOM) and Fused Deposition Modelling (FDM). The majority of RP processes involve the conversion of the CAD data into cross-sectional information and the model is built layer-by-layer. In the production of EDM electrodes many RP processes have been previously used. The most promising process involves the use of stereolithography and producing models as either positive or negative master patterns. Stereolithography (SL) uses information from a computer generated three-dimensional model to produce a solid three-dimensional model from various types of laser-curing polymer resins. The SL Apparatus builds the three-dimensional solid model layer by layer. The computer file is broken down to layers and the SLA reproduces the layer on the surface of the resin. The part is then lowered by the relative layer thickness, and the process is repeated until the completed model is produced. The SL Apparatus used is developed and marketed by 3D Systems Inc, Valencia, California, USA. The machines produce models with high detail and accuracy and have the ability to produce multiple parts simultaneously. Using the positive master pattern is termed as "Direct Electrode Manufacture" in that the SL pattern is plated with a conductive material and used as the electrode. Alternatively, using the SL pattern as a negative and removing the plated shell is termed as "Indirect Electrode Manufacture".

Research in the area of Direct Electrode Manufacturing process includes work from Arthur et al. [3-7] and Leu et al. [8]. Results using the direct manufacturing method have shown advantages in that the electrodes are comparable to traditional solid electrodes in finishing, semi-roughing and roughing machine settings and electrode production time is reduced as large quantities of electrodes can be produced simultaneously. The results also concluded disadvantages including the possibility of non-uniform distribution of electrodeposited material resulting in unknown plating thickness, EDM machining time is quite high, the SL master pattern is sacrificial and the electrodes are prone to premature failure if the plating thickness is less than 180 ⎕m. Alternatively the area of Indirect Electrode Manufacture has been researched and developed by Jensen and Hovtun [9], Rennie et al. [10] and Yarlagadda et al. [11,12] . Jensen and Hovtun were also able to show that the performance is comparable to solid electrodes. Jensen and Hovtun [9] found disadvantages that include unacceptably high wear rate, poor accuracy, long process time and internal details can be problematic. Rennie et al. [10] provided similar disadvantages in that narrow internal cavities are not plated to the same thickness as external features and failure still occurs with excess wear and uneven material distribution. Yarlagadda et al. indicated that different sections of the tool performed more work than other sections, triangular protrusions had split and tool failure occurred and course machining can deform the tool.

Table 1: Machine Settings or Finishing Semi-Roughing and Roughing Cuts

Machine Setting	C110	C140	C170
Discharge Pulse Duration **ON**	012	016	019
Quiescent Pulse Duration **OFF**	012	016	019
Quiescent Time **MA**	01	01	01
Peak Current **IP**	002.0	005.0	010.0
Servo Voltage **SV**	03	05	05
Polarity **PL**	+	+	+

3. EXPERIMENTAL DESIGN

The experiments in this research are based on a similar procedure to Leu et al. [8]. The procedure allows an indication of the difference in the performance of different manufacturing methods. Leu et al.

[8] provided a comparison between electroformed copper electrodes and traditional solid electrodes by running experiments at three different machine settings for a set time of ten minutes. There were a total of eight experiments per electrode type at each machine setting. EDM performance is dictated by the machine parameters and the optimisation of those parameters has been the basis of research by the majority of research groups in the field of EDM. Due to time and budget restrictions the number of experiments determined the type of analysis that could be done. The Taguchi method and neural network experiments require a large number of experiments to prove the methods and the budget didn't allow that size research. Leu et al. [8] completed eight experiments per machine setting for each electrode type and to get results that are comparable, within the budget, only two experiments for each machine setting and electrode type were conducted. A comparison of the three electrodes (solid copper, electroformed copper and spray metal copper) will be made using the same machining conditions and measuring the performance attributes. The performance attributes measured include material removal rate (MRR), tool wear ratio (TWR) and surface roughness (R_a). The electrodes will be tested under three machining conditions and measured to compare the performance attributes. The machining conditions include a roughing cut, semi-roughing cut and a finishing cut. Using the same machine parameters for all three electrodes will allow a good comparison to be made. The settings for the three different experiments involve the following parameter settings are described in table 1.

The values given are not actual values. They are machine setting numbers for the scale on the machine. The actual values for the machine settings are as follows:

Pulse Duration OFF			
Quiescent Time MA	X2	X2	X2
Peak Current IP	2A	5A	10A
Servo Voltage SV	35V	60V	60V
Polarity PL	+	+	+

To restrict the experimental machining time the cut depth will be reduced according to the cut type. The roughing cut will make a cut of approximately 1mm, the semi-roughing cut will be 1mm and the finishing cut will be 0.5mm. The machining time is measured on the EDM computer control unit and it measures to an accuracy of seconds. The electrodes and work-pieces will be measured before and after to determine the MRR, TWR and R_a. The MRR can be measured using a mathematical equation –

$$MRR = \frac{Electrode\ Area\,(mm^2) \times Depth\ of\ Cut\,(mm)}{Time\ of\ Cut\,(min)}$$
$$(mm^3/hr) \ ---- (1)$$

MRR can also be measured by the change in weight of the electrode and the work-piece. The mass of the electrodes and work pieces was measured on standard electronic scales which measures masses from 0 to 100g to an accuracy of 0.001g increments, masses from 100 to 500g to 0.01g increments and above 500g to 0.1g increments.

The TWR is measured by –

$$TWR\,(\%) = \frac{\Delta Volume^{Electrode}\left(mm^3\right)}{\Delta Volume^{workpiece}\left(mm^3\right)} \times 100$$
$$----------- (2)$$

The measurements can be made by weight and also the use of a coordinate measuring machine (CMM). CMM was chosen because of the accuracy attainable and also the availability of the machine itself. The CMM has the accuracy to measure down to 0.001mm in horizontal axis and vertical axis. The CMM is used to measure the vertical height and change of height at preset coordinates in the horizontal plane (x axis and y axis). Using the CMM, a grid is used to measure preset

Table. 2: Actual Settings or Finishing, Semi-Roughing & Roughing Cuts

Machine Setting	C110	C140	C170
Discharge Pulse Duration ON	80□sec	180□sec	350□sec
Quiescent	20□sec	20□sec	30□sec

points before and after experiments. The difference is used to determine the amount of wear or material removed from different sections and features of the electrodes and test pieces. The R_a is measured using a machine such as a Taylor Hobson Surtronic instrument. Several measurements are made on each electrode and test piece to give and average roughness of the whole machined surfaces. The surface roughness is measured to the very fine increments of 0.01☐m. The measuring probe scans a 4mm section of the surface and then determines the average surface roughness (R_a). Measurements for the experiments were made on equipment available but the measurements such as the masses, volumes and heights could have been measured to greater accuracy with more advanced machines. The volume is one method that was unable to be used but if a three dimensional scanner was available it would have been possible to measure the change of volume.

4. EXPERIMENTAL PROCEDURE AND RESULTS

The experimental results compare the performance of the different electrode manufacturing methods at the three different machine settings. The aim is to compare the electrode performance at different workloads on the electrode from roughing cuts, semi-roughing and finishing cuts. The three settings cut at different speeds so the depth of cut for the finishing cut was reduced. This was to prevent the machining time from climbing too high. The selection of electrode shapes (Figure 1) was to help compare different areas of tool performance. The three shapes used highlighted smooth curved surfaces, sharp corners, low draft angles and complex deep holes. The Electrodes were all set up in the same conditions and the similar shapes made the same cuts at the same settings. The depth of cut is measured from the top surface of the work piece and the experiments begin with the depth of the hole in the near net casting. The first four experiments are 1mm cut added to the previous measurement and the final two experiments are 0.5mm extra.

Fig. 1 – SLA Electrode Master Patterns

The electrodes and work pieces were measured before and after each experiment to determine the MMR, TWR and R_a. A total of six experiments were carried out. Due to manufacturing costs two sets of three solid copper electrodes, six sets of three electroformed electrodes and two sets of three spray metal electrodes were produced. Due to the porosity and uneven thickness in the spray metal electrode shells the backing material penetrated and made the electrodes unusable. The experimental conditions for a roughing cut used in the first set of experiments with the machine set on a standard machine setting of C170. This produced high MRR and R_a with low machining time and TWR. The machine and actual settings used for one of these studies are as follows:

	Nominal	Actual
Machine Setting:	C170	C170
Discharge Pulse Duration (ON):	019	350μsec
Quiescent Pulse Duration (OFF):	019	30μsec
Quiescent Time (MA):	01	X2
Peak Current (IP):	010.0	10A
Servo Voltage (SV):	05	60V
Polarity (PL):	+	+

The following is the depth of cut for the first set of experiments:

Cone Electrode – 28mm
Triangle Electrode – 26mm
Base Electrode – 19mm

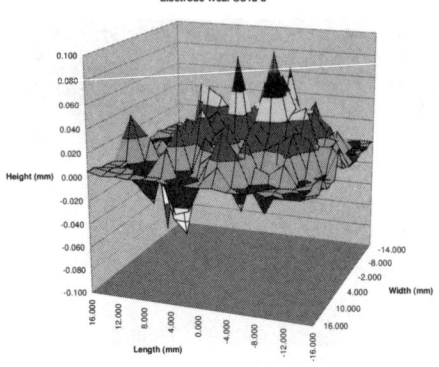
Electrode Wear SC1a-b

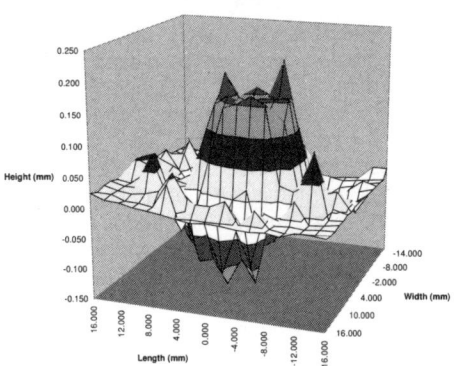
Electrode Wear EC1a-b

Fig. 2. Cone Electrode Wear Experiment 1 - Solid Electrode and Electroformed Electrode

(a) Work piece

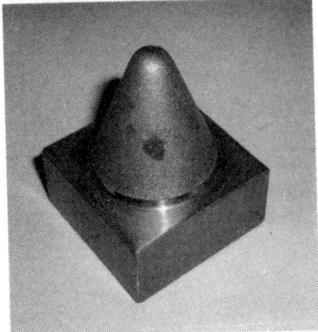
(b) Electrode

Fig. 3. Casting Inclusion and Electrode Wear

4.1 DAMAGE AND EXCESSIVE WEAR OF ELECTROFORMED BASE ELECTRODE (EB1)

The cone electrodes show similar characteristics as the base electrodes in that the solid electrode has less than 0.1mm wear and the electroformed electrode shows greater wear of over 0.1mm on the higher sections. The negative wear on the electroformed electrodes was caused by the deformation of the electrode. Heat from the EDM process builds up in the copper and is partially insulated by the back filled material therefore expanding the copper. Increased localised wear on the point of the electrode is also caused by the extra work performed by the tip. The work piece is a near net casting and the cavity has more material to remove at the base of the cavity until the hole is identical to the electrode shape. The CMM results for the solid cone electrode shows a negative wear in a small area near the front left of figure 2. The negative wear is the result of a carbon build up from an inclusion in the work piece casting. Figure 3 shows the inclusion that appeared after the first experiment and the black carbon build up on the electrode. The inclusion didn't appear to affect the MRR.

Triangle electrodes gave a very good indication of excessive wear when the electrode is needed to machine larger amounts of material. As shown in Figure 5.5 the solid electrode has lower wear than the electroformed electrode. The higher wear along two sides of the electrodes was produced by increased work rate. The cavity of the near net castings is slightly smaller than the electrodes and any vertical surfaces will be machined more than the surfaces that are more horizontal. From the current experimental investigation it can be stated that the solid triangle electrode performed better than the electroformed electrode in terms of the shape of the machined cut, because the electroformed electrode failed during the experiment. The sharp corners of the electrode wore through to expose the back filled core and therefore stopped machining in that small area.

4.2 PERFORMANCE COMPARISON OF MANUFACTURING METHODS

The machine settings for the three levels of machining as shown in Table 2 show that as the machining goes from C170 (roughing) down to C110 (finishing) the Pulse ON and OFF drops as does the Peak Current and Servo Voltage. As the parameters drop the machining time should increase, the MRR should decrease, the TWR should increase and the R_a should reduce. As the experiments in this work have shown that the results followed the expected trends in that the machining time increased, the MRR decreased and the Ra decreased. The TWR measured as expected for the electroformed electrodes but the solid electrodes performed against the expected trend.

5. CONCLUSIONS

Manufacture of three different shapes of electrodes in three different manufacturing methods was achieved. The solid copper and electroformed copper electrodes were manufactured successfully to the experimental stage however the spray metal electrodes were unusable. The experiments with the solid electrodes and electroformed electrodes were conducted with success at three different machines setting and comparisons were able to be made. The solid electrodes consistently performed better than the electroformed electrodes at all machine settings in Machining Time, MRR and TWR. Although the solid electrode has out performed the electroformed electrodes in the majority of the experiments, the solid electrodes are much more expensive to produce. The standard workshop is more likely to have a machining centre to machine solid electrodes as opposed to an electroplating system to produce electroformed electrodes so the convenience of the solid electrodes will often out way the use of electroformed electrodes.

The cost of electrodes becomes a major factor as soon as the electrode manufacturing process becomes more comparable. Even though the solid electrodes out performed the electroformed and spray metal electrodes, the cost of manufacture plays a vital role in the tooling process. This research has shown that the cost of solid electrodes is $810 each which is six times that of electroformed and spray metal electrodes at $130 each. Solid electrodes take approximately six hours to produce where as a single electroformed electrode will take up to 50 hours to produce. The cost of production is sometimes not the critical factor when rapid tooling is required. For low numbers of electrodes it is probably more economical in terms of time to use traditional machining. However when a large number of electrodes are required, electroforming will take a similar amount of time to produce one electrode as it will take to produce an infinite number of electrodes and therefore becoming faster as long as more than 10 electrodes are required. The electroforming process could be a viable option for the EDM process if the electrodes could be produced more robust and consistent shell thickness. Problems with the shell thickness produced warping and delamination on some of the larger flat surfaces. With greater control over the wall thickness and greater heat conductivity of the backing material would give better performance of the electroformed electrodes.

6. REFERENCES

1. **Semon, G.** (1975), *A Practical Guide to Electro-Discharge Machining.* p. 63-76.
2. **Jacobs, P.F.** (1992), *Rapid Prototyping and Manufacturing.* in *SME.* Dearborn USA.
3. **Arthur, A.** and **P.M. Dickens.** (1995). *International Symposium for Electromachining.* Lausanne, Switzerland.
4. **Arthur, A.** and **P.M. Dickens.** (1996), *5th Annual European Conf. on Prototyping.*
5. **Arthur, A.** and **P.M. Dickens.** (1997), *6th European Conf. on Prototyping.* 1997. UK.
6. **Arthur, A.** and **P.M. Dickens** (1998), *International Journal of Production Research*, **36**(9): p. 2451-2461.
7. **Arthur, A., P.M. Dickens,** and **R.C. Cobb** (1996), *Rapid Prototyping J.*, **2**(1): p. 4-12.
8. **Leu, M.C., B. Yang,** and **W. Yao** (1998), *Technical Paper - SME. MR.*
9. **Jensen, K.L.** and **R. Hovtun.** (1993). *2nd European Conference of Rapid Prototyping.* University of Nottingham.
10. **Rennie, A.E.W., C.E. Bocking,** and **G.R. Bennett** (2001), *Journal of Materials Processing Technology*, **110**(2): p. 186-196.
11. **Yarlagadda, P.K.D.V., P. Christodoulou,** and **V.S. Subramanian** (1999). *Journal of Malr. Processing Tech.*, **89-90**: p. 231-237.
12. **Yarlagadda, P.K.D.V., I.P. Ilyas,** and **P. Christodoulou** (2001), *Journal of Materials Processing Tech.*, **111**(1-3): p. 286-294.

GCMM 2004
Editors: Prasad K D V Yarlagadda and S Narayanan
Copyright © 2005, Vellore Institute of Technology, Vellore, India
Publisher: Narosa Publishing House Pvt. Ltd., New Delhi, India

Experimental Investigation into Electro Jet Drilling

Mohan Sen[*], H.S. Shan[**]

Research Scholar[*], Prof. and Head[**]
Mechanical and Industrial Engineering Department
Indian Institute of Technology Roorkee, Roorkee 247 667, INDIA.

Email: shanhfme@iitr.ernet.in

Abstract

Producing accurate submillimetre size holes in parts for use in aerospace, electronic, computer and medical industries necessitate the use of non-conventional machining methods. Electro Jet Drilling (EJD) is a promising technique, since it offers notable advantages that include better hole shape accuracy, good surface finish and absence of heat affected zone with the singular limitation that it can be used only for conducting materials that can be machined. This paper reports the experimental findings on the effects of different process parameters, such as applied voltage, electrolyte concentration and feed rate on the material removal rate (MRR) and radial overcut. The experiments are performed on SUPERNI 263A. The results indicate that better geometrically shaped small holes are achieved in the applied voltage range of 190 to 350V, electrolyte concentration and feed rate in the range of 13 to 17% and 0.2 to 0.5mm/min respectively. Scanning electron microscopy has been used to study the accuracy of the small holes machined by EJD.

Keywords
ECM, EJD, adial overcut.

1. INTRODUCTION

Electrochemical hole drilling processes involving the electrolyte jet have seen a resurgence of industrial interest in the last decade due to their enormous capabilities. These include absence of tool wear, stresses and thermal damage (i.e. heat affected zone), and the ability to machine holes of different shapes in any electrically conductive material regardless of its physical and chemical properties [1-3]. There are several variations of electrochemical machining (ECM) for producing small and micro holes. Electro jet drilling (EJD) is one such variant of ECM process. In EJD a negatively charged fast flowing stream of weak acid electrolyte is impinged on the workpiece from a finely drawn glass tube nozzle. The metal ions thus removed are carried away by the flow of the electrolyte. A much longer and thinner electrolyte flow path

requires much higher voltage (150-750V) so as to effect sufficient current flow [4,5].

The present study aims to find out the machining rate and the accuracy of the small hole produced by EJD. The radial overcut has been taken as the measure of accuracy of the hole. A set of experiments has been carried out to analyze the effect of the predominant process parameters such as applied voltage, electrolyte concentration, and feed rate on material removal rate and radial overcut so as to effectively control the EJD process for producing small holes.

2. THE INFLUENCE OF PROCESS PARAMETERS ON EJD PERFORMANCE

Based on the findings of the researchers [1,3,6] and the results of the brainstorming session, process variables for the EJD process can be grouped in four categories. These are:

1. *Electrolyte based parameters*: Type of electrolyte, pressure, flow rate, temperature, percentage concentration, contamination, composition, conductivity.
2. *Workpiece based parameters*: L/D ratio, hole geometry (shape and size), conductivity (high or low).
3. *Electrode based parameters*: cathode wire material, inter-electrode gap, nozzle feed rate.
4. *Power Supply based parameters:* Voltage, current.

The cause-and-effect diagram illustrating the relationship of the process parameters with the quality of hole is shown in Fig 1. Preliminary experiments indicated that out of several process parameters, applied voltage, electrolyte concentration, feed rate and electrolyte pressure greatly influence the quality of the small and micro holes produced by EJD process.

3. EXPERIMENTAL SETUP

An experimental setup for EJD has been designed and fabricated. It consists of the following major subassemblies:
(i) Machining unit
(ii) DC power supply and controlling unit,
(iii) Electrolytes supply system.
Fig.2 presents a schematic diagram of the various system components of the developed setup. The DC power supply unit for the experimental setup can provide 0-650V and can be regulated with the help of a variac. The rectifier unit changes the main 220V/50Hz power supply to 650V DC. In the designed setup the feed is imparted to workpiece against the stationary glass tube nozzle.

3.1 Machining unit

The main machining unit consists of the following elements: e.g. (a) Work holder, (b) Microprocessor based work feed control unit, (c) Nozzle holding assembly, (d) machining chamber and (e) the structural elements including the platform on which all these rests.

3.1.1 Workpiece holder

The work piece holder is designed as a mini-vice. The one face of the vice has a stainless steel block for carrying current to the workpiece. A metal screw provided on the metal block is used to connect it to the positive terminal of the power supply.

3.1.2 Workpiece feed system assembly

The purpose of the workpiece feed system assembly is to provide the flexibility in achieving different feed rates. It is designed to serve the following tasks: (i) To hold the workpiece rigidly and accurately positioned, (ii) To provide controlled linear feed (up to 1.0mm/min) to the workpiece with the help of Intel 8085 microprocessor 4. The main elements of the workpiece feed system assembly are stepper motor 13; spur gear train 14; reduction gear unit 15; and rack and pinion 5. The linear movement of the rack is controlled through a microprocessor unit based on Intel 8085 processor powered by a 12V DC supply. The output of the executing program is sent to the interface card unit through the input/output port of the microprocessor. The interface card unit supplies 12V power to the stepper motor depending upon the signal it receives from the microprocessor I/O port. The stepper motor can be stopped at any moment by pressing the RESET key on the keyboard.

3.1.3 Nozzle holding assembly

The nozzle holding assembly consists of the following components: (i) Glass tube nozzle 8 (ii) Nozzle fixture 9 and (iii) Nozzle manifold 10. The component parts were fabricated mostly from stainless steel and Perspex. The glass tube nozzle is made by controlled pulling the glass tube through a flame. The Nozzle fixtures are made from Perspex whilst the nozzle manifold is made up of stainless steel.

3.1.4 Machining Chamber

The machining chamber 16, which is made of perspex, covers the work piece and glass nozzle. The machining takes place inside this enclosure. The upper half of the chamber is openable for loading and unloading the workpiece.

3.2 Electrical power and drive system

The DC power supply unit **1** used in the setup can provide 0-650V and has a current rating of 5 Amperes. The mains power is converted to a variable voltage DC power supply by a step up/down transformer and a silicon controlled rectifier unit. A digital ampere meter and voltmeter have been used to measure the current and the voltage respectively.

3.3 Electrolyte Supply System

The main function of this system is to supply the acid electrolyte under desired pressure to the nozzle manifold. The main components of the electrolyte supply system are the following: (i) Electrolyte tank **20**, (ii) Electrolyte re-circulating pump **22**, (iii) Filter **21**, (iv) Electrolyte reservoir **23**, (v) Screw pump **24**, (vi) Speed gear box **25**, and (vii) Electric motor **26**. The electrolyte reservoir is fabricated from the perspex sheet. From the reservoir, the electrolyte is supplied under pressure to the nozzle manifold by a screw pump. Used electrolyte is returned to the reservoir by a re-circulating pump.

The screw pump and the centrifugal pump used for pumping electrolyte have all the wettable parts made of stainless steel. The pipes carrying acid electrolyte must be made of corrosion resistant material like reinforced nylon.

4. EXPERIMENTAL RESULTS AND DISCUSSION

Experiments have been carried out to determine the influence of some of the predominant process parameters on material removal rate (MRR) and radial overcut. These are discussed as under.

4.1 Effect of EJD parameters on MRR
4.1.1 Effect of applied voltage

An increase in applied voltage increases the removal rate. Fig.3 shows the relation for a representative set of values of other parameters like electrolyte concentration, electrolyte pressure, feed rate and inter-electrode gap. An increase in current increases the material removal. As it can be seen material removal increases rapidly in high voltage range (over 400V) as compared to low voltage range (100-350V). This is due to the low dissolution efficiency at low voltage range because of long and narrow electrolyte path. At higher voltage, the side machining on the return path of the electrolyte due to the greater charging of electrolyte enhances the material removal. Fig.4 shows a scanning electron microscopy of a hole machined by EJD at applied voltage 550V, electrolyte concentration 17%, feed rate 0.3mm/min, and inter-electrode gap 25mm. The shape of the hole machined at this parametric combination is not only inaccurate but largely oversize due to the side machining which could have taken place because of the excessive charging of the electrolyte.

4.1.2 Effect of electrolyte concentration

Fig.5 shows the effect of electrolyte concentration on MRR at a representative machining parametric combination. It is seen that material removal rate increases with increase in electrolyte concentration upto a certain limit which is nearly 20% beyond which material removal rate is little affected. An increase in concentration of electrolyte leads to increase in its electrical conductivity as a result of which more current will be available in the machining zone to remove more material. The nature of curve is almost linear in 10 -17% concentration zone. In this zone the increment rate of dissolution efficiency is almost constant. In higher concentration zone particularly between 22 to 25% no appreciable increase in material removal rate has been noticed as compared to the rate achieved for 10-20% concentration.

4.1.3 Effect of feed rate

Fig.6 shows the effect of feed rate on MRR at a representative machining parametric combination. It is seen that with in limits an increase in feed rate increases MRR. The increase in feed rate reduces the inter-electrode gap thus resulting in enhancing the flow of more electrolyzing current in the gap thus causing higher stock removal. Using too high a feed rate not compatible with the dissolution efficiency can result in breakage of the glass nozzle. Fig.7

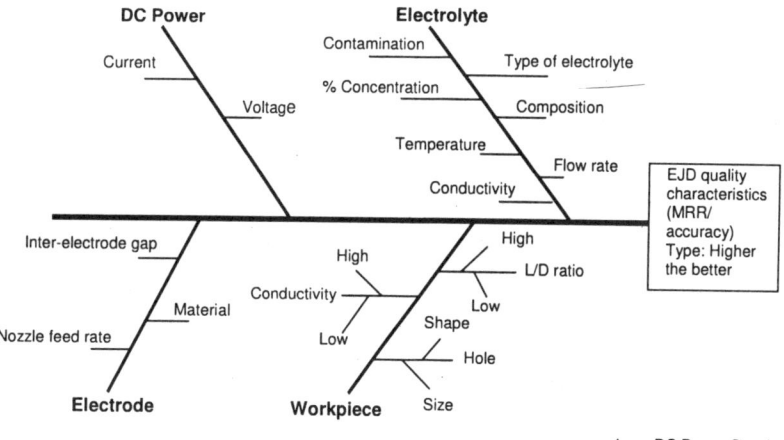

Fig.1 A cause-and-effect

1. DC Power Supply
2. Pressure Gauge
3. Temperature Indicator
4. Microprocessor
5. Rack and Pinion
6. Sample holder
7. Workpiece
8. Glass Tube Nozzle
9. Nozzle Holder
10. Nozzle Manifold
11. Flowmeter
12. Hand Wheel
13. Stepper Motor
14. Spur Gear Train
15. Gear Reduction Unit
16. Machining Chamber
17. Table (X-Y movement)
18. Platform
19. Pressure Gauge
20. Electrolyte Tank
21. Pump
22. Filter
23. Electrolyte Reservoir
24. Screw Pump
25. Speed Gear Box
26. Motor
27. Base

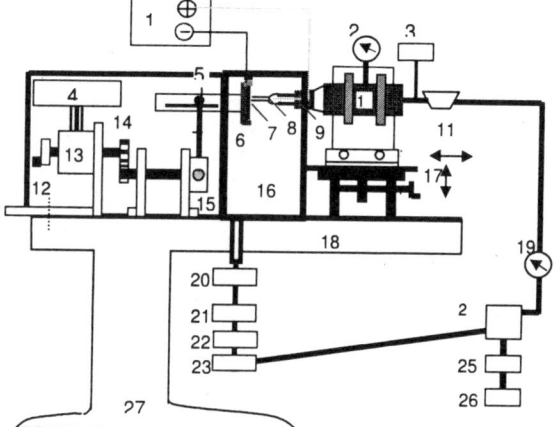

Fig.2 Schematic of Experimental Setup for Electro Jet Drilling

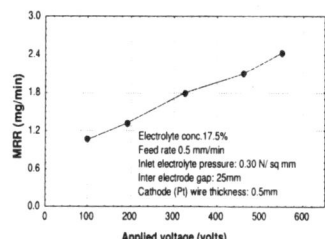

Fig.3 Relationship between MRR and applied voltage

Fig 4 SEM image of machined hole at a particular parametric combination 550V, 17%C, 0.5mm/min

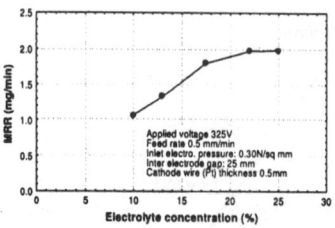

Fig.5 Relationship between MRR and

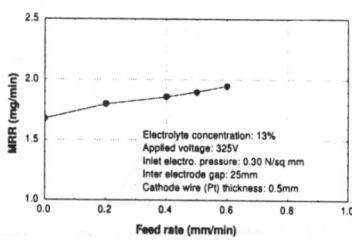

Fig.6 Relationship between MRR and

Fig.7 SEM image of machined hole at a
Particular parametric combination
190V, 13%C, 0.6mm/min

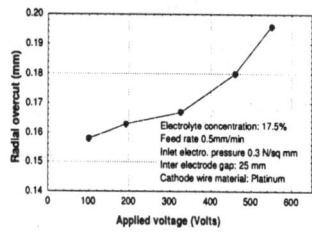

Fig.8 Relationship between radial
overcut and applied voltage

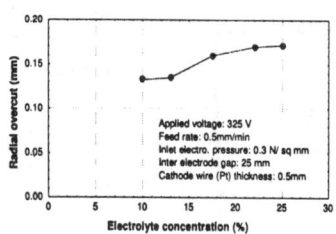

Fig.9 Relationship between radial
overcut

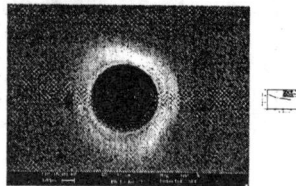

Fig 10 SEM image of machined
hole at a
particular parametric

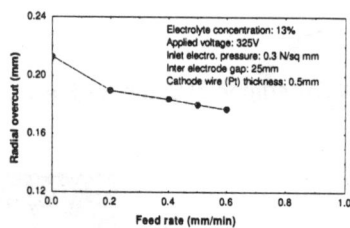

Fig.11 Relationship between radial
overcut and feed rate

shows a SEM image of hole machined at highest feed rate employed i.e. 0.6mm/min. It is noticed that the quality of the hole achieved is better (uniform shape) and MRR is higher.

4.2. Effect of EJD parameters on radial overcut

The radial overcut is an important criteria affecting the quality of the machined hole by EJD.

4.2.1 Effect of applied voltage

With the increase of applied voltage the radial overcut increases, Fig.8. The availability of higher machining current with increase in voltage results in greater charging of electrolyte. As a result, there is the possibility of side machining of the hole by the electrolyte on its exit path causing increase in radial overcut. Over 400V, the radial overcut is more pronounced.

4.2.2 Effect of electrolyte concentration

Fig.9 shows the effect of electrolyte concentration on radial overcut at a representative machining condition. It can be seen that increase in electrolyte concentration increases the radial overcut. As the concentration of electrolyte increases, charged ions in the machine zone increase in numbers, resulting in enhancing its electrical conductivity. As a result of which more charged ions are available for machining the material even on its return (exit) path thus increasing radial overcut. Fig.10 gives a SEM image of a hole machined by EJD at 25% electrolyte concentration. At these machining condition moderately highest MRR and largest overcut has been observed while the shape of the hole machined is not uniformly round.

4.2.3 Effect of feed rate

Fig.11 presents the relationship between the radial overcut and feed rate. It can be noticed that the overcut decreases with increase of feed rate. The increase in feed rate decreases the side machining effect due to the availability of less time during which stray or side machining occurs. Fig.7 shows a SEM image of a hole machined at a representative set of process parameters,

which has produced a better round shaped hole. At these machining condition low overcut has been observed.

5. Conclusions:

The following conclusions can be drawn from the present study:
1. Material removal rate is influenced by the applied voltage, electrolyte concentration as well as feed rate.
2. The increase in electrolyte concentration increases both the material removal and radial overcut. However beyond certain value, higher electrolyte concentration does not produce proportional increase in MRR and overcut.
3. Moderately higher MRR with low overcut has been achieved at the middle range of the parameters employed i.e. applied voltage 190-350V, electrolyte concentration 13-17% and feed rate 0.2 –0.5mm/min.
4. From the SEM image of the hole produced at highest voltage (550V) and highest electrolyte concentration (25%) it can be made clear that the highest values of these two parameters do not contribute in achieving the uniform shape of the hole.
5. Sparking occurs in and around the workpiece fixture during experiments over 550V.

6. ACKNOWLEDGEMENTS

The authors gratefully acknowledge the Defense Research and Development Organization, Project Office (materials) Hyderabad, INDIA for providing sheet material used for the experimentation.

7. REFERENCES

1. **Bannard, J.** (1978), "Fine hole drilling using electrochemical machining", *Proceedings of the 19th International Machine Tool Design and Research Conference*, Manchester, 503-510.
2. **Chryssolouris, G., Wallowitz, M.** (1984), "Electrochemical hole making", *Annals of CIRP*, 33(1), 99-103.
3. **Datta, M., Romankiw, L.T.** (1989), "Application of chemical and electrochemical micromachining in electronic industry", *Journal of The Electrochemical Society*, 136(6), 285C-292C.

4. **De Barr, A.E., Oliver, D.A.** (1975), *Electrochemical Machining*, Macdonald & Co. (Publishers) Ltd, New York.

5. **Shan, H.S.** *Advanced Manufacturing Processes*, Tata McGraw Hill, New Delhi (under publication).

6. **Kozak, J., Rajurkar, K.P., Balkrishna, R.** (1996), "Study of electrochemical jet machining processes", *Transactions ASME, Journal of Manufacturing Science and Engineering*, 118, 490-498.

GCMM 2004
Editors: Prasad K D V Yarlagadda and S Narayanan
Copyright © 2005, Vellore Institute of Technology, Vellore, India
Publisher: Narosa Publishing House Pvt. Ltd., New Delhi, India

Influence of Magnetic Assistance to Abrasive Media in Abrasive Flow Machining

Sehijpal Singh

Mechancial Engg Dept., GND Engg College Ludhiana, Punjab, India

Shan H S & Pradeep Kumar

Mechanical and Industrial Engineering Department,
Indian Institute of Technology Roorkee, ROORKEE- (India)

Abstract

In recent past, an effort has been made for the performance improvement of Abrasive Flow Machining (AFM) process by applying magnetic field assistance around the work piece. The present paper discusses some of the results based upon the application of magnetic field in to AFM. Taguchi experimental design approach has been employed to investigate the effect of various parameters on two surface characteristics i.e. surface finish and scatter of surface roughness. The input process parameters, taken for this study, are magnetic flux density, abrasive concentration, media viscosity, and polymer to gel ratio. L_8 (2^7) orthogonal array was chosen for conducting the experiments and analysis of variance was performed. Results of this study indicated that magnetic flux density and concentration have significant effect on surface roughness. The scatter of surface roughness is significantly affected by concentration and media viscosity. The interaction among various factors is also seen to be significant.

Keywords
AFM, Taguchi Experimental Design, Scatter of Surface Roughness, Surface Finishing

1. INTRODUCTION

Non-conventional machining processes were developed during past 50 years to cope with the ever-increasing demands for precision machining of exotic materials such as high performance alloys, high temperature resistance metals. Abrasive flow machining (AFM) is one of the non-traditional metal finishing technology, which was introduced during late sixties. AFM can produce surface finishes around 0.05 μm. The holes as small as 0.2 mm and edge radius from 0.025 mm to 1.50 mm can be successfully finish machined with this process [1].

In AFM, a semisolid media consisting of abrasive particles and a flexible polymer carrier is extruded through or across the component to be finish machined. The pressurized media uniformly abrades the surface coming in its contact since it acts as a flexible tool when restricted. The process is mainly used for finishing inaccessible areas where ordinary tools cannot reach. Some studies [2, 3] report the fundamental principles, mechanism of material removal, modeling of AFM. As in other non-conventional machining processes like EDM, AJM, the problem of low material removal is also present in AFM, which needs to be studied for the performance enhancement of the process. The use of ultrasonic has been explored in this direction and results were encouraging [4]. Recently, magnetic field has been employed as an external assistance for performance improvement of work pieces being processed by this process [5]. The present paper reports a part of this study for investigating the effect of some of medium related AFM parameters on surface characteristics of work pieces processed in the presence of magnetic field.

2. SELECTION OF PARAMETERS

The designation and range of parameters is shown in Table 1.

Table 1. Parameters and their values at different levels

S.N	Process Parameter	Range	Level 1	Level 2	
1	Magnetic flux Density, A, (Tesla)	0-0.8	0	0.8	**Response Parameters:** *Percentage improvement in surface roughens over initial roughness (ΔR_a) *Scatter of Surface roughness (SSR)
2	Abrasive concentration, B (% by weight)	33-67	33	67	
3	Media viscosity, C, (Qualitative)	low-high	low	high	**Constant Parameters:** Extrusion pressure = 30 bar Media flow volume = 250 cm^3 Number of cycles = 4 Work piece material = brass
4	Polymer to gel ratio, D, (% by weight)	33-67	33	67	Reduction ratio = 0.9 Abrasive grain size = 250 μm

3. SELECTION ORTHOGONAL ARRAY (OA)

In the present Experimentation, four parameters each at two levels have been selected. Each parameter has one (number of levels-1) degree of freedom (DOF). Therefore, the DOF for AB, and AC, is also 1. The total DOF for the four parameters and two interactions in this case will be 6. As the appropriate OA cannot have a DOF less than the total DOF of the experiment, L_8 OA (DOF=7) seems to be suitable for this experiment [6].

4. RESULTS AND DISCUSSION

The experiments were conducted on the set up developed for magnetic assisted AFM [6]. The magnetic Al_2O_3 abrasive particles mixed in a polymer based compound form the medium used in this work. The eight runs as specified by L_8 array were conducted. For each trial, the experiments were repeated thrice and the order of trials was randomized. The surface roughness was measured with the help of a Perthometer (Mahr P2). Scatter of surface roughness (indicator of uniformity of roughness over the surface) was computed on the basis of maximum and minimum value of surface roughness recorded on the work piece surface. The signal to noise ratio (S/N ratio) for both the response parameters was computed for each of the nine trials [6].

4.1 Percentage Improvement in Surface Roughness

The average values of % improvement in surface roughness (ΔR_a) and the S/N ratio for each parameter at level 1 and 2 are plotted in Fig.1. The application of magnetic field in AFM causes increase in ΔR_a. The simultaneous increase in MR [6] and ΔR_a indicates a unique behaviour of AFM when compared to other machining processes. This result supports the findings reported by Williams and Rajurkar [7]. One possible explanation for this could be that in AFM, the material removal takes place first from hills or peaks of the surface profile. Removal of more material produces smoother surface. In other words, more the material removal lesser would be the height of hills on the work surface and hence lesser would be the roughness on the surface. This holds good until the high hills are machined away and quite a smooth surface is produced. Fig.1 further reveals that the concentration of abrasives in media has a strong effect on ΔR_a. Higher concentration of abrasives causes more improvement in R_a. This may be because more number of abrasive particles causes more abrasion resulting in increase in ΔR_a. The media viscosity and the polymer-to-gel ratio have negligible influence on ΔR_a. This is because of the existence of the interaction between magnetic field and media viscosity (Fig. 2).

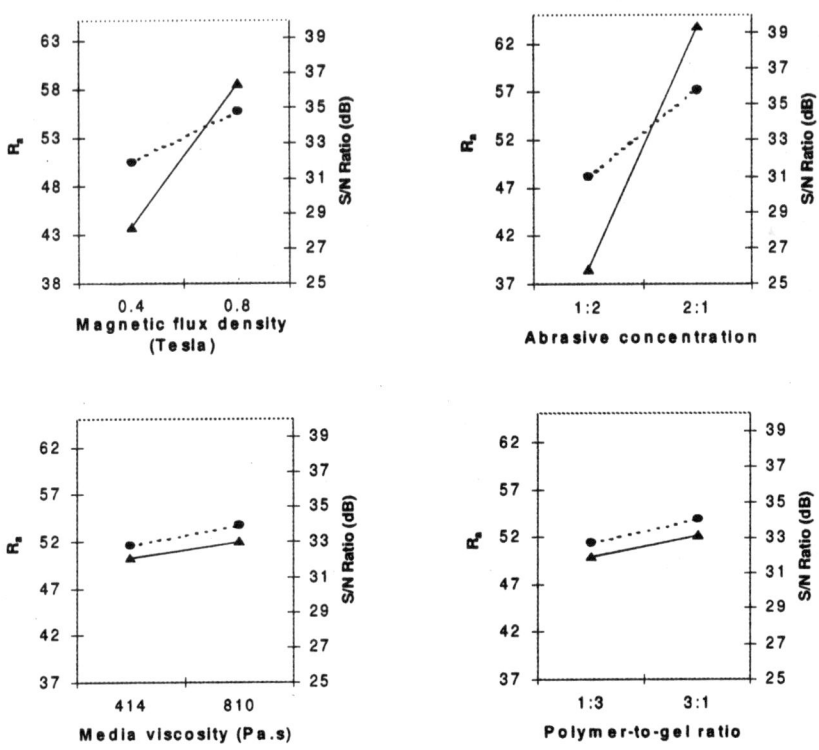

Fig.1: Effect of Process Parameters on % Improvement in R_a (ΔR_a) and S/N Ratio ($\blacktriangle$ - ΔR_a; $\bullet$ - S/N Ratio)

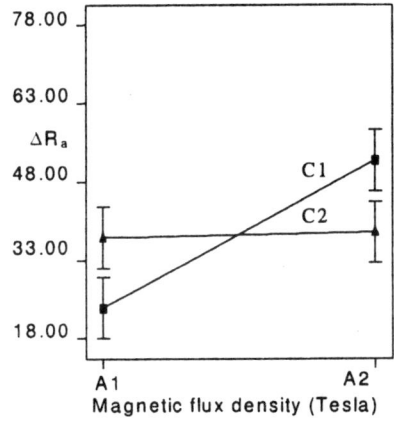

Fig.2: The Interaction between Magnetic Flux Density (Levels A1, A2) and Media Viscosity (Levels C1, C2) on % Improvement in R_a (ΔR_a)

4.2 Scatter of Surface Roughness

The average values of the scatter of surface roughness (SSR) on the workpiece surface and the S/N ratio for each parameter at levels 1 and 2 are given in are plotted in Fig. 3. It can be seen from Fig.3 that the increase in abrasive concentration and media viscosity lowers down the values of SSR. Also, higher levels of these parameters give higher S/N ratio. The increase in SSR at lower abrasive concentration could be due to the fact that the lower concentration of abrasive particles in media would cause less abrasion, thus there will be more chances of the presence of high peaks on the surface implying non-uniform work surface. On the other hand, greater concentration of abrasives would imply removal of more peaks in the same time, making the surface more uniform and hence less SSR. The same explanation holds good for the lower SSR at higher media viscosity, as higher viscosity media would hold the abrasive particles more firmly resulting in better abrasion. Another noticeable observation from Fig.3 is that at higher level of magnetic flux density and at lower level of polymer-to-gel ratio there is little reduction of SSR and slight improvement in S/N ratio. Though these trends are weak, they suggest a detailed study of the likely presence of interaction between magnetic field and polymer-to-gel ratio. It can be observed from

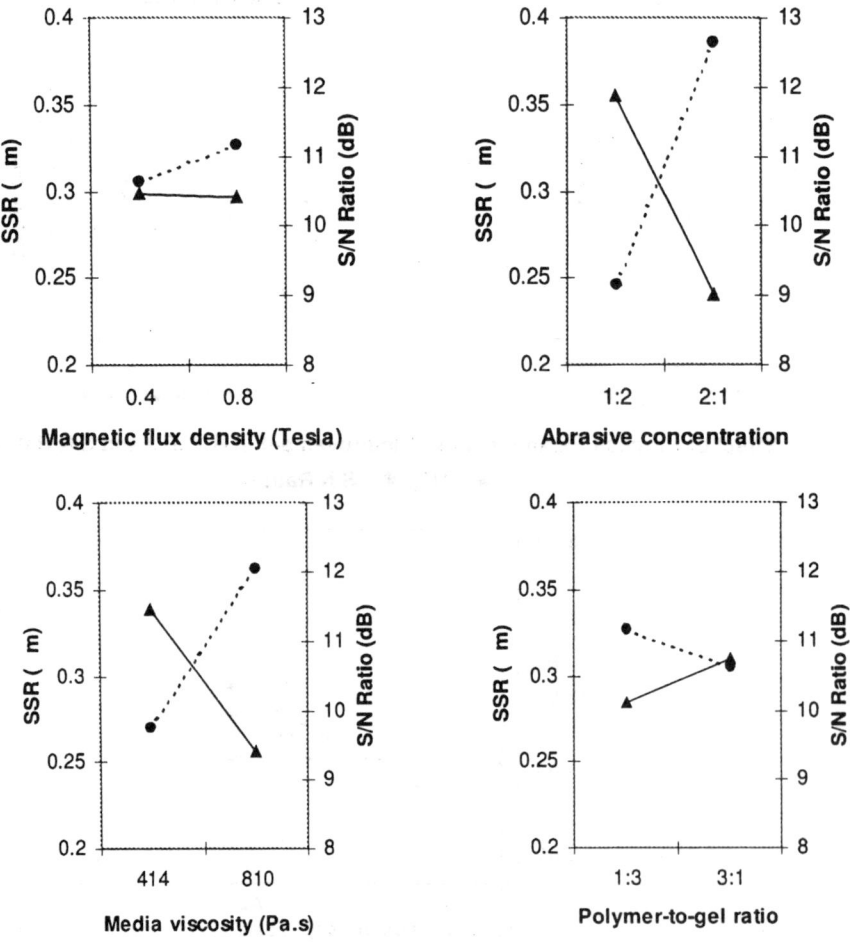

Fig. 3: Effect of Process Parameters on Scatter of Surface Roughness (SSR) and S/N Ratio
(▲- SSR; ● - S/N Ratio)

Fig. 4 that magnetic field and the abrasive concentration interact with each other to affect SSR. The combination of higher concentration and magnetic flux density reduces SSR because this combination results in greater abrasion.

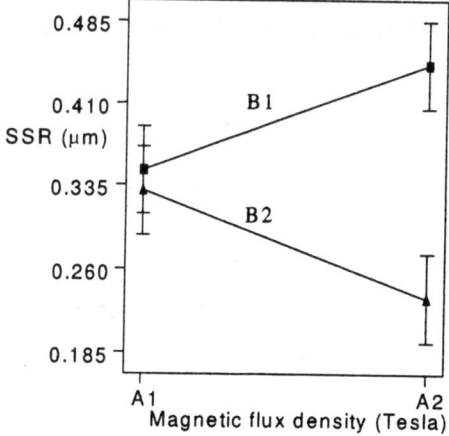

Fig. 4: The Interaction Between Magnetic Flux Density (Levels A1, A2) and Abrasive Concentration (Levels B1, B2) on Scatter of R_a (SSR)

5. CONCLUSIONS

Following conclusions can be drawn based upon this study.

1. The application of magnetic field in AFM and the increase of abrasive concentration in media cause percentage improvement in surface roughness over the work surface.
2. There is a strong interaction between magnetic field and the viscosity of media. While affecting % Improvement in Surface Roughness. The effect of magnetic field is more dominant in case of low viscosity media.
3. Polymer to gel ratio employed in the formulation of media for this work has negligible effect % Improvement in Surface Roughness..
4. Increase in abrasive concentration and media viscosity lowers down the values of SSR. Also, higher levels of these parameters give higher S/N ratio.
5. At higher level of magnetic flux density and at lower level of polymer-to-gel ratio there is little reduction of SSR and slight improvement in S/N ratio

6. REFERENCES

1. **Stackhouse J.**, Deburring by dynaflow, SME paper MR 75-484, 1975.

2. **Shan H.S, Dubey A.K,** (1997) Micro machining by flow of abrasives. Proceedings *17th AIMTDR Conference*, Warrangal, India. Pp. 269-275.
3. **Jain V.K, Jain R.K, and Kalra P.K,** Modeling of abrasive flow machining process: a neural network approach, Wear, 231 (1999) Pp. 242-248.
4. **Jones A.R., and Hull J.B.** (1998), "Ultrasonic flow polishing", Ultrasonics, Vol. 36, pp.97-101.
5. **Sehijpal, and Shan H.S.** (2002), "Development of magneto-Abrasive Flow machining Process", *International Journal of Machine Tool and Manufacture*, Vol. 42, pp. 953-959.
6. **Sehijpal, Singh**, "Studies on Metal finishing by magnetically assisted Abrasive Flow machining", Ph.D Thesis, Mech and Ind. Engg, IIT Roorkee, 2002
7. **William R.E and Rajurkar K.P.** (1989), "Performance characteristics of abrasive flow machining," SME technical paper No FC 89-806.

GCMM 2004
Editors: Prasad K D V Yarlagadda and S Narayanan
Copyright © 2005, Vellore Institute of Technology, Vellore, India
Publisher: Narosa Publishing House Pvt. Ltd., New Delhi, India

Variant EDM Processes for Micro Drilling and Sawing

Aleem Sadiq M A

Mechanical, Engineering Department
Deccan College of Engineering, Hyderabad – 500 001.

Murti V S R, Narayana P L, & Ramesh N N

Mechanical Engineering Department
Osmania University, Hyderabad – 500 007.

E-mail : drvsrmurti@yahoo.com

Abstract

This paper presents two variants of conventional electro discharge machining (EDM). One is electro discharge sawing (EDS) and the other elctro discharge microdrilling (EDMD) with minor adaptations of process parameters. EDS is associated with high machining rates with poor accuracy whereas EDMD characteristics are other way round. The experimental results have been accordingly presented and analysed.

Key words
EDM, EDS, EDMD, Machining rates, Accuracy.

1. INTRODUCTION

Electro discharge machining (EDM) finds extensive application for machining exotic materials and complex shapes. But its slow machining rates are a major limitation for its application for sawing of large billets or bar-stocks of high strength materials. Similarly in EDM drilling of holes is very difficult due to frequent short circuits from contamination of inter-electrode gap by erosion debris[1]. The problem is further compounded by high inaccuracy in the form of tapered surface. However by suitable adaptations the EDM process has been successfully developed to overcome these limitations. Fig.1 schematically illustrates the EDM process and its modified versions EDMD and EDS.

All the three processes employ high frequency spark discharges for material erosion. The tool and work piece form a pair of electrodes separated by a small spark gap which is flooded by a dielectric.

The power source is a square pulse generater. The pulse time has two parts i.e.ontime (Ton)and off time (Toff). The pulse voltage is generally not varied but the pulse energy is varied through cycle time and current. The basic EDM process employs kerosene dielectric in tank in which the tool-work electrodes are immersed. Kerosene has high deionisation property required for transient spark discharges. The electrode can be any conductive material but copper is preferred for its high conductivity and machinability.

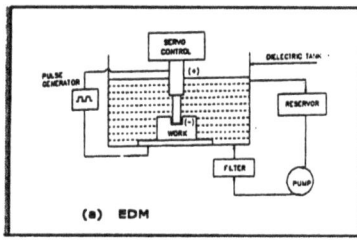

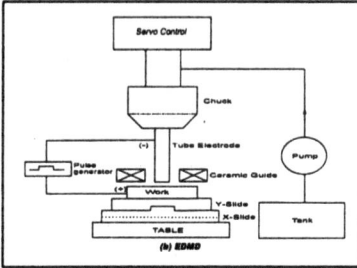

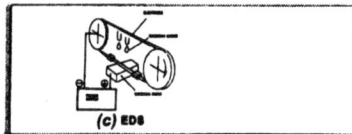

Fig.1: Schematic Sketch of EDM and its variant processes, EDS and EDMD

The EDMD process employs a tube electrode for flushing of dielectric which is distilled water with highly effective quenching and removal of eroded debris from spark gap. Brass is preferred over copper as electrode for better rigidity. Lateral deflection of the slender electrode is prevented by a ceramic guide assembly. Compared to EDM the current and voltage employed are smaller.

The EDS employs a mild steel belt as electrode with typical dimensions of 0.9x35x7450mm and guided through ceramic assemblies. The dielectric fluid is replaced by an electrolyte to promote arcing in place of sparking owing to poor deionisation characteristic of the electrolyte[2]. Consecutive sparks are located at the same spot and their shift occurs due to rotating belt electrode. The electrolytic reactions produce hydrogen at cathode which promotes ionisation and sparking and oxygen at anode leading to the formation of a passivating film. This is an important requirement and for this reason the electrolyte employed is silicic acid soda solution. For aluminium which

has high affinity to oxygen this non conducting film is formed by an oxide layer. Therefore for machining aluminium water dielectric can be used. The insulating film prevents a conducting path between electrodes. As the advancing electrode scrapes the work surface, a short circuit is established. The servo control reverses the electrode and a spark is initiated through the gap, promoted by the gaseous presence from the aforementioned evolution at the electrode[3]. The arc discharge from continuous sparking needs very low pulse off times thus the spark energy is high which is further boosted with the employment of very high current (up to 300 Amp) which facilitates high machining rates associated with sawing. This also enlarges the interelectrode gap extinguishing the arc. The resulting pause time reestablishes the passivation film on anodic work pieces and the cycle is repeated.

2. EXPERIMENTAL PLAN

The characteristic features of EDM, EDS and EDMD are analysed for machining rates, surface finish and accuracy. The relative evaluation is qualitative since the three processes have varying process parameters. The work material was high speed steel for its easy availability and corrosion resistance with 12mmx12mm cross section.

3. EQUIPMENT

EDM (Charmiles), EDS (Custom built by Electronica) and EDS (Sparkonix Disintegrator Microdrill).

In these two sets the electrodes were of similar thickness and diameter respectively. For demonstrating relative erosion rates of EDM and EDMD suitable pulse parameters (Current and pulse times) for matching levels of pulse energy were selected from the respective technology guide lines provided by the manufacturers [4]. Similarly for EDM and EDS, respectively highest and lowest pulse parameters were adopted. Erosion rates were estimated from material loss or machining times. Surface roughness was evaluated from Taylor Hobson Talysurf and accuracy of cuts from 3-D CMM and roundness analyser (THP TR31 Version 3.36).

4. RESULTS AND DISCUSSION

EDS Vs EDM

Relative erosion rates, roughness and accuracy of EDM and EDS are listed in Table 1. The findings are as expected but illustrate the considerably high erosion rates, surface roughness and inaccuracy (Kerf width and its variation from top to bottom) associated with EDS. The data belong to two levels of current and pulse on times(Low and high). Increase in either current or pulse on time results in higher erosion rates as well as roughness in both EDS and EDM. This is an obvious result of increase in pulse energy. The erosion rates are very high, nearly 8 to 10 times in EDS compared to EDM. This is attributed to higher currents and pulse times of EDS. Roughness also has similar trend and once again it is on expected lines. Higher energy sparks naturally produce larger size erosion pits leading to rougher surfaces.

Table 1. Erosion rate, Roughness and inaccuracy in EDM and EDS. Data arranged in ascending orders of pulse energy (Current and pulse on time).

S.No	Process	Erosion rate mg/min.	Roughness Ra (µm)	Inaccuracy Kerf width(mm)		
				Top	Bottom	Difference
1	EDS	178	4.0	1.80	1.05	0.75
	EDM	18.8	1.91	1.52	1.18	0.34
	(Low Current	_low pulse time)				
2	EDS	214	9.4	1.90	1.19	0.71
	EDM	21.6	2.02	1.60	1.21	0.39
	(Low Current	_high pulse time)				
3	EDS	234	7.6	1.96	1.18	0.78
	EDM	31.6	2.94	1.73	1.36	0.37
	(High Current	_low pulse time)				
4	EDS	268	12.2	2.02	1.35	0.67
	EDM	33.4	3.63	1.71	1.36	0.35
	(High Current	_high pulse time)				

The Kerf width represents the addition of spark gap on the two sides of the electrode. The higher spark gaps for EDS are the results of larger size erosion debris. The larger Kerf width at top compared to the bottom surface is due to higher concentration of erosion debris at top as they move out of the spark gap. A visual inspection of EDS surfaces exhibit remarkably even and turbulence free structure and considerably high accuracy compared to what one achieves from band saw and arc cutting which also suffer from burrs. This superior quality of machined surfaces with fast cutting rates renders electro discharge sawing a highly suitable process compared to conventional methods particularly for high strength and hard materials. The erosion being thermo electric , the tooling is simple. The surfaces from EDM and EDS bear considerable similarities. The erosion appears to be in molten form due to high energy densities of spark discharges. The erosion rates are so high in EDS, that the high energy pulses may not be the only reason but also short circuits between electrode and work surface with high current surge and resulting explosive force providing efficient expulsion of eroded metal. EDM, on the other hand, suffers from significant retention of molten metal at the pits or craters from the erosive effect of sparks.

5. EDMD Vs EDM

Similar results on the erosion rate, roughness and accuracy are listed in Table.2 for EDMD and EDM. The erosion rates were evaluated in terms of machining times required for drilling steps of 3mm depth. In EDM there is a considerable stalling of machining due to spark gap contamination and short circuits. The

Table.2 Machining time, Roughness, inaccuracy error in EDMD and EDM nominal hole diameters; 3 and 2mm with higher and lower current settings respectively.

S.No.	Process	Machining time for depth in mm				Ra (µm)	Inaccuracy/Hole dia (mm)		
		0-3	3-6	6-9	9-12		Top	Bottom	Diff.
1	EDMD	3'-38"	3'-42"	3'-56"	4'-49"	0.96	3.262	3.314	-0.052
	EDM	1'-15"	3'-52"	5'-25"	8'-32"	1.24	3.620	3.260	+0.360
2	EDMD	1'-10"	1'-19"	1'-22"	2'-10"	1.13	2.424	2.402	+0.022
	EDM	1'-29"	3'-26"	6'-16"	1'-46"	1.84	2.836	2.335	+0.301

electrode was reversed after every 3mm drilled depth and fed again. The timings were noted for machining each step of 3mm hole depth. As the hole depth increases the machining times for each subsequent depth of 3mm increases considerably. This highlights, the problem of spark gap contamination in cavity sinking and drilling in EDM and the need for effective gap flushing. In EDMD this is achieved by pumping the water dielectric at high pressure (about 100 bar) through the pipe electrode as well as its rotation for enhancing the fluid circulation. The eroded debris are effectively removed from the spark gap and machining is continuous and effective. There is only marginal increase in machining times with higher depths but the drilling continues uninterrupted. The roughness of machined surface is again witnessed as dependent on spark energies. The results on overcut are significant. As already pointed out in the preceding results on machining times, the gap contamination is a major problem in EDM, particularly in drilling. The eroded debris encounter resistance to flow from the narrow spark gap and their larger concentration at the mouth of the hole results in larger spark gaps and over cut at the top surface resulting in a tapered and over sized hole. An over sized hole occurs even in EDMD owing to the need of a spark gap. The excessive gap contamination witnessed in EDM does not occur in EDMD and the hole size is considerably uniform along its depth. Still there will be some uneven gap contamination and its effect on a larger hole size at the top surface. Paradoxically in some cases the hole dimension at the bottom surface was more. This can be visualized as the effect of a bend diflection in the tube electrode. Thus a revolving

electrode will create a larger hole. If this effect is more than that of larger debris concentration at the mouth of hole, the net effect will be negative taper or larger hole size at the bottom surface. In EDMD these two effects will generally cancel out each other which in combination with efficient gap flushing results in a uniform hole size along its depth. This is the attractive feature of the provision of electrode rotation in addition to forced circulation by pumping the dielectric through a hollow electrode.

6. CONCLUSIONS

1. Electro discharge sawing is essentially suitable for large bar stocks or ingots for fast, accurate and burr free cuts.
2. The arc discharges in EDS result in higher roughness and Kerf width compared to EDM.
3. The efficient gap flushing of EDS results in unform and uninterrupted drilling unlike EDM with poor flushing and extensive short circuits.
4. Effective gap flushing combining with tool rotation results in highly uniform hole diameter along its length where as in EDM the hole has considerable taper.

7. REFERENCES

1. **Paulo Carlos Kaminski, Marcelo Neublum Capuano,** Microhole machining by conventional electrical discharge machine, Int.Jl.Mach.Tools & manufacture V.43,2003.pp 1143-1149.
2. **I.M.Crichton and J.A. Mc Geough,** Theoretical, experimental and computational aspects of electrical discharge arc machining process, Annals of the CIRP, V.33, 1984, pp429-433

3. **I.M.Crichton, J.A. McGough, W.Munro and C.Whlte**, Comparative studies of ECM, EDM and ECAM, Precision Engg;1981,pp.155-159

4. Operation manual-Electronica, EDS and EDM systems,1994.

Simulation

GCMM 2004
Editors: Prasad K D V Yarlagadda and S Narayanan
Copyright © 2005, Vellore Institute of Technology, Vellore, India
Publisher: Narosa Publishing House Pvt. Ltd., New Delhi, India

Modeling, Simulation and Analysis of Flexible Assembly System using Petri Net

Pundlik V, Choudhari, Jadhav V S

Government College of Engineering
Karad,

E-mail: pundlik_er@yahoo.co.in

Abstract

This paper presents the new Generalized Stochastic Petri Net, which is more suitable for modeling and simulation of flexible manufacturing system. Petri nets are a graphical and mathematical modeling technique that is useful for modeling concurrent, asynchronous distributed parallel, nondeterministic and stochastic systems. The advantages of Petri net lie in the fact that their resulting models are not only simpler, intuitive but also of the more decisive power. In this study, a computer interactive simulation program is prepared in general purpose Visual Basic 6.0 environment. The performance evaluation of Flexible manufacturing Systems refers to estimation of various qualitative and quantitative performance measures. Qualitative performance measure includes liveness, safeness, boundedness and quantitative performance measure includes utilization, throughput rate, cycle time, average waiting time. These helps in decision regarding part mix changes, system modification, maximizing machine utilization, total no of work pieces in the system, rescheduling in case of breakdown. In this study, a representative form of flexible manufacturing system has been taken under consideration for performance evaluation through simulations modeling. The results were rigorously analyzed and thoroughly discussed, indicating the changes required in the system.

Keywords
Petri Net Modeling, FMS, Markov Chain Model, and Simulation

1. INTRODUCTION

In current manufacturing low Volume high Variety market, Flexible manufacturing system provides a better solution where life cycle of product is Very short and design changes rapidly. Flexible manufacturing system can accommodate these changes in product and produces a low Volume high Variety product simultaneously. This paper presents modeling, simulation and analysis of these flexible manufacturing system using Petri nets. Simulation is the most effective way to support the design and modification of an assembly line. By reproducing the

activities of the system, a simulation can provide insight into the systems overall behavior and performance potential. To facilitate the development of such simulation package, Generalized Stochastic Petri nets are used to specify the system and model its behavior because of their expressive power in modeling. Simulation models, based on Petri net theory, find better utility after the system design has reached an advanced stage, or in fact, when the system goes into production.

2. LITERATURE REVIEW

The concept of Petri nets has its origin in Carl Adam Petri's Ph.D. dissertation, submitted in 1962, to faculty of Mathematics and Physics in Germany. A Petri net is composed of the following four parts [1].

1. A set of places P represented on Petri net graph by circles
2. A set of transition T represented on a Petri net graph by straight lines
3. An input function I that consist of directed arcs from places to transition.
4. An output function O that consist of
5. Directed arcs from transition to places.

Formally, a Petri net C is defined as the five tuple C=(P, T, I, O, M). Transitions are the actions, which take place in the system, the occurrences of these transitions being controlled by the state of the system. The state of the system may be described as a set of conditions. A condition is a logical description of the state of the system. For a transition to occur (or to fire), it may be necessary for certain condition to hold, and these are termed as the precondition of the transition. The firing of the transition may cause other condition called post condition to become true. In Petri net graphs, preconditions are modeled by token residing in an input place(s) of a transition and post condition become true by placing a token in the output place(s) of a transition. The marking M is defined as an n-Vector M=(M1, M2...Mn). The number of token in place P1 is M1. This is also termed as execution of the modeled system.

A marking changes when transition fires i.e. when an event or activity occurs. Transition firing is equivalent to a state change and describes the Petri nets dynamic behavior. Define the set function I of input places and O of an output places for a transition t.

Viswanadhamn and Narhari [2] described the use of generalized stochastic Petri nets in the performance studies of automated manufacturing systems. They provide a procedure to analyze the developed GSPN model. They also pointed out the necessity of introducing time in classical Petri nets.

X.F.Zha et al. [3] used knowledge intensive Petri nets for design of robotic automatic flexible assembly system. The knowledge intensive Petri nets has been defined using object oriented programming for modeling, simulation and analysis of robotic automatic assembly system.

H. Yu et al [4] defined a new class of Petri nets for modeling FMS, which enhance the modeling technique for manufacturing system with features difficult to model. The automatic synthesis of Petri nets has been explained briefly using FMS modeling language.

As the complexity of the problem increases, manual construction of reachability tree during simulation of Petri net model becomes time consuming and difficult. Thus, there is an urgent need for preparation of software package for automatically generating the reachability tree and simulation of steady state probabilities for performance evaluation the flexible manufacturing system. Simulation allows the designer to experiment with different shop floor layout, product mixes and schedule without the cost that would be incurred in experimenting with real systems.

3. OBJECTIVES AND METHODOLOGY

The object of the present work has been oriented with following

➤ To Model Flexible manufacturing system with Generalized Stochastic Petri Net and generate the reachability tree. A computer package is developed to generate Reachability tee automatically.
➤ Analysis of the GSPN model using Markovian methods.
➤ Computation of performance measures like utilization, waiting time, throughput etc.

Algorithm to construct Reachability:

Reachability tree represents all the marking of the Petri nets, which can be obtained by all the combinations of transition firing. Firing all enabled transition and noting the marking construct the Reachability tree. Steps in generating Reachability tree [4]

1. The GSPN model of the system is prepared.
2. Initial marking of the model is denoted by M_0

3. The set of enabled transitions for this marking are computed by checking the input places to various transitions.
4. Using GSPN firing rules, one of the enabled transitions is fired. It is given a separate number thus forming a branch. From the marking there may be one or more transitions enabled, further forming branches.
5. Using step 4 all the possible enabled transition will be fired forming several branches.
6. Every time a new marking is generated, it is compared with existing markings. If such marking already exists, then no further branching takes places for this marking.

4. PROBLEMS AND MODEL FORMULATION

4.1 Problem Formulation for Flexible Manufacturing System

A flexible manufacturing system, which has been considered for analysis in this work, is as shown in Fig. 3.1. The FMS consists of two-manufacturing station MS-1 and MS-2. The material transport system consists of an AGV (Automated Guided Vehicle) system. The pallets with part carried by the AGV will be either routed to manufacturing station MS-1 or manufacturing station MS-2 or unloading unit according to certain probability. A raw part is loaded into the system only if there is an empty pallet. It is assumed that initially there are two pallets in the system, AGV is idle, MS-1 is machining one parts, and MS-2 the other part. Performance measures like throughput rate, utilization of MS-1, MS-2 and AGV, length of AGV queue is to be found out.

4.2 Design of Petri Net Model for Flexible Manufacturing System

In Petri net model conditions are modeled by places events are modeled by transition. The input of the transitions are the preconditions of the corresponding events, the output are the post conditions. The occurrence of the events corresponds to the firing of the corresponding transition. Holding of the condition is represented by a token in place corresponding to the condition. When the transition fires it remove the enabling token representing the holding of the precondition and create new tokens, which represent the holding of the post conditions.

Petri net model of this flexible manufacturing system is designed as shown in Fig. 1.

The interpretation of places and transitions in the model is given as follows:

Places Interpretation
P_1 Queue of the part waiting for transport
P_2 AGV available
P_3 AGV transporting a part
P_4 Part transferred by AGV
P_5 Queue of the parts waiting for MS-1
P_6 Queue of the parts waiting for MS-2
P_7 MS-1 available
P_8 MS-2 idle
P_9 MS-1 busy
P_{10} MS-2 busy

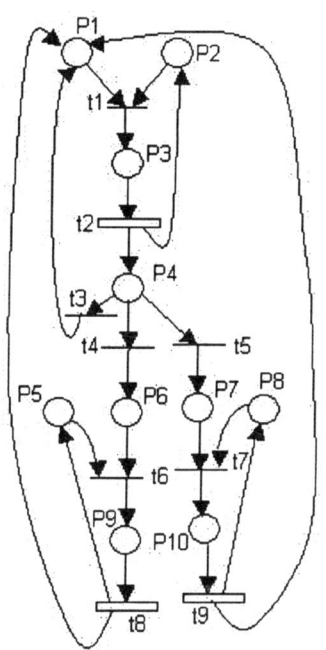

Fig. 1: Petri Net Model

Transition   Interpretation
T_1 AGV start transporting a part
T_2 AGV finishes transporting a part
T_3 Finished part unloading from system
T_4 Part entering queue for MS-1
T_5 Part entering queue for MS-2
T_6 MS-1 starts processing a part
T_7 MS-2 starts processing a part
T_8 MS-1 finishes processing a part
T_9 MS-2 finishes processing a part

4.3 Flexible Manufacturing System with change in Decision Rule

The above model can capture the change in decision rule dynamic routing scheme and change in architecture of the physical system. The modification required in the model to incorporate the change in routing decision is discussed here. In the above model if MS-1 and MS-2 both manufacturing station are available, the AGV assigned part to any one of the manufacturing station.

Lets make the following change in decision rule: If MS-1 and MS-2 are both available, the waiting part is assigned to manufacturing station MS-2 because MS-2 is faster than MS-1. If MS-1 alone is available or MS-2 alone is available, the part is assigned to the available manufacturing station. If MS-1 and MS-2 are currently busy, the part is assigned to one of the queue probabilistically. The model of Petri net with change in decision rule is constructed as shown in Fig. 4.2.

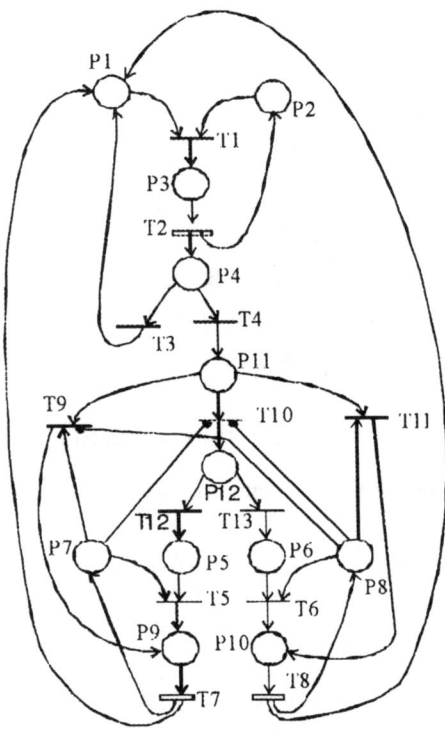

Fig. 2: Model with Change in Decision Rule

5. SOFTWARE ARCHITECTURE

The fourth generation language Visual Basic 6.0 has been used for front-end design, i.e. software interface, along with core part of programming. The database handling is done through the Database Management System (DBMS) Microsoft Access. The software consists of MDI form, input forms, processing forms, and data report and database tables. Using above explained tools and controls various modules in software named FASSimulator are designed and programmed. After running the software named FASSimulator MDI form with main menu is displayed as shown in Fig. 3.

5.1 Input Module

This module consists of two sub menus namely new and open. From the new menu new model can be entered in software. This menu consists of three forms namely input form1 and input form2 and initial status form. The different inputs fed through input form1 include the number of transition i.e. events or activities in the system, number of places i.e. logical condition and inhibitor arcs present in the system for modeling priority decision.

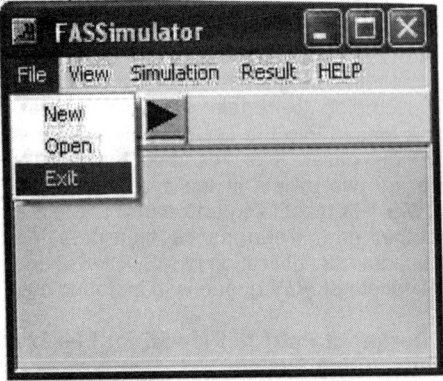

Fig. 3: Main Menu of software

5.2 Reachability Tree generation and Simulation Module

After feeding input information, simulation can be started from simulation menu. At first the enabled transition are checked from initial marking and stored in database. Then the enabled transition fired according to firing rules. All the marking generated, enabled transition in that marking are stored in database.

5.3 Generation of output reports module

This module finds out the steady state probability for each marking i.e. for each status of the system. From this generic performance measure are simulated using Monrovian techniques.

The following assumptions are made to ensure existence of unique steady state probabilities for the GSPN marking:
1. The GSPN is bounded i.e. the reachability tree is finite.
2. The GSPN model is proper and deadlock free.

The reachability set contains three types of markings. Tangible markings are those in which only timed transitions are enabled. In Vanishing markings, immediate transitions are enabled which are used to model logical condition of the system. Markings in which no transition is enabled are known as deadlock markings. The transition probability matrix of the Marko chain is calculated using firing rated of the timed transition. The ij^{th} entry in TPM denotes the probability of going from state i to state j.

Let Y be Vector of real number. Then the solution to

$$Y*A = Y \text{ and } \sum_{i=1}^{n} yi = 1 \text{ ----------(1)}$$

gives the stationary probabilities of reduced embedded Marko chain. This can be interpreted as the relative number of Visit to M_i. Let m_i be the mean sojourn time of the marking M_i and is giVen by

$$m_i \quad \frac{1}{\sum_{t_k \in t_i} F(M_i, t_k)} \text{ --------(2)}$$

Where T_i are set of enabled transitions in M_i. Let q_i be the steady state probability of marking M_i then

$$q_i = \frac{y_i * m_i}{\sum_{j=0}^{t} y_j * m_j} \text{ ----------(3)}$$

Once the steady state probabilities of the tangible states were calculated, different performance measures can be computed as below
1. Probability that particular condition C holds:

$$\Pr ob(C) = \sum_{j \in S_1} q_j \text{ ----------(4)}$$

Where S_i is the set of markings in which the condition 'C' is satisfied.
2. Probability that a place P_i has exactly k tokens:

$$\Pr ob)P_i, K) = \sum_{j \in S_2} q_i \text{ ----------(5)}$$

Where S_2 is the set of markings, which have exactly k tokens in place P_i
3. Expected number of token in a place:

$$ET(P_i) = \sum_{k=1}^{K} k \Pr ob(P_i, k) \text{ ----------(6)}$$

Where K is the minimum number of tokens P_i may contains
4. Throughput rate of a timed transition t_j

$$TR(tj) = \sum_{i \in S_3} q_i * F(M_i, t_j) * r_{ij} \text{ ----------(7)}$$

Where S_3 is the set of markings in which t_j is enabled
$r_{ij} = 1$ if t_j is not in conflict with any enabled transitions in M_i. Otherwise r_{ij} is the probability that t_j fires among the conflicting transition

6. RESULTS AND DISCUSSIONS

The matrix of input and output places to transition is fed to software. There are no inhibitor arcs in the model. If place represent precondition of the transition (activity) then enter "1" otherwise "0" in the matrix. The initial status of the system shows that the AGV is available, MS-1 and MS-2 doing the machining operation is given as an input matrix to software. In addition, the time transitions t_2, t_8 and t_9 that required nonzero times to fire in the model are given to software as a matrix. For timed transition we assign "1" otherwise "0" in the matrix. Firing rates (number of parts per hour) are entered to the software. Routing probabilities for t_3, t_4 and t_5 are 0.3, 0.3 and 0.4 respectively fed to software.

There are six tangible marking in the model. The interpretations of tangible markings are:

M1 (2 9 10) - MS1 and MS2 busy, AGV idle.
M2 (3 7 10) - AGV and MS2 busy MS1 idle.
M3 (3 8 9) - AGV and MS1 busy MS2 idle.
M4 (1 3 7 8) - AGV is busy and other parts waiting for AGV.
M5 (2 6 7 10) - MS2 is busy and other parts waiting for MS2.
M6 (2 5 8 9) - MS1 is busy and other parts waiting for MS1.

To see the effect of change in routing decision, the routing decision is incorporated in the model. Now there are inhibitor arc to model priority in the FMS model. Then the software simulates the performance parameter of the system. According to new decision the AGV assign the part to the faster assembly station if both assembly station are idle. When the change in decision rule is incorporated in model the tangible marking is reduced to four. The interpretations of the tangible markings are

M1 (2,9,10) AGV is idle, MS1 and MS2 busy
M2 (3,7,10)   AGV and MS2 busy, MS1 idle
M3 (3,8,9) AGV and MS1 busy, MS2 idle.
M4 (1,3,7,8)   Queue of part is waiting for AGV, AGV is transporting part, and MS1 and MS2 are idle.

Figure 4 shows graphical comparison of the utilization of the FMS after change in routing decision with initial FMS model.

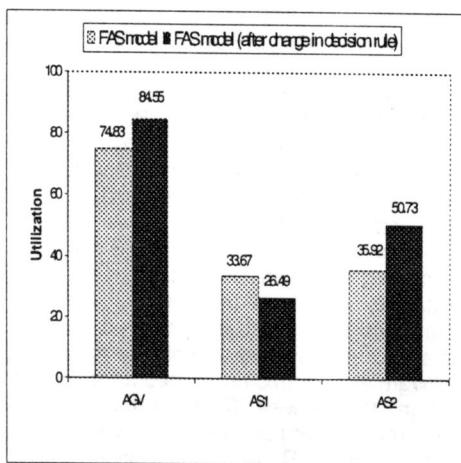

Fig. 4: Comparison of Performance Measure

The graph shows the utilization and throughput of FMS after change in decision rule increases. In the system, the utilization of resources is poor. This is because of routing decision and the number of pallet in the system is restricted to two. The numbers of pallets are restricted to two to minimize the work in process inventory. After application of priority decision utilization of AGV and manufacturing station MS-2 increases but the utilization of MS-2 decreases. The throughput rate of the system increases.

7. CONCLUSION

For hypothetical FMS software simulates the performance parameter such as utilization and throughput of the AGV, station MS-1 and MS-2. In first case, probabilities for routing the AGV toward station MS-1 and MS-2 are assigned. The throughput and utilization of resources in this case is poor. To improve the performance the priority decision is incorporated in the model.

Modified FMS model has simulated. The result shows that the utilization of AGV increases from 74.83% to 84.55 %. Utilization of MS-2 increases from 35.92% to 50.73%. But, utilization of station MS-2 decreases from 33.67 to 26.49 because AGV assigns part to MS2 if both stations are available. Throughput rate of FMS increases from 1.34 to 2.53 parts per hour. Hence, based on above quantitative discussion it is advisable to implement the new decision rule in actual system. Here, the effect of changes in the system can be analyzed without incurring cost and experimenting with real system.

By manipulation of model, knowledge about the modeled process can be obtain without danger, cost or inconveniences of manipulating the real process itself. By analyzing output of software, plan of design is prepared and implement the flexible assembly system successfully. Hence the software can be effectively used as a powerful decision making tool during design and expansion of FM

8. REFERENCES

1. **Peterson. J. L., 1981** " *Petri Net Theory and Modeling of System* ", Prentice Hall Inc., Englewood Cliff NJ.
2. **Viswanadham & Narhari Y,** *"Performance Modeling of Automated Manufacturing Systems"* Prentice Hall Inc., Englewood Cliff NJ 1992.
3. **Zha X.F. , Du H. and Lim Y.E.,** "Knowledge intensive Petri net framework for concurrent intelligent design of automatic assembly systems" *Journal of robotics and computer integrated manufacturing,* 2001, vol. 17, pp 379-392.
4. **Yu H., Reyes A., Cang S. and Lloyd S.;** "Combined Petri net modeling and AI based heuristic hybrid search for flexible manufacturing systems- part 1 Petri net modeling and heuristic search", *Journal of computer and industrial Engineering,* 2002 (in press).

GCMM 2004
Editors: Prasad K D V Yarlagadda and S Narayanan
Copyright © 2005, Vellore Institute of Technology, Vellore, India
Publisher: Narosa Publishing House Pvt. Ltd., New Delhi, India

Simulation Modelling and Analysis of a Job Shop Scheduling Problem with Sequence Dependent Setup Times

Sridharan R

Professor, Dept. of Mechanical Engg., National Institute of Technology Calicut, NIT Campus P.O., 673 601, Kerala, India.

Email:sreedhar@nitc.ac.in

Vinod V

Lecturer, Dept. of Mechanical Engg., N.S.S College of Engineering,

Palakkad - 678 008

Suresh kumar N

Sr Gr Lecturer,Dept of Mechanical Engg,College of Engg, Adoor,691551

Abstract

This paper presents the salient aspects of a simulation study carried out in a typical job shop in which the setup times are sequence dependent. A discrete event simulation model of the job shop system is developed for the purpose of experimentation. Scheduling rules from the literature are incorporated in the simulation model. Three new scheduling rules such as JSPT, JEED, JEMDD based on setup time are proposed and implemented. The performance measures considered are mean flow time, mean tardiness, proportion of tardy jobs, mean setup time per job and number of setups per job. It is found that the proposed scheduling rules are found to provide better performance than the existing rules.

Keywords
Scheduling, Sequence Dependent Setup, Simulation, Scheduling Rules.

1. INTRODUCTION

The job shop scheduling problem may be characterized as one in which a number of jobs, each comprising one or more operations to be performed in a specified sequence on specified machines and requiring certain amount of time, are to be processed. The objective usually is to find a processing order on each machine for which a chosen measure of performance is optimized. Many scheduling rules have been proposed and investigated by researchers using simulation [1, 2, 3, 4]. Blackstone et al. [5] and Maccarthy and Liu [6] provide a review of scheduling rules used in job shop production systems. A review of the literature shows that there has not been a significant amount of research done on scheduling dynamic job shops when the setup times are sequence dependent.

521

The present work investigates scheduling a job shop production system in which the setup times are sequence dependent. Some of the existing scheduling rules from the literature [7] are considered in the simulation study. New scheduling rules have also been proposed and implemented.

The paper is organized as follows. The following section provides the approach adopted in the present study. Then, the salient aspects of simulation model development are presented. The existing scheduling rules and the proposed scheduling rules are described in section four. The measures used for evaluating the performance of the system are presented in section five. The details of experimentation are provided in the next section. Subsequently, the results obtained from simulation are analysed. The last section provides conclusion.

2. APPROACH ADOPTED IN THE PRESENT STUDY

In the present study, a realistic job shop system is considered. Discrete event simulation model of the job shop system is used for the purpose of experimentation. The system consists of nine work centers each containing one machine, representing a multi-purpose, flexible machine that can process different types of jobs by changing the setup. The shop processes six groups (types) of jobs. Each of the six job types has an equal probability to be assigned to an arriving job. The time between arrivals of jobs is adjusted to maintain shop utilization at approximately 90%. The mean setup time for a job is 0.5 hrs and the proportion of mean setup time to the mean processing time is fixed at 20%.

The total work content (TWC) method of due date setting is used with a flow allowance factor of 3 representing tight due-date setting. From the past research (Blackstone et al. [3]), the TWC method is seen to be superior to other due date setting methods.

In the TWC method, the due-date is determined by

$$D_i = A_i + K (P_i + NOP * AST)$$

Where D_i denotes the due date assigned to job i, A_i arrival time of job i, K flow allowance factor,
P_i total processing time of job i, NOP Number of operations of the job and AST = Average Setup Time

The present study focuses on job shop configurations with the following assumptions:

1. A given operation can be performed by only one type of machine
2. Each machine can process only one operation at a time.
3. There is only one machine of each type in the shop.
4. Once an operation has begun on a machine, it must not be interrupted.
5. An operation may not begin until its predecessors are completed.
6. Setup times are known.
7. Each machine is continuously available for production.
8. The same type of jobs can be processed with the same setting of the machine. However, individual jobs within each type may differ in terms of processing requirements, routing and number of operations.

3. DEVELOPMENT OF SIMULATION MODEL

In the preset study, a discrete event simulation model is developed for the operation of the job shop production system. The initial status of the system is assumed to be idle and empty. Once an arrival event happens (as per the inter arrival time distribution), the simulation clock is advanced to the time of occurrence of this event and then attributes with regard to the arrived job namely, number of operations, machine routing, processing times and due dates, are determined. The machine required for the first operation of the arrived job is identified. The job is then processed if the machine status is idle, otherwise, the job waits in the queue in front of the machine. Once the processing is completed, the queue in front of the machine is checked. If there is no job in the queue, the machine is kept idle, otherwise a job is selected based on the scheduling rule and the machine starts processing that job. When all the operations of a job are completed, its performance measures are determined and the job leaves the system. The simulation is run for a sufficiently long period after achieving steady state. The overall logic of the simulation model is as shown in the Figure 1.

4. SCHEDULING RULES

A scheduling rule is used to select a job from among the jobs waiting to be processed at a machine, when the machine becomes free after processing a job.

4.1 Ordinary Rules

SPT (Shortest Processing Time): Choose the job with the shortest processing time.
EDD (Earliest Due Date): Choose the job with the earliest due date.
FIFO (First In First Out): Choose the job on first come first served basis.
CR (Critical Ratio): Select the job with the smallest CR.
CR = (Due date −Current time) / (Total remaining process time)
EMDD (Earliest Modified Due Date): Select the job with the earliest modified due date
MDD = [Maximum (Due date, Current time + remaining processing time)]

4.2 Setup Oriented Rules

SIMSET(Similar Setup): Select a job that requires the smallest setup time.
JCR (Job of Smallest Critical Ratio): Scan the queue to find a job identical to the job that finishes processing on the machine. When there is no identical job, select a job with the smallest CR.

4.3 NEW RULES PROPOSED IN THE PRESENT STUDY

JSPT (Job of Smallest Processing Time): Scan the queue to find a job identical to the job that just finishes processing on the machine. When there is no identical job, select a job with the smallest processing time.

JEDD (Job of earliest due date): Scan the queue to find a job identical to the job that just finishes processing on the machine. When there is no identical job, select a job with the earliest due date.

JEMDD (Job of earliest modified due date): Scan the queue to find a job identical to the job that just finishes processing on the machine. When there is no identical job, select a job with the earliest modified due date.

5. PERFORMANCE MEASURES

(a) Mean Flow Time
(b) Mean Tardiness
(c) Percentage of Jobs Tardy
(d) Mean Setup Time Per Job
(e) Number of Setups Per Job

6. EXPERIMENTATION

The simulation experiment has been conducted using the simulation model developed for the chosen job shop configuration consisting of nine machines and six job types. The routing for each job is different and generated randomly, with each machine having an equal probability of being chosen except that the successive operations on the same machine are prohibited. The number of operations for each job is uniformly distributed in the range 1 to 15. The processing times are drawn from the exponential distributions with a mean of 2.5 hours. The TWC method of due date setting is used in all experiments with an allowance factor of 3. Interarrival times of jobs are generated using an exponential distribution with a mean of 2.94 hours. There are ten experiments, one for each scheduling rule. Ten replications are made for each simulation experiment. Welch's procedure recommended by Law and Kelton [8] is used for identifying the steady state. It is found that the system reaches steady state at 7500 hours of simulation clock time. Hence, the simulation period corresponding to the first 7500 hours is considered as warm up period. The simulation is run for 10000 hours and the simulation outputs for the first 7500 hours are not considered for evaluating the performance measure values. Using the simulation outputs for the remaining period, the average values of the performance measures over the ten replications are determined.

Table 1 Summary of Simulation Results

Scheduling Rule	Performance Measure					
	Mean flow Time (hours)	Shop Utilization (%)	Mean Tardiness (hours)	Proportion of Tardy Jobs	Mean Setup Time	Number of Setups per Job
SPT	107.44	90.07	41.64	38.83	3.624	6.676
EDD	216.34	89.76	140.73	93.52	3.652	6.709
FIFO	228.09	89.41	152.61	92.82	3.653	6.732
SIMSET	118.13	84.75	48.81	63.05	2.209	4.493
CR	197.99	89.59	122.08	96.06	3.639	6.697
JOB_CR	117.6	85.26	44.04	79.28	2.342	4.306
JOB_SPT	105.67	85.69	35.97	73.06	3.624	6.686
JOB_EMDD	116.02	85.22	43.34	70.89	2.348	4.322

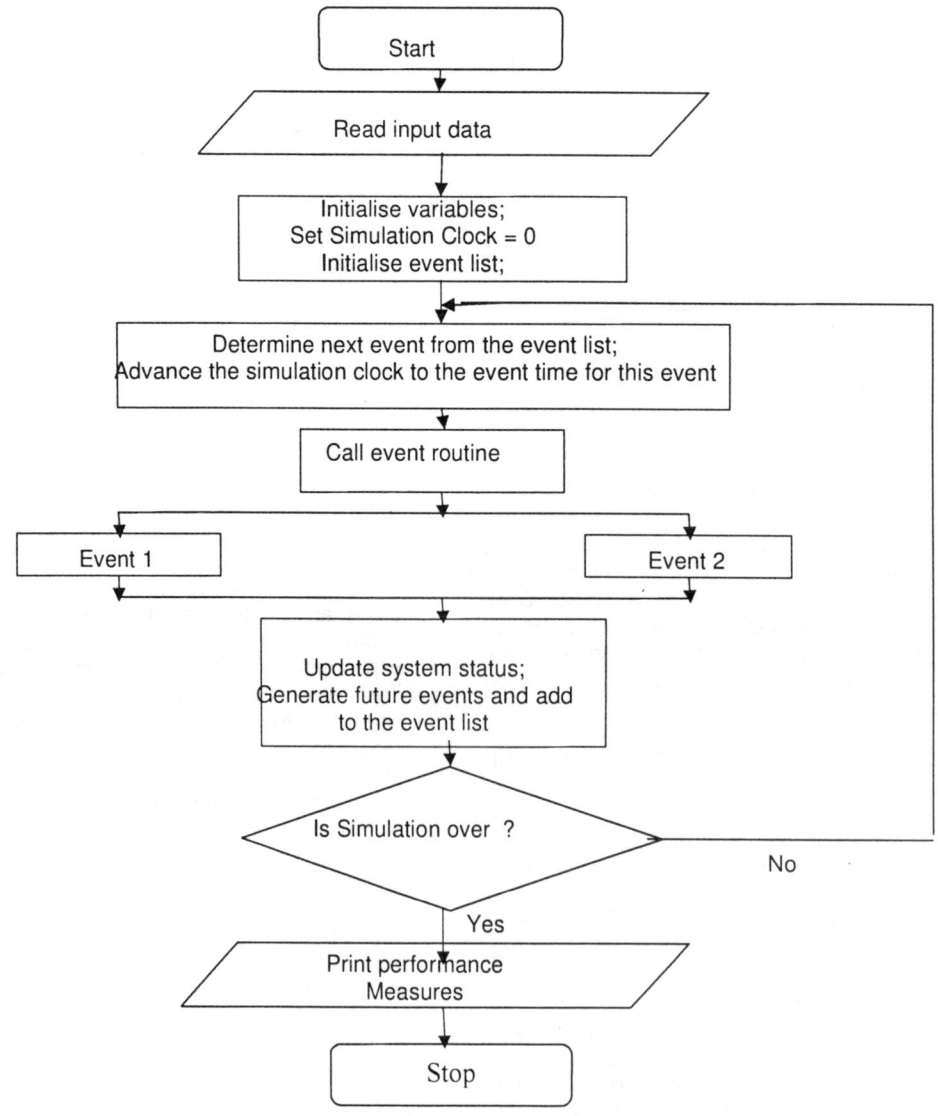

Fig.1: Flow chart of Simulation logic

7. RESULTS AND DISCUSSION

Table 1 shows the summary of the simulation results for the various scheduling rules. It is found that JOB_SPT rule provides the smallest values for mean flow time and mean tardiness. As expected, the simple rule SPT provides reasonable performance for all the measures. This is due to the fact that the shop operates under tight due date conditions (the flow allowance factor being used is 3). Among the setup time based rules, SIMSET provides minimum values for mean setup time per job and JOB_CR provides minimum value for number of setups per job. However, it is found that JOB_SPT rule out performs all the scheduling rules for the measures, mean flow time and mean tardiness. Hence it can be concluded that the JOB_SPT rule can be suggested as a suitable scheduling rule for the sequence dependant scheduling problem when the objectives are minimization of mean flow time and mean tardiness.

8. CONCLUSION

The sequence dependent setup time has a significant impact on the shop performance. The present study reveals that the proposed scheduling rules such as JSPT, JEDD and JEMDD perform better than existing rules such as SPT, EDD and EMDD. Among the rules tested, JOB_SPT rule performs the best for mean flow time and mean tardiness. Hence, considering the overall performance of the scheduling rules, the JOB_SPT rule can be suggested as a suitable scheduling rule for the sequence dependent scheduling problem.

9. REFERENCES

1. **Baker, K.R.**, "Sequencing Rules and Due Date Assignments in a Job Shop" *International Journal of Production Research*, 1984, Vol. 30, No. 9, 1093-1104.
2. **Jayamohan, S. and Rajendran, C.H.**, "New Dispatching Rules for Shop Scheduling: A Step Forward", *International Journal of Production Research*, 2000, Vol.38, No. 3, 563-586.
3. **Ramasesh, R.**, "Dynamic Job shop Scheduling: A Survey of Simulation Research", OMEGA: *International Journal of Management Science*, 1990, Vol. 18, No.1, 43-57.
4. **Askin, R.G., and Standridge, C.R.**, Modelling and Anaalysis of Manufacturing Systems, John Wiley & Sons, Inc., 1993.
5. **Blackstone,J.H., Philips, D.T., and Hogg, G.L.**, "A state-of-the-art Survey of Dispatching Rules for Manufacturing Job Shop Operations", *International Journal of Production Research*, 1982, Vol.20, No.1, 27-45.
6. **Maccarthy, B.L., and Liu, U.**, "Addressing the Gap in Scheduling Research: A Review of Optimization and Heuristic Methods in Production Scheduling", *International Journal of Production Research*, 1993, Vol. 31, No.1, 59-79.
7. **Kim, S.C., Bobrowski**, "Impact of Sequence Dependent Setup Time on Job Shop Scheduling Performance", *International Journal of Production Research*, 1994, Vol. 32, 1503-1520.
8. **Law, A.M., and Kelton, W.D.**, Simulation Modelling and Analysis, McGraw-Hill Inc., New York, 2000, 3/e

GCMM 2004
Editors: Prasad K D V Yarlagadda and S Narayanan
Copyright © 2005, Vellore Institute of Technology, Vellore, India
Publisher: Narosa Publishing House Pvt. Ltd., New Delhi, India

Visual Simulation of Robot Manipulator using VRML and Java

Kumaraswamy A & Janardhan Reddy K

Vellore Institute of Technology
Vellore-632 014

E-mail: janardhan_reddy@yahoo.com

Abstract

In a complex real world production line, usage of simulation systems for off-line program development is very much essential in industrial applications. The robotic simulation makes a great economic sense before going to implement, as there is a need for predicting the behavior of the robot manipulator to reach its specified spatial position and orientation for its predefined task. Graphical simulation will be an effective tool to accomplish the above task by providing the necessary visualization. This paper describes a VRML-Java based simulation system for a six-axis robot manipulator. This simulation system enables to display the robot configuration as a 3D solid model where the simulation and control of the manipulator is performed through Java programming. The Cosmo player and Java applet are embedded in a single HTML page that serves as complete Graphical User Interface (GUI). The Java applet is developed as an External Authoring Interface (EAI) that registers an applet to communicate by sending events between VRML environment and Java applet on dynamic basis.

Keywords
Visual Simulation, Robot Simulator

1. INTRODUCTION

Robotic simulation is the process of building and experimenting a computerized system model of a particular robot such that a specific purpose of the study is achieved through observing model's behavior under the defined assumptions [1]. Simulations are usually performed in a standalone environment for testing, experimenting, and studying a system or its prototype. Virtual reality is a high-end, human-computer interface that allows to interact with simulated environments in real time where it is widely used in areas such as architectural modeling, manufacturing, training in servicing complex equipment, and design of new plants. Virtual reality is being used in design of manipulators, programming of complex tasks and Tele-operation over large distances since many years [2].

The visualization occurs when the user interacts with three-dimensional objects in a virtual environment like one can move through the virtual world as desired, scrutinizing virtual objects from different positions, angles and orientations, where the environment is continuously updated according to the navigator's viewpoint [3]. In virtual simulation, one can interact with objects in a virtual world and the objects act like the real ones in response to unscripted user actions in the same way as they do in the real world. This results in ideal environment for evaluating the design of any systems.

During design process of Robot manipulator, predicting the desired spatial position in three-dimensional space for an end-effector depends on the solution of kinematics problem. Forward kinematics had proven to be a powerful technique for the interactive positioning and the animation of complex articulated structures. Main aspect in designing and fabricating a robot is its workspace analysis and the calculation of joint constraints limitations. This concept brings the possibility of generating imaginary robots and it is very much useful for training courses or demonstrations and also for consultation before taking purchase decisions. Thus computer-based simulation plays an important role in visualizing and predicting the behavior of physical objects in the virtual environment. The Visual simulation has become an increasingly important aspect of engineering, allowing us to predict the behavior of any articulated structure. Essentially it is a transformation of data into pictures, allowing us to harness our highly developed visual senses in order to 'see the unseen'. The basic aim is to develop robot simulation software for a robot manipulator of articulated arm with Roll-Bend-Roll (RBR) wrist configuration based on Forward kinematics in order to evaluate the spatial position of robot's end-effector. The platform independent design allows to manipulate the robot for the given input joint parameters.

It is an interdisciplinary approach where Robot kinematics, interactive computer graphics and software technologies such as Java, HTML and Virtual Reality Modeling Language (VRML) [4] are used to build the required Simulation environment and Graphical User Interface (GUI).

With this software, the Robot simulation can be done and the possibility of interference between various links can be detected before the manufacturing stage.

2. METHODOLOGY
2.1. Robot Kinematics

Kinematics is used to develop a mathematical framework for describing the relationships, in particular for the position. The transformation specifies the location (position and orientation) of the hand in space with respect to the base of the robot. If a coordinate frame is attached to each link for a serial link manipulator, the relationship between two links can be described with a homogeneous transformation matrix. The first homogeneous transformation matrix relates the first link to the base frame and the last homogeneous transformation matrix relates the hand frame to the last link. A sequence of these homogeneous transformation matrices is used to describe the transformation from the base to the hand of the manipulator, a sequence called the Forward kinematics transformation of the manipulator [5].

Based on the Denavit-Hartenberg principle, a systematic technique for evaluating the displacement matrix for each two adjacent links of a mechanism is formulated. This method is mainly implemented in robot manipulators, which consists of an open kinematics chain in which each joint contains one degree of freedom and the joint is either revolute or prismatic. The revolute and prismatic joints are considered as lower-pairs.
This paper deals with the Manipulator that is constructed for simulation consists of Articulated Arm with Roll-Bend-Roll (RBR) Wrist. In order to simulate the motion of a robot the kinematics structure of the particular robot is required to evaluate.

$$T_{Base}^{Gripper} = T_{Base}^{1} T_{1}^{2} T_{2}^{3} T_{3}^{4} T_{4}^{5} T_{5}^{6} T_{6}^{Grippe} \quad ------(1)$$

The homogeneous displacement matrix for joint is given by,

$$T_{i-1}^{i} = \left[\begin{array}{ccc|c} & R_{i-1}^{i} & & P_{i-1}^{i} \\ \hline 0 & 0 & 0 & 1 \end{array} \right] --------(2)$$

Where the upper left 3 x 3 portion of T_{i-1}^{i} is the rotation matrix R_{i-1}^{i} of link i with respect to link i-1 and three upper components on the right column of T^i_{i-1} are the components of the translation vector P^i_{i-1}.

3. VISUAL SIMULATION SYSTEM

Visual simulation provides the physical behavior of virtual objects. Java adds complete programming capabilities plus network access, which makes VRML fully functional and portable [6]. Proper blending of Java and VRML enables true multimedia, experiential and dynamic content on the Web, because of both are cross - platform standards. This is a powerful new combination, especially as ongoing research shows that VRML plus Java provide extensive support for building large-scale virtual environments where it can be optimally used with VRML to provide for Collaborative virtual environments [7].

The Java API is the specification of how to program an application to access the facilities of some object. Interfaces can be specified in Java and C++ using classes. Java also has a special interface syntax that allows interfaces that are more flexible than classes. API's available today are VRML EAI, Java3D, OpenGL++, Direct3D and Liquid Reality.

External Authoring Interface (EAI) defines an interface specification between a VRML world and an external environment [8]. It contains a set of functions of the VRML browser that the external program can call to affect (or get parameters from) the VRML world. This contribution deals only with interface between a Java applet on an HTML page and a VRML world opened in a viewer embedded in the same page. It is a set of classes with methods that can be called to control the VRML world. To VRML the EAI is a mechanism that can send and receive events. So in principle, the EAI is neither entirely tied to Java nor to a Java applet on the same HTML page. The basic operations followed are as shown in Fig.01.

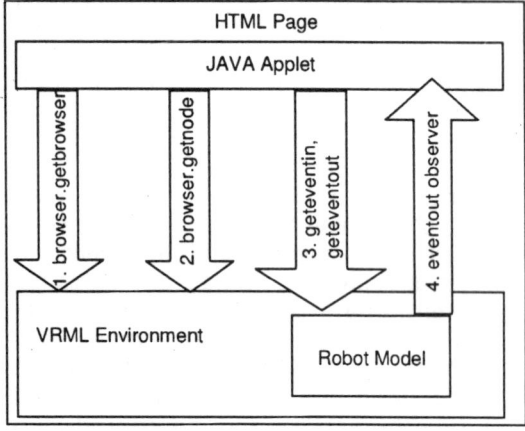

Fig. 1: Basic Operations

1. Getting a reference to a VRML node
2. Writing and reading values to the Event fields of a VRML node
3. Generating VRML from strings, replacing scenes, adding and removing nodes.
4. Receiving Events from the Scene

A Java class 'robot' that acts as abstract robot model, that contains all functions required for simulation of a robot. Afterwards a VRML model is added as graphic user interface for visualization of the robot, which is then connected in the Java object. This Java class is provided, which receives the joint commands from the GUI and then passes to compute the appropriate kinematics equations. On the basis of zero position the associated range of rotation is characterized around the z-axis by the two values min and max. These parameters are the constant attributes of the robot class. After the attributes of the robot class were defined, they must receive an interface from the user and permits the access to its kinematics status. For this purpose some methods are necessary, which can be applied to the object. The possibility of indicating to joint angle as parameters where the Forward kinematics is implemented and the position of the end effector is computed.

The implementation of VRML objects was divided into three separate VRML components, which forms the final unit. These components communicate over events with one another on dynamic basis.

These three components are interaction component, geometry component and the kinemath component. The geometry component displays the robot model on the screen, a kinemath component converts joint values to the positional values with Forward kinematics and finally an interaction component that enables the user to simulate the robot with six degrees of freedom. These three components are implemented as three different VRML objects and these are the essential components build together a fully functional interactive robot model. Each component of the arm moves in a coordinate system that is determined by the position of the previous components. This chain is modeled by a tree of nodes, where each node is a child of the previous node. The distances for assembling the kinematics chain are calculated from the Denavit-Hartenberg parameters. The geometry component stands in connection with the kinematics, which performs two-way communication with both kinematics and interaction components by communicating the changes in joint angles. Thus the geometry component works only on basis of the joint angles, the resulting matrix for the end effector is unknown to this component. Therefore only two events become needs in order to send or receive the joint angles to the kinematics component. The kinematics computations for the Forward kinematics are performed in kinemath component. Through an eventIn, a new joint position is indicated and produces one eventOut for the resulting transformation matrix for the given joint angles.

Finally the implementation ends with embedding VRML environment and Java applet in a single HTML page. A HTML file that has the embedded .wrls and applets, that is required only one semantic, mayscript in the applet tag so the applet can get the VRML plugin browser object instance from the browser. The mayscript field in the applet tag allows the applet to access Java Script methods built into Netscape Navigator and get an instance of the plugin object.

4. RESULTS

The robot was modeled using VRML and the functionality to this Robot model has been added through the Java programming. The EAI was implemented in order to communicate with the VRML environment on dynamic basis. The user input was fed to the system by entering the desired joint values in degrees through the text field of the Java applet. The simulation of the Robot for the given values of joint angles was visualized in the VRML browser and the corresponding spatial position of the end-effector was displayed in the Analyser panel. Thus the forward kinematics has been successfully incorporated in this software. The web page that has hyperlinks and will guide to the desired web page that includes simulator page was designed. All the information regarding this software development has been kept in these web pages. The same input joint angles were used in order to evaluate the forward kinematics equations manually and the evaluation was carried out successfully. Here various viewpoints have been added to the VRML environment, which allows to visualize the model in different views. This system allows to simulate by dragging the mouse on the desired link and the corresponding spatial position can be found out from the Analyser panel. The following figures depict the details the software development. The various Web Pages are shown in following Fig.

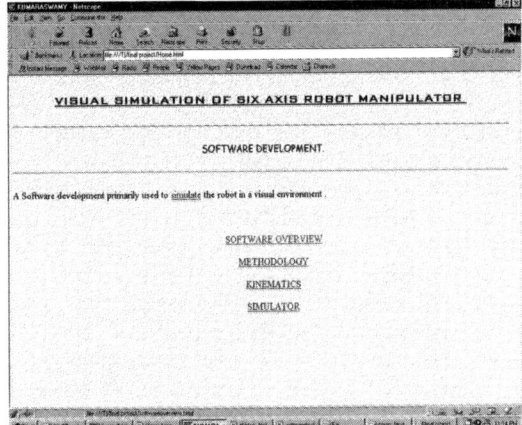

Fig.2: Visual Simulator Main Page

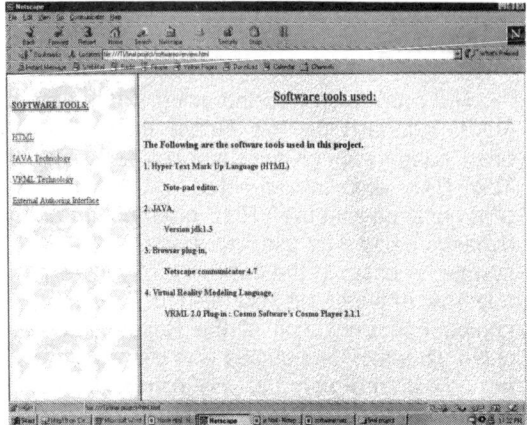

Fig. 3: Software Tools Page

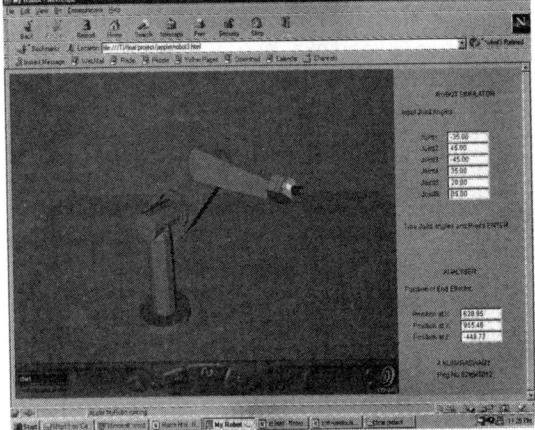

Fig. 4: Robot Simulator Page

5. CONCLUSIONS

Much effort was put into programming the graphics of the robot. A great deal of time was also spent on working through the required mathematical efforts to find the Forward kinematics required for the robot simulation which is the most important part of this software development. The resulting simulation is very realistic and works well. The development starts with developing a graphic model of the six axis robot manipulator with VRML 2.0 Specification, which can be manipulated based on joint angles as user input and also by dragging the mouse on the joints interactively. As the second step providing robot class in the Java programming, which represents a virtual robot and its kinematics by means of DH parameters. Objects of this class can

receive over an interface positioning commands and accomplish independently all necessary kinematic computations of the robot. Based on these two parts, VRML model and Java class, the EAI program is developed to connect the functionality of the Java object and the VRML model.

Now a days we hear much about "collaborative systems", It is such a system, where multiple users are engaged in particular shared activity, usually from remote locations. This kind of cooperation is very useful for dispersely located people to develop or consult their work without disturbing their physical locations. Another approach is to allow users to share interaction in 3D. As this system uses VRML and platform independent programming language Java, it can be incorporated in such collaborative environments through the Internet, which provides the communication background. This system allows to find out the way, how to control VRML browser for the particular parameters in the VRML scene, because it plays the main role in such collaborative systems.

As the future work, investigating some of the possibilities to the robot through providing the required modules, which will lead to the Telemanipulation over the Internet. This process will definetely helpful in educational purposes, collaborative working, remote operations etc. It can be extended to implement object-to-object collision detection using VRML. Even though it is a tedious process to implement, It is a great idea to implement such functionality since VRML does not support inter-object collision detection.This system development is based on a strict modular programming concept, which can be reused to another type of robot in its future development. This conceptual development can be adopted later to arbitrary robots with more or less than six revolute or linear joints. Here still many things can be added, such as Inverse kinamatics, to find out joint parameters based on given spatial positions and the programming of trajectories which can be implemented in future. The concept implemented by here can be served as for

530

development of more complex models. This can be expanded on environments with several cooperating robots and work cells. Thus a virtual robotics laboratory can be set for the production lines using VRML environments.

6. REFERENCES

1. **Chris Lattner and Ming-Shu Hsu,** *"Developing a Graphical Robotics Simulator",* School of Engineering, University of Portland, Portland.1995.
2. **Duffy B.R., O'hare G.M.P., O'donoghue R.P.S., Rooney C.F.B., Collier R.W,** *"Reality & Virtual Reality In Mobile Robotics",* Prism Laboratory, Dept. Of Computer Science, University College Dublin, Ireland, 2000.
3. **Calkin D.W., Parkin R. M., Safaric R., Czarnecki C. A.,** *"Visualization, Simulation & Control of A Robotic System Using Internet Technology",* Department of Mechanical Engineering, Loughborough University, The Gateway Leicester, UK, 1998.
4. http://tecfa.unige.ch/guides/vrml
5. **Yoram Koren,** *"Robotics for Engineers",* McGraw-Hill, 2001.
6. http://Java.sun.com/j2se/1.3 /docs
7. **Andre M.C.Campos,** *"Developing Visual-Interactive Simulations With Java And VRML",* Blaise Pascal University, LIMOS Computer Science & Modeling Institute, FRANCE, 1998.
8. www.frontiernet.net/eaifaq.html
9. **Craig Hennessey,** *"SCARA Robot simulator",* Course Project, Simon Fraser University.1999.
10. **Jiri Zara,** *"Distant Learning and Cooperation Using VRML",* Department of computer science and Engineering, Czech Technical University, Prague, Czec Republic,1999.
11. **Salman Yussof, Adzly Anuar, Azlan Zainuddin,** *"Web Based RV-2AJ Robotic arm Simulator and Manipulator",* CARs&FOF, Universiti Tenaga Nasional, Malasia, 2003
12. **Pal P.,** *"Kinematic Analysis of a SCARA Robot Arm with Roll-pitch-yaw gripper",* Department of production Engineering, Regional Institute of Technology, Jamshedpur-831 014, 2000.
13. **Kaveh E. Afshari and Shahram Payandeh,** *"Toward Implementation of Java/VRML Environment for planning",* Training and Tele-Operation of Robotic Systems, Experimental Robotics Laboratory (ERL) School of Engineering Science, Simon Fraser University Burnaby, Canada, 2000.
14. **Milan Kubec, Jiri Zara,** *"Remote VRML browser control using EAI",* Department of Computer Science and Engeneering, Czech Technical University,Prague, Czech Republic, 1999.
15. **William G. Beazley, and John B,** *"VRML Engineering Applications",* Chapman Information Assets, Inc. 5700 NW Central Dr. Suite 160, Houston, 1996.
16. **Rached Manseur,** *"A software package for computer-aided robotics education",* Electrical Engineering, University of West Florida, Pensacola, Florida.1997.
17. **Mikell P.Groover, Mitchell Weiss, Roger N. Nagel, Nicholas G.Odrey,** *"Industrial Robotics-Technology, Programming and Applications",* McGraw-Hill International Editions, 2001.
18. **Chris Marrin and Bruce Campbell,** *"Teach yourself VRML 2 in 21 days",* Techmedia publications,1999.
19. VRML reference www.rit.edu.
20. http://www.soton.ac.uk/rmc1/robotics/argeometry.htm
21. http://cosmosoftware.com/developer/eai.html

Process Control & Sensors

GCMM 2004
Editors: Prasad K D V Yarlagadda and S Narayanan
Copyright © 2005, Vellore Institute of Technology, Vellore, India
Publisher: Narosa Publishing House Pvt. Ltd., New Delhi, India

Automatic Thyristorised Control of any Electrical Load (Electric Furnace) from a Remote Area using an Optical Fiber Cable

Manikandan K V

Student, Vellore Institute of Technology-Vellore,

Haroon Ali K

Lecturer, Saranathan College of Engineering-Trichy,

Sankarraja P

Customer Engineer,HCL-Bangalore.

Email: kvmanikandan1@yahoo.co.in

Abstract

The Project is planned and executed as a base of yet to emerge 'Network Control System' (NCS) and well emerging Optical Fiber technology. The NCS is under excavation of the drawbacks of the present master 'Distributed Control System' (DCS) and NCS has gained its momentum to drop a full stop to DCS. This system controls and maintains the temperature of the electric heater, by controlling the gate pulse of the two anti parallel thyristors, given by an UJT pulse-triggering unit, controlled through an optical fiber cable. The UJT triggering provides pulses of relatively high amplitude and is not affected by loading. To maintain the temperature of the heater, a feed back circuit consisting of a thermistor, a voltage amplifier, comparator and a control unit are employed. Optical fiber provides greater isolation between power and control circuitry. OFC are not affected by electromagnetic interference. This concept of controlling can be utilized for any kind of electrical load.

Keywords

Furnace Control, Temperature Control, Remote, Thyristorised Control, OFC.

1. INTRODUCTION

Furnace temperature control is achieved by connecting the load parallel to anti- parallel thyristors. These thyristors are triggered using the UJT triggering unit, which in turn is controlled by the light source from the OFC. The electrical load can be located at a remote area, which is controlled through an Optical Fibre Cable (OFC). The temperature is sensed using a thermistor; the variation of this resistance is converted to variable voltage using voltage amplification circuit explained in section 2.5. This voltage is compared with the set voltage that is done by the comparator and control unit explained in section 2.6. When the voltage equivalent of the thermistor reaches the set value the relay circuitry is turned on so that the LED is turned off i.e. the gate pulse is cut off. When there are variations between the set voltage and thermistor equivalent voltage the gate pulse is turned on until it reaches the set value. Hence the temperature of the furnace is maintained constant.

2. PROTOTYPE

The prototype used here is temperature control of a room heater. The same electronic circuitry can be implemented for furnace of any power rating. The system units and different stages are explained as follows.

2.1 Voltage Step-Down Unit

The single phase 230V, 50 Hz, AC supply is taken from the mains which is stepped down to single phase, 12 V, 50 Hz, AC supply by the 230V/(12-0-12) V transformer. The 12 V AC supply is used for obtaining the dual power supply and is also used for the triggering circuit.

2.2 Dual Power Supply Unit

The 12-0-12 V AC power supply is rectified using bridge rectifier. The rectified output is filtered and fed to the regulator chips IC 7812 and IC 7912.The AC ripple component is further removed using capacitors as filters and the dual power supply of +12 V and −12 V is obtained.

2.3 Transmitter

The transmitter stage consists of an attenuator block and a single light source (LED) .The supply for the LED is given from .an attenuator circuit and the supply for it is +12 V DC taken from the dual power supply. The LED converts electrical signal into the light signal.

2.4 Triggering Unit

The light signal from the OFC is received by the LDR in the triggering circuit and converts light signal to an equivalent variable resistance and gives voltage to the UJT, which in turn triggers the pulse transformer. The pulse transformer gives pulses based on the value of the LDR resistance.

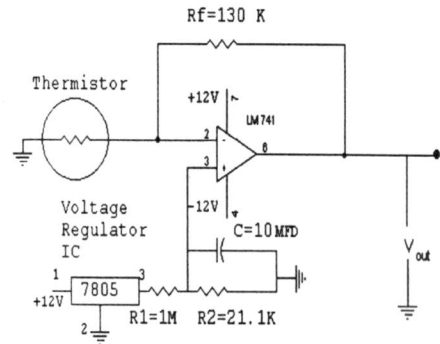

2.5 Voltage Amplification Stage

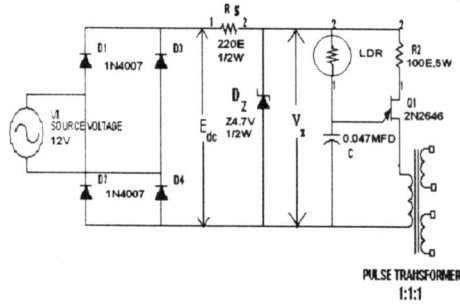

PULSE TRANSFORMER
1:1:1

The output of the thermistor is the variable resistance dependent on the temperature of the heater and hence the resistance has to be converted into a voltage, which is much easier for further processing. IC LM741 in the non-inverting amplifier mode has been employed for this purpose. The biasing voltages are taken from the dual power supply unit. At the non-inverting terminal of a constant voltage source of 0.1 V has to be applied. Hence a regulator IC 7805 and an attenuator circuit have been designed. The thermistor leads are connected to the inverting terminal and a feedback resistor improves the gain, which gives an output voltage as below

Voltage at pin- 6 of LM 741(approx) (V)	Temperature of the heater (approx)(^{o}C)
1.7	35
2.0	40
2.4	45
2.8	50
3.5	55

The temperature of the heater measured using a mercury thermometer.

2.6 Control Stage

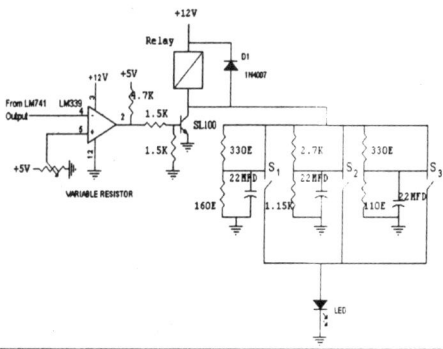

The temperature of the heater has to be continuously compared with the set value (temperature), set with the 4.7KΩ potentiometer. A dual comparator IC LM339,in the non-inverting mode has been employed as the comparator. The variable end of 4.7 KΩ potentiometer is connected to the non inverting terminal, one of the fixed end is given a supply of +5 V from the regulator IC 7805 and the other fixed end is earthed. The output of the IC LM741 is given to the inverting terminal of the IC LM339.The biasing are done from the dual power supply circuit. The output of the dual comparator is fed to the base of NPN transistor SL 100, connected in CE configuration. The collector terminal of SL 100 is connected to the12V DC relay coil in the other terminal of the relay coil is connected to the +12 V DC, from the dual power supply. A PN (1N4007) diode is connected across the relay to prevent the negative voltage reaching the transistor SL 100. When the main supply for the system is turned on the relay coil energizes and forms the NC contact. As the comparator output reaches zero the contacts changes to NO.

An attenuator circuit has been designed for three levels of voltage to be fed to the 12 V LED. The voltage and the switch setting are given below

- ❖ S1 closed; S2 and S3 open gives 3 volts.
- ❖ S2 closed; S1 and S3 open gives 3.5 volts.

- ❖ S3 closed; S1 and S2 open gives 4 volts.

  - • 3 V represents a lower rate of heating.
  - • 3.5 V represents a medium rate of heating.
  - • 4 V represents a higher rate of heating.

This is achieved by the change in LED intensity.

2.7 Electromagnetic Relays

Relays are electromagnetic switches, which provides contact between two mechanical elements. The relay has a coil that works on 12 V DC power supply and provides DPDT action as an output. In general relays provide potential free contacts which can be used for universal function like DC, AC voltage switching and to control larger electrical switchgears.

The characteristics of these relays have some limitation and are only used for simple and low cost protection purposes. For important and costly equipment installations, static relays are preferred.

The specification of the 12 V DC relay is O/E/N 57 DP-12-1C6.

2.8 Optical Fiber Cable

The LED light intensity passes through the OFC and reaches the LDR, which maintains the system operation.

The specifications of Optical Fiber Cable used here is given below

Fiber Optic Cable:

Connector Type - Standard SMA (Sub Miniature Assembly).

Cable Type- Step indexed multimode PMMA plastic cable.

Fiber Diameter- 1000 microns.

3. EXPERIMENTAL RESULTS

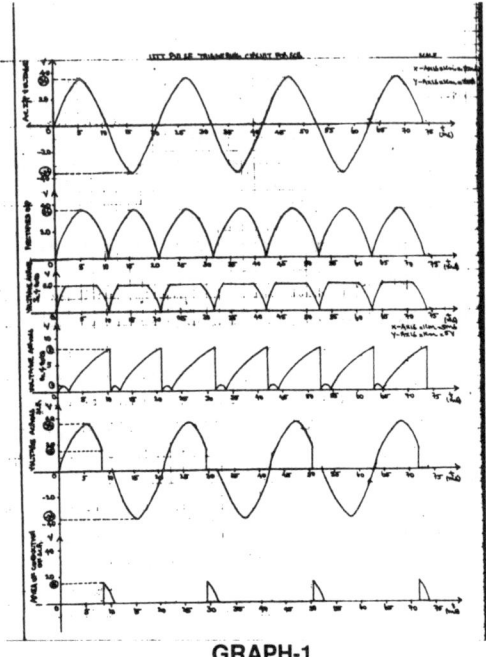

GRAPH-1

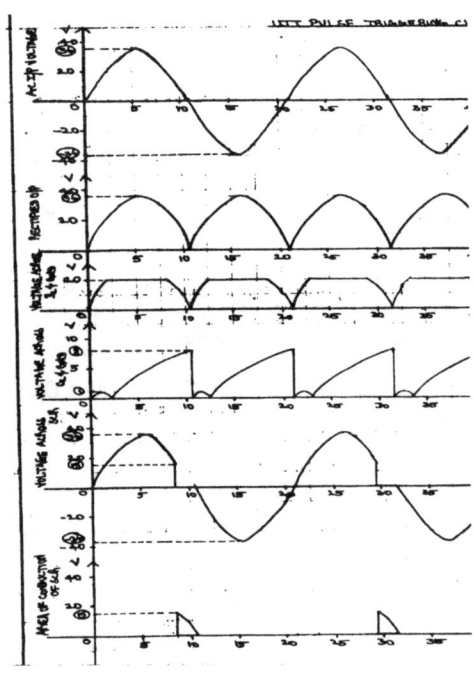

GRAPH-2

4. FUTURE DEVELOPMENTS

The importance of replacing the old technology with modern trends need not be emphasized. The technology is dramatically changing day by day. By switching over to the new trends it is possible to utilize the system more effectively. The concept of this project can be implemented to any type of electrical load, of any capacity, located at any distance and this gives a crystal clear idea of implementing the concept for yet to emerge NCS (Network Control Systems). The following improvements can be made for the better use of resources and there by making the system more efficient.

✓ As far now, only the temperature is controlled. By increasing the parameters to be controlled and monitored, it is possible for the user to understand even a minute change in the working area. The parameters such as flue gases, toxic gas content, charge inlet, and pressure can be controlled and monitored.

✓ Some hardware circuits can be included and controlled by software/ DSP/ PLCs / Fuzzy logic with protected access can also be done.

✓ The sensor used for sensing the temperature can be replaced by an Optical fibre, which is specially designed for that purpose.

✓ The multimode type of fibre cable can be replaced by duplex type of fibre cable for transmitting and receiving data through a single core of cable.

✓ Both, the voice data light pulse regarding the control strategy and the control parameter light pulses can be transmitted over a single core of cable and received at the other end for enhanced utility.

5. CONCLUSION

The **"Automatic thyristorised control of any electrical load (Electric Furnace) from a remote area using an Optical Fiber Cable"** is a system, which provides fast and accurate control of voltage.

The major limitation of the system is that the repeaters are to be employed after each 150 km, which increases the cost of the system considerably. Also, the cost of the cable increases with the distance. The advantages of the system have been already highlighted in the introduction.

The advantages over weigh the limitations and the system can be best adopted in any industry.

The working model is designed, fabricated and successfully tested on a 1000W room heater and the desired control is acquired. As for now only a part of the system has been implemented using fiber optic cable and the whole system can also be linked through the fiber.

Hence, the concept of controlling an electrical load using an optical fiber cable can be utilized for any kind of electrical load, of any capacity, located at any distance.

6. REFERENCE

1. **Bolton W.,** *Mechatronics*, Electronic Control System in Mechanical and Electrical Engineering, Second edition, Pearson Education Limited, Boston (2001).
2. **Singh M.D.,** *Power Electronics*, First edition, Tata Mc Graw Hill.
3. **Roychoudry D., Shailjain** (1996) *Linear Integrated Circuits*, New Age International Pvt. Ltd., New Delhi.
4. www.bannerengineering.com

GCMM 2004
Editors: Prasad K D V Yarlagadda and S Narayanan
Copyright © 2005, Vellore Institute of Technology, Vellore, India
Publisher: Narosa Publishing House Pvt. Ltd., New Delhi, India

Improving the Process Control in a Sugar Processing Industry through the use of Mamdani Type FIS

Gunasekaran N

Assistant Professor, Department of Mechanical Engineering,
Kumaraguru College of Technology, Coimbatore – 641 006, India.

Email:gunquality@rediffmail.com

Arunachalam V P

Professor and Head, Department of Mechanical Engineering,
Govt. College of Technology, Coimbatore – 641 013, India.

Email: vp_arun@yahoo.com

Senthil Gavaskar S

Assistant Professor, Department of Production Engineering,
PSG College of Technology, Coimbatore – 641 004, India.

Email: devadasan_srd@yahoo.com

Devadasan S R

ME(IE Student: 2000-2001 batch), Kumaraguru College of Technology,
Coimbatore-641 006, India.

Abstract

Many software engineering principles based on fuzzy logic such as artificial intelligence (AI) have emerged to reduce human skill required to produce products and offer services. However, interfacing them with the real systems is challenging because the knowledge of such process control techniques is to be educated and trained to the process engineers. An attempt has been made in this paper to build models using the Mamdani type Fuzzy Inference System (FIS) to provide comprehensive information and analysis on sugar processing. The quality of sugar is characterized by grain size, colour, ash content, moisture content and dextron content of crystals. Forty-five fuzzy rules have been developed to study the effect of these factors using a case study conducted in an industry situated near Erode, Tamil Nadu, India. The 'Matlab" software has been used to develop the fuzzy model. The fuzzy model built using these type of rules gives the graphical outputs. It enhances the understanding of process engineers about the process gap. Thus the quality of people is improved using the education and training to bridge the process gap in order to improve the quality of sugar.

Keywords

Mamdani Inference Engine, Fuzzy Rules. Process Control and Sugar Processing Industry

1. INTRODUCTION

The globalization has thrown a lot of impact on Indian manufacturing scenario. Modern manufacturing technologies are replacing the existing or conventional technologies so as to produce high quality products at a competitively low-price. Many techniques based on fuzzy logic such as AI are found to be emerging to reduce human skill required to produce the products / services. The introduction of fuzzy inferencing by Mamdani and Sugeno [4],[5],[6] has made a lot of impact in the complex manufacturing systems such as castings, cement and sugar. Controlling the quality of sugar is found to be difficult as they are affected by many factors [10],[14]. In this paper, the authors have made an attempt to study the quality of sugar and the factors influencing the same.

Intelligent computing has become reality because of neuro–fuzzy application[2],[8]. The neuro-fuzzy systems are found to be adoptive to the control of the process involved in manufacturing industries such as

fertilizers, sugar, cement etc. The robust control mechanisms have come due to the soft computing involving the use of neuro–fuzzy systems. The guiding principle of soft computing is to exploit the tolerance for imprecision, uncertainness and partial truth to achieve trace-ability, robustness and low solution cost. A fuzzy system is a non-linear mapping of an input data vector into a scalar output using a fuzzy logic. The mapping is performed using the fuzzification, fuzzy inference and defuzzification components.

2. PROBLEM DEFINITION

A brief introduction of sugar processing has been made in this section to define the problem focused in this paper. The detailed discussions are avoided to concentrate on the fuzzy based analysis of quality of sugar. A block diagram of manufacturing sugar is shown in Figure 1. The absence of the use of advanced control techniques in processing

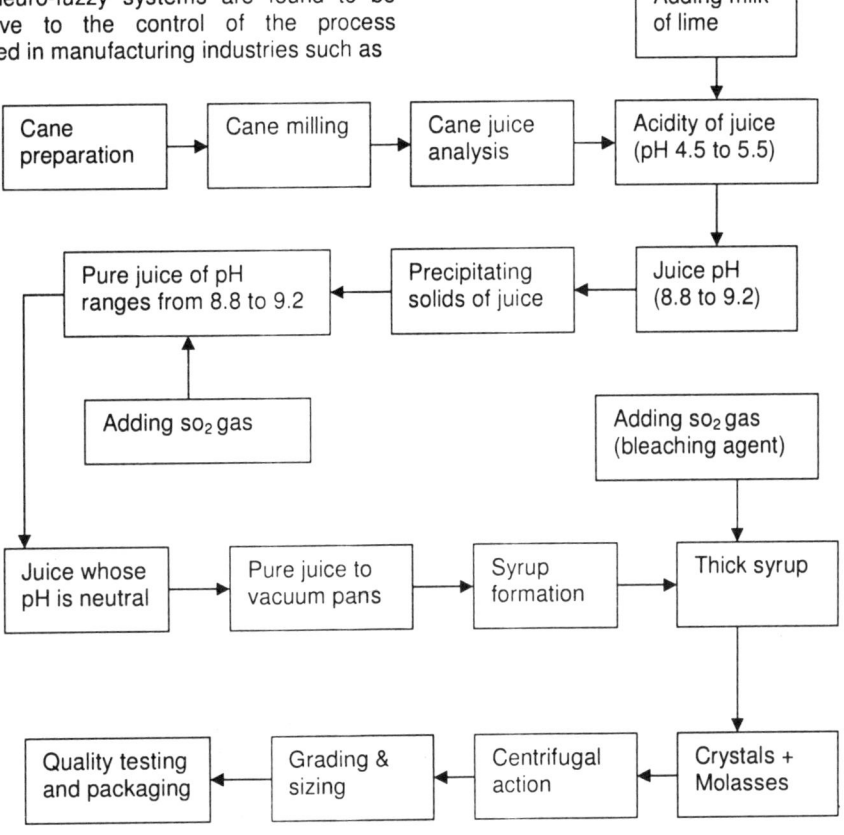

Fig. 1: Block Diagram for Processing Sugar

sugar is one of the reasons for not producing high quality sugar with competitively low price. The major problem in sugar processing industries is the control of pH value of cane juice. The milk of lime, sulphurdioxide, presence of impurities in cane juice, grain size of sugar, suspended matters, colour of the syrup, etc., affect the quality of sugar. The pH value of cane juice varies from 4.5 to 5.5 that are due to soil, climate, etc. There is an expert intervention needed to control the quality of sugar even though fuzzy based PID controls are used in some industries for processing sugar.

The process engineers and operators need to know the way the factors interact with regard to the output quality of sugar so that they could initiate actions to reduce or eliminate the process gaps.

3. FUZZY MODEL

A team of process engineers and operators was formed for this research study. The company was preparing to introduce automatic control systems for processing sugar. The understanding of control systems and the interrelationship of factors affecting the output quality of the sugar was a prerequisite to fully utilize the automatic control systems. It was decided to use the model for enriching the process knowledge. And hence, the brainstorming sessions had been conducted with the operators and process engineers to develop the fuzzy rules. A fuzzy model is formulated to analyze the effect of factors on the output quality of sugar.

The output quality of sugar is analyzed in detail in this model due to the factors grain size, colour, ash, moisture and dextron. Forty five 'If-then' rules are used in this model with five antecedents and one consequent. The AND operators are used as there is more than one antecedent in this model. The rule 'If grain size is Extracourse AND Colour is Pure White AND Ash is Acceptable AND Moisture is Acceptable AND Dextron is Unacceptable then Quality of sugar is Superior' is detailed below. Similarly, the other forty-four rules can also be detailed.

Antecedent 1: Grain
Range : (0-1.5)
No. of mfs: 3
Mf type : trimf

Mf1: Fine
Mf2: Standard
Mf3: Extra Course

Antecedent 2: Colour
Range : (40-150)
No. of mfs: 5
Mf type : trimf
Mf1: Pure White
Mf2 : White
Mf3 : Standard
Mf4 : Acceptable
Mf5 : Unacceptable

Antecedent : Ash
Range : (0- 0.15)
No. of mfs : 2
Mf type : trimf
Mf1 : Acceptable
Mf2 : Unacceptable

Antecedent 4: Moisture
Range : (0-0.08)
No. of mfs: 2
Mf type : trimf
Mf1: Acceptable
Mf2: Unacceptable

Antecedent 5: Dextron
Range : (0-200)
No. of mfs: 2
Mf type : trimf
Mf1: Acceptable
Mf2: Unacceptable

Consequent : Quality
Range : (0-100)
No. of mfs : 5
Mf type   : trimf
Mf1 : Highly Inferior
Mf2 : Inferior
Mf3 : Average
Mf4 : Good
Mf5 : Superior

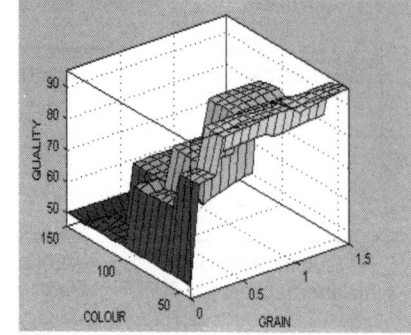

Fig. 2: Colour, Grain Vs Quality

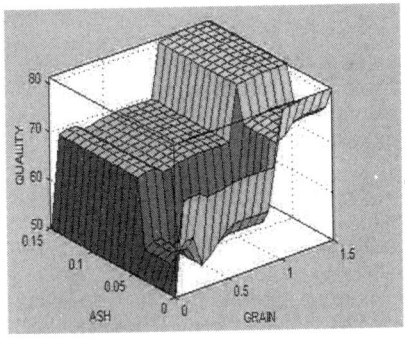

Fig. 3: Ash, Grain Vs Quality

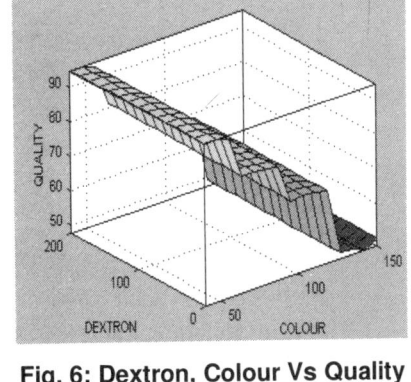

Fig. 6: Dextron, Colour Vs Quality

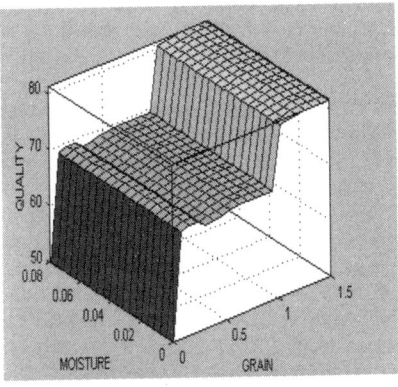

Fig. 4: Moisture, Grain Vs Quality

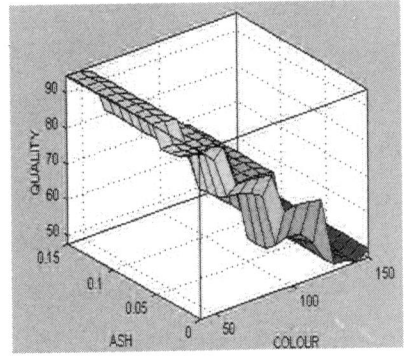

Fig. 7: Ash, Colour Vs Quality

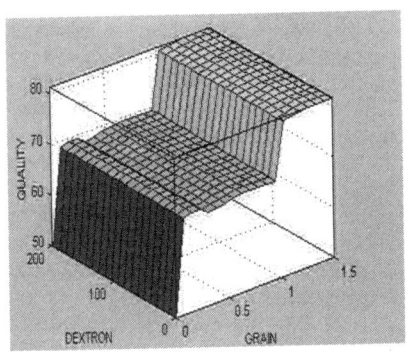

Fig. 5: Dextron, Grain Vs Quality

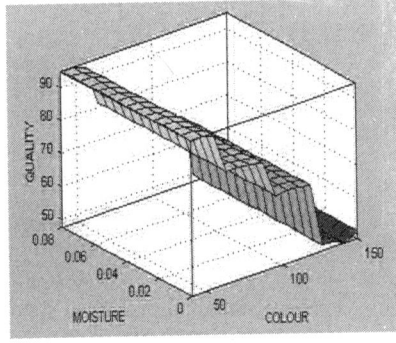

Fig. 8: Moisture, Colour Vs Quality

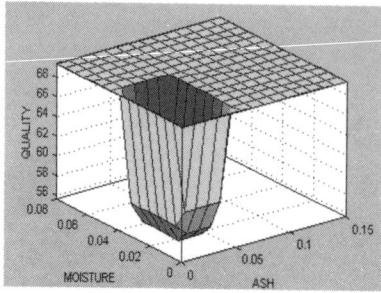

Fig. 9: Moisture, Ash Vs Quality

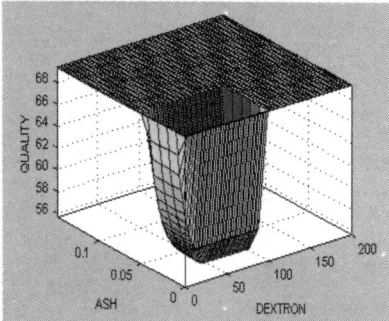

Fig. 10: Ash, Dextron Vs Quality

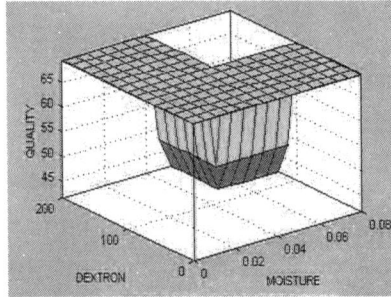

Fig. 11: Dextron, Moisture Vs Quality

4. RESULTS AND DISCUSSIONS

A fuzzy model is addressed in this paper to study the output quality of sugar in relation to the factors grain size, colour, ash, moisture and dextron. The other factors such as the effect of soil, irrigation are not taken for study.

The relationships of the factors grain size, colour, ash, moisture and dextron on the quality of sugar are evidently indicated in the plots. However at a time only two factors are considered. It is found from the Figure 2. that the quality of sugar is inferior if the colour is

greater than 120 and grain size is less than 0.25mm.On the other hand the quality of sugar is superior if colour is less than 50 and the grain size is around 1 mm.

The Figure 3. shows relationship between grain size, ash with quality of sugar. The quality of sugar is around 70% when the grain size is 0.5mm to 1mm even if the moisture is above 0.04%. The Figure 4. indicates that the moisture does not influence the quality of sugar if the grain size is greater than one. The effect of grain size and dextron on the quality of sugar is shown in Figure 5. If the grain size is greater than one, the quality of sugar is not much affected by the dextron content. The effect of dextron content is negligible on the quality of sugar if the colour varies between 40 to 90 (refer Figure 6.).

The quality of sugar is superior as shown in Figure 7. even if ash content varies from 0 to 0.15 while the colour varies between 40 to 60. The relationship of moisture and colour on quality is shown in Figure 8. The quality of the sugar is worst affected as shown in Figure 9. if moisture varies from 0 to 0.05 and the ash varies from 0 to 0.05.The quality of the sugar will be superior if dextron content varies from 100 to 200 and the ash content varies from 0.1 to 0.15(refer Figure 10.). Like wise the relationship of dextron and moisture on the quality of sugar is described in the Figure11.

The team comprising of operators and process engineers were involved in each stage of the development of the fuzzy model. The output of the fuzzy models were discussed with them. The different colours in the fuzzy output had shown them the factors and their relationship with the quality of sugar. Firstly, it has enhanced the understanding of the operators and process engineers about the factors influencing the processing of sugar. Secondly, the ranges of factors and their effects had been clearly appraised through the use of graphical outputs. The engineers were trained with understanding the fuzzy rules and fuzzy operators for getting the output.

Nevertheless, intensive training programmes were needed for preparing them to use the 'Matlab' software for formulating fuzzy models of their choice. Thirdly, the operators' gap which lies between the people (employees) and sugar processing and the process gaps which lies between the sugar processing and sugar were minimized using the fuzzy based control systems.

5. CONCLUSION

The continuous improvement of quality of the product or the process is the only way to meet the global competition. On the other hand, the cost of the product or process should be kept at competitively low-price. Many sugar manufacturers are using semi–automatic process control techniques. The knowledge of the process factors that are affecting the final quality of the sugar is essential. It is clear that many factors are contributing to the quality of the sugar. A change in variable may have serious impact on the output quality of sugar. It is very difficult to model the dynamic behaviours of such factors. The experts are needed to make use of such complex models. The fuzzy model developed using Mamdani type FIS is more simple to analyze the quality of sugar. It can be used to enhance the knowledge of the process engineers for producing superior quality of sugar.

An insight is given in this paper that how the factors such as grain size, ash content, moisture content, dextron content and colour influence the quality of sugar. It would be more useful for the process engineers to have knowledge of the factors and its influences over the quality of sugar. The generation of fuzzy rules by a neural network for the dynamic changes of factors in the system would be integrated into the conventional PID controllers for better control of the system. Further researches are needed to go in for the integration after simulating the entire system behavior.

6. REFERENCES

1. **Chiu,S.** (Sep. 1994), "Fuzzy model identification based on cluster estimation", *Journal of intelligence and fuzzy systems*, Vol.2, No. 3.
2. **Jang,J.S.R. and Sun C.T.** (March 1995), "Neuro -Fuzzy modeling and control", *Proceedings of IEEE*, Vol.83, pp. 378 - 405.
3. **Mamdani,E.H. and Assilian S.** (1975), "An experiment in linguistic synthesis with a fuzzy logic controller", *International Journal of man-machine studies*, Vol.7, No.1, pp. 1-13.
4. **Mamdani, E.H.**(1976), "Advances in the linguistic synthesis of fuzzy controllers", *International Journal man-machine studies*, Vol.8, pp. 669-678.
5. **Mamdani, E.H.** (1977), "Applications of fuzzy logic to reasoning using linguistic synthesis", *IEEE transaction on computers*, Vol.26 ,No – 12, pp. 1182-1191.
6. **Zadeh,L.A.** (1989), "Knowledge representation in fuzzy logic", *IEEE transactions on knowledge and data engineering*, Vol.1, pp. 89-100.
7. **Pivorika,P.and M.Findora,** (1998), "The alternative realization of fuzzy controllers", *Automatizace*, Vol.1, No. 10,11,12, pp. 31-38.
8. **Shin, Y.C. and P.Vishnupad** (1996), "Neuro – fuzzy control of complex manufacturing process", *International Journal of Production Research*, Vol.34, No.12, pp. 3291-3309.
9. **Solomon,S., K.Srivastava, B.L.Srivastava and V.K.Madan,** (1997), "Premilling sugar losses and their management in sugarcane",*Indian Institute of sugarcane research publications*, Lucknow, pp. 289 – 310.
10. **Lofti A. Zadeh,** (1995), *Fuzzy logic tool box for use with Matlab*, Version2, Berkley, CA.
11. **Cox E., (1994),***The Fuzzy systems hand book: A practitioner guide to building, using and maintaining fuzzy systems*, Cambridge,MA: A P Professional.
12. **James, A. Anderson,** (1999), *An introduction to neural networks*, Massachute Institute of technology, USA.
13. **Howard Demut,** (2000), *Neural network tool box for use with Matlab*, Version4, Mark Beale.
14. **Meade, G.P. and Chen J.P.C.** (1985), *Cane sugar hand book*, John Wiley & Sons.
15. **Verma,N.C.** (1988), "*System on technical control for cane sugar factories in India*", The sugar technologies association of India, Kanpur, India.

Finite Element Methods

GCMM 2004
Editors: Prasad K D V Yarlagadda and S Narayanan
Copyright © 2005, Vellore Institute of Technology, Vellore, India
Publisher: Narosa Publishing House Pvt. Ltd., New Delhi, India

Springback Analysis of Wiping Die Model using Finite Element Method

Natesan A & Ramesh B

Sri Muthukumaran Institute of Technology,Chikkarayapuram, Chennai-600 069.
India.

Email: natesan_a@rediffmail.com, ramesh_baskar75@yahoo.co.in

Abstract

With technological developments and increase in automobile and aircraft industries, the use of sheet metal has also increased. Due to increase in sheet metal more effort has been put in bending process to predict the dimensional accuracy of the sheet metal. Literature review of recent investigations on bending system has revealed that more attention being paid on spring back, which affects the dimensional accuracy. Hence in present investigation springback analysis of a wiping die bending model using FEM is attempted. The three dimensional analysis has been carried out for three materials of LF-21, LY-12 and SPCC which are mainly used in the automobile and aircraft industries. The factors, which affect the springback, have been analyzed. In addition, the compensation of springback-overbending has attempted to obtain the desired angle using LS-DYNA FEA software. The inferences indicate that the punch-die clearance and young's modulus are the predominant factors. The factors punch radius, thickness, punch-die clearance, pad force and young's modulus are inversely proportional to the springback except the die radius and the desired bend angle has obtained by the over bending approach.

Keywords
Wiping Die Bending, Springback, FEM

1. INTRODUCTION

The technology of sheet metal forming is an emerging field, which touches our lives everyday. Compared to other process, the sheet metal bending is solely responsible for lightweight and versatile shape due to low cost, good strength and formability. While reviewing the application areas, it is concluded that the dimensional accuracy is more important in the bending process. When the load is removed from the bend, the elastic recovery will be occurred. Due to this elastic recovery the accuracy of the bend angle is minimized. So that the part couldn't be used for the specific application. The elastic recovery is called springback. Wiping die bending is also called the L-bend. Factors affecting the springback are thickness, tolerance, and size of bend radius, speed, grain direction, friction and lubrication.

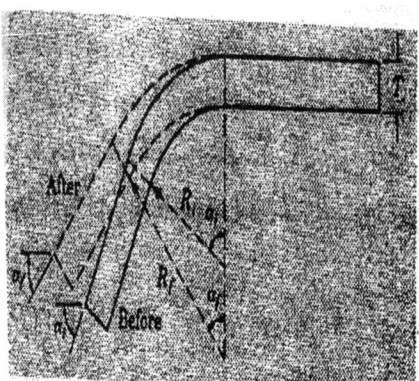

Fig.1: Measurement of springback

The springback can be calculated by,
$$\Delta\theta = \alpha_i - \alpha_f$$
Where,
$\Delta\theta$ = Springback angle in degrees
α_i = bend angle before springback in degrees
α_f = bend angle after springback in degrees

Bend force, pad force, bend radius, bend allowance are calculated to find the springback effect. Among the various compensation of springback, the over bending is applied to attain the desired angle. The FEA software LS-DYNA is used for this analysis. Because using CAE simulation tools, the manufacturing feasibility of the parts can be evaluated at the design stage; to explore alternative designs and evaluate trade offs and eventually to derive an optimized design using the right material processed in a cost effective and timely fashion.

2. REVIEW OF LITERATURE

The factors which affecting the springback were computed by the experimental analysis using OFAT (One Factor At a Time) method by Livatyali [1]. A quantitative method for calculating the springback on thin walled aluminum tubes was derived by Inamdar [2]. Wang et al [3] conducted experiments for springback of thick stainless steel. Xuchen li et al [4] carried out a finite element analysis for the effect of work hardening on the springback simulation accuracy. From the literature review it was revealed that the aluminum alloys and carbon steel are used for

bending and the development of CAE simulation is accurate and very less time consumption. Some 2D FE Analyses were carried out on springback and the attention on 3D is very less.

3. FORMULATION OF THE PROBLEM

The materials taken into the analyses are LF-21, LY-12 and SPCC. The first two materials are used for corrosion resistance and used in the marine atmospheric environment and the third material is used in the power steering assembly. The material properties are given in the table.

Table.1: Material Properties

S.No	Material Type	Young's modulus in Gpa	Yield strength in Mpa
1.	LF-21	159.048	246.05
2.	LY-12	70.085	91.41
3.	SPCC	67.339	60

The composition of the materials is given below.

Table.2: Composition of the Materials

S.No	Material Type	Composition in %
1.	LF-21 (Aluminum Alloy)	0.25 Cr, 2.5 Mg, Remaining Al
2.	LY-12 (Aluminum Alloy)	0.1 Mn, 5.2 Mg, 0.1 Cr Remaining Al
3.	SPCC (Carbon Steel)	0.9 to 1.03 C, 0.3 to 0.5 Mn, 0.04 P, 0.05 S

The 3D model of the bending system has been modeled. The computational domain for the analysis is shown below.

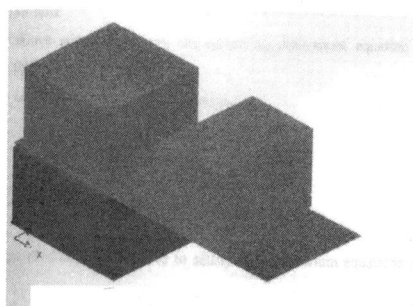

Fig.2:Computational domain of the bending system

The assumptions made in the analysis are three dimensional non linear structural problem, large deformation process, the displacement of the sheet metal after removal of loading, the tools are non-material dependent, friction force is neglected, temperature is constant and the lubrication is neglected.

The boundary conditions are the displacement of the die and pad are zero. The force needed to bend the sheet, pad force and the velocity of punch are calculated and applied.

4. SOLUTION METHODOLOGY AND EXPERIMENTAL VALIDATION

The springback analysis has been carried out by FEM using the software LS-DYNA. The entire model of the bending system is drawn using DYNAFORM and is solved by the solver LS-DYNA. The analysis has been carried out for each material and parameter viz., punch radius, die radius, punch-die clearance, thickness and pad force. Finally the results were obtained in the post processor.

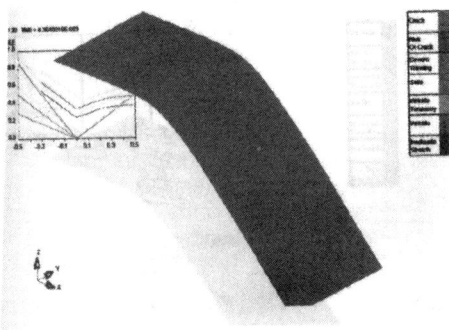

FIG.3: BENDING OF SHEET METAL WITH FLD

To assure the solution, one set of parameter has been validated with experimental results.

Table.3.Comparision of the results

S. N o	Material Type	Expt. Δθ (rad)	FEM Δθ(rad)	Prediction Accuracy in %
1.	LF-21	0.087	0.083	95.4
2.	LY-12	0.101	0.096	95.04
3.	SPCC	0.112	0.108	96.42

5. RESULTS & DISCUSSION

The wiping die bending model has been investigated for several cases and it was found that,

1. The punch radius is inversely proportional to springback. A small punch radius requires higher forces. So max. Energy is needed to bend the sheet. Thus the internal release will be decreased so that the springback is decreased.

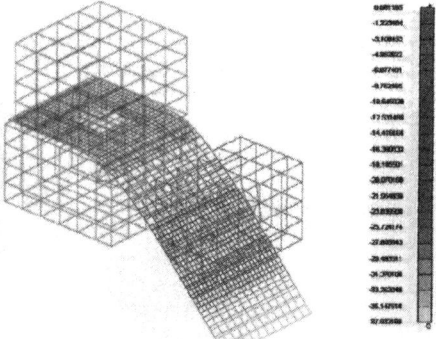

Fig.4: Displacement of LF-21 material sheet

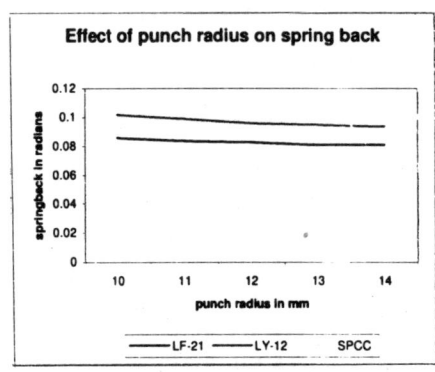

Fig.5: Comparision of Springback on punch radius

2. The die radius is directly proportional to the springback. If the die radius is small, the resistance to the flow of metal increases resulting in tearing of the metal and also it requires more bending force.

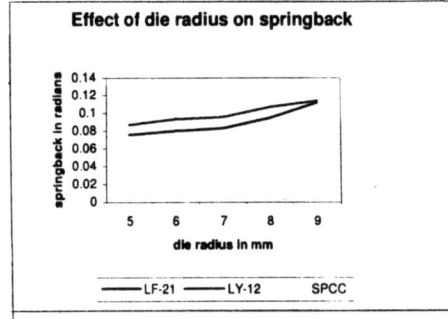

Fig.6: Comparision of Springback on die radius

3. The thickness is inversely proportional to the springback. It is because of the thinning % of the material and the thickness variation, when thinning % is increased, the thickness reduction is more, which causes more springback.

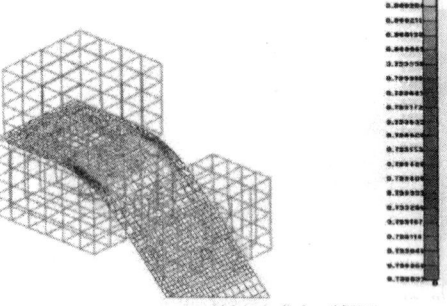

Fig.7:Thickness variation of LF-21 material Sheet

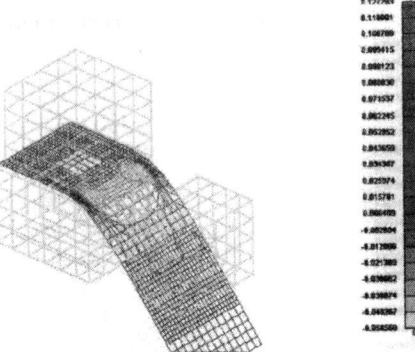

Fig.8: Thinning % of LF-21 material Sheet

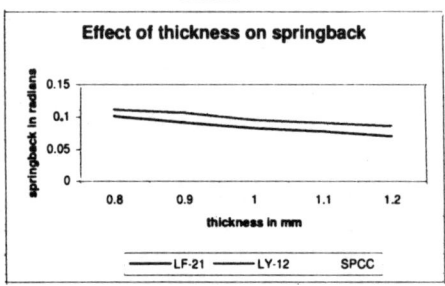

Fig.9: Comparision of springback on thickness

4. The punch-die clearance is inversely proportional to springback. A smaller punch-die clearance translates a large curvature (smaller radius) and thus a large force is needed to complete the bend.

552

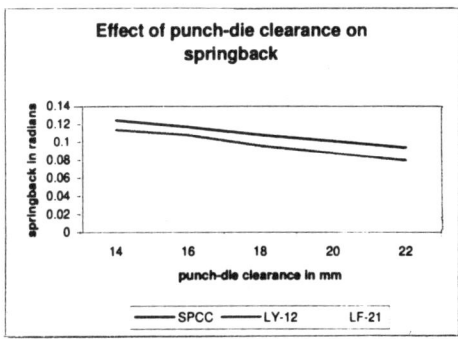

Fig.10: Comparision of springback on punch-die clearance

5. The pad force is inversely proportional to the springback while applying maximum pad force. The material flow from fixed end to free end will be getting reduced.

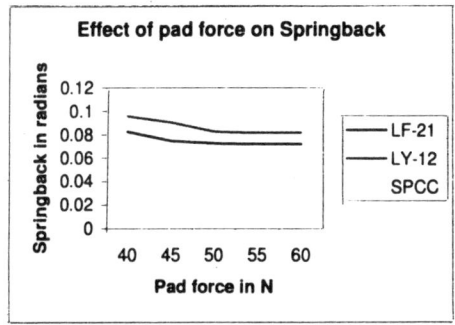

Fig.11.Comparision of springback on Pad force

6. Young's modulus is inversely proportional to springback. It is purely depends on material behavior and the maximum shear stress developed on it.
7. The optimized bend model has obtained by varying the punch-die clearance for over bending.

6. CONCLUSION

It is concluded that the punch-die clearance and young's modulus are the predominant factors, which affects the springback more. The springback is directly proportional to the die radius and inversely proportional to the other factors viz., punch radius, thickness, punch die clearance, pad force and young's modulus.

7. SCOPE FOR FURTHER WORK

Sheet metal forming is a never-ending process. Considerable effort has been made in this analysis. The following are the few to further think off:
1. The effect of friction lubrication and temperature may be taken into account.
2. Different compensation methods may be studied.
3. By implementing DOE approach, the effect of combined parameters on springback can be studied.

8. REFERENCES

1. **Livatyali.H and Altan.T**, Prediction and Elimination of springback in straight flanging using computer design methods- Part 1. Experimental investigations, *Journal of materials processing technology,* v 117 (2001), pp 262-268
2. **Inamdar.M.V, Date.P.P.,** and **Sabnis.S.V**, On the effects of geometric parameters on springback in sheet if five materials subjected to air vee bending, *Journal of materials processing technology,* v 123 (2002), pp 459-463
3. **Wang.C.T., Kinzel.G.L** and **Altan.T**, Mathematical modeling of plane strain bending of sheet and plate, *Journal of materials processing technology,* v 39 (1993), pp 279-304
4. **Xuechen Li, Yuing Yang, Yongzhi Wang, Jun Bao** and **shunping Li**, Effect of the material hardening mode on the springback simulation accuracy of bending, *Journal of materials processing technology,* v 123 (2002), pp 209-211
5. **Hul.Z** and **Li.J.Q.,** Computer simulation of pipe bending processes with small bending raius using local induction heating, *Journal of materials processing technology,* v 91 (1999), pp 75-79
6. **Al-Qureshi H.A.** and **Russo A.,** Springback and residual stresses in bending of thin walled aluminium tubes, *Journal of materials and design,* v 23 (2002), pp 217-222.

GCMM 2004
Editors: Prasad K D V Yarlagadda and S Narayanan
Copyright © 2005, Vellore Institute of Technology, Vellore, India
Publisher: Narosa Publishing House Pvt. Ltd., New Delhi, India

Static and Thermal Analysis of Radiator Fan Blade of Diesel Locomotive Engine of Indian Railways

Gopinath C V & Srinivasa Rao Ch

Associate Professor, Dept. of Mechanical Engineering
GITAM College of Engineering, Visakhapatnam 530 045 AP INDIA

E-mail: gopinathcv@yahoo.com, csr_gitam@yahoo.co.in

Abstract

Railway diesel locomotive engine contains a wide (66") radiator fan, whose primary function is to drive away excess heat from engine jacket cooling liquid. The radiator fan blades are of complex 3D shape and are made up of cast aluminum. This paper presents the analysis of the blade, to explore the causes of failure at junction of blade and flange and to suggest a suitable alternative material for the blade. Initially static and thermal analyses have been carried out separately. Coupled field analysis performed to study the effect of temperature of working fluid subsequently. Different load variations and material variations are employed to study and propose a suitable material to withstand structural and thermal loads. Fiber Reinforced Plastic (FRP) material is suggested to Railway Engineering authorities and it is under consideration and testing stage.

Keywords
Radiator Blade, Failure Analysis, Static Analysis, Thermal Analysis, Coupled Field Analysis, Wire Frame And Surface Design, Finite Element Analysis, Fiber Reinforced Plastic.

1. INTRODUCTION

The radiator fan is a device, which sucks the atmospheric air through the radiator panels and expels it to atmosphere to cool the engine coolant after discharge from the engine and maintains an acceptable operating temperature by transferring heat from the engine to the atmospheric air.

The radiator fan assembly is fitted at the rear end of the locomotive, which takes drive from the engine through horizontal shaft, eddy current clutch gearbox & universal shaft arrangement (Fig.1). The radiator fan assembly consist of a hub with six blades screwed on its periphery and is mounted on the fan shaft and bearing housing assembly. It is driven by a universal coupling through a eddy current clutch and right angle gear box unit which transfers the power from horizontal to vertical direction and raises the speed of the shaft in the ratio of 1: 1.312. The locomotive air compressor is connected to the radiator fan drive shaft by a rubber cushioned flexible rigid coupling. It consists of a rigid half, mounted on the fan drive shaft, made up of an inner and outer member using rubber blocks between the two members.

As an object moves through a fluid, the velocity of the fluid varies around the surface of the object, which induces a centrifugal force on the body. This centrifugal force on the fluid particles on the upper side i.e. convex side tries to move them away from the surface. This reduces the static pressure on this side below the free stream pressure. On account of this "suction effect", the convex surface of the blade is known as suction side.

This centrifugal force on the lower side i.e. concave side presses the fluid harder on the blade surface, thus increasing the static pressure above that of the free stream. Therefore, this side of the blade is known as the pressure side. The upward force on the blade is the cumulative effect if the positive static pressure on the pressure side and the negative pressure on the suction side. Due to this pressure difference lift and drag forces are created.

1.1 Drag Force

Drag is the force that opposes a fan motion through the air. Drag is generated by every part of the radiator fan assembly. Drag is generated by the interaction and contact of a solid body with a fluid (liquid or gas). Drag is not generated by a force field, in the sense of a gravitational field or an electromagnetic field, where one object can affect another object without being in physical contact. For drag to be generated, the solid body must be in contact with the fluid. Drag is generated by the difference in velocity between the solid object and the fluid. There must be motion between the object and the fluid. If there is no motion, there is no drag. It makes no difference whether the object moves through a static fluid or whether the fluid moves past a static solid object. Drag acts in a direction that opposes the motion.

As the fan moves through the air, there is another aerodynamic force present. The

air resists the motion of the fan; this resistance force is called the drag of the fan. Like lift, there are many factors that affect the magnitude of the drag force including the shape of the body, the "stickiness" of the air, and the speed.

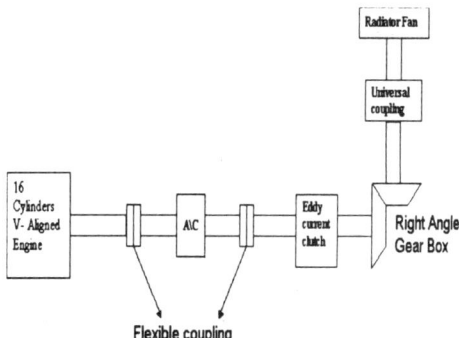

Fig. 1: Locomotive radiator fan drive system.

2. EXISTING APPROACHES IN ANALYSIS OF BLADES SUBJECTED TO FLUIDS

Pratt and White [1] described the main cause for failure of first stage turbine blades of Space Shuttle Main Engine (SSME). Inspection showed that up to 50% of the blades in several units had cracks in the inside hollow core of the leading edge tips of blades and the failure is a result of one of these cracks growing through the entire wall thickness of the blade. Metallographic inspection of the cracked surface verified that the cracks were due to high cycle fatigue, which can be an indicator of substantial dynamic stress.

Ilker Tari [2] discussed one of the important challenges in gas turbine design is cooling of the turbines due to high operating temperature uses. Je – Chin Han and Sandip Dutta [3] discussed the sophisticated cooling scheme for continuous safe operation of gas turbine with high performance. The paper focused on turbine blade internal cooling, this is achieved by passing the coolant through several rib enhanced serpentine passages inside the blade and extracting the heat from the outside of the blades. Gabor

Csaba [4] discussed the common failure mode for turbo machinery is high cycle fatigue of compressor and turbine blades, due to high dynamic stresses caused by blade vibration resonance with in the operating range of the machinery. Patric B. Lawless [5] has conducted experimental research program to improve the design capability for high-temperature turbines by providing a thorough, detailed understanding and data base of turbine flow fields and their effect on heat transfer.

C.C. Chamis [6] has evaluated the high velocity impact on the composite blade. The evaluation is focused on quantifying probabilistically the effects of uncertainties (scatter) in the variables that describe the impact, the blade make-up, (geometry and material), the blade response (displacements, strains, stresses, frequencies), the blade residual strength after impact, and the blade damage tolerance. Results show that the blade has relatively low damage tolerance at 0.999 probability of structural failure and substantial at 0.01 probability.

3. FAILURE ANALYSIS OF THE FAN BLADE

Even though the number of failures of a particular component may be small, they are important because they may affect the manufacturer's reputation for reliability. In some cases, particularly when the failure results in personal injury or death, it will lead to expensive lawsuits. In any failure analysis it is important to get as much information as possible from the failed part itself along with an investigation of the conditions at the time of failure.

The possible causes of failures in case of radiator fan blades are as fallows.
- Improper heat treatment of the radiator fan blade.
- Pressure variations along the length of the blade.
- Other sundry causes

3.1. Improper heat treatment of the radiator fan blade

Proper heat treatment must be done after casting process i.e., precipitation hardening, so as to increase the strength of the material. The purpose of precipitation hardening is to increase strength and hardness of heat treatable aluminum alloys, and is achieved through a sequence of solution heat treatment, quenching and natural/artificial ageing. However, certain alloys, which are relatively insensitive to cooling rates during quenching, can be precipitation hardened either by air-cooling or by water quenching directly form the elevated temperature shaping process followed by a ageing treatment.

By conducting certain laboratory tests it is observed that that the heat treatment is not done properly and some defects such as

- Pin holes/porosities have been revealed (in clusters at the critical zones and in scattered pattern over other locations of the fan-blades).

- Notches/deep dents have been noticed at and near by to the hub ends of the fan blades. One can notice that the fractured faces reveal two distinct zones having dull and bright in nature. Fractured faces of the broken blade are completely crystalline in nature.

3.2. Pressure Variations along the Length of the Blade

As the fan is rotating past the fluid (air), this fluid exerts some pressure variation along the cross-section of the blade, due to this pressure changes lift and drag forces will be created, these forces depends upon the design and operating conditions. For the radiator fan, lift force has to be minimum, otherwise it may lead to the breakage of the blade.

3.3 Other Sundry Causes
- The radiator fan of diesel locomotives is required to work in a very hazardous

environment with increase of oil dust and rain. It can be exposed to the roadside dust or fiber of various organic materials that can be in the environment of the locomotive operation such as, calcium carbonate, silica sand, aluminium, carbon black, fiber of various organic materials, oil, locomotives brake shoe dust, etc.

- Failures may occur due to cracks generated with the impact of tools, machinery items like clamps, pipes etc during engine overhauling(Fig. 2. a &b).

Fig. 2: (a)

Fig. 2(b)

4. DESIGN AND ANALYSIS

The radiator fan blade with the existing material is analysed first to verify the induced stresses are with in the safe limits or not. Further a better alternative material is studied with the same input parameters. The material is chosen in such away that it is least effected to the above said causes of failure. The first part of analysis is to calculate the various forces acting on the blade at different cross sections. Then the

blade model is created in CATIA and analysed in ANSYS.

Assumptions for the design
- The fluid (air) is considered to be incompressible.
- The turbulent effect i.e., stall conditions are neglected.

The profile geometry Calculations of aerofoil section for different radii of the fan and tabulated in Table.1.(Calculations available with authors, If required).

4.1. Forces Acting on the Different Sections of the Fan Blade

On account of considerable variation in the flow conditions and the blade section along the span, it is divided into a number of infinitesimal sections of small, radial thickness. The flow through such a section is assumed to be independent of the flow through other elements.

Velocities and blade forces for the flow through an elemental section are shown in fig.3. The flow has a mean velocity W and direction β (from the axial direction). The lift force ΔL is normal to the direction of mean flow and the drag ΔD parallel to this. The axial (ΔF_x) and tangential (ΔF_y) forces acting on the element are also shown, (ΔF_R) is the resultant force inclined at an angle ϕ to the direction of lift.

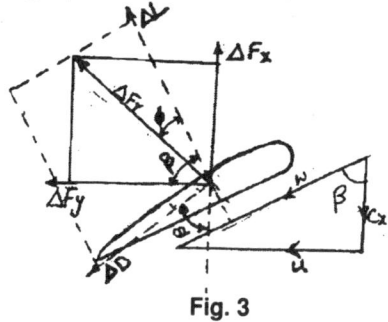

Fig. 3

Resolving the forces in the axial and tangential directions,

$$\Delta F_x = \Delta L \sin\beta - \Delta D \cos\beta \text{ -------(1)}$$
$$\Delta F_y = \Delta L \cos\beta + \Delta D \sin\beta \text{ -------(2)}$$

By definition lift and drag forces from the eq

$$\Delta L = \frac{1}{2} C_a \rho \omega^2 (ldr)$$
$$= 1/2 \times 0.4588 \times 1,225 \times 125.66^z \times 0.194$$

= 860.845 N

$\Delta D = \frac{1}{2} C_d \rho \omega^2 (ldr)$

= /2×0.0.335×1,225×125.66²×0.194

= 62.856 N

From these ΔL and ΔD values the ΔF_x and ΔF_y are calculated from the eq (1) & (2) as:

The axial thrust ΔF_x = 98.950 N

The torque force ΔF_y = 857.446 N

Table 2. Axial Thrust and Torque Forces at Different Radii of the Blade

R (mm)	ΔL (N)	ΔD (N)	ΔF_x (N)	ΔF_y (N)
835	860.845	62.856	980950	857.446
750	950.722	75.259	121.956	945.866
650	1078.388	93.781	160.536	1070.488
550	1241.838	121.493	216.744	1228.798
450	1453.648	149.992	315.124	1426.985
350	1730.256	202.359	460.688	1680.030
250	2073.600	268.328	690.958	1973.422
150	2361.815	342.306	913.246	2204.841

4.2. Analysis of Radiator Blade

Due to the complex geometry of the blade, the individual components are first created in CATIA. The 3D model of radiator fan assembly is as shown in Fig.4. For analysis a single blade is imported to ANSYS (Fig.5) in IGES format.

Fig. 4:Radiator fan assembly in CATIA

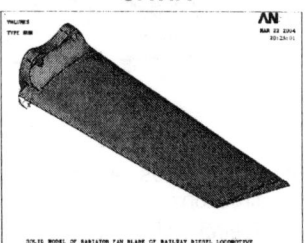

Fig. 5: Imported blade model in ANSYS

The blades are subjected to both thermal and structural loads. Coupled field analysis has been carried out to analyse the effect of maximum temperature of the engine jacket cooling water as well as lift and drag forces of the suction fumes on the blades. To conduct coupled field analysis, thermal analysis should be carried first. The blade is meshed with 3D 10-node tetrahedron thermal elements. The meshed model is as shown in Fig.6. The maximum temperature is applied on lower surface of the blade as the top surface is maintained at ambient air temperature. The obtained results are applied as an input to structural analysis. In structural analysis the blade is considered as a cantilever beam (flange end fixed to hub). The loads i.e. the lift and drag forces which are resolved in F_x and F_y directions are applied at various cross sections of the blade obtained (Table.2). The applied loads and boundary conditions on blade are presented in Fig.7.

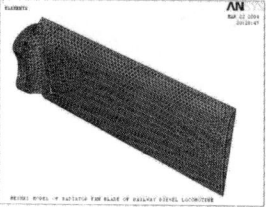 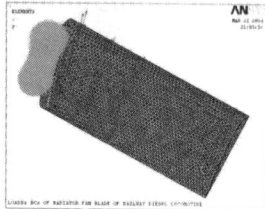

Fig. 6   **Fig. 7**

The analysis is first carried out with the existing blade material i.e. cast aluminium. The maximum deformation and von-mises stress contour plots for cast aluminium material are presented in Fig. 8 and 9 respectively. As an alternative material for radiator blade, Fiber Reinforced Plastic (FRP) is used to replace Cast Aluminium.

FRP radiator fan shall be manufactured from isopthalic resin reinforced with a combination of E-glass unidirectional roving, chopped strand mat and woven roving either by RTM (resin transfer moulding) or compression moulding process. FRP radiator fan shall be free from, blowholes, pinholes, porosities etc. Catalyst pigment and accelerator should suit the above resin. The color of the pigment shall be either blue or green. The glass reinforcement used shall not be less then 35% in content.

Table 1. Geometry Calculations

R Mm	U M/sec	C_u M/sec	W_∞ M/sec	$C_a l$	C_a	C_d	L Mtrs	β_∞	ϕ_∞	$\beta=\beta_\infty+\phi_\infty$
835	104.93	5.591	109.653	0.0891	0.4588	0.0336	0.194	10.759	4.187	14.9464
750	94.247	6.225	99.488	0.0983	0.4964	0.0393	0.198	11.873	4.531	16.404
650	81.681	7.182	87.694	0.1115	0.5439	0.0473	0.205	13.499	4.966	18.465
550	69.115	8.488	76.161	0.1284	0.6060	0.0587	0.214	15.591	5.535	21.126
450	56.549	10.375	65.041	0.1503	0.6450	0.0665	0.233	18.344	5.892	24.236
350	43.982	13.339	54.631	0.1789	0.7330	0.0854	0.245	22.005	6.672	28.677
250	31.416	18.674	45.605	0.2144	0.8060	0.1043	0.266	26.670	7.370	34.040
150	18.850	31.123	40.039	0.2442	0.9011	0.1306	0.271	30.746	8.245	38.991

Table 3: Static Analysis of Radiator fan blade – Maximum Deformations

Material	Deformation in mm			
	X	Y	Z	Resultant
Cast Al,2014-T6	0.102	0.417	0.015	0.421
Steel,ASTM-A514	0.036	0.148	0.004	0.148
Cast Iron,ASTM-A-48	0.103	0.420	0.005	0.424
FRP	0.106	0.433	0.008	0.437

Table 4: Static Analysis of Radiator fan blade – Maximum Stresses

Material	Maximum Stress in N/mm^2			
	Von-mises	Shear	Principal	Thrust direction
Cast Al	49.50	7.49	43.08	38.49
Cast Steel	52.01	7.93	42.52	37.94
Cast Iron	56.05	8.63	41.79	37.19
FRP	53.97	8.28	42.14	37.56

The above resin has been specified to obtain high tensile and flexural strength, in view of the fact that the standard deviation of tensile strength in FRP is very high. However the resin and reinforcement had to be chosen such that the mechanical properties specified in this specification are met. Fig.10 and 11 represent maximum deformation and von-mises stress contour plots for the considered alternative material Fiber reinforced plastic (FRP).

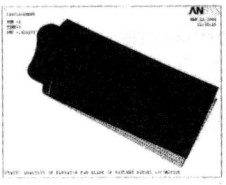
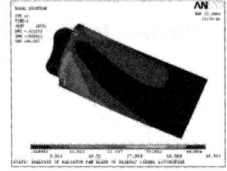

| Fig. 8 | Fig. 9 |

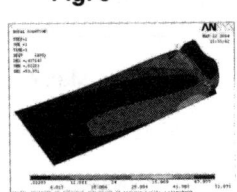

| Fig. 10 | Fig. 11 |

5. RESULTS AND CONCLUSIONS

The maximum deformations of the blade in Global X, Y, and Z directions for existing material and considered materials are presented in Table.3. The induced stresses are tabulated in Table.4. The marginal rise in stresses as well as deformations is observed in case of FRP. But the values are with in the safe limits. To prevent the failure of blades due to environmental and other sundry reasons as discussed in article 3, FRP can be considered as suitable alternate material.

6. ACKNOWLEDGEMENTS

The authors are grateful to Railway Engineering Department, DRM office, East Coast Railway, Visakhapatnam, for their kind cooperation in providing the necessary data regarding Radiator Blade.

7. REFERENCES

1. **Pratt and White** (1998), "Comprehensive Structural Dynamic Analysis of the SSME/AT Fuel Pump First-Stage Turbine Blade".
2. **Ilker Tari**, "3-D Simulation of Convection in Asymmetrically heated Turbine Blade Cooling Channels".
3. **Je – Chin Han and Sandip Dutta**, "Recent Developments in Turbine Blade internal Cooling", Department of Mechanical Engineering , Texas University, U.S.A.
4. **Garbor Csaba** (1998), "Modeling Micro slip Friction Damping and its influence on Turbine Blade Vibrations.
5. **Patric B. Lawless**, "Advanced Multi Stage Blade Aerodynamics, Performance, Cooling and Heat Transfer".
6. **C.C. Chamis** "Probabilistic Evaluation of Blade Impact Damage", Prepared for the *Air Force Structural Integrity Program Texas Dec, 2000.*

GCMM 2004
Editors: Prasad K D V Yarlagadda and S Narayanan
Copyright © 2005, Vellore Institute of Technology, Vellore, India
Publisher: Narosa Publishing House Pvt. Ltd., New Delhi, India

Thermal Stress Analysis due to Frictional Heating in a Dry Sliding System using Finite Element Method

Kumaravel A

Assistant Professor, Department of Mechanical Engineering,
R.R. Engineering College,Tiruchengode-637209, Namakkal (Dt).

Email: kumarave_l@yahoo.com

Sundaram S

Assistant Professor, Department of Mechanical Engineering,
Jeppiar Engineering College, Chennai.

Email: sundarakanagam@rediffmail.com

Senthil kumar. M

Lecturer, Department of Mechanical Engineering,
Vellore Institute of Technology, Vellore, India

Email: mskengg@yahoo.com

Abstract

The main objective of the present work is to study the temperature and thermal stresses near the regions of contact between flat sliding rings, such as the seal rings of mechanical face. The analysis was performed for various coating materials, material parameters and for different geometries. The analysis shows that frictional heating is the dominant contributor to high-localized temperatures and stresses around the contact region and that thermally induced stresses can be a major reason for coating failure. The thermal conductivity of the coating material is the most vital thermal parameter that controls the interface temperature. It was found that the stresses in the coating could be substantially reduced by operating at lower normal load or by achieving a lower friction coefficient.

Keywords
Contact, Finite Element Analysis, Dry Sliding Systems, Thermal Stresses

1.INTRODUCTION

The temperature rise due to frictional heating at the interface of tribocontacts has attracted the attention of engineers and tribologists in recent years. Friction and wear of dry contacts are dependent on the overall temperature increase at the interface.

Whenever relative sliding motion occurs between two contacting solids, there will be a loss of mechanical energy associated with friction. In most dry sliding situations it may be assumed that all of the energy loss resulting from friction is transferred to the contacting bodies as heat. This energy transfer, called frictional heating, is responsible for increases in the temperatures of the sliding bodies, especially in the immediate vicinity of the contact interface. The magnitude of the temperature on the contact surface can be large enough to have a considerable influence on the performance of the sliding system. Among the possible consequences of high sliding surface temperatures are the following:

- ignition of one of the contacting bodies
- surface melting of one of the contacting bodies
- oxidation and oxidation wear of metallic sliding components
- deterioration of solid or boundary lubrication films
- deterioration and increased wear of polymeric components
- formation of thermo elastic instabilities in the contact zone
- early thermo mechanical failure(e.g., thermo cracking or warping) of the sliding components

Thermo mechanical effects, such as the initiation of thermal cracks and the low cycle thermal fatigue failure in dry bearings and seals, are dependent on the heat dissipation mechanism and overall temperature rise. When two flat solids are placed in contact, the real area of contact is much smaller than the nominal or apparent contact area. It is within the real area of contact that the thermal and mechanical consequences of sliding friction occur, i.e. frictional heating, near-surface plastic deformation and wear of the contacting

bodies. These thermal and thermo mechanical contact phenomena can be responsible for failure of sliding mechanical components such as brakes, face seals and sleeve bearings through such mechanisms as thermo cracking and excessive wear[1].

In order to understand these failures it is necessary to study the temperatures, stresses and deformations that arise on and near the contacting surfaces as a result of friction. Contact spots are subjected to two types of loadings: mechanical loads consisting of shear and normal tractions at the contact interface, and thermal loading resulting from temperature gradient due to frictional heating. It is generally agreed that the interaction velocities during sliding are low enough to permit the use of uncoupled thermal stress theory in analyzing the phenomena [2]. Thus two solutions are required: the temperature distribution around a frictionally heated contact spot and the stress distribution due to combination of surface tractions and temperature gradients.

Floquet et al. [3] used a two dimensional Fourier transform method developed by Ling [2] to calculate the contact temperatures in dry bearings operating with a plastic liner. Floquet and Play [4] extended this technique to three dimensional problems. They showed that small changes in the design may bring large differences in contact temperatures and that to reduce the maximum temperature the rubbing surface must be as close as possible to a controlled temperature heat sink and must not be shielded by any thermal barrier. Gecim and Winer [5] extended the Fourier transform method to calculate steady temperatures in a rotating cylinder that had multiple surface heat sources and a variety of geometries

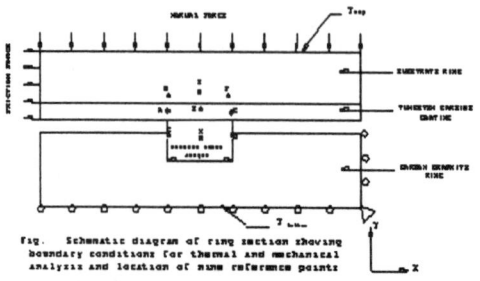

Fig. Schematic diagram of ring section showing boundary conditions for thermal and mechanical analysis and location of nine reference points

and thermal boundary conditions. Mihir K. Ghosh and David E. Brewe [6] studied the temperature and stress distribution due to frictional heating within a solid lubricated journal bearing was analyzed by using the Patran-Marc finite element program.

2. PROBLEM DESCRIPTION [7]

Contact between two flat conforming rings is concentrated in several (1-5) patches, with few small solid/solid contact spots within each patch. It was assumed that each contact spot was identical and that the contacts were equally spaced around the ring circumference. A ring could therefore be divided into as many sections as the number of contact spots and only one such section would have to be analyzed. If, for example, there were three contact spots located at 120^0 intervals, the section to be studied would include one-third of each ring and would have a small region of solid-solid contact between the two rings in center of the section.

The contact spots were approximately rectangular in shape extending further in the circumferential direction than radially. All tractions at the contact interface act in either circumferential (θ) or axial (y) directions. The most important temperature variations were those occurring in the θ-y plane. For this reason it was decided to analyze the problem only in the θ-y plane and to do a two-dimensional ring section is shown in Fig.1. A very fine grid is used in the contact region in the center of the mesh owing to the large temperature gradient. No contact between top and bottom rings was allowed except within the central contact region.

The boundary condition for the thermal solution included prescribed temperatures of the top face of metallic ring and bottom faces of the contact model.

Convection to ambient air was assumed at the free surface of the rotating ring and reasonable convection coefficients were chosen from the heat transfer literature. A heat flux equal to the product of contact pressure times friction coefficient time's velocity was input to the interface between

the two rings within the contact zone. The form of the contact pressure distribution had little effect on the temperature distribution, so uniform heat distribution was assumed. The ring section being analyzed was assumed to be identical to the ones on either side of it, and in order to insure this the nodal temperatures on the right hand edge of the model in Fig.1 were set equal to those on the left hand edge.

2.1 Stress Analysis

Analysis of the stresses around the sliding contact was done using ANSYS6.0. The boundary conditions for the analysis are shown in Fig.1. Since only one section of the ring was analyzed and it was assumed that the rings was composed of n identical sections, the friction and normal forces applied to the model were 1/n times the normal forces. The two contacting rings were analyzed together and no attempt was made to insure a uniform distribution of contact pressure or shear traction within the predetermined contact zone. The friction traction is everywhere equal to the normal force times the friction co-efficient. The stress field near a sliding contact is dominated by the thermal contribution, which is not significantly affected by distribution of surface tractions. The nodal temperatures evaluated from thermal analysis were applied as a body load.

3. GEOMETRIC MODELLING

The contact model taken as a baseline model [7] for this analysis was composed of a mild steel ring with a tungsten carbide coating in sliding contact with a ring made of carbon graphite. The axial thickness of the coated steel ring was 6.43mm, while that of carbon graphite ring was 10mm. The plasma-sprayed tungsten carbide coating on the contacting surface of the steel disk was approximately 0.2mm thick. The 50mm diameter rings were in solid-solid contact at two identical contact patches located 180^0 from one another. Thus a single ring section of circumferential length 79 mm could be analyzed. A typical contact patch was assumed to be 1mm wide in the circumferential direction and 0.5mm thickness in the axial direction. The metallic ring was sliding at a velocity of 4.71 m/sec relative to the stationary carbon ring. The details of material properties of baseline system are shown in Table 1.

3.1 Discretisation of the contact model

The contact model was discretized using four node, two dimensional rectangular element with 5200 elements and 5922 nodes. Contact pair was created between the interface of the sliding contact with 20 target and contact elements each. The discretized finite element contact model is shown in Fig 2. A very fine mesh is used in the contact region in the center of the mesh owing to the large temperature gradient and coarse mesh is used in other areas.

3.2 Boundary conditions [7]

1. A heat transfer coefficient 'h' equal to 58 Wm^{-2} $^{0}C^{-1}$ and reference temperature equal to $27^{0}C$ was assumed at the free surface of the rotating ring.
2. Steady state temperatures of the top face of the metallic ring and the bottom face of the carbon graphite ring were both assumed to be $150^{0}C$.
3. The normal force on a contact was assumed to be 100 N with coefficient of friction 0.1.
4. No axial and circumferential displacement boundary conditions in the carbon graphite ring were assumed.

Table. 1 Material Properties [7]

Material	Properties		
	Young's Modulus (GPa)	Thermal Expansion Coefficient($/^{0}C$)	Thermal Conductiviy(W/mK)
Carbon-graphite	23	3×10^{-6}	11
Tungsten carbide	614	4×10^{-6}	100
Mild steel	192	10.5×10^{-6}	51.9

Fig.2: Discretization of the contact model

4. RESULTS AND DISCUSSIONS

A steady state thermo elastic analysis of the base line system, the highest temperature occurred on the contact interface. The maximum temperature was $257.4^{0}C$ in this case, giving a temperature rise of $107.4^{0}C$ above the back face temperatures. The temperature distribution in the metallic ring was relatively symmetrical about the contact center.

4.1 Effect of Coating Thickness on Temperature Distribution

The temperature distribution of the contact interface extended from -5 to +5 mm for various coating thickness are shown in Table.2. It is observed that the peak temperature occurred at the center of the contact and the maximum temperature is decreased when increasing the coating thickness.

4.2 Effect of Contact Geometry on Temperature Distribution

The base line heat flux input to be applied at the interface of the contact model. It can be seen that the changes in the size of the contact patch also had a very significant effect on contact temperature. A smaller contact had a higher frictional heat flux, resulting in lower surface temperatures. The stress analysis was carried out by applying both the temperatures and mechanical loads. Here, nodal temperatures are applied as a body load. This is allowed to study of the contribution of mechanical and thermal loadings. Results are shown in Table.3 for nine points in the contact region, three each in coating, substrate and carbon.

Table.2: Temperature distribution at the interface for different coating thickness

Contact patch length(mm)	Temperature(^{0}C)		
	Coating thickness=0.2mm	Coating thickness=0.4mm	Coating thickness=1mm
-0.5	244.74	238.75	228.97
-0.4	249.92	243.46	233.35
-0.3	253.37	246.46	236.13
-0.2	255.68	248.44	237.91
-0.1	257.02	249.57	238.92
0	257.46	249.94	239.24
0.1	257.02	249.57	238.92
0.2	255.68	248.44	237.91
0.3	253.37	246.46	236.13
0.4	249.92	243.46	233.35
0.5	244.74	238.75	228.97

The location of the nine points is shown in Fig.1. A plane strain situation was assumed in this case. The results shown in Table.3 assumed purely elastic deformation. The effective stress determined in this analysis was rather large in both coating and substrate.

It can be seen that much of the coating in contact zone had a high effective stress, with the peak effective stress in both coating and substrate occurring near the point of maximum contact temperature. Thermal effects were found to be the major contributor to those high effective stresses. The most significant result of the stress analysis, however, is the very substantial tensile stress σ_{xx} which occurred in the coating. The temperature gradients near the contact produced a tensile stress in the coating and compressive in the much thicker substrate. The resulting tensile stress could be responsible for the radial cracks, called thermo cracks. The nature of stress distribution is validated with the available literature. But the absolute value of stresses is differed; it may be due to assumptions made for this analysis.

4.3 Effect of Material on Stress Distribution

An extensive series of analyses was carried out to study the influence of material properties, coating and contact dimensions, normal and friction forces that could lead to coating failure. Since the baseline analysis showed that the stress in coating and substrate were greatest for the thermo elastic case, and since the harder materials seem to be the most likely candidates for future contact applications, elastic behavior was assumed for most of the analysis. Results are presented in Table 4.

In each case in Table.4 a single material parameter was changed from its baseline value. The properties of most interest were the modulus of elasticity E, Coefficient of thermal expansion α, and thermal conductivity K of the substrate and coating materials. Since thermal conductivities of each material affect the temperatures, it is no surprising that an increase in thermal conductivity of either coating or substrate led to lower stresses in each of the components. A substantial decrease in coating stress could be brought about by choosing a more conductive substrate which could transfer more of the frictional heat away from the contact region. The effects of modulus of elasticity and coefficient of thermal expansion were quite large and can be explained by thermal deformation considerations. An increase in the elastic modulus of one of the two materials raised the stress in that material but had a much smaller influence on stress within the other material.

In the baseline analysis it was learned that the difference in thermal expansion between substrate and coating was primarily responsible for tensile stress within the coating. An increase in the coating material's expansion coefficient caused a

Table.3: Contribution of mechanical and thermal loadings to stress at various points in tungsten carbide coating, mild steel and carbon graphite mating ring – thermo elastic analysis

	Mechanical Loads + Temperature			
	σ_{xx} (MPa)	σ_{yy} (MPa)	σ_{zz} (MPa)	τ_{xy} (MPa)
Coating				
A	219.14 (198)	3.96 (-285)	-80.53(-575)	-2.40(-146)
B	230.77 (676)	-1.80(-42)	-101.58(-480)	0.160(-20)
C	213.15 (796)	-0.317(16)	-83.61(-326)	1.16(-16)
Substrate				
D	-39.67 (-181)	-0.337(-97)	-122.9(-518)	-7.09(-6)
E	-47.74 (-171)	-4.91(-26)	-139.19(-511)	0.831(-20)
F	-39.71 (-198)	-2.80(-52)	-123.73(-512)	6.471(-15)
Carbon graphite				
G	-0.131 (-29)	2.713(-96)	-2.248(-62)	0.5711(12)
H	-0.144 (+1)	-0.470(-44)	-3.59(-37)	-0.633(22)
J	-1.753 (+28)	-2.76(17)	-4.377(-11)	0.860(38)

Note: Coating thickness = 0.2mm; contact patch length = 1mm; Normal load = 100 N

Table.4: Effect of material properties on maximum temperatures and Stresses – thermo elastic analysis

Property changed from baseline value	Change in calculated values (%)			
	Maximum Temp(^{0}C)	Maximum effective stress(MPa)		
		Carbon	Substrate	Coating
$E_{coating}$ up by 100%	-	-10.0 (-8.1)	+37.0 (+0.9)	+47.7(+76.5)
$.E_{coating}$ down by 50%	-	+7.1 (+7.0)	-33.0 (-0.2)	-38.3(-44.4)
$\alpha_{coating}$ up by 100%	-	+12.1 (+8.1)	+1.5 (0.2)	+10.2(+35.8)
$\alpha_{coating}$ down by 50%	-	-6.4 (-4.1)	+29.0 (0.8)	+27.8(+4.2)
$K_{coating}$ up by 100%	-4.3	-5.8 (-3.5)	-12.9 (-3.5)	-6.0(-4.0)
$K_{coating}$ down by 50%	+8.4	+5.9 (+3.5)	+7.0 (1.8)	+1.1(+4.0)
$E_{substrate}$ up by 100%	-	+9.7 (+2.33)	+33.0 (72.0)	+21.9(+2.1)
$E_{substrate}$ down by 50%	-	-12.6 (-11.6)	-31.5 (-55.8)	-25.5(-17.5)
$\alpha_{substrate}$ up by 100%	-	+38 .0(+54.7)	+77.3 (+73.3)	+82.5(+79.5)
$\alpha_{substrate}$ down by 50%	-	-19.2 (-30.2)	-52.5 (-55.6)	-77.0(-36.2)
$K_{substrate}$ up by 100%	-11.9	-41.5 (-14.0)	-42.7 (-17.0)	-46.1(-36.2)
$K_{substrate}$ down by 50%	+18.2	+67.7 (24.4)	+58.9 (+26.7)	+71.3(+27.9)

5. CONCLUSIONS

1. It was found that the stress field around a sliding contact is tensile in nature. It is due to thermal contribution resulting from frictional heating. These tensile stresses could be large enough to cause cracking of the coating.
2. A reduction in coating stress could be achieved by having a thicker coating or a coating with lower modulus of elasticity or higher thermal conductivity. An increase in coating thermal expansion coefficient would result in lower tensile stress.
3. The properties of the substrate proved to be at least as those of the coating, with decreased coefficient of thermal expansion, decreased modulus of elasticity, and increased thermal conductivity of the substrate material leading to reductions in stress in both coating and substrate.

6. REFERENCES

1. **Kennedy F.E**, (1984), Thermal and thermo mechanical effects in dry sliding. *Wear* Vol.100,pp:453-476.
2. **Ling, F. F.**, (1973), Surface Mechanics, Wiley, New York.
3. **Floquet A., Play, D., and Godet**, M., (1977), Surface temperatures in distributed contacts. Application to bearing design, *ASME Journal of Lubrication Technology,* Vol. 99, pp.277-283.
4. **Floquet, A. and Play, D.,** (1981) Contact temperature in dry bearings. Three dimensional theory and verification, *Trans. ASME Journal of Lubrication Technology*, Vol. 103(2), pp.243.
5. **B.Gecim and W.O Winer,** *(1986)* Steady temperatures in a rotating cylinder – some variations in the geometry and the thermal boundary conditions. *Trans. ASME J.Tribol.* 108(3),pp: 446.
6. **Mihir K.Ghosh and David E.Brewe,** (1995), Temperature distribution and thermal distortion due to frictional heating in a dry shaft-bush tribosystem using the finite element method. *Int.J Mech Sci.* Vol.37, No.9 pp:1021-1034.
7. **Kennedy F.E and Hussaini S.Z.,** (1987), Thermo-mechanical analysis of dry sliding systems. *Computers and structures* Vol.26, No 1,2 pp:345-355.
8. **Cars law, H.S., and Jaeger, J.C.**, (1959), Conduction of heat in solids, 2nd Ed., Clarendon press, Oxford.
9. **Heinz K. Muller, Bernard S.Nau.,** (1998), Fluid sealing technology, Marcel Dekker Inc., New York.

Design and Product Development

GCMM 2004
Editors: Prasad K D V Yarlagadda and S Narayanan
Copyright © 2005, Vellore Institute of Technology, Vellore, India
Publisher: Narosa Publishing House Pvt. Ltd., New Delhi, India

Challenges in Product and Process Design in the Information Era

Jayant K Singh

Professor, Mechanical Engineering Dept., College of Technology,
Pantnagar- 263 145 (Uttaranchal), India

E-mail: jayantksingh@rediffmail.com

Abstract

Extraordinary changes are taking place in the business universe and go beyond an imbalance between supply and demand. In the period of modern industrial technology age, large corporations were growing up. The growing up is more or less based on efficiency of manufacturing, ability to mass production and specialized work. To-day the hub of the driving wheel is IT and the driving force comes from it. The information technology is therefore, one of the most powerful economic equalizer. One should know how to convert the challenges in to opportunities and we need to rethink the future and to change our mindset accordingly. To meet with the goal, systematic thinking warrants a comprehensive understanding of the system and the winner will be those who stay ahead. The tendency in most organization is to get good at doing what they have always done. Collaborative Product Commerce (CPC) integrate technologies to tie together product design, engineering and Sales /Marketing in to a global knowledge. The paper will discuss the four well established steps of challenges, where we are, the gaps and what next! for organizations to meet with the challenges of unpredictable future and to evolve innovative ideas.

Keywords

Challenges; Information Era, The gaps, What Next.

1. INTRODUCTION

Business houses[1] to-day agree that extraordinary changes are taking place in business universe. These changes go beyond an imbalance between supply and demand or the advance of new technology. In the period of modern industrial technology age (1920-1990), when Ford, GM, Du Pont and many other large corporations were growing up-there were several driving forces behind the success of every winning company. The most important was efficiency of manufacturing, the ability of mass- produce, specialized work and cut every cost down. Second, the winning companies learned to be effective mass marketers. A third attribute was rapid adoption of technology and fourth was financial acumen – the ability to analyze activity in detail to determine how to get the best rates of retune and keep capital moving. The fifth driving force was a set of people skill, which companies developed through sincere efforts[2]. All these forces gave momentum to the wave of modern industrial technology.

2. THE HUB – INFORMATION TECHNOLOGY

The greatest driving force to-day comes from IT. No matter which product we manufacture or service we provide, the hub of the driving wheel is IT. According to Peter Senge the 21st century unfolds the following[3]:

- Technology explosion
- Globalization
- Societal distortion

It is very clearly indicated that we need to challenge all our personal and organizational assumptions about the world we are heading into. We need to rethink the future. The road that we have been traveling for decades is coming to an end and from here journey to tomorrow will be an off-road experience and we need to change our mindset accordingly.

3. WHERE WE ARE!

In this environment where we stand today? This could be explained with respect to product and process in a simple 2x2 matrix fig. (1). The answer is we are at low end of product and process technology. The chart below speaks where we are to-day against world class standards Fig. (1).

Fig,1

Fig. (2) tell us about the world class performance standard Vs our performance standards.

Performance Measure	World Class Standards	Our Standards
Reject in Parts Per Million (%)	100	10000
Capacity Utilisation (%)	90	75
Break down loses (%)	1	5
On-time delivery (%)	100	75
Go through rate(%)	99.99	80

Fig.2: World Class Performance Standard Vs Our Performance Standard

3.1 What Does 99.9% Quality Mean

In U.S.A. it means:
- One hour of unsafe drinking
- Two unsafe landing at O' HARE airport each day
- 16,000 lost pieces of mail per hour
- 20,000 incorrect drug prescriptions each year
- 500 incorrect surgical operations each week
- 22,000 cheques deducted from wrong account each year
- 1900 new born babies dropped at birth each year

The question arises – Do we have capabilities! The answer is 'Yes' companies like Ford, GM and Chrysler have off-loaded their software related development work like CAD/CAM and other commercial application to Indian Software companies like Infosys, TCS, and Satyam. All the software development activities are being carries out in US as well as in India by Indians.

The information technology [4] is the most powerful economic equalizer. This may be the only business you can become successful and become wealthy. We should know how to convert the challenges into opportunities for growth. However, we are not efficient in systematic thinking. A systematic thinking warrants as comprehensive understanding.

4. WHAT ARE THE GAPS!

The chart in fig (3) speaks the status. In this new era, the winners will be those who stay ahead of the change curve, constantly refining their industries, creating new markets, new trials, reinventing the competitive rules and challenging the status quo.

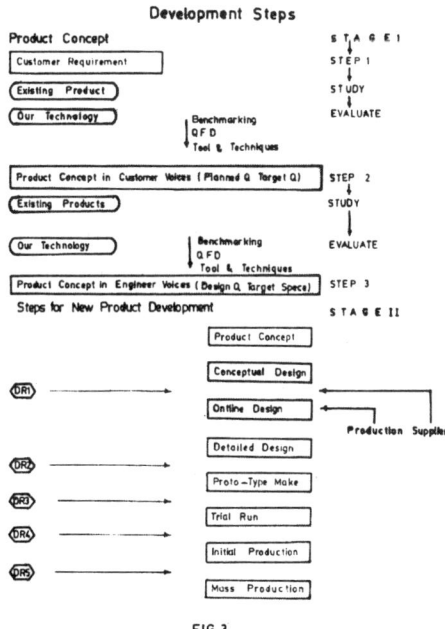

Development Steps

Product Concept — STAGE I
Customer Requirement — STEP 1
Existing Product — STUDY
Our Technology — EVALUATE

Benchmarking
QFD
Tool & Techniques

Product Concept in Customer Voices (Planned Q Target Q) — STEP 2
Existing Products — STUDY
Our Technology — EVALUATE

Benchmarking
QFD
Tool & Techniques

Product Concept in Engineer Voices (Design Q Target Specs) — STEP 3

Steps for New Product Development — STAGE II

Product Concept
Conceptual Design
DR1 — Online Design
Detailed Design — Production Suppliers
DR2 — Proto-Type Make
DR3 — Trial Run
DR4 — Initial Production
DR5 — Mass Production

FIG.3

5. COLLABORATIVE PRODUCT COMMERCE (CPC)

CPC is defined as " a class of software and services that used internet to permit individuals – no matter that their role in commercialization of a product, no matter what computer based tools they use no matter where they are located geographically.

CPC integrate technologies through Internet to tie together product design, engineering, sourcing (manufacturing and purchasing), sales, marketing, fields services, and customers in to a global knowledge net[5].

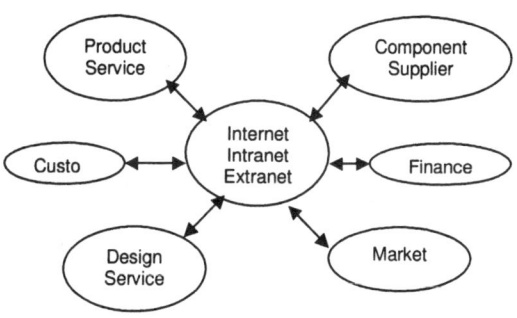

Fig. 4

6. E – LANCING

New organization culture is already on the anvil. It means freelancers get electronically connected with knowing even each other by face but work together to complete a project. After completion of the project the 'Team' dismantle and the freelancers are once again offering their expertise for another groups.

7. CONCLUSION

In conclusion, to meet the challenge of unpredictable future, we have to be Agile, responsive to change and should evolve innovative ideas. The definition of insanity is "Doing the old thing and expecting different results".

Learning from Hindu philosophy, about Brahma – the creator, Vishnu – the preserver , Siva – the destroyer, we can draw our circle of innovation. It is a cycle – creation, preservation and destruction. The organizations who does not realize the benefits of this principle, seems to be going down examples are Binny Mills, Dyanora etc. A role of successful organization can be only two -create customer and innovation.

8. REFERENCES

1. **Ravinder Reddy, P..**, "Business Process Reengineering for Organizational Success in an Industry", *Proceeding NCIET*, Tirupati, Jan 31-Feb 2, 1998.
2. **Evan Philip B, and Wurster Thomas S.**, "Strategy and the New Economics of Information", *Harvard Business*, Review, No. 5, Sep-Oct, 1997. pp 71-82.
3. **Muthu S., Devdasan, S.R.**, "QS 9000 Based Intelligent Maintenance Quality Systems", *Proceeding NCIET, SVU*, Feb 2, 1998.
4. **Pugh S.**, "Total Design - Integrated Mehods for Successful Product Engineering", *Addition-Wesley*, 1990.
5. **Jerry. L. Hamlin**, "Productivity Appraisal for a Maintenance Center", P.E. Cities Service Co., Tulsa, *Journal of Industrial Engineering* Sep. 1979.

GCMM 2004
Editors: Prasad K D V Yarlagadda and S Narayanan
Copyright © 2005, Vellore Institute of Technology, Vellore, India
Publisher: Narosa Publishing House Pvt. Ltd., New Delhi, India

Design and Manufacturing of Test Rig for Investigation of Improved Mechanical Peeling Methods of Tough Skin Vegetables

Emadi B, Kosse V & Yarlagadda P

Queensland University of Technology, School of MMME
Brisbane, QLD 4001, Australia

Email: bagher_emadi@yahoo.com
Email: v.kosse@qut.edu.au
Email: ẏ.prasad@qut.edu.au

Abstract

One of the important preparatory stages of fruit and vegetable processing is peeling. Low efficiency of peeling leads to high losses, and poor quality of final processed products. Although several methods of peeling had been developed for some kinds of fruits and vegetables, but there is no any adopted peeling method which can respond to all producer and consumer needs. Mechanical, chemical, and thermal methods are currently in use. Mechanical peeling methods are generally preferred because of keeping freshness and low harmful effects on edible portions of products. Low level of flexibility and efficiency for different size and shape of products are main limitations. This paper presents work done to design and manufacture of a test rig for investigation of improved mechanical peeling methods. High level of flexibility and manoeuvrability of test rig for different size and shape of products and peeling tools were considered in this design.

Keywords
Design, Peeling, Vegetable, Test rig

1. INTRODUCTION

Peeling is one of the important preliminary stages of fruits and vegetables processing. The quality and quantity of final processed products are influenced by this stage. Low quality of peeling leads to high loss and low quality of final product.

Mechanical, thermal, and chemical methods are most common peeling methods of fruits and vegetables [1]. Mechanical peeling is preferred method among current peeling methods. Keeping freshness and making minimum impact on the remaining flesh of products are main advantages of mechanical methods while the high loss is considered as important limitation.

There are different kinds of mechanical peeling methods that are used for different kinds of fruits and vegetables. Using abrasive devices [2-5], knives and tools with blades [6-13] are main commercial application of this method. Application of those devices is

574

accompanied with high losses especially when the product is of irregular shape.

In this paper a new test rig is described for investigation of different mechanical peeling methods of tough skin vegetables such as different varieties of pumpkin and melon. Facilitate to investigate of using different peeling tools for different size and shape of products are considered as benefits of the design.

2. PEELING METHODS OF VEGETABLES

For some kinds of vegetables only manual peeling is currently used. That stage is accompanied with high losses, labour cost, and is time consuming. Current methods of peeling can be classified into three main groups: mechanical, thermal and chemical peeling. In mechanical peeling, machines use mechanical tools to peel off the skin of fruits and vegetables. For example, machines equipped with abrasive, knife and sieve drum tools are commonly used in this group. Generally, the quantity of losses in this kind of peeling is high, but the quality of final peeled vegetables such as freshness is good.

To reduce the losses during mechanical peeling, chemical peeling is considered. In this method, skins can be softened from the underlying tissues by submerging vegetables in hot alkali solution. The quantity of solution and the exposure time are different for different kinds and varieties of vegetables. Generally, lye may be used at a concentration of about 0.5-3%, at about 93ºC (2000ºF) for a short period of time (0.5-3 min) [14]. The loosened skins are washed away by high velocity jets of water or compressed air. This method of peeling reduces the losses but it has harmful effects on the flesh of vegetables and also is not environmentally friendly.

Thermal peeling as well as chemical peeling is used for thick-skinned vegetables. This method can be performed by wet heat (steam) or dry heat (flame). The steam pressure that is used in wet heat is about 10 atm and it leads to the softening of skins and underlying tissues. When the pressure is suddenly released, steam under the skin expands and causes the skin to puff and crack. Then the skin is washed away with jets of water at high pressure (up to 12 atm)

[15]. Floros and Chinnan (1988) reports that the widespread application of steam peeling is due to its high level of automation, precise control of time, temperature and pressure by electronic devices to minimize peeling losses and reduced environmental pollution compared to chemical peeling [16]. In another kind of thermal peeling, some vegetables such as peppers can be peeled by dry heat (flame). In this method, vegetables are exposed to direct flame (for about 1 min at 1000ºC) or hot gases in rotary tube flame peelers. Here too, heat causes steam to develop under skins and puff them so that they can be washed away with water. Each heat treatment should be immediately followed by cooling in water. This method of peeling causes a cauterizing of the surface, wound areas, and small pieces of charred skin, which if not removed, give bad appearance to the canned product especially [15].

The capability of every peeling method as mentioned above is different. None of them can be considered as the ideal peeling method for all products. Generally mechanical methods are preferred because of keeping the freshness and low harmful effects on remaining flesh.

3. OBJECTIVE OF THE DESIGN
3.1 Adaptability for investigation of different mechanical peeling methods

Several mechanical peeling tools are currently applied. Using blades, knifes, and abrasive tools are important techniques. The possibility of investigation of these and other mechanical tools on the test rig was considered. Miller cutter, wire brush, abrasive ropes are some examples of interested peeling tools to investigate in the test rig.

3.2 Possibility of accommodation of different product size

As the variation in product size is considerable, it was attempted to design the test rig in which it would be possible to use different sizes of products. The range of product size variation was taken into account in designing the peeler head to cover the whole product in different sizes.

3.3 Possibility of peeler head position adjustment in three directions

To cover the whole surface of products of different sizes, it was necessary to enable the peeler head to adjust its position. It was desirable to adjust its position in three main directions: axial, lateral and vertical.

3.4 Possibility of installation of peeler tool in the vertical and horizontal planes

To enable investigation of different angles of acting forces on product by peeler tools, it was necessary to make possible positioning of peeler head in both the vertical and horizontal planes.

3.5 Facility of rotation of peeler tool at different angular velocities

In some methods, the rotation of peeler tool at different angular velocities is needed. Rotary blades and some abrasive tools require rotational movement to accomplish the task.

3.6 Facility of rotation of vegetable holder at different angular velocities

As the different angular velocities of product during peeling leads to different results, so the table with a product holder should be spun to achieve large range of speed variation.

3.7 Simplicity and low cost of manufacturing

Low cost of manufacturing is one of the objectives of every design. Attempts were made to reduce the number of components of the test rig. Corrosion resistance requires the use of stainless steel. Simple spring and screw mechanisms were used to provide necessary adjustments.

4. ENFORCEMENT OF THE OBJECTIVES
4.1 Chassis and Chamber

The chassis was designed as portable body equipped with one chamber at the top and expandable to two separate chambers. The spacious chamber was designed to accommodate large size products and the peeler head. The product holder was mounted at the base of the chamber and the peeler head was installed at the front side of

chamber (Fig.1). There are two possible positions of the product holder, on the centre line of the peeler head and offset in the lateral direction (fig.2). Such solution was selected for two reasons: firstly to enable handling of different product size, and secondly to enable peeling by both of just one side of the peeler head.

Fig.1: Test rig

4.2 Vegetable Holder

Product holder was designed as a rotating table that can carry the product (Fig.2). The product can be fixed on the disc by a three sharp blades that form a pyramid to provide access to sides and the top (Fig.3).

Fig.2: Product holder and two available positions

The drive is a 24V DC motor that produces up to 270 rpm depending on supplied voltage. The DC motor is installed outside under the base of the chamber. This assembly can be easily repositioned.

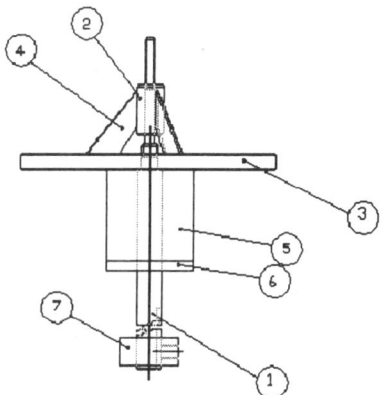

Fig.3: Product holder

1. Shaft, 2. Tube, 3. Plate, 4. Blade, 5,

7.Bush, 6.Teflon

4.3 Peeler Head

The mechanism of the peeler head was designed to produce adjustment in three different directions. Two vertical rods enable movement in the vertical direction (Z axis) in front wall of chamber (fig.1). Position adjustment in the longitudinal direction (X axis) is provided by a screw and spring mechanism. Resilient ability of the holder of peeling tools was needed to able tools follow the irregular shape of different products. Spring mechanism was preferred to use in these cases. Peeler tools can be installed on two different kinds of rotary plates. The first plate (Fig.4) contains six flaps with adjustable angular position with the plane of rotation parallel to the product and second one with the plane of rotation perpendicular to the product.

Fig.4: Peeler head (First Rotary Plate)

4.3.1 The First Rotary Plate

Each of the six flaps has ten holes placed in a spiral pattern to improve the yield of peeling production (fig.5). The angular position of flaps is adjusted from 0 to 30°. Flaps are adjusted by means of a screw mechanism that contains a spring and a lock screw. The springs 7 and 12 in fig.6 enable adjustment of angular position of flaps to accommodate different shape of a product. The main shaft is driven by a DC motor that can provide angular velocities up to 300 rpm. Different peeler tools can be installed on the flaps using holes and fixtures.

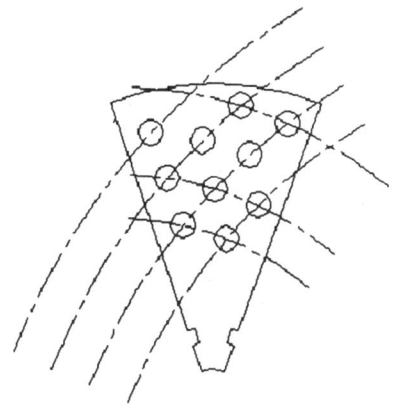

Fig.5: Flap with holes in spiral pattern

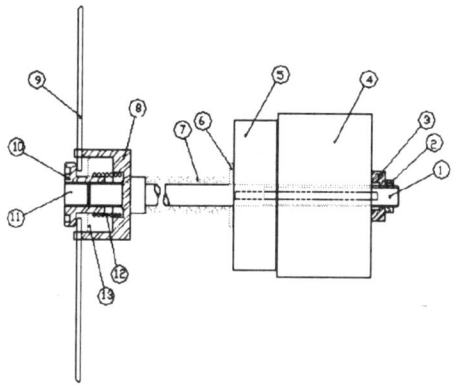

Fig.6: Details of the first rotary plate

1. Shaft, 2. Lock nut, 3. Nut, 4. Motor,

5.Block, 6,13. Washer, 7,12. Spring, 8. Bush,

9. Flap, 10. Nut Screw, 11. Grip screw

4.3.2 The Second Rotary Plate

It is basically three solid plates that can carry peeling tools in the plane perpendicular to the product surface. It was needed to increase the penetration ability of abrasive tools for some products which have irregular groovy surface. The speed of rotation can be adjusted up to 2000 rpm. The position of motor can be also adjusted in the longitudinal and lateral directions.

5. PERFORMANCE OF THE TEST RIG

As the test environment is acidic because of product juices, stainless steel was used as the material of the test rig. In application the test rig showed good performance and versatility enabling the use of different peeling tools and handling tough skinned vegetables of different size. Flexibility of the test rig and the ease of adjustment and installation of different peeling tools including abrasive, knife and blade tools were excellent. The test rig enabled access to the whole surface of product except the area engaged with the mounting table.

The test rig has shown ability to extend the range of application for investigation of new approach mechanical peeling tools. Also some other fruits and vegetables can be investigated by using this test rig in future.

6. CONCLUSION

Mechanical peeling methods are preferred method of peeling for vegetables and fruits. Among current main peeling methods such as chemical and thermal methods, mechanical methods can keep the freshness of remaining flesh and reduce the harmful effects on flesh. High losses encourage researchers to improve current mechanical methods or to propose new methods.

The test rig for investigation of new concepts of mechanical peeling methods was designed and manufactured. Some requirements regarding to different sizes of products and different prospect peeling tools were considered in design of the test rig. High flexibility and possibility of peeler head adjustments as well as simplicity and low cost of manufacturing enabled experimental verification of a wide range of mechanical peeling devices.

The test rig proved reliable easy to use. Those capabilities enable to extend the range of test rig application for more different kinds of products in future. It is also believed that investigation of new concepts of peeling tools is easily possible on available test rig.

7. REFERENCES

1. **Luh, B. S. and Woodroof, J. G.** (1988). *Commercial vegetable processing.* 2nd Edition. AVI Book, New York, USA.
2. **Jasper, A., Hhrig, J. r. and Warren L.** (2001). Electrically – operated hand fruit and vegetable peeler. *U. S. Patent No. 6186058B1.* U. S. Patent and Trademark Office, Washington, D. C.
3. **Zittel, D. R. (1991),** Method for treating a product. *U.S. Patent No. 5989614.* U. S. Patent and Trademark Office, Washington, D. C.
4. **Singh, K. K.** and **Shukla, B.D.** (1995). Abrasive peeling of potatoes. *Journal of food engineering,* 26, 431-442.
5. **Suter, M. L. (2002),** Peeling apparatus having feeder control based upon load and associated methods. *U. S. Patent No. 6431061B2.* U. S. Patent and Trademark Office, Washington, D. C.
6. **Shen Long, H.** and **Tardif, P.** (1999). Machine for peeling vegetables and fruits. *U. S. Patent No. 5957045.* U. S. Patent and Trading Office Washington, D. C.
7. **Harding, G. J. (2001).** Peeler for fruits and vegetables. *U. S. Patent No. 6324969.* U. S. Patent and Trademark Office, Washington, D. C.
8. **Gingras, M.** (2001), "Apparatus for peeling and optionally cutting vegetables", *U. S. Patent No. 6253670B1.* U. S. Patent and Trademark Office, Washington, D. C.
9. **Ridler, D. G.** (2000), "Fruit and vegetable peeling apparatus", *U. S. Patent No. 6082253.* U. S. Patent and Trademark Office, Washington, D. C.
10. **Martin, R.** (2000), "Fruit peeler", *U. S. Patent No. 6125744.* U. S. Patent and Trademark Office, Washington, D. C.
11. **Protte, C.** (1999), "Peeling machine", *U. S. Patent No. 5857404.* U. S. Patent and Trademark Office, Washington, D. C.
12. **Sommer, F.** (1997), "Device for peeling elongated vegetables", *U. S. Patent No. 5669293.* U. S. Patent and Trademark Office, Washington, D. C.

13. **Rouschning, K.** (2001), "Peeler for root vegetables", *U. S. patent No. 6167801B1*. U. S. Patent and Trademark Office, Washington, D. C.

14. FAO: vegetable specific processing technologies. [Online]. Available: http://www.fao.org/docrep/v5030E/v5030 E0q.html [Accessed 3 Aug.2002].

15. **Weaver, M., Huxsoll, C.** and **NG, K. (1980).** Sequential heat-cool peeling of tomatoes. *Food Technology.*, 34, 40.

16. **Floros, J. D. and Chinnan, M. S. (1988).** Microstructural changes during steam peeling of fruits and vegetables. *J Food Sci.*, 53, 849-853.

GCMM 2004
Editors: Prasad K D V Yarlagadda and S Narayanan
Copyright © 2005, Vellore Institute of Technology, Vellore, India
Publisher: Narosa Publishing House Pvt. Ltd., New Delhi, India

Development of an Innovative Vending Machine through Innovation and Creativity

Benjamin Wee & Prasad K D V Yarlagadda

School of Mechanical, Manufacturing and Medical Engineering
Queensland University of Technology, Brisbane, Q 4001, Australia

Abstract

In this paper, the concepts of innovation and creativity are explored, its relevance in engineering and its use in the conceptualization and design of a vending machine that dispenses hot food will also be illustrated. Methods to promote creativity and innovation will also be discussed.

Keywords

Innovation, Creativity, Vending Machine

1. INTRODUCTION

This paper outlines the conceptualization and development of a vending machine that dispenses hot food, it was part of a final year project for students from Mechanical, Electrical and Infomechatronics departments of QUT. It will highlight how creativity and innovation were used in this project.

Innovation and creativity are integral concepts to the advancement of engineering and society in general. Many studies have been done on the subject from psychologist and educators to engineers and scientist [3], [4].

Many times, the terms creativity and innovation are used interchangeably, we however believe they can be defined in more narrow terms.

We have taken creativity to be the use of new ideas and solutions to existing problems, usually through the application of existing technology within a field, and innovation as the use of solutions from other disciplines to problems from different fields.

The constant generation of new ideas and solutions should be always be promoted. Many a time, engineers are thought to be analytical and methodical, if this were the case, nothing new would have been created and the field would have stalled.

Products such as post it notes, where the materials; paper and glue are widely used, but when combined, form an innovative new product. Is just one example of an innovative product.

Besides just the need for innovation or creativity, how it can be promoted will also be explored. Methods such as TRIZ or lateral thinking are just a few such methods. From an organizational level to a more personal approach, creativity can be fostered by

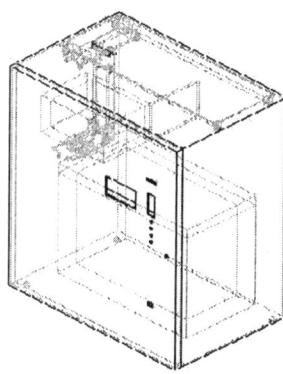

Fig. 1: Solidworks model of vending machine concept

constantly challenging the mind and promoting a climate not critical of failure [11].

From the initial idea to the final concept, the creativity was stimulated by several factors. One of these was that nothing was impossible or absurd until proven otherwise and constantly consulting external views. While constantly exploring new ideas and directions may be contradictory to the usual set train of thought that engineering be methodical, it should not be taken to the extreme. Creativity is to let no option be impossible until proven otherwise.

2. CREATIVITY AND INNOVATION

It has been said that Creativity and Innovation consists of "SEEING what everyone else has seen, THINKING what no one else has thought, and DOING what no one else has dared".

The recognition of need, is in itself a creative act. Though in this project, through our research, it was found that there have been other instances where others have sought to build such a machine and faced problems, it was our intention to try to overcome these limitations by applying creativity and innovating with problems encountered [9] [10].

Many studies have been done on creativity and innovation. Why is it some people have it,

and others don't. Can it be learnt? Can it promoted? It is our opinion that creativity can be promoted to some extent, while innovation takes more work. When questioned on creativity, many people think of artistes and other "creative" people. In many cases, engineers should be creative in their search for solutions. However, innovation is not so obvious. Innovation seems to strike at the strangest times and is only apparent to some people until explained to others. The idea of a squeeze bottle for tomato ketchup or sauces is a simple, innovative idea. So simple yet not obvious until explained.

Recently, an innovative can that will heat the drink by an exothermic chemical reaction was introduced. This does away with the need for an external heater to heat the drink. It was a little more complicated as it employed effects from different disciplines. This is another mark of innovation, that many innovations are a combination of different disciplines and as such to promote innovation, multi- disciplinary teams should work together to provide innovative solutions [5].

In summary, creativity is best served without any preconceived notions of the method, looking at the end result and then finding a solution is as useful as a rigidly structured approach. Although in this case, we did take a somewhat structured approach by researching the current state of the art in the field and critically reviewing the various alternatives. Innovation on the other hand, may use technology from other fields to improve a particular field of endeavor.

In this project, one objective was to bring together members from different engineering disciplines and levels of experience. This was to promote new thinking and innovative solutions.

Creativity on the other hand can be promoted. The more exposed a person is, the more creative his/her ideas may be as they draw on a wider range of possible solutions. This is not to say that the more experiences a person has, the more creative he/she will be. There must be the mindset of think out of the box and exploring different options.

The views on creativity and innovation in general varies depending on who is asked.

Students and the general public have different views from engineers or inventors.

When asked about what qualities creativity people possess, students would say novelty, open-mindedness, unconventionality, insightfulness, and attitude [3].

When practicing engineers are questioned about peers that are known to be creative, they usually mention their personal motivations- desire and fulfillment from being creative, environment- autonomy and support from superiors, as well as their knowledge and openness to new concepts [4].

It would therefore be safe to say that creativity can be fostered by a change in attitude [11].

3. CREATIVE AND INNOVATIVE EXAMPLE IN THE VENDING MACHINE

The very first act of creativity is the recognition of need. In this case, the fact was that many times, after hours, there was no hot food available on campus. The idea was to then develop a vending machine that would dispense hot food. There have been vending machines that dispense frozen food to be heated in an external microwave oven, usually beside it. However, this was prone to vandalism and abuse. The innovation was the use of existing technologies into a new solution, in this case, a vending machine that would dispense hot food. The initial components would be readily available; freezer, heating, etc. but a combination of these technologies in a way not used before was innovative. The creativity was in the execution of the ideas, the finding of solutions to practical problems.

The Storage system was a creative solution, since it would be better to have the heavier components at the base to provide better stability. To do this the conventional layout of the products being held in the upper compartments and being dispensed by gravity was changed. It was instead decided that the freezer that would hold the frozen product was to be located in the lower compartment. This in itself required a creative solution as the retrieval system would have to reach into the freezer to retrieve the package. The retrieval

system had to be compact to maximize the space available in the machine frame.

As an economic criterion was to have the machine hold as much stock as possible to reduce the maintenance required in restocking it. This was done by inverting the problem, and having the package come to the retrieval system and not have the retrieval system go down into the freezer to pick this up. This would have meant having a motion source within the freezer to move the packages up which was quite heavy and would have required a large motor, which would have taken up space in the freezer. In addition to that the freezer had to be at about -20°C. this would not be possible for conventional motors. To do this, it was decided that the force of gravity should be used. Since the freezer would be in the lower portion of the machine, having gravity acting directly on the packages would not be possible. Therefore an innovative solution had to be found.

After much consideration, including the use of conveyors that would be powered by the oncoming retrieval system, it was decided to use springs that would compress under the weight of the packages and push the packages up towards to retrieval gripper. It became obvious that if the spring was selected to be in equilibrium with the weight of the stack of packages, it would not move up. It was then decided to have the spring provide an up force greater then the weight of the packages. This would cause the packages to "pop" out of the freezer. This was another problem that had to be solved.

The solution to this was to have spring-loaded flaps hold the packages in place till the gripper was ready to pick it up. In this way, the weight of the packages compressed the springs and the excess force required to accelerate the packages was resisted by the spring-loaded flaps, and when these flaps were defeated by the oncoming gripper, the packages would "pop" out.

The Retrieval system was another solution that required creative thought. The usual configurations of a multi- jointed arm was discarded as it would be bulky and hard to control. A simpler solution along the lines of a Cartesian robot was selected. However due

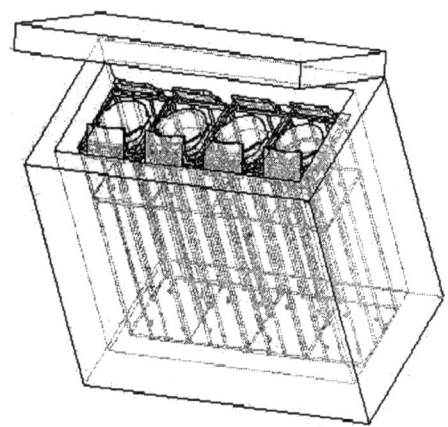

Fig. 2: Solidworks model of storage modules within the freezer.

to space constraints, the freezer door could not open fully, this prevented the Cartesian arm from reaching into the freezer fully to defeat the flaps. It was then decided that prongs would be attached to the gripper to act like a key to unlock the flaps and release the packages. A creative solution example.

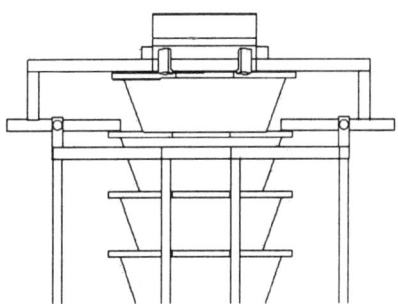

Fig. 3: Detailed view of Gripper and Storage module.

Other ideas that were explored were methods of rapid heating as well as means to keep the packages frozen. Unfortunately, since this was a prototype machine, it would have been unfeasible to develop any new methods of heating or cooling since it would not be cost effective.

Since then, advances in food technology have now allowed heating to be done in 90 seconds for some packaged foods. This again demonstrates how advances in another field may yield innovative results, and thus cross discipline collaboration may yield innovative ideas.

4. TOOLS AND METHODS TO PROMOTE CREATIVITY AND INNOVATION

Of the many tools that are available to designers/inventors/engineers is TRIZ, this is method developed by Genrich Altshuller [1] [8]. It gives a set of possible scenarios and a set of possible solutions. This matrix was developed by analysis of thousands of patents to find and synthesize the creative/innovative essence of these patents. It is a useful tool to get the mind moving towards a solution.

TRIZ research began with the hypothesis that there are universal principles of invention that are the basis for creative innovations that advance technology, and that if these principles could be identified and codified, they could be taught to people to make the process of invention more predictable. The research has proceeded in several stages over the last 50 years. Over 2 million patents have been examined, classified by level of inventiveness, and analyzed to look for principles of innovation. The three primary findings of this research are as follows:

1. Problems and solutions were repeated across industries and sciences

2. Patterns of technical evolution were repeated across industries and sciences

3. Innovations used scientific effects outside the field where they were developed

In the application of TRIZ all three of these findings are applied to create and to improve products, services, and systems. TRIZ is in use at Ford, Motorola, Procter & Gamble, Eli Lilly, Jet Propulsion Laboratories, 3M, Siemens, Phillips, LG, and hundreds more.

One of the creative examples is the use of inversion, that is, in the limited space available, inversion was used with the storage system. Instead of bringing the package to the gripper and have motors within the freezer to provide motion, it was decided to have the package fed upwards towards the gripper by using springs and have the power for motion of the flaps provided by the arm. This solved the problem of having to drill holes in the freezer and also of having motors within the freezer.

Brainstorming is where members of a team get together to suggest solutions to a problem. This is helpful in that sometimes, a idea may spark off another idea, or a modification of an idea may be a possible solution [1].

An off shoot of this is the nominal group technique, in this method, the ideas are silently written down and the group members each present their ideas before discussion [2].

In Lateral Thinking, the person is advised to not to think in a logical horizontal manner, where one idea is built upon another idea to reach a goal. They are instead told to think laterally, that is to let ideas flow in a linked manner to form a useful solution, somewhat like a concept map. These help by not letting the horizontal progression of things obscure a solution. Developed by Dr. Edward de Bono [6] [7] It advocates the "thinking outside the box" way of thinking. He advocates that to be creative, people have to break away from the usual perception of patterns. An example is, instead of stacking toy building blocks to make a tower which is a common perception of its use, lining up blocks to make a wall may serve a purpose as well. An example is the common perception that vending machines should have the heating system outside the machine. Creativity and innovation challenges that perception and seeks ways to provide a solution.

Cross discipline consultation would be very much like brain storming, except that instead of consulting within a group of the same discipline, a fresh outside view is given. These fresh ideas may help by offering an insight that may not otherwise be apparent

3-D modeling was heavily used in this project to better visualize ideas. This helps in that being able to see may better help provide a better solution.

A few methods have been suggested [ ] to promote creativity and innovation among them are;

- Immerse yourself in a problem- to learn all you can about the field in which it exist and become an expert in it.
- Be prolific- to generate as many ideas as possible without discounting any of them.
- Use tools for representation and thought- to keep logs or diaries of ideas or sketches, to use CAD packages or creative thinking tools that stimulate the mind
- Try looking at all levels, from abstract thought to practical views
- Do not settle for the first idea, keep looking for better ways to solve a problem
- Don't be afraid to be different
- Be open to new ideas
- Look outside you own field- new technologies in other fields may have applications in yours
- Reflect on your solutions, often on deeper introspect, a solution may be improved.
- Relax and have fun in creative thought

5. CONCLUSION

In conclusion, we have presented the ideas of creativity and innovation, shown why it is important within an engineering context, provided ways to promote creativity and innovation as well as shown how it was applied in a design.

6. REFERENCES

1. **Kosse V**, 2000, *Mechanical Engineering Design, Course Notes*, Part I MMB 281, QUT publication.
2. **Hurt F**, 1999, *Rousing Creativity; Think New Now!*, Crisp Publications, USA.
3. **Richards LG**, 1997, Student Perceptions of Creativity and Intelligence, *Journal of Engineering Education*.
4. **Klukken PG**, Parsons JR and Columbus PJ, 1997, The Creative Experience in Engineering Practice : Implications for Engineering Education, *Journal of engineering Education*, Vol. 86 No.2, pp133-138.
5. **Gorman ME, Kagawa J, Richards LG** and **Scherer WT**, 1995, Teaching Innovation and Design, Multi-disciplinary

Modules, *Journal of Engineering Education*, Vol. 84, no.2, pp175-185.

6. **De Bono E**, 1996,Serious creativity : using the power of lateral thinking to create new ideas, HarperCollins Business, London.

7. **De Bono E**, 1990, *Lateral thinking : a* textbook of creativity, Penguin, London .

8. **TRIZ and I-TRIZ**, Ideation International, 2004. http://www.ideationtriz.com/triz.asp

9. Vendtastic Ltd., 1999, http://www.vendtastic.com/

10. Hankers Vending Machine, 2004 http://www.hankers.com.au/

11. Big Ten Innovation Killers, Innovation Network,2004 http://www.thinksmart.com/ library/ BigTenInnovationKillers.htm

Metrology

GCMM 2004
Editors: Prasad K D V Yarlagadda and S Narayanan
Publisher: Narosa Publishing House Pvt. Ltd., New Delhi, India

An Approach to Evaluate Circularity using Co-ordinate Measurement Data

Ravindra K

R V R & J C College of Engineering, Guntur - 522 019

Email : ravindra_kom@rediffmail.com

Narayana Rao K N V·S & Madar Valli P

College of Engineering, GITAM, Visakhapatnam - 530 045

Nageswara Rao D

College of Engineering, Andhra University, Visakhapatnam - 530 003.

Abstract

Most of the machine components consist of circular form which should possess the required geometrical tolerance and should be checked for their acceptance. At the present scenario, the Coordinate Measuring Machines (CMMs) are considered to be reliable and capable to perform automated inspection on the manufactured parts. In CMMs, the measured data is processed using Least Squares Method to assess the form errors in the geometric features of the components. The error values assessed by CMM are not the minimum, there by resulting the rejection of the good parts. A simple approach is proposed to evaluate the circularity error in this paper and the results indicate the validity of the methodology. The results are at par with the other methodologies.

Keywords
Circularity, Minimum Zone Circle, Co-ordinate Measuring Machine.

1. INTRODUCTION

Most of the machine parts process circular features. The variations on the circular part feature occur due to imperfect rotation, erratic cutting conditions, tool wear, inadequate lubrication, defective machine parts, machine tool vibrations, misalignment of chuck jaws, fixturing, excessive feeds, inconsistencies in the work piece material etc.. These result in imperfections in the form of waves around the periphery of the part surface. It is very important to ensure the correct interpretation of the true deviation. Problems related with assembly, oil escapes, and vibrations in machines are due to non-maintenance of the tolerance specified by the designer. Accurate evaluation of the circularity error is very critical.

2. LITERATURE REVIEW

The International Standard ISO 1101 [1] defines the 'Circularity error' as: "the radial distance between two concentric circles separated by minimum possible distance and given geometric profile". It also recommends a minimum zone evaluation of form and

589

specifies that the 'Ideal or Reference' features containing all the measured points on the contour must be established from the actual measurement data such that the deviation between the actual feature and the 'Ideal' feature shall be the least value possible.

One of the established methods of evaluating circularity is by the least squares deviation. This has the advantage of uniqueness for linear systems. T.S.R. Murthy and S.Z. Abdin [2] proposed Normal least squares fit and numerical methods based on Monte Carlo technique, Simplex Search and Spiral techniques to evaluate circularity in terms of minimum zone deviation. M.S. Shunmugam [3] implemented this mini-max criterion by adopting numerical searching procedures of optimization. H.Chang and T.W. Lin [4] proposed a sampling technique using Monte Carlo simulation to calculate the out of roundness.

Nam-Hyun Kim and Seuing-Woo Kim [5] have developed an algorithm for the normal least squares evaluation for circularity. Jing-Yih Lai and Ing-Hong Chen [6], proposed a strategy for minimum zone evaluation of circles, which employs a non-linear transformation to convert a circle into a line. Dhanish and Shunmugam [7] developed an algorithm using discrete Chebyshev approximations and arrived at the minimum zone values. Lai and Wang [8] proposed a computational geometry technique to solve roundness problem using farthest Voronoi and Medial axis concepts. Roy and Zhang [9,10] developed a more comprehensive method using nearest and farthest Voronoi diagrams calculated over the convex hulls of the set. Olivio Novoski et. al. [11], proposed a program to calculate a MZC based on the concept of Voronoi diagrams and compared with the LSC. Timothy Weber et al. [12] proposed a unified linear approximation technique in evaluating the circularity and successfully tested on the form data collected on CMM. Dhanish, P.B. [13] proposed a simple algorithm to give a minimum value of circularity error using CMM data. Li-Min Zhu et al. [14] formulated the evaluation of circularity as an unconstrained optimization problem. G.L. Samuel et.al. [15] presented appropriate methods to handle two dimensional coordinate data obtained from CMMs for circular feature. Directly a circle is considered as the assessment feature while

evaluating the circularity error using CMMs data and a limacon [16] is considered while using the transformed data. The values of form error evaluated from the CMM data and

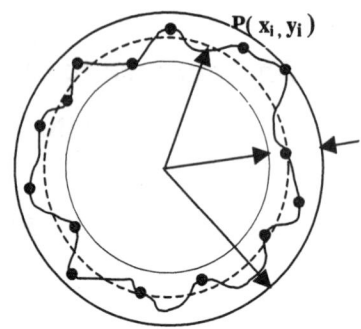

the transformed data are nearly the same. The present work aimed at a new approach to assess the circularity error from Co-ordinate Measurement data.

3. Least Squares Circle Method

The Least Squares fitting technique is the commonly used method in CMMs for Circularity evaluation [2,16]. The least Squares technique is efficient in computation and is widely used in Co-ordinate Measurement Machines.

For a circular feature, as shown in the Fig:1, having measurement data in Cartesian Co-ordinates as $P_i(x_i, y_i)$, the deviation of the point 'P_i' from the least squares centre (a, b) is represented by the following equation [11]:

$$e = R - r \qquad \text{--------- (1)}$$

Where r = minimum of r_c
R = maximum of r_c
r_c = radial location of the point from the LSC
$= [(x_i - a)^2 + (y_i - b)^2]^{1/2}$
$a = 2 \Sigma x_i / n$; $b = 2 \Sigma y_i / n$
i = 1 to n
n = No. of symmetrical points with uniform spacing

If the measurement data in Cylindrical Co-ordinates is taken on CMM as $P_i (r_i , \theta_i)$ and $O (a , b)$ is the least squares centre, the minimum zone value [5] is expressed as:

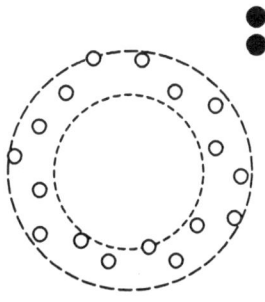

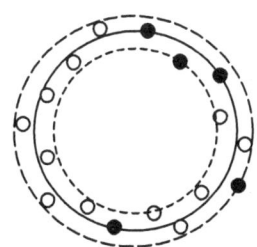

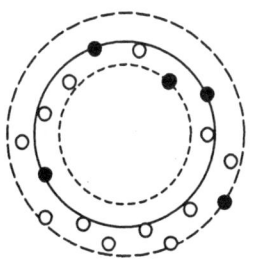

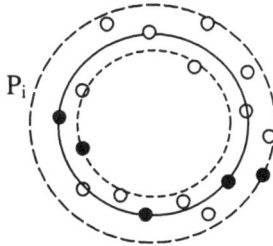

P_i

$$e = [\text{Max. of } (r_i - r_m)] - [\text{Min. of } (r_i - r_m)] \quad \text{--- (2)}$$

Where $r_m = \Sigma \, r_i \, / \, n$

The deviation of the actual feature from the least squares circle is given by 'e' ie... the 'Circularity or Form error'.

4. MINIMUM ZONE CIRCLE METHOD

Two concentric circles with minimum radial separation are assessed which contain the profile of the circular feature. This method is also known as Minimum Zone Circle (MZC) method. The radial difference between these circles is used to measure the Circularity error. Most of the current research work follows this category. The studies show that the minimum zone method yields more accurate fitting results because it evaluates smaller zone value than other techniques and it is more consistent with the standard definition of physical fittings [11].

5. PROPOSED METHODOLOGY

The proposed methodology evaluates the minimum circularity error. It processes the given co-ordinate positions of the points representing the contour of the circular feature. These data points P_i are obtained by scanning the contour of the circular feature on CMM. In this methodology, the centre of the reference circle is evaluated for which the radial deviation between the nearest and the farthest points lying on the contour is minimum.

Fig: 2a shows the scattered positions of the measured points of the contour. In each iteration process, it is assumed that a circle is passing through the randomly selected set having three points. Using the concept of three point circle method, the centre of the circle is evaluated.

Fig: 2b shows the circle which is passing through the selected points P_1, P_2, & P_3 and O_1 (a_1, b_1). The radial deviation (e_1) between the farthest and the nearest points from this center is evaluated. In the next step, another set of three points are selected. The new centre of the circle and the corresponding radial deviation between the farthest and nearest points is evaluated. Fig: 2c shows the new center $O_2(a_2, b_2)$ of the circle which is passing through the second set of points.

Fig: 2d shows the selected three points from the data set P_i (x_i, y_i), for which the center of the assessing circle as O_j (a_j, b_j). The radial deviation between the farthest and nearest points is 'e_j'. In this manner, the centers ($O_1, O_2, --- O_j$) and the corresponding radial deviations ($e_1, e_2 ---- e_j$) are evaluated for all possible combinations of point sets. From these centers, the center with minimum radial deviation is the Minimum Zone Centre. The radial deviation between the farthest and nearest points is the minimum radial deviation. This is the minimum 'Circularity or Form error' that can be assessed from the co-ordinate measurement data.

6. MATHEMATICAL MODELLING

CMM measurement data points $P_i(x_i, y_i)$ of a circular feature are processed to evaluate the center of the best fit circle and the minimum circularity error. Fig:3 shows the scattered points P_i of the circular feature. Let $P_1(x_1, y_1)$, $P_2(x_2, y_2)$ and $P_3(x_3, y_3)$ be the points through which the assessing circle passes and $O_j (a_j, b_j)$ be the centre of the circle.

The radial location of each point of P_1, P_2 and $P3$ is 'R' from the center O_j (a_j, b_j) for j = 1 and 'R' is expressed as:

$$[(x_1 - a_j)^2 + (y_1 - b_j)^2]^2 = R^2 \quad ----(3)$$
$$[(x_2 - a_j)^2 + (y_2 - b_j)^2]^2 = R^2 \quad ----(4)$$
$$[(x_3 - a_j)^2 + (y_3 - b_j)^2]^2 = R^2 \quad ----(5)$$

By solving the above equations, the centre of the circle $O_j (a_j, b_j)$ is evaluated. The radial distance of the points from the center $O_j (a_j, b_j)$ is

$$r_i = [(x_i - a_j)^2 + (y_i - b_j)^2]^{1/2} \quad ----(6)$$
$$\text{for i = 1 to n}$$

$$\text{Deviation} = e_j = R_j - r_j \quad ----(7)$$
$$\text{for j = 1 to nC}_3$$
Where $R_j = \max [r_i]$ and $r_j = \min [r_i]$

$$\text{Circularity} = e = \text{Min} [e_j] \quad ------(8)$$

Eq. 8 gives is the minimum zone solution for 'Circularity' error.

7. ALGORITHM

The computational procedure based on the proposed strategy has been developed in the following algorithm:

Step 1: Reads the number of data points 'i' and x_i and y_i coordinates of CMM data point set ' P_i '

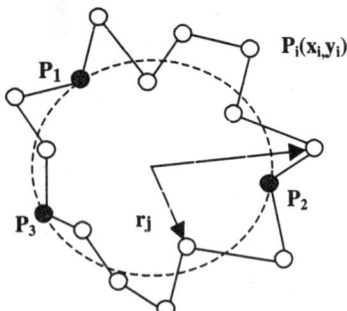

Fig. 3: Scattered points on the part feature

Step 2: Picks up three data points P_1, P_2 and P_3 randomly from data set to set subset ' j '

Step 3: Evaluates the centre of the circle O_1 (a_1, b_1) passing through the selected three points

Step 4: Evaluates the radial distances of the nearest point, min [r_i] and the farthest point, max [r_i] of the remaining data set

Step 5: Evaluates the radial deviation 'e_j' between the max [r_i] and min [r_i]

Step 6: Then selects another set of three points to form another subset and repeats the steps 2 to 5 to estimate the radial deviation 'e_j'

Step 7: Evaluates the minimum value of 'e_j' from the radial deviation values found from each of the nC_3 iterations. Min [e_j] is the circularity error

8. PERFORMANCE EVALUATION

To check the performance of the above algorithm, a computer program is developed in C – language. The coordinate measurement data sets are collected from the previous literature [12] to evaluate the circularity errors and are presented in Appendix. The evaluated values of the Circularity errors are tabulated in Table:1. The results are compared with those evaluated by Least Square Method and Linear Approximation Technique of T. Weber et. al. [12].

9. CONCLUSIONS

This procedure is simple and efficient. The evaluated Circularity errors by this method are 'more accurate' and 'at par' with the other methodologies. The same procedure can be extended to evaluate form errors in cylindrical features.

Table 1: Comparison of Circularities in 'mm'

Example	LSM	LAT[a]	OCM[b]
1	0.0006	0.0006	0.0006
2	0.0022	0.0018	0.0018
3	0.0012	0.0011	0.0011
4	0.0279	0.0253	0.0256
5	0.0009	0.0008	0.0008

[a] Linear Optimization Technique [12]

[b] Optimum Circle Method [Proposed Method]

Appendix :

CMM – Circularity data set [12] in 'mm'

Example : 1		Example : 2		Example : 3		Example : 4		Example : 5	
X	Y	X	Y	X	Y	X	Y	X	Y
-0.1690	0.3360	-0.0017	0.2476	-0.1512	0.2608	0.0812	0.2758	-0.1376	0.5963
-0.3631	0.1275	-0.1754	0.1905	-0.2890	0.1094	-0.1308	0.2308	-0.2504	0.5350
-0.3561	-0.1533	-0.2649	0.0676	-0.2615	-0.1691	-0.2745	0.1038	-0.3624	0.3896
-0.1233	-0.3620	-0.2748	-0.0807	-0.1517	-0.2701	-0.3318	-0.0706	-0.3865	0.1762
0.1925	-0.3177	-0.2409	-0.1658	-0.0096	-0.3050	-0.3193	-0.1956	-0.3455	0.0603
0.3494	-0.0985	-0.1980	-0.2188	0.1820	- 0.2328	-0.2798	-0.2890	-0.2083	-0.0810
0.3222	0.1613	0.0379	-0.2910	0.2786	- 0.0783	-0.2030	-0.3778	0.0765	-0.1212
0.1413	0.3364	0.1767	-0.2190	0.2799	0.0667	-0.0018	-0.4634	0.2180	-0.0496
		0.2461	-0.1078	0.2127	0.1940	0.1739	-0.4126	0.3264	0.0942
		0.2449	0.0687	0.0659	0.2840	0.2842	-0.3452	0.3234	0.3932
		0.1974	0.1518			0.3477	-0.2915	0.2773	0.4703
		0.1348	0.2064			0.4073	-0.1371	0.1810	0.5577
						0.3995	0.0148		
						0.3545	0.1096		
						0.2869	0.1860		

10. REFERENCES

1. **ISO 1101**, (1983), "Technical Drawings – Geometrical Tolerancing", 12-01.

2. **Murthy T.S.R. & Abdin S.Z.**, (1980), "Minimum Zone Evaluation of Surfaces", *International Journal of Machine Tool Research*, 20:123-136.

3. **Shunmugam M.S.**, (1991), "Establishing reference figures for form evaluation of Engineering Surfaces", *Journal Manufacturing Systems*, 10(4), 314-321.

4. **Chang H. and Lin T.W.**, (1993), "Evaluation of circularity tolerance using Monte Carlo simulation for Coordinate Measuring Machine", *International Journal of Production research*, 20 , 2079-2086.

5. **Nam-Hyun Kim & Kim S.W.**, (1996), "Geometrical Tolerances: Improved Linear Approximation Of Least squares Evaluation Of Circularity By Minimum Variance", *International Journal of Machine Tools & Manufacturing;*, 36(3), 355-366.

6. **Jing-Yih Lai & Ing-Hong Chen**, (1996), "Minimum Zone Evaluation of Circles and Cylinders", *International Journal Machine Tool Manufacture*, , 30, 435-451.

7. **Dhanish,P.B. and Shunmugam,M.S.**, (1991) "An algorithm for form error evaluation using the theory of discrete and linear Chebyshev approximation", *Computer Methods in Applied Mechanics and Engineering*, 92, 309-324.

8. **Lai, K. and Wang, J.** (1988), "A computational geometry approach to geometric tolerancing", *Proceedings of the 16th North American Manufacturing research Conference*, 376-379.

9. **Roy,U. and Zhang,X.** (1992), "Establishment of a pair of concentric circles with the minimum radial separation for assessing roundness error", *Computer Aided Design*, 24, 161-168.

10. **Roy,U. and Zhang,X.** (1994), "Development and application of Voronoi diagram in the assessment of roundness error in an industrial environment", *Computers Industrial engineering*, 26, 11-26.

11. **Olivio Novoski and Andre Luis Chautard Barczak**, (1997), "Utilization of Voronoi diagrams for circularity algorithms", *Precision Engineering*, 20; 188-195.

12. **Timothy Weber, Saeid Motavalli, Behrooz Fallahi and S. Hossein Cheraghi**, (2002), " A unified approach to form error evaluation", *Precision Engineering,* 26; 269-278.

13. **Dhanush, P.B.,** (2002), "A simple algorithm algorithm for evaluation of minimum zone circularity error from coordinate data", *International Journal of Machine Tools & Manufacture,* 42; 1589-1594.

14. **Li-Min Zhu, Han Ding, You-Lun Xiong,** (2003) "A steepest descent algorithm for circularity evaluation", *Computer Aided Design*, 35; 255-265.

15. **Samuel G.L. and Shunmugam M.S.,** (2003), "Evaluation of circularity and sphericity from coordinate measurement data", *Journal of Materials Processing Technology,* 139; 90-95.

16. **Samuel G.L. and Shunmugam M.S.,** (2000) "Evaluation of Circularity from Coordinate and Form data using computational geometric techniques", *Precision Engineering, ,*24; 251-263.

GCMM 2004
Editors: Prasad K D V .Yarlagadda and S Narayanan
Copyright © 2005, Vellore Institute of Technology, Vellore, India
Publisher: Narosa Publishing House Pvt. Ltd., New Delhi, India

Calibration of Wattmeter for the Measurement of Process Torque in an Experimental Brick Extruder

Ajay M Fulambarkar

Head of the Department of Mechanical & Production Engg.,
B.D. College of Engineering, Sewagram, Wardha, (M.S.), India.

E_mail : ajay_f@rediffmail.com

Askhedkar R D

Principal, K.D.K. College of Engg., Nagpur (M.S.), India.

Abstract

It has been noted through literature review that no systematic efforts have been made in the past to evolve the generalized theoretical as well as experimental models for motorized auger type brick extrusion machines for extruding flyash-clay bricks [1,2,3]. Therefore, it was necessary to generate design data to provide a systematic basis for designing motorized auger type brick extrusion machine. An experimental brick extruder was designed and fabricated for carrying extensive experimentation to generate design data for motorized auger type brick extrusion machine, extruding flyash-clay bricks[4,5].

During experimentation the measurement of torque on the auger screw in the process of extrusion of flyash-clay bricks was tried with the help of wattmeter.

This paper reports the methodology of calibration of wattmeter (replication technique)[6] used for the measurement of process torque in the process of extrusion of flyash-clay bricks in an experimental extruder. A calibration setup specially fabricated for the purpose has been explained. The statistical tools are applied to prove that the measurement of torque by wattmeter gives a reasonably accurate measure of torque on the auger screw of a motorized experimental extruder. The calibration curve for wattmeter plotted on the basis of calibration results has been presented.

Keywords

Calibration, Extrusion, Brick, Torque Measurement

1. EXPERIMENTAL BRICK EXTRUDER

The salient features and working principle of a specially fabricated experimental extruder having 1:3 scaled reduction of the full size motorized auger type brick extrusion machine are given below –

The isometric layout of an experimental extruder is shown in figure 1. A 3.7 KW, 1440 rpm, three phase induction motor (13) is used to drive the experimental extruder. The speed of auger shaft of experimental extruder is taken as 24 rpm. A speed reduction from 1440 to 24 rpm has been achieved through a combination of V-belt drive (12) and worm gear reducer (11). A speed reduction of 1:4 is obtained with the worm gear reducer giving a speed of 24 rpm to the auger screw.

The output shaft of worm gear reducer is coupled with the shaft of a torque sensor (9), the other end of which is further coupled with the auger screw.

Flexible couplings (8) are used to couple torque sensor shaft with the worm reducer shaft and auger screw. A torque sensor is used to measure the process torque on the auger screw during extrusion of brick column.

An auger screw (5) is supported at one end with the help of two taper roller bearings housed in the bearing housing (7). A properly prepared homogeneous mix of flyash and clay is fed through a hopper (6). Due to the rotation of auger screw the mix moves forward towards cone (3) and then through the die (2). The uniformly shaped brick column extrudes through a die which is connected to the cone. It is then collected on a simple cutting tray (1) having a slot through which a piece of wire can be inserted for cutting the bricks by wire-cut method.

2. MEASUREMENT OF PROCESS TORQUE

The basic criteria considered for optimizing the flyash-clay brick extrusion are,
1. Rate of extrusion of bricks.
2. Green strength of brick.
3. Torque on the auger screw i.e. the process torque.

During experimentation, the rate of extrusion was determined by measuring the length of brick column extruded per unit time and the green and baked strength of brick was measured on compression testing machine. It was attempted to measure the process torque for extruding bricks with the help of in-line rotating torque sensor. It was connected in between the output shaft of a worm gear reducer and the auger shaft with the help of flexible couplings. A digital torque indicator of the torque sensor gives a record of the process torque.

It was observed during experimental trials that the torque sensor continuously malfunctioned giving extremely fluctuating and erratic readings. Hence, an alternate method of measurement of process torque was adopted in which the torque on the auger screw was measured by connecting a wattmeter to the three phase induction motor. The wattmeter measures the power taken up by the motor for extrusion of brick column which in turn gives a record of torque on the auger screw of the experimental extruder extruding flyash-clay bricks.

3. CALIBRATION OF WATTMETER

It was necessary to calibrate the wattmeter against the known torque. A calibration setup was specially fabricated and installed. The wattmeter was suitably calibrated and the calibration curve as shown in figure 3 was obtained.

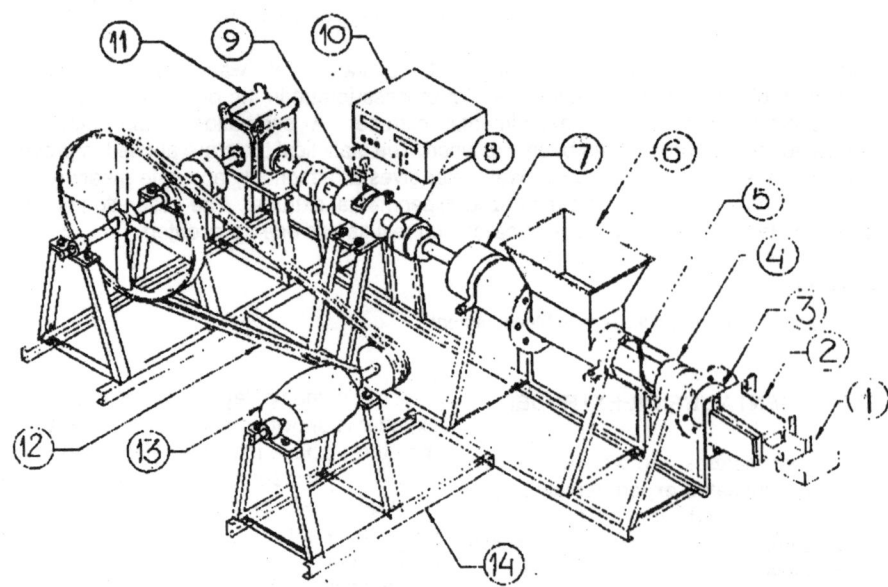

Figure 1: Experimental Brick Extruder

Description of Calibration Setup:

The isometric layout of the calibration setup is shown in figure 2.

A 3.7 KW., 1440 rpm, three phase induction motor (12) is used to drive the flat pulley of the calibration setup. The speed of the flat pulley is taken as 24 rpm. A speed reduction from 1440 rpm to 24 rpm has been obtained by a combination of the V-belt drive (11) and the worm gear reducer (10) having speed reduction ratio of 1:4 and 1:15 respectively.

A flat belt dynamometer was specially fabricated for the calibration of wattmeter. A flat pulley (6) is mounted on a M.S. shaft (7). The shaft is supported on a pedestal bearing mounted on a bracket (8). The shaft on which flat pulley is mounted has been coupled to the output shaft of a worm gear reducer.

A leather belt (5) is passed over a flat pulley. A spring balance (9) is hooked to one end of the flat belt to measure the tension on the slack side. The other end of the flat belt is connected to rope (2) which passes over a guiding pulley with bracket (3) mounted on ceiling hooks (4). A weight pan (1) is attached to the other end of the rope. The location of hooks is fixed in such a way that the angle of lap of the belt on the flat pulley is 180^0. A wattmeter to be calibrated is connected to the motor through proper electrical connections.

4. PROCEDURE OF CALIBRATION

The following procedure is adopted for the calibration of wattmeter -

i) Determination of no load torque : The power taken up by the motor which is measured by wattmeter represents the sum of the power required to overcome the belt friction and the losses in motor, V-belt drive and the worm gear reducer.

In order to account for the power losses in motor, V-belt drive and worm gear reducer, the wattmeter readings are taken at no load condition. The drive motor is switched on and wattmeter reading is noted. These no load readings are replicated for 30 times and the average no load torque T_0 is calculated which is found out to be 559.53 N-M.

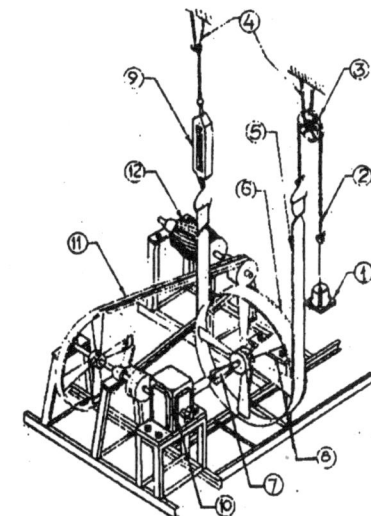

Fig. 2 : Calibration Setup

1)Weightt pan 2) Rope 3) Guiding pully with bracket 4)Ceiling hooks 5) Leather belt 6)flat pully 7) Shaft 8)Bracket 9) Spring balance 10)Worm gear reducer 11)V-belt drive 12) Motor.

ii) Calibration for frictional torque : A known torque T_A is applied by keeping the weights in the pan. Initially, a load of 231 N is kept in the pan. The drive motor is switched on. The power taken up by the motor to overcome the applied torque is measured by the wattmeter. The wattmeter reading is noted. Simultaneously, the speed of the flat pulley is measured by tachometer and the spring balance reading is also recorded. The motor is switched off. This procedure is replicated for 30 times for 231 N load. From the wattmeter readings, the measured torque T_M is determined. The belt frictional torque T is obtained as a difference between the torque measured by wattmeter T_M and the no load torque T_0, i.e.,

$$T = T_M - T_0$$

The above procedure is repeated for other loads like 447 N, 647 N and 847 N by replicating the readings for 30 times for each load and estimating the frictional torque T.

The torque measured by wattmeter T_M is calibrated against the known applied torque T_A. The readings of the calibration are given in table 1

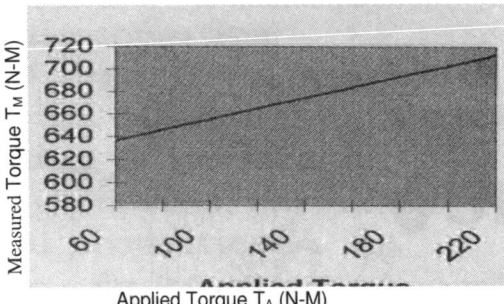

Applied Torque T_A (N-M)

Check For Normal Distribution

The deviation between the applied torque T_A and the frictional torque T for 30 replicated samples at each applied torque was checked for its normal distribution. This has been checked by applying the area property of the normal distribution curve [7] and further confirmed by applying the Chi-square test [8] to each set of data obtained during calibration.

The area property of the normal distribution curve have revealed that the said deviation (T_A-T) is normally distributed as shown in table 2, since the observed frequency is found out to be nearly equal to or greater than the expected frequency for all sets of load applied.

The Chi-Square Test

Each set of data is subjected to a Chi-square test with the null hypothesis that the fit between the actual applied torque and frictional torque measured by wattmeter is good. The results of the test have revealed that the estimated X^2(Chi-square) value for each set of data (applied torque) is much less than the standard tabulated value of X^2 (Chi-square) at 5% level of significance and 29 degrees of freedom as shown in table 3.

5. CONCLUSION

The result of the Chi-square test leads to the conclusion that there is no cause to suspect the hypothesis and the fit between the actual applied torque and measured frictional torque is good, i.e. the null hypothesis may be accepted. This proves beyond doubt that the deviation between applied torque and measured frictional torque follows a normal distribution and the measurement of torque by wattmeter gives a reasonably accurate measure of torque during experimentation.

Calibration Curve For Wattmeter

The calibration curve for wattmeter plotted on the basis of calibration results is shown in figure 3.

Table 1: Calibration Readings

Set No.	Applied Load (N)	Average applied torque T_A (N-M)	Average measured torque T_M (N-M)	No load torque T_O (N-M)	Average Frictional torque $T = T_M - T_O$	Average deviation $(T_A - T)$
1	231.00	63.023	618.656	559.53	59.126	03.897
2	447.00	122.878	682.320	559.53	122.790	00.088
3	647.00	173.593	721.655	559.53	162.125	11.468
4	847.00	225.230	688.134	559.53	128.604	96.626

Table 2: Check for Normal Distribution

Set No.	Applied Load (N)	Average deviation ($T_A - T$)	Standard deviation	Expected frequency			Observed frequency		
				-1σ to $+1\sigma$	-2σ to $+2\sigma$	-3σ to $+3\sigma$	-1σ to $+1\sigma$	-2σ to $+2\sigma$	-3σ to $+3\sigma$
1	231.00	03.897	0.5790	20	28.5	29.5	20	28	30
2	447.00	00.088	0.35366	20	28.5	29.5	22	29	30
3	647.00	11.468	0.81064	20	28.5	29.5	22	29	29
4	847.00	96.626	0.82839	20	28.5	29.5	23	29	29
					28.5	29.5			
					28.5	29.5			

Table 3: Chi-Square Test

Set No.	Applied Load (N)	Std. tabulated χ^2 at 5 % significance level and 29 degrees of freedom	Estimated value of χ^2
1	231.00	42.557	2.677
2	447.00	42.557	0.301
3	647.00	42.557	3.527
4	847.00	42.557	29.954

6. REFERENCES

1. **Goodson F. J.**, "Experiments in Extrusion",
2. Transactions of British Ceramic Society, Vol. 58, 1959,pp 158-182.
3. **Carley J. F.** and **Strub R. A.**, Ind. Engg. Chem., Vol. 45, No. 5, 1953, pp 970.
4. **Wadhwa S. S. and Srivastava L. K.**, "Factors affecting performance of augers for clay extrusion and their remedial measures", Interceram, NR 3, 1982, pp 198-203.
5. **Fulambarkar A. M., Askhedkar R. D.**, "Planning of experimentation on a scaled model of motorized auger type brickmaking machine", presented at *International conference on 'Signals, Data & Systems' ASME,* France, held at Hyderabad, India, 12-14 Dec. 94.
6. **Fulambarkar A. M.**, "Optimization of manufacture of flyash bricks through the development of motorized auger type brickmaking machine", Ph.D thesis, Nagpur University, Nagpur (India), Sept. 1998.
7. **Schenck Jr H.**.,"Theories of Engineering Experimentation", *McGraw Hill Book Co., Newyork*, 1961, pp 6.
8. **Gupta S.C.** and **Kapoor V. K.**, "Fundamentals of Mathematical Statistics", S. Chand & Sons, New Delhi (India), 1984, pp 471-473.
9. **Ray M. and Harswarup Sharma**, "Mathematical Statistics", Ram Prasad and Sons, Agra (India), 1978, pp 313-335.

GCMM 2004
Editors: Prasad K D V Yarlagadda and S Narayanan
Copyright © 2005, Vellore Institute of Technology, Vellore, India
Publisher: Narosa Publishing House Pvt. Ltd., New Delhi, India

Design of a Control Algorithm to Optimise Solar-Thermal Efficiency on a Parabolic Trough

Puramanathan Naidoo

Mangosuthu Technikon, Faculty of Engineering

Durban, South Africa

E-mail: Pnaidoo@julian.mantec.ac.za

Theo Van Niekerk

PE Technikon, Faculty of Engineering

Port Elizabeth, South Africa

E-mail: Theoian@petech.ac.za

Abstract
A rotational tracking error less than 3,5 milli-radians (0,2°) is assumed to be sufficiently accurate and results in good thermal efficiency on a parabolic trough. The control algorithm will be required to execute the PSA algorithm on a continuous basis in order to provide positional updates for the collector. These could either be used for "virtual" positioning of the trough in the presence of cloud, or for providing a back-up check on the fixed-rate tracking. Although it is unlikely that any significant error would be introduced by varying the trough position at the sun speed of 0,25° per minute, the temperature of the heat transfer fluid must be controlled optimally for effective thermal efficiency, for storage of thermal energy. The designed architecture positions the trough by means of self-adaptive control and utilises rule base control to regulate the temperature of the heat transfer fluid.

Keywords
Solar Parabolic Trough, Programmable Logic Control, Thermal Efficiency

1. INTRODUCTION

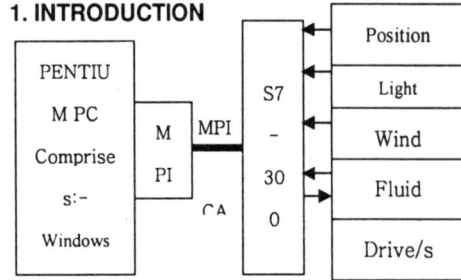

Fig. 1: Components of the Tracking and Control System

Tracking is particularly important in solar energy collection systems that operate under concentrated sunlight. The aim of the research project is to test the solar-to-thermal energy efficiency of a tracking line-focus solar parabolic trough. Accurate control of the collector is therefore crucial to the maximising of a solar parabolic trough's thermal efficiency. The main components of the tracking and control system are indicated in Figure 1. Two light sensors measures diffused and concentrated sunlight, two temperature sensors measure the collector inlet and outlet temperature, an encoder measures the position of the trough and an anemometer measures the wind speed.

2. TOLERANCE ERROR ANALYSIS FOR FIXED RATE CONTROL

A tracking error less than 3,5 mrad is assumed to be sufficiently accurate. The nature of tracking sensor errors is best illustrated graphically in figure 2. The sun's position is shown as it "moves" across the sky, first from position A to B and then C. The parabolic trough is perfectly aligned at position B. For position B the sun's rays will be reflected off the mirror surface and on to the focal point, in accordance with Snell's Law.

The tolerable error is 3,5 mrad, or 0,2° either side of position B. This means the trough can be positioned ahead (west) of the sun (at A in the sketch) and left standing until the sun moves through a total of 7 mrad, or 0,401°, which would take 69,12 seconds. Once the sun moves into position C, the DTCS must once more rotate the trough west through 7 mrad to reposition for A. The rotary encoder used in this project to provide feedback on the absolute angular position of the trough, has 2500 pulses per 360° of rotation, or 0,144° per pulse. A rotational movement of 0,007 rad, or 0,401° equates to 2,79 pulses. Since a discrete number of pulses must be used to position the trough, it is suggested that the trough corrections be made for 2 pulses, thus ensuring that the maximum allowable misalignment error is not exceeded.

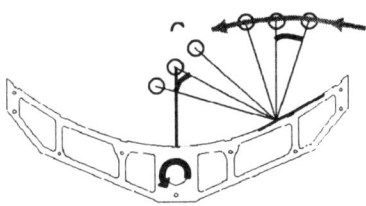

Fig. 2: Trough misalignment due to movement of the sun at 0.25 degrees/minute

Working backwards, two pulses correspond to an angle of 0,288°, which gives a maximum angular tracking error of $(0,5 \times 0,00503 \text{ rad}) = 2,513$ mrad or 0,144°. This represents the angular distance between A and B, or between B and C in figure 1. Having determined the number of

pulses to be used for each positioning step the behaviour of the Variable Speed Drive (VSD) must be defined. The VSD is capable of controlling motor drive speed from 685 rpm down to zero rpm, although for the sake of motor stability, speeds very near to zero are best avoided. At the same time, it is advisable to avoid a situation where the VSD has to switch on and off too quickly in order to cover each 0,288° step. The faster the trough rotates, the shorter the "on-time" of the VSD. VSD behaviour should therefore represent a compromise between these competing constraints. A reasonable "on-time" for the VSD-motor combination is 4 seconds. This would require a trough angular speed of $0,288°/4 = 0,072°/s$. Working back through the drive train, the gearbox input speed, or VSD output speed, would therefore equal 33,336°/sec or 5,556 rpm. Since the sun moves at 0,25°/min or 0,004167°/s the time interval between corrective steps would be 69,12 seconds. The VSD should switch on for 4 seconds at 5,556 rpm every 69,12 seconds. This would rotate the trough through exactly two pulses on the encoder.

3. PSA CONTROL

The Plataforma Solar de Almeria (PSA) algorithm, by means of mathematical calculations that is synchronised to the controller clock, locates the Sun's position to maintain the trough position. The value of the Sun's location is applied as an input to the control algorithm. The encoder detects the trough position and generates a counter data signal to the controller that is interpreted as an angle value and compared to the calculated position of the Sun. An output signal is applied to the drive that positions the trough to keep pace, as discussed with reference to figure 2. The trough is positioned in the North-South axis in order to track the sun in the East-West direction. The constants applied to the control algorithm are the longitude and latitude based on the geographical location of the trough and the variable will be the instantaneous universal time extracted from the processor of the controller. The counter was initially configured as a single rotary encoder. Due to the effects of the wind speed less than 10 knots, the counter generated a pulse signal indicating movement. This resulted in the control algorithm generating a corrective action thereby causing the trough to move out of position. Once the trough was positioned for maximum radiation it became impossible to control the position. This resulted in an efficiency curve that will slowly deteriorate as indicated in figure 3 until a corrected signal is generated. The counter was then configured as a quadruple rotary encoder in order to increase resolution. This not only resulted in a more stable control condition, but also made it possible to convert the 2,500-pulse encoder to a 10,000 pulse signal in the software. Another problem that was encountered is the final angle of the

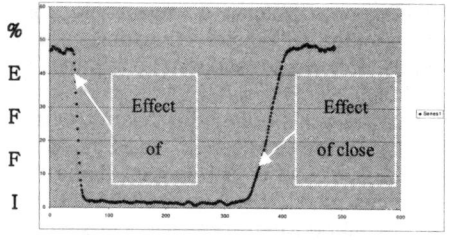

Fig. 3: The deterioration of efficiency that is corrected by the control algorithm

4. KNOWLEDGE BASED ALGORITHM

A fuzzy logic controller, an intelligent control algorithm that is knowledge based, will determine the output signal to the fluid pump, whilst the PSA algorithm determines the trough position. This mode of control is different in that it is knowledge-based and three inputs, i.e. fluid temperature, wind speed and light intensity are required to determine the flow rate of the fluid. After naming the inputs and outputs the membership functions had to be defined, for each input and output. The trapezoid form was used for the inputs, in order to increase the number of corner points, for clear distinction of one function from the other. The output was inserted as singleton. The rules were then edited in the inference engine, in either the rule table or rule matrix form. Only the fluid temperature, light intensity and the drive speed will be analysed under this section. Figure 3 represents the knowledge engineering process in a generic form.

The membership functions (procedural knowledge) for both, the inputs and outputs, were derived from the plant variables; Wind speed, diffused and concentrated sunlight, fluid temperature, variable speed drive, for the specified band. The rules (declarative knowledge) for the intelligent system were

trough. Due to a tangent mathematical function the x-axis and y-axis had to be checked by means of the control software. This was necessary to check the value of the angle if it was greater than 180 degrees. Although the control algorithm, using the PSA calculation, can control the trough position optimally, wind speeds greater than 10 knots create a problem. Since high wind speeds has the effect of cooling the heat transfer fluid a knowledge based system will be considered.

derived from the following control variables; Data communication signal from anemometer, pyranometer and pyrheliometer, thermocouples, and data communication signal to variable speed drive, for the specified band.

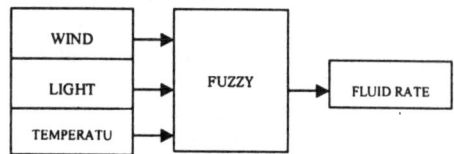

Fig. 4: Overview of the 3-input, 1-output controller

Table 1: Fluid Temperature (Actual)

MEMB. FUNCT.	V_h ot	hot	med	cold	v_cold
PT 1	30.0	44.6	59.2	70.8	88.3
PT 2	30.0	50.4	65.0	76.7	94.2
PT 3	44.6	59.2	70.8	88.3	100.0
PT 4	50.4	65.0	76.7	94.2	100.0

Table 2: Drive Speed

MEMB. FUNCT.	VALUE
V_slo	-100.0
Slo	-50.0
Stop	0.0
Fas	+50.0
V_fas	+100.0

Table 1: represents the edited input membership function in trapezoid form, for only fluid temperature. This facilitates fuzzification of a crisp value by scaling and mapping the input's domain, a linguistic variable, into an internal computer code. Table 2 represents the edited output membership function in singleton form, for the variable speed drive. This facilitates de-fuzzification of the internal computer code to a crisp value by scaling and mapping the output's domain. Table 3 represents all the assigned rules assigned. The system can be configured up to two hundred rules in total.

The facts and rules (declarative knowledge) are represented separately from decision-making algorithms (procedural knowledge). Rule#1states that *IF* the WIND_SPEED is weak and FLUID_TEMP is v_hot and LIGHT INTENSITY is high, *THEN* PUMP DRIVE = v_slo.

Table 3: Assigned Rules for the Knowledge Based System

Rule No.	Wind Speed	Fluid Temp	Light Intensity	Pump Drive
1	weak	v_hot	high	v_slo
2	strong	hot	high	v_slo
3	weak	cold	high	slo
4	strong	med	high	stop
5	weak	v_cold	high	v_fas
6	strong	v_hot	low	fas
7	weak	hot	low	slo
8	strong	cold	low	v_fas
9	weak	med	low	stop
10	strong	v_cold	low	v_slo

5. ANALYSIS OF RULE BASE

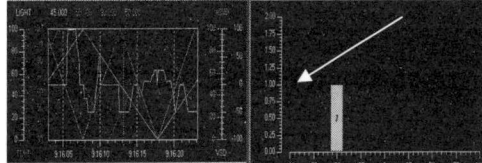

Fig. 5: 2-Dimensional analysis of Rule Base, indicating active rule

Figure 5 indicates that the active rule 7 is effective (indicated by the arrow in 1st diagram and represented by means of bar graph on 2nd diagram). Rule 7 states that IF wind speed is between 0.0-to-100.0 (weak) AND fluid temperature is between 88.3-to-100.0 (hot) AND light intensity is between 0.0-to-100.0 (low), THEN the variable speed drive must adjust to –50.0 (slo). The number 7 indicated on Figure 6 is rule 7 that is active in this region of the X-Y-Z axis. It can be seen that when the light intensity is *low* (the second membership function from the X-axis), and the fluid temperature is *hot* (the second membership function from the Y-axis), the drive speed is *slo* (the second membership function from the Z-axis. All the configured rules can be verified from Figure 6 in the same way. Along the X-axis is input one, wind speed. The adjoining areas that are slanted are the areas of the membership functions that overlap each other.

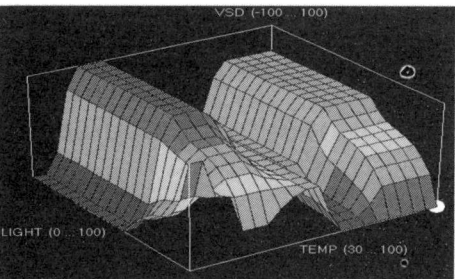

Figure. 6: 3-Dimensional analysis of Rule Base, in two views

6. CONCLUSION

Most solar tracking and control systems function in open loop mode. Using the PSA algorithm control is sufficient for the trough position but for stable temperature control of the heat transfer fluid an alternate control method is required. In the fuzzy control mode the light intensity, wind speed and the fluid temperature will be essential at various points to determine optimal solar-to-thermal conversion, for each available Watts/square metre solar energy. By regulating the fluid as efficiently as possible under varying light conditions, e.g. cloud cover, and varying wind conditions the available solar energy is converted with minimal wastage.

7. REFERENCES

1. **Glover J.D.**, **Sarma M**. *Power System Analysis and Design*. PWS. Boston. 1994.
2. **Johansson T.B**. *Renewable Energy*. Earthscan. London.1993. 213 – 296.
3. **Jamshidi M., Vadiee N., Ross T.J**. *Fuzzy Logic and Control*. Prentice Hall. Englewood Cliffs. 1993. 357 – 362.
4. **Kreith F., Kreider J.F. Principles of Solar Engineering**. HPC. New York. 1978. 203 – 309.
5. **Kosko B**. *Fuzzy Engineering*. Prentice Hall. Englewood Cliffs. 1997. 213 – 243.
6. **Markvart T.** Solar Electricity. John Wiley. New York. 2000. 75 – 110.
7. **Parsaei H.R., Jamshidi M**. *Design and Implementation of Intelligent Manufacturing Systems*. Prentice Hall. Upper Saddle River. 1995. 107 – 137.
8. **Ruan D.A**. *Fuzzy Set Theory* and *Advanced Mathematical Applications*. Kluwer. Netherlands. 1995. 245 – 262.
9. **Wang L. A** Course in Fuzzy Systems and Control. Prentice Hall. Upper Saddle River. 1997. 257 – 263.
10. **Wang L.** Adaptive Fuzzy Systems and Control. Prentice Hall. Upper Saddle River. 1994. 102 – 108.

GCMM 2004
Editors: Prasad K D V Yarlagadda and S Narayanan
Copyright © 2005, Vellore Institute of Technology, Vellore, India
Publisher: Narosa Publishing House Pvt. Ltd., New Delhi, India

Development of Computer Aided Tolerance Charting (G-CAT) From CAD Model

Sreeram Chand G, SuryaNarayana Rao K N V, Surendra Babu B, Madar Valli P*.

Dept. of Mechanical Engineering, College of Engineering,

GITAM, Rushikonda,

Visakapatnam – 530045, A.P.

*Email: drpmv@gitam.edu

Abstract

A tolerance chart is a graphical representation of a process plan and manual procedure for controlling tolerance stackup when the machining of a component involves interdependent tolerance chains. The tolerance chart has been used as an effective tool to ensure that, a specific processing sequence is appropriate for a product of the required dimensions. Manual computation of tolerance chart is both tedious and time consuming. This heuristic experience based method of planning sequencing based on tolerances of individual cuts of a process plan can be embodied in a computer based module. This paper presents a simplified approach for deriving a process sequence directly from a CAD model using G-CAT (Gitam-Computer Aided Tolerance Charting). This helps in reducing time by avoiding lengthy calculations by giving efficient process sequence.

Key Words
Tolerance, Tolerance stackup, Process tolerance, Dimensional matrix, Process tolerance matrix

1. INTRODUCTION

A basic concept of design and manufacturing is the transformation of functional requirements into proper descriptions in engineering drawings of individual components, followed by production of parts satisfying the specified dimensions. Because of the limitation of machine accuracy, manufacturing will produce parts whose dimensions are within certain ranges rather than specific quantities. Appropriate tolerances in the design phase based on functional requirements and manufacturing capacity can certainly relax the difficulties in production.

For effective integration of design and production, tolerance charts were introduced as a means of the manufacturing process. A tolerance chart [1] is a graphical representation of the dimensions of a work piece through a sequence of machining operation. In tolerance chart, based on information provided by engineering blue print, process planner copies relevant dimensions to the chart and then he assigns a machine tool, datum surface and machined surface for an operation. The planner should be aware of machine productivities and accuracy limitations from manufacturing database. With this knowledge the planner has to do some calculations before arriving for a proper sequence. But the difficulty is at tolerance stackup, i.e. the accumulation of tolerances of machining process and may exceed the blue print tolerances. To avoid this, process planner has to go through some series of calculations to obtain optimal sequence.

This paper presents a simplified approach for deriving a process sequence directly from a CAD model and consists two modules. First module consists of recognition of dimensions, dimensional tolerances and surfaces from an Auto-CAD 2D model. In second module, the data obtained in the first module is used. With this data, a dimensional relationship is developed between all the surfaces in matrix forms along with their tolerances. From these matrices number of possible sequence(s) are developed and an optimum sequence is selected.

2. LITERATURE REVIEW

In this section we present a review of the key operational dimensioning and tolerancing schemes proposed in the past. At the end of this sections we evaluate these schemes against the three criterion mentioned in the introduction.

Xiaoqing and Davies [2] proposed a matrix tree chain method for automatically tracing the dimensional chains instead of doing in manually as in tolerance chart. Mean working dimensions were then calculated similar to tolerance chart. Initial tolerance to each working dimension was assigned based on experience or industrial standards and iterative adjustments were then made until satisfactory results are obtained but this process is iterative. Whybrew et al. [3] proposed a rooted tree method based on graph theoretic approach to represent dimensional chains. It was assumed that stock removal and tolerance for each step is already known. It was just a method to check the allocated tolerances and mean working dimensions using an algorithm instead of doing it manually using tolerance chart. Mittal et al. [4] proposed a method of representing machining sequence graphically. An algorithm was then used for identifying the machining cuts which contribute to the stack up of

tolerances for every B/P dimension and stock removal. A LP model was then used to allocate tolerances to each individual machining cut. Ngoi and Teck [5] proposed a path tracing method to trace the process links and then represent then using linear equations. These linear equations were then solved to obtain working dimensions using gauss elimination technique. Tolerances were allocated based on a LP with sum of weighted tolerances as an objective function and blue print tolerances and process capabilities as constraints. Ji [6] proposed a method of allocating tolerances based on a LP model with an objective function of maximizing the sum of assigned tolerances. The stock removal, blue print tolerances and economic tolerance for each machining operation were used as constraints.

Tang et al. [7] proposed yet another LP model for the optimal allocation of process tolerances and stock removals. The objective function was to minimize the production cost with process tolerances and stock removal as decision variables. The constraints for the LP model were derived from the dimensional chains associated with tolerance chart. Ngoi and Fang [8] proposed a branch and link approach to work out machining surfaces after finding working dimensions. After finding out process links balancing of tolerances is done rather then finding out the optimal tolerance stackup. Its major drawback was directly balancing tolerances which may be avoiding the best process.

The literature review of tolerance allocation methods reveals that most of the methods formulate the problem as an optimization problem but are based on the principles of tolerance charting. Methods differ from each other in the choice of objective function and constraints. Most of the papers consider the cost minimization or tolerance maximization as an objective function. Design tolerance requirements, machining allowance etc are normally considered as constraints. To summarize, we can say that most of the methods try to automate the tolerance charting procedure by the method of linear or non-linear programming by considering working dimensions and stock removal, but no one has considered to have a process based on tolerance stackup which reduces most of computations and at the same time to obtain data automatically from CAD model.

3. TOLERANCE CHAINS AND TOLERANCE STACKUP

The most crucial work of in tolerance chart generation is the assignment of working dimensions. The difficulty originates from the tolerance stack-up problem. For a derived dimension in a dimension chain, the resultant tolerance is always accumulated from individual tolerances even through the resultant nominal (mean) size may be the summation or difference of individual nominal sizes. This is shown in the figure 1. The chains involved in the tolerance chart can be considered in terms of two classes. On one hand, the dimensions of each row in the process section compose a dimension chains. On the other hand, every balanced dimension can form another chain because it can be derived from the dimensions of preceding operations.

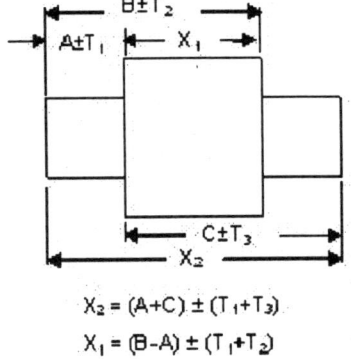

$$X_2 = (A+C) \pm (T_1 + T_3)$$
$$X_1 = (B-A) \pm (T_1 + T_2)$$

Figure 1: The nature of tolerance stack-up problem

4. TOLERANCE CHART

Used for decades, tolerance chart still remains the most powerful tool for tolerance allocation (or to be more accurate, for checking the stackup of tolerances). The main idea behind tolerance chart is to find the dimensional chains for the final blue print dimensions and then allocate the individual tolerances so that the blue print tolerance is not violated. The steps involved in constructing a tolerance chart can be summarized as follows (refer to [1] for a detailed procedure on constructing a tolerance chart):

1. List all the final (blue print) dimensions and tolerances.

2. Find out the dimensional chains involved in these final dimensions.
3. Allocate tolerances to all the individual links of these chains so as to achieve the tolerances associated with blue print dimensions, even in worst case.
4. Allocate tolerances to all other remaining cuts based on process knowledge.
5. From these allocated tolerances, find out the variation in stock removal for each machining cut.
6. Add a safety stock to get the mean stock removal for each cut.
7. Based on stock removal for each cut, work backwards from the finishing cuts, to find the working dimension for each of the pre-finishing cuts.

Looking into these seven steps it can be said that constructing a tolerance chart manually is quite a laborious task. For a complex part, this manual procedure could not only be inefficient but also error prone. For this reason, numbers of researchers in past several years have tried to automate the process of tolerance charting.

5. THE PROPOSED METHODOLOGY

This method mainly works by obtaining the blue print dimensions and tolerances from an Auto CAD 2D drawing and calculating the tolerance stackup. Process sequencing for a turning component is discussed to explain the method. Initially the required drawing is produced in AutoCAD in 2D with its details such as its dimensions, dimensional tolerances and datum. The turning component considered for explaining the process sequence is shown in the figure 2. As this component is axi-symmetric only the section above the center line is considered.

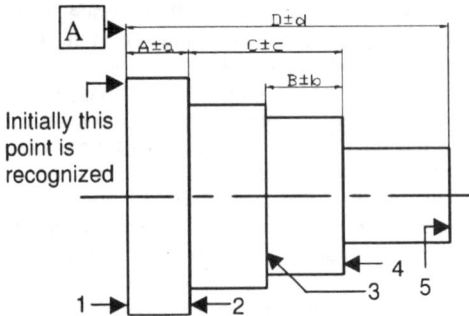

Figure 2: The turning component used for process sequence

From the figure show in the figure 2, the top left corner point 'A' is initially recognized. With help of this recognized point 'A' any entity associated with this point is taken and is checked for horizontality. If an entity is proved to be horizontal, then its length is obtained. And later, if any dimension and dimensional tolerances are associated with the horizontal entity, they are extracted. Now the vertical surfaces associated with the recognized horizontal entity's are recognized and numbered as 'i' for left side vertical surface and 'j' where j = i + 1 for right side vertical surface. These 'i' and 'j' represent surface numbers and numbering starts from one. At the same time the distance between the horizontal entity and the centre line is obtained and with this one, diameter of the surface 'i, j' is determined. The above process is repeated for next horizontal entity associated with vertical surface 'j' and numbering of vertical surfaces will be i=i+1 and j=j+1. This process is repeated for all horizontal surfaces above the center line. At the end, a vertical surface associated with primary datum is recognized. All the data extracted form drawing is stored in data file.

The stored data is then used to build dimensional relation matrix as shown in the table.1. Using mathematical calculations the final dimensional relation matrix is developed which gives dimensions between all the surfaces as shown in table.2. Process tolerances for all dimensions shown in table.3 are taken from ANSI Standard Tolerances based on lengths of the surfaces but small alphabets a, b, etc. represent design tolerances given in drawing. The process tolerances of all dimensions are shown in table.3. Each element (i, j) in the table.3 corresponds to the process tolerance of element (I, j) in final dimension matrix shown in table.2. Now possible sequences are generated with the help of permutations making the vertical surface which is associated with primary datum as a initial surface and sequence for other surfaces are generated. By using sequences generated, by order of surface numbers, the process tolerances are of these surface numbers are used to find their tolerance stackup. From the generated sequences, the sequence(s) having minimum tolerance stackup is taken and given as optimal sequence(s).

Table 1: Initial dimensional relationship matrix

Surface No.s	1	2	3	4	5
1	0	A			D
2		0	C		
3			0	B	
4				0	
5					0

Table 2: Final dimensional relationship matrix

Surface No.s	1	2	3	4	5
1	0	A	A+C-B	A+C	D
2		0	C-B	C	D-A
3			0	B	D+B-A-C
4				0	D-A-C
5					0

Table 3: Process tolerance matrix

Surface No.s	1	2	3	4	5
1	0	a12	a	a14	d
2		0	a23	c	a25
3			0	b	a35
4				0	a45
5					0

6. CASE STUDY

The above explained method is applied for the figure.3. By using Auto Lisp here initially top left corner point is recognized and stored as point 'pt1'. Now with the help of point 'pt1', the entities associated with this point are checked for horizontality and then a horizontal entity is taken. The vertical surfaces associated with this are numbered as 1 and 2. Later the length of the horizontal entity 20 is obtained with help of its starting and end points and dimension and its dimensional tolerance from the dimensional entity associated for this horizontal entity are also obtained. In the same way all dimensions and tolerances associated with all horizontal entites are obtained and at the same time the numbers of surfaces are also obtained. The surface associated with primary datum (here surface no. 1) is also recognized. During recognition of surfaces and dimensions, to know whether each required entity is recognized its colour property is changed. The total data obtained is written to a data file.

From the data file, with help of 'C' language dimensions are read along with their surface numbers and arranged into a matrix from. Now with these, the remaining dimensional relations with other surfaces are computed and given as shown in table 4. Based on the values of the dimensions and with the given design tolerances values, process tolerance matrix is developed as shown in table 5. The process tolerance values will be in micrometers. Here as surface "1" is primary datum it is produced initially. Using surface "1" as initial surface, possible sequences are generated along with their stackup values. From these sequences, the sequence(s) having the least stackup value is given as output.

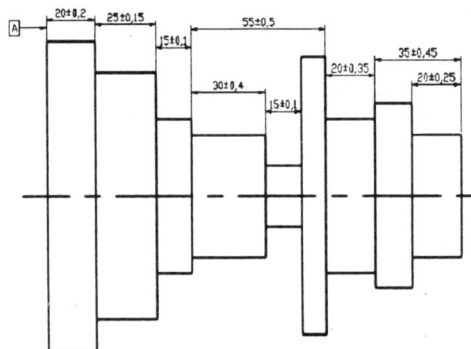

Figure 3: Example for case study

6.1 Output File from Auto LISP and Input File to C Program

The output file from Auto LISP and input for C program is shown here.

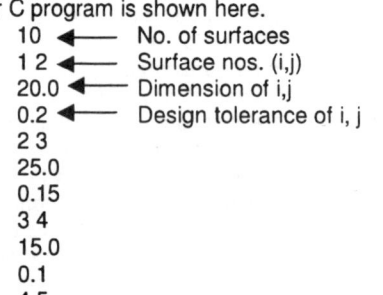

10 ◄——— No. of surfaces
1 2 ◄——— Surface nos. (i,j)
20.0 ◄——— Dimension of i,j
0.2 ◄——— Design tolerance of i, j
2 3
25.0
0.15
3 4
15.0
0.1
4 5
30.0
0.4
4 7
55
0.5
5 6
15.0
0.1
7 8
20.0
0.35
8 10
35.0
0.45
9 10
20.0
0.25
1 ◄——— Surface associated with primary datum

6.2 Output from C program

The below table.4 and table.5 are the output from C program and represents final dimensional relation matrix and process tolerance matrix respectively.

Table 4: Final dimensional relation matrix

0	20	45	60	90	105	115	135	150	170
20	0	25	40	70	85	95	115	130	150
45	25	0	15	45	60	70	90	105	125
60	40	15	0	30	45	55	75	90	110
90	70	45	30	0	15	25	45	60	80
105	85	60	45	15	0	10	30	45	65
115	95	70	55	25	10	0	20	35	55
135	115	90	75	45	30	20	0	15	35
150	130	105	90	60	45	35	15	0	20
170	150	125	110	80	65	55	35	20	0

608

Table 5: Process Tolerance Matrix (in μm)

0	200	160	190	220	220	220	250	250	250
200	0	150	160	190	220	220	220	250	250
160	150	0	100	160	190	190	220	220	250
190	160	100	0	400	160	190	190	220	220
220	190	160	400	0	100	130	160	190	220
220	220	190	160	100	0	150	160	160	190
220	220	190	190	130	150	0	350	160	190
250	220	220	190	160	160	350	0	250	160
250	250	220	220	190	160	160	250	0	250
250	250	250	220	220	190	190	160	250	0

With the help of both final dimensional relation matrix and process tolerance matrix the process sequences are generated and sequences with least tolerance stackup are given as:

Table 6: Sequences of surface no.s with their Stackup

Sequences of surface no.s	Stackup (μm)
1 8 2 10 3 4 6 5 7 9	1390
1 8 6 5 7 9 4 3 10 2	1390
1 8 5 7 9 6 4 3 10 2	1390
1 8 5 6 9 7 4 3 10 2	1390

7 CONCLUSION

The proposed method eliminates the heuristic process of tolerance chart and simplifies process sequences by directly using G-CAT which is based on 2D CAD drawing with the help of Auto LISP and C program. This method can be generalized for other formats of drawings like IGES, DXF, STEP etc.

8 REFERENCES

1. **Eary D.F. and Johnson G.E.** "*Process Engineering for Manufacturing*" Prentice Hall, Englewood Cliffs, NJ, 1962.

2. **Tang Xiaoqing and B. J. Davies** (1988), "Computer Aided Dimensional Planning", *International Journal of Production Research*, Vol. 26, No. 2, pp. 283-297.

3. **K. Whybrew, G. A. Britton, D. F. Robinson and Y. Sermsuti-anuwat** (1990), "A Graph- Theoretic Approach to Tolerance Charting", *International Journal of Advanced Manufacturing Technology*, Vol. 5, pp. 175-183,

4. **R. O. Mittal, S. A. Irani and E. A. Lehtihet** (1990), "Tolerance Control in the Machining of Discrete Components", *Journal of Manufacturing Systems*, Vol. 9, No. 3, pp. 233-246.

5. **Ngoi, B. K. A., and C. T. Ong** (1993), "A complete tolerance charting system", *International Journal of Production Research*, Vol. 31, No. 2, pp. 453-469.

6. **Ji, P.** (1993), "A linear programming model for tolerance assignment in a tolerance chart", *International Journal of Production Research*, Vol. 31, No. 3, pp. 739-751.

7. **Tang, G. R., R. Kung and J. Y. Chen** (1994), "Optimal allocation of process tolerances and stock removals", *International Journal of Production Research*, Vol. 32, No. 1, pp. 25- 35.

8. **B.K.A.Ngoi and S.L Fang** (1994), "Computer aided tolerance charting", *International Journal of Production Research*, Vol. 32, No. 8, pp. 1939-1954.

GCMM 2004
Editors: Prasad K D V Yarlagadda and S Narayanan
Copyright © 2005, Vellore Institute of Technology, Vellore, India
Publisher: Narosa Publishing House Pvt. Ltd., New Delhi, India

Magnetorheological Fluid and Smart Damper for Forced Vibration Control

Soundarapandian S & Nagendran N

*Dept of Mechanical Engineering, SACS MAVMM Engineering College, Madurai – 625 301

Rathinavel Pandian M & Alfin Leo A

3 4Dept of Mechanical Engineering, Vellore Institute of Technology, Vellore – 632014

Email: subashpandiyan@yahoo.com, alfinleo@rediffmail.com

Abstract

Conventional suspension system has the problem of limited damping effect and less life. In this project, we have taken Bajaj Chetak scooter shock absorber as a reference and we have found the problem in this shock absorber that high frequency of vibration and low damping effect. This project has given an idea to design a damper by using MR fluid. This system has not given only cushion effect and also absorbs shocks, which are not possible in conventional suspension system. MR (Magneto Rheological) Fluid is just like that a smart material, which transforms from a liquid state to solid state. These fluids because thicker (like colloidal gel) when it is magnetized and hence used as a most active damper. An electro magnet may be used to magnetize this fluid. Design procedure has given an idea to use MR fluid instead of SAE 20 W 40 oil. It absorbs shock greater than that of commercial shock absorbers. Magneto Rheological (MR) fluid properties and SAE 20 W 40 oil have been analyzed in ANSYS that shows better results. The system provide fast, smooth, continuously variable damping in a cost effective and reliable package that reduces body motion and increases tire road contact an all surfaces.

Keywords
Damping Effect, Shock Absorber, Magneto Rheological

1. INTRODUCTION

A vehicle suspension along with tyres and steering linkages is designed for safe vehicle control and to be free from vibrations. Therefore, suspension designs are a compromise between ride softness and handling ability. Suspension system therefore must not only absorb shock and support the automobile weight but it must keep the tyre in contact with the road to ensure vehicle control. Shock absorbers are a key component of all automobiles. They control the vehicle suspension movement to provide stable and comfortable ride, nowadays a novel suspension system has to be implemented which will react the shock. They have produced an electronically adjustable, active, intelligent suspension system. Intelligent suspension system has a each shock absorbers adjust its self, when a wheel hits a bump in the road surface in flashes a message in three hundred milli seconds to the electronic unit. Which updates the adjustments an each wheel. This produced an idle suspension based on road condition, speed and level of comfort required. For the auto engineers in this suspension allows quicker calibration and suspension turning for new vehicles. For drivers, in this system offers a flatter, smoother ride, enhanced later and longitudinal control of body movement, and better road isolation from the passenger compartment.

2. SUSPENSION SYSTEM

Early automotive suspensions have derived from the suspension system used on horse drawn carts. The primary function of the suspension is to isolate the vehicle and its occupants from shocks and vibrations generated by the road surface while maintaining steering control and stability at all times. The first task concerns the ride whereas the other two concern handling. It is to be remembered that ride is a measure of the ability of the suspension to handle mostly vertical forces applied at ground level, whilst handling is affected much more by horizontal forces acting on the center of gravity and by ground level couples. Generally speaking, a soft suspension gives good isolation from road irregularities whereas a stiffer suspension gives better handling characteristics. These traditionally opposed design requirements pose tremendous challenges to suspension system developers.

Hydraulic shock absorber develops resistance to the spring action by forcing a fluid through check valves and a small hole. There are two chambers in this type. The outer chamber serves as a reservoir. This outer chamber contains another inner chamber, which acts as a cylinder. The cylinder contains a piston and a valve, which are connected to a rod. This piston valve arrangement system divides the cylinder into upper and lower chambers. The upper chamber is called rebound chamber and the lower one is called compression chamber. When the road spring is compressed, the piston valve arrangement moves into the lower chamber of the cylinder thereby compressing the fluid in the chamber. The incompressible fluid opens the valve and enters in the upper chamber. Some of the fluid rushes into the outer chamber by opening the inlet compression valve lasted at the bottom of the cylinder. When the spring rebounds, the fluid resistance in the shock absorber produces its effect on it. When the

piston valve arrangement is pulled up, the valve in the piston is closed, and at this stage, due to increase in pressure, it opens in the other direction.

3. MR FLUIDS

Magneto rheological (MR) fluids belong to the class of controllable fluids. The essential characteristic of MR fluids in their ability to reversibly change from free flowing, linear viscous liquid to semi-solids having controllable yield strength in milliseconds when exposed to a magnetic field. This feature provides simple, quiet, rapid-response interfaces between electronic controls and mechanical systems.

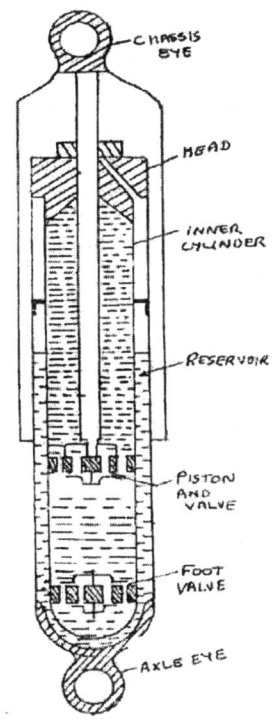

Fig.1: Components of shock absorber

MR fluid dampers are relatively new semi-active devices that utilize MR fluids to provide controllable damping forces. In the absence of a magnetic field, MR fluid flows freely or allows free movement. Upon application of a magnetic field, the fluid's particles align with the direction of the field in chain-like fashion, thereby restricting the fluid's movement within the gap in proportion to the strength of the field.

Table .1. Shows the Properties of MR Fluids

Max. Yield stress	50-100 kPa
Max. field	250kA/m (limited by saturation)
Viscosity	0.1-1.0Pa-s
Operable Temp. Range	-40 to +150 □ C (limited by carrier fluid)
Stability	Unaffected by most impurities
Response time	< milliseconds
Density	3-4 g/cm^3
Max. energy density	0.1 joule/cm^3
Power supply (typical)	2-25 V @ 1-2 A (2-50watts)

Under common flow conditions, no separation is observed between particles and the carrier fluid. A degree of separation may eventually occur under static conditions, but low-shear agitation (shaking or remixing) prior to use will easily re-disperse the particles into a homogeneous state. A typical MR fluid contains 20-40% by volume of relatively pure, soft iron particles, e.g., carbonyl iron; these particles are suspended in mineral oil, synthetic oil, water or glycol. A variety of proprietary additives similar to those found in commercial lubricants are commonly added to discourage gravitational settling and promote particle suspension, enhance lubricity, modify viscosity, and inhibit wear. The ultimate strength of an MR fluid depends on the square of the saturation magnetization of the suspended particles. The key to a strong MR fluid is to choose a particle with a large saturation magnetization.

4. METHODOLOGY

Conventional shock absorbers use oil passing through orifices to dampen suspension movement. When a tire hits a bump, the suspension moves up, moving the body of the shock absorber up too. So the conventional suspension system has the problem of limiting damping effect and less life. These problems have to be solved by changing the fluid in the system, Conventional suspending fluids have to be replaced in lieu of MR fluid in the shock absorber. Use of MR fluids in this system has to decrease the vibration of the vehicle. So the driving of vehicle and the passenger has felt that it is comfortable. This fluid can accommodate any road condition that shows from the analysis and result of this system.

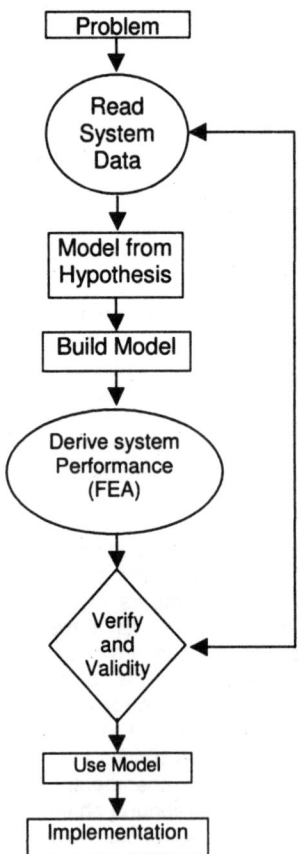

Fig.2: Algorithm for Magnetorheological Fluid and Smart Damper

5. RESULTS AND DISCUSSION
5.1 Design Procedure
5.1.1 Specification of spring

- Outer diameter (Do) = 60mm = 6 cm
- Coil diameter (d) = 7.5mm = 0.075 cm
- Number of coil spring (n) = 16
- Modulus of rigidity(G) = $84*10^9$ pa
- Vehicle unload condition = 96 kg [Bajaj chetak manual]
- Vehicle load condition (p)
  =96+60 = 156 kg
- One man on the vehicle assume the weight of the man = 60 kg (Assume)
  [The Bajaj Chetak vehicle has two shock absorber in the rear wheel
  [So the vehicle load is divided by the each one. The load is half of the total load]

Vehicle load, P = $\frac{156}{2}$ = 78 kg or 780N

Engine speed maximum = 5200 rpm (Bajaj Chetak manual)

5.1.2 Deflection of the Spring (δ)

$$\delta = \frac{8npD^3}{Gd^4}$$

D = Do-d = 60-7.5 = 52.5mm
D = 0.0525m

$$\delta = \frac{8(16).(780).(0.0525^3)}{84.(10^9).[(7.5).(10^{-3})]^4}$$

δ = 0.05436m

δ = 54mm

5.1.3 Stiffness of the Spring (S)

$$S = \frac{\cdot\ load}{Deflection} = \frac{780}{0.05436} = 14348.785 \text{ N/m}$$

5.1.4 Angular Velocity (ω)
$$\omega = \frac{2.\pi.N}{60} = \frac{2.\pi.(5200)}{60} = 544.542 \text{ rad / sec}$$

5.1.5 Static Force (F)
$F = m.\omega^2.r$
Mass of engine (m) = 18kg (bajaj chetak manual)
Stroke (l) = 57mm, Cank radius (r) = 57/2
= 28mm
r = 0.0285m (bajaj chetak manual) and F = 152.117 KN

5.1.6 Damping co efficient of MR Fluid
Damping coefficient (c) = $\frac{load}{velocity}$
For 20 ton MR fluid damper velocity
= 0.1 m/sec
$$c = \frac{20 \text{ ton}}{0.1} = \frac{20 \times (10^3)}{0.1}$$

For MR fluid (c) = $2 \times (10^5)$ N/(m/s)

5.1.7 Amplitude of Forced Vibration for SAE20W40 Oil (x_{max})

$$x_{max} = \frac{F}{[c^2\omega^2 + (s-m\omega^2)^2]^{0.5}}$$

[c = 1040 (assume)]

$$= \frac{152.117(10^3)}{[(1040.(544.542))^2 + (14348.8 - 156.(544.542)^2)^2]^{0.5}}$$

x_{max} = 3.29.(10^{-3})m

5.1.8 Amplitude of Forced Vibration for MR Fluid (x_{max})

$$x_{max} = F / [c^2\omega^2 + (s-m\omega^2)^2]^{0.5}$$

$$= \frac{152.117.(10^3)}{[\{(20\times(10^5))^2.(544.542)^2\} + \{14348.8156.(544.542^2)\}^2]^{0.5}}$$

x_{max} = 1.3955 x (10^{-4})m

Magneto-rheological (MR) fluid damper unsurpassed in its combination of controllability, responsiveness, and energy density. As a magnetic field is applied to the MR fluid inside, the damping characteristics of the fluid increase with practically infinite precision. Featuring straightforward controls, simple design, and quiet operation, this MR damper is especially well suited for suspension applications.

6. CONCLUSIONS

The significant conclusions of this work is presented here,

1. DEFLECTION OF THE SPRING
   : 54mm
2. STIFFNESS OF THE SPRING
   : 14348.785N/m
3. ANGULAR VELOCITY
   : 544.542rad/sec
4. STATIC FORCE
   : 152.117 x 10^3 N
5. DAMPING COFFICIENT (SAE 20W40 OIL) : 1040 N/m/sec
6. DAMPING COFFICIENT (MR FLUID)
   : 20 x 10^5 N/m/sec
7. AMPLITUDE OF FORCED VIBRATION (FOR SAE 20W40 OIL)
   :3.29 x 10^{-3} m
8. AMPLITUDE OF FORCED VIBRATION (FOR MR FLUID)
   : 1.395 x 10^{-4}m

Design procedure has given an idea to use MR fluid instead of SAE 20w40 oil. Magneto Rheological (MR) fluid properties have been analyzed in ANSYS that shows better results. The results obtain through the finite element method are gnizable and comparable (Results are Shown in Fig 2 to 5). MR fluids are to bring variable damping to high-performance levels currently unmatched in the industry. It helps overcome the traditional tradeoffs between ride and handling by delivering increased maximum damping forces with lightning-quick response. It also delivers ultra-quiet operation in a durable, cost-effective package.

MR fluids enables lightning-quick response and a valve-less damper design, resulting in never-before-seen levels of performance, virtually silent operation, and the elimination of electromechanical valves. In operation, of the system's electronic control unit continually sends electrical currents to electromagnetic coils housed in the dampers. The currents dictate the MR fluids yield stress, which in turn determines damping resistance.

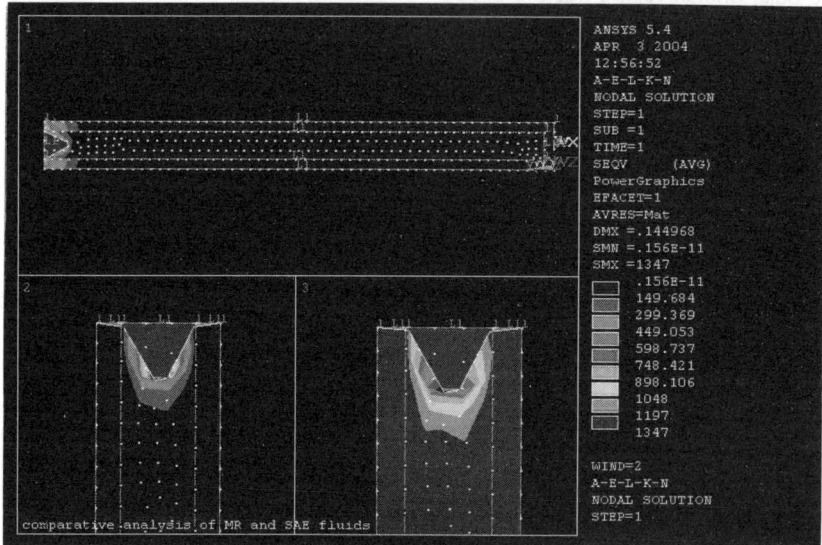

Fig . 3: Shows the Comparative Analysis of SAE20W40 and MR Fluids

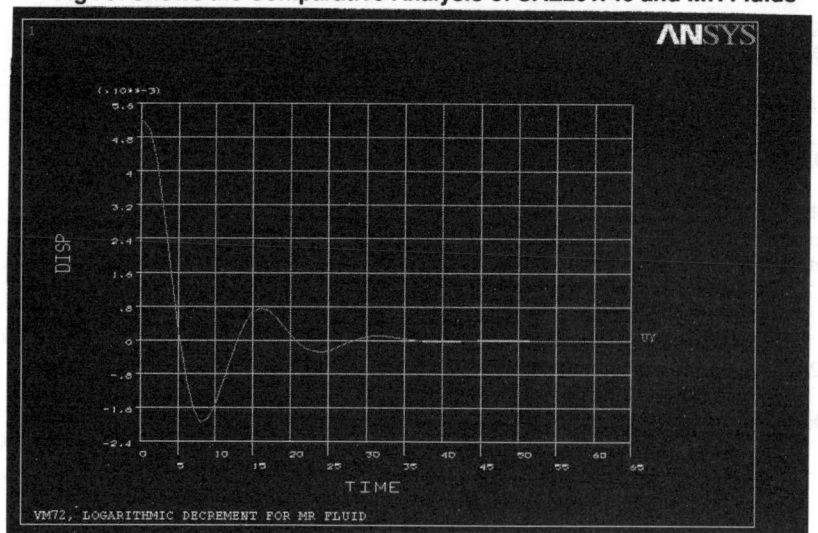

Fig . 4: Shows the Amplitude of forced vibration of MR Fluid

614

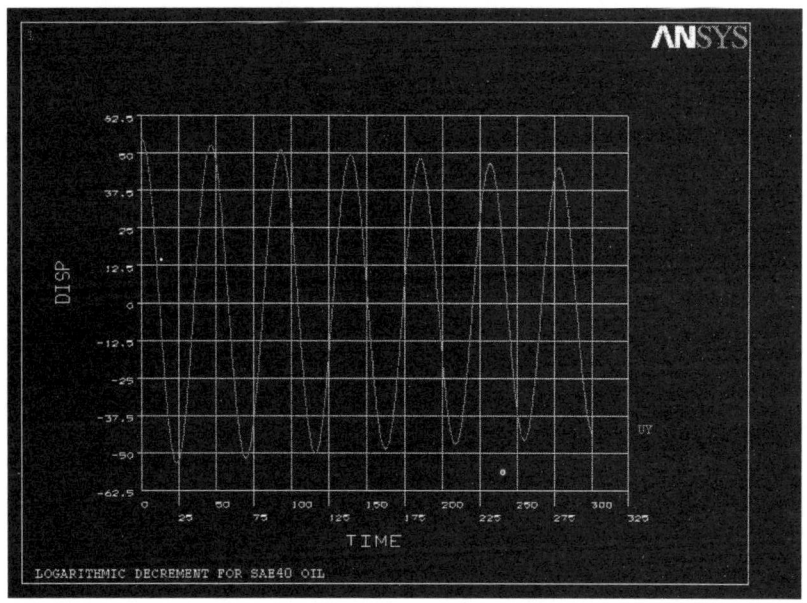

Fig . 5: Shows the Amplitude of Forced Vibration of SAE20W40

7. REFERENCES

1   **Fiona Lowrie, Markys Cain, Mark Stewart and Mark Gee**, "Time dependent Behaviour of Piezo-Electric Materials" , *NPL Report CMMT (A)* 151, March 1999.

2   **Sims N D, Stanway R and Johnson A R,** "Vibration Control Using Smart Fluids: A State of the Art Review", *The Shock and Vibration Digest*, 31(2), 195-203 (1993)

3   **Spencer B F** , " Phenonmenal model for Magneto rheological Dampers" *Journal of Engineering Mechanics* (3), 230 – 238, 1997

4   **Ramalingam K K,** "Automobile Engineering" *SciTech Publictions* (2001), *Journal of Engineering Mechanics* (3), 230 – 238, 1997

GCMM 2004
Editors: Prasad K D V Yarlagadda and S Narayanan

Predicting the Uncertainty of Multi-Axis Machines by Probabilistic Model

Sompoap Talabgaew, Ph.D.
Department of Teacher Training in Mechanical Engineering
King Mongkut's Institute of Technology North Bangkok
1518 Pibulsongkram RD., Bangkok, Thailand 10800
Email: sompoap@yahoo.com

Abstract

This research develops an alternative approach for the prediction of uncertainty of coordinate measuring machines (CMMs) using geometric error information in each axis or repeatedly measured coordinates. It also introduces a procedure to calculate the probability of accepting a measured position within a specified range. The developed model has resulted in an improvement in the probability of accepting a measured position, compared to previously published models and results. The model may also be used for determining an optimal tolerance for the manufacturing measurement processes and provides less costly approach for evaluating the performance of coordinate measuring machines.

Keywords: Uncertainty, Performance, Tolerance

1. Introduction

The performance of a coordinate measuring machine (CMM) may be simply defined as its ability to perform its measurement function effectively under specified operating condition [3]. To ensure valid measurement results, all measurements should be presented with their measurement uncertainty [12].

While moving, there are many noise factors affecting CMMs' probe head. For this reason, probe position at the workpiece surface may deviate from target position. Large errors at the measured position significantly deteriorate the accuracy of a CMM and adversely affect its performance. Uncertainty of CMM can be explained as the interval in which 95% of the measured values are placed [14].

2. Coordinate Measuring Machine Errors

Systematic error and random error are the two major errors in a CMM environment [10, 12].

2.1 Systematic error

Specifically, systematic error is defined as the worst possible error at a specified position [1]. The systematic errors can occur when an error in the relative position between the measured position and the probe exists. CMMs cannot perform an exact measurement on the workpiece because of the difference of coordinate systems as shown in Figure 1.

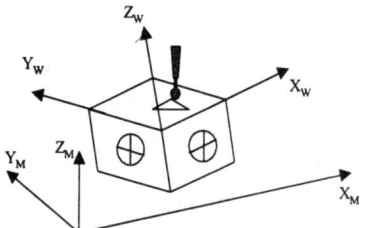

Figure 1: The relative errors caused by the different coordinate systems between the workpiece and CMM

2.2 Random error

Random errors or precision uncertainties vary under operating conditions for example the environmental conditions, the skill of operators, the imperfection of workpiece or CMM itself, etc. so it is safely assumed that every measured position cannot be determined without a certain degree of measurement uncertainty. Furthermore, a measurement between two arbitrary selected points in a workpiece surface, the systematic error between two randomly chosen points can only be treated as random because of the lack of specific knowledge of the existing errors and where they come from. By this reason, the error component relating to the total errors can only be treated as randomly independent.

3. The performance of CMM

The performance of CMM is defined as the ability to perform its function effectively under specified and operating conditions [2]. As known, the main function of CMM has been used for the purpose of workpiece inspection after machining and what industry highly expects from CMM is its accuracy. However, there are several measurement characteristics e.g. accuracy, repeatability, reproducibility and linearity involved when evaluating a CMM since the bias or accuracy of a CMM can be calibrated, the only remaining error is that due to uncertainty.

Recently, it has been said that all measurement results should be presented with their measurement uncertainty or precision [8]. In CMMs' operation, uncertainty can arise from various sources as shown in Figure 2 [7].

While a CMM is performing the measurement, there are many factors causing an error at the probe position. Theoretically, when probe head touches the target position on workpiece surface, the probe position at target position (in 2 or 3-dimension) is translated to be a reading position that is ideally assumed to be as same coordinate as the true coordinate in CAD or drawing. However, in reality, while probe head is moving, there are many noise factors e.g. probe systems, coordinate systems, environments and software & hardware affecting its performing, by this reason, probe position at workpiece surface may deviate from target position. The larger error at measured position, the worse accuracy of CMM and also the worse performance of CMM.

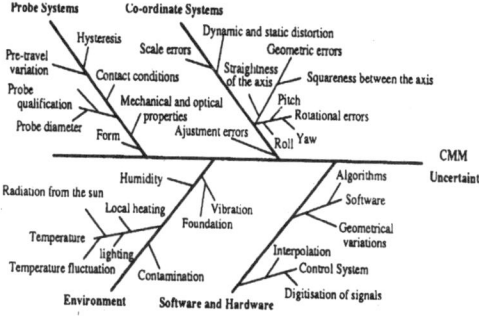

Figure 2: The potential factors contributing to CMM uncertainty

Theoretically, the precision of CMM can be explained as the interval in which 95% of the measured values are placed in this interval [9]. For example, in most cases, if a CMM repeatedly makes measurement and there are at least 95 % of all measured values lie within a tolerance zone of measurement specification, it can be said that this CMM has high performance (in term of tolerance zone specification). Figure 3 represents the outline of this relationship.

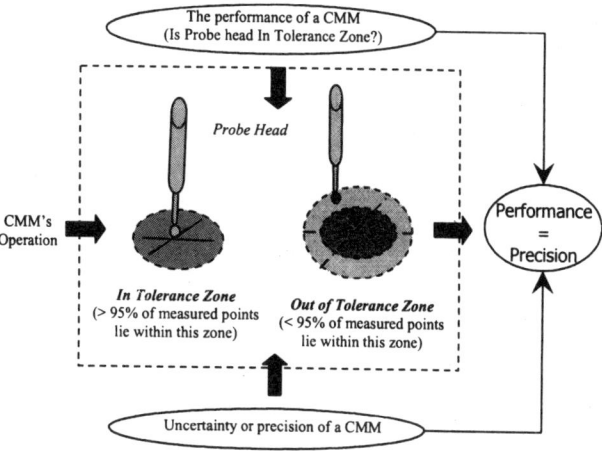

Figure 3: A relationship between the performance and precision of CMM

4. Uncertainty ellipse

From the relationship represented in Figure 3, an uncertainty region associated with the measured point coordinate has to be determined in order to estimate the CMMs' performance. As mentioned previously, there is the random error in the coordinates of each point within the measuring volume of the CMM. Hence, each point in the measuring volume can be viewed as having a "random errors cloud" associated with it. In general, firstly, these random error clouds will not be spherical because the uncertainty sources are associated with a particular axis of the CMM, which elongates the cloud along that direction. Similarly, the size of the cloud will vary from point to point within the measuring zone. The random errors cloud could be viewed as ellipsoid, as shown in Figure 4 and 5 [4, 6]. Secondly, the uncertainty of the measured coordinate (x, y, z) is statistically independent and distributed in a Gaussian. The set is an ellipse overlap with the coordinate (x, y, z).

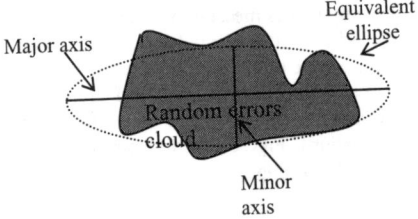

Figure 4: Equivalent ellipse for a random errors cloud

The random errors can be considered as an uncertainty of measurement. When the probe is moved to the destination, there will be the difference between the true position and the measured position. If a specific position is measured over and over (repeatability), the random space will be as ellipsoid with which the major axis will be parallel to the axis that is moving (see Figure 5). So the random error is similar to the uncertainty. The uncertainties are also likely present in the most mechanically accurate CMMs. The most commonly applied method of uncertainty evaluation is the Guide to the Expression of Uncertainty in Measurement (GUM).

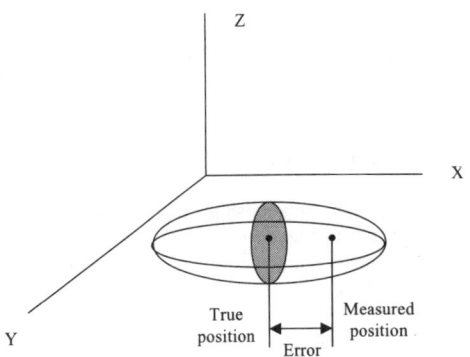

Figure 5: The three-dimensional random error in the coordinates

5. Probabilistic approach

Assuming that a measured point (P) on the workpiece surface can be treated as random position, therefore, the x, y coordinates can also be considered the random variables. It is assumed that uncertainty is normally distributed around the nominal value of the position. The probability that the magnitude of positional error within a certain value can be expressed by the probability of a randomly measured position P(x, y) within an allowable zone of uncertainty (Au). It can be given by the integration of the joint probability density function representing x and y as follows:

Pr (u) = Probability that a measured position lies within an allowable zone of uncertainty (A_u)

$$Pr(u) = \iint_{A_U} f(x, y) dx dy \qquad (5.1)$$

where,

$f(x, y)$ is bivariate normal joint probability density function of random measured position variables (x, y), in which $x \sim N(0, \sigma_x^2)$, $y \sim N(0, \sigma_y^2)$ and no correlation coefficient exists between the two random measured positions x and y.

The joint probability density function is given by:

$$f(x, y) = \frac{1}{2\pi\sigma_{\delta x}\sigma_{\delta y}} \exp\left[-\frac{1}{2}\left(\frac{x^2}{\sigma_{\delta x}^2} + \frac{y^2}{\sigma_{\delta y}^2} \right) \right]$$

$$(5.2)$$

where,

$\sigma_{\delta x}$ is the standard deviation of error in x – axis

$\sigma_{\delta y}$ is the standard deviation of error in y – axis

A contour of the joint probability density function is illustrated in Figure 6.

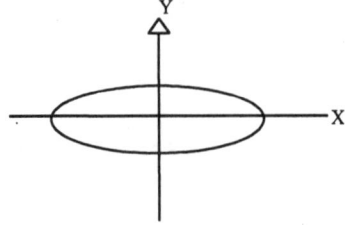

Figure 6: A contour of f (x, y)

Furthermore, specified tolerances on a part or its features can be interpreted as uncertainty of position. Therefore, knowing the uncertainty associated with the nominal position, the statistical distribution of uncertainty can be obtained. The boundary of uncertainty is an elliptical shape that has semi-major and semi-minor axes.

The probability that the measured position P (x, y) lies within an allowable area of uncertainty zone (Au) is, as shown in Figure 7, given by

$$Pr(u) = \iint\limits_{A_u} \frac{1}{2\pi\sigma_1\sigma_2} \exp\left[-\frac{1}{2}\left(\frac{x_1}{\sigma_1}\right)^2 - \frac{1}{2}\left(\frac{y_2}{\sigma_2}\right)^2\right] dx_1 dy_2$$

(5.3)

where,

$$\sigma_1 = \sigma_{\delta x}/a$$
$$\sigma_2 = \sigma_{\delta y}/b$$
$$x_1 = x/a$$
$$y_1 = y/b$$
$$a = \text{a semi-major axis}$$
$$b = \text{a semi-minor axis}$$

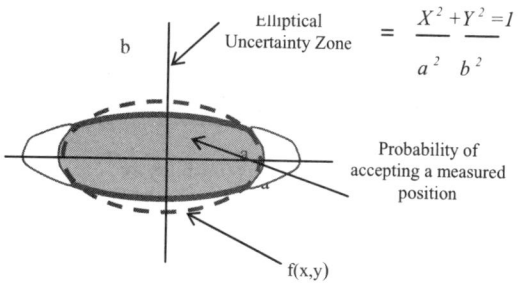

Figure 7: The probability of accepting a measured position P (x, y) lies within an elliptical uncertainty (Au)

However, the double integration model in (5.3) can be simplified to single integration in (5.4)

$$Pr(t) = \frac{1}{2\pi u} \int_0^{2\pi} \frac{\left\{1 - \exp\left[-(R/\sigma_x)^2 S(\theta,u)/2\right]\right\}}{S(\theta,u)} d\theta$$

(5.4)

where,

$$u = \frac{\sigma_{\delta_Y}}{\sigma_{\delta_x}}$$

$$S(\theta,u) = \cos^2\theta + \sin^2\theta/u^2$$

R = the radius of tolerance zone

6. Comparing the developed model

The developed model in this paper has been compared with the model done in previous research. Those who performed the research in this area are well known such as Lehtihet and Gunasena [5] and Shin and Wei [11].

The parameters used to calculate the probability of accepting a measured position P (x, y) that lies within an elliptical uncertainty (Au) are:

- the standard deviation of error in x – axis ($\sigma_{\delta x}$)
- the standard deviation of error in y – axis ($\sigma_{\delta y}$)
- the radius of tolerance zone (R)

6.1 Case 1: the geometric error for each axis of a CMM

Using all parameters given by Shin and Wei,

I. The standard deviation of geometric errors for x and y-axes are 0.11825 mm and 0.10549mm
II. The radius of tolerance zone (R) for measured position ranging from 0.00 mm to 0.40 mm

then, substitute I) and II) into (5.4). Finally, the results are shown in Table 1 and Figure 8.

Radius of tolerance zone for a measured position (mm)	Probability of accepting a measured position (Shin & Wei)	Probability of accepting a measured position (The developed model)
0	0	0
0.04	0.05	0.0621
0.08	0.207	0.2261
0.12	0.406	0.4379
0.16	0.604	0.6404
0.2	0.764	0.7971
0.24	0.875	0.8989
0.28	0.941	0.9554
0.32	0.975	0.9826
0.36	0.991	0.994
0.4	0.997	0.9981

Table 1: Comparing the probability of accepting a measured position with the same radius of tolerance zone between the developed model and Shin & Wei

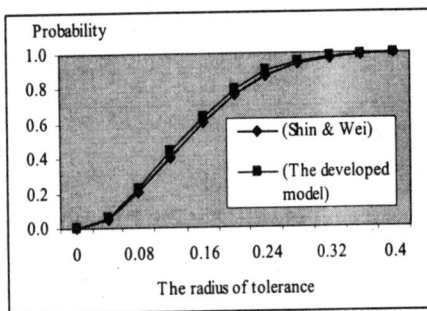

Figure 8: Graphical comparison of the probability of accepting a measured position at the same radius of tolerance zone between the developed model and Shin and Wei

From Table 1, at the same radius of tolerance zone, the probability of accepting a measured position calculated using the model developed is greater than those reported by Shin and Wei

By implementing this model, for example, it can be stated that the use a CMM with a standard deviation of geometric error for x axis, $\sigma_{\delta X}$ = 0.11825 mm, and a standard deviation for geometric error for y axis, $\sigma_{\delta Y}$ = 0.10549 mm, to measure a target position will guarantee that 98.3 % probability of the next measurement will lie within an uncertainty zone with R = ± 0.32 mm, as opposed to a

reported 97.5 % probability by research of Shin and Wei.

6.2 Case 2: the geometric error for each axis of a drilling machine

Using all parameters given by Lehtihet and Gunasena,
I. The standard deviation of geometric errors for x and y-axes are 0.0005 mm and 0.001mm
II. The radius of tolerance zone (R) for drilled position ranging from 0.0005 mm to 0.0045 mm

then, substitute I) and II) into (5.4). Finally, the results are shown in Table 2 and Figure 9.

Radius of Tolerance Zone for Drilled-Hole (mm)	Probability of accepting a drilled position Lehtihet & Gunasena (1990)	Probability of accepting a drilled position (The developed model)
0.0005	0.0446	0.2153
0.0010	0.3015	0.5901
0.0015	0.592	0.8351
0.0020	0.7989	0.9455
0.0025	0.9191	0.9853
0.0030	0.9735	0.9968
0.0035	0.9929	0.9995
0.0040	0.9986	0.9998
0.0045	0.9998	0.9999

Table 2: Comparing the probability of accepting a drilled-hole position with the same radius of tolerance zone between the developed model and Lehtihet and Gunasena

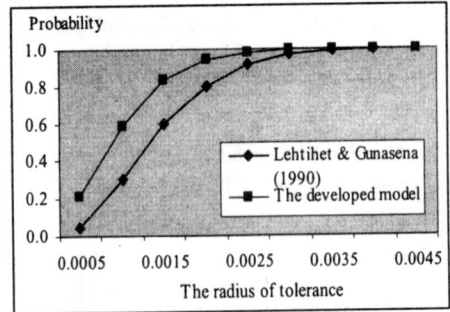

Figure 9: Graphical comparison of the probability of accepting a drilled-hole position at the same radius of tolerance zone between the developed model and Lehtihet and Gunasena

620

From Table 2 at the same radius of tolerance zone, the probability of accepting a drilled-hole position calculated using the model developed in this research is greater than those reported by Lehtihet and Gunasena.

By implementing the model, it can be stated that the use a CNC with standard deviation of geometric error for x axis, $\sigma_{\delta x}$ = 0.0005 mm and a standard deviation for geometric error for y axis $\sigma_{\delta y}$ = 0.001 mm, to drill a target hole position will guarantee that 98.53 % probability that the next drilling will lie within a tolerance zone with R = $\pm$ 0.0025 mm, as opposed to a reported 91.91 % probability by the research of Lehtihet and Gunasena.

7. Conclusion

Several methods can be employed to assess the performance of coordinate measuring machines. Using laser interferometer, ball bar, and artifacts for calibrating and enhancing the CMM performance have received wide acceptance in the research community dealing with performance evaluation of coordinate measuring machines and CNC machine tools. Although these methods are very effective, they are too costly and time consuming to make them implementable on the shop floor.

Recent research work has been dealing with the use of statistical models of error parameters to achieve faster results with less cost. The research work presented here is an extension to these recent research efforts. It has utilized the concept of measurement uncertainty in coordinate measuring machine to provide a faster and less expensive approach to assess CMM performance.

In summary, the developed models resulted in an improved probability of
7.1) accepting measurements and
7.2) indicating an improvement in the performance of CMM
7.3) providing an assessment of its capability and reliability

References

[1] Automotive Industry Action Group, "Measurement Systems Analysis", Reference Manual, Second Edition, MI, (1995)

[2] Drescher, J. D., "Assessment of Machine Tool Accuracy Using ISO-Guide to The Expression of Uncerainty in Measurement (GUM)", American Society For Precision Engineering", Vol. 16, pp. 61-64, (1997)

[3] Elshennawy, A. K. and Ham, I., "Performance Improvement in Coordinate Measuring Machines by Error Compensation", Journal of Manufacturing Systems, Vol. 9, No. 2, pp. 151-158, (1990)

[4] Hulting, F. L., "Method for Analysis of Coordinate Measurement Data", Computing Science and Statistics, Vol. 24, pp. 160-169, (1992)

[5] Lehtihet, E.A. and Gunasena, U. N., "Statistical Models for the Relationship between Production Errors and the Position Tolerance of a Hole", Annals of CIRP, Vol. 39, pp. 569-572, (1990)

[6] Liu, Z. Q., "Repetitive Measurement and Compensation to Improve Workpiece Machining Accuracy", International Journal Advance Manufacturing Technology, Vol. 15, pp. 85-89, (1999)

[7] Phillips, S. D., Borchardt, B., Sawyer, D., Estler, W. T., Ward, D., Eberhardt, K., Levenson, M. S., McClain, M., Melvin, B., Hopp, T. and Shen, Y., "The Calculation of CMM Measurement Uncertainty via The Method of Simulation by Constraints", American Society For Precision Engineering, Vol. 16, pp. 443-446, (1997)

[8] Rabinovich, S. G., "Measurement Errors and Uncertainties: Theory and Practice", Translated by Alferieff, M. E., Second edition, AIP Press, NY, (2000)

[9] Salomons, O. W., Jonge Poerink, H. J., Van Slooten, F., Van Houten, F. J. A. M. and Kals, H. J. J., "A Tolerancing Tool Based on Kinematic Analogies", Computer-Aided Tolerancing, Edited by Kimura, F., Chapman & Hall, NY, pp. 47-70, (1995)

[10] Shen, Y and Duffie, N. A., "An Uncertainty Analysis Method for Coordinate Referencing in Manufacturing Systems", Transactions of the ASME, Vol. 117, February, pp. 42-48, (1995)

[11] Shin, Y. C. and Wei, Y., "A Statistical Analysis of Positional Errors of a Multiaxis Machine Tool", Precision Engineering, Vol. 14, No. 3, pp. 139-146, (1992)

[12] Takatsuji, T., Osawa, S. and Kurosawa, T., "Uncertainty Analysis of Calibration of Geometric Gauges", Journal of the International Societies for Precision Engineering and Nanotechnology, Vol. 26, pp. 24-29, (2001)

[13] Weckenmann, A., "The Accuracy of Coordinate Measuring Machines", ACTA IMEKO, pp. 287-296, (1982)

[14] Weckenmann, A. and Rinnagl, M., "Acceptance of Processes: Do We Need Decision Rules? ", Precision Engineering, Vol. 24, No. 3, pp. 264-269, July, (2000)

Quality

GCMM 2004
Editors: Prasad K D V ,Yarlagadda and S Narayanan
Copyright © 2005, Vellore Institute of Technology, Vellore, India
Publisher: Narosa Publishing House Pvt. Ltd., New Delhi, India

An instrument for measuring Total Quality Management Implementation in Service-Based Business units in India

Saravanan R & Surya Prakasa Rao K*

*Anna University, Chennai

Email: rsaravanan72@yahoo.com

Abstract

In this era of globalization and liberalization, Indian industries have to face the global competition and survive in the international market successfully. Hence, the customer satisfaction has to be given prime importance by the industries. In this context, Total Quality Management (TQM) is introduced. TQM is a comprehensive approach to continuously improve the quality, reduce cost and ensure consistent on-time delivery of products and services. TQM is adopted by the companies to focus on creating economic value over the long-term. The results are influenced by profit margins, sales growth, market share and productivity. But TQM is still in initial stages in many organizations of our country. Hence it is appropriate time that our industries have to adopt TQM in their organizations to improve their business performance and to achieve customer satisfaction. The objective of the paper is to explain about the development of instrument to measure TQM implementation in service-based organizations in India. Through an extensive literature survey, this research identified 139 measures for quality management. After a pre-test with various academic experts, quality consultants and managers in service units; 118 measures were used to develop a questionnaire to measure the quality management practices in various service-based business units in India.

Keywords
Total Quality Management, Service Units, Instrument.

1. INTRODUCTION

TQM is an integrated philosophy of management by continuously improving the quality of products and processes to achieve customer satisfaction.

Bounds and Dewhirst [1] defined TQM as "Total quality management refers to a comprehensive approach to management which involves implementing strategies and organizational systems that continuously improve quality, reduce cost and ensure consistent on time delivery of products and services in order to provide superior value to customers.

Feigenbaum [2] defined TQM as the organization wide impact of Total quality control.
Oakland [3] defined TQM as "A comprehensive approach to improve

competitiveness and flexibility through planning, organizing and understanding each activity and involving everyone at each level. TQM ensures that management adopts a strategic overview of quality and focus on prevention rather than inspection."

2. LITERATURE REVIEW

Saraph et al.[15] collected data from general managers and quality managers of the companies in Minneapolis/St.Paul area and identified eight critical factors of quality management namely the role of management leadership and quality policy, role of the quality department, training, product/service design, supplier quality management, process management, quality data & reporting and employee relations. Operational measures of these factors were developed and were found to be reliable and valid.

Black and Porter [17] developed a model for total quality management which portrays visual information on various factors of total quality management, relationships between those factors, strength of those relationships and relative importance of those factors.

Powell et al. [18] concluded that quality training, process improvement and benchmarking may not be much useful for effective total quality management implementation but certain resources like open culture, employee empowerment and executive commitment are vital to win over their competitors with or without TQM level.

Ahire et al. [16] examined the relationships between company size and TQM implementation. The findings suggested that small firms with shortage of managerial expertise, inspection resources etc. can implement TQM with their strengths in flexibility and innovation than the large firms. Moreover he argued that successful firms get better operational results within first two to three years of its implementation.

Black and Porter [17] focused on the important elements of the Malcolm Balridge National Quality Award model and other established literature. They surveyed managers in United Kingdom organizations and identified ten critical components of TQM namely corporate quality culture, strategic quality management, quality improvement measurement system, people and customer management, operational quality planning, external interface management, supplier partnership, teamwork structures, customer satisfaction orientation and communication of improvement information.

Samson and Terziovski [19] covered eight Australian manufacturing and service organizations and found that no significant differences were there between manufacturing and service industries in most of critical management practices.

Suresh Chandar G.S. et al. [12] developed a conceptual model for TQM in service organizations. They identified twelve dimensions of Total Quality Service (TQS) as being critical for effective implementation of TQM based on extensive review of the vast literature on TQM and TQS. They are top management commitment and visionary leadership, human resource management, technical system, information and analysis, service culture, servicescapes, social responsibility, union intervention, benchmarking, customer focus, employee satisfaction and continuous improvement.

Dr.Mahajan.T.M. [5] proposed a model synthesizing the concepts of TQM, organizational learning and knowledge management. They identified seventeen key factors contributing to proposed model. A "self assessment knowledge based quality index" (SKQI) is being designed with the help of pair wise comparison of key factors.
Based on the survey of various industries they found that the knowledge based quality score for IT industries is the highest, for educational institutes is medium and Non-IT industries is the lowest. IT industries focused on current as well as future requirements whereas Non –IT industries focused on current requirements only.

Mc.Adam et al. [6] examined the key dynamics of an organizational transition from ISO 9000 to TQM in UK and Irish brewing sector and they concluded that TQM is to be best implemented within the controlled environment/quality assurance environment of ISO 9000.

Raju.R and Dr.Balasubramanian.N. [9] developed a TQM implementation model for Indian industries by analyzing the views of quality promoters, consultants, practitioners and academicians. They identified five individual variables, four cultural variables and four structural variables to implement TQM in industries using mean score as criterion. Using the same criterion, thirteen TQM success factors were identified as critical measure of TQM in Indian industries.

Prof. Sathyajit Majundar [10] studied the TQM (Business excellence) models and they compared the Malcolm Balridge National Quality award and European model for Total quality management.

3. DEVELOPMENT OF INSTRUMENT

The instrument has been developed after extensive literature survey. Further the items in the instrument developed by Suresh Chandar et al. have been considered and modified according to the requirements of automobile service stations and included in the present instrument. Also the factors that are not covered previously have been included in the instrument. A pilot study was conducted and the instrument was circulated to various academicians, researchers and practioners related to the service sector. The instrument has been refined further by incorporating the comments and suggestions from the experts in the field. After modification and refinement the instrument has been finalized with 118 items and is presented in the appendix.

4. CONCLUSION

This research work developed an instrument with 118 operating elements for measuring the TQM implementation in service industries in India. The instrument

has been developed after extensive literature survey. It was further modified by including the suggestions by experts in the field. The findings of this study may be useful for the practioners to understand the level of practice of various operating elements and to improve their business performance.

5. REFERENCES

1. **Bounds G.M. & Dewhirst H.D.** (1991), Assessing progress in managing for customer value", *The management of strategic systems*, Westport CT, Greenwood press.
2. **Feigenbaum A.V.** (1983), *Total Quality Control*, 3rd edition, New York, Mcgraw Hill Company.
3. **Oakland J,** (1993), *TQM,* Oxford Edition.
4. **Hartz Ove & Kanji Gopal K.** (1998), Development of strategies for total quality management in large industrial companies & small, *Total Quality Management,* July 1998, Vol 9, Issue 4/5, pp S 112, 4p.
5. **Mahajan.J.M. and Amit Ranjan** (2001), Knowledge based total quality management, *Industrial Engineering Journal,*Vol. xxx, No.4, pp 19-26.
6. **Mc.Adam et al.** 2002, A sectoral study of ISO 9000 and TQM transitions, *integrated manufacturing systems,* Vol 13 page 255-263.
7. **Mohd.Yusof Shari & Aspinwall Elaine M.** (2000), Critical success factors in small and medium sized enterprises-survey results, *Total Quality Management,* July 2000,Vol 11, Issue 4-6, pp 448, 15p.
8. **Munshi D.**(2000), Total quality management strategies for the armed forces, *Industrial Engineering Journal,* Vol xxix, No.2, pp 15-19.
9. **Raju R. and Balasubramanian N.** (2002), Total quality management Implementation model for Indian industries, *Industrial Engineering Journal,* pp 18-26.
10. **Satyajit Majumdar** (2002), Study of TQM (Business excellence) models, *Industrial Engineering Journal.* pp 23-30.
11. **Singh Saurabh & Deshmukh S.G.** (1999), Quality initiatives in the service

sector- A case, *Total Quality Management*, Jan 1999, Vol 10, Issue-1, pp 5, 12p.

12. **Suresh Chandar G.S.,Rajendran C. & Anantharaman R.N.** (2001), A conceptual model for total quality management in service organizations, *Total Quality Management*, May 2001, Vol 12, Issue 3, pp 343, 21p.

13. **Winchester et al.** (1997), Integrating Total quality management and computer integrated manufacturing in textiles, *Proceedings of world conference of the textile institutes*, Manchester, pp 155-178.

14. **Zhihai Zhang,** (2000), Developing a model of quality management methods and evaluating their effects on business performance, *Total Quality Management*, Jan. 2000, Vol-11 Issue 1, pp129, 9 p.

15. **Saraph J.V., Benson P.G. & Schroeder R.G.** (1989), An instrument for measuring the critical factors of quality management, Decision *Sciences*, pp 810-829.

16. **Ahire L.S., Golhar D.Y. & Waller M.A.,** (1996), Development and validation of TQM implementation constructs, *Decision sciences*, 27, pp 23-56.

17. **Black and Porter** (1996), Identification of the critical factors of TQM, *Decision Sciences,* 1-22.

18. **Powell C.T.** (1995), Total quality management as competitive advantage :a review and empirical study, *Strategic management journal*, pp 15-37.

19. **Samson D. and Terziovski M.** (1999), The relationship between total quality management practices and operational performance, *Journal of Operations Management*, 17, pp 393-409.

6. APPENDIX

The instrument to measure TQM has been developed to analyze the respondent's perception of the actual level of practice of TQM with respect to the items on a seven point Likert scale(1 = very low, 2 = low, 3 = slightly low, 4 = medium/moderate, 5 = slightly high, 6 = high and 7 = very high.)
The items that are developed are
• Level of practice of decentralized authority structure.

• Extent to which business vision forms the basis for strategic quality planning and decision-making.
• Degree of importance given to quality rather than cost by the senior management.
• Degree of top management commitment to the philosophy of quality management.
• Importance given by the top management for allocation of sufficient resources and time for quality improvement initiatives.
• Extent to which top management takes into account the competitor organizations and the element of risk in its strategic planning and decision-making.
• Attitude of the top management to consider employees as valuable assets to the organization.
• Extent to which the leaders properly guide their subordinates.
• Self-introspection by the leaders towards their commitment to quality management implementation.
• Attitude of the leaders to remove the root causes of the problems instead of firefighting with them.
• Building mutual trust and respect among the employees.
• Encouragement of participative management among the employees.
• Coordination skills of the supervisors with various department heads.
• Ability of the supervisors to bring consensus approach while solving the problems.
• Degree of importance given to quality consciousness of employees at the recruitment stage.
• Degree of importance given at the time of recruitment regarding experience related to quality management.
• Degree of importance given to develop communication skills in training programmes.
• Level of employee awareness of business goals of the service station.
• Training of employees in diagnostic and basic problem solving skills such as Cause and Effect analysis, Pareto analysis, Brainstorming, Quality Circles and Quality management systems such as ISO 9000.
• Effectiveness of inculcating quality culture among the employees.
• Extent of money budgeted each year for employee education, training and upgrading the use of technology.
• Degree to which the employees are encouraged to enrich their problem solving skills.
• Degree to which the employees are allowed freely to express their views and opinions about the service station.
• Extent to which the employees are given adequate authority to achieve the goals.

- Self-inspection of the vehicles by the mechanics/service personnel themselves without waiting for quality inspectors.
- Degree of importance given to employee suggestions and innovations.
- Effectiveness of Quality Circles (QC) and Cross Functional Teams with respect to evolution of quality improvement strategies and solutions to problems related to quality.
- Extent to which employees are involved in quality management programmes.
- Degree of coordination among various departments' personnel to achieve overall improvement in service quality.
- Extent to which the service processes are simplified and standardized so that the results are achieved without any delay.
- Emphasis on systematic documentation of service processes for easy traceability of mistakes and for taking corrective actions.
- Identification of critical processes and monitoring them regularly.
- Level of practice of fool-proofing the processes.
- Level of upgradation of available technology in the service station to compete in market.
- Redesigning the processes to reduce the cycle time of delivery of the vehicle by applying Business Process Reengineering concepts.
- Extent of work measurement by conducting time studies and motion studies.
- Level of enforcement of safety precautions among the employees.
- Periodic appraisal of the employees about the effectiveness of quality management processes undergone in the service station.
- Frequency of departmental meetings conducted to implement Plan-Do-Check-Action cycle for quality improvement programmes.
- Usage of quality management tools like bar charts and control charts to monitor the quality.
- Integration of customer-feedback data with the service design processes to improve the service quality parameters.
- Extent of evaluation of relationship between customer satisfacfion and business performance of the service station.
- Measurement of quality improvement efforts in terms of reduction of wastage.
- Level of progress-report analysis of the various departments.
- Amount of feedback provided to employees on their performance with respect to quality.
- Degree of importance given for market investigation with respect to the service station position in the market.
- Degree to which analysis of various types of costs, namely, prevention costs, appraisal costs and failure costs are done.

- Level of teamwork and good human relationship among the employees.
- Level of trust and openness among the employees.
- Level of Practice of Philosophy "Make it Right at the first time itself" in the service station by the employees.
- Feelings such as "Our Company" and "We work together to achieve common goals" among the employees.
- Realization and Practice of the motto "Service to Customers" in the service station by employees.
- Belief among the employees that quality management is very much essential for survival in the highly competitive market.
- Employees' resistance to change their behavior towards implementation of quality management concepts.
- Emphasis on benchmarking the level of servicescape (eg. aesthetics, comforts and the equipments), with those of other service stations.
- Emphasis on benchmarking the training and development programmes, with that of other service stations.
- Emphasis on benchmarking the employee satisfaction, with that of other service stations.
- Emphasis on benchmarking the employees' commitment to achieve customer satisfaction, with that of other service stations.
- Emphasis on benchmarking the customer satisfaction, with that of other service stations.
- Level of practice of benchmarking the business performance, with that of direct competitors.
- Level of providing services as per the promised delivery schedule.
- Extent to which analysis is done with respect to dissatisfaction in service quality.
- Level of goodness of employees who are consistently courteous and well behaved with the customers.
- Extent of adding new techniques in service activities; service innovation (e.g., payment by citicard, internet, registration for service of vehicles by e-mail, conducting service mela, etc.)
- Range of service period based on service charge, (e.g., quicker delivery of vehicle by paying higher service charge, normal delivery of vehicle by paying lower service charge, etc.).
- Degree of importance given to customer satisfaction and service quality in day-to- day operations.
- Level of the employees to clarify customers' doubts after servicing the vehicles thereby instilling confidence in them.
- Degree of doing services correctly at the first instance itself.
- Extent to which the customer-feedback forms are provided to the customers for the purpose of

continuous improvement.

• Level of technical capability of the staff to diagnose the critical problems in the vehicle and rectify them.

• Level of effectiveness of the employees to understand the needs and expectations of the customers' & delivering prompt service.

• Level of making customers to feel safe & secure in their business transactions.

• Extent to which service station's working hours and working days are convenient to the customers.

• Extent of giving caring & best attention to the customer by keeping customer delight in mind.

• Level of reliability of the service station in handling customers' grievances & redressing them through customer day, etc.

• Extent to which customers are informed/apprised about safety precautions while driving.

• Degree of availability of all types of facilities in all service locations.

• Effectiveness of employee-grievance redressal meetings conducted by the management.

• Extent to which employee-appraisal system is implemented.

• Degree of implementation of indirect benefits such as selection for training programmes, giving certificates for quality improvements, etc.

• Design of career-advancement programmes for all level of employees with requirements and expectations clearly specified.

• Giving monetary awards to employees for cost reduction and service innovation.

• Degree of importance given to job enrichment rather than job enlargement and job rotation.

• Group incentives for motivating the employees to achieve the desired level of performance.

• Emphasis of continuous improvement in all the activities done at various levels.

• Measurement/quantification of continuous improvement techniques on the basis of factors such as cost and time.

• Degree to which the service station believes that by implementing continuous improvement strategies, it can survive and serve better in the highly competitive environment.

• Extent to which quality is given more importance than quantity (e.g. service quality vs. number of vehicles serviced per day.).

• Level of effectiveness of work instructions given in the process sheet.

• Extent of efforts taken to have quality management systems such as ISO 9001:2000

• Extent of emphasis on quality-awareness programmes (such as Quality Day) for employees.

• Extent of implementation of vision/mission statement.

• Level of implementation of quality policy.

• Extent to which quality goals are achieved.

• Level of consideration of customer's requirements and expectations in formulating the service station's objectives, plans, strategies and actions.

• Extent to which inspection, review or checking of work is automated.

• Extent of using quality-department data to evaluate managerial and supervisory performance.

• Autonomy of the quality department in development and implementation of company-wide quality process and management.

• Level of appearance of employees who have a neat and professional look.

• Level of practice of Seiri(elimination), Seiton(orderliness),Seiso(cleanliness), Seiketsu(standardization), and Shitsuke(self discipline) in the service station.

• Extent of suitability of environmental factors such as temperature, ventilation, noise and odour to the employees.

• Degree of impact on customers by the boards displaying business vision and quality policy.

• Level of customer satisfaction with the existing service station layout and other facilities.

• Extent of display of product advertisement boards.

• Extent of display of service delivery status.

• Extent to which materials and colours used in the service operations are visually appealing.

• Extent of providing good service at a reasonable price without comprising on quality.

• Emphasis on disciplined behaviour among the employees with a sense of social responsibility.

• Level of satisfying customers beyond their expectations (service transcendence).

• Extent of treating all customers equally irrespective of their status in society.

• Extent of establishing service stations at all locations, viz. urban, semi-urban and rural areas.

• Level of practice of value added services service station.

• Extent of providing extended warranty to vehicles.

• Extent of sending reminder letters to customers for routine service and maintenance of the vehicles.

• Level of informing the customers of next due-date of service by telephone or emails.

• Degree to which indication of next due-date for service by means of coupons.

• Extent of effectiveness of quick repair service in the service station.

• Extent of providing free pollution control checkup/service to vehicles by conducting service mela.

GCMM 2004
Editors: Prasad K D V Yarlagadda and S Narayanan
Publisher: Narosa Publishing House Pvt. Ltd., New Delhi, India

Literature Mining on Zero Defects Manufacturing

Rajendran M, Pravinkumar M, Vaitheeswaran P, Muthukumar & Jagadeesan J

Government College of Technology, Coimbatore,
Tamilnadu, India.

Devadasan S R

P.S.G. College of Technology, Coimbatore,
Tamilnadu, India.

Abstract

Although the history reveals the emanation of zero defect concepts during 1960 s, its growth had not been phenomenal till today. In order to examine this state, the literature was systematically mined. The details of this mining process are briefly presented in the paper. The paper traces the work of the authors under four categories. These categories are termed as management based approach, technology based approach, unconventional approach and integrated approach. After citing inferences, it is pointed out that the model integrating all the categories of work are yet to be appear in literature. For this purpose, a model termed as 'Seven phase ZDM' has been designed and proposed. The paper is concluded by claiming that a financial accounting system to measure the performance of this model could motivate the management to support its implementation.

Keywords
TQM, Zero Defects, Six Sigma, Poka-Yoke, Taguchi's Quality Loss Function.

1. INTRODUCTION

The emanation of the principles of total quality management (TQM) instigated the aspect of questioning the credibility of various traditional concepts. Before TQM became popular, companies were complacent with quality control approach. TQM enlarged its scope, thereby companies started to concentrate on quality planning, quality evaluation and quality improvement activities. In addition to these, quality control activities are also carried out, but by the involvement of all the personnel and departments .On implementation of TQM programmes, in many companies, quality control department ceased to function independently. Rather TQM application was spread throughout the company. Companies came to a conclusion that carrying out the above activities was the sole and major part of TQM implementation. Whilst this major paradigm change was transforming the companies, one major and most important objective of TQM was pushed to the background. That is nothing but attaining zero defects not only in manufacturing but also in other functional activities of the company. Because some quality gurus like Deming and Crossby, [1] and ISO 9000 series standards emphasized upon statistical quality control approach, TQM researchers and practitioners failed to concentrate on developing programme that would lead to zero defects in companies. In fact, a search by the authors in the literature indicates that a zero defects programme was evolved in the Martin Company in Orlando plant in as early as 1960s under the leadership of their Director of Quality Mr. James F. Halpin [2]. A brief study of this programme indicates that it is similar to the TQM approach that is being followed today. There is little evidence in literature to indicate that this zero defects programme received any kind of favourable reception among the companies from 1960s to 1980s.

Because of the overwhelming thrust on SPC and SQC technique as part of ISO 9000 series quality system standards [3,4] implementation, no effective Zero Defects Manufacturing (ZDM) model emerged during the later part of twentieth century. However there was one particular point at which two American companies by names Motorola and General Electric brought out six-sigma programme. Basically six-sigma programme calls for allowing only 3.4 defects per million opportunities [5]. This number is approximately equal to zero and hence six-sigma programme can be considered as a ZDM model. Also a careful study of the six-sigma model would indicate that it is similar to the ZDM programme proposed by James F. Halpin. A bird's eye view on the literature and manufacturing scenario would indicate that there have been intensive efforts by many companies to implement six-sigma programme. This development indicates the thirst of companies for progressing towards ZDM. In fact many companies have also started to report success statistics of implementing six-sigma programme [5]. In other words, currently ZDM has been revived in the form of six-sigma programme.

While ZDM programmes were defunct during the years between 1960s and 1980s, different principles were brought out in shadowed forms of ZDM programme. One among them is the foolproofing principle in the design of processes, tools, jigs and fixtures. Foolproofing principles prevent the user from doing mistake [6]. Another popular concept that has emerged during the recent period is poka-yoke approach. Basically this approach is an advanced form of fool proofing which is characterized by the expansion of the scope towards the design and assembly functions. In fact poka-yoke is also addressed under the title "mistake proofing" [7]. This approach envisages the design of the components and products in

such a way that mistakes do not happen during their manufacturing and assembly. Particularly human weaknesses such as fatigue, tiredness, forgetfulness, carelessness etc. are taken into consideration while following Poka-yoke approach. Basically Poka-yoke tools are dependent upon the technological phase of manufacturing scenario.

A careful study of various ZDM approaches would indicate that, they differ considerably from each other with very little commonalties between them. An overview on literature would indicate that, the companies which implement technology based ZDM approaches do not implement management based ZDM programme and vice versa. As any manufacturing paradigm is composed of technology and management elements, ZDM approaches which deal with technology and management separately will not yield effective solution for achieving zero defect in totality. Hence, a consolidated approach in ZDM is imperative for achieving zero defects in organisational performance in today's companies. Before progressing in this right direction, it is necessary for the researchers to navigate the literature to estimate and assess the ZDM approaches that are currently under research and applications. In order to fulfill this requirement the authors of this paper carried out a literature mining exercise and derived inferences which would be useful to strengthen the research programme on ZDM .The details of this work are briefly presented in this paper.

2. METHODOLOGY

In order to mine globally the ZDM literature, it was decided to access international database by making use of internet technology. In the beginning,(to be precise, on December 23,2002) during the end of December 2002, the database maintained by United Kingdom based Emerald Library was searched. For this purpose, the site maintained by this library was visited (www.emeraldinsight.com). For the purpose of surveying ZDM literature, "zero defect manufacturing" was entered as key word. The result showed the availability of one paper. After that "zero defects manufacturing" was entered as keyword. The result showed the non-availability of papers against this keyword. Then, "zero defects" was entered as keyword. The result showed the availability of 20 articles. After that "zero defect" was entered as keyword and against this five papers were available. Some of the papers listed were coinciding with the above four slightly different keywords. In total 23 papers was listed under ZDM field. In most cases, the soft copies of the full text of the papers published after 1994 have been stocked by Emerald Library. Out of 23 papers, the full text of eight papers was available. The full text and the abstract of the papers have been referred to bring out the appropriate inferences concerning the ZDM programme.

3. CATAGORISATION

An overview on the papers collected indicated that the scant work that has been carried out on ZDM could be classified into three categories namely management based approach, technology based approach and unconventional based approach. Besides very few papers deal with the consolidation of all these three approaches. The review of papers under these four categories and the inferences drawn from these are briefly described in the following four sub-sections.

3.1. Management Approach

The papers that deal with management approach on ZDM mainly concentrate on achieving zero defects through participative programmes. For example Ripley and Ripley [8,9] propose empowerment as a major technique of promoting the employee involvement and hint that it would lead to zero defects in organisational performance through innovative approaches. Likewise Cuylenburg [10] hints the effect of quality action team as the means to achieve zero defects by enhancing motivation level of employees. King [11] discusses the introduction of Crossby quality system into a dairy crest by citing examples of aiming zero error and zero sickness. Meyer and Ferdows [12] indicate zero defects as one of the improvement programme which on implementation results in negative effects in the short run but can have positive effects in the long run. Crawford and Shutler [13] deal with the process of achieving zero defects in education, which would be indicated when every student in the class passes the examination at the first attempt. They have examined the validity of this approach by considering the implementation of Crossby

and Deming models in education. This work indicates the penetration of zero defect approach in educational system.

Some papers view six-sigma programme as mere equivalent to ZDM programme. Behara et. al. [14] have pointed out that zero defect is an approach which stresses the fact that all errors are preventable. Mainly Philip Crosely identified the concept more than three decades old. They have pointed out that the six-sigma approach leads to near zero defect results. They have also presented a case study in which six-sigma have been adopted to achieve customer satisfaction. Behara and Lemmink [15] have used six sigma as zero defect approach to benchmark field services. They have presented case studies to claim that by using six sigma approach there is an added advantage is being able to compare the performance to an attainable zero defects ideal.

Aboulnaga [16] has narrated the features ISO 9000 and ISO 14000 series standards. Although he has dealt with zero defect concepts only to a small extent, his observation with regard to zero defects is highly worthwhile to consider. For example, he has pointed out the existence of the 14-step approach to achieve zero defects, which is 30 years old. Also, he has indicated that the concept of accepted quality level is wrong because it leads to the belief that the error is inevitable. He has also presented the fundamental notion of management oriented zero defect programme which is based on the fact that the mistakes are caused by lack of knowledge and attention. On overcoming these causes with the support of top management, it is possible to achieve zero defects. Hill and Taylor [17] refer TQM and ISO 9000 as service sector models and describe them from the context of zero defects. Ngin and Chong [18] have viewed TQM as a means of eliminating defects and described the experience of implementing TQM in a company situated in Singapore. Thus although very little number of researchers and practioners have applied ZDM programme, they have indicated the imperativeness of management approach in attaining zero defects in organizations.

3.2. Technology based Approach

Technology based articles on ZDM are dominated by Poka-yoke approach. For example, Fisher [17] has addressed Poka-yoke as a quality methodology for achieving ZDM. He has pointed out that Poka-yoke involves the application of simple devices, which on application have promoted Japanese quality miracle. He has also criticized the use of slogan and exhortations using the advocation of Shingo (the creator of Poka-yoke techniques) and pointed that Poka-yoke applied through investigations have resulted in zero defects. In fact he has indirectly underestimated the effect of management approach of ZDM. Perona [19] has pointed out the contribution of Taguchi's quality loss function for achieving zero defects. He has used this model to instigate the technologists to develop and improve technologies continuously with the purpose of attaining ZDM. Hollingum and Stone [20] have addressed safety issues but have pointed out the efficacy of automation in achieving ZDM. Likewise Riley [21] has pointed out the application of assembly automation as a vehicle to switchover from traditional production to zero defect production. Thus, researchers and practitioners have applied three models namely poka-yoke, Taguchi's quality loss function model and automation for achieving ZDM.

3.3. Unconventional Approach

Some papers on ZDM are found to deal with unconventional approaches. Particularly, one paper is found to be dealing with a contradictory view of ZDM. Price [22] who has claimed that ZDM approach is admirable but neither always attainable nor appropriate in certain areas authors this paper. In fact he has criticized the ZDM movement. However, this view is held invalid by Aboulnaga [16] who has pointed out that the people are conditioned to believe that error is inevitable in any kind of activity. In coincidence to this paper, Smith [23] has pointed out that zero defects is a meaningful concept. However, he has pointed out that an approach called zero acceptance number plans is required to replace the conventional sampling plan in which acceptance number is more than zero. His claim is almost equivalent to the emphasis made by Taguchi's quality loss function approach. Xie and Goh [24] have also indirectly claimed that conventional three sigma based control charts are not suitable for achieving ZDM. In a nutshell, these unconventional ZDM approaches emphasize the need for attitudinal changes with regard to the process of achieving ZDM. Particularly, the authors of these papers advocate that researchers and practitioners must have to develop the trust upon the possibility of achieving zero defects by using models, which should be different from conventional three sigma interval based sampling plans.

3.4. Integrated Approach

Although ZDM is one of the approaches of TQM, it has not yet been applied widely in organisations. As indicated in the previous subsections, the researchers and practitioners associated with ZDM principles have worked in three different direction namely technological, managerial and statistical approaches. The contribution of these researchers and practitioners has not yet been synergised to evolve a holistic ZDM model. Presumably, on realizing this lacuna very few authors have presented ZDM models by combining any two or three of the approaches mentioned above. For example, Duffin [25] has presented an integrated approach in which he has combined both management and technological principles of ZDM under the terminology called zero quality control. Primarily he has presented these ideas by referring to the concept of zero quality control presented by Shingo. However, this approach is very general and he has not presented a procedure for implementation of ZDM.

4. INTEGRATED MODEL

The results of the literature survey on ZDM reported in this paper indicated that and its analysis indicated us no researchers and practitioner have brought out a model for implementing the ZDM with management and technological features. As mentioned in the previous section of this paper, majority of papers on ZDM deals with management aspects of attaining zero defects. Very few papers addressing technological aspects of attaining ZDM are available. This observation is coinciding with the remark of Juran and Deming [1]. Juran has claimed that the management personnel can avoid 80% of the errors related to quality whereas Deming has claimed that the management employees can avoid 94% of the errors related to quality. These findings indicate that ZDM programme shall comprise, majority of management principles with little thrust on technological principles. Another indication with regard to ZDM is that, a step-by-step, procedure cannot be arrived for ZDM will be a long journey. Hence it is possible only to evolve major phases of ZDM programme, which have to be applied by the companies on all occasions and on continual basis. Based upon these inferences, the authors of this paper are proposing here a seven-phase ZDM model. The phases of this model are given below:

* Motivation of the management
* Motivation of the employees
* Indoctrination
* Identification and rectification of impediments to quality
* Measurement of internal results
* Measurement of external results
* Recognition of achievements

Referring to James F.Halpin model and the contribution has drawn the above phases by other authors of ZDM papers that have been surveyed by the authors. In the above phases, except the phase titled as "Identification and Rectification of Impediments to quality", all other phases deal with management aspects. If equal importance is given to all phases, then the proportions of management application in the proposed seven-phase ZDM model is agreeable to the observations of Juran and Deming. This observation also tallies with the statistics of ZDM literature surveyed.

5.CREDIBILITY OF SEVEN PHASE ZDM MODEL

Although sounds powerful, the Seven phase model presented in the sections is prone to receive some vital reservation in the minds of management personnel of companies. The main reason is that all the seven phases demand financial investment. The management will be worried if those investments are not returned with premium. At this juncture, as indicated in the previous paragraphs the proposed Seven phase ZDM model will contribute not only financial benefits but also non-financial benefits. The benefits of applying ZDM are listed below.

Tangible quality improvement
Intangible quality improvement
Enhanced motivation of employees
Enhanced enthusiasm attained by the employees
Enhanced positive attitude of employees
Enhanced self discipline of employees
Enhanced work culture of employees
Enhanced team spirit of employees
Enhanced decision making ability of employees
Enhanced awareness (knowledge) of employees
Enhanced initiative attitude of employees
Enhanced union support

Although the above benefits will lead to smooth functioning of the company and increase profitability, the management would be interested to see the results in financial values. This is due to reason that, the majority of the inputs by the management towards ZDM programme are in financial form. Hence a system to financially account the proposed Seven phase ZDM model would be a major contribution to modern days organizations. The authors have ventured in his direction, but the details have not formed the scope of this paper.

6. CONCLUSION

The ultimate goal of TQM is to attain zero defects in all aspects of organizational performance. This shall be achieved through continuous quality improvement efforts. However the research works leading to attainment of this objective appear to be dismally low. This presumably due to the domination of statistical techniques, which recommend the dilution of zero, defects. However, few ZDM programmes under different titles have emanated during various periods of quality improvement era [16]. Some of them have thrived while the remaining have subsided. In this background, the literature mining reported in this paper assumes special significance. The literatures were drawn from Emerald Library, U.K. The credibility of Emerald Library is that most of their journals are listed in world's leading databases. Hence the authors are of the opinion that the inferences drawn from those papers on ZDM would represent the global scenario. Since the authors could not locate any integrated model, a generalised integrated model named as seven-phase ZDM model has been designed and proposed in this paper. Further it is claimed that a system to financially account ZDM programme is imperative, as management is more sensitive to financial results. The authors conclude this paper claiming that in the absence of such a financial accounting system, no ZDM programme will be able to motivate the management and thrive in today's organizational scenario.

7. REFERENCES

1. **Logothetis, N.,** (1997), -Managing for Total Quality- Deming to Taguchi and SPC-Prentice hall of India, India.
2. **Lal,H.,** (1990), *Total Quality Management - A practical approach,* Wiley Eastern Limited, New Delhi, India.
3. ISO, (1994), ISO 9000: 1994, ISO9001: 1994,ISO 9002:1994 and ISO9003: 1994 Standards.
4. ISO, (2000), ISO 9000: 2000, ISO 9001:2000 and ISO 9004:2000 standards.
5. **Bengt, K., Wiklund, Hand Edgeman, R.L.,** (2001), "Six sigma seen as a methodology for total quality management", *Measuring Business Excellence,* Vol.5, No.1 pp.31-35.
6. ASTM, (1959), *Tool Engineers Handbook- Second Edition,* McGraw Hill book company, NY.
7. **Fisher, M.,** (1999), "Process improvement by poka-yoke", *Work Study,* Vol.48, No.7, pp.264-266.
8. **Ripley, R.E., and Ripley, M.J.,** (1992), "Empowerment, the corner stone of quality: Empowering management in Innovative organisations in the 1990's", *Management Decision,* Vol.30 No.4, abstract.
9. **Ripley, R.E. and Ripley, M.J.,** (1993),"Empowering management in innovative organisations in the 1990s:Part 1", *Empowerment in organisations,* Vol.1 No.1, Abstract.
10. **Cuylenburg, P.V.,** (1991), "Why TQM," *Managing Service Quality,* Vol.1,no.1, abstract.
11. **King, T.,**(1990), "Quality - A Belief and Awareness", *Work Study* Vol.39, No.6, abstract.
12. **Meyer, A.D. and Ferdows, K.,** (1990), "Influence of manufacturing improvement programme on performance", *International Journal of Operation and production Managements* Vol.10, No.2, abstract.

13. **Crawford, L.E.D. and Shutler, P.,** (1999), "Total quality management in education: problems and issues for the classroom teacher", *The International Journal of Educational Managements,* Vol 13 No.2 pp.67-72.
14. **Behara, R.S., Fontenot, G.F. and Gresham, A.,** (1995), "Customer satisfaction measurement and analysis using six sigma", *International Journal of Quality and Reliability management,* Vol.12, No.3, pp.9-18.
15. **Behara, R.S. and Lemmink, J.G.A.M.,** (1997), "Benchmarking field services using a zero defects approach", vol.14, no.5, pp.512-526.
16. **Aboulanaga, I.A.,** (1998), "Integrating quality and environmental management as competitive business strategy for 21st century", *Environmental Management and Health,* Vol.9 No.2, pp.65-71.
17. **Hill, F.M. and Taylor, W.A.,** (1991), "Total quality management in higher education", *International Journal of Educational Managements, assemble automation,* Vol.5, Nno.5, abstract.
18. **Ngin, P.M. and Chong, C.L.,** (1997), "Achieving zero defects", *The case of star Union Engineering, Singapore., Employee relations,*Vol.19, No.4, pp.374-387.
19. **Perona, M.,** (1998), "Manufacturing conformity assessment through Taguchi's quality loss function", *International Journal of Quality and reliability Management,* Vol.15, No.8/9, pp.931-946.
20. **Hollingum, J. and Stone, C.,** (1998), "Safety products must be safe", Vol.18, No.2, pp.abstract.
21. **Riley, D.,**(2000)," Switch to zero defect production", *Assembly Automation,* Vol.20, No.3,page 11.
22. **Price,F.,** (1991), "Chasing perfection", *The TQM Magazine,* Vol.3, No.5, abstract.
23. **Smith, G.E.,** 1992, "Zero Acceptance Number Plans and Zero Defects", *International Journal of Quality and Reliability Management* Vol.9, No.3, abstract.
24. **Xie, M. and Goh, T.N.,** "Improvement Detection by Control Charts for High Yield Processes", *International Journal of Quality and reliability Management,* Vol.10 No.7.abstract.

GCMM 2004
Editors: Prasad K D V Yarlagadda and S Narayanan
Copyright © 2005, Vellore Institute of Technology, Vellore, India
Publisher: Narosa Publishing House Pvt. Ltd., New Delhi, India

Theory to Practice: Implementing TQM through Change Management

Debabrata Ghosh*, Ranodeep Sinha* & Sathish Rajamani**

* Students, Dept. of Mechanical Engineering, Vellore Institute of Technology
**Student, DLPD- Birla Institute of Technology, Pilani – Engineer, Oracle India Pvt. Ltd.

Abstract

In 21st Century, Organization change has become a way of life. Total Quality Management (TQM) had been widely accepted by many organizations as a change process and a 'Key to Success'. Yet, in many organizations, the 'change for the better' had not been smooth. An in-depth analysis of the various hurdles and the missing links in handling the 'Change Management' are analysed in this paper .A Holistic model is suggested to over come them in the successful implementation of TQM

Keywords
Total, Quality, Management, TQM, Change,

1.INTRODUCTION

Quality principles are a buzzword for today's organizations. Much has been said and written about the quality principles and the benefits it brings to the organizations. Numerous interpretations of Total Quality Management (TQM) in organizations have been made. TQM advocates company-wide approach to managing change. They seek to change the philosophy or culture of the organization and are intended to improve business performance.

However, McKinsey has reported that more than two-thirds of the Quality initiatives across organizations, over the past two decades have failed to realize the expected benefits. The very foundation of processes and organizations is shaken. "WHY" is the question that appears before us again and again and a working reality that comes in our minds is Managing Change in implementing Total Quality Management. This paper focuses on this key aspect of Change Management.

This paper is structured as follows. The Methodology used to identify the problem on Change Management is first explained along with an overview of the Change Management process. A discussion on the key factors of 'Change management' and the missing links, especially, in today's Indian Scenario is done. A holistic approach to overcome these hurdles is provided. Finally, the conclusions outline the main findings of this work.

2. METHODOLOGY

Interactions with employees of leading organizations in India over a period of time led us to identify the various problems faced in TQM implementation. Further research questions posed to them in the form as a questionnaire prepared by us helped to identify the problem. The Pareto analysis of the responses indicated that managing change in organizations from an Indian perspective poses impediments to the implementation and success of TQM. It is seen that the most difficult part of TQM process is managing and sustaining the methods of organizational change necessary to transform an organization, so that quality becomes a 'way of life'.

3. CHANGE MANAGEMENT

In today's business environment, organizations need to continuously adapt to new conditions and respond to competitive pressures. Especially, when TQM is thought of, change management plays a big role in its implementation in any industry. The basic problem of change lies with the fact that TQM brings in a change in the existing ORGANISATIONAL BEHAVIOUR. As a result of this huge change the workforce and the management are thrown off their regular way of life and a new way of life is established. To make the people adapt to this new way of life, is the major challenge of any TQM initiative.

We, as per our research believe that people must be made to believe the very fact and essence of TQM that Total Quality Management is "not to do different things but it is a way of doing things differently". The problem of change management is basically the problem of bringing a system out of the process i.e. "Defreezing" the existing system and then "Refreezing" the system in an entirely new way. This is possible only through a structured Change Management.

4. ANALYSIS

4.1 TQM as a change

TQM offers a company wide perspective on managing change that includes all members of an organization, from top management to the operational personnel. TQM is concerned with quality improvement on a company-wide basis. It is a comprehensive approach to improving competitiveness, effectiveness and flexibility through planning, organizing and understanding all the activities undertaken by people within an organization.

4.2 Key problem areas

Various problems and the missing links were identified during our research. They are:
- o Conventional mindset of the top management, which does not visualize the need for change.
- o The top management's lack of commitment to the TQM programme.

- o TQM as a cult or fad is imposed upon the work force, which does not inwardly accept it.
- o Viewing TQM as a short-term programme or as a system of Statistical Process Control with immediate returns.
- o Viewing TQM as an expense rather than an investment.
- o Viewing TQM as an extra burden and a basic.
- o Faulty training programmes.
- o Wrong interpretations of TQM techniques.
- o The basic desire to resist change in the existing system.
- o These problems were analysed in detail with reference to Indian Context and a practical approach is suggested.

5. A HOLISTIC MODEL

Based on our research we feel that the following 'Holistic Model of change management process' would be a practical way for successful TQM implementation.

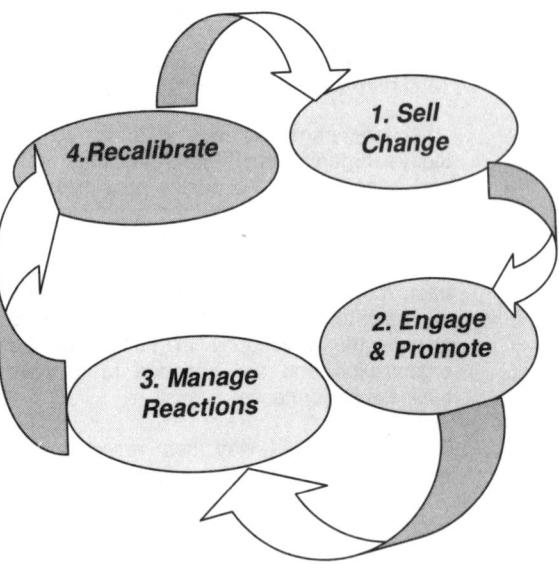

This simple model has 4 different steps. They are
- Sell Change
- Engage and Promote
- Manage Reactions
- Recalibrate

5.1 Sell Change

This is the basic step. This step should aim at winning the participation of all concerned. Necessary resource identification and allocation should be made in this step. It is easy to get the participation of all by having representatives from the employees who should play the role of a champion or a driver. The Champions should be involved in creating the blue print for implementation and in setting up the various deliverable targets. Important aspect is to start small and be realistic.

One example, which was commonly cited by the participants of our research, was the example of setting targets for Defects. The change management procedure becomes tough if you load the staff or operator suddenly with defined targets like "ZERO DEFECTS". He will feel overloaded and would resist the change whereas if you put the target as "REDUCE DEFECTS" and then introduce the ways it would be easier and the resistance would also be less.

5.2 Engage and Promote

This is a key step of change management, which focuses on providing clear goals and performance measures. The role of the Top management is critical in this step and their engagement level would determine the course of further actions. The people at the top should clearly differentiate between a Business Process Reengineering (BPR) and TQM. While TQM and BPR share a focus on customers and processes, they should understand the main difference. BPR gets a company where it needs to be, fast; TQM moves the company in the same direction but a bit slow. The Top management should be clear that TQM is not dramatic and it involves incremental adjustments. The fullest Engagement of the top management initially, helps TQM to be built into a company's culture and can go on working without much day to day attention from management in future

Communication gaps were cited as a reason for difficulties in change management. Good Communication system should be devised to update the employees on the developments in the journey of TQM. Poor communication structure spells the death knell for any TQM initiative undertaken. The poorer the communication the worse is the situation. A poor communication would make the employees feel that information is being hidden from them. Communication system should be used effectively as a method of Promotion of TQM philosophy.

Then come the actual promotional activities that includes employee training, motivating and inducing a sense of need for change.

Restructuring of the training programmes is necessary for acceptance of the change that is to be brought about. Flooding the trainees with principles they cannot understand leads to the failure of the training efforts. Instead a generic approach with examples of personal life improvements is ideal to set the programmes in flow. Small assignments and games to the trainees can set them rocking on the concept of change in TQM. The training activities should be redesigned to promote both Conceptual learning and operational learning. In other words, a Promotional learning needs to be devised. Rather than leaving the training activities to the external agencies, the Management should be engaged directly in the training activities with inputs from the agencies.

As a part of promotional efforts, TQM activities should become a part of In-house journals and magazines. Significant contributors should be rewarded. This in turn would motivate others to get into the TQM groove. Improvements should be depicted in simple and easy format with simple graphs or other visual control methods.

Tell the staff regarding the corporate performance and it should also show the performance standards of other competitors. This clearly shows them the need for change and would help in their engagement.

5.3 Manage Reactions

A literature on Change management explains that the reactions of an individual or a group to changes and their ability to cope to the changes can be viewed as a state of:
- Shock
- Defensiveness
- Acceptance
- Adaptation & Growth

The top management and the implementation teams including the TQM champions and drivers should be highly sensible to it. The Communication and Motivation programmes should be geared to handle each of these key aspects. Wherever required tailor-made approach should be devised to handle specific cases.

Davenport developed a concept of Process innovation. This was an ambitious management change programme, which fuses information technology and human resource management for improving business performance. The implementators should understand the power of the Collective human system. The Management needs to reinvent them by helping the people develop and refine new sets of interlinked skills and capabilities. This would help them to become powerful positive players in the dynamics of change thereby increasing the level of acceptance

5.4 Recalibrate

This step helps to find out the current status of the efforts made in the earlier steps and provides an opportunity to redefine the targets in line with the overall objectives of the organization. This step helps in channelising the learning and to go forward for much higher targets. It provides an opportunity to view change as a continuous process and make change a way of life. This in turn fosters organizational development.

6. CONCLUSION

This paper explored the different hurdles faced by the organization during the change management for implementing TQM. The missing links were analysed with live examples from Indian Industries. A four step, holistic approach is suggested which takes care of all the key aspects of Change management. It provides a guideline for the management to focus on. This model is based on the foundation of continuous improvement. If this model is followed in true spirit then we are sure that the Organization following this would be highly successful in their journey towards excellence.

7. REFERENCES

1. **Deming W E** 1982 Improvement of Quality and Productivity through action by management – *National productivity Review (Winter, 1982)*
2. **Kevin Dooley** - Perceptions of Success and Failure in Total Quality Management Initiatives," *Journal of Quality Management*, 3(2): 157-174.
3. **Jeff Dooley** – *Cultural Aspects of Systematic Change Management*
4. **F J C Martins** – *Change and its Management*
5. **Jeff Dooley** – *A Systematic approach to Organization Change management*
6. **Geoff Elliott** – *Business Performance Improvement*
7. **Davenport** 1993 *Process Innovation: Reengineering work through Information Technology*, Boston: Harvard Business Press
8. **Wendy Currie** – *Proceedings of the 2000 Winter Simulation Conference*
9. **Hammer and J Champy** 1993 *Re-engineering the Corporation: A Manifesto for Business Revolution*, London:Nicholas Brearley Publishing
10. **Rao** *TQM: A Cross functional Perspective*
11. **Kid Sadgrove** *Making TQM Work* Kogan Page Publishers
12. **John Okland**, *Total Quality Management - The Route to Improving Performance*, 2nd Edition, Butter Worth - Heinemann, Oxford
13. **D. H. Besterfield, C. Besterfield-Michna, G. H. Besterfield, and M. Besterfield**- *'Total Quality Management'* Second Edition, Pearson Education Indian Edition, 2003

GCMM 2004
Editors: Prasad K D V Yarlagadda and S Narayanan
Copyright © 2005, Vellore Institute of Technology, Vellore, India
Publisher: Narosa Publishing House Pvt. Ltd., New Delhi, India

Understanding the Six Sigma– A Breakthrough Strategy for Business Improvement

Arunachalam S

Senior Lecturer, School of Computing & Technology, University of East London, Longbridge Road, Dagenham, Essex RM8 2AS, UK

E-mail: s.arunachalam@uel.ac.uk

Thoburn J G

Director, Seven Sigma Training (UK), Coventry, UK

Email: graham.thoburn@seven-sigma.có.uk
www.seven-sigma.co.uk

Lenny Koh S C

Lecturer, Management School, University of Sheffield, UK

Email: S.C.L.Koh@sheffield.ac.uk

Abstract

Too many companies worldwide fail to make an appropriate financial investment in improvement tools to eliminate non value added activities or emphasise zero free quality attributes. Today, investing in quality improvements tools should be considered equally important to investment in equipment and machinery. The absence of continuous improvement efforts to enhance quality issues in business operations that equalize or exceed customer expectations, could mean that companies are unlikely to survive the fierce global competition. To reach world-class performance levels, businesses must find better ways to direct their corporate resource and efforts; one such approach is Six Sigma. Six Sigma is a disciplined methodology for improving organizations' processes, based on rigorous statistical analysis. In the recent years, there has been an increasing trend in companies adopting Six Sigma techniques both in manufacturing and service sectors. Six Sigma focuses on helping organizations produce products and services better, faster and cheaper by improving the capability of processes to meet customer requirements. This paper presents an overview of Six Sigma philosophy with reference to the methodology and its benefits to companies.

Keywords
Six sigma, Quality, Lean manufacturing, continuous improvement, TQM

1. INTRODUCTION

Globally, maintaining or exceeding customers' quality expectations has become an essential requirement to survive business for companies of all types and sizes. In the last twenty years, approaches like World Class Manufacturing (WCM), Just-in- Time (JIT), Flexible Manufacturing Systems (FMS), Total Quality Management (TQM), Statistical Process Control (SPC), Business Process Reengineering (BPR), benchmarking and business excellence have been suggested as the drivers of manufacturing success [1]. But lately, there has been an increasing interest in Six Sigma to achieve excellence in quality through intensive application of statistical techniques. It has been demonstrated that implementing Six Sigma into an organisation's corporate culture, improves processes and maximises business performance, thereby helping companies to achieve a distinct competitive edge through improved quality. Commitment to Six Sigma accomplishes this goal. Appropriate training and a top-down commitment of the organization makes Six Sigma effective [2].

Six Sigma identifies and eliminates activities and costs, which add no value to customers. Unlike simple cost-cutting programs, Six Sigma delivers cost cuts whilst retaining or improving value to the customer. Six Sigma is being used to improve key areas such as high scrap rates and costly waste, under-utilized capacity and slow cycle times due to high process variation.

Six Sigma was pioneered by Motorola in the 1980s as an approach to improving productivity and quality, and reducing costs in the face of overwhelming competition from Japan. The company recognized that technology at the time was so complex that it was rendering old ideas about acceptable quality levels obsolete, so it developed a quality philosophy based on a goal for process quality of Six Sigma, consequently changing its internal perception of 'acceptable' quality from parts per hundred to parts per million [3]

2. THE FOUNDATIONS OF SIX SIGMA

Six Sigma is a philosophy of continuous improvement and measurement to eliminate defects to a near zero level. Six Sigma emphasizes quality improvement, but is much more than statistics and tools. When properly deployed on carefully selected business projects, Six Sigma application virtually eliminates defects before they occur, which saves valuable corporate resources. That translates into immediate and dramatic financial profitability [4,5]. Six Sigma is a disciplined methodology for improving processes, using statistical data collection and analysis. The approach concentrates on manufacturing high quality products at a faster pace and lowers cost by improving the capability of processes specifically to meet customer requirements. Six Sigma identifies and eliminates costs, which add no value to customers. Unlike simple cost-cutting programmes, however, Six Sigma delivers cost cuts while retaining or improving value to the customer [6]. Six Sigma levels of performance are often expressed in 'Defects Per Million Opportunities' (DPMO). DPMO simply shows how many activities would emerge if a process was repeated 1 million times.

Sigma is a statistical measure of variability in a given process. The name Six Sigma is derived from a statistical heritage. Lower case Sigma (σ) is a Greek letter assigned to represent the amount of variation or inconsistency a measurable outcome exhibits. In manufacturing, for instance, it could be used to measure the number of sub-standard products. In a service industry, it could be used to quantify delays in delivery or other procedures. As a way of running a business, Six Sigma is a highly disciplined improvement system that helps individuals and companies eliminate costly problems, develop and deliver near perfect products or services [7, 8].

In Six Sigma, process variation is only half the width of the design tolerances for the process, i.e. the difference between the upper specification limit (USL) and lower specification limit (LSL) (Figure 1) 99.9997 per cent of the process output is contained by this natural spread. Clearly a process running at Six Sigma is highly capable of meeting the design specifications - only 3.4 parts per million will be outside these specifications [9, 10]. Controlling processes in the longer term so that they remain on target can prove difficult in many practical situations. A typical process is likely to

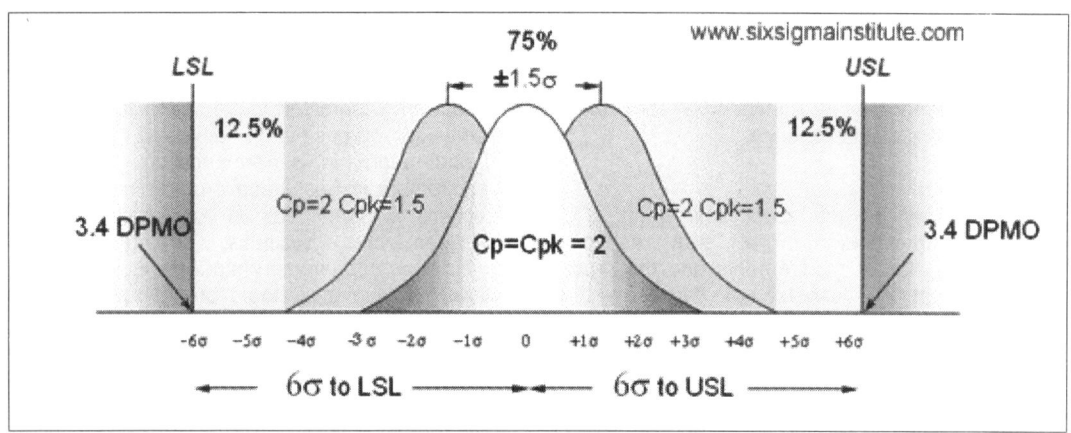

Fig.1: Six Sigma Performance

deviate from its natural centring position by up to one and half standard deviations. Applying this principle, longer-term capability of the process can be calculated based on the initial short-term capability of the process based on the initial specifications. The statistical basis of Six Sigma, in particular the 1.5 sigma shift, is not without its critics but this is outside our scope. Suffice to say the issue of process shifts and process capability is a practical problem in many industries [11]. Variation in the process behaviour leads to defects or poor quality and defects that reach the customer are significant problems to business.. Attaining a Six Sigma rate of improvement means the variation in the process has limited to a defects rate to 3.4 per million opportunities-virtual defect-free performances [12]. Leading global companies have attained Six Sigma; most companies, however, are operating at levels of around four sigma, or approximately 6,000 defects per million, according to estimates (Table 1)

Table 1: Sigma Conversion Table

Yield	DPMO	Sigma
30.9%	690,000	1.0
69.2	308,000	2.0
93.3	66,800	3.0
99.4	6,210	4.0
99.98	320	5.0
99.9997	3.4	6.0

3. SIX SIGMA METHODOLOGY

Six Sigma uses a project approach. It identifies a problem and uses appropriate statistical tools. One of the most commonly used methodology is – Define, Measure, Analyze, Improve, Control technique described below: (Figure 2) is based on the

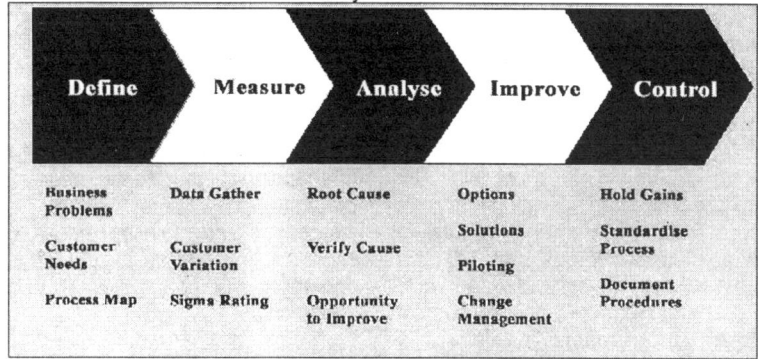

Fig. 2: DMAIC Approach

Shewhart Plan-Do-Check-Act cycle (PDCA) [13]. An organization's key business performances are enhanced by following the five phases in sequence.

Phase 1
- Defines the scope and goals of the improvement project with respect to customer requirements and the process that are capable of delivering these requirements

Phase 2
- Collects data on the selected problem and identifies key customer requirements, and product and process characteristics.

Phase 3:
- Analyses and identifies the gap between the current and desired performance. Once identified, problems are then prioritized and root causes are identified. Benchmarking the process outputs, products or services, against recognised benchmark standards of performance may also be carried out at this stage.

Phase 4
- Designs and carries out experiments to establish cause and effect relationships and optimizes the process.

Phase 5
- Implements improvement methods to processes identified from the previous phase. . Standards of operation are then documented in systems such as ISO 9000 and standards of performance will be established using techniques such as SPC. Process capability is calculated again to establish whether the performance gains are being sustained. The cycle is repeated, if further performance shortfalls are identified [14, 15].

4. PROVISION FOR SIX SIGMA

The key feature of a successful Six Sigma culture is the creation of an infrastructure that supports and invests in performance improvement. Six Sigma programmes involve major investment and must deliver bottom-line results. Successful Six Sigma programmes require a combination of the following characteristics [16]. One of the objectives of Six Sigma is to achieve business transformation; hence, it requires specific leadership qualities to make it happen. Committed leaders who have the clarity of purpose and drive to achieve breakthroughs in performance are a vital requirement in Six Sigma programmes. The success is dependent on the strong links between the business strategy and continuous improvement strategy. Six Sigma aims to achieve strategic breakthroughs in performance. Organizations that have successfully embraced it ensure that it supports their strategic objectives and key performance measures, and that it is well integrated throughout the organization. [17, 18].

4. BENEFITS TO COMPANIES

Applying Six Sigma in companies has lead to potential to deliver improved performance and increased profits through a wide variety of mechanisms. By striving to achieve a Six Sigma level of quality, companies reduce costs related to scrap, rework, inspection, and customer dissatisfaction. Other benefits include:

- o Cost reduction
- o Improvement in customer satisfaction
- o Increase in sales and sales force effectiveness
- o Drives operational and administrative process improvement, leading to cost saving, increased productivity and improved shareholder value.
- o Deeper understanding of business operations [19,20].

5. CONCLUSION

Every manufacturing company and many other organisations are under immense pressure to improve their business performance through improved profits, cost reduction and increased shareholder value, simultaneously delivering quality. Six Sigma methodology is considered to be a breakthrough strategy that establishes awareness and strive for continuous quality improvement efforts to enhance business operations that equalize or exceed customer expectations.

6. REFERENCES

1. **Andrew Cave**, Quality World January 2001
2. Anonymous, 1998, "The fundamentals of Six Sigma",Quality Progress, 31, 6,36-7.
3. **Randals,** Quality World January 2001
4. Bowman, R, 1997, "Best practices: the joy of Six Sigma", Distribution.
5. **Hendericks, C, Kelbaugh, R,** 1998, "Implementing Six Sigma at GE*", The Journal for Quality and Participation.*
6. **Tadikamala, P**, 1994, "The confusion over Six Sigma quality", Quality Progress.
7. **Kane, L**, 1998, "The quest for Six Sigma", Hydrocarbom Processing (International Edition), 77, 2.
8. The Breakthrough Management Strategy Revolutionizing the World's Top Corporations by **Mikel Harry]**
9. **Motorola** University,Quality World January 2001
10. **Eckes, G**., 2001, Making Six Sigma Last, Managing the Balance Between Culture andTechnical Change. John Wiley and Sons Inc.
11. **Minahan, T**, 1997, "Allied signal board by building up suppliers", Information Access Company, 123, 4, 38.
12. **Fortenot, G, Behara, R, Gresham, A**, 1994, "Six Sigma in customer satisfaction", Quality Progress.
13. **Smith, G,** 1993, "Benchmarking success at Motorola", Copyright Soceity of Management Accountants of Canada.
14. **Thompson, C,** 1994, "Operating the TQM way", Credit Union Management.
15. **Welch, J,** 1996, "GE quality 2000", Executive Speeches.
16. Anonymous, 1998, "What have been the results of Six Sigma?", Quality Progress, 31, 6, 39.
17. **Welch, J,** 1996, "Quality 2000", Executive Excellence.
18. **Breyfogle, F.W**., 1999, Implementing Six Sigma: Smarter Solutions Using Statistical Methods, John Wiley & Sons, New York, NY.
19. **Lazarus, I.R., Stamps, B**., 2002, "The promise of Six Sigma: getting better faster", Extra Ordinary Sense, 3, 3-29.
20 **Hoerl, R,** 1998, "Six Sigma and the future of the quality profession", Quality Progress, 31, 6, 35, 38.

Optimization

GCMM 2004
Editors: Prasad K D V Yarlagadda and S Narayanan
Copyright © 2005, Vellore Institute of Technology, Vellore, India
Publisher: Narosa Publishing House Pvt. Ltd., New Delhi, India

Optimization of Sliding Contact Characteristics of Unidirectional FRP Composites

Prabhu Raja V, Gomathinayagam A, Giriraj B, Thyla P R

Department of Mechanical Engineering,
PSG College of Technology, Coimbatore - 641 004.

E-mail id: prabhuraja_venu@yahoo.com

Abstract

The contact characteristics of unidirectional continuous fiber-reinforced plastic (FRP) composites are investigated based on Hwu and Fan's closed form analytical solution. The friction and wear behaviour varies with sliding direction, fiber and matrix material combinations, fiber volume fraction and fiber ply orientation. The optimum values of the contact parameters are obtained using Genetic Algorithm (GA). The optimization tool developed can be effectively used for the manufacture of composite components so as to realize maximum friction and wear resisting characteristics.

Keywords
Composite, Orientation, Contact Pressure, Genetic Algorithm

1. INTRODUCTION

Fiber reinforced polymer (FRP) composites are being increasingly used as alternatives for conventional materials primarily because of their high specific strength, specific stiffness and tailorable properties. In addition, the self-lubrication capabilities and low noise of the composites render them suitable for applications like seals, bearings, gears and artificial prosthetic joints.

FRP composite materials are comprised of fiber and matrix elements. The fibers provide necessary mechanical characteristics. The most common filled fiber reinforcements are glass, carbon (graphite) and aramid. The matrix material is used to bind the fibers together and to protect them from environmental conditions and handling. The most common matrix materials are epoxy and PEEK (Polyether ether ketone).

The fiber orientation has a significant influence on wear and friction behaviour of FRP composites [1,2,3]. For the purpose of fully utilizing the beneficial contact characteristics of FRP composites, it is necessary to obtain an in-depth knowledge of their contact behaviour. Hertzian and other fundamental contact theories are not valid for FRP composites due to their anisotropy. Fan and Hwu [4,5] derived a general closed-form solution for the sliding contact of bodies on anisotropic elastic planes.

Ning and Lovell [6] studied the sliding contact between the composite half-plane and a rigid cylinder. They have investigated that the friction and wear behaviour of FRP composites varies with sliding direction, fiber and matrix material combinations, fiber volume fraction and fiber ply orientation. Ning and Lovell [6] have also predicted that the composites have maximum wear resistance

649

when the contact pressure is maximum. This contact pressure is again a function of the above said parameters.

An optimization tool is needed to determine the contact parameters at which the contact pressure is maximum. In this work, the optimum values of the contact parameters are obtained using Genetic Algorithm (GA). The optimization tool developed can be effectively used for the manufacture of composite components so as to realize maximum friction and wear resisting characteristics.

2. PROBLEM FORMULATION

In this work, the unidirectional FRP composite is modeled as quasi-homogeneous, transversely isotropic elastic half-plane that is in contact with an infinitely long, rigid parabolic cylinder.

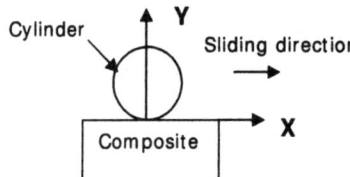

Fig.1: Contact model of a rigid cylinder on FRP composite

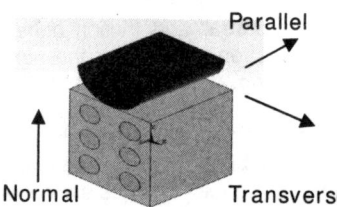

Fig.2: Contact model showing different sliding directions

The two-dimensional sliding contact pressure P(x) on the anisotropic elastic half-plane has been obtained using Hwu and Fan's [4,5] analytical solution as

$$P(x) = \frac{2\sin(\delta\pi)}{(\beta + \bar{\beta})}(b - x)^\delta (x + a)^{1-\delta} \quad ----- (1)$$

In the above equation, the contact pressure P(x) is a function of position (x), symmetry parameter (δ), contact patch [a,b] and anisotropy parameter (β). δ, a, b and β are given by

$$\delta = \frac{1}{2\pi} \arg\left(\frac{-\bar{\beta}}{\beta}\right); 0 \le \delta \le 1$$

$$a^2 = \frac{\delta(\beta + \bar{\beta})RF}{\pi(1 - \delta)} \quad -------- (2)$$

$$b^2 = \frac{(1 - \delta)(\beta + \bar{\beta})RF}{\delta\pi}$$

$$\beta = \frac{1}{L_{22}} - if\frac{S_{12}}{L_{22}}$$

where R is the radius of parabolic cylinder, F is the normal force applied and L_{ij} and S_{ij} are components of Barnett-Lothe tensors. The explicit expressions of L and S for orthotropic materials have been given in terms of the elastic components C_{ij} by Dongye and Ting [7] as follows:

$$S_{21} = \left(\frac{C_{66}(\sqrt{C_{11}C_{22}} - C_{12})}{C_{22}(C_{12} + 2C_{66} + \sqrt{C_{11}C_{22}})}\right)$$

$$S_{12} = \frac{-\sqrt{C_{22}/C_{11}}}{S_{21}}$$

$$L_{11} = (C_{12} + \sqrt{C_{11}C_{22}})S_{21} \quad -------- (3)$$

$$L_{22} = \frac{\sqrt{C_{22}/C_{11}}}{L_{11}}$$

$$L_{33} = (C_{44}C_{55})^{1/2}$$

The values of δ, a, b and β are the functions of elastic properties of the composites, their material properties and fiber ply orientation. The components of the stiffness may be expressed in terms of engineering constants as follows:

$$C_{11} = \frac{E_1}{1 - v_{12}v_{21}}$$

$$C_{12} = \frac{v_{12}E_2}{1 - v_{12}v_{21}}$$

$$\quad --------- (4)$$

$$C_{22} = \frac{E_2}{1 - v_{12}v_{21}}$$

$$C_{66} = G_{12}$$

If the fiber is assumed to be isotropic, the elastic constants can be determined using the elastic properties of the fiber and the matrix as presented by Rosen [8] and Hashin [9]:

$$E_3 = E_m V_m + E_f V_f + \frac{4V_m V_f (v_f - v_m)^2}{V_m/k_f + V_f/k_m + 1/G_m}$$

$$v_{31} = E_m v_m + E_f v_f + \frac{V_m V_f (v_f - v_m)(1/k_m - 1/k_f)}{V_m / k_f + V_f / k_m + 1/G_m}$$

$$G_{12} = G_m \frac{(\alpha + \beta_m V_f)(1 + \rho V_f^3) - 3V_f V_m^2 \beta_m^2}{(\alpha - V_f)(1 + \rho V_f^3) - 3V_f V_m^2 \beta_m^2}$$

$$E_1 = E_2 = \frac{4k_t G_{12}}{k_t + G_{12}(1 + 4k_t v_{31}^2 / E_3)}$$

$$v_{12} = E_1 / 2G_{12} - 1$$

$$\frac{E_i}{v_{ij}} = \frac{E_j}{v_{ji}}; (i, j = 1, 2, 3) \qquad \text{-------- (5)}$$

$$k_t = \frac{k_m k_t + (V_f k_f + V_m k_m)G_m}{V_m k_f + V_f k_m + G_m}$$

$$\alpha = (\gamma + \beta_m)/(\gamma - 1)$$

$$k_f = E_f / 2(1 - v_f - 2v_f^2)$$

$$k_m = E_m / 2(1 - v_m - 2v_m^2)$$

$$\beta_f = 1/(3 - 4v_f)$$

$$\beta_m = 1/(3 - 4v_m)$$

$$\rho = (\beta_m - \gamma \beta_f)/(1 + \gamma \beta_f)$$

$$\gamma = G_f / G_m$$

$$f = (V_f / f_f + V_m / f_m)^{-1}$$

For an angle lamina, the components of the stiffness matrix can be expressed as follows:

$$\overline{C_{11}} = C_{11}C^4 + C_{22}S^4 + 2[C_{12} + 2C_{66}]S^2 C^2$$

$$\overline{C_{12}} = [C_{11} + C_{22} - 4C_{66}]S^2 C^2 + C_{12}[C^4 + S^4]$$

$$\overline{C_{22}} = C_{11}S^4 + C_{22}C^4 + 2[C_{12} + 2C_{66}]S^2 C^2$$

$$\overline{C_{16}} = [C_{11} - C_{22} - 2C_{66}]C^3 S - \qquad \text{-------- (6)}$$
$$[C_{22} - C_{12} - 2C_{66}]S^3 C$$

$$\overline{C_{26}} = [C_{11} - C_{22} - 2C_{66}]CS^3 - [C_{22} - C_{12} - 2C_{66}]SC^3$$

$$\overline{C_{66}} = [C_{11} + C_{22} - 2C_{12} - 2C_{66}]S^2 C^2 + C_{66}[S^4 + C^4]$$

where C = Cos and S = Sin

3. GENETIC ALGORITHM

It is found from the equations (1) – (6) that the contact pressure depends on sliding direction (M), Young's modulus of fiber (E_f), fiber volume fraction (V_f), Young's modulus of matrix (E_m), applied normal force (F), radius of curvature of the parabolic cylinder (R) and fiber ply orientation (θ).

In this work, three sliding directions, four fiber materials, fiber volume fraction varying from 40% to 70%, two matrix materials and fiber ply orientation between 0 and 90 degrees are considered. A normal force of 30 N and radius of 8 mm is assumed. Hence, the contact pressure is taken as a function of M, E_f, V_f, E_m and θ. The values of E_f and E_m are related to fiber material number (N_f) and matrix material number (N_m).

An attempt has been made to optimize the above contact parameters with the objective of maximizing the contact pressure. The technique used here for optimization of the contact parameters is genetic algorithm (GA) [10].

The values assigned to M, N_f and N_m and the corresponding material properties are given in Table 1 to 3. In GA, all the variables are expressed by strings of bits. The values of different variables and corresponding number of bits required for binary representation are given in Table 4. Thus, a total of nineteen bits were required to represent an input string i.e. string length is equal to 19. Thus, the objective function has a solution space of size $2^{19} = 5, 24, 288$.

Table 1 Values of M

M	0	1	2
Sliding Direction	Transverse	Normal	Parallel

Table 2 Values of N_f and Material Properties

Nf	0	1	2	3
Fiber Material	E-Glass	Aramid	Stainless Steel	AS-4 Carbon
Modulus (GPa)	72	130	183	235
Poisson's Ratio	0.2	0.36	0.3	0.2
Frictional Coefficient	0.43	0.17	0.18	0

Table.3 Values of N_m and Material Properties

N_m	0	1
Fiber Material	Epoxy	PEEK
Modulus (GPa)	0.33	3.6
Poisson's Ratio	0.34	0.3
Frictional Coefficient	0.3	0.4

Table. 4 Values of Variables and Number of Bits Considered

Variables	Range of Values	No. of bits considered
M	0,1,2	2
N_f	0,1,2,3	2
V_f	40% - 60%	7
N_m	0,1	1
θ	0 - 90	7

The genetic operators namely reproduction, crossover and mutation are applied to the strings of length 19 bits, for the process of optimization. The crossover carried out here is three-point-crossover with 100% probability. The mutation is carried out with 3% probability. The population size is considered to be 50, with 50 population generations. Hence with the technique of genetic algorithm, the total number of objective function value calculations is reduced to 2,500 (50×50) from the space of 2^{19}. The processes in GA are explained in Fig. 3.

The objective function and constraints are given below:

Maximize

$$P = \frac{2\sin(\delta\pi)}{(\beta+\bar{\beta})}(b)^{\delta}(a)^{1-\delta} \qquad \text{-------- (7)}$$

subjected to

$$0 \le M \le 2; 0 \le N_f \le 3;$$
$$0.4 \le V_f \le 0.7; 0 \le N_m \le 1;$$
$$0 \le \theta \le 90;$$

M, N_f and N_m are integers

where $P = f(M, E_f, V_f, E_m, \theta)$
$= f(M, N_f, V_f, N_m, \theta)$

The optimum values of contact parameters obtained from the GA are given in Table 5. The sample output of GA for the optimization of contact parameters for the unidirectional FRP composites is shown in Fig. 4.

Table 5 Results of GA

Contact Parameter	Optimum Value
Sliding Direction (M)	2 (Normal)
Fiber Material (N_f)	3 (AS4-Carbon)
Volume Fraction (V_f)	70 %
Matrix Material (N_m)	1 (PEEK)
Fiber Ply Orientation (θ)	22.5° and 67.5°
Contact Pressure (P_{max})	67.21 MPa

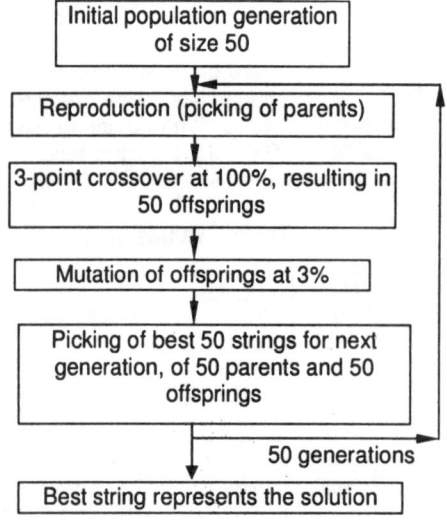

Fig. 3: Processes in GA

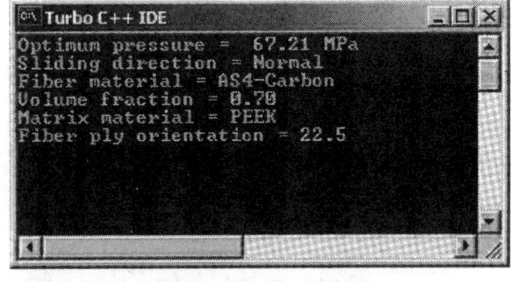

(a)

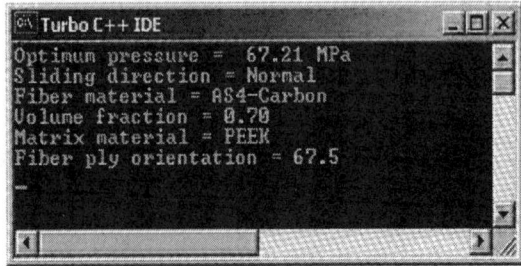

(b)

Fig. 4: Output of GA

4. CONCLUSIONS

Instead of studying the influence of contact parameters independently and identifying the optimum values, the GA directly gives the optimum values of the contact parameters. The findings obtained from GA are summarized below:

- The normal direction has more wear resistance because the fibers are carrying larger portion of the load in that direction
- In the case of material combinations, the materials with higher elastic modulus contribute more to the contact pressure
- If the volume fraction of the fiber is more, the contact pressure is also high
- The contact pressure is maximum at two values of fiber ply orientation i.e. $22.5°$ and $67.5°$
- The optimization tool developed can be effectively used for the manufacture of composite components so as to realize maximum friction and wear resisting characteristics

5. NOMENCLATURE

E_1, E_2 = Young's modulus of the transversely isotropic plane

E_3 = Young's modulus of the plane normal to the transversely isotropic plane

F = Applied normal force

G = Shear modulus

K = Bulk modulus

L, S = Barnett-Lothe tensor

P(x) = Pressure distribution

R = Radius of curvature of the parabolic cylinder

V = Volume fraction
= Poisson's ratio

f = Frictional coefficient
= Symmetry parameter
= Anisotropic characteristic parameter

f, m, t = Subscripts expressing the matrix, fiber and transverse respectively

6. REFERENCES

1. **Sung, N. H., and Suh, N. P.**, 1978, "Effect of Fiber Orientation on Friction and Wear of Fiber Reinforced Polymeric Composites", Wear, 53, pp. 129-141.

2. **Cirino, M., Friedrich. K., and Pipes, R.B.,** 1988, "The Effect of Fiber Orientation on the Abrasive Wear Behaviour of Polymer Composite Materials", Wear, 121, pp. 127-141

3. **Viswananth, B., Verma, A. P., and Rao, V. S. K.**, 1993, "Effect of Reinforcement on Friction and Wear of Fabric Reinforced Polymer Composites", Wear 167, pp.93-99.

4. **Hwu, C., and Fan, C. W.**, 1998, "Contact Problems of Two Dissimilar Anisotropic Elastic Bodies", ASME J. Appl. Mech., 65, pp. 580-587.

5. **Hwu, C., and Fan, C. W.**, 1998, "Sliding Punches With or Without Friction Along the Surface of Anisotropic Elastic Half-Plane", Q. J. Mech. Appl. Math., 51, pp.159-177.

6. Xinguo Ning and Michael R. Lovell, 2002, "On the Sliding Friction Characteristics of Unidirectional FRP Composites", ASME Journal of Tribology, 124, pp. 5-13.

7. **Dongye, C., and Ting, T. C. T.**, 1989, "Explicit expressions of Barnett-Lothe Tensors and Their Associated Tensors for Orthotropic Materials", Q. J. Mech. Appl. Math., 47, pp. 724-734.

8. **Rosen, B. W.**, 1973, "Stiffness of Fiber Composite Materials", Composites, 4, pp. 16-25.

9. **Hashin, Z.**, 1983, "Analysis of Composite Materials - A Survey", ASME J. Appl. Mech., 50, pp. 481-505.

10. **Rao, S.S.**, 1995, "Engineering Optimization Techniques", Wiley Eastern, New Delhi.

GCMM 2004
Editors: Prasad K D V Yarlagadda and S Narayanan
Copyright © 2005, Vellore Institute of Technology, Vellore, India
Publisher: Narosa Publishing House Pvt. Ltd., New Delhi, India

Study of Dynamic Behavior of Boring Tool Holder and Optimization of Tool Parameters using Computational Models

Alwarsamy T* & Balasubramanian R**

Antony Amal Raj*, Prasannaa. Shu*, Gopal Dass A***

*Assistant Professor, **Professor, ***Students

Government College of Technology -Anna University, Coimbatore, 641013, India

E-mail: alwar_samy@yahoo.co.in

Abstract

One way of improving the damping of the system is by adding damping to the tool side, since workpiece is a rotating structure in boring. The study includes the feasibility of using a damped tool holder for boring tools and other cost effective techniques to improve the stability during machining. **Finite Element Analysis** is performed to study dynamic behavior of EN 31steel tool holder and also replacing it by composite tool holder, lead filled EN 31steel tool holder. Modal analysis, Harmonic analysis and Transient dynamic analysis are performed and results are analyzed. In addition, to optimize tool parameters, a **Genetic Algorithm** is developed. The developed Genetic Algorithm gives the optimized value of the inertia mass of the boring tool holder. Based on the optimized value obtained using Genetic Algorithm, steel tool holder with lead at its core is modeled. Finally, boring tool holder with lead is designed and tested in CNC machining center. Surface finish of machined workpieces are measured and compared.

Keywords

Boring Tool, Finite Element, Genetic Algorithm.

1. INTRODUCTION

The standard boring tool made of EN-31 is modeled for finite element analysis to study its dynamic behavior. Also the boring tool filled with Lead is modeled to study its dynamic behavior. Modal, harmonic and transient dynamic analyses have been performed and the results are compared.

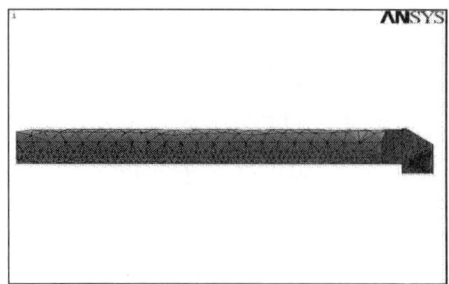

Fig.1:Finite element model of Boring tool

2. DETAILS OF MODAL ANALYSIS

The modal analysis is used to determine the natural frequencies and mode shapes of a structure. The natural frequencies and mode shapes are important parameters of a structure for dynamic loading conditions. Modal analysis is a linear analysis. Any nonlinearity, such as plasticity and contact (gap) elements, are ignored even if they are defined.

Type of an analysis - structural
Element type - solid 92
Shape of solid 92 - tetrahedron
Number of elements
For tool without Lead - 40,668
For tool with Lead - 1, 15,392
Clamping length - 70mm, 80mm, 90 mm, 100 mm,123mm

2.1. RESULTS OF MODAL ANALYSIS

From the result of modal analysis it is observed that using Lead filled tool holder, enhances the natural frequency. An increasing in natural frequency(as given in Table 1) implies an increase in dynamic stiffness of the body. Thus by using Lead filled tool holder, the overall dynamic stiffness and the stability have been improved. The mode shapes are shown in Fig.2 and 3.

Table 1- Natural frequencies for an overhang of 153 mm

Mode	Natural frequency of Tool without Lead (Hz)	Natural frequency of Tool with Lead (Hz)
1	1093.6	1204.4
2	1984.4	2097.4
3	5592.0	5653.8
4	8409.4	8642.3
5	9356.8	9513.8
6	9764.8	9953.1
7	10847.0	10962.0
8	12592.0	12754.0
9	12892.0	12974.0
10	13806.0	13982.0

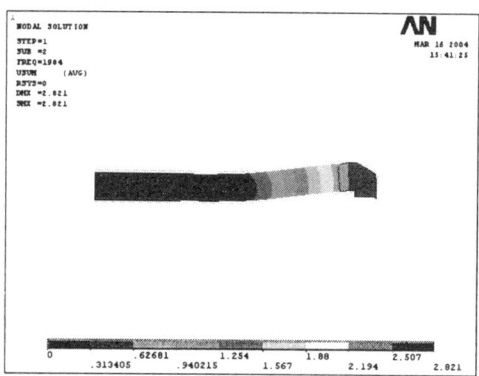

Fig.2:Second mode shape for the over hang 153 mm without Lead (f_n = 1984.0 Hz)

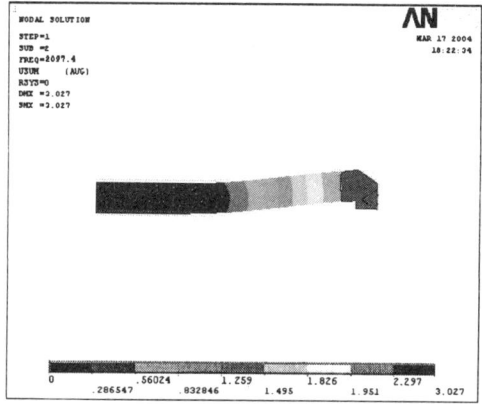

Fig.3: Second mode shape for the over hang of 153 mm with Lead (f_n = 2097.4 Hz)

3. HARMONIC RESPONSE ANALYSIS

Harmonic response analysis is technique used to determine the steady-state response of a linear structure to loads that vary sinusoidal with time and the Amplitude of vibration is recorded in Table 2. The results are evident with the graphs given in Fig. 4 and 5.

Table 2 - Computing result

Modal	Amplitude of vibration (μm)
Boring tool without Lead	5.468
Boring tool with Lead	5.368

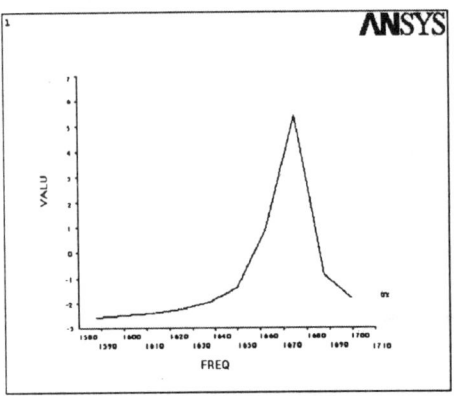

Fig.4:Result of harmonic analysis

(without Lead)

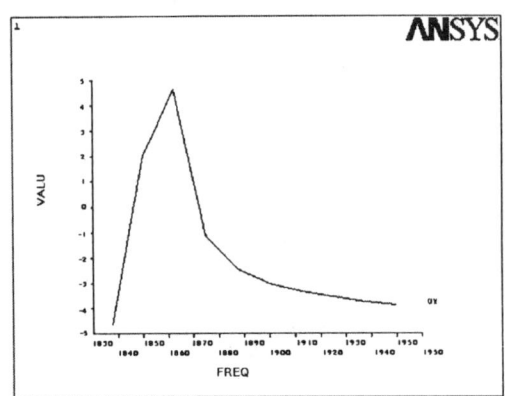

Fig.5: Result of harmonic analysis (with Lead)

4.0 TRANSIENT DYNAMIC ANALYSIS

Transient dynamic analysis is a technique used to determine the dynamic response of a structure under the action of any general time-dependent loads. The result of transient dynamic analysis is given in table It is observed that boring tool with Lead has significant improvement in its dynamic stability.

Stability Analysis	K_t	K_c	M_t	K_w	M_w
	kN/m	kN/m	kg	kN/m	kg
SGA	GA Test – With Mutation				
	5838	1681	1.0	665	2.59
	GA Test – Without Mutation				
	4218	1262	0.8	494	2.02

Table 3 - Results of transient dynamic analysis

Time taken to decay the amplitude	Seconds
Boring tool without Lead	0.50
Boring tool with Lead	0.42

5. GENETIC ALGORITHMS

Genetic algorithms are computerized search procedure based on the mechanics of natural genetics and natural selection that can be used to obtain global and robust solutions to optimization problems. Genetic algorithms are computational optimization schemes with an unconventional approach.

Simple genetic algorithm ()

Initialize population;
Evaluate population;
While termination criteria not reached
{
Select solutions for next iterations;
Perform crossover;
Perform mutation;
Evaluate population;
}
}

Table 4 - SGA Input Parameters

S. No	Input Parameters	Test 1	Test 2	Test 3	Test 4
1	Number of parameters	7	7	7	7
2	Maximum Generation	1000	1000	1000	1000
3	Chromosome length	14	14	14	14
4	Population size (POP)	20	50	30	20
5	Crossover Probability(P_c)	0.8	0.6	0.95	0.8
6	Mutation Prob.(P_m)	0.001	0.001	0.01	0

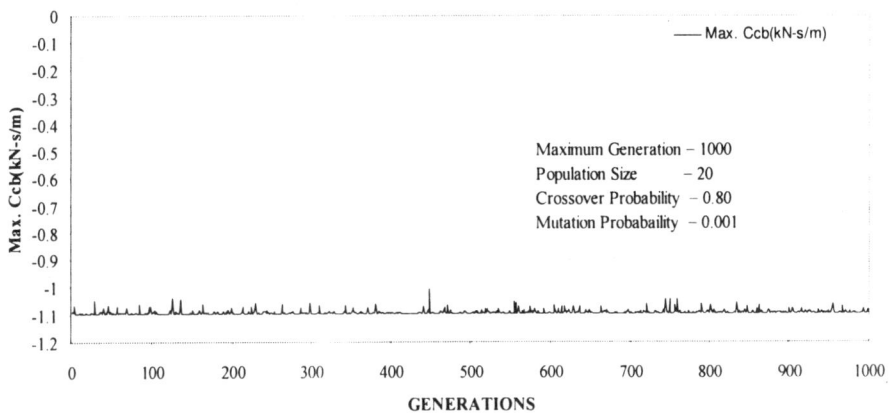

Maximum Generation – 1000
Population Size – 20
Crossover Probability – 0.80
Mutation Probability – 0.001

Fig.6: Generation Vs. Maximum stability boundary

The results of SGA test are shown in Fig.6

Cutting Parameter	Spindle Speed rpm (*n*)			
	850	900	950	1000
Cutting velocity, V_c (m/min)	114.77	121.52	128.27	135.02
Metal removal rate, $V(m^3/min)$	2.75	2092	3.08	3.24
Machining time, *t* (min)	0.31	0.3	0.28	0.27

Table 5 – SGA Results

6. MEASUREMENT OF SURFACE FINISH OF MACHINED COMPONENTS

In order to validate the proposed concept of optimal mass of tool holder cutting experiments are performed at various cutting velocity(as in Table 6) in CNC machining centre. After performing cutting tests, the surface finish of the workpieces are measured and compared as in Table 7 and 8.

Table 6 - Surface finish of machined workpiece by boring tool without Lead

Boring tool	Cutting velocity (m/min)	Surface roughness values (R_a)			
		Trial-1	Trial-2	Trial-3	Avg.
WOL-1	114.77	0.8	0.83	0.83	0.82
WOL-2	121.52	0.9	0.86	0.79	0.85
WOL-3	128.27	0.91	0.92	0.9	0.92
WOL-4	135.02	1.01	0.9	0.96	0.96

Table 7 - Surface finish of machined workpiece by boring tool with Lead

Boring tool	Cutting velocity (m/min)	Surface roughness values (R_a)			
		Trial-1	Trial-2	Trial-3	Avg.
WL-1	114.77	0.71	0.75	0.7	0.72
WL-2	121.52	0.8	0.73	0.75	0.76
WL-3	128.27	0.84	0.81	0.81	0.82
WL-4	135.02	0.8	0.78	0.76	0.78

7. CONCLUSION

Results of cutting test show that surface finish of machined components has been improved in boring. The results agree with the theoretical investigation. The optimized values obtained using Genetic Algorithm plays a vital role in getting improved results.

8. REFERENCES

1. **Rao S S**,1985, Mechanical Vibrations, Addison Wesley Limited
2. **Kalyanmoy Deb**, 2000, Optimization for Engineering design Algorithms and examples, *Prentice Hall India Limited.*
3. **David E. Goldberg**, 1999, Genetic Algorithms, Addison- Wesley Longman Inc.
4. **Rivin, E.I** and **Kang, H.L.**, 1989, "Improvement of Machining conditions by tuned dynamic stiffness of tool", Int. J. Mach. Tools Manufact, Vol 29, No.3, pp 361-376
5. **Cantu-Paz, E.** and **Goldberg, D.E.,** 2000, 'Parallel genetic algorithms: theory and practice', *Computer Methods in Applied Mechanics and Engineering.* New York: Elsevier.
6. **Mehdi, K., Rigal, J.F.**and **Play, D.**, 2002, 'Dynamic Behavior of a Thin-Walled Cylindrical Workpiece During the Turning Process, Part 2: Experimental Approach and Validation', *Transactions of the American Society of Mechanical Engineers, Journal of Manufacturing Science and Engineering,* Vol. 124, pp. 569-579.
7. **Melanie Mitchell**, 1996, *'An Introduction to Genetic Algorithms',* Massachusetts Institute of Technology Press, Cambridge, MA, U.S.A.

GCMM 2004
Editors: Prasad K D V Yarlagadda and S Narayanan
Publisher: Narosa Publishing House Pvt. Ltd., New Delhi, India

Topology Optimisation of Compliant Mechanisms for Displacement Amplification with FEA

Arun Kumar G & Srinivasan P S S

Department of Mechanical Engineering, Kongu Engineering College,
Perundurai-638 052, Tamilnadu, India.

Anantha Suresh G K

Department of Mechanical Engineering, IISC, Bangalore, India.

Abstract

A Topology Optimisation method is developed to design a displacement amplifying compliant mechanisms for induced strain actuators. Two optimisation methods are developed, one that maximises the stroke amplification or geometric advantage (GA) of the Mechanism, and another one maximises the mechanical efficiency (ME) of the mechanism. These formulations are implemented using two different solutions methods. Sequential Linear Programming and an Optimality Criteria (OC) method. Computation time and mechanism performances are compared for the two solution methods.

Keywords

Compliant Mechanisms, Mechanical Amplifier, Piezoelectric Actuator, Geometric Advantage, Topology Optimisation.

1. INTRODUCTION

One type of smart material typically used is a piezoceramic actuator, a solid state device that possesses a high energy density and a high output force. One limitation of this type of actuator how ever is that its output displacement is only about 0.1% strain, thus limiting its output stroke performance. To increase the effective stroke of these piezoelectric actuators compliant mechanism amplifier single piece jointless mechanism that employs elastic deformation to achieve motion and mechanical amplification can be used. Two design formulations have been developed to design compliant amplifiers for piezoceramic actuators based on topology optimization technique and the finite element method.

2. PROBLEM FORMULATION

The problem is posed as the design of compliant mechanisms coupled with input force provided by a piezoelectric actuator. The compliant mechanism is to act as a coupling structure, which amplifies the stroke of the piezoelectric actuator. When considering the design of compliant amplifiers there are two measures of performance. The resulting output displacement and the blocked force at the output of the amplifier. The ratio of output displacement to input displacement or geometric advantage (GA) is to be maximised. Consider a load f_a applied at an input point A representing the input force from the piezoelectric material as mentioned in figure1.

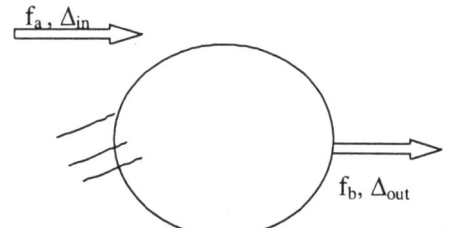

Fig.1: Geometric Advantage Design Problem

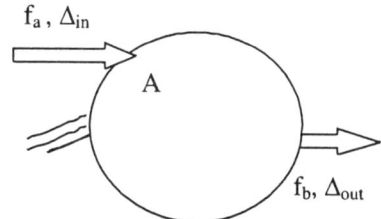

Fig.2: Mechanical Efficiency Design Problem

This force is proportional to the voltage applied to the piezoelectric material. It is desired that compliant mechanisms amplify the input deflection (Δ_{in}) while transferring it to an output point B. The deflection at the output point can be formulated by applying a unit dummy load f_b at an output point B in the direction of (Δ_{out}). This output deflection shown in the equation 1, is equivalent to the mutual potential energy (MPE), Which is simply the energy due to two different sets of loading.

$$\Delta_{out} = MPE = V_b^T K U a \qquad (1)$$

In equation 1, V_b is the deflection field due to the applied load f_b. U_a is the deflection field due to the applied load f_a applied at the input point A, and K is the global stiffness matrix. A similar expression is obtained for equation (Δ_{in}) in equation 2, where the input load is assumed to be a unit load.

$$\Delta_{in} = U_a^T K U a \qquad (2)$$

The objective function and constraints are then given by equation 3. Constraints on this problem consist of equilibrium equations, an upper limit on total material resource, and upper and lower limits on the design variables. In this case the ratio of the output to input displacement serves as the design objective.

$$Max\ (GA) = V_b^T K U_a / U_a^T K U a \qquad (3)$$

s.t. $f_a = K U_a$
$\quad f_b = K V_b$
Volume $< V_0$

To amplify the input displacement, both the force and deflection transmitted to the output location can be considered simultaneously by considering the overall mechanical efficiency of the compliant mechanism amplifier. The Mechanical Efficiency is defind as the ratio of the work provided by the compliant mechanism at the output location to the work provided by the PZT actuator material at the input location. The output work is the work done against a linear spring of stiffness Ks and the input work is simply the product of the input force and the input deflection (or) $fa^T \Delta_{in}$.

3. SOLUTION METHDOLOGY

The design formulations have been implemented using two different approaches: Sequential Linear Programming and Optimality Criteria methods (OC). In each case the problems are solved using a linear finite element analysis. To account for element bending, frame elements arranged in a uniform ground structure are used to discretize the given design domain. The design variables are the cross sectional areas of each element. To implement the SLP method, the user first specifies the location and direction of the input force f_a and output deflection (Δ_{out}).

The user also provides upper and lower designs limits on the cross-sectional areas of the frame elements. An initial starting point must be supplied for the algorithm as well as a maximum step size, which imposes a move limit when updating the design variables. The algorithm iterations proceed as follows. First the nodal deflections the structure are obtained using a linear finite element analysis. Then the sensitivities of the objective function are calculated and used to solve the constrained optimization problem.

a) Sequential Linear Programming Procedure
b) Computational process of Optimality Criteria Method

As an alternative solution method, the Optimality Criteria method is also employed. Since there is only one active constraint an OC method can be used to provide more rapid convergence. The Optimisation procedure will give an alternate optimality criterion.

The procedure involves the following steps:

1) The deflection of the structure is obtained using a linear finite element analysis
2) The design variables are resized based on the optimality criterion
3) A search direction, S is defined
4) A one-dimensional minimisation on the variable is used to find the maximum objective value along this direction while constraining the design variables to remain within their bounds.

This line search procedure is necessary to ensure that the algorithm moves toward a maximum rather than a minimum solution.

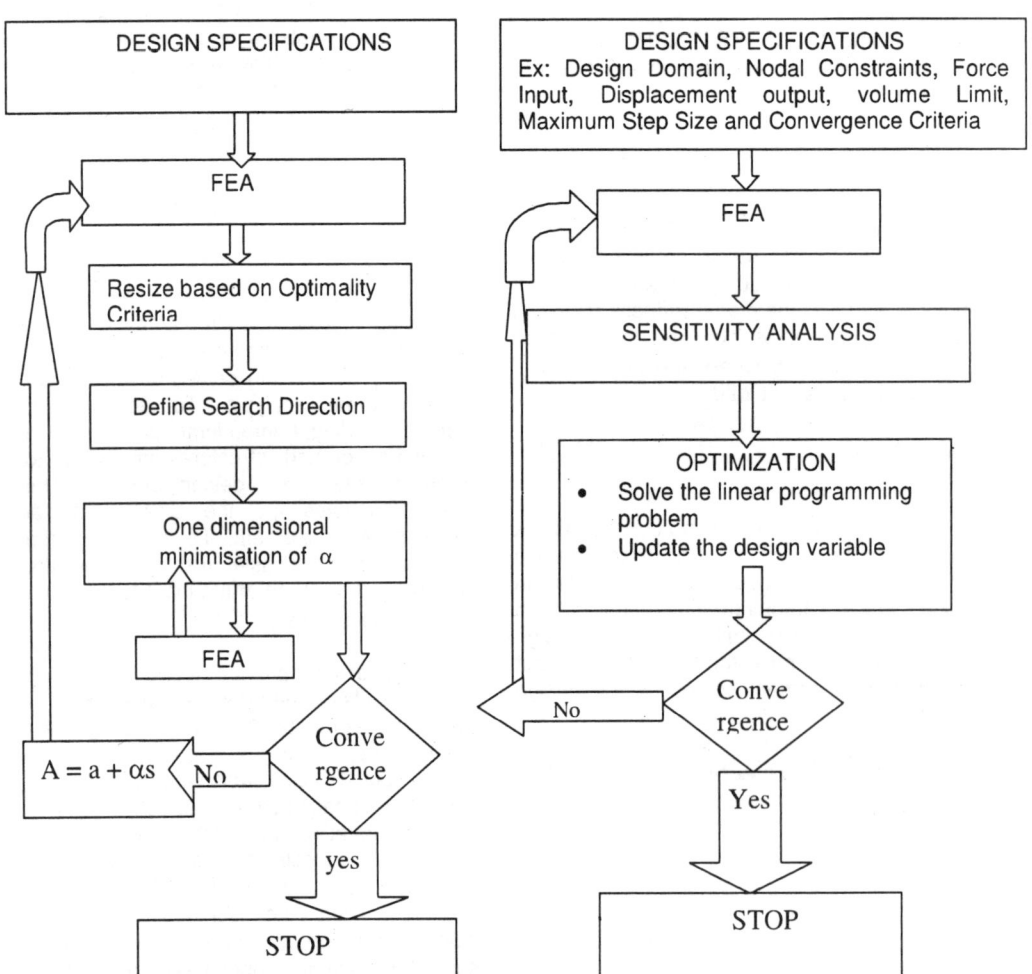

a) Optimality Criteria Method

b) Sequential Linear Programming

3.1 Example

The design domain, loading and constraint conditions of the specified design problem, where the input force and output deflection are in the same sense but displaced laterally from one another. The problem is solved with both the Max (ME) and Max (GA) formulations to illustrate the distinctions between them. The discretized design domain as well as the nodal constraints are defind.

4. MAXIMISATION OF MECHANICAL EFFICIENCY BY SLP

When using the max (ME) formulations, the algorithm converged to a solution a few mints. The maximum step size in the design variable update was set to 15% of the previous value to insure the linear approximation remained valid. The optimal topology is illustrated as a greyscale plot in fig, where frame members whose design variable reached the lower bound constraint are not shown. The deformed profile of the mechanism as well as the convergence history is plotted. At the convergence the resulting topology yields a stroke amplifications of GA 1.42.Additionally the mechanical advantage the ratio of input force to the amount of force available at the output) was found to be 0.63,resulting in a structure which is 89% mechanically efficient overall. So while this design only amplified the input displacement by 40% it did so while optimisation routine seeks to find a structure which transmits the most force to the output location while simultaneously maximising the deflection at that location.

5. MAXIMISATION OF (GA) BY SLP

In comparison when coupling the max (GA) formulation with the same SLP routine, the result after a runtime of 2.5 minutes on a Pentium III processor, is a design that amplifies the actuator stroke by more than four times. The optimal structure, deformed profile and convergence history are depicted. This resulting topology yields a compliant amplifier, which is 32% mechanical efficient, thus transmitting only a third of the work input by the piezoceramic elements. This maximisation of stroke amplification solution outperforms the Max (ME) formulation in terms of displacement amplification though it

is less efficient than the previous result, as efficiency is not taken in to account in the current solution.

5. COMPARISON OF SOLUTION METHODS-RESULT

Both the SLP and OC Methods do not guarantee that the solution obtained is a global Optimum values and solution runtimes resulting from the SLP and OC methods. The max GA formulation is solved again using the OC solution procedure stated previously. Employing the same initial ground structure as before, the optimal topology predicted by the OC method converges on a geometric advantage equalling 3.265 representing a 25% decrease in amplification from the previous optimum. Although the present example is not very computationally expensive, similar runtime gains can be extrapolated to problems with larger number of design variables.

6. CONCLUSIONS

(1) The differing optimal topologies using the SLP and OC solution methods illustrate the existence of several local optima. These results demonstrate that the choice of solution method given the same initial starting point plays a significant role in both computer performance and optimal design properties.

(2) The results presented in this paper illustrate that implementation of the max (GA) and max (ME) formulations yield functional topologies for design of complaint mechanism amplifiers for piezo electric actuators. The convergence histories indicate that in each case the design objective is Maximised while satisfying the constraints. There are limitations to these methods, however, In max (GA) formulation although the geometric advantage is to be maximised, there is no direct control over its value in the optimisation procedure.

(3) For a given set of input-output requirements, it may not be possible to achieve amplification at all, the maximum value of GA may be less than one.

(4) In the Max (ME) formulation, there is no direct control over the specific value of the ME or the Garth optimiser tends to converge to a results interms of overall GA and ME is the maximisation of the

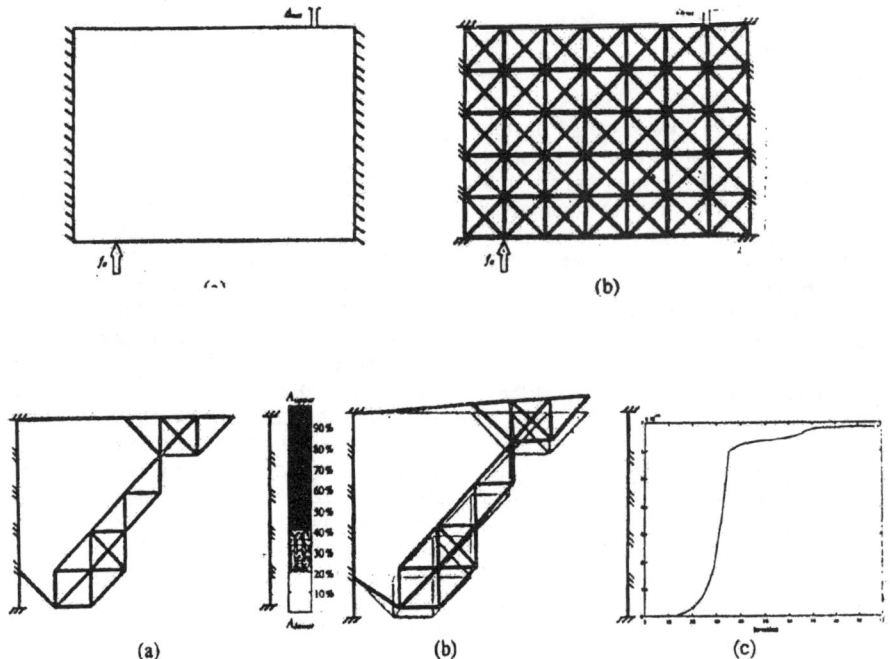

Figure 2 Maximization of ME using SLP (a) Optimal Topology (b) Deformed Profile
(c) Convergence History   GA=1.42   ME=0.89

mechanical efficiency subject to a specified GA.

(5) The optimisation formulations developed in this paper consider only the topology of the compliant mechanism amplifier while assuming that the piezo electric material provides a constant input force.

However it is widely known that the most efficient amplifier for a piezoelectric actuator is one in which its stiffness matches the stiffness of the piezoelectric material. Direct control of the overall stiffness in the topology optimization procedure is difficult. It is possible to prescribe the stiffness of the complaint mechanisms as a subsequent optimisation procedure.

7. REFERENCES

1) **Frecker, M., Ananthasuresh, G.K., Nishiwaki,N and Kota.S.,** ".Topological Synthesis of compliant mechanisms using Multi-Criteria optimisation". *Journal of Mechanical design, Transactions of the ASME*, Vol. 119, No.2 June 1997,pp.238-245

2) **Saxena A., Ananthasuresh, G. K.,** 1998,An Optimality Criteria approach for the topological synthesis of compliant mechanisms, *Proceedings 1998 ASME Design Engineering Technical Conference*, DETC98/mech-5937.

3) **Shield,R.T., and Prager,W.** 1970, Optimal structural design for given deflection.*Journal of Applied Mathematics and Physics* pp.513-523.

4) **Belegundu, A and chandrupatla,T,** 1999,Optimisation concepts and applications in engineering,upper saddle river,New Jersy,Prentice Hall. Piezoelectric Actuator, Topology Optimisation.

5) **Venkayya,V.B.,** Optimality criteria: A Basis for multidisciplinary Optimization, *Computational Mechanics,* Vol. 5,PP 1-21,1989.

6) **Saxena, A. and Ananthasuresh, G.K.,** Topology Optimisation of compliant mechanisms with strength considerations, *Mechanics of Structures and Machines,*29(2001),pp.445-467.

7) **Saxena,A. and Ananthasuresh,G.K.,** Topology Synthesis of Compliant Mechanisms for non-linear force-deflection and curved path specifications. *Journal of Mechanical Design ASME,*Vol.123,No.1,March 2001,pp.33-42.

8) **Yin, L. and Ananthasuresh, G.K.,** A Novel Formulation for the Design of Distributed Compliant Mechanisms, *Mechanics Based Design of Structures and Machines,* Vol.31, No.2, 2003.pp.151-179

8. ACKNOWLEDGEMENT

The authors gratefully acknowledge Canfield.S and Frecker.M for their work on "Topology Optimisation of compliant mechanisms" which helped us to mend and polish our work.

Education

GCMM 2004
Editors: Prasad K D V Yarlagadda and S Narayanan
Copyright © 2005, Vellore Institute of Technology, Vellore, India
Publisher: Narosa Publishing House Pvt. Ltd., New Delhi, India

Advanced Manufacturing System: Education and Training –

An Emerging Need of the New Economic and Globlisation Era

Vora Y D

Asst. Prof., Mech Engg, Government Engineering College
4th floor, M S Bldg, Gandhinagar-382 011, Gujarat, India.

E-mail- yd_vora@mailcity.com

Vasudevan P

Prof. Mech. Engg., Indian Institute of Technology, Mumbai.

Abstract

Presently, education and technology both are rapidly changing in the world. After globalization and new economic era, a greater demand to provide highly educated manpower in the area of advanced manufacturing system with certain level of competency is felt worldwide. This is required to produce quality goods in mass production at optimum (lowest possible) cost to face global competition. As a result of this, it has become necessary to update the present advanced manufacturing system education and training programme to cope up with the cyber edge to make the industries/service sectors enough competent – quality vise, economy vice and productivity vise internationally.

This paper deals with the planning and implementation of advanced manufacturing education program and training modules for different level personnel's considering the emerging requirements of industries and other sectors.

Keywords
Advanced Manufacturing, Education.

1. INTRODUCTION

True technological revolution has taken place when the world has entered in new economic era and globalization phase during the year 1990. Before this, industrial growth was confined in the hands of few corporate sectors and handful industries. For the multinational companies, floodgates were opened to participate in the economic activity everywhere after globalization. Thus, the industries are exposed to both – global and local competitions. Moreover, at the same time, the environmental protection is given prime importance and considered as one of the important aspects worldwide. The rules and regulations related to this issue are made strict and compulsory for the manufacturing industries.

1.1 Importance of Advanced Manufacturing Education and Training

In this changing scenario, the great need of technological requirements and services are demanded by the industries/service sectors to improve quality, productivity and economy to compete the global market. Due to this, an emerging demands to provide knowledgeable / skilled manpower with certain level of competency in the field of advanced manufacturing is created. This has forced to change present advanced manufacturing education system by implementing a new competency based advanced manufacturing education and training system. Hence, advanced manufacturing education and training is considered as one of the important issue in the information age.

2 PRESENT MANUFACTURING EDUCATION PROGRAM – AT A GLANCE

Looking to the present requirements of manufacturing industries the advanced manufacturing education program offered by the various institutions worldwide, can be categorize into three groups: -
(i)   Operators level program – Certificate program,
(ii)   Supervisory level program – Diploma / Degree program,
(iii)   Higher-level program –Post Graduate and Research.

The first, operators level programs are mainly designed for the persons connected with actual manufacturing activity and the prime importance are given to practical training with little basic technical information.

While, the supervisory level programs are made for supervisors and more emphasis is given to in depth technical information with management background.

The post graduate and research programs are planed with the main objective to develop / invent new technology, new processes and materials, etc. this requires high level technological knowledge with research and development attitude.

The present advanced manufacturing education programs are not capable to provide the required level of competency and knowledge / skills as needed due to the following reasons:

➢ Lack of planning / improper planning of advanced manufacturing education programs
➢ Lack of knowledge / information's regarding new technologies and the other areas including environmental policy, human behavior / psychology, administration, human resource development etc.
➢ Not revised to accommodate the present requirements i.e. level of competency, skill to be developed, etc.
➢ Missing link between advanced manufacturing education and work.

3. PLANNING A NEW COMPETENCY BASED ADVANCED MANUFACTURING EDUCATIONAND TRAINING PROGRAM

In real sense, it is a challenging task for planners / educators to plan to a new competency based advanced manufacturing education and training program, which can be proved techno-economical.

The planning of such program needs to follow a systematic scientific approach having due considerations of human values and sincere efforts in the right direction.

A systematically planned advanced manufacturing education and training program can only be matched with the industry and society, resulting from rapidly changing technology and other issues to manufacturing industries.

The planners should be capable to predict/visualize/identify the areas of development in advanced manufacturing education looking to the industrial development in the nearest future. According to this, they should forecast the manpower required-teaching staff, supporting staff, etc and other matters related to this area-finance, infrastructure facilities, etc based on the experience and the statistical data collected. They should visit the institutes, which are offering the same courses and try to collect the feedback from them. If they are first, then they should form a group of related expert persons from educational institute and industries.

The advanced manufacturing education programs can be of two types mainly -long term and short term. The result–oriented successful advanced manufacturing education and training program can be planned to make it more fruitful considering the following aspects / tools: -

➢ TQM approach in advanced manufacturing education system.
➢ Technology watch on education system and center for education research.
➢ Application of IT tools and communication technology for effective learning and teaching.
➢ Relating education with business and industry.

The detailed discussion regarding the mentioned aspects / tools are as under.

3.1 TQM Approach in Advanced Manufacturing Education

With the globalization of international economy, the introduction of the concept of Total Quality approach has become a necessity for survival not only for business and industry, but also for advanced manufacturing educational institutions. This believes that customer is the boss and hence the curriculum for advanced manufacturing education should be based on expectations and requirements of the customer i.e. industry.

Basically, TQM consists of mainly four elements as listed below: -

1) Employee involvement and teamwork.
2) Management leadership and commitment.
3) Concentration on customer needs and requirements.
4) Continuous improvement.

Finally, it is highly essential for all advanced manufacturing educational institutions to keep abreast of the emerging thrust on quality and relevance in advanced manufacturing education and take appropriate steps for continuous improvement.

Now, after effective planning of advanced manufacturing education, next important tool is technology watch and center for advanced manufacturing education research.

3.2 Technology Watch and Curriculum Development

New materials of manufacturing and construction, new processes, new concepts and new devices are being developed continuously in different parts of the world. Fiber optics, CAD / CAM / CAE technologies, robotics and automation, e-manufacturing, optical communication and the other new areas have changed the industrial scene and life styles, drastically. Thus, in last decade, the rapidly changing technology and consumer behavior had created a sea change among the industrial working environment. To bring new concepts and technologies into industry, an important step is the production and supply of knowledge / skilled manpower with certain level of competency. Hence, at this stage, it is felt that a there is a need for continuous technology watch to modify and upgrade the advanced manufacturing education system. The syllabus/curriculum of the advanced manufacturing education courses should be designed properly in accordance with industrial needs and other requirements. Moreover, it should be uniform in the state/regions in the country. It should be kept up-to-date and relevant as possible all times. A strong link is required between technology watch group, the industry and the curriculum development cell / agency.

An international professional society / body should be formed to associate with and co-ordinate the activities of these technology watch groups and helps to transmit new information to the institutions. Moreover, it also helps in creating an awareness among the staff / trainers about the new technologies and its impact on educational curriculum.

It is also necessary to establish few Centers for advanced manufacturing education Research and Development in each country according to their needs/expertise. The co-ordination of advanced manufacturing education activities is necessary among these centers and the advanced manufacturing educational institutions. The research reports or feedback reports made by such centers must be circulated to the concerned advanced manufacturing educational institutions so that the corrective measures can be taken within time. Such centers can also be used to update the technical as well as management knowledge in the thrust/developing areas.

3.3 Application of IT, Communication And Other Recent Technology In Education

In addition to planning of advanced manufacturing education, the next important point is Technology Enhanced Learning and Teaching (TELT).

Teaching is needed to facilitate, to create interest and to motivate a learner to learn some thing new, while learning is concerned with acquisition of new skills, knowledge and attitude. Teaching and learning depends upon systematic interaction between the learner, teacher and the environment.

In order to increase the effectiveness of learning and teaching process to uplift the competency level, it is required to adopt IT tools-internet technology, new communication and presentation aids-OHP projectors, multi media facilities and other recent technology. These provide opportunity to the students for: -

➢ Self-learning guided learning or structured learning.
➢ Keeps pace with technology change and capacity needed.
➢ Get education from any university on online mode.
➢ Team working through video conferencing.
➢ On-line assignments, tests, examinations, etc.
➢ Skill development through virtual lab, seminar, group working, etc.

This is applicable to both- teaching / non-teaching staff and students.

3.4 Relating Advanced Manufacturing Education with Industry and Business

To compete in the world market, co-ordination between know how, innovations, manufacturing and business skills are required. This can be only done by relating advanced manufacturing education with business and industry.

The advanced manufacturing education system should be developed in such a way that the industry and business become part of the education system. Presently, such concept is developed and known as industry - institute – symbosis, industry – institute interaction, etc. This will offer the benefit for qualitative development of advanced manufacturing education.

In fact, it is seen that so percentage of an employee's competence will be acquired only through planned on the job training. This is applicable to all levels of advanced manufacturing education discussed earlier.

In the areas like CAD/CAM/CAE, computer and software applications instrumentation, information technology, bio-medical instrumentation, mechatronics, manufacturing, etc such training programs planned with industries can be proved very much beneficial to all the concern-students, institute and industry.

4. WORKING AND ANALYSIS OF ADVANCED MANUFACTURING EDUCATION SYSTEM

Fig. 1 shows the various phases of advanced manufacturing education system for designing/developing any type of advanced manufacturing education programs and courses. These stages are as under: -

• Define objectives and planning of advanced manufacturing education system
• Implementation of systematically planned advanced manufacturing education system
• Programme Evaluation of advanced manufacturing education system programs and its review

4.1 Feedback

The course objectives must be defined clearly initially and then plan it critically considering various aspects-manpower, finance, human psychology, etc with creative thinking. Before implementation of the programs, one should think about the following things:

- Selection of course coordinator/chairman- their job functions, duties and responsibilities, etc
- Teachers/supervisors/non-technical staff - selection and their training in different areas
- Infrastructure facilities, etc

Programme evaluation and its review is a very important step of advanced manufacturing education system. Identify the strength and weakness of the program, which are to be overcome and solved. Get suggestions of the concerned persons and critically review it to improve the future programs. This is the real way of evaluating and reviewing program effectively. Redesign the existing programs considering valuable feedback.

5. CONCLUSION

Under the impact of ever changing and emerging technologies, the role of advanced manufacturing education assumes grater importance for the developing countries. Advanced manufacturing education has to adopt and responds to the advances in technology and emerging socio – industrial environment. It can be said that a new systematically planned competency based advanced manufacturing system education and training programs considering the four important aspects discussed earlier, is enough competent to face any challenges

resulted from rapidly changing technology, globalization and other issues.

Looking to the present emerging need of the new economic and globalization era all over the world, This is the right time to adopt new technology enhanced advanced manufacturing system education and training programme with improving the present education system to ensure better position in a global market as well as to increase the productivity.

6. REFERENCES

1. **George P. G.,** A primer for teachers and administrators of technical education, *ISTE publication,* New Delhi, Edition (1997).
2. **Shivram M. N.,** Training to competency based training – a metamorphosis role of technical education in the context of globalization of Indian Economy, *Indian J. of Technical Education,* vol – 18 (Jan – Mar, 1995).
3. **Natarajan R.,** Challenges and opportunities in the design of technical education for the future, *30th annual convention of ISTE (2000),* 19-25.
4. **Thete A. R.,** Relating technical education with business and industry, *30th annual convention of ISTE (2000)* 91-95.
5. **Robert V. Peltier,** Farouk Attia, A profile of the 21st century engineering technology graduate: an industry perspective, steward and Stevenson services, inc. / University of Houston.
6. **Vora Y. D.,** Faculty development program for technical education, *12th annual ISTE convention (1982).*

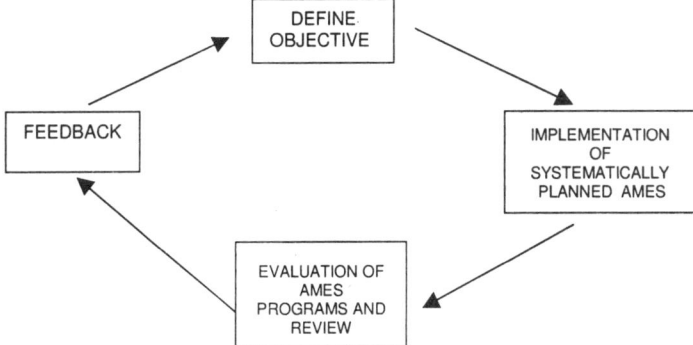

Fig .1: **Phases of Advanced Manufacturing Education System (AMES)**

GCMM 2004
Editors: Prasad K D V Yarlagadda and S Narayanan
Copyright © 2005, Vellore Institute of Technology, Vellore, India
Publisher: Narosa Publishing House Pvt. Ltd., New Delhi, India

Challenge Cycle: A Proposal for Manufacturing Engineering Program in Brazil

Claudio da Rocha Brito, Melany M Ciampi

COPEC- Council of Researches in Education and Sciences
Av. Dr. Epitácio Pessoa, 248 – 33. 11.045-300. Santos – SP - BRAZIL

E-mail: melany@copec.org.br

Abstract

In Engineering field among other few the necessity is a Manufacturing Engineer. To get the goal of forming good Manufacturing Engineers COPEC – Council of Researches in Education and Sciences has conceived a different kind of engineering program. It is a five years program of Manufacturing Engineering. For that it has been included in the program what is called "Challenge Cycle". They are extra classes of peculiar areas of human knowledge, specially selected to make the students to develop their abilities of applying their skills in the global context with success. It is a program that will fulfill the lack of this kind of engineer in the Atlantic Coast Region of São Paulo State, which has a natural vocation to fishing industries due to its large portion of seashore and large number of fishing cooperative communities besides the industries located at the Industrial Park of Cubatão.

Keywords
Challenge Cycle, Extra Classes, Supervised Internship, Work in Projects.

1. INTRODUCTION

For Developing Countries like Brazil it is very important to form engineers committed with science and technology research principally in manufacturing field, because despite of all problems of policy nature of the Country it has many fields that are not behind any other one like USA and France, for example. In a country like Brazil it is very important to form professionals committed with the creation and development of science, principally in engineering field, because Brazil despite the low investment in education system, it is a Country, which among others in biological and engineering areas are not behind other developed Countries. Many representatives groups, leaderships and agencies have been implemented programs to prepare the engineers to increase the efficiency of research system, experimental development, engineering, producing system and market.

This new demand of better quality of professional has motivated the coordinating team of COPEC – Council of Researches in Education and Sciences that has conceived a different kind of approach to a Manufacturing Engineering Program that has been named "Challenge Cycle". It consists in the inclusion of extra classes of peculiar areas of human knowledge, specially selected to make the students to develop their abilities of applying their skills in the global context with success. It is a five years program, morning and/or afternoon classes and supervised internship is a requirement to get the diploma.

2. COPEC WORKING FOR THE FUTURE

COPEC means Council of Research in Education and Sciences. It is constituted by scientists of the several areas of human knowledge and citizens committed with education. Citizens and scientists who believe that education is the main beam in the construction of a better society and that also believe in research and in the development of sciences and technology as the big agents in the fostering of progress and the welfare of human being.

It is a council, which works have the goal to enhance and to maintain relations between universities, institutions of education, enterprises and the society of the several countries for the discussion of education, technology and sciences directions.

The history of COPEC has started with an idea shared by some professionals of sciences and technology. It was the idea of creating a non-governmental organization to foster the research mainly in education and sciences. This idea seized proportions and after some meetings the Council became reality.

Although very young this Council through its very active members has already a history of participations in scientific events in education and technology, also sponsoring conferences and developing projects since 1994, with the goal of enhancing discussions about education, technology and science congregating specialists of the five continents. Its mission is to stimulate and to foster the efforts to bring an international perspective in education. It aims to establish and maintain the interchange among institutions, educators of educational institutions in Brazil and in the several

countries worldwide. It is a council that seeks the improvement of communication and the interchange of researches in education field and sciences between the countries.

It also aims the development of an apprenticeship community and the development of education and sciences areas constituting in an intelligent way of collective knowledge for the integration with social and economic agents of community.

3. THE PROGRAM

The new paradigm of education preaches that the capital is the intellect and people are the most important, but by the other hand it is still difficult the total absorption of this new model of development [01]. Changes have been happening and many of them are successful. COPEC proposal program for engineering education is one of the successful new kind of forming good engineers prepared to face next century.

The producing of goods and services in every part of the world has changed dramatically in the last years of XX century and beginning of XXI century. To maximize efficiency while minimize the costs is the main target of new enterprises. A good example of this new management philosophy is the big corporations spread over the world that have found ways to get efficiency and lower costs to produce the goods in Countries where labor is cheaper, higher quality and/or where government policies are more liberal and easier to get agreements.

Manufacturing is rooted in physics, mathematics and chemistry. It is the application of a systematic, quantitative, and integrative way of thinking about and approaching the solutions of problems important to process development, materials usage, work safety, and operating management. It advances fundamental concepts, creates knowledge for the maintenance of producing systems and develops innovative manufacturing processes, generating alternatives for implementation of operating equipment and for improving safe reliable work place.

4. REASONS FOR THE PROJECT CONCEPTION

Santos is a city, more specifically an island located in the Atlantic Coast Region of São Paulo State close to São Paulo the capital city. São Paulo is the most industrialized State of Brazil concentrating the larger number of industries in the Country. Santos has the largest Sea Port of Latin America and is also close to Cubatão city where is the Largest Industrial Park of Latin America. So geographically there are many reasons and possibilities to start a project in education field to attend the market demand of industries and enterprises installed in the region [02].

5. THE PROJECT

The manufacturing engineering program proposed by COPEC has been conceived and developed as a project of under graduation, five years, which main characteristic is the inclusion of new courses and the effective work in projects [03]. So besides the basic science courses, basic engineering courses and specific mechanical engineering courses, other two blocs of engineering courses were added and they are:

- Industrial Engineering: Involves the development of techniques and methods for optimization in producing system;
- Environmental Engineering: Essentially the research of methods and process to reduce the negative impacts in environment.

The specific courses of mechanical engineering are distributed along the last two years of the program [04]. These courses allied with the basic science courses and the basic engineering courses can provide to the students a new kind of formation, which is much more dynamic and general [05].

6. THE CURRICULUM

The subjects that are part of the curriculum were chosen in order to attend a minimum of the resolution 48/76 of April 27 of 1976 from CFE – Federal Council of

Education about the curricula directress [06]. And in the last two years of the program the students will have the "Work Term" or the "Supervised Internship", which is a period of four months at the end or in the beginning of the last two years. It is a period when the students work effectively in an industry or research center. A professor altogether the supervisor of the institution supervises the students' work in part of a project. The student has to accomplish her/his work so that another student that will replace her/him in the project can perform the next step.

The effective work in projects exposes the students to the real manufacturing environment and problems, and this provides the interface of the theory and the practice. It is believed that the seeking for the right solution for such problems enlarges their academic horizons considerably.

7. THE "CHALLENGE CYCLE"

It is visible that each time, more and more we watch the gigantic growth of human knowledge that it is escaping of human control. More important than cumulating information, it is to have the general ability of setting and dealing the problems, having in mind the organizing principles that allow connecting the knowledge giving it sense. The proposal named "Challenge Cycle" is a very simple one. It consists in the inclusion of extra classes of areas related to manufacturing and industrial engineering fields. The main goal is to make the students to develop their abilities of applying their skills in the global context with success. The courses last a period of four months each and the professionals are invited and hired specially for this program. They can be industrial or mechanical or even environmental engineers.

At the end of the program the student will be a professional with strong knowledge in physics, mathematics and environment, management, economy and law and possessing great Manufacturing process bases. S/he will be professional with full formation in Mechanical Engineering, which is necessary because of the effective Education Law in Brazil.

8. THE EVALUATION CRITERION

The coordinating team of the project considers that the flexibility for evaluation criterion is very important for the success of it. So it is up to the teacher that is responsible for each course the kind of evaluation to adopt [07]. It can be done by means of works, seminars and tests or any other method. This policy [08] is important because of the objective of the courses, which is to give the student an opportunity to develop their abilities of create solutions in according to the demands of manufacturing and management environment, helping to decrease the impact of progress over nature and men. For sure a minimum score is required to the approval for next year [09].

Besides good faculty members, the students can count with well-equipped Libraries, Internet access and a staff of technicians specially trained for helping.

9. CONCLUSIONS

Presently the Atlantic Coast Region necessities are a new kind of professional, capable to think global without loosing the dimension of local and vice-versa. It is not easy to form this kind of professional although it is known exactly what is needed.

Recognizing the importance of engineering in world scenery Brazil has been working to get and keep the competitiveness of national goods and services by means of projects of professional qualification through continuing education and by means of new laws to improve the quality of engineering programs.

A paradigm of education that promotes the future of a Country's youth is the one that is dimensioned to attend the needs of a population viewing the whole aspects of present society. It is basically the adoption of a new science education policy, making possible the learning and principally the creation of concepts completely new. So

engineering education institutions in Brazil are, let's say, running fast to form a new engineer. New programs have been conceived, new approaches, new laboratories and so on. Changes have been happening and many of them are successful. COPEC proposal of program for manufacturing engineering is one of the successful new kind of forming good engineers prepared to face XXI century.

10. REFERENCES

1. **Chevalier, G.** (1998), "La gestion opaque de la recherche universitaire", *La Recherche*, 306 (12).
2. **Hernandes, V. K.** (1997), "Confluências externas e internas", *Psicologia Ciência e Profissão*, 17, pp. 44-52.
3. **Brito, C. da R.; Ciampi, M. M.; Valle, E., Molnar, J.** (2003), "K12 Initiatives: A Path to the Future of Citizenship". *Proceedings of International Conference on Engineering and Computer Education - 2003*. São Vicente: ICECE, Volume I, p. 216-219. (also in CD-ROM).
4. **Brito, C. da R.; Ciampi, M. M.; Valle, E., Molnar, J.** (2003), "The Fortress of Knowledge – Social Dimension in Engineering Education". *2003 American Society of Engineering Education Annual Conference Proceedings*. Nashville: ASEE. (in CD-ROM).
5. **Brito, C. da R.; Ciampi, M. M.; Valle, E., Molnar, J.** (2003), "New Projects to Foster Engineering Education: a rush to the future". *2003 International Conference on Information Technology Based Higher Education and Training Proceedings*. Marrakech: ITHET. (in CD-ROM).
6. **Brito, C. da R.; Ciampi, M. M.** (2003), "Rio Declaration: Enhancing International Experience in Engineering Education". *Global Engineer: Education and Training for Mobility. 2003 SEFI Annual Conference*. Porto: SEFI. (in CD-ROM).
7. **Brito, C. da R.; Ciampi, M. M.; Valle, E., Molnar, J.** (2003), "The Fortress of Knowledge on an Island: K-12 Initiatives to foster Engineering Education". In: **Fischer, W.; Flückiger, F.** (Hrsg.)

Information-Communication-Knowledge Engineering Education Today.

8. Alsbach/Bergstraße: Leuchtturm-Verlag, p. 196-202.

9. **Brito, C. da R.; Ciampi, M. M.; Valle, E., Molnar, J.** (2003), "K12 in XXI Century: a Challenge for the Developing Countries' New Society". *2003 ASEE/IEEE Frontiers in Education Annual Conference Proceedings.* Boulder: FIE, v. 2, p. F3B-7. (also in CD-ROM).

10. **Brito, C. da R.; Ciampi, M. M.** (2004), "Fishing Engineering Program at the Atlantic Coast Region". *Proceedings of World Congress on Engineering and Technology Education - 2004.* Guarujá: CETE. (in CD-ROM).

GCMM 2004
Editors: Prasad K D V Yarlagadda and S Narayanan
Copyright © 2005, Vellore Institute of Technology, Vellore, India
Publisher: Narosa Publishing House Pvt. Ltd., New Delhi, India

Manufacturing Engineering Program - A View to the Future

Claudio da Rocha Brito, Melany M Ciampi

COPEC- Council of Researches in Education and Sciences
Av. Dr. Epitácio Pessoa, 248 – 33. 11.045-300. Santos – SP - BRAZIL

E-mail: cdrbrito@copec.org.br

Abstract

The characteristics of the work market of this new Century that are extremely competitive and mutable are impelling professionals and enterprises as well as institutions of higher education to run fast not to loose the track with the risk of becoming obsolete. COPEC - Council of Researches in Education and Sciences has conceived and applied a Manufacturing Engineering Program, under graduation, five years, which contains in its curricula the so-called "free period". It is a time the students have to attend classes in the several other areas of knowledge, in one of the Units of University. They are free to choose among the many options like: environment issues, nursery, photography, design, fashion, languages, art, etc, whatever. They can choose as many areas as they want along the five years, at least one per two years. At the end of each period they have to present a report about their development.

Keywords
Communication Skills, Flexible Period, Free Period, Management.

1. INTRODUCTION

The goal of this paper is to show a project developed for a School of Engineering in Brazil that is a Manufacturing Engineering Program, which contains in its curricula a flexible period that is a time the student can attend in the several areas of human knowledge, in one of the other Schools. A distance education course is included among their choices and the experience has showed that this kind of education is one step further in engineering education.

Technology must be comprehended in the context of social relations, in its historical development. It is the scientific knowledge transformed in technique, which amplifies the possibility of producing new scientific knowledge, too. So the major challenge of· science is to promote the technological development with positive results, principally because it depends also of the scientific qualification of society members. To get this scientific qualification it is necessary a scientific and technological education. It is not possible to think about technology only as a result and a product, but also as conception and creation, and so it is necessary also to have minds to conceive it and so education to form these minds. Attempt to that, in 1996 the Education Ministry of Brazil published the Federal Law no. 9.394, known as LDB - Basis and Directress Law of Education. With this

Law educational reforms have started, with the objective to increase the quality of superior education in the Country. Although the reforms are associated to a political project of the present team of Republic, the real motivation is due to the necessity of the education to attend the new social and technical postindustrial paradigm recognized, simply as "globalization". Among all the characteristics of this new productive model, the most interesting one may be the intense use of information technology as an aggregation factor of people and markets.

2. ENGINEERING EDUCATION IN BRAZIL: A HISTORY OF SUCCESS

Brazil is five hundreds years old with a history of races meeting to the construction of a peoples' identity marked by the diversity and cultural richness. Five hundred years that brings the challenge of starting this new millennium building up a new Brazil, a Country where quality of life in daily basis is a concept of its 166.113.000 in habitants and not only of a minority. Having a look at the present history of humanity it is easy to notice the importance of engineering and engineers in the development of science and technology, which have shaped a new social world order having as a straight consequence the new life style and so a new way of thinking.

These aspects added by the formation of economic blocs have been changing the profile of engineers and in Brazil it could not be different once it is involved in the Mercosul. It is the economic bloc of Countries in South cone of Americas and the Countries participants are Brazil, Argentina, Paraguay and Uruguay.

With a GNP of US$ 767.568 and a total GDP of US$ 561.781 Brazil is the largest Country and has the strongest economy of Mercosul and it is the most interested one in making it work [01]. This is an economic bloc that considers the educational and cultural aspects as part of the union. Since 1995 it is a reality and the phases for the accomplishment of the objectives are being kept despite the problems and they will culminate in 2006.

Recognizing the importance of engineering in world scenery Brazil has been working to get the competitiveness of national goods and services by means of incentive to create projects of qualification of professionals through continuing education for example and others. Many representative groups, leaderships and agencies have been implemented programs to prepare the engineers to increase the efficiency of research system, experimental development, engineering, producing system and market.

3. COPEC WORKING FOR THE FUTURE

COPEC means Council of Research in Education and Sciences. It is constituted by scientists of the several areas of human knowledge and citizens committed with education. Citizens and scientists who believe that education is the main beam in the construction of a better society and that also believe in research and in the development of sciences and technology as the big agents in the fostering of progress and the welfare of human being.

It is a council, which works have the goal to enhance and to maintain relations between universities, institutions of education, enterprises and the society of the several countries for the discussion of education, technology and sciences directions.

The history of COPEC has started with an idea shared by some professionals of sciences and technology. It was the idea of creating a non-governmental organization to foster the research mainly in education and sciences. This idea seized proportions and after some meetings the Council became reality.

Although very young this Council through its very active members has already a history of participations in scientific events in education and technology, also sponsoring conferences and developing projects since 1994, with the goal of enhancing discussions about education, technology and science congregating specialists of the five continents. Its mission is to stimulate and to foster the efforts to bring an international perspective in education. It aims to establish and maintain the interchange among institutions, educators of educational institutions in Brazil and in the several countries worldwide. It is a council that seeks the improvement of communication and the interchange of researches in education field and sciences between the countries.

It also aims the development of an apprenticeship community and the development of education and sciences areas constituting in an intelligent way of collective knowledge for the integration with social and economic agents of community.

4. THE "FREE PERIOD"- STUDENTS' CHOICES

Science and Technology are together, not only in terms of structured and based knowledge but also in terms of effective practice. The Manufacturing Engineering Program was elaborated so that it is possible any change in the curricula that is necessary to modernize the program [02].

The program contains in its curricula what was named "free period". It is called so because it is a time when the students have to attend classes in the several other areas of knowledge in one of the Units of University [03]. The main characteristics of this program are:

- The students are free to choose among the many options like environment issues; management, computer design, marketing, languages, art, and many others, whatever they want;
- They can choose as many areas as they want along the five years, at least one per two years;
- At the end of the each period they have to present a report about their development;
- The report is showed and discussed with a council compounded of a psychologist, a pedagogue, an engineer professor and the coordinator of the program [04].

The students can attend anyone, a short time program of Computer Design, for example, or a long time program like Marketing. In a long time formation program

they can choose to attend the whole program or only some courses, it is up to them. This flexibility is necessary because the goal is to foster their abilities and to enlarge their cultural knowledge.

It is a five years program, under graduation, morning or afternoon classes. The students have the basic science courses, basic engineering courses and specific engineering courses besides the courses they choose to attend during the "free period" and also the internship when they can get practical experience. The curriculum was elaborated in according to the curriculum directress established by the Federal Law No. 9.394 known as LDB - Basis and Directress Law of Education, of 1996 [05].

5. THE MANUFACTURING ENGINEERING PROGRAM CURRICULUM

To make the Manufacturing Engineering Program more dynamic the curriculum was elaborated so that any change can be made with the goal of modernizing the program constantly. So the blocs of courses were conceived and implemented to accomplish the project in a way the students can get the best formation. It is about a formation that considers the requirement of Education Ministry for Higher Education Programs and also pursues innovation in the field. So the students have the basic science courses, basic engineering courses and specific engineering courses. The goal is to increase their perception of human dimension and how much it implies in the search for answers to the several problems of engineering. It is about the construction of an education that does not fall apart the science and technology of man's day by day, exploring and clarifying the implications of the new social relations.

This proposal of Manufacturing Engineering Program, as mentioned before is to form Manufacturing engineers with solid knowledge of Management to act in the future work market.

6. THE MANUFACTURING ENGINEER PROFILE

The project aims to form a professional with solid theoretical knowledge - hardware and software - having also the notions of economy, management and law. S/He is prepared to specify, to conceive, to develop, to implement, to adapt, to produce, industrialize, to install and maintain producing systems, as well as to complete the integration of physical and logical resources necessary to take care of the production system, computer and automation necessities and general organizations [06].

S/He is a professional with training in new management methodologies by means of physics, mathematics and chemistry. It is the application of a systematic, quantitative, and integrative way of thinking about and approaching the solutions of problems important to process development, materials usage, work safety, and operating management [07].

To have a good performance and in terms of work market, our engineers have a larger knowledge in management so that s/he can be a candidate in development of equipment for industry, flying companies, construction manufacturing. Added to this the "free period" is a great opportunity for them to refine their knowledge about humanity necessities, the local and global context in which they are immersed, all aspects of a new vision that can enrich their professional activities.

7. CONCLUSION

This kind of education is one step further in engineering education once it provides the students a great opportunity to improve their knowledge of the several areas of human science, without the damage of time waste. The proposed program has its philosophical basis in the conception of a "transforming and progressive instruction" that goes further a new education proposal. It is more than that; it is the teaching/learning process that results in to know-how to think and to create [08]. A process that does not end in the transmission of knowledge, but that starts in the search of knowledge that makes possible to transform and to overcome the skills and the instructions. Besides they have the basic science courses, basic engineering courses and specific engineering courses. It is believed that the simple legal demand does not guarantee the effective development of a new education. The most important is to reflect about the role of education, which is one agent of transformation of society, the greatest builder of human history.

The impact of this flexible period has been such that some teachers are paying more attention to this contributing to the betterment of students' choices helping them to take the maximum of it. They suggest them to take this or that course and distance courses have been far one of the best options for many students.

8. REFERENCES

1. **Taraman, K. S.** (2002) "The Competitiveness of a Union of the Americas". *Proceedings Interamerican Conference on Engineering and Technology Education - 2002.* Santos: INTERTECH, vol. I, p. 255-263. (also in CD-ROM).
2. **Brito, C. da R.; Ciampi, M. M.; Botari, A.** (2003) "Distance Learning challenging present Computer Engineering Program". *2003. Proceedings International Conference on Engineering and Computer Education -2003.* São Vicente: ICECE, Volume I, p. 10-11. (also in CD-ROM).
3. **Brito, C. da R.; Ciampi, M. M.** (2003) "Internationalization of High Education: A New Option for Engineering Education". *2003 American Society of Engineering Education Annual Conference Proceedings.* Nashville: ASEE. (in CD-ROM).
4. **Brito, C. da R.; Ciampi, M. M.** (2003) "The Invisible Continent and Engineering Education". *2003 International Conference on Information Technology Based Higher Education and Training Proceedings.* Marrakech: ITHET. (in CD-ROM).

5. **Brito, C. da R.; Ciampi, M. M.** (2003) "Rio Declaration: Enhancing International Experience in Engineering Education". *Global Engineer: Education and Training for Mobility. 2003 SEFI Annual Conference* Porto: SEFI. (in CD-ROM).

6. **Brito, C. da R.; Ciampi, M. M.** (2003) "Dazzling for Engineering Education Programs Of XXI Century". In: **Fischer, W.; Flückiger, F.** (Hrsg.) *Information - Communication - Knowledge Engineering Education Today.* Alsbach/Bergstraße: Leuchtturm-Verlag. pp. 190-195.

7. **Brito, C. da R.; Ciampi, M. M.** (2003) "Enhancing Engineering Education in Iberian-American Countries". *2003 ASEE/IEEE Frontiers in Education Annual Conference Proceedings.* Boulder: FIE, v. 2, p. F3B-8. (also in CD-ROM).

8. **Brito, C. da R.; Ciampi, M. M.** (2004) "Web based Extra-Curricular Classes for Engineering Programs". *Proceedings of World Congress on Engineering and Technology Education - 2004.* Guarujá: WCETE, 2004. (in CD-ROM).

Organizing Committee

Chief Patron

Mr. G. Viswanathan, Chancellor, VIT, Vellore.

Patrons

Mr. Sankar Viswanathan, Pro-Chancellor (Acad.), VIT, Vellore.
Mr. G.V. Sampath, Pro-Chancellor (Admin.), VIT, Vellore.

Conference Chairman

Prof. P. Radhakrishnan, Vice-Chancellor, VIT, Vellore.

Key Committees and Chairs

Chairman, International Committee

Prof. Prasad KDV Yarlagadda, QUT, Australia.

Chairman, Logistics Committee

Prof. M. Adithan, VIT, Vellore.

Organizing Secretary

Prof.S.Narayanan, VIT, Vellore.

Advisory Committee

Prof.B.V.A.Rao, VIT, Vellore
Prof.M.V.Krishnamurthy, VIT, Vellore
Mr.A.Venkatachalam, VIT, Vellore
Prof.Anand A. Samuel, VIT, Vellore
Prof.A.Kanda, IIT, Delhi
Prof.S.Wadhwa, IIT, Delhi
Prof.S.G.Deshmukh, IIT, Delhi
Prof. D.K.Banwet, IIT, Delhi
Prof. Subash Babu, IIT, Mumbai
Prof.T.T.Narendran, IIT, Chennai
Prof. C.Rajendran, IIT, Chennai
Prof.V.Jayabalan, Anna University, Chennai
Prof.C.Gajendran, CMTI, Bangalore.
Dr.Thomas Mathew, SFIMR, Mumbai
Dr.S.Pandey, IIT, Delhi

Dr.A.K.Kaushik, DRDL, Hyderabad
Dr.P.J.Mohanram, HMT, Bangalore
Mr.N.Kumar, Sanmar, Chennai
Mr.A.Ramkrishna, L & T, Chennai
Mr. P.Jagannathan, BHEL, Delhi.
Mr.C.R.Swaminathan, PSG, Coimbatore
Mr. D.Jayavardhanavelu, LMW , Coimbatore
Dr.D.R.Prasada Raju, DST, New Delhi
Prof.R.Pannerselvam, Pondicherry University
Prof. M.S.Shanmugam, IIT, Chennai
Prof.A.B.Chattopadhyay, IIT, Kanpur
Prof.S.G.Dhande, IIT, Kanpur
Prof.H.S.Shan, IIT, Roorkee
Mr.P.Selvaraj, ADA, Bangalore
Dr.G.Ranganathan, Roots Industries, Coimbatore

GCMM Board

President

Dr.Jong Seong Gim   President, Balzers Korea Coating Company,Korea

Board Members

1. Australia — Prof. Prasad KDV Yarlagadda, Program Leader, Product Design & Manufacturing, Queensland University of Technology.

2. Brazil — Dr.C.Brito, President, Council of Research in Education and Science.

3. Canada — Dr.H.ElMaraghy, Director, Intelligent Manufacturing Systems Center, University of Windsor.

4. China — Dr.P.Ding, Vice President, Society of Mechanical Engineers

5. Egypt — Dr.H.Elwany, Chairman, Production Engineering, Alexandria University.

6. France — Professor S.Tichkiewitch, Deputy Director, 3S Laboratory, Domaine University.

7. Germany — Professor Dr. Ing. P.Gumpel, Vice President, R & D Fachochschule Konstanz.

8. India — Mr.N.Ravi Chandran, Executive V P - Operations, Lucas-TVS Ltd.

9. Japan — Dr.S.Fujii, Professor of Systems Engineering, Kobe University.

10. Mexico — Professor C.Acosta, Mechanical Engineering Dept. Universidad de las America – Pueba.

11. Netherlands — Dr.E.De Bruijn, Professor, Technology & Management, University of Twente.

12. Philippines — Dr.D.Dizon, Coordinator Consortium of Engineering Education, Manila

13. Singapore — Prof.A.Y.C.Nee, Director, Singapore – MIT Alliance, National University of Singapore.

14. Spain	Dr.E.Tovar, Professor, Facultad de Informatica Universidad Politechnica de Madrid.
15. Switzerland	Dr.T.Schelker, Professor, Swiss College of Agriculture.
16. Thailand	Dr.S.Butdee, King Mongkut's Institute of Technology, North Bangkok.
17. USA	Prof. K.S.Taraman, Chair-Professor Manuf. Engg., Lawrence Technological University.

GCMM Honorary Board Members

1. Dr.T.Boonyasopon, President, King Mongkut's Instt. of Tech., Thailand.

2. Dr. C.Chambers, President, Lawrence Technological University, USA

3. Dr.Jong Seong Gim, President, Balzers Korea Coating Co.Ltd., South Korea

4. Ir. Hadiwaratama, Retired Director, POLLMAN- ITB, Indonesia

5. Dr.J.Lee, Professor, Seoul National University, Korea

6. Dr.H.Ohta, Professor, Osaka Prefecture University, Japan

7. Mr.G.Viswanathan, Chancellor, Vellore Institute of Technology, India.

International Organizing Committee

Chairman: Dr.Prasad KDV Yarlagadda, QUT, Australia

Australia	Dr. R.Mahalinga Iyer
	Prof. S.Masood
	Dr. Adekunle Oloyede
	Prof. Joseph Mathew
Brazil	Dr.C.Brito
	Mr.R.Camenho
	Prof.M.Ciampi
Canada	Dr.H.El Maraghy
China	Dr.P.Ding
Egypt	Dr.H.Elwany
	Dr.K. Abdel Ghany
France	Prof. S.Tichkiewitch
Germany	Dr.Ing. P.Gumpel
Hong Kong	Dr.Kamineni P.Rao
India	Mr.N.Ravichandran
Ireland	Prof.M.S.J.Hashmi
Japan	Dr.S.Fujii
Korea	Dr.Jong Seong Gim
	Dr. B.Y.Kang
	Prof.III Soo Kim
	Prof.Man Kyung Ha
	Prof. Tae Jo Ko
	Prof. Sung Chung Kim
	Prof. Dong Woo Cho
U.K.	Prof.S.Arunachalam
	Prof.S.K. Battacharya
	Prof..James Gao
Mexico	Prof.C.Acosta
Netherlands	Dr.E.de Bruijn
Papua New Guinea	Prof.W.C.K. Wong
Philippines	Dr.D.Dizon
Singapore	Prof.A.Y.C. Nee
	Dr.M.Chandrasekharan
	Prof..V.Radhakrishnan
	Dr. L.C.Lee
Spain	Dr.E.Tovar
Switzerland	Dr.T.Schelker
Thailand	Dr.S.Butdee
U.S.A	Prof.K.S.Taraman
	Prof.V.M.Rao Tummala
	Dr.Venkitaswamy Raju
	Dr. Maniam Ramkumar
	Prof.Robert C. Creese
	Prof.Perry W.Carter
	Prof. R.Lal Tummala
	Dr.M.Al Ubaidi
	Dr.R.Radharamanan
	Dr.S.Taraman
	Dr.Shantakumar palanisamy
	Prof.A.Gunasekaran
Malaysia	Prof. Vellore C.Venkatesh

Local Organizing Committee

Prof. V. Sinagaravelu
Dr. K. Chidambaram
Dr. K. K. Ray
Dr. K. T. Rengamani
Dr. K. Ganesan
Dr. D.V. S. Bagavanulu
Dr. R. Sundaresan
Dr. A. Senthil Kumar
Mr. K. Manivannan
Mr. P.V. Srihari
Mr. K. Annamalai
Dr. R. Ajit Kumar
Mr. K. Raja
Mr. K. Janardhan Reddy
Mr. V.G. Sridhar
Mr. M. Anthony Xavier
Mr. Sivaprasad Darla
Mr. C.D. Naiju
Mr. P. Parthiban
Mr. M. Senthil Kumar
Mr. K. Udayakumar
Mr. K. Gokul Kumar
Mr. G. Vijayakumar
Mr. Solomon Bobby
Mr. K. Muralidharan
Mr. Khalid Hussain Syed
Mr. S. Anivel

Mr. S.K. Sekar
Dr. P. Ganesan
Mr. C. Allen Rajdas
Mr. R. Murugavel
Mrs. D. Thiripurasundari
Mrs. E. Anupriya
Mr. S. K. Jayakumar
Mr. A. Balasenthilnathan
Mr. S. Sivabalan
Mr. P. Kalyanaraman
Mr. V. Sairam
Ms. P. Vijayapriya
Mrs. Margret Announcia
Ms. Swarnalatha
Mr. A. Ruban kumar
Mr. P. Anbarasan
Mr.R. Rajkumar
Mr. M. Govindaraju
Mr. V. Senthilkumar
Mr. L. Saravanan
Mr. R. Oyyaravelu
Mr. P.A. Jeeva
Mr. E. Visvanathan
Mr. K. Sukumar
Mr. Solomon Rajendra
Mr. V. Rajendran
Mr. R. Palani
Mr. Hari Krishnan

Author Index

MODERN

UPHOLSTERY

CONTENTS

MODERN

MICAELA SHARP

Discover the joy of
transforming your furniture

UPHOLSTERY

Hardie Grant

BOOKS

INTRODUCTION

'Have you thought about taking an upholstery course?' When my friend Claire asked me this question in 2016, it instantly set my mind racing with possibilities and made me smile. That question changed the trajectory of my life. Thank you Claire!

Growing up, nothing was ever broken in my house for long. My grandad, John, was a carpenter who could fix anything. I spent hours in his home workshop (our garage) making small carpentry projects and generally slowing him down. On our family vacations to the British seaside, I ran wild collecting shells and stones to use in crafting projects back home. From jewellery making to candle making, I wanted to try everything and loved learning how items were made.

While my grandad focused on carpentry and repairs, my nan, Janet, added a softness to our lives through her sewing projects. She dreamed up beautiful clothing and homewares, bringing her visions to life with the skill of a professional tailor, teaching me how to sew along the way. I took to altering her vintage clothes into one-off creations. The pieces of hers still hanging in my wardrobe are some of my most treasured possessions.

When I eventually realised that upholstery is carpentry plus sewing, I wished I'd figured it out before as it spoke to me so strongly. After my conversation with Claire, I hurried off and enrolled in an evening class at my local adult education centre. Too excited to wait for the start date, I began watching YouTube videos and teaching myself the basics. Many upholsterers take a more traditional route by studying an official three-year course, but that wasn't for me – I had already completed a degree and, as a dyslexic person, I didn't want to return to the classroom in that capacity. I prefer hands-on environments and wanted to be behind a work table, tools in hand, not sitting behind a desk. But here I am writing a book! Upholstery quickly became a dream job for me, crafting and making something seemingly out of nothing.

My grandad helped me strip down my first item – a piano stool – expertly guiding me to fix the frame in the garage workshop we had shared when I was younger. And I knew in that moment I was going to commit the next chapter of my life to upholstery. I had an instant affinity with the processes and the physicality of it. He saw the first two projects I completed, but then sadly passed away. With the inheritance from my nan and grandad (my nan had passed a few years before) I launched my first business. This upholstery service was built on the skills they taught me and was driven by the wisdom, determination and commitment to hard work that they shared.

Today, I'm a multi-hyphenate creative, which is really to say that as well as being an upholsterer, I'm also an interior designer, magazine columnist and television broadcaster. The common thread between all of these roles lies in answering the question, 'how can thoughtful design elevate our lives, allowing us to share more of who we are with the world?'.

I'm passionate about saving items from landfill and encourage a creative solution to sustainable interior design through all aspects of my work as a designer and TV presenter. Sustainability can seem overwhelming; there's a lot of jargon used and guilt mongering placed on us as individuals. But it doesn't have to be scary. By first looking at the items you already have and choosing to reupholster them you are already being more sustainable. You don't have to be an expert to take part in the journey towards sustainable living. Sometimes it can seem like you have to do it all – be zero waste, carbon neutral and self-sustaining. Instead, I encourage you to slow down before buying new items, consider what you already have to see if it can be repurposed and make intentional changes that feel in alignment with you.

Back as far as I can remember, my nan would take us into charity shops not only to donate clothes we had grown out of but also to buy 'new' things. I've always loved the quality of vintage clothes and embrace the fact that I'm far less likely to see other people in the same items as me. I love finding individual items full of personality and charm, and that applies not just to fashion but to homeware too. The patina on vintage pieces and their stories cannot be rivalled by newly made items. There's a charm to teak wood, coloured glass and paisley prints in my opinion.

I started buying second-hand fashion and progressed to homeware when I moved into my first rented flat in South London many years ago. The flat was furnished entirely with charity shop finds; it was very granny chic with chintzy floral two seaters and teak woodwork everywhere, but it was mine and I loved it. I've since moved several times but continue to expand my collection of vintage homeware.

Beyond the thrill of finding a fun vintage piece, buying second-hand or vintage is usually a more affordable way to shop, and because of this I think it's easier to make adjustments. Whether it's taking up the hem of a dress or repainting a chest of drawers, upcycling an item to make it more appropriate for your needs and your own personal style is such a thrill. I understand that upholstery can seem like a daunting task. I myself came to it late in my thrifting/upcycling journey, but I'm here to tell you, you can do it!

I am so excited to share my love of upholstery with you and hopefully inspire you to transform your furniture at home with confidence.

The Joy of Upholstery

When I think of my cherished memories with my grandparents a lot of them revolve around upholstery in a roundabout way: the sofa my nan and I used to snuggle up and watch TV on; the armchair my grandad would sit in to listen to his favourite music (Nat King Cole ... and Celine Dion for balance because I don't want him to sound too cool); the embroidered Spanish tablecloths from our lunches on the Costa del Sol.

When people bring me their family heirlooms to be redesigned they rarely tell me about the practicalities of the piece. More often than not they share stories of grandma's nursing chair being passed down, or grandad's favourite armchair for reading. The textures, the smells, the faded patterns all make up the fabric of our lives and our memories.

I try to always bear that in mind when choosing fabric for my own creations. Will my family and friends say 'she loved green velvet' or will they say they remember me being vibrant and cheerful and this fabric reflected my spirit, hence the bold choice of pattern?

When I ask people about fabrics they can remember from childhood, usually they reference bold patterns or particularly soft textures. They very rarely talk about plain cottons or linens. It's important to remember that when we are choosing fabrics for our home now. Let's be bold and choose fabrics that will pad our future memories with softness and colour.

One of the boldest fabrics we had growing up were the striped curtains in our dining room. The room was a teal and pink concoction of florals, stripes and a patterned carpet. We only really ever used the room for birthdays and Christmas lunch so the special occasions in my life were always surrounded by bold, chunky colours. At the time I always felt the mix wasn't to my taste, it was quite full on in that room. But now I miss those stripes!

Our furniture takes on more of us than we realise. Whenever I strip back a sofa, I find things that point to how the owner lives: biscuit crumbs from teatime snacks, Lego from playtime or receipts from forgotten purchases. Inevitably our furniture holds tiny mementos of our lives in its frame ready for the next owners (or your upholsterer) to unearth.

Usually the first thing we do when we go to a friend's house is take a seat. I think a soft chair can determine how long we stay. A comfortable dining chair can extend the end of a dinner party into hours of chatting and laughing, rather than squirming on a hard wooden seat. A cosy garden sofa can help us decide an extra coffee is in order after all. A comfortable bed is the best excuse for a lie-in! So let's build our furniture to be as comfortable as possible; I'm going to show you how.

Understanding how furniture is made has many benefits. First, you can make better decisions about what to buy and whether it's truly value for money. Being aware of different shapes, raw materials and fabrics will give you this insight, even if you decide to purchase a new sofa rather than upholstering your existing one. It will definitely help to avoid items that aren't made to last. Secondly, when we understand how things are made and the time and energy it takes to make them I believe we take better care of our things. We are the custodians of these items after all. Once they're made there's no getting rid of them. We can only pass them on to someone else or break them down into the raw elements to be recycled or reused.

Mastering reupholstery will give you a new appreciation of furniture and I hope it will inspire you to look for the castoffs, the rejects and the unwanted items and to transform them confidently into items you and those around you will cherish for years to come.

Upholstery comes in so many different forms and has evolved throughout the ages. I won't pretend to be an historian but it's clear to see that examples of antique furniture that are seen from the 16th and 17th centuries have morphed dramatically into modern-day pieces. Gone are the ornate hard wooden frames and delicate silks, replaced by modular lounge chairs and durable fabrics. And our furniture really is a sign of the times. Where once people perched upright listening to a home piano recital, we now lounge while watching a TV series.

Contemporary furniture has to work hard to meet a lot of requirements. We want comfort, durability, vibrancy, safety, individuality, storage and multipurpose items. When you can make your own furniture, or at least re-cover existing furniture, you can start to fulfil more of these needs. And upholstery is not just for chairs and sofas. Once you have mastered adding fabric to classic shapes, there is no end to what can be upholstered. Palaces and chateaux with upholstered walls led the way in redefining where we expect to see fabric, and upholstery projects can also take the form of dressing tables, cupboard fronts and even mirror frames. The skills are so versatile, don't be afraid to experiment with them!

This book aims to share modern upholstery skills, techniques and projects that will teach you the foundations. No two upholstery projects are the same (unless you're doing a pair) and so with each new project you will hone new skills. There is always a new technique to learn and really it's about having the confidence to give something a try, as mistakes can usually be easily salvaged. I want to demystify upholstery so that you can transform your furniture in affordable and sustainable ways yourself.

This is a practical guide to getting stuck in and giving your first projects a go. I'd love you to upholster with confidence and create furniture that brings you joy. These unique custom-made pieces are for you and you alone, so go wild with fabric and trim and embrace your own personal style. *Modern Upholstery* aims to go beyond the internet hacks to help you redesign furniture that will stand the test of time and stand out for all the right reasons.

I would *love* to see pictures of your finished items and invite you to send them to me on Instagram.

@micaelasharpdesign #modernupholsterybook

There's lots to cover ... so let's get to it!

HOW TO USE THIS BOOK

Upholstery is an amazing craft with a multitude of applications and ways of working. This makes it super exciting, but also a bit daunting. To get the most from *Modern Upholstery*, follow this directory to find the right bit of information wherever you are on your journey.

SOURCING AND PLANNING

This section outlines the first things you'll want to consider when embarking on your upholstery journey, from fabric and trim selection to thinking about how your piece will be used and the best ways to source furniture.

TOOLS AND MATERIALS

Discover the tools and materials you'll be working with in this chapter. It's important to note that you won't need all of these immediately. The essential ones are marked with an asterisk so you can see what a starting toolkit would consist of.

PROJECTS

There are four projects to select from. Each of them will help you to develop different skills and offer different challenges and opportunities. They will draw on the material from the core and decorative technique chapters to help give context and clear instructions.

CORE TECHNIQUES

The methods covered in this section will be at the heart of many upholstery projects. Starting with stripping back and including different methods for webbing and finishing corners, these are the building blocks of upholstery. Not every technique will be needed on every project so you will hop around a little, but will discover much on your way.

DECORATIVE AND FINISHING TECHNIQUES

This is where you'll learn how to embellish and finish your project in a whole host of different ways. You can learn how to add frills and piping to your project, as well as discover how to create a fluted chair.

MAKE DO AND MEND

This section will offer up suggestions of what to do with any offcuts you may have from your projects, to avoid them being wasted. Information on how to repair your upholstery throughout its life can also be found here.

SOURCING & PLANNING (PAGE 12)

TOOLS & MATERIALS (PAGE 38)

PROJECTS (PAGE 58)

CORE TECHNIQUES (PAGE 116)

DECORATIVE & FINISHING TECHNIQUES (PAGE 192)

MAKE DO & MEND (PAGE 234)

CHAPTER ONE

Sourcing & planning

PLANNING
YOUR PIECE

Finding exciting fabrics and furniture is often the impetus to wanting to learn upholstery. An interestingly shaped fluted armchair that was irresistible at a car boot fair, or the vintage floral fabric from a charity shop are quick to snap up but perhaps slower to use and transform. Spending time planning what to do next is key to making that transformation a reality.

When thinking about how to tackle your chosen piece you'll be considering a number of different factors including things like how long it might take you, what tools and materials you'll need as well as the order that you'll need to work in.

A vital part of this order will be established during the stripping back process, which will allow you to assess the inner layers, understand how the piece was made and what needs to be replaced. Stripping back an item is undoubtedly the nerve-racking part! Taking something functional and breaking it a bit – scary stuff! But it is a necessary part of understanding the processes and techniques that will be needed to successfully cover it. Ensure you read Stripping back your item on page 120 to correctly document and label everything. Do not throw anything away until you have completed the project so that you can refer back to it if needed. In many cases the original upholstery will act as a template for your new project, so it's vital you hang on to it!

The photos opposite gives you an overview of the stages involved in a typical armchair upholstery project. There will be places where your chosen piece may diverge, especially when it comes to choice of finishing materials and methods, but it gives you a sense of the fun journey ahead.

Armchair overview

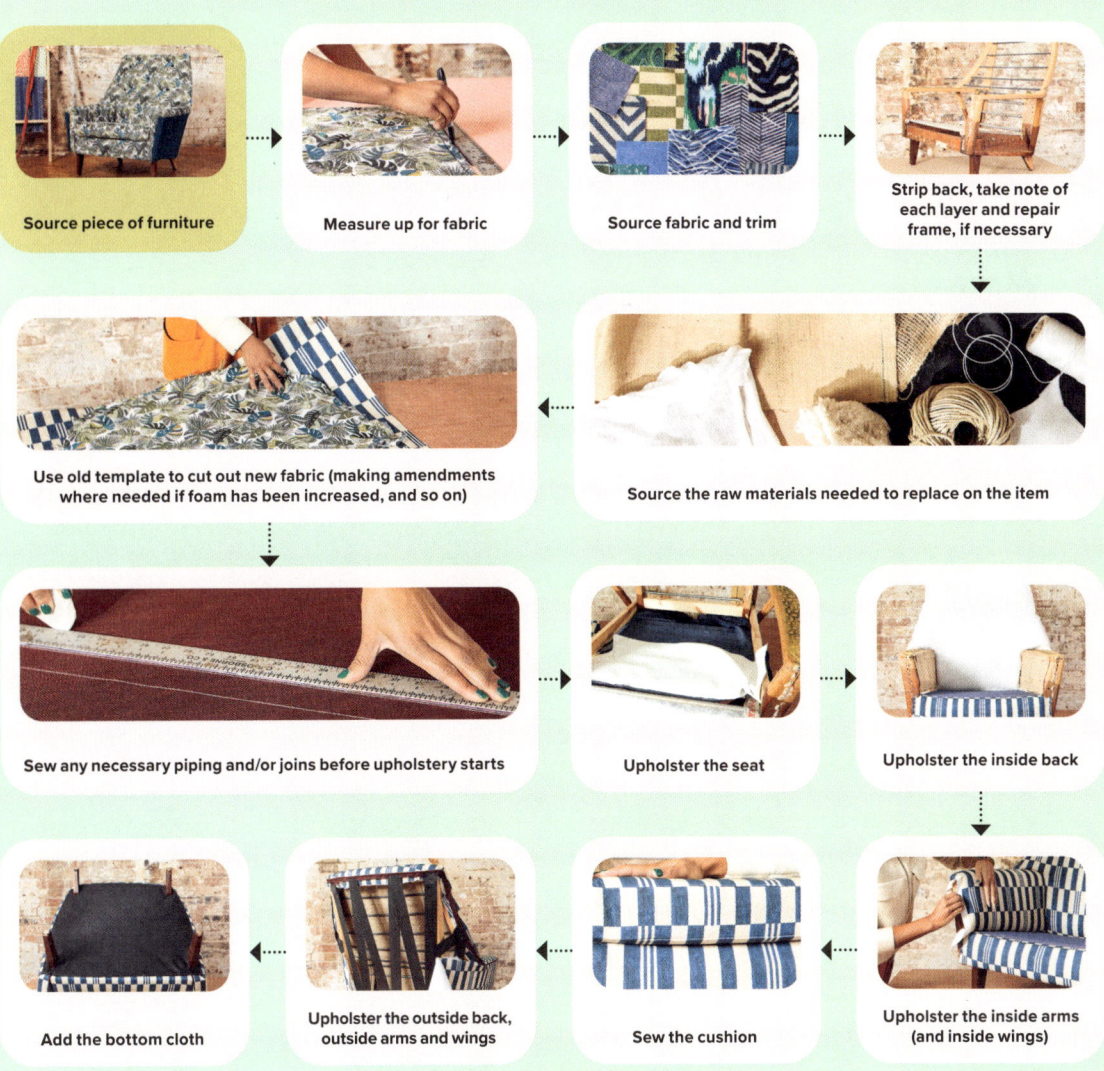

Source piece of furniture

Measure up for fabric

Source fabric and trim

Strip back, take note of each layer and repair frame, if necessary

Use old template to cut out new fabric (making amendments where needed if foam has been increased, and so on)

Source the raw materials needed to replace on the item

Sew any necessary piping and/or joins before upholstery starts

Upholster the seat

Upholster the inside back

Add the bottom cloth

Upholster the outside back, outside arms and wings

Sew the cushion

Upholster the inside arms (and inside wings)

The end!

METHODS OF UPHOLSTERY

Upholstery generally falls into two categories: traditional and modern.

The differences between the two are largely down to the materials used. Traditional upholstery uses more natural fibres such as horsehair and cotton felt, which are held in place with tacks. These materials are gradually layered up to create the desired shape between sheets of hessian, which are then hand tied with twine in sections to compact them. As a result, traditional upholstery is more time-consuming than using modern methods and will also be more expensive when outsourcing. It does tend to be more environmentally friendly, as using natural materials such as cotton felt (as opposed to synthetic materials such as polyester wadding) brings down the piece's carbon footprint.

These centuries-old techniques are trickier to work with; building the even, comfortable layers of hair and natural fibres isn't as easy as working with foam layers, and it can be quite tough on your hands doing all the hand stitching and pulling the twine tight, although it should be noted that sheet materials for fibre layers are now available to speed up the process.

I would always advise keeping antique furniture upholstered using traditional methods and materials. You can usually tell from the age of a piece if it will be traditionally upholstered: you will generally find that items over 100 years old are traditionally upholstered, whereas pieces less than 100 years old use modern techniques. You can also sometimes tell from feeling or sitting on the item as traditional upholstery tends to be firmer.

If you strip a piece back and find it has been traditionally upholstered, consider the next step carefully. You can swap traditional materials for modern ones, but you lose a bit of the integrity of the piece. If it's a 150-year-old antique, adding foam doesn't feel completely right. It should be noted that iron or metal frames require traditional techniques to be used, as you cannot staple into the metal and so everything has to be hand tied.

Modern upholstery favours modern materials such as foam, polyester and staples. It's therefore quicker to build up the layers, as foam comes in predetermined, even sheets. Stapling with an air gun is also more efficient and so usually modern upholstery costs less than traditional upholstery (if paying a professional). Vintage and modern furniture tend to favour these modern techniques and raw materials. The feel is softer as foam and synthetic materials aim to create comfort rather than structure.

We'll be demonstrating modern upholstery methods in this book, as I believe that people just starting out on their upholstery journey will find that these techniques pack the biggest punch, both in terms of timeframe and resources required. Modern materials are easily sourced online or from local suppliers and are more affordable than traditional materials. You will be able to move more quickly through the various projects, build your confidence and master an array of skills, which I hope you will continue to explore.

Armchair anatomy: Modern

A – Arm rail
B – Fascia
C – Scroll arm
D – Wing
E – Jute webbing
F – Hessian
G – 1.5 inch (4 cm) blue foam
H – FR layer
I – Polyester
J – Fabric
K – Polyester
L – FR liner
M – 0.5 inch (1 cm) pink foam
       and 2 inch (5 cm) blue foam
N – Hessian
O – Lashed-down coil springs
P – Hessian
Q – Black and white webbing

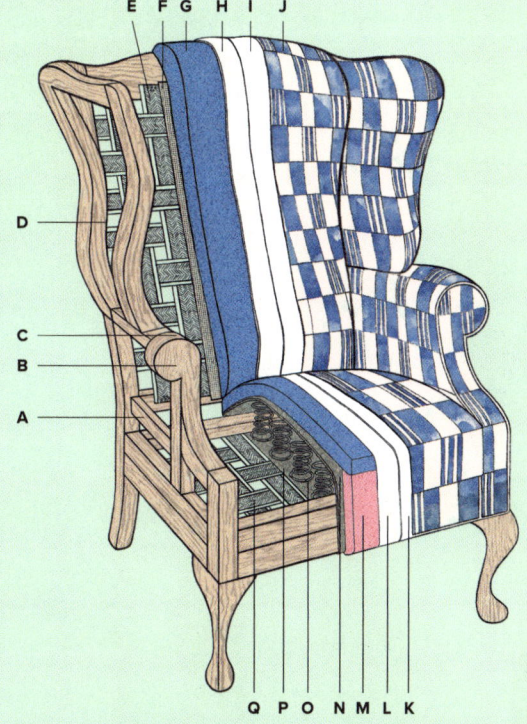

Armchair anatomy: Traditional

A – Uncovered armrest
B – Open frame
C – Jute webbing
D – Hessian
E – Hair fibres
F – Hessian
G – Cotton felt
H – Calico
I – FR layer
J – Fabric
K – Covered armrest
L – Fabric
M – FR liner
N – Calico
O – Cotton felt
P – Hessian
Q – Lashed-down coil springs
R – Hessian
S – Black and white webbing

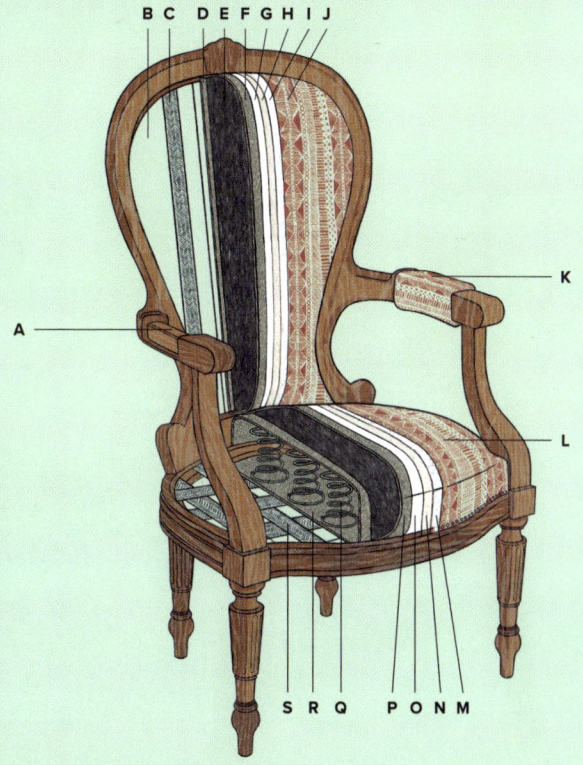

SOURCING FURNITURE

This is such a fun part of the planning process, but it can be easy to fall in love with an item and get carried away and pay over the odds for it. When sourcing furniture it's good to be mindful of the place and the vendor you are dealing with. Are they selling to trade (trade markets), do they want to shift stock quickly (charity shops) or do they price their items for the end user and therefore they sell at a much slower rate (curated vintage stores)?

Designer furniture

Stylish vintage homeware stores are great for buying finished items as they have often already been upholstered and restored, but you are paying a premium for this. Shop owners in these types of curated stores expect to be selling to an end user who doesn't want to do any work to the piece. These stores are great for finding inspiration, learning about different designers and building an understanding of various price points. I often write notes on mid-century designers I like so that I can look for cheaper pieces online. And it's helpful to know that a Bentwood chair is a more affordable version of Jindřich Halabala and what the differences in design are in case you find a Halabala set going cheap, so you can snap it up.

If you are looking for high-end designers, online vintage specialists such as 1st Dibs, Vinterior and Design Market can be great. But again there is a trick to buying from these sites. They take around a 20 per cent commission on all sales and often the vendors will add this on top of their usual price. So to avoid paying this extra 20 per cent you can google image search the items you want or search for the vendor's own website to buy your items directly.

Affordable pieces

When you're first learning upholstery you may find it less daunting to start on pieces that are more affordable. Rather than sourcing at stores that have already invested in refurbishing pieces, it's best to focus on shops or markets selling items that are seen as less desirable because they're worn, damaged or dated. I favour car boot fairs (flea markets), charity shops (thrift stores) and online marketplaces to find bargains in this way.

Sites like eBay and Facebook Marketplace are great places to source affordable furniture. But I would say that searching by designers and keywords usually returns items with higher prices, as the sellers know what they have and have done some market research. It's important to note that often things are misrepresented by accident where someone has seen a similar shape and thought they had a designer item, but they don't. So do your research before you buy designer pieces on these platforms. Designer pieces usually have stamps on the frame underneath with either the initials, name or year of manufacture. You could also cross-reference the images with others online to see if the shape and size match. There are some reproduction items of iconic furniture (such as egg chairs) that are newer and have far less provenance, so be wary. Sometimes if the price is too good to be true, it's not a genuine designer piece.

I sourced this vintage Parker Knoll 970 armchair from Smith and Halls in London.

Instead, online I generally search by very generic, broad terms such as 'wooden armchair' and trawl through the hundreds of listings, glancing at the images to decipher key shapes and hopefully spot a mid-century bargain. This obviously takes longer, but is more likely to show results for people getting rid of granny's old chair that to them looks dated and worn, but to you is an upholstery project with huge potential.

Don't be put off by the fabric! You will be changing this and you can always strip an item back to the frame and replace all the foam and other layers. If it's worn, it's a great chance to get a good price. If it's ripped, even better!

I once bought a chaise longue for £25 because someone had drawn a smiley face on it in permanent red marker pen. I also bought an Art Deco-style real leather sofa for £1 – yes only £1! The leather seat cushions were ripped and so I replaced the tops with a contrast fabric, et voila! As good as new – well better because now it's one of a kind.

And let's not overlook free items! Freecycle (a website where you can advertise unwanted free items from people in your local area), looking in skips and finding items on the roadside can be a bit scary at first and our tendency is to worry about germs, but strip them back to the frame and you will alleviate any concerns. If the frame has been wet or has had woodworm you can easily use a liquid sealant to kill any surviving worms before you start to reupholster it.

The key is looking for items that other people see less value in. These are the projects that garner the most reward in terms of transformation. And keeping the cost of your item low will allow you to spend more on fabric and trims and experiment more confidently, as you won't be worried about damaging a 16th-century heirloom.

SOURCING FABRIC

A mix of plain and patterned fabrics from various suppliers (see page 249 for details about each swatch).

Perhaps the most exciting part of planning is starting to imagine what your newly transformed furniture will look like and the fabric is a huge part of this. One of the many benefits to reupholstering your own furniture is that you can customise every element to ensure it is perfect for your home. With endless fabrics available, you're sure to find a colour and pattern to work well with your interior design scheme.

I would invite you to look beyond neutral blocks of colour and typical fabrics found on the high street. When brands are marketing their mass-produced furniture, they want to sell large quantities and part of that is appealing to as many people as possible, so typically what we see are lots of greys, creams and beige. The most daring modern shapes may showcase blocks of colour in jewel tones such as sapphire, emerald and ochre, but rarely ever pattern. Textures are also generally limited to velvets and linens. Try to set aside the things you are used to seeing, otherwise you can quite quickly be sucked into the trap of looking at different shades of grey for your own projects.

Instead, look to the major fabric houses such as Sanderson, Linwood and Colefax & Fowler for example in the UK. These suppliers create new ranges every year with very on-trend colour palettes and patterns. More high-end fabric houses like Pierre Frey and Christopher Farr are often the fabrics chosen by interior designers, which you may even recognise from interiors magazines. These high-end fabrics are often best sourced as end-of-roll via discount outlets. Smaller suppliers such as Haines Collection offer limited quantities of fabrics that have been discarded by the makers and sell them at hugely discounted rates. A more sustainable way to shop!

Sustainable fabrics

When choosing sustainable fabric I would consider natural fibres such as cotton, flax and wool. There is a lot of discussion about which is truly the most sustainable due to the processes needed to manufacture each. But natural fibres will at least return to the earth when they are changed in the future. You also have the option to explore fabrics made from recycled materials. This is becoming a lot more popular, so don't be afraid to ask the major fabric houses about their sustainable ranges.

Alternatively, you can shun newly made fabrics altogether and focus your attention on vintage fabrics, often best sourced online. Just be sure to buy enough, as often you won't be able to source more later on.

Other sustainable ways of upholstering include using old denim, repurposing curtains and even tablecloths. Just ensure your fabrics are thick enough for upholstery, as you want them to be as durable as possible so they stand the test of time. You will also need to add a fire-retardant layer with these. I would not advise using fashion fabrics for upholstery as they are stretchier, thinner and generally a lot less hard wearing.

The power of pattern

The world of fabrics is ever expanding with every colour combination, pattern and texture you can dream of available. There are brands with iconic looks which are instantly recognisable such as Liberty, Svenskt Tenn, William Morris and House of Hackney. There are timeless prints such as stripes, ginghams and checkerboards. There are styles to suit every need from Art Deco to maximalist. And there are so many shades of colour it's easy to be overwhelmed but I believe there is a pattern out there for everyone. Even Scandi, minimal interiors benefit from a checkerboard or stripe.

Often a small pattern repeat, like a ticking stripe or polka dot, helps to break up larger items of furniture such as sofas. So try not to think of pattern as 'busy' because sometimes it helps move the eye around the room, rather than fixating on one large section of colour. Instead of having a large block of navy, for example, you have a softer navy look which, up close, reveals a subtle colour combo of navy, cream and black.

And then there is the mix-and-match approach where not all parts of the item are covered with the same fabric. Often you'll see the outside back in brighter, more intricate designs such as embroidered fabric. This is because the outside back generally has the least wear as it's not sat on or leant against so the Martindale rub count (the measure of durability used for fabric) can be lower here. Embroidered fabrics aren't suitable for high-traffic areas like sofas, but they are great for impactful low-traffic pieces like headboards.

I would encourage you also to consider the smaller independent brands. The UK has an abundance of textile designers offering everything from modern vintage patterns (Poodle & Blonde) through to reimagined florals (Ellen Merchant). There are marble experts (Suzie Bellamy), Art Deco icons (Interior Curve), Cottage-core queens (Ottoline Devries), geometric goddesses (Bethie Tricks) and quirky colour lovers (Annika Reed). Social media is a great place to find these independent brands. I have included a list of my favourite global brands in the Fabric Suppliers (see page 248) index.

Left: A mix of plain and patterned fabrics from various suppliers (see page 249 for details about each swatch). Above, right: An assortment of Linwood fabrics.

Practicalities

There are lots of elements to consider alongside colour and pattern. When choosing your fabric you may want to consider the usage and therefore practicalities required: where it's going in your home, who it will be used by, if you need stain resistance or hard wearing fabrics. You are the one choosing the fabrics, so make sure you prioritise your needs! Nowadays many upholstery fabrics are inherently fire-retardant so you don't need to add an additional layer when upholstering. Stain resistant fabrics are also very prominent now and do not absorb liquids which is great if you have children and/or pets at home or are a bit messy like me! You can also use scotch guard to make fabrics more durable. There are outdoor fabrics which are more colour-fast and water-resistant.

Upholstery fabrics are generally very durable and this is reflected in something called the Martindale rub count. The score is determined by the fabric being rubbed until the first thread breaks. The score will be in the thousands. I generally aim for a minimum of 35,000 Martindale for frequently used domestic upholstery, such as armchairs and sofas. For headboards and occasional use items you can lessen this at your own discretion. For commercial fabrics I tend to aim for 100,000 depending on the usage (restaurants, bars, and so on).

ALL THE TRIMMINGS

Anywhere there is a seam or an edge, there is an opportunity to add a trim!

Mostly you will see piping/welt used as trim and commonly it's made from the same fabric as the rest of the item. We call this 'self-piping'. But you can use a contrast fabric to highlight different details as well as the shape of the item (as piping is usually found around the edge of the shape).

Better yet, why not add a totally different type of trim? There are so many to choose from: brush fringe, tassels, pom-poms, scroll gimp, beading, ribbon, braid, lace, galloon, bullion fringe and more! These trims are either sewn in or glued on, so it's important you know the distinction as they are not all suitable for all areas of the furniture.

Long trims look great along the bottom edge of armchairs and sofas and can be used in place of skirts. You can glue or sew ribbon into box cushions.

Frills can be stapled along the edge of the outside back and brush fringe can be used around the edge of a shaped headboard (one of my favourite trims!). It's important to consider whether the area you're adding trim to is going to be a high-traffic area and therefore will the trim be squashed by people sitting on it? The front edge of a seat box cushion, for example, would mean a frill would be flattened over time.

The possibilities to add colour and texture really are endless so do not stop your design at the fabric alone. Be sure to explore all the trimmings!

A collection of trims sourced from a haberdashery in Malaga, Spain (Merceria el Torcal), including leather fringe, ribbon, cotton bullion fringe, passementerie, frills and brush fringe.

MEASURING UP FOR FABRIC

Measuring up for fabric can seem a bit daunting at first. You won't want to overestimate the quantity needed as it can add a lot of unnecessary cost onto your project. Equally, underestimating will leave you with a partly uncovered item.

Fabric considerations

The first thing to take into account is the width of the fabric you have chosen. Usually fabrics are 138–143 cm (54–56 in) wide. Sometimes brands make double width fabrics so we can avoid seams on larger items.

The next thing to note is the pattern repeat size. This is the distance between the same part of the pattern. For example, if you have a fabric patterned with different birds, the pattern repeat would be the distance between two of the exact same birds. This is important because you will usually want to match your pattern on various parts of the item or have it centred. For example, you may want to match box cushion borders to the top fabric, have matching arms on an armchair, or centre the pattern on the inside back and continue it down onto the seat. Every time you need to pattern match or centre a specific part of the pattern you can lose useable fabric. This is because in order to pattern match perfectly you must add a seam allowance to each piece for sewing, or an allowance for pulling the fabric through the frame for fixed upholstery

(see Pulling, smoothing & stapling fabric, page 126). If you are centring the design you will end up with smaller, unusable pieces either side. So for example, if you're cutting out box cushion pieces, you would need to use the same part of the pattern twice in order to allow for the seam allowance either side. The space in between is then wasted unless it can be used for other smaller sections. I recommend using the offcuts for less important sections such as zips and piping (if there is enough to still cut diagonally on the bias).

Small patterns with only a few centimetres pattern repeat size (or plain fabrics) have little to no waste between each section. Some pattern repeats can be up to and over 1 m (39 in) long. These large patterns generally require a larger amount of fabric to be bought in order to pattern match and generally larger patterns cost more to begin with, so this can be a costly exercise.

Usually fabric is printed with the pattern running up and down the roll. It will be sent with the front of the fabric inside the roll as you pull out a section. That means the maximum width of a patterned fabric is the width of the fabric, i.e. 140 cm (55 in); this includes the selvedge, unless the print is 'railroaded' (see Laying out on page 30). So if your sofa or headboard is wider than this, you will need to sew sections equally either side to increase the width and this will need to be pattern matched.

Rough quantities of fabric needed

Here are loose guides as to how much fabric you would need for each of these pieces of furniture, but you may need more for large pattern repeats. It's also possible to lay the fabric on the item and roughly gauge how much is needed that way.

Remember to add 1 m (1 yd) to make piping if needed.

- **A – Foot stool with border, skirt and piping 7 m (7 3/5 yd)**
- **B – Dining chair 2 m (2 1/10 yd) (with excess)**
- **C – Show wood chair with double-piped edge 3 m (3 1/5 yd)**
- **D – Mid-century chair with fascias 4 m (4 1/3 yd)**
- **E – Armchair with capped-on scroll arms and box cushion 9 m (9 4/5 yd)**
- **F – Mid-century armchair with floating buttons and footstool 7 m (7 3/5 yd)**
- **G – Wingback chair with skirt 10 m (10 9/10 yd)**
- **H – Two-seater sofa with piped box cushions 13 m (14 1/5 yd)**
- **I – Mid-century banana sofa with piping 9m (9 4/5 yd)**

A

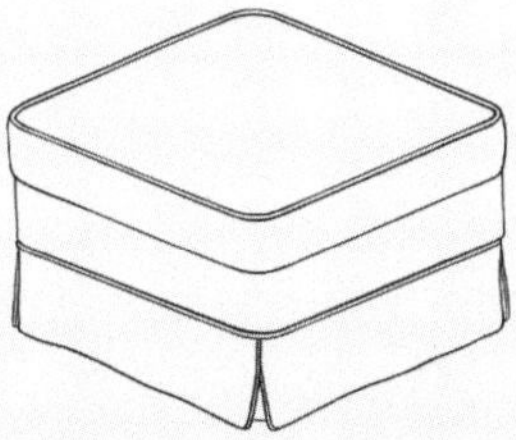

B

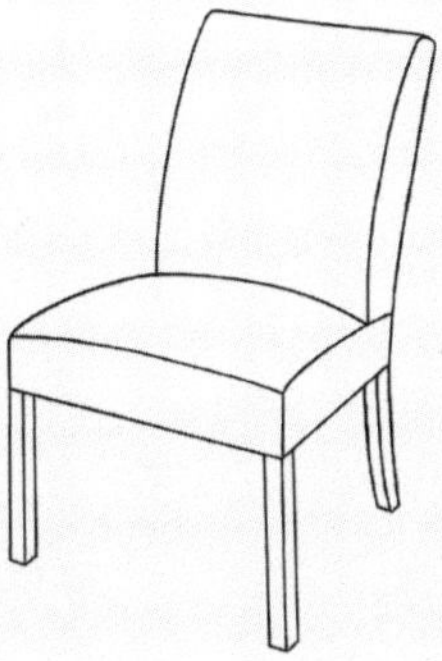

C

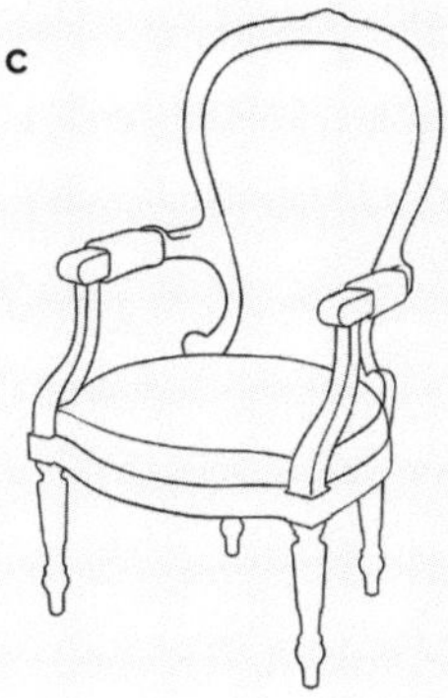

D

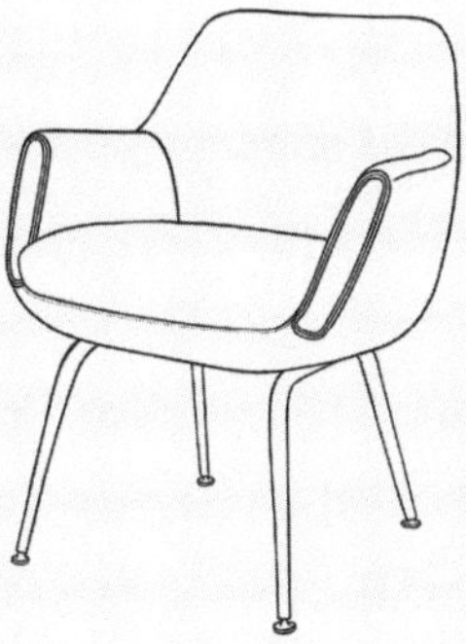

E

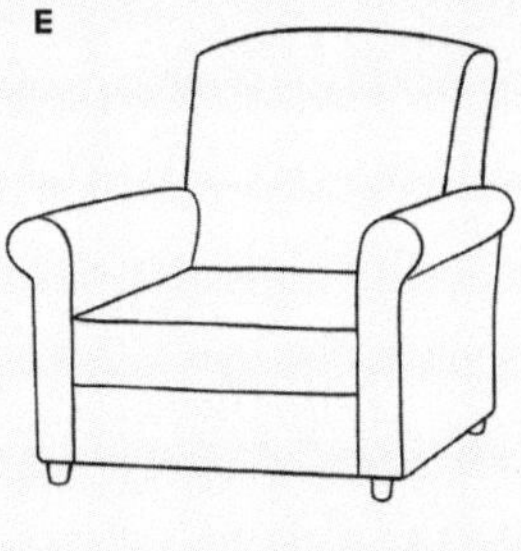

F

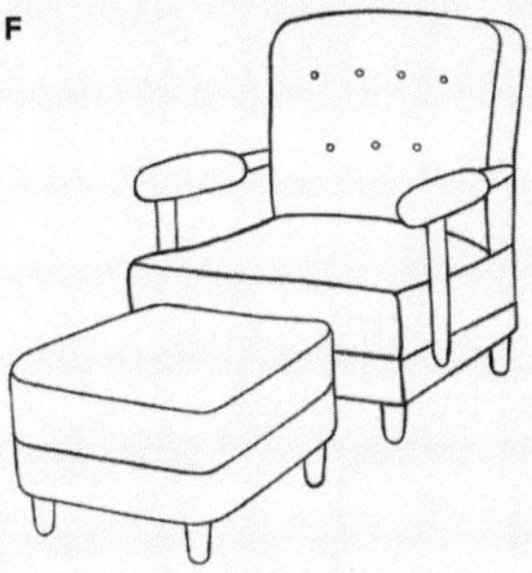

G

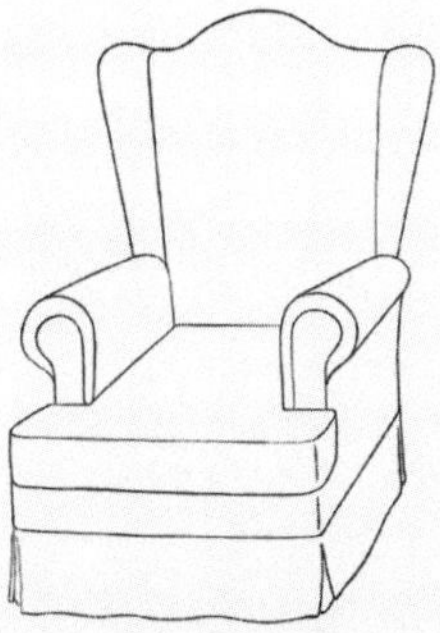

H

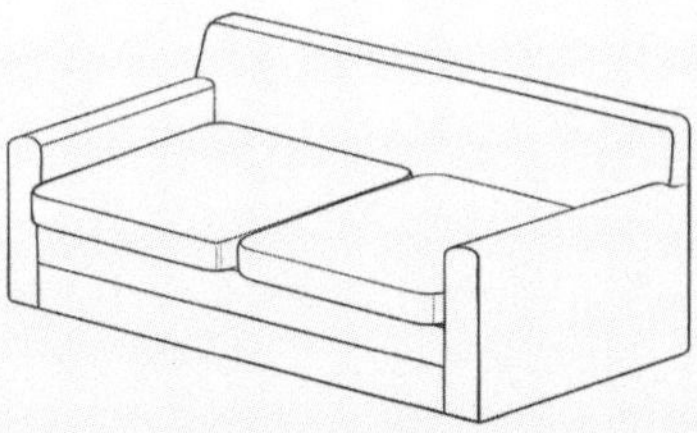

I

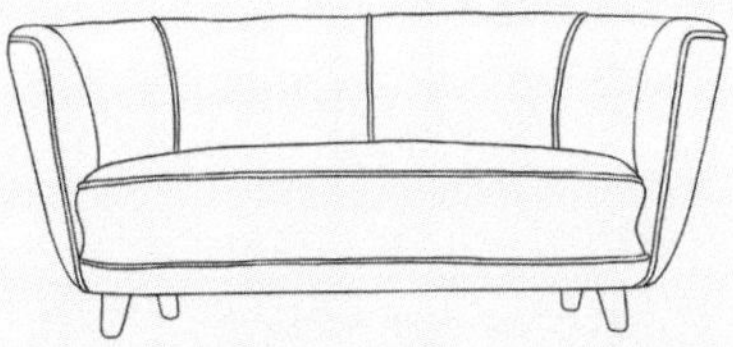

Sketching or stripping back

There are two ways to work out how much fabric you'll need: sketching and measuring, or stripping back. If you do not want to strip your item back yet you can sketch out each section in a notepad and add the dimensions. It's important to note there will be areas of fabric you cannot see, for example the inside arm fabric stretches back to the frame in two directions in order to be secured – at the back and the bottom of the arm. You can either slide your hand into the frame with your tape measure or estimate the necessary length.

ADDING A FLY

Sometimes for the parts that aren't seen we add what is called a 'fly'. On vintage pieces especially, or items with expensive designer fabric, a fly is added to keep the quantity of expensive/patterned fabric down. For the inside arm for example, only the visible section will have the main fabric. The part that is pulled into the frame and isn't visible at the bottom and towards the back has a cheaper fabric sewn on, and this is used to staple and secure the piece into place. If for any reason you cut a piece too short you can also add a fly in order to extend it. Use either the same fabric or a different one, but ensure the seam is out of sight.

The easiest way to understand how much fabric you'll need is to first strip your item back by removing the old fabric (see Stripping back your item, page 120). You only need to remove the fabric for this stage, not the other layers. Carefully remove each section of fabric, trying to keep it intact and unpick any sewn seams. Follow the directions on page 121 for how to label your item before you do this so that your template is easily identifiable later.

Mark your template, or annotate your sketch, with each raw edge. Either it is sewn and therefore you know the exact allowance you need to cut (the standard 1 cm [⅜ in] seam allowance) or it has been stapled onto the frame. Where it has been stapled you will need to leave more fabric, about 10 cm (4 in) more, to allow for pulling and stretching it onto the frame. The excess is cut away, so the template pieces you're looking at will have been cut down – ensure you add this extra back in to your template and understand each piece before cutting anything out.

Laying out

Now you can begin configuring your template on the fabric or in your notebook, making sure you're laying the pieces the right way around. Each piece must remain the right way around to ensure the pattern and the pile of the fabric go the right way. The exception here is if you have a plain or semi-plain fabric and a long item where you are avoiding having additional seams. You want to 'run' or 'railroad' the fabric in these cases, which means cutting it sideways, so the selvedge edges are at the top and bottom. If you are ordering from a small independent supplier sometimes you can request they print the fabric this way around so that you can cut long lengths.

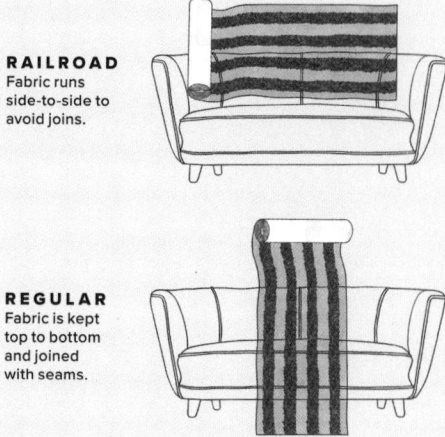

RAILROAD
Fabric runs side-to-side to avoid joins.

REGULAR
Fabric is kept top to bottom and joined with seams.

LAYING OUT TIPS

- Each piece of the template must remain the right way up with the top facing upwards, otherwise your finished pieces will be inside out.

- Lay items together or sketch them side by side with your fabric width in mind, usually 138 cm (54 in).

- Keep laying them up the imaginary roll of fabric until all the pieces are accounted for.

- For piping you will need to cut along the roll diagonally (see Making single piping, page 198). This is to ensure it's flexible enough to navigate corners without puckering or creasing.

I have cut out the new fabric for the inside back (the blue and white geometric fabric underneath) with a fly sewn on at the bottom (blue fabric). The old cover is laid on top. Note that I have kept the new cover square.

Laying out *continued*

Now measure the length of all the pieces laid out, or drawn out, continuously and you will know how much fabric is needed. I usually add 50 cm (19 ¾ in) extra or round up to the nearest whole metre to account for any discrepancies. Some upholsterers add more and make cushions with anything remaining after the project is completed. You may feel more confident having 1 m (39 in) extra. But generally if you sew something wrong or upholster something not quite right, you can unpick your work and adjust it without needing a whole new piece of fabric. The most important thing is not to cut your template out incorrectly! So measure it all twice, or even three times, before you order your fabric or cut it out. Fabric houses usually accept a minimum order of 1 m (39 in). They also accept 50 cm (19 ¾ in) increments, i.e. 2.5 m (2 ¾ yards).

Opposite are some examples showing the pieces you would need to cut for a box cushion and an armchair.

Box cushion

YOU WILL NEED TO CUT:

A – Top
B – Bottom
C – Front border
D – 2 x side borders
E – 2 x zip borders
F – Piping

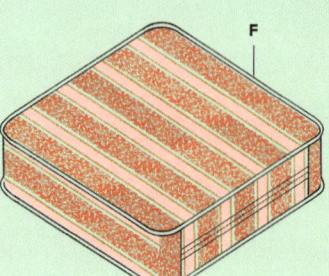

Armchair

YOU WILL NEED TO CUT:

A – Inside back (IB)
B – Seat
C – Inside arm right (IAR)
D – Inside arm left (IAL)
E – Outside arm right (OAR)
F – Outside arm left (OAL)
G – Outside back (OB)
H – Any additional borders
       or pieces (follow your
       templated sections)
I   – Piping

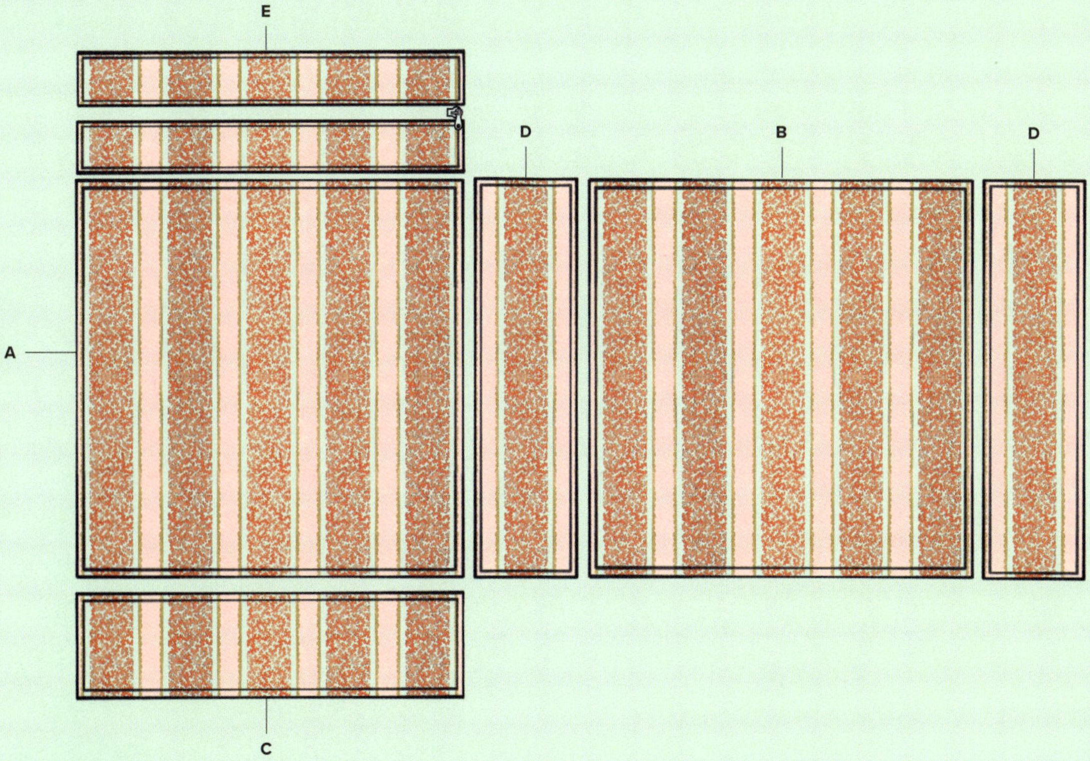

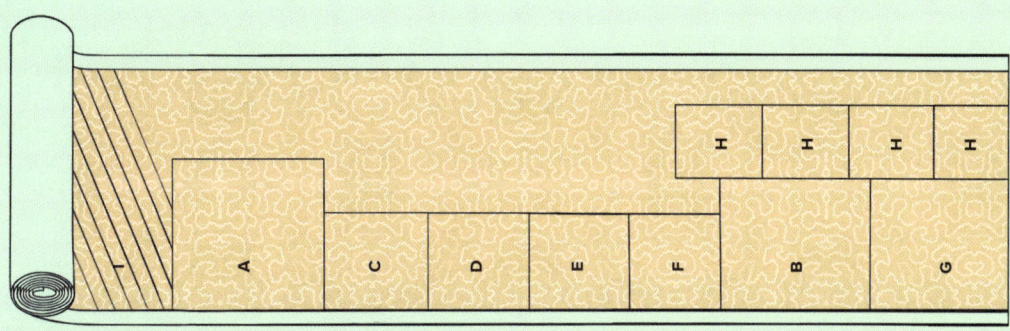

WHAT TO CHANGE & WHAT TO KEEP

Whilst it's best practice when professionally reupholstering an item to strip it to the frame and replace all the raw materials, it's not always completely necessary.

Identifying what needs to be replaced and what can be reused is a more economical approach, especially with your own at-home projects.

If you have information about the age of your item it will help you make an informed decision about what to replace and what to keep. The older the item the more likely you will need to replace all the upholstered layers. Antique pieces will likely be upholstered with traditional materials and not foam. Speak to your vendor to find out the age, or if you have no luck there, search the internet for similar items for sale that have more detailed descriptions of their age. Newer items may not need total reupholstery, rather just a replacement cover.

Foam

As a rule, I always replace the foam if I can see it has started to flake. Foam can be steamed to fluff it out more if it has flattened, but once small pieces have started to break off I would say it should be replaced entirely. When going to great lengths to reupholster something the main focus is to make it comfortable and so replacing the foam ensures this. If anything is ripped or hanging down it should be replaced entirely, i.e. if hessian is torn or worn in one area it should be replaced wherever else it is used in the piece.

The frame

When you strip your item back, before you start upholstering it, you should take a minute to assess the frame. It may benefit from some wood glue and new dowels or screws to fix any wobbles or squeaks. Always ensure the chair is upright and that all four feet are on level ground when clamping the frame together whilst the glue is setting – sometimes the frame can twist slightly if clamped in other positions so you may find the feet no longer touch the floor. You won't need to fill holes or small chips to the frame from the staples that have been removed as these will not be visible once polyester has been added and the new fabric is in place.

Whilst the frame is bare, it's also a good time to decide on the finish for the wood. Perhaps you want to sand it back, revarnish or paint it? It's best to do this before your new fabric is added. The quickest way to paint the wood is to lightly sandpaper it and then use chalk paint. This requires far less preparation than say changing the wood colour with paint stripper and wire brushes. For simple touch-ups on chipped varnish, I would recommend using a varnish pen in the matching colour – they're handy to have around the house for all furniture!

The stripped-back frame of the Parker Knoll armchair for our project. This frame has tension springs on the back and seat, which are all in good condition.

WORKSPACE

Before beginning your chosen upholstery project at home, there are a few health and safety considerations to have in mind.

It's best to work on trestles with an MDF board on top to form a solid and flat work base. If you don't have trestles you could work on a large table, but please note that as you slide the furniture around to upholster it, there's a danger you may damage the table underneath. There are also instances where you might need to clamp an item to your table (when webbing for example, so that it doesn't move each time you try to pull the tension tight), so you'll want to be working on a surface that can accommodate clamps. Though you could add some foam and/or old fabric between the table and the item being worked on to prevent surface damage, trestles are more appropriate as they are at a better height to work on.

When stripping back an item, staples will likely fall onto the floor, and could cause injury to people walking around without shoes on, or pets. I try to work neatly by disposing of each staple as it's pulled out. Or you can have a dust sheet underneath your workstation, which can be gathered up when you are finished and the staples can be shaken out into the bin.

If using a compressor and air gun stapler, the compressor can be quite loud (unless you opt for a silent model, which isn't usually completely silent) so considerations may need to be made around the times it is used and be mindful of who could be disturbed by it.

Some items are quite difficult to manoeuvre, such as large headboards, so you may need someone to help you lift it onto your workbench and flip it over each time you need to access the back/front.

Best practice & safety

Whenever you are operating machinery or using tools you should be alert and aware of your surroundings. Please consult the safety protocols of each tool used as you may need to wear goggles, gloves, ear defenders and/or a mask. You may also opt to wear a mask when stripping back an item to avoid breathing in the dust and micro particles that are released. When using solvents such as paints, wax, spray adhesive and varnish you will need to ventilate the area and wear the appropriate clothes and protective gear.

Upholstery is not a small-scale craft and you will be moving heavy objects around. Be really careful when doing so and know that you may require help sometimes.

CHAPTER TWO

Tools
&
materials

TOOLS

Upholstery tools are generally quite inexpensive as the craft mainly requires a few hand tools and a staple gun. When tackling your first project I would advise buying the entry-level options I have outlined so that you can get started with minimal outlay (marked with an asterisk* on the following pages). As you progress and take on more projects, and possibly more complicated projects, you may decide to upgrade your staple gun, foam cutter and even sewing machine so that you can move through the projects quicker.

I usually opt for wooden handles over plastic as they are more durable, although they may cost a small amount more in the first instance. Most of these tools are not specialist and so can be found in general hardware stores. Specialist tools such as web stretchers can be ordered with your local upholstery supply company or found online. If I can source vintage hand-held tools at car boot fairs and markets then I do, as I love the patina and knowing that the tool already has a long history.

My most prized tool is one I rarely need for upholstery but holds sentimental value. It's my grandad's hammer. I remember him using it on countless DIY projects at home and for some reason it became synonymous with him fixing things (although a hammer is more for smashing than fixing!). I keep it in my tool box as a reminder of my grandad, his influence on me and also of my journey so far.

Over the years, I've upgraded my sewing machine. Now instead of a domestic sewing machine I use an industrial Juki DU1181N which handles thick fabrics easily.

1/ TACK REMOVER*

This will be your most used tool! Not least of all because of stripping down upholstery projects but also for undoing temporary tacks and errors along the way. There are two main types: a spade-like head or a two-prong head. I prefer the two-prong tack remover but they both do the same job.

2/ SHARP SCISSORS*

Tailor's scissors come in a variety of sizes. My kit always includes 20 cm (8 in) and 30 cm (12 in) pairs. The larger pair I only ever cut fabric with. The smaller pair are used for all other materials such as polyester, fire-retardant (FR) lining, etc. Keeping your scissors clean is good practice so as to ensure you're getting a crisp line as you cut and will help you avoid transferring any marks to your main fabric (when cutting polyester you will find spray adhesive gets on the blades). Never cut paper with your fabric scissors as this will blunt them.

3/ ROTARY CUTTER

A rotary cutter is not essential as you can always use scissors but I added this to my tool kit for when I need to cut multiple layers of fabric at once. The circular blade can cut up to a 2.5 cm (1 in) thickness. It's rare that you will need to cut multiple layers as usually you will be upholstering one item at a time. But this tool has been great for long lengths of piping, patchworks and precision cutting.

4/ RULER*

A long ruler is essential for marking out your fabric and for making piping, using a short ruler takes longer and will cause more errors. Investing in a ruler that is the thickness of the piping you will usually make (the width of the cord, plus your seam allowance, multiplied by two) will make these long lines a lot quicker to draw out and therefore more efficient. I use a 6 cm (2¼ in) wide ruler to cut my piping.

5/ MALLET*

This is needed for tapping your tack remover when removing staples and tacks. A wooden mallet is best but if you want to protect the handles of your wooden tools you can use a rubber mallet.

6/ PINCERS/PLIERS*

You'll need pincers or pliers to remove staples. Staples often break as you remove them so pincers which can get in close to the wood are best. I advise investing in some with a rubber grip as stripping back old upholstery can take a while and can be tough on your hands. If there are tiny fragments of staples that you can't get out, hammer them back into the frame so they are not sticking out.

7/ STUDS / GIMP PINS

Studs are often used to finish an item in a decorative way. They come in all shapes, sizes and colours from brass to matt black, square to floral shaped. The key is to think about the proportions of the stud in relation to the size of the item. For example, large studs work well on large headboards but not so much on small dining chairs.

Gimp pins are more subtle and a less decorative type of pin or stud. They are usually used to hold pleats or corner folds in place. They come in a variety of colours to be matched with the fabric and somewhat camouflaged. I often buy white gimp pins and then colour them with a permanent marker so that I don't have to store lots of different colours.

8/ SHARP BLADE OR STANLEY KNIFE

This blade is useful for opening seams when stripping back. It's also better than scissors for cutting away excess fabric on the frame, in corners or underneath before the bottom cloth goes on. It's especially helpful if you have show wood and need to cut accurately along the frame edge to cover the staples with piping.

1 & 2/ WEB STRETCHERS

There are three types of web stretchers: slotted (1), gooseneck (2) and spiked (not pictured). I favour the slotted web stretcher which is used by threading a loop of webbing through the slot and securing it with a peg. The gooseneck stretcher is spiked and uses a lever to pull the webbing tight. Finally, the spiked web stretcher is smaller than the gooseneck and also has spikes which go through the webbing in order to gain purchase and pull the webbing tight.

Needles & Pins

3/ REGULATOR

A regulator needle is flat on one end. This tool is great for achieving a crisp edge in pleats, corners or folds. The sharp end can be used to hold fabric in place (instead of a pin) before adding gimp pins or studs. It is a very versatile item.

4/ CURVED NEEDLE

The curved needle is used for upholstery instead of a straight needle, as when sewing to a fixed surface, like a chair back, it's easier to thread back out of the furniture. Otherwise you're in danger of losing it in the layers. Curved needles come in varying sizes; I favour a 5 cm (2 in) size for small slip stitches.

5/ CURVED SPRING NEEDLE

These are more heavy duty than a standard needle and with a much sharper and sturdier tip to sew through hessian and traditional upholstery layers. The needle eye is also wider so that twine can be threaded through for sewing springs into place and lashing them.

6 & 7/ BUTTONING NEEDLE

This is a double-ended needle with a sharp point at each end. Only one end can be threaded with twine. Both ends are sharp so that when buttoning an item the needle can be pushed through from underneath using the back end of the needle or from the front using the normal tip.

PINS*

Pins are needed to hold fabric together before you sew. They are particularly useful before you slip stitch the outside back in order to secure your fabric and ensure there are no wrinkles. I also use pins to mark out the spacing of studs to ensure even spacing as they are easily moved and don't leave a mark like chalk or pen.

8 & 9/ STAPLE GUNS*

This is potentially the biggest investment in your tool collection, but will depend on the type of staple gun you want to use.

The most affordable option is a hand-held gun that can take 8–12 mm (5/16–1/2 in) staples (8). The side of the gun will always outline the type of staples suitable and it's best to have this range as you'll need longer 12 mm (1/2 in) staples when working with thick upholstery fabrics. A hand-held gun can be quite tough on your hands after a while. Sometimes you may find the staples aren't lying flat on the wood or frame so you may need to press and hold the gun down with more force.

The mid-range option is an electric staple gun. This allows you to fire at a more rapid pace which, when you're working on larger items, can be very useful. It will also secure the staples further into the wood or frame with less effort.

The most professional option is an air compressor with an air gun (9). This has the most rapid fire release so you can work most efficiently. Some air guns have a safety catch which has to be pushed to the side before you can fire them and some don't. Familiarise yourself with the brand and the release mechanism before you plug it in to avoid any injuries.

10 & 11/ FOAM CUTTERS*

There are several different ways you can cut foam. It will largely depend on which tools you want to buy and how much you'd like to spend. The most affordable option is a serrated knife. This works well on straight lines and curves but can leave a rougher edge when cutting thick foam.

I advise using an electric carving knife (10) as they are fairly inexpensive but get much better results than a serrated knife. The cord is usually quite short so it's best to pair it with an extension lead.

And finally, if you'll be tackling lots of projects and want to invest in professional tools I use a Bosch foam cutter (11). It has various blades for cutting really thick foam and can give a smooth finish when you need to chamfer an edge or cut with millimetre precision. But the electric carver is a very close second!

1/ TACK HAMMER

This is a double-sided hammer used for hammering in tacks. One side is thinner and magnetic for quickly picking up an individual tack and tapping it lightly into place. Then you turn the hammer around in your hand and hammer it into the frame with the wider end. Most modern upholstery techniques can be done with a staple gun, but tacks are advised for securing springs.

2/ NYLON-TIPPED HAMMER

This is very similar to a tack hammer but one side has a nylon tip. This is used for hammering in studs and the nylon tip stops the stud from being scratched or damaged as you hammer it in place.

3/ STUD/NAIL SPACER

You can use a spacer tool to help position studs evenly and avoid hammering your fingertips. One side lets you space five studs evenly which is great for doing straight rows. The other side aligns one at a time which is good for curves. To use it, place the studs in the allocated slots and hammer them lightly into place. Remove the tool to hammer the studs down fully. It's not an essential tool. You can also position the studs by eye, which is what I do.

PNEUMATIC DECORATIVE NAIL GUN

If you plan to stud a lot of items you might want to invest in a nail gun specifically for studding to speed up the process. This is optional. I do my studs with a hammer.

4 & 5/ BUTTON MAKING MACHINE AND MOULDS

These can be bought online and usually come with a variety of different die sizes to make varying size buttons. I personally opted for a vintage machine as I love the patina. Usually button machines need to be mounted to a surface and clamped into place in order to be used. They are quite weighty, especially the vintage ones.

You can switch out the function to either use the cutter circles to cut the fabric (make sure to use the correct size for the buttons you are making), or the button press to secure the fabric onto the moulds. You will need to purchase the button moulds in the sizes required (both the front cup part and back loop part).

See the instructions of your specific machine on how to make a button.

6/ DRILL

You need this to drill out the holes in foam for deep buttoning. Other than that, a drill is only needed if the frame of your item needs fixing. You may need to drill new holes for dowels or add some hidden screws to a frame to make it more secure.

7/ FOAM CUTTER BIT

These drill bits come in lots of sizes and can be found in your hardware store or online. You will need one the size of the button you are using or ever so slightly bigger. Each time you cut a hole the foam will stay inside the drill bit; after a few cuts you may need to empty this. Switch the drill off before doing this and be careful.

8/ GLUE GUN

This is needed for glueing trim and double piping in place. Alternatively, you can use studs or small gimp pins.

9/ CLAMPS

If you are fixing the frame you may need clamps to hold it in place when glueing it back together. You may also need to clamp the item down in order to work on it safely and securely when you are upholstering if you find it is moving around a lot.

TACKS

Tacks are often used in traditional techniques, instead of staples, to secure a material to the frame. As we are following modern techniques generally we will opt to use staples. When lashing springs into place I favour the older technique and use large improved 20 mm (¾ in) tacks as this method ensures the cord is not damaged and can be pulled tight before it is fastened off.

1/ SEWING MACHINE*

Most domestic sewing machines will be fine for sewing upholstery projects, although generally they are best for thinner fashion fabrics. If you can source a heavy-duty machine this will be better equipped for thicker upholstery fabrics. I use an industrial machine (a Juki 1181N) which is table-mounted. These machines are best for long use and are well-equipped for thick upholstery fabrics as they have a walking foot (also known as an even feed or dual feed foot) which helps guide multiple layers of fabric through together.

ZIP FOOT

Traditionally used for attaching zips. I don't use a zip foot for my method, I use the standard pressure foot. But a zip foot is an option if you want to sew your zip in a different way.

2/ SEAM GUIDE

This is a handy little tool but totally optional. It's a magnetic guide that sits next to the needle to guide your fabric through at your exact seam allowance. Alternatively, you can stick some tape to the machine to remind you of your seam allowance.

3/ PIPING FOOT

A piping foot is for sewing piping cord. It has a ridge underneath to allow the cord to pass underneath the foot and be sewn between the piping fabric. They come in various sizes depending on the cord size you use.

4/ EXTRA BOBBINS

It's good practice to have a few bobbins (and cases if your machine uses them) so that you can either keep some filled and ready or fill them up as you go. I usually keep a few full bobbins in the most commonly used thread colours (cream, grey and black).

5/ TAILOR'S CHALK OR MARKER PEN*

As a general rule, I usually only use tailor's chalk on fabric in whichever colour shows up best (usually chalk is available in white, black, blue and red). That's so that if mistakes are made when marking, they can be rubbed off. However, I would advise making a small mark on the fabric to check it doesn't leave a permanent mark before using it all over.

Permanent marker pens are good for drawing your shapes onto foam.

Fabric markers (permanent) and vanishing markers (which can be erased) are other options for marking your fabric. Be careful when using permanent pens on your expensive fabric.

6/ SEAM RIPPER/PACKING KNIFE

A seam ripper is essential for unpicking either your own sewing when errors are made, or the original sewing when you're trying to use the existing cover as a template. I often interchange between a seam ripper (when I need to be careful with the fabric) and a packing knife (when I'm being less precise).

OVERLOCKER

An overlocker machine is not essential but you may decide to use one as it neatens raw edges and helps prevent fraying. You can add this finishing touch to items with loose covers such as box cushions or scatter cushions. If the covers are washable, overlocking is a great way to protect the sewing and make the covers as durable as possible. But if fabric is dry clean only or not washable it is not essential to add this step. For your own personal use it's not essential to overlock your work, but for clients I usually add this in for a more professional finish.

You will need a heavy-duty industrial machine to cope with multiple thick layers. Or you can overlock the edges of each piece when it's cut out, before you sew them together. Be careful as the overlocker will cut away excess fabric, so if you have cut your pieces to size, ensure you are not cutting them smaller as you complete this step.

OLD SOCKS

This is a fun one and not essential! Old socks come in handy for a few reasons. One use is to protect the feet or legs of an item you are reupholstering. To do this, put the sock on and secure in place with elastic bands. When the item is being worked on and is moving around the bench the socks will stop scratches on visible areas of wood and varnish. Secondly, if you are waxing or repairing intricate turned wooden legs, socks can be good for polishing or evenly distributing the wax or varnish (you will need a latex glove underneath to protect your skin).

MATERIALS

Modern upholstery materials are more affordable and easier to source than traditional materials which is, in part, why modern techniques are better for beginners.

I source all my supplies and tools from my local upholstery supplier in the UK, Martins Upholstery Supplies. I would recommend finding a local specialist because the materials work out cheaper this way and can be sent more economically than buying individual things online. Building a rapport with your suppliers also means you can ask questions about different materials and broaden your knowledge over time. Every time I visit the warehouse I see new things that inspire me (such as new trims) or raw materials I hadn't heard of before. For years I would use a permanent marker pen to colour my staples dark before stapling on the bottom cloth before I realised you can buy them black! This type of supplier will also be able to custom make cushion inners for your projects (if you need feather-wrapped box cushions, for example), advise on replacement materials and different types of foam, etc. They are a fountain of knowledge so don't be afraid to ask questions.

If you don't have a local supplier, you could ask a local upholsterer where they source their materials. They may even sell you small quantities of foam and offcuts and finding someone with shared interests can only be a positive thing! Alternatively, you can of course source all of the materials online. I would encourage you to check where they are based so that you can source as locally as possible.

As with everything, there are always a few different options for upholstery materials. Whether you opt for pink or blue foam will come down to preference. Whether you choose cotton felt or polyester wadding is up to you. This book aims to provide you with the basics to get started, but finding materials you favour is part of your own personal journey.

FOAM

There are lots of different foam options. There are two main things to consider when choosing foam for your project. The first is how thick you want the sheet of foam to be. Foam in the UK is often measured in inches, which can be confusing when using metric measurements elsewhere. Usually we replace like-for-like so if removing 2.5 cm (1 in) foam, replace with a new 2.5 cm (1 in) foam. The second point to consider is how soft or firm you'd like the foam to be. This is graded by numbers but also categorised into colours. Generally I stick to three types of foam but there are many more available: blue (firm – for seats), pink (soft – for back and arms) and chip foam or reconstructed foam (very dense and firm – for banquette seating). But there are also orange (medium soft), lilac (soft) and white (very firm) densities to choose from. Foam can be layered together so you could have a firm foam underneath and a thinner layer of soft foam on top for comfort.

You can now buy eco-foam, which is fully recyclable and made from mostly recycled materials. In the UK this is called SpringBond Ultraflex. Latex foam is another solution for materials made from more natural fibres.

If you are making outdoor furniture consider using outdoor foam, which is more lightweight and dries faster.

1 – 6lb soft chip foam – orange
2 – 10lb chip foam – blue
3 – Medium seat – green
4 – Soft seat – pink
5 – Very firm seat – white
6 – Medium seat – orange
7 – 5lb chip foam –yellow
8 – Firm seat – blue
9 – Very soft back –pale blue
10 – Soft headboard back – lilac
11 – 8lb chip foam – pink

1–3/ SPRINGS

Depending on the type of frame you have, different springs will be used. There are zigzag (1), coil (2) and tension springs (not pictured). Zigzag spring clips (3) are needed to secure the zigzag springs safely to the frame. Mid-century pieces may also have sprung units, which is a series of springs attached within a metal frame. A sprung base is more comfortable than webbing and foam alone.

4–8/ WEBBING

Webbing sets the structure for the upholstery by providing a strong base when pulled tight and/or woven together. Webbing comes in four main types: black and white (for seats – 4), jute (for arms and backs – 5), elastic (versatile), plastic (for outside backs – 6) and pirelli (7). Pirelli is a thick rubber webbing used mainly in mid-century furniture and needs to be secured with pirelli clips (8).

If you are making a deconstructed chair where the back is left open so that you can see the inside layers, you may want to use a decorative webbing which comes in various colours and designs. With all webbing the most important thing is to pull it tight and get strong tension.

SPRAY ADHESIVE

Spray glue can be bought from any hardware store. You want a strong glue to stick foam and polyester wadding layers into place, but your fixed upholstery fabric will also reinforce this. When glueing foam you will need to spray both the foam and the surface it's going to stick to. But when you glue polyester wadding only one surface needs to be covered.

There are more sustainable options available, such as Naturlatex, a latex glue, and Aquatack, a water-based glue, which are painted on.

9/ BACK TACK CARD

A roll of thin cardboard about 1 cm (½ in) wide used to secure borders and outside backs into place with crisp straight lines.

10/ PLY GRIP

A metal claw-like material that comes on a roll and is used for closing gaps, often between an outside arm and outside back. It can be used in place of slip stitching. The types indicate how many spikes are on each claw, two or three. I generally use three prong. Be careful when using this, it's very sharp!

> Using the correct webbing and springs will form a really solid and comfortable foundation for your item, and help it stand the test of time.

1/ POLYESTER WADDING

Polyester wadding, sometimes called dacron or terylene, is used between the fabric and the foam. It stops the fabric sticking to the foam and creasing over time. It also fills out the cover to make it look more full, fluffy and professional. Polyester wadding comes in different thicknesses. I tend not to use really thick layers as over time when they flatten they can leave the cover looking flat. I generally use 4 oz, 70 cm (27 in) wide polyester wadding. You can glue together polyester wadding to make longer lengths.

Eco options are available, made from recycled materials which use fewer chemicals.

2/ COTTON FELT

Cotton felt can be used instead of polyester wadding, as a more natural fibre. It's mainly used with traditional upholstery but can be mixed with modern techniques if you prefer it to synthetic polyester wadding.

3/ FIRE RETARDANT (FR) LINER/FR CALICO

You will only need to add a fire-retardant (FR) liner if your fabric is not already FR treated. There are different types available. I favour FR felt liner which has the UK standard rating of CRIB 5.

This level is suitable for residential and commercial use. It's easily glued or stapled into place and is thick, which adds a bit of extra padding underneath the polyester wadding and fabric. There are also calico and cotton options. They all do the exact same thing, which is make the item fire safe to various degrees (depending on the category you choose).

Check your government's guidelines about fire safety regulations and the requirements for upholstery in your area.

4/ STOCKINETTE

This is the mesh material that wraps around a box cushion foam and polyester wadding. It keeps the polyester wadding compact and allows the cover to go on without clogging up the zip with fibres. It is not essential, but gives a professional finish. If you plan to take the covers off to swap them over or clean them a lot this layer is advised.

5/ LAID CORD

Laid cord is used to lash the springs down to the frame across the top of the spring.

TWINE

Flax twine is used when sewing coil springs into place at the seat bottom.

6/ DIPRYL/BOTTOM CLOTH

This is used to cover the base of the finished item. It stops dust falling out of the chair over time and prevents creatures getting inside the item. Dipryl is the most affordable option for this but you can use anything on the bottom of the chair. Cotton bottom cloths offer a bit more of a high-end finish and come in various colours.

Dipryl is also useful for making templates.

PLATFORM LINING

A thicker, plain lining fabric used on the seat platform of armchairs or sofas. It allows less main fabric to be used on the parts under the box cushions which are not seen.

7 & 8/ HESSIAN

Hessian is the layer that covers the webbing. It stops foam and other materials from being forced through the holes of the webbing over time. Hessian comes in various densities and widths. I tend to use 12 oz, 183 cm (72 in) wide hessian. Other options are 7 oz, 10 oz and 12 oz with the heavier option having a more closed weave. The width needed will depend on how large your item is. Sofas generally need the wider 72-inch option but smaller chairs will be fine with 40 inch. If you need longer sections, pieces can be sewn together.

9/ BUTTONING TWINE

Nylon twine or buttoning twine is used for sewing in buttons.

1/ ZIP & ZIP PULLS

Zips come on a continuous roll with the pull separate. Choose the colour most appropriate for your make. I stick to neutrals such as black, cream and tan because the zips are not visible on the finished items, so don't need to be an exact colour match like they do in fashion sewing. Open one end of the zip and cut the corner away on one side to slide the pull into place.

Try to avoid fashion zips as these are not strong enough for upholstery fabrics and use.

2/ PIPING CORD/WELT

Piping cord, also called welt, comes in different sizes which should be matched to the piping presser foot size used. I use a more flexible cotton cord (pre-shrunk) without a coating as I think it gives a better finish for corners. I use pre-shrunk cotton piping cord numbers 8 (4mm) and 10 (5mm) depending on how wide I'd like the piping to be. You can also use plastic cord or paper cord if you need a really stiff piping. Double piping cord is also available or you can sew two rows of single cord together using a double piping presser foot.

3 & 4/ THREAD

The thread I use comes on large spindles, which are suitable for my industrial machine. The type is terko thread 36 with 4000m of thread, but any suitable for industrial machines are fine. It's more durable and so does not snap when sewing.

For domestic machines you want to use an extra strong thread to ensure it's durable.

Always colour-match the fabric colour and make a few bobbins before you get started.

If your machine is overheating and the thread keeps breaking, you can spray a small amount of non-silicon lubrication spray on the needle to cool it down.

If using an overlocker to finish the edges and prevent fraying (mainly for cushion covers), the threads are slightly thinner.

STAPLES

The staples used will need to match your staple gun. Usually in either a 52 or 71, my air gun takes 71s. Then choose the length of the staple (between 6–12 mm [¼–½ in]) depending on how many layers you are securing to the frame. For thin fabrics and single layers I use 8 mm (5/16 in). For a few layers of fabric I'll use a 10 mm (3/8 in). For webbing and attaching ply grip to the outside back I use 12 mm (½ in).

5/ BUTTON MOULDS

These come in two parts (wire backs and tops) and a range of sizes ready to be covered with fabric for bespoke buttons. You will need a button-making machine to be able to use these.

BUCKRAM, SKIRTEX OR VALANCE STIFFENER

This is used to stiffen the skirt on a piece. It's inserted into a sewn skirt cover to help hold the shape, and is available in various widths. It has a stiff, almost cardboard-like texture with a fuzzy feel that flexes slightly. It can also be used to make thin, lightweight pelmets.

> I try to colour-match thread to fabric to make it less visible. When that's not possible, I use neutrals like grey, cream or black.

CHAPTER THREE

Projects

PROJECTS

The great thing about upholstery is that the projects are always different. That means if you upholster 10 armchairs they will probably be totally different, unless you have matching pairs, and every slightly new shape requires slightly different techniques. Upholstery is really about mastering different skills and then problem solving on each item to decipher which skills are needed for that particular project. I love this way of working because it keeps me on my toes and I feel there's always more to learn. If you come up against something new there is usually a workaround solution where you can replace something you don't know with something you do; for example, if you haven't mastered sewing a frill you can use piping and if you haven't mastered that you could do a plain seam.

Here I'll walk you through how to tackle your first upholstery projects. If your items are slightly different from mine, use the techniques section to guide you. For example, if your armchair has a fluted back follow the flutes techniques (see page 210) rather than following along for a plain back. Or if you want to use ply grip (see page 184) instead of slip stitching (see page 220), opt for that technique.

Upholstery is all about giving it a go and building your confidence. Most things can be readjusted or redone so get started and assess your progress every so often to make sure you're happy with the look as it comes together. I find the most unnerving part is stripping an item back as that's the moment you commit to redressing it, however long it takes.

I love to get into the zone with a good playlist whilst sewing on my machine.

HEADBOARD

OK ... so a headboard might seem like an odd place to start if you've never upholstered anything before, but you have to trust me here.

Usually, upholstery lessons will start with a drop-in dining seat – a flat rectangular shape that can be popped out of the dining chair frame and upholstered separately before being reattached. But that is just one seat and usually you'll have a set of at least four chairs. You diligently learn how to upholster your seat and step back to admire your creation only to realise you have to do another three! And let's not mention the fact that they're tucked underneath the table for most of their life.

Instead, I propose starting with a headboard. In a bedroom it can be the most impactful piece when the right fabric is chosen and it's proudly displayed on the wall for all to see. When you've finished your headboard you won't have three more to make to complete the set ... unless you decide to make some for more bedrooms (which I hope you will). Making just one is triumph enough. Be bold and experiment with different shapes, trims and designs to make your headboard a one-of-a-kind masterpiece.

The only problem is, you'll want to have it in your living room to make sure every guest sees your mastery! If that's the case, fear not. Making a headboard requires exactly the same skillset as making a backrest for a banquette seat, so you can apply these skills to various projects around the home.

My headboard is upholstered in Colours of Arley midi stripe fabric (colours peach and lilac) with a frill in Linwood Juno (colour blush). Cushions and lampshades by Studio Janettie.

TO MAKE THE FRAME:

MATERIALS NEEDED

- 2 full sheets (2.44 m x 1.22 m (8 x 4 ft) of 18 mm thick MDF or plywood
- Wood glue
- 25 mm (1 in) screws (the screw should be shorter than the thickness of both boards together)
- Webbing (if using)
- Large piece of bottom cloth or scrap fabric, slightly larger than you want your headboard
- Struts (optional for smaller headboards)

TOOLS NEEDED

- Jigsaw
- Circular saw
- Foam cutter
- Marker pen
- Screwdriver
- Sandpaper (optional)
- Tailor's chalk
- Web stretcher (if using webbing)

TO UPHOLSTER THE HEADBOARD:

MATERIALS NEEDED

- 4 cm (1½ in) thick foam full sheet (203 x 159 cm [80 x 63 in])
- Back tacking card
- Polyester wadding
- Spray adhesive
- Thread for sewing machine
- Fire-retardant (FR) lining (if needed)
- Fabric

TOOLS NEEDED

- Long ruler
- Mallet
- Tack remover
- Pincers
- Sharp fabric scissors
- Sewing machine
- Staple gun and staples
- Piping foot for sewing machine (if adding piping)
- Presser foot for sewing machine (if adding frills)

SKILLS NEEDED

- Pattern matching (page 162)
- Measuring & cutting foam (page 152)
- Adding a fire-retardant (FR) lining (page 160)
- Adding polyester (page 158)
- Temporary staples (page 122)
- Pulling, smoothing & stapling fabric (page 127)
- Sewing on piping or trim (page 198)
- Back tacking (page 178)
- Corners (page 166)
- Adding bottom cloth (page 188)

Before you start

If you have an existing headboard to reupholster skip over to page 69, but if you'd like to learn how to make your own frame, read on ...

Headboards don't have to be rectangular, so start by considering the shape you want to make. Straight lines are of course easier, but concave shapes, like a semicircle, are next in line. Most difficult are extremely convex lines, as the fabric needs to be pulled into the curve and smoothed out. Consider your shape carefully.

The shape I have drawn out is based on a design by Ensemblier London, a company I admire who specialise in traditional upholstery and natural materials. I've made it my own by adding a frill!

Another thing to consider is whether you would like a pillow stop. This is a flat part of the headboard (without foam) that sits behind the mattress. If you are using struts to attach your headboard to a divan base, the headboard will need to sit above the divan but overlap with your mattress for stability. If you are mounting the headboard to the wall with a split batten (sometimes called a French cleat), a pillow stop is optional. A split batten is made of two angled pieces of wood that slot together. One attaches to the frame and one to the wall in order to hang the item securely. If you want the full height of the wood to make a really tall headboard then opt out of a pillow stop and hang the headboard in line with the top of your mattress.

Making the frame for your shape is much simpler than you would expect, as outlined in the following pages. I usually opt for using a split batten to attach the headboard to the wall. With larger headboards (UK king size and above) or tall shapes, they can end up being quite heavy so two split battens may be needed. To cut the weight down you can also cut out holes in the frame to remove some wood. These holes are then covered with jute webbing and hessian before continuing to upholster the frame as normal.

To work on the headboard I use two trestles but if you don't have those you can use a large sturdy table covered with a thick sheet or some foam to protect it. There will be lots of movement to turn the headboard over and around which you may need help with.

Alternatively, you can ask a local carpenter to cut out your frame.

The back of the headboard frame with the split baton not yet attached in the recess/void

Making the frame

1. Using a large piece of bottom cloth or scrap fabric, mark out your desired shape with a marker pen. To ensure you get a symmetrical design, use tailor's chalk to draw over one half of your shape and then fold the fabric in half together so that the chalk line transfers over. Make sure you're happy with your shape and then cut it out.

2. Transfer the design onto both sheets of MDF or plywood with a marker pen.

3. Cut out one shape from the MDF with the jigsaw. If you are reducing the weight of the board by cutting out holes do this now. Leave a 15 cm (6 in) allowance above the pillow stop line (if you are having one). Do not cut all the way to the edge as you want your frame to still be sturdy. Web and hessian over the holes before foaming it (see webbing a seat, page 130, and adding hessian, page 150). You can use jute webbing as the headboard won't need to bear any weight like a chair, but weave them in the same way as you would with black and white webbing.

4. The second uncut board forms the frame at the back of the headboard. To fit the battens, create a hollow centre by marking out a 15 cm (6 in) border inside your shape. Cut out both lines.

5. Glue both pieces of the wooden frame together. Secure with some screws, making sure the screws don't come through the wood all the way from the back. Place one screw roughly every 30 cm (12 in). If you're using 18 mm (¾ in) wood the total thickness is now 36 mm (1½ in), so your screws need to be longer than 18 mm (¾ in) but slightly shorter than 36 mm (1½ in).

6. If your two frames match up, success! If not, sand down the edges until they are in line.

7. Use the offcuts of wood to make your split battens using a circular saw. Angle it at 45 degrees and cut through your length. Then cut a straight line roughly about 8 cm (3¼ in) either side of the angle to make your battens. Cutting it in this order means it is easier and safer to hold, as you aren't trying to cut an angled line through a thin piece of wood.

8. Add one side of your split batten to the frame, with the straight side at the top and the angle overhanging on the front edge at the bottom (ready to hook onto the wall piece).

9. If you are opting for struts for a smaller headboard, add them to the frame at the end, otherwise they will be in the way as you're upholstering and may get damaged.

A more lightweight option, showing webbing and hessian.

Back of the frame

A – Back of headboard frame
B – Split batten
C – Webbing and hessian

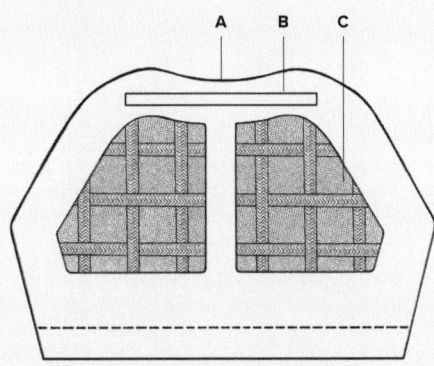

Preparing a ready-made headboard

Preparing the frame

1   If you are reupholstering an existing headboard you will need to strip it back (see Stripping back, page 120) and assess whether or not you want to keep the foam.

2   Use the stripped fabric as templates for your new fabric, and buy new foam if replacing, ensuring it is a similar thickness to what you removed. If reusing the old foam, skip to step 3 opposite.

1   Add an oversized piece of foam by spraying the foam and the front of the headboard frame with spray adhesive (if you would like to add studs do not spray adhesive right to the edge). Press the foam to the board.

2   With the foam sheet secured, turn the headboard over and trim the edge with the foam cutter, leaving a 0.5 cm (¼ in) overhang, which will aid in softening the edge of the board (see Measuring and cutting foam, page 152). If you intend on studding your headboard leave the edge of the board free of foam by at least the width of your studs plus 2 mm (1/16 in) (see Adding studs, page 208).

3   If needed, add your FR lining now (see Adding a fire-retardant lining, page 160). Trim the excess level with the edge of the foam.

4   Add polyester wadding – tear off the desired length of wadding. Spray the glue onto the foam. Then stretch out the wadding and stick into place. If you need to join a few pieces together, do so by spraying glue to the foam and the edge of wadding that is already stuck down. Ensure the wadding is pulled tight to avoid creases. Trim the excess level with the edge of the foam.

5   Depending on the width of your headboard, you may need to sew the fabric together to make it wide enough. If your fabric is plain or doesn't have a pile you can run it sideways (also called 'railroading', see page 30) to avoid needing seams but this method doesn't work for patterns that need to stay the right way up. See Pattern matching on page 162 to sew any extra pieces of fabric together.

6   Mark out the required amount of fabric with tailor's chalk and a ruler. Ensure you are happy with the position of the pattern; you may want part of the pattern centred. Add 15 cm (6 in) on each side to give you enough fabric for pulling and stapling (this accounts for the MDF and foam).

7   Label top and bottom on the back of the fabric. Cut the length of fabric out. You won't need to cut the exact shape of the headboard, keep your fabric rectangular for now.

Upholstering
the frame

1   With the foam facing up and the bottom edge
    towards you, staple the bottom, starting in the
    middle of the fabric along the bottom edge of the
    frame using temporary staples. Keeping the fabric
    straight, pull it taut along the line from corner to
    corner and ensure there is enough overhanging
    on each corner; we have allowed for 8 cm (3¼ in).

2   Turn the headboard around so the top is facing
    you or standing up on the floor with something
    to lean on. Smooth the fabric over the frame and
    foam. Check you are happy with the positioning
    before starting to staple the top edge.

3   Starting in the middle, pull the fabric taut and add
    some temporary staples. Pull to the top corners
    and add temporary staples to secure the fabric.
    Check the pattern is straight before adding any
    permanent staples. We are adding a border,
    which will separately cover the edge of the frame,
    so the staples can be placed in the side of the
    frame at this stage, not on the back. This also
    gives the fabric more flexibility to be manipulated
    around your shape. It's necessary to do it this way
    for most shaped headboards, but if you would
    prefer a plainer look you can opt out of adding the
    piping and use the same fabric for the border.
    If you are adding a border but no piping you will
    cover the headboard in the same way. If you are
    not adding a border you can staple the fabric
    on the back of the board at this stage.

4   Starting from the middle of the top, place a few
    permanent staples into the centre and work your
    way along one side towards the corner. Remove
    the temporary staples as you work along. See
    Pulling, smoothing & stapling fabric, page 127.

WORKING AROUND CURVES

CONCAVE CURVES

In order to manipulate the fabric into concave
sections, cut into your fabric at the back, as close to
the staple line as possible without going over it (the
fabric can rip, so you keep a little distance in case of
this). The closer together the cuts are, the more the
fabric will be flexible, so loose curves do not need
many cuts. Tight curves on the other hand will need
a lot of cuts very close together. Ensure your cuts are
not too long as you don't want them to be visible on
the front of your headboard. Start with smaller wider
cuts and add to them as you need to.

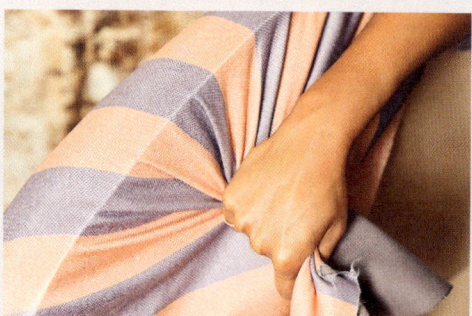

CONVEX CURVES

If your shape is convex (shapes such as semicircles),
you will find the opposite to be true: rather than tight
fabric you will have a lot of excess. To avoid creasing
in the front, you can take a fistful of fabric and as
you pull it tight, twist it slightly. You will see creases
appear on the back or side edge, which is fine. Check
there are no creases on the front and when you're
happy that it's smooth, staple it into place.

3

3

4

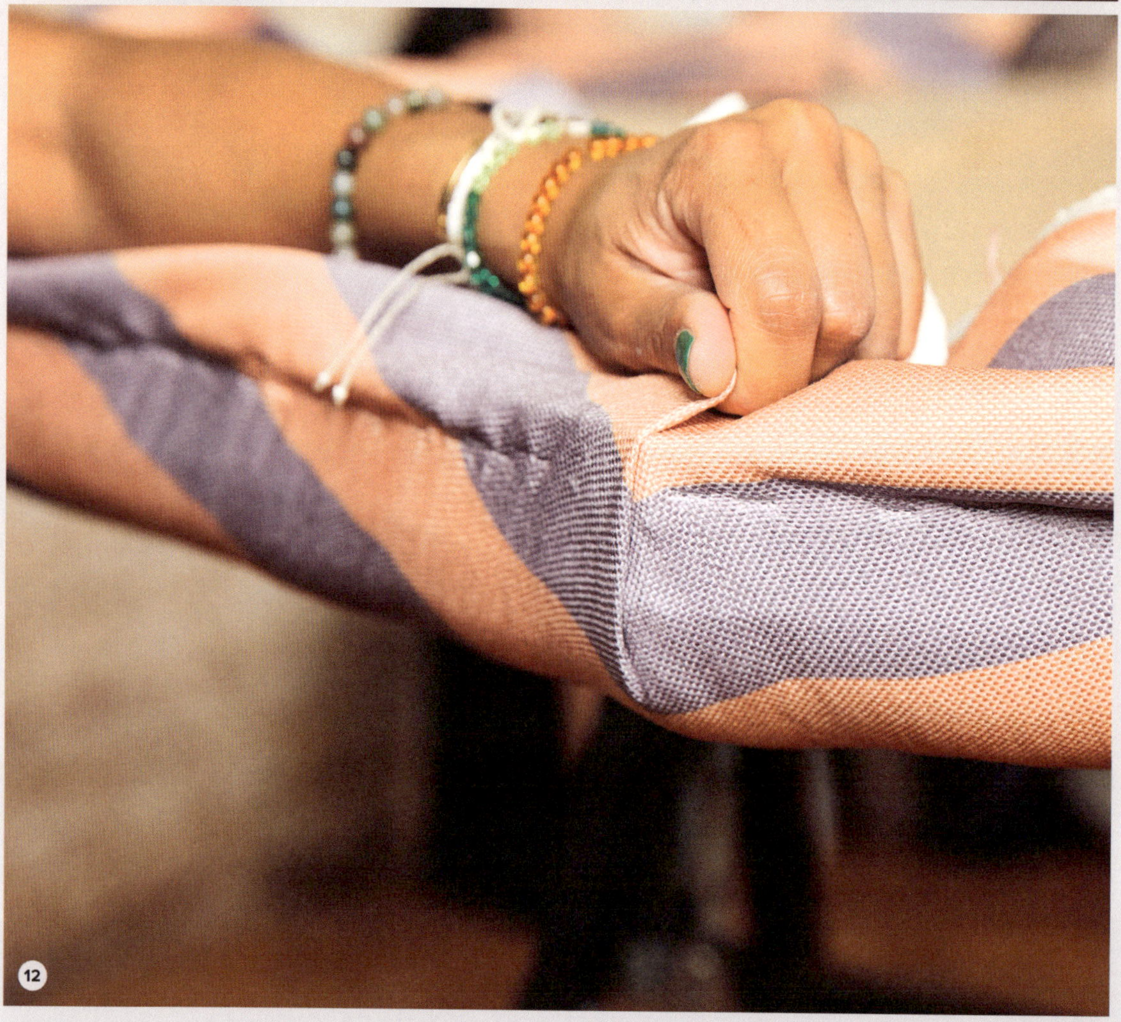

Upholstering the frame

Continued

5 As you are working, ensure the tension in the fabric is the same all the way along by smoothing the fabric over the front of the foam and pulling it taut.

6 When you get to the corner, leave the length of about three staples free. Then start back at the middle towards the other corner.

7 With your top edge done, check you are happy with the finish at the front. Lightly pull your fabric at the sides to ensure you can pull out any remaining creases. If you need to make any adjustments do so now.

8 Now replace the temporary staples along the bottom edge with permanent staples. Do this in small sections so that you don't lose the tension on the fabric.

9 Begin working on the sides. Put a temporary staple in the middle of one side to stop you from pulling the pattern off-centre. The tension from the top and bottom is tight enough that the sides shouldn't need to be pulled too hard.

10 Start to secure the opposite side with permanent staples, working from the middle to the corners.

11 Repeat on the last remaining side, removing any temporary staples.

12 Close the corners (see Finishing corners, page 166).

TROUBLESHOOTING

- **Wrinkly fabric** – the fabric needs to be pulled tighter. You may need to pull diagonally to reduce the crease and cut some relief cuts into the back to allow it to lie flat. Try also pulling the sides slightly tighter to pull out any creases.

- **Spray glue on fabric or other items** – glue can be wiped off fabric with a little white spirit on a cloth.

Adding trim and decorative elements

1   Cut and sew the piping or trim. I'm using a frill that I've sewn (see Sewing on piping or trim, page 204, or Sewing a frill, page 202). It's not necessary to add trim to the bottom edge as this won't be visible when the headboard is behind the mattress and pillows. Only calculate the sides and the top edge (plus 15 cm [6 in] extra).

2   First, close the end of the frill by folding it inside itself to hide the raw edge.

3   Attach the frill using staples to the side edge of the headboard frame. Make sure it's level all the way around, ensuring the sewn line is never over the edge of the frame (otherwise it will be visible on the finished item). Make any cuts necessary so that the trim lies flat.

4   The border will be back tacked over the trim so don't worry about stapling too close together at this stage. It's just about getting the trim straight and roughly secured.

5   Cut out your border fabric. Be mindful to pattern match along straight edges, if using a matching patterned fabric for your border. You cannot pattern match on curved edges. Cut the borders double the depth of the thickness you are covering. If the area is 8 cm (3¼ in), cut 16 cm (6¼ in). Decide if you want to sew the border pieces together (best if you have long, sloped edges) or join with overlaps in separate pieces (best if your shape is very curvy or has sharp-angled corners). If sewing together, do this now.

6   Back tack the borders on all sides of your frame (see Adding back tacking card, page 178).

7   Attach a thin strip of polyester wadding to the border using spray adhesive and cut it down level with the edge of the frame.

8   Pull and smooth the fabric border over the edge of the frame and staple it securely on the back. Ensure the polyester wadding is lying flat behind.

9   Where joining the border pieces (if not sewing together in step 5), overlap one piece and staple into place. Then fold back the piece that will lie on top for a crisp seam. This join can be slip stitched closed.

10 Finish the corners (see page 166).

11 The headboard is nearly done. To finish it off, use the fabric from your template to cover the back (see Adding bottom cloth, page 188).

12 Well done! You have made a bespoke headboard. A complete one of a kind!

DEEP-BUTTONED FOOTSTOOL

Deep buttoning (or tufting in America) is perhaps one of the most iconic upholstery designs. The classic diamond shape is most notably recognised in Britain on Chesterfield sofas and armchairs.

For a plain footstool you can apply the same skills as upholstering a headboard, because essentially they are both flat objects. So, to build on your skills we're moving on to deep buttoning here. It's also easier to deep button a footstool for the same reason: it's rectangular and flat, rather than starting to learn on, say a Chesterfield sofa with a curved back and springs underneath. But once you have mastered deep buttoning a footstool, you will be ready to move on to buttoning all sorts of more complicated items.

I'm using floral fabric from my Studio Janettie range with buttons in a contrasting yellow velvet from Linwood, (omega maize).

MATERIALS NEEDED

- 5 cm (2 in) foam with 1 cm (⅜ in) overhang on each side of the footstool
- Back tacking card
- Polyester wadding
- Spray adhesive
- Thread
- Buttoning twine
- Button moulds or pre-made buttons (I'm using 28L [18mm])
- Fire retardant (FR) lining (if needed)
- Main fabric
- Marker pen
- Ruler
- Fabric

TOOLS NEEDED

- Tailor's chalk
- Long ruler
- Mallet
- Tack remover
- Pincers
- Sharp fabric scissors
- Staple gun and staples
- Drill and foam hole cutter bit, slightly larger than the size of the button used (I'm using 20 mm)
- Buttoning needle
- Button-making machine (if making custom buttons)
- Measuring tape
- Staple gun and staples

SKILLS NEEDED

- Stripping back your item (page 120)
- Adding a fire-retardant (FR) lining (page 160)
- Adding bottom cloth (page 188)
- Webbing (page 128)
- Adding hessian (page 150)
- Measuring and cutting foam (page 152)
- Making a button (page 194)
- Adding buttons (page 196)
- Finishing corners (page 166)

Always be bold with your fabric choices! A patterned fabric will sit well alongside plain sofas, but will also add interest to the room as a whole. You could also make scatter cushions in the same fabric to help tie it all together. Don't be afraid to layer different patterns together. See page 249 for supplier information on each swatch pictured.

This is the original upholstery for the footstool featuring floating buttons.

Before you start

A large footstool or ottoman is a great way to add colour and pattern to a living room. I love styling them with a tray, beautiful books (ahem, this one!) and candles. Think about the type of fabric you want to use, as some of the pattern will be lost in the folds of the buttoning.

For added design drama, why not consider upholstering the wooden legs of your footstool. To do this, lightly glue the fabric into place and sew it closed (inside the leg where it's least visible) with a slip stitch. This is easiest for straighter legs and can be done before you cover the sides so that the fabric tucks neatly under the cover.

Preparation

1   Strip back your item carefully (see Stripping back your item, page 120), removing the foam and replacing any necessary webbing and hessian (see Webbing a seat, page 130, and Adding hessian, page 150).

2   Glue the foam to the base by spraying adhesive to the foam and the base. Trim so there is a 1 cm (⅜ in) overhang on all sides. I have layered foam together to get the desired 5 cm (2 in) thickness.

3   Prepare the new foam. With a pen and ruler, mark out the diamonds. The usual proportions are 12.5 cm (5 in) wide and 18 cm (7 in) tall. You can tweak this slightly if your item is small. Think about the positioning of the holes as each hole will have a button inside and it's best not to have them too close to the edge. If needed, leave some holes off so as to avoid having them within 4 cm (1½ in) of the edge.

4   Attach the foam cutter bit to your drill and drill through the foam where marked. The holes need to be big enough for the buttons to fit inside with 0.5 cm (¼ in) excess. Don't make the holes too big compared to the buttons. I'm using a 20 mm hole for a 18 mm button.

5   If your footstool was not deep buttoned before, you will need to drill holes in the board underneath if it has a solid base, so that the buttoning threads can pass through. They should be directly underneath the drilled foam holes. Use the foam as a guide if needed.

6   Add an FR lining if needed (see Adding a fire-retardant (FR) lining, page 160) and cut the buttoning holes out with scissors.

7   Add the polyester wadding by spraying the foam with glue and pulling the polyester tight over the FR liner and foam. Then poke the holes out with your finger.

8   Make all the buttons (see Making a button, page 194) and cut out the scrap fabric (if securing buttons through webbing).

Planning the diamond spacing

Spacing is 12.5 cm (5 in) wide and 18 cm (7 in) tall with 4 cm (1 ½ in) gap around the edge.

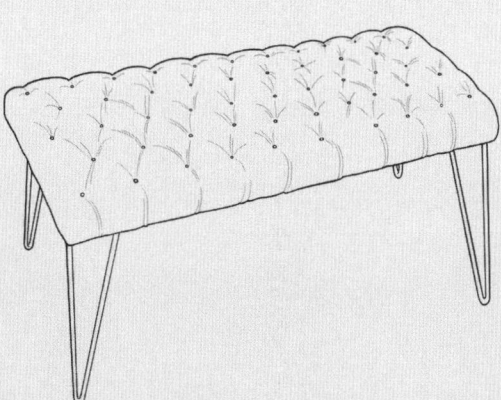

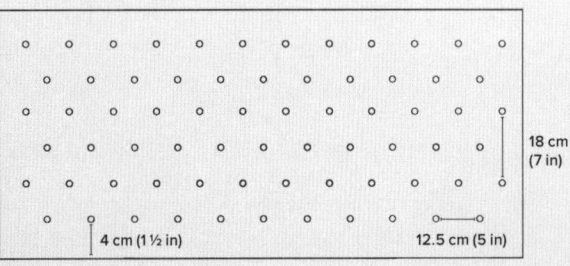

18 cm (7 in)

4 cm (1 ½ in)   12.5 cm (5 in)

Upholstering
the frame

1   Cut out the main fabric. To calculate this, use a
    measuring tape to measure between the buttons
    holding the ends inside the holes, to see how
    much extra fabric will be used pulling the fabric
    into the design (this will depend on the thickness
    of foam used), plus a fold for the diamond. The
    diamonds may be 12.5 cm (5 in) × 18 cm (7 in) but
    the fabric used may be 18 cm (7 in) × 23 cm (9 in)
    per diamond. Add this extra allowance to your
    fabric quantity, allowing some extra to cover
    all four sides, and pull underneath the frame
    to secure (this measurement will depend on
    the depth of your footstool). Doubling the total
    dimension of your item should give you enough
    fabric with some left overhanging on all sides.

2   Cut the buttoning twine. Each button will need
    one piece of twine that is at least quadruple the
    depth of the board.

3   Lay the fabric over the footstool. Begin working
    at the top left corner. Thread a button onto some
    buttoning twine and pull to the middle so both
    ends of the twine are even. Then thread both
    ends of the twine through the buttoning needle
    eye. Pull the buttoning needle through the first
    hole halfway and ensure you have a safe grip
    on the needle as it can take some force to pull
    it through (see Adding buttons, page 196).

4   Pull the needle all the way through the frame
    and remove it on the other side, leaving the
    button in place. Pull both ends of the twine to
    ensure the button lies flat on the frame. You may
    need to push the button down at the front as well.

5   Staple off the twine at the back in a 'z'
    configuration to stop the threads coming loose.

TIP

If you have a webbed back you will need to tie a
slipknot (see page 197) with the threads and insert
a scrap piece of fabric to stop the knot pulling back
through the foam. Roll the scrap fabric up and place
it inside the slipknot loop before you pull it tight.
A piece about 5 x 5 cm (2 x 2 in) will be enough.

Upholstering the frame

Continued

6   Smooth the fabric into a diamond shape, making a pleat at each straight edge. Use the holes beneath as your guide. Check you're happy with the tension of the fabric and sure the fabric is still lying straight.

7   Take the needle and thread a button through the next hole underneath the first button.

8   Pull the button tight and secure as before.

9   Now find the hole to the right side to start making a half diamond shape. Smooth the fabric until there are no creases in the centre of the half diamond. You may need to adjust the pleats in the fabric to get a clear and even diamond design. Ensure all the folds face downwards so the pleats do not collect dust and they all fold in the same direction so that it looks neat.

10 Then pull a button through the hole and secure it in place with staples or a roll of offcut fabric and a slipknot.

11 Keep moving along the board making all the diamonds one by one and adjusting the pleats as needed. Keep an eye on the overhanging fabric – this should stay straight and evenly spaced as you move along, otherwise it's an indication that you are going off course.

TROUBLESHOOTING

- The pleats are not lying flat – use a regulator needle to manipulate the fabric into the right configuration. If the buttons are in the correct position, the diamond shape should be fine. You may need to pull the buttons tighter – they should be pulled as tight as possible.

- The fabric doesn't cover the entire piece – you can add more fabric using the Van Dyke method by joining it without sewing. Overlap the new fabric with the old along the pleats and use the buttons to secure both layers. You will need to cleverly cut the fabric in your diamond design to ensure the join is not visible and the overlap only occurs along the diamond pleats. Tuck the new layer behind the existing fabric.

- Where to add a button – If you prefer, you can mark the back of the fabric with chalk to indicate where each button should go by calculating one diamond, i.e. when the fabric is pulled into the design fully the distance between buttons on the fabric is 18 cm (7 in) wide × 23 cm (9 in) high. So you draw lines along and across, which cross at these measurements to indicate where to put the buttons.

Finishing off

1   Once the buttons are all in, it's time to finish the edges. Working along one side, pleat the fabric at each button and take the pleat straight out to the edge, making sure to fold in the same direction all the way along.

2   Then staple the fabric to the back of the frame (or the edge of the frame, depending on the design of your footstool and how it was originally made). Adjust the pleats to be parallel to each other and neat. Repeat on all sides.

3   Finish the corners (see Finishing corners, page 166).

4   Depending on the style of your piece you may be adding a piped border (see Attaching piping or trim with staples, page 206). Then back tack the border (see Adding back tacking card, page 178). If you'd like studs see Adding studs, page 208.

5   With the sides totally finished you can add your bottom cloth (see Adding bottom cloth, page 188).

Mastering deep buttoning is an impressive skill. Well done!

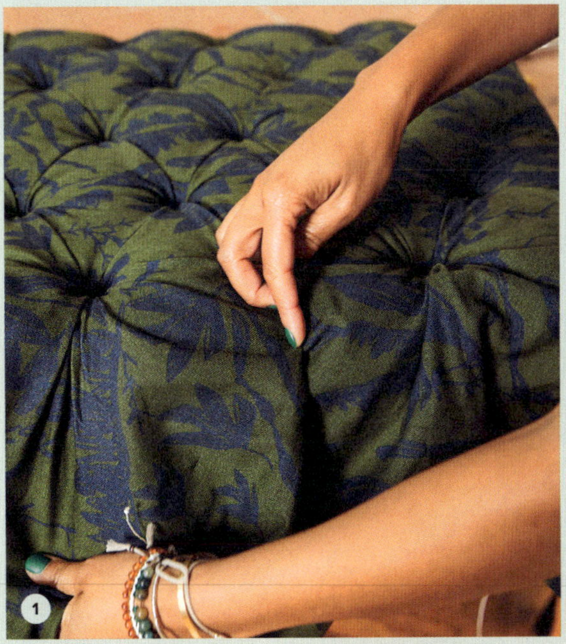
1

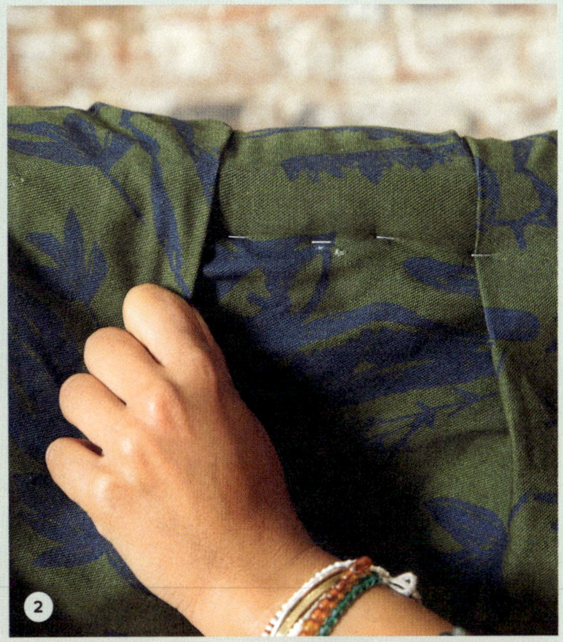
2

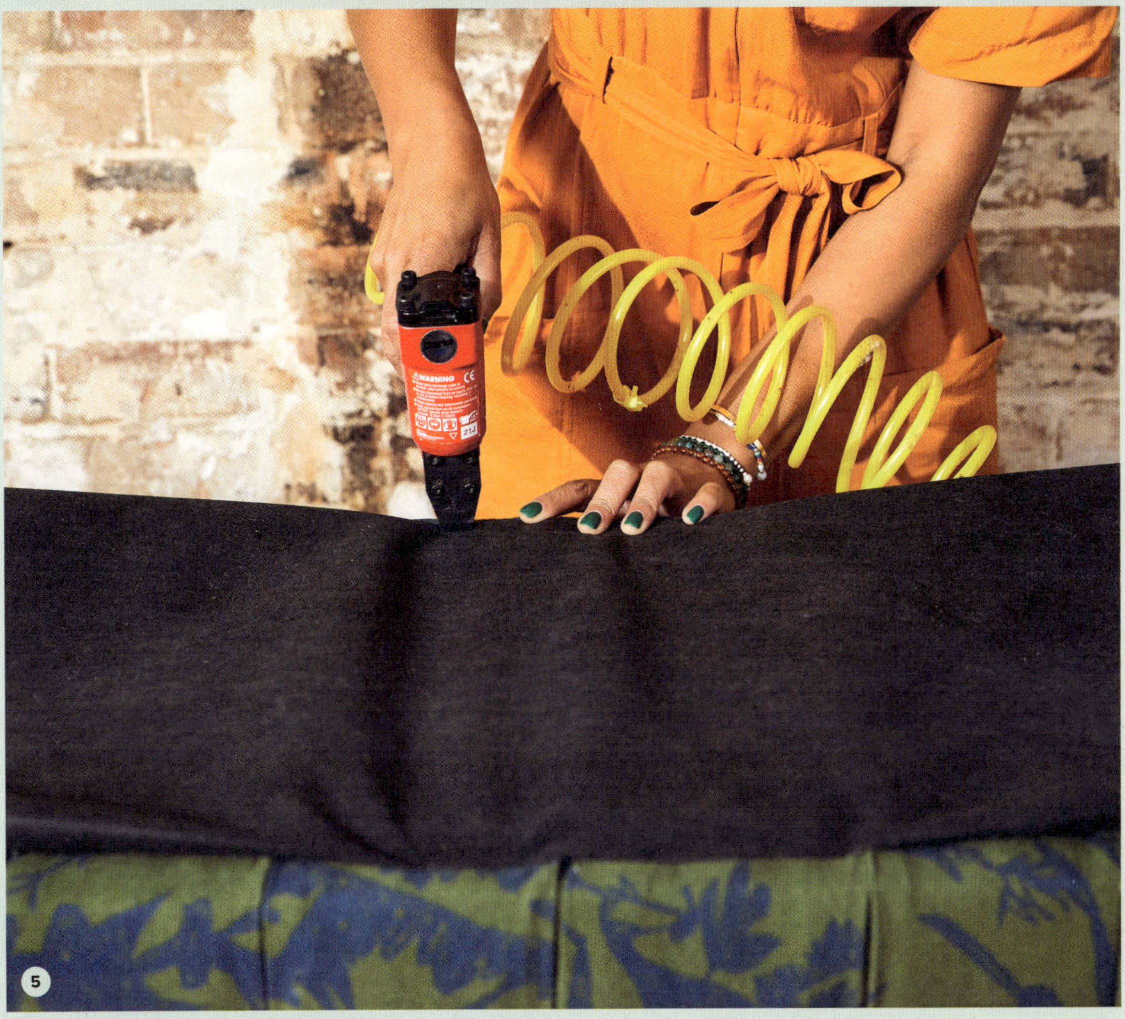
5

WINDOW SEAT BOX CUSHION

Fabric by Interior Curve -
Rodeo Drive on lovely
linen in colour Green on
Jade. The piping is linen
by Linwood, Juno Ocean.

A well-made bespoke box cushion can really elevate a window bench and it's one of the commissions I get the most enquiries for.

This method is, I think, the most versatile, so whether you're sewing a perfect square or an asymmetrical shape, the method will be the same. I've chosen this because often bay windows, for example, can be quite irregular shapes, so between slightly wonky walls and joinery that's not quite perfect you'll invariably find yourself needing to create a bespoke template.

This method of sewing a box cushion can be applied to so many upholstery projects, whether it's new covers on garden furniture or even new sofa seat cushions. Mastering the art of sewing an unusually shaped box cushion will also mean you can tackle the seats for wingback armchairs, which are often more T-shaped.

This method allows you to easily square up the border fabrics to ensure the seams are exactly where they should be on the corners.

A T-shaped box cushion – often seen on wingback armchairs.

MATERIALS NEEDED

- Foam (in the desired thickness)
- Piping cord
- Polyester wadding
- Spray adhesive
- Zip and zip pull
- Stockinette
- Bottom cloth to make
  a template (if needed)
- Fire-retardant (FR) lining
  (if needed)
- Fabric

TOOLS NEEDED

- Tailor's chalk
- Long ruler
- Sharp fabric scissors
- Sewing machine and thread
- Piping foot (if adding piping)

SKILLS NEEDED

- Stripping back (page 120)
- Measuring & cutting foam
  (page 152)
- Adding a fire-retardant (FR)
  lining (page 160)
- Adding polyester & stockinette
  to a foam cushion (page 158)
- Sewing on piping or trim
  (page 204)
- Sewing a zip (page 190)
- Seam allowance (page 122)
- Pattern matching (page 162)
- Adding bottom cloth (page 188)

Window seat box cushion

Before you start

If the area you're creating your cushion for isn't totally symmetrical, you will find that the resulting cushion you make won't be reversible (in that you won't be to turn the cushion over). Knowing this can save you money as you can use a plain, cheaper fabric for the underneath of the box cushion, rather than the more expensive main fabric. If doing this, I usually add a lip of fabric to the front bottom edge to avoid the cheaper fabric being visible.

In core techniques, I take you through cutting out a foam inner to use as your cushion (see page 152) – if you prefer a different filler such as feather or down (or a mix of foam with a feather topper) you will need to have this specially made. Make the template as outlined below, neatly label it with 'front', 'top', etc, as well as what type of inner you would like and send this to your supplier. Be sure to write down whether or not the seam allowance has been added and if you want the cushion made exactly that size or sightly bigger to fill the cover.

There are lots of different foam thicknesses to choose from. I usually say at least 7.5 cm (3 in) for a window seat cushion, as anything thinner can look a bit meagre. Pink foam is softer than blue so also consider how firm you would like the support (see Foam, page 50). My finished cushion is filled with a custom foam inner, wrapped in feathers.

Remember to consider the design before you start. Here I added piping but you may opt for an alternative seam with additional sewing (see French seam/top stitching, page 230) or perhaps you want to add an alternative trim such as frills, fringe or ribbon to the seam or border. You may opt to finish the cushion using a French mattress edge which is a slightly different technique (see French mattress edge, page 232).

Making a template

As you're making a new cushion you won't have an old cover to use as a template, so you'll need to make one. If, on the other hand, you have an old cover, carefully unpick it and skip ahead to cutting the fabric.

1   Take a piece of bottom cloth large enough to cover the whole area of where the cushion will go and lay it flat, making sure it hangs over every side by a few centimetres. Using tailor's chalk mark the edge of the frame. Label the front edge on the template.

2   Before you cut out the template, add the seam allowance to every side, otherwise your cushion will be too small for the area. Use a ruler to mark out straight lines. Cut this new larger shape with sharp scissors. The zip panels will be cut in two, a piece of fabric either side of the zip itself (see page 190). For these pieces cut half the border panel height with added seam allowance on all sides.

3   Calculate the fabric needed and make templates for the borders and zip panels including the seam allowance on each side. For the border you will need three separate pieces: front and two sides. Use the same width as the top/bottom template at the front edge and the sides. For the height, add your seam allowance to the thickness of the foam plus add the seam allowance either side (so you're adding the seam allowance on all sides). See Making a new template (page 118) .

4   Transfer this template to your fabric and cut out both the top and bottom pieces of your box cushion. Think about whether your fabric is going to run sideways or be joined with seams if the cushion is longer than the width of your fabric. Think also about the fabric positioning; perhaps you want a specific part of the pattern centred? See Pattern matching (page 162) if you need to sew pieces together.

Cutting the fabric

5   Cut out the border pieces of your box cushion. Consider if you are pattern matching here, especially for the front border. Mark the 'top' of each. If your cushion is very large and you need to sew the border pieces together along the short sides, do that now.

6   Cut out your zip borders and sew the zip with a standard presser foot on the sewing machine (see Sewing a zip, page 190).

7   Calculate how many meters of piping is needed and cut and sew the piping (see Making single piping, page 198).

Making the foam inner

8. Transfer the template onto your foam and cut this out (see Measuring & cutting foam, page 152). You can include the seam allowance in the foam dimensions (using the template exactly) as you want the foam to be slightly bigger than the cover. This is so that the cover stays full and without creases. If later your cushion won't lie flat, you may need to trim the foam slightly. Conversely, if the foam is too small and the cover is baggy you can always glue the foam together with additional pieces to make it bigger.

9. Wrap the foam in a fire-retardant lining, if needed (see Adding a fire-retardant (FR) lining, page 160). Add polyester wadding and stockinette if you choose (stockinette is optional). See Adding polyester & stockinette to a foam cushion, page 158.

TROUBLESHOOTING

- The foam inner is too big for the cover – you may need to trim the foam slightly, or remove some polyester wadding.

- The foam inner is too small – you can glue on more foam. Check the cover against the frame before altering the foam as another option is to adjust the cover on the sewing machine.

- The cover is twisted – this could mean a few things. The foam might be slightly too large inside and not lying flat. Have a play around to manipulate the foam inside the cover or trim it down slightly. Otherwise it may mean the sewing isn't quite right, in which case you may need to unpick it and resew.

- Sewing a leather or vinyl cover – you will need to add air vents to the back of the cushions to allow air to escape when the cushions are sat on to avoid burst seams. You can purchase these online.

Sewing your cover

1   Sew the piping to the top section of the cover. You will need the piping foot for this. Start at the back towards the corner so that the piping join will be less visible. Don't start exactly at the corner as it's difficult to join the piping here. Keep the piping straight, pulled tight and crease-free. See Sewing on piping or trim, page 198.

> If your piping has the same seam allowance as your cushion pieces, you can lay the edges of the top piece, piping and border together and sew them together at the same time. Repeat for the bottom piece.

2   When you reach a corner, keep the needle down and reposition the fabric. Cut some snips into the piping edge so that the piping will continue to lie flat.

3   Sew along each side until you reach the start. Then close the piping cord.

4   Sew the piping in the same way to the bottom piece of your cover.

5   Now it's time to assemble the box cushion and sew it all together, starting with the front border. Pin or hold the front border to the top piece, making sure the edge marked 'top' is oriented the right way and you pattern match.

6   Sew the front border on, leaving about 2 cm (¾ in) free at the start and the end to sew the corners closed later. If you need to sew around corners or angles, do so by keeping the needle down and manoeuvring the border fabric to align with the piped edge. Keep the fabric edges lined up.

7   Join the side borders in the same way, making sure each one is the right way up and pattern matched.

8   For large box cushions it's best to take the zip border around the corners so that the cushion has more space to go inside.

9   Join the zip border in the same way as the other borders by sewing the top edge. Make sure the zip is left open so that you can turn the cushion the right way around once it's sewn closed.

10 Once the borders are attached all the way around the top section of the cushion, you can join them to the bottom in the same way.

11 Sew all the vertical seams of the borders, and the corners, making sure to pin and sew where they will meet on the corner of the top and bottom pieces.

12 Press the vertical seam of the border open with your fingers. Then sew the 2 cm (¾ in) opening you left at each corner closed (between the top and bottom fabric and border fabric). Do this for both the top corners and the bottom corners. This method ensures you have a seam lined up with each corner perfectly.

Finishing off

1   Turn the cushion the right way out.

2   Add your foam cushion inner. Make sure each of the corners are full and the foam is lying flat.

3   Ta-da! You're ready for a cuppa on your new comfy box cushion!

MID-CENTURY ARMCHAIR

Inevitably the item you will want to start with is an armchair. I've been asked by so many people over the years if they can tackle this as a complete novice and the answer is 'Yes', you can if you really insist on starting here. However, I would recommend doing a headboard first as you will master valuable skills on a flatter project and gain confidence. Then you'll have a better understanding of how to approach a chair with more angles, sides and techniques.

The great thing about mid-century design is the furniture is usually made of materials we consider more modern – foam for example. If you start on older, more antique pieces they will often use traditional techniques and, whilst you can replace traditional methods and materials with modern ones, I would not recommend it for pieces with provenance. Also, if you are changing the materials in this way it's hard to know what to replace them with as you won't be able to follow what was there before. Stripping back hair and fibre to replace with foam can be confusing if you're new to upholstery. Mid-century shapes are also very often made up of slightly straighter lines and have far less ornate show wood (see page 180) so they're perfect as a starting chair project.

Mid-century furniture is also great for beginners because you can create some stunning transformations. Brown was hugely popular in the 1960s and, as it has fallen out of favour (although I must say I prefer warmer brown tones to cooler grey ones), it means that changing the fabric on these items gives them an instant style update. From brown to brilliant! This style of furniture was frequently upholstered in wool and so you will find many of the original covers in patterned or plain wools. But as you already know from the sourcing fabric section, you can replace the old upholstery with any fabric texture you wish, so be bold and choose something eye-catching.

This armchair is a Parker Knoll 970. I added rails to the arms in order to show the usual method of webbing an arm and covering it.

Fabric is Romo checkerboard in kingfisher; piping is an offcut.

MATERIALS NEEDED

- Foam in desired thickness to replace inside back and arms
- Foam in desired thickness for cushion
- Back tacking card
- 4oz Polyester wadding
- Spray adhesive
- Stockinette
- Ply grip
- Fire-retardant (FR) lining (if needed)
- Dipryl
- Fabric
- Piping cord or trim (if using)
- Zip (for box cushion)

TOOLS NEEDED

- Tailor's chalk
- Long ruler
- Mallet
- Tack remover
- Pincers
- Sharp fabric scissors
- Staple gun and staples
- Curved needle (if slip stitching)
- Sewing machine and thread
- Piping foot for sewing machine (if piping)

SKILLS NEEDED

- Stripping back your item (page 120)
- Pattern matching (page 162)
- Sewing a zip (page 190)
- Making single piping (page 198)
- Sewing on piping or trim (page 198)
- Measuring & cutting foam (page 152)
- Adding a fire-retardant (FR) lining (page 160)
- Adding polyester & stockinette to a foam cushion (page 158)
- Adding back tacking card (page 178)
- Using ply grip (page 184) or Slip stitching (page 220)
- Adding bottom cloth (page 188)

Armchair sections

A – Inside back
B – Seat platform
C – Inside arms
D – Outside arms
E – Box seat cushion
F – Outside back

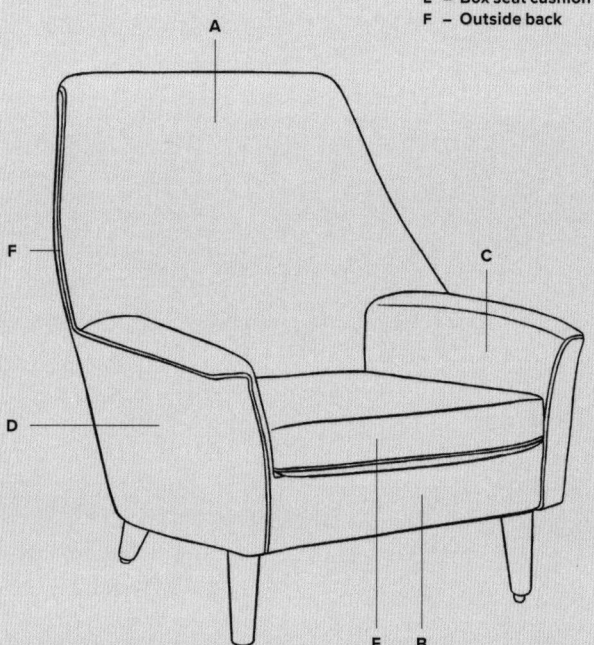

Before you start

This chair may take you a few weekends to complete and so it's really important to clearly document the chair both before you strip it back and during the process to remind yourself of the layers and where things were stapled, etc. If you're anything like me, you will convince yourself that you'll remember everything, but three weeks later you have forgotten! So take lots of pictures to refer back to and clearly label the old cover.

Your chair will be a slightly different shape to mine so start by identifying the similarities and the differences. Your chair may have wings, a fixed seat platform without a cushion, different springs, etc. Use the Core Techniques chapter where needed to adapt the method according to your specific chair.

You can also adapt the design. If your item had floating buttons in the back and you don't want to replace them you can leave them out. Decide on whether you want to add flutes, buttons or trim. Do you want a piped seam or a plain seam? Feel free to adapt the design to your own taste.

Depending on the use of your chair, you will have different requirements for the fabric. You may need it to be stain resistant or more durable. Refer to fabric practicalities on page 25 to help decide which fabric is best for you.

One thing to note with very degraded items is that it's often impossible to measure the foam inside, as it will have disintegrated. Instead, look at the cover and the sewn border depth to determine the size of foam that once filled the cover. Often, the wear on the fabric and the discolouration can indicate where the angles were and help you figure out the depth of foam needed.

Remember that when using the old cover as a template, you may need to add extra fabric for pulling. When it was upholstered onto the piece initially, it would have had excess fabric cut away along the staple line. For example, the fabric that is stapled along the bottom edge would have been trimmed away to remove excess bulk before the bottom cloth was added. Therefore, when using the old cover as a template, you will need to make an allowance and add more fabric in order to have enough to pull onto our newly foamed shape (see pieces of an armchair, opposite).

If your chair is bolted together remember to leave the holes free of all layers, including polyester wadding and fabric, so that the bolts can be rejoined.

This mid-century sofa is upholstered in a very similar way to the armchair in this project (but with varying techniques around the arms with show wood). Here you can see examples of matching floating buttons.

Preparation

1. Strip back the chair using the principles on page 120. Remember to clearly mark the old cover and take lots of reference images to refer back to.

2. Write down all of the materials used which will need to be replaced before you dispose of them (e.g. 5 cm (2 in) pink foam for the back, 1.5 cm (½ in) blue foam for the arms, etc).

3. Before you cut out the new fabric using the old cover as a template, note if you will be adding thicker foam anywhere as the template will need to allow for this.

4. Cut out the fabric and any additional pieces needed for flies (see page 30) or seat platforms, except the seat cushion. Mark it out, but do not cut the fabric at this stage. You may need to adjust the size of the cushion once all the foam and upholstery is in place on your chair.

5. Sew everything apart from the seat cushion now, including the piping and any seam or joins that need to be attached. Alternatively, you can sew each section together as you move through the project and make adjustments as you see the section on the frame.

Upholstering the seat platform

1 Always start with the seat platform. If the original seat was webbed, you should replace the webbing as the seat takes most of the weight for the chair and you want this to last as long as possible (see Webbing a seat, page 130).

2 This chair doesn't have webbing, instead it has tension springs. Assess the springs to see if any need replacing. See the spring section for how to replace and assess each different type (pages 138–149). These tension springs are intact and in good condition, but note that I have added some jute webbing to the back to secure the tension of the springs.

3 Add a layer of polyester wadding to the front edge to soften the fabric's appearance on the wooden frame. Spray the glue on to the desired area and stick the wadding in place. Trim it down as needed on the item. You can add very thin foam (0.5 or 1.5 cm [¼ or ½ in]) as well if you prefer, but because the seat here has a thick box cushion it's not necessary to add a lot of foam to the seat platform as the cushion will ensure comfort.

4 Sew the front border fabric (which usually is only visible on the front edge) to the platform lining (usually a plain cheaper fabric in thick cotton) with a straight line across to join them together, then add jute webbing if needed (see Sewing a seat platform, page 176).

5 Position the fabric on the frame ready to be stapled in place. Pull the platform lining back through the frame and onto the top of the seat platform. Ensure enough of the fabric is covering the front and the top edge of the seat platform to hide the join with the platform lining. Staple the lining in place along the back of the seat platform. Then, pulling it tight to the front, staple it in place along the underneath the front of the seat platform. Ensure the pattern is centralised ready to match the seat cushion.

Upholstering the seat platform

Continued

Preparing the inside arms

6   If needed, add extra staples on the sides of the front border to secure the front fabric to the side. The arm fabric will cover these staples.

7   Smooth the fabric to the sides and pass it underneath the arm frame. Then pull it upwards and staple it in place on the back of the arm frame. You may need to cut around some supporting struts. Always use a V-shaped cut to avoid the fabric splitting when it's sat on (see V-cuts, page 124). You will need to cut and fold the fabric around the corners to get a tight fit and crisp lines. Do this by cutting a 45-degree snip towards the corner. The end of the cut should be in line with the corner of the frame. Do not pass this point, otherwise the cut will be visible.

8   Cut away any excess fabric.

1   Assess the arms of your piece and decide what needs replacing. This frame didn't have the usual arm struts so I have added them in to teach the more common way of upholstering arms.

2   If the frame is open at the arms, use webbing to close the void and start to create a structure for your fabric to sit on top of. Using a web stretcher and jute webbing, web the arms with vertical webs (see Webbing an inside back or arm, page 133).

3   When you reach the back, ensure the webbing only leaves a small gap for the fabric to tuck into without leaving a void in the arm.

4   Add hessian.

Upholstering the inside back

1   Begin working on the inside back. If you are adding flutes (page 210) or deep buttons (page 196), refer to those techniques. If you are adding floating buttons, follow along here and add them once the inside back is upholstered (before the outside back goes on).

2   Start by webbing the inside back with jute webbing vertically (see Webbing an inside back or arm, page 133).

3   Add hessian. If your back is sprung, follow the instructions for the type of springs first, then cover them with hessian, using a pleat to allow the springs to move without ripping the hessian open.

4   Either reuse the foam that was there if it's in very good condition or attach new foam using spray adhesive. Use the same thickness of foam as you removed, unless you adjust your fabric template to account for thicker foam. Overestimate the foam for the back as you want it to really push up against the foam on the arms and the seat to avoid gaps.

5   Trim the top edge of foam to size once glued in place. You may need to smooth the foam over the top edge by stapling it in place or attaching dipryl and pulling that tight (see Securing foam on the edge, page 154). Here the sides have been secured with staples for a smooth edge.

6   Add the fire-retardant (FR) lining, if needed (page 160).

7   Then add the polyester wadding by glueing it into place and trimming away any excess.

TIP

If your chair has wings, cover these before you start the inside back. If your wings had piping on the edge that joins the arm, sew that in place first on the sewing machine. Follow the shape of your old template. Add the jute webbing and hessian to the wing as you did with the arm. Then attach the foam and polyester wadding. To cover them, staple the fabric to the frame along the side keeping the fabric straight. Smooth the fabric out towards the edge of the frame and staple into place. Pull and smooth the fabric to the top last. See Upholstering wings, page 174.

Upholstering the inside back

Continued

13   As you work your way along the top edge, pull and smooth the fabric tightly into place. If needed, adjust the bottom of the fabric to ensure it's tight and lies flat and crease-free. Ensure the tension of the fabric is even as this too can create creases. Some creases might be best pulled out across the sides. Only staple the sides in place when you are happy with the top and the bottom. But you can stretch the fabric from side to side to check if the creases will be pulled out with this motion.

14   Smooth and pull the fabric to either side and staple it into place.

15   Finish by securing the top corners. Depending on the shape of your item you may need pleats or, if the corners are more rounded, you can smooth the fabric out without pleats (see Finishing corners, page 166).

8   Begin to attach the fabric. Starting in the middle of the inside back, use temporary staples to staple the bottom of the fabric into place along the back rail, found through the gap of the inside back, and the seat at the back of the frame. Usually the fabric is stapled up onto the back rail but if the gap is too wide on the frame (and the gap is visible from the front of the chair), you may need to staple the fabric down onto the seat rail. This will close the gap.

9   If the inside back on your chair is curved, pay particular attention to the fabric to avoid creases and wrinkles. You may need to cut relief cuts into your fabric (at the bottom edge and the top edge) to allow it to lie flat and crease-free (see Cutting & relief cuts, page 124).

10   Staple all the way along in both directions towards the corners. You may need to make some v-cuts around the rails and frame. My fabric has a fly sewn on (see page 30).

11   Then pull and stretch the fabric to the top of the inside back. You want the fabric to lie tightly against the polyester wadding and foam so that it doesn't look baggy over time.

12   Starting in the middle of the top, staple the fabric into place. Ensure the pile and/or pattern are straight. You should be stapling onto the back edge of the top rail. Note where the holes are from the old staples and staple there. Avoid stapling too close to the top edge as you want to cover these staples later with piping and/or the outside back. You may need to make small relief cuts in the fabric to ensure it lies flat.

Upholstering the inside arms

7   Ensure the pattern matches with the inside back.

8   When you are happy with the position of the fabric, and that the pattern is straight and the pile is running down, pull the fabric under the rail for the armrest, through the gap between the seat platform and the arm. Do this all the way along. Using temporary staples, start stapling the fabric to the outside of the arm at the back of the arm frame. Refer to the pictures taken when stripping the chair if needed, to ensure you are upholstering to the right area; sometimes the holes in the frame from the previous staples will guide you. Once the fabric is through this gap it is not seen so if you have a fly sewn on, ensure the seam is beyond this point.

9   Smooth the fabric upwards and pull it tight towards the top of the arm. Staple along from the front to the back of the armrest (on the back of the arm frame), ensuring there are no wrinkles. Do this all the way along. Adjust any staples that do not hold the fabric tight and crease free. If you have any sewn seams, ensure they are aligned to where they need to be on the frame. Leave the side edges open so that you can make your cuts to release the fabric around the frame later on.

10   Make the necessary cuts to manoeuvre the fabric around the frame. Be very careful with these cuts to ensure you don't have visible holes on your finished items. Always cut less than is needed at first and check it. You can easily extend a cut line but you can not close it back-up if you cut too much.

1   Either reuse the foam that was there if it's in very good condition or attach new foam using spray adhesive. Overestimate the foam and trim it down on the piece to ensure the shaping is spot on. Cover the frame in the same way it was covered previously using the same thickness foam (unless you are adjusting your fabric template to account for thicker foam).

2   Add the fire-retardant (FR) lining, if needed. The FR layer is a great place to practice your v-cuts. Then add polyester wadding by glueing it in place and trimming away any excess.

3   Tuck the foam, FR lining and polyester wadding underneath where the inside back joins the arm.

4   Begin to add the fabric. If the arms on your armchair have a different shape to mine with pleats, fascias or panels sewn to the cover, you'll need to adjust the method using the techniques section.

5   If your arm is sewn together (with or without piping) and capped on, see page 182. Ensure the seams are lying flat when you place the fabric onto the frame. Staple it first at the front of the arm to ensure the seams are all in the right place. Then pull towards the back of the frame and staple it into place.

6   Start by laying the fabric over the arm. Ensure it covers all the necessary areas. You need enough to wrap around the support under the arm and fix inside the frame. You also need enough at the front and top to cover the section of the frame needed, and the back to reach the frame.

Upholstering the inside arms

Continued

11 Now move back to the bottom edge and secure the fabric with permanent staples. Remove the temporary staples a few at a time to replace them without freeing the fabric entirely. Smooth and pull the fabric to ensure the fabric is as tight as possible. You should be pulling the foam down slightly to soften the edges.

12 With the fabric pulled tight from top to bottom, you only need to smooth it softly over the side edges. Do not pull too tight here. Staple into place.

13 Find the part of the frame that connects the arm to the seat platform at the front. Cut from the bottom edge of the fabric diagonally in towards that point in the frame, always cutting a V-shape to stop the fabric ripping. This edge is the same one that is stapled to the underneath arm which was left slightly open. You may need to start the cut from the back of the arm where the staples are. You want to avoid a cut that is visible on the inside arm or on the front of the arm.

14 Take note of where the staples were before and staple along this line. Put a few staples at the top of the straightest part of the arm, and then pull the fabric to the bottom to ensure it's straight and to avoid wrinkles.

15 If you need to add pleats to the top of the arms do it now.

16 Finally, you need to pull the fabric to the back of the frame and staple it. Again, follow where it was fixed previously. You may need to make relief cuts around the rails and frame for the fabric to lie flat.

17 If the back of the arm connects to a wing or the inside back, ensure there is enough fabric to tuck underneath this section when you come to upholster it. Pull the fabric through the frame and staple it into place on the back of the frame. You may need to slip stitch the join between the wing and the arm.

18 Repeat the process on the other arm. Ensure the pleats are symmetrical if you are adding them. If your chair has arm fascias, you can cover them now but do not attach them until the arm is covered on all sides, as they will sit on top of the raw edge to hide it.

Making the box cushion

1 Now with the seat, inside arms and inside back complete we can check our loose box seat cushion. It's important to wait until the other sections are done as the foam may make the area in the middle smaller or bigger, so you want to check the old cushion in the remaining space. Assess if it's the right fit, you don't want a gap around the sides but equally it shouldn't be pushing into the sides too much either. Mark any adjustments you want to make to the chalked-out fabric.

2 Cut out and sew the box cushion. See the box cushion project on page 88. Make sure to pattern match the front border to the seat platform, and the top of the cushion to the inside back so the pattern runs continuously down the chair.

3 Make any adjustments if needed, by either reshaping the foam or the cover.

Upholstering the outside arms and outside back

1 Begin by cutting away any bulky excess fabric from the outside back, sides and top.

2 If you are piping the outside back, first staple the piping into place in one long continuous length, making any necessary cuts to ensure the piping lies flat at the corners (see Attaching piping or trim with staples, page 206).

3 To close the voids of the frame and create a base for the fabric, add plastic webbing along the outside arms and the outside back (see Webbing an outside back or arm, page 134).

4 Position the fabric for outside arms. Fold over the top edge and add a few staples to the wrong side of the fabric.

5 Flip the fabric back over and check the positioning is correct and the pattern is aligned.

6 Fold the fabric over and add the FR layer. Rather than glueing it into place, staple it to the edge of the frame to secure it.

7 Using spray adhesive, glue the polyester wadding in place.

8 Back tack the top of the fabric into place (see Adding back tacking card, page 178). If the shape slopes down to the arms you will only be able to back tack the top edge.

9 Lightly pull and smooth the fabric to the bottom edge and staple it underneath the frame and into position. Check the tension is tight enough all the way along and round all the curves of the frame.

Upholstering the outside arms and outside back

Continued

10   Pin the front edge to the piping or inside arm fabric ready to be slip stitched.

11   Staple the back of the outside arm to the frame at the back. Ensure the staples will be hidden by the fabric where it joins the outside back. Cut away any excess fabric.

12   Slip stitch the front edge in place (see Slip stitching, page 220).

13   Repeat on the other arm.

14   Begin working on the outside back. Follow steps 3–9 now for the outside back. Secure the fabric at the top to check the pattern is aligned before adding back tack card.

15   Add FR lining, if needed, and polyester wadding.

16   The sides of the outside back can either be closed with ply grip (page 184) or slip stitch (page 220) depending on your preference.

17   Cut away any excess fabric at the bottom of the frame.

18   Finally, cover the bottom with dipryl or bottom cloth, cutting it where necessary around the legs of the chair (see Adding bottom cloth, page 188).

19   There you have it! You have transformed a tired mid-century armchair into a unique masterpiece. I hope you'll proudly present this armchair in your home and take much comfort and joy from it.

Sofas are made in this same way but with wider seat platforms and inside backs. Now you have mastered these skills you can apply them to projects of all sizes and shapes.

TROUBLESHOOTING

- Section of fabric cut too short – you may be able to add a fly to one end using scrap fabric. (See sewing a fly, page 30). A fly can only be added where the fabric will not be seen on the finished item, i.e. where the fabric sits within the frame.

- Cover not sitting as it should – undo the staples on the areas that aren't lying flat and re-pull the fabric. If the corners aren't full you could add some fistfuls of polyester wadding to fill the cover out.

- Puckering or wrinkles – there can be a few different reasons for this. Usually you need to make more cuts in the fabric in order to allow it to lie flat. Start with small cuts to ensure they are not visible on the finished item. You may also need to pull and smooth the fabric in alternative directions to pull the creases out – try pulling diagonally. See Pulling, smoothing & stapling fabric, page 126.

Core techniques

MAKING A NEW TEMPLATE

If you're making a new item or can't use the old fabric as a template because it is too worn, you will have to make your own template.

You can either use dipryl if you're upholstering something flat such as a window bench (dipryl is a cheap fabric that has a paper-like quality so it's ideal for this type of use), or calico if it's a piece of curved furniture. Calico best resembles finished fabrics, such as cotton, so can be manipulated, sewn and pinned more easily than dipryl.

For a box cushion, simply lay the dipryl across the area where the cushion will sit and chalk around the edge. If there is space on the dipryl, add your seam allowance to the template before you cut it out. If there isn't space, cut the template out and then add the seam allowance when marking the template out on the fabric before cutting. If you're upholstering a piece of furniture without any fabric on (perhaps the item didn't have a cover when you bought it, or it was too damaged), you can't just make a template from the bare frame, as the pieces won't fit once the foam is added. You need to do the upholstery up to the point where you have added the foam (you do not need the polyester on).

Lay the calico for the template on the item in the same sections you would expect to find an individual piece of fabric, i.e. inside back, seat, arm, etc. When it's crease free, pin it in place. Chalk out the edge where you would expect to see a join or where the frame is. Cut along these lines. Continue to do this for each section until the whole item is covered. Clearly annotate each section before you remove the pins. Use these sections to cut out your fabric, adding a seam allowance, fly or extra fabric to pull onto the frame where needed.

Templating
a bay window

A – Chalk line
B – Seam allowance

STRIPPING BACK YOUR ITEM

Arguably the most important part of every project is the stripping-back stage. This process not only gives you the first insight into what needs to be changed and replaced on your item, but it shows you exactly how it was made.

Getting started

- Label each piece of fabric before anything is removed. Label the top (T) of each section using a permanent marker (chalk will rub off over time). Mark any seams by drawing lines to any corners or joins to annotate them. Also mark any corners or the frame where there aren't joins, i.e. if a piece wraps around the side and front of an arm without a join. It's important to mark the cover so you can see clearly where the corner of the frame sits. Label each piece: right inside arm (RIA), left inside arm (LIA), inside back (IB), outside back (OB), seats, etc. These pieces will be used as templates to cut your new fabric so you need to know what each piece is and which way around it goes.
- In the coming days or weeks you may forget what went where, so take lots of photos of where layers were stapled, which order they were in and any joins or seams.
- Remember to replace like for like. If you had 7.5 cm (3 in) foam on the back of a chair, for

example, you want to replace it with the same thickness so that your new cover fits. Keep a list of the materials removed if you intend on replacing them i.e. 5 cm (2 in) pink foam for the inside back, 6 mm (½ in) blue foam for the arms. If you amend foam depths you will need to adjust your templates accordingly. If you're unsure how thick the old flattened foam was, look to the cover for clues. The cushion border shows the thickness of the foam inside, for example.

TOOLS:
- Seam ripper or sharp blade
- Mallet
- Tack remover
- Pincers
- Permanent marker pen
- If fixing the frame: clamps, wood glue, drill and screws

1. Label each piece carefully, noting where it joins or wraps, where it sits and the top of the piece.
2. Using a tack remover and mallet, knock each staple loose from the frame to release the old fabric. You can also use the pincers to remove staples and pull gently at the fabric to release it.
3. Use a seam ripper or sharp blade to undo each seam without cutting away any fabric on the old cover, so that each piece can lie flat to be used as a template. Take your time stripping back the item to ensure each piece of fabric is kept whole (to use it as a template you need the piece in its entirety). It's important to see where there was a sewn seam as you will need to allow the same

allowance for your sewing. If the raw edge was stapled straight onto the piece, you need to know to allow extra fabric to pull your new cover into place, as usually excess fabric is cut away after the upholstery is stapled.

4   Once the item is stripped back assess your frame. You may need to glue and clamp joins to strengthen them if you have any wobbly joints or movement in the frame. If you are glueing the frame, make sure all four legs are always on the ground while it dries. Avoid clamping the chair on its side as sometimes the legs shift and when it's dry the legs won't be level. You may also decide to sand and revarnish the legs and visible wood. Do this when the frame is clear before you start to reupholster.

Labelling your piece

A – Inside back
B – Seat platform
C – Outside back (not seen)
D – Outside arm right
E – Outside arm left
F – Outside wing right
G – Outside wing left

H – Inside arm right
I – Inside arm left
J – Inside wing right
K – Inside wing left
L – Right fascia
M – Left fascia

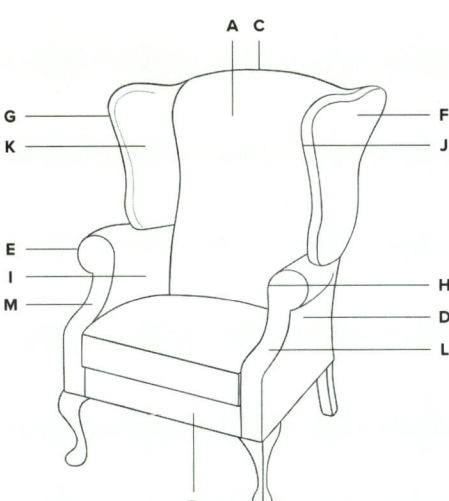

TEMPORARY STAPLES

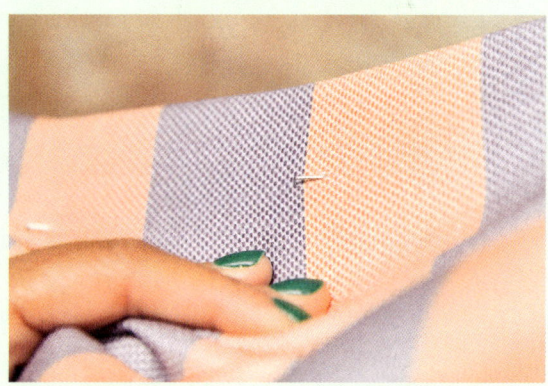

Temporary staples or temporary tacks are there to hold fabric in place while we pull and smooth. Place them at an angle and slightly raised so they can easily be removed without marking the fabric. Shorter staples are easier to remove so I opt for 8 mm (⁵⁄₁₆ in) usually, but you may need longer staples if your layers are particularly thick. I use them most often when securing a large piece of fabric to ensure the pattern is straight and the positioning is correct before my final tight pull, and to staple it securely. Temporary staples do not need to be as close together as the final staples. I usually do a temporary staple every 25 cm (9 ¾ in) or so.

SEAM ALLOWANCE

A seam allowance is the distance between the sewn line and the edge of the fabric. The most common seam allowance is 1 cm (⅜ in) but you can adjust this if you prefer.

You can mark where your seam allowance should be on your machine either using a magnetic guide or with a simple piece of tape. This will allow you to always ensure you're sewing your seam in the correct place. To mark the seam allowance on your machine, first turn it off and then measure outwards from the needle with a tape measure and mark the distance with your preferred method (magnet or tape). You may need to lift the presser foot and lower the needle.

Fabrics designed by Charlotte Beevor for our Studio Janettie range.

CUTTING & RELIEF CUTS

TOOLS:
- Scissors
- Chalk
- Upholstery regulator (optional)

Making cuts in the fabric as you are upholstering is a very nerve-racking part of the process. Getting it wrong can be costly, particularly if additional fabric is then needed to patch up any mistakes. It's also difficult to demonstrate as a singular technique because every item is different and so has different angles, rails and frames to work around.

The fabric should always be attached to the frame before you start making cuts (usually at the front and back). This is because you need a certain amount of tension in the fabric before you can see where to make the cuts.

The biggest mistake when cutting into the fabric around arms and other parts of the frame is to cut at the wrong angle. You can use a chalk line on the back of the fabric to test different angles and ensure there is enough fabric either side to cover the frame. If you're still not sure where to cut, you can use scrap fabric. Temporarily staple the fabric in place and practise the cuts to ensure there is enough fabric on either side of the cut to cover the frame.

V-cuts (or Y-cuts)

When making a cut to fabric that will hold weight or tension (such as a seat or inside back) you want to avoid the fabric ripping when used. So instead of cutting a straight line, end the cut with a small V to distribute the weight and protect the fabric from ripping.

1. Attach the fabric at the front and back of the piece.
2. Using chalk, make a line on the back of the fabric to test the angle.
3. Pull the fabric and see if the line is exactly to the corner of the rail or not.
4. When you're happy, make the cut. Always stop cutting about 3 cm (1¼ in) before the frame itself. Pull the fabric into place and check how it looks. If it's creasing then you will need to cut in closer, little by little until the fabric lies as it needs to. Doing this will help you avoid mistakes.
5. You can use a regulator to tuck the fabric around the frame, especially to tuck in the V and help with folds.
6. Cut away any excess leaving 2 cm (¾ in) to fold underneath. Get a crisp line along the frame when folding the fabric and pulling it underneath to be stapled.

Relief cuts

Relief cuts refer to making small snips in the fabric to allow it to lie flat on a wider angle. These may be made in piping to manoeuvre it around a corner, or in the main fabric to help pull it over the edge on a more convex shape. On a convex shape the fabric has further to stretch, and so small straight snips can help open the fabric up. On concave shapes you will have excess fabric so cutting out small Vs will help smooth the fabric and avoid wrinkles.

Different ways
to create cuts

A – V-cuts around a rail (for example)
B – Straight cut around a corner
block (for example)
C – Star cut around a leg (for example)

V-cut

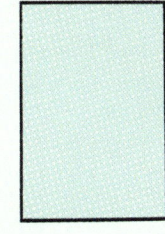
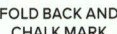
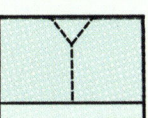

FOLD BACK AND
CHALK MARK

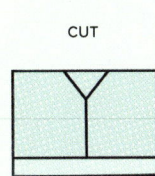
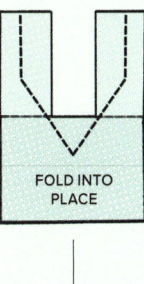

CUT

FOLD INTO
PLACE

A

Straight cut

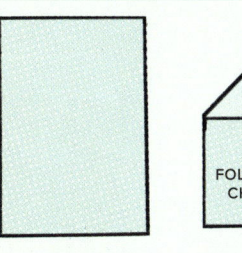

FOLD BACK AND
CHALK MARK

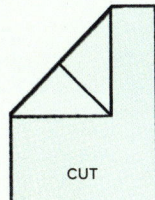
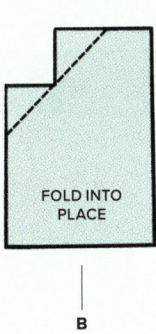

CUT

FOLD INTO
PLACE

B

Star cut

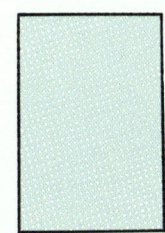
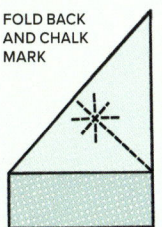

FOLD BACK
AND CHALK
MARK

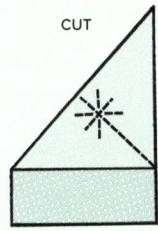
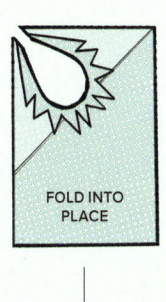

CUT

FOLD INTO
PLACE

C

PULLING, SMOOTHING & STAPLING FABRIC

How you pull the fabric whilst upholstering can have a huge effect on the finished look. Pulling the wrong way, without enough force or pinching the fabric in small sections can lead to ripples appearing. Not having enough tension on the fabric can lead to it sagging over time.

1   Grip the fabric with your dominant hand and pull it away from the side it is stapled on. With your other hand push down and smooth the fabric towards the side you will be stapling.

2   Continue to push the air out of the cover and push down on the foam underneath, smoothing the fabric in an upward motion (towards the hand doing the pulling) until there are no visible creases and the fabric is tight.

3   To achieve a professional finish, flatten the foam down at the edges of the piece so you don't leave an obvious square edge of foam visible. The only exception to this is if you have a sewn border that needs to sit on the corner edge of the foam.

4   Start by adding temporary staples every 25 cm (9¾ in) or so.

5   Begin adding permanent staples, stapling in the middle and working towards the corners, completing one whole side before moving to the other. As you work towards the corners, pull slightly diagonally in the direction you're moving in, away from those first centre staples. This diagonal motion will help eradicate creases.

6   The fabric on a curved surface (such as a curved inside back, for example) needs to be manipulated more significantly to get the fabric flat on the shape. You will need to create relief cuts before big diagonal pulls can be made. If you're upholstering a very long edge, put some temporary staples on these diagonal pulls towards the corners to help smooth the fabric and keep the pattern straight. Remove them as you add the permanent staples.

7   You may see what we call tack ties: small creases on the front where each staple is holding the fabric in place. This happens when the staples are too far apart, so smooth the fabric over and add more staples. Pulling diagonally also helps get rid of these.

8   Don't be afraid to pull out staples that aren't right. Use a tack remover, mallet and pincers to remove the staples and replace them.

9   Make adjustments as you go along or at the end of each section if you notice the fabric isn't lying perfectly. At the end of each section it is important to assess the overall look and make any necessary adjustments. It can be hard to fix the fabric later on in the upholstery process, i.e. once you've added piping or back tacking.

WEBBING

This layer is the foundation of your item. The webbing holds all the tension and weight, and is the first step towards building the shape. The hessian, springs and foam all sit on top of your webbing so it needs to be taut. It's often this layer that wears fastest and bows underneath an old chair or rips to reveal the springs.

There are different types of webbing and which type you work with depends on where it's being used on your piece:

- **Black and white (1 – strongest):** used for seats as they take the most weight.
- **Jute (2 – medium):** used for the inside back and inside arms, which take less weight but are still leant against.
- **Black plastic webbing (3 – light):** used for the outside back and outside arms to hold the shape of the cover without taking any weight and without adding any bulk.
- **Pirelli (4):** a thick rubber webbing found on mid-century pieces under box cushions.
- **Elastic (not pictured):** used for seats and backs often instead of pirelli.

You may need to clamp your item to the workbench in order to web it so that it's not moving around.

Webbing a seat

YOU WILL NEED:
- Black and white webbing
- Staple gun
- 12 mm (½ in) staples
- Web stretcher
- Clamps (optional)

1   If necessary, clamp your frame to your work bench. Using black and white webbing, measure out how many webs will fit across your frame. Leave a gap between each, which is slightly less than the width of your web. Use the old holes as a guide for where the webbing will go and how it's spaced. Do not cut the webbing yet.

2   Load your stapler with long staples to give the webbing the maximum support. I use 12 mm (½ in) staples.

3   Starting in the middle of the frame at the back, fold the webbing back on itself and staple both layers into your frame with long staples. Use at least six staples (two rows of three staples) to secure this.

4   Pull your roll of webbing to the front of the chair and over the top of your frame.

5   Thread a loop of webbing through the slot on the web stretcher and secure with the toggle. With the groove against the frame and holding the long end of webbing together with the web stretcher, pull it tight with your non-dominant hand (your staple gun will be in your dominant hand).

6   Pull your webbing as tight as you can to get rid of all slack. When it's as tight as it will go, staple it into place on the front edge through one layer. Use at least six staples across the whole width of webbing.

7   Cut your webbing, leaving a 4 cm (1½ in) end. Fold it back and staple off the excess to mirror your start.

8   Do this all the way along your frame from the back of the frame to the front. Leave a 2 cm (¾ in) gap at each corner.

9   Now begin webbing side to side. Secure the end as before, then thread the webbing up and over the webs already running front to back to create a lattice effect. Threading them like this helps secure the strongest configuration of webbing.

10 Stretch each web and secure them in the same way all the way along, leaving at least a 2 cm (¾ in) gap at each corner.

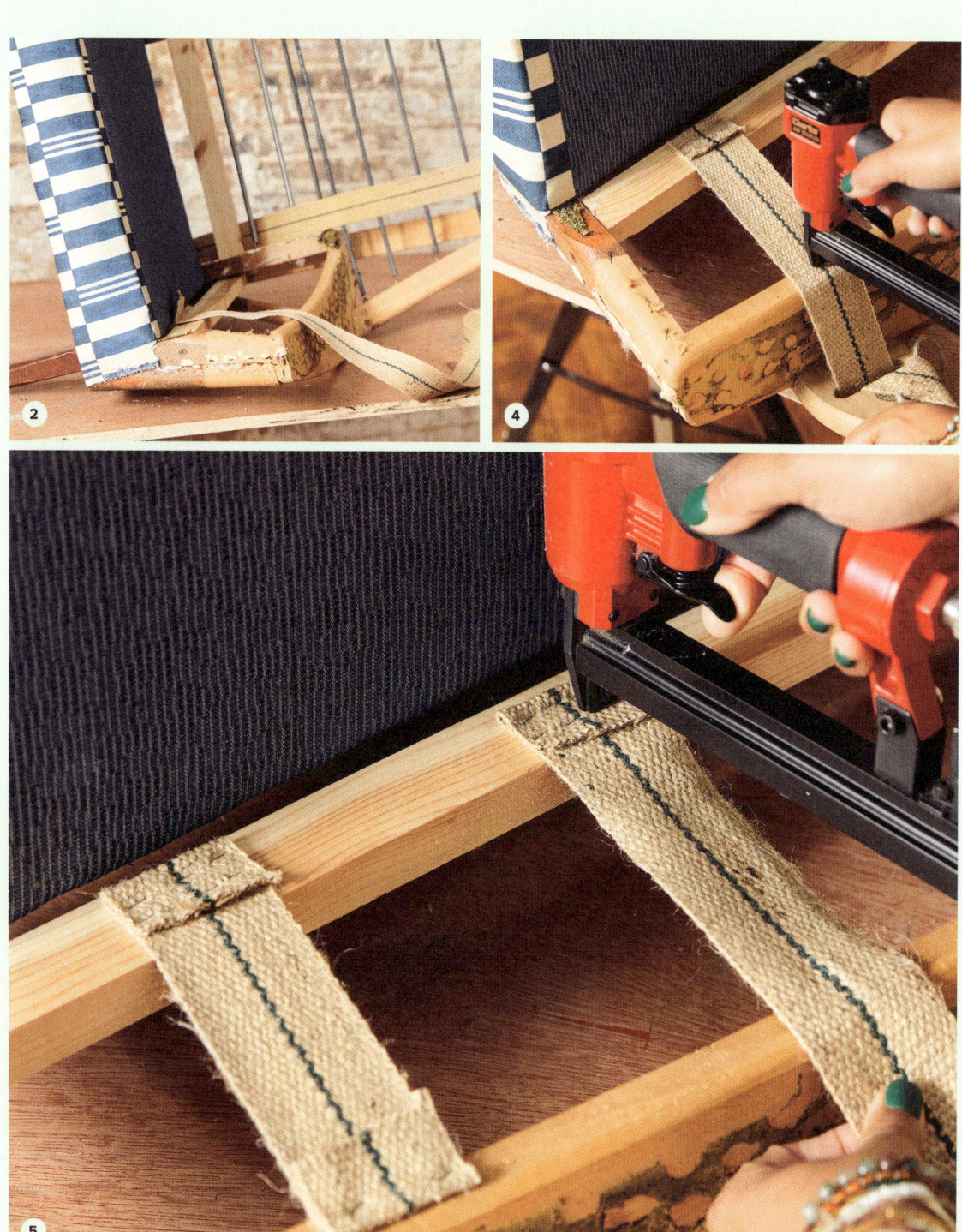

Webbing an inside back or arm

The main difference when webbing a seat to webbing the inside back using jute webbing is that the webs are only needed from top to bottom and not side to side. This is because we don't need as much tension in the arms and back. Depending on your chair, you may find it easier to work with it on its side for this stage.

YOU WILL NEED:
- Jute webbing
- Staple gun
- 12 mm (½ in) staples
- Web stretcher

1 Plan out the spacing of your webs. For inside backs you'll need more webs in order to hold the shape when leant on. The space in between webs should be about the same width as the webbing itself. Arms need fewer webs as they don't take any weight.

2 First, fold back the webbing and attach it with 12 mm (½ in) staples to the front of the base of the back or arm.

3 Pull upwards with your web stretcher to the top of the arm or back. You may need to use a clamp or a weight to keep your chair in place while you pull.

4 Staple the webbing as tight as you can using the web stretcher.

5 Cut the webbing, leaving a 4 cm (1 ½ in) end. Fold back and staple the excess into place.

6 If webbing an arm, make sure the last web is close to the back, leaving only enough space for two layers of fabric and polyester wadding to pass through.

6

Webbing an outside back or arm

When working with plastic webbing it's not necessary to use a web stretcher. This webbing does not take weight, it merely holds the shape of the cover and fills any large voids. It's used for outside arms and the outside back.

YOU WILL NEED:
- Plastic webbing
- Staple gun
- 8 mm ($^5/_{16}$ in) staples

1 Starting in the top left corner, staple the folded end of the plastic webbing using 8 mm ($^5/_{16}$ in) staples.
2 Pull down the webbing at an angle and staple in place on the bottom edge of the frame. Do not cut the webbing.
3 Pull the webbing back to the top of the frame at an angle (making a 'v' shape) and staple into place.
4 Continue working in this way, zigzagging the webbing up and down (instead of cutting individual pieces), pulling it taut as you go and stapling it at each side. Be sure to zigzag evenly until the void is covered.

PIRELLI WEBBING

Pirelli webbing is a thick rubber webbing that comes in various colours and widths. It's commonly found on mid-century chairs to support the inside back or seat platform where a box cushion will be. Over a long period of time Pirelli webbing degrades and flakes, eventually breaking or snapping.

Replacing Pirelli webbing is different to other types in that you will not need a web stretcher as it is not stapled to the frame. Usually it is held in place with Pirelli clips (matching the width of the web).

Sometimes replacing Pirelli webbing can be expensive as usually you have to buy a whole roll. Alternatively, you can replace it with elastic webbing. If you take care when opening the clips you can usually reuse them, but replacement clips can be bought online (along with the webbing). I don't recommend stapling the webbing on, as it causes damage to the frame.

Pirelli webs are not usually crisscrossed on small armchairs; instead, there is only one row so they are placed closer together. Larger sofas with Pirelli may be crisscrossed (in the same way that black and white seat webbing is done). Always replace like for like – meaning the same width of webbing, the same number of webs and the same direction of webbing.

To replace pirelli webbing

YOU WILL NEED:
- Flat head screwdriver
- Pirelli webbing
- Pirelli clips (if replacing)
- Pliers
- Hammer

1 The chair frame will have a long groove (or individual grooves) to house the Pirelli clips and allow the lip of the clip to sit flat. Pull one end of the webbing up and out of the groove to release the tension. Pull all clips and webbing off the frame.

2 Carefully open the clips with a flat head screwdriver. One side of the clip has a lip to sit flat into the frame, so take care not to bend this. Use your screwdriver to twist open the clips, avoiding the teeth so that you do not flatten them. When the clip is open wide enough, unhook the old Pirelli webbing from the teeth and slide it out.

3 Cut the new Pirelli webbing to the desired length. You want the webbing to be taut to support the weight of someone sitting in the chair without too much sagging. Cut it 5 cm (2 in) shorter than the distance the web is filling as you will need to stretch it in place to achieve a tight structure (rather than cutting the web the same length and slotting it into place with ease). You can always adjust the Pirelli by cutting it a little shorter and reattaching the clip, so start a little longer than expected and test the first piece until you are happy with the tension. Then, if the grooves of

your chair are parallel in length so all the clips are the same distance, you can cut the remaining strips to the same length.

4 Using the pliers, close the clips around the end of the new Pirelli webbing. Carefully tap the clip with a small hammer to make sure it is fully closed (ensure the lip is over the edge of your bench when doing this so that it is not bent). Check the clip is closed all the way along and kept straight so it will fit back into the groove of the frame. Replace the clips in the grooves, taking care to ensure they are the right way around at each end and facing up, as shown in the illustration below.

On some frames the Pirelli webs are looped at the end, secured with a rivet gun and a small dowel is inserted into the loop to hold it in place within the hole in the frame. These are replaced in the same way but instead of clips you will need a rivet gun and some dowel rods.

Pirelli webbing in place

A – Silver clip
B – Groove
C – Pirelli webbing x 6
D – Frame
E – Pirelli web
F – Flat side of clip
G – Silver clip
H – Flat edge on inside edge of frame
I – Webbing
J – Clip

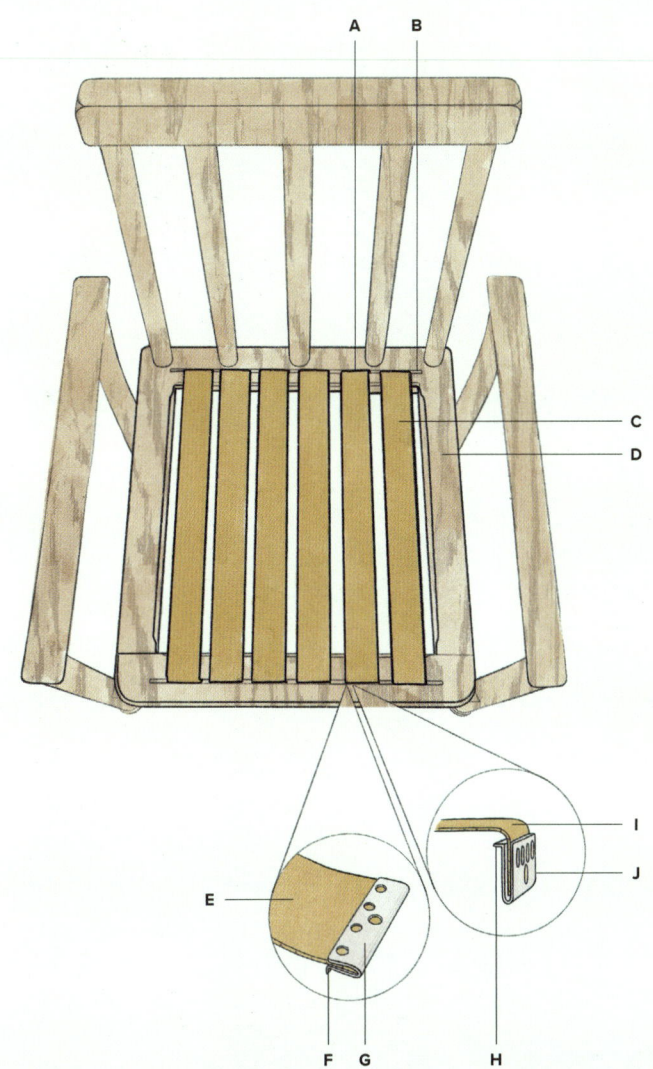

TYING & LASHING COIL SPRINGS

To be totally honest, tying and lashing coil springs is my least favourite part of the upholstery process! It takes a lot of energy to secure the springs and get the right tension and shape. However, it's a really important part of the process because all the other layers sit on top of the springs. When working with coil springs you'll be using traditional upholstery techniques involving tacks and a tack hammer instead of a staple gun, because this gives a better way to pull the twine tight. Also, staples can flatten and snap the twine, whereas tacks do not.

Often you'll be able to re-use the existing springs, but if they're broken then you'll need to replace them and you should always use the same size as the original spring.

Most pieces will only require being tied in from front to back and side to side, however, if you're doing larger pieces of furniture you may need to do further diagonal ties so that the springs stay secured down.

Securing the springs at the bottom

TOOLS:
- Springs
- Marker pen
- Twine
- Curved needle

1   Position your springs on top of the newly webbed seat, following the configuration the springs previously had. Refer back to the images you took when stripping the item back to see the placement and spacing. Usually the springs will be in rows.

2   Best practice for new springs is to ensure the joins on the springs all face the same direction, towards the back right corner. Here I am reusing the old springs, so following the shape of the previous lashing, putting them in the same position so they slope the correct way.

3   Use a marker pen to draw around each spring onto the webbing. Then remove them from the frame.

4   Place one spring back on the marked area. Using a large, curved needle and twine, sew the base of the spring to the webbing underneath. Start with a slipknot.

5   Tie three knots over each spring into the webbing. Ensure each knot is tight and secure in order to hold the spring firmly in place.

6   Some springs will overhang the gaps between the webbing, so focus on tying the knots on the areas where webbing is available. Keep the springs aligned with your pen marks.

7   Continue to tie in all the springs, working towards the back of the frame first. Then back towards the front on the next row, tying three knots on each spring into the webbing to secure them.

8   If you reach the end of the twine, but haven't secured all of the springs, tie it off with a secure triple knot and sew in a new piece of twine to the webbing.

Lashing the springs at the top

This process ties the springs to the frame at the top while compressing them down slightly. This prevents the springs from moving around when the item is used and creates a supportive base for the structure.

TOOLS:
- Laid cord
- Improved tacks
- Hammer
- Staple gun
- 12 mm (½ in) staples

1   Cut a long length of laid cord at least three times the depth of the frame.
2   Place your first two improved tacks (with round heads) next to each other on the front edge of the frame, in line with the middle of the spring on the front left side (alternatively, staple the cord to the frame in the same place using long 12 mm (½ in) staples). Place two more at the back edge in line with these.
3   Next create a bow or figure of eight in your cord containing two loops, leaving a 15 cm (6 in) length at the start to secure when finished. Hook each loop over one of the tack heads and hammer them down into place.
4   Work in a straight line from front to back. Wrap the cord up and over the second rung of the spring at the front. Pull the cord tight to remove the slack without pulling the spring out of line. Tie a tight knot around the spring.
5   Wrap the cord up and over the top rung of the back of the spring. Pull the tension tight and tie a knot. As you are working, hold the cord to the spring with one hand keeping it in place while you tie and move the cord with the other hand. This will help to keep the tension in the cord.
6   Wrap the cord over the front of the next spring on the top rung and tie a knot.

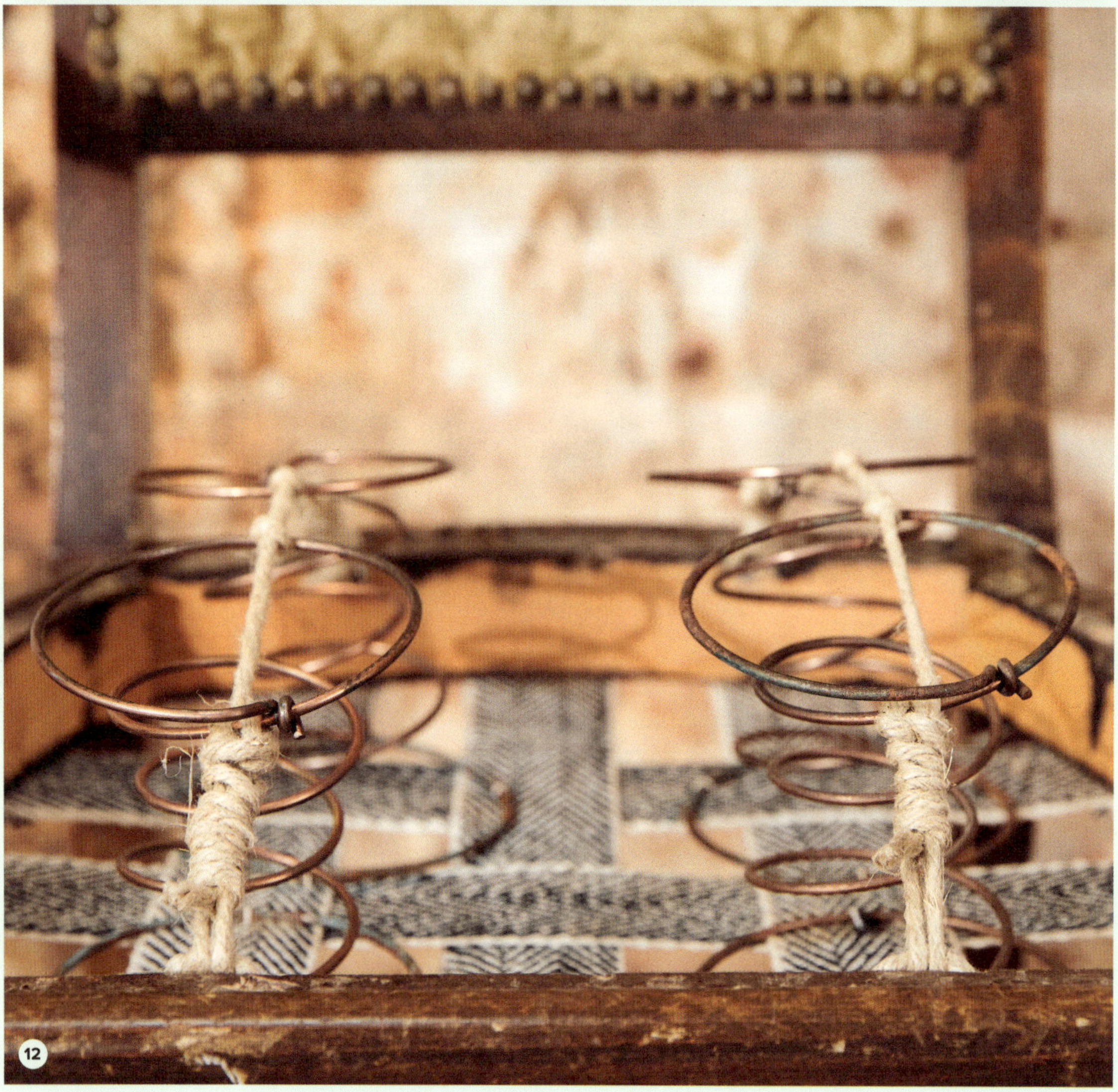

Lashing the springs at the top
continued

7   Then tie the cord to the back top edge of the spring.

8   Keep tying the top edges of the springs until you are at the spring at the back.

9   Tie the back spring on the top of the front edge. Then drop down to the second rung of the back of the spring and tie a knot (as we did at the front).

10 Create a bow as in step 3 and hook the loops over the tacks and pull tight.

11 Hammer into place. If using staples, pull the cord to the frame edge and staple into place while keeping the tension in the cord.

12 Trim the cord leaving a 15 cm (6 in) end. Wrap the cord around itself a few times and tuck it in to secure it. Do this at both ends.

13 Continue to the next row of springs, working front to back to tie the springs in place.

14 Next do the same, but working side to side. The only difference is that when crossing an existing cord (running front to back) tie the cords together. Then continue to tie on the springs as normal.

15 With the springs secure you will then add a layer of hessian (see Adding hessian page 150). The top of the springs will be sewn to the hessian in the same way as Securing springs at the bottom on page 139, to ensure no movement within the frame.

14

POCKET SPRING UNITS

Pocket spring units are often found in mid-century sofas and armchairs. The units are made up of series of coil springs, which are fused together within a metal structure. It's a faster way of using coil springs, as they don't need to be individually hand tied into place.

Often you can reuse spring units. Check it is still securely fastened to the frame. If not, you may need to hammer in some new U-shaped nails. If you need to replace a whole unit, you can contact your local upholstery material supplier. They are made to order in particular dimensions and you can specify how tall you would like the springs to match the existing unit.

To install a new spring unit, first remove the old unit. Lay the new unit in place and use new U-shaped nails to hammer the unit in place onto the frame. You may want to place the nails in different locations to the original nails so that you have the best grip between the nail and the frame instead of using old holes.

Because the structures are all metal there can be some squeaking. This can be solved with some lubricant spray.

ZIGZAG SPRINGS

Zigzag springs are most commonly found on newer sofas. They are generally very durable and so don't need to be replaced. They are also quick and easy to install, hence they are commonly used for mass-produced furniture.

A tighter zigzag provides a firmer tension. These are used for the seat platform where there is a large weight to support. Wider zigzags provide less support and are used for the inside backs where there is less weight and pressure.

Zigzag springs are pulled tight and held in place by a metal clip at either end. This tension makes them a little dangerous to work with as they will retract quickly if you release them from the clip. Sometimes larger items will have silent tie wires across a few of the central springs to ensure they do not warp or cross over each other.

TOOLS:
- Pliers
- Hammer
- Nails
- New zigzag spring and clip (if originals are broken)
- Mallet
- Tack remover
- Pincers

Reattaching a zigzag spring

If the spring has come out of the clip, it is possible to reattach it from underneath the furniture if the clip is still in place and not broken.

1   Begin by removing the bottom cloth using a mallet, tack remover and pincers.
2   Carefully pull the spring taut and attach it back into the clip. You may need pliers and a hammer to help hold and pull the spring and then lightly tap it into the clip as the clip is already closed.

Replacing a broken clip

If the clip has broken or is open, it's best to fix it from the top of the frame.

1   Carefully remove the upholstery (see Stripping back your item, page 120). If you are planning to reattach the fabric afterwards, be extra careful not to damage it when stripping back.
2   Remove the broken clip. Hammer the new clip into the same location so that the spring will be straight.
3   Reattach the spring as detailed opposite.
4   Hook the spring over the clip and hammer closed. Nail down to secure.

Replacing a zigzag spring

1   You will need to strip the upholstery back carefully in order to reveal the springs. Keep it intact so that it can be reattached once the springs are replaced.
2   Measure one of the other springs and order that size.
3   Remove the pieces of the old spring. Ensure both clips are secured into place either side of the frame and slightly open for the new spring to be attached. Replace the clips if needed.
4   Attach one end of the spring to the clip furthest away from you. Hammer the clip closed and add round head nails.
5   Using your body weight, pull the spring towards you until it reaches the second clip on the frame. Use a hammer to tap it into the clip if needed before securing the clip closed with round head nails.

Anatomy of zigzag springs

A – Frame
B – Flat head nail with large head
C – Open clip. Needs to be nailed down
D – Closed clip. Hammered closed
      and secured with nails

TENSION SPRINGS

These springs are commonly found on mid-century armchairs with box cushions from brands such as Parker Knoll and Cintique. Often the springs are encased in fabric and over time this fabric can wear, but it's not necessary to replace the whole spring just because the fabric case has degraded. The springs have a hook on each end and attach to the frame, either onto U-shaped nails or onto eyelets on a grosgrain ribbon that is stapled to the frame. These types of frames are usually angled and so the springs are slightly longer at the front than they are at the back. If you need to replace a spring, measure the length carefully. You will need a little tension to pull the spring into place, so you want to order a centimetre or so shorter than the gap (you can confirm this with your supplier).

Be aware that often newer springs are encased in rubber rather than fabric so may not match exactly.

If the piece has a U-shaped nail that is damaged or missing, you can replace it with another U-shaped nail or by screwing in a long hook. If it uses grosgrain ribbon with eyelets and those are damaged, remove the ribbon completely and replace with a metal plate that the springs can hook onto (the ribbon is very hard to find these days). These frames may also have a thin cover over the edge of the spring on either side. This protects the cushion fabric (which will sit on top) from catching on the hook of the spring and potentially ripping. It can be replaced with a double layer of thick canvas fabric sewn along the free edge and back tacked into place.

BOX CUSHION WITH SPRINGS

If the box cushion you are reupholstering has a spring unit inside, I would always advise reusing this rather than replacing it with all foam. Depending on how firm you would like the seat, you can replace the materials around the spring unit with firmer or softer foam as well as a fire-retardant (FR) liner (see page 160) and a polyester wadding layer. You can add these layers according to your preference, but ensure you account for the new depth of the cushion when you are sewing your cushion border, i.e. if you have made the cushion thicker with more foam you will need a wider cushion border and zip border when you are cutting out the cover. If you need to replace the spring unit you can order a new one from your upholstery material supplier by giving them the measurements.

These are vintage tension springs with a worn fabric casing. These can still be reused. The grosgrain ribbon and eyelets are also intact.

PARKER-KNOLL

ADDING HESSIAN

The hessian layer is the first full layer without any holes. The hessian lies between the webbing and the next layer (the foam or springs) to stop any fall out through the bottom of the item. Foam, although solid, would eventually work through the gaps in the webbing, so the hessian forms a barrier to protect the foam from degrading in this way.

The hessian needs to be pulled tight and flat over the webbing. If your hessian is going over springs it will need a fold/pleat (overlapping around 5 cm [2 in]) to allow for the movement of the springs. We add the fold so the hessian can move with the springs without ripping. If adding a fold to a seat, add the fold front to back. For an inside back add the fold top to bottom.

Hessian fabric frays very easily so always fold it back and staple through two layers when attaching it to the frame.

YOU WILL NEED:
- Hessian (8 oz)
- Staple gun
- 10 mm (⅜ in) staples

1 Cut your hessian larger than the area you are covering by at least 3 cm (1¼ in) on each side.
2 Lay the hessian over the area you are attaching it to. Follow the weave of the hessian to keep it straight.
3 Starting at the back of the seat or the base of the back, fold the hessian over by 2–3 cm (¾–1¼ in) and staple through both layers, first in the middle and then work towards the corners.
4 Pull the hessian tight to the front (or top) and staple into place. Again, start in the middle and work towards the corners.
5 Fold the front edge and staple the fold.
6 Smooth over the sides and staple in the same way from the middle to the corners along one side first, and then the other.
7 Fold the sides and staple them in place. Depending on the shape of the chair you may need to cut or fold your corners in order for the hessian to lie flat. You may also need to make cuts around the legs, for example.

MEASURING & CUTTING FOAM

The most important thing to remember when cutting foam is that if your edges are wonky, wobbly or uneven it will show through the upholstered cover, so take your time to get crisp lines. Usually you want to focus on holding the blade of your foam cutter upright to ensure the edge isn't skewed and is the right dimensions on both the top and bottom edges. Sometimes it's necessary to angle the blade to chamfer the edge or angle the foam.

Do not try and cut the foam to a different thickness. Large machinery is required to do this precisely. If you need 2.5 cm (1 in) thick foam, don't buy 5 cm (2 in) thick foam thinking you'll be able to slice it cleanly in half and have two pieces. We can only shape the foam by cutting the width and length.

YOU WILL NEED:
- Foam
- Long ruler
- Marker pen
- Foam cutter
- Spray adhesive

1   Start by carefully measuring and planning. Usually cushions are cut 0.5 cm (¼ in) wider on each side than the finished cover so that they don't look too small — we want to avoid a baggy cover. Think about where the foam is going on your item. If it's going to be glued onto the frame of the piece (for backs and arms for example) you'll want to make it slightly larger than the frame (about 1.5 cm [½ in]) to avoid the edge of the wood being visible or felt. I often cut the visible top edges when it's in place to ensure the foam is exactly 1.5 cm (½ in) above

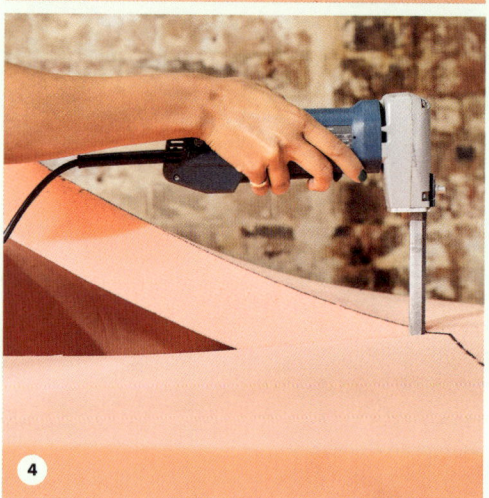

LAYERING FOAM

the frame. Err on the side of caution by cutting your foam larger than you need and trying it in place, without glue.

2   Mark out your measurements on the foam using a long ruler and marker pen. Never include the fused edge of the foam as it has a different texture to the rest of the foam. Cut this off to ensure a smooth pad. Be strategic with how you mark out the shapes on your foam so that you're getting the most out of it.

3   Mark the foam so you know which is the front (F) and top (T) as not all shapes will be perfectly square. If cutting multiple pieces, also mark where each will go on the item, i.e. 'seat', 'back', 'L arm', etc.

4   Holding your blade upright, cut along the lines.

5   For fixed pieces of foam, check you're happy that the frame is covered and you have the right dimensions.

6   If you need to angle the sides (because the cushion is smaller at the top than the bottom or your frame is angled) turn the foam upside down and mark out the measurements for the bottom. Then angle your blade accordingly, keeping the lower edge of the blade at the original line while the top is on the new line.

7   Glue your foam into place by spraying adhesive on the foam itself and the area you want to attach it to. Both areas need glue to ensure it sticks.

8   If you are rounding your foam, you can chamfer the edge of the foam all the way around. You can do this by eye or mark out where you'd like to cut with a marker pen and ruler.

You can glue layers of foam together to make thicker foam. Sometimes for banquettes or long stretches of fixed seating (especially in commercial settings) it's best to use dense chip foam underneath to hold the shape, but with a softer blue or pink foam on top for comfort. When glueing foam together in layers like this I will usually overestimate how much foam is needed.

YOU WILL NEED:
- Foam
- Spray adhesive
- Long ruler
- Marker pen
- Foam cutter

1   Take two pieces of foam, larger than the finished size you need. Glue the pieces together, spraying adhesive on both pieces.

2   Once they are stuck together, mark out the exact shape and size needed and cut it out. This ensures the edges are perfectly aligned.

SECURING FOAM ON THE EDGE

Sometimes glueing the foam into place isn't enough and the curved shape of the frame requires stapling to ensure the foam moulds to the edge well. You can usually tell this will be needed when stripping back a piece and seeing that the old foam was stapled into place. You won't need to use these methods if your cover has a sewn border which needs to sit squarely. But if you need to pull the foam tightly to the frame to be upholstered, use one of these methods.

Staple along the edge

This method ensures the foam sits exactly on the edge of the frame. It's best when the foam is no thicker than 5 cm (2 in). Handheld staple guns may struggle with this task – electric or air compressor guns with longer noses are best.

YOU WILL NEED:
- Foam
- Staple gun
- 12 mm (½ in) staples

1   Hold the gun at roughly 45 degrees to the cut edge of the foam and staple down into the frame. You will need to push the staple gun quite hard (you may need to hold the back of the gun as well). This gives a rounded edge and closes the raw edge of foam onto itself. Ensure the staples are firmly in the frame and not floating in the foam. Use long staples to penetrate through the foam. If they keep popping out you could try longer staples.
2   Do this all the way along, keeping the angle of the gun and position of the foam the same to get a good finish.

Staple 1

Dipryl 3

5

Dipryl the edge to bind the foam to the frame

This method allows you to get a smooth edge on thick foam and will pull the foam down flat. The dipryl will be covered by the usual FR liner, and polyester wadding. It won't be felt through the layers.

YOU WILL NEED:

- Dipryl
- Spray adhesive
- Foam
- Staple gun
- 8 mm (⁵⁄₁₆ in) staples

1   Cut a piece of dipryl. It should be wider than the foam you are covering by 5 cm (2 in) on either side and about 23 cm (9 in) long.
2   Spray some adhesive along the edge you want to shape. Ensure the glue covers the area from the edge to about 5 cm (2 in) into the foam.
3   Stick down the dipryl, leaving an end about 18 cm (7 in) long over the edge of the foam. Let it dry slightly to bond.
4   Pull the dipryl tightly down to compress the foam and mould it to the shape of the frame.
5   Staple the dipryl into the back of the frame, working from the middle to the corners.
6   Trim the excess dipryl close to the staples.

DOMING FOAM

Sometimes flat foam just won't cut it! There are shapes that require more of a domed effect (like footstools, so large areas don't look too flat) and there are a few ways to achieve this. You can also use this method if you want to create a lumbar support in the backrest for example. Simply position the foam you are using for the lumbar where you would like to push the foam out in the lower part of the inside back.

The first method is to bevel the edge of the foam to cut away the corner edge and create a more domed look (see steps 2 and 3). This works well for smaller items. It also works well if your cover is going to be pulled tightly down to further curve the foam and flatten the edge.

On larger items this does not always create enough of a domed look in the centre of the foam. For more of a domed look, you can place thinner layers of foam together in smaller sizes with a bevelled edge.

YOU WILL NEED:
- Foam
- Spray adhesive
- Foam cutter

1. First, cut a smaller piece of foam to help push up the centre and create a domed effect. Using 2.5 cm (1 in) or 4 cm (1½ in) foam (depending on the shape of dome you are trying to make) cut the foam 4 cm (1½ in) smaller than the frame all the way around.
2. Bevel the edge of the foam by marking a line 2.5 cm (1 in) in from the edge along each side on the top. Place the foam in line with the edge of your workbench.
3. Using a foam cutter (not a serrated knife) angle the blade until the top of the blade is on the line and the bottom of the blade is on the bottom corner of the foam. Cut along the line on all sides (if you want a dome effect on all sides).
4. Stick the smaller surface of bevelled foam onto your hessian in the centre, with the larger part overhanging at the top.
5. Glue all the way to the edge and stick the foam down. This will create a slope along each side.
6. Cut the next piece of foam larger than needed (3 cm (1¼ in) on all sides) and place it over the top. If needed, you could use two layers of foam in this way but generally I find one is sufficient.
7. Glue the foam into place.
8. Ensure the edges are cut down to size in line with the frame edge.

3

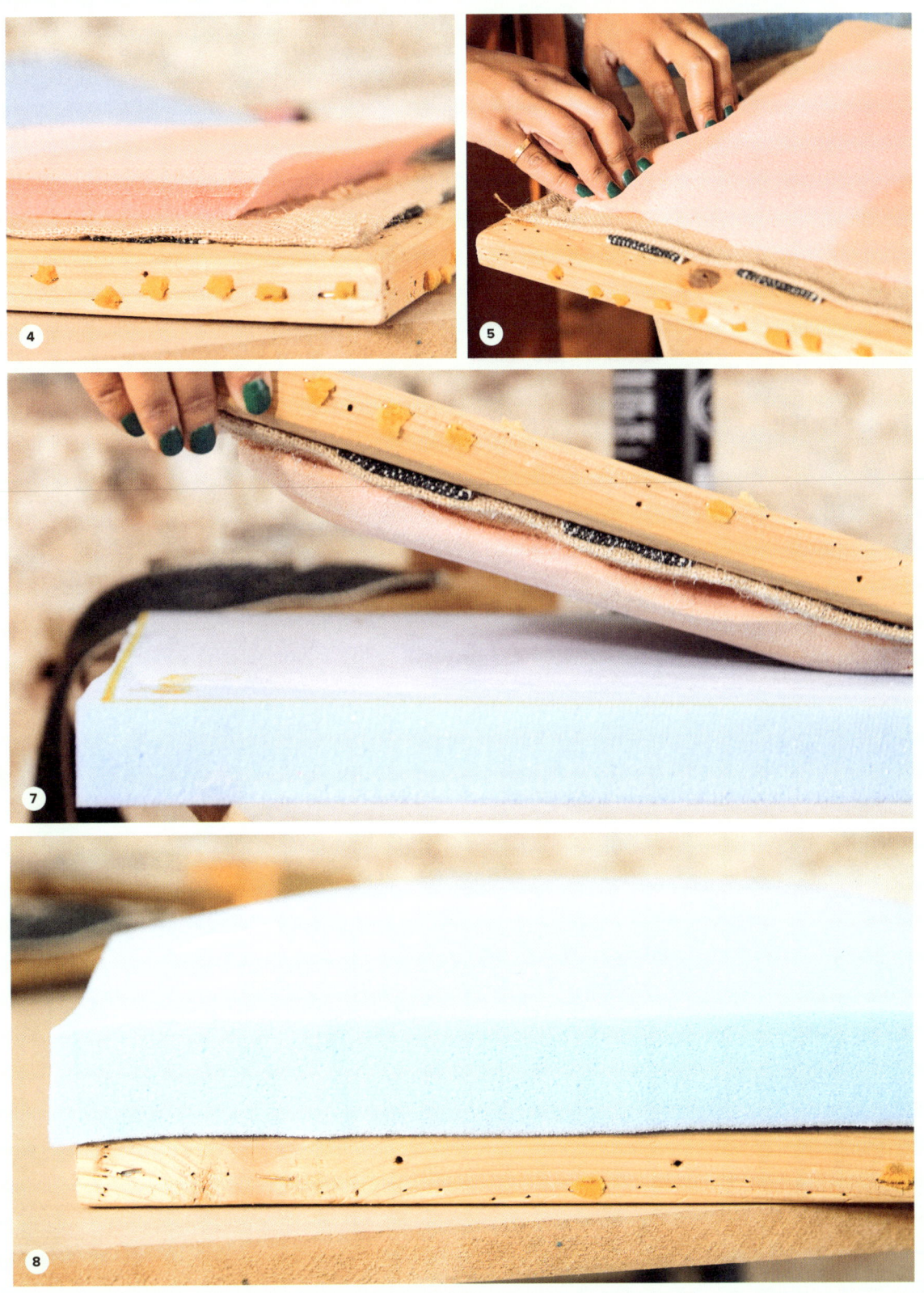

ADDING POLYESTER & STOCKINETTE TO A FOAM CUSHION

Once your cushion foam is cut (see Measuring & cutting foam, page 152) it's time to wrap it in polyester wadding in order to fill out your shape, make it smooth and stop your fabric cover from sticking to the foam and creasing. The thicker the polyester wadding, the softer the cushion, but this will also change the size of your finished item ever so slightly. Usually for box cushions I use 4 oz or 6 oz wadding. You can also add stockinette if you wish, which makes it easier to take the cushion covers off.

YOU WILL NEED:
- Polyester wadding
- Spray adhesive
- Stockinette (optional)
- Scissors

1. Wrap the cushion in polyester wadding. Usually the back, where the zip is, should be kept free of wadding to avoid it getting caught in the zip.
2. Before you start glueing, think about the edges you want the glue/joins to be on. Joins can be a little more bulky and uneven so it's best to place the joins at edges that are less visible, i.e. towards the back of the cushion or the bottom edge.
3. Spray adhesive on the foam to stick the wadding down, starting at the front. Try to have as few joins as possible.
4. Use spray adhesive to stick the edges together and slightly stick the polyester wadding to itself. You can leave the zip edge free of polyester wadding for box cushions that will not have stockinette attached.
5. If using stockinette, cut it twice the width of the cushion. If you're making a very long window seat you won't need as much excess, so cut around 25 cm (9¾ in) extra at each end.
6. Insert your cushion into the stockinette and position it in the middle of the length with the open ends on the least visible sides (usually the sides of the cushion – as the front and top edges are the most visible).
7. Open one side. Spray adhesive onto a large area of the side of the cushion, inside the edge you are sealing.
8. Pull the stockinette tight and gather it onto the glue. Wait a few minutes for it to start drying.
9. Spray the glue on the other side (on the cushion inside and polyester wadding layer).
10. Pull the stockinette tight and gather it onto the glue.
11. Once semi-dry, spray more adhesive underneath the gathered section of stockinette. Stick down some of the excess and cut the rest away. Stick down any fraying ends.
12. Wait until the glue is completely dry before putting your cushion in the cover.

To avoid a visible line when joining pieces of polyester, fluff out the polyester along the glue line. If trying to create a rounded edge, pull the polyester over the edge of the foam and stick down. If you are trying to create a square edge, join two pieces of polyester along the corner using glue, keeping the line straight.

ADDING A FIRE - RETARDANT (FR) LINING

Depending on the country, there will be different regulations around fire-retardant (FR) fabrics for both domestic and commercial use (commercial spaces require a higher standard of fire safety). Most large fabric houses offer fabrics that already have a fire-retardant treatment within the fabrics so you won't need an additional layer. For that reason, these are favourable as there are fewer materials to buy and layers to upholster.

If using a vintage fabric or something that is not inherently fire-retardant, you will need to add a liner. There are various liners available from cotton and calico to wool felt.

I prefer to use the wool felt as it can be glued into place on top of the foam quickly, before the polyester wadding. The felt I use is CRIB 5 (the UK standard for commercial spaces) and I tend to use this even for domestic jobs as it's the quickest to secure.

YOU WILL NEED:
- Fire-retardant fabric
- Spray adhesive
- Staple gun and staples (for fixed upholstery)

1   Using spray adhesive, glue the FR liner to the foam, covering all the edges. Spray the glue onto the foam and then pull the FR layer into place
2   Pull the liner tight to get rid of any creases.
3   If you are covering a cushion be sure to cover all sides. If you are covering fixed upholstery the sides can be stapled down in the same places your top fabric will be stapled, either underneath the frame or on the edge.

This is a good time to practice your v-cuts as this layer will not show through the polyester wadding if the cuts are wrong.

PATTERN MATCHING

Pattern matching is about creating a seamless join between two pieces of the same patterned fabric. It is an important skill to master as it can really elevate your project and give it that professional finish. Much like when you wallpaper, the aim is to marry up the pattern either side of the seam so perfectly that the seam becomes almost invisible with the pattern continuing from one side to the other.

With plain fabrics and fabrics with very small patterns and frequent repeats (such as very thin stripes, polka dots or ticking) there is no need to pattern match in a specific way; you simply join the fabric wherever it's needed. However, with patterned fabric you want to celebrate and showcase the pattern as much as possible so it can shine. This means thinking carefully about the pattern placement on your item and also pattern matching any seams.

Railroading the fabric is where you run it lengthways to avoid joins. This is fine with plain fabrics or fabrics without a pile. Patterned fabrics, however, don't always work when they are used sideways. Patterns with animals on, for example, won't look good if they aren't used the correct way round. And because the fabrics are only generally 140 cm (55 in) wide, you will need to sew additional panels either side to make a wider useable piece.

To do this you need to be able to locate the pattern repeats. The pattern repeat is the amount of fabric from where a pattern begins until that exact part begins again. So if you have a pattern with a figure, it's the distance from the start of the figure until the same figure appears again. Some patterns repeat a lot, for example, thin stripes or small polka dots repeat so frequently you barely lose any fabric

in between trying to match them. Others have large patterns such as woodland scenes, or my favourite Liberty floral, where there is a lot of distance between the start of each pattern repeat. With these you will find there may be a lot of wasted fabric when pattern matching, so make sure to plan carefully when purchasing (see Measuring up for fabric, page 28).

When adding fabric and sewing pieces together, generally I avoid having a seam in the middle of the item. On a headboard, for example, I would sew a smaller piece on either side (so you end up with three pieces of fabric sewn together and the seams are at the side) rather than two pieces sewn together with the seam in the centre.

Matching when sewing

It is important to note that when sewing pieces together to pattern match, you need to add seam allowance to any sides you're sewing together.

FOR EACH JOIN YOU WILL NEED:

- Fabric
- Tailor's chalk
- Scissors
- Pins

1   Cut the first piece with seam allowance added to the side you will be sewing the second piece to.
2   To cut the second piece, move up the roll until you find the identical part of the pattern. Cut this out, making sure the pattern flows correctly from the side you are sewing (to the left or the right as you've planned it), adding the seam allowance.
3   You can lay the first cut-out piece on top to check that the pattern placement matches.
4   Lay the first piece of fabric flat on your bench, right side up. Lay the second piece on top, right sides together.
5   Fold the second piece back by the seam allowance, checking the pattern is perfectly aligned. Then pin along the seam allowance. The sewn seam will need to be exactly right for the pattern to appear continuous.
6   Carefully sew the two pieces of fabric together along the pinned line. Remove each pin as you come to it to avoid breaking the needle.
7   You may need to unpick and resew any parts where the pattern is not perfectly aligned. Take your time to get it right and achieve a well-matched seam. The more you practise this skill, the better you will become at it.

Matching on fixed upholstery

If you are pattern matching fixed upholstery (for example, you want to continue the pattern from the arm to the inside back), you will need to cut more fabric either side so that you can play around with it when it's on the frame – positioning it until you are happy with it. The fabric will extend past the visible line (where the fabric goes past where it is seen and into the frame) with either the same fabric or a fly (see page 30).

The main difference between pattern matching when sewing versus fixed upholstery, is the precision. When pattern matching on the fixed upholstery you can move the fabric around until you are happy with it, only stapling it to the frame when the pattern is aligned and straight. You can remove staples and re-pull the fabric if the pattern needs to be adjusted. This makes it easier, in my opinion, as long as you have cut a big enough piece of fabric to allow for this movement.

You will still need to cut out the fabric in the same way, moving up the roll to find the same part of the pattern again for the second piece. Plan which side of the pattern will go on which side of the frame, i.e. the top of the jungle scene on the inside back and the bottom of the jungle scene on the seat.

If pattern matching a border which will be back tacked, ensure you are happy with the location by using temporary staples first. When you are satisfied that everything is perfectly aligned you can add a few permanent staples and start attaching the back tack card. But once the back tack card is on, it's impossible to move the fabric and you may have made larger holes in the fabric, so getting the alignment right before you back tack is essential.

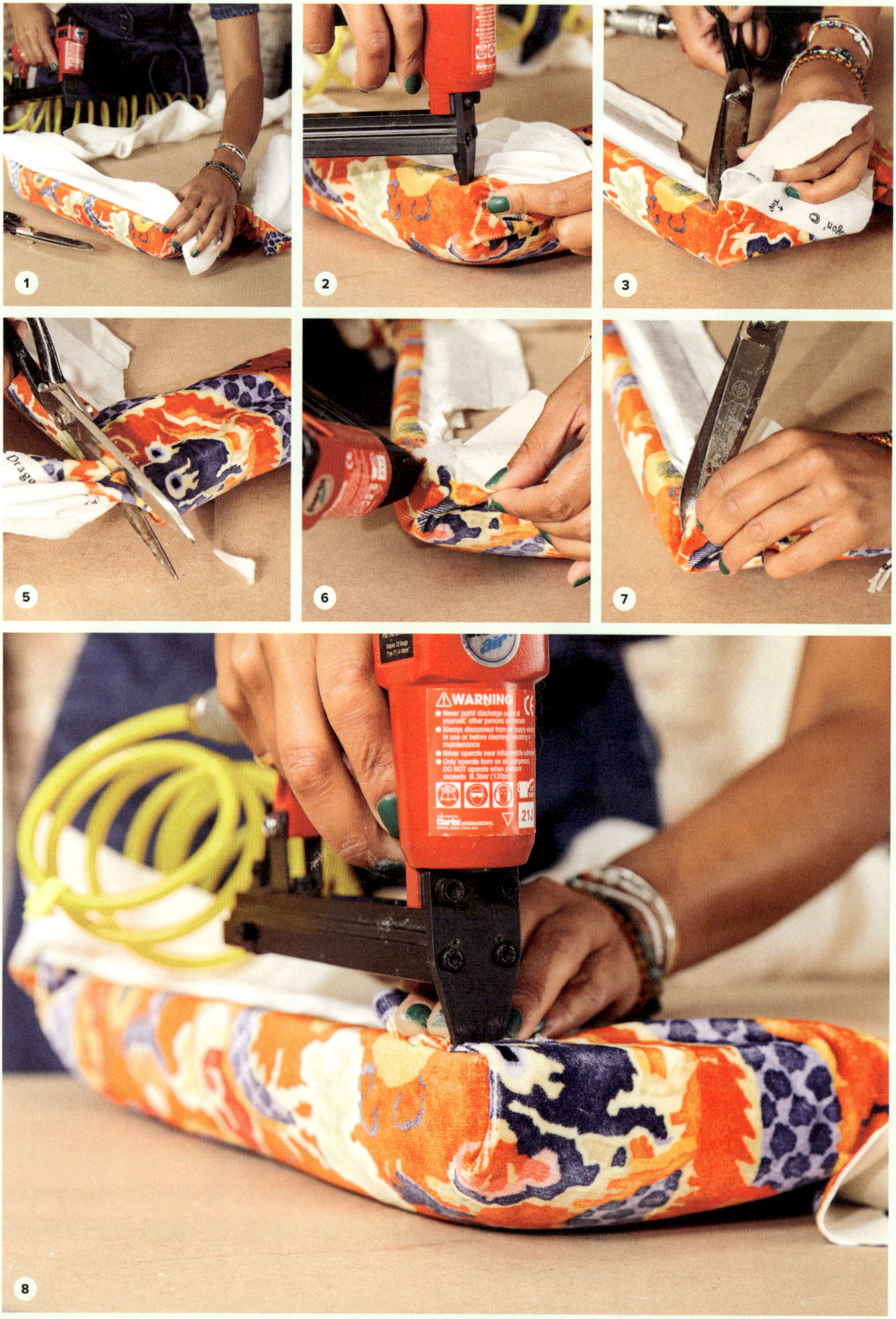

1

2

3

5

6

7

8

FINISHING CORNERS

To me, corners are the most important part of any upholstery project. It is the area where I can quickly see if a project has been completed professionally or not, so it's important to take your time to get them to the highest standard. The main thing to note is that you want to avoid bulky corners with lots of excess fabric folded underneath itself. To achieve flat corners it's important to cut away excess fabric. Do this carefully so that you do not accidentally cut away necessary fabric. It's also important to match all your corners on the piece so they're identical. Decide if you are doing a single or double pleat and the angle of the pleat and repeat this for each corner. Before you start any corner you will need a space of about the length of three staples in either direction to allow room to pull and manoeuvre the fabric. Once the corner is complete, you can add any necessary additional staples either side of the corner to secure the fabric.

YOU WILL NEED:
- Staple gun
- Staples
- Scissors

Single pleat

1   Start by deciding which side you would like the pleat to be visible on. Staple all the way into the corner on this side, leaving a distance of three staples to the corner.
2   For the last staple, pull the fabric around the corner slightly so that it's tight and staple at a 45-degree angle into the corner.
3   Cut away the excess on this first side and into the diagonal staple.
4   Now fold the fabric back down, to the position it will eventually be in.
5   Leave a small overhang and cut away any excess fabric outside of the frame.
6   Fold your fabric as needed so that it is straight on the edge of the frame. You may need an optional staple in the side of the frame to hold the pleat.
7   Check for any excess fabric and trim away as needed.
8   Pull the pleat tight and staple into place.
9   Trim away any remaining excess.
10 If the pleat in the fabric is very long you may need to slip stitch it closed (see page 220). I would advise doing this for anything over 3 cm (1¼ in).

Curved corner

Curved corners are fun to do. The temptation is to add a pleat the same way as on a right angle, but it's not always needed. I prefer to take a fistful of fabric at the back, gathering the fabric in my hand. Then pull it hard towards the back of the frame, twisting it slightly to gather the fabric at the back. Do this until all of the gather is on the back of the frame out of sight. There should not be any visible wrinkles on the front of your item or along the visible side edge. When you're happy, staple the fabric into place.

If any adjustments need to be made, you can smooth the fabric at the front and staple the back into pleats or gathers until the finish is to your liking.

You may need to undo some staples either side of the curved corner to have enough space to gather it all together. If the sides of your fabric are not tight enough this technique may not work. It works best when the foam has been pulled down tightest. If you have left a baggy cover it's hard to match the exact tension with this technique. If the cover has been pulled tight all the way along, it's easier to match the tension of the corner by continuing to pull to the maximum tension.

Double pleat

A double pleat is a more decorative option as you have two visible pleats. Whether you choose this or a single pleat is a personal preference.

1   Start by pulling the corner of the fabric diagonally over the corner of the item. Staple it into place at a 45-degree angle across the corner.
2   Cut away any excess parallel to the staple.
3   On one side make a small pleat in the fabric and pull it tight. Staple into place.
4   Do the same on the other side.
5   Cut away any excess fabric.

1

2

3

4

UPHOLSTERING A CIRCULAR SHAPE

If the piece you're working on doesn't have straight edges, I would advise upholstering it in a different way to ensure the tension is even all the way around. Usually we would secure the front with temporary staples, then pull to the back and secure the fabric, reset the front with permanent staples and smooth over the sides. That's hard to do when there aren't really any separate sides. However, we can use the same principle of working between opposite points to achieve the same result.

YOU WILL NEED:
- Staple gun
- Staples

1   Cut the fabric out as a square with enough overhang either side to pull it into place. As you start to upholster the shape, ensure the fabric is positioned where you want it with your pattern centred (if you have one).
2   Put two staples in the top (at 12 o'clock) and two directly opposite them at the bottom (at 6 o'clock).
3   Turn the item 45 degrees and repeat step 2, putting two staples opposite one another, in between the first two sets.
4   You should now have four sides secured down (at 12, 3 , 6 and 9 o'clock). Check the fabric is still centred and make any necessary adjustments before you continue.
5   Keep rotating the item and working in the middle of the remaining gaps, always pulling to the opposite side. Keep doing this until all the gaps are filled.
6   Cut away any excess fabric.

This fabric design is by
William Morris & Co.

UPHOLSTERING A FASCIA

Fascias are normally found on the arm of a piece – a thin wooden board cut to shape and then upholstered, often finished with piping.

They are held in place either with thin nails (fired through the fabric) or plugs that fit into matching holes on the frame. You will need to redo whichever method is already in place, either by hammering in new nails or reusing the existing plugs.

The most important thing about re-covering a fascia is to get it as flat as possible. There should not be excess bulk or fabric on the back of the fascia, because you need it to sit flat against the frame when it is reattached. This means it's essential to strip it back properly, removing the old fabric and staples, and also to cut away excess fabric on the frame where the fascia will lie.

If your fascia board is very thin you will need to use short staples to cover it. If your short staples still show through the board, use spray adhesive at the back to secure the fabric in place instead of staples.

To cover the fascia you will upholster it in the same standard way (FR liner first, then polyester wadding). Cut these level with the edge so they don't reach the back to avoid excess bulk. Then add your fabric. Start at the middle of one of the long sides and work your way towards the corners. Then pull to the opposite side and, starting in the middle, secure the fabric, working towards the corners. Smooth over the shorter sides and staple the fabric into place. If you want to add piping this is stapled onto the edge of the fascia (and not to the frame). Line the piping up with the edge and staple it into place. See steps 11–13 in Sewing on piping or trim on page 204 for how to tackle joining the two ends together. Cut away any excess before reattaching the fascia to the frame using the original method.

Fascia

A – Holes for plugs
B – Fabric and single piping
C – Piping
D – Plugs
E – Fascia board
F – FR layer and polyester

UPHOLSTERING WINGS

The wings of an armchair or sofa are usually quite straightforward to cover. The main thing to get right is the order in which they're covered in the project – after the arms but before the inside back. This makes sure the fabric is layered in the right order.

The wing is webbed with jute webbing and upholstered in the same way as the arms. Hessian, foam, FR liner and polyester should all be added before the fabric.

If your old cover was sewn together you will need to sew the wing fabric (and piping if using) to the arm cover before you upholster the arm and wing together. This gives the best finish. Alternatively, you can sew the piping just to the wing fabric and then hand sew the opening underneath the piping closed, once the wing is upholstered.

YOU WILL NEED:
- Foam
- Jute webbing
- Piping
- Main fabric
- Staple gun
- Staples
- Mallet
- Pincers
- Tack remover
- FR layer
- Polyester

1   If using piping where the wing meets the arm, sew it to the bottom edge of the wing fabric first.
2   Lay the fabric on the wing, ensuring it's straight. It should be straight compared to the floor and the rest of the chair, not the wing itself, which may be angled.
3   Staple along the inside part of the wing where it joins the frame of the inside back, usually the long edge of the wing.
4   Pull and smooth the fabric to the outside edge and staple into place.
5   Pull and smooth to the top and staple, being careful not to pull the fabric off line.
6   For the base of the wing (which joins the arm), you may need to slip stitch (see page 220) the piping or cover to the arm. Small stitches will ensure the best line.
7   Repeat on the other side for the second wing.

Anatomy of a wing

A – Top of the wing
B – Frame of the wing
C – Back of the
jute webbing
and hessian
D – Side of the wing
E – Inside left wing
F – Opening through
which the fabric
is pulled between
the inside back
and the wing
G – Outside edge
of the wing

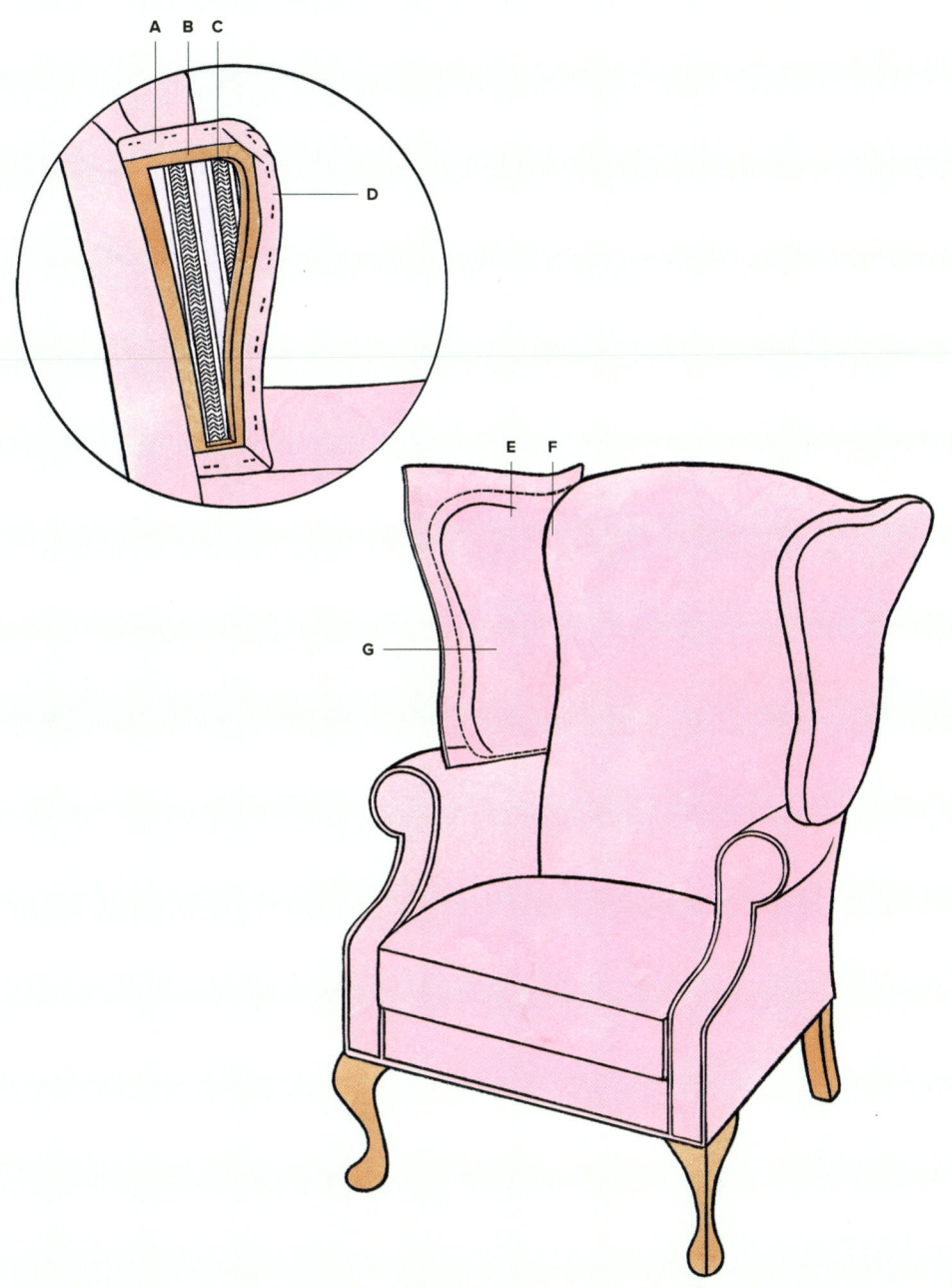

SEWING A SEAT PLATFORM

Wide armchairs and sofas often have the seat platform sewn in place to stop the fabric in the centre moving and appearing to sag, or from hanging down away from the frame. This method is usually applied underneath a box cushion.

YOU WILL NEED:
- Front border fabric
- Platform lining fabric
- Jute webbing
- Buttoning needle
- Buttoning twine

1   Pin together the front border fabric to the platform lining as per your template with a row of jute webbing on the inside of the platform lining. The jute webbing acts to reinforce the seam between the border fabric and the platform lining.
2   Sew the three layers together with the standard seam allowance.
3   Lay the finished sewn piece onto the frame and line it up as needed, following the previous sewn line from the old cover.
4   Fold back the front fabric until the webbing is visible.
5   Using a long buttoning needle and buttoning twine, sew the webbing through the frame and foam. Pull it down slightly to create a very small ridge in the foam and staple the buttoning twine onto the frame underneath, or sew through the webbing to secure it in place. Do this all the way along at 10–15 cm (4–6 in) intervals.
6   Finish by upholstering the seat platform as normal. Pull and smooth the front border and staple it underneath the front edge of the frame.
7   Then pull the lining to the back through the rail between the back and the seat, and staple onto the back rail.
8   Finally smooth the sides and staple them under the rail between the arm and the seat platform. You may need to make v-cuts around some rails.

Sewing a seat platform

A – Seat frame
B – Polyester or FR lining
C – Main fabric folded back on itself
to reveal jute onto which it's sewn
D – Seat lining
E – Long needle through frame
F – Twine
G – Jute webbing

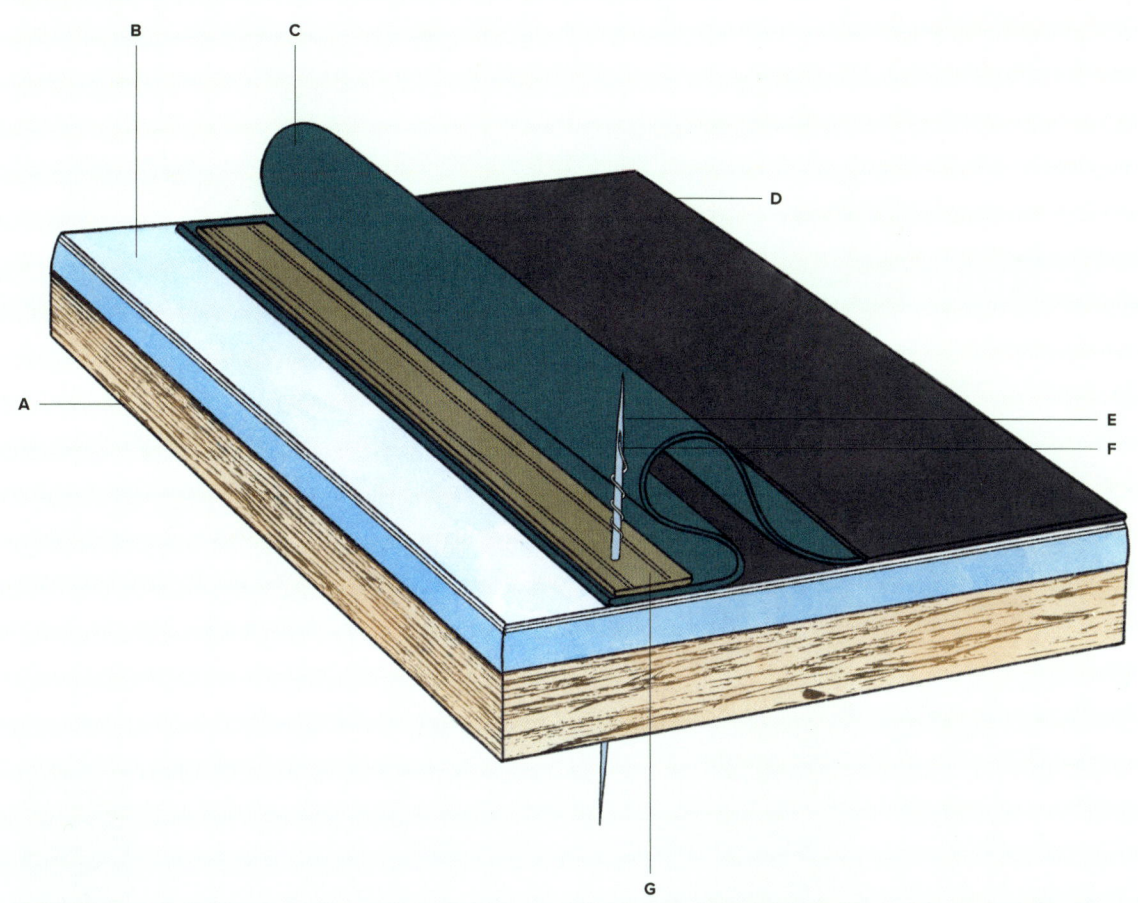

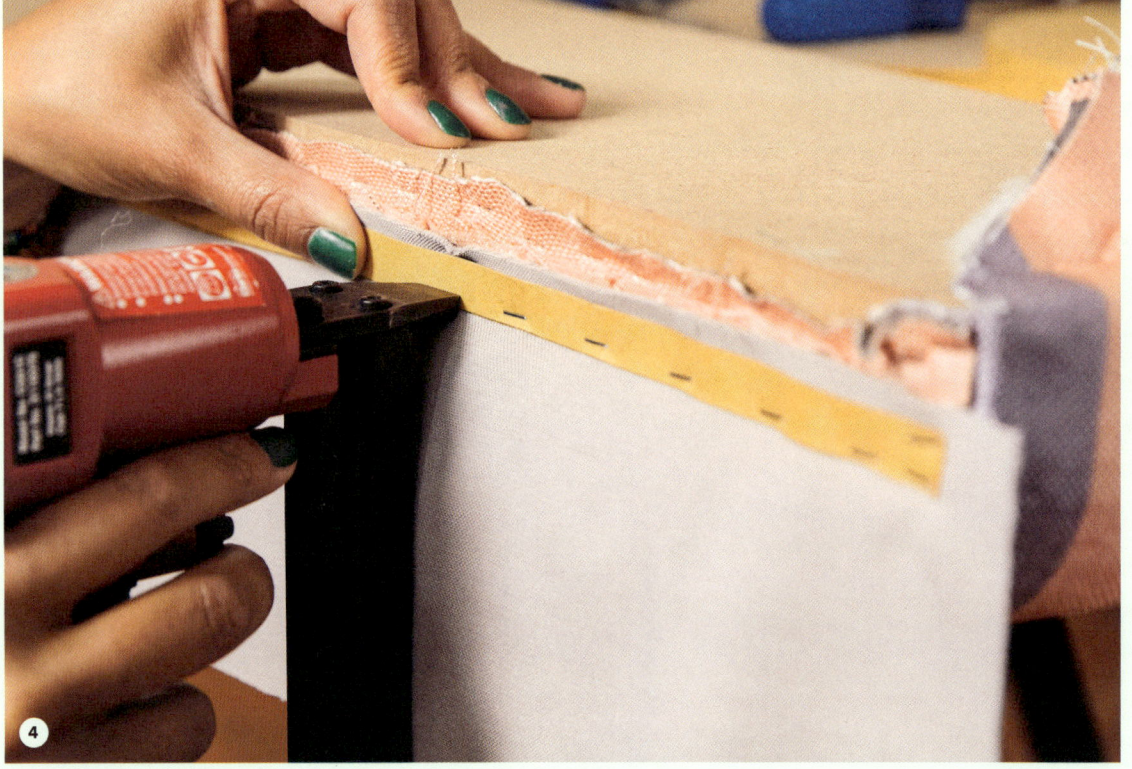

ADDING BACK TACKING CARD

This method is used predominantly on straight edges (or minimally curved edges) to get a crisp, tight join between two pieces of fabric. It is most commonly found at the top of an outside back, outside arm or to attach a border. It's a very secure way of attaching a piece of fabric to the frame that won't allow it to slip down over time, like hand sewing might.

You'll need back tack card, which is a 1 cm (⅜ in) wide cardboard on a continuous roll. It's stapled into place along the back of the fabric to secure the fabric in place and give a crisp line. The card stops the staples showing when the fabric is then pulled into place.

The most important thing about back tacking is to get the card straight and equidistant from the edge all the way along.

YOU WILL NEED:
- Back tacking card
- Staple gun
- 12 mm (½ in) staples

1   Cut a piece of back tacking card a few centimetres longer than the edge you are covering.
2   First, roughly staple your fabric into place, wrong side facing up, with the bulk hanging away from where you want to attach the back tacking card. Ensure it's straight and the staples aren't too close to the edge.
3   Take your back tack card and secure to the frame through the fabric with one or two staples. You will be covering the staples that are roughly holding the fabric in place. If you're doing a long edge like on a headboard, start at the end, leaving about 0.5 cm (¼ in) from the corner (however, if you were adding it to an outside back, you would begin in the middle). Then pull the card to the other corner firmly, ensuring it's the same distance from the edge and staple into place. Make sure the card doesn't hang over the edge, but equally ensure it's not too far set back either.
4   Check you are happy with the line of the card and the fabric positioning. Add staples all the way along the card on the edge closest to the join, spacing them about 1 cm (⅜ in) apart. Remove any staples that cross past the edge of the card. You'll need enough staples that when the fabric is pulled over the card and firmly pulled down, there is no movement.
5   If you are using back tack card around a curve, you will need to make relief cuts in the card all the way along the curve.
6   If you have cut the back tack card too short, you can add more by simply stapling a new piece in line with it.
7   Avoid back tacking corners (leave a gap about 0.5 cm (¼ in) from the corner). It is tricky to back tack two edges that are at right angles to each other, as the fabric needs to be pulled back in order to attach the card. If you have multiple edges to close, I advise back tacking the top edge and slip stitching or ply gripping the sides.

WORKING WITH SHOW WOOD

When tackling a project that has a lot of ornate show wood, there is a slightly different approach to upholstery.

Show wood is part of the wooden frame that remains visible after the upholstery is completed, often around the back and the arms. This means that the staples used to secure the fabric in place will remain visible and not underneath the frame as usual, so they need to be covered by trim or piping. Often double piping is favourable as it's wider, so can hide more variation in staple placement (see Making double piping, page 201).

If the piece is antique it is most likely upholstered traditionally, so consider this at the start. If it's a reproduction piece it will likely have foam and modern materials used.

First, it's important to avoid damaging the frame and wood when stripping the item back. Remove the staples slowly. Avoid levering the tools against the ornate wood as this will dent or break it. Instead, favour the side of the frame that will be hidden when upholstered.

You'll need a staple gun with a nose or long nose in order to be able to get into the crevices of the frame to secure the fabric over the foam. Handheld staplers don't have this feature and so can be tough to manoeuvre in these tight spaces.

When upholstering this type of item, the fabric isn't pulled around to the back to be stapled; it's finished at the front edge with a visible line of staples (later hidden by piping or trim). Focus on getting the tension even all the way along. Having well-secured foam will help, so I advise stapling the edge of the foam (see Securing foam on the edge, page 154).

Ensure the staples are close enough to the edge so that your piping or trim will cover them all.

Use a very sharp blade to cut away excess fabric once the fabric is in place.

The item will be finished off with double piping or trim, which is glued in place along the edge to hide the staples. You could also use studs and hammer them into place.

The fabric used here is by Febrik.

Capting on

A – Outside left arm which would be upholstered with plastic webbing, polyester wadding, back tack and ply grip as normal.

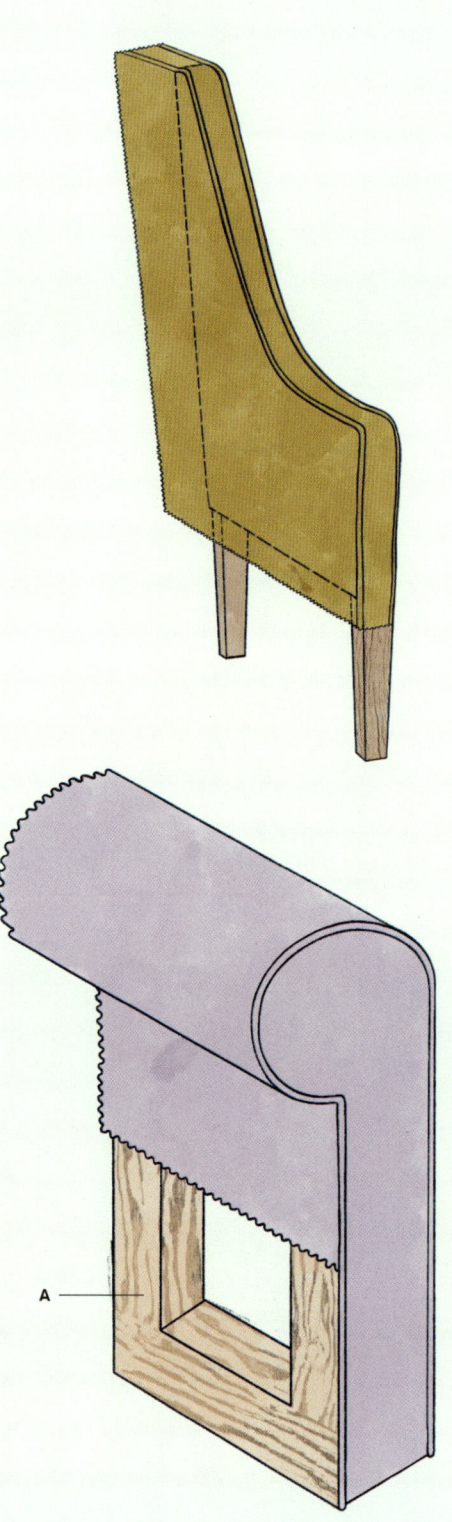

This arm section is pre-sewn together with piping. The inside arm, outside arm, border and piping are all sewn together, then stapled onto the frame.

This scroll arm is capped on. The fabric that sits on top of the arm is sewn around the fascia in one big continuous piece then stapled into place. The outside arm is then attached separately with back tack and ply grip as normal.

CAPPING ON

This is a very simple technique for when you have sewn a cover together, almost like a box cushion, but with an open side to pull over the frame and slide in place.

This might be for an arm with a front fascia sewn in, or a scroll arm with a flat front fascia. Different shaped arms will be sewn together in different ways, so remember to follow the old cover as a template. All you need to do is staple it in place, but there are a few things to remember.

First, check the fit is correct once you have sewn your cover together. Do this by sliding the cover on the frame, once it is fully ready with foam, FR and polyester. Check the seams are the correct width and sit in line with the edge of the frame. If it's too big or too small, make the necessary adjustments to your sewing.

When it's ready to be attached, ensure the seams are pressed open. You won't need an iron; usually upholstery fabric can be pinched open with your fingers. When the cover is on the piece but not yet stapled into place, slide your hand inside and ensure the seam is lying flat all the way along. This will avoid any wiggly looking seams.

Finally, as you start to staple the piece to the frame, focus on getting the tension even so as not to pull the seams out of alignment. If you have a very prominent seam that will be visible, pay attention to this first and place some temporary staples to hold this in line so that you don't pull it off-centre as you pull the fabric into place.

You will still need to tackle the corners as usual (see Single pleat, page 167) but you might find that opening up the seam with a blade on the back of the frame (the part that is not visible on the finished item) will allow you to cut away excess and get a crisp, flat corner. Keep an eye on the tension to ensure it's the same all the way along and you haven't over pulled the corners.

USING PLY GRIP

Ply grip is a metal strip with claws that you staple in place and then the fabric is pushed into the claws, which are hammered closed to hold it in place.

When I first started upholstering I was always scared of ply grip, mainly because it's sharp and I would catch my skin in the claws while unravelling the roll. I've since realised how useful it is, and not just for closing the side of the outside arms and the outside back. It can be used in any area in place of slip stitching; for example, if you want to add a liner to the inside of an ottoman. Once mastered, it's an extremely satisfying and quick way to finish off any item.

As I mentioned, the claws themselves are sharp, so be careful when handling the roll. It also tangles really easily, so cut as much as you need and then secure the roll with ties so it stays neat.

As with back tacking and slip stitching, the most important thing is getting a straight line that is equidistant from the edge all the way along. I use ply grip for straight edges or those with a minimal curve. When I have a very curved shape I secure it with a slip stitch.

Usually you will have back tacked the top edge and will be ply gripping the sides. Ply grip works best with medium to thick fabrics and the claws can be hidden by piping. Thin and delicate fabrics should be attached with a slip stitch. Staple guns with a nose navigate ply grip the best, as they can get into the claw. Flat handheld guns may be tricky so you might need to open the claws wider to get the staple gun inside.

YOU WILL NEED:
- Ply grip
- Staple gun
- 10 mm (⅜ in) staples
- Regulator needle or skewer
- Hammer

1   Before applying ply grip to the sides, back tack the top, web the opening with plastic webbing and glue on your polyester wadding. The bottom edge should also be secured in order to get tension on the fabric. The wadding should not cover the edge where the ply grip will be stapled, as it will get caught in the teeth and stop the fabric from securing properly.

2   Cut the length of ply grip needed. I usually cut one or two grips extra so it's a little long. If applying to two sides, cut both now.

3   Pull the fabric back at the sides so it's out of the way and reveals the polyester wadding.

4   Start at the top and position the open claws facing the outside edge. The side with a round hole should lie flat on the frame with the claw side up. The start of the claws should be 0.5 cm (¼ in) from the corner.

5   Find the hole and place one staple to the left and one to the right of it (parallel with the length of ply grip). Avoid shooting though the metal as this may damage your gun and cause the staple to contort, resulting in injury. If your staples are not flat, remove them and retry.

6   Once the end is secured you can pull the ply grip straight and secure the opposite end, keeping it in line with the edge of the frame.

7   Then work methodically along, attaching two staples on each claw (either side of the hole).

8   With the ply grip secured, the next step is to trim the fabric edge. Take a long needle or skewer and, holding one corner of the fabric, score the fabric into the claw using long sweeping motions. It doesn't have to be perfect, but it should be straight and tight when compared to the back tacked top edge.

9   Pull the fabric back out of the claw (careful not to damage the fabric in the claws themselves). The fabric should show a crease where the claw was. Leave an overhang of 0.5 cm (¼ in) and cut away any excess. Be careful not to over trim as you won't have enough fabric to hold in the claw. Equally, too much fabric will look bulky. You can trim some fabric away and then try it back in the claw using the needle or skewer until you're happy.

10 Once you're happy that enough fabric has been trimmed off, push the fabric inside the claw. Ensure your top corner (which meets the back tack card) is crisp and neat. When it's straight, close the claw with a hammer. I always use some offcuts of fabric to cushion the hammer so that I don't damage the fabric. Tap the claws closed, ensuring you close them all straight. You should not be able to see any metal once the claw is fully closed. If any corners of the claw show through, you can unhook the fabric with your skewer or needle so that the metal is hidden.

11 Ply grip the other side in the same way.

12 Finish off the bottom corners with staples under the frame where needed.

ADDING BOTTOM CLOTH

This final layer underneath a chair, sofa or behind a headboard serves a few purposes. First, it collects any dust that is created from the foam over time. Second, it makes the project look neat and tidy. Third, it stops any little creatures from easily damaging the underneath of the chair. Although it's rarely seen, given its position, it's definitely worth adding in order to finish off the item professionally.

I usually use a black cotton bottom cloth or dipryl (it's a thinner, cheaper material) but you can use anything really. Don't use your best fabric, as a large piece that would cover the bottom of a chair or sofa is best used for a cushion or another project (see Using your fabric offcuts, page 240).

YOU WILL NEED:
- Bottom cloth or dipryl
- Ruler
- Tailor's chalk
- Staple gun
- Staples

1   Measure out how much is needed to cover the bottom of your item. Add at least 5 cm (2 in) on either side to fold the fabric under and avoid a frayed edge. Use a ruler and tailor's chalk to mark the fabric and cut your piece.

2   Start by folding the edge under by roughly 5 cm (2 in). Tuck the folded side in towards the frame. Ensure it will lie flat when pulled tight and will cover the entire area necessary. Starting in the middle of the back, staple the fabric down as close to the folded edge as possible so that the fabric doesn't hang down, spacing your staples at 5 cm (2 in) intervals (the spacing can be wider than when stapling fabric into place as there is less tension here).

3   Pull the cloth to the front edge and fold under any excess until you are happy with the shape.

4   Start stapling in the middle and work your way out towards the corners. For now, leave the corners open.

5   When the front and back are completed, smooth the fabric over the sides gently and staple it in place. I usually put one staple in one side and then staple the other side entirely. This ensures I'm not pulling the fabric off-centre. You won't need to pull very hard, but ensure there aren't any wrinkles or creases. If the fabric is loose it will sag down and be seen, so ensure it is taut.

6   Make small cuts to shape the fabric around any legs.

7   You can fold where necessary. Depending on the shape of your item and the types of legs, there are different ways to tackle the corners. The aim is for a neat finish so try to cover as much of the space around the legs as possible, but remember this isn't really visible.

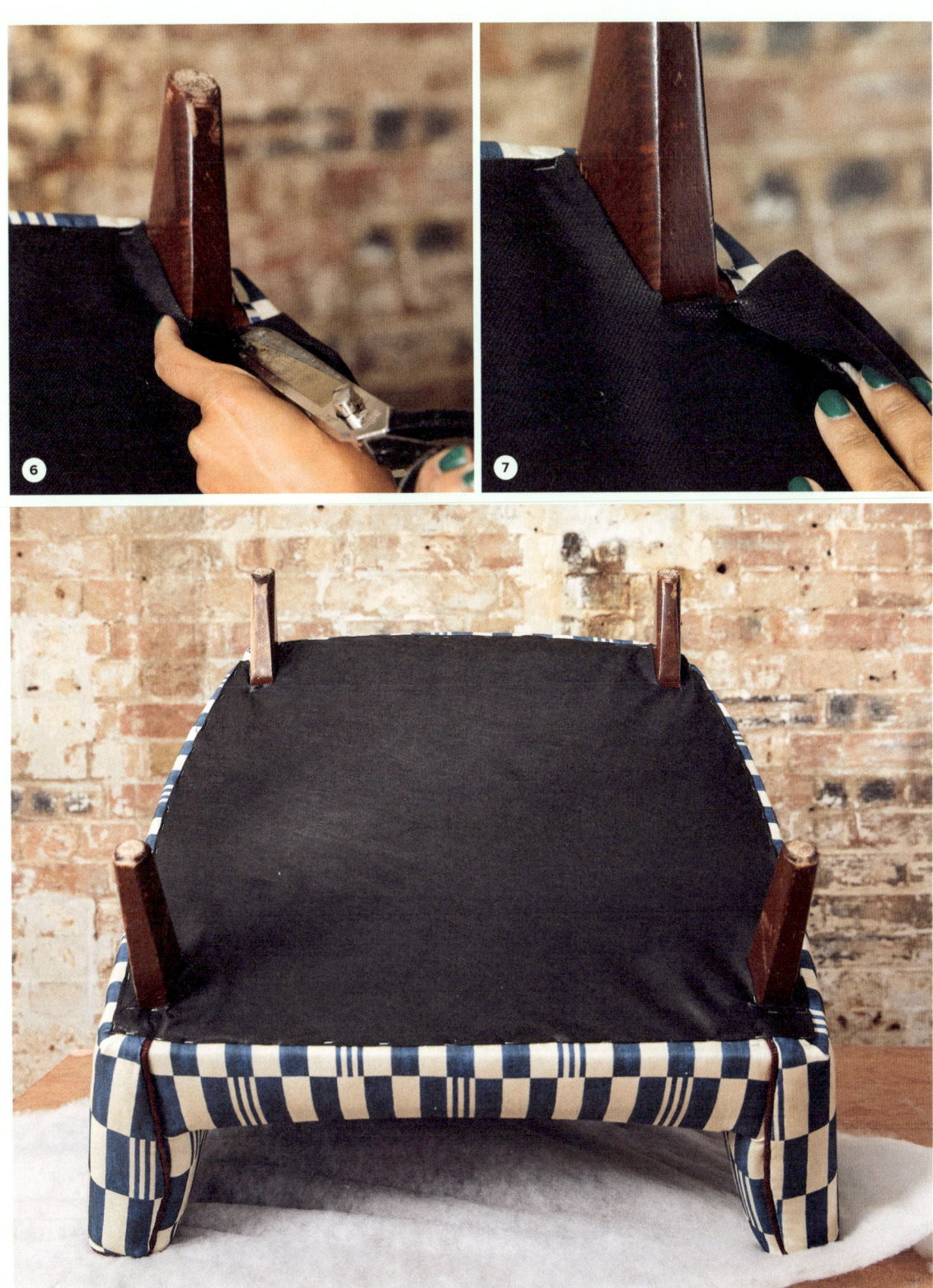

SEWING A ZIP

There are so many ways to sew a zip but I tend to stick to just one method. It makes sewing them fast and I always opt to cover the zip with a lip of fabric.

Upholstery zips are more durable than fashion zips so definitely make sure you buy the right kind. Otherwise, when the air is forced out of your cushion if someone sits or jumps on it, the zip may break. Also there's often more tension in upholstered pieces, as the aim is to fill the cover out completely and avoid it being loose or wrinkly.

The zips I use come in a continuous roll with the sliders separate. This way I can cut long lengths of zip for large cushions and get exactly the right amount. I prefer this to matching the colour (which is what's favourable on clothing), as my method of sewing covers the zip anyway and the zips in upholstery are more often than not at the back and not seen.

If adding a zip to a really large cushion for, say, a window bench or sofa cushion, you may want to take the zip around the back two corners rather than just the straight edge. Only do this if it won't be seen on the finished design. Doing this will help to fit the large foam inner inside the cover.

If you really want to avoid sewing a zip you can sew your cushion closed with a slip stitch (see page 220). This will mean you can't take the cover off to wash it, but if that is your preferred choice then go for it. I know zips can be intimidating so don't let that put you off completing your project! If you do try sewing a zip and it's not perfect, keep at it. The more you sew the better you'll become.

Cutting the zip borders needs careful consideration in order to get the sizing right. You can always cut the borders deeper than needed and trim them down once the zip is sewn.

YOU WILL NEED:
- Zip tape
- Zip pull
- Zip borders (cut from your main fabric)
- Sewing machine
- All-purpose foot

1 Cut out your zip borders, taking into account how long they will be and that your seam allowance needs to be wider on the side where the zip is sewn in place – to accommodate the zip cover. Instead of the usual 1 cm (⅜ in) allow 3 cm (1 ¼ in).

2 Cut a length of continuous zip at least 10 cm (4 in) longer than needed.

3 To add the zip pull, you will need to open one end of the zip slightly (about 4 cm [1½ in]). Cut away 1 cm (⅜ in) of zip from one side. Thread the zip pull onto the long end first, followed by the shortened side. As soon as it catches, stop, as it's easier to sew the zip with the pull out of the way at one end.

4 Fold back 3 cm (1¼ in) of fabric along the first edge that will be sewn to the zip. Check your pattern is the right way around. Pin the fabric into place on the zip; the edge of the fold should press up against one side of the zip teeth.

5 With an all-purpose foot, sew the zip to the fabric.

6 Turn the zip around and pin the other side into place. Fold back 3 cm (1¼ in) but in this case cover the zip teeth completely. Pin in place.

7 Sew the fabric to the zip all the way along.

8 Move the zip pull into the centre of the zip and open it ever so slightly. It's now ready to be attached to your cushion and the pull is in the right place to ensure it will open.

CHAPTER FIVE

Decorative & finishing techniques

MAKING A BUTTON

I find making buttons quite therapeutic! Perhaps because I have a vintage button press and the weighty metal and slow process of making each button individually force me to be very present. If you are unable to make your own fabric buttons you can send fabric to companies who will make them for you. You could ask your local upholsterers to make you some. Or you could source ready-made buttons in a contrasting fabric or go with something different, like a crystal or metal finish.

MATERIALS AND TOOLS:

- Button maker
- Fabric cutter or scissors
- Button moulds (front and back)
- Fabric offcuts
- Wooden board

1   First you will need to create circles of fabric in the right size, depending on the buttons you are making. If using a circle cutter attachment, each cutter is numbered and correlates to the button moulds you have chosen. The circle should sit inside the lip of the mould you have chosen. If you have a robust circle cutter attachment for your press, you can fold the fabric back on itself and cut out about eight layers at a time. Ensure the fabric does not twist and warp, as you will need perfect circles for the buttons. Place a wooden board underneath your fabric before making the cuts (this protects the cutter from grinding against the metal underneath). If you want a specific part of the pattern on each button, take your time planning your circles and cut carefully. You can also cut the fabric with a separate fabric circle cutter or with fabric scissors, but this does take a bit longer and may not be quite as precise.

2   Take a circle of fabric and place it face down in your button press. Add a button front with the rounded side down and push into place using a wooden rod or pencil.

3   Add the back of the button (the side with the loop) to the other half of the press.

4   Join both halves of the button press together by rotating the handle. Turn the button press two or three times to full capacity, which will press the button together securely.

5   Undo both halves to reveal your custom button. Ta-da!

6   Repeat as needed. I always make one or two extra, just in case!

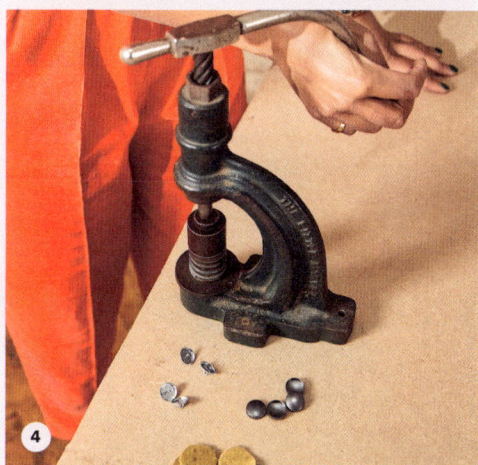

ADDING BUTTONS

Now that you've made your bespoke fabric-covered buttons, it's time to attach them. The key thing to focus on here is to get a uniform tension for all the buttons. You'll want to pull them so that they sit at the same depth in the foam and cast the same shadows. Note that to attach floating buttons (these sit on top of the fabric without pleats, whereas deep buttons sit within diamond pleats/folds) to a solid wooden board like a headboard, you will need to drill holes on the frame for the needle to pass through. It's best to do this before you attach the foam.

MATERIALS AND TOOLS:

- Buttons
- Buttoning twine
- Pins
- Long buttoning needle
- Staples and staple gun
  (if attaching to wooden board)
- Offcuts of fabric (if attached through webbing)

1   Cut long lengths of buttoning twine. You will need a length that is at least quadruple the thickness of the foam, for example, if the foam is 10 cm (4 in), cut at least 40.5 cm (16 in) of twine. I usually make mine even longer, just to be on the safe side.

2   Mark out where your buttons will go using pins if you are adding floating buttons. Do not use a marker or fabric pen in case you need to adjust the position or measurements; a pin can be easily moved and won't damage your fabric. For floating buttons check the spacing is even and symmetrical. For deep buttons you'll know to add the button into the pre-cut hole in the foam.

3 Thread your first button onto a single thickness of twine.

4 Thread both ends of the twine through your long buttoning needle.

5 Push the needle through all layers of foam and fabric, keeping it straight. Pull it out fully to the other side, being careful of the super sharp point. If you are buttoning onto a wooden board, the needle will come through a pre-drilled hole in the board. Take the needle off the twine.

6 If working with a wooden board, use 8 mm (^{5}/$_{16}$ in) staples to staple the twine ends together three times, zigzagging back and forth to stop the tension releasing over time.

7 If you are securing your threads onto the back side of webbing, roll up a small piece of offcut fabric and place it between the twine ends, next to the foam. Tie a slipknot over the fabric and pull tight (see Tying a slipknot, below). Cut away any excess twine.

8 Repeat for all of your beautiful buttons.

9 If any adjustments are needed to make sure the tension of all the buttons is the same, simply cut the twine off and use a new piece. Make sure to secure the buttons tightly so they do not become loose over time.

Tying a slipknot

A – Hold both loose ends of twine

B – Wrap the right piece clockwise twice around your thumb and the twine

C – Thread the wrapped piece down into the loops made where your thumb is

D – Pull tight

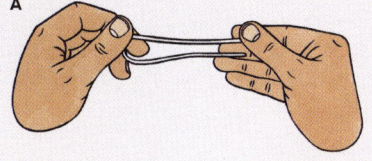

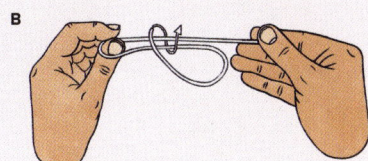

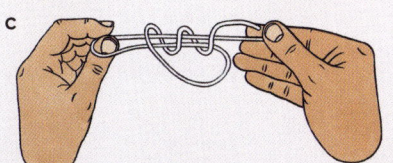

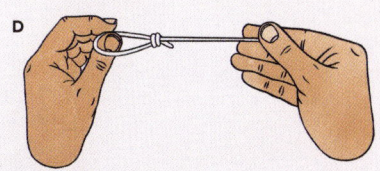

MAKING SINGLE PIPING

Once I'd mastered making piping, I felt like a true upholsterer. That probably sounds quite silly, but piping is so common in upholstery that it makes sense to learn how to create it, and it can really elevate the finish of your piece. Traditionally, piping matches the main fabric, but I love using contrasting colours.

Piping is always cut on the bias (the diagonal of the fabric) so if you're sewing a stripey fabric it will not match up to the main pattern, but that's totally standard.

MATERIALS AND TOOLS:

- Fabric
- Tailor's chalk
- Long ruler
- Piping cord
- Piping foot
- Scissors or fabric cutter

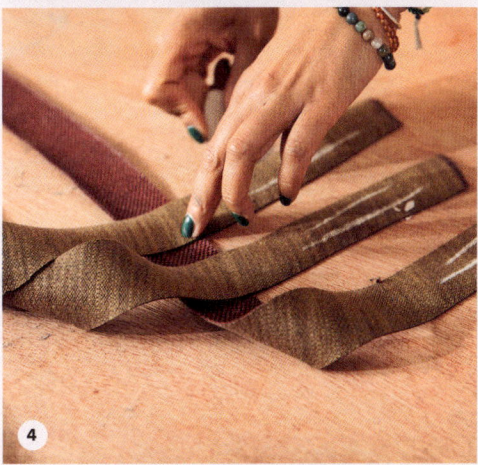

1 Calculate the amount of piping needed by measuring the length of all the edges where the piping will go, and then add an excess of 50 cm (19¾ in) to allow for joins.
2 Using tailor's chalk and a long ruler, mark out parallel diagonal strips on your fabric. They should be 4 cm (1½ in) wide to sew a classic 8 mm (⁵⁄₁₆ in) piping. The rough edge should match your seam allowance of 1 cm (³⁄₈ in). Always cut piping diagonally as the bias of the fabric has more stretch, which is necessary for corners and curves. It will also stop your fabric from puckering when you attach the piping to the piece.
3 Carefully cut out all your strips.
4 Before moving the strips, mark the back of the fabric just at one end. You will be joining your strips together – one marked end to an unmarked

end. This will ensure that the pile/pattern is continuous.

5 Take two strips and match up one marked end to the unmarked end of the other. Place them right sides together and at right angles. I have chalked a diagonal line to show where to sew these together.

6 Using an all-purpose foot, sew diagonally across the line shown. Cut away any excess leaving a 1 cm (⅜ in) seam allowance.

7 Repeat until all your strips are joined in one long piece.

8 Swap to a piping presser foot on the sewing machine and use a matching coloured thread so it won't be as visible on your finished item.

9 Place the piping cord inside the length of fabric at one end. Fold the fabric over it ready to sew (the right side of the fabric will be facing outwards). Use the piping cord straight off the roll without cutting it to avoid bulky joins of cord inside your piping. If you need to join more piping cord, simply glue the ends together, keeping any excess bulk to a minimum.

10 Sew the piping closed. As you feed it through the machine, continue to fold the fabric around the cord lining up both edges.

11 When you sew over a join in the fabric, open the seam so it lies as flat as possible, ensuring it isn't too bulky.

12 When you reach the end of the fabric, cut your threads and the piping cord.

If you're using a particularly thin fabric, you may find that once you've sewn your piping, it's appearing too baggy. If it feels loose, you may find that as you assemble the piece, sewing the piping first to the cover and then the borders, the extra layers of fabric make it tighter each time giving you a better finish.

MAKING DOUBLE PIPING

Double piping is not as flexible as single piping. Instead of being sewn into place, it is usually glued along the edge of an item with a glue gun to cover staples, as an alternative to trim or studs.

MATERIALS AND TOOLS:

- Fabric
- Tailor's chalk
- Long ruler
- Piping cord
- Double piping foot
- Scissors or fabric cutter

1 Calculate the amount of piping needed by measuring the length of all the edges where the piping will go.

2 Mark out, cut and sew the fabric strips as you usually would for single piping (see Making single piping, page 198). For double piping you will need to cut the fabric strips wider than the usual 4 cm (1½ in); I tend to cut 7 cm (2¾ in).

3 Join the ends of the fabric strips together (see steps 5 and 6, opposite).

4 Swap to a double piping presser foot on the sewing machine.

5 Sew the first row of piping cord inside the fabric, aligning it on one side with enough fabric to cover the cord. It should not be in the centre of the fabric as with single piping.

6 Add a second row of piping cord next to the enclosed first row and fold the fabric over to encase it. Hold these together as tightly as possible.

7 Sew along the cord, holding the folded material as tightly as you can to ensure even piping.

8 Trim away any excess overhanging fabric.

SEWING A FRILL

Frills are a lovely addition to upholstered items. They add a certain cottage core look and a softness which only fabric can achieve. You can add frills to the outside back or bottom of an item. Just remember that if it's an area that will be sat on, eventually the frill will be flattened or squashed.

As with piping, a frill can match the main fabric or be in contrasting or complementary colours and textures. I usually sew my frill before I attach it to the item. More experienced sewists may prefer to sew the frills and folds as they attach it to the main fabric for efficiency.

MATERIALS AND TOOLS:

- Fabric
- Tailor's chalk
- Long ruler
- Standard presser foot
- Scissors or fabric cutter

1 First, decide how wide you would like the frill to be. The fabric is folded back onto itself to make a double-sided frill, so double this figure and then add the seam allowance on each side.

2 Calculate how long the frill will be by measuring the edges it will be attached to. To allow for the fabric that is lost in each fold, multiply this measurement by 1.5. This sum is the length of fabric to cut out.

3 Mark out the strips for the frills using a ruler and tailor's chalk. Unlike piping, you do not need to cut the fabric diagonally – you can cut it horizontally or vertically, depending on how you want the pattern to run.

4 Before you cut out your strips, mark the back of the fabric at one end. When you come to join your strips, you will match a marked end to an unmarked end, which will ensure that the pile/pattern is continuous.

5 Cut out the strips.

6 Lay two pieces right sides together (one marked end to an unmarked end – see step 4 on page 199) and sew them together along the end with the usual 1 cm (⅜ in) seam allowance to create a long strip of fabric.

7 Once all your pieces are joined together, you are ready to start sewing the frill.

8 Fold the fabric lengthways, wrong sides together, matching the raw edges. Press the fold with your hands.

9 Sew along the raw edge of the fabric, using a slightly narrower seam allowance of 6 mm (¼ in) so the stitching doesn't show when sewn to the final piece with a 1 cm (⅜ in) seam allowance. To add the folds, start with the needle down, fold the fabric over the desired amount and then guide the fold until it has been sewn. Repeat this as frequently as desired (I usually aim for around every 4 cm [1½ in]).

My limited edition chair for Studio Janettie (co-founded with Charlotte Beevor).

SEWING ON PIPING OR TRIM

Now you're ready to attach the piping cord to your project. These same steps will apply for all types of trim being sewn onto fabric. The goal is to get the piping to lie flat without any wrinkles. If you can see wrinkles in the fabric over the cord, this will show at the end so pull it nice and tight as you sew and keep it as flat as possible.

MATERIALS AND TOOLS:
- Piping
- Piping foot

1. Attach the piping foot to the sewing machine.
2. Make sure the piping measures 1cm (⅜ in) from the sewn line to the raw edge. That way you can match the edges while you sew for ease. If your piping is wider you'll need to trim it down. If it's narrower make sure you follow the seam allowance on the main fabric.
3. Start sewing your trim at the least visible point of your item, as where you begin is where you'll have a join to close the piping. If you're sewing a box cushion, for example, I advise starting at the back towards one side. You don't want to start in the corner as it's tricky to join the piping and sew the corner at the same time.
4. With the fabric right side up, line up the raw edge of the piping with the raw edge of the fabric.
5. Place the piping foot over the piping, leaving approximately 2.5 cm (1 in) free before the needle. Sew straight towards the corner.

6 About 10 cm (4 in) before the corner, stop sewing and keep the needle down. Cut small snips in the piping border where it will go around the corner, approximately 4 cm (1½ in) before and after the corner. Do not cut past the sewn line or you'll create a hole and be able to see the piping cord.

7 Continue to sew the piping slowly towards the corner. Stop with the needle down at the corner.

8 Turn the fabric 90 degrees towards the direction you want to sew. Match the piping with the raw edge. Continue sewing.

9 Continue all the way around, repeating for all other corners.

10 When you are back to where you started, leave a gap of 5 cm (2 in). Cut any excess piping, leaving a 7.5 cm (3 in) end.

11 To close the piping cord you will need to find the point where the two lengths of piping overlap. First open the end of the piping cord using a seam ripper.

12 Trim the piping cord and fabric on the end you started with (this is still enclosed in the fabric). Then trim just the cord in the open end so that it matches up to make one long continuous length of piping without any bulky overlap and without a gap between cords.

13 Fold the open fabric back on itself to hide the raw edge. Place the enclosed end inside.

14 Close the fabric and sew into place to make a continuous length of closed piping. The join will be straight here, unlike the joins sewn previously when making the piping, which are diagonal.

If you're sewing a curve you will need to make snips in the fabric for any curved areas to ensure the piping is flexible enough to lie flat as you sew.

ATTACHING PIPING OR TRIM WITH STAPLES

When you're attaching piping to an outside back, headboard border or any other area that is stapled on, the main difference is that it doesn't matter how wide the piping has been sewn. You won't need to trim it down if it's wide, unlike when you're sewing it on. Usually areas where the piping or trim is stapled on are open-ended, meaning they will not need the piping ends joined together at the end to form a continuous loop of piping.

MATERIALS AND TOOLS:
- Piping
- Staple gun
- Back tack card (optional)

1   Start at one end, the left if right-handed. Staple the piping to the wooden frame, ensuring that the cord is matched up to the edge. It should not be over the edge or have a gap. Try to make it as flush as possible all the way around.

2   Work around the piece, ensuring the piping is pulled tight lengthways to remove any creases or wrinkles. Pulling it lengthways will also ensure straight lines.

3   Make snips when you reach corners or any curved areas in order for the piping or trim to lie flat.

4   If adding back tack card to attach the next layer of fabric, these initial staples can be placed beneath the sewn line and can be quite spaced.

5   If you are not using back tack card, ensure the staples are close enough together that the piping won't pull away from the frame in any areas. Usually a 1 cm (⅜ in) gap between each will suffice.

ADDING STUDS

Studs are a great way to add some shine and interest to a piece. They accentuate the shape and lead the eye around the item. Studs come in all sizes and colours so if the classics aren't your style, consider larger studs in matt or colourful shades.

Studs work particularly well around the edge of headboards. If you plan to stud the edge of a headboard, leave the area free of foam (the same width as the studs you're using). It's hard to stud through thick foam, so I'd advise only adding studs to a foam with a maximum thickness of 1.5 cm (½ in). Otherwise they will pop out and will look bumpy.

Remember if you are going to add studs (to the outside back of an item in particular) that you won't want lots of staples in the way. Instead use a few temporary staples to hold the fabric in place. Then use the studs, instead of staples, to hold the fabric (removing the temporary staples as you go).

If your studs aren't going to be continuous and you've opted to space out the studs, you'll need to plan the spacing. As with buttons do not mark the fabric with pen or chalk; instead use pins.

For a row of continuous studs there is the option to use strips of faux studs. The strips are already in long rows and you simply add a real stud between three or four faux ones to hold them in place. They can be bent around curves or corners as needed. Use scissors to cut where needed. I usually make sure all the corners are real studs and not the faux ones so that they lie flat on the bulky areas.

The trickiest part of adding studs is tapping them in and keeping them straight. If they bend as they go in, the spacing will not be even. If you're adding studs to a hard piece of wood you may want to drill tiny pilot holes (thinner than the point of the stud itself) on your pinned marks so the studs go in easier. Do not drill big holes because the studs won't stay in.

Using a nylon-tipped hammer will protect the studs from scratching. If you're using coloured studs or coated studs a nylon-tipped hammer is essential.

A stud spacer tool will help you keep your studs in straight lines. The wider end allows five to be held in line at once in a continuous line. The thinner end is for replacing one at a time.

1: If studding through the fabric, cut two separate pieces of foam, leaving a gap between, wide enough for the studs you want to use.

2: If studding the edge, leave it free of foam by the width of the stud you are using. This example has been left open at the end to demonstrate this.

1

2

FLUTES

Flutes (sometimes called channels) are one of my favourite upholstered elements for their impact on a piece. They add an element of texture and structure which I think speaks to a certain level of craftsmanship.

They have definitely come back into fashion recently for both traditional and contemporary pieces. You'll see fluted backs everywhere from banquette seats in high-end restaurants to headboards in boutique hotels.

There are so many ways to achieve this look. Many novice upholsterers, when tackling a fluted headboard, make individual boards and hang them closely side by side to give the illusion of flutes. This is a great solution if your flutes are quite wide and you haven't yet mastered other upholstery techniques to give a more refined finish. Because a headboard hangs on the wall, this method disguises the fact that each panel is separate. But flutes on furniture cannot be done like this.

It's worth noting that the kind of flutes I'm teaching here are deep, where the groove goes into the foam and back as far as the frame, the same way it would for deep buttoning. You will probably have seen some flutes on mass-produced furniture where the cover was sewn – which gives a faint illusion of flutes, but actually the fabric lies very flat. This is kind of a cheat on flutes which works well for mass-producing items because it's much quicker to sew through the fabric plus a thin foam. To achieve this, simply sew the fabric through the polyester wadding to a piece of 1.5 cm (½ in) or 0.5 cm (¼ in) foam with a bottom cloth on the back and upholster as normal.

Here, I'm going to teach you one of the many ways to achieve a deep flute which is more complicated, but totally worth it in my opinion.

Fabric by Linwood, 'double dragon' in hot orange

Fluted headboard or banquette

For a flat board such as a headboard or bench backrest, the technique is to back tack each section. This allows you to ensure each flute is parallel and equal and there will be no movement in the fabric. It can take a little longer but it's a very durable and sturdy way to upholster and the finish will last for years.

You will want to decide how deep the flutes will be. I usually use 4 cm (1½ in) or 5 cm (2 in) foam. These thicknesses can be glued in without a bevelled edge and pulled down to create a domed effect as you pull the upholstery tight. Thicker foams are quite tricky to handle as they may need to be bevelled.

MATERIALS AND TOOLS:
- Fabric
- Wooden board
- Foam (5 cm (2 in) thick or less)
- Long ruler
- Marker pen
- FR liner (if using)
- Polyester wadding
- Staple gun
- Back tack card
- Spray adhesive

1   Start by measuring the length of your item and deciding how wide each flute will be so they are equal all the way along. Larger flutes will be quicker as there are fewer to make. Decide if you want a scalloped top edge by taking the foam over the top edge. Alternatively, you can finish the foam level with the top for a straight edge (always cut the foam 1 cm (⅜ in) longer than needed to hide the wooden edge at the top).

2   Mark the foam, using a long ruler and a permanent marker, at the decided width for each flute (see Measuring & cutting foam, page 152). The length of each flute will be the total height of the back plus the depth if you want to take the foam over the top edge for a scalloped edge. Cut these out so you have a piece of foam for each individual flute. Feel free to cut them slightly longer, as you can trim them down later. Ensure your cuts are really straight (especially along the long edge) because wobbly foam will make wobbly flutes.

3   Mark the flutes onto the wooden board with a marker pen, taking the line over the edge on the top and bottom. This helps keep the lines straight. Also mark the top and bottom of the board so you know which way to fit it. You can do this on the front (for reference as you're upholstering) and the back (for when you need to fit it to the frame or wall).

4   There are two options to cut out your fabric. The first is in one long continuous length. If you are using a plain and/or a fabric with no pile this is the best option. Cut the height as needed, but add 7.5 cm (3 in) at either end so that you can wrap it over the top and bottom edge – check this is enough to cover the thickness of your foam plus the thickness of the board at each end. Alternatively, if you have a pattern that needs to be upright or a pile in your fabric, cut enough fabric pieces to cover each foam flute. Do not sew them together; instead you will join the fabric in the crease of the flutes so it's hidden. These still need to be longer than the board, so add 7.5 cm (3 in) at either end.

5   Start at one end and glue the first piece of foam in place, keeping it in line with your markings on the board. The bottom edge of the foam should be flush with the edge of the board, with the top edge going slightly over.

6   Add the FR liner, if using (see Adding a fire-retardant (FR) layer, page 160).

7   Glue polyester wadding into place over the flute, exactly even with the edge of the foam.

8   Take your fabric and, starting at the side edge of the board, staple all the way along on the back. No need for temporary staples. Ensure the fabric runs straight and has enough at the top and bottom to cover the ends of the foam and board.

9   Next, pull the fabric sideways across the foam flute with equal tension from top to bottom and staple the fabric in place just past your next marked line on the board. Start in the middle and work your way up and down. To ensure it's tight enough, you will need to push the foam down and pull the fabric taut. You're working sideways here and leaving the top and bottom open until the very end.

5

6

9

10 With that flute done, it's time to prepare for the second. Fold the fabric back on itself and back tack the fabric along the marked line on the board, which is now slightly covered by fabric but visible at the top and bottom edge (see Adding back tacking card, page 178). Ensure your back tack is always lined up on the same side of the line to ensure your flutes stay even.

11 Check you are happy that the lines are parallel before you move on.

12 Repeat the process of sticking down your foam, FR liner and polyester wadding before stapling your top fabric into place. Do this all the way along. When you need to join a new piece of fabric, start by folding it back on itself and back tacking it into place. Then continue as normal by pulling the flute sideways and securing it into place with even tension. You may want to think about pattern matching when adding new pieces of patterned fabric. If you are working with individual pieces of fabric for each flute, staple the fabric into place along the first edge and secure with back tack card before sticking your foam, FR liner and polyester into place.

13 For the last flute your fabric will be finished off over the edge of the board on the back. You can then cut away any excess fabric from the side.

14 Close the corners on the top and bottom of one end (see Finishing corners, page 166).

15 Begin finishing the top and bottom edges, working away from the completed corners. Whether you are taking the foam over the top edge or not, the process is the same. Start by stapling the fabric closed above and below the centre of the flute. Continue stapling, working towards the flute groove.

16 Fold the fabric under itself at the groove until you have a neat fold that continues straight from either the top or bottom of the flute. You want a nice straight line so your flutes stay looking evenly spaced. Pull the fabric as tight as possible and staple it at the back. If you need to cut away any excess fabric to achieve neat, straight folds, do this.

17 Work your way along the top and the bottom, then cut away any excess fabric.

18 Close the final two corners (see Finishing corners, page 166).

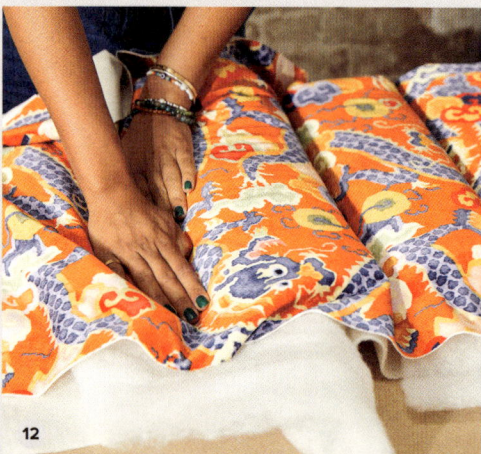

15

Fluted chairs

The difference when making flutes for a chair is the curved back. Rather than a headboard where the flutes are all even and parallel, on a chair you need to taper the flutes so they are slightly narrower at the bottom and allow more space at the top to curve around the shape, but also to curve over the top edge. Flutes on furniture like this need to be sewn rather than back tacked. Thin flutes are more complicated to make as there are more of them and they can be harder to stuff full.

If your item was previously fluted you can unpick these carefully, labelling each one, and use the old cover as a template. Before you unpick it, transfer the lines and shape to a scrap piece of fabric or bottom cloth – this will be used as the back piece to sew your channels.

MATERIALS AND TOOLS:
- Fabric
- Dipryl or old fabric (for planning)
- Bottom cloth or scrap fabric (for the template/backing)
- Tailor's chalk
- Piping cord
- Piping foot
- Polyester wadding
- Pins

MAKING A TEMPLATE FOR NEW FLUTES

1 If you need to make a new template because you are adding flutes, first start by pinning a piece of old fabric or dipryl to the inside back. It will need to cover the entire area including the top edge. Decide how many flutes you would like on the piece.

2 I would advise having a flute in the centre rather than either side of centre. Use tailor's chalk to start to map out your faint lines. Once you have completed a rough plan, take the fabric off and use a ruler to check the flutes are evenly distributed and straight. They will be wider at the top.

3 Use a different colour to mark your final lines. Place the fabric onto the furniture to check you are happy with the template and transfer the lines of the top and bottom edge of the frame to the template fabric.

4 Transfer this plan onto another piece of fabric exactly as it is. Later we will sew this piece to our front flutes to make pockets, which will be filled. This can be scrap fabric or bottom cloth as it will not be seen.

5 Number each channel and label the top of each. Use this template to mark out your fabric but remember to add your seam allowance to each side (not the top and the bottom), as well as the allowance for the filling. Your seam allowance for this will be bigger than the standard as later piping cord needs to be sewn to each seam. Allow a 3 cm (1¼ in) seam allowance. The allowance for the filling is usually an extra 1.5 cm (½ in) either side. Mark with chalk on each piece where the top and bottom of the frame is for each flute. Add an extra 15 cm (6 in) of fabric at the top and bottom of each flute to cover the frame and have enough to pull into place. Before cutting the fabric, ensure you have enough at the far edge of your first and last piece to wrap around the frame.

Templating flutes

A – Template fabric

B – Pins

C – Central line to measure from

D – Final lines drawn on clearly from top of frame to bottom including the shape around the top edge

E – Flute design transferred to main fabric

F – Top edge shape also transferred to each flute

G – Wide side panels to allow fabric to go around the frame. Dotted line illustrates where the edge of frame will be

H – Waste fabric

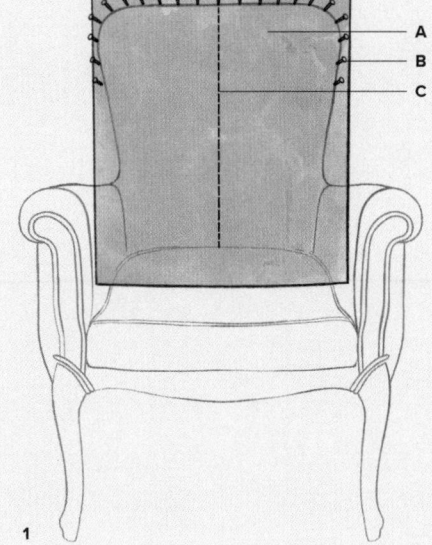

1

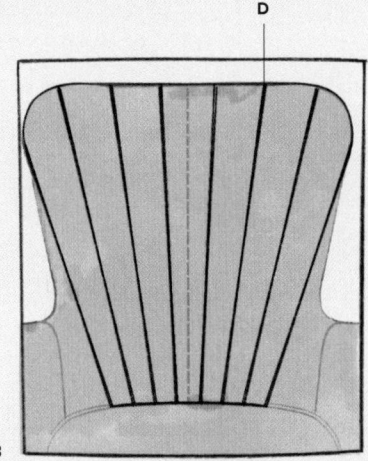

3

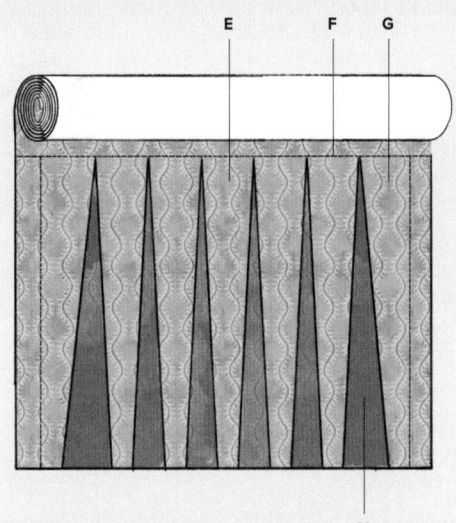

5

SEWING THE FLUTES

1 Label and cut out each piece.
2 Sew all pieces together using the wider 3 cm (1¼ in) seam allowance. Sew the full length of the channel together from end to end.
3 Sew piping cord to each seam using the piping foot attachment on the sewing machine. The piping cord should start at the point marked for the top of the frame and end at the bottom of the frame (do not sew to the extra 15 cm [6 in] of fabric either end). Leave 15 cm (6 in) of cord at either end for pulling.
4 Take the scrap fabric or bottom cloth previously marked out with the flute design. Sew this to the flutes by matching the lines together. Sew one flute at a time with the fabric folded back on itself to avoid visible stitching on the finished item.
5 Begin to fill the pockets. Roll lengths of polyester wadding into tubes then feed them through the flutes until they poke out at either end. This can be tricky to do with thin flutes. You may need to use a ruler or stick to push the filling through the channels.
6 Trim the wadding at the bottom of each flute in line with the mark for the base of the frame.
7 Now you are ready to upholster your fluted fabric onto your frame. Start by stapling the back fabric into place at the bottom in the middle only. Ensure the fabric lies flat and central following the curves of your piece. Starting with the bottom of the inside back, line up the centre and pull the fabric through the gap in the frame towards the back.
8 Work your way towards the sides, pulling the fabric taut as you go.
9 Along the bottom edge gently pull the piping cord on each seam and staple this securely into place. You will be pulling against it later on so it needs to be secure.
10 Now work along the top edge. Pull the piping cord on the top edge firmly, making sure the lines are straight and on your marked points. Pull them firmly and staple them into place to secure. Start in the middle and work your way towards the edges, ensuring the spacing is correct for each flute as you go until you are happy with the tension from top to bottom of each flute.
11 To secure the top fabric, you will need to cut away some of the overhanging wadding filling. Do this evenly for all flutes.
12 Pull your top fabric over the top edge, making sure you're happy with the shape of the flute at the top (add more filling if needed, or cut more away). Then staple into place. For the seams, cut away any excess and ensure the folds are in line with the flutes. You may need to unpick the seams to get this to lie flat (as the sewing extends 15 cm [6 in] past the frame).
13 Smooth the sides over and upholster as normal.

Sewing the flutes

A – Left side panel with
wider fabric to go
around frame
B – Next flute lying face to
face to be sewn together
C – Wider sewing allowance
of 3 cm (1¼ in)
D – Piping sewn into place
E – Back of the chair
F – Bottom of the inside
back secured in place
G – Top flutes stapled in
place by pulling the
piping cord tight and
pulling and smoothing
the fabric in place
H – Open flute with
wadding cut down
level with frame, ready
to be stapled closed

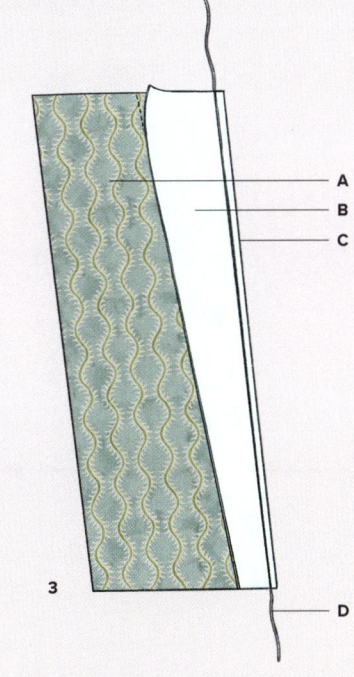

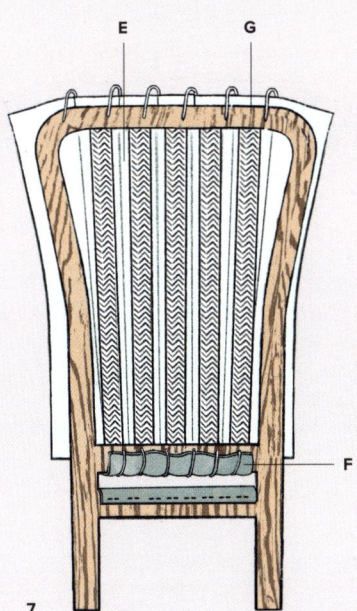

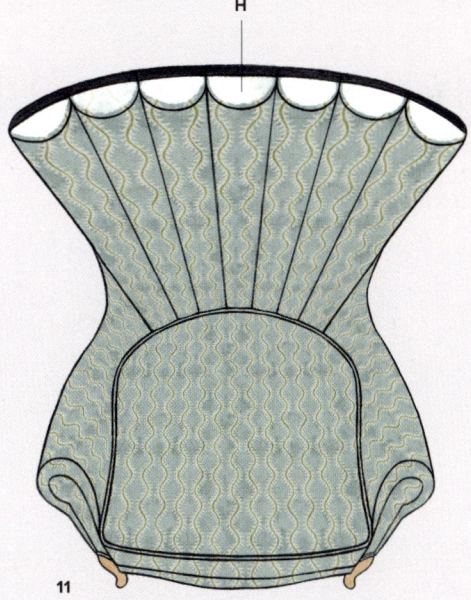

SLIP STITCHING

This is the best way to attach the outside back fabric along the sides. This method is great for fabrics of all thickness and furniture of all shapes, especially where the sides are not straight as, unlike ply grip (see page 184), this method handles curves well. The aim is to sew an invisible stitch to hold the fabric in place.

It's best to use a curved needle as it comes back out of the fabric easily when sewing as opposed to a straight needle, which you'll lose in the fabric. Unlike embroidery you do not have access to the other side here to push the needle back out. You can find curved needles online and also in Afro-Caribbean hair shops, as they're used for sewing weaves, general fact for you there!

MATERIALS AND TOOLS:
- Curved needle
- Thread
- Pins
- Scissors

1   Cut a long double length (about 1 m [39 in]) of thread and thread it through your curved needle, tying the ends together.

2   Begin by pinning the fabric in place. Make sure you fold any excess fabric underneath or cut it away to leave just a 1–2 cm (⅜–¾ in) fold. Pay particular attention to the corners to ensure they are not too bulky and as much excess is cut away as possible, especially where the side fold meets your back tacking (see page 178) at the top.

3   If sewing the outside back, that has been back tacked at the top, start sewing at the top corner and move downwards. This will ensure you don't have any wrinkles as you smooth the fabric down towards the open end at the base. Make sure the knot is hidden in a part of the fabric which will not be seen, close to the area you want to start. Then pull the needle out at the start point through the fabric, which is fixed down with staples.

4   Insert the needle into the opposite fabric, directly across from the point it just came out of. A top tip to avoid any visible thread is to sew ever so slightly above the initial hole on the opposite side. Move the needle down inside the fabric, and bring it out further down. Repeat the action, inserting into the first side and then bringing it out again further down.

5   Work your way down the pinned edge, matching the sewing either side. As you work, pull the thread tightly to close the seam.

6   Secure the final part by sewing a small knot. I usually knot three times before pushing the needle through and out of a part of the fabric underneath that cannot be seen. Staple the threads in place and cut the needle free to finish.

FINISHING FABRIC AROUND LEGS

Fixed legs which are flush to the corner of an item (such as on a dining chair) create a small issue because the staples would be seen if you upholster in the standard way.

The fabric can't be secured in the traditional way, but does need to be held down to avoid movement when the item is being used. To combat this there are a few options.

Gimp studs

The simplest way is to use small gimp studs. I buy white gimp studs and use a permanent marker in a matching colour to colour the head to make it as invisible as possible. Then, using a nylon-tipped hammer (so as not to damage the tack head), tap it in as close to the edge as possible.

Upholstery studs

A small number of upholstery studs can be used in a row to secure the corner. Avoid using a strip of faux studs as the purpose here is to secure the fabric, so individual studs are better. Use a nylon-tipped hammer to avoid scratching the studs as they are hammered into place.

Piping

Alternatively, you can staple some piping into place. Ensure it is in line with the bottom edge of the fabric so the corner will look straight. Finish the piping ends off neatly. The staples should be close to the sewn line and relatively close together to avoid any movement in the fabric when the item is used. Then sew your fabric to the piping using a slip stitch.

Trim

You can also staple the fabric in place and glue a trim of your choice over it to hide the staples (similar to Working with show wood, page 180).

Scroll arms

A – Saddle arm with pleats
B – Ruched arm with fascia.
     Ruched pleats around
     the outside and a piped
     fascia in the centre
C – Modern scroll arm.
     Inside arm fabric is
     finished on the outside
     edge (covering the top
     and front of the arm).
     One pleat. With piping
     along the outside arm
D – Pleated scroll arm.
     Pleats add more interest
     to a plain scroll arm.

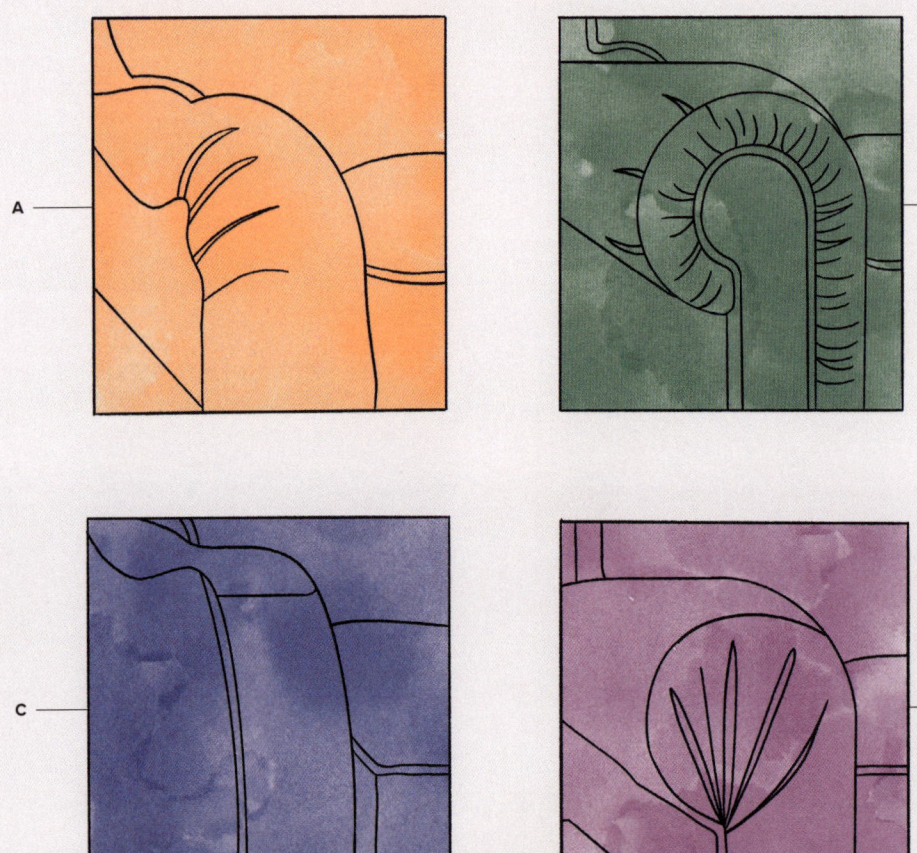

SCROLL ARMS AND PLEATS

Scroll arms and other curved areas are often upholstered with matching pleats. The key is to measure your pleats to achieve even spacing and a symmetry on both sides of your item.

You can take a template of the first arm, reverse the paper (by turning it to face away from you and extending your marked lines onto the back side) and use it to match your pleats on the other arm if you find this easier.

Remember your pleats should always be folded underneath so that they are closed if you're smoothing the item from top to bottom. We want to avoid pockets where dust will gather or things will get caught.

If you are adding pleats to corners it is the same process. Fold them underneath so the top is closed. Then measure the placement or make a template and replicate this on the other side(s).

SKIRTS & VALENCES

Skirts are a more traditional finish to a piece of furniture to hide the legs and opening underneath. When used on a bed, they are called valences.

They can make the furniture appear denser. If your item had a skirt on before, you can decide whether you want to replace this or remove it to reveal the legs. Furniture without skirts allows more light to pass underneath and can therefore create the illusion of more space in small rooms. If you are adding a skirt to the item, avoid using too much padding on the bottom where the skirt will hang when you are upholstering the frame.

Skirts usually match the overall fabric but you can do a contrast fabric if you prefer. You can also play with the shape to achieve a scalloped or wavy edge if you want to avoid traditional straight lines; or add a contrast fabric at the corner gussets which peeks out, to add a pop of colour or pattern.

There are a few different ways of making skirts. I usually add the skirt last when the item has been fully upholstered rather than building it into the cover itself. Using this method allows each side of the skirt to be made and attached separately to align them perfectly.

You will need a backing fabric for the skirt (a plain cotton cloth is fine) and, depending on the stiffness of your main fabric, you may also need to insert buckram or Skirtex (the correct width for the skirt you are making) so that it holds its shape.

The difference for a valence is you'll need a large piece of fabric to sit over the bed base to which you'll attach all of the pieces.

Standard kick pleat

MATERIALS AND SPECIAL TOOLS:

- Main fabric
- Backing fabric
- Already made piping (enough to go around the base of the piece of furniture)
- Buckram or Skirtex to stiffen the skirt
- Pins
- Tailor's chalk
- Piping foot
- Back tack card

1 First measure each side of the item and make a note of each length. If you are pattern matching the fabric, make sure you know which side is which as they probably aren't all equal. You may also want to break up the panels on the long sides, so decide this while in the planning stage.

2 Work out the height of the skirt you want to make. Measure on your item of furniture, leaving 1.5 cm (½ in) between the floor and the bottom of the skirt. The skirt should sit at least a few inches higher than the top of the foot or leg, usually about 12.5–18 cm (5–7 in) tall. Using pins, mark the height of the top of the skirt. When you've done this all the way around, you can faintly mark the corners with tailor's chalk to reinforce this line.

3 Pin the piping into place along the line of pins where the top of your skirt will be. The piping seam should sit on the pin line.

4 Using chalk, mark on the piping where the pleats will go, in the corners on each side and any between panels on the long sides (if you're making multiple panels for them). Put

Skirt

A – Slipper chair
with skirt

B – Piping and line to
measure for skirt
width and height

C – Box pleat

D – Measure and
pin piping here

E – Place pin
perpendicular on
piping to show
corner positioning

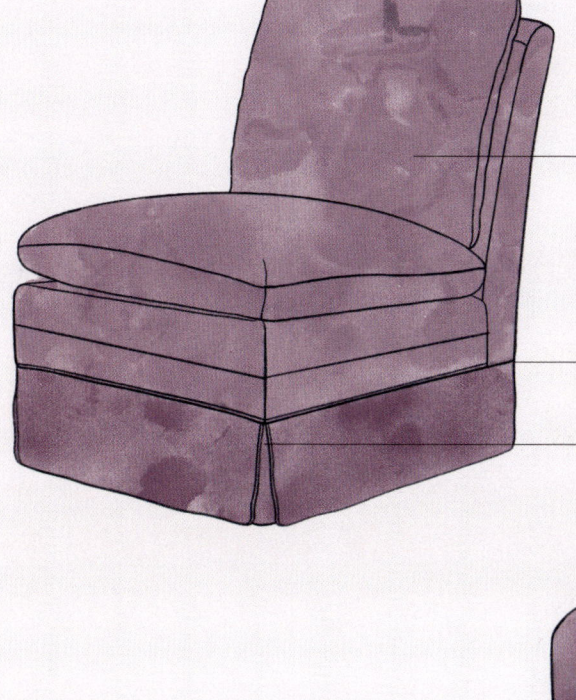

Instead of a kick pleat
you could sew a frilled
or gathered skirt. See
Sewing a frill, page 202.

Sections of skirt

A – Skirt with buckram
B – Gusset without buckram
C – Skirt with 5 cm
  (2 in) border
D – Liner
E – Gusset with bottom
  border only

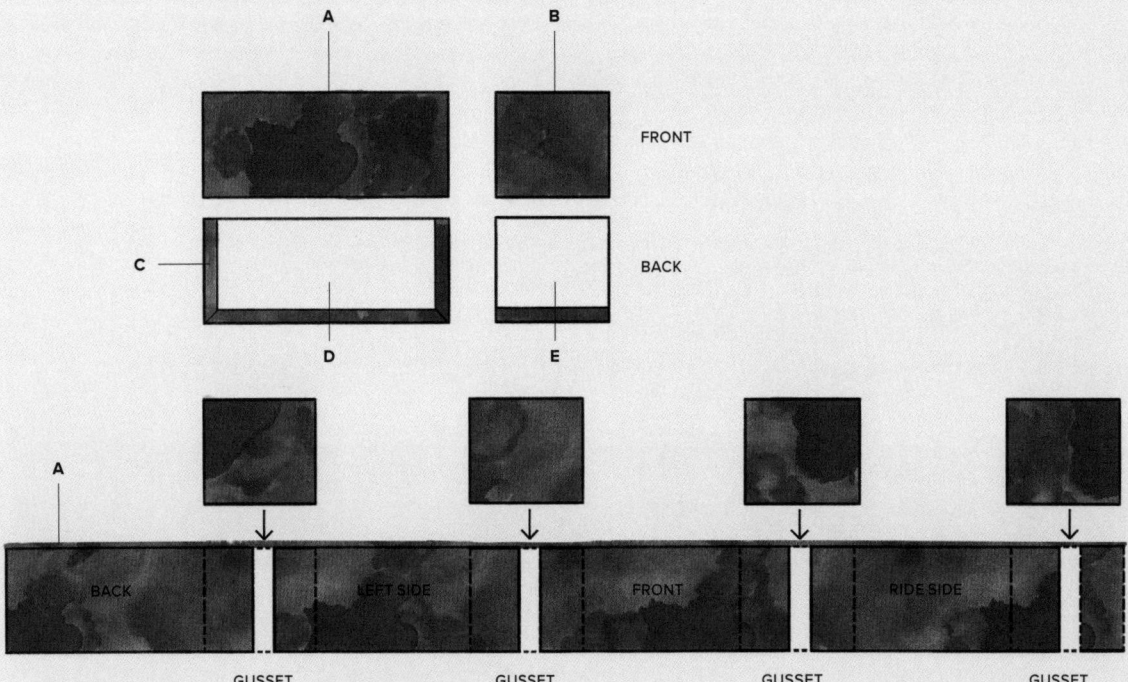

perpendicular pins on the piping to highlight these lines.

5   Mark where the piping will be sewn closed to form a continuous loop. I usually put the join at the back of the item.

6   Remove the piping from the piece but leave the pins in and the marked chalk lines at the correct height.

7   Cut the main fabric out for each skirt panel, adding 10 cm (4 in) to the height, and the seam allowance plus 5 cm (2 in) to either side of the panel. Cut the backing fabric minus 3 cm (1¼ in) to the height (this will give a border of 1.5 cm (½ in) on the back) and the same width as the main fabric.

8   Cut out buckram pieces for each panel the same size as the desired finished panel minus 0.5 cm (¼ in) either side to comfortably sit within the sewn skirt.

9   Cut the main fabric and liner for the gussets (for between each join). These can be in a matching or contrasting fabric. You do not need to cut buckram for these. You will want around 10 cm (4 in) either side of the corner so cut these around 20 cm (8 in) wide and the same heights as the main and liner for your other pieces.

10   With right sides facing, sew the bottom edge of the main fabric and liner for the skirt panel together.

11   Using an iron, press open the seam.

12   Match the tops of the main fabric and liner. There should be a 1.5 cm (½ in) border of main fabric along the bottom of the back.

13   Match the sides and sew them closed. Snip the corners and cut away any overhanging fabric to get rid of the bulk. Turn the panels right side out.

14   Use the iron and a regulator needle to press the side seams. Ironing it correctly will help it sit flat later on the item.

15   Place the buckram inside and press the skirt section to ensure it's flat and the buckram fits inside without twisting.

16   Fold the sides in 5 cm (2 in) each and press.

17   Repeat for each panel.

18   Sew the gusset panels together in the same way, following steps 9–14. These will not have the borders on the sides, only at the bottom on the back.

19   Match up your pinned piping with the correct skirt panels, placing gusset panels in the middle of each join (they should sit underneath the panels,

perfectly centred to the join). Make sure the panels and gussets are placed so they will hang the desired finished length.

20   Attach the piping foot to the sewing machine and sew all the pieces together.

21   Finally, you are ready to attach the sewn skirt to the furniture along your chalk line. Start at the front to ensure the corners are aligned and the skirt is centred and repin the skirt in place.

22   Lift up the panels and staple in place on all sides using 16 mm (⅝ in) staples, removing the pins as you go. The staples can be quite spaced out at this stage. Check you are happy with the positioning and it is straight.

23   Once positioning is correct, staple it into place with back tack card to ensure a crisp line. Push the back tack card up against the piping on the underside, avoiding the corners. Check the skirt hangs down without distortion. You may need to slightly tap it with a rubber mallet if it is kicking up anywhere.

24   The skirt should lie flat with no twists or creases, but steam if needed.

25   Join the piping in the same way as explained in Sewing on piping or trim, but instead of sewing it closed you will staple it closed. See Attaching piping or trim with staples, page 206.

FRENCH SEAM/ TOP STITCHING

This technique is a way of finishing a seam so there is a visible line of sewing. It's decorative but also practical as it allows the seam to lie flatter and makes it more durable (if you sew it with grosgrain ribbon, even more so). It's very commonly found in car upholstery or on box cushions.

MATERIALS AND SPECIFIC TOOLS:
- Basting tape
- Grosgrain ribbon
- Decorative thread

1   Sew your seam as normal, but go slowly to ensure a straight line.
2   Cut a piece of basting tape and grosgrain ribbon the length of the seam. Stick the tape to the grosgrain.
3   Use your fingers to press the seam open.
4   Peel off the backing on the basting tape and stick the grosgrain in place along the middle of the seam.
5   Turn the fabric over. Line the edge of the presser foot up with the seam and sew either side. This line of top stitching should be thinner than your seam allowance to catch the seam fabric underneath. The sewing should pass through the double layer of fabric and grosgrain.

TIP

If you have a right and left edge guide presser foot you can use this to glide along the existing seam and keep your sewing straight. Without this presser foot you can use a regular presser foot and sew slowly to ensure a straight line.

You may want to adjust the stitch length for a slightly longer, more decorative stitch.

FRENCH MATTRESS EDGE

French mattress edges are used to accentuate the seams on a box cushion. This style of cushion usually has buttons or toggles in the middle. As the buttons or toggles hold the cover in place (and would need to be cut off to release the cover) these cushions are usually sewn closed and do not have zips.

The cushion can be filled with foam, fibre or feathers. I think softer filling, such as feather or fibre, give a better, more authentic look than foam does. Make the soft fibre or feather inner slightly larger than the cover (by 2.5 cm [1 in] all the way around) to make sure it's full. A French mattress edge looks great on outdoor furniture or large box cushions for window benches.

You can also add tufting or buttons if you wish. These are added in the same way as adding buttons on page 196, but tie a button onto the back as well so that the cushion can be reversed.

French mattress edge cushion

MATERIALS AND TOOLS:
- Box cushion outer (see page 88)
- Cushion inner
- Pins
- Large curved or straight needle (if sewing by hand)
- Decorative thread

1. Cut the cover 2.5 cm (1 in) wider on each side to allow for the extra sewing if you are using a sewing machine. If hand stitching, make the cover the usual size to fit the inner.
2. Sew the box cushion together as normal, sewing the borders to the top and bottom sections (see page 94).
3. Leave an opening big enough to get the cushion inside.
4. Turn the cover the right side out.

Here you have the option to either sew on the machine for a small mattress effect, or by hand for a more full and rounded edge. Personally, I prefer the look of the hand-sewn finish.

SEWING ON THE SEWING MACHINE

1   Pinch the seam together with the seam edge centred. If needed, you can pin the fabric together. Remove the pins as you sew so that you do not sew over them, which may break the sewing machine needle.
2   Sew 1 cm (⅜ in) in along the seam to create the French mattress edge.
3   Do this on all the seams.
4   Insert the cushion inner.
5   Pin the opening together and sew it closed either on the sewing machine or with a slip stitch.
6   Then sew the French mattress edge over this seam so that it matches the other seams.
7   If you are adding buttons or toggles add these at the end in the same way as floating buttons (see page 196), but with a button or toggle on both sides of the cushion. You can add the buttons in either a square or diamond design.

SEWING BY HAND

1   The top line will be 2.5cm (1 in) above the seam. The bottom line will be about 2.5 cm (1 in) below the seam on the side border. Use pins to mark out the points at which you want to sew, usually spaced about 5 cm (2 in) apart (depending on the size of your item). The pins on the border should be between the ones on the top edge.
2   Starting at the back edge, use a large curved needle (or a long straight needle) and a thread colour of your choice (it will be visible) and start to sew on the marked points connecting the top with the border. Leave about 3 mm (⅛ in) of visible thread on top of the fabric for each mark.
3   Sew through the soft fibre or feather filling so that the filling creates a soft, rounded edge.
4   Pull the thread tight to scrunch the border. Keep an even tension all the way along so that your French mattress edge is even.
5   Do this on the top edge and the bottom edge of the box cushion. Ensure the border markings and sewn line are directly over each other to give a square effect along the border.
6   If you are adding buttons or toggles add these at the end in the same way as floating buttons (see page 196), but with a button or toggle on both sides of the cushion. You can add the buttons in either a square or diamond design.

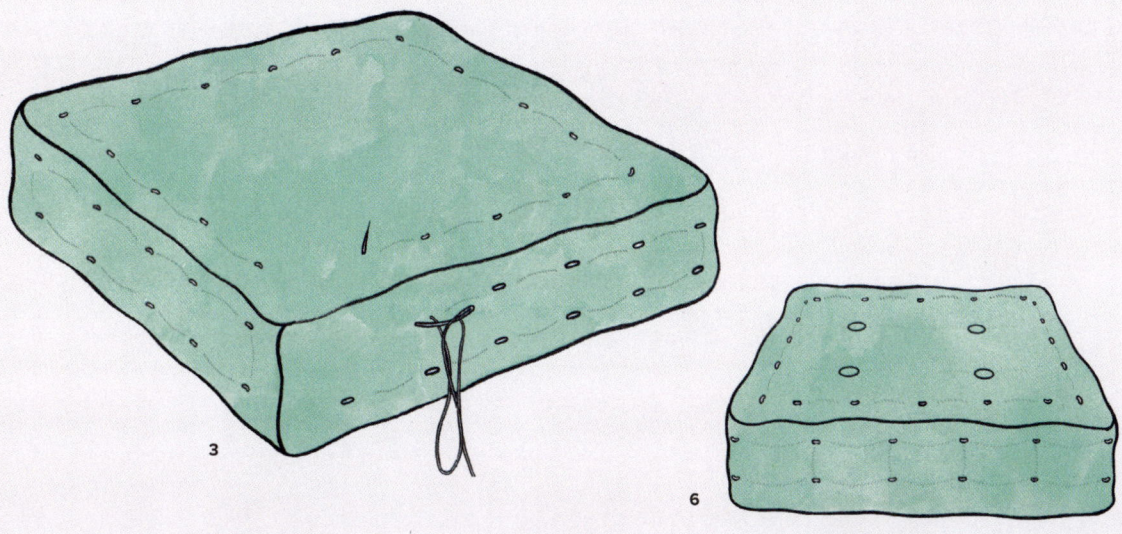

CHAPTER SIX

Make do
&
mend

MAKE DO AND MEND

I guess you could argue that all reupholstery falls into the category of 'make do and mend' but I want to give you other, more cost-effective ways to fix your furniture. These small solutions are great for addressing small cuts, tears and stains in order to make your furniture as long-lasting as possible.

You may have heard of *Kintsugi*, the Japanese art of fixing broken ceramics with gold, where the philosophy is to embrace the repair as part of the new history of the piece. I believe this can be applied to upholstery as well. Repairs do not always have to blend into the affected area; sometimes it's best to embrace it with a contrast fabric or thread, which celebrates the solution and the new stage of life.

Darning

For small holes in the top fabric, darning is a great solution. You will need a curved needle (if working on a fixed piece of upholstery, or a straight needle if

working on a removable cover) and thick thread or yarn to either match or contrast your fabric (depending on if you want to blend or highlight your fix). Decide whether you want a square, circle or organic shape and bear this in mind with your thread placement. First, stitch across the hole going sideways, sewing slightly beyond the hole on either side. Keep the threads close together until they cover the hole and tie off your thread when you are done. Now sew top to bottom, weaving the threads between the existing sideways stitches to form a thatch, keeping them close together to cover the hole in both directions. Again, tie off the thread when you are done.

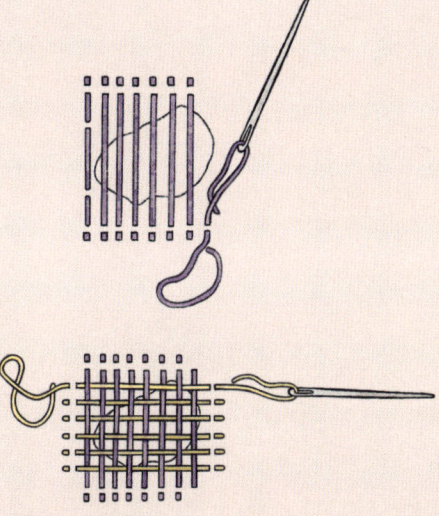

I adore this mended chair by the talented Sarah Neubert. Visible mending celebrates the history of a piece by not trying to hide the mends.

Patching

The other option for small holes or rips is to sew a patch on. Again, why not embrace a contrasting fabric. You can glue a small piece of fabric inside the hole to help stop the fabric from tearing more. Then cut a patch and fold the edges underneath so the cut edges are not visible. Sew on the patch using a slip stitch. You can use a decorative stitch to create visual interest, if you prefer. Patching is a great option for cat scratch areas on furniture, as you can use more durable fabrics to make the patches.

Fixing seams

If a seam has started to open revealing a hole, you can simply use a slip stitch to close it back up. First, pin the seams back together and then follow the slip stitch method on page 220.

Replacing cushions

Often box cushions go flat over time as either the feather and down flatten or the foam degrades. For replacement foam wrapped in polyester you can follow the steps to making a new cushion inner on page 93. Alternatively, you can order cushion inners made to size online with your choice of filling (feather and down, polyester, foam or a mix). To get the correct size, make sure to measure the size of the cover, not the degraded inner. Be specific with the supplier that you are supplying the exact size of the cover so they will know whether to add a tiny allowance to fill the cover or not. If they are feather wrapping the cushion it will be very full, so usually extra foam is not added. For soft foam they may add a little extra to ensure the cover is filled out.

You do not have to replace like for like. If you had foam cushions but you would prefer feather, you can swap.

Steaming

Steaming is a great option for cleaning upholstery but be careful. Not all fabrics can handle steam well; silk, for example cannot withstand high temperatures.

Professional upholstery cleaning services can clean your items on site, but always check your fabrics in advance and communicate your findings with the company. If your fabrics are dry-clean only, or have water-repellent, stain-resistant or other treatments, they will have different finishes and not all can be steamed or cleaned. Check before washing or steaming any upholstered covers, as many upholstery fabrics should not be cleaned with water.

Steam can also help revitalise the foam inside if it has flattened over time.

Looking after your items with regular cleaning, using the correct products, will help prolong their life.

Linwood Arlo fabrics
(above). Febrik samples
(left), which I have
sewn together to
create a patchwork.

USING YOUR FABRIC OFFCUTS

Keeping leftover pieces of fabric is an obsession of mine. I hate throwing away usable pieces and always try to avoid waste and sending things to landfill. But offcuts come in all shapes and sizes, so it can be difficult to know what to make with them. As upholsterers, we are used to making large pieces of furniture so smaller pieces can seem unusable. Here I share some of my favourite makes for smaller items!

Patchwork

Making a patchwork is by far the best solution for small offcuts, as you can cut small squares of the same size and sew them together to make a new larger piece of fabric. Mixing patterns and colours together works well for patchwork, and you can even start to make your own patterns within the layout if you like. A rotary cutter is perfect for this as you can layer the offcuts together and cut all the squares out at the same time.

1   If you have a desired layout, arrange your squares before sewing. Make piles in the order you want them to appear in your strip for however many squares long you would like the patchwork to be (for example, 10 squares long).
2   Take two of the squares from the first pile and sew them together with a 1 cm (⅜ in) seam allowance. Do the same with the other squares, joining them all together in one long strip.
3   Repeat with the other piles until you have several strips of sewn squares.
4   Press open each seam with an iron (this helps when joining in the next step).
5   Join each strip together. This is more tricky as you will need to match up each seam to ensure your patchwork sewing is straight in all directions. I do this by holding the cross sections together as I sew each section, but you may prefer to pin them together.
6   Press open the new long seams with an iron.
7   Your patchwork is ready for use! You can make many things with it, including cushion covers, or use it to upholster another project.

Drawer scents

These are a very easy make and a cute way to use herbs and scents at home. Using dried lavender, cedar or mint will help protect against moths. You can sew the scent bags in whatever way you want, as either bags or little cushions for drawers or something to attach to a hanger for your wardrobe.

Doll's house items

If you have or know children with a doll's house, offcuts are perfect for making tiny versions of the furniture you have already reupholstered. You can even make tiny curtains, tablecloths, cushions or doll's clothes. Let yourself get carried away with the possibilities, and if you can recreate your whole home in miniature form, you get bonus points!

Doorstops

In a similar way to the drawer scents, you can sew this in whatever design you want and then add small stones or pebbles to weigh the bag or cushion shape down in order to hold open a door. It's lovely to use fabric in unexpected ways like this throughout your home. If using heavy pebbles, you may want to line the shape before sewing your main fabric. You can even add a thin layer of foam to the bottom to protect your floor.

Trim for other projects – frill or piping

Long offcuts are great to put towards making a contrasting or complementary trim for another project, so always keep hold of them. Long lengths of offcuts are great for frills and diagonal lengths are great for piping on other projects, especially if you need a contrast colour or pattern. If you have long lengths of piping leftover, these are great for using on scatter cushions.

Scatter cushions with different front and back

Plain fabric offcuts can be used for the backs of scatter cushions, thus saving your chosen patterned fabric for just the fronts. Remember that scatter cushions don't always need to be square; try sewing rectangular lumbar shapes or even round bolsters.

Picture frame covers or mounts

I would love to have a totally upholstered room, where everything is covered in fabric! And adding fabric to mirror frames and picture frames is my attempt at starting this phenomenon. Add a thin layer of polyester if you want a more padded look. For thin frames you may need to glue the fabric into place rather than stapling it on.

Buttons

Tiny scraps can be used to make fabric-covered buttons using your button press, which is great if you want contrasting buttons for a project. I usually keep a selection of mismatching buttons in my kit ready to trial on projects that may benefit from floating buttons.

Donate them

Finally, if you don't think you will get around to using your offcuts, you can donate them to people who will use them. Local schools or craft centres may take them, or larger pieces can be donated to charity shops that stock craft materials. I once donated my offcut leather to a crafter who made small leather items such as purses and key rings, so there is always someone out there who will be grateful for free materials, and it's best to avoid sending them to landfill when they can be used.

Lampshades

Long strips of fabric can also be made into drum
lampshades with a drum lampshade kit (bought online).
Alternatively, you could sew a pleated or gathered
shade. One thing to bear in mind is the density
of the fabric, as it may not let much light through,
but for directional up or down light it's perfect.

SUCCESS! HERE'S TO YOU!

It's no easy feat, but you did it! You've made your own bespoke furniture that's completely unique to you and your home. I hope it will colour the memories you make using it with joy and vibrancy.

I hope you've really enjoyed getting to grips with your first upholstery projects using this book as your guide. It can be really daunting disassembling something and reimagining it; getting over that hurdle is the hardest part and deserves acknowledgement. The hard work you have put into mastering these new upholstery skills can be applied to lots of projects and I hope you will continue to explore different shapes, techniques and fabrics. If you want to extend your learning, you can explore traditional upholstery techniques to gain a deeper understanding of the craft and its history.

I believe that having more understanding of how your everyday furniture is made will help you make more informed decisions around what you buy, what you tackle yourself and the materials used. Once I realised I could redesign chairs and sofas, I started designing all sorts of furniture and homeware. I hope your creativity has shone whilst making these projects and continues to bring you joy.

I'm sure that those around you will be impressed with your creations! I hope this will also encourage you to continue your upholstery exploration with confidence.

I came to upholstery in the same way, finding joy creating my own furniture before tackling projects for friends and family, and eventually starting my own business. Who knows where these new skills will lead you!

Me, aged about 7, ready to build things; plus, my prized tool — my grandad's hammer.

FABRIC SUPPLIERS

	TERRITORY			TYPE			SELLING				
	AUS	UK	USA	Small Indie	Large Fabric House	Discount fabrics	Fabric	Leather	Faux Leather	Outdoor Fabric	Trim
Annika Reed		✓		✓			✓				
Bethie Tricks		✓		✓			✓				
Bev's Remnants House	✓					✓	✓				
Bute Fabrics		✓			✓		✓				
Camira Fabrics	✓	✓	✓		✓		✓		✓	✓	
Christopher Farr Cloth		✓	✓		✓		✓			✓	
Claire Martin Design	✓			✓			✓				
Cloth Fabric	✓				✓		✓				
Colefax and Fowler	✓	✓	✓		✓		✓			✓	
Crest Leather		✓			✓			✓	✓		
Crevin			✓				✓				
Eco Outdoor	✓				✓					✓	
Ellen Merchant		✓		✓			✓				
Fabric Trader	✓						✓				
Fermoie	✓	✓	✓		✓		✓			✓	✓
Haines Collection		✓				✓	✓				
Home Upholsterer	✓				✓		✓				
House of Hackney		✓	✓		✓		✓			✓	
Imogen Heath		✓		✓			✓				✓
Ink & Spindle	✓			✓			✓				
Interior Curve		✓		✓			✓				
Knoll			✓		✓		✓	✓	✓	✓	
Kvadrat	✓	✓	✓		✓		✓			✓	
Leffler Leather	✓				✓			✓			
Liberty Fabrics		✓			✓		✓				✓
Linwood Fabric	✓	✓	✓		✓		✓		✓		
No Chintz	✓				✓		✓				
Molly Mahon		✓		✓			✓				
NSW Leather Company	✓				✓			✓			
Ottoline de Vries		✓		✓			✓				✓
Poodle & Blonde		✓		✓			✓				
Pierre Frey	✓	✓	✓		✓		✓			✓	
Redelman Fabrics	✓				✓		✓				
Romo	✓	✓	✓		✓		✓			✓	✓
Sanderson	✓	✓	✓		✓		✓			✓	
Schumacher		✓	✓		✓		✓			✓	✓
Soane		✓	✓		✓		✓			✓	
The Stripes Company	✓	✓			✓		✓			✓	
Verve Outlet	✓				✓		✓				
Warwick Fabrics	✓	✓			✓		✓			✓	
Morris & Co.	✓	✓	✓		✓		✓				
Willie Weston	✓				✓		✓				
Zepel Fabrics	✓				✓		✓				
Zimmer + Rohde	✓	✓	✓		✓		✓			✓	

CREDITS

Every reasonable effort has been made to acknowledge the copyright holder of any artworks, fabrics and furniture in this volume. Any errors or omissions that may have occurred are inadvertent, and will be corrected in subsequent editions provided notification is sent in writing to the publisher.

PAGE 23
1   Nomad, Ellen Merchant
2   Bell, Mimi Pickard
3   Malachite Marbled, Susi Bellamy
4   Cosmati Embroidery Serpentine, Zoffany
5   Leaf, House by Hazel
6   Tribal Stripe Palm, Rapture & Wright
7   Alchemy, Bute
8   Tucson, Poodle & Blonde
9   Omega Prints II Emerald, Linwood
10 Omega Prints II Navy, Linwood
11 Tango Weaves, Linwood
12 Stone Moorish Washable, Villa Nova
13 Omega Prints II Indigo, Linwood
14 Aria Indigo, Imogen Heath
15 Strata, Bute
16 Miami Fabric, Siobhan Murphy
17 Lost and found, Christopher Farr
18 Clan Stewart, Bute
19 Chameleon, Bute
20 Abstract 1928 Serpentine, Zoffany
21 Caimano, Pavoni

PAGE 24
1   Sage Marbled, Susi Bellamy
2   Welbeck Acacia, Clarke & Clarke
3   Food Babies in Blossom, Poodle & Blonde
4   Money Tree, Poodle & Blonde
5   Evergreen, Imogen Heath
6   Clan Sinclair, Bute
7   Pencil, Bute
8   Small Prints, Linwood
9   Tottenham Dalmatian, Poodle & Blonde
10 The English Garden, Linwood
11 Braemar, Bute

12 Joy, Mimi Pickard
13 Bibi, Linwood
14 Chain of Fools, Poodle & Blonde
15 Wild Life, Linwood
16 Storr, Bute
17 Danube, Linwood
18 Kami, Linwood

PAGE 79
1   Small Prints, Linwood
2   Synergy, Camira
3   Somerset Stripe, Annika Reed Studio
4   Lilo, Bethie Tricks textiles
5   Bibi, Linwood
6   Identity, Bute
7   Annika Reed Studio
8   Bamboo Brights, Siobhan Murphy
9   Storr, Bute
10 Tango Weaves, Linwood
11 Heather, Imogen Heath
12 Botanica, Pierre Frey

PAGE 96
Artwork by Karl Davis.

INDEX

ABOUT
THE AUTHOR

Micaela Sharp is an upholsterer, interior designer and broadcaster from South East London. After attending an upholstery course, Micaela quickly learned the tricks of the trade and set up her own business in 2017. She has an online upholstery masterclass with Create Academy. Micaela appeared on *Interior Design Masters* (BBC2 and Netflix), where she made it to the semi-finals. She was the first-ever black interior designer on *Changing Rooms* (Channel 4) and features regularly on design shows such as *Woodland Workshop* (Discovery+), *Make it at Market* (BBC1) and *Love Your Weekend with Alan Titchmarsh* (ITV). She is passionate about sustainability, vintage and pattern. She also writes a monthly column for *Reclaim* magazine and co-founded a limited edition homeware brand with Charlotte Beevor called Studio Janettie.

Find her online: @micaelasharpdesign and micaelasharpdesign.com.

ACKNOWLEDGEMENTS

To Claire, who so brilliantly suggested I try an upholstery course. You started my journey in a new and exciting direction and I am forever grateful for your wonderful suggestion, open heart and true friendship. You also believed in me enough to commission not one, but two chairs and a footstool from me right at the start – thank you. To Wayne, Claire, Elijah, Jade, Robyn and Skye – you are my chosen family and I love you deeply.

To Nads, Denise, Caroline and Steve – working with you over the years has been a joy and a privilege. You are so dear to me and I value all your hard work, support and friendship. I am forever grateful that you came into my working life and enriched it!

To my nan and grandad – I wish you were here to see this. I've written a book! Thank you for everything you taught me, not least of all, resilience and hard work; for the opportunities you afforded me to be curious, learn and have space to change my mind. And for the love you instilled in my heart. I miss you every day. This is for you.

The Team

Wow! Writing a book takes a village – is that the saying?! I had such enormous support with bringing this book to fruition, I would be remiss not to thank the talented people who shared their expertise. Firstly, and perhaps most importantly, Chelsea, the project manager at Hardie Grant whose patience and expert guidance elevated every aspect of this project. Chelsea, your job title doesn't do your skillset justice. From a mere concept to an actual book and I credit you for that almost entirely. Thank you for keeping me on track, for patiently editing my dyslexic copy, for bringing such joy to every interaction and for the energy you have graciously shared over 18 months getting this over the line. Please be on all my projects in future!

Heather, Sara and Megan, my agents, who navigate my contracts and calendar with grace and ease. With you by my side I feel confident to take on these new exciting opportunities.

Charlotte, my business partner at Studio Janettie and the creator of all our beautiful prints, used here as chapter headings. You are my colour guru.

Thanks to Issy and Hardie Grant for commissioning the book and seeing both the potential in me and in upholstery. Thanks also for allowing me to make it as beautiful as I wanted!

Layouts and design are credit to Claire who added colour and vibrancy to every page. Emli, my wonderful photographer – the book would not work without your stunning photography. It's not easy to photograph staples but you made it look effortless! Thanks to creative genius Veva for her expert lighting and photography assistance.

Kind-hearted Raafaye, your meticulously accurate illustrations are a triumph. Thanks to detail-oriented Rachel for checking everything through so brilliantly. Styling was expertly overseen by Jen, who perfectly understood my aesthetic. Kasia and Jason, thank you for your muscle! Michael, as ever, thanks for your logistical help and patience. And thanks to every friend who read sections for me, sharing feedback and insights – with a special shout out to Alyssa for her brilliant suggestions.

Published in 2024 by Hardie Grant Books,
an imprint of Hardie Grant Publishing

Hardie Grant Books (London)
5th & 6th Floors
52–54 Southwark Street
London SE1 1UN
hardiegrantbooks.com

British Library Cataloguing-in-Publication Data.
A catalogue record for this book is
available from the British Library.

Modern Upholstery
ISBN: 9781784887278

10 9 8 7 6 5 4 3 2 1

Publishing Director: Kajal Mistry
Commissioning Editor: Isabel Gonzalez-Prendergast
Senior Project Editor: Chelsea Edwards
Design: Claire Warner Studio
Illustrator: Raafaye Ali Sheikh
Photographer: Emli Bendixen
Photographer's assistant: Genoveva Arteaga-Rynn
Stylist: Jennifer Haslam
Location assistants: Jacob Pryce, Kasia
Bevan and Michael Frimpong
Copyeditor: Rachel Malenoir
Proofreader: May Corfield
Indexer: Vanessa Bird
Senior Production Controller: Gary Hayes

Colour reproduction by p2d
Printed in China by C&C Offset Printing Co., Ltd.